Encyclopedia of
Women and Baseball

ALSO BY LESLIE A. HEAPHY

The Negro Leagues, 1869–1960
(McFarland, 2003)

Encyclopedia of
Women and Baseball

Edited by LESLIE A. HEAPHY *and*
MEL ANTHONY MAY

Foreword by Laura Wulf

McFarland & Company, Inc., Publishers
Jefferson, North Carolina, and London

LIBRARY OF CONGRESS CATALOGUING-IN-PUBLICATION DATA

Encyclopedia of women and baseball / edited by Leslie A. Heaphy
and Mel Anthony May ; foreword by Laura Wulf.
p.   cm.
Includes bibliographical references and index.

ISBN-13: 978-0-7864-2100-2
ISBN-10: 0-7864-2100-2 (illustrated case binding : 50# alkaline paper)

1. Women baseball players— United States— Encyclopedias.
2. Baseball for women — United States— Encyclopedias.
3. All-American Girls Professional Baseball League — Encyclopedias.
I. Heaphy, Leslie A., 1964–   II. May, Mel Anthony.
GV880.7.E63   2006   796.357098'03 — dc22   2006008719

British Library cataloguing data are available

On the cover: 1918 New York Bloomer Girls
(National Baseball Hall of Fame Library, Cooperstown, NY).

Manufactured in the United States of America

McFarland & Company, Inc., Publishers
Box 611, Jefferson, North Carolina 28640
www.mcfarlandpub.com

To all those who have been and
continue to be involved in the
great game of baseball

Acknowledgments

In writing any book there are always many people who make the whole thing possible. The first and most important group that has to be acknowledged consists of all the women who have played baseball throughout the years and continue to play today. They are the reason for this encyclopedia, and their stories need to be recognized as a part of the history of baseball. Without them the history of America's national pastime is incomplete.

There are many individuals who deserve special thanks for their help in gathering materials, starting with Cecilia Tan, who is herself a player. Cecilia provided information not only about her own experiences but also about the 24-hour benefit game in Arizona. Most importantly, she provided contacts with a couple of hundred other ball players. This help has been invaluable in constructing the more recent history of the game. Special thanks also go to Justine Siegal, who first introduced Leslie to a number of the people who wrote entries for this book. Justine invited her to be a part of the first Women's Baseball Leadership Conference, and that opened doors to many who have had a long history with the game, such as Jim Glennie and Dorothy Mills. Jen Hammond, Ashley Nicholls and Deb Bettencourt provided an array of photos to round out the book. Dick Clark and Larry Lester have continually provided us with new information

and articles that they found in their own research; this has been invaluable in filling in the details. Larry has also been a great source of encouragement as this project has taken shape: he has edited entries, provided photographs, filled in when entries were needed and, most importantly, just been supportive.

As always the National Baseball Hall of Fame has been incredibly cooperative, through the help of Tim Wiles. Women's baseball is one of Tim's own interests, and he has done a great deal to see that the story is being properly preserved. The Players Association for the AAGPBL helped track down players, answered questions, and provided a regular newsletter. The Minnesota Historical Society sent all their materials on Toni Stone and her involvement in the game. The reference staff at the Indiana University of Pennsylvania library provided a huge amount of assistance in putting together the story of Bernice Gera. The Wisconsin Historical Society provided us with the microfilm covering the years 1946–49 in the history of the Racine Belles. Laura Wulf gave us access to her photographs of women's baseball since the creation of the Silver Bullets, and that is truly a wonderful addition. Jim Glennie, who has been instrumental in the recent history of women's baseball, has provided lots of articles and photographs to help document the history.

In addition to all the libraries, universities

and other groups who have helped, we would also like to thank the authors who contributed to this encyclopedia. Their work made this text possible.

And finally, the idea for this book originated in the Women in Baseball Committee of SABR (Society for American Baseball Research). We spent a long time trying to figure out what kind of project we could get involved in and this is the end result. The committee had a smaller idea in mind for a book about the top 25 women in baseball, but it became apparent that there were too many to limit the list. Thanks to all the committee members and SABR for their help in getting this encyclopedia off the ground.

Table of Contents

Foreword

by Laura Wulf

In the early 1970s I developed a passion for baseball. I might have seemed an unlikely candidate. My mother was English, my father preferred football, my sister and only sibling had little interest in sports, I went to an all-girls school and I lived in Manhattan, where baseball diamonds were few and far between. Still, the New York Mets became my team. I bought baseball cards on my way home from school, checked the stats and the standings every day in the newspaper, tucked a transistor radio to my ear at night when I was supposed to be sleeping, and cried when Rusty Staub, my favorite player, was traded to the Montreal Expos. My uncle was a sporting goods salesman and he gave me a blue leather glove, which I had till it wore out. I played "pitch 'n catch" with my dad on the sidewalk in front of our apartment building, as well as across England and France on a summer trip. When I couldn't get my dad or a friend to play with me, I threw tennis balls against the side of the building to simulate grounders, and up onto the roofs of vacation houses to simulate fly balls. One summer I even got to play baseball, in a recreational league in the northwest corner of Connecticut where my family was on vacation. That summer was an initiation into the joys and perils of being a girl who loved a game that wasn't quite ready to love her back. I was 11 years old and these are some of my diary excerpts from that month:

> Monday, June 30, 1975
> I am going to play (I think) baseball with Claudia. It is [for] 6–9 year olds but the coach said we should go because 10–12 is too rough. I think that I could probably play with the 10–12s but Claudia said it was all boys. So?

I was always told that I "threw like a boy" so why shouldn't I think that I could play with the boys? But it's clear that I already had an inkling that we wouldn't be entirely welcome.

> Tuesday, July 1, 1975
> The baseball thing stunck [sic]. We're going to the 10–12 tryout tomorrow.... I hope that tomorrow the baseball thing is good and I hope that I am good to [sic]. Everybody said that the coach is a chauvinist and he wanted no girls in 10–12.

I remember being so angry after that first tryout. I felt humiliated at having to try out with the younger kids. I was insulted, as only a young person can be, not yet hardened to life's disappointments. But I went back the next day, made the 10- to 12-year-old team, and let the four-week season become my whole life.

> Wednesday, July 7, 1975
> In baseball I hit 2 for 5 with a single and a double. We had a grounders contest. Actually we had 2. It

1

was girls against boys. The first game was a tie. Then the second it was one boy against one girl (me). We won!

Friday, July 18, 1975
Didn't have baseball on Monday because of rain. On Weds hit 5–5, all singles, but 3 turned into doubles because of overthrows. Hit 3–6 today, all singles. Phil asked why I wasn't in the Little League because I was good enough. Ricky said that I was the best of the girls. Bill said that I am hitting .600. The National League beat the American League 6–3 in the All-Star Game. YAYYYY.

Monday, July 21, 1975
I hit 2 for 4 today. Rozie played too. And she hit something like 6 for 7. WOW. She was on a different team and they (her team) won 30–16. Slaughter.

Rozie was a school classmate who came to visit for a week. She was also an avid Mets fan and would make up baseball quizzes for me during classes with questions like "Who is the manager of the Detroit Tigers?" She'd pass them to me and I'd answer them and pass them back to her. We also sent letters to each other that summer. Hers were addressed to Laura "Rusty Staub" Wulf, and my letters to her were addressed to Rozella "Felix Millan" Floranz. Mostly we wrote about how the Mets were faring, how many home runs Dave Kingman had and perhaps, as an afterthought, how we were, or were not, getting along with our respective siblings.

Wednesday, July 23, 1975
Today I hit 6 for 11. I played 3rd base. I had 3 chances to get someone out at 1st but only got 1 out. I LOVE playing third base. I got a lot of action…. I think baseball ends on the 28th. BOOOOO HOOOOOOO.

I consider myself lucky to have had that opportunity to play. Many girls were denied access to the game altogether. It was only in 1972 that the Supreme Court ruled it unconstitutional to bar girls from playing Little League. Boys had the opportunity to play the game from the time they were old enough to hold a baseball. There was tee ball, Pony League, Little League and Babe Ruth League. There were traveling teams, high school and college teams, recreational park and senior leagues, and of course the minor leagues and the majors. When a girl wanted to play baseball she had to challenge the dominant thinking that girls played softball and boys played baseball. She was faced with questions: Why does she want to play baseball? Why does she want to play with the boys? Why does she want to be different?

Baseball and softball are similar in some ways, but baseball has a mythology and a history that softball lacks, and that are part of the allure of the game. I knew a lot about the game of baseball when I was a kid. I read about the history, the cast of characters, the great moments and the "unbreakable" records. I read *The New York Times Book of Baseball History*, *Ball Four* and books with titles like *My Greatest Day in Baseball* and *Great Infielders of the Major Leagues*. I didn't know anything about softball or its history, so the game didn't resonate for me. And softball didn't have cards that you could buy at the corner stationery store that offered up trivia, photos and stats, and were covered with the sweet smell and gritty texture of bubble gum and sugar. The only experience I had with softball was from playing at school, mostly indoors, with a squishy ball that neither rolled nor bounced. Softball was not an alternative. It was an altogether different game and I never claimed it as mine, nor did it claim me.

My relationship with baseball changed in 1977, when the Mets traded Tom Seaver. I was 13 years old, and was in England for the summer with my grandparents, when my father sent me the newspaper articles about the trade. I was devastated. I felt betrayed and let down, by a team that could trade its star player, and by a player that could even think about pitching in any other uniform. It made no sense to me. I took it hard and turned my passions elsewhere. I became a fixture on the tennis courts, emulated the players on the men's and women's professional circuits, went on to play varsity sports in high school and college and forgot about my shoebox full of baseball cards. But in my 13-year-old heart something was left unfinished, because the first time that I saw the Colorado Silver Bullets play, I became a baseball fan all over again. Just like that. When I saw nine women take the field at Fenway Park in July of 1994, I was 30 years old, and even though they only played seven innings, and even though they lost, I was hooked. Watching the Silver Bullets play ball, I reconnected to how much I loved everything about the game. The arc of the ball, the silence during the throw. The waiting and then the action. The rhythm. The stats. The soft field. Contact. The infielder's feet crushing earth. The silent flight of the ball. Sometimes it takes the presence of the unexpected to reveal the absence of the ordinary. That afternoon I sat in the stands at Fenway Park with tears in my eyes. I'd never seen a woman play baseball and had barely wondered where the women were. Well, there they were. I decided then and there to follow and photograph the team as much as I could. I'd been working as a photographer for almost ten years at that point, and with my baseball background it seemed a perfect match. And so, over the next four years, I photographed two dozen of their East Coast games. I also went down to Florida for two of their spring training camps. It was extraordinary to witness first-hand the players honing their skills and learning to play hardball.

Preface

Baseball enthusiasts recognize the names Babe Ruth, Cy Young, and Lou Gehrig. The more serious know the career achievements of players such as Addie Joss, Wally Pipp and Joe Torre. How many can tell a thing about Donna Mills, Dolly Brumfield or Isabelle Baxter? Most would ask the more likely question, who are these women and what do they have to do with baseball? Are they softball players? The answer is that since baseball began in the United States, women have participated recreationally and at the amateur, semi-pro and professional levels. This surprises most people who believe that baseball is and has been a primarily masculine endeavor. Even today, in the twenty-first century, most people think men play baseball and women play softball. This assumption often goes a step further, to the belief that women know little or nothing about baseball. In interviewing many women to put this book together, that idea was proven wrong again and again.

In the pages that follow readers will be introduced to hundreds of women who have been involved in the game of baseball from the mid–nineteenth century until 2005. There have been hundreds of teams and innumerable leagues for women, and women have been involved as umpires, owners, broadcasters, general managers and groundskeepers. Since the release of the movie *A League of Their Own*, people have become a bit more aware of women's roles in baseball during World War II. A few of the better-informed baseball aficionados are aware of the Colorado Silver Bullets of the 1990s, and some know about the women in the Negro leagues because of the recent attention paid to those leagues. These examples represent the tip of the iceberg. The story of women in baseball is stronger and deeper. One of the present-day players, Lily Nyland, says there is nothing like the game of baseball and women should just get out there and play.

The book is set up alphabetically. Some entries have little more than the player's name, while others are pages in length. This shows readers and researchers how much we know and how much there still is to find out. Generally the women are listed under her maiden name with her married name in parentheses, if known.

The entries are also not all identical in writing style and tone because they have various authors, who are identified in the individual entries. If there is no author listed, the article was written by editor Leslie A. Heaphy.

A series of appendices follow the main text. Appendix A is made up of the rosters of all the teams in the All-American Girls Professional Baseball League. Appendix B presents the teams, champions and batting champions of the AAGPBL. In the rosters the bold type indicates that there is an entry in the encyclopedia for that individual. Appendix C includes the rosters of all the teams and lists all the players from all over the world we have been able to find and identify to date. Appendices D and E both deal with the Women's World Series since 2001; D provides the World Series results and E provides rosters for all teams taking part in the World Series, from 2001 through 2004. Appendix F includes the rosters of the teams participating in the 2004 women's World Cup. Appendix G is a chart of all the various women's baseball tournaments in recent years and the results, since most of the recent teams play more traveling games than any other type of contest.

There are also extensive notes to help researchers and fans find out where this information came from and where they can go to find out more. The bibliography is the most comprehensive to date on women's baseball. It is broken down according to the encyclopedia's entry headings, and it includes related terms to indicate when other sections of the bibliography can be consulted for additional or related sources. For instance, the "Afterman, Jean" entry in the bibliography directs readers to the "Management Personnel" entry for other sources that are of interest.

Our goal in putting together this text has been to inform readers and to encourage researchers to fill in the gaps. We look forward to hearing from readers with new information and details to continue to improve our knowledge about women and the national pastime.

Leslie A. Heaphy *and*
Mel Anthony May

THE ENCYCLOPEDIA

Abbott, Velma "Abbie"

(b. 29 May 1924, Regina, Saskatchewan; d. 1 January 1987) 2B/3B 1946–47, Kenosha Comets, Peoria Red Wings, Rockford Peaches, Fort Wayne Daisies

Velma Abbott got the chance to play in the All-American League after getting noticed while playing softball in Alameda, California. She played on two world championship teams and then moved to the Midwest to play baseball. During her rookie season she played for three different clubs before playing her second and final season with Fort Wayne. In 1947 she had the best fielding percentage among the league's second basemen at .978. She played in 149 games and hit only .155, though she walked 38 times and stole 31 bases. {AAGPBL Baseball Cards, 2000.}

Acosta, Melissa

Long Beach Aces

Melissa Acosta played softball at Cal State, Dominguez Hills, before trying out for the Colorado Silver Bullets. At Dominguez she set the record for most hits in a single game. In 1997 she joined the Long Beach Aces of the Ladies Professional Baseball League. {"Women's Baseball Joins Professional Ranks," PRNewswire, 25 June 1997.}

Adams, Allison

(Millersville, Maryland) 2B/3B Baltimore Blues

After attending Dickinson College Allison Adams got a job coaching softball at Severna Park High School in Maryland. She played baseball for the Baltimore Blues as part of the Eastern Women's Baseball Conference, and that is how she was invited to join Team USA in 2001.

Adams, Evelyn Edell "Tommie"

(b. 16 November 1923, Richmond, Virginia; d. 14 August 1999) SS 1943–47, Fort Wayne Daisies, Grand Rapids Chicks

Evelyn Adams grew up in Richmond. She earned the nickname Tommie because of all the sports she played. She participated in basketball, field hockey, tennis, baseball and softball. She even played for the Frickles, Virginia's only girls' baseball team at the time. Adams was a switch-hitter with good speed, so she was often called on to bunt to start or keep a rally going. Adams left the AAGPBL in 1947 due to acute asthma, but she continued to play fast-pitch softball for the Virginia Dairy team and the Pollyannas. As time passed she gave up the fast-pitch and moved to Polly's Pals, a slow-pitch team. She was inducted into the Virginia Softball Hall of Fame in recognition of her many accomplishments. {Jenifer V. Buckman, "'Tommie Adams' Funeral Is Today," Richmond Times-Dispatch, 16 August 1999, B3; AAGPBL Baseball Cards, 1995.}

Adler (Calenda), Adriane

(b. 26 May 1970, Yonkers, New York)

Growing up, Adler played Little League as soon as she was allowed to sign up. Playing baseball with her dad and brothers had given her an early love of the game. After Little League Adler continued to play through Pony League before having to switch to softball. She then played softball and basketball at J.F. Kennedy High School and continued playing varsity softball and JV basketball at Fordham University. Her baseball career began in 1994 with the Philadelphia Strikers. The Strikers were organized by Mary Cattolico from Philadelphia, with Adler's assistance. They played each weekend and had two special events at the close of the season. They played an all-star team from Michigan at Doubleday Field in Cooperstown and followed that with a game in Fishkill, New York, at the Hudson Renegades' minor league park. Adler got her next chance with the New Jersey Diamonds in 1998 in the Ladies Professional Baseball League while at the same time playing in the Men's Adult Baseball League of Northern New Jersey. Adler played in the men's league from 1996 to 2002. In 2000 and 2001 she participated in the New England Women's Baseball League as a member of the Waterbury Diamonds. In 2002 Adler signed on with the Parsippany Yankees of the East Coast Women's Baseball League. In her first season with the Yankees Adler had ten hits in 25 at-bats; she knocked in eight runs in the summer and then was 9–21 in the fall. When asked to describe her favorite memory of playing baseball, Adler said it was opening night in July 1998, when she came

Adriane Calenda watching practice at camp in 1998 (courtesy Laura Wulf).

to bat for the first time with the New Jersey Diamonds. She laid down a perfect sacrifice bunt that moved the runner from second to third and then slid headfirst into first base so she was also safe. The roar of the crowd was exciting and made all the hard work pay off. As a player Adler contributed with the bat and on the mound. For example, in her senior year at Fordham she hit back-to-back home runs, and then in 2000 she hit an RBI double to score the go-ahead run for the Waterbury Diamonds in the Citrus Blast Championship. In 2002 she threw a two-hitter for the Yankees. In addition to playing baseball, Adler helped found the East Coast Women's Baseball League and works in television production. {Adriane Adler, correspondence with Leslie A. Heaphy, North Canton, Ohio, 9 February 2004.}

Afterman, Jean

(b. 1957, San Francisco, California) Management personnel

Jean Afterman joined the staff of the New York Yankees in 2001 as their assistant general manager. She replaced Kim Ng, who moved on to the same office with the Los Angeles Dodgers. In 2003 Afterman received an additional title from the Yankees: that of vice-president, with a contract through 2007. Before joining the Yankees, Afterman worked from 1994 to 99 with agent Don

Adriane Calenda taking batting practice during a tryout for the New Jersey Diamonds in 1998 (courtesy Laura Wulf).

Nomura. Their clients included well-known players such as Hideki Irabu and Hideo Nomo. The Yankees brought her on board because of her experience in this area. Afterman graduated from law school in San Francisco in 1991. {Ken Davidoff, "Pioneering Spirit Serves Yanks Assistant GM Well," *Newsday*, 18 April 2004; Mark Feinsand, "Batting Around with Jean Afterman," <MLB.com>, 30 January 2003; "New York Yankees Promote Jean Afterman," *AP Online*, 11 February 2003; "Yankees Hire Afterman as Asst. Gm," *AP Online*, 5 December 2001.}

Aguilar, Marcie

(b. 22 December 1969) IF 1996, Colorado Silver Bullets

Marcie Aguilar graduated from the University of Arizona in 1992 following the 1991 crowning of the Arizona Wildcats softball team as the national champions. She joined the Silver Bullets in their third season, 1996. {*Silver Bulletin*, March 1996.}

Ahrndt (Proefrock), Ellen "Babe"

(b. 8 November 1922, Racine, Wisconsin) 2B 1944, South Bend Blue Sox

In high school Ellen Ahrndt played softball and basketball, earning honors in both sports. She played in city league basketball and county softball as well. Though she played less than ten games in the All-American League, she enjoyed the experience. She got married in 1947 and raised two boys. She taught in a junior high school and continued to play a variety of sports to stay active. {AAGPBL Questionnaire, National Baseball Hall of Fame.}

Ajax

The Ajax club belongs to the Central Ontario Girls Baseball League, along with 11 other squads. They have three divisions within the league for Peewee, Bantam and adult women players. The Ajax are a team for those 17 and older. They have played since 2002. In 2004 their manager was Dave Watson. Their typical season lasts from May until the end of July.

Albright, Eileen

P/2B/3B 1948, Chicago Colleens

Eileen Albright joined the traveling team in 1948 in order to develop her skills and be placed on one of the regular teams in the All American League.

Alderfer (Benner), Gertrude "Gert"

(b. 21 September 1931, Kulpsville, Pennsylvania) 1B 1949–50, Springfield Sallies, Chicago Colleens, Muskegon Lassies

Gertrude Alderfer graduated from high school in 1949, a time when women's sports were limited. She did play field hockey, basketball and softball in school. She played on a playground team for two years before joining the All American League. Most of her time in the AAGPBL was spent on the two touring teams, though she did stay with Muskegon for five weeks in 1950. Traveling around the Midwest was an experience she would not have had if not for baseball. She was recruited to play for another season for Kalamazoo in 1951, but her mother took ill and she decided to stay home and care for her. Among Alderfer's favorite baseball memories are playing in two big league stadiums—Yankee Stadium and Griffith Stadium. Alderfer believed the toughest pitcher she faced was Doris Sams and the best player she saw in action was Dottie Schroeder. She played in 54 games and hit .236. After leaving baseball she worked at Ameter, Inc., for over 40 years. She married in 1955. {Gertrude Alderfer, correspondence with Leslie A. Heaphy, North Canton, Ohio, March 2004 and September 2004; AAGPBL Questionnaire, National Baseball Hall of Fame; AAGPBL Newsletter, October 1993, 16.}

Alexandria Baseball

Miss Allison organized the first ladies' baseball team at Lee-Jackson High School for the purpose of competing in the Fairfax County League with the boys' teams. She hoped that her team would encourage others to join the league. {"Lee-Jackson Girls Form Ball Club," *Washington Post*, 27 March 1935, 18.}

All-American Girls Professional Baseball League (AAGPBL)

By Grant Provance

In May of 1943 a significant event in the sporting history of the United States occurred: For the first time in the nation's existence there were all-female professional baseball teams engaged on the field. The All-American Girls Professional Baseball League was an organization that existed between 1943 and 1954. It was the predecessor of modern day women's professional sports leagues, such as the WNBA (Women's National Basketball Association). The focus of this article is twofold: first, to determine the events and circumstances that altered the traditional American ideal of womanhood, allowing women to compete on the playing field in front of a paying audience; second, to give a basic history of the league itself, provide details about the league's formation, teams, and key figures, and examine how the league played a unique brand of baseball.

The world of American athletics has always been geared toward the male portion of the population. For the majority of American history prior to the 1940s, women were expected to concern themselves mainly with matters of family. There are a few significant movements and events that helped put American women in a position to

play professional ball. One early factor was the effort of the women's physical education movement, which became prominent in the years following the Civil War. Educators such as Senda Berenson instigated a change in the traditional notion that women were not equipped to participate in strenuous physical activity. Acting as director of physical education at Smith College, she was responsible for the creation of sets of modified rules specifically designed for women's games. A growing number of women attending universities took up these games. Berenson and her contemporaries reasoned that "intellectual activity ... depleted women of vital energy.

Women physical educators countered that properly regulated exercise could restore energy, reduce nervousness common to women, and prevent traumas to the female's reproductive system" (Rader 1999, 209). These were the first steps that led women into the realm of athletic competition.

Women were encouraged to participate in events such as dancing, basketball, swimming, tennis and various other activities designed to improve fitness. As early as 1866 (at Vassar College), female students formed baseball clubs. As time passed, more clubs like the one at Vassar were sporadically found around the country (Gregorich 1994, 3). As the century drew to a close, women were beginning to participate in competitive sporting events. However, they were only encouraged to compete in games that allowed the participants to be in line with America's cultural ideals of femininity. Noncontact team sports such as softball and early women's basketball (a sport that barely resembles the game we see being played today) were two examples of games appropriate for women to play. The rules for these games were designed to lessen the physicality of the contests, therefore making them suitable for female participation.

Following the First World War, arguably the most widespread women's game was softball. The larger ball and smaller playing field made the game more acceptable for women to play, as pundits felt it was

OFFICIAL 1952 PROGRAM
Price 10 Cents

All Home Games Played At BEYER FIELD
(15th Avenue High School Stadium)

The cover from the 1952 program for the AAGPBL Rockford Peaches.

less demanding than hardball. By 1943 there were 40,000 semiprofessional women's softball teams in the U.S. and Canada, often playing in front of enthusiastic local crowds (Galt 1955, 11). The rise in popularity of women's softball coincided with the national success of female athletes.

In the 1920s America was introduced to gifted female athletes who gained recognition for their athletic prowess. One of these early stars was Mildred "Babe" Didrikson. "The Babe" was a multifaceted athlete who gained a measure of fame by excelling in a variety of sports including track and field, tennis, golf and baseball. Didrikson's baseball talents were good enough to earn her the opportunity to pitch in spring training exhibition games against major league players in 1934 (Gregorich 1994, 75). The success and fame of Didrikson and other pioneering women such as Gertrude Ederle helped to normalize the image of the female athlete in American minds. World War II would alter the experience of American women and be the catalyst that led to the organization of the AAGBL.

The onset of American involvement in the war created a situation that altered the traditional view of the female role in society. The expectation that "a woman's place was in the home" had fallen by the wayside. Women were now needed to fill the roles of men in society, who were drafted into the military. Rosie the Riveter, a strong, determined and feminine character created by the American propaganda effort, was to be the embodiment of the patriotic wartime American woman.

The war had a tremendous impact on every sector of American business, and the national pastime was not immune: "The men's minor leagues, the farm teams upon whom they [Major League Baseball] depended for new talent, had been largely wiped out by the military draft. Half of the players for the sixteen big-league teams had joined the war effort, and stars like Joe DiMaggio were putting on Army uniforms" (Johnson 1994, xix). In late 1942 the Office of War Information announced to the owners of Major League Baseball that they were considering canceling the 1943 season. This announcement led Chicago Cubs owner Philip Wrigley, along with other major league figures such as Branch Rickey, to devise a plan for the creation of a professional women's softball league.

Spurred by the need to provide the public with an alternative to men's pro ball, Wrigley was the key figure in the creation in 1943 of what he initially called the All-American Girls Softball League. At the time of the league's creation it was called the All-American Girls Baseball League (AAGBL) or just the All-American Girls League. The word "professional" was added after the creation of the Players Association in the 1980s. Since that is the name most recognized for the league, readers will generally see the acronym AAGPBL being used. In an effort to attract fans to the sport, Wrigley and company decided to revamp the game of softball so that it more closely resembled baseball. For example, the distance between base paths, and between home plate and the pitcher's mound, were increased, and the league dropped the number of players on the field from softball's traditional ten-player unit to baseball's standard team of nine. In addition, they broke with conventional softball etiquette by allowing base runners to lead off, steal bases and slide. These rule changes, largely initiated by MLB Hall of Famer and AAGBL manager Max Carey, created a game that in today's baseball vernacular would be described as "small ball" (Galt 1995, 12).

Even though the 1943 men's major league season went on unimpeded, Wrigley and his cohorts decided to proceed with the plan, as they believed that the games would provide communities with low-cost entertainment. The league would further shift towards baseball soon after its inception in large part because "league management, always concerned with what the public wanted, concluded that what fans liked most of all was a live ball — one that traveled fast and far and resonated with a resounding crack" (Gregorich 1994, 85). Another factor that contributed to the change was the feeling of a number of outspoken managers in the league who wanted to play baseball because it was a far more intricate game than softball.

The managers of the AAGPBL were usually men. There are a few instances of women managing teams, but usually these positions were short lived. Mary "Bonnie" Baker, who entered the league as a player in 1943, had the longest tenure of any woman manager, acting as skipper for the Kalamazoo Lassies for the majority of the 1950 season (Johnson 1994, 185). In 1943, the leagues founders made the decision to hire men who had a background in highly competitive male athletics. In an effort to gain public attention and fan credibility, Wrigley hired as managers a pair of ex–big league players, Bert Niehoff for the South Bend Blue Sox and Josh Billings for the Kenosha Comets; an ex–minor league catcher named Eddie Stumpf, for the Rockford Peaches; and Canadian hockey star and softball coach Johnny Gottselig for the Racine Belles (Galt 1995, 28). The league would continue to hire former major leaguers as managers throughout its existence. The managers of the AAGPBL were charged with taking the talent provided by the league's thorough scouting process and forming professional caliber teams.

Wrigley's plan was to form and disperse a group of scouts around the country to search for women interested in playing in the league. These scouts scoured the amateur softball fields of America for women who could perform at a high level of competition, but this was not the only criteria Wrigley's scouts used. They were equally interested in finding women who fit with the league's image of the type of girl they wanted for their product. Susan E. Johnson, in her book *When Women Played Hardball*, quotes from the league manual.

> Every effort is made to select girls of ability, real or potential, and to develop that ability to its fullest power. But no less emphasis is placed on femininity, for the reason that it is more dramatic to see a feminine-type girl throw, run and bat than to see a man or boy or a masculine-type girl do the same things. *The more feminine the appearance of the performer, the more dramatic her performance* [Johnson 1994, xxi; italics Johnson's].

This overt effort to maintain traditional standards of femininity illustrates the decision of the men organizing the league to compromise the product, in terms of player quality, by omitting women with talent who did not fit their vision of the feminine woman.

The financial strength of Wrigley's chewing gum fortune funded the league and offered women a very respectable wage that ranged between 50 and 100 dollars a week. Although this wage was above the national average, the women of the AAGPBL were expected to conduct themselves in a manner that would reflect the feminine image that the league was so intent on maintaining. From the beginning, the women of the AAGPBL were held to a much more rigid code of conduct than their male counterparts.

Male major league players were notorious for their crass off-the-field behavior. Womanizing, drinking and generally rowdy behavior was the calling card of the pro baseball player. There would be measures taken by the league's front office to ensure that the players of the AAGPBL did not carry the same off-the-field image. Players were not allowed to drink alcohol, wear revealing clothing, or indulge in any activities that would reflect anything but the American vision of wholesome femininity. To ensure that the players would be equipped to conduct themselves in the proper "feminine" manner, they were required to attend finishing school. "There they learned correct posture, how to speak politely to gentlemen callers, how to cross a room in high heels, and when sitting, to cross their feet at the ankles" (Galt 1995, 18). To enforce the strict behavioral guidelines of the organization, chaperones were assigned to each team. The organizers of the AAGPBL were as interested in providing the public with players who fit the era's description of femininity as they were in providing high-quality baseball.

With Philip Wrigley, a Chicago businessman, in firm control of the league, it was logical that he would operate out of the Midwest. Following the intense scouting sessions, over 200 women were invited to a final tryout at Wrigley Field, home of the Chicago Cubs. From that group, the first 64 players of the AAGPBL were selected. The league originally consisted of four franchises: two in the state of Wisconsin, the Kenosha Comets and the Racine Belles; the Indiana-based South Bend Blue Sox; and the Rockford Peaches of Rockford, Illinois (Madden 1997, 3). The league chose towns that were small markets, to borrow a more recent term. This assured that these teams were one of only a few entertainment options for the people of these communities. This strategy paid dividends, as in its first year the league made almost $200,000.

Prompted by the large fan response to its initial campaign, the league experimented with the idea of expanding to larger markets. In the following year, the Milwaukee Chicks and the Minneapolis Millerettes were added to the league. Before the end of the 1944 season, a combination of factors—including travel costs for the other teams and poor box office receipts from the Millerette home games—resulted in that team being required to play all of its games on the road. Appropriately, they played out the year under the moniker "the Orphans." The following year the expansion teams were relocated, with the Milwaukee franchise heading to Grand Rapids, Michigan, and the Millerettes moving to Indiana, where they would be called the Fort Wayne Daisies (Galt 1995, 30). The effort to expand to larger markets was unsuccessful. This did not stall the progress of the league, which continued its expansion efforts, and at its peak in 1948 the AAGPBL had ten franchises, including one in Chicago (the Colleens).

The league's formula of femininity and skilled players was received well by the small Midwestern cities that hosted teams. When the teams of the AAGPBL finally took the field, they were required to wear long dresses and makeup during games. The choice of uniforms was a poor one; as any former ball player could relate, skirts are not the ideal uniform for a baseball team. The skirt-uniform was a constant throughout the league's history; it played an important role in the feminine characterization of the league's players. As author Susan Johnson points out, "The skirted-uniform was an important part of the image management had chosen in order to market the league: this woman's baseball league would be family entertainment where fans could see girls who looked like girls play baseball like men" (Johnson 1994, 139).

The players of the AAGPBL were to exude traditional feminine characteristics for the specific purpose of marketing. The league organizers "believed there was nothing unusual or noteworthy about tomboys being able to play baseball. Tomboys, being 'masculine-type girls' could of course do masculine-type things. But where was the show in that" (Johnson 1994, 141).

The exclusion of women from the league on the basis of unfeminine appearance was not the only form of discrimination that existed within the structure of the AAGPBL. African-Americans had been prevented from participating in the men's major leagues until Branch Rickey's April 1947 signing of Jackie Robinson shattered the color barrier (Rader 1999, 294–295). Not surprisingly, the women's game followed the pre–1947 precedent set by their male counterparts. The exclusion of nonwhite women from the AAGPBL is the result of several factors. First, the social climate of the 1940s was one of racism and inequity, as evidenced not only by professional sports practices, but also by segregation within the U.S. military. Black women were not seen as equal to their white counterparts and were not capable, in the eyes of the majority of white Americans, of achieving the level of femininity that the league required from its players. Keep in mind that when the league formed in 1943, racial segregation was an accepted practice in American society. For the founders of the AAGPBL to include black players would have been a public relations scandal. In a league that was built so heavily on appealing to the white demographic, the last thing that was needed was to alienate the fan base.

Attracting fans to the games was always the main objective of the founders of the AAGPBL. During the course of the league's existence, the rules of the game were tweaked along the way to keep fans interested. What started in 1943 as a modified version of softball would, over time, evolve into baseball. During the 12 years of the league's existence, several features of the game were changed to complete this metamorphosis.

The size of the ball, for example, shrank from 12 inches in circumference in 1943 to 10¾ inches in 1948. In the final year of play it measured 9¼ inches, approximately the size of a men's baseball. In the first three years of play, pitchers were required to use an underhand delivery. Nineteen forty-six saw the introduction of sidearm deliveries and, by 1948, the league had adopted the men's overhand pitching style. Other facets of the game that changed included the ever-expanding distance between the pitcher's mound and home plate, as well as that between the bases. The largest AAGPBL diamond was used in the 1953 season. The mound was 60 feet from home plate, and 80 feet separated the bases. Not surprisingly, the smallest field was used in the 1943 inaugural season, measuring only 40 feet between the mound and home plate and 65 feet on the base paths (Gregorich 1994, 89). The alteration of on-the-field rules was accompanied by a constantly changing organizational structure.

The league operated under the control of Philip Wrigley only for its first two seasons of play. He sold the organization in 1945 to Arthur Meyerhoff, an advertising guru in the Chicago area, who held the reins of power until the 1951 season. In these first two phases of ownership, franchises were obligated to funnel the gate receipts of their games directly to the league office, which dispersed the funds. Under the direction of Meyerhoff, the league flourished until 1948, when he made the decision to expand the league to ten teams. When two of the expansion franchises, the Chicago Colleens and the Springfield Sallies, failed to attract significant numbers of fans, the rest of the teams were left to offset the losses they incurred. The true change in organizational structure came prior to the 1951 season as Meyerhoff sold his rights to the league to the individual team owners (Gregorich 1994, 85–86). From 1951 to 1954, the franchises of the AAGPBL were in control of their own financial destiny.

From the beginning, the league was molded to attract fans who were accustomed to men's professional baseball. During the 1943 season the league followed the major league formula that included a midseason All-Star Game at Wrigley Field. The game was not held in either of the next two seasons, but it was held again in 1946 (Madden 1997, 3). The idea of having an all-star team goes hand in hand with the promotion of the game to the general public. What better way to associate fans with a sports league than to highlight the best players and market them in the same manner as the men's game did? In 1946, Don Black, a writer for a national publication called

Major League Baseball Facts and Figures, "had the league managers vote for an all-star team, and the 1946 edition of the publication featured pictures and statistics about the All American Girls" (Galt 1995, 53). This type of exposure was key to the increased popularity of the league, but it would not have occurred if there were not all-star caliber players to market.

There were a number of standout performers in the AAGPBL, and many of these players put up stats that would be impressive in any baseball league. While it would be impossible to mention every standout performer, several players are worthy of individual attention. In a game that was centered around pitching and defense, one of the greatest offensive players in the league's history was Dorothy Kamenshek. Kamenshek played over 1,000 games at first base and in the outfield for the Rockford Peaches between 1943 and 1953 (she did not play in 1952 due to injury). "Kammie" was a multifaceted player who excelled both at the plate and in the field. She ranks highly in several career statistical categories and is the league's all-time leader in hits with 1,090. Perhaps her most impressive stat is that in 3,736 career at-bats, she only struck out 81 times (Madden 1997, 124).

While Kamenshek was arguably one of the league's best all-around performers, Sophie Kurys' base-stealing records are some of the most impressive baseball statistics ever seen. Kurys primarily played the outfield and second base for the Racine Belles between 1943 and 1950; she also played during the 1952 season for the Battle Creek Belles. Her best year was the 1946 campaign, which author Barbara Gregorich terms "the year of Kurys. She played in 113 games, rapped out 112 hits, drew twenty-three walks, and was hit by ten pitches. Reaching base 215 times, she attempted 203 steals, succeeding a monumental 201 times" (Gregorich 1994, 122–123). Her base-stealing prowess earned her the moniker of the "Flint Flash," and by the time her career ended she had stolen a remarkable 1,114 bases and finished with a highly respectable .260 batting average (Madden 1997, 140). In a league that relied heavily on the running game to produce runs, Sophie Kurys was one of the most formidable offensive weapons.

Perhaps the most proficient hitter in the history of the AAGPBL was Joanne Weaver of the Fort Wayne Daisies. Weaver's playing time was limited in her first two seasons, the first year because she was only 14 years old, and the following year due to injury. The 1953 campaign was Weaver's first full season, and the 16-year-old responded by posting a .344 batting average and leading the Daises to the pennant that year. It was, however, her accomplishments during the final year of league play that make Weaver a noteworthy figure in AAGPBL history. In the 1954 season her stat line was arguably the best of any player (regardless of gender) in the history of professional baseball during the twentieth century. It included a .429 batting average, 29 home runs, 79 stolen bases, and 109 runs scored. It should also be noted that midway through the final year of league play, the AAGPBL adopted the official men's size baseball, which boosted offensive numbers (Madden 1997, 258–259). What if the change to a regulation baseball had come earlier? Perhaps the women's game would not have evolved into the strategic brand of ball that was unique to the AAGPBL.

Much like softball, play in the AAGPBL was often dominated by defense and pitching. Along with the phenomenal offensive players previously mentioned, there are several pitchers whose accomplishments should be noted. First and foremost is the South Bend Blue Sox right-handed hurler Jean Faut. In her eight-year career (1946–1953), she became the only pitcher in the overhand era of AAGPBL play to throw a perfect game, a feat she accomplished twice. Working with a four-pitch arsenal, she was able to dominate her competition. Compiling an impressive 140–64 career record with an equally impressive 1.23 earned run average, Faut was named AAGPBL Player of the Year in 1951 and 1953. Her best single season came during the 1951 campaign, when she posted a 20–2 record with a miniscule 0.93 ERA (Gregorich 1994, 141–145). Faut also played the outfield and third base for the Blue Sox and amassed over 300 career hits.

Another notable player is Connie "Polish Rifle" Wisniewski. A member of the Milwaukee Chicks in 1944, she moved with the franchise to Grand Rapids, where she continued to play from 1945 to 1952. While Faut was the league's premiere overhand pitcher, the distinction for the best underhanded delivery arguably belongs to Wisniewski. During the course of her eight-year career, she amassed a record of 107–48 with an ERA of 1.48. She also earned the nickname "Iron Woman" for her durability, often pitching both games of a doubleheader. The 1945 season was her best, as she won 32 games with a scant ERA of 0.96, pitching a superhuman 391 innings. Wisniewski was also a formidable offensive presence, posting a career batting average of .275 in 2,165 at-bats (Madden 1997, 273–274). Skilled players such as Wisniewski, Faut, Weaver, Kurys, and Kamenshek, along with a host of women not mentioned here, helped lead their respective teams toward the AAGPBL Championship Series.

The league had a postseason playoff its very first year. The first team to capture the title was the Racine Belles, which swept its opponents three games to none in the best-of-five series. For its efforts, the team was awarded 60 percent of the gate receipts from the series, a championship flag, a plaque to be kept at the city hall and a $1,000 scholarship to the University of Wisconsin. The scholarship was to be awarded to a female high school girl to "encourage athletics among women for health and recreation" (Galt 1995, 30). The Belles would win the pennant again in 1946.

The most dominant team of the AAGPBL was the Rockford Peaches, which captured its first title in 1945. The Peaches reclaimed the title during the 1948 season; it was the first of three consecutive titles the team captured. Ranking second behind the Peaches, with three series wins, were the Milwaukee/Grand Rapids Chicks, who were champions in 1944, 1947 and 1953. The South Bend Blue Sox won back-to-back titles in 1951 and 1952, while the final championship in 1954 belonged to the Kalamazoo Lassies (Gregorich 1994, 131). These five franchises accounted for the 12 AAGPBL titles, leaving several teams without a championship.

To explain the ever-changing makeup of the teams that composed the AAGPBL is a bit complicated. Expansion, contraction, and relocation make it almost impossible to merely give a list of franchises that were part of the league. It is best to start with the two teams that were 12-year institutions in their respective cities, the Rockford Peaches and the South Bend Blue Sox. The Racine Belles first moved to Battle Creek for the 1951-52 seasons and then to Muskegon, Michigan, where they played their final season in 1953. The Kenosha Comets played from 1943 to 1951 before they folded. The franchise that began as the Milwaukee Chicks in 1944 moved to Grand Rapids, Michigan, where the team competed until the league dissolved. The Fort Wayne Daisies were in existence from 1945 to 1954 but actually played the 1944 season as the Minneapolis Millerettes. The Muskegon Lassies played from 1946 to 1950 before moving to Kalamazoo to play the 1952 to 1954 seasons. The Peoria, Illinois, Red Wings were in the league from 1946 to 1951. A pair of clubs, the Chicago Colleens and the Springfield Sallies, participated only in the 1948 season, and the following year they were both traveling teams with no affiliation to the league (Gregorich 1994, 95). These ten franchises were the components of the AAGPBL, which at the peak of its popularity drew almost one million fans in a single year.

In the inaugural season, the original four teams played a 108-game schedule that attracted 176,000 fans. The enthusiastic support of small Midwestern communities continued to grow, and the league grew as a result. By the 1946 season the league had expanded to eight teams and attendance shot up to 754,000 (Galt 1995, 49). During the late 1940s the AAGPBL reached its zenith. Despite the fact that World War II had ended, the league was still thriving, the result being that the league expanded for a final time in 1948. Then, as abruptly as the league had skyrocketed to become a regional phenomenon, the crowds began to taper off as the decade of the fifties began. In 1954, the final season of play, the league drew only 270,000 fans, its lowest total in a decade (Johnson 1994, xxiii). The downfall of the AAGPBL was the result of a combination of factors, both internal and related to changes that occurred within America's cultural landscape.

There were several front office decisions that contributed to the demise of the AAGPBL. One problem, which has already been addressed in part, had to do with the league's expansion effort in 1948. Although then-league-boss Arthur Meyerhoff's intentions were probably pure, the decision to expand to ten teams created several problems within the framework of the league's franchise owners. The expansion in 1948 was ultimately "a move that many felt diluted the talent and caliber of play and that within one month resulted in the financial failure of the two new teams" (Gregorich 1994, 86). The rest of the league's franchises were forced to offset the two failed teams' losses, and the whole experience created a division between franchise owners and Meyerhoff. Not surprisingly, this led to the sale of the league to the individual team owners, who chose to cut down on their expenses: "Cutting back on spring training and on publicity and promotion in a time when league attendance was dwindling, the board of directors found themselves running out of players, fans, and viable franchises all at once" (Gregorich 1994, 86). The mismanagement of the league was only one of the problems that faced the league; equally important were the changes in American life created by technology after World War II.

The 1950s saw a boom in technology that has forever altered life in America. The widespread distribution of television, advances in travel technology, and other new opportunities for leisure activities cut directly into the league's fan base. There was also a shift in the American idea of femininity, which during the previous three decades had seemed to be becoming more liberal.

Television and advertising created the "June Cleever" image, and American women began to conform to it. Author Benjamin Rader gives a thorough explanation of the change in the perception of women in America that occurred in the fifties: "A more restrictive conception of femininity, one revolving around marriage, home, and family, once again won public favor. The revived cult of domesticity along with a rising postwar homophobia that identified female athletics with lesbianism dampened the enthusiasm for women's sports" (Rader 1995, 221–222). The combination of these factors led to the downfall of the AAGPBL following the 1954 season.

Looking back at the AAGPBL, there are several key components to the league's historical significance. What began as a temporary diversion for a nation in the grip of war ended up being a quasi-successful professional sports league that lasted a dozen seasons. The women of the league were given the opportunity to earn a living playing baseball, essentially as a result of the "Rosie the Riveter" image of women that developed during World War II and the war's effect on major league baseball. What was at first a softball league was abruptly transformed into a unique brand of baseball that emphasized strategy and the philosophy of "small ball." In the final analysis, the AAGPBL offered over 500 women the opportunity to play professional baseball. However, in return for their handsome salaries, the girls were forced to comply with a list of rules that robbed them of much personal freedom. The AAGPBL was granted a measure of respect from the baseball community in 1988 when the Baseball Hall of Fame in Cooperstown, New York, dedicated a permanent exhibit to the league. Perhaps as a result, the early 1990s saw interest in the league translate into a number of books on the topic, as well as the motion picture *A League of Their Own*.

All-Star Bloomer Girls

Under manager F.C. Schmeltz, this team of 16 included 12 ladies, three men and their manager. The ladies ranged in age from 17 to 24 and hailed from all over the country. They relied on the three men for pitching and catching duties. According to news accounts of them in 1913, they traveled all over the country in their own Pullman car and had done so since at least 1904. They also carried their own canvas fence as did a number of other ladies' clubs. This allowed them to enclose the grounds and charge regular rates to all attending. In 1904 their travels took them through Elyria, Ohio, to play a local men's club at the fairgrounds.

After defeating a Kings College team from Bristol, Tennessee, they found themselves in Maryland playing back-to-back games in Frederick and Hagerstown in 1913. The All-Stars were in Georgia early in 1914, playing the Atlanta Federals in April. {"Bloomer Girls," *The Elyria Chronicle* (Ohio), 23 June 1904, 1; "Bloomer Girls to Play High School Cadets," *The Frederick Post,* 2 June 1913; "Bloomer Girls Play Feds on Saturday," *The Constitution* (Ga.), 29 April 1914, 10.}

All-Star Ranger Girls

This team, owned and managed by Maud Nelson, started barnstorming across Pennsylvania and Ohio in 1927. One of their first games was against the Greensburg Generals, and they lost badly. One good thing came out of the game: Nelson recruited two new players for her team, Margaret Watson and Alice Lopes. Lopes stayed with the team for two years before leaving to take care of her ailing mother. The team came to Elyria, Ohio, to play in June 1927. Their visit marked the first time a bloomer team had been in Elyria since 1916. It was hoped by the local promoters that the novelty would bring out a large crowd. One of the stars of the squad in the 1930s was Margaret Gisolo. The shortstop for the club was Lee Chandler. He later went on to play with the Triple A club of the Chicago White Sox. {Betty Sarafin, "Women in Baseball: Destined for the Big Leagues," *Focus*, 10 July 1994, 6, 7; "Bloomer Girls to Play Here June 8th," *The Chronicle-Telegram* (Ohio), 20 May 1927, 21.}

Allard, Beatrice "Bea"

(b. 10 July 1930, Muskegon, Michigan) P 1949, Muskegon Lassies

Bea Allard grew up with a father who loved the Detroit Tigers and taught his daughter to love the game. Allard graduated from high school in 1948. She had a chance to join one of the Lassies youth teams before actually entering the league in 1949. She went to the tryouts in Chicago to keep a friend who wanted to play company rather than with any plans to play herself. League president Max Carey was impressed and offered her a contract instead of her friend. She pitched in 19 games for the Lassies with a 2–2 record and hit .200. One of the highlights of her career was earning a save in the season opener. She came into the game with the bases loaded and no one out and got out of the inning without any damage. She struck out two, and the third batter popped up to end the inning quietly. She developed shoulder trouble and could not return to the league for a second year. After her baseball career ended she spent three years in the army and then worked for 30 years for the Michigan Employment Security Commission. {Beatrice Allard, correspondence with author, October 2004; "Bea Allard Interview," The Diamond Angle Web site; AAGPBL Baseball Cards, 1995.}

Allen, Agnes Lorraine "Aggie"

(b. 21 September 1930, Alvord, Iowa) P/OF 1950–53, Springfield Sallies, Kalamazoo Lassies, Battle Creek Belles

While attending St. Mary's High School in Larchwood, Agnes Allen played softball and city league basketball. When she got a chance to join the traveling Springfield team Allen took the opportunity to see some of the country. She did not always like the traveling but loved the game, the fans and the confidence playing gave her. After getting her start with the Sallies in 1950, Allen spent most of her four years in the league playing for Kalamazoo. She played in 75 games though she only pitched with a recorded decision in 54 games. Her winning percentage stood at .426 with a 23–31 won-loss record. Her first and last seasons were both above .500. After finishing her playing career, Allen went to work as a physical therapist after completing college at Augustana College and Western Michigan University as well as attending the Mayo Clinic School of Physical Therapy. To stay active she played tennis and golf while coaching a variety of sports. {AAGPBL Questionnaire, National Baseball Hall of Fame.}

Allen, Peggy

2B

Peggy Allen played Little League baseball in Rancho Penasquitos, San Diego. She played for seven years in that organization, mostly at the minor division with the North League White Sox. When she tried to move up to the major level her application was denied. Her parents, Jack and Teresa, have been supportive of her desire to play baseball rather than softball. {Ken McMillan, "The Double Standard," Real Sports, May/June 2001, 28–30.}

Allington All-Americans/All-Stars

The Allington All-Americans played from 1954 to 1958. Bill Allington, a manager in the AAGPBL and a scout, coached the team as they traveled across the country playing baseball. Most of the players were former members of the AAGPBL who wanted to keep playing after the league folded at the end of the 1954 season. In 1955 they played 90 games and in 1956 managed 65 games. They traveled over 40,000 miles that included 150 cities, 23 states and one Canadian province. Players who joined the tour included Maxine Kline, Ruth Richard, Joan Berger, Joanne Weaver, Dottie Schroeder, Dolores Lee, Jean Descombes and Jean Smith. Two new players joined in 1958 who had no connection to the AAGPBL. They were Mary Taylor and Charlene Smith. {Allan White, "Touring All-American Girls Prove Baseball's Still Anybody's Game," The Lima News, 14 June 1956.}

The club liked to involve the communities where they played their games. It helped their attendance and created long-term support. In order to accomplish that goal they often played in benefit games or used local girls as their bat girls. For example, in June 1956 at a game in Kalida, Ohio, they used a local Lima girl, Carla Sue Roush, as their bat girl. The night of the game was her eighth birthday. The games were organized by local Toledo sports promoter Hank Rigney. {"All-American Girls to Play at Kalida," The Lima News, 3 June 1956, 2-D.}

In a game against the Brownsville Charros in 1957, the All-Americans lost 7–2. Then they tied the Texas Lone Tigers 7–7 in 12 innings at Lions Park in Texas. Maxine Kline, Katie Horstman and Terry Young did the bulk of the pitching. They found themselves in small towns such as Menasha, Wisconsin, on their travels. While there they played the Menasha Macs. Often when they played these exhibition games to raise interest the clubs would switch batteries so that the men pitched for the ladies and vice versa. {AAGPBL Souvenir Program, 1986; "All American Club to Play Here Tonight," Valley Morning Star, 10 May 1957, A8; "All-American Girls Squad to Be in Town Sunday to Vie with Menasha," Appleton Post-Crescent, 14 June 1958, 20; "Baseball Belles Find Sun Hot in Valley Workouts," Valley Morning Star, 1 May 1957, 12; AAGPBL Touring Teams File, National Baseball Hall of Fame; "'Queen for a Night,'" The Lima News (Ohio), 17 June 1956.}

Allington, William "Bill"

(b. Van Nuys, California) Mgr. 1944–54, Rockford Peaches, Fort Wayne Daisies

William Allington managed two of the best franchises in the All-American League. His Peaches won the league in 1945, 1948 and 1950 while Fort Wayne did the same in 1953 and 1954. He came to the league after managing championship softball teams in California for many years. He recruited a lot of his players to come with him and play in the AAGPBL. After the league folded in 1954 he kept some of the ladies together as part of the Allington All-Stars, who played through 1957. {AAGPBL Baseball Cards, 2000.}

Alvarado, Linda

(b. 1952, Albuquerque, New Mexico) Management

Linda Alvarado made a name for herself in the usually all-male field of construction work. She founded and owns Alvarado Construction in Denver, Colorado. In addition, she is the president of Palo Alto, Inc., Restaurant Company and was a co-owner of the Colorado Rockies during the 1990s. In 2003 Alvarado was inducted into the National Women's Hall of Fame for her accomplishments in business.

Growing up in a family with five brothers, Alvarado never felt pushed into stereotypical women's roles. She liked working outdoors and felt supported in all she did by her parents. She decided to form her own company in 1976 after a couple of years as a construction site manager. She turned to the banks for a loan and was turned down by them all, so her parents lent her the money to get started. She started small and gradually the company grew, taking on more and more complex projects. The company Alavarado founded built and runs over 150 restaurants across the Southwest.

Alvarado has received all kinds of awards and honors over the years for her hard work. In 1979 she was asked to become a member of the board of Norwest Bank and since then has been invited to sit on many other boards. In 1996 she was named Revlon Business Woman of the Year and also received the U.S. Hispanic Chamber of Commerce Business Woman of the Year award. The National Minority Supplier Development Council gave her a business leadership award in 1996. In 2001 she received the Horatio Alger Award and was inducted in 2002 into the Colorado Women's Hall of Fame. These are just a few of the many recognitions Alavarado has received and continues to be awarded each year. {Entry for the National Women's Hall of Fame; "Parties the Flower in May," *New York Times*, 26 May 1996; Presentation by Jean Ardell, SABR Annual Meeting, 2003; "Homerunner: Linda Alvarado, Empresaria," *Latina*, August 1999.}

Alvarez, Isabel

(b. 31 October 1933, Havana, Cuba) P/OF 1949–54, Chicago Colleens, Fort Wayne Daisies, Battle Creek Belles, Kalamazoo Lassies, Grand Rapids Chicks

Before coming to the United States to play baseball, Isabel Alvarez played for the Estrellas Cubanas, a girls' all-star team in 1947 and 1948. She came to the U.S. in 1949 at her mother's urging and got the chance to join the traveling Chicago Colleens. Her mother felt America offered better opportunities than Cuba did. As a member of the Colleens she became the youngest Latina player in the league. She pitched for two years with the Colleens as she learned the skills and then got traded to the Fort Wayne Daisies. She had three teammates in Chicago who were also from Cuba, so they could help one another with the language and other customs. When she moved to the Daisies she had no one who really spoke the language, which made the adjustment a bit tougher. At Fort Wayne Isabel pitched in 13 games during the 1951 season and then found herself on the move again, this time to Kalamazoo and then Grand Rapids. She returned to the Daisies in the league's final season. Alvarez played in 105 games during her career and hit .250. Many years later she returned to Cuba to visit her family and to try to locate some of the early players, in order to make a documentary titled *Cuba on My Mind: The Baseball Journey of Isabel Alvarez*. The film was made possible with support from the Indiana Humanities Council. It was shown in 1996 at the Allen County Public Library. Alvarez became a U.S. citizen eight years after her arrival to play baseball. {AAGPBL Newsletter, May 1996; Hispanic Research Center, University of Texas at San Antonio; Larry Fritsch Cards, 1995.}

Amado, Jeanette "Jet"

(b. 12 December 1965, Tucson, Arizona) OF 1994–95, Colorado Silver Bullets

Growing up in Tucson, Jeanette Amado played softball at Cholla High School and then at the University of Arizona. While at Arizona, Amado compiled a .310 batting average and helped the Wildcats to a third-place finish in the 1988 NCAA World Series. In 1990 and 1991 Amado led her teams offensively and defensively. Her achievements in college resulted in an invitation to one of the 12 tryouts held by the Bullets across the country in 1994. Amado, along with 47 other players, got a further invitation to spring training in Florida. When the final roster was announced in April, Amado had made the team. With the Silver Bullets Amado came to be relied upon as a hitter who got on base, having the second highest on-base percentage on the team at .388. She was fast and had a cannon for an arm, which made her valuable in the outfield. {"For the Love of the Game," Colorado Silver Bullets souvenir program, 1995, 30; Dave Kindred, *Colorado Silver Bullets: For the Love of the Game* (Atlanta: Longstreet Press, Inc.), 60; Linda Helser, "Ms. Baseball Lives Dream of Playing in Pros," *Arizona Republic*, 28 April 1994.}

Amateur Athletic Union Women's Baseball (AAUWB)

In 2003, women's baseball became the thirty-ninth sanctioned sport in the Amateur Athletic Union (AAU), after a year as a probationary sport in 2002. The successful vote rested on the registration of over 400 athletes, five tournaments and a national championship in 2003. The AAU recognizes eight geographic regions for women's baseball and over 40 teams. The probationary board that helped push for this recognition included Jim Glennie, president of the American Women's Baseball League. The new chairman for the executive committee is Tom Giffen, and Chris Hill of the California Sabres became the new vice-chair. Each will serve a two-year term along with a youth chairperson and several at-large members. By joining the AAU, women's baseball has become part of an organization that has been around since 1888. {AAU Women's Baseball, <www.uswb.org>.}

Amazons

In 1889 a game took place between a men's team called the Danforths and a women's club that the reporter and players dubbed the Amazons, though no one seemed to know what their real name was or where they had come from. They played a baseball game at Windsor Beach won by the Amazons 20–17, but clearly the Danforths had allowed the umpires to make questionable calls in the girls' favor. The reporter described the player's uniforms in great detail but only mentioned by name their pitcher, Emily Howard, who gave up a lot of hits. The team uniforms consisted of red and black striped dresses, jockey caps and black stockings. The skirts of their dresses could be used to stop a ball and to protect the ladies when they slid. {"Female Ball Players," *Rochester Union and Advertiser*, 9 September 1889.}

American Athletic Girls

The American Athletic Girls were co-owned by Maud Nelson and Rose Figg. This was the first club Maud Nelson owned. The club consisted of six women and three men. In 1923 a local Ohio paper reported them losing a game 4–1 to a men's squad from Newcomerstown. {"Bloomer Girls on Losing End Here," *Coshocton Tribune*, 1 July 1923, 14; Barbara Gregorich, *Women at Play*, 36.}

American Bloomer Girls

Accounts of this team are found in papers from 1906. E.J. Christman traveled with the ladies to arrange all their games. The club went from place to place in style since they had their own private car on the train. They even brought a canvas to create a fence for the field and cushions for fans to sit on to watch them play. Ohio was one of their many stops; they played in Coshocton and Zanesville in early August. They also traveled to New Jersey to play some teams in Newark. Admittance to the games there cost 25 cents. {"Bloomer Girls Play Beaches on Hill Wednesday," *Coshocton Daily Age*, 6 August 1906.}

American Female Baseball Club

During 1893 the American Female Baseball Club played exhibition games both in the United States and in Almendares, Cuba. During a game against a Cuban men's team, a riot broke out among fans who felt the women were not serious ballplayers and therefore wanted their money back. According to the coverage in the *New York Times*, the women were pursued off the field and into a private home. The police had to be called to disperse the crowd. In the ensuing trouble one member of the club, Emily Forrester, was slightly injured. In addition the crowd set fire to the ballpark fences and broke many of the seats. {"Riot on the Ball Field," *New York Times*, 7 March 1893, 1; "Women Ball-Players Mobbed," *Atlanta Constitution*, 9 March 1893, 2.}

American Women's Baseball Association (AWBA)

This league was founded in July 1988 by Darlene A. Mehrer in Glenview, Illinois. The first coach for the AWBA was Randy Hundley, a 13-year major league veteran. The league has been centered in the Chicago area from 1988 to 2004. There were two original member teams, the Daredevils and Gators. The league expanded to three in 1989 by adding the Knights. They then added a fourth, but by the mid–1990s there were again only three teams, though the league branched out to try and start affiliates in Michigan and Florida. One attempt the league made to connect with baseball history was to invite local veterans of the AAGPBL to throw out the first pitch or to come for special ceremonies honoring their achievements. The typical season ran from June through August. All games were played at Elm Park on Saturday mornings, since so many of the players worked regular jobs during the week. The Knights won the 1989 title for the league with a 5–1 record while the Daredevils were 4–3 and the Gators were 0–5. {Lindsey Willihite, "Women Play Hardball in Association," *Daily Herald*, 20 August 1989; Cheryl TerHurst, "Women Have Few Chances to Play Ball," *Daily Herald*, 14 August 1991, 3.}

Mehrer passed away from cancer in 1990 but Judi Kahn, who also played shortstop, took over as president and worked with a five-member board of directors to keep the league going. {Bill Beuttler, "The Girls of Summer," *Sports Illustrated*, 6 September 1993, 139; *Sports Collectors Digest*, 2 September 1988, 126.}

American Women's Baseball League (AWBL/USWB)

This umbrella organization was created in 1992 to help promote women's baseball in the United States and around the world. The founder of the league was Jim Glennie. The league began as the Michigan Women's Baseball League in 1992 and then in 1997 became to the AWBL to give broader representation to the growing efforts in women's baseball. Glennie developed a newsletter and Web site to help promote the various events and teams that began to show up in the United States and in other countries. In 2001 the AWBL merged their operations with those of the Roy Hobbs organization to create a new set-up known as United States Women's Baseball (USWB). Jim Glennie continued his association with this new league but turned most of his time to the Women's International Baseball Association, which plans the Women's World Series. Tom Giffen was chosen as the executive director of the USWB and Ellen Giffen became the vice-president. They work with a board of directors that includes Glennie and Roy Hobbs as members. Some of the duties of the USWB included selecting the national team for the Women's World Series, operating the national championship at the

Roy Hobbs tournament, and developing leagues and teams around the country.

Amodeo, Alexis Rae

(New York) 2B/3B, Team WBL

Alexis Rae Amodeo plays second base on a local men's team with her uncle. In 2002 she traveled to Australia to play in an international women's tournament. When she is not on the baseball diamond Alexis works at a day care.

Amundsen, Elaine

(b. 1969) P/OF, Waterbury Diamonds, Colorado Silver Bullets, Team USA

Elaine Amundsen had a stellar softball career before getting the chance to play baseball. She made the all-state team while at Jonathan Law High School. She went to the University of South Carolina on a softball scholarship before transferring to the University of New Haven. Amundsen was named Female Athlete of the Year for Connecticut in 1987. She pitched for the Waterbury Diamonds tournament team in 2000–2001 and was on Team USA in both 2000 and 2001. The Diamonds won the 2001 Citrus Blast and were second in the Roy Hobbs World Series. Amundsen tried out for the Silver Bullets in 1994 at Westpoint, New York, but hurt her arm and did not get to play. Diamonds coach James Alberto named Amundsen the starting pitcher for the inaugural game of the 2000 season. She beat the Boston Blitz in a two-hitter and struck out 12 batters. By the end of their first season Amundsen hit .273 and had compiled a 5–4 record with a .873 ERA. In the Diamonds' first game in 2001, Amundsen worked with Adriane Adler to pitch a three-hitter. She struck out seven members of the New York Traffic in that win. When not on the ball field Amundsen works as a private investigator. {Waterbury Diamonds Web site.}

Anderson (Perkin), Janet Margaret

(b. 21 November 1921, Montreal, Quebec) P/RF 1946, Kenosha Comets

Janet Anderson grew up at a time when sports for women were limited, but she did not let that keep her from being active. While attending Bethune High School in Saskatchewan, Anderson participated in softball, tennis, basketball, hockey, track and field, and curling. Her academic success earned a scholarship to the University of Saskatchewan from 1938 to 1942, where she earned a teaching degree. In college Anderson had the chance to play what was the equivalent of today's intramural types of sports in basketball, and track and field. She also played on the university's tennis and hockey team. In 1946 Anderson traveled to the United States to play in the AAGPBL. She loved the travel and the chance to watch major league games.

After her one year in the league she returned home to teach and got married in 1950. She raised two children, taught, and kept active with bowling, golf, softball and especially curling. In recognition of her accomplishments she was selected for membership in the Saskatchewan Baseball Hall of Fame and the Alberta Amateur Softball Association Hall of Fame. {AAGPBL Questionnaire, National Baseball Hall of Fame and Museum.}

Anderson (Sheriffs), Vivian M. "Andy"

(b. 21 April 1921, Milwaukee, Wisconsin) 3B 1943–44, Milwaukee Chicks

Vivian Anderson attended West Division High School in Milwaukee and played baseball and basketball. She also played softball for local teams in the city of Milwaukee before joining the Milwaukee Chicks as their third baseman. She learned the skills of the game from manager Max Carey but her career was cut short because of broken fingers. While playing and going to school she worked as a secretary to make ends meet. After leaving the AAGPBL she worked as a loan closer and for a long distance moving company as their dispatcher. She also stayed active playing field hockey and semi-pro baseball. She made her mark in bowling as a member of the 600 club. {AAGPBL Questionnaire, National Baseball Hall of Fame and Museum; AAGPBL Baseball Cards, 1996.}

Andry, Mary Ann

1948, Chicago Colleens

Mary Ann Andry needed to develop her skills a bit more before getting a chance to play in the All American League, so she was assigned to the Chicago Colleens, one of their two traveling teams, in 1948.

Appier, Jeri

OF/P, Boston Blitz

One of the founders of the New England Women's Baseball League in 1999, Jeri Appier joined the Boston Blitz and served as the league's primary financial officer. She even got her brother, Oakland A's pitcher Kevin Appier, to donate equipment for the league when it began. Appier got her former Bentley College roommate Chris Lindeborg to join her as the league commissioner. Jerry Dawson worked with Lindeborg and was convinced to sign on as well. When she is not playing baseball Appier is a CPA in Allston, a Boston neighborhood. {Barbara Huebner, "A New League of Their Own," *Boston Globe*, 12 May 1999; Dick Dahl, "Out of His League," *Boston Globe Magazine*, 12 September 1999, 20, 2229.}

Applegren, Amy Irene "Lefty"

(b. 16 November 1926, Peoria, Illinois) P/1B 1944–53, Rockford Peaches, Muskegon Lassies

Amy Applegren got her start in softball by age 11 with a team called the Farrow Chicks in Peoria. She joined the Peaches when she was only 17, when the league was still using underhand pitching. As a left-handed pitcher she filled a need on her squad. She later moved to first base as the league shifted to overhand pitching. In 1946 while with the Lassies, Applegren played in 30 games and batted a solid .258. She only got the plate 66 times with 17 hits. She played in the National Girls Baseball League in Chicago for three years after leaving the AAGPBL. She worked for Caterpillar Tractors in the computer department. In 1993 Amy received word she had been selected for membership in the Greater Peoria Sports Hall of Fame. {AAGPBL Newsletter, January 1994, 5, and May 2002, 27.}

Aquino, Rita

Pawtucket Slaterettes

Rita played for the Pawtucket Slaterettes before switching to softball at St. Raphael's Academy. Aquino plays there with teammates Nancy Guay, Maura O'Brien and Mindy MacLane from the Slaterettes.

Arai, Junko

CF, Team Japan

Junko Arai helped her team beat Australia to win the 2003 Women's World Series. Arai knocked in two of Japan's four runs in their 4–1 victory. Arai hit .417 in four games and stole four bases in four attempts. {Australian Baseball Federation, <www.baseball.org.au>.}

Arakawa, Yoko

P, Team Japan

Yoko Arakawa played in four games in the 2003 Women's World Series. She had five at-bats and was held hitless. She did get on base once and stole second. Arakawa also pitched to one batter and walked the hitter.

Arbour (Parrott), Beatrice M. "Bea"

(b. 2 December 1920, Somerset, Massachusetts) SS 1947, Racine Belles

Bea Arbour attended Somerset High School and played softball for St. Patrick's. She had a bit of baseball experience with the American Legion boys' teams in Somerset. While playing for Racine she had a number of different jobs during the off-season to pay her bills; one of the more interesting was working in an apple orchard. Her time with Racine resulted in her playing in less than ten games. She got married in 1952 and raised four children. {AAGPBL Questionnaire, National Baseball Hall of Fame and Museum.}

Archer, Janice

GM, Kingsport Mets

Janice Archer served as the general manager for the Kingsport Mets, the minor league affiliate of the New York Mets. {Dottie Enrico, "Breaking the Grass Ceiling," *Newsday,* 27 March 1994.}

Arizona Peppers

The Arizona Peppers were one of the original four members of the Ladies Professional Baseball League in 1997 and remained as one of the six entrants in 1998. They finished the 1997 with a record of 9–20 under the coaching of Dan Hughes and assistant coach Jeff Nugen. The team had 18 players on the roster and usually tried to carry four pitchers who also played other positions.

Arlington (Stroud), Elizabeth "Lizzie"

P

Elizabeth Stroud, better known during her playing days as Lizzie Arlington, grew up in Mahonoy City, Pennsylvania. She played her first professional baseball game for the Philadelphia Reserves in July 1898 for a reported sum of $100 a week. She pitched four innings for the men's squad and gave up six hits and three unearned runs. Then she moved on to play for Reading in the Atlantic League for the rest of 1898. On July 5 she pitched one inning against Allentown and gave up two hits but no runs. Atlantic League president Ed Barrow had given the ok for her to pitch. In 1900, records indicate she was pitching for a men's team in Wapakoneta, Ohio, before she joined a series of bloomer teams. {Barbara Gregorich, *Women at Play*, vii, 13, 15.}

Armato, Ange "Lil Bonnie"

(b. 27 October 1929, Rockford, Illinois) 2B 1953, Kalamazoo Lassies

Ange Armato played for the Lassies in 27 games during the 1953 season. She only had two hits in 26 at-bats but was a sure-handed fielder. The Lassies ended the season in third place. Armato did not return for the league's final season but returned home, where she went to work in an advertising agency. {AAGPBL Baseball Cards, 1995.}

Armstrong, Charlotte T. "Skipper"

(b. 17 June 1924, Phoenix, Arizona) P 1944–45, South Bend Blue Sox

Charlotte Armstrong played for two seasons with the Blue Sox. During her short career she pitched two extra-inning games and won them both with shutouts. This feat earned her a spot on the *Ripley's Believe It or Not* TV program. Her career totals included a record of 39–37 with a 1.76 ERA. After leaving the Blue Sox Charlotte continued to play and even got the opportunity to be a part of a national championship softball club. She took up painting and made that her career. {AAGPBL Baseball Cards, 1996.}

Arnold, Lenna "Sis"

(b. 29 October 1930, Fort Wayne, Indiana) P 1946, Fort Wayne Daisies

Lenna Arnold got a chance to play for one season with her hometown Daisies in the All American League. She pitched in the city softball league and was recruited from there. She went on to teach physical education at the high school level. {AAGPBL Baseball Cards, 2000.}

Arnold, Louise Veronica "Lou"

(b. 11 May 1923, Pawtucket, Rhode Island) P 1948–49, 1951–52, South Bend Blue Sox

Lou Arnold grew up as the youngest of 13 children, which gave her lots of opportunities to play ball with her brothers. She played shortstop for a number of local softball teams including the Riverside Townies, and this got her noticed for the AAGPBL. She played for two championship teams in 1951 and 1952. Her best individual season came in 1951 when she was 10–2 with a 2.62 ERA. Her career numbers included a 23–16 won-loss record with a 3.02 ERA and 75 strikeouts. After leaving the league Lou worked for the Bendix Corporation in South Bend for nearly 40 years. {AAGPBL Questionnaire, National Baseball Hall of Fame and Museum; AAGPBL Newsletter, May 1996, 10; Rick Harris, "Women, Baseball and Rhode Island," In *Rhode Island's Baseball Legacy, Vol. I.* (Rhode Island: Rick Harris, 2001), 16–31, 25.}

Arnold (Witzel), Norene "Blondie"

(b. 21 November 1927, Oregon, Illinois; d. 27 January 1987) P 1949, Springfield Sallies, Muskegon Lassies

Norene Arnold pitched for one season in the All American League. She spent the first half of the year touring with the Sallies and then settled in with the Lassies for a few games to finish out the year. {AAGPBL Baseball Cards, 1995.}

Asay, Amanda

(b. 16 May 1988) C/DH, Canadian National Team

Amanda Asay joined the Canadian team that traveled to Havana, Cuba, in 2005 for a series of games. Unfortunately only four games were played before the competition was interrupted by Hurricane Dennis. Asay got the chance to catch a few innings and batted as the designated hitter. At only 17, Asay was one of the younger members of the team. {Harpreet Sidhu, "Tropical Vacation," *Prince George Free Press*, 20 July 2005.}

Asis, Monica "Monika"

(b. Argentina) 1B/OF 2004, Motown Magic

Monica Asis began to play baseball in 2004 for the Magic after moving to the United States in 2000 from Argentina. She is known for her solid defense and sense of humor. {Motown Magic Web site.}

Australian Baseball

According to the baseball archives in Australia, records have been found dating back to the 1920s showing women playing baseball. In 1934 New South Wales even played host to a baseball fair for women's clubs from Victoria and Queensland. Women appear to have played regularly until the 1960s; then there are no records until the 1990s. New South Wales started women's contests again in the early 1990s while Western Australia started their competition with eight squads in 1995. The Victoria Baseball Association put out an inquiry for women's clubs in 1994 and got enough responses to create over 40 ball clubs. This led to the creation of the Australian Women's Baseball Championship in 1999. From this competition a national squad is picked to represent Australia in various international tournaments. This began with the first Women's World Series in Toronto in 2001.

The team representing Australia at the first Women's World Series was coached by Grant Weir from Victoria and his assistants, Kane Longstaff and Denise Griffiths. Twenty players were chosen for that team from Victoria, New South Wales and Western Australia. They finished in third place. In the 2002 series the Aussie Stars, under head coach Chris Norrie, defeated Japan 8–6 to bring home the championship.

At the 2003 Women's World Series Australia took the silver medal and in 2004 came home with the bronze. In addition, the Australian team also placed fourth at the first women's World Cup event in Edmonton, Canada, in 2004. {Australian Baseball Federation, <www.baseball.org.au>.}

Australian National Team

This team is selected from the various squads that participate in the Australia's National Women's Championship. With an 18-member roster, it competes in the Women's World Series and took part in the first women's World Cup in 2004. The team is coached by Grant Weir.

Autry, Jacqueline Ellam "Jackie"

(b. 2 October 1941, Newark, New Jersey) Owner

Jackie Autry married into ownership of the California Angels through her husband, actor Gene Autry. She served as executive vice-president starting in 1990 and maintained that role until the Walt Disney Company bought up 25 percent of the team in 1996. Her husband asked her to step in and help the team with its finances since she had a banking background. She became noted during her tenure for her stingy financial policies as salaries began to soar; she encouraged the club not to re-sign some high salary stars such as Jim Abbott and Wally Joyner.

Jackie grew up in New Jersey. She was an active child until she contracted polio at the age of eight. She took up swimming to strengthen her legs. Her father George died when she was four and her mother Madeline remarried when Jackie was 17, moving the family to Palm Springs. She graduated high school and went to work as a bank teller, working her way up to vice president which is how she met her future husband. Jackie married Gene Autry in 1981 when she retired from banking and began to take control of his financial holdings. They were married for seventeen years before he passed away in 1998. Jackie has remained active with the Autry foundation and a variety of other community organizations. {"Jackie Autry Began with Three Strikes Against Her," *St. Louis Post-Dispatch*, 2 June 1996; "Jackie Autry Upset, Ponders Moving Angels," *Los Angeles Daily News*, 16 March 1996.}

Jackie Autry was the only female ever to be on the executive council of Major League Baseball. She also spent time on the oversight committee and on the board of directors.

Baker (George), Mary Geraldine "Bonnie"

(b. 10 July 1918, Regina, Saskatchewan, Canada; d. 17 December 2003) C/Util. Inf. 1943–50, 1952, South Bend Blue Sox, Kalamazoo Lassies

By Kathleen Birck

Mary Geraldine George, "Bonnie" Baker, was born 10 July 1918 in Regina, Saskatchewan, one of ten children. She began her sports career early and was a natural from the beginning. In elementary school, she was said to have thrown the ball a record 105 meters (Walton 2003). She played basketball, softball, and track while in high school. After high school, she worked in army and navy department stores during the day and played on company-sponsored softball teams in the evenings (Browne 1992, 34).

In 1943, she traveled to the United States to compete in the World Softball Championships, where multiple scouts were able to see her and others compete. A former resident of Regina, Saskatchewan, Johnny Gottselig, had coached multiple women's softball teams over the years. Baker was reading the newspaper in a coffee shop when she saw a picture of Mrs. Wrigley and Mr. Gottselig advertising the new baseball league. Later on that day, she got a call from Hub Bishop, one of Mr. Gottselig's sports friends and a Regina hockey scout, asking her if she would play (Browne 1992, 34).

She then was sent back to Canada to recruit other players (Helmer 1993, 18). During the 11-year history of the AAGPBL, over 20 women from Saskatchewan were recruited to play, including Baker and her sister Gene McFaul (Solomon 2003, 13). Beginning in the AAGPBL at age 25, she later came to symbolize the league image of a female baseball player and was one of the most publicized players in the league (Browne 1992, 44). A reporter gave her the nickname "Bonnie" after he saw her radiant smile one day (Browne 1992, 35).

Bonnie's husband was overseas, serving with the Royal Canadian Air Force, at the beginning of her professional baseball career. The year before, Baker had given up a chance to play in Montreal because her husband insisted she stay home. However, with her mother-in-law's support, she joined the league and told her husband only after she became one of the best players. He always told her, though, that when he came home from the war, she must come home from baseball (Browne 1992, 38). Baker, a catcher and later a second baseman, played parts of nine seasons in the league, beginning with the South Bend Blue Sox and making the all-star team in her first season. One teammate admired the grit and determination with which Bonnie played. In her first game with the team, she recalled Bonnie making it clear who she was and where she played. This rookie got an elbow in the face as Bonnie said, "Don't you know the catcher always takes pop flies?" Baker played through multiple injuries in her career, including getting knocked unconscious in one game and having her hand broken twice (Sue Macy, *A Whole New Ball Game: The Story of the All-American Girls Professional Baseball League*. New York: Henry Holt & Co., 1993, 25; Browne 1992, 116).

In 1946, her husband Maury came home, and she planned on quitting baseball and returning to him. He realized, however, how unhappy she would be not playing baseball, and he told her to go back (Browne 1992, 38). She was again selected to play in that year's All-Star Game after stealing 94 bases and batting .286. In 1947, the South Bend Blue Sox played the Grand Rapids Chicks in the playoffs, Baker led all players with a .389 batting average for the series. In the fourth game of the series, she stole home for her team's only run (Galt 1995, 64).

Having played with the Blue Sox for over eight years, Baker was traded midway through the 1950 season to play for and manage the new Kalamazoo Lassies team. This unpredictable move came about after the previous male manager failed to meet expectations (Browne 1992, 182). The year before, the Lassies had finished last and moved from Muskegon to Kalamazoo. When the league asked Baker to take over as manager, the Blue Sox club president, Harry Dailey, debated whether to let the heart of his team go or gain the chance to boast about his team giving the league their first female manager.

Baker indeed left and made sweeping changes to help the Lassies. She began to acquire new players and had high expectations for what her girls should know about the game of baseball (Galt 1995, 75). Under Baker's leadership, the team climbed to fourth place by the end of the 1950 season. As a result, many fans came back to see the Lassies. She became the first woman (and was the only one at that time) to manage a baseball team. The following year, in 1951, a ban was placed on women managers in the AAGPBL due to complaints from multiple male owners, though Baker did move into an executive league position (Browne 1992, 182). Multiple explanations have been proposed as to why club directors were largely against female managers. Some thought making former players into managers meant taking talent off the field. Some wanted to hire only well-known male ballplayers as managers, and female managers may have been seen as a threat, especially if they did well. Money may also have been an issue. Managers made more money than players, and thus teams found it more costly to pay a manager's salary than a player's (Browne 1992, 183).

As a star in the league, Baker often posed in advertisements at various stores in South Bend and Kalamazoo (Macy 1993, 79). She was a media darling, combining beauty and charm (Helmer 1993, 18). Baker was popular with the fans and always obliging in signing autographs. As a manager, she would do radio shows and store promotional events to sell baseball to fans (Galt 1995, 75). She appeared on the front cover of the 4 June 1945 issue of *Life* magazine and made an appearance on the television show "What's My Line" (Vanstone 2003, 35). She was said to have "glamour-girl looks" that offered her "steady flashbulbs from the press (Walton 2003)." It was said that Baker made substantially more than the other players in the league: Other veteran top hitters made about $100 a week while Baker probably made about $200 to $300. Her excellent catching skills, hot bat, and popularity with the fans probably contributed to this (Galt 1995, 72). She also tended to be the player most written about in the news headlines — the price of stardom for her meant getting showered with praise for routine

pop flies as well as receiving negative attention when she made a mistake (Browne 1992, 44).

Bonnie left after the 1950 season to have a baby and then returned in 1952 to play and manage one final season with Kalamazoo (Galt 1995, 75). After leaving the league, she returned home to Regina. Her husband died several years after her baseball career ended, after which she went to work as a radio sports news director and took care of her then nine-year-old daughter. She also coached an American Legion women's softball team that participated in the world championships (Solomon 2003, 13). She later became a sportscaster and, in 1986, began managing a curling rink in her hometown of Regina before retiring (Browne 1992, 198). She was inducted into the Saskatchewan Baseball Hall of Fame, the Saskatchewan Sports Hall of Fame, and the Canadian Baseball Hall of Fame (Solomon 2003, 13).

Mary "Bonnie" Baker died 17 December 2003 at her home in Regina from respiratory failure. The four-time AAGPBL all-star was 84 years old.

Baker (Wise), Phyllis Joyce

(b. 3 June 1937, Marshall, Michigan) P 1952–54, Muskegon Lassies, South Bend Blue Sox, Fort Wayne Daisies

Sports were not a real option for women while Phyllis Baker attended Marshall High School. They did have regular field days, and she always took part in events such as the softball throw and the high jump. Baker played basketball in the local city league and then got a chance to join the AAGPBL for its last season. Due to her age and school attendance she was unable to play earlier. One of her favorite memories was of meeting Babe Zaharias. After her baseball days ended Baker played fast-pitch softball until she was almost 50. Her club won a number of league championships and she was the team MVP. She helped her husband coach softball at Marshall High School while she worked at State Farm Insurance. {AAGPBL Questionnaire, National Baseball Hall of Fame and Museum.}

Ballentine, Kelly

C 1992–2001, Maryland Barncats

Kelly Ballentine played softball in college and earned All-American Honors. She went on to become the owner of PetBarn, the sponsor of the Maryland club she starred on for almost ten years. In 2001 she received a Hall of Fame Award from the National Women's Baseball Hall of Fame.

Ballingall, Chris

(b. 17 May 1932, Ann Arbor, Michigan) 1B/OF/ C 1953–54, Muskegon Lassies, Kalamazoo Lassies

Chris Ballingall learned to play baseball by catching for her twin brother. She signed to play in the All-American League at the age of 21 after waiting for six years to play. She had originally been offered a contract at the age of 15 but her father did not want her to play then. She played in 162 games during the league's final two seasons and hit .218. She hit 17 home runs in 1954 and shared the nickname "Home Run Twins" with teammate Carol Habben. In that same season the Kalamazoo club won the playoffs. {Chris Ballingall interview, the Diamond Angle Web site; AAGPBL Baseball Cards, 1995.}

Baltimore Black Sox Bloomer Girls

Playing in the Baltimore area in the 1920s, this local African-American women's team received periodic reports in the *Baltimore Afro-American*. They reported a game they won 10–4 over the Excelsior Girls of Sparrow Point on 9 September 1921. They beat them again 34–11 at Maryland Park on 16 September 1921. This followed a loss to the same Excelsior club in August 1921 by a score of 17–14 at Druid Hill Park. They also played to a tie at 29–29 at the end of August. They called the game in the ninth inning because of darkness. About 1,000 fans came out to see the girls' play and were treated to some heavy hitting as four home runs were hit. The roster for the 1921 squad consisted of the following players: M. Sparks (RF), Clarke (RF), M. Winn (LF), Williams (LF), G. Clark (CF), Burke (CF), S. Johnson (SS), P. Myers (3B), Banks (3B), G. Davis (2B/1B), Matthews (1B/3B), M. Johnson (2B), Williams (C), R. Taylor (CF), M. Taylor (C), and B. Taylor (P).

No other reports have been found for 1921. The next report found is for the end of the 1922 season. The Black Sox lost 48–2 to the N.Y. Bloomer Girls in August 1922 at Maryland Park. A Miss Taylor was the losing pitcher for the Black Sox. Catching duties were shared by a Miss Slaughter and a Miss Elkins. Relief pitching was carried out by Miss Morris who also played second base. The outfield consisted of Misses Cook, Banks and Duffin. The remaining infielders were Cook at third, Cockerell at first and Downey at short. Marion Watkins was listed in the newspapers as the man to contact if you wanted to play the Black Sox. In 1928 the Baltimore ladies were listed as the premier women's team in the South, and they lost 51–2 to the New York Bloomer Girls and their star pitcher, Helen Demarest. {*Baltimore Afro-American*, 12 and 26 August 1921, 9 and 16 September 1921, 19 May 1922, 18 and 25 August 1922; "Bloomer Girls to Play," *Frederick Post*, 7 August 1928, 3.}

Baltimore Bloomer Girls

In 1913 a women's team called the Baltimore Bloomer Girls got caught perpetuating a fraud during a game in Washington, D.C. The fans realized early on that the team they came to watch was actually a group of men rather than women as the team had been billed. They chased the "ladies" off the field but did not get their money back because the promoter disappeared in all the confusion with about $500 in a suitcase. {"From All Accounts," *Frederick Post*, 21 July 1913.}

Baltimore Blues

The Blues belong to the Eastern Women's Baseball Conference and play under manager Jo Ann Richardson and coach Dave Kruger. In 2004 they struggled to a last place finish in the five-team league, winning only a couple of games.

Baltimore Stars/Cantina Banditas

The Baltimore Stars finished the 1999 season with a record of 8–2 and one tie. The Stars were formed in 1998 by Kerry Keller and for two seasons belonged to the WMBWL but they left the league in 2000 to join the Eastern Women's Baseball Conference. They finished the 2000 season with a 1–3 record in the league. In 2004 they became the fifth entry in the Eastern Women's Baseball Conference under the leadership of Kelli Presnell. They finished third in the league in 2004.

Baltimore White Sox Bobbies

E.L. Taylor became the business manager of the Baltimore Bobbies in 1926. He organized a local team to play all challengers, both male and female clubs. {"Girls' Nine Seeking Players and Games," *Washington Post*, 3 January 1926, 19.}

Bancroft, Dave "Beauty"

(b. 20 April 1891, Sioux City, Iowa; d. 9 October 1972, Superior, Wisconsin) Mgr. 1948–51, Chicago Colleens, South Bend Blue Sox, Battle Creek Belles

Dave Bancroft came to the All American League in 1948 after having played from 1915 to 1930 with the Philadelphia Phillies, the New York Giants and the Boston Braves. He played shortstop for the World Series winners in 1921, 1922 and 1923. His career numbers included 1,913 games, 2,004 hits and 7,182 at-bats. His play led to his induction into the Baseball Hall of Fame in 1971. He managed the touring Colleens in 1948 for the All American League and then moved up to the Blue Sox in 1949 and finished with the Belles in 1951. In 1949 the Blue Sox hosted a "Dave Bancroft Night" at Playland Park. A committee of local businessmen and citizens under the direction of Frank Helvie planned the event with the Shriner Band as the centerpiece followed by a ceremony to honor Bancroft for his 40 years in baseball. {"Manager of South Bend Blue Sox Holds Major League Record for Shortstops," *The Lima News*, 18 May 1949, 17; AAGPBL Baseball Cards, 2000; OBBHOF Newspaper Collection; National Baseball Hall of Fame Stats.}

Barbaze, Barbara

(Toronto, Ontario) OF 1948, Springfield Sallies

Barbara Barbaze needed to better develop her baseball skills and so in 1948 she joined one of the two traveling teams for the All American League, the Sallies.

Barber, Perry Lee

(b. 1953, Manhattan, New York) Umpire

Growing up in New York City, Barber was encouraged by her mother, Jackie, to follow her dreams. She attended the Harry Wendelstedt Umpire School in 1982 with her twin sister, Warren. She talked Warren into going with her so she would not be the only female in attendance. She returned in 1983 and 1984. Though she had started in 1981 umpiring Pee Wee games, her first experience umpiring had been a less than stellar outing as she volunteered even though she really knew nothing of the rules. She simply wanted to be involved in baseball while the strike in major league baseball was going on. That opening experience convinced her to attend an umpiring school, and it was what kept her going back, because she really wanted to learn the game. She then moved up to Little League — umpiring for games in California in 1982 and in Utah in 1983 — CYO and high school games. With the advancement into college ball she umpired in the Atlantic,

Southern, South Florida and Eastern College conferences. {Gregg Sarra, "Following Their Call," *Newsday*, 24 September 1996.}

One of the real highlights of her career came during spring training in 1985 when she served as home plate umpire for an exhibition game between the New York Mets and the Chicago White Sox (she was still umpiring Mets exhibition games in 2001). By 1987 she was umpiring in the Empire State League. In 1989 she was invited to go to Japan and umpired two games for the Orix Braves. She received the invitation from Kazuo Sayama, a fellow member of the Society for American Baseball Research. She worked both home plate and the infield. Her first game behind home plate was nationally televised and made her a celebrity throughout Japan. In 1996 Barber was chosen as an alternate for the Olympic Games in Atlanta. During the season of 1996–97 she coordinated all the umpires for the Junior Olympics. She worked from 1998 to 2001 as one of ten full time umpires for the Atlantic League. Barber umpired for 21 years at all levels through the professional ranks. In 1993 she won the New York State Golden Diamond Amateur Baseball Woman of the Year Award, sponsored by the Topps Company.

In addition to her umpiring duties Barber has also worked as a color commentator at RNN-TV at Duchess Stadium in New York. She reported on the games of the Duchess County Renegades. Barber got the chance to work for RNN after appearing on Brian Kenny's program *Sports Line* as a special guest.

Barber graduated from the Hewitt School in Manhattan and tried one semester at Arizona State University, but she did not like it. She also spent time at the Sorbonne studying English literature. She became a freelance writer and musician when she was not umpiring. A number of articles written by Barber appeared in the *International Baseball Rundown* between 1989 and 1998. For example, she wrote one titled "Hank O'Day's Famous Ruling" concerning a call he made back in 1908. She also wrote about umpires she knew, such as Lee Weyer. Her article on Weyer came out after he died of a stroke. Barber also appeared on *Who Wants to Be a Millionaire?* and won $10,000 on *The Challengers*. She writes her own music and plays the guitar. One writer described her music as being in the "modified country vein." She has been on stage with Bruce Springsteen and written songs for Bette Midler and Carly Simon. She sang the national anthem at Shea Stadium, belonged to a band named Crayon and has recorded songs about baseball. {Matt Damsker, "Brenner Humor

Hits Home," *The Evening Bulletin*, 10 April 1975, 40A.} Barber is married to Tom Vris and has two stepdaughters, Tracy and Courtney. The family lives in Connecticut. {Perry Lee Barber, "The Men (and Women) in Blue," *International Baseball Rundown*, March 1996, 12, 20; Rudy Lanini, "Belle of the Ballfield Umpires and Dreams," *Star-Ledger*, 14 June 1998; Bob Pacitti, "Mets Hitters Hit Their Stride," *The Tribune*, 28 February 2001; Perry Barber file, National Baseball Hall of Fame; Dave Rosner, " Look Behind the Mask," *New York Newsday*, 14 July 1985; Umpires file, OBHOF; Women Umpires file, National Baseball Hall of Fame.}

Barker, Lois Anna "Tommie"

(b. 7 April 1923, Dover, New Jersey) RF/3B 1950, Fort Wayne Daisies, Grand Rapids Chicks

While growing up, Lois Barker got to watch her father coach baseball teams and her brother's career as an Olympic track athlete. In fact, her family thought she would be a boy and had a name all picked out, Thomas Henry. When Lois arrived her family started calling her Tommie and the name stuck. In such an athletic family it was no surprise that Barker won a high school letter award and was MVP for her intercounty softball league in 1956. She graduated from Roxbury High School, where she played softball. After hearing about the All American League she wrote and asked about a tryout. She was invited to New Jersey and got an offer to sign with Fort Wayne. Before the season started, her contract was traded to Grand Rapids, where she spent one season. Her first game was memorable because she lost the first ball hit to her in the lights. Her playing career in the AAGPBL was cut short because of a family illness, and she had to return home. She played in 32 games with a .125 average and a .944 fielding average. She then worked as a supervisor for the WaveGuide department at NASA for 40 years. {AAGPBL Questionnaire, National Baseball Hall of Fame and Museum; AAGPBL Baseball Cards, 1995; Brenda S. Wilson, *Nicknaming Practices of Women in a Nontraditional Occupation: Female Professional Baseball Players*, MA Thesis, 1991, 66.}

Barnard College

Assistant professor of physical education Edgar Fawver started the first women's baseball teams at Barnard in 1909. By 1910 the team had developed to the stage where it could play other colleges such as Vassar. In one reported contest against

Vassar the Barnard team won behind the heavy hitting of Millicent Ormsby, who drove in four runs with a home run. {"American Girl as Ballplayer," *Washington Post,* 5 June 1910, MS4.}

Barnes (McCoy), Joyce N.

(b. 18 October 1925, Reno County, Kansas) P 1943, Kenosha Comets

Joyce Barnes joined the Comets when she was only 17, which is why she played for only a single season. In 1944 she returned to high school to play basketball, softball, volleyball, and track and field while finishing school. She went to work as an optician during the war and then got married in 1947. Her family moved to a farm in Partridge, Kansas, where she continued to play softball and also took up golf. {AAGPBL Newsletter, May 2001, 35; AAGPBL Questionnaire, National Baseball Hall of Fame and Museum; AAGPBL Baseball Cards, 2000.}

Barnett, Charlene "Barnie"

(b. 13 March 1928, Elgin, Illinois; d. 25 November 1979) 2B 1947–50, Grand Rapids Chicks, Chicago Colleens, Rockford Peaches

Charlene Barnett started her career in the All American League at the age of 19. She played her rookie season with Grand Rapids and then was assigned to the touring Chicago Colleens to develop her skills. Her career totals include playing in 355 games and hitting .175. She was known not for her hitting but for her fine fielding. {AAGPBL Baseball Cards, 2000.}

Barnett, Pearl

1B 1917, Havana Stars

Pearl Barnett played first base for the semipro Havana Stars in 1917, under manager Bean. At the time she was the only African-American woman playing baseball on a semipro men's club. {*Chicago Defender*, 12 May 1917.}

Barney, Edith Louise "Little Red"

(b. 3 February 1923, Bridgeport, Connecticut) C 1948, Grand Rapids Chicks

While attending Bassick High School, Edith Barney played basketball, soccer and softball. She also participated in industrial league softball and basketball. She joined the Chicks when they won the divisional championship in 1945. Unfortunately, they lost in the playoffs. Barney's career lasted only one season because she was a backup catcher. She appears to have played in only four games and batted four times without a hit. After the AAGPBL she went to work for Raybestos-Manhattan, Inc., for over 35 years. Raybestos had a number of industrial teams for their employees, and Barney bowled and played basketball, softball, and golf for the company. In 1954–55 she won the Outstanding Female Athlete Award for Raybestos and in 1973 received the Veteran Athlete Award for Recreational Program Achievement for the company. {AAGPBL Questionnaire, National Baseball Hall of Fame and Museum; AAGPBL Baseball Cards, 2000.}

Barr, Doris "Dodie"

(b. 26 August 1921, Winnipeg, Manitoba) P/OF
1943–50, South Bend Blue Sox, Racine Belles, Springfield Sallies, Muskegon Lassies, Peoria Red Wings, Kalamazoo Lassies

Doris Barr played for six different ball clubs in the AAGPBL, pitching and playing the outfield. She often pinch hit as well, because she was a solid hitter. Her highest single-season average was .269 and she knocked in 18 runs that same year to help South Bend. In 1945 Barr won 20 games against only eight losses. One of those wins was a no-hit, no-run game against Fort Wayne; the final score was 2–0. She also helped herself with her fielding, committing only 38 errors in her career. She pitched in 218 games and compiled a record of 79–96 with an ERA of 2.80. She struck out 572 batters but also walked 959.

After playing baseball she stayed in Kalamazoo for a number of years before returning to Winnipeg and working in the finance division of the local hospital until her retirement in 1985. She kept herself active by taking up golf, curling and bowling. She was inducted into the Manitoba Baseball Hall of Fame and Museum in July 1998. {AAGPBL questionnaire; AAGPBL Newsletter, May 2001, 41.}

Barringer, Patricia

(b. 14 September 1924 New Carlisle, Ohio) 2B
1947, Chicago Colleens; chaperone, 1948–50, Chicago Colleens, Battle Creek Belles

Barringer played only one season on the AAGPBL but remained involved after her playing career. She went on to serve the league for three more years as a chaperone for the Chicago Coll-

eens and the Battle Creek Belles. As chaperone Barringer had the duty of supervising the activities of her players on and off the field. Chaperones were necessary to help keep up the proper image for the league. {AAGPBL Baseball Cards, 1996.}

Bartlet, Denise

1998, Arizona Peppers

Denise Bartlet attended Arizona State University on a softball scholarship and then in 1998 joined the Peppers of the Ladies Professional Baseball League. {*Baseball Girls*, 1995, produced by the National Film Board of Canada, directed by Lois Siegel.}

Barton, Meredith

Team USA

In five games during the 2003 Women's World Series Barton hit .182 with a 2–9 performance and four strikeouts. She only made two errors in the field while completing 28 put outs and two double plays.

Baseball Canada

Canada developed a national team to send to international events such as the Women's World Series which began in 2001 and the Women's World Cup in 2004. They played in the bronze medal game in the 2002 Series, eventually losing to the United States. They lost again in the same round to the U. S. in 2004. The official Baseball Canada team was created in 2004 like Team USA to play in the World Cup.

In 2005 the national club went to Cuba to play an exhibition series with the Cuban National team. The team was led by their manager Andre Lachance. Unfortunately the series was interrupted by a hurricane that cut short the trip. The team is chosen from regional tryouts around Canada. The 2005 squad included at least nine returning players from the previous season. Melanie Harwood led the Canadian team with five RBIs while Karine Gagne scored six runs in the World Cup. They came away with the bronze medal, defeating Australia 8–3.

The roster for Baseball Canada is a group with lots of experience. One of the players who played both seasons is catcher Genevieve Beauchamp. Karine Gagne, Melanie Harwood, Katherine Hannah, Erin Forman and Samantha Magalas all returned as position players too. The pitching staff also had three veterans in 2005 in Martine Nadeau, Kate Psota and Ashley Stephenson.

Bason, Katie "KB"

(North Carolina) C/3B/P 2002 Chicago Storm, Team WBL

Katie Bason played baseball on her high school team and then after graduation started playing for the Chicago Storm in the Great Lakes Women's Baseball League. She also played for Team WBL when they traveled to Australia in 2002 to play in an international tournament. In the 2003 AAU National Championship series, Bason pitched in two games for the Storm and won one with a 2.45 ERA. She is attending Wake Forest University to earn a teaching degree.

Batikis, Annastasia "Stash"

(b. 15 May 1927, Kaukauna, Wisconsin) CF 1945, Racine Belles

Growing up at a time when girls did not play sports, Annastasia Batikis took advantage of the few things Washington Park High School provided. All girls' sporting activities were either intramural or play days; there were also a few club sports. Her participation earned her a letter for All-Girls Sports. After graduation in 1945 she got the chance to join the Racine Belles as a utility outfielder. She played in only five games but thought it was a great experience to have that opportunity to play and travel.

After one season she went to work for the school system until she went back to school at Lacrosse State College in 1948. She graduated with a degree as a physical education and recreation major with a minor in science. She returned to the University of Wisconsin, Lacrosse, in 1957 to earn an MS degree. When not playing in the AAGPBL, Batikis participated in city league basketball, softball and badminton. She also played in every sport the college offered and joined all the honorary societies she could to stay active.

For 38 years Batikis worked as a physical education teacher in Manitowoc and Racine, and coached all kinds of sports. Her accomplishments have resulted in numerous awards and recognition over the years. In 1985 she received the VFW Award for Outstanding Service to Youth. She was selected for membership in the Washington Park H.S. Hall of Fame in 1987 and in 1998 she was added to the University of Wisconsin, Lacrosse, Wall of Fame. In 1997 she was inducted into the Southeastern Wisconsin Education Hall of Fame. {AAGPBL Questionnaire, National Baseball Hall of Fame and Museum; AAGPBL Newsletter, January 1994, 5, and May 2002, 26.}

Battaglia, Fern G.

(b. 6 January 1931, Chicago, Illinois; d. 8 March 2001) 2B/SS 1950–51, Chicago Colleens, Springfield Sallies, Battle Creek Belles

Fern Battaglia attended Immaculata High School in Chicago before going on to Wright Junior College and DePaul University. When she joined the AAGPBL she got the chance to travel with the Colleens and Sallies, but her favorite experience was playing in Yankee Stadium. She also played for half a season in Battle Creek but had to return home because of a family illness. After playing baseball Battaglia coached and taught physical education in the Chicago public school system for nearly 30 years. {AAGPBL Questionnaire, National Baseball Hall of Fame and Museum.}

Battle Creek Belles

The Belles took over the franchise from Racine in 1951 before turning the club over to Muskegon in 1953. In their first season they compiled a record of 30–80 while in their last season they did a little better at 43–67, though they were still in the cellar. Their managers included Guy Bush, who had pitched for the Chicago Cubs in the National League; Dave Bancroft, also a former major leaguer; and Joe Cooper. {"Bush Joins Girls," *Syracuse Herald-American*, 22 July 1951, 56.}

Baumgartner, Mary Louise "Wimp"

(b. 13 September 1930, Fort Wayne, Indiana) C 1949–54, Springfield Sallies, South Bend Blue Sox, Peoria Red Wings, Kalamazoo Lassies

Baumgartner started her baseball career in 1949 with the Springfield Sallies before going on to join the South Bend Blue Sox in 1951 and 1952. She was selected as the catcher for the all-star team in 1953. While she was with South Bend in 1951 and 1952, the team was in the playoffs. In 1953 she broke her thumb and had to play with a metal brace, which made catching exceedingly difficult. Before joining the traveling Sallies in 1949, Mary had had no baseball experience but had played volleyball and basketball in and around the Fort Wayne area. She earned a BS degree in 1957 from Indiana Central College and an MS degree in physical education in 1961 from Indiana University. She worked as a teacher for 28 years at Jimtown and Leo high schools before retiring. In recognition of her many accomplishments, Baumgartner was elected into the University of

Indianapolis's Hall of Fame in 1989, the first female athlete named. In 1990 she was elected vice-president of the AAGPBL Players Association and then served as president for eight years. {AAGPBL Questionnaire, National Baseball Hall of Fame and Museum; University of Indianapolis Hall of Fame Web site; AAGPBL Newsletter, May 1996.}

Baxter, Isabelle

(Cincinnati) 2B, Cleveland Giants

Baxter played second base for the Cleveland Colored Giants in 1932 when they challenged the Henny Mason All Stars. According to a news report about the game, she was scheduled to play three innings at first base for the men's team, in the first game of a double header. In addition to playing baseball Isabelle was noted as a swimmer, bowler and tennis player. She was again listed in the papers as playing for the Giants in 1933. She played in the opening game of the season against the Canton Clowns and handled all her fielding chances. At the plate she went one for three as her club won 14–8. {"Girl Ball Player Aids Cleveland 9," *Chicago Defender*, 17 June 1933, 11; "Girl to Play 2nd Base," *Cleveland Plain Dealer*, 27 August 1932; *Cleveland Call and Post*, 29 May 1948.}

Bays, Betty

c 1950, Springfield Sallies

Betty Bays caught for the traveling Springfield Sallies in 1950.

Beare, Kathryn "Katie"

(b. 7 November 1917, Syracuse, New York) C 1946, South Bend Blue Sox, Fort Wayne Daisies

Kathryn Beare played in 1946 for the Daisies in Fort Wayne. She played in 24 games and hit .111. She then went on to play softball for many years in the Syracuse area. In 1993 the National Organization of Women presented Beare with the Unsung Heroine Award of Honor for her achievements in sport. {AAGPBL Newsletter, January 1994, 8; AAGPBL Baseball Cards, 1995.}

Beatson, Nora

Nora Beatson played for the Virginia Boxers in 2002 and was asked to join the DC Thunder as a tournament team representing the EWBC. The Thunder lost to the North Shore Cougars in a Maryland tournament in which Beatson hit .500 after batting a solid .270 for the season.

Beaty, April

(b. 1958) Umpire

In 1996 April Beaty became a rookie umpire in the Shawnee Umpires Association. She started umpiring while attending Wichita State for nursing. She worked during the summers to earn money for school. After college she went to work in the intensive care unit at KU Medical Center. {"A Conversation with April Beaty," *Star Magazine*, 9 June 1996, 4.}

Beauchamp, Genevieve

(2 September 1981, St. Jerome, Quebec) C 2002–05, Team Quebec, Team Ontario, Team Mississauga, Team Canada

Genevieve Beauchamp was selected for induction into the National Women's Baseball Hall of Fame in 2004. This came after she played in the 2004 Women's World Cup, where she hit .375 with one run knocked in and played flawlessly behind the plate. She had previously played in the 2002 Women's World Series in Australia and then won the MVP award at an international tournament in 2003 for Team Quebec.

Beauchamp got her start in baseball with Little League at age seven. She then played with boys' teams until 2002. In 2002 with Ontario she hit .386 in twenty games. The following season with Quebec Beauchamp hit .612 in 20 games. During the 2004 season she played for three teams in a total of 50 games including tournament play. For those three clubs she hit .523, .452 and .508 respectively. {Baseball Canada 2004 Women's National Team Media Guide.}

Beck, Amanda

(b. 1982, Pleasantville, New York) SS, Queens Cyclones

Amanda Beck is the shortstop for the Queens Cyclones and played softball at Bates College in Maine (2001–03). She played in 83 games in college with a .149 batting average and 12 RBIs. She had not played baseball since she was 12 and had been forced out of Little League because it was a boys' sport. In 2004 she continued to play in the NYWBA. She is also attending the College of Veterinary Medicine at Kansas State. {Michael Malone "Throwing Like a Girl," *New York Sports Express*, n.d.; Bates College Web site; Stephanie Kornfeld, "Finding a League of Their Own," *The Rivertowns Enterprise*, 5 September 2003, 8; Anthony Garzilli, "Recreation Baseball," *The Patent Trader*, 9 September 2004.}

Beck, Lottie

(Jackson, Michigan) C 1946, Fort Wayne Daisies

Lottie Beck joined the Daisies of the All American League for only one season before hanging up her cleats.

Becker, Donna M. "Beck"

(b. 6 August 1932, Kenosha, Wisconsin) P 1951, Kalamazoo Lassies

Donna Becker grew up in family of athletes. Her three brothers all played semipro baseball and her sister played in the city league. Becker pitched during one year in the AAGPBL after playing baseball, basketball and volleyball at Mary D. Bradford High School. She only pitched in three games. She also played in the local city league before going on to get a BS in elementary education and psychology from Carthage College in Wisconsin. She taught for 25 years as an elementary school teacher. {AAGPBL Questionnaire, National Baseball Hall of Fame and Museum.}

Becker, Kate

Kate Becker pitched for a series of bloomer teams that barnstormed across the country in the 1910s. One reporter described her as the best female pitcher in the country at the time.

Beining, Tina

Tina Beining wanted to play Little League ball growing up, but could not because she was female. Later she got the chance to play in Florida with the Daytona Beach Sharks and the DeLeon Springs Diamonds. She also played in a senior men's baseball league in Jacksonville with three different squads. She tried to start a league in Jacksonville for ladies age 17 and older, without much luck because she could not get any sponsorship. {AAGPBL Newsletter, "Baseball Veteran Hopes to Form League of Her Own," May 2002, 27.}

Beishline, Jennifer "JB"

P, New Jersey Nemesis

In 2000 Jennifer Beishline pitched for the New Jersey Nemesis in the Eastern Women's Baseball Conference. She defeated the Baltimore Blues 11–3 for one of her team's eight victories that season.

Bell, Justene

(b. 20 March 1982) IF/P 2003, Queensland

Justene Bell grew up playing softball but switched to baseball in 2000 for a change. Bell got one at-bat in the 2003 Women's World Series and had one assist in the field. She also pitched in two games and picked up one loss. She gave up eight runs in only five innings of pitching.

Bell, Virginia "Ginger"

(b. 30 July 1927, Muskegon, Michigan; d. 19 April 1994) P/OF 1948, Springfield Sallies

Nicknamed Ginger, Bell stood only 5'3" tall but had a solid bat and loved the thrill of being on the mound. Her club was filmed during spring training in 1948 by World-Pathe News and the program was shown across the United States. After her short career, Bell served for two years with the WACS in Japan and then went on to work for Boeing Aircraft after studying mechanical engineering. {AAGPBL Newsletter, May 1994, 11; AAGPBL Baseball Cards, 1996.}

Bellini, Alexandra

(Ottawa) 3B

Alexandra Bellini played third base for Ottawa in the 2004 Little League World Series. She never realized until the series who had made it possible for her to be there to play, but the Little League headquarters decided to honor the women pioneers at the 2004 series. That was when Bellini first heard about Maria Pepe and her efforts to play baseball in the early 1970s. {"Little League Honors Female Pioneers," *Grand Rapids Press*, 22 August 2004; Dan Lewerenz, "Girls, Women Featured Prominently at this Year's LL World Series," *Associated Press*, 21 August 2004.}

Bellman (Balchunas), Lois "Punkie"

(b. 11 September 1926, Berwyn, Illinois) 2B/OF 1949, Chicago Colleens

Lois Bellman played one year with the touring Colleens. She did not return after her one season of travel but married in 1951 and raised three daughters. {AAGPBL Baseball Cards, 2000.}

Belman, Jo Jo

DH/Util. 2004, Motown Magic

At only 17 Jo Jo Belman became the youngest member of the Motown club, in 2004. Belman joined the team for the camaraderie and the chance to learn the game of baseball rather than softball.

Benedict, Gertrude Edita "Geri"

(b. 30 October 1909, Seattle, Washington; d. 17 August 2003, Auburn, Washington) P

Gertrude Benedict was the only daughter of Jim and Mathilde Harty, who owned the New Washington Hotel in Seattle. Her father taught her to pitch a baseball and she played for the Seattle Indians in 1932 in the Northwestern League. She was reported as the only girl playing in that league. She also traveled for exhibition games for many years. Benedict worked for Montgomery Ward as a cashier and married Porter William Benedict. {"Gertrude Edita Benedict," *Seattle Times*, 21 August 2003.}

Benefit Games

In October 2003 women from all over converged on Tuscon, Arizona, for a 24-hour marathon baseball game designed to raise money for AIDS victims in Africa. While many of the women who played participate in other leagues during the year, there were also some who came to play for the first time. The participants ranged in age from 13 to 80, and they were helped out by honorary coach John Denny, a former major leaguer, and members of the AAGPBL. Seventy-two women took part in the game, and they raised over $60,000. The women came from 16 states, plus Japan and Australia. The event was organized by Rob Novotny, vice-president of American Women's Baseball. Before the game itself there were two days of professional instruction, run by Kevan Burns of Live the Dream Athletics, Inc.

The game began at 12 noon at Tucson Electric Park. Stacey Brownewell from Illinois threw out the first pitch for the Red-Eye Nights. The final out came just over 24 hours later, when Kris Ward made the final putout. Nanaei Chiba from Japan pitched 20 innings during the game and there was one inside-the-park home run. The African Gray Birds defeated the Red-Eyes 127–110 in 65 innings. {Manny Correira, "Area Players Recall 'Big Game,'" *The Providence Journal*, 5 February 2004, C-01; Nancy Haggerty, "Women to Play a 24-Hour Game to Benefit AIDS Victims in Africa," *The New York Times*, 21 September 2003; Jack Magruder, "Pitching In for a Good Cause," *Arizona Daily Star*, 20 October 2003.}

Bennett, Catherine

(Regina, Saskatchewan) P 1943–44, Kenosha Comets, South Bend Blue Sox

Catherine Bennett played for the first two years of the All American League.

Berger (Brown), Barbara Ann "Bergie"

(b. 6 December 1930, Maywood, Illinois) C 1949–50, Chicago Colleens, Racine Belles

Barbara Ann Berger attended Proviso Township High School, graduating in 1948. While in school Berger was unable to participate in any girls' sports that required competition against other schools, because this was not allowed. She did play tennis and badminton as well as softball in some local clubs. She got a chance to play in 1949 with one of the traveling teams for the AAGPBL, which took her out of the state for the first time. Unfortunately she broke a bone in her throwing hand, cutting short her playing time. She played in 11 games with the Belles during the 1950 season. Her sister Norma played in the AAGPBL with her. During the off-season Barbara worked in a factory to earn money to attend the University of Illinois, where she earned a BS and a master's degree. She worked as a physical education teacher and camp counselor for many years after her baseball career ended. Her main physical activity continued to be badminton as a participant in the Chicago Badminton Club. {AAGPBL Questionnaire, National Baseball Hall of Fame and Museum.}

Berger (Knebl), Joan "Bergie"

(b. 9 October 1933, Passaic, New Jersey) RF/2B/SS/3B 1951–54, Rockford Peaches

While growing up, Joan did not have any chance to participate in school sports because there were no girls' teams. Her father started a girls' baseball team to play men's clubs in the area. When she joined the league in 1951 Berger joined one of the top teams, and they made the playoffs during three of her four seasons. In 1952 Joan made the all-star team at second base. After the league folded in 1954 she played four more seasons with the Allington All-American traveling team. She enjoyed the touring and the chance to continue to play baseball. She stopped playing when she got married in 1959, and she and her husband Andrew raised three boys. She worked for Feraro Chocolates as a supervisor. In recognition of her accomplishments Joan was elected to the Lodi Hall of Fame in 1993 and the Garfield Hall of Fame in 1996. {AAGPBL Questionnaire, National Baseball Hall of Fame and Museum; AAGPBL Newsletter, May 2005, 24.}

Berger, Margaret "Sunny"

(b. 24 December 1922, Homestead, Florida) P 1943–44, South Bend Blue Sox

Nicknamed Sunny, Berger played two full seasons in the AAGPBL. She pitched in a total of 88 games, winning 46 and losing only 30 for a .605 winning percentage. In those same 88 games Berger only hit .153 with 18 RBIs but only had six strikeouts in 222 at-bats. {AAGPBL Baseball Cards, 1996.}

Berger (Taylor), Norma "Bergie"

(b. 22 December 1932, Maywood, Illinois; d. September 2004) P 1950, Springfield Sallies

Norma played in the league with her sister Barbara. She spent a year traveling with the Sallies, pitching in 18 games with an 8–8 record. {AAGPBL Baseball Cards, 1995.}

Bergeson, Dawn

RHP Cactus Wrens, 1996 Colorado Silver Bullets

In 1994 Bergeson pitched for the Cactus Wrens and compiled a 12–0 record with 1 save and a 1.11 ERA in 76 innings pitched. Bergeson came to camp as a rookie in 1996 for the Bullets. She played in 30 games and hit .665 with five home runs. She also struck out 289 batters. {Silver Bulletin, March 1996.}

Bergmann, Erma M. "Bergie"

(b. 18 June 1924, St. Louis, Missouri) P/OF 1946–51, Muskegon Lassies, Springfield Sallies, Racine Belles, Battle Creek Belles

By Joan M. Thomas

A member of the AAGPBL from 1946 through 1951, pitcher Erma Bergmann tallied an impressive 2.56 ERA during those years. Throwing sidearm, she began her professional career with the Muskegon Lassies in 1946 and went to the Springfield Sallies in 1948. After playing for the Racine Belles in 1949 and 1950, she completed her last year in the AAGPBL with the Battle Creek Belles in 1951. Her career highlights include hurling a no-hitter against Grand Rapids on 22 May 1947, and helping Muskegon win the pennant that same year.

Born in St. Louis, Missouri, on 18 June 1924, Bergmann grew up in the city's then-working-class Soulard neighborhood. She lived with her parents, Otto and Sophie Bergmann, and her two younger brothers. A German immigrant from a small town near Nuremberg, Otto made a living as a packing house butcher. Erma attended

Erma Bergmann standing in front of the St. Louis County Library during the week of her seventy-ninth birthday (Joan Thomas).

Lafayette Grammar School and earned her high school diploma at McKinley High School, graduating in January of 1942. She then learned secretarial skills, attending the Midland Institute of Commerce in St. Louis for one year.

Bergmann always enjoyed the outdoors. Though her parents knew little about baseball, she learned by playing sandlot games with her brothers and other neighborhood kids. As a teenager, she started playing third base in St. Louis' Amateur Softball League since other opportunities at school were limited. She continued for eight years, playing at the St. Louis Softball Park, now known as Fox Park. She then joined the pro ranks, signing with the AAGPBL in 1945, where she was converted to a pitcher. The following years of professional baseball provided her with some of the happiest memories of her life.

Reflecting on those times while in her twilight years, Erma recounts little about the unpleasant aspects of playing with the AAGBPL. The scrapes and bruises, the strict rules and the long bus

Erma Bergmann at a vintage baseball game in June 2003. The game was held at Lafayette Park in St. Louis (Joan Thomas).

remains grateful and humble. A proponent of a strong work ethic, she said in a personal interview that a person is born with talent, but needs to develop the skill. About pitching, she advocates teamwork, saying, "You are only as good as your backup ... nobody's an island."

Following her years with the AAGPBL, Bergmann spent three years with another girls' league, the Chicago Professional Baseball League. In 1952 she played with the Chicago Bluebirds, and from 1953 through 1954 she played with the South Side Queens. Finally retiring from baseball in 1955, she then returned to St. Louis. There she took a Civil Service test and landed a job as a clerk in the city assessor's office. Still seeking a career, she noticed the police station near her place of employment. Realizing that she had the basic requirements for the job, she joined the St. Louis Police Department in 1956.

A single woman in her early thirties needing a reliable means of support, Bergmann then began a career that would last 25 years. She was among the first women to become commissioned police officers in St. Louis. She excelled at the academy and qualified as expert on the pistol range. Her strong ability to focus helped her to pitch professionally and contributed to her fine marksmanship. It also helped her to function calmly under the pressures of police work. Starting out in the juvenile department downtown, she later worked in various other positions, including the decoy squad. In the late '50s, she appeared on a local TV show assisting her sergeant in a judo exhibition.

In addition to her physical prowess and self-discipline, an even temperament and the ability to take orders allowed her to stay on the force until her retirement in 1981. In spite of the fact that a policeman has to take a lot of verbal abuse, she says that she never allowed herself to retaliate. When asked if the men on the force resented women being admitted, she downplays that aspect, admitting that they were somewhat resentful at first. Including herself when describing the first women police officers, she says, "We were trailblazers."

Now that she's retired from both baseball and police work, Bergmann enjoys a variety of leisure pastimes, including bowling, cooking, gambling and reading — especially the sports pages. As a St. Louis native, she naturally follows the hometown Cardinals. Although she does not admit to having a favorite player, when asked during the 2003 season, she mentioned Albert Pujols' name with verve. Her ardor for the outdoors is as intense as ever, as now her favorite pastime is taking long walks. Still close to her family, she shares a home with her brother and keeps in touch with her niece

rides were minor inconveniences to her. But her eyes always light up when she relates one of her proudest moments: when in 1946 her parents and brothers came to see her pitch in Peoria. With the game tied in the top of the ninth, she drove in the winning run with her only career home run, assuring her victory as the pitcher and her team's 2–1 win. Naturally, she also beams when telling about her 1947 no-hitter against Grand Rapids.

In addition to the fact that she loved playing baseball, Bergmann appreciated the accompanying sidelights. In several interviews, including one with reporter Kathleen Nelson that appeared in the 21 June 2003 *St. Louis Post-Dispatch*, she recalls how one year it was an honor to go to Cuba for spring training at the same time as the major league Dodgers. She notes other benefits of professional baseball, such as getting to compete with some of the nation's best players, and getting to travel and get an education, all the while getting paid for doing something she loved to do. While discussing her professional baseball career, she and two nephews. She also anxiously anticipates the reunions of her former AAGPBL teammates.

Since the media brought the history of the AAGPBL to the attention of modern baseball fans, Bergmann is often honored by groups such as the St. Louis Cardinals. In 2003, she threw out the first pitch at a St. Louis Perfectos Vintage Base Ball game. In 1996, she was inducted into the St. Louis Softball Hall of Fame. When she spoke at a SABR (Society for American Baseball Research) meeting, she told a favorite story that always gets a laugh: after her parents saw her play in Peoria, she asked her mom (who knew practically nothing about the sport) what she thought of the game. Her mother responded, "Well, it looks like you stand out there and throw a while, and the other team swings. Then, they throw a while, and you swing." Sounds pretty simple, but basically, that's baseball. {Erma Bergmann, interview with Joan M. Thomas, 2003.}

Berthiaume (Wicken), Elizabeth "Betty"

(b. 26 May 1927, Regina, Saskatchewan) 1945–46, Grand Rapids Chicks, Muskegon Lassies

Betty Wicken moved south to try out for the All American League in 1945 and was sent to Grand Rapids. During her first season her fiancé came home from the navy on leave and they got married. She played one more year before returning home and taking up golf to stay active. While in the league she developed a reputation as a stellar defensive outfielder who only made seven errors. She played in 117 games, hitting .182 with 17 extra-base hits. {AAGPBL Baseball Cards, 1995.}

Beschorner (Michaelson, Baskovich), Mary Lou "Bush"

(b. 18 September 1929, Sandwich, Illinois) CF/RF 1949–50, Grand Rapids Chicks, Peoria Red Wings

While attending Plano High School, Mary Lou Beschorner never had a chance to play school sports because there were none for women. Her school involvement consisted of membership in the National Honor Society. She did play softball for one year for the Dekalb Hybrid club, and they won a local championship. She spent two years in the All American League patrolling the outfield for the Chicks and Red Wings. She played in 85 games, hitting .156 with 14 RBIs. After her playing time ended she worked in a local factory and as a grocery clerk for over 30 years in Plano, Illinois. She kept active as an amateur golfer, winning a number of local competitions. {AAGPBL Questionnaire, National Baseball Hall of Fame and Museum; AAGPBL Baseball Cards, 1995.}

Bestudik (Rudis), Mary

Chaperone, 1949

Mary Bestudik worked for one season as a team chaperone in the All American League, helping to teach the girls manners, dress, responsibility and other things necessary to promoting a proper feminine image.

Bettencourt, Debbie "Deb"

Pawtucket Slaterettes

Deb Bettencourt started playing for the Pawtucket Slaterettes in 1981. She joined the league's board in 1989. She has traveled all over as a player and as a spokesperson for women's baseball. Bettencourt has also coached in the boy's program for the U.S. Scholar Athlete and is one of the founders of the Rhode Island Women's Baseball League. In 2003–04 she became the general manager of the new league.

Bevis, Muriel "Breezy"

(b. 7 October 1928, Corona, New York) P/OF 1950, Kenosha Comets

Growing up in West Hampton Beach, New York, Muriel "Breezy" Bevis often found herself playing softball at Cedarhurst Stadium. It was during one of those many games that a scout for the AAGPBL saw her play and recruited her for the Kenosha club in 1950. Bevis was offered a contract for $400 for the season and she took it. She then went on to play professional softball and tried her hand at golf, but an automobile accident cut short that effort. She also competed in the Senior Olympics on a number of occasions. {AAGPBL Newsletter, January 2001, 19; AAGPBL Baseball Cards, 2000.}

Bilby, Danielle

(b. 8 June 1980, New South Wales) IF 2001–03, New South Wales

Danielle Bilby played on the 2001 and 2002 National Women's teams. During the 2001 tournament Bilby hit .438 to lead her team. She had seven hits, of which three were doubles and two were sacrifice flies. She led all runners in the series with nine stolen bases in nine attempts. In the 2003 Women's World Series she hit .267 in the five games she started. She stole two bases in two attempts, walked four times and only struck out once. {Australian Baseball Federation, <www. baseball.org.au>.}

Binet, Louise "Lou"

(b. 16 February 1979) P/3B 2003, New South Wales

Louise Binet played in the Australian National Tournament in 2003.

Binks, Emma

(b. 10 December 1972) P/3B 2002–05, Lady Mariners, Australian National Team

At the 1999 International Friendship Series, Emma Binks hit .125 with two RBIs and one walk. During the 2003 Women's World Series, Binks hit .250 for her club. She played in two games, though she only started one of them. She helped her team in the gold medal game as the designated hitter. Binks played for Victoria in the 2004 National Women's Championship, which her club won 12–1 over New South Wales. As a result she also got named to the Victoria team in 2005. When she is not playing baseball Binks enjoys cooking and gardening. {Andrew Johnstone, "Favourites Tag Is No Obstacle," *Progress Leader*, 14 January 2003, 42; "Binks, Stokes on Vic Women's Side," *Caulfield Glen Eira Leader*, 28 February 2005, 50.}

Birchmount

The Birchmount Peewee club won the 2003 Ontario Peewee Championship tournament for the Central Ontario Girls Baseball League. The Peewee division is for ages 11–13 and is one of three that exists in the league. There are 12 teams altogether in the three divisions.

Bird (Phillips), Nalda

(b. 11 February 1927, Los Angeles, California) P/OF 1945, South Bend Blue Sox

Nalda Bird started playing baseball when she was only ten. She found herself in the All American League for only one year before she got married. She pitched in 31 games and compiled a record of 13–17 with an ERA of 2.70. {AAGPBL Baseball Cards, 1995.}

Bittner, Jayne "J.B."

(b. 17 March 1926, Lebanon, Pennsylvania) P 1948–54, Grand Rapids Chicks, South Bend Blue Sox, Muskegon Lassies, Fort Wayne Daisies

Though J.B. pitched four and a half seasons for the Grand Rapids nine, she also pitched one season with Muskegon and one and a half with Fort Wayne. In 169 games Bittner pitched almost 1,100 innings and was just under .500 with a 65–67 win-loss record. She helped her team get into the championship series in both 1952 and 1953. In recognition of her achievements she was inducted into the Pennsylvania Sports Hall of Fame. {Midwest League All Star Game program, 1999; AAGPBL Baseball Cards, 1996.}

Bjorklund, Chelsea

IF 2004, San Francisco Fillies

Chelsea Bjorklund played one season in the California league with the San Francisco Fillies.

Black, Ella

Sportswriter

Ella Black was a sportswriter during the nineteenth century who wrote for a number of Pittsburgh papers. *The Sporting Life* reported that she was the first lady to join the baseball writers and that she had displayed a thorough knowledge of the game. {*The Sporting Life*, 14 February 1890.}

Black Hawks

The 2002 season was the Black Hawks' first in the Sydney Women's Baseball League. By 2003 they made it to the league semifinals before losing to the Stealers. They ended in second place with an 8–3 record. The team they fielded in 2004 included a number of returning veterans and three rookies. The club operates under the direction of Janenne Vickery. {Sydney Women's Baseball League Annual Report 2003, 11, 17; SWBL Annual Report 2004.}

Blair, Maybelle

(b. 16 January 1927, Redondo Beach, California) P 1948, Peoria Red Wings

While in high school Maybelle Blair played every sport her school had for female athletes. She served as president of the Girls' Athletic Association and won the Best Athlete Award from Leuzinger High School. Before joining the

AAGPBL, Blair played professional softball in a league in Chicago for the Chicago Cardinals. After her time in the AAGPBL she continued to play softball for the New Orleans Jax. In addition to playing softball Maybelle worked for Northrop A/C as the manager of highway transportation. For many years, she was one of the few female managers the company employed. {AAGPBL Questionnaire, National Baseball Hall of Fame and Museum.}

Bleiler (Thomas, Seitzinger), Audrey

(b. 12 January 1923, Philadelphia, Pennsylvania; d. 20 June 1975) 3B/SS 1950–52, South Bend Blue Sox

Audrey Bleiler stood at 5'7" tall, and that gave her an advantage playing at the hot corner for most of her three seasons in South Bend. She did not wield a heavy bat but played because of her strong fielding. In 103 games she only hit .180. She did participate in a rare event during a game in 1950 when South Bend defeated Muskegon 14–6. She caught a line drive off the bat of one of the Lassies and threw to Baker at second to get the runner there; then the throw went to third to complete the triple play. {AAGPBL Baseball Cards, 1996; Ohio Baseball Hall of Fame newspaper collection.}

Blois, Annaliese

As a catcher for the Dominion Bantam Girls Hawks in 2003, Blois continued her sporting excellence. Blois learned a lot of her baseball skills at a camp in Japan in 1999. She also won a silver medal for softball at the Eastern Canadian Championships in 2002. Blois' athletic prowess also gained for her two provincial championships in hockey.

Blondes and Brunettes

In 1875 the *New York Clipper* announced the formation of two female teams called the Blondes and the Brunettes. The teams were formed in Springfield, Illinois, by Frank Myers, S.B. Brock and Thomas Halligan. Their motivation was solely to make a profit from this novelty. The rosters of the two teams were listed as follows:

Blondes	*Brunettes*
Estella Brown — C	Maude Levy — C
Jenny Wyman — P	Mollie Broden — P
Nettie Glidden — 1B	Ella Burgan — 1B
Eva Sheppard — 2B	Lotta Clark — 2B

Blondes	*Brunettes*
Lizzie Sheppard — 3B	Annie Wilson — 3B
Lydia Lambert — SS	Molly Young — SS
Mollie Foster — LF	Josie Spencer — LF
Kate Tinley — CF	Lou Chafer — CF
Emma Staeckling — RF	Georgie Avery — RF
	Carrie Renfro — Sub
	Amy Bell — Sub

Their first game took place on 11 September 1875 on a field specially set up for a women's game. The bats and ball were lighter and the bases were only 50 feet apart rather than 90 feet. The report indicated the Blondes were victorious but no score was given. This appears to be one of the few games that the *New York Clipper* gave coverage to for the Blondes and Brunettes in 1875. A second contest was reported on September 25. The Brunettes won the game by a score of 41–21. Another group of ladies using the same names appeared in Manayunk, Pennsylvania, in April 1884 to play one another, but again no account of the game followed the original announcement. Another announcement appeared for a game on May 17 but the team did not show up and no reason was given for the failure. {*NY Clipper*, 12 April and 17 May 1884.}

In 1879 the *Washington Post* reported a game between two local groups of ladies playing on an open field at 59th and Madison Avenue. Both groups had been practicing for a number of weeks in preparation for the game but there were still a lot of muffs and poor base running reported. The uniforms were highlighted by red and blue stockings and matching jockey caps. The Blondes defeated the Brunettes by a score of 45–31. The organizer of the event claimed this was to be the beginning of regular sporting events for ladies so that they could develop their physical constitutions. He also told the reporter from the *Journal* that this was just the beginning of new opportunities for women in baseball and other sports as well. {"Feminine Base Ball," *Albany Journal*, 12 May 1879.}

Brunettes	*Blondes*
Laura Gray — C	Lillie Richmond — C
Millie Melville — 1B	Jennie Melville — 1B
Gracie Clinton — 2B	Annie Adams — 2B
Georgie Lostbaum — 3B	Lou Shepherd — 3B
Lottie Drake — SS	Mary Adams — SS
Maude Tremaine — CF	Gipsey Melville — CF
Minnie Mollenhauer — RF	Josie Arnold — RF
Sadie Howell — LF	Tessa Banguers — LF
	Alice Lingard — P

{"Red and Blue Legs," Washington Post, *12 May 1879, 1*; Chicago Times, *12 July 1879, 3.*}

The *New York Times* ran an account of a game between two teams at the Manhattan Athletic Club in 1883. About 1,500 fans came out to watch the Blondes and Brunettes compete. The Brunettes wore red uniforms while the Blondes had blue dresses. Pitching for the Brunettes was a Miss P. Darlington, who surrendered three runs in the first inning. Her team came roaring back with 15 runs in their half of the first inning. The final score was reported at 54–22 after five innings, with the Brunettes the winners. {*New York Clipper*, 18 and 25 September 1875; 12 April 1884; *New York Times*, 23 September 1883.}

The *New York Clipper* continued to have periodic articles about various blonde and brunette clubs in 1883 and 1884. It seemed that most of the teams came from the Philadelphia or Baltimore area, though they traveled extensively, playing opponents in places such as New Orleans; Easton, Pennsylvania; and Omaha, Nebraska. {*New York Clipper*, 22 and 29 September 1883; 8 and 29 December 1883; 12 April 1884; 17 May 1884; 12 July 1884; 25 October 1885 and 1 November 1884.}

In 1884 a group of blondes and brunettes from Philadelphia arrived in Baltimore, Maryland, to play at Oriole Park. Emile Gargh arranged this game for the ladies and a second at Monument Park, but he disappeared before the ladies got paid and so they had to appeal to the mayor for help to get home. The club consisted of Nina Sherman, Tillie Baseman, Ida Dickson, Susie Lincoln, Eva Ellis, Nina Temple, Daisy Muir, Sadie Rich, Maggie Wagner, Annie Temple and Amy Hall. {12 July 1884, *New York Clipper*.}

Bloomer Girls

Developed in the late nineteenth century, bloomer girl teams gave women the chance to play the game of baseball. While baseball at the time was primarily a man's sport, there were a number of colleges that hosted women's teams, such as Vassar and Smith. For others the only option became the bloomer teams. Many of these early squads had two or three men on the team, often the pitcher, the catcher and the shortstop, since these were considered essential positions and required the most skilled athletes. The significance of these teams is that they allowed women to participate in a man's sport and world. This was happening at a time when the general feeling was that women were physically inferior and had no business out in the public world. Their realm focused on home and hearth. Women's baseball seemed to be either a curiosity or allowed when mixed audiences were not present.

Bloomer girl teams appeared across the country. The name was used in Chicago and New York and all points in between. The origin of the name is tied to suffragette Adelaide Jenks Bloomer and not the pants that bore that name, though some teams did wear the bloomer style pants. These

1918 New York Bloomer Girls (National Baseball Hall of Fame Library, Cooperstown, NY).

A wire-service photograph of Amy Hill, a bloomer girl from Brooklyn, New York, in the 1920s or early 1930s. She is identified as a member of the Bedford Community Center Beauty Club.

with Maud. Local papers reported the team playing in Mansfield, Ohio, in 1901 with Nelson still pitching for them. By 1907 when the club played in Nashua, Nelson was no longer listed but the squad still carried six ladies and three men. Claud East was listed as the manager by 1914 and the team was traveling through Georgia. One of the new stars was Selma Welbaum, their first baseman. She appeared to have a strong bat and solid fielding. They played a series of games against the Atlanta Federals, splitting the contests. According to the roster reported in the paper at that time, the team seems to have been all women. The roster included Ethel Maloney (c), Margaret Camingham and Hattie Crowe (P), Selma Welbaum (1B), Hattie Murphy (2B), Elizabeth Pearl (3B), and May Arbaugh, Mary Diern and Mildred Dodge as outfielders.

The Chicago Bloomer Girls received coverage in Cincinnati, New York, Boston and Chicago as they traveled the country. In 1905 their manager announced the team would be taking a two-year world tour, with destinations including Australia and Cuba. Whether they did or not is unclear because no accounts of these games have been uncovered.

A Western bloomer girl team came to Harrisburg, Pennsylvania, in 1913 to play a local men's team, the Brandons. Victory belonged to the men with a 10–4 final score but the highlight of the game for the fans was the pitching of a Miss Kate Becker. The reporter covering the game called her "the greatest female pitcher in the world." {"A Shut Out," *Delphos Herald*, 3 September 1900; "The Bloomer Girls Play at Baseball," *Mansfield News*, 12 July 1901; "Bloomer Girls Play Feds Today," *The Constitution* (Georgia), 2 May 1914, 10; "Atlanta Federals Down Bloomer Girls," 3 May 1914, 11A; "Nashua 16-Bloomer Girls 1," *Nashua Reporter* (IA), 8 August 1907; "Kate Becker, Woman Pitcher, Had Drop That Fooled Local Players," *Williamsport Sun*, 27 May 1913.}

In 1919 the Bosworth Bag Company of Memphis, Tennessee, sponsored a bloomer team with 12 ladies on the squad. They wore white blouses with dark bloomers and stockings. The name Bosworth was stitched on the front of the blouses. The company seems to have advertised the team with postcards.

Many of these teams sported the names "Blondes" and "Brunettes" in different cities. The only way to tell the teams apart was by the color of their skirts and stockings; most commonly they were blue and red. Instead of playing men's teams as many bloomer clubs did, these contests were usually set up with the Blondes and Brunettes playing each other for fun or sometimes for charity.

teams played all comers as they barnstormed across the United States. Their opponent one night might be an amateur club, while the next it might be a semipro squad. This was the reason many promoters brought in a few men to play with the ladies. The games were more competitive when the team had a topper or two. "Topper" was the title attached to male players who wore curly wigs atop their own hair.

Some of the best known teams played throughout the 1880s and the early twentieth century. *The Boston Herald* carried an account of a 1903 game that starred Maud Nelson. Nelson became one of the most famous of the female players, renowned for her hitting, fielding and pitching.

Nelson's name can be found in 1900, pitching for a bloomer girls team as they played in Ottawa and Cloverdale, followed by stops in Napoleon and Delphos. There were three men on that club and a Miss Lindsey who shared pitching chores

These early teams helped lay the foundation for the later development of the All-American Girls Professional Baseball League (AAGPBL). The AAGPBL of the 1940s and 1950s gave women role models and ideas about what was possible. Though none of these ventures continued permanently, the bloomer girls showed that it was possible for women to play baseball, a men's sport, and to play it well. {*Chicago Tribune*, 18 May 1877; *Sporting News*, 20 September 1890.}

Blue Stockings/Red Stockings

Much like the blondes and brunettes, the use of "Blue Stockings" and "Red Stockings" team names was popular in the nineteenth century. Many clubs going by these names appeared in different cities, making it difficult to track all the teams playing. Often articles gave no player names to help with identification, and sometimes not even a city. For example, there was a San Francisco club known as the Blue Stockings who played the Red Stockings of Chicago in 1886 while a Philadelphia Red Stockings club got stuck in Chicago in 1883 and another Red Stockings team appeared in 1884 without attribution. It could have been one of the above mentioned clubs or an entirely separate team. A Delaware set of Reds and Blues played together in 1910 while they were guests at the Glenwood Hotel, but nothing more is known about them except the Blues won one contest 16–5. The team names were simply chosen based on the color of stockings the players wore with their uniforms or the ribbons they attached to their bonnets. {"Women's Baseball Teams Play a Closely Contested Game," *New York Times*, 21 August 1910, C11.}

The Chicago Times reported a game in 1879 between two clubs known simply as the Reds and Blues. The Reds came from New York while the Blues were from Philadelphia. The uniforms for both clubs were loose dresses with lots of buttons and covering the girls' knees. The trim was either red or blue as was the trim on the jackets worn over the dresses. The stockings were red or blue, and each girl wore a jockey cap. Lottie Drake captained the Philadelphia nine, who defeated the Reds 50–34. The rosters given in the report for the two clubs were as follows (no positions were given):

Reds	Blues
Laura Gray	Lottie Drake — captain
Minnie Neville	Jenny Meyerberry
Retta Howard	Josie Howard

Reds	Blues
Eva Clifford	Alice Lingard
Tillie Sheldon	May Carter
Georgie Lostbaum	
Georgie Bell	
Josie Arnold	
Minnie Stacey	
{Chicago Times, 12 July 1879, 3.}	

The Rochester paper talked about a contest in 1879 at Hop Bitter's field where the Reds and Blues played before a decent crowd of about 1,000. The reporter was not all that favorably impressed with the style of play; he referred to one player as the "dizzy little blonde" with a "womanly throw." The Reds triumphed in the end by a score of 23–10. {"Feminine Field Fun," *Rochester Democrat and Chronicle*, 13 August 1879, 4.}

In 1883 the *New York Clipper* reported on a game involving teams from Philadelphia who came to town to play at the Manhattan Athletic Club. The Blues won the five-inning game by a score of 45–20. Over 100 errors were reported for the contest, which is why the fans got bored and became a bit abusive toward the female contestants. Later in the year the teams got stuck in Chicago after an indoor game did not bring in enough receipts to pay their way back to Philadelphia. {29 December 1883, *New York Clipper*.}

One of the things that began to help the traveling teams was the development of baseball nines at some of the country's colleges. This gave some women the chance to be introduced to the game and also gave the game a bit more legitimacy for women. For example, in 1897 the University of Chicago decided to add baseball to its list of activities for young ladies. The teams would be organized and trained by Amos Alonzo Stagg. {*New York Clipper*, 29 December 1883, 12 July 1884, and 20 February 1886; "Girls at Base-ball," *New York Times*, 19 August 1883, 2; "Girls Play Base Ball," *Brooklyn Daily Eagle*, 4 January 1897, 12.}

Blum, Jennifer

Scranton Diamonds

Jennifer Blum played Little League ball while growing up in Oakland, California. As was typical of many young girls she then switched to softball at Indian Hills High School until her graduation in 1992. She played four years at Ithaca College. She intended to try out for the Colorado Silver Bullets but heard about a league in Pennsylvania called the U.S. Women's Baseball League. She attended a tryout and made the roster of the Scranton Diamonds. The league had four teams, and it was run by Sal Algieri. {Joe Chessari, "Oakland Woman Ready to Play Hardball," *The Record* (Bergen County, N.J.), 8 August 1996.}

Blumetta, Catherine Kay "Swish"

(b. 1 May 1923, North Plainfield, New Jersey) P/1B/OF 1944–54, Minneapolis Millerettes, Milwaukee Chicks, Grand Rapids Chicks, Peoria Red Wings, Fort Wayne Daisies, Kalamazoo Lassies

Kay Blumetta played for six different clubs in the AAGPBL during a successful ten-year career. She received a great deal of encouragement to play from her mother but not her father.

Bohle, Mabel

1B

Mabel Bohle started playing baseball at age seven and eventually joined a number of women's traveling teams, primarily playing first base. She even played in a game for the Cooke's Colts when they needed a first baseman. Her teammates had never played with a woman before but were pleasantly surprised as she handled 14 chances in the field flawlessly and scored their first run in an 8–5 victory. In addition to playing baseball, Miss Bohle was a local celebrity at the ice rinks, winning all kinds of medals. {"Girl Baseball Player Who Saved Day for Cooke's Colts Team," *Chicago Tribune*, 20 April 1915, 10.}

Bolden-Shorter, Hilda

(b. 31 July 1904, Darby Pennsylvania; d. March 1986 Cambridge, Maryland)

By Bijan Bayne

Hilda Bolden was the only child of Ed and Nellie Bolden. She was born in Darby, Pennsylvania. One of her early loves was playing the piano, which her mother taught her. She graduated from Darby High School as valedictorian and then attended the University of Pennsylvania. After graduation she went on to Meharry Medical College and the University of Chicago. She became a pediatrician and worked her residency at Chicago Provident Hospital. She also worked for the International Health Office and went to Liberia as part of a medical mission in 1946. She received a gold medal for her service when she returned to the United States in 1947. She never gave up the piano, and while in West Africa she gave a benefit concert to help raise money for building a school.

When her father Ed died he left her his ballclub, the Philadelphia Stars. She kept control of the club from 1950–52 with manager Oscar Charleston running the day-to-day operations. Eddie Gottlieb tried to buy the ball club from her in 1951 and eventually did. In addition to her baseball duties and her medical practice, Bolden belonged to the NAACP and a number of societies related to the sciences and medicine. {Bolden Papers; *Philadelphia Tribune*, 16 January 1951.}

Bonilla, Geena Marie

WBL Sparks

In 2004 Geena Bonilla got the chance to play baseball at the World Children's Baseball Fair, one of five girls chosen from the United States. In 2005 Bonilla, from San Francisco, was chosen to play for the Sparks at the Cooperstown tournament for those 12 and under. The Sparks are the only girls' team to play in the tournament, and 2005 will be their third year in attendance.

Borchert, Idabell

Owner

Idabell Borchert took over the ownership of the Milwaukee team in the American Association after the death of her husband Otto. Mr. Borchert died at a banquet being held in his honor. His wife decided she would maintain control of the ball club. She indicated she planned on making no significant changes in the way the ball club was run but would listen to the advice and counsel of attorney Henry J. Killilea, a good friend of her husband's. {"Woman to Take Over Ball Club," *Los Angeles Times*, 3 May 1927, B1.}

Borders, Ila

(b. 18 February 1976, Downey, California) LHP

Ila Borders began playing softball and baseball at an early age. She started at age seven with Little Miss Softball in La Mirada, California. By the following year she was playing for an all-star traveling squad and then by age ten was pitching for the Minor A Little League. Her first full season of Little League came at age 11 when she also hit her first home run. Upon entering junior high school Borders, with her parents' support, decided to attend Whittier Christian Junior High in order to be able to play baseball and continue in the junior division of Little League. By her second year in junior high Borders was also playing for a semipro men's team though she was only 15. After junior high Borders went on to attend Whittier Christian

High School, though it was not connected to the junior high school. Her father had interviewed the local school coaches to see who would give his daughter a fair chance to play. At Whittier Borders pitched her way to being named the Most Valuable Player and an all-league selection in her senior year. She finished her four years with a 2.31 ERA in 147 innings and a 16–7 record. The decision for college followed the same process as high school: determining where she could play that she was wanted and not let on the team because someone ordered them to play her. She started at Southern California College under manager Charlie Phillips and got her first victory on 15 February 1994, beating Claremont-Mudd 12–1 on a five-hitter. Borders retired the first ten batters she faced and carried a shutout into the eighth inning. She gave up a home run to Gabe Rosenthal for the only score. She also struck out two batters, the first being Jake Schwartz. Southern California competed at the NAIA Division I for college sports. When Phillips left, Borders' playing time was cut and she transferred to Whittier College. At Whittier Borders pitched in 81 innings with a 4–5 record and a 5.22 ERA.

Following college Borders signed in 1997 with the St. Paul Saints before being traded just a few weeks into the season to the Duluth Superior Dukes, where she remained through 1999. Manager George Mitterwald used her mainly in relief appearances. In 1999 she was traded in June to the Madison Black Wolf squad under manager Al "Dirty" Gallagher. There she pitched 32.1 innings with a 1.67 ERA. Borders relied on a decent fastball, a strong curve and an occasional screwball. Her final pitching days were spent with the Zion Pioneerzz in Western baseball's Southern Division. She pitched in only five games for 8⅔ innings with a 9.35 ERA before calling it quits. After retiring from active playing, Borders hoped to put to use her kinesiology degree. {Ila Borders Web site; "Borders Makes History," *Press-Enterprise*, 16 February 1994; Rick Lawes, "First Female College Pitcher Has Major Goal," *USA Today Baseball Weekly*, 23 February–1 March 1994, 13; Samantha Stevenson, "Sister Strikeout Does the Job Well," *New York Times*, 23 February 1994, B10.}

Borg (Alpin), Lorraine Madeline "Borge"

(b. 18 July 1923, Minneapolis, Minnesota) C 1944, Minneapolis Millerettes

Lorraine Borg attended West High School in Minneapolis and played sports in the local city league since the school had none for female athletes. Her favorite sports were basketball, softball and bowling. After a short stint in the AAGPBL as a second string catcher, Borg managed a restaurant and raised five children. She played in 23 games, hitting .133 but making only ten errors behind the plate. {AAGPBL Questionnaire, National Baseball Hall of Fame and Museum; AAGPBL Baseball Cards, 1995.}

Born, Ruth L.

(b. 8 August 1925, Bay City Michigan) P 1943, South Bend Blue Sox

At an early age Ruth Born fell in love with sports and started playing softball on the local sandlots. By age 12 she was playing for her school and the following season she joined a Moose Lodge club. She continued to play softball and basketball at Bay City Central until her graduation in 1943. She wrote and was invited for a tryout, after which she was assigned to South Bend in 1943. She pitched in 11 games before giving it up and deciding she wanted to go to college. Born got her bachelor's degree from Valparaiso University and her master's from Loyola University. She worked in the child welfare department for the federal government for 23 years after graduation. She remained active, taking up golf as her new sport. {AAGPBL Newsletter, May 2001, 40; AAGPBL Questionnaire, National Baseball Hall of Fame and Museum.}

Boston Blitz

Coached by Paul Harrington and Dick Dahl, the Blitz were one of the original teams of the WNEBL. One thing both coaches learned early on was that most of the women had limited baseball experience, if any. Most of the players were fast-pitch softball players who had good hands and instincts but little power. There seemed to be an abundance of infielders but not many true outfielders and even fewer catchers. One catcher for the Blitz was Katia Pashkevitch from Russia, one of the best female hockey players anywhere. She was the head coach of the women's team at MIT. She decided to try baseball after watching it on television. Catching appealed to her because hockey is such a physical sport. She became the second-string catcher for the Blitz in 1999. Harrington brought to the job a wealth of coaching experience at the adult and youth levels, but had always worked with men's teams. His wife Naomi worked as the official statistician for all the

WNEBL teams. {Michael O'Connor "The Local Women Are ... Playing Hardball," *The Boston Herald*, 28 May 2000.}

Boston Bloomer Girls

As early as 1895 the Boston Bloomer Girls could be found traveling across the United States in their own railroad car. A Fresno paper reported a game in November 1897 between the Boston ladies and a local nine chosen by Ralph Thompson. The Boston club arrived with much fanfare, as a regimental band played for the crowd that gathered. Among the many spectators could be found Mayor Dennett and State Commissioner Dante Prince. The roster for the ladies included third baseman Julia Marlowe, pitcher Maud Nelson, pitcher Maud Dellacqua, second baseman Annie Jennings and Georgia Devere. In the news account of the game the ladies were praised for their fine teamwork and solid hitting, but the big weakness was their throwing. The Bloomer Girls won the contest 13–12, though it was reported that the umpire, Charley Burleigh, gave the ladies a number of breaks. Their next game was reported for the following day in Selma. {"Women Ball Twirlers," *The Fresno Weekly Republican*, 5 November 1897, 8; "Woman Pitcher Dies," *Reno Evening Gazette*, 16 February 1944, 12.}

Scheduled to play a game in Duluth, Minnesota, against the hometown team in 1895, the Bloomer Girls were disappointed when Mayor Lewis called off the game. He said that no girls in bloomers would play in his city on a Sunday. The news report indicated a large crowd came out to see the ladies play. In 1897 the Boston club found itself invited to play a local team in Nebraska called the Semi-weeklies. They were invited because of their stellar record and the hope that the novelty of seeing women play would draw a large crowd. The Boston team would be led by pitcher Maud Nelson and catcher Alice Hall. The outfield consisted of Carrie Ellis, Frankie Ormsdale and Ada LaBeau. The infielders were Georgia German, Laura Ellis, Emily Forester and Annie Jennings. In 1901 the Boston squad defeated a local Fort Smith, Arizona, women's club 2–1 in ten innings. Manager W.P. Needham brought the team on their own rail car from their game in Fayetteville, which they also won. The general manager for the team was a gentleman named S.S. Stout while P.A. Gilmore handled the secretarial duties. Gilmore took care of publicity for all games. He came up with fancy placards and posters with the girls' pictures on them, advertising the beauty of the young ladies. In 1901 the Boston club turned up in Arizona and helped arrange a series of games to raise money for the local hospitals. Fifteen cents' admission was charged, with the proceeds divided between two hospitals. Three teams were to be involved, the Boston ladies and two men's teams, the Leaps and the Fats. In 1904 the team turned up in a local account by a Wisconsin newspaper, losing to the Hartford club 7–6. The loss came as a result of a wild throwing error in the seventh inning. The Boston nine defeated a local Santa Barbara club 5–3 in 1909. {"The Semi-weeklies," *Nebraska State Journal*, 2 August 1897; "Another Baseball Game for Blood Next Saturday," *The Arizona Republican*, 31 July 1901; "Boston Bloomer Girls," *The Arizona Republican*, 27 July 1901; "Girls in Bloomers Can't Play Ball," *Chicago Tribune*, 22 September 1895, 1; "Amateur Baseball," *The Daily Northwestern*, 1 May 1904; "Girls Victorious," *Los Angeles Times*, 22 November 1909, I15; "Bloomer Ball Players," *The Arizona Republican*, 30 July 1901, 4; "Another Baseball Game for Blood Next Saturday," *The Arizona Republican*, 31 July 1901; "Ungallant Pastimes," *The Syracuse Herald*, 24 January 1908.}

Boston Blue Sox

The Boston Blue Sox were founded to give young ladies the opportunity to play baseball in and around the Boston area. The team belonged to the United States Women's Baseball organization. The Blue Sox developed after the New England Clippers disbanded following the 2000 season due to financial difficulties. The team was coached by Ron Scroczynski, who had previous experience with the Bay State Express in the New England league. He also coached Team USA at the 2001 and 2002 Women's World Series. His wife Deb pitched for the Blue Sox along with fellow World Series MVP Judy O'Brien. {Boston Blue Sox Web site.}

Boudreau, Bethanie

(b. 1979) Pawtucket Slaterettes

As early as age five Bethanie Boudreau wanted to play baseball. She had seen a picture in the paper of a girl playing with the Slaterettes. She played for 14 years in the various divisions before calling it quits after the 1997 season. While playing, Boudreau won two MVP awards. When her playing days ended Boudreau turned to coaching and took over one of the senior league teams. {Sumathi Reddy, "Girls League Celebrates 25 Years of Baseball," *Providence Journal*, 11 August 1998, C-01.}

Bowers, MaryAnne

2B

At age ten MaryAnne Bowers played for the Hawks Little League team. She played second base and was one of the best base runners on her squad. Her parents encouraged her to play, with her dad Jack being the one responsible for finding the umpires for the league in Lowell, Massachusetts. Her mom, Joan, encouraged Bowers to get out and play with her four brothers. {Nancy Tuttle, "Their Heart's in the Highlands," *Lowell Sun*, 30 May 2004.}

Boyce, Ethel "Boycie"

(b. Vancouver, British Columbia; d., n.d.) 1946, Kenosha Comets

After her year in the league Boyce returned to her work in the RCAF from 1954 to 1963. After that she went to work for the federal penitentiary system until her retirement in 1982. {AAGPBL Newsletter, January 1996, 21.}

Boyd, Michelle

Victoria Provincial Team

In the 2001 Australian National Tournament, Michelle Boyd hit .417 for her Victoria team.

Braatz-Cochran, Leah

3B 1998, Arizona Peppers

Leah Cochran played softball at the University of Arizona until her graduation in 1998. She helped her team win two national championships and one runner-up trophy. She was named an All-American in 1995, 1997 and 1998. After graduation she joined the Arizona Peppers in the Ladies Professional Baseball League. She was expected to help the club rebound from a 9–20 finish in 1997.

Braatz-Voisard, Kimberly Rae "Braatzy"

(b. 13 July 1969, Santa Ana, California) CF 1994–97, Colorado Silver Bullets; 2004, USA National Team

Kim Braatz graduated from Estancia High School in Santa Ana, California, where she played softball growing up. She continued her play at the University of New Mexico through her graduation in 1991. At New Mexico Braatz received second team All American honors in 1990. Braatz played for a professional softball team in Navaro, Italy, in 1993 and hit .466 for the season. Braatz was invited to try out for the inaugural Silver Bullets team in 1994, one of only 22 athletes chosen for the first tryout. Then the team held open tryouts across the country and over 1,100 women tried out. After making the team and starting in right field in 1994, Braatz hurt her back diving for a ball and was told she would never play again. After a lot of hard work and rehabilitation, Braatz returned and made the team again in 1995. She even had a 12-game hitting streak, batting .375 during those games. She played in 43 games for the Bullets in 1995. She hit the first home run for them in 1996 against the Cape Cod League All Stars. The team had a 23–22 record in 1997 against men's ball clubs. During that season she made a mark in the history books for another reason, inciting a bench-clearing brawl in a game on June 10. She had been beaned in the ribs in the ninth inning of a game they were losing, and after the pitcher laughed at her, she went after him. {Tony Jackson, "Role in Brawl Still Haunts Silver Bullets Outfielder," *Denver Rocky Mountain News*, 3 July 1997; "For the Love of the Game," Colorado Silver Bullets souvenir program, 1995, 31; David Kindred, *Colorado Silver Bullets: For the Love of the Game* (Atlanta: Longstreet Press, Inc., 1995), 62.}

During the 2004 World Series IV, Braatz-Voisard led the United States into the championship game versus Japan. Though Team USA came away with only the silver medal, Braatz-Voisard received the honor of being selected Best Offensive Player of the series. She hit .538 with six runs scored and six runs batted in. She also played every inning of all the games, hit third and patrolled right field. Kim helped Team USA win the gold medal at the 2004 women's World Cup event even though she only hit .167. Kim still drove in three runs and made no errors in the field. Kim and her husband Mark, who played baseball in the Colorado Rockies organization, have two children, Madison and Franklin. {<www.USABaseball.com>; USA Baseball 2004 Media Guide.}

Bradford, Katy

P, Baltimore Stars

Katy Bradford pitched for the Stars, a member of the Washington Metropolitan Women's Baseball League.

Brannon, Jody

2B, Virginia Boxers

When not manning second base for the Boxers, Jody Brannon is working on a Ph.D. at the University of Maryland.

Laura Brenneman
Infield

Chevy Chase, MD

Infielder Laura Brenneman for Team USA. Photographer John Lypian (courtesy Jim Glennie).

Brenneman, Laura

(Rockville, Maryland) SS, Virginia Boxers; Virginia Flames; 2002–03, Team America; 2004, USA National Team

Laura Brenneman attended Williams College from 1995 to 1999. She played soccer, basketball and softball, earning All-American honors as a soccer goalie. She also received all-league, all-New England honors in softball and all-league/NCAA tournament honors in basketball. At the end of 2002 Brenneman joined the DC Thunder to take part in an invitational tournament in Silver Spring, Maryland. She led all batters with a .633 average in the four games. Her season average was .556. Her regular team from 2001 to 2003 was the Virginia Boxers in the Eastern Women's Baseball Conference. She was the conference MVP from 2001 to 2003. In 2004 she joined the Virginia Flames as their shortstop. She hit .647 for the season. She also played for Team America in the second through fourth Women's World Series. In the 2004 series Brenneman hit .500 with four runs scored. She also led the team with four stolen bases in four attempts. Laura hit .500 in the 2004 women's World Cup as the United States won the gold medal. She stole four bases and knocked in one run to help her team. At the conclusion of the 2004 season Brenneman received major honors by being named the 2004 IBAF Woman Player of the Year and winning the 2004 World Cup MVP award. When not playing baseball Brenneman is working on her Ph.D. in astrophysics at the University of Maryland. {USA Baseball 2004 Media Guide.}

Briggs, Rita "Maude"

(b. 27 March 1929, Ayer, Massachusetts; d. 6 September 1994) C/OF 1947–54, Rockford Peaches, Chicago Colleens, South Bend Blue Sox, Peoria Red Wings, Battle Creek Belles, Fort Wayne Daisies

Rita Briggs played for seven seasons in the All American League and spent most of that time behind the plate because of her strong arm. She could also play the outfield and keep the runners from advancing. She made the all-star team in 1953 when she hit .231 in 80 games. She participated in eight double plays from behind the plate that same year. Her career numbers included 749 games, a .218 batting average and 274 runs scored. She worked for 26 years for Michigan Bell Telephone Co. before retiring. {AAGPBL Newsletter, September 1994, 5; AAGPBL Baseball Cards, 1996.}

Briggs, Wilma Hannah "Willie," "Briggsie"

(b. 6 November 1930, East Greenwich, R.I.) RF/LF/1B 1948–54, Fort Wayne Daisies, South Bend Blue Sox

While growing up, Wilma Briggs loved sports and would play any chance she got. There were 11 children in her family so there were always others to play with at home or at school. For example, in junior high school she played pickup baseball games during her lunch hour with the boys on the playground. While attending East Greenwich High School Briggs played basketball, was on the gymnastics team and, in her senior year, played on the boy's baseball team. She was captain of the basketball team and the gymnastics squad. She went on to Barrington College, earning an elementary education degree. She also played softball and basketball in college and was named MVP for the softball team. After school Briggs still found time to play in the East Greenwich Twilight Baseball League and on her father's baseball team, the Frenchtown Farmers.

Wilma Briggs was invited to tryouts for the AAGPBL and joined the Daisies in 1948. Most of her time was spent in the outfield, though she did play 14 games at first base in 1952 because the team needed her to fill in. There were many highlights to Briggs' career, including the nine home runs she hit in the 1953 season. Briggs hit the only home run at Playland Park during the 1949 season, in the ninth inning of a game to defeat the Blue Sox 5–0. It was her only hit in five at-bats. Another highlight was helping her team win the league championship in 1952. In 1954 she hit a grand slam home run while playing for South Bend, and her parents were there to see the game. In the field one of the best plays she made was when she robbed Connie Wisniewski of a home run in a playoff game. Her career numbers included an average of .258 in 691 games. She knocked in 301 runs on 633 hits and 43 home runs.

After her playing days were over Briggs kept active in a variety of sports but primarily softball and basketball, winning all kinds of awards and recognition. She coached and played in a slow-pitch league for over 35 years. In 1990 she became the first female inducted into the East Greenwich Athletic Hall of Fame and received the Game of Legends Award in 1991 for contributions to softball. In 2000 Briggs received the further honor of being inducted into the International Scholar-Athlete Hall of Fame. When not playing Briggs worked at the Colonial Knife Company and taught as an elementary school teacher for over 20 years. {AAGPBL files, OHBBHOF; AAGPBL Questionnaire, National Baseball Hall of Fame and Museum; Rick Harris, "Women, Baseball and Rhode Island," in *Rhode Island's Baseball Legacy*, *Vol. 1* (Rhode Island: Rick Harris, 2001), 26–27; Susan E. Johnson, 51–52, 41; Heinie Martin, "Connie May Be Pitching Her Last Year," *The Grand Rapids Herald*, 6 August 1946.}

Bright, Amy

Umpire

Amy Bright started umpiring boys' baseball games in 1994 to help pay for college at Bowling Green. Following her graduation from North Ridgeville High School in 1995, Bright began umpiring five days a week in the North Ridgeville city league program. She switched over to baseball because of a shortage of umpires. During her first season she just umpired the base paths but in 1995 began to also umpire behind the plate. While in school Bright played softball and was a cheerleader for basketball and football. In addition

to umpiring baseball games Bright also calls softball games because of her playing background. {Jerry Rombech, "She Calls Strikes in Ridgeville," *The Chronicle-Telegram*, 1 July 1995, B7.}

Britton, Dominisha Ariel "Nisha"

P, San Francisco Fillies, 2004, USA National Team

Dominisha Britton won all kinds of honors while playing basketball and softball in high school. She was selected as conference MVP in basketball and received the honor of being named *Fairfield Daily Republic* Female Athlete of the Year as a senior. She attended Morgan State University on a softball scholarship. From 1999 to 2001 she participated on the AAU Women's National Championship team in softball. She also earned first team all-county, all-City and all-league honors in basketball. She was named female athlete of the year and conference MVP. In 2004 she attended tryouts and was selected to play for the USA National Team. She came out of the Women's World Series with a 2.74 ERA and six strikeouts in just over 12 innings of pitching. She pitched twice against Canada and Taiwan and once against the team from Japan. She also pitched five innings in the first World Cup in 2004 and gave up zero runs. {USA Baseball 2004 Media Guide}

Britton, Helene Hathaway Robison

(1879–1950)

By Joan M. Thomas

Born in 1879, Helene Hathaway Robison grew up in an affluent Cleveland, Ohio, suburb. There she was educated at Hathaway-Brown, a private all-girls school for primary through the upper grades still operating in the twenty-first century. In 1899, Helene's father, Frank Robison, and his brother Stanley purchased the National League baseball franchise that soon adopted the name Cardinals. Although there is no indication that she ever played the sport, all evidence points to the fact that Helene had a keen appreciation for baseball. She did, however, learn to play billiards and other sports at her male relatives' encouragement. After her father's death in 1908, she frequently accompanied her uncle on the Cardinals' road trips. That exposure helped to cultivate her interest in scorekeeping. Her closeness to her father and uncle undoubtedly added to her comfort level in all-male gatherings. So, when her uncle Stanley passed away in the spring of 1911, she had no compunctions about taking over the family baseball enterprise bequeathed to her and her mother. In her early thirties and married with two children by then, she slipped into her new role with ease.

Keeping in mind the times, it is remarkable that Helene, a well-bred young woman, did not simply sell out, or at least turn matters over to her husband, lawyer Schuyler Britton. Following her father's death, she had managed the family's affairs for her mother. Since her uncle was a bachelor, she was like a daughter to him. Already in a position of responsibility, she easily took on more upon his demise. However, she admittedly did not relish the idea of meeting with the press. Shortly after the news of a woman taking over the Cardinals helm broke, a female reporter from the *St. Louis Post-Dispatch* managed a lengthy interview with Helene at her Cleveland home. The writer, Marguerite Martyn, was certainly an accomplished journalist to both land the assignment and earn Helene's confidence. The two women, both pioneers in then-male-dominated fields, must have formed a bond, as Martyn's second interview with Mrs. Britton the following year resulted in another full page story.

In 1911, no one could have predicted that Helene would maintain her baseball enterprise until 1917. She even moved her family to a home in St. Louis in 1913. From the beginning, sports writers and cartoonists made gibes about the female presence in the hierarchy of the national game. But Helene remained undaunted and secure in her position. She even took it upon herself to fire Cardinals manager Roger Bresnahan following a number of heated arguments with him. Moreover, she encouraged other women to adopt an interest in the sport. Though her husband, Schuyler, was named president of the Cardinals organization in 1913, records reveal that it was really Helene who called the shots. Fred Lieb, in his book first copyrighted in 1944, *The St. Louis Cardinals*, says "the Cards went under petticoat rule, as Mrs. B, as the league called her, was the head and made all the decisions."

The year before Helene sold the Cardinals to a group of investors, she divorced Schuyler after separating from him several times. She also took over as club president then. Most stories about the marriage breakup only hint at Schuyler's bad behavior. Some even suggest almost jokingly that his carousing was just a boys-will-be-boys thing. But her first divorce petition reveals that he not only spent much of their family income on his drinking sprees, but also physically abused his wife.

Following the sale of her baseball holdings, Helene eventually remarried and moved to Boston. In 1950, she passed away at her daughter's Philadelphia home. As time passed, her name sank into obscurity. Yet, she was the first woman to own a major league baseball club.

{"Baseball Moguls Are Gathering in Gotham," *Washington Post*, 9 February 1913; "Bresnahan Will Manage Cards Again — Mrs. Britton," United Press, 12 September 1912.}

Brody, Leola Mae

IF 1943, Racine Belles

Leola Mae Brody played one season with the Belles in the All American League.

Brooklyn Female Baseball Club

The Brooklyn club played mainly in New York City. Their manager was Thomas Kelly. {"Insulted Woman Ball Player," *Brooklyn Daily Eagle*, 5 September 1901, 7.}.

Brown, Patricia I. "Pat"

(b. 23 April 1931, Boston, Massachusetts) P 1950–51, Chicago Colleens, Kenosha Comets, Battle Creek Belles

Pat Brown graduated from Winthrop High School in 1948 and went to work for Rustcraft Publishing Company. Brown spent one year traveling with the Colleens and then a season pitching for Battle Creek. She pitched in 23 games with a 9–9 record. She also hit .298 in 57 at-bats with ten runs scored and another six knocked in. After her playing days ended, Brown got a BA from Suffolk University in 1955. She earned her law degree in 1965 and was immediately admitted to the bar as an attorney. In 1970 Brown returned to school and earned an MBA followed by a MTS from Gordon Conwell in 1977. {AAGPBL Baseball Cards, 1995.}

Brownell, Katelyn "Katie"

P (New York)

Katie Brownell has played Little League baseball since she was nine years old in upstate New York. She made a name for herself in 2005 when she shut out the Yankees 11–0 at Oakfield Town Park. What really made the game special was that she pitched a perfect game, striking out every batter she faced. The local Batavia paper picked up the story first, explaining the rarity of this feat by this sixth grader. In addition to her superb pitching, Katie also batted over .700 for her team. She is the only girl on her Dodgers roster. Earlier in the season Brownell also pitched a one-hitter. {Thomas Lueck and Ben Beagle, "Shy Smile. Mean Fastball," *New York Times*, 19 May 2005, C23.}

Brownewell, Stacey

In 1999 Stacey Brownewell made history in Kane County when she became the batgirl for the Cougars in the Midwest League, the only girl to do so. She carried that responsibility for three years. She had started playing tee ball at the age of five and at 16 claimed she wanted to be the first woman to play major league baseball. When she started high school she tried out for the Wheaton Warrenville South High School freshman team but did not make the roster. She turned to playing fast-pitch softball as a result, and she took over centerfield. Stacey got a chance to work on her baseball skills when her family hosted various Cougars players in their home. She finally got a chance to join the Chicago Storm in the American Women's Baseball League (AWBL), playing in the infield. {Deborah Kadin, "A League of Her Own, Warrenville Teen Determined to Make It in Male Dominated Field of Baseball," *Daily Herald* (Ill.), 15 August 2002.}

Brucker, Victoria

During the 1989 Little League World Series, Victoria Brucker got the first hit for a girl.

Brumfield (White), Miriam Delores "Dolly"

(b. 26 May 1932, Prichard, Alabama) 1B/2B/3B/OF 1947–53, South Bend Blue Sox, Kenosha Comets, Fort Wayne Daisies

Dolly Brumfield got an early start in the AAGPBL, trying out in 1946 when she was only 13. Max Carey thought she was still a little too young, but she was invited to spring training in Havana in 1947 with South Bend. In the intervening time she joined her first softball team at Brookley Air Force Base in Mobile, Alabama. She also played city league basketball. Her first manager in the AAGPBL was Chet Grant, who mentored new players well. Brumfield was assigned her own chaperone, Daisy Junor, and she roomed with Shoo Shoo Wirth, the Blue Sox shortstop. She turned 15 while with the Blue Sox, and the club

Former AAGPBL player Dolly White (courtesy Dolly White).

made a big deal out of her birthday with a cake, singing and gifts before the game that night. In 1948 Brumfield joined the Comets and then was reassigned to Fort Wayne for her final two years after Kenosha folded. Under manager Bill Allington in 1952 and 1953, the Daisies won the league championship.

Brumfield's individual accomplishments were many, including finishing second in the league in batting in 1953. She led the Comets in hitting in 1951. She only played second base for one season in 1952, because she did not like the position and preferred first base.

After leaving the league she completed her BS in 1954 at Alabama College. She went on for her MS at the University of Southern Mississippi in 1959 and in 1969 completed her Ed.D. degree at the same university. Brumfield's work experience was varied but included a lot of coaching in basketball, tennis and track and field. For 31 years she taught at Henderson State Teacher's College (now known as Henderson State University). She retired from the HPERD department in 1994. In 1998 Brumfield was elected to the board of the AAGPBL Players Association and then in 2003 became president of the group. As for her athletic activities, Brumfield stayed involved in softball and bowling. She coached and played in recreational leagues for many years. {Miriam Brumfield, correspondence with Leslie A. Heaphy, North Canton, Ohio, March 2004; AAGPBL Newsletter, May 2001, 24; AAGPBL Questionnaire, National Baseball Hall of Fame and Library.}

Brun, Patti Jane "PJ"

(b. 1971, San Francisco) OF/P 1997–98, San Jose Spitfires

The cleanup hitter for the San Jose Spitfires, Brun played center field and pitched in relief. Originally from San Francisco, Brun joined the team in 1997 at age 26. In 1997 Brun pitched the opening game of the season against the Arizona Peppers in Arizona. Brun also attended the University of Hawaii, where she played softball. {Video.}

Bryant, Lori

P/C 1996–2001, South Bend Blue Sox

Lori Bryant started in the Great Lakes Women's Baseball League as a catcher and then developed into a solid pitcher. In 2000 she had a 1.000 fielding percentage and hit .333 to help her club. {<www.baseballglory.com>.}

Bryson, Marion

P 1946, Peoria Red Wings

Marion Bryson played for one season with the Red Wings of the All American League.

Bucior, Florence

(Jackson, Michigan) 2B 1946, Peoria Red Wings

Florence Bucior played for one season with the Red Wings of the All American League.

Buckley, Jean "Buckets"

(b. 4 December 1931, Boston, Massachusetts) CF/RF 1950–52, Kenosha Comets, Rockford Peaches

Growing up in Massachusetts gave Jean Buckley plenty of opportunities to play sports. She played softball in Boston and Catholic Youth Organiza-

tion games as well. She attended tryouts in South Bend in April 1950 and got assigned to Kenosha, where she played until 1952. She was a strong hitter who usually filled the fifth spot in the order but could also fill in at cleanup if needed. She played in 255 games and hit .200 with 77 runs scored and another 88 knocked in. In 1954 her whole family moved to Redwood City, where she continued to play softball. She attended San Francisco State College and then taught in elementary and junior high school. {"Jean Buckley Interview," *The Diamond Angle* Web site; AAGPBL Baseball Cards, 1995.}

Buckman, Alice

Alice Buckman made the boy's baseball team at her high school in Griswold, Iowa, in 1928. She played in the outfield for two seasons. {"Some Young Lady May Soon Break into Big Lineups," *The Messenger* (Athens, Ohio), 10 August 1928, 2.}

Burch, Yvonne

Yvonne Burch played Babe Ruth baseball in North Carolina in the early 1970s until the national headquarters threatened to revoke the local charter and she was told she could no longer play. The reasoning was that it was better to deprive one girl than over 200 boys of the chance to play. {"People in Sports," *New York Times*, 17 May 1973.}

Bureker (Stopper), Geraldine "Gerry"

(Portland, Oregon) OF 1948–49, Racine Belles

Geraldine Bureker played for two years with the Racine club as part of the All American League.

Burke, Kitty

In 1935 Burke made a name for herself after heckling the outfielders during a game between the Reds and the Cardinals. One of the players jokingly yelled back at Burke sitting in the stands and told her to grab a bat and see if she could hit better. She took the challenge literally and ran down to the on-deck circle, grabbed a bat from Babe Herman and went to the plate against Paul "Daffy" Dean. The umpire called for the pitch and Burke hit a soft grounder to first. The out and at-bat did not count against the Reds since she was not an official player, but she did bat during a major league game. {"This Woman Did Bat in the Major Leagues," *Albany Times-Union*, 31 July 1935.}

Burkovich, Shirley "Hustle"

(b. 4 February 1933, Pittsburgh, Pennsylvania) INF/OF 1949–51, Springfield Sallies, Rockford Peaches

Though she attended three different high schools, Shirley Burkovich played basketball and field hockey wherever she went. She also played basketball for the Westinghouse Girls Basketball League. She played baseball with her brother and his friends on the local sandlots. Shirley signed with the AAGPBL when she was just 16 and still attending high school. Her mom went with her to meet the chaperone and manager before she would let her daughter play. She played in 37 games with a .229 average. After playing for three seasons she went to work for Pacific Bell Telephone for 30 years. She also played amateur softball and golf and bowled to stay active. {AAGPBL Questionnaire, National Baseball Hall of Fame and Library.}

Burlingame, Sherry

3B, Arizona Baseball

Burmeister (Dean), Eileen "Burmy"

(b. 30 November 1924, Milwaukee, Wisconsin; d. 23 March 1990) OF/C/IF 1943–44, Rockford Peaches

Eileen Burmeister found herself a valuable player in the All-American League because she could play so many different positions. Anywhere you put her on the field, she excelled. She also wielded a powerful bat for the Peaches, with 60 runs batted in on only 113 hits. {AAGPBL Baseball Cards, 1996.}

Burnett, Alison

(b. 14 June 1974) 1B/OF 2003, New South Wales

Alison Burnett played in the 2003 Australian National Tournament for New South Wales.

Burnham, Elizabeth

(b. 28 December 1970, Norfolk, Connecticut) C 1995, Colorado Silver Bullets

Elizabeth Burnham grew up playing basketball and softball at Oxbow High School. She graduated in 1988. While attending the University of Connecticut in 1989, she continued to play before transferring to Lyndon State College, where she was named Conference Player of the Year in basketball in 1993. She tried out for the Silver Bullets at one of their camps in 1994 and made the 1995 squad. She caught 27 games for the Bullets in 1995 and had no passed balls, while throwing out five base stealers. {"For the Love of the Game," Colorado Silver Bullets souvenir program, 1995, 31; David Kindred, *Colorado Silver Bullets: For the Love of the Game* (Atlanta: Longstreet Press, Inc.), 64; Jim Shea, "An Ever Expanding Field," *The Hartford Courant*, 5 June 1994, C7.}

Burnham, Kendall

2B

During the 2003 baseball season Kendall Burnham and her husband Jake were signed by the San Angelo Colts of the independent Central League, becoming the first husband and wife team playing professional baseball together. She spent four weeks with the Colts and started one game at second base while going 0–7 at the plate. She was put on waivers when the team needed an open roster spot, but she continued to travel with the ball club in case another spot opened up. Jake Kendall was traded to Quebec in June 2003 and his wife went with him, though she was not signed on to play. {"Burnham Released by Minor-League Team," *The Register-Guard* (Oregon), 18 June 2003; "Colts Let Go of Burnham," *San Angelo Standard-Times*, 22 June 2003.}

Kendall Burnham played in the Women's Professional Softball League and worked as an assistant softball coach at University of Nevada-Las Vegas before joining her husband on the Colts roster. {Kostya Kennedy and Mark Bechtel, eds., "For the Record," *Sports Illustrated*, 26 May 2003.}

Burrill, Christina

INF, Outlaws, Falcons, North Shore Lady Spirit

Christina Burrill has played ball for a couple of teams in the North American Women's Baseball Association (NAWBA). She was even chosen as the captain of the Falcons. In 2004 she traveled with the Lady Spirit to the Dominican Republic for a four-game goodwill tour. In game two Burrill had two hits to help lead her club to a 12–4 victory. {Jean DePlacido, "Lady Spirit a Big Hit in Dominican Republic," *The Salem News*, 18 November 2004.}

Butcher, Lori

1B/P, Cactus Wrens

Lori Butcher played for the Cactus Wrens in 1994 and hit .575 while pitching in 4.2 innings.

Butcher (Marsh), Mary A. "Butch"

(b. 12 October 1927, Berne, Indiana) P 1945–46, Kenosha Comets, Grand Rapids Chicks

Mary Butcher graduated from Jefferson High School in 1945 and got a chance to play in the AAGPBL. She had a bit of experience playing softball for General Electric in Decatur, Indiana. Most of her time spent in the All American League involved her pitching batting practice. She pitched in one regular game and did not record a win or a loss. After her playing career ended, Butcher worked for a time as a medical records clerk in Carson Tahoe Hospital. She got married in 1955. She raised three children and stayed active with a bit of softball and bowling. {AAGPBL Questionnaire, National Baseball Hall of Fame and Library; AAGPBL Newsletter, September 1994, 21; AAGPBL Baseball Cards, 1995.}

Cactus Wrens

The Arizona Cactus Wrens formed in 1994 as part of WNABA. The Wrens won the league championship in 1994 and 1995, leading the league with a 14–1 record in the inaugural season. They led again in 1995 with a 13–1 record. Dawn Bergeson was their leading pitcher in 1994, recording wins in 12 of the team's 14 victories. When the NWBA formed in Phoenix in 1995, the Wrens took a hiatus from playing for the 1996 season. They planned to start up again in 1997 but the Ladies League was formed and seven former Wrens joined that league. In 1998 the Wrens came back to the league and finished their first fall back in the league at 4–4. The Wrens continued to play each year through 2004 as a traveling team going to tournaments, when they could field enough players. The Wrens have operated since their inception under the direction of Richard Hopkins. {Richard Hopkins, correspondence with editor, February 2001.}

Cain, Nicole

OF, Victoria, 2004 Australian National Team

Nicole Cain led her team in hitting during the 2003 Women's World Series, hitting .714. She knocked in eight runs and scored another four. She also stole five bases in six attempts. She made no errors in eight chances in the field. {Australian Baseball Federation, <www.baseball.org.au>.}

Caitlin (Doyle), Emily

P, Senators

In 1987 the Washington Senators planned to sign Emily Caitlin to pitch for their minor league team, the Raleigh Rallies. Caitlin was a softball player by background and a nurse by profession. General manager Elliot Suskind arranged for the tryout, some claimed to save the Senators, who were hurting financially. {Peter Carlson, "Senators Unveil Surprise Stopperette," *Washington Post*, 19 July 1987, A1.}

Cal Sabres

The Cal Sabres are the traveling tournament team in the Southern California Women's Baseball League, based in San Diego. Their season runs from June through August each season, with Saturday games locally to prepare for tournament play. Over the years they have had a number of veteran ball players such as Alex Sickinger, Jo Curone and Pam Conro lead them to various finishes. For example, in the 2001 Roy Hobbs Tournament the Sabres lost in the finals to the Ocala Lightning 2–1. At the 2002 tournament they came in third behind the Lightning and the Chicago Storm.

Calacurcio (Thomas), Aldine "Al"

(b. 8 June 1928, Rockford, Illinois) SS/UTIL. 1947, Rockford Peaches

Aldine Calacurcio played one season of baseball for her hometown Rockford Peaches in 1947. That was also the season the league held its spring training in Cuba, so Al got to travel even more than usual that season. {AAGPBL Baseball Cards, 2000.}

California Women's Baseball League (CWBL)

The California Women's Baseball League began in 2002 to help promote women's baseball in the San Francisco Bay Area, for women age 14 and older. The main entrants in the league are the Peninsula Peppers, the Alameda Oaks, the San Francisco Fillies and the San Jose Spitfires. League president Melanie Laspina also plays in the league. The league hosts a fall tournament, won in 2003 by the Bay Area All Stars. Each team has 14 players on its roster, and they play a ten-game season. League games are played at Mission College in Santa Clara, California. Players range in age from 14 on up.

Callaghan (Candaele, St. Aubin), Helen "Cally"

(b. 13 March 1923, Vancouver, British Columbia; d. 8 December 1992, Santa Barbara, California) OF 1944–48, Minneapolis Millerettes, Fort Wayne Daisies

Helen Callaghan and her sister Margaret grew up in Vancouver, British Columbia. Callaghan played a solid outfield but was best known for her hitting. She won her only batting title in 1945 with a .299 average for 122 hits in 111 games. In 1946 with the Daisies, she stole 114 bases in only 111 games. Unfortunately she had to sit out the 1947 season due to illness, and then came back to play only part of the 1948 season after giving birth to her son. She hit .257 and also stole 354 bases in her career. After leaving the league she and her husband settled in Lompoc, California, and she became a cleaning staff supervisor. Her son Casey played for the Montreal Expos and always talked about learning the game from his mother. He even made a documentary about his mother's baseball career. {Kelly Candaele, "Mom Was in a League of Her Own," *New York Times*, 7 June 1992, S9.}

Callaghan (Maxwell), Margaret

(b. 23 December 1921, Vancouver, British Columbia) 2B/3B 1944–51, Minneapolis Millerettes, Fort Wayne Daisies, South Bend Blue Sox, Peoria Red Wings, Battle Creek Belles

Margaret's play with Minneapolis made her a part of the first sister combination in the league. Her sister Helen played in the outfield at the same time. While in high school Margaret and her sister participated in every sport they had for girls, ranging from field hockey to track and field. Margaret also played city league basketball, softball and lacrosse. Before signing with the AAGPBL, she worked for Boeing Aircraft because of the war.

When Callaghan joined the AAGPBL she quickly established a reputation for being a fine fielder. She led the league in fielding average for third basemen in 1944 and 1945. She also led the league in put outs in 1946. Her favorite experience was getting to travel down to Cuba for an exhibition trip. She played in 672 games by the time her career ended. She batted .196 but stole 283 bases and walked 371 times. She helped her team with her speed on the bases and her solid defense.

After her playing career ended, Callaghan remained active in basketball and softball. Her basketball squad won the Canadian championship in 1951 and in softball they won a number of local series. In addition to playing she did a lot of coaching and worked in a drug store, a department store and a care home. She was married in 1952 and raised two boys, Guy and Dale. In recognition of all her athletic accomplishments Margaret was inducted into the South Hill Sports Hall of Fame in 1990 and in 1993 entered the British Columbia Softball Hall of Fame. {AAGPBL Questionnaire, National Baseball Hall of Fame and Library; Kelly Candaele, "Mom Was in a League of Her Own," *New York Times*, 7 June 1992, S9.}

Callaway, Natalie

Natalie Callaway pitched as a freshman for the South High baseball team in Denver, Colorado. She got to pitch in one game and she struck out nine players from the Adams City team. Adams City athletic director Fred Applewhite launched a protest after the contest, and Callaway was told she could not play anymore. Applewhite cited a rule that said if a female player played softball in the fall she could not play spring baseball. South had to forfeit the game. Natalie was allowed to stay with the team as a manager but could not play. {Carol Kreck, "The Girls of Summer Distaff Players Shortstopped by Obscure Rule," *The Denver Post*, 15 May 1996, G-01.}

Callison, Leslie

Announcer

Leslie Callison was the play-by-play announcer for the Springfield Capitals; they claimed she was the only female lead announcer in the country at the time. Before joining Springfield, Callison worked for two years with the Ozark Mountain Ducks as their promotions director. While attending Evangel College she played tennis and golf. Her major was broadcasting and marketing.

Callow, Eleanor "Squirt"

(b. 8 August 1927, Winnipeg, Manitoba, Canada; d., n.d.) LF/P 1947–54, Rockford Peaches, Peoria Red Wings

Eleanor Callow spent seven years in the league with the Rockford Peaches after a season with Peoria as a rookie. She made the all-star team in 1951, 1952 and again in 1954. For her career she knocked in 407 runs, the third highest total in the history of the league. She holds the career home run title with 55 and hit a solid .273 in 778 games. {AAGPBL Baseball Cards, 2000.}

Calloway, Ruth

Ruth Calloway was reported as the star of the Portsmouth Black Sox, an all-men's team. She played second base for the club, which was under the direction of Harold "Yellowhorse" Morris. Morris had played for the Detroit Stars of the Negro leagues before moving to Portsmouth. In 1933 a reporter stated that Calloway batted .275 and was a "mighty fine one" at second base. {*Detroit Tribune Independent*, 29 July 1933, 7.}

Campbell, Jamie

(Lacrosse, Indiana)

Jamie Campbell got a chance to play on the Lacrosse High School boys' baseball team when she was a sophomore because the school did not have a girls' softball team. She and Fonda Robinson were the two girls on the boys' squad. Jamie also was a cheerleader, runner and volleyball player. {Richard Grey, "No League of Their Own," n.p., n.d.}

Campbell, Janice

(b. 3 July 1981, Dartmouth, Nova Scotia) 2B/ DH 2004, Team Canada

Janice Campbell played in the 2004 women's World Cup, hitting .286 to help Canada win the bronze medal. Earlier, Campbell had a chance to represent Canada in the 1999 Junior Softball Championships held in Taiwan. Her club finished seventh. Then she played softball for four years at Ball State University in Muncie, Indiana, where she covered second base until her graduation in 2003. She was an All-American Scholar Athlete from 2000–2003. In 2004 she went back to school to study sports management at the University of Windsor. {Jody Jewers, "Nova Scotia Women Trying Out for National Baseball Team," *Halifax Daily News*, 21 May 2004, 47; Jewers, "Campbell Will Make History with Team Canada Tonight," *The Halifax Daily News*, 30 July 2004.}

Campbell, Jean

1946–47

Jean Campbell had a short career in the All-American league with the Fort Wayne Daisies.

Campbell, June

P/OF, Manhattan Giants, Elmwood Park Angels

In the fall 2002 season, Campbell was 12 for 37 with eight runs scored for the Giants. Campbell made her pitching debut for the Elmwood Park Angels on 27 April 2003 and lost 16–4. Normally Campbell played in the outfield. Her excellent outing put her into the bull pen as a relief pitcher for the remainder of the 2003 season.

Canadian Female Umpires

By Margaret Hart

Don Gilbert, the supervisor of umpires for Ontario and Canada, strongly believes that the spring of 1997 was the most significant time for the female umpires' program. He had been instructing at a level 2–3 clinic in Norfolk County. Living in Windsor, Ontario, he had a long drive home, which allowed him time to reflect on the events of the day. This particular clinic was no different from others except that something kept jumping around in his mind. Betty Opersko was the sole woman umpire in the midst of about 40 men. She sat there, listened, wrote her exam, got her card and went home. Don honestly believed that she may have had many questions but did not want to ask them because of the all-male environment. This played on his mind. During his two-hour drive home, he kept wondering — how many more female umpires were there in this position? That was when the idea popped into his head: an all-female umpire's clinic! He decided to take a risk.

He phoned Lisa Turbitt (an accomplished umpire and Baseball Ontario Board member), shared his idea and explained that he would need her help. They decided that, since Don had access to all the Ontario clinic registrants, they could contact the women listed on the clinic registration forms. They gathered as many names as possible and invitations were sent out for the "first ever all female umpires' clinic" to be held in London, Ontario. Don remembers the phone calls from Lisa saying that the response wasn't as good as they had anticipated. He and Lisa were far more excited about it than their potential participants seemed to be. This didn't dissuade Don; he was adamant that if even only one person attended, they would hold the clinic. As he said, it was like throwing a party and not knowing if anyone would come.

It turned out to be the right decision. With an overwhelming response from 21 women, the first annual all-women umpires' clinic was held in Guelph, Ontario, in November 1997. They were a varied group of women, ranging in ages from 18 to 60-plus. The youngest traveled from Antigonish, Nova Scotia, well over a thousand miles away. The oldest was a retired school teacher who officiated several different sports almost full time. They didn't know it then, but they were about to embark on a learning experience they would always remember.

Friday evening started out slow but once the ladies felt comfortable, their questions, comments and concerns were nonstop. The emotional atmosphere was a combination of apprehension and excitement, for this was the first opportunity of its kind ever offered to them. This, they hoped, would be the light at the end of the tunnel, not another obstacle on their way to improvement and equality.

For most, this was the first time that they had ever met other female umpires. The thread that wove them together was that it was difficult to be accepted in a male dominated avocation and to obtain the proper training they so desperately sought. Not knowing what to expect, most were prepared for another boring clinic, sitting for hours, half listening to stories about people of whom they had no knowledge. But quite the opposite was true; this turned out to be the best clinic they had ever attended.

One of the clinicians was Lisa Turbitt, who had been umpiring since the age of 11 and had worked her way up the ranks. She was a very skilled umpire. Most sat in awe as her credentials were presented. At that time, she had already umpired in provincial and national tournaments at the Bantam level. That was great, but was that a realistic goal for the others? The women gravitated strongly towards Lisa. There seemed to be an immediate bond and respect for her that exists to this day.

Saturday was spent in a sports dome that had been converted into an indoor baseball diamond just for this clinic. The participants were divided into crews and put through basic drills, such as set positioning, proper out and safe calls, and the first base pivot. For the majority of them this was all very new, but they couldn't get enough of it. For the first time, they were being taught how to properly and professionally umpire. Pitching machines were set up, and everyone was videotaped working the plate. Given the fact that they had never been shown the proper mechanics, it was extremely exciting and rewarding for not only the umpires but also for the clinicians to see how quickly they accepted instructions to change and improve.

Sunday was spent on rule interpretations, how to deal with conflict and difficult situations, where

to drawn the line for ejections, and so forth. The wrap-up in the afternoon was very emotional for all. The women had formed new and solid friendships based on their common bond. Don Gilbert and the clinicians had accomplished something bigger then they had ever imagined. This inaugural clinic was so successful that everyone involved committed to advancing the program. The groundwork for the future of female umpires had been established. Quality umpiring is always needed. The ability of the female umpire had finally been recognized, and was now being supported at the highest level. The "first ever" was a huge success. What made this clinic better than any other Don had attended? Simply put the enthusiasm. That's what separated the female clinic from any male or co-ed clinic that he had been to. As a result of this, Don determined that Lisa would take full control of the female clinic.

The next summer, as a direct result of that clinic, eight of the original 21 participants were selected to umpire in the Girls' Bantam Baseball Summer Games (provincial tournament) held in Guelph, Ontario, in August 1998. Most of them couldn't believe that they had been selected. They were excited but very nervous, for this was the first time that the majority of them had umpired at such an important tournament, and they were concerned about their abilities.

The umpires who worked that tournament, all from Ontario, were Lynda Archibald, Bolton; Dana Williams, Windsor; Margaret Hart, Mississauga; Betty Opersko, Waterford; Carol Giffen, Creemore; Nikki Ross, Mississauga; Tosha Winters, Windsor; and Lisa Turbitt, Burlington. Don Gilbert and Ray Merkley supervised the tournament, providing positive feedback after each game so that the umpires had the opportunity to immediately make corrections to their mechanics. They willingly accepted the critiquing, and were able to incorporate it in their subsequent games.

History was made during that tournament. As far as was known, that was the first time in Canadian baseball history that exclusively all-female crews umpired a provincial girls' baseball tournament.

Other opportunities soon appeared on the horizon. Nikki Ross and Lynda Archibald were selected from Ontario to umpire at the first Women's Nationals held in Winnipeg, Manitoba, in August 1999. Quebec sent Melanie Pascal. The highlight of the tournament came when four women were chosen to work the gold medal game, British Columbia vs. Ontario. The ball from the first pitch was removed from the game and sent to reside in the Canadian Baseball Hall of Fame in St. Mary's, Ontario.

Don Gilbert may have planted the seed, but the women's program flourished under Lisa Turbitt's direction. They were starting to realize that although it would take hard work and dedication, they were making gains into a male dominated field.

Lynda Archibald vividly remembers her first women's clinic and how far they have all progressed since. She can recall how bad they looked when they took the field: mismatched pants, white shoes and socks. Some had no hats; they wore skinny belts and old hand-me-down equipment. They were very intimidated by Don Gilbert, and by Ed Quinlan, the rulebook guru. Then there was Jim Cressman; he had umpired at the Olympics. When they spoke, the women listened. When they were shown even little things, they learned. They absorbed the knowledge like sponges; they were that keen and thirsty for knowledge. They learned how to go into the hand-on-knees set position, even how to stand behind the plate. They were taught to yell, "Yes, he did" and "No, he didn't." Most importantly, they learned to have faith in their own abilities and in the abilities of their fellow lady umpires. They celebrated each other's successes and suffered with each other's mistakes.

Ben Mercier, 41, of Welland, Ontario, was one of the clinicians who joined the program in its second year. He came with extremely high qualifications: he holds his Level 5 (International) umpire's certification; he is a master course conductor for Baseball Canada; he sits on the Baseball Ontario Umpires' Committee; and is an umpire clinician for Baseball Ontario. He has been a crew chief and plate award winner at tournaments of many levels, including Bautam, Peewee, Junior, Senior, and Olympic qualifying games. In the beginning, he felt that a separate women's program was not necessarily a good idea. He believed that an umpire is an umpire is an umpire, and that women should not be treated any differently. At his first clinic, he soon realized that the women's thirst for knowledge was going to be an important part of the weekend. Knowing that baseball is male dominated Mercier soon recognized the advantages of having a women-only clinic. They could learn at their own pace, free from being shy and intimidated by their male colleagues. It helped greatly that the chief organizer, Lisa Turbitt, was and continues to be an asset not only to the women's program but to Baseball Ontario and Baseball Canada as a whole. She continues to be one of Canada's best umpires.

Over the years it has been possible see the quality of umpiring improve from this group of individuals. Many have gone on to umpire the Women's World Series, Ontario Summer Games, Baseball Canada National Championships and the recent women's World Cup. It is a great testament to these women who continue to attend this clinic, as there is always something to learn. Mercier firmly believes that if it weren't for this program, there would not be as many good qualified female umpires in the province. He has supervised, evaluated and worked with many umpires throughout North America. Without making any distinction between the genders, he believes that Ontario-trained umpires are the best that Canada has to offer to amateur baseball at the national and international level.

When Nikki Ross was growing up, girls weren't allowed to play baseball and organized softball didn't exist, so she was relegated to helping her father coach her brothers' teams.

Fast-forward 15 years: She joined a fast-pitch team shortly after her son was born. When he was three years old, she signed him up for tee ball. His team didn't have a coach, so rather than have it disband, Ross took it on, as well as sitting on the board of directors for her local association. That first year, she coached both a house and a rep league team. She continued to coach her son up to the Junior level (18- and 19-year-olds).

In 1996, she became an umpire. Her son wanted to become an umpire to make some extra money, and she thought it would be fun to do it together.

By the end of her first year, she had become the umpire-in-chief of her association, working with 257 umpires. She feels very fortunate to have been involved with Baseball Ontario and its women's program over the past several years. It is this affiliation that has given her the great pleasure of meeting and knowing some of the most interesting women in the amateur ranks. Lisa Turbitt, who has devoted much of her life to umpiring, and who serves as the head of the women's program, is an inspiration to many. Judy Zarubick, Carol Giffen, Lynda Archibald, Laura Pfanner and Margaret Hart were all there that first year. Nikki states that she has had the pleasure of watching these women grow and learn and become accomplished umpires. After initiating the mentorship program, they were all proud to watch the likes of Jacqui Klas, Shanna Kook, Jen Golding, Amanda McCrae, Becky Bruce, Megan Lem and Jenna Johnstone grow into very fine young umpires who were able to benefit from the roads that were cleared by the pioneers. Although Ross was thrilled to have been invited to two nationals and two Ontario Summer Games, her biggest pleasure has been her involvement in the mentorship program.

In 2000, Ross was selected to sit on the Women's Baseball League Board of Directors as the supervisor of umpires and to travel to Florida for meetings and clinics. Lisa Turbitt and Ross promoted the women's umpire program at a Girl Scouts "Girls N Play" one-day jamboree at Disney's Wide World of Sports in February 2002. They ran an umpires' clinic and taught over 600 young girls basic umpire positioning in group sessions. Ross also supervised at the Women's World Series in Florida. It was at this tournament that Shanna Kook was noticed by Major League Baseball and invited to go to the Harry Wendelstedt Umpire School.

In 2004 Shanna Kook, from Toronto, Ontario, was only 22 years old and in her second year as a professional umpire in the Pioneer League. In September 2002, she traveled to St. Petersburg, Florida, and was the crew chief at the Women's World Series. Teams from Canada, the United States, Japan and Australia competed. (One of the nicest stories to come out of that tournament was that the Japanese participants gave financial assistance to the Australian team to ensure there were four teams involved.) The games were played at the Tampa Bay Devil Rays' spring training diamond, with finals at Tropicana Stadium. It was there that Kook was scouted by Major League Baseball. She graduated from the Harry Wendelstedt Umpire School in 2003, where she was nominated for the Top Student Award.

Kook had started umpiring at the age of 16. She had attended a level-one clinic that gave her the opportunity of a job right away with her community center. She learned so much and asked so many questions that she was awarded a ball bag, indicator and brush for being the most enthusiastic student. She was exceptionally interested in knowing more about the rules, and more about her favorite game. The clinician was also her umpire assigner, and he gave her as many games as she was willing to take, working at the Tyke and Peewee levels. For the first few years she did not feel a need to do higher level games. But, when she was 17, she learned that one of the boys who had attended that same first clinic with her was now doing Bantam and Midget baseball. That gave her the incentive to progress.

However, when she was 18, Shanna was accelerated through high school and skipped a grade. Needing money to go to university a year earlier than planned, she had to go to work full time and was unable to umpire that season. She returned to Toronto for the summer after her first year at McGill University in Montreal, Quebec. Hanging out at the baseball diamonds at High Park watching games, she approached one of the community center employees and asked him if she could umpire for them. He took down her information and said that he would have the umpire supervisor contact her. Shortly after, George Smilka called her and arranged to take her onto a field to assess her abilities and review fundamentals. He told her about a professional umpires' school that he had recently attended. That was the start of her dream of becoming a major league umpire. Shanna located the last level-three clinic of the season and convinced her father to drive her there which was over an hour away. She was overwhelmed with all the information provided and felt as if she knew nothing. She realized she was in no way prepared to work any higher level games. Although she received her level-three certification, Shanna was unsuccessful at being assigned to work Midget League games. There was only one scheduler for Midget and higher games and he was unwilling to provide her the opportunity. About a week later, scheduled games were cancelled because no umpires were available. This really angered her. She lived only a block and a half away from the park. Shortly after that, hearing that another game would be cancelled due to lack of umpires, she took her equipment to the park and worked her first Midget game alone. After the game, the convener of the field approached her and said that she had worked a good game. He said he hoped that he would see her there again. The following week she worked her first Junior double header, by herself. That was when she realized she was capable of umpiring at a much higher level.

Kook met Nikki Ross that same season. After working a girls' Peewee game together, Shanna learned that there were other women in the same situation: struggling to obtain assignments and recognition. She recognized that she wasn't alone.

Ross convinced her to attend the women's clinic that fall. She returned to university in Montreal, but traveled back to Ontario for that scheduled weekend just to attend it. She learned so much at that clinic that when she returned to school she became obsessed with umpiring. She read everything she could find about women who were professional umpires in the minor leagues. She decided that she too could do it. She convinced her parents to let her leave school for one semester to attend the one-week course at the Jim

Evans Academy of Professional Umpiring in Florida. It was there that she was told to give professional umpiring serious consideration. While waiting at the airport for her return flight, she decided to go back for the five-week course. Instead of continuing with university, she took a job in the off-season and umpired games during the summer to apply what was learned at pro school. Her mentor, Chris Teliatnik, helped her prepare for the five-week course by working numerous games with her.

This time, she decided to attend Harry Wendlestedt's school. Her outstanding abilities resulted in her being advanced to the Professional Baseball Umpire Camp's 10 Day Evaluation Program. She knew she had a good chance for a professional career when Wendlestedt himself gave Shanna her evaluation. He told her that she was the best female to ever come out of his umpire school. She was offered a job right out of Professional Baseball Umpires Camp, and was ranked high enough to get an advanced rookie placement. This was in March 2003. She is the first Canadian woman, and the sixth in baseball history, to umpire professionally.

In the off-season, Kook, Margaret Hart, Jen Golding, and Amanda McCrae assist Nikki Ross as clinicians at her eight-week umpires' clinic.

When Margaret Hart's son began playing tee ball in the early eighties, quite often the umpires would not show up for the games. Rather than have the kids go home without playing, she "stepped up to the plate" and volunteered to umpire. After this had happened several times, the umpire in chief asked her if she would be interested in becoming a regularly scheduled umpire. She decided to give it a try, and as her son moved up to regulation baseball, so did she.

Hart was one of the umpires who received an invitation to the first all-female umpires' clinic. At that time, she had been umpiring for about 15 years, and refereeing tackle football for ten. In the early eighties, umpiring was a volunteer job. One tee ball tournament that Margaret and her husband were asked to work awakened her to the injustices between the genders. The convener, who was also the umpire in chief, told her that she could not umpire any games because they did not allow female players or umpires in that league. It was only after a severe shortage of male umpires during that tournament that she was grudgingly permitted to work third base in a couple of games. Her husband had one year less experience, but he went on to umpire the plate in the semifinal game. During the following off-season, several like minded individuals got together to rewrite the rules of tee ball to include female players. Consequently, a new league was formed that opened the doors to all players, regardless of gender. This had an impact on the original league to the point of extinction. Mothers, who in the past could only watch their sons play, were now able to participate as umpires or coaches for their sons' and daughters' games. And they became involved with the overall running of their local associations.

As the years progressed, Hart was required to attend annual clinics to obtain her certification. In all those years, she had never once met another woman umpire, although she was constantly asked if she knew one by the name of Nikki Ross. Apparently, she lived in the same city, but they had never crossed paths. The clinics Hart had attended over the years were all in-class sessions, usually listening to the clinician as well as the male umpires devoting the majority of the time bragging about games they'd done, or telling "war stories." It was very boring, but mandatory if she wanted to continue umpiring.

Now, with more that 20 years' experience, Hart can attribute her success to some specific people and events. The first women's clinic was the real start for her. Up to that point, she was just going through the motions, but really did not know the proper mechanics for either the bases or home plate. She knew she enjoyed what she was doing, but had always felt inadequate on the diamond. After attending the women's clinic, she realized just how little she knew, but was determined to work hard and improve her skills. Support and encouragement from the likes of Don Gilbert and Ed Quinlan and others at the provincial and national level, as well as from Michael Grove, the umpire in chief of the local association, and her mentor, Ron Herd, has been invaluable to her. Her dedication and hard work has paid off. She has worked the 1998 Summer Games, several women's international tournaments, and the 2003 and 2004 Canadian Nationals.

Jennifer Golding was only 13 when she started umpiring softball; she already knew most of the rules and it seemed like a good way to make a little bit of extra money. After only two years, though, she grew tired of the politics and of not getting paid on time, so she gave up softball, and thought that she might be interested in umpiring baseball. Her younger brother played baseball and she knew that the rules for the two sports were very similar, so she decided to give it a try. Looking for a summer job, he decided try it too. For a 15-year-old, it was a good paying summer job. The next year, she attended a local clinic in the area to become a better umpire. She has continued to try to better herself ever since. Jen is a very competitive person and always wants to excel. She admits that she is her own worst enemy when it comes to critiquing her performance. Over the past several years, she has gone on to umpire higher levels of ball, having started out at the Peewee level (12- to 13-year-olds). She now umpires players who are older than she is. She assists the clinicians at the same eight-week course at which she had originally been a student.

Golding has umpired at a couple of the provincial championships in Ontario for the boys at different age groups, but she enjoyed it more when she umpired the girls and women at various tournaments. She has worked two Ontario Summer Games for girls' baseball, and umpired in Florida with Nikki Ross and Shanna Kook at the Women's International Tournament. In August 2004, she umpired at the Bantam Girls' Nationals in Sherbrooke, Quebec.

What made Roberta Hornak from Mississauga, Ontario decide to start her umpiring career in 2004 at the age of 48? Her boyfriend had umpired for around 20 years, and she started going to his games to watch him. She could plainly see the enjoyment and gratification he got from doing the plate and working together with the kids. He had earned respect from the coaches, players and parents. One night after he finished a game he asked her to consider taking an umpiring course so they could work together, as a team. Margaret Hart was the clinician and Hornak said she made it all look so easy. She was a great teacher, very enthusiastic and informative.

Hornak started umpiring with her boyfriend the very next week, doing the bases. It was very nerve wracking for her, but he made her feel as though she had been out there with him for years. He was very supportive, coaching and guiding her. She enjoyed being out there and calmed down very quickly. There were a few times when she forgot where she should have been, but he inconspicuously directed her into position.

There are many different reasons for doing things. Hornak saw umpiring as one more thing she and her boyfriend could do together. Many of the coaches specifically requested them to umpire their games because they performed so well as a team; they were always consistent and fair. Hornak looks forward to many more years of umpiring, especially with this special teammate.

Carol Giffen remembers clearly why she decided to become an umpire. She had been coaching her son's team for a couple of years,' he was mosquito age then. During one particular game,

a batting-out-of-order situation arose. Giffen replaced the batter before he became a runner, but the opposing coach told the umpire that the batter should be out. The umpire decided that the coach was correct, and ruled the batter out. Giffen's team lost the game then and there.

Giffen was very unhappy about the way the game ended, but there was nothing she could do about it at the time. At that moment she decided that the only way to make sure this would not happen again was to become an umpire herself. She promised herself she would do her best to ensure that the game was played according to the rules and umpired within the spirit of the game, with fairness to all.

The next spring Giffen signed up for a course and began her career as a minor league baseball umpire. She admits that although she thought she knew the rules, she very quickly found out that she still had a lot to learn. She spent the next few years learning the hard way—from her mistakes.

In the late '90s, Giffen also received an invitation to attend the clinic designed specifically for women. She was nervous about going; the clinic was being held over an entire weekend and she wouldn't know anyone there. However, she feels that the decision to go was one of the best she has ever made. She was very quiet throughout the course, and absorbed all of the knowledge the clinicians were providing. At times she felt as if she were back at boot camp. Being ex-military, she can realistically make that comparison. But she survived. It couldn't have been that bad, since most of the women come back year after year to the clinic.

Giffen cherishes the friendships and camaraderie that have evolved from attending those clinics. As good as the clinics were, though, she was not prepared for how thick-skinned she had to become for a number of years. She was called various unkind names and endured many games where she was not welcome because baseball was "a man's game."

It appeared to her that many people had a difficult time comprehending why women would ever want to umpire. She has always enjoyed sports, and she loved being an umpire. She feels she has the best seat in the house because there are no fans obstructing her view. She understands the strategy of the game, and can tell a player "well done" when they've made a good play.

Giffen remembers one game in which her partner wanted nothing to do with umpiring with a woman. He had never met her, or any other female umpire, before. She can still see him standing in the field with his arms crossed, not moving at all — no signals, no talking, no moving. It was one of the toughest games she had ever worked. However, several years later this man and Carol were scheduled as partners for two seasons. They actually could talk together, discussing signals, mechanics, and the game in general. The best thing to come out of that partnership was that they earned each other's respect.

Umpiring has given Giffen memories that she will treasure forever. Solid friendships have been made. She has earned the opportunity to umpire at higher levels of ball than most. She has umpired four Ontario Summer Games in a row, two Nationals, and the Women's World Series in Toronto in 2001 in the SkyDome, the home field of the Toronto Blue Jays.

Giffen is proud of her accomplishments. She has proven that "girls" can umpire, and do it well. She remembers a Peewee game that she umpired, in which her son was playing. After the game, the coach of the visiting team admitted that when he realized she would be umpiring the plate, he was afraid that she would favor the home team. But he told her he thought that she was extremely fair, and that she had called a good game.

Players and coaches have learned a few things about Giffen. She is a competent and confident umpire. They know better than to argue with her about the wrong things. She will not tolerate inappropriate behavior from anyone. She's a mother and does have eyes in the back of her head. Even if she is busy taking lineup changes, she really can see that coach trying to warm up his pitcher without a face mask on. If it's 33 degrees Celsius outside and she has all her plate equipment on, she cannot be swayed by being given water.

Giffen umpires for the right reasons. This is not a power trip for her. She does it for the love of the game. And she loves being loud. Her petite frame has always belied her ability to bellow with the best of them. God, and everyone else at the ball diamond, knows when there is an infield fly. She is proud of being fair, consistent and dependable. It has taken her many years to overcome the obstacles that she, like the other female umpires, faced. She has earned the reputation of being a fair umpire. When she retires from umpiring she knows that she will still be at the top of her game — but always willing to learn more.

In July 2001, Toronto, Ontario, was the host for the Women's World Series. Games were scheduled on various local diamonds, but the highlight was umpiring at the SkyDome, the home of the Toronto Blue Jays. Teams from the United States, Canada, Japan and Australia participated in the Women's Under 30 International All Star Tourna-

ment. Laura Pfanner, 38, from Kitchener, Ontario, was one of the umpires. In 1996, she had been looking for a part time job and answered a help wanted ad in the local newspaper. She had never played or coached baseball before, but had played softball for many years. She currently does Midget AAA ball in Waterloo, Ontario. She is thankful to have received support from her home association; they've always encouraged and helped her. And she feels extremely lucky as far as Ontario Baseball Association's support goes — she's received many coveted assignments.

Pfanner believes that her real start came at the women's clinic. She says that the highest accomplishment for her was umpiring at the SkyDome during the Women's Under 30 tournament, although working the plate on the bronze medal game at the 2003 Canadian Nationals Tournament and doing first base on the gold medal game at the 2004 Nationals were also high points.

Umpires for the Women's Under 30 tournament were selected based on their mechanics, rules knowledge, game control and attitude. Those chosen had demonstrated a willingness to learn and improve by attending various other clinics. For example, Nikki Ross attended the one-week course in Florida at the Jim Evans Academy of Professional Umpiring in 2000, followed by Jen Golding, Kelly Murphy, Margaret Hart and Lynda Archibald in January 2001. Amanda McCrae of Etobicoke, Ontario, went the following year.

When Lynda Archibald's son played baseball many years ago in Bolton, Ontario, she felt that the umpires were lacking in rules knowledge. Since she had already been umpiring softball for a while, Archibald decided to go into baseball, with the intention of improving the quality of the umpiring in her son's association. Until that first women's clinic, she found it hard to learn the skills and mechanics required to become a better umpire. It was next to impossible to learn positioning at a one day's clinic with 30 men, whose attitude indicated that they already knew it all.

Support and encouragement from her local association was nonexistent except from two brothers, who were graduates of the Jim Evans Academy of Professional Umpires. Ed Quinlan and Don Gilbert had a very positive influence on Archibald when she first started attending the women's clinics. It was a new experience to have high level officials such as Ed and Don telling her that she could do it, continually raising the bar, and having 100% confidence that she was up to the challenge.

Archibald is currently a level-four umpire and has worked numerous provincial and international tournaments as well as the 1999 and 2003

Canadian Nationals. She has a mentor by the name of Peter Skrypka, a 6'4" policeman and level-four umpire. Peter offers suggestions, not criticisms, and praise when she nails a call. He can always find the positive side of things. He has helped her maintain her self-confidence and faith in her umpiring abilities. She has worked very hard and now feels that she is a competent level-four umpire. She didn't get there just because a token female was needed.

Geneviève Laflamme, 25 years old, is from St.-Rédempteur. It's a little town on the south shore of Quebec. She currently lives and works in Quebec City. She started umpiring in 1996, when she was 16 years old. She never played, never coached. She umpires Peewee to Midget BB and AA levels. In 2005 she umpired Junior AA games.

Her highest accomplishment is being chosen to work second base for the gold medal game at the Bantam Girls' National Tournament in Sherbrooke, Quebec, in August 2004. It is a very big accomplishment considering where she was in 2003.

Laflamme has always loved baseball, playing it throughout her childhood but never on an organized team. When her younger brother joined a league, she decided to become the scorekeeper. In the province of Quebec, game scoring is taken very seriously. Participants are required to go to clinics, and are paid for doing it; it's a very good summer job. Many girls who enjoy baseball become scorekeepers.

As a scorer, Laflamme met many umpires and after two years, decided to become one herself. She wanted to be more a part of the game. At first, she felt that being a girl made no difference. Maybe it even helped a little; coaches were hesitant to argue with her; they were a lot more polite. When she progressed and started doing higher level ball, that all changed; the coaches weren't any different but the others umpires were. They seemed to perceive her as a threat. The male umpires she had originally started officiating with were doing higher level ball while she remained at the same level for many years. At the age of 22, she was umpiring with 17-year-old partners. She was about to give up umpiring when she received a phone call from the president of the umpire's committee for the province of Quebec. He was looking for umpires to go to Windsor, Ontario, for the 2003 Bantam Girls' National Tournament, and asked if she would be interested. Of course, she said yes. She had no experience working tournament games of this caliber. She had never umpired in crews. She was nervous, inexperienced and had never been supervised. She learned a lot during that tournament.

She learned that there were at least 11 other women who loved the game as much as she did. She learned that she could umpire until she was 50 and beyond. And she learned that with a little supervision, and a lot of work on her part, she could improve. The Windsor Nationals were the experience of a lifetime.

When she returned home to Quebec City, she was motivated and determined to work hard. When she was selected to officiate in Sherbrooke, Quebec, for the 2004 Bantam Girls' National Championships, she went with a completely different attitude. Although she was nervous, she was much more confident. Laflamme's goals were achieved when she received a positive evaluation and was assigned to work second base in the gold medal game. This time when she returned home, she was immediately assigned to higher level games—finals for the Bantam and Midget AA, and university baseball. And her spot on the Junior AA umpiring staff for the following year was assured. She wasn't a girl anymore, she was an umpire.

Katrina Cadotte of Port Lambton, Ontario, had something to achieve. She started playing fastball and softball at the age of 11. As a young adult, she became frustrated at being struck out on pitches over her head. The umpires seemed not to know what a strike looked like. She felt that it was her duty to demonstrate how it should be done.

Cadotte loves the game of baseball. Every year her goal is to play and umpire more games than she did the previous year. She never tires of being on a baseball diamond, learning new rules and improving her mechanics each season. She uses her knowledge of umpiring to her advantage when she plays softball. Her umpiring skills have transferred over to her professional life. As a teacher, she shares her experiences with her students and it has helped her with classroom control. She enjoys sharing her umpiring stories with her students. She finds it is a way to have a connection with them. She uses her umpiring as an example to her students that they can achieve anything they want if they work at it. Cadotte is proud to be the only female umpire in her area.

Attending the women's clinic in 2000 and receiving continual support from other umpires within the program as well as the other level-three umpires in Wallaceburg (her home association) has been instrumental to her success. After every game in tournaments they discuss what went well and which areas need improvement.

Cadotte was selected to umpire a base in the gold medal game at the 2002 Ontario Summer Games. The highlight so far in her career was being chosen for the 2004 Bantam Girls' Nationals in Sherbrooke, Quebec.

Jacques Goyette lives in Magog, Quebec. He has 36 years' experience as a baseball umpire, and still has fun doing it. He has coached up to the Midget AA level. He has been the local and regional president of Baseball Quebec, and has sat on the provincial committee of umpires at Baseball Quebec since 1997. He has been in charge of supervision for major provincial championships, and since March 2004, in charge of the female umpire program in Quebec. At the provincial level, he has umpired in ten tournaments, and he has supervised the umpires in about 20 of them. He is a level-four umpire and a master course conductor. He has umpired at two nationals, in 1995 and again in 1996. The year 2004 marked his fifth as a supervisor for Baseball Canada. That year also provided a new challenge for Goyette. He was asked to supervise the female umpires at the Bantam Girls' Nationals in Sherbrooke, Quebec. He was amazed at how quickly the group accepted him and his assistant supervisor, Stéphane Durocher.

Goyette noticed some differences between all-male and all-female championships. With the men, everything was a big competition: who was the best, who would be chosen to do the gold medal plate. With the women, he noted they tended to work as one group. Some competition existed but it was not the most important thing. When providing feedback and evaluations, he found that he had to deal a little more with feelings and emotions, and as a male supervisor he had to be more aware of how he approached sensitive issues. Jacques feels strongly that female umpires have their place in baseball at any level because, regardless of the sex of the person, a good umpire is a good umpire. After this positive experience of supervising the female umpires, Goyette states that Baseball Canada can assign him with them anytime.

When Stéphane Durocher, who lives in St.-Sauveur, Quebec, found out he would be the assistant supervisor for the 2004 Bantam Girls' Nationals in Sherbrooke, Quebec, he became a little anxious. This would be his first nationals as a supervisor, and it would be with the females. Were they going to accept him as their supervisor? How experienced were they? What would be different from other tournaments? Now he can answer all of those questions. He has been involved in baseball since 1993 in various roles. He was in charge of all the Laurentides umpires for the 2000 and 2001 seasons. Since 2002, he has sat on the Provincial Committee of Umpires for Baseball Quebec. He heads up all the level-one, -two and -three clinics for umpires, and is responsible for the

training of instructors. He runs the Minor Provincial Championship and the Jeux du Québec (Provincial Summer Games). He has been working with Jacques Goyette in the development of their female umpires program. He is a level-four umpire, as well as a master course conductor. He has umpired at several provincial championships, as well as being the umpire supervisor for approximately 12 championships (minor, major and Jeux du Québec). With all of these credentials behind him, it is difficult to understand why he would be apprehensive about his first national championship as a supervisor with the female umpires. It turned out to be the greatest championship that he had experienced to date. He faced new challenges on two levels: it was his first nationals, and secondly, it was with the female umpires. He soon realized that he was accepted immediately as their supervisor, and together they experienced some very memorable moments.

Durocher feels that the biggest difference between male and female is mental. With the men, a national championship is a big competition between each of the umpires: who will be the plate umpire for the gold medal game. They did not work as a team like the women did. The female umpires all worked as a unit; they helped each other. He is aware that competition for the gold medal plate existed, but it was not the most important thing for them. They wanted to learn and improve, and have some fun along the way.

Durocher has had the opportunity to supervise and evaluate some very good umpires during various championships. He is a strong supporter of the women's program, appreciating that they have their place in baseball as umpires. As a male supervisor, he had to change his approach during evaluations. He learned that it's not the same dealing with male and female umpires. He had to work more with the emotional side. He experienced some very emotional situations that he had never had before with the men. This affected both him and Goyette on a very personal level. They had all worked together very closely for seven days. Durocher was amazed at the women's performance. He recommends that everyone should have the opportunity to become a supervisor in a female championship at least once in their life to have this unique experience.

The year 2004 marked the eighth anniversary of the all-women's umpire clinic, and they have come a long way. For some of the veterans, it may soon be time to hang up the masks and chest protectors for good. Some might chose to leave the game completely, but most will probably continue to be involved by contributing in other ways, through recruiting, mentoring and the training of new umpires. Whether they carry on or not, they will always have memories of the good times they have shared, and the great friendships that have been made, not only in Ontario, but throughout the continent. They are extremely proud of their pioneering achievements, making the way that much easier for those who follow. They will remember and cherish that what they have accomplished is extraordinary.

When Don Gilbert left the position of supervisor of umpires for Ontario to become the supervisor of umpires for Canada, Ed Quinlan took over the female program and it climbed to new heights. Ed is a no-nonsense guy who demands perfection in the umpiring world. He treats the women no different than he does their male counterparts.

With the continuance of Lisa Turbitt's influence and dedication to the female program, and Ed Quinlan's ability and penchant for detail, the female umpires are moving onward and upward. They have earned the respect they never had in 1997. They were generally relegated to Peewee or lower classification ball. At that time, they probably deserved that ranking. Since then, they have received the proper training. They now look the part. The most noticeable change is how they approach their avocation: with a confidence in themselves and their ability that was lacking before.

Lisa Turbitt umpired at the International World Cup of Women's Baseball in Edmonton, Alberta, in August 2004. The tournament was played at Telus Field, which is the home of the Triple A Edmonton Trappers. Five countries participated: Canada, the USA, Japan, Taiwan, and Australia. The International World Cup of Women's Baseball was the first sanctioned women's baseball event ever. The women played baseball with regular major league distances (90-foot bases, 60'6" pitching distance) and overhand pitching, just like the major leagues.

Ten umpires worked that tournament. Six were Canadians (three women and three men) and the four remaining were all men from the United States, Australia, Taiwan, and Japan. Lisa Turbitt has normally umpired men's baseball but as women's baseball has started to emerge worldwide, she has been involved with several women's tournaments. But this was the first sanctioned IBAF international tournament. Turbitt was assigned the plate on the second day of the tournament. History was made: she was the first woman to umpire a plate in an International Tournament.

According to international rules, umpires are not assigned to the gold medal game if the umpire's country's team is playing. Canada had lost the semifinals to Japan but ultimately won the bronze medal. Turbitt was assigned the plate in the gold medal game. Of the three base umpires, the women worked second and third, and the U.S. umpire did first.

The USA defeated Japan 2–0 to win the gold medal. There were over 3,600 people in the stands. It was the highlight of Turbitt's umpiring career! After the game, the Australian coach (who had lost the bronze game) told her she did an outstanding job. He was so impressed that he presented her with his National Team warm-up jacket. Ironically, this was the same coach that Turbitt had ejected in a game during the Canadian Women's International Tournament in 2001.

Don Gilbert, supervisor of umpires for Canada, recently spoke to Richard Runchey, the supervisor (United States) for the first International World Cup of Women's Baseball, and he stated that it had been his intent to showcase the female umpires. Case in point: he believed Lisa Turbitt had earned the gold medal plate, and therefore he assigned it to her. He assigned the base positions to the two women umpires for the same reason. It is his intention to have all women at the next world tournament.

Turbitt has been a tremendous asset to the umpire development program at the provincial and national levels for over 24 years. Her dedication and commitment to improving umpiring in general, and to fostering women in umpiring in particular, has lead to many improvements in Baseball Ontario's programs.

Not only focused on improving the national program, she is actively involved in the grassroots development of Canada's future umpires. She has excelled in a male dominated program, and has devoted countless hours to the development of women in umpiring at the local, provincial and national levels.

In 2002, Turbitt was inducted into the Women's Amateur Baseball League Baseball Hall of Fame for her contributions to the development of women in the sport.

From their very modest and incompetent beginnings in 1997, barely able to umpire at the Peewee level, these women have evolved into confident, competent officials, capable of taking on the world of baseball, from local to provincial, national, international, and even professional levels. Some have chosen to advance their skills by becoming clinicians. Others have had the opportunity to be supervisors at provincial and national tournaments.

Don Gilbert started something that would turn female umpiring into something no one else would have ever dreamed of. He feels that this is the one significant mark he has left during his term as the supervisor of umpires for Baseball Ontario, and he is extremely proud of it.

Thanks to the dedication of people like the visionary Gilbert (now supervisor of umpires for Canada, who umpired at the 2004 Olympic Summer Games in Athens, Greece), Ed Quinlan (currently supervisor of umpires for Ontario), Lisa Turbitt, Ben Mercier, Blair Hains, Jim Cressman and Czaba Vegh (clinicians), and many others, these clinics have continued to improve each year. So have the women umpires.

Tournament Championships in Which the Women Umpires Have Participated

Year	Event	Location
1997	Bantam National Championships	North Bay, Ontario
1998	Ontario Summer Games (Bantam Girls)	Guelph, Ontario
2000	Ontario Summer Games (Bantam Girls)	Ajax, Ontario
2000	Women's International Tournament	Toronto, Ontario
2001	Women's International World Series	Toronto, Ontario
2001	Bantam National Championships	Windsor, Ontario
2002	Midget National Championships	St. Albert, Alberta
2002	Women's International Tournament	Toronto, Ontario
2003	Midget National Championships	Windsor, Ontario
2004	International Women's World Cup	Edmonton, Alberta

The governing body of Baseball Ontario annually recognizes the efforts of its umpires by selecting a senior and junior umpire of the year. In 2002, the recipient of the junior award was Jacqui Klas of Mississauga, Ontario, and her prize was a trip to the one-week course at the Jim Evans Academy of Professional Umpiring.

Canadian National Baseball Team

This team won the Saskatoon Ladies League championship in 1921. The manager was a Mr. F. Duhamel and the team's catcher was also a man, J.M. Taylor. This was typical of the era; many bloomer teams used men as catchers and pitchers because those were considered the key positions.

Canadian National Team

The Canadian National Team operates under the umbrella of Baseball Canada, an organization that has been in existence since 1971. The women's team is managed by Andre Lachance with assistance from Brad Lawlor. The 2004 team had 18 players representing six Canadian provinces and ranging in age from 16 to 36. This team played in the first IBAF-sanctioned World Cup event for women in 2004, held in Edmonton, Canada, and won by the United States. {Baseball Canada 2004 National Team Media Guide.}

Cardin, Julie
Pawtucket Slaterettes

Julie Cardin started playing baseball for the Pawtucket Slaterettes when she was five years old. She stayed in the league as long as there were girls' teams and then joined the adult division when it began in 2001. She became the recording secretary for the league at the same time. In 2003 she took over as the director of transportation for the Rhode Island Women's Baseball League. {Rhode Island Women's Baseball Web site.}

Carey, Mary "Pepper"
(b. 8 September 1925, Detroit, Michigan; d. 1 January 1977) 3B/2B/SS 1946–54, Kenosha Comets, Peoria Red Wings, Kalamazoo Lassies, Muskegon Lassies, Rockford Peaches, South Bend Blue Sox

Mary Carey spent nine seasons playing in the All American League. She found herself on a number of different teams over the years because she could play so many positions in the infield. She had a strong arm but only hit .186 in 840 games. She walked 263 times against 255 strikeouts and also stole 198 bases. Mary also helped her teammates out on their long bus rides by playing the harmonica to entertain them and pass the time. {AAGPBL Baseball Cards, 2000.}

Carey, Max
(b. 11 January 1890, Terre Haute, Indiana; d. 30 May 1976, Miami, Florida) OF

Max Carey was an outfielder for the Pittsburgh Pirates and Brooklyn Dodgers. His career lasted from 1910 to 1929. He also managed the Dodgers from 1932 to 1933. He was inducted into the Indiana Baseball Hall of Fame and elected to the National Baseball Hall of Fame in 1961. His two great claims to fame were his speed and his fielding. He led the league in stolen bases for ten seasons. He ended his career with 738 stolen bases and held the career record until Lou Brock broke his record in 1974. He managed the Milwaukee Chicks and Fort Wayne Daisies in the AAGPBL. The Chicks won the championship in 1944. Carey also held the role of league president from 1945 to 1949. {National Baseball Hall of Fame plaque; AAGPBL Baseball Cards, 2000.}

Carnes, Jo Ann

In 1976 Jo Ann Carnes tried out for her high school baseball team and made the squad. Carnes was then told by the Tennessee Secondary School Athletic Association that regardless of the decision by the Wartburg coaching staff, she could not play under state law, which prohibited co-ed teams in contact sports. Carnes sued for the right to play. The court ruled in her favor and she was placed back on the team, but there was only one game left in the season so her victory was limited. {"Girl's Prep Baseball Career Over Quickly," *Los Angeles Times*, 14 May 1976, A13.}

Carr, Jennifer

lf/c DC Thunder, Maryland Barncats

Carson, Helen

P

As a nineteen year old, Helen Carson got the starting nod for a summer baseball squad in Britton Woods, New Hampshire in 1938. She helped her team at the plate because she was a switch hitter. On the mound she had a variety of pitches she threw, including a drop ball. {John Kovach, *Women's Baseball*, Arcadia Publishing, 2005, 42.}

Carter, Melanie

CF 1998–2000, South Bend Blue Sox

Melanie Carter roamed center field for the Great Lakes Women's Baseball League Blue Sox under manager John Kovach. In 1999 she was nominated by Kovach and then selected by the National Women's Baseball Hall of Fame to receive the 1999 MVP Award. She hit .378 for the season and led the Blue Sox in six different offensive categories. For the 2000 season she was named captain of the club. {*Fame Forum* 2, no. 43 (6 November 1999).}

Carter, Melissa

RHP 1996, Colorado Silver Bullets

The year before Melissa Carter was invited to the Bullets' spring training camp, she pitched for the San Diego Diamonds. The Diamonds were an amateur all-star team with the National Women's Baseball Association (NWBA). {*Silver Bulletin*, March 1996.}

Carveth (Dunn), Betty

(b. 13 April 1925, Edmonton, Alberta) P 1945, Rockford Peaches, Fort Wayne Daisies

After one season with Rockford and Fort Wayne, Betty Carveth did not return to play because she got married and stayed home to raise her three boys. She played in 21 games and had a 4–11 record. She did coach a Little League team in the 1950s and 1960s in Edmonton. She also got involved in curling and cross country skiing. {AAGPBL Baseball Cards, 1996.}

Castillo (Kinney), Ysora "Chico," "Pepper"

(b. 16 May 1932, Havana, Cuba) 2B/3B 1949–51, Chicago Colleens, Kalamazoo Lassies, Kenosha Comets

Ysora Castillo learned her baseball skills from her father, Argelio del Castillo. She began playing third base for the Habaneras at age 15. This opportunity led to other teams and eventual selection to the Cuban national women's team known as Las Cubanos. This team traveled in Venezuela in 1948 and played against some of the AAGPBL members. As a result, Ysora got the chance to come to America in 1949, where she played in 71 games with the Colleens. She played another two years with Kalamazoo and Kenosha before marrying Raymundo Kinney and retiring. Her career batting average was only .128 but she walked over 100 times while only striking out 70. {"Colleens Win in 14; Play Again Tonight," *The Austin American*, 6 July 1949; Hispanic Research Center, University of Texas at San Antonio; AAGPBL Baseball Cards, 1995.}

Catarino, Jill

(b. 24 July 1981, Summit New Jersey) 3B

Jill Catarino played softball and tennis in high school. While attending the University of Arizona she got a degree in elementary education. She traveled to Arizona in October 2003 to play in the 24-hour marathon baseball game. Catarino played third base and had four consecutive hits in the game. She works at the Scottsdale Resort and Conference Center to help pay for her schooling. {Jill Catarino, correspondence with Leslie A. Heaphy, North Canton, Ohio, March 2004.}

Catford, Angela

OF, New South Wales, 2004 Australian National Team

Angela Catford played for Team Australia at the 2004 Women's World Series and World Cup of Women's Baseball. She was chosen primarily for her solid hitting, as shown by her .643 average in Australia's National Women's Championship. She also boasted a 1.036 slugging percentage with 21 runs scored on 18 hits.

Catskill Nine

The Twin Mountain House in the Catskills hosted a baseball game between a men's and women's team that the women won. The women's roster included Mrs. Connerty, Mrs. McKeon, Miss Byrne, Miss Quinn, Miss Brinker, Miss O'Neil, Miss Dempsey, Miss O'Hagan, Miss Orlowsky and Miss Dietrowski. {"Women's Baseball Team Defeats the Men's— Recent Arrivals," *New York Times*, 6 August 1911, X4.}

Cella, Anna

C/SS, 2003 WBLS Parks

Anna Cella plays Little League baseball in the Chicago area with the strong encouragement of her mother Laura. In addition to her eight years of playing baseball, beginning when she was about four, Cella got a chance to play for the Sparks. The Sparks are an all-girls' team that has played in the Cooperstown tournament since 2003. {Julie Ferraro, "Baseball for Girls?" *South Bend Tribune*, 19 March 2005, B7.}

Chambless, Tammy

OF, Ocala Lightning

Tammy Chambless has not only played softball but has also coached in the Ocala area for over 19 years. Her other coaching duties include overseeing cross-country teams. She attended the University of South Florida and earned All-American honors in softball in 1981. When the Ocala Lightning was formed, Chambless became one of the team's starting outfielders. She played in the 2000 Roy Hobbs championship series and saved a no-hitter by throwing out a runner from center field at first base.

Champeens Female Chicago Nine

The Champeens traveled to Philadelphia for a game on the Athletics grounds, which they won 23–14 over an all-men's team called the Duffers. According to the reporter the team would have won by an even greater score, but apparently a couple of the players stopped on the field to fix their uniforms before continuing their runs. Emma Howard was the winning pitcher while her sister May was the catcher. Allie Allison, the center fielder, walked all three times she came to bat, while the left fielder, Belle Fuller, was considered the team's hardest hitter. {*Philadelphia Inquirer*, 8 October 1889.}

Champion Ladies Club of Cincinnati

While under the direction of W.S. Franklin, this team of nine ladies was arrested in June 1890 for playing a game against the Danville Browns in Illinois. Franklin entered guilty pleas for each girl for their Sunday game and paid the $100 in court costs. The men were also arrested and fined $7 each. {*Chicago Tribune*, 10 June 1890.}

Charest, Amanda

P

Amanda Charest was one of the Junior League's toughest pitchers in 1999, when she led the league with 110 strikeouts.

Charleroi Bloomer Girls

In 1920 the Charleroi Bloomer Girls arrived in Monessen, Pennsylvania, to play the local American Legion team. The team included eight women and one man as the catcher. Miss Pulce did all the pitching for the Bloomers while Miss Shaw handled first base duties. The rest of the infield included Miss Rogers at short and Miss Johnson at third. The outfield duties were handled by Miss Poundstone, Miss Ryan and Miss Webster. James Buchanon managed the club. Some of their previous games included a contest against the Westinghouse Bloomer Girls and a semipro team from Vandegrift. {"Bloomer Girls Base Ball Team to Play Legion Here Friday," *Monessen Daily Independent* (Pa.), 30 August 1920.}

Charpia, Billy Jo

(b. 27 August 1971, Charleston, South Carolina) P 1995, Colorado Silver Bullets

Billy Jo Charpia played varsity softball for three years at Summerville High School and then continued to play at Baptist College. While there she hit .392 to lead the team and drove in 41 runs also to lead her club. Charpia worked primarily in relief for the Bullets in 1995, earning one save in 11 appearances. Her save came in a 7–4 victory over Briles' Bucs All-Stars on July 15, 1995. {"For the Love of the Game," Colorado Silver Bullets souvenir program, 1995.}

Charron, Anne

SS, North Shore Cougars

Anne Charron grew up playing softball but finally got a chance to play baseball with the creation of the Women's New England Baseball League. She became the starting shortstop for the North Shore Cougars in 1999. She found that the biggest adjustment came in trying to hit a baseball because of the speed and movement on the ball. In addition to playing softball in school, Charron also played field hockey. After she finished school she went to work in the financial department for Boston Medical Center. {Michael O'Connor, "The Local Women are ... Playing Hardball," *The Boston Herald*, 28 May 2000.}

Chequer, Natasha

(Geelong, Australia) 3B/P, Team Australia

Natasha Chequer's ball playing experience before 2002 stemmed from fast-pitch softball. She played in an international women's tournament held in Geelong, Australia, in 2002.

Chester, Bea

(Brooklyn, New York) 3B 1944, Rockford Peaches

Bea Chester played one season in the All-American League with the Peaches as their third baseman.

Chiarolanza, Stacy

Stacy Chiarolanza played for the Mets in 2002 and had ten hits in 21 at-bats while scoring nine runs. She also walked seven times while only striking out twice.

Chicago Black Stockings

This team traveled to Canada in 1891 to play a series of games in the Maritime provinces. The two promoters for the team were M.J. Raymond and William Burtnett. They went ahead of the ball club to secure guarantees of games. The organizer of the trip was a New Yorker named W.S.

Franklin. In 1890 Franklin advertised in the *New York World* for players to start a women's league. In response to his call five clubs were created, but only three lasted the summer, one of them being the Black Stockings. The club's uniform consisted of red and black striped dresses, black stockings, light colored blouses, and jockey caps to match their dresses. The manager of the club was W.F. Phillips, who had previous experience with the Reds and Blues run by Harry H. Freeman. The girls in the Black Stockings were expected to play a musical instrument as well, so they could organize their own parades when they entered a town. The first game on this barnstorming tour took place in Fredericton and was reported in the local paper as an event that was disappointing. Fans discovered the ladies were not as well versed in the game as they had hoped. It seemed that many of the young ladies were only interested in the chance to travel and see a bit of the world rather than in learning the finer points of the game. There were strict rules of conduct created for the ladies, and any infraction would result in a fine. Repeated trouble would get a young lady removed from the club. An example of the rules when they traveled was that the women were to stay in their rooms or the ladies' parlor, or else be fined 25 cents. The rules were designed to help promote a positive image of "lady" ball players. {"Introducing Females into Professionalism," *The Sporting Life*, 30 August 1890; "Young Lady Baseballists," *The National Police Gazette*, 20 September 1890; "Gendered Baselines: The Tour of the Chicago Blackstockings," in *Northern Sandlots*.}

Chicago Bloomer Girls

The Chicago Bloomer Girls traveled all over in a search for opponents to play. The earliest record of the club found so far comes from 1901, when they were playing in Pennsylvania. On 20 August 1901 they played in Blossberg against the Arnot nine. The Arnot club defeated the visiting Bloomers 12–4. Maud Nelson pitched for the Chicago team. Manager Clayton Orser ran the club from 1905 to 1908. One of their trips in 1908 found them playing a couple of games against a team from Santa Ana. The Bloomers lost 4–2 and 12–10 at Chutes Park. The highlights of the game involved the fielding of their center fielder, Blanche Orrie, and the hitting of their captain, Birdie Carlton. Carlton had been playing baseball since 1893, when she took a team called the New York Stars to Cuba to play. The losing pitcher was a Miss Winslow, who gave up seven hits and hit two batters.

The leading base stealer over the three years for

the club was third baseman Fay Howard. Elsie Erickson, the left fielder, was considered the fan favorite for her looks and her pleasant personality. The team also had four men on the squad who dressed in the same attire as the women, and even wore wigs to give the crowd a chance to wonder where the men were playing. Some of the other places the team played included Vancouver, Washington and Oregon, Salt Lake City, Utah; Fresno, California; and Massillon, Ohio. On each of their stops they attracted a large turnout in the stands because of the novelty of seeing women play the game and because of their uniforms. The ladies wore red bloomers, short skirts, red blouses, red and black hose, and variegated caps. {"Baseball at Blossberg," *The Wellsboro Agitator* (Pa.) 21 August 1901; "Fair Bloomer Girls to Play Ball Here," *Los Angeles Times*, 16 September 1908, I7; "Bloomer Girls Great on Squeeze Play," *Los Angeles Times*, 19 September 1908, 16; "Bloomer Girls' Game," *Los Angeles Times*, 21 September 1908, I12; "Bloomers Beaten," *Los Angeles Times*, 20 September 1908, V17; "Manly Maidens," Massillon *Independent*, <www.newspaperarchive.com>.}

Occasionally a problem developed for these bloomer teams when others borrowed their name. For example, in 1913 a large group of fans paid to see the Chicago Bloomers play a local team in Washington. The publicity before the game encouraged the fans to come out and see this team of lovely ladies. Unfortunately the fans found they had been duped when the club arrived: it quickly turned out the Bloomer Girls were actually men in dresses and wigs. The game took place at Union Park. The first clue came when one of the outfielders threw a strike from deep to home plate on the fly. During the excitement generated by the discovery, the gatekeeper absconded with all the money from the tickets. {"Ball Crowd Angry When It Is Discovered 'Bloomer Girls' Men," *Lincoln Daily News*, 21 July 1913; "Bloomer Girls Are Real Men," *Sheboygan Press*, 22 July 1913; "Bloomer Girls Were Chewing Navy Plug," *The Fort Wayne News*, 21 July 1913.}

Chicago Blue Notes

The Blue Notes were a charter member of the Great Lakes Women's Baseball League and won the league championship in 1996 under the leadership of Sharon Ephraim.

Chicago Colleens

The Colleens were an expansion team created for the 1948 season. When the club looked like it would fold, the league made it a traveling squad for the 1949–50 seasons. The purpose was supposed to be player development, but the concept did not last. (The Springfield Sallies were the other traveling team.) There were 50 players chosen by Lennis Zintak for the original touring squads. They played 71 games in 1949 and were expected to play the same in 1950. Pat Barringer and Bobbie Liebrich served as team chaperones while Walt Fidler drove their bus. The business manager and publicity person was Murray Howe. The young ladies got $25 a week plus $3.50 a day for meals.

In 1948 the Colleens had a 126-game schedule. They began the season with a three-game series against the Rockford Peaches. The series was played at their home park, Shewbridge Field, located at 74th and Aberdeen streets. Their games were broadcast on WJOB out of Hammond, Indiana, and WBKB televised their Friday night home games. Dave Bancroft managed the team in 1948 and had 18 players on the roster, including Gene Travis at first base, Esther Hershey in the outfield and Greta Cogswell in the outfield. {"Colleen Games to Be Televised, Broadcast," *Chicago Tribune*, 5 May 1948, B4; "Colleens Open Season Tonight at Rockford," *Chicago Tribune*, 9 May 184, A5; AAGPBL souvenir program, 1986.}

Chicago Gems

The Gems started play in 2003 and became full members of the Great Lakes Women's Baseball League in 2004. The team is open to all women without regard to age, though all minors must have parental permission to play. The ages of players in the league range from 14 to 50. In their first season the Gems played in the Labor Day tournament in South Bend and finished at 2–2. Other contests have included a doubleheader against the Detroit Danger and a game with the South Bend Blue Sox.

Chicago Star Bloomer Girls

John B. Olson Jr. owned the Chicago team by 1902 and hired as his main attraction pitcher Maud Nelson. In 1903 the team traveled to Georgia and played a game against the Crescents at Brisbane Park in Atlanta. The arrangements were made by the Bloomers' advance agent, Tom Tracy. Maud Nelson did the pitching though no final account of the game has been found. Another short news account found the team playing in 1913 in Washington, D.C., against the Columbias. The game took place at Union League Park with Margaret

Members of the WIMNz club. Front row, from left: Ashley Nicolls, Jodi Irlbeck, and Theresa Williams. Back Row: Kristy Smith, Sarah Stenroos, Rae Lundberg, Georgina Gorecki, and Megan Elm (courtesy Ashley Nicolls).

Cunningham pitching and May Walsh handling the catching duties. {"Bloomers to Play Here," *The Constitution* (Ga.), 25 March 1903, 9; "Bloomer Girls to Play Here," *Washington Post*, 7 June 1913, 9.}

Chicago Storm/Lightning

The Chicago Storm was founded in 1997 as a part of the Great Lakes Women's Baseball League by Charlene Wright. At that time they were called the Chicago Lightning. The Storm journeyed to Florida to take part in the Citrus Blast in 2002 and came away with second place. They lost the championship game to the Ocala Lightning 5–4. They won the Great Lakes Wood Bat Invitational over Labor Day weekend in 2002, beating South Bend 6–0. Katie Korecek led the way with two hits while catcher Jen Hughes knocked in two runs. The winning pitcher was Charlene Wright. In 2003 the Storm won their first national title, the 2003 AAU Roy Hobbs Championship in Ft. Myers, Florida. The Storm were undefeated in the series, winning all seven of their contests. They shut out the New England Spirit 1–0, in an extra-

inning game, to capture the title. {Chicago Storm Web site.}

Childress, Thelma

Thelma Childress played for the Grand Rapids Chicks in the All American league in 1946.

Chin, Jackie

(b. 1976) OF Florida Lightning, Florida Legends, Cal Sabres

In the 1998 South Florida Diamond Classic, Jackie Chin helped lead her team to victory with two doubles in the final game. The Lightning was a traveling all-star squad in the league. That same season Chin had played regularly with the Florida Legends in the

Outfielder Jackie Chin for Team USA (courtesy Jim Glennie).

Ladies Professional Baseball League. In 2001 Chin helped her new club, the Cal Sabres, to a second-place finish at the Roy Hobbs Tournament. She shared MVP honors with Alex Sickinger. {Pascale Etheart, "Blazing the Trail for Women in Baseball League," *Miami Herald*, 19 July 1998; Barry Jackson, "Women's League Puts Team in Homestead," *Miami Herald*, 9 April 1998.}

Christ, Dorothy "Chris"

(b. 19 September 1925, LaPorte, Indiana) OF 1948, South Bend Blue Sox

Dorothy Christ never actually played in a single game for South Bend. She signed a contract to join the Blue Sox in mid–1948 but got traded to Fort Wayne before she even reported. Then she was traded again to Rockford. After six weeks of this type of travel Christ gave up and went home. {AAGPBL Baseball Cards, 2000.}

Christianson, Jerrika

SS 2000, South Bend Blue Sox

Jerrika Christianson hit .333 as a rookie with South Bend. She also knocked in three runs and became known for her solid defensive play and strong arm. {<www.baseballglory.com>.}

Christy, Emily

P

Christy started her playing days by joining the local Little League squad in Falmouth, Maine, and then switched to softball. She went on to play softball at Princeton until her graduation in 1998 and then became a pitcher in the New England Women's Baseball League while attending MIT. {Chad Konecky, "Return to Pitching Reinvents Former Princeton Softballer," *The Somerville Journal*, 12 September 2002.}

Chu, Ling-Yin

P, Taiwan

Ling-Yin Chu pitched in four games for her Taiwan club during the 2004 women's World Cup event. She gave up seven earned runs in 14 innings but had an 0–3 record. She walked five batters while striking out only three.

Chu, Yu-Chin

P, Taiwan

Yu-Chin Chu pitched four innings for her country in the women's World Cup in 2004 in Edmonton, Canada. She gave up six hits and four earned runs while striking out one batter.

Cindric, Ann "Cindy"

(b. 5 September 1922, Muse, Pennsylvania) P 1948–50, Muskegon Belles, Peoria Red Wings, Springfield Sallies

Ann Cindric attended tryouts for the women's league in Allentown, Pennsylvania, and was chosen for spring training. After playing in the league for one year with Muskegon, Cindric joined the Sallies for two more years of touring. Her career ended more quickly than she would have liked because of a recurring hand injury. Ann entered a Dominican convent for five years but did not renew her vows. She went to work in a nursing home for 25 years. {AAGPBL Newsletter, September 1994, 20, and May 2005, 21; AAGPBL Baseball Cards, 1995.}

Cione, Jean "Cy"

(b. 23 June 1928, Rockford, Illinois) P/1B/OF 1945–54, Rockford Peaches, Kenosha Comets, Battle Creek Belles, Muskegon Lassies

Jean Cione started her playing career with her hometown Peaches and finished her career with them in 1954. She started when she was only 17 and still in high school. In between those two seasons Cione played for three different ball clubs, pitching in a total of 170 games. A highlight of her career was throwing two no-hitters in 1950. In 1952 she made the all-star squad with a 2–5 record but she also sported a 3.24 ERA in only nine games. After the league folded, Cione took up teaching physical education and eventually became a professor of sports medicine at Eastern Michigan University. {AAGPBL Newsletter, May 2002, 24; AAGPBL Baseball Cards, 1996.}

Ciulla, Stephanie

(b. 1967) P/SS 1996–1998, Montgomery County Barncats; 1999–2004, Virginia Flames

Stephanie Ciulla pitched for the Virginia Flames from 1999 to 2003 and was inducted into the National Women's Baseball Hall of Fame in 2003. Behind her solid pitching the Virginia Flames won league titles in 1999, 2000, 2003 and 2004. She was also noted for her strong hitting. When the Flames won in 1999, Ciulla pitched an 18–0 shutout and went 4–6 at the plate. Before joining the Flames, Ciulla helped the Barncats win their league championship in 1996. Ciulla won championships with two different teams in the league. Her number, seven, was retired by the Flames after the 2004 season.

Ciulla grew up playing softball and even some basketball, but not baseball. She played softball at George Mason University. When she is not on the ball field she works for the Pentagon in Washington, D.C. {Eastern Women's Baseball Conference Web site.}

Civiello, Annette

IF/OF/P 2001–04, Detroit Danger, Motown Magic

Annette Civiello has played alongside her sister Marie for the Danger and the Magic. Her greatest asset is her versatility, as she can play just about any position on the field except catcher. When she is not playing baseball Annette is a middle school teacher in Ohio.

Civiello, Marie

P/OF/IF 2000–2004, Detroit Danger, Motown Magic

Marie Civiello has played for the Danger and Magic, convincing her sister Annette to join her. Like her sister, Marie is a versatile player with a great deal of experience. Her first game came in 2000 at Tiger Stadium against the Canadian all-star squad.

Clark, Corrine

(b. 28 September 1923, Yorkville, Illinois) Util. 1949, Peoria Red Wings

Corrine Clark played less than one full season with the Red Wings before returning to Chicago to play softball. She later earned her BS from Illinois State and her MA from Columbia University. She also got her P.Ed. from Indiana University and worked for the University of Wisconsin at Whitewater. She served as chair of the Physical Education and Recreation Department as well as associate dean of the College of Education. {AAGPBL Baseball Cards, 2000.}

Clark, K.C.

(b. 10 October 1969, Sierra, California) CF, Colorado Silver Bullets

K.C. Clark got her start in baseball playing Little League from age 7 to 14. At age 12 Clark pitched a no-hitter in the Sacramento Tournament of Champions. She became an outfielder for the Colorado Silver Bullets in 1994. She found her spot in center field because of her exceptional speed. Prior to joining the Bullets, Clark played softball at Cal. State, Fullerton, from 1991 to 1992. {Susan Fornoff, "Playing Hardball," *The Sporting News*, 30 May 1994; Steve Jacobson, "Living the Dream," Newsday, 8 March 1994; David Kindred, *Colorado Silver Bullets: For the Love of the Game* (Atlanta: Longstreet Press, Inc.), 66.}

Clarke, Diane

Victoria Baseball

Diane Clarke played in the 2001 National Tournament for Victoria, hitting .556 and scoring seven runs.

Clarke, Lynn

(Geelong, Australia) P/C/Util.

In addition to playing baseball, Lynn Clark works as a nurse and has three girls to raise. In 2002 she played in the International Women's Baseball Tournament held in Geelong, Australia. She gained her experience playing on men's teams.

Clays, Adah "Tomboy"

P

Hailing from Utah, Adah Clays developed a reputation as a tough pitcher to face on the sandlots because she could throw with either hand. She also wielded a pretty fair bat from both sides of the plate. She played against local men's teams though her own team was an all-women's high school team. The other two stars were Lucille Dixon and Pearl Adderly. Clays began playing baseball in her home town of Bingham when she was only six years old. {"Girl a Baseball Star," *Washington Post*, 11 February 1917, E9; "Girl Baseball Star is Two-Handed Twirler," *Washington Post*, 27 May 1917, 19.}

Clayton, Cassie

Etobicoke All Stars

In 1999 Clayton helped her team to two victories in the USA Baseball Championship series. She also won the home run derby with the farthest hit. {"Canada Shows Well in USA Baseball Championship," *AWBL Baserunner*, November 1999, 3.}

Cleary, Katie

Alameda Oaks, Outlaws

Katie Cleary got into two games of the 2003 World Series. She came up to bat four times and was held hitless. In 2004 she was named Most Valuable Player in the North American Women's Baseball League while playing for the Outlaws.

Clement, Amanda

(b. 20 March 1888, Hudson, South Dakota, d. 20 July 1971, Sioux Falls, South Dakota)

Clement became the first female umpire when she began officiating both amateur and professional games in South Dakota in 1904. She developed her interest in the game because of her brother Hank and her cousin Cy Parkin, who let her tag along with them and even play on occasions when they were short players. She moved from playing to umpiring as a bit of an accident. For one game between a local team and a club from Canton, no umpire showed up, so Amanda took over the duties. She learned to deal with the ribbing and baiting that goes with her job while captaining the basketball team at Yankton College until her graduation in 1907. In addition to basketball Miss Clement played baseball and took part in track and field events, as well as gymnastics. She set the world record in the baseball throw by a woman at 197 feet, and also held records in hurdles and high jumping. She broke her own record in 1912 with a recorded throw of 275 feet. She went on for two more years at the University of Nebraska, graduating in 1909 with a degree in physical education. After umpiring for six years she taught in the Dakotas and Wyoming before returning to Hudson to care for her mother. Amanda worked as the city assessor, a police matron, a justice of the peace, a drugstore clerk and as a newspaper typesetter. In 1934 she moved away and settled in Sioux Falls where she went to work for 30 years as a social worker. In between, she worked as a director of the YWCA in La-Crosse, Wisconsin. She organized all kinds of classes and special programs for the women of the community and even gained fame for saving a man's life while swimming at a local park.

Clement became a highly sought-after umpire. Teams in the Dakotas, Iowa, Minnesota and Nebraska began to request her presence. She was billed as "South Dakota's Great Woman Umpire." Reporters and fans acknowledged that she knew the rules thoroughly and showed no favoritism no matter what game she umpired. She made firm decisions and stuck by them, and for this she earned the respect of players and managers. Though she never umpired at the professional level, Clement traveled and earned a living as an umpire. She often worked as the only umpire for a series of games that paid her travel expenses. For example, she traveled to Oaks, North Dakota, to umpire a game behind home plate while a man umpired the bases. Before the game the next day, the fans wanted the male umpire to leave and let Amanda control the game alone. They even took up a collection to pay the man $15 and sent him away. On occasion she did get heckled and not all the press she received was positive. For example, at one point questions were raised about her abilities as a wife and homemaker due to her athletic antics. Others responded to the editorial, claiming she could do all her homemaking duties and umpire and lose nothing. By 1908 Clement also refereed basketball games. In 1964 Clement was inducted into the South Dakota Sports Hall of Fame for her achievements. She became the second woman inducted, joining 1973 inductee golfer Marlene Hagge.

Clement earned the respect of players and fans for her knowledge of the rules and her fairness in applying them. She also made a good living, earning up to $25 a game for her services and umpiring about 50 games a summer. Her paychecks helped put her through school as a physical education major at the University of Nebraska. She continued to umpire while in school except when she broke a bone in her left knee playing catch. League presidents Ban Johnson and Harry Pulliam both tried to recruit Clement to umpire games at the major league level. Clement's acceptance at the turn of the century is especially impressive given the difficulties female umpires have had in more recent decades. Part of the reason had to do with the belief that a lady umpire would help clean up the image of the game. In keeping with this idea, she never umpired on Sundays, stayed with local ministers' families when she traveled on the road and did not tolerate swearing from the players or managers. {Amanda Clement file, South Dakota Sports Hall of Fame; Amanda Clement scrapbook, National Baseball Hall of Fame and Museum; Sheri Roan, "The 'Lady in Blue': a Long-Forgotten First," *Sun-Sentinel*, 8 July 1981, 1C, 5C; Denver Howard, "The True First Female Ump," *The Bryan Times*, 15 November 1997, 11, and "Umpire Myth Denounced," *The Bryan Times*, 2 January 1998, 4.}

Cleveland Comets

The Comets joined the Great Lakes Women's Baseball League in 2004.

Cline Maid Bloomer Girls

In 1916 the Cline Maid nine played in a benefit game against the Desmond Blue Beauties to raise money for the family of Arthur Day, who was killed in a car wreck. Day had been a pitcher for the Desmond club. The Cline Maids would rely on the pitching arms of Hortsman, Newmyer and Hogg and the catching of a Miss Stein for the contest. The rest of the club included 1B, Ida Delaney; 2B, Lenora Bevione; 3B, Margaret Butler; SS, Louise Bevione; LF, Amelia Jackson; CF, Rose Sousa; and RF, Margaret Butler or H. Smith. {"Benefit Game Sure Success," *Los Angeles Times*, 29 October 1916, VI17.}

Coats, Sal

1997–98, San Jose Spitfires, Alameda Oaks

Sal Coats attended Chico State University to play softball and then joined the Ladies Professional Baseball League in 1997, playing for the San Jose Spitfires as they won the league championship.

Coben, Muriel

(Saskatoon, Canada; d., n.d.) P 1943

Muriel Coben was considered one of the best softball pitchers in the Canadian provinces. She tried to make the adjustment to baseball in the U.S. but went home after one year of struggling. She continued to dominate the softball scene and in 1979 she was inducted into Saskatchewan's Sports Hall of Fame. Some of the teams she played for were inducted into Saskatoon Sports Hall of Fame. In 1998 Coben received further recognition when she joined a group of women inducted in the Canadian Baseball Hall of Fame in St. Marys, Ontario. {Induction program, 1998.}

Cohen, Rhianna

(b. 25 January 1980, Lowell, Massachusetts)

Rhianna Cohen grew up at a time when girls played softball and never thought she would get the chance to play baseball. When she did, it was a dream come true. While attending Lawrence Academy in Groton, Massachusetts, Cohen participated in field hockey, ice hockey, basketball, track and field, cheerleading and softball. She continued her extensive sports involvement while studying at St. Lawrence University in New York, where she received a BS in biology. Cohen played a bit of field hockey, water polo for a year, and three years of softball. She even went to the Olympic tryouts for softball in 1998. Cohen

traded her softball uniform for one year with the Boston Blitz as their third baseman in 2001. She hurt her shoulder playing college softball and had to take two years off, but hopes to return again in 2004. When not playing baseball Cohen works at the Center for Cancer Research at MIT and is a volunteer softball coach for the Bay State Bandits, an 18- and-under softball team. She also helps coach at Lawrence Academy in softball, field hockey and ice hockey. {Rhianna Cohen, correspondence with Leslie A. Heaphy, North Canton, Ohio, April 2004.}

Colacito (Appugliese), Lucille "Lou"

(b. 27 December 1921, Florence, Colorado) C 1944–45, Kenosha Comets

Before joining the AAGPBL, Lucille Colacito had limited softball experience since Horace Mann–North High School had no girls' sports. She played amateur softball in the local area. She made the roster for the Kenosha Comets in 1944 and played under former major leaguer Max Carey. Her favorite part of the whole experience was the traveling the teams did. After leaving the league Colacito continued her activities as a golfer and won several local awards over the years. She got married in 1941 and raised one son. She was also elected to the Denver Softball Hall of Fame. {AAGPBL Questionnaire, National Baseball Hall of Fame and Museum; AAGPBL Baseball Cards, 1995.}

Cole, Amy

OF, Colorado Silver Bullets

Collinsworth, Jessica "Sam"

Nicknamed for an uncle, Sam Collinsworth played baseball for the Cal Lutheran High School baseball team in 1978. The club went 3–8 while Collinsworth had one hit, four walks and no errors in her time on the field. The school population only registered 80 students so no girls' softball team existed. Coach Rod Frieling welcomed her presence and that of freshman Andy Parker to the club. Both play right field and second base. {Steve Brand, "Girls' Best Friend: Prep Diamond," *San Diego Union*, 29 April 1978.}

Colorado Silver Bullets

By Laura Wulf

The Colorado Silver Bullets were the result of an attempt by Bob Hope, a former Atlanta Braves executive and the owner of a public relations firm in Atlanta, to field a women's team in the minor leagues. He organized and held tryouts for a team called the Sun Sox in the mid–1980s, but the minor league system would not allow them into the league, so Mr. Hope decided to put together a team outside of professionally organized baseball. He secured about two million dollars in sponsorship from Coors Brewing Company and, with Phil Niekro on board as the manager of the team, held tryouts across the country. The team played 44 games during its first season in 1994, and 195 games over a four-year period.

The Silver Bullets barnstormed the country playing men's all-star, amateur and semipro teams from 1994 to 1997. Their coaches were mostly former major leaguers, including Joe Pignatano, Johnny Grubb, Al Bumbry, Joe Niekro and their manager, Phil Niekro, who was inducted into the National Baseball Hall of Fame in 1996, surrounded by his new and loyal team. Most of the players were top college softball players. Many had played some baseball as young girls, but most had been excluded from playing past the age of 12. There were a few exceptions such as Lee Anne Ketcham and Julie Croteau. Ketcham played baseball right through high school in Alabama but switched to softball for college because of scholarships. Julie Croteau went to court to play baseball at her high school in Virginia and lost, but went on to become the first woman to play and eventually to coach baseball at the college level.

In their first two seasons, the Bullets did not win a lot of games, though their record did improve each year. And it was not until their fourth and final season that they managed a winning record. It was ironic that just as they began to win, they lost the sponsorship of Coors. But anyone who measured the team's success only by the win-loss column completely missed the point. Those who dismissed the team on the basis of their record showed no understanding of the significance of women getting a real opportunity to play and learn the game of baseball. The players received high quality coaching from dedicated men who were willing to pass down their knowledge and experience to a hungry, appreciative and previously ignored group of prospective ball players.

The Silver Bullets broke a lot of new ground and were recognized by the Hall of Fame in Cooperstown. After the 1994 season, Lee Anne Ketcham and Julie Croteau became the first women to sign with the class A and AA men's Hawaii Winter Baseball League. In 1996, four players hit home runs, and Pam Davis, in a guest appearance with the AA Jacksonville Suns, pitched a scoreless inning of relief against the Australian Olympic men's team. In 1997, three players hit over .300 and the team dramatically won their final game to finish with a record of 23–22, for their first winning season. Phil Niekro described that final game as being as exciting as a World Series game.

In their first season the team's batting average was .141, and their opponents hit .336 against them. The pitching staff's ERA was 5.82 and opponents had a 1.27 ERA-against. The top individual batting average on the team was .200, shared by Stacy Sunny and Michelle MacAnanay, who each had just over 100 at-bats. Lee Anne Ketcham lead the pitching squad with a 4.80 ERA, and 63 strikeouts over 77.1 innings pitched. They finished with a record of 6–38.

Shortly into the start of their second season it was decided that the Silver Bullets would switch from wooden to aluminum bats. This decision came after they started the season at 2–8, with their two victories coming against teams from Greenville, South Carolina, and Greensboro, North Carolina. That season saw the team batting average rise to .183 while opponents batted .294 against them. The team ERA dropped to 5.08 and their opponents' ERA rose to 2.64. The top individual batting average for that second season was .246, hit by Stacy Sunny over 130 at-bats. That year Missy Coombes led the team with an ERA of 3.90 and 48 strikeouts over 85.1 innings. They won 11 games that season and lost 33.

With two years of playing under the belt of many of the returning players, the 1996 season saw dramatic improvements all around. The team's batting average finished at .241, five players hit over .250, and the top individual batting average was .308, compiled by Laura Espinoza-Watson, over the course of 214 at-bats. As a team the Silver Bullets had 68 doubles, as compared with 28 over the previous season. The team ERA for the 1996 season was 5.94 but their opponents' ERA jumped to 4.40. The team turned 47 double plays, as compared with 19 in their first year. Lee Anne Ketcham had the lowest ERA among the pitchers, finishing off at 2.27 over 43.2 innings pitched. Missy Coombes posted 82 strikeouts over 111.1 innings of work. They finished with 18 wins and 34 losses.

In their final season, the team batting average was .252, with their opponents hitting .313. Once again five players hit over .250, but that year three came in above .300, including Jenny Dalton-Hill, Toni Heisler and Tammy Holmes, who finished with an individual batting average of .341 in 170 at-bats. The pitching staff's ERA was 5.38 and their opponents' ERA was 4.48. Six members of the pitching squad had ERAs under 5.00, Lee Anne Ketcham leading with an ERA of 3.35 over 51.0 innings pitched. Christine Monge only walked four batters over 32.2 innings of work, while striking out 27. Their final record was 23–22. This season also included their first brawl in a game in Albany, Georgia, against the Americus Travelers. Kim Braatz-Voisard got hit by a pitch in the ninth inning of a losing effort, 10–6, and when the pitcher laughed the benches cleared.

After the conclusion of their fourth season and despite their winning record, Coors Brewing Company, which had been providing the team with about two million dollars a year to operate, decided not to continue with their sponsorship. Some rumors had it that Coors did not want people to think of Coors as a "women's beer," but the official reason was not made public. Despite much effort the Silver Bullets were unable to secure alternate funding and so were forced to disband. But their impact was undeniable. They were a catalyst and a point of convergence for girls and women who dreamed of playing baseball. Today, in 2004, there exist a number of amateur women's baseball leagues across the US, Canada, Australia and Japan and there are numerous national, as well as international, tournaments. {Henrietta Hay, "Girls Can Admire Silver Bullets," *The Denver Post*, 2 October 1996, B-11; "Texas Host of Silver Bullets Open Tryout," *BW SportsWire*, 18 March 1997; "Silver Bullets in Brawl with Teenage Boys' Team," *The Denver Post*, 14 June 1997, C-02; "Silver Bullets Play Exhibition," *The Frederick News*, 8 June 1995, D-8; "Silver Bullet to Hold Open Tryouts in Los Angeles," *BW SportsWire*, 17 February 1997; Tom Saladino, "Battle of the Sexes," *The Chronicle-Telegram*, 14 June 1997, D6.}

Colorado Women's Baseball Association (CWBA)

The Colorado Women's Baseball Association in 1995 was an affiliate member of the large Women's National Adult Baseball Association (WNABA). The president of the local Denver league was Howard Rollin and the league commissioner was Dean Tsutsui. The league planned a 12-game schedule in their inaugural season, with the opening game played 18 June 1995 at Horizon High School in Denver. The four teams in the league were simply designated as East, West, North and South. On opening day, the North beat the South team 16–8 while the East defeated the West 8–5. Theresa MacGregor managed the North squad while Allison Knudson took charge of the South nine. Nancy Popenhagen carried the managerial burden for the East and Sheri Smith did the same for the West. In game two the West defeated the North and the East triumphed over the South. The North had to forfeit their game because of a lack of players for the contest. In the third contest the North shut out the East 16–0 while the West beat the South 16–3. The winning pitcher for the North was Teresa Maraia with some relief help from Anna McCarty. During the fourth week the North recorded another shutout, this time against the East, 11–0, while the South squeaked out an 11–9 victory over the West. Teresa Maraia got the shutout victory, giving up only two hits and striking out six. The offensive outburst for the North was led by catcher Simona Errico. The South was led to victory by the solid pitching of Angie Morales, Allison Knudson and DeeDee Hoemann. In their fifth game the North gave up their first run in three games and came away the winner 17–1 over the South, while the West triumphed over the East but no score was reported. The victory for the North again went to Teresa Maraia as she gave up only two hits. The hitting was led by Carol Bishop's two hits. The final score of the second game was not reported because of an injury that resulted in some confusion on the field. Tammy Bernardi collided with first baseman Heather Wright and suffered a broken nose. In week six the North continued to dominate with a 12–9 victory over the South and the West again beat the East. Allison Knudson announced her resignation as manager of the South squad and Debbie Ross took over as the new skipper. Teresa Maraia picked up her fourth victory and her catcher Simona Errico again led the offensive output with a triple. In a come-from-behind victory the North defeated the East 10–9 in week seven and the South triumphed over the West 9–7. Anna McCarty got the win in relief, and the winning run was knocked in for the North by Maddy Russell. Due to weather and other complications, week eight saw no game played but a doubleheader was played in week nine. The North split their games, winning the first 8–4 over the West and losing the second 11–7 to the West. The East also split their games, winning game one 20–6 and losing game two 16–3 to the South. Teresa Maraia won the North's game while Cyndi Harrington took the loss. Anna McCarty lost the second while Natasha Castillo picked up the win for the West.

The league chose an all-star squad that played against the over-40 men's North American Baseball Association team and lost 6–3. Chosen as all-stars were Tammy Bernardi, Heather Wright, Carol Adams, Nanette Martin, Natasha Castillo, Kelly Docks, DeeDee Hoemann, MaryAnn Kurtinaitis, Theresa MacGregor, Teresa Maraia, Laira Hickman, Anna McCarty, Kerry Kramer and Jennie Mikkelson.

Following the week of the All-Star Game the North came back and won two games. They defeated the East 9–1 and the West 9–3. Teresa Maraia got hurt and was unable to pitch for the North. The South lost to both the East and the West. Though the North went into the championship series heavily, favored the winner of the CWBA was the South after defeating the North 11–1 and then the West 7–6. DeeDee Hoemann got the final victory for her club against Cyndi Harrington.

In 1996 a fifth team was added to the league, known simply as the Central team. Opening day games took place on 5 May 1996 with the North beating the East 11–3. The Roasters of the North were led at bat by Gayle Gallagher and Jodi Long. Over the Memorial Day weekend the league put together a team called the Colorado Rookies to represent them at the Las Vegas tournament. Included on the Rookies roster were Nancy Popenhagen, Beth Kelly, Gayle Gallagher, Carol Puehlhorn, Kerry Prebble, Kay Easthouse, Tracy Hanton, Amy Pomering, Jodi Long, Theresa MacGregor, Terri Scott (manager of the East squad), Teresa Maraia and MaryAnn Kurtinaitis. The North beat the new Central squad 10–4 on June 2 on a game-winning hit by Lori James. The winning pitcher was Theresa MacGregor. On June 7 the East beat the South 15–7. After week five the standings were reported with the East on top at 3–1 followed by the North at 2–1 with one tie. The West had yet to win a game, with an 0–3 record with one tie.

Week six saw the East triumph over the Central nine, 4–3 in extra innings. At the end of the eighth week the East clobbered the West 23–1 and the North beat the Central 6–2 to remain in second place at 4–1–1. As the North continued to win, the East lost their second game of the season to the South 7–5, thereby ending in a tie with the North at 6–2 at the close of week ten. Week 12 saw the East fall behind with a 13–10 loss to the West and then in the final standings the North stood alone atop the league with a 8–2 record, while the East came in second at 6–4 followed by the South at 5–5. The Central and West ended tied at 3–7. {CWBA Newsletters, February 1995–August 1996.}

1995 Rosters

North (Indigo Peak Roasters)
Errico, Simona — C
Kurtinaitis, MaryAnn — LF
McCarty, Anna — P/1B
Maraia, Teresa — P

South (Jackson's Hole)
Adams, Carol — 3B
Brown, Dawn
Carlton, Bobbie
Crawford, Colette
Hoemann, DeeDee — P
Knudson, Allison — Mgr/P
Lilak, Terry
Morales, Angie — P
Moriarty, Michelle
Ross, Debbie — Mgr
Sohnen, Barb

East (Arctic Wolves)
Docks, Kelly — CF
Kramer, Kerry
Wright, Heather — RF

West (Old Chicago)
Bernardi, Tammy — 2B
Castillo, Natasha — P
Dobson, Dawn
Harrington, Cyndi — P
Kissell, Robin
Logue, Theresa
Martin, Nanette — C
Mikkelson, Jennie
Pinelli, Charlene
Prebble, Kelly
Schultz, Jennifer
Smith, Sheri — Mgr.
Whitney, Trixie

1996 Rosters

North
MacGregor, Theresa — P/MGR
Maraia, Teresa "Tree" — P
Kurtinaitis, MaryAnn

South
Hoemann, Dee Dee — P
Brown, Dawn
Todd, Amy

East
Docks, Kelly
Galloway, Rita
Wright, Heather

West
Castillo, Natasha — P
Mikkelson, Jennie "Turtle"
Whitney, Trixie

Central
Bossio, Dara — P
Gaschler, Michelle

The league was reorganized in 1997 as the Westminster Tuesday Women's Baseball League (WTWBL), with a ten-week schedule. Oversight of the league fell to the City of Westminster Department of Parks, Recreation and Libraries. Members of the WTWBL were the Arctic Wolves, the Northern Sluggers, the Reds, the West and the Yankees. They played seven-inning games at Wolff Run Park. The season opener on 13 May 1997 found the Wolves defeating the Sluggers 11–5 and the West triumphing over the Yankees 8–5. In week two the West beat the Yankees 6–5 and the Wolves-Reds game was called with no decision. By the end of week six the Yankees stood atop the standings with a 4–1 record while the Sluggers held down the bottom spot with a 1–3 record and one no-decision game. Results for the remainder of the season have not been found.

Rosters

Arctic Wolves	Northern Sluggers
Sussman, Tiffany — P	Hight, Terri — IF
	MacGregor, Theresa — SS/2B/P
	Meddaugh, Sam — 3B

Reds	West
Hoemann, DeeDee — P	Castillo, Natasha
Mendiolz, Sue — CF	

Yankees

Bossio, Dara — P
Nunns, Jill — SS
{*WTWB News*, 13 May–1 July 1997.}

Columbia High School Baseball

A Columbia high school girls' baseball team in Michigan beat Grafton 18–11. They played a seven-inning game and expected to play again the following week. Unfortunately the news account gave no indication of players or how the runs were scored. {"Baseball Notes," *The Chronicle-Telegram*, 13 October 1931.}

Conniff, Taylor

(Phoenix, Arizona)

Taylor Conniff started playing baseball at the age of five. She likes the game because it is more competitive for her than softball. She plays for local teams in the Phoenix area that attend tournaments around the country. She attends Phoenix Christian High School and plays sports there. {Jose E. Garcia, "Women Play the Game Too," *The Arizona Republic*, 16 July 2004, 6.}

Conro, Pamela

(b. 13 September 1965) P, Colorado Silver Bullets
Pamela Conro played Little League baseball in

Vista la Mesa, California, in 1975 but did not return to her baseball roots until 1995. In 1995 she pitched for the San Diego Diamonds, an amateur all-star team with the National Women's Baseball Association (NWBA). {*Silver Bulletin*, March 1996.}

Cook, Ashley "Cookie"

(b. 1986, Lynn, Massachusetts) P, 2004 USA National Teams, Sea Hawks, Cougars, Lady Spirit

Ashley Cook was only 15 when she was invited to join Team USA as their youngest player in 2001. She was playing high school basketball at the time for Boston Latin Academy and also traveled with the Boston Blue Sox tournament team during 2001 and 2002. She started playing baseball when she was only five years old. She played for three years on Parkway's Mike Melling Traveling Baseball Team. Cook played for Team USA in the first three Women's World Series and in 2004 was selected to join the first official USA National Team. During the regular season in 2003 and 2004 she played for the Cougars in the New England league and the Sea Hawks in the North Shore league. Michelle Cunningham says that Cook is the toughest pitcher she has faced.

During the 2003 World Series Cook lost one game, pitching five and two-thirds innings and giving up two earned runs. She also had two at-bats and was held hitless. In the field she had three assists and one error. {USA Baseball Web site;

Seahawks pitcher Ashley Cook showing off her form (courtesy Laura Wulf).

Leslie Heaphy, correspondence with Michelle Cunningham, April 2004.} In 2004 Cook got two victories in relief as Team USA took the silver in World Series IV. She also is playing softball at the University of Massachusetts beginning in 2004. Joining the North Shore Lady Spirit in 2005 gave Cook the chance to play the Australian women's team in an exhibition series. She helped her club win game two in extra innings with two hits, and she scored the tying run in the ninth after walking. She also pitched the Lady Spirit to a 10–7 victory in the first game. {"Lady Spirit Take Two Game Lead Over Aussies," *The Salem News,* 21 July 2005; <http://www.USABaseball.com>.}

Cook, Clara R. "Babe"

(d. 23 July 1996, Elmira, New York) P, Rockford Peaches, Kenosha Comets, Milwaukee Chicks

Clara Cook got her start in sports playing softball, as most women did, since there was no baseball team for her to play on. Her brothers let her come out and play with them. She played for the Precision Tool Nine and Remington Rand in Elmira, New York. The Rand club won the New York State softball title in 1939. In 1943 Cook signed on with the Kenosha Comets and then spent three years with the Rockford Peaches before finishing her baseball career with the Milwaukee Chicks. After returning to Elmira she helped organize and run two traveling softball teams, the Elmira Comets and the Coca-Cola Queens. {AAGPBL Newsletter, May and September 1996.}

Cook, Donna "Cookie"

(b. 24 May 1928, Muskegon, Michigan) P/OF 1947–54, Muskegon Belles, Fort Wayne Daisies, Chicago Colleens, Grand Rapids Chicks, Battle Creek Belles, South Bend Blue Sox, Rockford Peaches

Donna and her sister Doris were one of a number of sets of sisters who played in the AAGPBL. Donna pitched in 99 games and compiled a record of 28–37 with an ERA of 3.08. She also played in 480 games and hit .191 while driving in 82 runs. Donna was a versatile athlete with a strong arm and good defensive skills. {AAGPBL Baseball Cards, 1995.}

Cook, Doris "Little Cookie"

(b. 23 June 1931, Muskegon, Michigan) OF/P 1947–53, Chicago Colleens, Springfield Sallies, Kalamazoo Lassies, South Bend Blue Sox

Doris Cook began her playing career in 1947 with the Chicago Colleens touring club. She began as an outfielder but shifted to pitching in 1950. Her sister Donna also played in the league. Doris's stats include information for 136 games she played in. She batted only .130 with 42 hits. {AAGPBL Baseball Cards, 1995.}

Cook, Dorothy

(St. Catherines, Ontario) SS 1946, Fort Wayne Daisies

Dorothy Cook joined the Daisies as their backup shortstop for one season.

Cooke, Colleen

(b. 30 April 1985, Uxbridge, Ontario) C/P, 2004 Team Canada

Colleen Cooke started playing baseball at the Bantam level in 2001 with Team Ontario. In 2002 she got chosen to play for Canada in the Roy Hobbs World Series. In 2003 she played for the Whitby Eagles in Ontario while also perfecting her softball skills so she could receive a scholarship to play at Northwood University in Midland, Michigan. She is majoring in sport and promotion management with plans to graduate in 2007. In 2004 she joined Team Canada at the World Cup in Edmonton, Alberta. {Baseball Canada 2004 Women's National Team Media Guide.}

Cool Hands Cafe Boxers

The Boxers won only two games in 1999 against nine losses.

Coombes, Melissa "Missy"

(b. 7 June 1968, San Gabriel, California) LHP 1994–97, Colorado Silver Bullets

Missy Coombes finished the Silver Bullets inaugural season with an 0–10 record but pitched solidly and got better with each outing. She pitched seven complete games in 1995 for the Bullets, led the team in strikeouts with 21 in 47 innings pitched, and compiled a 5–8 record to lead the club. In a game against the Capitol Rockies on 22 June 1995, Coombes struck out eight and walked none in a complete-game 6–2 victory. She helped herself with the bat, hitting .222 to lead the club. In another game against the NY Mets old-timers, she pitched three innings and gave up seven hits and two unearned runs in a losing effort. Before joining the Bullets she was a first team All-American at Fullerton State in 1989. In college she played first base but, going back to her days in Little League, Coombes had always been a pitcher. She started playing when she was seven years old and tried out for Little League with 30 boys. {"For the Love of the Game," Colorado Silver Bullets souvenir program, 1995; David Kindred, *Colorado Silver Bullets: For the Love of the Game* (Atlanta: Longstreet Press, Inc.), 68; Jason Molinet, "Bullets Beaten: Mets Oldtimers Edge Women's Team," *Newsday*, 18 June 1995; Bill Parillo, "The 4–15 Silver Bullets Are Winning Fans Over," *Tribune News Service*, 2 July 1995.}

Coombes, Rebecca Georgina

(b. 25 October 1983) P 2001–02, Australian National Team

Rebecca Coombes pitched at the top of her sport for the Australian team in the inaugural Women's World Series in 2001 in Toronto. Australia came home with the bronze medal. Coombes started playing baseball with the Chelsea tee ball program and then progressed through the various levels of play. {"Coombes Pitches In for Stars," *Mordialloc Chelsea Leader*, 11 December 2002, 58.}

Cooper, Tracey

Pawtucket Slaterettes

Tracey Cooper forged a path her sisters have followed as each of them has joined the Pawtucket Slaterettes. Their father, Steve, has served the league as president of the executive board. He got involved when Joe Thibeault encouraged him to support his daughters. Thibeault had been the league president for a number of years because his daughter played baseball too.

Corbus, Vada

A team from Joplin, Missouri, made history in 1931 when they signed a 19-year-old player to their roster. What made this player notable? The new catcher hit right-handed and threw right-handed, but her name was Vada Corbus. She became the second female player to sign a professional contract in 1931. The other was Jackie Mitchell with the Chattanooga Lookouts. Corbus would join the Joplin Miners in the Western Association. Her brother Luke played in the same league for two years. Vada started playing baseball as a young girl with her brothers and their friends. A club official stated they signed her because she

could hit and run and she knew how to handle pitchers. Prior to joining the Miners, Corbus played in the local city league for three seasons, playing wherever they needed her fielding skills. {"Girl Catcher is on Joplin Ball Club's Payroll," *South Bend News-Times*, 20 April 1931; "Girl of 19 Signs with Joplin as Catcher," *New York Times*, 18 April 1931, 28; "Joplin Signs Girl Catcher, 19 and Blond," *Chicago Tribune*, 19 April 1931, A2.}

Cordes (Elliott), Gloria "Cordie"

(b. 21 September 1931, Staten Island, New York) P/1B 1950–54, Kalamazoo Lassies, Racine Belles, Battle Creek Belles

Gloria Cordes pitched in the All American League for five seasons. Her standout year was 1952, when she pitched in 24 consecutive complete games. Cordes made the all-star squad from 1952 to 1954. She pitched in 128 games with a record of 49–51 and an ERA of 2.54. At the plate she averaged about 60 at-bats a season without much production. Cordes made the league after attending an open tryout and was invited to join one of the traveling teams that folded in 1951. When she joined the Lassies she made $50 a week; she had been making $30 as a clerk. She spent 18 years managing one of her town's Little League teams. {Patricia Vignola, "The Patriotic Pinch Hitter," *Nine*, March 2004; AAGPBL Baseball Cards, 1995.}

Cornett, Betty Jane "Curly"

(b. 24 November 1932, Pittsburgh, Pennsylvania; d. 18 March 2006) 3b/p 1950–51, Rockford Peaches; Springfield Sallies; Kalamazoo Lassies, Battle Creek Belles

Betty Cornett grew up in Troy Hill after the death of her father. She was the youngest of eleven siblings. She started her professional baseball career with the Peaches when she was only 16. She started as a pitcher and then shifted to third base as the style of pitching moved from underhand to overhand. The Peaches assigned her to Springfield her first season to improve her skills. She got paid $55 a week and traveled all over the country. She played in 113 games and hit .183 with 43 RBIs. She also had an 0-1 record as a pitcher. After her baseball days ended she worked for the H. J. Heinz Company for 24 years, retiring in 1985. {Harry Lister, "You've Come a Long Way Baby," News Record/Valley News, 4 July 1992, B1; Betty Sarafin, "Women in Baseball: Destined for the Big Leagues," Focus, 10 July 1994, 7; "Obituary"

Pittsburgh Post-Gazette, 26 March 2006; AAG PBL Baseball Cards, 1995.}

Cortesio (Papageorgiou), Maria "Ria"

(b. 1977, Rock Island, Illinois) Umpire

Ria Cortesio grew up in the Midwest, taking dance classes and playing Little League, as many young girls do. Her family owned a wine import business and this allowed her the luxury of traveling all over the world. She knows as much about wine and languages as she does about baseball rules. While in college at Rice University, Cortesio enrolled in the Jim Evans Academy for umpiring and finished the course in time to be assigned to her first job in the pioneer league in 1999. She graduated in the top ten percent of her class and became affiliated with the Professional Baseball Umpires Corporation, which is associated with minor league baseball. In 2004 she got an invitation back to Rice to umpire the alumni game after she had returned to Rice to get a degree in sports management. She was promoted to the Midwest League in 2001, where coach Jeff Carter of the River Bandits expressed the idea that she might have what it takes to make it to the big leagues. Then she was promoted to the Florida State League in 2002. In order to move up to the double A level, Cortesio needed to bump some other umpires: the competition was quite intense since there are fewer spots available than there are umpires. 2004 marks her second season in the double A Southern League. The travel is extensive, the accommodations not always the best and the pay not that high, but Cortesio has said that there is no better way to watch a game than from behind home plate. Cortesio knows the rules from having played semipro baseball in the Houston NABA league. She pitched and played first base. {Steve Batterson, "Calling Her Own Game," *Quad City Times*, 13 May 2001, D1, D6; Kexin Baxter, "The Lady is an Ump," *The Miami Herald*, 5 August 2002; Karen Crouse, "Female Umpire Hears All, Calls All," *Palm Beach Post*, 19 May 2002; Patrick Lastrapes, "Ria Cortesio Breaks the Mold, Calls 'Em Tough," <ExaminerNews.com>, 5 May 2004; Scott Mansch, "Ria Cortesio Feature," *Great Falls Tribune*, 14 July 2000; Candace Rondeaux, "Not All Boys of Summer," *The Cincinnati Post*, 10 April 2003.}

Coughenour, Cara

(b. 12 May 1967, Sioux City, Iowa) 1B/DH/P 1995, Colorado Silver Bullets

Cara Coughenour attended the University of Iowa and was named to the Mid-East All-Regional team for softball in 1989. For her achievements in college she was selected for membership in the Iowa Girls High School Athletic Union Hall of Fame in 1994. Coughenour played in 34 games in 1995, splitting her time between first base and designated hitter. She stole three bases in three attempts during those 34 games. {"For the Love of the Game," Colorado Silver Bullets souvenir program, 1995.}

Courtney, Patricia "Pat"

(b. 8 October 1931, New York City, New York) 3B 1950, Grand Rapids Chicks, Chicago Colleens, Springfield Sallies

Pat Courtney graduated from Everett High School in Massachusetts in 1949. She also attended Bentley School of Accounting and Finance. Her athletic experiences before joining the AAGPBL involved the Catholic Youth Organization and Everett city league where she was coached by Ed English, brother to Maddy English, who also played in the AAGPBL. Courtney played for one month with Grand Rapids before being released. She was later chosen for the roster of the traveling Chicago Colleens. One of her favorite memories was playing in Yankee Stadium and getting to meet Connie Mack. After the Colleens folded Courtney stayed active as a bowler, golfer and basketball player. She also coached girls' softball. Her career after baseball was in the accounting department for the IRS. {AAGPBL Questionnaire, National Baseball Hall of Fame and Library; Patricia Brown, "Patricia Courtney," in *A League of My Own* (North Carolina: McFarland and Company, Inc., 2003), 161–63; AAGPBL Baseball Cards, 1995.}

Coutts, Lynn

Lynn Coutts got the chance to play against the Colorado Silver Bullets in 1996 when they traveled to Maine. Coutts and Tammy Silveira were the women chosen to play with the Cape Cod All Stars when they played the Bullets on July 20, 1996. {"Coutts to Play Against Silver Bullets," *Bangor Daily News*, 2 July 1996.}

Cox, Theresa

(b. 1961) Umpire

In 1988 Theresa Cox umpired two Southern League games at Hoover Metropolitan Stadium. She became the Southern League's first female umpire when she took up her space at third base. She made three calls in her first game, two on fly balls and one at third. During the 1989 and 1990 seasons Cox worked as an umpire in the Arizona Rookie League, making her the fourth female umpire to work in organized baseball. While trying to break into the professional ranks regularly, Cox umpired college and high school games. She graduated from the Joe Brinkman Umpiring School after she sold her business in Houston to pursue umpiring full time. She moved to Alabama to take a chance on getting into the Southern League. {Rubin Grant, "Female Umpire Makes First Appearance," *Birmingham Post-Herald*, 4 June 1988, B1, B6; Ken Gurnick, "It's a Field of Dreams Few Have Realized," *The National Sports Daily*, 19 June 1990, 18–19; Wayne Martin, "Lady Ump Makes Successful Debut at the Met," *The Birmingham News*, 5 June 1988, 1B, 8B; "Woman Ump Set for Weekend Duty at the Hoover Met," *The Birmingham News*, 2 June 1988, 1D, 7D.}

Coyne, Colleen

P

Colleen Coyne grew up playing sports. One of her loves was baseball, and she played one year of J.V. ball at Tabor Academy before she graduated in 1989. She played lacrosse, soccer and hockey for all four years while at the academy. Coyne tried out in 1994 for the Silver Bullets and made it to the cut of 48, but the roster only called for 24 players. The next 24 were on reserve in case a player got hurt. After hurting her shoulder she thought her pitching days were done, but in late 1994 Coyne became the first woman to pitch in a Cape Cod League baseball game. She pitched one inning in an exhibition game for the Wareham Gateman club just to see if her arm was healing properly. Coyne played for Team USA in hockey and played in the 1992 and 1993 world championships, losing to Canada both times. Coyne took time off from the University of New Hampshire to play hockey and try out for the Silver Bullets.

Craig, Kelly

C

Kelly Craig had the distinction of playing in the 1990 Little League World Series for British Columbia. She caught for her club in that competition.

Cramer, Jennifer

1B San Diego Stix, 2002, Virginia Flames

In 2002 Jen Cramer hit .429 for the Flames after joining them from the San Diego Stix. Cramer also contributed to the Flames' success with her outstanding defensive play at first base.

Cramer, Peggy

(b. 22 July 1937, Buchanan, Michigan) C 1954, South Bend Blue Sox

Peggy Cramer had age working against her since she joined the league in its final season, and she was only 16 and still in high school. Since she had to finish school she did not get to play the full season. After the league folded Peggy continued her schooling and became a school teacher, working for 28 years. {AAGPBL Baseball Cards, 1995.}

Crawford, Monica

Monica Crawford pitched for East High School's baseball team in Denver, Colorado, for two years before a protest was launched and she was not allowed to pitch any longer. The protest came in 1996 after another local female pitcher, Natalie Callaway, pitched against Adams City; their athletic director Fred Applewhite launched a protest. He cited an obscure Colorado High School Athletic Association rule that stated no female who played softball in the fall could play baseball in the spring. Her coach and athletic director supported her playing but did not want to see all their games forfeited. Crawford said she would continue to play softball because that is where the scholarships for female players were. {Carol Kreck, "The Girls of Summer Distaff Players Shortstopped by Obscure Rule," *The Denver Post*, 15 May 1996, G-01.}

Crawley, Pauline Marie "Hedy," "Pat"

(b. 11 September 1924, Phoenix, Arizona; d. 17 September 2003, Geneva, New York) OF 1946, 1951, Peoria Red Wings, Battle Creek Belles

Before joining the AAGPBL, Pauline Crawley played softball in the Phoenix city league. One of her teams, the Ramblers, won a number of state championships. Pauline played for one year in the AAGPBL before joining the Chicago Professional Softball League from 1947–50. Her career with the Red Wings was cut short by a knee injury and resulting surgery. She played for the Bloomer Girls, who won two championships. She did return to play for Battle Creek in 1951 before hanging up her spikes. All total, she played in 125 games and hit only .160. She played all sports in high school but did not continue them when she attended college. She worked for Goodyear during the Second World War and then worked for United Airlines for 32 years after earning her BA from California State University, Los Angeles. {AAGPBL Newsletter, May 2004; AAGPBL Questionnaire, National Baseball Hall of Fame and Museum; AAGPBL Baseball Cards, 1996.}

Cress, Missy

(b. 20 May 1970, Burbank, California) C 1994, Colorado Silver Bullets

Missy Cress graduated from Royal High School in 1988 and went on to attend the University of California at Northridge and play softball there, hitting .333 in 1993. In 1994 she caught 19 games for the Bullets, with her biggest highlight coming in a game against Bellingham, Washington, on August 21. In that game she caught three base runners stealing. When not playing for the Bullets, Cress worked as a driver for UPS. {"For the Love of the Game," Colorado Silver Bullets souvenir program, 1995; Ross Newhan, "A Dream of Their Own," *Los Angeles Times*, April 30, 1994, C1, C11.}

Crews, Mary Nesbitt

P 1944–45, Racine Belles

In 1945 Mary Crews led the All-American League in hitting with an average of .319, beating out runner-up Helen Callaghan, who hit .299. She played for two years with the Belles.

Crites, Shirley "Squirrely"

(b. 21 August 1934, Cape Giardeau, Missouri; d. 28 December 1990) 3B, Fort Wayne Daisies

Shirley Crites played one season with the Daisies after playing softball in her hometown. She played in 47 games, hitting only .129. Deciding not to return for a second season, she went to work for Motorola and worked her way up to a supervisory position. She also golfed in Chicago and Arizona. {AAGPBL Baseball Cards, 2002.}

Croteau, Julie

(b. 4 December 1970, Prince William County, Virginia) 1B

Julie Croteau came to national attention in 1988 when she tried out for her school's varsity baseball team, the Yellow Jackets, in Manassas, Virginia, and she was cut. Her claim was that she did not get

a fair trial because of her gender. So she and her parents sued Osbourn Park High School and the baseball coach Rick Fair for sex discrimination. Croteau wanted the court to put her on the team and award monetary damages, but she lost the case.

Croteau started playing baseball when she was six years old and got invited to play on a local tee ball club. She did get to play Little League, and she compiled a .300 batting average while fielding solidly at first base under coach William Hair. She played on the Big League team for 16- to 18-year-olds, and the manager, Larry Poplin, praised her skills at first base. She also participated in a series of baseball clinics run by Ron Natolli, Catholic University's baseball coach, to hone her skills. In tenth grade Croteau made the school's junior varsity squad but sat on the bench most of the season even though she beat out the boy playing first base. In eleventh grade she did not make the team when the coaches changed. The new coach, Rick Fair, thought she should go back to playing softball, a game she had never actually played. After visiting the school superintendent and principal her parents encouraged her to file a lawsuit, which she did. She lost the case because it was hard to prove that her tryout was a sham. Judge Tim Ellis III issued the final verdict and in ruling against Croateau, said that no constitutional right to play baseball existed. {Jane Leavy, "Hey, Fans, Guess Who's on First?" *Washington Post*, 16 May 1988, B1; Caryle Murphy and Peter Pae, "Judge Rejects Claim of Girl Cut from Baseball Team," *Washington Post*, 24 March 1988, D1, D4.}

Croteau then joined the semipro Fredricksburg Giants, an all-men's team, at the invitation of their manager Mike Zitz. The Giants played in the semipro Virginia Baseball League and had won two league championships prior to Croteau's trying out. She played with the Giants for five years and hit .261. In 1993 she had her best year, hitting .308.

Croteau attended St. Mary's College and played for three seasons before resigning from the squad because of ongoing sexist practices. During her three years she played first base and hit .171. She played in her first game against the Spring Garden College Bobcats in 1989 and went down in the history books as the first woman to play in an NCAA college baseball game. She played five innings and committed no errors at first, while grounding out three times at the plate. Her coach Hal Willard believed everyone should be impressed with her abilities. {"Flawless at First," *New York Times*, 19 March 1989, S1.}

In 1994 Croteau played a whole winter season for the Maui Stingrays with Lee Anne Ketcham of the Silver Bullets. Croteau also played the inaugural season for the Silver Bullets at first base. Her numbers at the end of the season were not impressive at the plate, where she only hit .078 with two runs batted in. She did walk 13 times and score five runs. In the field she only made two errors at first.

Her life outside of baseball has included being a television baseball analyst for Liberty Sports in 1995 and working for Major League Baseball. In the fall of 1993 she was the assistant baseball coach at Western New England College in Springfield, Massachusetts. From 1995 to 2000 she served as the assistant baseball coach at the University of Massachusetts, Amherst. Her primary duties were as hitting instructor, and handling team conditioning and infield drills. {Alice Diglio, "Girls Sues to Play Ball," *Washington Post*, 17 March 1988, A1, A20; Tony Kornheiser, "Julie Croteau's Play Deserves to be judged on the Baseball Field, Not in a Court Room," *Washington Post*, 19 March 1988, D3; Mary H. J. Farrell, "Say it ain't So," *People Weekly*, 6 June 1994; Nicholas Dawidoff, "Resigned: From the Baseball Team at St. Mary's College of Maryland, Junior First Baseman Julie Croteau," *Sports Illustrated*, 17 June 1991, 98; "Julie Croteau Profile," <http://www.spalding.com/croteau.html>; "Croteau Turns Passion to Coaching," *USA Today Baseball Weekly*, 1–7 May 1996, 35; "Girl Cut from H.S. Baseball Team Sues," *Base Woman Newsletter*, June 1988, 1–2; Robert Collias, "Hawaiian League Reloads with Pair of Silver Bullets," *USA Today Baseball Weekly*, 12–18 October 1994, 8.}

Cruz, Kayla

Pawtucket Slaterettes Junior Division

Kayla Cruz played for the junior division in the Slaterettes organization in 1999. She led the league in home runs with four, having tied Kristen Langevin for the lead. {Greg Botelho, "Pawtucket Slaterettes Having Another Banner Year," *Providence Journal*, 28 June 1999, C-03.}

Cubs

The Cubs joined the Phoenix league in 1994 and finished with a 5–9 record. They did not improve much for the 1995 season, ending with a 4–10 record.

Cunanan, Susie

3B, Fillies

During the 2003 season in 19 at-bats Susie Cunanan had eight hits and scored seven runs.

Cunningham, Michelle

(b. 22 December 1976, Cooperstown, New York) P/SS

Michelle Cunningham started her baseball career playing Little League in Mobile, Alabama, as a pitcher and shortstop for the team representing Knollwood Park Hospital. She played softball, volleyball and basketball in high school. Her accomplishments earned her the chance to play volleyball and softball at Eastern Connecticut State University. She earned second team All-American honors in softball in 1998 at third base and was Rookie of the Year in volleyball. She also was named All-Region and All-New England in volleyball for all four years, 1996–99. In 2003 she became the softball coach at Randolph-Macon Women's College after serving as the volunteer assistant coach for three years. Cunningham also worked as the assistant basketball coach for four years and assistant volleyball coach for three years. During the 2003 baseball season Cunningham pitched for the Falcons in the New England Women's Baseball League. As a part of her involvement she traveled with the all-star team to Canada and South Bend to play in tournaments. The squad won both tourneys. {Christopher L. Gasper, "Playing the Game They Love," *Boston Globe*, 13 July 2003, 1, 11; Michelle Cunningham, interview with Leslie Heaphy, 2004.}

Curiosities

Introducing young ladies and fans to women playing baseball was indeed a difficult thing to do from the beginning of the sport. Often the idea was complicated by various sorts of games that either made fun of the notion or concentrated more on the attire of the young ladies than on the play. While there were many regular teams that developed, researchers can find lots of single articles about one-time games obviously played for curiosity and nothing more. One such took place in 1883 in Manhattan: two teams of eight ladies entertained a crowd of 1,500. The teams were dressed in red and blue respectively and more attention was drawn by their loose fitting dresses than by their skills on the diamond. The game was filled with lots of wild plays and errant throws leading to a final score of 54–22 in only five innings. {"A Base-Ball Burlesque," *New York Times*, 23 September 1883.}

Just after the turn of the century there were an increasing number of women's baseball games reported that were not played by the Blondes and Brunettes of the previous century or the Bloomers of the teens and 1920s. Instead most of these games appear to have been staged solely as curiosities, to give the fans something to enjoy in small towns and resort areas. In South Jamesport, Long Island, for example, a group of young women played nine men and won 27–20, but the men had to play with one arm tied behind their backs. The girls were led by pitcher Mabel Pearce and catcher Sira Joseph. In a similar style of play was a game played in Patchogue, Long Island, at the Cliffton Resort. The young men had to play the game wearing skirts and had their right arm tied to their right leg. The reporter also indicated that a tennis ball rather than baseball was used and that they played seven innings with the girls triumphing in the end. Every one of the ladies scored at least one run and the pitching of Hazel Elliott kept them in the game. The catcher, Mary Connor, was applauded for her fine play while Miss Pitsche covered a lot of ground in center field and scored more than once because of her daring base-running. The Cliffton game was called early to avoid tiring out the ladies. These kinds of games made it difficult for women who wanted to play the game seriously. {"Girls' Team Won," *Brooklyn Daily Eagle*, 4 August 1900, 15.}

Other types of games relied on ridiculous handicaps for the men's teams to create a sense of competition. Fans reacted positively to most of these games, as long as they were advertised properly. For example, over 500 fans came out to watch a game at the McKinley Manual Training School between the female students and the boys, who had to play left-handed. In another contest on Staten Island the young men dressed in skirts so that an equal handicap would be faced by all the players. {"Amateurs in Skirts on Baseball Field," *New York Times*, 2 October 1906, 7; "Grammar School Games," *Los Angeles Times*, 11 December 1907, 16.}

Curone, Jo

OF 1999, San Diego Stix, Cal Sabres

In the 1999 national championship series Curone hit .556 with eight runs knocked in and another ten scored. She was selected to the All-Tournament team for her accomplishments as the Stix won the title. In 2001 Curone led a veteran pitching staff for the Cal Sabres as they came in second in the Roy Hobbs Tournament, losing 2–1 to the Ocala Lightning.

D'Amato, Michelle

(b. 1966) 1B 2002, Indians

Michelle D'Amato grew up playing softball but switched to baseball in 2002 with the formation of the new East Coast Women's Baseball League (ECWBL). She became the first baseman and coach for the Indians, one of four entries in the league. In college D'Amato had played third base at Stockton State College. {Wayne Witkowski, "Pioneers Are in a League of Their Own," *Asbury Park Press*, 25 September 2002.}

D'Angelo, Josephine "Jo Jo"

(b. 23 November 1924, Chicago, Illinois) OF 1943–44, South Bend Blue Sox

Josephine D'Angelo graduated from Harper High School in 1942. While attending she played softball in a local women's league since the school did not have a team. D'Angelo developed a reputation as the best contact hitter around. In 1943, for example, she struck out only three times during the season, once every 119.3 at-bats. She also stole 53 bases in 104 games. She played in the first All-Star Game at Wrigley Field in 1943. In the field she handled 61 chances and made no errors. D'Angelo went on to college after her ball-playing days and completed her bachelor's at DePaul University in 1948 and then went back to school for a master's at Chicago State University, graduating in 1966. Josephine worked in the steel mills in 1942 and 1943 as her first job after high school. She taught physical education for 24 years in the Chicago public school system. This led to her working for ten years as a guidance counselor. {AAGPBL Newsletter, May 2001, 40; AAGPBL Questionnaire, National Baseball Hall of Fame and Museum; AAGPBL Baseball Cards, 1996.}

Daetweiler, Louella "Daets"

(b. 30 April 1918, Lynwood, California) C, Rockford Peaches

Louella Daetweiler caught for one year for the Rockford Peaches after having played a number of years in softball. She returned to fast-pitch softball after her one year stint. She also taught, coached and officiated at Compton Community College in California. She played in 33 games for the Peaches with 38 putouts and 12 errors. Her hitting was not strong either and accounts for her limited playing time. {AAGPBL Baseball Cards, 1996.}

Dailey, Mary

(b. 5 December 1928, Lexington, Massachusetts; d. 5 December 1965) P/OF Peoria Red Wings, South Bend Blue Sox, Battle Creek Belles

Mary Dailey primarily caught during her two seasons in the All-American League but did get a chance to pitch in three games while with Peoria. She played in 114 games and hit only .162. In her three pitching starts she had only one decision and that was a victory. In addition to playing baseball Mary also played golf and tennis and bowled. {AAGPBL Baseball Cards, 2000.}

Daily, Elizabeth

Chaperone

Elizabeth Daily served as the chaperone for the Peoria Red Wings in 1949. Her responsibilities ranged from making sure the girls had no overnight male visitors to teaching them how to deal with the press. In addition, Daily was a registered nurse and served from 1940 to 1945 in the Army Nurse Corps. {Merrie Fidler, *The Development and Decline of the All-American Girls Baseball League, 1943–1954*, Master of Science thesis (Department of Physical Education: University of Massachusetts, 1976), 249.}

Dalton-Hill, Jenny

(Glendale, California) 3B, Colorado Silver Bullets

After playing softball at the University of Arizona, Jenny Dalton-Hill was invited to the Silver Bullets' spring training in 1997. While at Arizona, Dalton-Hill was named an All-American in 1994, 1995 (second team) and 1996, and she won the College World Series MVP in 1996. She was also named National Player of the Year in 1996. She set eight NCAA softball records in her career while batting a career high .412. In 1997 Dalton-Hill had the third highest average for the Bullets at .308. {"Arizona Standout to Join Silver Bullets in Spring Training," BW SportsWire, 22 April 1997; "Silver Bullets Future Uncertain," *Wisconsin State Journal*, 27 August 1997; University of Arizona softball Web site.}

Danaher, Sue

P, Lady Mariners

Sue Danaher pitched for the Lady Mariners in Australia and started the 2004 season primarily as a relief pitcher.

Dancer, Faye "Fanny"

(b. 24 April 1925, Santa Monica, California; d. 22 May 2002) OF/1B/P 1944–50, Minneapolis Millerettes, Fort Wayne Daisies, Peoria Red Wings

By Tim Wiles

Known as "All the Way Faye" for her exuberance both on and off the field, Faye Katherine Dancer was a complete ballplayer who featured baseball's traditional five tools: she could hit, hit for power, run, throw, and catch. Moreover, she was a fan favorite who thrived in the spotlight and displayed good humor and *joie de vivre* both on and off the field.

Born 24 April 1925 in Santa Monica, California, she was the youngest of two children born to Lloyd Augustus Dancer and Olive Victoria Pope Dancer. She grew up excelling in sports, particularly softball, playing on semiprofessional softball teams along with LaVonne "Pepper" Paire Davis, with whom she was recruited by Bill Allington for the AAGPBL in early 1944.

The five-foot, six-inch freckled blonde, who batted and threw right-handed, was assigned to the Minneapolis Millerettes in 1944. As an 18-year-old rookie, she batted a career-high .274 (third in the league), with two home runs— both grand slams—a career high 48 RBI, and 63 stolen bases. "She was that rare breed of ballplayer who could lay down a perfect bunt, and then steal second base," recalled Pepper. "Then, the next time up, she could hit the long ball."

The Millerettes moved to Fort Wayne, Indiana, for the 1945 season, and were renamed the Daisies. Dancer played in 108 games, leading the league with three home runs. The Daisies finished in third place in the six-team league, but won their first-round playoff series against the Racine Belles, with Dancer hitting .308, with two homers and eight RBI in the four-game series. The Rockford Peaches took the championship round, though Dancer kept up her torrid pace, hitting .286 in that series.

As outfielder and first baseman, Dancer continued to star for the Daisies in 1946, playing in 110 games and racking up a career-high 257 total bases. But Dancer also debuted a new facet of her game, going 10–9 with a 1.93 ERA as a pitcher. Early in the 1947 season, she was traded to the Peoria Red Wings along with Alice DeCambra for Thelma "Tiby" Eisen and Kay Blumetta, in the largest trade in league history up to that point.

After a so-so season in 1947, Dancer returned to form in 1948, leading the Peoria Red Wings into the playoffs. She recorded career highs in six offensive categories: 122 games, 89 runs scored, 109 hits, 6 home runs, 55 walks, and 102 stolen bases, second only to base-running wizard Sophie Kurys. Her home run and runs scored totals were also second in the league.

A headline from that season reads: "Dancer is High Test Fuel That Makes Wings Explosive." Despite three hits in three games by Dancer, the Red Wings were swept in the first round by the Racine Belles.

She did not play in 1949, perhaps due to lingering injuries caused by her all-out style of play. Dancer would slide headfirst — although she was particularly adept at hook slides as well — crash into outfield fences, and dive for balls. One sportswriter dubbed her a "fly catching genius," and Pepper recalled that she could fire strikes to the plate from center field after catching balls over her shoulder. On the bases, she was aggressive and fearless. "I loved to slide," she once remarked, rejecting the notion that skirted play might cause players to be conservative about hitting the dirt.

She returned to the Red Wings in 1950, retiring after the season due to a ruptured disc caused by sliding. She returned to California and worked as an electronics technician for many years.

The free-spirited Dancer didn't just entertain fans with baseball heroics, however. She also turned cartwheels and caught fireflies on the field, and once called an official time-out to get a drink of water. "I was forever having fun, raising my skirt up for the fans, doing the splits and handstands when the games got quiet," she recalled. "Faye had her share of admirers, but her nickname really came from her all-out style of play," remembered Pepper. "On the ball field, there wasn't anything she wouldn't do to win."

Indeed, June Peppas recalled a game, down by two runs in the eighth, where she came to bat with two runners on base. Peppas belted a home run over the center field wall, to put the Racine Belles up by a run. Or did she? Dancer managed to convince the umpire that the ball had bounced over the fence, and Peppas returned to second with a double and one RBI. Peoria won the game, and later that night at a restaurant, Dancer approached Peppas to apologize for the trick play.

Off the field, Dancer was a merry prankster, who enjoyed initiating new chaperones. She recalled replacing the filling in their Oreos with toothpaste, spreading Limburger cheese all over their light bulbs, or smearing peanut butter on their toilet seats. She also kept chaperones and managers busy worrying over her whereabouts, as she liked to go out and drink beer, often enlisting more well-behaved teammates in capers like drinking beer in cemeteries, where no one would come looking for them. She also enjoyed stealing the ubiquitous blowfish which hung from the ceilings in taverns. Her exits from hotels via fire escapes and returns via staff elevators were legendary. In the off-season, she traveled with Jim Thorpe's all-female barnstorming team, the Thunderbirds, members of the National Softball Congress.

Dancer was superstitious, always closing her door three times before a ball game, and collecting glass eyes from stuffed animals and carousel horses, which she then passed around for good luck. She enjoyed a good rapport with fans, and spoke to them on her way on and off the field. One fan in Peoria, who happened to be a Mafia kingpin, took a shine to her and tried to ply her and her family with meals and gifts. "One time he even asked me if I wanted anyone killed," she recalled. "I told him, 'Maybe the umpire.'" She added that she made sure he knew she was kidding.

Dancer never married, as the love of her life was killed during World War Two, according to Pepper. She did settle down, however, and quit drinking almost 30 years before her death. "At some point you make a promise to yourself," she commented. She became a board member of the AAGPBL Players Association, and served as an advisor for the filming of the movie *A League of Their Own*. It was widely reported that she was the inspiration for the character played by Madonna.

In 2000, she was diagnosed with breast cancer, and she died at the age of 77 on 22 May 2002 of complications related to cancer surgery.

In her six-year career, she recorded 488 hits in 591 games. She drove in 193 runs, hitting 53 doubles, 14 triples, and 16 home runs. She tallied 1,080 total bases along with 352 steals, and her career batting average was .236. As a pitcher in two seasons, she was 11–11 with an ERA of 2.28. "I'll probably be remembered as a crowd favorite, a little crazy," she once said. "I always had fun." {John B. Holway, "Confessions of an All-American Girl," *Nine*, Fall 2000, 267 ff.; "Faye Dancer," <Historicbaseball.com>.}

Danhauser (Brown), Margaret L. "Marnie"

(b. 9 June 1921, Racine, Wisconsin) 1B 1944, Racine Belles

Margaret Danhauser spent one short year with the Racine Belles.

Danz, Shirley

(b. 16 August 1926, Oak Park, Illinois) OF 1949–50, Chicago Colleens, Racine Belles

Shirley Danz spent one year tuning her skills on the Colleens touring club before joining the Belles for one season. She left the league after a short season that saw her in only 23 games and went on to manage fast-pitch softball teams. Then in 1961 she took up professional bowling and continued that until 1969. {AAGPBL Baseball Cards, 1996.}

Dapkus (Wolf), Eleanor "Slugger," "Ellie"

(b. 5 December 1923, Chicago, Illinois) OF/P 1943–50, Racine Belles

Eleanor Dapkus went to Fenger High School in Chicago and played every sport available to girls, but they were all of the playground variety, not varsity competition. Both before and after she joined the AAGPBL, Dapkus worked in a variety of jobs. Most of her early work was clerical except for during the Second World War when she spray-painted airplane parts at the Pullman Aircraft factory. Dapkus was chosen as the utility outfielder for the 1943 all-star team after belting ten home runs for the Belles. Dapkus earned the nickname Slugger in 1943 for setting the league batting record. Racine also won the league championship in both 1943 and 1946. For the 1946 team, Dapkus hit .253 and drove in 57 runs. In 1948 the Belles decided to move her to the pitching mound, and she was successful. She won 53 games in three seasons and only lost 34 games. She struck out 397 batters and had an ERA of 1.97. She spent her eight years in the league with Racine before leaving to get married on 30 September 1950. She worked for over 25 years as a legal secretary and enjoyed bowling and golfing in addition to playing baseball. In 1952 she also played for one season with the Music Maids, a softball team. {AAGPBL Newsletter, May 2001, 31; AAGPBL Questionnaire, National Baseball Hall of Fame and Museum.}

Darden, Leandra

3B, Virginia Flames

Leandra Darden debuted for the Flames in 2002 at third base. In her first game in June she was 1–3 with one RBI. Darden was only 14 when she started for the Flames.

Daredevils

This team was an entry in the American Women's Baseball Association.

Dark, Amanda

(b. 12 April 1985) IF 2003, Queensland Rams

Amanda Dark played for the Rams at the Australian National Championship series.

Dauvray, Helen

During the second half of the nineteenth century Helen Dauvray was a comedic actress in New York and Paris. She was also an avid baseball fan who married John Montgomery Ward. In 1887 she offered a silver cup to the winner of the series between the National and American Association clubs. The cup continued to be handed out through 1893 even though Dauvray's marriage lasted only two years. She also commissioned gold badges for each player on the winning team. {"Helen Dauvray Remarries," *Brooklyn Daily Eagle*, 30 April 1886; J.G. Floto, "Thumbnail Sketches of Female Baseball Pioneers," *The Diamond Angle*, summer 1997, 44.}

Davidson, Alison

(b. 1987, Melbourne, Australia) P/3B/1B, Doncaster Dragons

Alison Davidson plays baseball in the Victoria Baseball Association. In 1997 and 1999 she played in the Victorian provincial championships and participated in the 2002 International Women's Baseball Tournament in Geelong, Australia. She plays the fiddle in her family's bluegrass band when she is not playing softball at her high school. {Karen Hodge, "Winding Up for Success," *Manningham Leader*, 2 July 2003, 8.}

Davidson, Stella

Owner

In 1956 the *Sporting News* reported that Mrs. Stella Davidson had become the owner of the Yuma ball club in the Arizona-Mexico League. She bought out the stock of John Carleton in order to save the Tijuana team. She hired a new manager to help the club, Whitey Wietelmann, a former infielder for the Boston Braves. When not at the ball park Mrs. Davidson worked at the San Carlos Hotel cocktail lounge. In addition to these business pursuits she also owned the Call of the Canyon Lodge in Oak Creek Canyon, Arizona. Mrs. Davidson's sports interest developed while she attended Mrs. Goodson's School for Girls in Fresno, California. {Ben Foote, "'Mom' Spiked Yuma Shift by Becoming Sole Owner," *The Sporting News*, 25 July 1956.}

Davis, Gladys "Terry"

(b. 1 September 1919, Ontario, Canada) SS/OF/ 2B 1943–47, Rockford Peaches, Milwaukee Chicks, Muskegon Lassies

Before joining the AAGPBL, Davis played in the Toronto softball league during the 1930s. She became the league's first batting champion in 1943 when she hit .332. She was also selected to the all-star team at shortstop in 1943.

Davis, Pamela

(b. 17 September 1974) P 1995–96, Colorado Silver Bullets

Pamela Davis first came to people's attention as a baseball player when she pitched in the Junior League World Series in 1988, becoming the first woman to do so. The U.S. club from Florida beat Canada 7–3. She played second base and pitched for Lake Mary High School in 1989. She played softball at the University of South Florida. Davis also pitched in an exhibition game for the Jacksonville Suns against the Australian National Olympic Team. The Suns were a Class AA affiliate of the Detroit Tigers. She pitched one inning in relief, throwing ten strikes out of 18 pitches and helping her team win 7–2. She gave up a double to Peter Vogler but retired the rest of the side on two ground ball outs and a strike-out of Michael Dunn. Over 1,000 people came out to see her pitch, and her manager, Bill Plummer, gave her a chance in the fifth inning of a 6–0 game at that point. Her performance with the Suns did not make her the first woman to pitch in the minor leagues but it did place her in elite company with such players as Jackie Mitchell. In 1995 she was second on the Bullets roster with 39 strikeouts and had a 2–7 record with a 5.94 ERA. In 1996 she had a 2–2 record with a 1.88 ERA for the Bullets. {*The Silver Bulletin,* July 1996; "For the Love of the Game," Colorado Silver Bullets souvenir program, 1995; "Davis Works Inning of Scoreless Relief," *Detroit News,* 5 June 1996; "Out of the Bullpen, into the Record Books," *New York Times,* 5 June 1996, B15; "Silver Bullets Defeat Shreveport Team," *The Advocate,* 2 June 1997, 9E.}

Davis, Rachel

Umpire

Rachel Davis started playing softball when she was six but did not like it, so she switched to Little League baseball and found she liked it. When she turned 12 her schedule did not allow her to play any longer so she made the change to umpiring. She umpired all through school in the West Hills–Knapp Ranch League as the only female among the 42 umpires employed by the league. She started officiating tee ball and then moved up to the seven- to nine-year-old division. After two years she moved up to the nine- to ten-year-old group and even got to officiate behind the plate. As a sophomore in high school she also returned to playing as an outfielder and second baseman for the Junior Division in Woodland Hills. In addition to her baseball duties Davis played soccer and played trombone for the Calabasas High School Marching Band. {Rizza Yap, "Girls Gets Chance to Make Calls," *Los Angeles Daily News,* 25 June 1998.}

Davis, Sherry

Public Address Announcer

In 1993 Sherry Davis became the public address announcer for the San Francisco Giants. The initial reaction to her being given the job was not all that positive from many fans, but she earned their appreciation with her knowledge and love of the game and quickly became a fan favorite. {J.G. Floto, "Thumbnail Sketches of Female Baseball Pioneers," *The Diamond Angle,* summer 1997, 45.}

Dearfield, Norma

(West Mifflin, Pennsylvania) 2B 1949–50, Chicago Colleens, South Bend Blue Sox

Norma Dearfield got a chance to try out for a team in the AAGPBL in 1949 at Renzie Hauser Field. She was first assigned to one of the league's traveling teams and then in her second year joined the Blue Sox.

DeBenedictis, Lois

Lois DeBenedictis plays in the Philadelphia Women's Baseball League, which was organized in 2004 with three clubs. Her husband John plays on one of the men's teams that the women's clubs often play against, and her two children regularly come out and watch mom play. Against her husband's pitching in their first game she lined a double in her first at-bat. {Doug Lesmerises, "Men vs. Women on the Diamond," *The New Journal,* 25 June 2004.}

DeCambra, Alice G. "Moose"

(b. 18 August 1921, Somerset, Massachusetts; d. 19 June 1988) 2B/SS/P 1946–50, Fort Wayne Daisies, Peoria Red Wings, Kalamazoo Lassies

Alice DeCambra joined her sister Lillian in the All American League. She pitched in 31 games with an 11–8 record. She also played in another 490 games, hitting .198 and driving in 105 runs. {AAGPBL Baseball Cards, 1995.}

DeCambra, Lillian

(b. 21 November 1925, Somerset, Massachusetts) IF 1947, Fort Wayne Daisies

Lillian DeCambra joined her sister playing baseball. She served in a utility role for the Daisies during spring training in 1947. Lillian played basketball and ice skated as well. {AAGPBL Baseball Cards, 1995.}

Dedieu, Lauren

Dominion Bantam Hawks

In 2003 Dedieu played for the Dominion Bantam Hawks. Before joining this baseball team she played softball for seven years. She likes all positions on the field. She also likes to act and sing in school.

Deegan, Mildred "Millie"

(b. 11 December 1919, Brooklyn, New York; d. 22 July 2002) P/OF/2B 1944–52, Rockford Peaches, Kenosha Comets, Springfield Sallies, Fort Wayne Daisies, Peoria Red Wings, Rockford Peaches

Millie Deegan played nine seasons in the All American League. She pitched in 146 games, winning 66 against 59 losses. Her ERA was a low 2.26 though she walked more hitters than she struck out. Millie played in another 533 games, hitting .217 and driving in 152 runs while scoring another 175. She struck out only 100 times in 1,560 at-bats, so she made good contact. Deegan was inducted into the New Jersey Hall of Fame for softball and into the Union County Baseball Men's Hall of Fame for her career achievements. In addition she was selected for membership in the National Softball Hall of Fame in Oklahoma City. Deegan coached the Linden Arians in New Jersey for 22 years. She died of cancer in 2002. {AAGPBL Newsletter, May 2001, 37; "American Heroes," <Baseballhistorian.com>; AAGPBL Baseball Cards, 1995.}

Deemer, Audrey

Util. Ft. Wayne Daisies, Grand Rapids Chicks

Audrey Deemer played softball with her brother and his friends growing up in Steubenville, Ohio. She heard about the baseball league and attended a tryout in McKeesport, Pennsylvania. She made the cut and played for Fort Wayne and Grand Rapids primarily as a utility player.

Delarco, Brooke

(b. 24 November 1964, Nyack, New York) P/1B/2B, Metz, Fillies, Boxers

Brooke Delarco grew up playing softball and participating in track and field at Kingston High School in New York. Her love of baseball led to her involvement beginning in 1987, when she owned the Tigers, an American Legion team for men over 18. She threw batting practice and acted as scorekeeper through the 1989 season. In 1991 she helped found the Washington Metropolitan Women's Baseball League (WMWBL) and acted as president from 1991 to 1995. In addition to her administrative responsibilities, Delarco pitched for the Tigers from 1991 to 1997. In 1993 she also pitched and played first base for the Metz in the WMWBL. By 1994 she was not only playing but also managing the Boxers; this continued until 1997. After a few years away from the game Delarco came back to the Fillies in the CWBL in 2003. She also took part in the 24-hour game in Arizona in October 2003. She pitched and played first base for the Gray team. Her favorite memories of playing baseball include pitching a perfect inning and striking out her ex-catcher. Brooke attended Georgia State University. {Brooke Delarco, correspondence with author, May and June 2004.}

Deleon, Tamara

1B, Peninsula Peppers

During the 2003 season Tamara Deleon led the Peppers in hitting with ten hits in 23 at-bats. She also walked three times and scored six runs.

Delloso, Michelle

(b. 12 January 1969, Lansdale, Pennsylvania) 2B/Util. 1994, Colorado Silver Bullets

Before joining the Silver Bullets, Michelle Delloso was a softball player for three years at the University of South Carolina. While there she compiled a .320 batting average and 121 RBIs. With the Bullets she was best known for her steady fielding. This made her a valuable member of the team because she could play almost any position on the field. {David Kindred, Colorado Silver Bullets: For the Love of the Game (Atlanta: Longstreet Press, Inc., 72.}

Delmonico (Surkowski), Lena "Lee"

1946, Rockford Peaches

In 82 games in 1946 Lena Delmonico hit only .200 for the Peaches.

DeLuca, Christina "Nuke"

P/IF 1997–98, Phoenix Peppers, Arizona Cactus Wrens

Christina DeLuca played softball at the University of Oklahoma, where she was known for her power hitting. She led the club in nearly every category from home runs to RBIs and on-base percentage. She earned Academic All-Big Eight awards from 1993 to 1995. She joined the Arizona Peppers in the Ladies Professional Baseball League in 1997 and in 1998 she was the opening day pitcher against the San Jose Spitfires. {"Women's Baseball Joins Professional Ranks," PRNewswire, 25 June 1997.}

Dennert (Hill), Pauline "Denny"

(b. 8 April 1926, Hart, Michigan) OF/Util. 1947, Muskegon Lassies

Pauline Dennert attended Hart High School, graduating in 1944. From there she went on to Western Michigan University, where she played field hockey and tennis. When she was not in school Pauline worked as the summer recreation director and swim instructor in Hart. She also did a bit of umpiring for the men's softball league. Though she did not get to play a lot in the league, Pauline was part of the Lassies' winning team in 1947. They lost the playoffs to Grand Rapids.

After graduating from college in 1949 Pauline became a teacher and coach at Owosso High School until her retirement in 1986. She also got married in 1950 and raised five children. On 2 May 1995 the new softball field was dedicated as the "Pauline (Denny) Hill Field." {AAGPBL Questionnaire, National Baseball Hall of Fame and Museum; AAGPBL Baseball Cards, 2000.}

Dennis, Christene

(b. 1984, Masaryktown, Florida) IF/P, Orlando Fire

At age 17, Christene Dennis got the chance to play for Team USA in 2001. She brought with her a number of years' experience playing in the adult men's leagues in Florida and one season of pitching for the Orlando Fire in the Florida Women's Baseball League. She started playing baseball when she was only six years old and continued to play softball and baseball at Hernando High School. She received honorable mention for the all-state team in softball.

Denton, Mona

P

Mona Denton played in the All American League and then went to nursing school and earned her LPN.

Derouin, Stephanie

(b. 3 April 1975, Boise, Idaho) IF/P, Washington Stars

Stephanie Derouin grew up playing softball and baseball every chance she got. Mostly she played softball because the opportunities for women to play baseball were limited. Her grandfather was a former professional player, and he taught her the fundamentals of the game of baseball. While attending Bellarmine Prep High School in Tacoma she played soccer, basketball and softball. When she went on to college at Washington State, Derouin only played recreational softball because the school had no fast-pitch softball team. While at Washington, Stephanie earned a degree in recreation administration with a minor in business, graduating in 1998.

Her baseball and softball experience is extensive, starting with youth baseball in Boise. She moved on to CYO baseball and softball in Tacoma while also playing in high school. She played for the Stingers' elite team and traveled with them to Oklahoma for the world tournament while she was still in high school. Her most recent baseball playing has been with the Washington Stars in 2003 and 2004. Derouin is the captain of the Stars. In October 2003, she traveled to Arizona to play in the 24-hour benefit game for AIDS. This experience introduced her to other women playing baseball around the country and gave her practical knowledge, as the players had a chance to learn more from one another and the coaches.

When Derouin is not playing baseball she works for Amazon.com. Her real hope is that women's baseball will take off and the Washington Women's Baseball Association will become her full-time job. Stephanie believes that baseball is a different sport from softball and that young girls should have the chance to choose which game they want to play. This is a common sentiment among women ball players. {Stephanie Derouin, correspondence with Leslie A. Heaphy, North Canton, Ohio, May 2004.}

Descombes (Lesko), Jean "Lefty"

(b. 28 March 1935, Ada, Ohio) P 1953–54, Grand Rapids Chicks

Jean Descombes graduated as valedictorian of her class at Lake View High School in 1953. She traveled with the local men's team and worked as their bat girl. She found out about the league from one of the players who told her about tryouts coming up in Battle Creek, Michigan, in 1953.

She joined the Chicks after graduation and in the off-season started college at Ohio Northern University. Jean was a math major who wanted to be an atomic scientist. She also hoped to get a Fulbright Scholarship after graduation in order to travel to Europe for further education. In between semesters, Descombe pitched for Grand Rapids as they won the championship in 1953 and came in third in the league's final season. She compiled a 10–9 record in the league. She then went on to a short professional golf career before returning to baseball. After the league folded, Bill Allington invited Descombes to join his All-American team as they toured the country. She pitched for them from 1955 to 1957. In her first season she finished with an 11–8 record against mainly men's baseball clubs. In one 1956 game against the Jim White Chevrolets, Descombes switched batteries and pitched against the ladies, giving up nine hits en route to an 8–4 victory. {"Jean Descombes Has Plenty on the Ball," *The Lima News*, 17 June 1956, 2-D; AAGPBL Baseball Cards, 1995; Allan White, "Touring All-American Girls Prove Baseball's Still Anybody's Game," *The Lima News*, 14 June 1956.}

In 2003 Descombes helped to organize the Washington Women's Baseball Association with one team, the Washington Stars. She coaches the

Jen Hammond and Jen Lesko relaxing in the dugout.

women, who range in age from 14 to adults. She also plays in the outfield for the Bellevue Bulldogs Co-ed Senior softball team. {Sherry Grindeland, "Pursuing a League of Her Own," *The Seattle Times*, 13 August 2004, B1.}

DeShone (Rockwell), Nancy "Lefty"

(b. 22 March 1932, Elkhart, Indiana) OF 1948, South Bend Blue Sox

Nancy DeShone attended Roosevelt High School in Elkhart, Indiana, where she won a number of ribbons participating in the local school sports for girls. She pitched in the CYO league and for Miles Laboratory in a fast-pitch league. While pitching in a championship game she was approached by a scout to join the AAGPBL. She joined while still in high school. After her baseball career ended she worked in sales and management and got married in 1950 to Rodney Rockwell. She raised four children and did a bit of coaching in slow-pitch softball and tee ball leagues. {AAGPBL Questionnaire, National Baseball Hall of Fame; AAGPBL Newsletter, May 1995, 5; AAGPBL Baseball Cards, 1995.}

Detroit Danger/Renegades

In 2000 the Renegades joined both the Great Lakes Women's Baseball League and the Michigan Women's Baseball League. The team was founded by Shawn Macurio and managed by former Detroit Tiger player Barbaro Garbey. The team changed its name to the Danger in 2001. Recognition came to Macurio with her 2003 selection to the National Women's Baseball Hall of Fame. In 2004 the Danger came under the umbrella of the AAU Women's Baseball Division and came in first place in the Great Lakes Women's Baseball League with a 10–4 record. {Detroit Danger Web site.}

Dettweiler, Helen

(b. 1926; d. 1990) Broadcaster

Helen Dettweiler became the regular baseball broadcaster for 69 different radio stations in 1938. Her base was in North Dakota, but she had a roving assignment to follow games in the West. Dettweiler was a Maryland State record holder in golf and a good athlete overall. She won three state titles in four years. In 1939 she left the amateur ranks to become a professional golfer along with others such as Babe Didrikson and Marion Brown. She went to work for Wilson Sporting Goods Company. During the Second World War, Dettweiler served in the WASPs from 1943 to 1944. She flew B-17s and also worked as a cryptographer. {Johanna Mary Beers, "Golf Queens Show How to Hit Ball," *Iowa City Press-Citizen*, 24 October 1941, 9; "Helen Dettweiler to Appear at Country Club on Tuesday," *Union-Bulletin* (Wash.), 27 July 1952, 11.}

In 1949 Dettweiler was the first woman in the country to design a golf course when she set up a nine-hole course at Cochran Ranch in Indio, California. As a result, in 1950 Dettweiler became the first vice-president of the new Ladies Professional Golf Association, which she helped found with 12 others. Dettweiler got a little taste of Hollywood in 1949 when she secured a role in the film *Pat and Mike*, starring Katharine Hepburn and Spencer Tracy. Babe Didrikson Zaharias also had a role in the film. {Larry Bohannan, "LPGA Celebrates 55 Years in the Valley," *The Desert Sun*, 13 October 2004; *Bismarck Tribune*, 19 July 1938, 6; Merrell W. Whittlesey, "H. Dettweiler Turns Pro for 'Good Will' Job," *Washington Post*, 11 May 1939, 21.}

Deutsch, Kelly

P 2002–03, Cal Sabres

Kelly Deutsch pitched for the Cal Sabres when they attended the Roy Hobbs tournaments and the West Coast Classic.

Devils

Lena Caruso coached the Devils to the semifinals in their second season in 2003 as part of the Sydney Women's Baseball League. The club had four players selected to the all-star squad. Their final record stood at 6–5. Caruso also acted as league president. She had help from secretary Stacy Warren and treasurer Oriel Webster. In 2004 the club played under coach Pip Marks. {League Annual Report 2003, 9, 17; Annual Report 2004, 7.}

Diamond League

This league began in 1994 as an offshoot of the Lakewood Baseball Club in Tacoma, Washington. The league had four divisions: Bronze, Silver, Gold and Platinum, for girls aged nine to 16. Marty Shaw served as the league registrar while Greg Arnette helped with the organization and scheduling. {Diamond League brochure.}

Dickinson, Amy

Amy Dickinson played Little League in New Jersey in 1974 after a court ruling required the local clubs to allow girls to try out. She was the first draft choice out of 150 players by all the coaches when she attended the tryouts. {Joseph Treaster, "Girls a Hit in Debut on Diamond," *New York Times*, 25 March 1974, 67.}

Didrikson (Zaharias), Mildred Ella "Babe"

(b. 26 June 1914, Port Arthur, Texas; d. 27 September 1956)

Growing up in southern Texas, Mildred "Babe" Didrikson wanted to play sports but found at the time that the opportunities for women were limited. Every activity she tried, she did well at, whether organized sports or playground games. She played basketball in high school and then switched her attention to track and field, where she earned the chance to represent the United States at the 1932 Olympics in Germany. She came home a success, winning all three of her events. She won gold medals in the javelin throw and the hurdles and a silver medal in the high jump. This success was typical of the results Didrikson achieved when she put her mind to any task. She would practice for hours every day at whatever activity was her priority at the time. For example, in track she had two hours of practice every day; then she would go out again on her own in the evening until it got too dark to continue. In golf she would hit 1,000 golf balls at a time to practice her swing.

She took up golf as her next major sport. Initially she was refused entry into the amateur tournaments because of her barnstorming tours with the "Babe Didrikson All Stars" and the time she spent pitching for the House of David club. She was considered a pro and therefore ineligible. She earned her nickname "Babe" after hitting five home runs in one baseball game. She pitched in an exhibition game against the St. Louis Cardinals. In 1934 she appeared with the House of David against Westinghouse Electric in Mansfield, Ohio. She was expected to show off her skills in an exhibition before the game and then pitch one inning of the regular game. {"Babe Didrikson is Exonerated," *The Mansfield Journal*, 23 December 1932, 11; "Westies Host to House of David Club," *Mansfield News Journal*, 18 August 1934, 6; "Babe Wants to Play," *The Oshkosh Northwestern*, 5 February 1937, 18.}

After her marriage in 1938 to George Zaharias she could afford to forgo paying events. She began entering the major tournaments and winning. She got an invitation to the 1938 Los Angeles Open but did not make the cut. She returned to that tournament again in 1945 and made the first cut. In 1945 she finished forty-second in the Tucson Open. During the 1946–47 golf season she won 17 amateur tournaments in a row, including the British Amateur in 1947. She became the first American to do so since the championship had begun in 1893. {"Didrikson a Threat in Women's Western," *Oshkosh Daily Northwestern*, 28 June 1940, 19.}

In 1950 she helped found the Ladies Professional Golf Association. She won her first major golf tournament that same year, entering the All-American Open in Chicago. She became one of the first four women inducted into the LPGA Hall of Fame in 1951. She received the Vare Trophy in 1954 and the USGA Bobby Jones Award in 1957. She was inducted into the National Women's Hall of Fame in 1996 for her many athletic achievements. Over the years the *Associated Press* has named a Woman Athlete of the Year, and Zaharias received that honor six times between 1931 and 1954. Zaharias died in 1956 at the age of 42 from cancer. Following her death a foundation was begun in her honor that hands out scholarships to outstanding female athletes at Lamar University. A movie, *Babe*, was made about her life, starring Susan Clark and Alex Karras. {"'Babe' Premier Slated Oct. 11 in Beaumont," *Port Arthur News*, 29 August 1975, 9; Paul Gallico, "SI Flashback: Farewell to the Babe," <CNNSI.com>, 8 October 1956; "Play Team of Beards Under Arcs," *Mansfield News-Journal,* 18 August 1934, 6; Jerry Potter, "Brash Babe 'Showed the World,'" *USA Today*, 20 May 2003, 10C; "Babe Zaharias Dies; Athlete Had Cancer," *New York Times Magazine*, 28 September 1956.}

Dobrint, Alexandria

IF, Alameda Oaks

Alexandria Dobrint played in the Ladies Professional Baseball League.

Doerer, Valerie

IF, San Jose Spitfires

Valerie Doerer played in the Ladies Professional Baseball League.

Doherty, Darcy

NAWBL Saints

Darcy Doherty was named Best Offensive Player at the NAWBL Labor Day Tournament.

Dokish, Wanita "Lee"

(b. 6 April 1936, Van Meter, Pennsylvania) 3B/OF 1954, Battle Creek Belles, Rockford Peaches

Wanita Dokish only played in 27 games in the All-American League because she was a senior in high school in 1954. She played after school finished for the year and then the league folded. She hit only .114 in her short stint with the Peaches. {AAGPBL Baseball Cards, 1995.}

Dolbel, Narissa

(b. 14 July 1980) P/OF New South Wales

Narissa Dolbel played in the Australian National Tournament.

Dole, Shawna

(b. 1990, Dubuque, Iowa) P

Shawna Dole started playing baseball with the Astros in a Dubuque, Iowa, independent league in 2000. Her brothers Jake and Shane also played for the same ball club. One of her victories in the 2004 season came against the league's leading team, the Brewers. In addition to playing baseball Dole has played basketball for Jefferson Junior High School. When she started at Dubuque Senior High School she switched to playing softball, which she liked because she was not the only girl on the field. {Erik Hogstrom, "Baseball Diamonds Are This Girl's Best Friend," *Telegraph Herald*, 13 June 2004, E1.}

Dolly Vardens 1

The Dolly Vardens 1 were an African-American team from the Chester area (NY) who were scheduled to play the Dolly Vardens 2 from Philadelphia. One of the players on the team was identified as Ella Harris, who was the team captain. Mollie Johnson played first base while Miss Harris took responsibility for shortstop. Sallie Johnstone was identified as the second baseman while Lizzie Waters played third. The outfield was made up of Rhoda Scholl and Agnes Hollingsworth while the catcher was Ella Thompson. No center fielder was named. According to the news article the Philadelphia team never showed up for the game, so the spectators simply saw a practice by the colorfully attired Chester club. Each girl wore a different-colored dress with stripes, but they each wore a small red and white cap to identify them as the same team. {"Miss Harris's Baseball Nine," *New York Times*, 18 May 1883.}

Dominguez, Carmen

P, Virginia Flames

Carmen Dominguez led the Flames in hitting in 2002 with a solid .484 average based on 15 hits in 31 at-bats. Dominguez also played for the DC Thunder in tournaments representing the EWBC. In a four-day championship series in Maryland she hit .500. She followed that in 2003 by getting off to a fast start with a five-for-six performance in the season opener when the Flames beat the Banditas 14–5. By 2004 Dominguez was one of the veteran leaders on the team.

Dominion Bantam Girls Hawks

This team played out of Cape Breton in 2003 and hosted the first Nova Scotia Girls Youth baseball team. The team played at the Canadian Youth National Championships in Windsor in the summer of 2003. The age of the young ladies on the club ranged from 13 to 18.

Donahue, Terry

P. (b. 22 August 1925, Melaval, Saskatchewan) Util. 1946–49, Peoria Red Wings

Donahue began her career as a softball player for the Moose Jaw Royals club from 1942 to 1945 under the direction of owner William Passmore. During her first year with the team they won the Western Canadian Championship, and in 1943 they won the provincial championship. She also played hockey for the United Cancer Fund. Donahue joined the AAGPBL in 1946 with the Peoria Red Wings, remaining through the 1949 season. Though she could play nearly any position, most of the time she caught. The first game she caught actually went 19 innings. During the off-season she returned to Moose Jaw to work in the army and navy department store. Then she joined a professional softball league in Chicago and stayed there rather than returning to Canada. In 1951 she caught and played in the infield for the Chicago Music Maids. When she finally gave up softball she became an avid golfer, and a skater in the winters. In 1998 she was inducted into the Canadian Baseball Hall of Fame. {Induction program, 1998; AAGPBL Questionnaire, National Baseball Hall of Fame and Museum; AAGPBL Newsletter, January 2002, 15.}

Donald (Clark), Pamela

(b. 28 March 1970) OF/P, Melbourne, 2002 Australian National Team

Pamela Donald played for Melbourne in the 1999 International Friendship Series. She pitched five innings and struck out four batters. She was also 3–6 at the plate.

Dowler, Chris

1997, San Diego Stix

Chris Dowler played for the San Diego Stix in the Ladies Professional League in the mid–1990s.

Doyen, Darreth

Pawtucket Slaterettes, Robins

Darreth Doyen started playing with the Slaterettes in 1986. She has played in all the divisions including the adult division, added in 2003. In addition to playing, Doyen coaches and directs the senior division program. In 2002 she traveled to Cooperstown, New York, to try out for Team USA along with 12 other Slaterette players. In 2000 and 2001 Doyen expanded her playing to join the Lowell Robins in the NEWBL to improve her skills. She did not return to the Robins in 2003 because the travel became too hard. Doyen's father coaches in the league as well. His involvement began when Doyen was in high school at St. Raphael's academy. After graduation Doyen went on to Rhode Island College to study criminal justice. She worked as a bank teller when not playing ball, to pay for her schooling. {Chris Shott, "Sports," *Warwick Beacon*, 8 August 2002.}

Doyle (Childress), Cartha Lynn "Duckie"

(b. 12 October 1929, Knoxville, Tennessee) 2B 1947, Rockford Peaches

While attending Young High School, Cartha Doyle played basketball her senior year. She also played basketball and softball in the city league. She joined the AAGPBL while still in high school, for one season. The nickname "Duckie" was a shortening of the term "duck soup," which players got called when they were an easy out at the plate. Cartha continued to play fast-pitch softball and basketball after graduation. She also coached. She was inducted into the Knoxville Sports Hall of Fame in 1990. She married Albert Lee Childress in 1947 and raised one daughter. {AAGPBL Questionnaire, National Baseball Hall of Fame; Brenda Wilson, *Nicknaming Practices of Women in a Nontraditional Occupation,* master's thesis, University of North Carolina at Greensboro, 1991, 42.}

Doyle, Snookie

(b. 4 February 1924, Los Angeles, California) SS 1944–50, Rockford Peaches

Snookie Doyle excelled at the plate and in the field. She was selected for the all-star team five times in her career and led the Peaches in RBIs for three straight seasons from 1948 to 1950. While she was with the Peaches, the club won four pennants. Her lifetime batting average was .228 with 306 RBIs and 229 stolen bases.

Drew, Cheryl-Lee

Western Australia

In the 2001 Australian National Tournament Cheryl-Lee Drew hit .500 for Western Australia, second highest in the club. She knocked in eight runs and scored seven more.

Drinkwater (Simmons), Maxine Edna "Max"

(b. 19 May 1936, Searmont, Maine) 1B/2B 1954, South Bend Blue Sox

Immediately following Maxine Drinkwater's graduation from Camden High School in 1954 she joined the Blue Sox in the AAGPBL. She only got to play one year because the league folded after the 1954 season. Maxine had wanted to play earlier but she had to wait until she finished school. After playing she graduated from nursing school and worked until she was married in 1965 to Charles Simmons Jr. She coached girls' basketball and Little League for a number of years in Camden, Maine. She also stayed active by playing tennis and golf and bowling. {AAGPBL Questionnaire, National Baseball Hall of Fame; AAGPBL Baseball Cards, 1995.}

Dufficy, Pat

(b. 2 July 1961) C, Colorado Silver Bullets

Pat Dufficy joined the Silver Bullets in 1996 after playing for the USA national softball team and the Raybestos Brakettes. The Brakettes belonged to a major fast-pitch league in Connecticut. {Silver Bulletin, March 1996.}

Dunlop, Frances

Frances Dunlop played in a minor league game in 1936 without any publicity announcing her performance. This lack of coverage is what allowed her to play without baseball's officials being able to stop her. She played in a Class D game between the Fayetteville Bears and the Cassville Blues. Dunlop played for the Bears, who were a part of the Arkansas-Missouri League. {Gai Berlage, "Transition of Women's Baseball," Nine, September 2000.}

Dunn, Betty

P, Fort Wayne Daisies, Rockford Peaches

Betty Dunn pitched for both the Rockford Peaches and Fort Wayne Daisies. In 1998 she was inducted into the Canadian Baseball Hall of Fame. {"Pioneers of the Diamond," Alberta Report, 8 June 1998.}

Dunn, Gertrude "Gertie"

(b. 30 September 1933, Sharon Hill, Pennsylvania; d. 29 September 2004) SS 1951–54, South Bend Blue Sox

Gertie Dunn started in the AAGPBL in 1951 at age 18 after graduating from Sharon Hill High School. She was selected Rookie of the Year in 1952. She finally began to feel comfortable just as the league was folding. She played in 344 games and hit .261. She knocked in 105 runs and scored another 154 while only striking out 46 times in 1,226 at-bats. In addition to her baseball playing, Gertie played for the U.S. Field Hockey Team and the U.S. Lacrosse Touring Team in the 1960s and 1970s. Gertie had the honor of being inducted into the West Chester Athletic Hall of Fame in 1960. She won the honor of being the Delaware State golf champion in 1980. In 1983 she received the Margaret Crozier Fox Memorial Cup from the Women's Golf Association in Philadelphia.

Dunn attended West Chester University where she majored in physical education, graduating in 1960. She went on to teach and coach in West Chester following her graduation. Dunn died in 2004 in a plane crash. She had taken up flying in the late 1980s to give her more flexibility in travel and because she wanted a challenge. {Kathleen Brady Shea, "Friends Mourn 'A Real Pioneer' Killed in Small-Plane Crash," Philadelphia Inquirer, 1 October 2004; AAGPBL Baseball Cards, 1996.}

Dupre, Kristen

Pawtucket Slaterettes

After playing for the Slaterettes since 1986, Dupre decided to try out for Team USA in 2002.

Dustrude, Beverly "Dusty"

(b. 24 October 1926, Beloit, Wisconsin) 2B
1947, 1949, Rockford Peaches, Springfield Sallies

Beverly Dustrude joined the Peaches in time
to travel to Cuba for spring training in 1947.
She did not get much playing time and did not
return for the 1948 season. She tried again in 1949
with the touring Sallies but only played in ten
games altogether. In addition to softball and baseball, she played golf and bowled. {AAGPBL Baseball Cards, 2000.}

Dyer, Ashley

P, Queensland

At age 15, Ashley Dyer played for the Australian
Senior Women's team. She was chosen after helping Queensland win one game at the national
championships. Being the youngest player on the
2005 squad does not bother Dyer, because that
has been true for all her baseball career so far.
{"Teen in National Team," *Northside Chronicle*, 25
May 2005.}

Earp, Mildred "Millie"

(b. 7 October 1925, West Fork, Arkansas) P
1947–50, Grand Rapids Chicks

Mildred Earp made the all-star team in her
rookie season, as she finished the year with
a record of 20–8 and a league-leading ERA of
0.67. She pitched in 108 games and compiled an
overall record of 54–38 with a 1.35 ERA. On certain days when she pitched, Mildred could be
nearly unhittable. {AAGPBL Baseball Cards,
1996.}

East Coast Women's Baseball League (ECWBL)

The East Coast league was created in the summer of 2002 through a partnership between Mitch
Miles and Adriane Adler. Miles had long been involved with local men's leagues and Adler was the
first woman to play in one of the men's leagues in
northern New Jersey. Adler also played in the earlier Ladies Professional Baseball League. The
ECWBL began with three teams and added a
fourth for the fall season. They played a ten-game
season in 2002. All the games were played on five
different fields in the New York–New Jersey area.
A three-game championship series took place between the Indians and Parsippany Yankees. The
other teams were the Madison Mets and Elmwood

Park Angels. The rules for the league were made
to match the men's league, with a few exceptions.
For example, the games are only seven innings,
not nine. The season lasts from April through
September. The players come from all over and
range in age from 13 to 53. {Wayne Witkowski,
"Pioneers Are in a League of Their Own," *Asbury
Park Press*, 25 September 2002; <scorebook.
com>.}

Eastern Women's Baseball Conference (originally Washington Metropolitan Women's Baseball League)

The Eastern Women's Baseball Conference was
founded in 2000 to provide opportunities for
women to play baseball. It replaced the Washington Metropolitan Women's Baseball League,
which started in 1990 under the direction of Lydia
Moon, a graphic artist from Rockville, Maryland.
The original league had pickup games in 1990,
and then three teams began official play in 1991
when Brooke Delarco stepped in to provide new
leadership. In 1992 the number of clubs dropped
to two and then expanded to four in 1993 after
receiving some press coverage because of the
movie *A League of Their Own*, released in 1992.
In 1995 Delarco moved away and JoAnn Milliken
took over as league president. By 1996 the league
expanded to six clubs and then declined to four in
1997. They play their games by the same rules as
the men's game with just a few minor adjustments. Games are only seven innings or two and
one-half hours in length, and the players pay a
yearly fee to be a part of the league. The games
are played at regulation distance and with professional umpires. The four main teams in the
league are the Baltimore Stars, the Montgomery
County Barncats, the Virginia Boxers and the Virginia Flames. {"Diamonds Are a Girls Best
Friend," Chris Slattery, *Gazette.Net*, 20 July 2001.}

In 2004 a team called the U.S. Lightning was
added for girls under the age of 17. They play in
tournaments since they are the only such team in the
Washington, D.C., area. This team was added to
give the younger girls from the Olney team a chance
to continue playing. The Olney girls' club was
added to the league in 2002 for nine- to ten-year-
olds. Two teams were created from the girls who
tried out that first year. Coaches were provided
from the Barncats and the Boxers. They played their
games at Ednor Field in Silver Springs, Maryland.

In 2004 the Virginia Flames won the league with
a record of 10–2, the Barncats coming in second at

7–4 and one tie. The Baltimore Blues found themselves at the bottom, only winning three games against nine losses. Also in 2004, four girls represented the Lightning at the Mustang Machine Pitch All-Star Game. They were Vanessa Newman, Megan Descalzi, Sierra Stephens and Lauren O'Connell. {EWBC Web site.}

Edmonton North Stars

The Edmonton North Stars are a team in the Canadian League.

Eisen, Thelma "Tiby"

(b. 11 May 1922, Los Angeles, Calif.) CF/P 1944–52, Milwaukee Chicks, Grand Rapids Chicks, Peoria Red Wings, Fort Wayne Daisies

Thelma Eisen grew up playing softball and was already participating at the semipro level by age 14. In 1944 Eisen traveled east to Chicago to try out for the AAGPBL and was signed to a contract with the Milwaukee Chicks. This decision to play baseball came after a failed attempt to participate in a professional women's football league that was banned by the city. The Chicks won the league championship that year as Eisen stole 91 bases to help her team. In 1946 the Chicks moved to Grand Rapids and Eisen made the all-star team, but in 1947 she was sent to Peoria where she continued to show off her speed by stealing 128 bases. Eisen finished out her career with the Fort Wayne Daisies. All together Eisen played in 959 games and batted lead-off for every team she played for because of her speed. In 1949 she went with a group from the league on a tour of Central America. Her career numbers included 966 games, hitting .224 and stealing 674 bases. She had 85 doubles, 23 triples and walked 372 times which made her a threat on the bases all the time. After baseball Eisen went to work for Stateham Instruments until she moved to California and took up softball again. She also got involved in softball, field hockey and bowling. She helped her softball team, the Orange Lionettes, win the world championship. {Barbara Gregorich and Debra A. Shattuck, "All American Girls Baseball Register," in *Total Baseball Total Baseball IV*, edited by John Thorn and Pete Palmer (New York: Viking Press, 1989), pp. 623–625; AAGPBL Newsletter, January 2002, 28; AAGPBL Baseball Cards, 1995.}

Emerson, June "Venus"

(b. 4 June 1924, Saskatchewan; d. 1 October 1990) OF/1B 1948–49, Chicago Colleens

June Emerson played in the AAGPBL on one of the two touring teams, the Chicago Colleens. She played in 68 games and hit only .164. The best-known story about Emerson involved her place in history as the only player to provide an assist on a double play without using her hands. During a game she got hit in the head with a fly ball that then bounced into the glove of the second baseman, who then threw to first base to double up the runner there. This is also how she earned her nickname in honor of the armless Greek statue known as the Venus de Milo. {AAGPBL Baseball Cards, 1996; Brenda S. Wilson, *Nicknaming Practices of Women in a Nontraditional Occupation: Female Professional Baseball Players*, MA Thesis, 1991, 45.}

Emery, Anna

OF 2003–04, San Francisco Fillies

Anna Emery had the second highest hit total for the Fillies in 2003, with 12. She knocked in two runs with one homer and scored another three.

Emry, Elizabeth "Betty"

(b. 20 January 1923, Manistique, Michigan; d. 18 April 1995) SS/P

Betty Emry spent two seasons in the All American League. She started as a shortstop but because she had such a strong arm they tried her as a pitcher; she was 7–4 as a rookie. After two seasons she went to work at Briggs Aircraft Plant during the Second World War. {AAGPBL Baseball Cards, 1996.}

Engel, Heather "Blaze"

C/OF 2001–2004, Detroit Danger, Motown Magic

Heather Engel earned her nickname in baseball because of her speed on the base paths. She is always a threat to steal, causing havoc for opposing pitchers. She is also known for her strong defensive play behind the plate.

Engle, Eleanor

(b. 1928) IF

Eleanor Engle became the first woman to sign a modern-day baseball contract, in 1952, when she was signed by the Harrisburg Senators at age 24. The Senators were a member of the Class B Inter-state League at the time, resting in seventh place. Her contract was voided by the minor league commissioner, George Trautman, before she ever played a game, though there was no rule barring women from playing. Trautman threatened the Senators and other clubs with heavy penalties if they tried to sign women players. He called the signing of Eleanor Engle a "travesty on baseball."{"Trautman Bars Woman Players, Censures 'Travesty' on Baseball," *New York Times*, 24 June 1952, 38.} Trautman's decision was upheld by the commissioner of baseball, Ford Frick. Engle simply loved the game and wanted a chance to play. {John Pagey, "Shapely Young Gal Not Cut Out to be Star on Diamond," *Mansfield News-Journal*, 20 June 1952, 9.}

A number of people around the league were also asked their opinion of the move by a local reporter. Most were opposed because they saw it only as a publicity stunt. Bill Veeck told one news reporter that though he had pulled a number of stunts in baseball he would not sign a woman ball player because he had never seen one who was good enough. At the same time he also believed that Trautman could do little to stop the move if the Senators really wanted her to play. Oscar Fraley wrote a column for the *Redlands Daily Facts* in California stating that baseball needed to change with the times. He wrote that women had moved out of the kitchen into all kinds of new jobs and baseball should be next. {Oscar Fraley, "Women Should Play Says Fraley, They Look Better," *Redlands Daily Facts*, 24 June 1952, 9.}

By profession Engle was a stenographer with the Pennsylvania Public Utility Commission and had previously played only softball. One of the places she played was in Harrisburg, Pennsylvania. She helped the Harrisburg entry beat the Newberry Sluggers in a 1951 tournament at Pottstown. When her contract did not get honored she went back to her job as a stenographer. {"Harrisburg's Girl Slugger Known to Newberry Sluggers," *Williamsport Sun*, 25 June 1952; "Bill Veeck Predicts Minors Can't Stop Girl Ball Player," *Harrisburg Patriot*, 23 June 1952; Marjorie Turner, "Pro Baseball World Gets Shock," *Syracuse Herald-Journal*, 24 June 1952, 23; "Woman Signs with Baseball Team, May Not Get to Play," *Redlands Daily Facts*, 23 June 1952, 7.}

English, Madeline Catherine "Maddy"

(b. 22 February 1925, Everett, Massachusetts; d. 24 August 2004) 2B/SS/3B 1943–50, Racine Belles

Maddy English graduated from Everett High School in 1943 and planned on staying home to help her parents since her siblings were off at war. She got offered a chance to join the Belles and her parents encouraged her to take the opportunity. She had grown up following her brother to his baseball games and begging him to teach her. Maddie spent her entire eight years in the AAGPBL with the Racine Belles. Three times she was selected to the all-star team and regularly led her team in fielding percentage at third base. She hit .171 for her career in 836 games. Not known for any real power, she did hit 13 home runs but also stole 397 bases. She developed a reputation as a solid fielder who could hit, run, slide and steal. After her playing career ended, English attended and graduated from Boston University with bachelor's and master's degrees in education. Then she taught in the Everett public school district for 27 years at Parlin Junior High School. She also played softball and basketball into her thirties. In October 2003 the district dedicated their newest school, the Madeline English School. Her name was chosen in an essay contest by students and the winning entry came from Tiffani Macarelli, an eighth grader. English was inducted into the New England Women's Sports Hall of Fame and the Boston University Sports Hall of Fame for her achievements in baseball. She died of cancer at Whidden Memorial Hospital in 2004. {AAGPBL Newsletter, September 2000, 10; May 2001, 32; May 2004; AAGPBL Questionnaire, National Baseball Hall of Fame; Patricia Brown, "Madeline English," in *A League of My Own* (North Carolina: McFarland and Company Inc., 2003), 164–69.}

Ephraim, Sharon

(b. 1963) AWBA Daredevils

Sharon Ephraim grew up playing softball since that was what girls were supposed to play. She organized a fast-pitch team while attending Connecticut College and then played locally when she returned to Chicago to get her MBA at the University of Chicago. She stayed in town to work at Continental Bank and so she joined the local women's baseball league. In 1992 she was second in the league for the AWBA in hitting, with a .484 average for the Daredevils. {Bill Beuttler, "The Girls of Summer," *Sports Illustrated*, 6 September 1993, 139.}

Erickson (Sauer), Louise Elaine "Lou"

(b. 2 June 1929, Whitehall, Wisconsin) P 1948–50, Racine Belles, Rockford Peaches

Lou Erickson joined the Racine Belles as a rookie in 1948 and then moved to Rockford for her final two seasons in the AAGPBL. She graduated from Arcadia High School in 1946 and went to work in a local bowling alley. She did not play any sports in school because there were none for girls. She did coach in a summer softball league before joining the Belles. Her only experience came from playing with the neighborhood boys. She made the all-star team in 1949 after posting a 17–6 record with seven shutouts. Her last season she had a 16–10 record and also hit .239 to help her club. These numbers earned her selection to the all-star team again. The Peaches won the league championship both seasons Erickson pitched for them. After leaving the league, Erickson got married in 1950 to Burton Sauer and raised two children. She also took up bowling and kept that up for over 30 years. She worked as a grocery store clerk for over ten years. {AAGPBL Questionnaire, National Baseball Hall of Fame.}

Erickson, Whitney

(Danville) P/SS/2B Sabres

At age 15 Whitney Erickson, though only a sophomore in high school at the time, found herself as the youngest member of Team USA at the 2002 Roy Hobbs Women's Baseball Championships. She pitched 13⅓ innings while hitting .300 and driving in four runs. Whitney started playing Little League ball at the age of eight in West Los Angeles. She played for a team named the Bad News Bears in the 9- to 10-year-old division and received the Levis Amateur Athlete of the Month Award from ESPN.com. After she turned 11 the league no longer let her play, so she coached third base.

Ermis, Andi

C/OF 1999–2003, South Bend Blue Sox

Andi Ermis caught for the Blue Sox in 2003 and led off for the club at bat, connecting for a .333 average. In addition to good speed and solid contact Ermis also has some power, with a number of extra-base hits to her credit. She scored 15 runs and stole eight bases. Her play in 2003 led to her selection as MVP by the National Women's Baseball Hall of Fame. She has a career average of .340.

Espinosa, Wendee

(b. 29 June 1971) 1B/P, Colorado Silver Bullets

Before joining the Silver Bullets in 1996,

Wendee Espinosa played softball for the University of the Pacific in Stockton, California, from 1990 to 1993. While playing there she was named a second team All-American. {Silver Bulletin, March 1996.}

Espinoza-Watson, Laura

(b. 5 February 1973) 1B 1996, Colorado Silver Bullets

Laura Espinoza-Watson played for the Colorado Silver Bullets and hit one of the team's three home runs in 1996, a 420-foot shot, longest of them all. She led the team in hitting that same year with a .244 average, which included one stretch in May where she hit safely in nine of 14 games. Before joining the Silver Bullets, Espinoza-Watson played softball at the University of Arizona, where she was named the PAC-10 Player of the Year and College Sports Magazine National Softball Player of the Year in 1995. She hit .437 with 128 RBIs and 75 runs scored to earn those accolades. Her career average was high at .366, and she set the all time NCAA home run and RBI records with 85 homers and 315 RBIs for her career. She was a Second Team All American at shortstop in 1993. {"Questions for Laura Espinoza-Watson," New York Times, 6 October 1996, SM34; The Silver Bulletin March and July, 1996; "Arizona Standout to Join Silver Bullets in Spring Training," BW SportsWire, 22 April 1997.}

Etobicoke All Stars

The All Stars traveled to the U.S. in 1999 to take part, with six other teams, in the USA Baseball Championship. They won two games, defeating the Stix 6–2 in one before final losing to the Michigan Stars. Ruth Lancashire led the team in pitching while Cassie Clayton was the leading hitter. {"Canada Shows Well in USA Baseball Championship," AWBL Baserunner, November 1999, 3.}

Excelsior Bloomer Girls

In 1921 the Excelsior Bloomer Girls from Sparrows Point played a number of games with other local bloomer teams. They beat the Oakdale Bloomer Girls from Maryland 25–5 behind the pitching of Miss Jones who struck out 17 batters. They played the Baltimore Black Sox Bloomer Girls to a 29–29 tie in a game called after nine innings because of darkness. The game featured some heavy hitting by the ladies who connected for four home runs. They lost a second contest to the Black Sox team 32–21 though they did pull off a triple play. And in a final report in the Baltimore Afro-American the girls lost 34–11 to the Black Sox who were led by Miss Taylor's two home runs, Miss Banks solo home run and the fine pitching of Miss R. Taylor. {*Baltimore Afro American*, 19 and 26 August and 9 and 16 September 1921.}

Fabac (Bretting), Elizabeth "Betty"

(b. 6 April 1922, Detroit, Michigan) 2B 1945–48, Kenosha Comets

Betty Fabac played four seasons with the Comets. She played in 321 games, hitting .179 with 47 RBIs. Fabac's strength was not her hitting but her steady defense. After leaving the league she kept active through golf. She won eight straight championships in Jackson, Michigan. {AAGPBL Baseball Cards, 1995.}

Fadul, Melissa

Melissa Fadul grew up playing Little League but eventually switched to softball since there were few opportunities for girls to continue playing baseball. It was easier to play softball because this was the accepted sport for women. She finally got the chance to play baseball in the North Shore league.

Fairhurst, Suzanne "Sue"

(b. 9 July 1974, Illawong, New South Wales) IF

Sue Fairhurst played on the Olympic softball team before turning her skills to baseball in 2002. At the Australian National Championships in 2002 she hit .714 and knocked in 16 runs. She also hit the first home run of the tournament off Kerron Lehane. At the Women's World Series in 2002 she was named co–MVP with teammate Simone Wearne. In addition to playing baseball and softball Fairhurst is also a solid golfer. {"Olympic Softballer Changes Code," Media Release, 9 May 2002, Australian Baseball Federation; "Fairhurst Hits First Home run," *Gold Coast Bulletin*, 1 April 2002.}

Fairies of the Field

A team calling themselves the Fairies of the Field reported losing a game to a men's team in St. Paul, Minnesota, in 1885. They lost the game 14–4. The team was composed of all women except the catcher, who was a man. {*New York Clipper*, 12 September 1885, 403.}

Faralla, Lillian "Lil"

(b. 29 July 1924, San Pedro, California) P/2B/OF 1947–51, Fort Wayne Daisies, South Bend Blue Sox, Kalamazoo Lassies

Lillian Faralla played five seasons in the All American League and spent most of that time with South Bend. She was traded back and forth a couple of times when other teams had injuries; she was able to fill in since she played a number of positions. She pitched in 140 games with a record of 55–55 and an ERA of 2.00. She walked a lot of batters compared to her strikeouts, 392 to 238. At the plate she hit .209 in 266 games. She drove in 63 runs and scored another 43. {AAGPBL Baseball Cards, 2000.}

Farren, Patricia

Patricia Farren grew up playing Little League with her brothers but ended up on the high school softball team because there was no baseball team for girls. Farren played softball, basketball and field hockey in East Windsor, Connecticut, but no organized baseball. She played softball at Southern Connecticut State and then got married and moved to Virginia. She played for three seasons in the Washington Metropolitan Women's Baseball League, taking trips for tournaments to Florida. After her family moved back East, Farren continued her career with the Lowell Robins in the NEWBL in 2000. {Julie Kaster, "Baseball Diamonds This Girl's Best Friend," *Eagle-Tribune*, 25 July 2000.}

Farrow (Rapp), Elizabeth "Liz"

(b. 10 August 1926, Peoria, Illinois) P 1944, Rockford Peaches, Minneapolis Millerettes

Elizabeth Farrow joined Rockford as a rookie in 1944 and spent part of the season with the Peaches before being traded to Minneapolis. She played in 20 games with a .167 average but also pitched in 19 games, though she only recorded one victory. {AAGPBL Baseball Cards, 1996.}

Faut (Winsch, Eastman, Fantry), Jean

(b.17 January 1925, East Greenville, Pennsylvania) P/3B 1946–53, South Bend Blue Sox

Jean Faut grew up in a large family and developed her love of baseball at an early age. She loved to practice throwing by tossing stones at telephone poles but her real training came from the players on the East Greenville Cubs, a semipro baseball team in her home town. She learned to pitch from the players and often got the opportunity to pitch in exhibition games for the Cubs. While attending East Greenville High School, Jean played field hockey and basketball and participated in track and field. She went to work right after graduation in a clothing factory until a scout from Allentown, Pennsylvania, told her about the AAGPBL in 1946.

Faut was considered one of the best pitchers in the history of the league. In 1949, for example, she had a 24–8 record, a 1.10 ERA and hit .291. Her impressive pitching record included a league-leading 12 shutouts. In 1950 though she only won 21 games, she did pitch 29 complete games. Faut pitched two perfect games during her career, one in 1951 against Rockford and the other in 1953 against Kalamazoo. She pitched four no-hitters in total. She made the all-star team four times and was also named Player of the Year in both 1951 and 1953. She finished her career with a record of 140–64 and a 1.23 ERA. In 1949 Faut led the league in hitting with a .291 average. She led the league in ERA in 1950, 1952 and 1953. She later took up bowling and joined the Professional Bowling Tour. She worked for the University of Notre Dame as an executive secretary and then for Miles Laboratories. {Merrie Fidler, *The Development and Decline of the All-American Girls Baseball League, 1943–1954*, Master of Science thesis (Department of Physical Education: University of Massachusetts, 1976), 338–340; Jim Sargent, "Jean Faut," <www.AAGPBL.org>; AAGPBL Baseball Cards, 1995}

Feeley, Sarah

Pawtucket Slaterettes

Sarah Feeley played for the Pawtucket Slaterettes until she reached the age limit for their teams. In 2002 she joined the new adult league and became a board member as well. Her daughter began play for the tee ball team in 2003 at the age of four. Sarah is the director of operations for the Rhode Island Women's Baseball League. {Rhode Island Women's Baseball Web site.}

Feeney, Kate

Kate Feeny worked for Major League Baseball as the director of public relations for the National League. She is the daughter of former NL president Chub Feeney.

Felker-White, Tammy

(b. 1965)

In 1996 Tammy Felker-White resigned as the general manager of the Tucson Buzz of the Pacific Coast League. Felker-White was with the Buzz for seven years, five of those as GM. At the time she was the only female GM at the Triple A level. {Joe Baird, "Buzz Win on Night They Lose GM," *The Salt Lake Tribune*, 2 June 1996, C1; Dottie Enrico, "Breaking the Glass Ceiling," *Newsday*, 27 March 1994.}

Fellows, Julia and Romi

New South Wales

Sixteen-year-old twins Julia and Romi Fellows play baseball for the New South Wales club. In 2005 they accompanied their team to the Australian women's baseball championships. During the regular season they play for a new team from Illawarra. {Peter Rowe, "Illawarra's Baseball Diamonds," *The Sunday Telegraph*, 3 April 2005, 78.}

Female Baseball Club
of Philadelphia

According to the *Washington Post* of 1885, this women's club found themselves playing a men's club known as the Neenahs. The women found themselves on the winning end of an 8–7 score behind the excellent pitching of Miss Royalston. One of the leading hitters for the nine was Genevieve McAllister, who led off for the women. Others on the team included Agnes Macfarlane, the starting catcher; the shortstop, Florence McKusick; the first baseman, Agnes McDonohue; the third baseman, Clara Belle Corcoran; and the left fielder, Gertrude Bagley. The reporter attending the game described the ladies' uniforms as striped skirts with red hose. As was typical of the time period he also spent much of the article discussing the beauty and deportment of the ladies rather than their ball playing skills. For example, catcher Agnes Macfarlane is described as "the exquisite and amiable change catcher" for the club. {"Baseball Among Girls," *Washington Post*, 13 September 1855, 6.}

Fenton, Peggy L.

(b. 12 October 1927, Chicago, Illinois) 1B/RF 1948, Muskegon Lassies, South Bend Blue Sox

Peggy Fenton played baseball and basketball and ran track and field while attending two different high schools. She eventually got her GED in 1955 through the U.S. Marine Corp Reserves. She graduated from Loyola University in 1970. Her athletic prowess carried over to the 1944

Olympic trials, where she won the broad jump. Unfortunately, the Olympics were cancelled because of the war. She played one season in the All American League. She started in spring training in 1948 with the Lassies in Florida and then played some exhibition games in Cuba. She finished out her season with the Blue Sox. She worked for 26 years in the U.S. Marine Corps and retired in 1981. {AAGPBL Questionnaire, National Baseball Hall of Fame; AAGPBL Baseball Cards, 2000.}

Fereno, Cindy

(b. 14 August 1971, Fairfax, Virginia) C/P/2B, Virginia Flames

While attending high school, Cindy Fereno played fast-pitch softball. She then attended Northern Virginia Community College. She played baseball for eight years with the Virginia Flames. Fereno has played every position on the field except first base, because of her height. In 2001 Fereno was named MVP by the National Women's Baseball Hall of Fame; in 2002 she batted .444; and in 2003 she hit .714. Her solid hitting helped the Flames win the EWBC Championship for the 2003 season. In October 2003, Fereno traveled to Arizona to take part in the 24-hour marathon game for AIDS victims. Fereno says that the toughest pitcher she has ever faced is Stephanie Ciulla of the Barncats, and the best player she has seen is Laura Brenneman of the

Getting their pictures taken with the real stars of the AAGPBL are Jen Hammond, Cindy Fereno, Ann Meyer, Dolores Dries and an unidentified player.

Boxers. When not playing baseball, Fereno works as a program analyst for the U.S. Treasury Department. {Cindy Fereno, correspondence with author, March 2004.}

Ferguson (Key), Dorothy "Dottie"

(b. 17 February 1923, Virden, Manitoba, Canada; d. 8 May 2003) 2B/3B/OF 1945–54, Rockford Peaches, Peoria Red Wings

Dottie Ferguson played for ten seasons with the Peaches and during that time was on four championship teams. She played in 950 games with a career average of .201. She did not strike out much, only 281 times, compared to 396 walks in 3,216 at-bats. Before she took up softball she was named the North American women's speedskating champion in 1939. Only the coming of the Second World War kept her from competing for Canada in the Olympics. In 1949 she married Donald Key, a member of Canada's Olympic track and field team. In 1998 Key was inducted into the Manitoba Baseball Hall of Fame. In May 2005 she was also inducted into the Manitoba Softball Hall of Fame along with Audrey Daniels. {AAGPBL Baseball Cards, 1995; "Dottie Ferguson Key," <Historicbaseball.com>.}

Fermaints, Erika

Queens Cyclones

Fermaints helped her team most with her power at the plate, knocking one ball clear out of the field during one game in 2003. {David Abromowitz, "Another League of Their Own," *Newsday*, 13 August 2003, A56.}

Ferretti, Danielle

(Moodus, Connecticut) 1B, Waterbury Diamonds

Danielle Ferretti played softball for seven years before taking up baseball. While playing softball at Georgian Court College from 1996–98 she played in the NAIA World Series and received All-Region and All-American honors.

In 2001 Danielle Ferretti was chosen from the Diamonds to play for USA Women's Baseball in the first Women's World Series, held in Toronto, Canada. After the 2000 season with the Diamonds, Ferretti hit .462 with 20 RBIs.

Figlo, Josephine

OF, 1944 Milwaukee Chicks

Josephine Figlo played in the early years of the AAGPBL as an outfielder with the Milwaukee Chicks.

Filarski (Steffes), Helen "Fil"

(b. 11 May 1924, Detroit, Michigan) 2B/3B/OF 1945–50, Rockford Peaches, Peoria Red Wings, Kenosha Comets, South Bend Blue Sox

Helen Filarski grew up dreaming about being a professional athlete and was supported in all her efforts by her mother, who never had the chance to play sports because girls were not supposed to be too physical. In fact, while attending Detroit's Holy Name Grammar School she had to write on the blackboard that young ladies did not play ball games with boys. After high school Filarski went to work for the Briggs factory and played baseball after work. During a local tournament she was invited to a tryout for the AAGPBL in Chicago. She took the contract with the league because the money was so much better than she could make in the factories. Filarski played for the Rockford Peaches starting in 1945 and helped them win the pennant that year. In the series she got knocked out and lost her two front teeth. She also traveled to San Juan, Puerto Rico, for a baseball tournament. She did not return to the league after the 1950 season because in 1951 she married Tom Steffes and raised six children. She also coached a Mt. Clemens softball team for 30 years. Her career numbers include playing in 534 games, hitting .189 with 141 RBIs. {AAGPBL Newsletter, September 1994, May 1996 and September 2000; Bud Poliquin, "Diamond Celebration," *Syracuse Post-Standard*, 11 September 2003; AAGPBL Baseball Cards, 1995.}

Fillies

The Fillies captured last place in the Phoenix league in 1994 and 1995. Their combined record for the two seasons was 3–24. In 1998 the Fillies beat the Firebirds to stay out of last place but ended with a 3–5 record.

Firebirds

As a part of the Phoenix league, in 1994 the Firebirds finished with a 6–8 record and one tie to take second place. In 1995 they fell to third behind the new addition to the league, the Stealers. The Firebirds ended the season at 9–5. In 1998 the Firebirds fell to the cellar with a 0–8 record.

Fischer, Alva Jo "Tex"

(b. 23 August 1926, San Antonio, Texas; d. 13 August 1973) P/SS 1945–49, Rockford Peaches, Muskegon Lassies

Alva Jo Fischer pitched and played the infield during her career. She pitched in 91 games with 34 victories. She hit .223 in 387 games and knocked in 131 runs. In 1946 while playing for the Muskegon Lassies, Fischer hit .309 while driving in 11 runs. She played in 42 games for the Lassies that season. She left the league after the 1949 season following the death of her father. {AAGPBL Baseball Cards, 1996.}

Fiscus, Darlene

Growing up in western Pennsylvania, Darlene Fiscus found there were few opportunities to play baseball and so she took part in softball. She grew to love baseball because it was a different game from softball.

Fisher, Brenda

C/1B

Brenda Fisher played baseball in the Colt League while living in Emmitsburg, Maryland. When her family moved she had to make a choice about commuting to play baseball or switching to softball, since Thurmont had no girls playing baseball. She started playing baseball when she was 11 and generally was treated well by the boys. She made the all-star team her first year playing. {Molly Dunham, "LL Softball Doing Well in Thurmont," *Frederick Post*, 31 July 1980.}

Fisher (Stevens), Lorraine "Fish"

(b. 5 July 1928, Detroit, Michigan) P/OF 1947–49, Rockford Peaches, Grand Rapids Chicks

Lorraine Fisher was known for her defense and her control as a pitcher. She ended her career with 33 victories against 26 losses and an ERA of 2.52 in 70 games. She also played 131 games in the outfield and hit .138. {AAGPBL Baseball Cards, 1995.}

Fitzgerald (LeClair), Meryle "Pinky"

(b. 1925) P 1946, Fort Wayne Daisies

Meryle Fitzgerald got a lot of support at home to play sports. By age ten, for example, she served as the mascot and batgirl for the Lead, South Dakota, team that her father managed. After moving with her family to Oregon she played softball while attending Roosevelt High School in Portland. Her club, the Lind-Pomeroy Florists, won many honors and championships both locally and nationally. She also played for the Pasadena Ramblers softball team after her family moved again, this time to California. In 1946 she signed a contract and pitched one year with the Fort Wayne Daisies. {AAGPBL Newsletter, May 1996, 15.}

Flaherty, Colleen

(b. 1974, Somerville, Massachusetts) OF, North Shore Cougars

Colleen started playing baseball with the West Somerville Little League and then played on the Somerville High School softball squad, graduating in 1992. She also ran the 300- and 400-meter dash in track and field. After graduation she attended Burdette Business School in Boston and played softball in the Medford Women's League. She finally got her chance to return to baseball when she joined the North Shore Cougars in the NEWBL in 2002 and in nine games hit .385 with four RBIs. When not playing baseball, Colleen works as a project coordinator for an international consulting firm. {Chad Konecky, "Somerville Resident Shines in Women's Baseball League," *The Somerville Journal*, 5 September 2002.}

Flaherty, Mary

(b. South Ozone Park, Queens, New York; d. 30 March 2000, Vero Beach, Florida) P/3B, Racine Belles

Mary Flaherty got the chance to play in the AAGPBL when a scout saw her playing softball in New Jersey. She played for Racine for two seasons before going to work for General Motors in New York City. {AAGPBL Newsletter, September 2000, 7.}

Fleck, Karen

Detroit Renegades/Danger

Karen Fleck joined the Great Lakes Women's Baseball League and played for the Detroit Danger.

Florida Hurricanes

The Hurricanes took part in the South Florida Diamond Classic in 1998 and lost in the finals to the Florida Lightning. LuAnn Myatt was the losing pitcher for the Hurricanes. {"Florida Lightning Win South Florida Diamond Classic Second Time," *Baserunner*, October 1998.}

Florida Legends

The Florida Legends became the newest entry in the Ladies Professional Baseball League in 1998, the league's second season. The Legends played their home games at Homestead Sports Complex, Miami. The Legends had previously played in Los Angeles but were moved when the league could not renew their lease for a stadium at UCLA. Manager Bridget Wold moved with the team, but many of the players were new. One of their leading players was veteran pitcher Tina Nichols. Their season was from July to September with 28 games. {Pascale Etheart, "Blazing the Trail for Women in Baseball League," *Miami Herald*, 19 July 1998; Barry Jackson, "Women's League Puts Team in Homestead," *Miami Herald*, 9 April 1998.}

Florida Lightning

In 1998 the Lightning beat the Hurricanes to claim their second South Florida Diamond Classic. Pitcher Debbie Mitchell won the championship game. The hitting was led by Jackie Chin, who had two doubles in the game. LuAnn Myatt was the losing pitcher for the Hurricanes. The year before, Myatt had won the championship game for the Lightning. {"Florida Lightning Win South Florida Diamond Classic Second Time," *Baserunner*, October 1998.}

Florreich, Lois "Flash"

(b. 29 April 1927, Webster Grove, Missouri; d. 11 September 1991) P/OF/3B 1943–50, South Bend Blue Sox, Kenosha Comets, Rockford Peaches

As a rookie for South Bend in 1943, Florreich patrolled the outfield. In 1945 she moved to Kenosha and took over playing third base. While playing with Kenosha in 1946 Florreich only hit .234, but the team counted on her not for her bat but for her fielding. After a change in rules for pitching in 1947, Florreich made the switch to the mound and in 1949 led the league with a 0.67 ERA. She won 64 games against 25 losses in three seasons, and her final pitching record stood at 86–60. She made the all-star team in 1950 with a 20–8 record and 171 strikeouts to lead the league. She pitched game three of the 1950 championship series for the Peaches. She batted in 504 games and hit .192 with 139 RBIs. {AAGPBL Baseball Cards, 1995; Susan E. Johnson, *When Women Played Hardball* (Seattle: Seal Press, 1994), 46–47.}

Folder (Powell), Rose Marie "Rosie"

(b. 12 May 1926, Auburn, Illinois) OF/P 1944, Kenosha Comets

After graduating from Feitshans High School in 1944, Rose Folder got a chance to play in the AAGPBL. She played one season for the Comets before getting hurt. She returned home, married Edward Powell in 1946, and raised six kids and ran a day care center. Prior to playing baseball she played softball, as most of the players in the league did. She came to Chicago originally to play softball for the Tungsten Sparks for $35 a week and work part-time in a spark plug factory. She heard about the tryouts for the AAGPBL and decided to try to make the league. She also attended Illinois State Normal University. {AAGPBL Questionnaire, National Baseball Hall of Fame; AAGPBL Baseball Cards, 1995.}

Foley, Kate

(b. 23 January 1974) 1B 2003, New South Wales

Kate Foley played in the Australian National Tournament.

Foody, Jen

Parsippanny Yankees

Jen Foody played for the Parsipanny Yankees of the East Coast league in 2002 and led the league with 14 hits in 24 at-bats for the summer season. She scored 12 runs and knocked in six. She used her speed to steal eight bases to also lead the league. In the fall she was seven for 16 with eight runs scored.

Forkin, Chelsea

IF, Western Australia, 2004 Australian National Team

Chelsea Forkin played for Team Australia in the 2004 Women's World Series and World Cup. She had 13 hits during the Australian National Women's Championship to help out her club, six of which were doubles to lead all hitters.

Forman, Erin

(b. 12 December 1977, Grimsby, Ontario) SS 2004, Team Canada

Erin Forman graduated from Spring Harbor University in Michigan in 2000. While there she was named Conference Player of the Year and an All-American. She is married and teaches high school at Columbia International College. In 2004 she was selected as one of 18 baseball players to represent Canada at the first IBAF-sanctioned World Cup event for women. {Baseball Canada 2004 Women's National Team Media Guide.}

Fornoff, Susan

(b. 1958, Baltimore, Maryland) Sports writer/ Official scorer

Susan Fornoff started as a sports reporter in 1979 with the *Baltimore News American*, then worked for *USA Today* and finally covered the Oakland A's for the *Sacramento Bee*. She also worked as an official scorer for the A's and the San Francisco Giants. In 1986 she helped found the Association for Women in Sports Media and from 1987 to 1988 she served on the board of directors for the Baseball Writers' Association of America. Fornoff graduated from the University of Maryland in 1979 with a degree in journalism. She moved to California in 1985. {Susan Fornoff, *Lady in the Lockerroom* (Champaign, Illinois: Sagamore Publishing, 1993).}

Fort Wayne Daisies

The Fort Wayne Daisies belonged to the All American League from 1945 until the league folded after the 1954 season. They enjoyed their greatest success from 1952 through 1954 when they won the regular season title, but then lost each year in the playoffs. The Daisies enjoyed a long tenure in the league because of strong fan support. As a result the Daisies got involved in the community and often had benefit games and special nights to recognize their fans.

The Daisies had a lot of fine players on their rosters over the years. Betty Foss played first base for the club and was considered one of the league's best hitters. In fact, in 1952 Foss led the league in runs scored, hits, doubles, triples and total bases. She came in second in the league in batting average to fellow Daisy Jo Weaver, who hit .344. Dottie Schroeder played shortstop for the Daisies and regularly made them one of the best fielding teams in the league. {"Girls Baseball Team to Appear in Benefit," *The Marion Star*, 5 May 1953, 17.}

The Daisies had a junior league that included a team called the Redwings. Their Junior Girls Baseball League was designed to give young ladies a chance to develop their skills so they could play for the Daisies later in their careers. The Junior league continued on for a number of years after the All American League folded.

Fort Wayne Phantoms

The Phantoms were a charter member of the Great Lakes Women's Baseball League and played under the leadership of Christa Cook.

Fortin, Allison "Pookie"

In 1974 Allison Fortin wanted to play Little League baseball in Rhode Island. When they excluded her, she and her parents took the league to court and lost. The U.S. District Court of Rhode Island said that safety had to be the primary concern and girls could get hurt playing with boys. Fortin appealed the case, and the U.S. Court of Appeals First Circuit overturned the earlier decision. Fortin's father was a doctor, and he used his expertise to refute the claim that girls were physically not as fit as boys at age 12.

Foss, Anita "Nita"

(b. 5 August 1921, Providence, Rhode Island) P/2B 1948–49, Springfield Sallies, Muskegon Lassies, Rockford Peaches

Anita Foss joined the AAGPBL after her husband was killed in the navy. She played in only 28 games and was described as a scrappy hitter and good fielder. After leaving the league she went to work for Douglas Aircraft, becoming their first female supervisor. {AAGPBL Baseball Cards, 1996; Rick Harris, "Women, Baseball and Rhode Island," in *Rhode Island's Baseball Legacy*, Vol. 1 (Rhode Island: Rick Harris, 2001), 28.}

Fox, Pamela

(b. 1986, Sherwood Park, Alberta, Canada) CF, Team Alberta

In 2004 Pam Fox received one of two $1,000 scholarships awarded to current players on behalf of Betty Dunn and Millie Warwick-McAuley, both of whom played in the AAGPBL. Fox was named the MVP of the national team in November 2003 at the amateur baseball championships in Florida. She has been playing baseball since she was nine years old and played for Team Alberta for five years. In 2004 she attended tryouts and made the squad for Team Canada. When she is not playing baseball Fox is a student at New Sarepta Community High School. {Collin Gallant, "Outfielder Wins Bursary, Eyes Women's Selection Camp," *Edmonton Journal*, 9 March 2004, D5; Norm Cowley, "At Last, a Championship Team of Their Own," *Edmonton Journal*, 1 December 2003, D2.}

Foxx, Jimmy

(b. 22 October 1907, Sudlersville, Maryland) Manager

Jimmy Foxx came to the All-American League to manage the Fort Wayne Daisies. He brought with him a great deal of experience from his 19 years with the Philadelphia Athletics under Connie Mack. He hit .325 for his career with 534 home runs and led the league in RBIs for 13 years. Foxx received the highest recognition in baseball with his induction into the Hall of Fame in 1951. His Daisies benefited from his tutelage and always hit well as a team. In 1952 the team average, for example, was .257. {AAGPBL Baseball Cards, 2000; National Baseball Hall of Fame plaque.}

Fradette, Nathalie

(b. 26 October 1969, Montreal, Quebec) 3B 2004

Nathalie Fradette was chosen as one of 18 women who would represent Canada at the 2004 Women's World Series in Japan. Fradette played third base for the Canadian National Team. Before joining the club much of her experience came from playing softball. She played on the National Team from 1998 through 2001. With that squad she played in the Pan-Am games in 1999 and 2001 and represented Canada at the 2000 Olympics in Sydney, Australia. {Shi Davidi, "Team of 18 Women to Tune Up for World Cup," *Canadian Press*, 12 June 2004.}

Francis, Betty "BF"

(b. 7 July 1931, Chicago, Illinois) OF 1949–54, Muskegon Lassies, Kalamazoo Lassies, South Bend Blue Sox

Betty Francis joined the AAGPBL in 1949 by starting on the touring Colleens before moving up to the "big leagues" when a roster spot opened at Muskingum. Betty made the adjustment to baseball quite easily because she was a strong athlete, having won a round of awards in track and field from 1946 to 1948 in Chicago. {AAGPBL Baseball Cards, 1995.)

Frank (Dummerth), Edna "Frankie"

(b. 15 June 1924, St. Louis, Missouri) C 1944, Minneapolis Millerettes

Edna Frank spent one season in the AAGPBL with the Millerettes, as their backup catcher. When they traded her midway through the season to the

Racine Belles, Frank decided to join the navy instead. She later married and raised eight children. She played in 16 games during her short time in the league and hit only .109. {AAGPBL Newsletter, January 2002, 29; AAGPBL Baseball Cards, 1996.}

Franks, Hermina "Irish"

(b. 7 September 1920, Oconto, Wisconsin) P 1946, Kenosha Comets

Hermina Franks served in the Army Air Corps for three years during World War II. Part of that time she spent in England and France repairing planes. She joined the All American League for one year in 1946. After leaving the Comets she stayed active with biking, hiking, and cross-country skiing. {AAGPBL Baseball Cards, 2000.}

Frazer, Megan

Management personnel

Megan Frazer began working for the Charleston Alleycats in 1996 following her graduation from the University of Michigan. She came to the club with some public relations experience from the International Hockey League and the 1996 Summer Olympics. She moved through the organization to become the vice-president and general manager by 2003. The Alleycats play in the South Atlantic League and are under the ownership of Tom Dickson and Sherrie Myers. They play in Watt Powell Park but one of the projects Frazer was in charge of was the building of a new park to increase fan attendance. In 2003 Frazer was one of only two female GMs in minor league baseball. {Jack Bogaczyk, "Charleston's New General Manager Has Plenty of Experience Behind Her," *Charleston Daily Mail*, 27 March 2003.}

Freeman's Females

One of the difficulties in following women's teams during the nineteenth century is the lack of consistent coverage and the similar names many of them used in their local areas. Freeman's Females fall into that category, as it appears that Harry H. Freeman organized two different teams with the same name in 1885. His first club fell apart under disputed circumstances. According to the *New York Clipper* the players claimed Freeman did not pay them, while Freeman says the players deserted him, leaving him no choice but to form a new club. Freeman reorganized the club in New Orleans and planned to take the team on a barnstorming trip through Florida, Texas,

Arkansas, Tennessee, and Kentucky. Following the team's travel it seems they ran into financial difficulties in Hot Springs, Arkansas, and had to disband. Freeman reorganized the club in Cincinnati in June, and the final account of their travels came in Omaha, Nebraska, in October. They were scheduled to play a local men's team but that was cancelled when the wives of some of the players refused to let their husbands play a game against women. No further accounts of this club appear in the *Clipper*. The only two players receiving any mention were Pearl Emmerson and May Lawrence. {*New York Clipper*, 24 January 1885, 21 March 1885, 23 May 1885, and 31 October 1885.}

Frese-Khramov, Janelle

RHP 1996, Colorado Silver Bullets

Janelle Frese-Khramov played softball for the University of Nebraska before coming to spring training with the Silver Bullets in 1996. While at Nebraska from 1986 to 1988 her team won the Big 8 Championship. Frese also played for the Los Angeles Legends. {*Silver Bulletin*, March 1996.}

Fretto, Jackie

C 1996, Colorado Silver Bullets

Before joining the Bullets in 1996 Jackie Fretto gained some baseball experience playing for the Orange County Edge baseball team in 1994 and 1995. She hit .690 and had a 0.59 ERA. {*Silver Bulletin*, March 1996.}

Friend, Lauren

(b. 16 July 1979) 2B 2003, New South Wales

Lauren Friend helped New South Wales beat Queensland in the 2003 Women's National Championships. She hit one home run in the series to help her team.

Fritz, Zoe

(b. 10 March 1982) 1B/OF 2003, Queensland Rams

Zoe Fritz played in the Australian women's league.

Froning (O'Meara), Mary

(b. 26 August 1934, Minster, Ohio) OF 1951–54, South Bend Blue Sox, Battle Creek Belles

Mary Froning played for four years in the All American League, starting when she was only 17.

A scout saw her while she was playing CYO soft-ball and invited her to a tryout. Her parents took her to her first tryout, in South Bend, because of her age. There were over 100 girls there trying out for five roster spots, and Froning got one of them. Her parents helped her get settled in South Bend and she signed a contract for $50 a week plus travel money. Just as she found her feet in the league, the league folded, but she did go on to tour with the Allington All-Stars in 1955. She ended her career having played in 209 games, with her best season at the plate being in 1954, when she hit .231. She drove in 46 runs and scored another 95 with 58 stolen bases. She worked as an airline stewardess for American Airlines until she married Tom O'Meara in 1958 and moved to Wisconsin. She spent many years coaching her children's teams and then played softball, tennis and golf. {AAGPBL Newsletter, May 2005, 26–27; AAGPBL Baseball Cards, 1995; Jeni Leis, *History of the All American Girls Professional Baseball League,* Master of Science thesis, Mankato State University, 1998, 44–46.}

Fuchs, Lee

C/MGR 1988, Daredevils

In 1988 Lee Fuchs caught and managed the Daredevils in the new AWBA.

Gacioch, Rose "Rosie," "Rockford Rosie," "Grandma," "Petunia"

(b. 31 August 1915, Wheeling, West Virginia; d. 12 September 2004) P/RF/1B/2B 1944–1950, South Bend Blue Sox, Rockford Peaches, Grand Rapids Chicks

By Ryan Bucher and Kerri Bottoroff

Rose Gacioch had one of most successful ca-reers in the AAGPBL and possibly the most well-rounded career of any female ballplayer. In the AAGPBL, she was one of the best all-around play-ers, excelling at bat, in the field, and on the mound. Gacioch's longevity was also extraordi-nary: she played professionally in three decades and is often cited as linking the barnstorming bloomer teams of the 1920s and 1930s with the AAGPBL of the 1940s and 1950s. {Gregorich, 82.}

Gacioch was born on 31 August 1915 in Wheel-ing, West Virginia. Her father was killed in a fac-tory accident before she was born. Her mother grew up in Poland, where women were expected to conform to traditional gender roles. By con-trast, Gacioch was a tomboy as a child and was introduced to baseball at a young age. Her mother

discouraged her ball playing and diligently tried to raise Gacioch as a more traditional woman. Her mother was also often ill, and Gacioch missed a lot of school while caring for her. She only finished the seventh grade. When Gacioch was just 16 years old, her mother died of cancer.

Gacioch once skipped school to see Babe Ruth and Lou Gehrig on one of their barnstorming tours. She joined a boy's baseball team herself in 1931 when she was just 15 years old. Her profes-sional career began in 1934 when she joined the All-Star Ranger Girls, a barnstorming team owned by Maud Nelson. This team was the last of the bloomer girls teams, made famous in the 1920s and 1930s by their uniforms as well as their play. When the team folded after the 1934 season, Gacioch returned to Wheeling, took a factory job, and played on a few barnstorming softball teams.

Gacioch saw an ad for the AAGPBL in 1944 and told her friends that she was going to play in the league even though she was much older than most of other women and had not played professional baseball for a decade. The 28–year-old Gacioch was invited to join the South Bend Blue Sox as an outfielder. She soon distinguished herself as one of the team's best players. Despite her fine play, in 1945, Rose was traded to the Rockford Peaches, where she spent the rest of her career. According to the president of the South Bend team, she was traded "because she used poor English." {Barbara Gregorich, *Women at Play: The Story of Women in Baseball* (San Diego: Harcourt Brace & Co., 1993), 210; Susan E. Johnson, *When Women Played Hardball* (Seattle: Seal Press, 1994), 82.}

Gacioch went on to help the Peaches win the AAGPBL championship in four of the next six sea-sons and established herself as one of the league's best and most versatile players. In addition to being an outstanding infielder and outfielder, Gacioch developed into a dominating pitcher. She won 20 games in two different seasons and threw a no-hit-ter in 1953 against her former team, South Bend. Her best season on the mound came during the 1951 season. She was the league's only 20–game winner, going 20–7 with a 1.68 ERA.

In addition to finishing her career with a 2.48 ERA and a .603 winning percentage on the mound, Gacioch set a league record with 31 outfield assists in 1945, a mark she equaled in 1947. She also led the league in triples and RBIs in 1945. Gacioch was cho-sen to the all-star team in three years: in 1952 and 1954 as a pitcher and in 1953 as a utility infielder.

The winter before the 1954 season, Gacioch proved that her athleticism was not limited to the ball diamond, as she and her partner Fran Sten-nett won the national women's doubles bowling championship. After her baseball career ended in 1954, Gacioch remained in Rockford, where she retuned to factory work. She never married, and when she retired she moved to Detroit to be close to her remaining family.

In 1988, Gacioch and her niece celebrated the opening of the Women in Baseball exhibit at the National Baseball Hall of Fame in Cooperstown, New York. Of her experiences in Cooperstown, she told one interviewer, "It was a good feeling, seeing that exhibit at the Hall of Fame. ... now I got something on Pete Rose. I got there before he did!"

Gagne, Karine

(b. 15 December 1983, Granby, Quebec) OF/SS
2004, Team Canada

During the 2004 Women's World Cup, Karine Gagne led all batters by scoring six runs and batting .529 to help her team to the bronze medal. Though they lost the first game of the series to Japan, Gagne scored the first run on a single by Stephanie Topolie. Gagne gained her baseball experience playing at the Midget and Junior levels of Baseball Canada. In 2001 her team made it to the Canada Games at the Midget level and in 2002 they made it to the nationals. In 2003 Gagne moved up to the Junior level and again Team Quebec made the nationals. When she is not practicing or playing, Gagne can be found studying for her classes at Vanier College. {"Women Open Series with Loss to Japan," *The Record* (Ontario), 19 July 2004; Baseball Canada 2004 Media Guide.}

Gallegos, Luisa

P 1948, Peoria Red Wings, South Bend Blue Sox

Luisa Gallegos played one season in the All American League and split her time between Peoria and South Bend, and was traded because of pitching needs.

Gallina, Marita

1997, San Diego Stix

Marita Gallina played for the San Diego entry in the Ladies Professional Baseball League.

Ganote (Weise), Gertrude I. "Gertie," "Lefty"

(b. 17 February 1920, Louisville, Kentucky) 1B/P
1944–45, Kenosha Comets, South Bend Blue Sox

Getrude Ganote graduated from Louisville Girls High School and worked for a local printing company. She decided to drive to Chicago in 1944 to try out for the AAGPBL with Ann Hutchison. She learned her skills from her father Joe, who played minor league ball with the New Orleans Ziffers. She made the cut and was assigned to the Kenosha Comets as their starting first baseman and occasional pitcher. She won six games in her career and only hit .160 while stealing 33 bases, but none of that really mattered. She was considered one of the best, if not the best, fielding first basemen in the league. She finished playing after 1945 because she got married in 1946. She worked at Walgreens for 29 years. {AAGPBL Newsletter, January 1996, 15, and January 2002, 27; AAGPBL Questionnaire, National Baseball Hall of Fame; AAGPBL Baseball Cards, 1995.}

Garber, Jillian

Jillian Garber has played baseball since she was five years old. She developed her love for the game while attending Oakland A's games with her father, Alan Garber. When she got old enough to enter junior high school Garber never considered switching to softball but kept with baseball. She played for the Piedmont Junior Varsity baseball team as well as the North/South Oakland Little League squad. She patrolled the outfield for Piedmont's victory over their archrival, St. Mary's, 11–10 in June 2003. When she is not out fielding grounders Jillian is involved in ballet, attending rehearsals at the Piedmont Light Opera Theater. {Laura Casey, "Girl is one of the Guys Playing Baseball," *Oakland Tribune*, 22 June 2003; "High School Player Also Sports Dancing Shoes," *The Daily Review* (Calif.), 22 June 2003.}

Garcia, Adelina

Adelina Garcia played for the Cubanas all-star squad in Venezuela in the spring of 1948. She joined AAGPBL players Ysors del Castillo and Georgiana Rios.

Garcia, Bekki

IF/P Alameda Oaks

Bekki Garcia played for the Alameda entry in the California Women's Baseball League.

Garelick, Jackie

INF, Montgomery County Barncats

Garman (Hosted), Ann

(b. 11 March 1933, Avilla, Indiana) 1B 1953, South Bend Blue Sox

Ann Garman played only one year in the All American League before it folded. She played in 21 games and had 195 putouts against only seven errors. Her hitting was her weak spot, as she hit only .154 with seven RBIs. {AAGPBL Baseball Cards, 1995.}

Gary, Rachell

Team USA, Alameda Oaks

Rachell Gary played in two games of the 2003 Women's World Series. She came to bat three times and was held hitless, but she also walked three times and scored two runs. She also played for the Alameda Oaks.

Gascon, Eileen V. "Ginger"

(b. 1 December 1931, Chicago, Illinois) LF/3B 1949, 1951, Springfield Sallies, Grand Rapids Chicks

At Austin High School, Eileen Gascon played basketball and also played city league softball. In 1949 after the baseball season ended she played AAU Basketball and won the Indiana state championship. She toured with the Springfield Sallies in 1949, joined the rival Chicago league in 1950 and then joined Grand Rapids in 1951 at the hot corner. Later she graduated from Northeastern Illinois State University with a bachelor's in education. She got her master's degree from Chicago State University. With her degrees she ended up teaching for six years and then was a high school guidance counselor for 27 years. {AAGPBL Questionnaire, National Baseball Hall of Fame; AAGPBL Baseball Cards, 1995.}

Gascon, Sarah

(Rancho Palo Verdes, California) IF 2004, USA National Team

Growing up in California, Sarah Gascon played Little League baseball until the age of 11, when she switched to softball. Up to that point she had always been the only girl in her league. While attending Southeastern Louisiana University, Gascon earned All-conference honors in softball all four years. She earned the same honors in volleyball. These accomplishments led to her invitation to try out and her selection for the USA National Team in 2004. She helped her team to win the gold medal over Japan in the World Cup by knocking in the first run in the championship game. Her single in the fourth inning scored Laura Brenneman to make the score 1–0, and the final score was 2–0. During the 2004 women's World Cup Gascon hit .364 with three runs knocked in and two stolen bases. {"Former SLU Softball Player Helps U.S. Win Women's Baseball Gold," *The Advocate* (La.), 16 August 2004, 5–D; USA Baseball Web site and 2004 Media Guide.}

Gasior, Kim

Bacchus Marsh Tigers

Kim Gasior played for the Tigers in the Victorian Baseball Association. They played 18 games in 2002 and won 12 of them. Gasior always seemed to help her team's cause with her bat. In one game, for example, she had two triples. {"Home Diamond Final," *Melton Moorabool Leader*, 26 February 2002.}

Gators

This team belonged to the American Women's Baseball Association in the 1990s.

Gausch, Celeste

2B/OF, San Jose Spitfires

Celeste Gausch played in the Ladies Professional Baseball League with the Spitfires.

Gay, Lindsey

(Marion, Massachusetts) IF 2001, Lowell Robins

A native of Marion, Massachusetts, Lindsey Gay played softball and soccer while attending Old Rochester Regional High School. She began her baseball career with the Robins in 2001 as an infielder. Her previous baseball experience came while playing Little League. She did try out for the high school baseball team but hurt her knee and did not make the squad. {J.L. Barnes, "ORR Alum Finds a League of Her Own," *The Standard-Times*, 27 July 2002, A1.}

Gaynor, Katie

(b. 30 August 1977) C/OF New South Wales, 2004 Australian National Team

Katie Gaynor played for New South Wales in the 2004 Australian National Championships and helped her team to a second place finish with two sacrifice flies and six stolen bases.

She only got caught stealing twice and led all players with 34 at-bats in the series.

Geatches, Allison

(b. 19 November 1963, Mt. Clemens, Michigan) 1B/RF, Colorado Silver Bullets

Allison Geatches played a variety of sports growing up but not baseball. While in high school she played basketball, softball and volleyball, earning All-State honors for each sport. She also played some basketball in Europe before joining the Silver Bullets. She split her time between first base and the outfield. {David Kindred, *Colorado Silver Bullets: For the Love of the Game* (Atlanta: Longstreet Press, Inc.), 74.}

Geissinger (Harding), Jean Louise "Dutch," "Squeaky"

(b. 25 June 1934, Huntingdon, Pennsylvania) 2B/SS/CF/P 1951–54, Fort Wayne Daisies, Grand Rapids Chicks

Jean Geissinger attended Lower Camden County High School in New Jersey and lettered in sports all four years. She also attended Michigan State University, earning a certificate in special education. Geissinger enjoyed success in the field and at the bat. In 1953 she led the league in RBIs with 81. She was selected as the all-star second baseman in both 1953 and 1954. In the 1953 All-Star Game Geissinger hit a game-winning home run. In 1954 she led the league with 91 RBIs. Since her playing days she has kept active with golf, volleyball, fastpitch softball and speed walking. Her softball team won three state championships between 1969 and 1985. In recognition of her contributions Geissinger was elected to the Michigan Softball Hall of Fame in 1993 following election to her high school hall of fame in 1989. In April 2005, Harding joined a number of former All-American players as a member of the Northeast Indiana Baseball Association Hall of Fame. She married Russell Harding in 1959 and raised three daughters. {AAGPBL Questionnaire, National Baseball Hall of Fame.}

Gelman, Robin

P, Montgomery County Barncats

Growing up in Queens, New York, Robin Gelman had many chances to play baseball informally but she also developed quite a musical talent as well. In fact, Gelman earned an MA in classical music from Juilliard, playing the bassoon. During the 2000 season she helped her team to a number of victories including a 7–4 triumph over the Virginia Flames in June. In addition to pitching for the Barncats, Gelman also works for Lockheed Martin as a billing analyst. {Chris Slattery, "Diamonds Are a Girl's Best Friend," <Gazette.Net>, 20 July 2001.}

George (McFaul), Genevieve Mary "Gene"

(b. 22 September 1927, Regina, Saskatchewan; d. 11 March 2002) 1947, South Bend Blue Sox

Genevieve George grew up in a household with nine children, which gave her plenty of playmates as she got older. She began playing softball at age 13 and in 1947 went to a tryout for the All American League. The highlight of her one year with the Blue Sox came with an unassisted triple play. After that one season she returned to Saskatchewan and played softball through the mid–1950s, even winning a championship in 1951. She was inducted into the Saskatchewan Baseball Hall of Fame. {AAGPBL Newsletter, May 2002, 31.}

George, Patty "Mayo"

P, South bend Blue Sox, Chicago Storm

Patty George enjoyed a pitching career that saw her on the roster for the Blue Sox and the Storm in the Great Lakes Women's Baseball League. She went on to medical school in Baltimore and continued to play in the Washington Metropolitan League. {Kovach, 94.}

Georges, Beulah Anne "Scoop"

(b. 10 May 1923, Columbus Ohio; d. 4 January 2005) P/IF 1948, Chicago Colleens, Fort Wayne Daisies, Chaperone

Anne Georges served in the navy during World War II and played for one year in the All American League. She got minimal playing time so she came in back in 1949 as a chaperone for the Colleens. She liked being around the game and enjoyed the travel. She continued to play fastpitch softball after she left the league. {AAGPBL Baseball Cards, 1996.}

Gerring, Cathy

Cathy Gerring made a name for herself as an LPGA golfer but in 2004 she was honored at the Little League World Series with a group of female pioneers. Growing up, Gerring played in the Senior Division of Times Corners Little League. She received induction into the Little League's Hall of Excellence in 2004. {"Little League Set to Honor City's Gerring," *The Journal Gazette*, 22 August 2004.}

Gersztyn, Barb

P 1997–1999, San Diego Stix

In 1999 Barb Gersztyn helped pitch her team to a national championship and she was named to the All-Tournament team for her efforts. She finished the series at 2–0 with a 0.0 ERA. She pitched ten innings and gave up only three unearned runs.

Geyer, Veronica

Veronica Geyer helped establish the New York/New Jersey Women's Baseball League in 2000 with one traveling team, the New Jersey Nemesis. Geyer not only works on the administrative end but also plays baseball, though she grew up playing softball because that was all that was available for girls. Geyer was also elected to the National Women's Baseball Hall of Fame, which was created in 1999. {Michael Gasparino, "Playing Hardball," Long Island Sports Online, LISOnline.com, 15 June 1999.}

Gianfrancisco (Zale), Philomena Theresa "Phil," "Frisco"

(b. 20 April 1923, Chicago, Illinois; d. 18 January 1992) OF 1945–48, Grand Rapids Chicks

Philomena Gianfrancisco graduated from St. Mary's High School before playing in 21 games in 1945 and then 98 games in 1946 for the Chicks and batting only .225. She did hit the longest home run hit in the Chicks Park, a 300–foot shot. By the time she finished playing after the 1948 season she had played in 265 games with a .205 average. She married boxer Tony Zale and managed his career until her own death in 1992. {AAGPBL Baseball Cards, 1996.}

Gibbons, Melissa

2B, Blue Crush, NJ Diamonds

While growing up in Mechanicsburg, Pennsylvania, Melissa Gibbons played baseball on the local Little League teams. At Pennsbury High School she tried out for the baseball team and was told to go try softball. She found a local team called the Atlantic Pride that let her play when she was 15. At Slippery Rock University she ran into the same trouble and gave up on the sport until she joined the New Jersey Diamonds. Then she moved on to play second base for the Blue Crush in the new Philadelphia league. {Don McKee, "She's Creating a Place to Play Hardball," *Philadelphia Inquirer*, 9 March 2004; Eileen O'Donnell, "Covering All the Bases," *Philadelphia Inquirer*, 15 July 2005.}

Gibson, Lisa

IF, Phoenix Peppers

Lisa Gibson played with the Peppers in the Ladies Professional Baseball League in the 1990s.

Gilchrist, Jeanne

(b. 13 June 1926, New Norway, Alberta) C 1946, Peoria Red Wings

While attending Duke of Connaught High School, Jean Gilchrist played a variety of sports. She took part in softball, basketball, volleyball, grass hockey and an ice skating relay team. In addition, she also played in the city softball league beginning in junior high school. She was chosen for the all-star team in 1945. After leaving the Red Wings, Gilchrist continued to play softball and also picked up curling and golf. She did a lot of coaching in addition to her teaching after earning a degree in education from the University of British Columbia. {AAGPBL Questionnaire, National Baseball Hall of Fame; AAGPBL Newsletter, May 1995, 3; AAGPBL Baseball Cards, 2000.}

Gilham, Kaley

(b. 8 February 1988, Rocky Mountain House, Alberta) P/OF, Team Alberta

Kaley Gilham has played for Team Alberta's Bantam squad since 1999. In the summer of 2003 while playing for Rocky Mountain House, her squad won the western Canadian Bantam AA championship. At the Bantam championships Gilham had 19 strikeouts and even three RBIs at the plate to help her own cause. Gilham played for Team Canada at the AAU National Championships in 2003 as well. At most of the tournaments she has played in, her talents have been recognized with MVP awards and other honors. She works on her pitching technique by training with the Canadian men's coach and has pitched for a boys' Bantam team. Gilham also played for Canada in the 2004 Women's World Series.

One of her strongest pitching performances came in a victory over South Korea. At 16 she was the youngest player on the Canadian squad and the tallest at 6′1″. She attended St. Matthew's High School through her sophomore year and started her junior year at Red Deer. {Dan Carle, "Tall Future for Rocky Teen," *Edmonton Sun*, 5 August 2004, SP4; Norm Cowley, "At Last, a Championship of Their Own: Team Canada Evaluation Camp Held for Inaugural World Cup of Women's Baseball," *Edmonton Journal*, 1 December 2003, D2.}

Girouard (Vaslet), Valerie

Pawtucket Slaterettes

Valerie Girouard was one of the AAGPBL's original players. Her father helped found the league so she could play baseball instead of softball. She played in the league until she entered Tolman High School. Years later her own two daughters, Shana and Erin, played in the league as well, while Valerie turned to coaching. {Sumathi Ready, "Slaterettes Shine on the Diamond," *Providence Journal*, 27 April 1998, C–01.}

Gisolo, Margaret

(b. 21 October 1914, Blanford, Indiana)

By Shawn Selby

During the 1920s, Blanford, Indiana, was a town of coal mines and little other economy of any substance. Like children in the vast majority of Midwestern towns in the first quarter of the twentieth century, Blanford's youngsters looked to baseball to help relieve the drudgery of school and chores. It was into this world that Margaret Gisolo was born on 21 October 1914. Although her two sisters were cool to the idea of pursuing the sporting life, Gisolo was quickly hooked on baseball. She learned the game from her brother, Toney, himself a semipro and minor league baseball player. Toney's love of the game was contagious, and Gisolo soon showed promise in softball as well as baseball. In 1925, in an effort to build American citizenship as well as athletic prowess, the American Legion organized a junior baseball program. When competitive play began the next year, there were leagues in 15 states, and by 1929 every American Legion department boasted a team. Under the direction of Commissioner Kennesaw Mountain Landis, the American and National leagues contributed between $20,000 and $50,000 to American Legion Junior Baseball each year. It turned out to be money well spent, since by 1946 the American Legion program had graduated 161 players to the major leagues. {Susan E. Johnson, 214.}

Blanford created its own American Legion team within the first years of the league. Eager to demonstrate her ability in something other than sandlot ball, Gisolo jumped at the chance to participate in an organized league. She quickly demonstrated her prowess on the field, leading her team, the Blanford Cubs, to victories in nearly all of their early games. Unlike their namesake, Blanford's Cubs cut a swath through their league, reaching the state championship series in their first year of existence. On their way to the state

tournament, the Cubs played the team from neighboring Clinton, Indiana in the county championship. With the game tied at seven apiece going into the twelfth inning, Gisolo stepped to the plate and drove in the winning run. An ecstatic Blanford team was soon dismayed to learn that Clinton was challenging their victory on the grounds that Margaret's being female violated the league's rules of competition. The American Legion rulebook clearly stated that "any *boy* is eligible to play" (emphasis added). While the matter was being deliberated by A.V. Stringfellow at the local level, the case was passed on to the state arbiter. In the meantime Margaret was suspended for six days pending the outcome of the decision. {Johnson, 214.}

Indiana American Legion athletic officer Robert Bushee and the legion's state director, Dan Sowers, conferred several times over the matter. Unable to reach a conclusion themselves, they appealed to the highest power in the baseball universe at the time, baseball commissioner Kennesaw Mountain Landis. The three men eventually ruled that, although the rules of the American Legion's National Baseball Program did state that any boy was eligible, it did not specifically state that girls were not. In fact, they argued, the legion "did not contemplate the participation of girls" in the first place. Extreme circumstances call for extreme solutions, and Gisolo was reinstated in time for the finale of the county championship. Landis himself issued the press release on 30 June 1928. Ironically, the Cubs were stripped of their first victory in the series not because Gisolo played, but because another Cubs player was over the age limit of 17. The best of three series thus came down to a decisive third game, which Blanford won 5–2. {Johnson, 214.}

Although Gisolo herself was largely unaware of the controversy surrounding her participation, the media chided the Clinton Baptists for their lack of sportsmanship. The team's hometown paper, the *Daily Clintonian*, even went so far as to say that with the loss, the team would "lay claim to the unique distinction of being the first ball club to ever be beaten by a safe hit off a girl's bat in a championship affair." Whether or not the media covered the story as they did simply because the novelty of a girl ballplayer would sell papers is unclear. In addition, there is the distinct possibility that the American Legion's reasons for deciding in Margaret's favor were somewhat less than noble. The negative publicity generated by their exclusion of a female, even in the society of the 1920s, would have been significant, while positive reporting could only bolster the league's reputation. In any case, the matter was apparently resolved to the satisfaction of at least one of the protagonists and Gisolo's Cubs advanced.

As the Cubs moved up the tournament ladder, Gisolo rapidly became the player everyone wanted to see. While her gender was certainly a novelty for many fans, her skill at second base and at the plate won the most press coverage. She led her team — unbeaten — through the county, district and sectional tournaments, soundly thrashing all who opposed them. In addition, they took time out to play exhibition games, winning each of them as well. By the time the seemingly invincible Cubs reached the Indiana State Championship series, Gisolo was dominating the game. The Cubs won the state tournament 14–12 over the Gary Yankees to advance to the interstate regional championship to be held at Comiskey Park in Chicago. But the Cubs' dreams of a national championship were not to be. They were eliminated from the tournament with a 12–5 loss to Marine Post 273 of Chicago. During their tournament run, however, Gisolo put up impressive numbers, batting .429 and fielding her position with ten putouts, 28 assists and no errors. Even a newspaper as prestigious as the *New York Times* covered Gisolo's success on the field, saying she "starred in defeat." Clearly, here was a rarity — a girl who could beat men at their own game.

Even as the Cubs began looking forward to the upcoming season, the American Legion office issued a surprise ruling stating that henceforth girls would not be permitted to join any youth league sponsored by the legion. Gisolo was devastated. But, never one to shrink from a challenge, she soon landed on her feet with the American Athletic Girls, a barnstorming team owned and operated by Rose Figg. During the course of the 1929 season, Figg's team allowed the 14-year-old Gisolo a chance to play the game she loved. The paycheck of $75, to be paid monthly to either Gisolo or her mother, was certainly an added bonus. Leaving the American Athletic Girls at the end of 1929, she signed on with Maud Nelson's All-Star Ranger Girls in 1930. It is unclear why she changed teams, although money considerations were often factors in such decisions during the early days of the Great Depression. She stayed on with the barnstorming Ranger Girls until 1934 (graduating from Clinton High School in 1931) and saved enough money to attend college.

Gisolo attended Indiana State Teachers College in Terra Haute and graduated in 1935 with a BS in physical education. In 1942 she earned her masters' degree in physical education with an emphasis on administration. Like many Americans at the time, she was eager to help in the war effort and so joined the WAVES, eventually reaching the rank of lieutenant commander at the time of her discharge. Hired by Arizona State University in 1954, she expanded the dance department from part of the physical education curriculum into one of the most highly respected dance programs in the nation.

After retiring in 1980 as a full professor, Gisolo entered the world of competitive sports once again. She took up senior tennis and won gold medals in doubles at the Senior Olympics in both 1989 and 1991. In 1990 the United States Tennis Association's *Tennis Yearbook* ranked her number two in the nation in singles and doubles play at the senior level.

Gisolo made a lasting mark in the history of women in sports. She was the first woman to participate in organized junior baseball, and the media coverage her successes brought opened America's eyes to the role women could play in sports. Her talent on the field and her determination off it paved the way for women athletes in baseball. She was a precursor to the glory days of women's baseball during the All American Girls Professional Baseball League in the 1940s and 1950s. {Barbara Gregorich, *Women at Play: The Story of Women in Baseball* (New York: Harvest, 1993), 62.}

Glaser, Rose Mary "Hap"

(b. 22 October 1921, Cincinnati, Ohio) OF/P 1944, Kenosha Comets

Rose Mary Glaser played softball in the Cincinnati area before joining the Comets for one season. She returned to softball after her short stint. She played softball with a number of other former All-American girls from the Cincinnati area including Marie Lang, Marie Wegman and Marion Wohlwender. For her athletic accomplishments she was inducted into three halls of fame: at the University of Cincinnati, Caldwell University and Reading High School. {AAGPBL Baseball Cards, 2000.}

Glassman, Cari

(b. 1961) P, AWBA

Cari Glassman joined the AWBA when it first began in 1987 and was still playing for the league in 1993. During the filming of the movie *A League of Their Own*, Glassman finally got some training regarding her pitching from one of the former All-American pitchers. {Carrie Muskat, "Playing Hardball's a Down and Dirty Escape from Real Life," *Chicago Tribune*, 27 June 1993, 1, 11.}

Glennie, Jim

Organizer, Manager, Coach

Jim Glennie has been the driving force behind the upsurge in women's baseball since the 1980s. He works as assistant attorney general for the state of Michigan, but in baseball he has been involved in every major effort to promote the women's game. He is the founder of the Women's International Baseball Association and president and founder of the American Women's Baseball League.

Godwin, Sue

1997, San Diego Stix

Sue Godwin played in the Ladies Professional Baseball League in the 1990s with the San Diego Stix.

Goldberg, Kirsten

RF, Montgomery County Barncats

Kirsten Goldberg played in the outfield for the Barncats in the EWBC.

Goldsmith, Bethany

(b. 6 October 1927, Elgin, Illinois) P 1948–50, Kenosha Comets

Beth Goldsmith played for three seasons in the All American League and got the chance to participate in their Central American tour. She pitched in 87 games with a record of 34–34 and an ERA of 2.72. She also batted .160 with 24 runs scored. {AAGPBL Baseball Cards, 1995.}

Gomez, Korine

IF 1998, Arizona Peppers

Before joining the Ladies Professional Baseball League, Korine Gomez attended Southeastern Louisiana University to play softball.

Gonzales, Eulalia

IF 1947, Racine Belles

Eulalia Gonzales came from Cuba for part of 1947 and played with the Belles before returning to Cuba.

Goodall, Kristin

C 1997, San Diego Stix

Kristin Goodall played in the Ladies Professional Baseball League in the 1990s with the Stix.

Goodwin, Jeanette "Jen," "Goody"

(b. 3 September 1974, Quincy, Massachusetts) 1B/3B Baystate Express, Boston Blue Sox, Team USA

Before graduating in 1992 from Braintree High School, Jen Goodwin played soccer, basketball and softball for four years. She wanted to continue playing sports and found a chance to play baseball with the Bay State Express in the NEWBL in 1999. Though she had never played organized baseball before, Goodwin had grown up tagging around behind her brother when he went to the ball park. She helped the Express win the league title their first year. She played with the Express through 2001 and also joined the New England Clippers in 2000 and 2001. The Clippers were a select team that traveled to tournaments to compete. She also joined the Boston Blue Sox from 2002 to 2003. Goodwin played for the USA National Team in 2001 and 2002, and then in 2004 joined the New England Sox.

Since she started playing in 1999, Goodwin has collected a number of individual awards as well as team trophies. In 1999 she got a WNEBL Gold Glove for her fielding at first base. Her team won the WNEBL in 1999 and 2000. They also won the first Women's World Series in 2001, defeating Japan in Toronto. Goodwin also played in the 2002 Women's World Series and in November 2004 her team won the Roy Hobbs tournament. {Jeanette Goodwin, correspondence with Leslie A. Heaphy, North Canton, Ohio, November 2004.}

Goodwin graduated from Bridgewater State College with a degree in physical education. Goodwin played softball for Bridgewater State College under coach Dee Dee Enabenter. While at Bridgewater, Goodwin set the record for highest single-season average in 1993 at .504. She also holds the highest career average at .464 from 1993 to 1996. When not playing herself, Goodwin was the head softball coach at Simmons College and took on the job of assistant softball coach at San Jose State University in 2004. {Bridgewater State College Athletics Web site.}

Gordon, Mildred

Mildred Gordon was a local ballplayer in the Muskegon, Michigan, area in the 1920s. She was an infielder for the Conklin baseball nine. One reporter said she could "throw like a man," that she ran the bases with fair speed that she and was learning to hit all types of pitching. {"Girl Star," *Muskegon Chronicle*, 1 August 1925.}

Gosser, Ponch

1997, San Diego Stix

Ponch Gosser joined the Stix in the new Ladies Professional Baseball League.

Gosstray, Narelle

(b. 5 November 1969) P/2B, Australian National Team

During the 2003 Women's World Series, Gosstray only hit .167 in four games. She also had two errors in the field for a fielding percentage of .875. In 2004 she played for New South Wales in the Australian National Championships and helped out her team with 14 runs scored and eight walks.

Gottselig, John

(b. 24 June 1909, Odessa, Russia; d. 15 May 1986) Manager

John Gottselig coached softball in Canada before coming to the All American League. He was able to recruit a lot of Canadian players during the off-season to come and play for the league. He managed the Racine Belles to their championship in 1943, and in 1946 he became a scout for the league. His own playing experience did not come from baseball but hockey. Gottselig played with the Chicago Blackhawks from 1928 to 1941 and 1942 to 1946. {"Hockey Manager Signed to Scout Girls' Loop," *Waukesha Daily Freeman*, 24 May 1946, 7; AAGPBL Baseball Cards, 2000.}

Gouthro, Laurie

(b. 9 August 1968, Olongapo City, Philippines) IF 1994–95, Colorado Silver Bullets

Laurie Gouthro graduated from Miramar High School in 1986. She was named Player of the Year for the state of Florida as she led her high school with a .590 batting average. Gouthro played in 21 games for the Bullets in 1995. In two of those she started at second base. Before joining the Bullets, Gouthro attended Florida Community College and the University of South Florida. She was an All-American at Florida Community College, where she hit .505, and also was a bronze medalist in team handball at the U.S. Olympic Festival. In addition to playing baseball Laurie works at Worcester State College and Worcester Tech coaching volleyball and softball. {"For the Love of the Game," Colorado Silver Bullets souvenir program, 1995; Tom Foreman Jr., "Silver Bullets," *Associated Press*, 6 May 1994.}

Grace, Lynsey

Lynsey Grace became the first girl to play in the Greater New Bedford Pony League when she pitched for the White Sox against the Fairhaven Lumber team at Pope Park. She started playing catch with her aunt when she was two and never looked back. She played at every level of baseball available, including four years with the Verdean Vets in the New Bedford Little League. {Buddy Thomas, "Not Just One of the Boys," *Standard Times*, 14 May 1998.}

Grace, Mary

Mary Grace tried out for the 1995 Silver Bullets squad but did not make the team. She was a player in, and manager of, an amateur baseball team in South Dakota. {Sharon Ginn, "A Baseball Dream Come True," *The Press-Enterprise*, 27 June 1994, D5.}

Graham (Douglas), Mary Lou "Lou Lou"

(b. 15 August 1936, Chicago, Illinois) P, 1952–54, South Bend Blue Sox

While attending John Adams High School, Mary Lou Graham played volleyball, basketball and baseball. She started in the league as a bat girl for the Blue Sox in 1952 and then was offered a contract in 1953. She only pitched in ten games during her time in the AAGPBL. After the league folded in 1954, she joined a semipro softball and basketball league from 1955 to 1957. She bowled for the Bendix Corporation where she worked, and also picked up golf. {AAGPBL Questionnaire, National Baseball Hall of Fame.}

Graham, Melissa

(b. 2 May 1968) P/OF 2003, Queensland Rams

Melissa Graham played for Queensland in the 2003 Australian National Tournament.

Grambo (Hundeby), Thelma Josephine

(b. 28 October 1923, Domremy, Saskatchewan; d. 30 July 2001) C 1946, Grand Rapids Chicks, Racine Belles

Thelma Grambo graduated from Northern Light High School and attended the University of Saskatchewan. She did not get much chance to play sports except for joining the Saskatoon Pats.

She played one year in the AAGPBL and remembers getting to catch for Connie Wisniewski as a big thrill. Her career was cut short when she broke the index finger on her throwing hand. After leaving the league she returned to Canada and played softball for the Saskatoon Ramblers. She is a member of the Saskatoon Baseball Hall of Fame and the Saskatoon Sports Hall of Fame. She got married in 1947 and raised seven children. {AAGPBL Questionnaire, National Baseball Hall of Fame; AAGPBL Baseball Cards, 2000.}

Granahan, Nora

(Pennsylvania) P/2B/OF, Team WBL, Philadelphia Clash

Nora Granahan played for Team WBL in Australia when she was 14 years old. She plays basketball, baseball, and field hockey and runs track at Strath Haven High School in Delaware County. She also plays the cello.

Grand Rapids Chicks

The Grand Rapids Chicks were one of 14 teams to play in the All American Girls Baseball League. The team provided needed entertainment for the city during the 1940s and 1950s. Families could watch the Chicks play at South Field or Bigelow Field. The club represented the city from 1945 to 1954. The Chicks won the league championship in 1947 and again in 1953. They finished the season in 1947 with a record of 65–47 and in 1953 they were 62–44.

Their roster included such stars as Dolly Konwinski and Earlene Risinger. Marilyn Jenkins caught for the Chicks and was the only native playing on her hometown team. Before taking over as catcher in 1952, Jenkins had been bat girl since 1945.

In July 1950 the Chicks made a special appeal to their fans for donations to help keep the ball club in Grand Rapids. According to club president Melvin D. Anderson, the team would require $6,000 to be able to stay in the city.

The club was inducted into the Grand Rapids Sports Hall of Fame in 2001 as the only team in the hall. {Howie Beardsley, "Chicks Rule as First Team in GR Sports Hall of Fame," *Grand Rapids Press*, 17 June 2001.}

Grant, Chet

(b. 22 February 1892, Defiance, Ohio; d. 24 July 1985) Mgr 1946–48, South Bend Blue Sox, Kenosha Comets

Chet Grant managed the Blue Sox for two seasons and then spent a final season as manager of the Kenosha Comets. Chet graduated from South Bend High School in 1912 and went on to play basketball, football and baseball at Notre Dame. He quarterbacked for Knute Rockne in 1916. He left college to serve during World War I and then returned to finish at Notre Dame in 1920 and 1921. His father and uncle both played and managed at the minor league level in baseball. {AAGPBL Baseball Cards, 2002.}

Grant, Marion

OF, Aussie Diamonds

Marion Grant played in 1998 for the Aussie Diamonds and later turned up on the roster for the Australian team that played in the World Series in 2001 and 2002. She also hit .500 for Victoria in the 2001 National Women's Tournament held in Sydney.

Grant, Olga

(Calgary, Canada)

Olga Grant played in 1944 in the AAGPBL.

Third baseman Beth Turkin and shortstop Laura Tatar prepare for anything hit their way.

Great Lakes Women's Baseball League (GLWBL)

The Great Lakes Women's Baseball League began in 1996 with five teams and a 12–game schedule played from June through August. League games are played in South Bend, Detroit, Chicago and Winnipeg. The teams in the league

Flor Jiron in center field.

Brenda Mendoza warms up

include the Chicago Gems, the Winnipeg Taffy, the South Bend Blue Sox, the Cleveland Comets, the Detroit Danger and the Chicago Storm. The age range of the players has been from 14 to 50.

Greckol-Herlich, Naomi

C, Etobicoke All Stars

In 1999 Naomi Greckol caught for the All Stars in the National Baseball Championship series and was named to the all-tournament team. She hit .417 with three runs knocked in for the series.

Naomi Greckol-Herlich and her coach Ken Perrone. Perrone is the head at Salem State College, as well as coach for the Lady Spirit and Ravens (courtesy Laura Wulf).

Green, Dorothy "Dottie"

(b. 30 April 1921, Natick, Massachusetts; d. 26 October 1992) C 1943–47, Rockford Peaches; chaperone 1948, 1950–53

Growing up in Natick, Massachusetts, Green had the opportunity to play a number of sports while attending Natick High School. She served as captain of her school's softball, basketball and field hockey teams. After her graduation Green played semipro softball for a team known as the Olympettes, who played around the Boston area. Green began her career in the AAGPBL as a catcher but injuries ended her playing days. As a catcher she was known for her strong arm and her ability to handle pitchers. She played in 280 games with a career .140 average. She drove in only 43 runs but had a .957 fielding percentage with only 55 errors. She played in 12 playoff games during her career and hit only .088 but fielded flawlessly. She then became the club's chaperone in 1948, taking over responsibility from Millie Lundahl. She was responsible for the conduct and behavior of the players, particularly off the field. There were 23 duties listed for team chaperones. When her playing career ended Green worked as a recreation officer for the Framington state prison for women. {Susan E. Johnson, 105; Robert McG. Thomas Jr., "Dottie Green, a Baseball Pioneer in Women's League, Dies at 71," *New York Times*, 28 October 1991, D21.}

Green, Henryne

By Bijan Bayne

Henryne Green was owner of the Baltimore Elite Giants following the death of her husband Vernon in 1949. In April of 1948, "Candy Jim" Taylor (another brother-in-law of Olivia Taylor) was slated to take over as Elites manager, but died. Jesse "Hoss" Walker became manager for Ms. Green.

After the demise of the Negro National League, the Elites entered the Negro American League, where they won the 1949 pennant under Green. Lennie Pearson managed the championship club, which boasted Henry Kimbro and pitchers Leon Day and Joe Black. Green gave power of attorney to her late husband's close associate Dick Powell in 1951.

After the 1950 season, she sold the Elites to William Bridgeforth. At the February 1950 league meeting, noted promoter Syd Pollock represented the Elites. {*Baltimore Afro-American*, 22 February 1950.} Due to stadium problems at Bugle Field, Baltimore folded in 1951. In those twilight years of black baseball, Ben Taylor (another brother to Candy Jim), Olivia's legal rival, sold programs at Bugle Field.

Greiner, Harold

(b. Fort Wayne, Indiana) Manager

Harold Greiner coached softball for ten years before taking the reins of the Fort Wayne Daisies in 1949. He helped bring the Daisies to his home town

in 1945, served on their board of directors and then managed the club. Some of his players from the Bob Inn softball team joined him when he took over the Daisies. He owned the Bob Inn restaurant and his softball team won the state championship in 1945. {AAGPBL Baseball Cards, 2000.}

Griffith, Michelle

C, 1995, Sanford Ice

Michelle Griffith finally got the chance to play baseball in 1995 in a new Florida league. She joined the Sanford Ice as their catcher. In order to play she often drives long hours to get to games and practices. Griffith hit .330 for the Ice in 1995. When she is not on the diamond Griffith works as an accounts manager for a local mortgage firm. {Doug Carlson, "Plant City Woman Showing the Drive to Play Baseball," *Tampa Tribune*, 7 September 1995.}

Guidace, Kristin

Mgr./P, Virginia Boxers

Kristin Guidace played for and managed the Virginia Boxers. In addition she served the league as the vice-president. Growing up, Guidace played Little League baseball in Annandale, Virginia, and then moved to softball at Shippensburg University in Pennsylvania. Before the Virginia team came along, Guidace also played in an over–30 men's league. In 2002 Guidace played for the Boxers and the DC Thunder, a tournament team. In one four-day series she hit .462 after batting .538 during the season. Guidace has played a number of roles for the Virginia Boxers throughout the 1990s. Her excellent play led to her induction into the National Women's Baseball Hall of Fame in 2003. The Boxers won league titles in 2001 and 2002. She also helps out the league as assistant commissioner. {National Women's Baseball Hall of Fame Web site.}

Gunn, Kellie

(b. 20 September 1981) P, New South Wales, 2004 Australian National Team

Kellie Gunn played for Australia at the 2004 Women's World Series and for New South Wales at the Australian National Women's Championships. She helped her team to a second-place finish behind Victoria.

Gurley, Katherine

P/1B, Ocala Lightning

Growing up in Painesville, Ohio, Katherine

Gurley was able to play baseball during all four years of high school. She got a scholarship to play basketball at Loyola University and then was invited to join Team USA in 2001. She also played for the Akron Fire and the Ocala Lightning.

Gutz, Julia "Gutzie"

(4 December 1926, Storm Lake, Iowa) C 1948–50, Springfield Sallies, Muskegon Lassies, Kenosha Comets

Julie Gutz caught for three seasons, starting with the touring Lassies and ending her career in Kenosha. During one stretch she caught in 110 consecutive games and never missed an inning. Her fielding was her strength, as she only hit .175 in 235 games. She did score 62 runs and drove in another 44. {AAGPBL Baseball Cards, 1995.}

Haas, Jill

IF/P, North Shore Navigators, Boston Blitz, Team USA, NJ Diamonds

Jill Haas attended CSU Sacramento and earned Division I All-American honors in both volleyball and softball. She played for the Boston Blitz and pitched a no-hitter on opening day of the

Jill Haas at spring training in 1998 for the New Jersey Diamonds, a member of the Ladies Pro League (courtesy Laura Wulf).

inaugural season for the New England Women's Baseball League. She joined the New Jersey Diamonds in 1998 in the Ladies Professional Baseball League and played for Team USA in 2000 and 2001. In addition to her baseball career, Haas is the assistant women's volleyball coach at the University of Rhode Island. When she started playing baseball Haas was the only girl in her Little League district in the 7–12 age group.

Habben, Carol

(b. 15 May 1933, Midland Park, New Jersey; d. 11 January 1997, Ridgewood, New Jersey) CF/C 1951–54, Rockford Peaches, Kalamazoo Lassies

Growing up in New Jersey, Habben played baseball at Midland Park High School and sandlot ball in Rahway. She signed a contract for $250 a month with Rockford in 1951 and then in 1954 was traded to the Lassies. She started playing while still in high school, so she had to take her exams early in order to make it for the start of the season. Her career average was .231 and she knocked in 65 runs. After retiring from baseball Habben worked

Jill Haas pitching for Team USA (photographer Phil Dimarzio, courtesy Jim Glennie).

as a credit manager for Merck and Company for 35 years. She was also an avid golfer. {"AAGPBL Star Carol Habben," *Sports Collectors Digest*, 7 March 1997, 10; "Female Ex-Baseball Player Dies," *Associated Press*, 13 January 1997.}

Habetz, Alyson

(b. 17 December 1971, Crowley, Louisiana) P/1B 1995–97, Colorado Silver Bullets

Alyson Habetz started her baseball career at Notre Dame High School when she became the first girl on an all-boys team in the state of Louisiana. She played first base and pitched while also earning a variety of honors on the basketball team before graduating in 1990. Habetz played softball and basketball for four years at the University of Southwest Louisiana. She attended on a basketball and academic scholarship. Her softball squad came in third in the 1993 Women's World Series. She earned Third Team All-American honors in softball. In basketball she scored over 1,000 points in her career. She started three games for the Bullets in 1995 and won her only game on August 23 against the Puget Sound Mariners. She pitched 6.2 innings and gave up one earned run in a 7–2 victory. She remained with the Bullets for two more seasons before the team folded. She then went on to play for the Long Beach Aces in 1998 as a pitcher and first baseman. In September 1998 she became an assistant coach at the University of Alabama, working under head coach Pat Murphy. {University of Alabama Web site.}

Haefner, Ruby

(Gastonia, North Carolina) C 1947, Fort Wayne Daisies

Hageman (Hargraves), Johanna "Jo"

(b. 17 December 1918, Chicago, Illinois; d. 10 February 1984) 1B 1943–45, South Bend Blue Sox, Kenosha Comets; chaperone 1946–49, Kenosha Comets

Johanna Hageman played first base for three years in South Bend and Kenosha. Though not a strong hitter, Hageman stayed in the lineup because of her fielding. She had a .983 fielding percentage over her three seasons. She hit .167 in 320 games and then left the field to become the Comets' chaperone. {AAGPBL Baseball Cards, 2000.}

Haggerty, Nancy

(Somers, New York) C, Westchester Yankees

Before joining the Yankees in 2003, Nancy Haggerty's baseball experience was limited to occasional games with the over–30 men's Cortland Alleycats. In addition to playing baseball Haggerty also plays hockey for the Westchester Wildcats. {Rick Carpiniello, "A League for Those Who Say Softball Isn't Enough," *The Journal News*, 9 June 2003.}

Haine (Daniels), Audrey "Audie," "Dimples"

(b. 9 May 1927, Winnipeg, Manitoba) P 1944–48, 1951, Minneapolis Millerettes, Fort Wayne Daisies, Grand Rapids Chicks, Peoria Red Wings, Rockford Peaches

By Lou Parotta

Audrey Haine pitched for a number of teams in the AAGPBL after convincing her mother to let her leave Canada at the age of 17 to join the league. One of her best performances was a no-hitter in her rookie year, a 1–0 shutout for the Millerettes. She finished her baseball career with a 72–70 record and a 3.48 ERA. She was inducted into the Manitoba Baseball Hall of Fame and Museum in July 1998. {Phil Hicks, "The Girls of Summer," *The Chronicle-Telegram*, 26 July 1994, D1.}

Canada had quite a presence in the AAGPBL. A total of 64 women who were born in Canada suited up to play for teams such as the Rockford Peaches and the Fort Wayne Daisies. One of those players was a former softball player named Audrey Haine.

Born in Winnipeg, Canada, in 1927, this teenage star gained attention as a young softball pitcher who, according to writer John Lott, had a "wicked rising fastball" while playing on the softball diamond in the early 1940s. "On several occasions in the early '40s, she struck out 21 batters in a seven-inning game in her district league." Her husband, Bud Daniels, commented to Lott that "it was not uncommon for her to strike out 18 or 19 in a seven-inning game." She was a hot commodity in 1943 even at age 16.

When Haine's mother finally gave in and let her go to play professional baseball in the AAGPBL, she signed a contract for $65 per week, a nifty sum at that time, and headed off to Minneapolis to play for the Millerettes. That first season was everything but good for the teenage hurler. Loaded with homesickness due to being so far away from home for the first time, she finished with a horrific 8–20 record and 4.85 ERA. She managed to pitch in 36 games despite her losing ways, but over the course of the 230 innings she threw, she allowed 171 runners to score (124 of those were earned) and walked an astounding 209 batters, hit nine and threw 29 wild pitches. The Fort Wayne Daisies must have seen something they liked because they acquired Haine after the season to play for them in 1945.

A year older at 18, Haine looked significantly better in 1945 in Fort Wayne. Her ERA dropped nearly in half to 2.46, and she managed to turn her win-loss record around to 16–10. She walked 50 fewer batters, did not hit any, threw half the wild pitches she threw in 1944, and only gave up 61 earned runs. This proved that her 1944 season, a flop in every sense, was probably just due to her youth and inexperience. Haine turned her winning percentage around from a paltry .286 to an above-average .615, and she became one of the most consistent throwers of her time.

Haine fully intended to play the entire 1946 season in Fort Wayne, but was traded during the season to the Grand Rapids Chicks. There, she continued her model of consistency, finishing the season at 14–11 with 120 strikeouts (her most by far) and an ERA of 4.11. Her hits-allowed total reached a career high, but despite that she remained three games over .500 in the win-loss record.

Traded again during the 1947 season, Haine went on to Peoria to play with that city's Red Wings. Staying the rest of the season and all of the 1948 season, Haine had two of the best seasons of her career. Appearing in 61 games over the two seasons, she went 30–26 with ERAs of 2.89 and 2.92 respectively. She pitched in well over 400 innings, gave up only 138 earned runs, walked 182, and struck out an uncharacteristically low 140. Her wildness returned a bit, which was probably a direct reflection of pitching nearly 1,100 innings in five years, and she hit 55 batters and threw 27 wild pitches.

Sensing that her career was slipping, Haine retired from professional baseball and got married and decided to settle down. Three years into her retirement, however, Haine got an itch to return to the AAGPBL as a player. She signed on to play for the now-famous Rockford Peaches. She appeared in only ten games, but she pitched well. She finished at 4–3 — which allowed her to leave the game with a winning record as a professional — pitched 66 innings, and allowed 37 earned runs for a wonderful 3.82 ERA to close out her career.

When all was said and done on the playing field, Haine pitched in 167 games, went 72–70 for a .507 winning percentage, threw 1,154 innings, gave up 638 runs (of which 446 were earned), walked 835 batters, struck out 493 batters, hit 82 batters and threw 96 wild pitches. Her career ERA was 3.48, a dramatic turnaround from her first season in Minneapolis.

On 4 June 1998, Haine was honored for her accomplishments on the field for the AAGPBL by being inducted as an honorary member of the Canadian Baseball Hall of Fame in St. Mary's, Ontario, along with other former players. The players were nominated for induction by AAGPBL master researcher Bill Rayner who, according to Lott, introduced the women at the ceremony by saying, "It's hard to imagine these sweet ladies were once the terrors of the baseball field."

When the movie *A League of Their Own* came out in 1992, the general, non-research public was introduced to these "terrors," played by the likes of Madonna and Rosie O'Donnell. People got to see, albeit through Hollywood's tinted lens, some of the adventures these ladies went through. An instant phenomenon was born, and recognition of their accomplishments flooded in.

As with most former members of the AAGPBL, Haine has been traveling around the United States to promote the women who played baseball and the movie. Since the making of the movie, much has been written to revive the memories of these women of the game. Alumnae such as Haine, who were advisers in the production of the film to make it as realistic as they could, are the sole links between the game of nearly 50 years ago and the players of today. If not for these women, who were supposed to just be an attraction but became much more, then the breaking of some gender barriers might never have taken place. According to Haine, "The AAGPBL was a first. I don't believe any of us realized that we were breaking barriers for women in sports. We were pioneers then living a dream, having fun doing what we loved to do— playing baseball."

Haller, Jodi

(Kersey, Pennsylvania), P

Jodi Haller grew up playing baseball with her father and two brothers. She pitched in Little League and American Legion ball because her high school had no baseball team. To help improve her skills and control as a pitcher, Haller attended Doyle Baseball School in Florida and a baseball camp held at Shippensburg State University. She pitched for St. Vincent College in Pennsylvania in 1990, becoming the first woman to pitch in a college game. It appears from the scant records kept by the team that Haller pitched once as a reliever and once as a starter. She then went on to pitch one year for Meiji University in Japan in 1995. Haller became the first female college player in Japan. Meiji University beat Tokyo 4–0 in her start. {Rick Lawes, "Haller Was First of Coed Hurlers," *USA Today Baseball*

Weekly, 2–8 March 1994, 32; Jon Cook, "Nabozny Breaks New Ground." *Slam!Sports*, 17 June 1999; *Silver Bulletin*, March 1996.}

Halloran, Erin

1B, Philadelphia Women's League

Growing up in Massachusetts, Erin Halloran played baseball, but then as so many girls did she switched to softball. She also played hockey. While attending Temple University to get her Ph.D. in sports psychology she heard about a women's baseball league and she immediately joined up. When she is not in classes or on the diamond Halloran continues to play hockey with a women's team in Delaware. {Eileen O'Donnell, "Covering All the Bases," *Philadelphia Inquirer*, 15 July 2005.}

Hamilton, Patty

In 1974 Patty Hamilton turned old enough to play Little League baseball, only to find out that girls weren't allowed to play. She had begun playing catch with her dad and at the school playground to get ready for signing up. Her parents encouraged her to sign up if she really wanted to play. After voting at the local level to not let her play, the league did offer to talk with the family and other interested parties about setting up a separate baseball league for girls. {Judy Stone, "Little League Rebuffs Girls," *Edwardsville Intelligencer*, 20 April 1974, 1.}

Hamilton, Samantha Jane

(b. 8 April 1973) 1B, Doncaster Dragons, Victoria; 2003–04 Australian National Team

Samantha Hamilton played in five games during the 2003 Women's World Series. She was held hitless in 17 at-bats but walked three times and scored one run. In the 2004 World Cup event, Hamilton helped her team with both her bat and fielding. {John MacKinnon, "No Worries for Aussies," Edmonton Journal, 28 July 2004, D1.}

Hammond, Jennifer Rebecca

(b. 10 November 1980, Alexandria, Virginia) SS/3B/2B/OF/P Virginia Flames, DC Thunder

Jennifer Hammond grew up in Virginia, attending West Potomac High School and being home-schooled. She played softball her freshman year and then joined a variety of community leagues where she also played tennis. In 1997 she won the Pioneer Youth Softball League All Star Game MVP Award. She later joined the Eastern Women's Baseball Conference and switched her playing allegiance to the game of baseball.

During the 2002 season Hammond was 12 for 28, hitting .429 for the Flames. Hammond's solid fielding was often noted as helping to secure victories for her team. As a result of her all around play she was invited to join the DC Thunder, a tournament team. She batted .417 in the DC Invitational, which the Thunder lost to the North Shore Cougars. One of her favorite experiences as a player came when she got a chance to participate in the 24–hour game in Arizona in October 2003. She got to meet many other women ballplayers, both past and present. Hammond returned to the Virginia Flames in 2004 for another season. They were led to victory by a strong roster that included Carmen Dominguez, whom Hammond considers one of the best players she has seen, and teammate Laura Brenneman, who represents the highest level of play. The Flames won their league championship in 2004.

Jen Hammond getting some pointers from former All-American player Delores Lee "Pickles" Dries.

Hammond returned to school in 2005 to pursue a master's degree in history at George Washington University. Hammond is also a graphic artist and works in an animal hospital in Alexandria when she is not on the diamond. {Jennifer Hammond, correspondence with Leslie A. Heaphy, May–June 2005}

Hampton, Giavanna

P/3B

Gia Hampton has played baseball in Elk Grove, California, since she was five years old. She has played at all levels and has excelled at each step. In the ten-and-under division she led all pitchers with strikeouts and helped her club to a third-place finish in the state tournament. She won the Kyle Bristow State Sportsmanship Award for her play. One of her career highlights so far was a grand slam home run in June 2005 to help her club beat the best team in the division. She will play baseball at Franklin High School in the fall of 2005. {<http://www.womensbaseball.com>.}

Hannah (Campbell), Helen

(b. 25 September 1915, Pico-Rivera, California)
Chaperone 1947–51, Muskegon Lassies

Helen Hannah Campbell attended Whittier Union High School (along with Richard Nixon) and later served as a chaperone for the Muskegon Lassies before becoming the general manager for the ball club. As a chaperone her job was to make sure the ladies acted properly. There were rules to follow when traveling, rules for male visitors, and charm school to attend. As the general manager she had to deal with contract disputes, marketing, stadium leases and spring training issues. Campbell seemed perfect for the job since she had spent much of her early life traveling with a ball team because her father, Harry "Truck" Hannah, caught for the New York Yankees and the Detroit Tigers. Campbell graduated from Woodbury College and even went to high school with Richard Nixon at Whittier Union. Campbell also served for 32 years in the U.S. Marine Corps as a master gunnery sergeant. In fact, she did not join the league until 1947 because she served in the marines during World War II. {AAGPBL Newsletter, September 2000, 29; SABR Interview 2004; Patricia Brown, "Helen Hannah Campbell," in *A League of My Own* (North Carolina: McFarland and Company, Inc., 2003), 155–161; Hap Everett, "Helen Hannah Front Office Boss of Club," *Los Angeles Times*, 25 February 1950, B3.}

Hannah, Katherine "Kat"

(b. 7 September 1982, Kirkland Lake, Ontario)
P, 2004 Team Canada, Outlaws, Falcons, Saints, New England Spirit

Katherine Hannah played baseball for a number of teams leading up to her participation in the World Cup in 2004. From 1998 to 2000 she played in the Roy Hobbs World Series, which Team Ontario won in 1998 and 2000. From 1996 to 1997 and again in 1999 and 2000, Team Ontario won their local championship. In 1997 Hannah became the first female to play on an all-male team at the Baseball Canada championships, when she pitched for Team North. In 2003 she played for the New England Spirit and was named as the team MVP. She pitched in two games for Canada and got one victory. She struck out ten in 12 innings but also walked five batters. Kat also pitched for her club at the NAWBL Labor Day Tournament and was named Best Pitcher for her 17 strikeouts and a 1–0 shutout. She also only walked one batter intentionally. In the World Cup she pitched five innings against Japan in a game that eventually went into

Pitcher Katherine Hannah for Team Canada (photographer Phil Dimarzio, courtesy Jim Glennie).

extra innings before Japan won. In an earlier game, Hannah pinch-hit to help Canada win 2–1. She also beat the U.S. in a complete game victory, giving up only one run. Hannah is studying psychology at Lindenwood University in Missouri and intends to continue on for a master's degree. She is at the school on a hockey scholarship, playing center on the varsity women's club. She received All-American honorable mention in 2003 and 2004. {Collin Gallant, "Hannah Wants the Ball Again," *Edmonton Journal*, 5 August 2004, D1; NAWBL Web site; Baseball Canada 2004 Women's National Team Media Guide.}

Hardy, Giselle

Giselle Hardy played in the 1991 Little League World Series for the European team. She is from Saudi Arabia.

Harnett, Ann

(b. 10 August 1920, Chicago, Illinois; d. 1960s) 3B/C/OF 1943–47, Kenosha Comets, Peoria Red Wings

Ann Harnett was chosen as the all-star third baseman in 1943 after being the first player to sign a contract for the new AAGPBL. After playing the hot corner for two years, Harnett moved to catching to fill a need for her team. Her playing time dwindled by the second year. By 1946 she only played in 16 games and batted a lowly .224. Then she moved into the outfield for her final season. She played in 424 games and hit a respectable .231 with 28 triples and seven home runs. She became a nun after her playing days ended and even coached the boys' Catholic high school baseball team. {AAGPBL Baseball Cards, 2000.}

Harney, Elise "Lee"

(b. 22 July 1925, Franklin, Illinois) P 1943–47, Kenosha Comets, Fort Wayne Daisies

Elise Harney pitched for five seasons, mainly with the Comets. She had 19 wins in her rookie season against 19 losses in 45 games. She also had a career-high 102 strikeouts that year. During the off-season she attended the University of Wisconsin and graduated in 1947. She pitched in a total of 172 games with a record of 63–85 and an ERA of 2.78. {AAGPBL Baseball Cards, 2000.}

Harrell (Isbell, Doyle), Dorothy Harriet "Snookie"

(b. 4 February 1924, Los Angeles, Calif.) SS 1944–52, Rockford Peaches

By Kerri Bottoroff

Whether judged by her bat or her glove, Dorothy Harrell was one of the best middle infielders of the AAGPBL. Fellow players, when asked to list their all-time AAGPBL teams, often list Harrell as their choice for the best all-around shortstop.

Harrell was born on 4 February 1924 in Los Angeles, California. She was invited to join the AAGPBL in 1943, but her employer at the time, Bank of America, refused to let her go. The following season, she joined the league as a member of the Rockford Peaches. Harrell played second base and shortstop for the Peaches, forming a potent double-play combination with Dorothy Kamenshek, one of the best-known players of the league. She was often at odds with the manager of the Peaches, Bill Allington, as were other teammates. One day, Allington suggested a way for her to improve her fielding. She replied, "Bill, I haven't made an error in thirty-five games." {Lois Browne, *Girls of Summer* (Toronto: Harper Collins, 1992), 80.}

Harrell was considered one of the league's best shortstops, both offensively and defensively. She was frequently among the league leaders in putouts and assists at shortstop, and she often led all shortstops in hitting. Along with Kamenshek, Rose Gacioch, and other stars, Harrell helped the Peaches capture four championships in six seasons, from 1945 to 1950. During the 1950 playoffs, she hit two triples and three singles in one game. She was selected to the all-star team in four consecutive seasons, from 1947 to 1950.

Harrell got married in 1943 to Leonard Isbell and remained married through 1946. In 1949, Harrell married David Doyle. She played the rest of her career under her married name, Dorothy Doyle. Her husband died in 1963, and she never remarried.

Once her baseball career ended, Harrell was inspired to return to school by some of her former teammates. She attended Long Beach State (Calif.) and earned her bachelor's degree after earning an associates degree from El Camino Junior College. She then began a 26–year-long career as a counselor and physical education teacher. After retiring in 1984, Harrell joined the Golden Diamond Girls, a group of former players who made frequent appearances at reunions and card shows. She also became an avid golfer and remained close friends with Kamenshek, living next door to her in California for many years. In addition to her teaching Harrell remained active in softball, playing for a number of different teams until 1960. She even took a nine-week trip through Asia playing softball against the service personnel stationed in various countries. {Lois Browne, *the Girls of Summer* (New York and Toronto: Harper Collins, 1992), 199; W. C. Madden, *The Women of the All-American Girls Professional Baseball League* (Jefferson, N.C.: McFarland and Company, Inc., 1997), 101.}

In 1999, Harrell became the subject of a piece of artwork at the Seattle Mariners' new ballpark, Safeco Field. Harrell was unhappy with a draft of the piece, noting that her nose looked too big, and she asked if it could be changed. The artist, Tina Hoggatt, happily complied with the request and gave Harrell a shorter nose. {Regina Hackett, "Making Art for Safeco Field," *Seattle Post-Intelligencer*, 10 September 2003; AAGPBL Questionnaire, National Baseball Hall of Fame.}

Hart, Susan

Susan Hart played baseball when she was in Little League but had not played since, until she heard about the New York league and decided to try. She has two daughters who also play Little League baseball. {Stephanie Kornfeld, "Finding a League of Their Own," *The Rivertowns Enterprise*, 5 September 2003, 8.}

Harwood, Melanie

(b. 14 February 1980, Newmarket, Ontario) P/IF 2000–2004, Team Ontario

In the 2004 World Cup Melanie Harwood led all hitters by knocking in five runs while batting .462. In a 12–2 victory over Hong Kong, Harwood had a single, double and triple in her three at-bats to help her club win. Harwood began playing for Team Ontario in 2000 and has won a number of MVP awards since then, and has been named to the World All-Star squad in 2003. She works for Daimler Chrysler when she is not playing baseball. {"Japan Joins US, Australia in World Series Baseball Semis," *Agence France Presse*, 19 July 2004; "Canada Scores Nine in Baseball Romp," *The Star Phoenix*, 20 July 2004, B3.}

Hatfield, Karla

Util., Phoenix Peppers

Karla Hatfield played a number of positions for the Peppers when they were a part of the AWBA.

Hatzell (Volkert), Beverly

(b. 19 January 1929, Redkey, Indiana) P 1949–51, Chicago Colleens, Racine Belles, Battle Creek Belles, Peoria Red Wings

Beverly Hatzell pitched for three seasons in the All American League. She started with the touring Colleens to develop her skills and then joined Racine. She pitched in 38 games with a 5–21 record. She had a strong arm and good defensive skills on the mound. As a hitter she only batted .069 for her team. {AAGPBL Baseball Cards, 1995.}

Havenor, Mrs. Agnes

Owner

Mrs. Agnes Havenor took over the franchise for the Milwaukee entry in the American Association after her husband Charles died on 3 April 1912. She was elected president of the club and expected to take an active interest in the affairs of the team. She married Charles Havenor in 1908 after working for many years as a milliner in Chicago where she grew up. As Miss Molloy, she attended a Jesuit School and Chalmers Public School with her sisters in Chicago. {"Mrs. Havenor Chicago Girl," *Chicago Tribune*, 14 April 1912, C2.}

Havlish, Jean Ann "Grasshopper"

(b. 23 November 1935, St. Paul, Minnesota) SS 1951–54, Kalamazoo Lassies, Fort Wayne Daisies

While attending Washington High School, Jean Havlish played all the sports offered for girls. She also played city league softball and speedskated. She played basketball and softball in a commercial league too. The Rice-Lawson team she played on won the city division in 1947.

Havlish joined the AAGPBL right after graduating from high school. She tried out for the Kalamazoo Lassies but never heard from them, so then she tried out again for Fort Wayne, and that's where she played during the league's final two seasons. She played in 193 games and hit .218. She got her chance when the Daises traded their starting shortstop, Dottie Schroeder, and needed a replacement.

In addition to being a fancy fielding shortstop in the AAGPBL, Havlish won a number of local honors in speedskating in St. Paul, Minnesota. Her greatest sports accomplishments came in bowling, where she established herself as one of the best ever. She won the Minnesota State All-Star crown in 1962 and 1963 and in 1964 she became the first woman ever to win the singles and overall events crown at the Women's International Bowling Congress (WIBC). Today she is a member of the WIBC National Bowling Hall of Fame in St. Louis for having won the Women's International Bowling Congress singles title in 1964 with a 690 in a three-game event. In 1988 she was inducted into the Minnesota Sports Hall of Fame for her bowling trophies; there is no mention of her baseball experience on her Hall of Fame plaque. {AAGPBL Newsletter, September 2000, 34 and May 2005, 25; AAGPBL Questionnaire, National Baseball Hall of Fame; Kathleen C. Ridder, "A Win at Wimbledon in '59," *Ramsey County History*, Summer 1998, 13–16.}

Hauwert, Rachel

(b. 7 April 1970) P/Util. 2001–03, Queensland

In the 2001 Australian National Tournament Rachel Hauwert batted .529 to lead Queensland. She led all batters with nine hits including one triple.

Hay, Leola "Lee," "Bubbles"

(d. December 1997) 1B/OF/P, Racine Belles

After Leola Hay's baseball career ended she taught bowling at the Golf Mill Bowling Alley and worked as a physical therapist. {Kenan Heise, "Leola Hay, Played for Bloomer Girls," *Chicago Tribune*, 17 December 1997.}

Hayes, Kendra

OF

In 1994 Kendra Hayes played in 11 games for the Kentucky Rifles in Pikeville, Kentucky. The Rifles were an independent club in the Frontier League. Hayes' career in the outfield was short because she was 0–10 at the plate with one walk and eight strikeouts. {Jon Cook, "Nabozny Breaks New Ground," *Slam!Sports*, 17 June 1999; dick Dahl, "Out of His League," *Boston Globe Magazine*, 12 September 1999, 20, 22, 29.}

Hayes, Melissa

IF 2000, South Bend Blue Sox

Melissa Hayes played with South Bend in the Great Lakes Women's Baseball League. She joined the team as a rookie in 2000.

She played fast-pitch softball in college and made second team all-conference at third base.

She batted leadoff for the Blue Sox because of her speed. {<www.baseballglory.com>.}

Haylett, Alice Marie "Al," "Sis"

(b. 2 April 1923, Coldwater, Michigan) P/OF 1946–1949, Grand Rapids Chicks

Alice Haylett attended Coldwater High School but did not play sports there. Instead, she played basketball and softball and bowled in Battle Creek, Michigan. Before joining the AAGPBL she worked for a couple of local companies that had softball teams on which she played. After joining the league in 1946, Haylett led the league in pitching in 1948 with a 25–5 record and a league-leading 0.77 ERA for the Grand Rapids Chicks. Her numbers got her elected to the all-star squad in 1948. It was her pitching that kept her in the league and not her hitting. For example, in 104 at-bats in 1946 she only hit .221. The Chicks won the league championship in 1947. She compiled a career record of 70–47 in 128 games with an ERA of 1.92. After leaving the league Haylett became a golfer and worked in the packing room for Kelloggs. {AAGPBL Questionnaire, National Baseball Hall of Fame.}

Hazelwood, Nadine

(b. 3 July 1982, Toronto, Ontario) OF 2002–2004, Team Ontario

Nadine Hazelwood played for Team Ontario from 2002 through 2004. She was chosen in 2002

Canadian pitcher Nadine Hazelwood (photographer Laura Wulf, courtesy Jim Glennie).

to play in the Women's World Series in Australia and then again in 2004. She attends Centennial College with plans to graduate in 2004 so she can go to work planning children's recreational programs. {Baseball Canada 2004 Women's National Team Media Guide.}

Heafner, Ruby "Rebel"

(b. 5 March 1924, Gastonia, North Carolina) C 1946–51, Rockford Peaches, Fort Wayne Daisies, Racine Belles, Battle Creek Belles

Ruby Heafner played for six seasons in the All American league. During her tenure she developed a reputation as a strong defensive catcher and a clutch hitter. She played in 342 games, hitting only .178, but she had 21 extra-base hits and drove in 57 runs. {AAGPBL Baseball Cards, 1995.}

Heim (McDaniel), Kay "Heime"

(b. 21 August 1917, Athabaska, Alberta) C 1943–44, Kenosha Comets

Kay Heim had a short career in the AAGPBL because she got married and decided not to return for the 1945 season. She played in 58 games and hit only .154. Her hitting is not what kept her in the lineup, but rather her solid defensive play and her strong arm behind the plate. {AAGPBL Baseball Cards, 1996.}

Heisler, Toni

(b. 6 May 1969, Sacramento, California) SS, Colorado Silver Bullets

Toni Heisler played basketball and softball while attending Elk Grove High School. She was all-league in basketball for three straight seasons. She played softball at Sacramento State and set a school record for doubles with 14. Then in 1992 she went to Italy, where she played for a year. Heisler hit .448 for the Italian squad. Heisler helped the Bullets mostly with her bat. She had 17 hits in 38 games in 1995, including a five-game hitting streak. She got base hits at Three Rivers Stadium and at Jacobs Field. She also took part in completing 19 double plays and led the team in assists with 97. In 1997 she became one of three players to hit over .300 for the squad, batting a solid .316 behind Tammy Holmes and ahead of Jenny Dalton-Hill. {*The Silver Bulletin* 12/95; David Kindred, *Colorado Silver Bullets: For the Love of the Game* (Atlanta: Longstreet Press, Inc.), 76; "For the Love of the Game," Colorado Silver Bullets souvenir program, 1995.}

Hekimian, Catherine

While attending Julius West Middle School, Catherine Hekimian could only play softball. The same held true at Richard Montgomery High School in Rockville, Maryland. Though she played three sports, baseball was not one of them. Hekimian earned a softball scholarship to Swarthmore College in Pennsylvania. She finally got a chance to play baseball when she joined the Washington Metropolitan Women's Baseball League at age 31. {Alan Greilsamer, "Making Up for Lost Time," n.d., n.p.}

Henley, Rocky

San Francisco Fillies

Rocky Henley had 12 hits in 28 at-bats in 2003. She walked another five times and scored ten runs for the Fillies. {CWBL Web site.}

Henry, Jenifer

1997 Colorado Silver Bullets

Henry, Lauren

Pawtucket Slaterettes

Laura Henry led the junior division for the Slaterettes organization in 1999 with a .722 average. She also led the way in hits and doubles. {Greg Botelho, "Pawtucket Slaterettes Having Another Banner Year," *Providence Journal*, 28 June 1999, C–03.}

Herbst, Terri Lynn

(Massapequa, New York) OF, Waterbury Diamonds, New Jersey Diamonds, Team USA, NJ Nemesis

A traveling ballplayer, Terri Lynn Herbst makes her living as a professional photographer. She played for local men's teams in Long Island after switching from softball to baseball. In 1998 she had the opportunity to join the New Jersey Nemesis, a member of the Ladies Professional Baseball League. Tryouts were held in Augusta, Georgia, for the clubs. After an unsuccessful tryout in 1997 with the Silver Bullets she wanted to try again, and so she joined a men's team to get ready for another opportunity. When she made the Nemesis it was a dream come true. After the Nemesis folded she went back to playing in the Men's Senior Baseball League. She joined Team USA in 2000 and again in 2001. In Tokyo she helped lead the U.S. squad with two RBIs. She has also played for the New Jersey Diamonds. In 2004 she coached the East Coast Stars, an entrant in the North American Women's Baseball League, and received the Coaches Award for Leadership, Team Play and Sportsmanship at the NAWBL Labor Day Tournament. {Terri Lynn Herbst, "The Women's Pro Game," *Elysian Fields Quarterly*, 1998.}

Herlick, Naomi

North Shore Lady Spirit

Naomi Herlick went to the Dominican Republic in 2004 with the Lady Spirit. They played a four-game exhibition tour. In game two Herlick helped her team win 12–4 with two base hits. {Jean De-Placido, "Lady Spirit a Big Hit in Dominican Republic," *The Salem News*, 18 November 2004.}

Herring (James), Katherine B. "Katie"

(b. 11 July 1933, Altus, Oklahoma) Util. 1953, Grand Rapids Chicks

Katie Herring grew up in a baseball family. Her uncle Arthur Herring played in the major leagues from 1929 to 1940 for five different clubs. Her brothers William and Arthur played minor league baseball. In high school Herring played basketball rather than softball. Her career in the AAGPBL only lasted three months before she went back to playing softball for a couple of years. She married Paul James in 1954 and raised two boys. {AAGPBL Questionnaire, National Baseball Hall of Fame.}

Hershey (Reeser), Esther Ann "Zan"

(b. 5 January 1928, Nine Point, Pennsylvania) OF 1948, Springfield Sallies

Esther Hershey did not get to play sports while attending Scott Senior High School in Coatesville, Pennsylvania, because there were no organized teams for girls. Her softball experience came on local teams, where she was always the pitcher. When she was not out on the softball diamond Esther worked for her father in his general store. She married Edward Reeser in 1948 and had three children, which is why she did not return to the league for a second season. {AAGPBL Questionnaire, National Baseball Hall of Fame; AAGPBL Baseball Cards, 2000.}

Hess, Lisa

1997, San Diego Stix

Lisa Hess played in the Ladies Professional Baseball League in the 1990s with the Stix.

Hickey, Lillian

(British Columbia)

Lillian Hickey played in 1946 in the AAGPBL as one of the many Canadian ballplayers who came south to play baseball.

Hickson, Irene "Choo-Choo," "Mae"

(b. 14 August 1915, Chattanooga, Tennessee; d. 24 November 1995) C 1943–51, Racine Belles, Kenosha Comets

Irene Hickson was selected to the all-star team in the league's first season, 1943. Hickson played in 621 games but hit only .171. She played because of her defensive abilities and her speed more than her hitting. With 2,388 putouts and 561 assists, Hickson only committed 130 errors. After the league folded Hickson stayed in Racine and ran a restaurant called Home Plate. Then she worked for 22 years for Zayre's Department Store. {AAGPBL Newsletter, January 1996, 11.}

Hickson, Leslie

1997, San Diego Stix

Leslie Hickson played in the 1990s in the Ladies Professional Baseball League with the Stix.

Higgins, Isabelle

(b. 21 October 1969, Montreal, Quebec) 2B, Team Canada

Isabelle Higgins is a police officer in Montreal but she is also a baseball player. She played softball for many years at the local and national level before joining Team Canada in 2004 to play at the World Cup event in Edmonton, Alberta. {Baseball Canada 2004 National Women's Team Media Guide.}

Hill, Angela

OF 2003–04, San Francisco Fillies

Angela Hill played in the California Women's League with the Fillies.

Hill, Chris

1B 1999, San Diego Stix

In 1999 Chris Hill helped her team win the national championship and she was named to the all-tournament team. She hit .579 with 11 runs batted in.

Hill (Westerman), Joyce E.

(b. 29 December 1925, Kenosha, Wisconsin) C/1B 1945–52, Grand Rapids Chicks, Fort Wayne Daisies, Peoria Red Wings, Racine Belles, South Bend Blue Sox

Joyce Hill did not play any sports at Kenosha High School because they had none for girls. She got her softball experience playing in the county softball league for 12–to 15–year-olds and then in an industrial league for two years. She grew up working on a farm with her brothers so thought nothing of playing what were considered boys' games. Hill joined the AAGPBL in 1945, making $50 a week. They played every day and often a doubleheader on Sundays. Travel was tough but teams had their own bus to make it a little easier on the ladies. Hill moved around a lot during her career because each spring the league would move players to try to keep teams competitive so that fans would want to come out and watch whoever was playing. In 1952 Hill helped the Blue Sox win the championship. She played in 531 games and hit .228 with 167 RBIs and 191 runs scored. {AAGPBL Baseball Cards, 1995.}

After baseball, Hill went to work for the postal service, retiring in 1985. She played fast-pitch softball from 1960 to 1975 and won a number of championships. She married Raymond Westerman in 1950 and had two daughters. In 2000 Hill was inducted into the Oldtimers Baseball Association of Chicago and in 2001 into the Kenosha County Baseball Hall of Fame. {AAGPBL Newsletter, September 1996, 24, and May 2002, 22; AAGPBL Questionnaire, National Baseball Hall of Fame.}

Hockenbury, Mary G.

(b. 1903, Philadelphia) 1B, Chicago All Star Athletic Girls

Mary Hockenbury grew up in a family of ten kids at a time when it was common for children to go to work at an early age to help the family. She went to work for Fleisher's at age 12 and played on their Bloomer Girl team until 1918. In 1922 her name can be found in the reports about the Chicago All Star Athletic Girls. She later married and had five children. Three of her boys ended up playing minor league baseball. {Barbara Gregorich, *Women at Play*, 50–51.}

Hoffman, Bonnie

P/INF Virginia Boxers, DC Thunder, NJ Nemesis

Bonnie Hoffman pitched and played the infield for the Nemesis in 1999 and the Thunder in 2002. Both those clubs were tournament teams, picking up players from other areas to play. Hoffman also spent time on the roster of the Boxers in the East Coast League.

Hoffman, Margaret Barbara

(b. 18 January 1931, Belleville, Illinois) 3B/2B 1951–52, South Bend Blue Sox

Barbara Hoffman attended Belleville Township High School but played softball on independent clubs because there were no teams at school. She played for the Belleville Southsiders and the Londoffs, who played in St. Louis, Missouri. When she joined the AAGPBL she made the all-star team in 1952 and hit a home run in the game. She started working for the Bendix Corporation in 1952 and decided to stay after the season and not return to baseball. Her career numbers included 95 games, an average of .192 and 31 runs scored. She remained active playing basketball for the South Bend Rockettes, bowling, and playing softball. {AAGPBL Questionnaire, National Baseball Hall of Fame.}

Hofknecht, Brenda

3B, Pawtucket Slaterettes

Brenda Hofknecht played for the Pawtucket Slaterettes from the age of eight until 17. In her early thirties the league started offering adult opportunities and she got the chance to play baseball again along with her two daughters, who play in the instructional and minor divisions for the Slaterettes. {Patricia A. Russell, "Girls of Spring," *Providence Journal Bulletin*, 29 April 2003, C–01.}

Hogan, Kim

P, Florida Lightning

Kim Hogan played in the South Florida Diamond Classic in 1999. She pitched for the Florida Lightning, an all-star team sent to represent the league in the series. Hogan won her first game 6–4 with her arm and her bat. She drove in the go-ahead run with a two-run base hit in the bottom of the seventh inning. {Elizabeth Clarke, "Nothing Soft about the Play at South Diamond Classic," *Palm Beach Post*, 25 April 1999.}

Hohlmayer (McNaughton), Alice "Lefty"

(Springfield, Ohio) P 1946–51, Kenosha Comets, Muskegon Lassies, Kalamazoo Lassies, Peoria Red Wings

Alice Hohlmayer got a chance to hone her athletic skills while attending Ohio State beginning in 1943. While playing in a tournament in Cleveland in 1945 she was seen by a scout for the All American League. In 110 games for Kenosha in 1946, Alice Hohlmayer batted only .223 because she tended to strike out a lot. In 372 at-bats she struck out 63 times while only walking 24 times. Her best season came in 1951 with the Red Wings, when she hit .267 and went 17–11 on the mound with a 2.02 ERA. After the 1951 season she returned home to help her family with their Laundromats. Later she married and moved to California where she taught school and worked for the local recreation department.

Holderman, Ashley

P/RF 2000–03, South Bend Blue Sox

Ashley Holderman pitched for the South Bend Blue Sox from 2000 through 2003. In addition to her solid pitching Holderman is a contributor with the bat as well as in the field. Her versatility as a player allowed her to play every position except catcher and center field. She once went 27 games without an error while playing seven different positions. When the Blue Sox added a team to teach girls ages 10–13 baseball skills, Holderman acted as the coach. Holderman pitched two complete games for the Blue Sox in the 2003 Citrus Blast. {<www.baseballglory.com>.}

Holderness, Joan

(b. 17 March 1933, Kenosha, Wisconsin) OF/SS 1949–51, Kenosha Comets, Grand Rapids Chicks

Joan Holderness got her start with the AAGPBL at the young age of 15 while still attending Mary D. Bradford High School. She joined the Kenosha Comets in 1947 and 1948 as the bat girl before taking her spot on the roster in 1949. In 1950 she moved to Grand Rapids and stayed with the Chicks into the 1951 season before quitting to help her family, since her sister had polio. She played in 119 games but only hit .151 with 43 hits. She took up bowling, golf and fishing after her playing days ended and is a member of the Clearwater–St. Petersburg, Florida, Hall of Fame.

{AAGPBL Newsletter, September 2000, 24; AAGPBL Baseball Cards, 1996.}

Holgerson (Silvestri), Margaret "Marge," "Mobile"

(b. 28 January 1927, Mobile, Alabama; d. 23 March 1990) 2B/P 1946–52, Rockford Peaches, Muskegon Lassies, Grand Rapids Chicks

Margaret Holgerson played in the All American League for seven seasons. In 1949 she got married and continued to play under her married name of Silvestri. She pitched in 168 games with a 76–69 record. Her ERA was 1.99 and she struck out 599 hitters in 1,241 innings. After leaving the league Holferson stayed involved with baseball by becoming an umpire. She worked in both men's and women's leagues. {AAGPBL Baseball Cards, 2000.}

Holien, Ella

(b. 31 January 1981) P, Springvale Lady Lions, Australian National Team 2004

In the 2002 Women's World Series Ella Holien pitched a complete game in the finals to defeat Japan 8–6. She gave up eight hits but only walked two batters. At the 2004 National Championships for Australia Holien hit .667 and gave up only one earned run. In the 2004 World Cup Holien led all pitchers with two victories and no losses. {Press release, 9 September 2002, Australian Baseball Federation.}

Holle, Mabel B. "Holly"

(b. 21 March 1920, Jacksonville, Illinois) OF 1943, Kenosha Comets, South Bend Blue Sox

After playing for just one year in the AAGPBL Mabel Holle went back to school and got a bachelor's degree (1942) and master's degree (1955) from MacMurray College in Jacksonville, Illinois. While in college she played field hockey, volleyball and basketball. She taught physical education for 45 years at Waukegan High School. In addition to her teaching she coached softball and assisted with basketball and volleyball. Mabel was one of the original 60 players signed for the inaugural season of the AAGPBL. Her one season gave her the opportunity to play in 90 games and hit .199 with 21 RBIs. After that one year she stayed in Chicago to play fast-pitch softball. She was elected into the Illinois Girls Coaches Hall of Fame in 1988 and the MacMurray Athletic Hall of Fame in 1993. Her election to these two halls was based on more than just her playing, teaching and coaching: she also made a lasting impact on girls' sports in Illinois. She chaired the first committee of the Illinois High School Girls' Track and Field Committee, which organized the first track meet in 1973. She also helped establish the Interscholastic Athletics Committee for Women in Illinois and was involved with the initial preparations of drafting Title IX legislation. A Mabel Holle Golf Tournament was begun by MacMurray College in 2004 and is expected to become an annual event. It is designed to raise money for women's athletics. {AAGPBL Newsletter, May 2001; AAGPBL Questionnaire, National Baseball Hall of Fame; MacMurray College News, Press Release 2004.}

Hollywood Bloomer Girls (sometimes called the Hollywood Stars too, but not the same team as listed below)

This team from the West Coast came to Reno, Nevada, in 1931 to play the Reno Garage Team at Threlkel Park. They came into town the evening before the game to enjoy a street parade and ball at Tony's Spanish Ballroom in their honor. The ladies on the roster included Pauline Garon, Vivian Pearson, Shannon Day, Virginia Pearson, Mary Ann Jackson, Jackie Hooray and pitcher Ruth Reuther. All of these ladies also had various roles in Hollywood. For example, Virginia Pearson could often be seen acting alongside Lon Chaney. Lucille Wilson handled the shortstop duties while Jenni Lee covered the hot corner and Peggy O'Neil roamed the outfield. The most famous ballplayer on the club was first baseman Margaret Gisolo, who had first come to notice for her skills in 1928. By August the team found itself on the East Coast playing the Frederick, Maryland, Athletic Club. Their touring lasted for over 14 weeks and they played 88 games, winning 39. The club had 15 players on the roster under the direction of manager Paddy Ryan. {"Filmland's Baseball Team to Arrive Tonight," *Reno Evening Gazette*, 26 May 1931, 9; " 'Movie Star' Baseball Team to Meet F.A.C. at Local Park Friday," *The Frederick Post*, 26 August 1931, 3; "Will Show Garage Nine How to Slug Pellet," *Nevada State Journal*, 26 May 1931, 7.}

Hollywood Stars (were also called Bloomer Girls in some papers)

The Hollywood Stars were a barnstorming women's team in the 1920s and 1930s that played all over the United States. One of their trips took them to Williamsport to play the Duboistown Cardinals at the local Arch Street stadium. The Stars lost the game 2–0, giving up seven hits and no walks. The team included Edith Houghton at shortstop and Ruth Bard as catcher. The starting pitcher, Miss Smith, gave up seven hits but also struck out three of the Cardinals. The Stars only managed two hits in the contest, one by Bard and the other by Houghton.

By the early 1930s the Stars were billed as one of the best female clubs in the country, with a number of players having 6–10 years of ballplaying experience behind them. They were led by their star pitcher, Harriet Smith, and their biggest attraction, center fielder Dot Warren. One sportswriter compared Warren to Babe Ruth himself. Almeda Bard caught for the club while the infield included Agnes O'Neil, Edith Ruth, Edith Houghton and Alma Stack. The remaining outfield spots went to Josephine Gessing and Harriet Seifret while their manager was Evelyn Church. {"Large Crowd Sees Maiden Tossers Bow," *Williamsport Sun*, 27 August 1931.}

In September 1931 the Hollywood team played a benefit game at Griffith Stadium against the Pullman Athletic Club. Before the game the leading ladies of Hollywood had an opportunity to meet President Hoover. The proceeds from the contest were given to the family of local sandlot player Frank Cinnoti to pay his hospital costs. They lost the contest 6–5 on 13 hits. The club was led in the field by the fine play of center fielder Peggy O'Neil and at the hot corner by Miss Blood. O'Neil was also the leading hitter on the team, with a reported .346 average. A newcomer to the club was Evelyn Lynch, who pitched and played left field, though the loss went to Miss Fargo. Lynch was a local who received a tryout during this game. Her previous experience included three years of playing with the New York Bloomer Girls. {"Hollywood Girls Bow by 10–6," *Washington Post*, 2 September 1931, 15.}

Holmes, Tammy

(b. 2 June 1974) OF 1996, Colorado Silver Bullets

Tammy Holmes began as a Little Leaguer at age nine with a team called the Cubs and by 1986 was already an all-star. She hit .369 but even more impressive was her slugging percentage of .507. When she went on to high school she moved from baseball to volleyball and basketball. She was a four-time All-American and MVP in both sports at Albany and Berkeley High Schools. In 1992 while at Berkeley her basketball team won the state championship. She went on to attend UC-Berkeley and played for the Silver Bullets while in college. In her rookie season she was one of the leading hitters on the team, with a .214 average. She also displayed some power when she hit an inside-the-park grand slam home run in the top of the ninth inning of a game on May 13 at Foley Field in Georgia. Her home run helped the Bullets come from behind and defeat the Atlanta Mustangs 14–11. Midway through the 1996 season Holmes was leading the team in hitting and extra-base hits. In their tenth victory of the season she drove in three runs as they beat the KJR All-Stars 8–4. She hit .341 in 1997 for the Bullets to help them to their best record in four years. Holmes played for the Michigan Stars in 1997 and scored the winning run in the NWBA Tournament to help her team to victory. {*The Silver Bulletin*, 3/96 and 7/96; "Cal Rookie Blasts Historic Home run," *San Francisco Chronicle*, 15 May 1996; Tony Jackson, "All-Stars Dodge Bullets, Escape with 4–3 Victory," *Rocky Mountain News*, 4 July 1997.}

In 1999 Holmes tried out for the Mad Dogs, a team in the Northern League. She was trying out for the American Basketball League at the time she got the call from the Mad Dogs' general manager, Mike Kardamis. Kardamis acted on behalf of team owner Jonathan Fleisig when he called Holmes. Her manager was George Scott and in her tryout he was impressed with her ability to dig in at the plate and not be intimidated. She played in her first game against Allentown and went 0–4 with a groundout, a fly ball and two strikeouts. {Mark Murphy, "The Madwoman of Lynn — Holmes Mixes It Up with the Men on Mad Dogs," *Boston Herald*, 6 June 1999.}

Hong Kong Baseball

Women's baseball in Hong Kong is a new phenomenon. The women's teams are a part of the Hong Kong Baseball Association (HKBA), which was formed in 1992. There is a women's tournament held in Hong Kong each year and in 2004 they will be taking part in the Women's World Series for the first time. The HKBA holds a basic skills course each year to help build the pool of female players. In addition, the association decided to form a tie in 2002 with women's baseball in Taiwan because there are two local teams in Taipei. {Women's International Baseball Web site.}

Hoover, Alice R. "Pee Wee," "Sniffles"

(b. 27 October 1928, Reading, Pennsylvania) 2B/3B 1948, Fort Wayne Daisies

While attending high school Alice Hoover played every sport they had for girls. She also played softball in the local area for the Kauffman Maids. She played one year in the AAGPBL and then went back to work as a sewing machine operator for the Wide Awake Shirt Company until they shut down the plant. Then Alice worked for AT&T until she retired in 1994. {AAGPBL Questionnaire, National Baseball Hall of Fame.}

Horstman, Catherine T. "Katie," "Horsey"

(b. 14 April 1935, Minster, Ohio) 3B/P/C 1951–54, Fort Wayne Daisies

Katie Horstman played a lot of softball growing up in Minster, Ohio. A scout saw her play and visited her family to secure the teenager's services for Fort Wayne. Katie did not graduate from Minster High School until 1953. She also played CYO Softball while in school. Horstman was 15 at the time and needed her mother's permission to play. She played in 308 games and pitched in 49 during her career. She compiled a 29–11 record and a 2.50 ERA. She hit .286 with 150 runs knocked in and another 164 scored. She helped her team in many different ways and got the ultimate recognition when she played third base in the 1953 All-Star Game. After the league folded Horstman joined the Allington All-Americans as they toured the country from 1954 to 1957. In a game against the Jim White Chevrolets in 1956, Horstman had two hits and handled her catching duties without error against the men. {Allan White, "Touring All-American Girls Prove Baseball's Still Anybody's Game," *The Lima News*, 14 June 1956.}

After her baseball career she started playing slow-pitch softball for the Ohio Cardinals. Horstman got her BS degree in 1965 from DePaul University and then her M.Ed. in 1968 from Miami University in Oxford, Ohio. She went to work at Minster High School and coached girls' track. Her team won eight state titles and was runner-up for four years. She later received recognition for her coaching with her selection into the Ohio Track and Field Hall of Fame. She also was named National Coach of the Year and from 1976 to 1989 was the M.A.C. League Track Coach of the Year. In 1998 she was honored with other All-Americans before a Texas Rangers game. {AAGPBL Newsletter, January 2001, 21; AAGPBL Questionnaire, National Baseball Hall of Fame; AAGPBL Baseball Cards 1996; Jeni Leis, 47.}

Hosbein, Marion Ruth

(b. 29 January 1937, Coloma, Michigan) OF/P 1954, South Bend Blue Sox

Marion Hosbein grew up in a small town in Michigan where sports opportunities were minimal at best. Her organized sport experience was limited to church league softball and city league tennis tournaments. Hosbein had a short career in the AAGPBL, joining the South Bend Blue Sox in their final season in 1954. She played in fewer than ten games. The Blue Sox finished the season in second place with a 48–44 record. After playing baseball Hosbein worked in data processing and worked for the U.S. Postal Service as a letter carrier before retiring in Kalamazoo, Michigan. {AAGPBL Questionnaire, National Baseball Hall of Fame.}

Hotta, Miki

LF/P Japan

In game three of the 2003 Women's World Series, Miki Hotta helped lead her team to an 8–4 victory over the United States. Hotta had three hits in four at-bats and drove in one run. She played left field flawlessly. During game four Hotta had one hit and drove in one run as Japan lost to Australia 10–9. Hotta also pitched to one batter and gave up a hit. Game seven gave Japan a victory over Australia, with a score of 10–2. Hotta led the way with three hits, two RBIs, two runs scored and two sacrifice hits. In the semifinals against the U.S. Hotta knocked in another run with one hit. Her final series average was second on the team, at .500. Hotta also pitched a third of an inning and gave up six runs. {Australian Baseball Federation, <www.baseball.org.au>.}

Hottendorf, Nicole

Nicole Hottendorf played Little League in New Jersey in 1974 after a court ruling required the integration of all teams. In her first practice she hit two home runs, caught a fly ball in the outfield and even did a little pitching. She wanted to play because her brothers got to play and she wanted to play with them. {Joseph Treaster, "Girls a Hit in Debut on Diamond," *New York Times*, 25 March 1974, 67.}

Hough, Jade

IF, Doncaster Dragons, Victoria, 2004 Australian National Team

In six games during the 2003 Women's World Series, Jade Hough hit a measly .154. She did knock in two runs with her two hits. She led the team with three errors and a .786 fielding percentage. She only walked one time but also only struck out once. {Australian Baseball Federation, <www.baseball.org.au>.}

Houghton, Edith

(b. 12 February 1912)

By Shawn Selby

Edith Houghton was born in Philadelphia on 12 February 1912, the same year the Titanic sank and fans in Boston and Detroit were blessed with two spectacular new ballparks. Houghton was the youngest of ten children and loved baseball, it seemed, almost from the time she could walk. Not content to play the game during the day, she would often sit in her parents' bedroom at all hours of the day and into the night and watch the activity at the neighborhood ball field below their window. By the time she was eight, Houghton was the regular mascot for the Philadelphia police teams and got to sit next to the city's mayor during games. Within a year she was regularly putting on displays of hitting, fielding and throwing before police games. Such informal exhibitions were not sufficient for Houghton, though, and when she was ten she signed on to play shortstop for the newly created Philadelphia Bobbies team.

The Bobbies were an all-girl team started in 1922 by Mary O'Gara. It usually fielded players between the ages of 13 and 20. Houghton was easily the youngest girl on the team, yet she soon distinguished herself on the field. Too small for her uniform and hat, she used safety pins to adjust her cap and poked extra holes in her belt so she would look good on the field. Her play on the diamond won her high praise from local newspapers, who considered her performance to be the highlight of many Bobbies games.

Houghton, nicknamed the Kid, was the Bobbies' 13–year-old star shortstop when, in 1925, the team was invited to play in Japan. It was the chance of a lifetime for the girls. They would play 15 games against men's college teams and would receive a handsome paycheck of $800 per game. On the way, the girls played eight exhibition games throughout the mountain states, finally arriving in Seattle where they picked up their new uniforms and two former big leaguers who would serve as the team's battery in Japan. Earl Hamilton, who had split his 14 years between the Pirates and the St. Louis Browns, and Eddie Ainsmith, who had caught the great Walter Johnson during his 15–year career, would handle the pitching and catching duties overseas. The Bobbies sailed aboard the President Jefferson and arrived in Yokohama on 18 October 1925, where they began drawing large crowds eager to see the young girls, known by the Japanese as "the American team."

Japanese papers commented on their dress, noting they wore "sports shoes instead of high heels and all members look like real sports persons." Papers also expressed admiration for Houghton's play. Although she was "only a slip of a girl," Houghton played well, even catching a Japanese player for the Nippon Dental College team off the bag with "the famous Hans [sic] Wagner 'hidden ball' stunt." Houghton's age, in particular, caused catcher Eddie Ainsmith to worry about her ability to catch his throws if he should need to pick off a runner trying to steal second. Houghton assured him that she could handle the throw but when Ainsmith, still unconvinced, offered her an extra incentive of one yen per catch, she readily accepted. Over the course of the Bobbies' time in Japan, she took him for "plenty of yen." {Gai Berlage, *Women in Baseball: The Forgotten History* (Westport, CT: Praeger Publishers, 1994), 41; Gregorich, 59 and 55.}

The promise of the initial games was soon dimmed, however, as it became clear to the fans that, on the whole, the Bobbies were not exceptionally fine ballplayers. Apart from the occasional standout (most often Houghton), the team was rather subpar. It was not until the Bobbies played a team consisting of Japanese actors that they tallied their first victory. Attendance soon dwindled, causing the team's American sponsor to remove its backing and renege on its agreement to pay for the games. The team found itself stranded in Japan when the sponsor refused to pay their passage back to the States. Ainsmith and Hamilton soon left for Formosa (present-day Taiwan, R.O.C.) along with some of the Bobbies, leaving the rest of the girls under owner Mary O'Hara's guidance in Kobe. Things looked bleak until a hotel owner took pity on the girls and offered to pay their way back to Seattle; they arrived home in Philadelphia in early December 1925.

Houghton, somewhat disillusioned by her experiences with the Bobbies in Japan, quickly left the team and began playing for various clubs around Philadelphia. She eventually would play every position on the diamond, even pitcher and catcher. Soon, she was invited to play on the other premier girls' team on the East Coast, Margaret Nabel's New York Bloomer Girls. Jumping at the chance to earn $35 a week playing the sport she loved, Houghton began commuting from Philadelphia to New York three times a week. A year later, when she was 19, she was invited to barnstorm through Texas and

Oklahoma as a part of the Hollywood Bloomer Girls team, again for $35 a week.

By 1932, the year after Houghton's trips to the Southwest, opportunities for women's baseball had dwindled substantially. Still hungry to play, she boldly went to the Fisher A.A.s, a men's semi-pro team in Philadelphia, and asked for a tryout. Although she never could remember what she said to convince them, Houghton got the tryout and the job playing first base. By the mid–1930s, even the few remaining options for girls to play baseball had all but disappeared, forcing her to suffer the indignity of playing softball. It took her a few years to get the hang of the larger ball and smaller field, but she was soon distinguishing herself once again as a part of the New York Roverettes in the famed Madison Square Garden.

As was the case with millions of American women, Houghton's life was changed dramatically with the United States' entry into World War II. She joined the WAVES (Women Accepted for Volunteer Emergency Service) as a part of the U.S. Navy and, while working as a clerical assistant in supplies and accounts, she successfully tried out for the department's baseball team. Her talent and the paucity of pitching allowed Houghton to hit .800 during stretches of the season. One navy newsletter praised her ability, saying, "enlisted WAVE Houghton ... can make any ball team in the country." {Gregorich, 58.}

Frustrated by the lack of options for a woman baseball player, Houghton approached owner Bob Carpenter's last-place Philadelphia Phillies and offered her services as a scout. Leaving her baseball scrapbook with Carpenter, she probably assumed that the Phils had absolutely nothing to lose by signing a female scout. Carpenter evidently agreed, and a few days later Edith got a call asking her to come aboard as the first woman scout for a major league team. Carpenter knew he might take some heat for signing her, but figured he would have the last laugh when she signed a prospect someday. Over the next six years, Edith scouted hundreds of young men, signing 16. Although none ever made it to the majors, two did play in Class B ball. This does not necessarily reflect poorly on Edith's skill as a scout because, as she rightly points out, if she thought the player had talent, "you can bet your buttons ten others are after him, too." {"Phillies Sign Girl Talent Hunter," *Waukesha Daily Freeman*, 15 February 1946, 9; "Woman Scout Signed by Philadelphia Phillies," *Walla Walla Union-Bulletin*, 15 February 1946, 6.}

Unfortunately, little public record exists of her life after being discharged from the Navy after her call-up during Korea. Like so many figures in women's sports history, Edith Houghton's achievements both on and off the field of play are little remembered, and her life after baseball, even less so. It should always be remembered that these women were not simply ballplayers; their lives beyond baseball were just as worthy of remembrance as their exploits on the diamond.

Housman, Joanne

(b. 1962)

Joanne Housman helped organize the Florida Women's Baseball League in 1993 with three original clubs. Housman put together the league after another attempt failed in 1992, because she did not want to return to playing softball. The teams played their games at Jose Marti Park. {John Hughes, "Women Get a Chance to Play a Real Game of Baseball," *Fort Lauderdale Sun-Sentinel*, 4 June 1993.}

Howey, Becky

Util., Detroit Danger

Becky Howey started her baseball career playing Little League through the Midget level. She switched to fast-pitch softball during her junior high and high school years. She earned All-State and All-Region honors in 1995 and 1996 while playing softball at Macomb Community College. At the conclusion of the 1995–96 season Howey was named Athlete of the Year at Macomb. She joined the Detroit Danger and hit cleanup for them because of her power. {<www.baseballglory.com>.}

Hu, Nancy

Announcer

Nancy Hu started her athletic career as a ballerina at age seven and went on to become the deputy general manager for TVIS Television in Taiwan. One of the projects she worked on was the live broadcasts of the Chinese Professional Baseball League. The station also put Hu in charge of the Golden Dragon Tournament founded in 1995 to provide an outlet for the best high school players in Taiwan. {Tine Lee Odinsky, "Nancy Hu–From Ballet to Baseball," *International Baseball Rundown*, March 1996, 14–15.}

Huang, Ching-Yung

2B, Taiwan

Ching-Yung Huang played second base for Taiwan in the 2004 women's World Cup. She hit only .167 but did drive in two runs and she only made one error in the field.

Hudson, Renee

1B/P/OF 1998–2004, Virginia Flames, Montgomery Barncats

Renee Hudson was selected for membership in the National Women's Baseball Hall of Fame in 2004 after playing for six years in the Eastern Women's Baseball Conference. She has pitched and patrolled the outfield for the Virginia Flames and the Barncats. Her coach Richard Bender described her as a player who would play any position to help her team win. Her biggest assets to the teams she has played on have been her dedication and determination. In 2002 the Barncats selected her as their team MVP. Hudson played for the DC Thunder in a July 4 tournament and pitched a one-hit shutout in the first game to win 11–0. Growing up, Hudson played softball and basketball and then volleyball in school. Since she graduated she also took up running and has participated in a number of marathons and triathlons. After graduating from the University of Maryland she got a job teaching first grade at Jackson Road Elementary School in White Oak, Maryland. She also has a master's degree from Arizona State University. Hudson also coaches girls' baseball and basketball to pass on her love of these games to other young women. She is married to Tom Hudson and they have three children. {EWBC Web site.}

Hughes, Jennifer "Taz," "Jenn"

OF 1999–2003, Chicago Storm

Jennifer Hughes played the outfield for the Storm in the Great Lakes Women's Baseball League in the 1999 through 2003 seasons. She played in the 2000 Women's World Series and hit .400 over her first two seasons in Chicago. Her real reputation as a ballplayer has been built around her speed on the base paths, where she stole 62 bases in 66 attempts. This percentage earned her nickname. In 2003 she again played in the World Series in six games. She had three hits in 20 at-bats, and three strikeouts. In the 2003 AAU National Championship Series Hughes pitched one inning and gave up three earned runs for the Storm. When not playing baseball Hughes is a village engineer in Lincolnshire, Illinois. {"Village Engineer Throws a Mean Fast Ball," *Lincolnshire Review*, 26 June 2003; <www.baseballglory.com>.}

Hughes, Wendy Hoppel

Management Personnel

Wendy Hoppel Hughes was promoted by the Cleveland Indians in 1999 to the position of director of baseball administration. Hughes started working for the Indians in 1983 in the Baseball Operations department, overseeing the administrative duties of player development. Her primary duties include managing the budgets for the Indians for their player development system and the Latin American operations in the Dominican Republic and Venezuela. Hughes also plans all the travel and living arrangements throughout the season for all six minor league clubs. {Indians Press Release, 1 June 2000.}

Hunger, Karen

C, Ocala Lightning

Karen Hunger had over 20 years of baseball experience when she joined Team USA in 2001. She started as a Little League player at age eight and continued to play, mainly in the Florida Women's Baseball League in the mid–1990s. She caught for the Tampa Bay Thunder, the Pepsi Extreme and the Tampa Bay Diamondz. When that league ran into difficulties Hunger signed on with the Ocala Lightning and ended up catching for the 2001 championship team.

Hunolt, Alicia

Alicia Hunolt played in the Little League World Series in 1999, becoming the seventh girl to do so.

Hunt, Emily

P, NAWBL Saints, North Shore Lady Spirit

Emily Hunt pitched for the Saints in the championship game of the NAWBL Labor Day Tournament. She gave her club five strong innings to defeat the Seahawks. It was her first pitching experience since she had injured her arm during spring training. She also had four base hits. She earned the tournament MVP award. In 2004 she flew to the Dominican Republic with the Lady Spirit for a goodwill exhibition. They won all four games but more importantly had the chance to give away lots of equipment, food and other needed things. In their first win, 8–7, Hunt had two hits and got the save. {Jean DePlacido, "Lady Spirit a Big Hit in Dominican Republic," *The Salem News*, 18 November 2004.}

Hunter, Dorothy "Dottie"

(b. 28 January 1916, Prince Alberta, Canada) 1B/Chaperone 1943–54, Kenosha Comets, Racine Belles, Milwaukee Chicks, Grand Rapids Chicks

Emily Hunt pitching for the Eagles (courtesy Laura Wulf).

Dorothy Hunter started out as a softball player in Winnipeg, Canada, and was friends with Olive Little, who also played in the AAGPBL. Hunter played one year before becoming the first player to serve as a chaperone for the girls. She played in 82 games and hit .224. { Merrie Fidler, *The Development and Decline of the All-American Girls Baseball League, 1943–1954*, Master of Science thesis (Department of Physical Education: University of Massachusetts, 1976), 250.}

Hurley, Cristine "Cris"

(b. San Jose, California) Management

Cris Hurley joined the Los Angeles Dodgers organization in 1998 as their director of finance. Within less than two years Hurley was their chief financial officer. She oversees an annual budget that exceeds $250 million. At the time she began, she was one of only three women holding such a position in major league baseball. Hurley is a CPA and graduated with a BA in 1989 from Northeastern.

Hurley grew up traveling from place to place until her family settled in Connecticut, when she entered Staples High School. She played soccer and softball and liked to be active but never played baseball. After graduation she started work with Ernst and Young in Boston and then transferred to their Los Angeles office. In 1992 she left that job to work for the Walt Disney Company because she loved their films and musicals. {Gary Libman, "The Natural," *Nu Magazine*, March 2002.}

Hutchison, Anna May "Hutch"

(b. 1 May 1925, Louisville, Kentucky; d. 1998)
C/P 1944–49, Racine Belles, Muskegon Lassies

Growing up in Louisville, Anna May Hutchison played in the Girls Athletic Association (GAA). She also played for Camera Corner in the city league. When they won the Louisville city championship, the team was invited to play in the regionals in Fort Wayne. There were scouts present in Fort Wayne, and that was where Hutchison was discovered for the AAGPBL. She started out as a catcher for Racine before moving to the mound in 1946. During her pitching career Hutchison set a number of league records including the most games pitched in one season, with 51. She also pitched a 19–inning game against Peoria in 1946, the year she made the all-star team. Racine won the championship in 1946 and Hutchison pitched in eight of the 11 games. In 1947 she started 40 games and had a 27–13 record, making the all-star team for the second straight season. She pitched 360 innings and gave up only 230 hits. She also had 12 shutouts that year. After retiring from baseball in 1950, Hutchison went on to be a respected golfer and bowler. She also worked as a teacher in Kenosha, Wisconsin, until she retired. {"Ex-Belles Pitcher Dies at 73," *Associated Press*, 1 February 1998; Helmer, "Belles of the Ballpark." *Sports Collector's Digest*, 2 September 1988, 118–120; AAGPBL Questionnaire, National Baseball Hall of Fame.}

Hutfilz, Gloria

AWBA

Gloria Hutfilz gave up slow-pitch softball to play in the AWBA in 1993. She drove to Chicago from Lafayette, Indiana, to make the opening game of the season. Since the ten-game schedule included all Saturday contests, Hutfilz planned to make the drive each week for this once-in-a-lifetime opportunity. {Carrie Muskat, "Playing Hardball's a Down and Dirty Escape from Real Life," *Chicago Tribune*, 27 June 1993, 1, 11.}

Hutson, Jordan "Jordi"

2B 2001, Team Canada

Jordi Hutson appeared in the 2001 Women's World Series as Canada's youngest player, at 14. She played second base in the second game and though she went 0–2 at the plate she did help turn a needed double play.

Hyang-mi, An

P, South Korea

An Hyang-mi was the first female pitcher in South Korea, in 1999. She played for a team associated with Duksoo Information in Seoul. One coach, Jung Byung-kyu, said she got the chance to pitch in the quarterfinal game of the President's Cup because she had worked so hard to be able to play in school. This was seen as her reward though her team lost 9–6. While playing in high school her coach would not let any of the other players talk to her, but she did not give up playing. She tried out for two teams in Korea before finally moving to Japan in 2002 to play for a semipro women's team called the Tokyo Dream Wings. She generally plays third base and bats cleanup for the club. {Kim Taegyu, "Female Baseballer Can't Give Up the Diamond," *The Korea Times*, 25 February 2003.}

Hyde, Barbara

1B, Montgomery County Barncats

After playing softball her whole career, Barbara Hyde joined the Barncats as their first baseman. She works at the National Institute of Standards and Technology in Gaithersburg, Maryland, when she is not on the ball field.

Indianapolis Bloomer Girls

The Indianapolis team came to Atlanta, Georgia, in 1914 to play the Atlanta Federals. The game took place at Ponce Park. They came to Atlanta after a series of games in Eastman, Georgia. Claude East managed the ball club, and his roster included all ladies. Ethel Maloney handled the catching duties while Margaret Cunningham pitched to her. Katie Orr, Selma Welbaum, Hattie Murphy and Elizabeth Pearl took care of the infield while May Arbaugh, Mildred Dodge and Mary Diern roamed the outfield. Hattie Crowe served as a relief pitcher. {"No-Hit Pitcher to Face Bloomer Girls," *The Constitution* (Georgia), 1 May 1914; "Bloomer Girls Play Here on Saturday," *The Constitution* (Georgia), 23 April 1914, 10.}

International Women's Baseball

By Jim Glennie

Modern competitive international women's baseball play began when Japanese organizers sent

Team Energen to Ft. Lauderdale, Florida, to participate in the American Women's Baseball League's 1999 South Florida Diamond Classic. The AWBL had established contact with Japanese teams through a Web site developed by AWBL organizer Jim Glennie.

Japan has three separate organizations that support baseball for girls and women. The three groups are high school, university and summer recreational leagues, which operate distinctly as different associations. The university and summer recreational organizations meet in a tournament. This tournament would roughly equate to a national championship, although it is not publicized as such.

The United States had approximately 20 women's baseball teams playing around the country. Several teams would meet each spring and fall to compete in national tournaments organized by the AWBL. These tournaments were publicized on the Internet through the AWBL Web site.

Through contact made by Japanese organizers with the AWBL, it was agreed that the Japanese organizers would put together an all-star team from Japan to participate in a spring women's baseball tournament in Ft. Lauderdale, Florida. The Japanese all-star team would be called Team Energen. The sponsor was a pharmaceutical company, Otsuka Pharmaceutical, which marketed a sports drink called Energen.

At the 1999 South Florida Diamond Classic, Team Energen showed they could play at the top level of women's baseball and vowed to return home to develop an even stronger team. At a meeting between Japanese and AWBL officials following the tournament, plans were initiated for a contest between a national women's baseball team from the United States and Team Energen in Tokyo.

In May of 2000, a United States national women's baseball team flew to Tokyo and played the first competitive* international women's baseball game on May 1 in the Seibu Dome against a nationally selected Team Energen squad. The Japanese team defeated the United States team in front of 3,000 enthusiastic fans. The American and Japanese organizers developed a plan to continue this international competition with a Women's World Series to be held in the United States or Canada in the summer of 2001. After discussions with women's baseball program organizers within the American Women's Baseball League, Baseball Ontario, the Victorian Baseball Federation (Australia) and Japanese organizers

over the summer, plans were developed for the 2001 Women's World Series in Toronto.

Representatives from the AWBL, Baseball Ontario and Baseball Canada flew to Tokyo in April of 2001 for discussions with the Japanese baseball organizers. After several rounds of discussions the formation of the Women's International Baseball Association (WIBA) was formalized in an agreement between representatives from Canada, the United States and Japan. Although Australia was unable to send a representative for discussions, its representative had indicated their willingness to play in international competitions. A press conference was held in Tokyo on April 10 to announce the formation of the WIBA and Japan's participation in the 2001 Women's World Series in Toronto on 4–8 July 2001.

The cornerstone for attracting the Australian and Japanese teams to North America was the 2001 Women's World Series. This international competition, the first of its kind, involving national women's baseball teams from four countries, provided an attractive platform for seeding the long overdue development of international women's baseball play. The Toronto Blue Jays agreed that several games, including the championship game of the 2001 Women's World Series, would be played in the Toronto SkyDome between July 4 and July 8. This proved to be an irresistible venue for attracting Japanese and Australian teams to North America.

Before 2001 Canada had girls' baseball teams on which girls could play until age 16. There were no organized leagues for adult women. Often Canada's older talent played with teams in the United States in order to continue their participation in baseball. Baseball Ontario organized Team Ontario to play in the women's baseball competitions in the United States. As early as 1997 a Team Ontario representative team played in the fall AWBL championship in Tucson, Arizona. Team Ontario, which then essentially represented the best women's baseball played in Canada, added players from other provinces of Canada to form Canada's entry in the 2001 Women's World Series.

Women's baseball began seriously in Australia when the Victorian Baseball Association decided to see if there was interest from women to play baseball. A tryout to determine interest in 1994 resulted in the formation of almost 30 teams. These teams were organized as sister clubs with then-established men's adult baseball clubs. Approximately 60

---

*In 1997 an Australian team from Victoria visited southern California, playing local recreational teams in the San Diego and Los Angeles areas. A local recreational team from San Diego reciprocated by competing in the Victoria national tournament in 1998.

women's teams now play in Australia. In 2001 the Australian Baseball Federation sanctioned the development of a national women's baseball team to represent them in international play. The Australian team was selected mainly from the Victorian Baseball Association, supplemented from a few players in other states including New South Wales, Queensland and Western Australia. The Australian national team competed in the 2001 Women's World Series in Toronto, taking the bronze medal. In 2002 the Aussie Stars won the gold medal, beating Japan in the 2002 Women's World Series in St. Petersburg, Florida.

Japan also committed to play in the 2001 Women's World Series and sent their national team, Team Energen. The Japanese organizers selected their team from national tryouts held in Tokyo during the first week of December 2000. The tryouts attracted several hundred players from across their country. Team Energen came as an experienced international entrant. They had played in the 1999 South Florida Diamond Classic and hosted a United States national team in Tokyo in May 2000. Team Energen has been in the Women's World Series championship game twice but has come away with the silver medal both times.

The American Women's Baseball League (AWBL) with the help of the Roy Hobbs baseball organization selected and organized the 2001 United States team through tryouts held in several areas of the country. A team ranging in ages from 15 to 41 represented the United States well, eventually winning the inaugural 2001 Women's World Series. The AWBL selected and sponsored the 2002 American All-Stars in the 2002 Women's World Series. The United States entrant finished third at St. Petersburg.

The 2003 Women's World Series was awarded to Australia and was played on the Gold Coast in Queensland at the Australian Baseball Federation national training site, Palm Meadows Baseball Complex. The dates were August 25–30. Originally Japan was to host the 2003 event but the SARS virus foreclosed that venue. Invitations have been extended to Australia, Canada, the United States and China.[†]

It is hoped that the Women's International Baseball Association will create a network in which countries and other baseball organizations can nurture and develop strong women's baseball programs. Already the International Baseball Federation (IBAF) has taken notice and scheduled the first women's World Cup for baseball. This event has been awarded to the Edmonton International Baseball Foundation and will be played in late July 2004. Also the Australian Baseball Federation has hosted their first International Women's Baseball Tournament in Geelong from 16–22 December 2002. The fourth Women's World Series also took place in 2004, with more participants than in the past.

Ivie, Tamara

(b. 19 July 1972, Anaheim, California) 1B 1995, Colorado Silver Bullets 1995

Tamara Ivie played softball at California State, Northridge, after playing basketball and volleyball at Norco High School. She was Norco High School Athlete of the Year in 1990 when she graduated. Her softball honors included being named to the All W.A.C. First Team and First All-West Regional team for Northridge. Over the course of the 1995 season, Ivie played well enough to establish herself as the starting first baseman for the Bullets. She hit safely in nine of the final 16 games and had a number of multiple-hit games. {"Bullets Set for San Bernardino," *The Press-Enterprise*, 28 June 1997; *The Silver Bulletin*, 12/95; "For the Love of the Game," Colorado Silver Bullets souvenir program, 1995.}

Jackson, Gloria Jean

Gloria Jackson tried out for the Pittsfield Senators in August 1971 but did not make the team. Jackson decided to try out for the club after reading about the team's difficulty in attracting fans. She thought her playing for the team might help increase attendance. Jackson's baseball experience before her tryout was nonexistent; she had only played softball. She played first base and fielded well in her tryout, but hitting was a lot more difficult because the ball was smaller and had more movement. {Roger O'Gara, "Gloria Jean's Tryout Proves Pretty Failure," *The Sporting News*, 4 September 1971, 41.}

Jackson, Kim

P 2002, Mets

Kim Jackson had a 5–2 record in 2002 with an ERA of 3.44. She struck out 53 while walking only seven. Jackson also pitched five complete games and had one shutout for the Mets in the East Coast Women's Baseball League.

†*Both Hong Kong and Taiwan have women's baseball leagues.*

Jackson, Lillian N. "Bird Dog"

(b. 14 August 1919, Nashville, Tennessee; d. 30 October 2003) OF 1943–45, Rockford Peaches, Minneapolis Millerettes, Fort Wayne Daisies

Lillian Jackson played basketball while attending Isaac Litton High School. She took classes at Nashville Business College and played on their softball team. Jackson started with Rockford but was one of four players sent to other teams to help balance the league. She patrolled the outfield for three seasons before returning to softball in Chicago. Her speed in the outfield saved many a game for her team. She earned her nickname from teammate Faye Dancer, who told her she covered left field like a bird dog. She played in 120 games, hitting only .161, but she scored 47 runs and drove in 31. After baseball she played for the Parichy Bloomer Girls softball team for two years before going to work for Sunbeam. She worked for Sunbeam for 25 years before retiring. Lillian took up bowling and golf after her softball days were over. {AAGPBL Newsletter, May 2001, 39, and May 2004, 16; AAGPBL Questionnaire, National Baseball Hall of Fame.}

Jacobs (Badini), Jane "Jake"

(b. 16 June 1924, Cuyahoga Falls, Ohio) P 1944–47, Racine Belles, Peoria Red Wings

Jane Jacobs began playing baseball when she was only 12 years old, and this led to her being signed by the Racine Belles in 1943 as a pitcher. For her services she earned $250 a week and got to travel. During her first season Jacobs established herself as a quality starter and relief pitcher with a 2.82 ERA in 230 innings. Before the 1947 season Jacobs and the other players got the opportunity to travel to Cuba for spring training. She retired from the league in 1948 when the rules for pitchers changed from underhand to overhand pitching. She finished her career having pitched in 88 games, with a record of 24–43 and an ERA of 2.70. She walked double the number of batters she struck out and that may have accounted for some of her troubles in winning. In 1994 she became the first woman to be inducted into Akron's Baseball Hall of Fame. {AAGPBL Newsletter, September 1994, 9; May 1996, 11; AAGPBL Baseball Cards, 1995.}

Jacobs (Murk), Janet B. "Jay Jay"

(b. 31 October 1928, Englewood, New Jersey) SS/CF 1945, Racine Belles

While in junior high school, Janet Jacobs played baseball with the boys, and in eighth grade she made the boys' basketball team. She became the first girl to play baseball in New Jersey when she made the Dwight Morrow High School team in tenth and eleventh grade. In college she swam and played tennis. At the University of Miami, Florida, Janet set the United States record in the 50–yard freestyle in 1947. When she was not playing sports, she did some reporting on local sports for the *Bergen Evening Record* and the *Hudson Dispatch*. She played in 38 games in the All American League, batting .170 with six runs scored. After playing in the AAGPBL she coached Little League from 1951 to 1959 and continued to play tennis. She worked as a chemist for Allied Chemical after earning her BS in chemistry from Purdue University in 1950. {AAGPBL Questionnaire, National Baseball Hall of Fame; AAGPBL Baseball Cards, 1995.}

Jagielski, Katie "Jag"

(b. 31 March 1980) 2B/SS, Detroit Danger

Katie Jagielski started playing baseball with her family when she was five years old. She played Little League ball in Redford Township, Michigan. When she reached high school Jagielski played three sports: softball, volleyball and basketball. She became the captain of each squad by her junior year and in 1998 she was named Catholic League Softball Player of the Year.

Jagielski joined the Danger in 2004 and led the club with 27 runs scored. She stole 13 bases but was only caught once. She also led the club with five doubles and two triples, putting her speed to good use. She batted .360 and earned a reputation as a solid fielder. She earned recognition for her play with a 2004 National Baseball Women's Hall of Fame MVP Award. {Detroit Danger Web site.}

Jameson, Shirley

(b. 29 March 1918, Dundee, Illinois; d. 29 December 1993) OF 1943–46, Kenosha Comets

Shirley Jameson played in the outfield for the Kenosha Comets of the All American League after Wrigley signed her as the league's second player. Though only 4'11" tall, Jameson covered a lot of ground because of her speed. She stole 401 bases in her career while hitting .229 in 385 games. She had 41 extra-base hits and also walked 279 times. In 1947–48 Jameson worked for the league as a scout. She worked as a physical education teacher during the off-season and started a master's degree at Northwest. {"Power Plus," *Reno Evening Gazette*, 10 August 1945, 14; AAGPBL Baseball Cards, 1996; Jeni Leis, 35.}

Jamieson, Janet "Jamie"

1948, Kenosha Comets

Janet Jamieson played for one year with Kenosha and enjoyed the travel she did with the club.

Janssen, Frances "Fran," "Big Red," "Little Red"

(b. 25 January 1926, Remington, Indiana) P/ Mgr./Chaperone 1948–52, South Bend Blue Sox, Grand Rapids Chicks, Chicago Colleens, Peoria Red Wings, Kalamazoo Lassies, Fort Wayne Daisies, Battle Creek Belles

Fran Janssen joined the AAGPBL in 1948 with the Grand Rapids Chicks. She had graduated from high school in 1943, where there were no sports for girls. Instead she and some of her friends formed a fast-pitch softball team to play other local towns. Following her graduation Fran moved to Fort Wayne and began attending the International Business College. Her sport while in college was basketball for the Lincoln National Life Insurance team. After trying out in the spring of 1948, Fran made the South Bend squad. She pitched three games for them before the league shifted her to Grand Rapids. In 1949 she was assigned to one of two new rookie traveling teams. During that season the two clubs traveled more than 10,000 miles across the United States. In addition to pitching for the Chicago Colleens, Janssen became the team manager and chaperone in mid–July for the Springfield club. Due to her solid pitching (16–6) she was asked to join the Red Wings for the 1950 season. By midseason she was on the move again as she shifted to pitch for the Daisies. Though she started the 1951 season with the Daisies that did not last, and by season's end she had been traded three times, ending the year at Kalamazoo. She spent her final year with Battle Creek before calling it quits because the league was declining and she could not find a permanent team.

She pitched in 80 games during her career and had a 13–18 record. After leaving the league Janssen worked as a secretary and then moved to South Bend in 1955. She became a member of the Rockettes basketball squad and helped her club win five national championships in the Women's Basketball Association. She also played volleyball for the Turner club that won the national championship in 1966. {Jim Sargent, "Fran Janssen," <www.AAGPBL.org>.}

Japanese Women's Baseball

By Michio Takeuchi

History of Baseball in Japan

In the Meiji Period (1868–1912), about 130 years ago, baseball was introduced into Japan along with many other Western sports. At first, baseball in Japan was introduced into schools as an extracurricular activity. The first school in Japan to adopt baseball was the First Middle School (original of Tokyo University) or Kaitakusi-kari-Gakko (original of Hokkaido University) around 1872 or 1873.

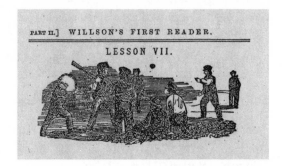

Baseball as depicted in *First Reader* (1863) by Marcius Willson (top) and in a *Textbook of Japanese Elementary School* (1872).

Horace Wilson (1843–1927), an English teacher at the First Middle School, introduced the game. He became an inductee of the Baseball Hall of Fame in Tokyo in 2003. The illustration of children playing baseball was carried in a school textbook of the early Meiji period (1873).

THE WIDESPREAD POPULARITY OF BASEBALL

Many sports such as Japanese archery (kyudo), Judo, Japanese fencing (Kendo), tennis, boating, bicycling, apparatus gymnastics and baseball

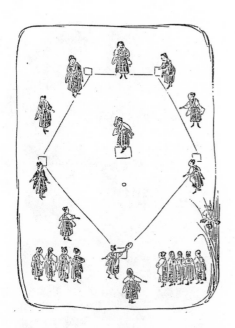

"Base" applied from Roundball in Nippon Women's High School, 1902 (Baba, 1990).

gradually became part of middle school sports activities all over the country. Above all, baseball became the most popular sport imported as part of the Meiji Restration (1868). The special character of the development of baseball in middle school education came through its connection to the spirits of the Japanese martial arts (Budo). In playing baseball, the main point was not the pleasure and liberation of body and soul, but rather the formation of the spirit of self and group control and the unity of the team. The spirit of totalitarianism strongly dominated in baseball.

The term "baseball" was interpreted as "Yakyu" by Kanoe Chuman (1871–1932) in 1895. Baseball is now the national pastime in Japan. People usually use the term "Yakyu," not "Baseball," indicating that the game has become Japanese and does not look like the American game of baseball.

Women's Baseball in Japanese Baseball History

When and where did women's baseball begin? The origins are uncertain. In literature we can see that the first game was played at Nippon Women's University in 1902. Kikujiro Shirai, a physical education teacher, improved on the English game of rounders. Students played by hitting a soft rubber ball with a tennis racket on a pentagonal field.

The second oldest women's baseball reference was a book at Kyoto First Elementary School in

1903. The title is *How to Play Baseball for Little Girls*. This book says baseball is a good sport to foster group spirit, individual responsibility, an independent mind and a healthy body.

Female students played by almost the same rules as today. A pitcher threw a soft ball with an underhand motion. We can see a lot of baseball terms used today already in use at the beginning of the twentieth century. They are as follows: play ball, strike, ball, hit, out, safe, double play, runner, grounder. We have lots of Japanese-English baseball terms today as well. Two examples are "four ball" ("walk" in English) and "full base" ("bases are loaded").

The Rise of Kitten Ball and Playground Ball

After World War I, the cultural philosophy of liberalism was introduced into the various areas of academics and sports in Japan. Tennis, handball and figure skating were introduced into Japan. Several physical education schools were established, and some sports magazines were also published. The first professional baseball team was organized in Tokyo in 1921. The first game of kitten ball was introduced to Nagoya Women's High School by the principal Yamato Koshihara in 1916.

In 1918, kitten ball also began in Aichi Shukutoku Women's High School in Nagoya and Imabari Women's High School in Ehime. Kitten ball was called "playground baseball" or "indoor baseball" or "Yakyu" or simply "base" at that time. Kitten ball is what some people today call softball.

Koshihara emphasized the necessity of women's physical education, and indoor ball fit the bill nicely in helping to develop their physical and mental health. He stressed the merits of baseball, which developed brain function, better behavior, physical strength, stronger personality and mental strength. He was one of the pioneers of women's physical education in modern Japan. From 1923 through 1925, six baseball tournaments were held in Nagoya, Central Japan. Nagoya Women's High School won three times.

Unique Japanese Baseball

Great numbers of people play baseball in Japan today using a rubber ball that is not so hard as the leather ball, but softer and more elastic. This ball was invented by the members of Kyoto Boys' Baseball Association in 1919. Sakae Suzuka and Asajiro Itoi, as the leading members, invented the ball as appropriate in size, weight, safety, and price for schoolboys and girls.

There are four kinds of rubber balls used in Japan. They are called A, B, C and H balls. The "A" ball is for men's baseball of adult, college and

Baseballs old and new. Top row, left to right: MLB ball, present day; ball from 1920s–1930s; ball used in 1950s. Bottom row, left to right: A, B and C ball.

high school level (140g weight), the "B" ball is for middle school and women's leagues (135g weight), and the "C" ball is for the elementary school level (130g weight). The "H" ball is for adult men's and college teams only; the ball is hard like the leather ball, however the ball is not empty inside, and the outside is made of rubber (148g weight).

Women's Baseball Begins

In 1922 baseball teams, using the rubber ball mentioned above, were established. They were at Wakayama Women's High School, Hashimoto Women's High School and Kokawa Women's High School, Wakayama Prefecture, near Osaka. Soon after, Ichioka Women's High School and Sennan Women's High School in Osaka developed their own baseball teams as well. The year 1924 became the history-making year in the history of women's baseball in Japan. The First National Olympic Athletic Meet was held in Osaka in June 1924. Wakayama Women's High School defeated Kokawa to win the championship at that meet.

Ms. Shigeyo Yanagi, a catcher for Wakayama, told Micheo Takeuchi about women's baseball at that time: "Our teacher intensively instructed the baseball rules, techniques and terms of Baseball English. We made up our uniforms and played at least one hour a day." However, just as baseball became popular, the Education Authority tried to stop women's baseball in Wakayama in 1926. The command was carried out in some other Prefectures as well. The reasons given to stop women's baseball were doubtful and mysterious.

Two Japanese players from previous generations of players (courtesy Jim Glennie).

Through a thorough search and inquiry at the Prefectural Education Office it was determined that all data related to these orders was abolished. We can guess some reasons from the newspapers and the magazines at that time. It may have been thought that baseball was not appropriate to women's bodies and that there was some danger of infertility. These same ideas had existed in the United States as well. Doctors tended to think too much physical exertion was not good for women.

Women's Baseball in Japan after World War II

Women's baseball had been a minor sport in Japan. However, the All Yokohama Women's Baseball Meet joined four teams including the Nissan Automobile Company, Victor Recording Company and others for a contest held in Yokohama in 1947, just two years after WWII. By 1949 the first professional women's baseball team, the Romance Bluebirds, was organized. The All Japan Women's Baseball League was established in 1950. Twenty-five professional teams joined the league; it was a golden age just like that of the All American Girls

Professional Baseball League in the U.S. from 1943 to 1954.

In 1952 the league was dissolved and restarted as a semiprofessional league to save money. The team representing the Hisamitsu Pharmatical Company visited Taiwan, Korea, the U.S. and Brazil to play men's teams and came home with a winning rate of over 80 percent. However, all semiprofessional teams dissolved again until 1982. They could not seem to gain enough support to keep playing.

THREE KINDS OF LEAGUES IN TODAY'S JAPAN

The All Japan College Women's Baseball League was established in 1987 and they have held the national meet every August. The Seventeenth Annual Tournament Meet was held in August 2003 in Uozu, Toyama Prefecture. This college league has the longest history of a women's baseball league in the world. About 30 university and college teams play baseball in this league using the unique Japanese rubber ball.

An All Japan Women's Baseball League was founded as the second league for women in 1990. The members of the teams in this league came from club teams of adult women and college and high school students. It is a mix of semiprofessional and

Representatives from two Japanese teams during international series played in Japan (courtesy Jim Glennie).

professional. They also use rubber balls at their games. Women players in these two leagues use official metal bats at all games. The last women's league is the newest one and is the Women's High School League, established in 1997. Only about ten teams join the Annual Meet every year. They use the leather hard ball.

Japan has a lot of problems promoting and sustaining women's baseball, just as do other places around the world. First, there was a lack of instructors; second, there was a lack of playground and sports facilities. Third, there are very few documents and little historical data on women's baseball. We have to hurry to fill in the blanks of the history of school physical education, sports history, and baseball history before it is too late and the people involved are all gone.

Jenkins, Marilyn M. "Jenks"

(b. 18 September 1934, Grand Rapids, Michigan) C 1952–54, Grand Rapids Chicks

Marilyn Jenkins graduated from South High School in 1952 and immediately joined the AAGPBL. She did not play sports in high school because there were none available to girls. Marilyn served as the Chicks' bat girl from 1945 to 1951, and that was how she learned the game. The players challenged her to try out after she graduated high school and she made the team in 1952. She was a part of the 1953 championship team. She played in 141 games and hit only .192, but she was in the game not for her hitting but for her ability to call pitches and keep runners on first. She continued to play amateur softball until 1967 and then took up golf. She graduated with an associate's degree from Grand Rapids Community College in 1968 and took some classes at Western Michigan University. She worked as a medical technologist, a legal assistant and in estate sales. {AAGPBL Questionnaire, National Baseball Hall of Fame; AAGPBL Baseball Cards, 1995.}

Jennings (McCarty), Mary L. "Mick"

(b. 8 June 1931, Flint, Michigan) P/OF 1951, Peoria Red Wings

Mary Jennings won a sports letter for three straight years from 1947 to 1949 while attending Central High School. In 1947 she was named the first Girl Athlete of the Year for the school. Mary played Class A basketball in the city and her club won the championship three years running. She also played softball from 1948 to 1950 for a semi-pro team in Flint. Mary played one year in the All

American League, and then her contract was sold to Grand Rapids for the 1952 season as Peoria folded and she did not return. After leaving the AAGPBL Jennings continued to play basketball and took up golf and bowling. She also refereed in the Genesee County basketball league. The Greater Flint Sports Hall of Fame inducted her in 1996. She married Gerald McCarty in 1951. {AAGPBL Questionnaire, National Baseball Hall of Fame.}

Jester-Lipski, Loretta "Sticks"

RF, Philadelphia Bobbies

Loretta Jester-Lipski played right field for the Philadelphia Bobbies from 1924 to 1927. She helped the Bobbies win a national championship in 1925 and went with them on a tour of Japan. She was best known for her power at the plate.

Jewitt (Beckett), Christine

(b. 3 August 1926, Leeds, England) OF 1948–49, Peoria Red Wings, Kenosha Comets

Christine Jewitt immigrated with her family to Canada in 1927 where she eventually became a softball player for the Regina Bombers in the Class A Inter-City League at age 15. She played for the Bombers for five seasons. In 1948 Jewitt joined the Kenosha Comets and hit .314. She had the honor of hitting the first home run in the team's new ballpark. While playing with Peoria she knocked in 50 runs in 202 games. Jewitt went to Havana, Cuba, for a five-game exhibition tour. She remained in the league for only two years before leaving to get married and raise a family. She hit .213 in 202 games with 50 runs batted in and another 70 runs scored. She continued to play softball in Saskatchewan for nearly 25 years. {Canadian Baseball Hall of Fame program; AAGPBL Baseball Cards, 1996.}

Jochum, Betsy "Sock 'Um"

(b. 8 February 1921, Cincinnati, Ohio) OF/1B/P 1943–48, South Bend Blue Sox

Betsy Jochum started playing softball by the time she turned eight. During her high school years at Hughes she took part in all intramural events offered for girls: basketball, track and field, and softball. By the age of 13 she had moved up to fast-pitch softball, playing on a team from Kentucky. Then she moved to the H.H. Meyer Company and played on their softball squad. That team made it all the way to the

nationals held in Detroit in 1940. She tried out for the AAGPBL in 1943 at Wrigley Field. A highlight for her came in 1944 when the Blue Sox played a night game at Wrigley field under the temporary lights Wrigley had installed for the contest. That was also the season Betsy led the league in hitting with a .296 average in 112 games. That was the best hitting season of her career. She also scored 72 runs and stole 127 bases. Since she had so much speed, Jochum generally batted lead-off in her first season, and after that she hit cleanup. In 1946 Betsy tied Dotty Kamenshek for the lowest strikeout total, ten. In 1947 Jochum was with the group that traveled to Cuba for spring training. Jochum remembers players receiving gifts from fans for good hits or defensive plays. She got a radio and record player for some of her best plays.

At the beginning of the 1948 season as the pitching rules changed her manager, Marty Mc-Manus, asked her to give pitching a try; she won 14 games. After a stellar season she was traded to Peoria, but since she did not want to leave South Bend she retired instead.

Betsy ended her career with a .246 average in 645 games. She stole 354 bases, walked 177 times and struck out 107. She did not have a lot of power but did score 307 runs while knocking in 232. After her playing career was over Jochum went to school for her bachelor's degree at Illinois State University and her master's degree at Indiana University. She taught junior high school for 26 years and retired in 1983. She was inducted into the Ohio Baseball Hall of Fame in 1999. {AAGPBL Newsletter, May 2001, 41; Jim Sargent, "Betsy Jochum," <www.AAGPBL.org>.}

Johnson (Noga, Stuhr), Arleene Cecilia "Johnnie"

(b. 1 January 1924, Ogema, Saskatchewan) 3B/SS 1945–48, Fort Wayne Daisies, Muskegon Lassies

Arleene Johnson played softball, basketball and volleyball during her senior year at Ogema High School. Johnson started playing city league softball in 1944 for the Meadows Diamond team of Regina, where she was scouted by Hub Bishop. Bishop recommended her for the league and she joined the Fort Wayne Daisies in 1945. After only 15 games she moved to the Muskegon Lassies, where she played in all 112 games. Though her career average was only .164, Johnson excelled in the field. In 1946 and 1947 she set the league records for fielding at third base, .928 and .942. In

1947 Johnson traveled to Cuba for spring training, the farthest she had ever been from home. She returned to Regina in 1949, married Harvey Stuhr, and played or coached softball for another 30 years. She remarried in 1963 to Ron Noga and they had two children. Johnson was inducted as a member of the Saskatchewan Baseball Hall of Fame in 1988 and their Sports Hall of Fame in 1989. {Canadian BBHOF; AAGPBL Questionnaire, National Baseball Hall of Fame.}

Johnson, D.J.

OF, Orlando Dragons

D. J. Johnson played in the outfield for the Orlando Dragons. The Dragons were a tournament team for a number of years, playing in events like the WBA World Series (which they won in 1996), and beat the San Diego Stix 12-1 in a 1997 tournament.

Johnson, Jude

Detroit Renegades, Motown Magic

Jude Johnson played for the Detroit Renegades before taking over as manager of the Motown Magic in 2004. {Kristin Karpscuk, "Motown Magic Calling on a Few Good Women," *Daily Oakland Press*, 14 April 2004.}

Johnson (Goodman), Mamie Lee "Peanut"

(b. 27 September 1935, Ridgeway, South Carolina) P, Negro leagues

Mamie Johnson of Ridgeway, South Carolina, grew up playing ball games. Her mother, Della Belton, told her she got her skills from her father, Gentry Harrison. Johnson grew up in South Carolina under the care of her grandmother until she was eight and then she moved to New Jersey to live with an aunt and uncle. There she got the chance to join the Police Athletic League (PAL) teams and was the only girl on the local baseball team. She continued to play in these local leagues during the summers after she entered high school. She graduated from Long Branch High School in 1949 and spent a bit of time at New York University before moving back to Washington, D.C. {Jean Hastings Ardell, "Mamie 'Peanut' Johnson: The Last Female Voice of the Negro Leagues," *Nine*, September 2001.}

Mamie got into the league as a pitcher who had to earn the respect of the players because of her gender and her size, hence the nickname "Peanut." She claims to have learned her curveball from Satchel Paige, and after that there was no turning back even though the idea of a woman ball player still went against the normal view of staying home and taking care of the family. Buster Haywood made sure Mamie pitched at least once on every stop they made because it helped ticket sales.

Johnson attended a tryout out for one of the teams in the AAGPBL in 1952, but did not get to try out. In a recent book about Johnson, she recounts that one of the coaches in charge of the tryout told her to go home; she was in the wrong place. Interestingly, the AAGPBL signed four Cuban players in 1949. That failed experience turned her toward the Negro leagues and her unique place in history. She received a tryout from the Clowns on one of their swings through Washington, where Johnson spent many days playing with local semipro clubs such as the Alexandria All-Star and St. Cyprian Nine at Banneker Field. After her playing days ended Johnson worked as a nurse for 30 years at Sibley Hospital in Washington, D.C. Today she helps manage a Negro leagues memorabilia store in the capital. She also raised one son. {Leah Latimer, "A Game of Her Own," *The Crisis*, March/April 2003; "Interview: Mamie 'Peanut' Johnson Discusses Her Baseball Career in the Negro Leagues in the 1950s," NPR Morning Edition, 18 February 2003; Tom Mashberg, "'Peanut' a Big Deal, Was Negro Leagues Pioneer," *Boston Herald*, 23 July

Mamie "Peanut" Johnson cooking at home (courtesy Noirtech research).

2000; Michelle Green, *A Strong Right Arm* (New York: Dial Books, 2002), 42–46.}

Johnson, Margaret "Peggy"

(b. 5 August 1917, Lansing, Michigan) Chaperone 1948, Chicago Colleens

Margaret Johnson graduated from the University of Michigan and then took on the job of chaperoning for the touring Chicago club in 1948. She took responsibility for her players on and off the field. {AAGPBL Baseball Cards, 1996.}

Johnson, Melissa

RHP 1996, Colorado Silver Bullets

Melissa Johnson played softball at Union University in Jackson, Tennessee. Her hitting exploits earned her all-conference and offensive MVP honors while there. Her softball skills helped her when she tried out and made the Silver Bullets roster in 1996. {*Silver Bulletin*, 3/96.}

Johnston (Massar), Kathryn "Tubby"

(Corning, New York) 1B

Kathryn Johnston challenged the unspoken bias against girls playing Little League in 1950 when she tried out and made a local team. She played first base until she told her coach that she was female. Though the boys on her club did not seem to mind, Little League's rules prohibited girls by 1951. Kathryn tried out for the local Corning, New York, team with her brother Tommy and signed up under the name "Tubby," a character from the comic strip *Little Lu Lu*. A local news report in 1950 indicated that the player on the King's Dairy roster named "Tubby" was the daughter of Mr. and Mrs. Malcolm Johnston. She was attending North Street Junior High School at the time. She then went on to play softball and eventually became a nurse in the Air Force, where she met her husband, Cyril Massar. She is generally credited with being the first girl to play Little League baseball. {Lance and Robin Van Auken, *Play Ball! The Story of Little League Baseball* (University Park, Pa.: Pennsylvania State University Press, 2001), 154–56.}

Johnston, Lindsay

SS/P, Pawtucket Slaterettes

Lindsay Johnston for a time was known as part of the "gruesome twosome" with teammate Nicole Servant. In 1999 the two played for Rhode Island Petroleum in the junior league. Their team ended in a tie for first place with a 9–6 record. Johnston started playing baseball in elementary school and prefers it to softball, which is a slower game. The one thing she and others especially like about the Slaterettes is being able to play with other girls rather than as the one or two girls in the boys' leagues. {Greg Botelho, "Pawtucket Slaterettes Having Another Banner Year," *Providence Journal*, 28 June 1999, C–03.}

Johnston, Rikki

P, Blue Jays

Rikki Johnston pitches for the Blue Jays in the Victorian Baseball Association. She played in the Claxton Shield Tournament for Victoria. There were five teams present at the tournament including Johnston's club. {"Coombes Pitches In for Stars," *Mordialloc Chelsea Leader*, 11 December 2002, 58.}

Jones, Clara Marie

By Bijan Bayne and Leslie A. Heaphy

Clara Jones was listed as the president of the Boston ABCs in 1935. The club was said to be the best in the city at the time. Boston city directories of 1935 did not list Jones, therefore we do not known her profession of record, or her marital status. The one news report that mentioned her involvement said she refused to allow her club to play on Sundays. Her club beat the Homestead Grays in 1935, 4–1, and lost to them 4–0. They also defeated a white ball club in Henderson, North Carolina, by a score of 17–0 in 1935. The ABCs were the premier black team in Boston in the mid–1930s. That followed a period during which Bob Russell and A.A. Johnson's Boston Tigers were the elite of local black baseball. Like the Tigers, the ABCs fielded a roster of both local and Southern players.

Of Jones, the *Philadelphia Tribune* stated that she was "president of the Boston ABC Club … the best all-around in Hub City." The ABCs played a high level of baseball in New England and the South. The team was owned by a local black promoter, Clem Mack.

Games against the powerful Grays, and the integrated game in Henderson, imply that Jones ran a well-respected, organized ball club. Her best players were Leroy Powell (who also played with the Washington Black Sox), Speedball Syms, and North Carolinian Jimmy Rhem (of the Mohawk Giants and Edgewater Giants). Though little else is known about her she is worthy of further study. (Even less is known of Harriet Smith, who in the 1930s was a starting pitcher for another Boston semipro team, the Pullman Porters.) {*Philadelphia Tribune*, 7 March 1935.}

Jones (Davis), Marguerite "the Lady"

(Regina, Saskatchewan) 1944

Marge Jones played one season in the All American League.

Jones (Doxey), Marilyn Charlotte "Jonesy"

(b. 5 April 1927, Providence, R.I.) P/C 1948–54, Kenosha Comets, Fort Wayne Daisies, Chicago Colleens, Rockford Peaches, Battle Creek Belles, Muskegon Lassies

Marilyn Jones earned her sporting experience before joining the AAGPBL on an independent softball team called the Riverside Townies. She played for them from age 14 until she was 20. At the same time, she played in an industrial softball league for the Monwatt Electric Company. When she entered the AAGPBL, Marilyn was used mainly as a backup catcher, though she pitched for Battle Creek after they acquired another catcher. Her switch to pitching kept her in the league, since she was only a career .158 hitter. She pitched a no-hit, no-run game against the Peaches on 10 July 1952 and won 1–0. In another memorable game she lost to Jean Faut and South Bend 1–0 in 1952. Jones walked 14 batters and hit one but only allowed one run. In 1954 while pitching for Fort Wayne, Jones gave up two grand slam homers in one game. Her career pitching number included a 31–26 win-loss record with a 2.79 ERA. After the league folded, Jones continued to play softball for another ten years and worked for the Michigan telephone company until her retirement in 1983. She married Homer Doxey in 1969 and raised two stepsons. She remained active as a bowler and golfer. {AAGPBL Questionnaire, National Baseball Hall of Fame; Rick Harris, "Women, Baseball and Rhode Island," in *Rhode Island's Baseball Legacy*, Vol. 1 (Rhode Island: Rick Harris, 2001), 30; Susan E. Johnson, 12–14, 17, 21; AAGPBL Baseball Cards, 1995.}

Jorgenson, Dallas

C 1996, Colorado Silver Bullets

Dallas Jorgenson grew up in Canada and was a three-time all-district catcher at Simon Fraser University from 1990 to 1993. In addition, she played for the White Rock Renegades, who were the two-time Canadian softball champions. That experience helped her make the roster of the Silver Bullets. {*Silver Bulletin*, March 1996.}

June, Kim "Kimmer"

3B 2000–04, Detroit Renegades/Danger, Motown Magic

Kim June played softball growing up and received All-State honors in high school. She played for a year in an international slow-pitch league in Senegal, Africa, before joining the Detroit club in 2000. She plays solid defense and gets on base regularly. In addition to playing baseball Kim also plays in the women's football league for the Detroit Demolition. When not out on the field Kim is a teacher. {<www.baseballglory.com>.}

Junior Racine Belles

During the existence of the All American Girls League the league hosted a four-team junior division for players age 14 and older. The program began in 1948 with the Junior Belle Reds, Grays, Greens and Golds. They often played before the Racine Belles home games and their uniforms were exactly like the Belles' but with different colors. A local business, Western Printing and Lithographing Company, donated the uniforms. Some of the players included first basemen Jackie Meinert, Mary Green and Dorothy Leuker; pitchers Rosemary Bonner, Joyce Rohde and Betty Schmidt; and third baseman Emma Collova. {AAGPBL Newsletter, January 2002, 19.}

Junor, Daisy

(Regina, Saskatchewan) LF 1946–49, South Bend Blue Sox, Springfield Sallies, Fort Wayne Daisies

While growing up in Canada, Daisy Junor played a lot of softball, and that was how she was discovered. A scout went up to watch the Western Canada Softball Tournament and Junor's team won. She was invited to come to spring training in 1943, but she had just gotten married so she turned the offer down. Her sister Ruby did go and ended up playing for the Racine Belles. By 1946 Daisy had heard enough to know she wanted to play and so she went to spring training in Mississippi and was assigned to South Bend. She enjoyed the adventures though the travel did get a bit hectic at times. The team worked under manager

Chet Grant and chaperone Lucille Moore. In 1947 Junor returned to go to Cuba for spring training. Though complete stats are not available for her four years in the league, Junor was known for her defense and her speed. She was always a threat to steal and covered a lot of ground in the outfield. Her fielding percentage stood at .971. In recognition of her playing experiences Junor was selected for membership in the Saskatchewan Sports Hall of Fame and the Saskatchewan Baseball Hall of Fame. {Carmen Pauls, "Daisy Junor," <www.AAGPBL.org>; AAGPBL Baseball Cards, 1996.}

Jurgensmeier (Carroll), Margaret "Jurgy"

(2 September 1934, Rockford, Illinois) P 1950, Rockford Peaches

Margaret Jurgensmeier played for only one season with the Peaches at the age of 16. She then got married and decided not to return to the league. {AAGPBL Baseball Cards, 1996.}

Kaatskills

A team made up of nine ladies, called the Kaatskills, was reported to have played two games at Lake George in 1883. They played the Sheldons, another team made up of women who were vacationing in the area. Though no scores were reported, the article indicated each team won one game. {Savannah Weekly Echo, 26 August 1883.}

Kabick, Josephine "Jo"

(b. 27 March 1922, Detroit, Michigan; d. n.d.) P 1944–47, Milwaukee Chicks, Grand Rapids Chicks, Kenosha Comets, Peoria Red Wings

Jo Kabick pitched for four years in the All American League. She pitched in 151 games, compiling a record of 74–72 with a 2.33 ERA. She pitched an amazing 1,213 innings, which averages out to just over eight innings per game. {AAGPBL Baseball Cards, 2000.}

Kahn, Judi

(b. 1957) 3B/SS, AWBA Gators

Judi Kahn is a Chicago lawyer who turned her talents to baseball, becoming the president of the American Women's Baseball Association after the death of founder Darlene Mehrer in 1990. The AWBA had been in existence from 1987 through 2003 with three teams in 2003. Kahn herself played third base for the Gators. Kahn attended John Mar-

shall Law School and then decided to give baseball a try after her graduation. The teams played a ten-game schedule each season at Dee Park.

Kahn grew up in a baseball family. Her grandfather played semipro ball and taught his grandkids how to enjoy the game. Though she played softball growing up, after trying baseball she did not want to switch back. {Carrie Muskat, "Playing Hardball's a Down and Dirty Escape from Real Life," Chicago Tribune, 27 June 1993, 1, 11; Bill Beuttler, "The Girls of Summer," Sports Illustrated, 6 September 1993, 139.}

Kalamazoo Lassies

The Kalamazoo Lassies enjoyed their greatest success in the All American League in 1954, the league's final season. They won the Shaughnessy Championship Series on 5 September 1954 behind the strong pitching of their all-star June Peppas. The Lassies beat the club from Fort Wayne to win their only title. They got into the title series by beating out South Bend. Nancy Warren and Elaine Roth hurled the team to victories in the second and third games of the series.

In 1953 the Lassies were expected to contend for the league title, being led by players such as Doris Sams from Knoxville, Tennessee. Sams led the way with 12 home runs in 1952. Dottie Schroeder at shortstop helped the Lassies by taking part in 38 double plays the previous season. {"Girls Baseball Team to Appear in Benefit," The Marion Star, 5 May 1953, 17.}

The lineup for the 1954 Lassies had some impressive players, who all combined to help the Lassies to a 48–49 record that season. June Peppas was their star at first base and on the mound. Jean Lovell took over first when Peppas pitched. Nancy Mudge was an all-star second baseman, and Chris Ballingall hit 17 home runs to power the squad. Dottie Schroeder gave them solid defense at short while Fern Shollenberger was a four-time all-star at the hot corner. Carol Habben was the second half of the home run twins for the Lassies, as she hit 15. Jenny Romatowski was their all-star catcher and Mary Taylor was a relative newcomer in the outfield. The pitching staff included Peppas, Nancy Warren, Elaine Roth and Gloria Cordes. {Jim Sargent, "June Peppas and the All-American League: Helping the Kalamazoo Lassies Win the 1954 AAGPBL Championship," The National Pastime, January 2002.}

June Peppas arrived in Kalamazoo in 1951 as their new first baseman, though she pitched regularly as well. She made the all-star team at first base for two years with Kalamazoo while also forging a solid pitching record.

Management of the Lassies fell to Mitch Skupien in 1952; he had previously managed Grand Rapids. Their games were generally played at Reynolds Field. Every so often the Lassies would play in benefit games, as did most of the AAGPBL teams. They wanted to give something back to their communities. {"Kalamazoo Raps Rockford, 16–0," *The Dixon Evening Telegraph*, 25 May 1954.}

Kamenshek, Dorothy "Dottie," "Kammie"

(b. 21 December 1925, Norwood, Ohio) 1B 1943–51, 1953, Rockford Peaches

Dottie Kamenshek grew up watching the boys in her neighborhood play baseball and only occasionally got a chance to play herself. They let her in the games when they were short a fielder. Kamenshek played for ten years with the Rockford Peaches in the AAGPBL. While with Rockford, Kamenshek won back-to-back batting titles in 1946–47 and was selected for seven All-Star

Dottie Kamenshek of the Rockford Peaches. Kamenshek was one of the all-time great hitters of the All-American Girls Professional Baseball League (National Hall of Fame Library and Museum, Cooperstown, N.Y.).

games, in 1943 and from 1946 to 1951. One of her reasons for success at the plate was her incredible patience. In 1950 a club from the Florida International League tried to purchase her contract. They appealed to the president of the AAGPBL at the time, Fred Leo, but the offer was turned down. Leo and the board of directors made the decision, saying that the league could not afford to lose one of their best players. Leo made further comments that indicated he did not think women could compete in baseball with men. {"Real Pro," *Ironwood Daily Globe* (Michigan), 9 August 1950, 12.}

By the end of her career Kamenshek had batted 3,736 times and only struck out 81 times. She had a career average of .292 with 304 RBIs and also 657 stolen bases. She holds career records for the league in hits with 1,090, in double plays with 360, and in putouts with 10, 440. {Dorothy Kamenshek file, National Baseball Hall of Fame and Museum, Cooperstown, New York.}

Kapenas, Jennifer

IF/OF, Bay State Express, Boston Blue Sox

Jennifer Kapenas grew up in Townsend, Massachusetts, and played volleyball, flag football and golf before taking up baseball with the Bay State Express in the NEWBL. She graduated from Fitchburg State College with a degree in biology.

Kardon, Robin

1B, AWBA

Robin Kardon joined the AWBA in 1988 as a relative newcomer to baseball. She had played pickup games until she was 14. In 1970 she and a friend tried to sign up for Little League in Bayside Hills but were not allowed. By profession, Kardon is a lawyer. She attended New York University and American University College of Law. Before moving to Chicago she practiced in Washington, D.C. {"Met Fan — What's She Doing on First?" *Base Woman Newsletter*, June 1988, 3.}

Kasagami, Yuka

2B, Japan

Yuka Kasagami played second base for the Japanese national tram at the 2004 women's World Cup in Edmonton, Canada. She hit .222 with four RBIs.

Kataoka, Ayumi

2B/P, Japan

Ayumi Kataoka helped her team defeat the

United States 11–0 in game eight of the 2003 Women's World Series. She drove in five runs and scored another three as she led her team to victory. Her series batting average was .467 for five games. {Australian Baseball Federation, <www.baseball.org.au>.}

Kato (Kosaka), Mineko

1B, Osaka Diamonds

After playing softball in school Mineko Kosaka got the chance to play for Osaka in the 1950s. The government started a series of women's baseball teams to generate positive publicity after the war. The Diamonds were a professional team, which she joined at age 17. After the team disbanded Kosaka continued to play amateur baseball for the Flowers, a team sponsored by a local department store chain. {"Onetime Female Pro Baseball Player to Make Comeback," *Japan Economic Newswire*, 12 July 2005.}

Kaufman, Joan Eleanor "Jo"

(b. 9 November 1935, Rockford, Illinois) 2B/3B 1954, Rockford Peaches

Joan Kaufman attended Winnebago High School and played all the sports they had for girls, which were all intramurals. Her competitive athletic experiences came when she played for the Winnebago girls' softball team and for the Rockford Ko-Eds in baseball and basketball. These two teams were semipro squads. In 1954 she got the chance to join the Peaches and earned Rockford Rookie of the Year honors. Joan joined the air force the year after the league folded and played softball and basketball there. {AAGPBL Questionnaire, National Baseball Hall of Fame.}

Kawaho, Maya

C, Japan

In five games during the 2003 Women's World Series, Maya Kawaho hit only .133 but did knock in two runs.

Kawamoto, Yu

SS, Japan

Yu Kawamoto played shortstop for the Japanese National team at the 2004 women's World Cup in Edmonton, Canada. She hit .375 with two stolen bases and only one error in the field.

Kazmieraczak, Marie "Skeets"

(b. 14 February 1920, Milwaukee, Wisconsin; d. 4 January 2000) OF 1944, Milwaukee Chicks, Racine Belles, Kenosha Comets

Marie Kazmieraczak played for one season in the All American League and managed to spend time with each of the three clubs from Wisconsin. Growing up she had played any sport that the neighborhood kids played. She loved playing baseball on the diamond in West Alle, Wisconsin. After her one year in the league she returned to playing ball and went to work first at a golf resort and then at the Eagle River ranger station. {AAGPBL Newsletter, May 2002, 11.}

Keagle, Merle "Pat"

(b. 21 August 1923, Tolleson, Arizona) OF/3B/P 1944, 1946, 1948, Milwaukee Chicks, Grand Rapids Chicks

Merle Keagle started with Milwaukee in 1944 but took a year off before returning in 1946. In 1946 Keagle hit .284 while playing for the Grand Rapids Chicks. She played in 112 games, stealing 107 bases while scoring 69 runs. She made the all-star team that year. Keagle decided not to return to Grand Rapids after the season in order to be with her son and family in Phoenix, Arizona. In 1948 she made a comeback, playing the full season before retiring. Keagle played in 337 games, hitting .266 and driving in 133 runs. {AAGPBL Newsletter, October 1993, 9; AAGPBL Baseball Cards, 2000.}

Keener, Allyson

(b. 6 August 1980, Walnut Creek, California)

Growing up in California gave Allyson Keener the chance to play in a variety of sports in high school and college. High school sports kept Keener busy in volleyball, soccer, basketball, softball, baseball and track and field. At James Madison University she played basketball while studying integrated science and technology. Keener also attended Georgia Tech for her master's degree in systems and industrial engineering. Keener's baseball career includes two years on a Lafayette Pony team and one year at third base for the Chicago Storm. In 2003 the Storm won the Roy Hobbs National Championship, and Keener had the game-winning hit in extra innings to win the game. One of the other highlights of her career was a combined 18–strikeout no-hitter in Little League. {Allyson Keener, correspondence with author, March 2004.}

Keller, Kelly

Mgr., Baltimore Stars

Kelly Keller started her playing career in Little League but then switched to softball when there was no more baseball for her to play. In the air force Keller pitched for a fast-pitch softball team that traveled around Europe playing other military clubs. In 1997 Keller joined the Barncats as her first women's team. Then, in 1998 Keller founded the Baltimore Stars and piloted them to a league championship their first year. The following year the Stars came in first for the season and second in the championship series.

Keller, Rita Ann

(b. 21 January 1933, Kalamazoo, Michigan) SS/LF 1951–52, Kalamazoo Lassies

Rita Keller attended St. Augustine High School through the eleventh grade. She had to quit to take care of her mother following her father's death. She did play softball in the city league before getting a chance to play for her hometown team, the Lassies. She continued to play in the city league after leaving the AAGPBL. Rita worked for 35 years for NWL Control Systems, retiring in 1993. {AAGPBL Questionnaire, National Baseball Hall of Fame.}

Kelley (Savage), Jackie "Babe," "Scrounge"

(b. 11 November 1926, Lansing, Michigan, d. 12 May 1988) Util. 1947–53, South Bend Blue Sox, Chicago Colleens, Peoria Red Wings, Rockford Peaches

Jackie Kelley was considered an outstanding fielder for the Rockford Peaches during her career. Her solid fielding made her a valuable utility player who could play anywhere on the field and did. She was named to the all-star team in 1950. By the end of her career Kelley had played 80 games as an outfielder, pitched 53, caught 52, and played 20 at first base, 21 at shortstop, 43 at second base and 58 at third base. She was instrumental in helping Rockford win their fourth championship. Kelley drove in the tie-breaking run and later scored the winning run in the final game in 1950. After leaving the league Jackie joined the marines, where she met her husband. She died in 1988 of lung cancer. {"Jackie Kelley," <www.AAGPBL.org>; Susan E. Johnson, 100.}

Kellogg, Vivian Caroline "Kelly"

(b. 6 November 1922, Jackson, Michigan) 1B 1944–50, Minneapolis Millerettes, Fort Wayne Daisies

Vivian Kellogg graduated from Jackson High School in 1943 and was noticed by a scout of the AAGPBL when she was playing softball for the Jackson Regent Café in 1943. After school she had played basketball, volleyball, tennis, and field hockey in addition to softball on the local sandlots. She received a contract offer for $75 a week plus food money, and she took it because she was only making $37.50 a week for the phone company at the time. She joined the new Minneapolis Millerettes in 1944. Due to the lack of fan support and close competition, the Millerettes struggled and spent the second half of the season as a road team before folding. In 1945 Kellogg joined the Daisies in Fort Wayne. Kellogg played for seven years in the AAGPBL, earning a reputation as one of the best first basemen in the league. Her career high in RBIs came in her final season, when she knocked in 49 runs in 1950. Her favorite memories include the spring the league trained in Cuba and exhibition games they played in different army camps.

She retired after the 1950 season following knee surgery and the realization that she would not be playing at the same level. She moved back to Michigan and went to work as a dental assistant for 30 years. She also became an excellent bowler and was elected into the Jackson Bowling Hall of Fame in 1992. In 2002 Kellogg was inducted into the Fort Wayne Hall of Fame as recognition of her contributions to the Daisies. Brooklyn, Michigan, named a ball field in her honor in 1994. {AAGPBL Newsletter, September 2000, 15; AAGPBL Questionnaire, National Baseball Hall of Fame; Susan Johnson, 81; Joyce M. Smith, "Vivian 'Kelly' Kellogg," <www.AAGPBL.org>; AAGPBL Newsletter, January 2002, 27.}

Kelly, Jodie

P, Bundoora Firsts

Jodie Kelly pitched in a 17–16 win for the Firsts over Ferntree Gulley in the Bundoora Women's League in Australia. {Sarah Benic, "Wins a Bonus for Improving Teams," *Diamond Valley Leader*, 27 October 2004, 33.}

Kelly, Kaitlin

P, Pawtucket Slaterettes

Playing for Lotti's Auto and A/C in the Minor division, Kaitlin Kelly led the league with a .697

average. She also displayed good power, leading the league with seven home runs and three triples. Kelly could be counted on in the clutch as well when she led the league with 41 RBIs. Her pitching stats matched her batting prowess, as she finished the 1999 season with a 6–0 record and an ERA of 0.56 to lead the league. She also struck out 78 hitters. {Greg Botelho, "Pawtucket Slaterettes Having Another Banner Year," *Providence Journal*, 28 June 1999, C–03.}

Kelly, Linda

P 1995, Colorado Silver Bullets

Linda Kelly joined the Bullets on the 3 August 1995. Her late start did not give her much chance to pitch but she came in as a reliever and as a designated hitter. {*The Silver Bulletin*, December 1995.}

Kelly, Tracy

1998, Arizona Peppers

Tracy Kelly, though originally from Omaha, Nebraska, played softball at Creighton University and then joined the Peppers in 1998.

Kelm, Melisanne

Melisanne Kelm tried out for the Silver Bullets, hoping to make the 1995 squad even though she was only 16 at the time. She made the first cut but did not gain a spot on the roster because the required age was 21. Kelm came to the Bullets with some skill because as a sophomore she played for the Riverside Bethel Christian School baseball team. She started in right field and hit .500 with ten runs batted in. {Ginn.}

Kemmerer, Beatrice "Betty"

(b. 23 February 1930, Center Valley, Pennsylvania) C/SS 1950–51, Fort Wayne Daisies, South Bend Blue Sox

Though she only played two seasons Betty Kemmerer played on two different teams in her first season because the league had a rule requiring every team to have at least one rookie who played.

Kennaley, Kathryn "Kathy"

WBL Sparks

Kathy Kennaley started playing baseball in Milton, Canada, and then for the Peewee club in Burlington. As a result of her participation there, she was chosen along with 11 other girls to join the WBL Sparks to play in a tournament in Cooperstown, New York, in 2003. This team was the first all-girls team invited to play in the 64–team tournament. {"Burlington Girls Get Taste of Baseball Fame," *The Hamilton Spectator*, 26 July 2003.}

Kenosha Comets

The Kenosha Comets joined the All American League in their inaugural season, 1943, and stayed through the 1951 season. In their first two years of play they enjoyed their best success, as they won the second half in 1943 with a 33–21 record. They followed that in 1944 by winning the first half of the season with a 36–23 record. They lost to Racine and Milwaukee in the playoffs.

Josh Billings managed Kenosha in its inaugural season. He brought with him a world of experience as a catcher in the majors. After the team's first meeting it was decided a contest would be held to name the team and $25 would go to the person providing the winning choice. Mrs. Hazel Templeton came up with the eventual choice, the Comets.

The Comets had 15 players on their roster that first year. The players ranged in age and ability, most having played only softball previous to their tryouts. Helen Westerman came on to catch while Janice O'Hara took on the first base chores. Her grandfather had been a major league ball player, so she knew a bit more than some about the game. The team's third baseman, Ann Harnett, was the first player signed by Philip Wrigley for the new league in 1943. The roster had one local girl, Darlene Mickelson, who played right field. The pitching staff was led by Helen Nicol.

The season began on May 30 with a game at Lake Front Park against the Racine Belles. To kick off the new venture properly, the American Legion provided musical entertainment and a Memorial Day service. The Comets won that first contest behind the strong hitting of Mickelson and the arm of Nicol. The fans loved what they saw and came out regularly to support their team. At midseason when the first all-star team was chosen, it included six Comets.

In 1944 the league expanded to six teams, and Marty McManus took over as the new Comets manager. He also brought big league experience with him, as a player and manager. Much of the original team returned for a second season, including star pitcher Helen Nicol. Nicol finished the 1944 season with a record of 17–11 which included one no-hitter. Mary Pratt and Lee Harney also pitched no-hitters for the Comets. They lost in the playoffs to the Milwaukee Chicks, partly because Nicol had developed a sore arm.

George Metten coached the Comets from 1945 to 1948 and spent many hours teaching the players how to slide while wearing skirts. Lake Front Stadium was the scene of many afternoon practices before an evening game. The secret Comet players learned was to slide in on their hip. Metten taught the players from his own experience as a semipro ballplayer. One of the people he played with was Eddie Stumpf, who later managed the Comets and used Metten as a coach. Metten only worked with the team at home and did not travel with them because he also worked for American Brass. Metten had begun playing baseball in 1914 when he pitched for St. George School. By age 19 he was playing shortstop in the Chicago Midwest Semi-pro League with the Simmons ball club. In 1922 he joined a club from Danville, Illinois, in a league that went bankrupt three weeks later. From 1922 through 1937 Metten barnstormed around the Midwest, playing wherever he found a team that needed a short stop or a pitcher.

With a new manager there were high hopes in 1945, but they did not pan out. The Comets ended the season in the cellar. Fans even began staying away, which hurt the team's financial success. As the 1946 season got underway, new manager Press Cruthers joined coach Metten and hoped to improve the team's standing. The Comets moved up to seventh place, which was not much of an improvement.

The highlight of the 1947 season began with spring training in Cuba. Ralph Shinners also joined the club as their new manager. Unfortunately for the Kenosha club, they again finished the season in the basement. This led to a decision in 1948 to move their playing field to Simmons Field. They started the new season with a bang as Millie Deegan pitched a no-hitter over the Chicago Colleens. They finished the season in fourth place. Audrey Wagner won the league batting title with a .312 average.

Johnny Gottselig became the new manager in 1949 and the club got a few new additions, including Ernestine Petras, Helen Callahan and Christine Hewett. They managed to squeak out another fourth-place finish with a record of 56–55. Gottselig returned in 1950 and the squad ended in third place before they lost to the Peaches in the playoffs. Jean Cione pitched a 12–inning no-hitter during the season, and the team had an 11–game winning streak to finish strong.

The Comets began their final season in 1951 with Gottselig returning for his third year as manager. Irene Hickson joined as the new catcher when Julia Gutz left to join the Chicago Girls National Baseball League. It became apparent as the season progressed that the fans were no longer coming out to support the team, and a decision was made to play their final home game on 25 July 1951. They averaged just over 450 fans a game that final season, when they needed closer to 800 to break even. The Comets ended their tenure in Kenosha with a 25–42 record.

In 2000 the city of Kenosha honored the Comets by declaring a day in their honor, touched off by a ceremony at Simmons Field. {Debbie Luebke Metro, "In a League of His Own," *Kenosha News*, 29 September 1992; AAGPBL Newsletter, September 2000, 21.}

Kerferlis, Donna

(b. 1971) 2B/C, AWBA Gators

Donna Kerferlis played for the Gators in the AWBA in 1992 as a second baseman and in 1993 as a catcher. Her mother and sister came out regularly to watch the team play even though her mother came all the way from Buffalo and the games were in Chicago. {"Women Play Hardball," *Daily Herald*, 8 July 1992; Bill Beuttler, "The Girls of Summer," *Sports Illustrated*, 6 September 1993, 139.}

Kerrar, Adeline "Addie"

(b. 31 August 1924, Milwaukee, Wisconsin; d. 4 July 1995) C 1944, Rockford Peaches

Adeline Kerrar had a short career with the Rockford Peaches because of injuries. After her one season she went on to work as one of the first female postmen in the country. {AAGPBL Baseball Cards, 1996.}

Kerrigan, Marguerite "Kerry"

(b. 24 July 1931, Lacrescent, Minnesota) P/Util. 1950–51, Rockford Peaches

Kerry Kerrigan played for two seasons with the Rockford Peaches. She developed a reputation for being a long ball hitter and had a strong pitching arm. She continued to remain active after her two seasons by playing softball, basketball and volleyball. {AAGPBL Baseball Cards, 1996.}

Kerwin, Irene Helen "Pepper"

(b. 3 November 1925, Peoria, Illinois) C/1B 1949, Peoria Red Wings

Irene Kerwin only played one full year in the

AAGPBL because she realized the league might fold and she needed to pay for college. She left the AAGPBL to join Chicago's pro softball league for four years instead. She made enough money playing to attend Illinois State University. She played basketball during her four years at Illinois and led her team in scoring every year. She continued to play softball until the early 1970s, and coached a variety of elementary and high school teams while teaching physical education in Farmer City. She has over 200 medals from the Senior Olympics and was elected to the Greater Peoria Sports Hall of Fame. {AAGPBL Questionnaire, National Baseball Hall of Fame; "She's No Stranger to Olympic Glory," *Touching Bases Newsletter*, January 1997, 21; AAGPBL Baseball Cards, 1996.}

Ketcham, Lee Anne "Beanie"

(b. 18 November 1969, Tallahassee, Florida) P 1994–95, Colorado Silver Bullets

Lee Anne Ketcham played a year of varsity baseball at Vestavia High School in Alabama. She finished with a 12–5 record and six saves. Lee Anne switched to playing softball at Oklahoma State. She was the team's shortstop but moved to the mound when she joined the Bullets. She played shortstop for the Big Eight champions and earned a degree in mechanical engineering. During the Bullets' inaugural season Ketcham pitched seven consecutive complete games and struck out 14 in their first win in St. Paul, Minnesota. They beat the Richfield Rockets in St. Paul in 1994 by a score of 7–2. The Rockets were an over–35 men's team. They finished the season at 6–44. Ketcham's record for that first season was 5–9 with a 5.26 ERA. She pitched 75.2 innings with 62 strikeouts and only 19 walks. At the conclusion of the 1994 season, Ketcham joined fellow Bullets player Julie Croteau in the Hawaii Winter Baseball League. In its second season the HWB had its pick of players and invited the two Bullets to join the Maui Stingrays. While with the Stingrays she pitched only nine innings in 52 games. Ketcham came back to the Bullets and finished the 1995 season at 0–9 with a 5.72 ERA. She pitched 61.1 innings and struck out 26. {"In Focus," *Game Face, Indian Scorebook Magazine*, 12; *Silver Bulletin* December 1995; David Kindred, *Colorado Silver Bullets: For the Love of the Game* (Atlanta: Longstreet Press, Inc.), 78; Robert Collias; Donna Carter, "Beaning Barriers: Silver Bullets Pitcher Strives to Open Doors So More Women May Chase Baseball Dreams," *The Denver Post*, 14 May 1995, B-1.}

Ketola (LaCamera), Helen "Pee Wee"

(b. 30 September 1931, Quincy, Massachusetts) Util. Inf. 1950, Fort Wayne Daisies

Helen Ketola first heard about the ladies' baseball league from her junior high school gym teacher, Mary Pratt, who had played in the league. She loved baseball because her brother played and as a little girl she wanted to do everything he did. LaCamera played for the Fort Wayne Daisies in 1950. She made a name for herself, though only 18 at the time, for her stellar fielding at third base. She got paid $55 a week for playing a game she loved. LaCamera did not return after one season because she met her future husband and stayed in Massachusetts. She and her husband had two children. Her career after baseball was as a bus driver and coaching softball in Edgewater, Florida. {Cindy F. Crawford, "Daisies Diamond Days," *The Daily Journal*, 6 April 2003, 1, 2; AAGPBL Baseball Cards, 1996; Susan E. Johnson, 33, 41.}

Keyes, Erma D. "Erm"

(b. 1 August 1926, Philadelphia, Pennsylvania; d. September 1999, Exton, Pennsylvania) RF 1951, Peoria Red Wings, Battle Creek Belles

Erma Keyes graduated from high school in 1943 and went on to earn a bachelor's degree in mathematics from Ursinus College in 1947. She got her master's degree from Lehigh University in 1961. While at Ursinus, Keyes lettered in basketball, softball and field hockey. In addition to her high school and college sports experiences, Erma played in the Delaware County Girls Softball League and the Women's Suburban Baseball League. In 1974 she was inducted into the college's hall of fame. She also won a number of amateur golf championships. For 35 years she taught mathematics and worked in school administration before retiring in 1983. She spent one year in the AAGPBL, patrolling the outfield for Peoria and Battle Creek. Though offered a contract to return in 1952, Erma decided to return to school and finish her education. {Dominic Sama, "Erma D. Keyes; Educator; Athlete," *Philadelphia Inquirer*, 28 September 1999; AAGPBL Questionnaire, National Baseball Hall of Fame; AAGPBL Baseball Cards, 1996.}

Keyser, Allisyn

Allisyn Keyser got a chance to play in the 24-hour benefit game in Arizona to raise money for doctors in Africa. Participating in that game gave her the opportunity to see and learn from lots of other women playing baseball around the country and even the world.

Kidd, Carly

(b. 25 June 1974) C/3B 2003, New South Wales

At the 2003 Australian National Championships, Carly Kidd had two hits to help her club defeat Queensland on the way to the finals. She knocked in one of the team's 26 runs.

Kidd, Glenna Susan

(b. 2 September 1933, Choctaw, Arkansas) P/1B/OF 1949–54, Springfield Sallies, Muskegon Lassies, Peoria Red Wings, South Bend Blue Sox, Battle Creek Belles

Sue Kidd joined the AAGPBL as soon as she graduated from Clinton High School, where she did get a chance to play one year of baseball on the boys' team. She was voted Outstanding Female Athlete all four years of high school. Outside of school sports Kidd got the chance to play on her father's baseball team. When Sue joined the AAGPBL she moved around a bit, as the league shifted players as needed to help teams stay afloat. When she did not pitch she played first base. She made the all-star team in 1953 and participated in the league championships in 1951 and 1952. She is in the record books for the league for pitching one no-hitter in 1949. She pitched in 117 games with a record of 47–45 and an ERA of 2.49. {AAGPBL Newsletter, May 2002, 15.}

After the league folded she went back to school and earned bachelor's and master's degrees in health and physical education from Arkansas State Teacher's College. While there she played basketball and volleyball. In 1953 she joined the South Bend Rockettes and played basketball with them until 1960. They won three national championships. She taught and coached for many years before retiring and getting involved in a dog grooming business. {AAGPBL Questionnaire, National Baseball Hall of Fame; Darren Ivy, "No Skirting the Issue, Arkansans Like Sue Kidd and Mildred Earp Pitched In to Make Women's Professional Baseball a Short-Lived Hit a Half Century Ago," *Arkansas Democrat-Gazette*, 17 September 2003, 23.}

Kik, Cheryl

IF, San Jose Spitfires

Cheryl Kik played for San Jose in the California league.

Kimberling, Shannon

(b. 12 February 1970, Fort Worth, Texas) C 1995, Colorado Silver Bullets

Shannon Kimberling caught for her high school team and then did the same while attending Oklahoma State. She caught 18 games for the Bullets in 1995. One of her season highlights was catching two runners stealing in one game on July 5. {*The Silver Bulletin*, December 1995.}

Kimbrell, Anna

C, Fort Mill Junior High School

Anna Kimbrell made the boys' baseball team in her hometown of Fort Mill, South Carolina. According to a state athletic official, this is acceptable because softball and baseball are seen as entirely different sports and therefore no equivalent to baseball exists for girls. Kimbrell catches for the Fort Mill Junior Varsity squad. Kimbrell is an eighth grader at the middle school; she loves the New York Yankees. She learned the game playing with her two older brothers, starting to play at age five in tee ball. She also played for the AAU Sparks at Dreams Park in Cooperstown, New York. In addition to playing baseball Kimbrell competes on her school's swim team. Her teammates seem to accept her one of the guys, contributing in each game she plays. The team has two catchers and they play a lot of doubleheaders, with Kimbrell starting one game and Michael Baker the other. {Barry Byers, *HeraldOnline*, 4 April 2005.}

King, Carolyn

In early 1974 Carolyn King attended the signups for Little League baseball in Ypsilanti, Michigan. After her tryout, she made the team as their center fielder. Then she was told she would probably not be able to play because Little League was for boys, not girls. King got support from the local community and especially from William Anhut, president of the local organization and an attorney. They planned to file a suit against the Little League headquarters to get the restriction against girls lifted. {Ira Berkow, "Sexism and Little League: A Summer with Controversy," *The Herald*, 27 June 1973.}

King, Dawnielle Renee

LHP 1996, Colorado Silver Bullets

Dawn King attended Sacramento City College and hit .355 with ten stolen bases to earn MVP honors and the chance to play in the California Junior College State Tournament in 1988. {*Silver Bulletin*, March 1996.}

Kirby, Lisa

P, Queensland

Lisa Kirby played for Team Australia in the 2002 Women's World Series. Kirby won the Redcliffe Leagues–Leading Edge Sports Award for her pitching excellence with Queensland in October 2002. {"Lisa, Kylie Lead Way for Awards," *Redcliffe and Bayside Herald*, 4 December 2002.}

Kishimoto, Mari

P, Japan

Mari Kishimoto pitched for her national team in the 2004 women's World Cup in Edmonton, Canada. She pitched four innings during two games, giving up three earned runs and six hits.

Kissell (Lafser), Audrey Susan "Pigtails," "Kiss"

(b. 27 February 1926, St. Louis, Missouri) 2B 1944, Minneapolis Millerettes

Audrey Kissell's brothers all played baseball and so she learned from them. Her brother Les had a chance to play for the Giants, but served in World War II instead. Audrey played softball, basketball and volleyball while attending Hancock High School. She captained each of those teams. She played only one year in the AAGPBL because she got married in 1945 to Frederick Lafser; he was in the navy, stationed in the U.S., and so Audrey could travel with him. That is what she decided to do rather than continue playing baseball. Kissell was inducted into the Hancock Hall of Fame and each year presents the Audrey Kissel/Lafser Athletic Award to the best female athlete at Hancock High School. She played in 102 games and hit .189 for the Millerettes. {AAGPBL Questionnaire, National Baseball Hall of Fame; AAGPBL Newsletter, January 2002, 26.}

Kitsutaka, Kazuyo

3B, Japan

Kazuyo Kitsutaka played third base for Japan at the 2004 women's World Cup. She hit .385 and drove in three runs. In the field she only made one error.

Kleinhans (Sommer), Shirley Marie

(b. 2 November 1928, Town Herman) P

Shirley worked on her parents' farm growing up and did not play sports. She graduated from Howards Grove High School in Wisconsin in 1946. Her career in the AAGPBL was cut short because of a back injury. She went on to play underhanded dart ball for 17 years and work at the Winnebago Indian School in Wisconsin. She married George Sommer in 1957 and raised two children. She and her husband raised cattle and farmed rabbits. {AAGPBL Questionnaire, National Baseball Hall of Fame.}

Kline (Randall), Maxine "Max"

(b. 16 September 1929, Addison, Michigan) P 1948–54, Fort Wayne Daisies

Maxine Kline grew up on a farm in Addison. She was the second youngest of ten children. She played basketball and ran track and field while attending North Adams High School. She averaged 23 points a game for her basketball team and led them to three undefeated seasons. Immediately after graduation she joined the AAGPBL. During five of her seven years in the league Kline was selected to the All-Star Game (1950–54). In 1950 she pitched the first, fourth and sixth games of the championship series for the Daisies. That same season she also led the league in victories with a 23–9 record. After the league folded she continued to play with the Allington All-Americans until the end of the 1957 season. Her career numbers included a record of 116–65 with a 2.34 ERA while only hitting .194.

In 2002 Randall was inducted into the Fort Wayne Hall of Fame in recognition of her pitching prowess with the Daisies. North Adams Village redid all the signs coming into town so that they now read "The Home of Maxine Kline, Hall of Famer." After the league folded Maxine went to work in the Jonesville Products factory for 20 years. She married Robert Randall in 1973. {AAGPBL Questionnaire, National Baseball Hall of Fame; Susan E. Johnson, 129–36.}

Klosowski, Dolores

(b. 28 April 1923, Detroit, Michigan) 1B/2B 1944–45, Milwaukee Chicks, South Bend Blue Sox

Dolores Klosowski had a short career in the All American League after she broke her leg during her rookie season and never fully recovered. She played in only 39 games and hit .197. After she left the league she stayed active in fast-pitch soft-ball and bowling. {AAGPBL Baseball Cards, 1996.}

Klusek, Sarah "Klu"

(b. 5 April 1977, Detroit, Michigan) OF/P/2B, Detroit Danger

Sarah Klusek started her softball career at age eight and continued to play all through high school. She earned All-District honors during her four years and also ran cross-country. She played softball for two years at Saint Joseph's College while earning her degree in political science. She worked in Washington, D.C., before moving back to Michigan to go back to school. She joined the Detroit Danger in 2005. {Danger Web site.}

Knezovich (Martz), Ruby

(b. 18 March 1918, Hamilton, Ontario; d. 1 August 1995, Regina, Saskatchewan) C 1944–45, Racine Belles

Ruby Knezovich caught for the Belles in 1944–45 and then in 1946 played for the Chicago Bloomer Gals in a local league. Her sister Daisy Junor also played in the league. {AAGPBL Newsletter, January 1996, 10.}

Knights

This team belonged to the American Women's Baseball Association in the 1990s.

Kobayashi, Chihiro

P, 2003 Japanese National Team

In game four of the 2003 Women's World Series Chihiro Kobayashi gave up seven runs in a losing effort against Australia. Japan eventually lost the game by a score of 10–9. Kobayashi picked up the victory in game eight with four solid innings against the United States. In two appearances Chihiro gave up only four hits and had a final ERA of 1.28 which earned her the Golden Arm Award. Kobayashi gained her pitching experience on a university team in Japan. {Australian Baseball Federation, <www.baseball.org.au>.}

Kobuszewski, Theresa "Koby," "Tracy"

(b. 28 April 1923, Wyandotte, Michigan; d. 22 March 2005) P 1946–47, Kenosha Comets, Fort Wayne Daisies

Before she joined the All American League, Theresa Kobuszewski pitched softball for 15 years. She played ball in the Detroit area for a team known as the Keller Girls at Mack Field and then in 1942 she joined the Women's Army Corps (WAC). Her softball experience made her an excellent underhand pitcher for the league, but she could not adjust when the league shifted to overhand pitching in 1948. She pitched in 51 games and had a 14–24 record in her two seasons. Her ERA stood at 2.53 with 103 strikeouts. She batted a solid .242 in 52 games. She left the league to join the professional softball league in Chicago. She rejoined the air force in 1951 and stayed until her retirement in 1975. While in the service Kobuszewski's softball teams won a number of championships. {AAGPBL Baseball Cards, 1996; "Touching Bases" AAGPBL Newsletter, September 2002, 31.}

Koehn, Phyllis "Sugar"

(b. 15 September 1922, Madison, Wisconsin) P/Util. 1943–50, Kenosha Comets

Phyllis Koehn spent six years in the AAGPBL. She started as a pitcher but moved away from that when the league changed from underhand to overhand pitching. She pitched in 124 games and played in another 587 before her career ended. She had a pitching record of 48–54 and an ERA of 3.43. A sportswriter once referred to her as "sugar cane" in an article because of the sound of her last name. Her teammates shortened this to her nickname Sugar. After playing baseball she went to work for Zenith Electronics for 34 years. Koehn stayed active as a bowler and golfer. {AAGPBL Newsletter, May 2001, 35; Brenda S. Wilson, 45.}

Kolanko, Mary Lou "Klinky"

(b. 16 May 1932, West Virginia) CF 1950–52, Springfield Sallies

Growing up with five brothers gave Mary Lou Kolanko many opportunities to play baseball with them. She played softball in her local city league since Weir High School had no real sports for girls. Then she read in the paper about the AAGPBL. She had never played baseball but was considered by everyone a tomboy, and so she thought she would give the game a try. During all the traveling the Sallies did, one of the best places they got to play was in Yankee Stadium. Kolanko batted lead-off during her career because of her speed and bunting ability. She played in 45 games with a .285 average and 36 runs scored. After leaving the league Kolanko worked at a bank for two years and then became a nun and taught at a Catholic school for 17 years. {AAGPBL Newsletter, January 1994, 10, and January 2002, 17.}

Kon, Yukiko

1B, Japan

Playing in the 2003 Women's World Series, Yukiko Kon helped her team to a 10–2 victory over Australia in game seven. Though her bat had been pretty quiet Kon had two hits, knocked in two runs and scored another in the win. By the close of the series Kon hit .429 while driving in six runs. {Australian Baseball Federation, <www. baseball.org.au>.}

Konishi, Mika

P, Japanese National Team

In the 2004 Women's World Series Mika Konishi pitched Japan to victory over the United States in the final game, 13–4. {"Japan Downs United States 13–4 to Take Gold Medal in Women's World Series Baseball," *AP Worldstream*, 22 July 2004.}

Konwinski, Dolly

SS 1943–54, South Bend Blue Sox, Springfield Sallies, Grand Rapids Chicks; umpire

Dolly Konwinski was an infielder for the South Bend Blue Sox starting in 1943. She was traded to the Grand Rapids Chicks in 1949. After her baseball career ended due to an automobile accident Konwinski decided to become an umpire. She attended umpire school in the 1970s as one of three women out of 160 attendees. After completing the training she became a member of the Western Michigan Umpires Association in 1976 and umpired for 15 years. She worked mainly high school and college softball games. Dolly also became a professional bowler. {AAGPBL Files, OBBHOF.}

Kook, Shanna

Umpire

Originally from Toronto, Shanna Kook grew up around the game of baseball. By the age of seven Shanna had started memorizing the rules, and in 2003 she began her career in the Rookie Pioneer League. She started umpiring local games at age 16. She attended McGill University as a music major but dropped out during her second year to pursue a career umpiring. She first at-

tended the Jim Evans umpiring school but did not have enough real experience, and so she went home and continued umpiring. She then returned to the Harry Wendelstedt Umpire School in Florida, where she received high praise from Wendelstedt and others who observed her working. {Jerome Holtzman, "Woman Umpire Set to Begin Career," <www.MLB.com>, 16 May 2003.}

Korecek, Katie

During the 2001 baseball season Katie Korecek played on the freshman boys' baseball squad at Antioch High School. She was the only girl on the team. Her coach, Paul Petty, said she had all the basic skills and he made her the team's second baseman. After playing that one season Katie switched to softball because of the chance for scholarships and future playing time. {Bill Pemstein, "Baseball Gave Korecek an Edge," *Lake Villa Review,* 22 April 2004.}

Kotil, Arlene "Riley"

(b. 22 May 1934, Chicago, Illinois) 1B 1949, Chicago Colleens, South Bend Blue Sox

Arlene Kotil joined the AAGPBL while she was still in high school and played for the touring Colleens in order to develop her skills. One of her highlights was hitting an inside-the-park home run against the Springfield Sallies to tie a game at 7–7 in the eighth inning. She played in 83 games and hit .205. {AAGPBL Baseball Cards, 1996.}

Kotowicz, Irene K. "Ike"

(b. 10 December 1919, Chicago, Illinois; d. 24 January 2002, Elk Grove Village, Illinois) CF/P, Rockford Peaches, Racine Belles, Kenosha Comets, Fort Wayne Daisies

Irene Kotowicz attended Schurz High School in Chicago and played softball, field hockey and basketball. Before joining the All American League she played for the Rock-Ola Music Maids softball team and worked in the American Gear War Plant. Kotowicz started in the league as an outfielder, but after a knee injury hurt her speed she switched to pitching. One of her highlights involved pitching a one-hitter for 12 innings for Racine against Kalamazoo. Kotowicz pitched in 96 games and batted in 188. She compiled a record of 34–47 with an ERA of 2.73. She only batted .141 but she scored 45 runs and knocked in another 32. After playing for the league for six years, she worked for Sears and Roebuck for 33 years and became a golfer. {AAGPBL Questionnaire, National Baseball Hall of Fame; AAGPBL Baseball Cards, 1995.}

Kovach, Irina and Marina

The Kovach sisters are twins who play baseball together in and around their home town. Their father, John, coaches and organizes teams for boys and girls. Usually the two girls are the only females on their teams, but they enjoy the chance to play baseball rather than having to play softball because there is no alternative. {Julie Ferraro, "Baseball for Girls?" *South Bend Tribune*, 19 March 2005, B7.}

Kovalchick (Erwin, Roark), Dorothy Ann "Dottie," "Dot"

(b. 31 December 1925, Sagamore, Pennsylvania) CF 1945, Fort Wayne Daisies

Dottie Kovalchick learned to play baseball with her father and brothers while growing up in the coal mining regions of Pennsylvania. By 1941 she was the official scorer for her father's team, the Kovalchicks. When they needed a fill-in her father put her in right field and eventually moved her to first base. She played for the Fort Wayne Daisies in 1945. She stayed for three months before returning to her father's team. Dottie graduated from high school in 1943 and went to work for her father at the Sagamore Hotel, which he owned until 1948. She worked in real estate, sales and accounting after her playing days ended. Though she played no other sports competitively she remained active in cycling, dancing, hunting, shooting, skating and horseback riding. In 1977 the Armstrong County Sports Hall of Fame inducted her. In 1996 she won an award from the International Quilter's Association. She took home the second-place award in the crazy quilt category. {AAGPBL Questionnaire, National Baseball Hall of Fame; "Dorothy Roark Shares Memorabilia with Hall of Fame," *Touching Bases* newsletter, January 1997, 9, 15; AAGPBL Baseball Cards, 2000; Bob Fulton, "The Queen of the Diamonds," *The National Pastime*, 1999, 72–74; AAGPBL Newsletter, May 2002, 25.}

Kowalski, Jalene

P, Pawtucket Slaterettes

Pitching in the minor division in 1999, Jalene Kowalski ended the season with a 5–2 record and an ERA of 2.78. {Greg Botelho, "Pawtucket

Slaterettes Having Another Banner Year," *Providence Journal*, 28 June 1999, C–03.}

Kramer (Hartman), Ruth "Rocky"

(b. 26 April 1926, Limekiln, Pennsylvania) 1946–47, Racine Belles, Fort Wayne Daisies

Ruth Kramer received a chance to try out for the league when she was a sophomore in college. Manager Max Carey visited her in Rhode Island, after which she took the train to join the Racine Belles. She quickly moved on to join the Fort Wayne Daisies for the 1946 and 1947 seasons. Most of her time in the league she pitched batting practice, and generally only got in a game when they needed a good bunter. After playing in the league she graduated from East Stroudsburg State College with a physical education degree. She took a job in Reading, Pennsylvania, where she also coached girl's softball. Her teams won the city and district championships as well as being state runners-up twice. {AAGPBL Newsletter, January 1994, 9; AAGPBL Baseball Cards, 1995.}

Kreppold, Christina Lia

(b. 13 January 1984) 3B, Western Australia, 2004 Australian National Team

In the 2002 World Series, Christina Kreppold made a game-saving catch in the final contest to help her club beat Japan 8–6. Her catch kept Eriko Nagano from scoring on Ayumi Kataoka's screaming line drive. {Sam Santurf, "Australia Jells Fast to Capture World Series," *St. Petersburg Times*, 9 September 2002, 2C.}

Kreyche, Cathy

1B DC Thunder, Virginia Boxers

Cathy Kreyche has played in the infield for the traveling DC Thunder and the Virginia Boxers, a team in the EWBC. Kreyche also played in the 24-hour benefit game in Arizona

Krick, Jaynie "Red"

(b. 1 October 1929, Auburn, Indiana) P/IF 1948–53, South Bend Blue Sox, Battle Creek Belles, Peoria Red Wings, Grand Rapids Chicks

Jaynie Krick pitched in 61 games while in the AAGPBL. She developed a reputation for wildness, hitting Connie Wisniewski four times in one game. She had 17 wild pitches during her career. She also walked 189 batters while only striking out 97. As a rookie she won her first game over

South Bend by a score of 7–4. She compiled a career record of 8–22 with an ERA of 3.37. {AAGPBL Baseball Cards, 1995.}

Kroc, Joan (Smith)

(b. St. Paul, Minnesota; d. 12 October 2003)

By Joan M. Thomas

Joan Kroc had humble beginnings. Yet, the time arrived — 1998 — when *Forbes* magazine ranked her eleventh among America's top 25 philanthropists. Known more for her many humanitarian causes than as a woman who owned a major league baseball club, she was also recognized as an extremely private person. That reticence renders it difficult to sketch her biography. It also makes every known aspect of her life enticing.

Born Joan Smith in St. Paul, Minnesota, she attended Humboldt High School there. She later "studied piano and organ at the McPhail School of Music in Minneapolis." Newspaper stories from the *St. Paul Pioneer Press* reveal that in her early years she worked at Hafner's Restaurant, a popular eatery and bowling alley on St. Paul's east side. She was also known to use her musical talents to support herself by performing in a St. Paul area cocktail lounge. From all reports, it was her experiences as a young woman that prompted her empathy for those in need, inspiring her generosity when she later gained financial independence.

Joan continued to perform professionally for many years. Additionally, she became the music director for KSTP-TV in Minneapolis. In 1969 she married McDonald's restaurant magnate Ray Kroc. The couple had a common musical background, as Ray once made extra money moonlighting as a piano player. That was when he worked as a salesman. But he had already made a fortune selling hamburgers by the time he and Joan wed. He became so wealthy that in January 1974, he was able to buy a major league baseball club — the San Diego Padres. Living in the Chicago area at the time, the Krocs then made San Diego their permanent home.

Several years after her husband bought the Padres, Joan founded Operation Cork, one of her early efforts "to promote awareness of chemical dependence and its impact on the family." Her experience with that project led her to establish an employee assistance program for the Padres. That program was so successful that it served as a "model for professional sports franchises."

When Ray passed away in January of 1984, Joan found herself in the position of being the Padres' owner and board chairwoman. While she accepted that responsibility, she kept a low profile, and was "said to be a background figure." The team honored her husband's memory by capturing the National League pennant that same year.

While heading the Padres, Joan continued her charitable works. In 1986, she founded Ronald McDonald House Charities, to which she donated over $100 million. Nevertheless, the energy she expended toward her many causes did not prevent her from maintaining her baseball concern. It was not until 1990 that she finally sold the club. In an *Associated Press* release in late 1989, she was reported to say "she wanted to retreat from public life and spend more time with her family."

Although she probably was able to devote more time to her daughter Linda, her son-in-law and four granddaughters, she still had time to give aid to thousands in need. Known to have experience with the delays created by politics, she chose her own charities and donated untold millions, earning the title of "angel." In 1997, Grand Forks, Minnesota, received $15 million for flood relief from an anonymous donor. No one was surprised when the "Angel of the Red River Valley" was discovered to be former Minnesota resident Joan Kroc. She also provided the funds for the Salvation Army's enormous community center in east San Diego. In 1999, her generous gift for the establishment of the Joan B. Kroc Institute for International Peace was joyously welcomed by the University of San Diego.

Joan B. Kroc died of brain cancer at her home in the San Diego suburb of Rancho Santa Fe on 12 October 2003. She was survived by her daughter, four granddaughters and four great-grandchildren. During her life she was never one to grant interviews, but her actions spoke volumes. She obviously had some liking for baseball, or she would not have kept the Padres as long as she did. Moreover, there is no doubt that she was a caring and giving individual. Early in 2004 it was announced that her estate left $1.5 billion to the Salvation Army to be used to build and operate more than two dozen community centers across the country. {Padres PR; Trausch 1989, 73; Lanpher 1997, 1B.}

Kroemer, Joy

IF 1996, Colorado Silver Bullets

Joy Kroemer played softball at Lake Michigan College and in 1993 was the team's MVP as they won a national championship. She went on to play at Western Michigan in 1994 and 1995 where she was co-captain of the Broncos. In 1996 she tried out for and made the Silver Bullets roster. Her softball experience helped her, especially in the field. {*Silver Bulletin*, March 1996.}

Kropke, Keri

(b. 23 September 1971, Montebello, California) LF 1994–95, Colorado Silver Bullets

In high school Keri Kropke helped St. Paul win the CIF Championship in 1988. By the time she graduated in 1989 she had been named All-League and All-CIF for four straight years. She pitched ten no-hitters and three perfect games for St. Paul's. Kropke made the Bullets team in 1994 and 1995 and was best known for her stellar fielding often making catches in the field that caused the crowd to gasp in awe. She played the entire first season without an error. Kropke used her speed at bat as well. She was 5–5 in stolen base attempts and was second on the team with 15 RBIs. She also had three multiple-hit games and a six-game hitting streak during the 39 games she played in 1995. She came to the Bullets with only a softball background, having played at the University of California at Berkeley, where she was an All-American every year. {*Silver Bulletin* December 1995 and March 1996; David Kindred, *Colorado Silver Bullets: For the Love of the Game* (Atlanta: Longstreet Press, Inc.), 80; "For the Love of the Game," *Colorado Silver Bullets souvenir program*, 1995.}

Kruckel, Marie "Kruck"

(b. 18 June 1924, New York City, New York) OF/P 1946–49, South Bend Blue Sox, Fort Wayne Daisies, Muskegon Lassies

Marie Kruckel grew up in New York City and played on a variety of amateur softball teams when she was not attending James Monroe High School. She played the outfield for two years in the All American League and then switched to pitching for two more. She had a 10–11 record while batting .148. She went to college at New York University and finished her degree at East Stroudsburg State College. She became a teacher in South Bend, Indiana, and coached the girls' swimming team for ten years. Her teams compiled a 123–9–1 record and lots of state titles. She is a member of the Athletic Hall of Fame at East Stroudsburg State College. {AAGPBL Questionnaire, National Baseball Hall of Fame; AAGPBL Newsletter, May 2005, 18.}

Kung, Stephanie

(b. 7 December 1965, Queens, New York) C/3B, Queens Cyclones, Traffic

Stephanie Kung has been the catcher for the Queens Cyclones and the Traffic. She is cheered on the field by her two daughters. In 2003 Kung was named the MVP for the NYWBL league. When she is not on the ball field she works as an environmental specialist. Her bachelor's degree is in geology and her master's from New York University is in environmental occupational health and safety. Kung also participated in the 24–hour game in October 2003 to benefit AIDS research in Africa. Kung played for over seven hours and cheered the rest of the game. She caught, played shortstop and even did a little relief pitching in the course of the game. {Stephanie Kung, correspondence with author, March 2004; Michael Malone, "Throwing Like a Girl," *New York Sports Express*, n.d.}

Kunkel (Huff), Anna "Kunk"

(b. 18 March 1932, Wescosville, Pennsylvania) RF 1950, South Bend Blue Sox

As a rookie in 1950 Anna Kunkel covered a lot of ground in the outfield with her speed. She got carried off the field during a game in May 1950 when she sprained her ankle catching a fly ball. Her speed made her a danger with the bat as well, since she could hit and bunt as well as be a constant threat to steal a base. Unfortunately her career was cut short when she suffered a knee injury during spring training in 1951. {OBBHOF newspaper collection.}

Kurys, Sophie Mary "Soph," "Flint Flash," "Soph"

(b. 14 May 1925, Flint, Michigan) CF/2B 1943–50, 1952, Racine Belles, Battlecreek Belles

Sophie Kurys ran track and field, and played softball and basketball while attending Northern High School. She worked at a dry-cleaning store and as a cashier before and after she joined the All American League. In her rookie season Kurys earned her nickname and place in the history of the league with 44 stolen bases. She followed that feat in 1944 with 166 stolen bases out of 172 chances. Kurys was named Player of the Year in 1946 when she stole 201 bases out of 203 tries. She also hit .286, walked 93 times and scored 117 runs. By the time she retired after the 1950 season Kurys had stolen 1,114 bases and scored 688 runs. She made the all-star team from 1944 to 1949. After the Belles moved in 1950, Kurys switched to fast-pitch softball and joined the Admiral Music Maids of Chicago. They won the championship for the National Women's Softball League. In 1952 she returned to baseball, joining the Battlecreek Belles for 17 games. In 1955 Kurys played one season for the A–1 Queens in Arizona. When not playing baseball Kurys worked for a Apex Machine Products, Inc., where she stayed until her retirement in 1972. In addition to playing baseball Kurys became an avid golfer, even attending Scottsdale Community College on a golf scholarship. In 1986 Kurys was recognized for her achievements with her selection into the Greater Flint Area Sports Hall of Fame. {AAGPBL Newsletter, May 2001, 30; AAGPBL Questionnaire, National Baseball Hall of Fame.}

Rebecca Chacon giving high fives to Erin Layton as she is introduced for the New Jersey Diamonds (courtesy Laura Wulf).

Ladies' Days

Ladies' days were adopted in the nineteenth century by a number of teams not only to increase general attendance but, more importantly, to help improve the behavior of those in the stands. In 1884 the Brooklyn team was pleased to see a large number of ladies in attendance, as it showed that the ladies were aware of what was happening in the national game. {"Base Ball," *Brooklyn Daily Eagle*, 15 August 1884, 2.}

Ladies of Hallsport

A baseball club of nine ladies from Hallsport was established in 1867 and encouraged to play by the local paper, which claimed baseball was a better sport than other current pastimes for ladies. {"The Ladies of Hallsport," *Rochester Evening Express*, 21 September 1867.}

Ladies Professional Baseball League

A league founded in 1997 as the first professional women's baseball league since the 1950s. The founder was Michael Ribant, owner of Trinity Capital in San Diego, California. Part of Ribant's motivation came from his own daughter, who wanted to be a cheerleader. Ribant wanted to show her there were other alternatives for girls. The other league officials were Rob Schupp,

vice president; Marizza Paoli, the director of promotions; and Ken Jacobs, the director of business operations. This league had four original teams: the San Jose Spitfires, the Los Angeles Legends, the Phoenix Peppers and the Long Beach Aces. Each team had 20 players on their roster and a 60–game schedule was planned. The league only lasted one 30–game season before folding shortly into the second year due to low attendance. The league had tried to expand in 1998 to New York and New Jersey while also moving one of the California teams to Florida. The league also got a boost when nine former members of the Colorado Silver Bullets joined the league after the Bullets folded. One of the nine was Kim Braatz-Voisard, who came on

Nikki Gwinett holding a runner at first for the New Jersey Diamonds in 1998 (courtesy Laura Wulf).

board to help coach the Buffalo Nighthawks. The other new teams were the Florida Legends and the New Jersey Diamonds. Ribant made these moves in an effort to increase the fan base. The costs of running the league included umpires, renting a stadium, publicity, airfare and hotels for the players, and salaries. {David Dorsey, "Pro League Bolstered by Ex–Silver Bullets," *USA Today*, 9 July 1998; R.S. Eldridge, "Our Home-grown Professional Sports League," *San Diego Metropolitan Magazine*, March 1998; Barry Jackson, "Women's League Puts Team in Homestead," *Miami Herald*, 9 April 1998.}

One of the other things that finally hurt the league was the conviction of founder Michael Ribant on fraud charges. In 1999 Ribant pled guilty to defrauding investors of over $2.8 million through Trinity Capital, his brokerage firm between 1993 and 1998. The expected sentence was to be 30 months in prison and being barred from dealing with any brokers in the future. {Michael Learmonth, "Ruthless Babes," *Metroactive*, 21–27 August 1997; "Founder of Women's League Michael Ribant Pleads Guilty to Fraud," *Associated Press*, 24 September 1999; "Ladies Professional Baseball Has Struck Out," *Long Beach Press Bulletin*, 30 July 1998.}

Lafirenza, Chris

P 2003, Alameda Oaks

Chris Lafirenza tried out for the Silver Bullets in 1994 and has played on an old-timers men's team with her husband Steve since 1998. In 2003 she joined the Alameda Oaks of the California Women's Baseball League at age 42. {Steve Herendeen, "Women Who Love Diamonds," *Alameda Times-Star*, 21 February 2003.}

Lagocki, Jolene "Jo"

(b. 30 October) P/IF, Detroit Danger

Jo Lagocki played for the Detroit Danger in 2005 after having played softball at Southlake High School. {Danger Web Site.}

Lakasik, Sue "Rookie"

P/OF 2000–01, Chicago Storm

Sue Lakasik played for the Chicago Storm in the Great Lakes Women's Baseball League in 2000 and 2001. She was elected to the National Women's Baseball Hall of Fame in 2000 based primarily on her outstanding hitting. For example, during her two seasons with the Storm she hit .466. {<www.baseballglory.com>.}

LaMarine, Karen

(Fitchburg, Massachusetts) OF, Boston Blue Sox

Karen LaMarine patrolled the outfield in 2001 for the Boston Blue Sox. She graduated from Salem State College and works as a physical education teacher.

Lamb, Madison

(Halfmoon Bay, British Columbia) P/Util., Team British Columbia, Team Canada

From 2002 through 2003, Madison Lamb played for her hometown baseball team, even winning MVP honors in 2002 at the Western Canadian Championships. In 2003 she played for Team Canada at the AAU National Championships.

Lamm, Kate

SS, Miracles

Growing up, Kate Lamm always played softball because that was all that was available to her. She got her first chance to play baseball in 1993 with the Miracles. Lamm also worked as an English professor at Nova University. {John Hughes, "Women Get a Chance to Play a Real Game of Baseball," *Fort Lauderdale Sun-Sentinel*, 4 June 1993.}

Lammert, Sue

SS/P, AWBA Knights

Sue Lammert played for the Knights in 1992 and got the chance to be an extra in the film *A League of Their Own*. There she met some of the pioneers that made it possible for her to play. {"Women Play Hardball," *Daily Herald*, 8 July 1992.}

Lancashire, Ruth

(b. 18 May 1982, Etobicoke, Ontario) P, Etobicoke All Stars

In the 1999 USA Baseball Championship, Ruth Lancashire pitched her team to one victory over the San Diego Stix, 6–2. She gave up seven hits in a complete game effort. At the conclusion of the 2000 season she was named Etobicoke Senior Athlete of the Year. She played for Canada in the 2001 Women's World Series, where she lost to Japan. In 2002 she was the MVP for the All-Star Tournament, winning her game against the WBL All-Stars. She also pitched for Canada in the 2004 Women's World Series against South Korea. She is attending the University of Toronto, majoring in education. She plays lacrosse and basketball at the university. {"Canada Shows Well in USA Baseball Championship," *AWBL Baserunner*, November 1999, 3; "Canada Scores Nine in Baseball Romp," *The Star Phoenix*, 20 July 2004, B3.}

Land, Kimberly

Kim Land was invited to the initial round of tryouts for the inaugural Silver Bullets club. She was a relative newcomer to the game of baseball, since she had played basketball in college. In 1993 she tried out for and made the roster of one of the seven teams playing in the Florida Women's Baseball League. She hit .663 to lead all batters. Her play in that league got her the invite to the Bullets tryouts. She did not make the team in 1994. {*Gettysburg Times*, February 1995.}

Landeweer, Kathy

P 1988–89, Daredevils

Kathy Landeweer pitched for the Daredevils in 1988 and 1989. The Daredevils belonged to the American Women's Baseball League. Landeweer helped her club win the league's inaugural game 11–6 with a homer and a single that she used to drive in four runs. {Bob Gordon, "Daredevils Win Women's Opener, 11–6," *Daily Herald*, 17 July 1988.}

Lang, Margaret "Margie"

(b. 19 February 1924, Cincinnati, Ohio) 1B/P 1943, South Bend Blue Sox

Margie Lang played sparingly during the Blue Sox inaugural season and then returned to playing softball in Chicago, Phoenix and New Orleans. {AAGPBL Baseball Cards, 2000.}

Langevin, Kristen

During the 1999 season Kristen Langevin led the junior league in RBIs, making her one of the most feared hitters in the league. {Greg Botelho, "Pawtucket Slaterettes Having Another Banner Year," *Providence Journal*, 28 June 1999, C-03.}

Langley, Julianne

(b. 20 November 1973) OF, Western Australia

During the 2001 Australian National Tournament, Julianne Langley had the third highest batting average at .545. Her slugging percentage was 1.000 while she scored eight runs. She led the se-

ries with five doubles and stole five bases. {Australian Baseball Federation, <www.baseball.org. au>.}

Langston, Sandra

C 1997–98, Arizona Peppers

Sandra Langston provided the big bat for the Peppers, hitting over .400 in their inaugural season. She attended New Mexico State University on a softball scholarship.

Lantrip, Kay

Management

In 1992 Kay Lantrip worked for the George Hyman Construction Company in Bethesda, Maryland. Her baseball involvement resulted from her role as stadium project manager for the Camden Yards project in Baltimore.

Largent, Bessie Hamilton

Scout

Bessie Largent scouted for the White Sox from 1925 to 1943 with her husband Roy.

Laspina, Melanie

C/1B, San Jose Spitfires

Melanie Laspina played a number of sports at Prospect High School including softball, basketball, and volleyball, and she threw the shot put for track and field. She caught for her high school team and earned MVP honors from 1989 to 1991. Her play earned her a scholarship to Miami University in Oxford, Ohio, as a first baseman. In 1994 she worked as the head coach for Westmont High School's league championship softball squad. She played in the now-defunct Ladies Professional Baseball League and helped start the California Women's Baseball League. While with the Spitfires they won the 1997 championship. Her role with the league is as president and commissioner. In 2003 Laspina also traveled to Arizona to play in the 24–hour marathon game to raise money for AIDS. Laspina used places such as Japan and Canada as her model since women's baseball is much bigger in those countries. When she is not involved with baseball Laspina is a sales manager for the entertainment magazine *The Wave*. {Melanie Laspina, correspondence with Leslie A. Heaphy, North Canton, Ohio, March 2004; Steve Herendeen, "Women Who Love Diamonds," *Tri-Valley Herald*, 21 February 2003.}

Laurie, Jen

3B, Manhattan Giants

Jen Laurie is the third baseman for the Manhattan Giants and is known on the team for her solid hitting. {Michael Malone, "Throwing Like a Girl," *New York Sports Express*, n.d.}

Lawson, Marie

1993, AWBA Gators

Marie Lawson played for the Gators in 1993, paying the $35 admission fee to be a part of this league. {Carrie Muskat, "Playing Hardball's a Down and Dirty Escape from Real Life," *Chicago Tribune*, 27 June 1993, 1, 11.}

Lawson, Mary

OF 1946, Peoria Red Wings

Mary Lawson played for one year with the Red Wings in the All American League.

Leatherwood, Cherie

P, California Sabres

Cherie Leatherwood has been involved in women's baseball as both a player and a board member. In 2003 she served on the AAU Women's Baseball Committee as it met to organize women's tournaments. She played for the Sabres in 2002 and 2003, and pitched for them at the Roy Hobbs AAU National Championships both years. She beat the Chicago Storm in a 2002 game 6-2 and went 1-3 at the plate. {Roy Hobbs Web Site.}

Leduc (Alverson), Noella "Pinky"

(b. 23 December 1933, Graniteville, Massachusetts) P/OF 1951–54, Peoria Red Wings, Battle Creek Belles, Muskegon Lassies, Fort Wayne Daisies

Noella Leduc grew up in a small town where all the kids played together. During the summer they played baseball and in the fall they played football; and that included the girls. After graduation Leduc joined the All American League and had some wonderful experiences. For example, she hit home runs in back-to-back games in 1954 and pitched a 14–inning game in 1952. She played in 144 games and pitched in 67 where she compiled a 15–23 record. She hit only .195 but did score 33 runs in only 52 hits. After the league folded she went to work for the Millipore Filter Company in Bedford, Massachusetts, and got

married in 1964 to George Alverson. They had one daughter, Betsy. {AAGPBL Questionnaire, National Baseball Hall of Fame; AAGPBL Baseball Cards, 1995.}

Lee (Harmon), Annabelle "Lefty"

(California) P/1B 1944–50, Minneapolis Millerettes, Peoria Red Wings, Grand Rapids Chicks, Fort Wayne Daisies

Annabelle Lee grew up in a household that knew baseball. Her father Bill played for the Hollywood Stars in the Pacific Coast League and her mother's nephew Bill pitched for the Boston Red Sox. Her mom Hazel played softball, as did Annabelle. She was playing in a Hollywood league when one of the scouts for the AAGPBL saw her play and invited her to tryouts in Illinois. She made the league and received her first assignment to Minneapolis, where she pitched a complete game for them on July 29. Her career numbers included a 63–96 record with a 2.25 ERA in 186 games pitched. She also played in 230 games and batted only .147. After her days in the AAGPBL ended, Lee played softball in California for a number of years and went to work for an electronics company. She gave up playing after injuring her rotator cuff, and then she got married in 1957. {AAGPBL Baseball Cards, 1996; Diane Pucin, "This 'Lefty' Is Right on the Mark," *Los Angeles Times*, 23 December 1998; AAGPBL Newsletter, January 2002, 26.}

Lee, Deanne Maree

(b. 26 June 1973, Victoria) OF, Victorian Women's Baseball Club, 2004 Australian National Team

Deanne Lee has been playing baseball for various Australian teams from the Victoria region since 2000. She traveled with her clubs to the United States, Canada and Japan. She grew up playing baseball and softball as did her sister Vanessa. Deanne started playing when she was seven and has played on men's and women's teams over the years. She liked playing with the men because it improved her skills and made her a better ball player in the women's league. In 2001 she was chosen to be one of 20 players on the Australian National Team that represented Australia in the first Women's World Series in Toronto. She was chosen the Victoria Division One MVP in 2001–02 and helped lead Australia to victory in the 2002 World Series with three RBIs in the final 7–1 victory. In the 2003 series

Lee hit .333 in six games with runs batted in. {"Lees' Sibling Rivalry," *Diamond Valley Leader*, 10 March 2004, 27; Sean Callander, "Bundoora Slugger," *Diamond Valley Leader*, 25 September 2002; Australian Baseball Federation, <www.baseball.org.au>.}

Lee (Dries), Dolores Margaret "Pickles"

(b. 21 April 1935, Jersey City, New Jersey) P/IF 1952–54, Rockford Peaches, Allington All-Stars

Dolores Lee grew up in the Garfield region of New Jersey and was discovered while still attending St. Dominic's Academy. She tried out and made the AAGPBL, went back to finish high school, and then started playing at age 16. Though her school had no sports for girls the local area provided a range of opportunities through the CYO leagues. She played basketball from 1948 to 1952 for St. Paul's. She also played baseball, stickball and basketball with her brothers and the other boys in the neighborhood. She started playing baseball competitively at age 12 for Al Santora's Village Boys club and for the Garfield Flashettes. She found out about the Flashettes while playing for the Santora club. A policeman saw her playing and introduced her to a girl on the squad. She played with the Flashettes for five years. The manager and coach of the team happened to be Slim Berger, father of AAGPBL player Joan Berger. He took her to Rockford for a tryout when she turned 16. In 1953 Dolores played a full season and was named Rookie of the Year. She made an appearance on the television program *What's My Line* because of that honor. She pitched in 53 games with a record of 23–22 and an ERA of 3.01. {AAGPBL Newsletter, January 2002, 18.}

Two former All-American ballplayers, Ann Meyer and Dolores Dries, reminiscing about their glory days.

After playing for three years in the AAGPBL, Lee toured for another four years with Bill Allington's team. After her baseball days ended Lee became the first female police officer in the Jersey City police department, joining the force in 1958. She married fellow officer Johannes Dries Jr. in 1963 and divorced him in 1971. They had one son, Johannes Dries III. Lee was inducted into the Hudson County Athletic Hall of Fame for her achievements in 1995. {AAGPBL Newsletter, May 1995, 8; AAGPBL Questionnaire, National Baseball Hall of Fame: AAGPBL Baseball Cards, 1995.}

Lee, Laurie Ann

(b. 3 January 1931, Racine, Wisconsin) P 1948, Racine Belles

Laurie Ann Lee grew up watching the Belles and finally got invited to spring training at age 17 in 1948. Unfortunately, she broke her finger during spring training and never got a chance to play in the regular season because it did not heal correctly. She went into the military and then managed an electronics manufacturing firm for 30 years. She also owned and managed a company in the swimming pool business. {AAGPBL Baseball Cards, 2000.}

Lee, Vanessa

(b. 1976) P, Lady Mariners

Vanessa Lee played for the Victoria Lady Mariners in Australia. Her sister Deanne also played baseball.

Legge, Derika

SS

Having played softball for many years, Derika Legge was invited in 2003 to join the NYWBA when her team folded. Legge became the starting shortstop for the Queens Cyclones. When she is not playing baseball Derika is an executive in the sales department for Heinekin. {Michael Malone, "Throwing Like a Girl," *New York Sports Express*, 28 August–3 September 2003, 15.}

Lehane, Kerron

P 2003, Australia

Kerron Lehane pitched for Australia in the 2003 Women's World Series. She made two appearances and pitched just over eight innings, giving up 15 hits and 12 runs. Only six of the runs were actually earned so her ERA was 6.86.

Lemasters, Keri Michelle

(b. 29 August 1975, Panorama City, California)
2B/SS/P, Los Angeles/Florida Legends, 2001–2003
Team America, 2004 USA National Team

Keri Lemasters graduated from Canyon High School in 1993 and attended Michigan State University on a softball scholarship. While there she earned a variety of honors as the club's shortstop and second baseman. She started every game (234) during her four years at MSU and set the single-season record for hits, doubles, extra-base hits and runs scored. She set career records in triples, doubles, hits, extra-base hits and runs scored. She received recognition by being named to the All–Great Lakes Region and All–Big Ten teams all four seasons. In 1996 she was also named an NCAA All-American. From 1997 to 1999 she played on the USA National Softball Team and then in 2001 began play for Team America in the first three Women's World Series. At the 2002 series Lemasters played third base instead of shortstop after Donna Mills was injured. At the plate she helped the USA beat Australia in the first round with three RBIs and a 2–4 night at the plate. In 2004, coaches selected her as a member of the USA National Team. She came out of the fourth World Series event hitting .364 with two RBIs. She hit in six of nine games and had extra-base hits in two of those games. She followed that performance with a .250 average in the 2004 women's World Cup. Lemasters works a police officer when she is not playing baseball. In fact, she had been on the police force in North Carolina but moved to Massachusetts so she could join the NEWBL. {Adam Gilgore, "A Grass Roots Campaign," *The Boston Globe*, 11 June 2004; Sam Santurf, "Injury Subs Lead Team USA Past Australia in Series," *St. Petersburg Times*, 4 September 2002, 3C; USA Baseball Web site.}

Lenard, Josephine "Jo," "Bubblegum"

(b. 2 September 1921, Chicago, Illinois) OF 1944–53, Rockford Peaches, Muskegon Lassies, Peoria Red Wings, Kenosha Comets, South Bend Blue Sox

Josephine Lenard played for ten years in the All American League. By the time her career in the AAGPBL ended, Lenard had knocked in 351 runs to place her ninth on the career RBI list for the league. A typical season for Lenard was 1947, when she played in 111 games for the Lassies and hit .261 while knocking in 38 runs. She also stole 83 bases and only struck out 30 times. Her career numbers included 1,000 games, a .221 batting average and 465 runs scored. She stole 520 bases and walked 481 times against only 234 strikeouts. In just over 3400 at-bats she only had one home run. After her baseball career Lenard went back to school and graduated from Chicago Teachers College, and then taught health and physical education for 25 years. {AAGPBL Newsletter, January 2002, 29; AAGPBL Baseball Cards, 2000.}

Lent, Sue

(Peekskill, New York) OF

Prior to the 2003 baseball season Sue Lent had played slow- and fast-pitch softball but never baseball. Lent found the game of baseball faster but liked the pace and the concentration it required. {Rick Carpiniello, "A League for Those Who Say Softball Isn't Enough," *The Journal News*, 9 June 2003.}

Leonard (Linehan), Rhoda Ann "Nicky"

(b. 31 January 1928, Worcester, Massachusetts)
2B/RF 1946, Fort Wayne Daisies

Rhoda Leonard graduated from Somerset High School in 1946 where she played basketball since it was the only sport available to girls. She also played softball in a summer league for six years and then she went on to college. In between her high school graduation and the start of college in the fall of 1946 Leonard played for the Fort Wayne Daisies. Her start in the league was a bit rocky, as she struck out her first time up and made an error on her first fielding chance, but the team did not send her home. She ended up playing in nine games and batted 21 times, though she only had two hits. She graduated from Bridgewater State College with a BS in education and became an elementary school teacher. She played softball, basketball and tennis in college, though the girls played mostly among themselves rather than against other schools. She got married to Edward Linehan in 1953 and they had two children. She received a great honor from her high school when they inducted her into the Somerset High School Hall of Fame. A photograph of her and the glove she played with are displayed in the New England Sports Museum in Cambridge, Massachusetts. {AAGPBL Questionnaire, National Baseball Hall of Fame; AAGPBL Baseball Cards, 1995.}

Lequia (Barker), Joan "Joanie"

(b. 13 March 1935, Negaunee, Michigan) 3B/P 1953, Grand Rapids Chicks

Joan Lequia saw limited action with the Chicks in 1953, playing in fewer than ten games which meant no statistics were kept. She left the league to play fast-pitch softball in the Marquette, Michigan, area, leading her teams to two state championships over the years. She hit .390 in her softball career. {AAGPBL Baseball Cards, 1995.}

Lessing, Ruth Elizabeth "Tex"

(b. 15 August 1925, San Antonio, Texas; d. 26 October 2000, San Antonio, Texas) 1944–49, Minneapolis Millerettes, Fort Wayne Daisies, Grand Rapids Chicks

Ruth Lessing played a number of sports while attending Jefferson High School. She also played on the local sandlots for teams such as the Alamo Jewelry Company. She left home at 18 to join the Minneapolis Millerettes and then the Grand Rapids Chicks, where she stayed until she retired after the 1949 season. One of Lessing's more famous moments in the league came when she was fined $100 for slugging umpire George Johnson. The fans took up a collection to help her pay the fine, and she was able to do that and give a substantial sum to charity. Lessing played in 112 games in 1946 but batted only .215. In 1947 she again played in 111 games but hit only .205. Her career numbers included 559 games, hitting .191 and driving in 164 runs. She also made the all-star team in 1946, 1947 and 1948. Lessing was an incredibly durable player, holding the league record for most games for a catcher in a single season, with 125. She also had the record for the highest fielding percentage for a catcher, at .982. Her career got cut short in 1949 when she injured her shoulder and had to quit. {AAGPBL Newsletter, January 2001, 29; AAGPBL Baseball Cards, 2000; Helmer, 124.}

Leveque, Nancy

(Streamwood, Illinois) AWBA

While growing up in the 1940s and 1950s Nancy Leveque did not play sports, because there were none for girls. She joined the AWBA in its first season, hoping to play and manage. When not playing baseball Leveque is a veterinarian. She attended Michigan State, the University of Illinois and the University of Pennsylvania. She has practiced in Lake Tahoe, Houston and Las Vegas. {"She's a Vet — In More Ways Than One," *Base Woman Newsletter* (June 1988) 3.}

Lewaine, Rochelle "Shelley"

(b. 1971, Hawaii) San Jose Spitfires

Rochelle Lewaine became the lead-off hitter for the San Jose Spitfires because of her small stature and speed. Standing only 5′1″ and weighing in at 110 pounds, Lewaine had the smallest strike zone on the team. She was a constant threat to get on base and when she did she caused havoc for opposing pitchers.

Liao, Pei-Chun

1B, Taiwan

Pei-Chun Liao played first base for Taiwan in the 2004 women's World Cup. She hit .455 and drove in four runs. In the field she handled all her chances flawlessly.

Liebrich, Barbara "Bobbie"

(b. 30 September 1922, Providence, Rhode Island) 2B/3B 1948–49, Springfield Sallies; 1952–54, Kalamazoo chaperone

Barbara Liebrich grew up in a baseball-playing household. Her father pitched for many years and she played softball for the Auburn Royals, the Monowatt Electric Company and the Riverside Townies. She played for two years in the All American League and then stayed on as a chaperone — because she did not want to end her connection to the league — until the league folded in 1954. {Rick Harris, "Women, Baseball and Rhode Island," in *Rhode Island's Baseball Legacy*, Vol. 1 (Rhode Island: Rick Harris, 2001), 29; AAGPBL Baseball Cards, 1996.}

Lillywhite, Shae Amanda

(b. 19 January 1985) SS/2B, Springvale, Victoria, 2004 Australian National Team

Shae Lillywhite hit .438 during the 2003 Women's World Series. She started five games and scored nine runs on seven hits and six walks. She also made only two errors in the field, for a .931 fielding percentage. At the 2004 Australian National Women's Championships she stole six bases for the second highest total during the series. In the 2004 World Cup she led all hitters by batting .556 with five hits in nine at-bats.

Limoges, Andrea

(b. 30 September 1979, Edmonton, Alberta) 2B/OF, Team Canada

Andrea Limoges played for Canada in the 2002 Women's World Baseball Championship played in Geelong, Australia. In addition Limoges has played for Canada in each of the four Women's World Series since that series began in 2001. When not playing baseball Limoges is getting a Ph.D. in physical therapy from Regis University in Denver, Colorado. She had attended the University of Alberta and then Oklahoma Panhandle State University on a softball scholarship. Limoges actually got her introduction to baseball after she moved to Colorado in 2002 and found a league there; she played for the Denver Suns. Before playing baseball Limoges played softball from 1998 to 2002 in Edmonton, Alberta. {Norm Crowley, "Playing Women's Baseball Has Its Perks, Limoges Discovers," *Edmonton Journal,* 8 June 2004; Baseball Canada 2004 Women's National Team Media Guide.}

Lindeborg, Chris

(Pawcatuck, Connecticut) P/1B, Boston Blue Sox

Chris Lindeborg played tennis, soccer and basketball while growing up, in addition to softball. She graduated from Bentley College with a degree in business communication and currently works in sales. Lindeborg took up baseball with the founding of the NEWBL, which she helps run. She also plays for the Bay State Express and the Boston Blue Sox. {Boston Blue Sox Web site.}

Line, Cassandra

(New Lowell, Ontario) 2B, Team Canada

Cassandra Line played baseball on a boys' Midget League squad and hopes to someday play baseball at a university. In 2003 she played for Team Canada as a 15–year-old in the AAU National Championships.

Little, Aimee

Bantam Hawks

In 2003 Aimee Little played her eighth season of baseball with the Dominion Bantam Hawks. Her main position was second base for the club. Little also plays basketball and won a regional championship in that sport.

Little, Alta

(b. 21 May 1923, Muskegon, Michigan) 1B 1944–46, Muskegon Lassies, Fort Wayne Daisies

Alta Little got the chance to play in the All American League when a scout saw her playing softball near Grand Rapids and invited her to a tryout. After playing for three seasons at first base Little got actively involved in bowling. She eventually became the Texas director of operations for Don Carter's All Star Lanes. In 1995 she was invited to Arlington stadium to throw out the first pitch before a game between the Rangers and A's. {AAGPBL Newsletter, January 1996, 14; AAGPBL Baseball Cards, 1996.}

Little (Bend), Olive "Ollie"

(b. 17 May 1917, Poplar Point, Manitoba; d. 2 February 1987) P 1943, 1945–46, Rockford Peaches

Though small in stature Olive Little was a powerful pitcher who was not afraid of any hitter. She never hesitated to pitch inside, even breaking the wrist of one batter for crowding the plate. Before joining the Rockford Peaches, Little pitched for two provincial softball championship teams. In 1943 she made the all-star team and pitched the AAGPBL's first no-hit, no-run game. Her lifetime ERA was 2.41 and the fans of Rockford loved her for it. They hosted two "Olive Little" nights while she played for the Peaches. She received a final recognition of her outstanding play when she was inducted into the Canadian BB Hall of Fame in 1983. {Canadian Baseball Hall of Fame; AAGPBL Baseball Cards, 2000.}

Little League

By Tim Wiles

The fight to allow girls to play Little League baseball in the early 1970s is a little-examined and highly significant chapter in the history of females in the game. Between 1970 and 1975, as many as 57 separate lawsuits were filed in 20 different states on behalf of girls who were prohibited from playing youth baseball, in Little League proper and also in independent municipal leagues. The male resistance to the participation of girls is not only significant in itself, but also suggests a pervasive antipathy toward females participating in baseball at any level. At the height of the controversy, Little League baseball in New Jersey shut down over 2,000 local leagues rather than comply with a state order to allow girls to play. It is useful to examine the chain of events leading up to this battle of the sexes in youth baseball.

The earliest known instance of a girl competing in a youth baseball league is the 1928 saga of Margaret Gisolo, of the Blanford, Indiana, American

Legion team. American Legion Junior Baseball, which may have been the first organized youth baseball program in the country, was founded in 1925. By 1928, 13–year-old Gisolo played second base for Blanford all season long, without controversy. But in the first game of tournament play, her game-winning single in the twelfth inning caused the opposing team to cry foul, citing rules which, while they did not expressly prohibit girls, noted that "any boy can play." It is noteworthy that her success in a playoff game fueled the controversy surrounding her play. Again and again, we will see that it is not simply participation that males object to, but particularly, successful participation, which seems to bother some males.

The protests escalated, as did national media coverage of both her success and the ensuing controversy, as the Blanford Cubs reached ever higher levels of play. Within a few weeks, national American Legion officials, in consultation with Major League Baseball commissioner Kenesaw Mountain Landis, had ruled her eligible to continue playing. The Cubs won the Indiana state championship, and Margaret finished the seven-game state tournament with a batting average of .429 and no errors in the field. However, in 1929, American Legion Junior Baseball prohibited the participation of girls, ruling that separate locker rooms, hotel rooms, and chaperones would prove financially prohibitive. This rationale for prohibiting girls to play was one of several that would reappear throughout the history of girls attempting to play baseball, and some would see it as a sham. "Apparently it was [okay] for Margaret to play second base for the opposition until she got too good," opined the *Indianapolis Times*.

In 1950, the first known case of a girl playing Little League baseball occurred in Corning, New York. When her brother announced his intention to try out for Little League, Kathryn Johnston indicated she would be joining him. He told her that she couldn't try out because she was a girl. Kathryn, a self described tomboy, tucked her short hair under a cap and tried out as "Tubby Johnston," borrowing the nickname from a male character in her *Little Lulu* comic books.

She made the team and played first base for a couple of weeks before revealing her true gender to the coach, who vowed to keep her on the team, as she was a good player. Her playing garnered mild publicity in Corning, and some parents complained about her presence on the field, but she finished the season. The next year, Little League headquarters in Williamsport, Pennsylvania, instituted a rule that stated, "Girls are not eligible under any conditions." Lance Van Auken,

a spokesman for Little League and the author of a history of the organization, says that there is no direct evidence that Little League passed the rule because of Kathryn, but that Little League officials were aware of her, and the timing of the rule change was probably more than coincidental.

A UPI news photo from 1960 identifies ten-year-old Trudy Shea as "the only girl little leaguer in New England," and celebrates her "rare accomplishment" as "one in a million." Trudy played catcher for a Little League team called the South End Settlement House in 1960, and the accompanying caption states that her male teammates, "in all candor, say she is as good a baseball player as they are."

In 1963, Nancy Lotsey played baseball in the New Jersey Small Fry League. While not affiliated with Little League, this youth baseball league was similar in scope. Initially rejected because of her sex, Nancy came back a second year and was placed on a team. She was the winning pitcher and hit a home run in her debut. "I loved it," she said. "There was no danger, no psychological damage. I could play better than most of the boys on the team." No psychological damage for Nancy, anyway. Some of the boys and their parents may have disagreed. While no one wanted to admit it, one of the underlying stories was the idea of boys getting humiliated, struck out by, or losing to, a girl.

Carol Tobias of Rock Hill, South Carolina, played baseball on a local boys' Little League team in 1966. While Carol's coach had to persuade other league officials to allow her to play, "The boys on the team agree that adding Carol to the squad was their smartest move, and the record supports them. The team credits Carol with contributing consistently to the high scores it achieved in the season's record of nineteen wins and only one loss." Her father adds, "It's just like having another boy, the way she goes for baseball, and I'm really proud of her." Her brother Neal echoed the sentiment: "I think she's great, and I'm glad I had a hand in her training. She's almost like a brother to me." Carol herself said, "I just like to play baseball. If they don't want girls to play Little League with the boys, they ought to have a girls' league."

Another interesting case occurred in Charlotte, North Carolina, in 1966–67. Charlene Rowe, ten years old in 1966, was told that she could not play on a boys' Little League team. Rather than deprive his daughter of the chance to play baseball, Ralph Rowe, who incidentally was employed that summer as the manager of the minor league Orlando Twins of the Florida State League, simply started a team for his daughter, and recruited the other players. The team took on all comers. The second year, the team lacked a sponsor, and 11–year-old Charlene took it upon herself to contact Phil Howser, president and general manager of the Charlotte Hornets, a professional team in the Southern League. The Hornets agreed to sponsor the Junior Hornets, and the uniforms looked just as good as they might have in Little League. Jack Williams, coach of the Junior Hornets, said, "She's as good as any of the boys. None of the boys we play against would dare kid her. They know they can't beat her."

The cases of Kathryn, Nancy, Carol, and Charlene are the only four known cases of girls playing in Little League or similar youth baseball programs in the 1950s and 1960s. Each generated press coverage at the local or national level, and their stories were found rather easily in the files on women in baseball kept at the National Baseball Hall of Fame library. No one knows how many more girls attempted to play in such leagues during the '50s and '60s, but it stands to reason that there were others. In reading the press coverage of these four girls, it is striking that they generated far less controversy than the girls who would follow them onto the diamond in the 1970s. The general tone of the coverage is bemused tolerance of the "tomboy" nature of the girls in question. It is implied that they would grow out of their love of the game, and soon would engage in more feminine pursuits. While it is noted that the girls in question were usually skilled players, few notes of objection were raised in any of these four cases. This would change in the 1970s.

The first girl to play Little League in the '70s was 12–year-old Sharon Poole, of Haverhill, Massachusetts. Sharon was recruited in 1971 to play on the Indians by coach Donald Sciuto after another player headed off for summer vacation. She took the field for a game against the Twins, whose coach Donald Daggett immediately protested. The local league, Riverside-Bradford League, was unaffiliated with Little League Baseball Incorporated, and no specific rule barred girls from playing.

Sharon batted cleanup against the Twins and walked once, scored once, knocked in a run with a single, and struck out. She fielded well in center field, and the Indians won 7–5. A few days later, she played in a 2–1 Indians victory over the Yankees. The league's ten managers called a meeting after this game and ordered Sharon to leave the Indians, declaring the games she played null and void. The league also dismissed Indians manager Sciuto. The league coaches insisted that Sharon

was not dumped because she was a girl, but rather because she was an illegal player, on the basis of the fact that she had never tried out and participated in the league draft. According to the other coaches, six undrafted players remained available. They should have been recruited before anyone else. Sciuto disputed that claim.

The case drew press attention from the *Boston Globe* and the *New York Times*, whose article included a consultation with Dr. Creighton Hale, a physiologist and director of research at Little League Baseball headquarters in Williamsport, Pennsylvania. Dr. Hale cited "fundamental physical and metabolic differences between growing girls and boys," as well as "slower reaction time" for girls, and a lower "compression breaking load" for the bones of young females versus males, in saying that "there are certain activities in which girls should not participate against boys." The American Medical Association's committee on the medical aspects of sports declared in the same article that it knew of no such studies. The story ended with the sentence, "Sharon, meanwhile, denied speculation that the experience would make her join women's liberation." Clearly the charged climate of the early 1970s made Sharon more newsworthy than her predecessors.

The next weekend, the *New York Times* editorialized on the incident, comparing Sharon's dismissal to an employment law case, saying, "No one contended that she lacked proficiency or even that her personality jarred on her working colleagues. She was fired because she was female, though a few technical and quickly refuted pretexts were advanced to cover up an otherwise blatant defense of the male ego." The editorial went on to criticize the whole atmosphere surrounding youth baseball, saying that the parents "seemed to take themselves almost as grimly as they take the game." Lastly, the *Times* sounded a word of warning: "No doubt Sharon Poole, at age 12, is ahead of her time. So was Satchel Paige. If it is any comfort to her, that great Negro pitcher of long ago is now being belatedly admitted to baseball's Hall of Fame. It is improbable that Sharon has any such objective; but if sex discrimination is on her mind, as well it might, she won't have to wait nearly as long as Satchel for vindication." By comparing Sharon's case both to employment discrimination and the long exclusion of African-Americans from baseball, the *Times* set the stage for a major battle in the "war between the sexes," fought on little green diamonds across the USA.

In 1972, 12–year-old Maria Pepe of Hoboken, New Jersey, tried out for and made the Young Democrats Little League team. The pitcher-outfielder played in three games before Little League Baseball headquarters in Williamsport notified the local league that its charter would be revoked if Pepe were allowed to continue playing. Charter revocation carried with it the loss of affiliation with the national program, which meant that the local league would lose the right to send teams to regional tournaments and to the Little League World Series. It also meant the local league could no longer purchase insurance through the national organization. Faced with this censure, the local league removed Maria from the team.

The Essex County chapter of the National Organization for Women (NOW) filed suit on Maria's behalf in May 1972, before the New Jersey Division of Civil Rights. The suit contended that Little League, while technically a private organization, utilized public facilities and public funds in carrying out its local programs, and as such, was required to forgo discrimination on the basis of sex. The legal process took more than a year, and at one point, Little League's Dr. Creighton Hale testified, repeating his concerns about girls' likelihood of injury due to what he saw as their physical inferiority. Other doctors testified that there were no substantial physical differences between boys and girls of Little League age.

On 7 November 1973, New Jersey Hearing Officer Sylvia B. Pressler ruled on the case, rejecting both the notion that Little League was not a public accommodation, and the notion that girls were physically inferior to boys and thus needed to be protected from the possibility of injury when competing with them. Her finding stated that "Little League is as American as hot dogs and apple pie. I am perfectly satisfied that there is absolutely no basis ... why that piece of public Americana should be withheld from girls." Pressler also noted that "the sooner little boys begin to realize that there are many areas of life in which girls are their equal and that it is no great shame, no great burden to be bested by a girl, then perhaps ... we come that much closer to the legislative ideal of sexual equality as well as to relieving a source of emotional difficulty for men."

The ruling came too late for Maria Pepe, who was 13 and too old to play Little League by November 1973, but it was set to open Little League's doors, both locally and nationally, to girls in the spring of 1974. Except that Little League still wished to fight. That spring, they asked the New Jersey courts to stay Pressler's decision, and sent a letter to 330 leagues in New Jersey, representing 2,000 or more teams. After characterizing Pressler's decision as "an outrageous and punitive order conceived in vindictive and prejudicial fashion," the letter went on to encourage local officials to "become articulate," to seek "equal time on television, radio, and in newspapers," and to warn the public that "Little League is in danger of being destroyed by a power-mad current combine of ambitionists who have overreached themselves."

While the letter helped generate grassroots opposition to the court decision—an attempt was made to present a petition with 50,000 signatures against girls playing Little League—the appellate division of New Jersey Superior Court ruled against Little League, and ordered the season to begin, with girls. In May of that year, many New Jersey girls tried out for Little League, and many played. Media accounts vary, with some highlighting the athletic ability of specific girls, and others suggesting that most of the girls were prodded into trying out by their feminist mothers. Judith Wenning, the national task force coordinator on sports for NOW, said the organization hoped the ruling would set a national precedent on the subject of girls playing baseball. At least two other high profile cases were pending in other states, including Carolyn King's attempt to play in Ypsilanti, Michigan, and Jenny Fulle's case in Mill Valley, California. Attempts continued to stop or delay girls' participation, and a bill was introduced in the New Jersey State Assembly hoping to delay girls' participation by one year, ostensibly to give local branches time to implement new policies and procedures to handle both girls and boys. In early April 1974, that bill, which would have been vetoed by Governor Byrne, lost by a 39–38 vote. In early May, after many leagues had already admitted girls, New Jersey threatened to hold the league presidents of five local Little Leagues in contempt of court if they continued to exclude girls. In June of 1974, Little League headquarters in Williamsport announced that it would "defer to the changing social climate," and abandon its fight—in New Jersey and other jurisdictions—against girls playing Little League.

While New Jersey had made it clear that girls could play, other cases dragged on in other states. In mid–December 1974, President Ford signed a bill that changed Little League's congressional charter so that the word "boys" was replaced by "young people" wherever it appeared. The change was requested by Little League, which sought to bring its charter in line with its new position of admitting girls. By the next spring, the landscape was significantly quieter, as girls played without major incident in New Jersey and elsewhere.

But in a move many saw as contradictory to the spirit of the recent court-mandated guarantee of girls' participation in Little League baseball, Little League formed a softball division in 1974 as well. This struck many as an attempt to channel girls into softball rather than baseball, and some compared the move to the establishment of a "separate, but equal" accommodation, a concept that had been discredited by the Brown vs. Board of Education Supreme Court decision of 1954. Initially, the softball program generated 30,000 participants nationwide — many more girls than were playing baseball. (Little League has never collected data on the number of girls playing baseball.) The softball programs grew and now comprise nearly 400,000 girls — and a few boys — playing softball annually. Advocates of baseball for girls and women continually wonder what the baseball landscape might look like today if a significant number of those 400,000 girls were developing baseball — rather than softball — skills at a young age.

Livernois, Kimberly "8 Mile," "Berly"

(b. 6 June) OF, Detroit Danger

Kim Livernois grew up in Michigan and started playing softball when she was seven. Her coach was former AAGPBL player Helen Steffes. She wanted to play baseball but was told that girls only played softball. She graduated from Southlake High School and went on to get a degree in computer science from Davenport University. After working for several years in the information technology field Livernois has gone back to school at Wayne State in forensic science.

Livernois's first chance to play baseball came in 2004 when she attended the Tigers Fantasy Camp for two weeks. That experience convinced her to join the Detroit Danger for the 2005 season. {Danger Web site.}

Lohmann, Tammy

SS 1998, Arizona Peppers

Tammy Lohmann played softball for Arizona State University before joining the Arizona Peppers in the Ladies Professional Baseball League.

Lonetto, Sarah "Tomato"

(b. 9 June 1922, Detroit, Michigan) IF/OF/P 1947–49, Racine Belles, Muskegon Lassies

Sarah Lonetto pitched in 20 games and played in another 102 during her time in the All American League. The real highlights for her came with the chance to go to spring training in Cuba in 1947 and to be a part of the South American tour in 1948. She hit only .142 and had a pitching record of 3–9. {AAGPBL Baseball Cards, 1995.}

Long Beach Aces

Coached by Don Barbara, the Long Beach Aces received excellent community support while they were an entrant in the Ladies League, organized by Michael Ribant. Their home games were played at Blair Field. This was made possible by the work of Angie Avery and Ralph Crider, who worked for the city's Department of Parks and Recreation. They paid for the use of the field for the whole summer since the schedule included 48–60 games. {Bob Keisser, "L.B. Adds Another Women's Team to Lineup," *Press-Telegram*, 5 June 1997.}

Long, Sue

CF, San Francisco Bay Sox

Sue Long grew up around the game of baseball because her father, Dick Aylward, was a catcher in the Pacific Coast League and for a short stint with the Cleveland Indians. She played softball in the San Diego Bobby Sox Girls League, starting when she was nine years old. As an adult, when not playing baseball, Long worked in a brokerage firm. {Dwight Chapin, "Believe It or Not: A Fledgling Ladies Baseball League," *San Francisco Examiner*, 11 July 1997.}

Looney, Shelly

WNEBL

Shelly Looney joined the Women's New England Baseball League in 1999 after playing on the 1998 gold medal Olympic hockey team.

Lopez, Celia

South Florida

Celia Lopez grew up playing baseball until she was 11 and her father told her she could not play anymore because she was a girl. In 1992 she returned to the baseball diamond with the South Florida team in the American Women's Baseball Association. The New York Mets and Montreal Expos donated balls and other equipment for the new team. {Judy Battista, "Baseball Lures Would-Be Women Stars," *The Miami Herald*, 14 September 1992.}

Los Angeles Legends

The Legends were an entrant in the short-lived Ladies Professional Baseball League, run by Michael Ribant. They played their home games at Jackie Robinson Memorial Stadium and at the VA Hospital grounds in UCLA. The Legends were led by pitchers Gina Satriano and Janelle Freese-Khramov and manager Bridget Wold. In 1998 the team was moved by the league to Homestead, Florida, because they could not renew their stadium leases. {"Women's Baseball Joins Professional Ranks," PRNewswire, 25 June 1997; Barry Jackson, "Women's League Puts Team in Homestead," *Miami Herald*, 9 April 1998.}

Lotti, Danielle "Boo"

P, Pawtucket Slaterettes

Danielle Lotti had a good season in 1999 with a 6–1 pitching record. Her ERA was 2.29 and she struck out 65 batters. {Greg Botelho, "Pawtucket Slaterettes Having Another Banner Year," *Providence Journal*, 28 June 1999, C–03.}

Lovelace, Ann-Marie

(Tennessee) 1B/SS/2B/P, Team WBL

Ann-Marie Lovelace has played baseball since she was five years old. In 2002 she played for Team WBL at an international tournament in Australia. She is a student at the University of Tennessee at Martin in education.

Lovell (Dowler), Jean "Grump"

(b. Conneaut, Ohio; d. 1 January 1992) C/P 1948–54, Rockford Peaches, Kalamazoo Lassies, Kenosha Comets

Jean Lovell played primarily as a catcher in the All American League, though she did get the opportunity to pitch in 18 games and compiled a 3–10 record with a 4.18 ERA. She played in 470 games and hit .229. In 1954 she had a break out season with 21 home runs when previously she had only hit four in her career. She also hit .286 with a previous best of only .246. In the field she handled almost 1,400 putouts with only 77 errors for a .955 fielding percentage. Unfortunately for Lovell the league folded just as she seemed to be hitting her stride as a player. Lovell played in 15 playoff games and hit .321 with seven RBIs. She saved her hitting for the big games. {AAGPBL Baseball Cards, 2000.}

Luckey, Lillian

(b. 9 July 1919, Niles, Michigan) P 1946, South Bend Blue Sox

Lillian Luckey pitched in eight games for the Blue Sox, winning two and losing four. She enjoyed the chance to play and travel but left the league to return to softball, where her clubs won three Michigan state championships over the years. {AAGPBL Baseball Cards, 1995.}

Ludtke, (Lincoln) Melissa

Sportswriter

Melissa Ludtke wrote for *Sports Illustrated* in the 1970s and made a name for herself when she sued the Yankees for denying her access to the locker room. She sued on the grounds that it was sexual discrimination. Commissioner Kuhn said they broke no laws and that there were plenty of opportunities for female reporters to get their stories.

Luhning, Brittany

(Lumsden) 3B/P, Team Saskatchewan

In 2004 Brittany Luhning played for Team Saskatchewan in the Canadian Bantam National Tournament.

Lukasik, Sue

(b. 1962) P/C/OF/1B 1988–2003, Knights, Chicago Storm

Sue Lukasik has played first base primarily for the Chicago Storm of the Great Lakes Women's Baseball League though she did also play in the American Women's Baseball Association in 1991 as a pitcher, catcher and outfielder. In 2000 Lukasik received the honor of being named to the National Women's Baseball Hall of Fame for her achievements. She also got a chance to be involved in the film *A League of Their Own*. {Lindsey Willihite, "Women Have Few Chances to Play Ball," *Daily Herald*, 14 August 1991.}

Luna (Hill), Betty Jean

(b. 1 May 1927, Los Angeles, Calif.) P/OF 1944–1950, Rockford Peaches, South Bend Blue Sox, Chicago Colleens, Fort Wayne Daisies, Kalamazoo Lassies

Lychak, Kim

OF Alameda Oaks

Kim Lychak led the Oaks in hitting in 2003

with six hits in 15 at-bats. She scored three runs and knocked in two more.

Lynch, Evelyn

1B/P/OF

Evelyn Lynch started her baseball career playing on the New York bloomer team but later joined the Cabin John men's team in the Montgomery County League. In one game against a Bethesda nine, Lynch saved the day with a spectacular catch in the tenth inning. She had already contributed at the plate with a single and a walk. Before playing for Cabin John, Lynch could be found at first base for St. Mary's Celtics. She helped them defeat St. Joseph's 4–3 and handled 11 chances in the field without incident. The game was designed as a benefit for Harry Hall, a local sandlot star.

Lynch also caught for a time for a team called the Linworth Insects and received 50 cents a game for her services. In 1931 she got a chance to try out for the Hollywood Stars when they came to her home town for a benefit game at Griffith Stadium.

{"Girl Is Leader in Cabin John Triumph," *Washington Post*, 2 July 1934, 18; "Girl Plays for Celtics Against St. Joe Team," *Washington Post*, 15 September 1932, 14; "Hollywood Girls to Play Baseball at Stadium Today," *Washington Post*, 1 September 1931, 15; "St. Joseph's Wins from Celtics, 4–3," *Washington Post*, 17 September 1932, 12.}

Lytle, Eleanor

P, Malone Athletics

Pitching for the Malone Athletics of Malone, Wisconsin, Eleanor Lytle quickly made a name for herself as a tough competitor. In her first game against a team from Alburgh, Vermont, the opposing players thought the game would be an easy win for them but changed their tune when Lytle struck out the first two batters. Lytle learned her technique from her father, who was also a pitcher. When she was not practicing her pitching Lytle could be found working on her drawing. {"Girl Pitcher Hurls Way to Mound Fame," *Washington Post*, 28 July 1935, 8.}

MacGregor, Theresa

(b. 1965, Colorado) 2B/SS/P/OF, Denver White Sox, Northern Sluggers

Theresa MacGregor graduated from Heritage High School in 1983. Before joining the San Jose Spitfires in the Ladies League, MacGregor tried out for the Silver Bullets five times. She also played for a number of different Colorado teams before signing on with the Spitfires. MacGregor worked for nine years as a bank teller. She married Dirk MacGregor. Theresa MacGregor joined Team USA in 2001 with eight years of baseball experience behind her. She was invited to the Silver Bullets tryouts in 1995 and started in the outfield for the San Jose Spitfires in 1997–98. After leaving the Spitfires she played for the Northern Sluggers in the Colorado women's league. In 2002 she helped coach Team WBL at the International Women's tournament in Australia. In the 2003 Women's World Series MacGregor hit .357 in five games. She drove in two runs and stole four bases in four attempts. {Australian Baseball Federation, <www.baseball.org.au>.}

MacLane, Mindy

Pawtucket Slaterettes

Mindy MacLane started playing for the Slaterettes when she was eight. She played in the instructional division, the juniors and the seniors. Upon entering high school she made the St. Raphael Academy fast-pitch team because of her baseball skills.

MacLean (Moore, Ross), Lucella "Frenchy," "Lucy," "Lu"

(b. 3 January 1921, Lloydminster, Saskatchewan) C/OF 1943–44, South Bend Blue Sox

Lucella MacLean graduated from Lloydminster High School in 1940. While in school she played basketball and field hockey and ran track and field. Softball belonged to the town and city leagues, where MacLean played from 1935 to 1942. Her teams always seemed to win the Provincial Trophy. When she was not on the ball diamond Lucella worked as a telephone clerk until 1943. In 1944 Lucella came south to join the All American League and was a participant in the league's first triple play that year. She played in a total of 101 games, hitting .204 and driving in 25 runs.

In 1946 she joined the Chicago National Softball League and played through the 1952 season. She stayed in the States, working, until 1959 and then returned to Canada. She married Jesse Moore in 1951 but he died in 1957. She got remarried in 1960 to George Ross. In recognition of her athletic contributions Lucella was inducted into the Saskatchewan Baseball Hall of Fame in 1991 and is also in the Alberta Fastball Hall of Fame. {AAGPBL Questionnaire, National Baseball Hall of Fame.}

MacLeod, Jenna

(Collingwood, Ontario) OF/IF, Team Canada

Jenna MacLeod played for Team Canada in the 2003 AAU National Championships.

MacNeil, Lindsay

Bantam Hawks

Lindsay MacNeil joined the Dominion Bantam Hawks in 2003 in order to be eligible to play for the national championship in Windsor, Canada. In addition to baseball MacNeil also plays for the provincial soccer team during the winter.

MacPherson, Katie

(b. 1991, Burlington, Ontario) P, WBL Sparks

In 2003 Katie Macpherson became one of 12 girls invited to play for the WBL Sparks in Cooperstown. They would be the first girls' team to play in the annual Cooperstown tournament. Macpherson played first and second base, was a consistent hitter and a good base stealer. Katie started playing baseball when she was only six years old as part of the Burlington Organized Minor Baseball Association on their Peewee clubs, for girls aged 10–13. {"Burlington Girls Get Taste of Baseball Fame," *The Hamilton Spectator*, 26 July 2003; Allen Pulga, "Talented Elite Girls' Baseball Team a Shock to the Boys," *Hamilton Spectator*, 14 August 2004, SP08.}

McAnany, Michelle

(b. 15 November 1963, Inglewood, California) 2B, 1994–97, Colorado Silver Bullets

Michelle McAnany played basketball and tennis at Culver High School. She was a two-time All-American softball player at California State University at Northridge before she made the Silver Bullets roster. In 1989 she was a member of the gold medal team at the China International Games. McAnany hit in the lead-off spot for the Bullets in 1994 and 1995. In the Bullets' inaugural game Michelle had one of only two hits for the club, a single off former major league pitcher Dennis "Oilcan" Boyd. In 1995 she was the only member of the squad to play in all 44 games, leading the team in runs scored with 22 and in walks with 50. Her fielding helped the team up the middle as she turned 13 double plays. In a game against the New York Mets old-timers, McAnany scored the team's first run after doubling off Mike Torrez. After the team folded McAnany returned to playing softball with the Georgia Pride in the Women's Professional Fastpitch League. {Paul Newberry, "Out of Action," *Rocky Mountain News*, 19 July 1998.}

McAnany came by her skills and love of the game through a family tradition of ballplayers. Her father Jim played for the Chicago White Sox (including in the 1959 World Series) and the Cubs, while her brother Jim was drafted by the California Angels. Her cousin, Tim Layana, pitched for the Cincinnati Reds and the San Francisco Giants. She chose her number, three, because that was her father's number when he was with the White Sox. When she is not playing baseball McAnany teaches physical education. In recognition of her outstanding athletic career she was inducted into the Northridge and Culver City halls of fame. {*Silver Bulletin*, December 1995; Laura Blumenfeld, "The Girls against the Boys," *Washington Post*, 24 April 1994, F1; David Kindred, *Colorado Silver Bullets: For the Love of the Game* (Atlanta: Longstreet Press, Inc.), 84; "For the Love of the Game," Colorado Silver Bullets souvenir program, 1995.}

McCann, Amy

(b. 19 December 1978) OF, Doncaster Dragons, Victoria, 2004 Australian National Team

During the 2004 women's World Cup, Amy McCann fielded flawlessly but did not help much with the bat as she struck out twice and walked once. During the earlier Women's National Championships she scored 14 runs to help Victoria win the series. At the 2004 World Series McCann was selected for the all-world team after the series ended. {Sarah Benic, "Dragons Live World Series Dream," *Manningham Leader*, 25 August 2004, 34.}

McCann, Rachelle "Rocky"

(b. 1968) San Jose Spitfires

Hailing from San Francisco, Rachelle McCann joined the Spitfires in 1997 as one of the few players with any baseball experience after Little League. McCann also played for the Silver Bullets in 1994. While attending San Francisco State University McCann was named MVP of the softball team in 1991. {Karen Townsend, "Making Dreams Come True on a Diamond." *Lesbian News* 23, September 1997.}

McCauley, Millie

(b. Edmonton, Alberta) 3B 1943–44, Rockford Peaches

Millie McCauley played for $75 a week in 1943

and 1944 for the Rockford Peaches. In 1998 Mc-Cauley was inducted into the Canadian Baseball Hall of Fame. She is also a member of the Saskatchewan Baseball Hall of Fame. {"Pioneers of the Diamond," *Alberta Report*, 8 June 1998.}

McComb, Joanne E.

(b. 1 March 1933, Avonmore, Pennsylvania) 1B 1950, Springfield Sallies

Joanne McComb traveled with the Sallies in 1950 at the age of 16. One of her best memories is of a game they played in Yankee Stadium before the Yankees played the Philadelphia Athletics. McComb tried out for the AAGPBL after seeing an advertisement in the paper. Unfortunately at the time she was only 15, so she had to wait a year to play. She was still attending Avonmore High School, where she played varsity basketball for four years. After her experience in the league Mc-Comb finished high school and then attended Slippery Rock University, graduating in 1954. She also received an MS degree from Pennsylvania State University in 1966 and took classes at East Stroudsburg State College and West Virginia University. She went on to become the associate athletic director of Bloomsburg University. The university created a scholarship in her honor called the Joanne McComb Outstanding Female Athlete Underclassman Award. This recognized her contributions to the AAGPBL and also her long athletic career after 1950, her coaching and her years working with the athletic department at Bloomsburg. {AAGPBL Questionnaire, National Baseball Hall of Fame.}

McCutchan, Lex

(b. 4 November 1910, Regina, Saskatchewan) Chaperone, 1944, Kenosha Comets

Lex McCutchan played softball and ice hockey while in junior high school. She became the chaperone for the Comets in 1944. {AAGPBL Baseball Cards, 1996.}

McFadden (Rusynyk), Betty Jean "Mac," "Red"

(b. 22 October 1924, Savanna, Illinois) P 1943, South Bend Blue Sox

Betty Jean McFadden attended Savanna High School, graduating in 1942. While there she played basketball, softball and volleyball. Her favorite sport was softball, which she started play-ing when she was 11. Every year she played she made the all-star squad. After one year in the AAGPBL, McFadden played softball for eight years with the Savanna, Illinois, All Stars and five years for the Lakewood, Ohio, Rangers. She also played for Lakewood's basketball team. The basketball squad won the AAU championship three years straight. After marrying Michael Rusynyk, Betty Jean had three children to raise, and most of her athletic endeavors involved coaching her children's teams though she did take up golf as well. {AAGPBL Questionnaire, National Baseball Hall of Fame; AAGPBL Baseball Cards, 1995.}

McGraw, Krista

2000–01, Team Canada

Krista McGraw helped Team Canada defeat the Waterbury Diamonds at the 2000 Roy Hobbs Tournament, scoring the winning run in the championship. She also played for Team Canada in the first Women's World Series in 2001.

McIntosh, Lacey

(b. 26 September 1982, Oak Bluffs, Martha's Vineyard, Massachusetts) Edgarton Eagles

Like many young ladies, most of Lacey McIntosh's playing experience has been on the softball diamond. She played varsity softball for four years at Martha's Vineyard Regional High School, winning the MVP award and serving as team captain. In addition to softball McIntosh played field hockey and basketball in high school. She did play for two years in the outfield for the Edgarton Eagles, a baseball team in the area. In addition, she played in the 24–hour marathon game in October 2003. {Lace McIntosh, correspondence with Leslie A. Heaphy, North Canton, Ohio, March 2004.}

McKeague, Andrea

(b. 1987, Calgary) 1B/C, Team Alberta

In 2004 Andrea McKeague received one of two $1,000 scholarships awarded to current players on behalf of Betty Dunn and Millie Warwick-McAuley, both of whom played in the AAGPBL. McKeague played for Team Alberta in the Western Canadian Championships in 2002 and received the MVP Award. In 2003 she played for Team Canada at the AAU National Championships. {Collin Gallant, "Outfielder Wins Bursary, Eyes Women's Selection Camp," *Edmonton Journal*, 9 March 2004, D5.}

McKenna, Betty "Mac"

(b. 31 May 1931, Lisbon, Ohio; d. 24 February 1992) 3B 1951–53, Fort Wayne Daisies, Battle Creek Belles, Peoria Red Wings, Muskegon Lassies

Betty McKenna got off to a slow start in the AAGPBL and found herself on three different clubs during her rookie year. She graduated in 1949 as the salutatorian of her class and worked as an assistant librarian at the Lepper Library before taking up baseball. In 1952 she only played in 11 games before she finally started to settle in at the plate. Her playing improved in the field with Muskegon in 1953, and then the league folded the following year. She played in 166 games and hit .186, though in 1953 she raised her season average to .215. Her parents supported the idea of her playing just as they did with her two brothers, who played football in college. {"Lisbon Lass Plays 3rd for 'Big League' Club," *East Liverpool Review,* 30 May 1951, 10; AAGPBL Baseball Cards, 1996.}

McKenna, Janet

CF 1992, Gators

Janet McKenna patrolled center field for the Gators of the American Women's Baseball Association in 1992. {"Women Play Hardball," *Daily Herald,* 8 July 1992.}

McKenna, Jenny

(Didsbury, Alberta) OF/C, Team Canada

Jenny McKenna started playing baseball on a Midget boy's team, getting encouragement and training from her father, who played minor league baseball. In 2003 she played for Team Canada in the AAU National Championships.

McKesson (Gibbs), Molly

(b. 1986, St. Petersburg, Florida) P

Hailing from Florida, Molly McKesson began playing baseball when she was eight. She played on the American All-Stars and helped them win the Australian National Championship when she was 12. She also pitched for the Gibbs High School varsity baseball team for four years. She has a fastball in the mid–70s and throws a pretty good curveball as well. Later she joined the Ocala

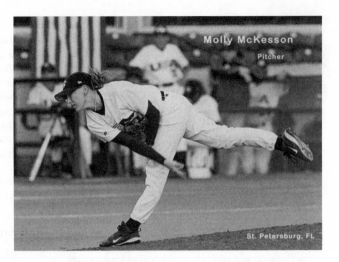

Pitcher Molly McKesson for Team USA (photographer John Lypian, courtesy Jim Glennie).

Lightning and threw a no-hitter during the Roy Hobbs World Series in 2000. In 2001 she helped Ocala win the national title at the USWB Championships. In the 2002 World Series she pitched against Japan in an 8–4 loss. During the 2003 World Series Molly pitched in one game and gave up nine runs in two innings. She also came to bat six times and was held hitless. That was her third World Series for the U.S. She also played for the first USA National Team in the fourth Women's World Series and first World Cup. During the 2004 World Series, McKesson pitched against Japan and Taiwan and picked up one victory in three innings pitched. In the fall of 2004 McKesson began to play baseball on scholarship at Christian Brothers University in Memphis, Tennessee. She got in her first game against Bethesda College of McKenzie, Tennessee and pitched two scoreless innings. {Australian Baseball Federation, <www.baseball.org.au>; USA Baseball 2004 Media Guide; Lenora LaPeter, "Women's World Series," *St. Petersburg Times,* 7 September 2002, 1B; Nancy Morgan, "Woman Keeps Adding to Her Baseball Success," *St. Petersburg Times,* 20 June 2004, 4.}

McKinley (Uselmann), Therese Mary "Terry"

(b. 28 February 1928, Chicago, Illinois) OF 1949, Muskegon Lassies

Therese McKinley played intramural basketball and volleyball while attending Notre Dame Academy in Chicago. There were no other sporting opportunities available for girls at that time.

In addition to the school experience, Therese played for six years in the Chicago Park District leagues and one year in an industrial softball league for men. She joined the AAGPBL in 1949 as a rookie and got to play in the playoffs that year against Grand Rapids, who won.

After that one year in the league Therese went on to college and earned her BS in 1958 from Depaul University and her MA in 1963, also from Depaul. She held a teaching job in Chicago for 30 years and also coached a variety of different teams. This work led to her selection for the Chicago Sports Hall of Fame. She married Duane Uselmann in 1960 and they had five children. {AAGPBL Questionnaire, National Baseball Hall of Fame; AAGPBL Baseball Cards, 1995.}

McNally, Lucia

Management

Lucia McNally took over the job of administrative assistant for baseball administration for the San Francisco Giants in 1993.

Machado (Van Sant), Helene "Chow"

(b. 17 April 1926, Venice, California) OF 1946–47, Peoria Red Wings, Fort Wayne Daisies

Helene Machado played for two years with the Red Wings and Daisies. She patrolled the outfield for both clubs, making 261 putouts in 163 games. She hit .204 and drove in 37 runs while scoring another 39. She did not play again in 1948 due to her father's declining health, but remained at home and took up selling real estate. {AAGPBL Baseball Cards, 1995.}

Machnik, Kris

WNEBL

Kris Machnik grew up playing Little League baseball but then had to switch in high school to playing softball. She became a national amateur player in the sport but always liked baseball better. She finally got a chance to return to the game in 2000 with the formation of the WNEBL. {Michael O'Conner, "The Local Women are ... Playing Hardball," *The Boston Herald*, 28 May 2000.}

Macurio, Shawn

(b. 19 August 1971, Big Rapids, Michigan) C/3B 1999–2004, Lansing Stars, Detroit Danger

Shawn Macurio developed an early love for baseball while watching her friends play the game. Her one attempt to try out came when she was a sophomore in high school, but the coach told her that girls did not play baseball. Instead, Macurio spent most of her early years playing hockey. She was the starting catcher for her high school softball team. She made the Wayne State University fast-pitch team as a walk-on but never actually played for them.

Macurio started playing baseball in 1999 with the Lansing Stars (a team started in 1992 by Jim Glennie), and then moved on in 2000 to join the Detroit Renegades. She had tried out for the Colorado Silver Bullets in 1994 with her sister and for Team America in 2001. Macurio convinced former Detroit Tiger Barbaro Garbey to become the manager of the new squad. This club became the Danger in 2001. Macurio was a league all-star. In 2003 Macurio played for the American Snappers at the Colorado Classic Women's Baseball Tournament, where she was named tournament MVP. While with the Renegades/Danger squad Macurio put together a .414 career average. Not only does Macurio love to play baseball but she is passionate about teaching the game. Towards that goal she also created *Planet Baseball Magazine*, an online journal about women's baseball. Shawn also received the honor of being inducted into the National Women's Baseball Hall of Fame in 2003 and received an MVP award in 2004. She has won many other honors and accolades as a player. When she is not on the diamond or working on league business, Macurio works as a graphic designer. She graduated from Wayne State. {http://www.detroitdanger.com; www.baseballglory.com; Richard Jaffeson, *Fame Forum Newsletter*, 9 October 2003.}

Madison Mets

The Madison Mets belong to the East Coast Women's Baseball League. They play under managers Bonnie Finkeldey and Nancy Peralta. Both managers also play for the team, with Nancy pitching and playing second base while Bonnie catches, plays the hot corner and roams the outfield.

Magalas, Samantha

(b. 9 April 1982, Burlington, Ontario) 1B/OF, Team Canada

Samantha Magalas hit .333 during the 2004 women's World Cup, helping Canada to win the bronze medal. In the bronze medal game Magalas had two hits and two RBIs. Magalas brought a wealth of athletic experience to the 2004 games, having won seven MVP awards starting in high school in hockey, basketball, and track and field at Assumption Secondary School. In 2000 and again in 2002 she was named Burlington Athlete of the Year. At the Team Ontario Tournament at the SkyDome she received the Top Hitter Award in 2001 and 2002. Her fielding has also been recognized with a Gold Glove Award at the 2002 World Series in Australia. Her awards show that Magalas is an all-around player who can hit, field and run. {Baseball Canada 2004 Women's National Team Media Guide; Robert Tychkowski, "Canada Rules Aussies," *Edmonton Sun*, 9 August 2004, SP5.}

Magill, Pamela

In 1973 Pamela Magill wanted to play Little League baseball in her home town in Pennsylvania. The Avonworth Baseball Conference did not allow her to play, so her parents sued the ABC, claiming her rights had been violated. In the initial case the judge decreed that the league was not a state actor but a private one and therefore not subject to Fourteenth Amendment protections. The ABC had claimed they worried girls would get hurt, or that boys would quit if girls were allowed to play. {M.J. Yelnosky, "If You Write it, (S)He Will Come: Judicial Decisions, Metaphors, Baseball and 'the Sex Stuff,'" *Connecticut Law Review*, 1996, 813–54.}

Maguire (McAlpin), Dorothy "Mickey"

(b. 21 November 1918, LaGrange, Ohio; d. 2 August 1981) C/OF 1943–49, Racine Belles, Milwaukee Chicks, Grand Rapids Chicks, Muskegon Lassies

Dorothy Maguire played for seven years in the All American League. She moved around a bit because she was not the strongest hitter, but she was a durable catcher. For example, Maguire only batted .218 for the Lassies in 1946 but she played in 101 games. She made her hits when they counted, because she knocked in 47 runs and scored another 42. When she played with the Milwaukee club she started in 55 of the team's first 56 games. She also got to play in the championship series with Racine in her rookie year. For her career she hit .194 in 595 games with 243 stolen bases and 222 runs scored. {AAGPBL Baseball Cards, 1995.}

Mahon, Elizabeth Bailey "Lib"

(b. 18 November 1919, Greenville, South Carolina; d. 27 October 2001) 2B/OF 1944–52, Minneapolis Millerettes, Kenosha Comets, South Bend Blue Sox

Lib Mahon attended Parker High School through the eleventh grade. When she finished school in 1937, South Carolina schools did not yet go to the twelfth grade. She took part in all the intramural sports that were offered because there were no other competitive sports. She played in an industrial league from age 12 to 17, taking part in basketball and softball. While she attended Winthrop University from 1938 to 1942 she played on all their class sports teams and worked in the cotton mill. She taught school in 1942–43 and worked for the post office before joining the All American League in 1944 with the Millerettes. In 1946 while with South Bend, Mahon played in 112 games and batted .276. She only struck out 15 times but walked 64 times. That was the first year she made the all-star team. She made the all-star squad again in 1947, 1948 and 1949. She helped South Bend win the league championship in 1951. The following season she and five teammates quit the club two weeks before the end of the season because of the way the manager treated one of the other players. She hit .248 during her ten-year career.

Mahon started teaching in the off-season in 1947 and stayed with the South Bend school system until she retired in 1981. To stay physically active she became a golfer. In May 2005 Mahon earned the distinction of entering the South Carolina Hall of Fame for her lifetime contributions to women's sports. {AAGPBL Questionnaire, National Baseball Hall of Fame; AAGPBL Baseball Cards, 1995; Jim Sargent, "Elizabeth 'Lib' Mahon," AAGPBL Newsletter, January 2002, 34–35.}

Mahoney, Katie

Florida Lightning

Katie Mahoney grew up playing slow-pitch softball but discovered the game of baseball when the South Florida Diamond League was created to let women play. She catches for the Florida Lightning. When she is not playing baseball Mahoney is the coach of the Cardinal Newman softball team. {Elizabeth Clarke, "Nothing Soft about the Play at South Florida Diamond Classic," *Palm Beach Post*, 25 April 1999.}

Mahoney, Marie "Red"

(b. 21 September 1924, Houston, Texas) OF

Claudia Amato meeting former AAGPBL player Marie "Red" Mahoney (courtesy Keira Amato).

1947–48, South Bend Blue Sox, Fort Wayne Daisies

Marie Mahoney played for two years in the All American League. In 1948 she made the all-star team after making only two errors all year in the outfield. She played in 103 games and made only seven errors. She also only hit .177 but did score 31 runs to help her teams. After leaving the league she worked for Kodak and became an avid golfer. {AAGPBL Baseball Cards, 1995.}

Maldonado, Wanda

Wanda Maldonado played second base for the Toa Baja Llaneros in Puerto Rico. By playing for the Llaneros she became the first woman to play at that level of amateur baseball in her country.

Maliszewski, Danielle

C, Virginia Flames

In 2002 for the Flames, Danielle Maliszewski was 9 for 20 at the plate, hitting .450. Her catching abilities earned her the honor of defensive player of the game on more than one occasion during 2002.

Maly, Rochelle

(b. 1968) P, AWBA Knights

Rochelle Maly played softball growing up and earned a scholarship to St. Xavier University. Though she works during the school year as a high school math teacher, Maly joined the AWBA and in 1992 helped the Knights win the league

with a 9–1 record. She led the league in hitting at .500 and also in ERA at 2.48. Maly got the opportunity to be an extra in the film *A League of Their Own* because they were looking for women who could play baseball. {"Women Play Hardball," *Daily Herald,* 8 July 1992; Bill Beuttler, "The Girls of Summer," *Sports Illustrated,* 6 September 1993, 139.}

Mandella, Lenora "Smokey"

(b. 4 May 1931, McKeesport, Pennsylvania) P/IF 1949–51, South Bend Blue Sox, Springfield Sallies, Peoria Red Wings

Lenora Mandella got a chance to try out for the AAGPBL in 1949 when local councilman Andy Jakomas arranged for local tryouts to be held at Renziehausen Park. Mandella started in the league as an infielder but in her second season her manager decided to turn her into a pitcher because of her arm strength. One highlight she recalls is pitching a one-hitter and receiving a dozen roses and a watch as a gift from one of the fans for her performance. She played in 60 games and hit only .127. After her baseball career ended Mandella managed softball teams and refereed basketball games. She also worked as an accountant and general manager of a union. {Patricia Brown, "Lenora 'Smokey' Mandella," in *A League of My Own* (Jefferson, N.C.: McFarland, 2003), 169–71.}

Manitoba Taffy

The Manitoba Taffy belong to the Great Lakes Women's Baseball League and the Amateur Athletic Union, and are affiliated with American Women's Baseball. They joined the Great Lakes group in 2003 and finished their first season at 8–4 in second place. The title went to the Chicago Storm. The team was designed to allow women between the ages of 16 and 30 a chance to play baseball. The team plays under head coach Russ St. Germain, whose son Adam also acted as bat boy. {Manitoba Taffy Web site.}

Manley, Effa

(b. 27 March 1897, Philadelphia, Pennsylvania: d. 18 April 1981, Los Angeles, California) Owner, Newark Eagles

Effa Manley co-owned the Newark Eagles of

the Negro National League from 1935-48. Her own background growing up is one that still generates controversy today since she is believed to be the illegitimate daughter of Bertha Ford Brooks and John Bishop, both white. She grew up in a household with six other racially mixed siblings and her mother married two black men. This led most to believe that Effa was a light-skinned black herself. She got involved in black baseball with her husband Abe Manley when he bought the Brooklyn Eagles in 1935. Effa ran the team on a day-to-day basis while her husband recruited players. Abe moved the team to Newark in 1936 to improve the club's fortunes. Abe served the NNL as treasurer and Effa attended all league meetings with him. In addition to her involvement in baseball she took an active role in civil rights actions as well. For example, she started a "Don't Work where you can't buy campaign" to force white owners to hire black workers. She worked hard to integrate the Eagles into the local community, holding benefit games and inviting local leaders as their guests to watch the Eagles play. She never sat back and passively watched events happening around her. Later, when baseball started to move toward integration Effa was a loud voice in the efforts to get compensation for Negro League owners for their players signed by major league ball clubs. She wrote columns for the newspapers and later to the Hall of Fame and *Sporting News* for recognition for the ball players. She also wrote her own history of black baseball entitled, *Negro Baseball: Before Integration*, published in 1976. In 2006 Effa Manley became the first woman to be inducted into the National Baseball Hall of Fame. {Effa Manley and Leon Hardwick, *Negro Baseball: Before Integration*, Chicago: Adam Press, 1976; James Overmyer, *Effa Manley and the Newark Eagles*, Metuchen, NJ: The Scarecrow Press, Inc., 1993.}

Mansfield (Kelley), Marie M. "Boston"

(b. 4 November 1931, Jamaica Plain, Massachusetts) P/1B/OF 1950–54, Rockford Peaches, Battle Creek Belles

There were no sports to play at Roslindale High School in Boston, but Marie Mansfield played one year of CYO softball before joining the All American League. When she made the Rockford roster in 1950, Mansfield took a spot mainly as a pitcher. She spent all but two weeks of her career with the Peaches. In 1952 she was sent to Battle Creek for two weeks and then was sent back. She

pitched in 92 games compiling a record of 34–42. Mansfield also played in 253 games in the outfield and hit .130. She married William Kelley in 1959, and they had a daughter, Marie. {AAGPBL Questionnaire, National Baseball Hall of Fame; AAG PBL Baseball Cards, 1995.}

Manzie, Kelli Anne

(b. 18 April 1973) C/P, Springvale, Australian National Team, Chicago Storm

During the 2002 World Series in Florida Kelli Manzie helped Australia win the gold medal and then got the chance to be a special guest out on the field during a major league game. At the 2003 AAU National Championship Series Manzie pitched in one game for the Storm, giving up two hits and one walk in two innings of pitching. {"Queens of Baseball," *Bayside Leader*, 23 September 2002, 46.}

Marklew, Shelli

(b. 23 February 1967) OF/P, Lady Mariners, Victoria, Australian National Team

During the 2001 Australian National Tournament Shelli Marklew hit an even .500 with an .833 slugging percentage, the second highest in the series. Her excellent play led to her selection to the Aussie Stars, who played and won the gold medal in the 2002 Women's World Series in Florida. {"Queens of Baseball," *Bayside Leader*, 23 September 2002, 46.}

Marlowe (Malanowski), Jean "Mal," "Jeanie"

(b. 28 December 1929, Scranton, Pennsylvania) P/IF/OF 1948–54, Springfield Sallies, Kenosha Comets, Kalamazoo Lassies

Jean Marlowe grew up in Scranton, Pennsylvania, and heard about the All American League through an ad in the local paper. She went and tried out, and played for six years in the league. She could play just about any position on the field, which made her a valuable asset to her team. She played in 314 games and hit .199 with 68 RBIs. She also pitched in 145 games, compiling a record of 56–79 with an ERA of 3.19. During one season local newspapers reported that Marlowe had a 10–7 record by mid–July 1950. She came home to Pennsylvania to pitch before her family and friends on July 17 before returning to Kenosha. Before the game the local drum and bugle corp entertained the fans. They wanted to celebrate their hometown celebrity. Marlowe was inducted into the Northeast Pennsylvania Sports Hall of Fame. {"Sallies Outscore Colleens, 9–4," *Scranton Times*, 17 July 1950.}

Marrero, Chico

(b. Cuba) P

Chico Marrero came to the United States with three other female players to join the All American League. They were initially all assigned together so they could help each other adjust to the new culture, language and other differences.

Marrero, Mirta

(b. Cuba) P 1948–53, Chicago Colleens, Kalamazoo Lassies, Fort Wayne Daisies, Battle Creek Belles, Muskegon Belles

Mirta Marrero came from Cuba to play in the All American League and quickly became a favorite with her fellow players. She was described by many as a lively, energetic player. She quit baseball when she got married because her husband did not want her playing. Her best year came in 1951 with Fort Wayne. She won 17 games that year. Before coming to the United States, Marrero had played throughout Cuba and had even been pictured on the front of one of Cuba's magazines *Bohemia*. She signed a contract with Max Carey in 1948 when he brought players from the league to Havana for spring training. {Bill Douthat, "League of Her Own," *Palm Beach Post*, 12 September 2003; "For Daisies Against Belles," *Washington Post*, 3 May 1951, 16.}

Marshall, Michelle

2B, Alameda Oaks

Michelle Marshall scored 11 runs on 11 hits for the Oaks in 2003.

Marshall, Theda A. "T"

(b. 24 April 1925, Denver, Colorado) 1B 1947–48, South Bend Blue Sox, Chicago Colleens

There were no school sports to play for girls when Theda Marshall attended Garden Home–Westwood school. Instead she played basketball and softball in a local Denver league. After graduation Marshall went to California to play softball and work in the defense industry. When she made the All American League, Marshall did a great deal of traveling and was paid nearly $100 a week. She had been working as a bank teller for just

under $30 a week when she got the contract with South Bend. In 1947 she went to spring training in Cuba and in 1948 she joined the traveling Colleens to get more training. She played in 238 games but only hit .141. Her fielding was solid, as she made 80 errors with over 2,600 putouts. Marshall also played professional basketball and coached in Denver for about seven years. She played professional softball in the Phoenix area until 1951, when her mother had a stroke. She worked for the air force for nearly 30 years before retiring. {AAGPBL Questionnaire, National Baseball Hall of Fame; Bill Johnson, "Old Baseball Player Was in a Special League," *Rocky Mountain News*, 6 August 2000; Gary Massaro, "Cooperstown Now on Deck," *Rocky Mountain News*, 12 October 2002; AAGPBL Baseball Cards, 1995.}

Martin, Kelly

In 1998 Martin played for Riggs Construction under coach David Brassard.

Martinez, Lisa

(b. 23 July 1964, Stockton, California) P 1994–95, Colorado Silver Bullets

Lisa Martinez was named Texas State Athlete of the Year in 1981. She played softball at Texas A&M as well as at Cal State Berkeley. She became the first Bullets pitcher to pitch a no-hitter when they beat the Summerville Yankees 6–0 in Charleston, South Carolina, in 1995. Martinez used an underhand pitching motion that confused the batters. In her first game for the Bullets she came in as a relief pitcher and struck out Darius Gash, a Class AA player. Her experience before joining the Bullets had been limited to her university softball. When not playing baseball, Lisa works as a science teacher. She took a leave of absence from Liberty High School in Stockton, California, to join the Bullets. {"In Focus, Game Face," *Indian Scorebook Magazine*, 12; *The Silver Bulletin* December 1995; David Kindred, *Colorado Silver Bullets: For the Love of the Game* (Atlanta: Longstreet Press, Inc.), 82; Claire Smith, "Belated Tribute to Baseball's Negro Leagues," *The New York Times*, 13 August 1991, A1, B9.; Sam Donnellon, "Silver Bullets," Knight-Ridder Newspapers, 9 May 1994; Bonnie DeSimone, "Playing Hardball," *Cleveland Plain Dealer*, 8 May 1994, 1D, 9D.}

Martinez, Pat

IF, San Jose Spitfires

Pat Martinez played in ten games for the

Spitfires in the 2003 California Women's Baseball League. She had 18 hits in 38 at-bats and scored ten runs to help her team.

Martino, Nan

(b. 10 March 1966, Washington, D. C.) 1B/3B
2001-2005, Montgomery County Barncats

Nan Martino played soccer and softball growing up. She even earned High School All-American Honorable Mention in soccer. After graduating with a BS from James Madison University in 1987 and an MS from the same university in 1992, Martino became a teacher and coach. From 2001 to 2005 she played baseball for the Montgomery County Barncats. One of the highlights of her baseball career was a come from behind win against the Sparks. Martino hit a triple to spark the rally. She also said the toughest pitcher she faced in her career was Renee Hudson. Martino is the head soccer coach at Montgomery College and also is the co-ed volleyball coach at Einstein High School. {Personal correspondence with Leslie A. Heaphy, No. Canton Ohio 2006.}

Marzetta, Angie

(b. 18 October 1972, Virginia Beach, Virginia)
OF 1995–96, Colorado Silver Bullets

Angie Marzetta came to the Bullets after an outstanding softball career at the University of Washington and at Taft High School. At Taft she was the first female to play football; she also played tennis and volleyball. While at the University of Washington she hit .425 and set a PAC–10 record for stolen bases in a single season with 59. At the 1994 Olympic Games she hit .550 with 11 hits. Marzetta played in 40 of the Bullets' 44 games during the 1995 season. While Marzetta was mainly known for her hitting, she also threw out a runner at home at Jacobs Field. She was third on the team in batting at .221, including at least three multiple-hit games and a five-game hitting streak. Marzetta was the only switch hitter on the club and had the second four-hit game for the Bullets on 28 July 1995 in Geneva, Illinois. By mid–1996 Marzetta led the Bullets in stolen bases and had broken the team record for being hit by pitches, which had been five. The new record was 11, set in a game against the Reno Diamonds. Marzetta prepared to charge the mound but was stopped by the umpire and the catcher. {*The Silver Bulletin* December 1995 and March 1996; "For the Love of the Game," Colorado Silver Bullets souvenir program, 1995; Sheldon Spencer, "Sil-

ver Bullets Bring Tour Back to Area Game Tonight in Everett," *Seattle Post-Intelligencer*, 6 August 1996.}

Masako, Ogawa

P, Japan

Ogawa Masako pitched her club to a victory in game five of the 2003 Women's World Series. Masako held the United States scoreless for five innings en route to a 3–0 victory.

Matlack (Sagrati), Ruth "Matty"

(b. 13 January 1931, Cromwell Heights, Pennsylvania) LHP 1950, Fort Wayne Daisies

Ruth Matlock pitched one season for the Daisies and ended up with a record of 0–4. Since she had such a solid bat she often got used as a pinch hitter, batting .361 in that capacity. She started working in an office in 1952 and stayed with that organization in various capacities until her retirement in 1985. To stay active Ruth golfed, bowled and waterskied. {AAGPBL Newsletter, October 1993, 16.}

Matson, Karen

(b. 1982) C

In 2003 Karen Matson tried out for Team Canada in order to play for the first world cup in women's baseball, and made the squad. Her background in sports was in fast-pitch softball, not baseball. When not playing baseball, Matson is a student at the University of Alberta. {Norm Cowley, "At Last, a Championship of Their Own: Team Canada Evaluation Camp Held for Inaugural World Cup of Women's Baseball," *Edmonton Journal*, 1 December 2003, D2.}

Matsumoto, Ayano

P, Japanese National Team

Ayano Matsumoto played for Japan in the 2004 Women's World Series in Uozu, Japan.

Mattson (Baumgart), Jacqueline "Jackie"

(b. 16 November 1928, Waukegan, Illinois) C
1950–51, Springfield Sallies, Kenosha Comets

While growing up, Jackie Mattson played sports with the boys because there were no real opportunities for girls. When her family moved to Milwaukee in 1942, when she was a teenager,

Mattson got the chance to play in the city leagues, which had not existed in her home town in Illinois. In 1945 her fast-pitch softball team, sponsored by Majdecki Foods, won the state championship 1–0. In 1949 she was catching for the Milwaukee Jets when a scout saw her and invited her to a tryout in 1949 in Newark, New Jersey. The following spring she came to South Bend for spring training and found herself on the roster of the Sallies. Mattson earned the respect of fellow players and fans for her fine play behind home plate. After playing in the AAGPBL Mattson became a teacher in Milwaukee.

{Patricia Brown, "Jacqueline Mattson," in *A League of My Own* (Jefferson, NC: McFarland, 2003), 172–74; Courtnay Charles Brummer, "Girl's Baseball League Made History Decades Ago," *Brookfield News*, 16 June 1994, 1, 14.}

Mazin, Robyn

C, Falcons

In 2003 Robin Mazin caught for the Falcons after having played softball for St. Mary's College. {Christopher L. Gasper, "Playing the Game They Love," *Boston Globe*, 13 July 2003, 1, 11.}

Meacham, Mildred "Meach"

(b. 5 May 1924, Charlotte, North Carolina) 1B 1947–48, Racine Belles, Springfield Sallies

Mildred Meacham grew up playing basketball and softball in high school. Her first baseball experience came with the champion Racine Belles in 1947. In 1948 she joined the touring Sallies in an effort to develop her skills. Her career numbers include playing in 97 games with a .179 average. She scored 26 runs and drove in another 10. {AAGPBL Baseball Cards, 1995.}

Mehrer, Darlene

AWBA Founder

In 1988 Darlene Mehrer went looking for some other women who wanted to play baseball in the Chicago area. She thought she might find a few but she found 30, so she founded the American Women's Baseball Association with two teams, the Daredevils and the Gators. In 1989 they added a third team, the Knights. Mehrer ran the league but also played for the Daredevils until her death from cancer in 1990. {Bob Gordon, "Daredevils Win Women's Opener, 11–6," *Daily Herald*, 17 July 1988.}

Meidlinger, Meg "Meggie"

P

Meggie Meidlinger pitches for her Dominion High School baseball team in Virginia. She also pitches for the East Coast Yankees in tournament play under manager Adriane Adler. She began playing the game at age five and has never stopped. Before joining the Dominion squad as a sophomore Meidlinger pitched for Potomac Falls JV team. Her first appearance for Dominion came in relief of starter Anthony DeMott. She relieved him in the fourth inning of a game in 2004 versus Randolph Macon Academy, and she struck out the batter. In the fifth she did give up one run, but her team came from behind to earn a victory for her. Meidlinger relies on a fastball and curveball to get batters out. Her coach, Jay Raines, has no problem with her gender because he just wanted a pitcher who could throw strikes, and she does. {Carl Lukat, "Dominion Pitcher's Big Win," Loudon *Times-Mirror*, 31 March 2004.}

Meier, Naomi "Sally"

(b. 17 November 1926, Fort Wayne, Indiana, d. 15 July 1989) LF 1946–53, Rockford Peaches, Fort Wayne Daisies, Peoria Red Wings, Chicago Colleens, Kalamazoo Lassies, Battle Creek Belles, Muskegon Lassies, Racine Belles

Naomi Meier played for eight seasons in the All American League. She found herself playing for a number of different teams because she sometimes struggled at the plate. In 1946 Meier hit .249 for the Peaches, though at midseason she was battling Mary Baker for the batting lead. Both were hitting .308 in early July. She played in 103 games and had one home run in 374 at-bats. She was not known for her bat in her career, but for her speed and coverage in the outfield. By 1948 she became a solid hitter for Peoria, always making good contact and getting on base. She only struck out 277 times in her career while walking 219 and stealing 206 bases. {"350,000 See All-American Girls' Games," *Chicago Tribune*, 21 July 1946, A4; Susan E. Johnson, 47; AAGPBL Baseball Cards, 1996.}

Meisner, Jessica

Jessica Meisner played for the Siegel and Soper Little League team in Cranbury, Connecticut, which started its leagues in 1960. Her parents encouraged her to sign up even though the league had a ban on girls' joining. The league commissioner, John McMahon, tried to push Jessica toward the local softball league, but she wanted to play baseball. He allowed her father to register her, but then the Cranbury Community Athletic Association claimed he violated the league's bylaws and McMahon resigned. Two days before league play was to begin in 1983, Vincent DePanfilis, president of the athletic association, told the family Jessica could not play. Her mother Lydia contacted their local congressman, Stewart McKinney, and that prompted a meeting with the State Human Rights Commission. Jessica's manager, Ken Varga, put her in the lineup on opening day and the umpire declared the game a forfeit. Two days later the association reversed their decision and allowed Jessica to play, though they did not remove the ban on girls from their bylaws. Jessica also played the piano and violin while attending Tracey School. Her favorite ballplayers were Lou Gehrig and Babe Ruth, because she grew up a fan of the Yankees. {John Cavanaugh, "Girl Stirs Up League," *New York Times*, 5 June 1983, CN8.}

Melbourne Spirit

This is a team that was formed for women over 35 in 2003. The players who joined the club came from the Victoria Baseball Association teams.

Mercatante, Andrea "A-Rod"

(b. 4 February 1983, Detroit, Michigan) P/SS/3B, Detroit Danger

Andrea Mercatante started playing ball as soon as she could hold a bat. She earned All-League and All-Area honors while playing high school softball. She developed a reputation as a strong defensive player. She became a tennis instructor after high school before going to school at Wayne State University. She joined the Danger in 2005. {Danger Web site.}

Merhige, Phyllis

Management

Phyllis Merhige worked as the director of public relations for the American League while Kate Feeny did the same job for the National League.

Meriwood, Trinity

RHP 1996, Colorado Silver Bullets

While attending Thomas Jefferson High School, Trinity Meriwood pitched for the JV baseball team for two years. She compiled a 3.41 ERA in 26.6 innings pitched. When she started college she moved away from softball to soccer and bas-

ketball at Seattle University before returning in 1996 to baseball. {*Silver Bulletin*, March 1996.}

Metes, Beatrice P

Beatrice Metes joined her brother's American Legion team in 1948. At age 19 Metes became one of the starting pitchers for the St. Joseph club while her brother caught for the team. {Kovach, 86.}

Metesh, Bernice B. "Bernie"

(b. 9 August 1929, Joliet, Illinois) Util. 1948, South Bend Blue Sox, Rockford Peaches

Bernice Metesh grew up in a family with a bit of athletic prowess. Her brother Jim played hockey in Canada in 1960 and 1961. She joined the Blue Sox in 1948 and midway through the season was traded to the Peaches. At the end of that one year she decided not to return but went home to Joliet, where she pitched for an all-male baseball team in the Joliet City Park League. She pitched for the St. Joseph's American Legion Post club. In her first game with St. Joseph's they lost 8–6 due to five errors in the field. {AAGPBL Baseball Cards, 1996; "Joliet Girl, 19, Wins Semi-Pro Pitching Job," *New York Times*, 22 July 1948, 28.}

Metrolis, M. Norma "Trolley"

(b. 5 December 1925, Kittery, Maine) C 1946–50, Muskegon Lassies, Racine Belles, South Bend Blue Sox, Peoria Red Wings, Fort Wayne Daisies

Norma Metrolis moved a fair amount as she was growing up, attending school in Washington, D.C.; Maryland; Maine; and Sarasota, Florida until she graduated in 1943. No matter where she went she participated in whatever athletic opportunities were offered for girls. Her Sarasota high school named her Outstanding Woman Athlete when she graduated. She also played softball in the Orlando, Florida, city league from 1940 to 1945. Her strong play in that league got her a tryout in Chicago for the All American League. Though only in the league for five years, she played for five different teams, being reassigned — as players often were — as the league tried to level out the competition. She tore the cartilage in her knee while playing in 1948 but hung on until her release in 1950. Her career numbers include playing in 60 games with only a .160 average. It was her fielding that made her valuable to her team. She continued to play softball until 1957 for the Orlando Rebels and was the all-state catcher. She worked for the U.S. Department of Agriculture for 30 years, retiring in 1986. {AAGPBL Questionnaire, National Baseball Hall of Fame; AAGPBL Baseball Cards, 1995.}

Meyer (Petrovic), Anna L. "Pee Wee"

(b. 17 November 1928, Aurora, Indiana) SS 1944, Kenosha Comets, Minneapolis Millerettes

While attending Aurora High School Anne Meyer played softball for a local industrial league. She learned her baseball skills from her five brothers, who used her as a target — she had to learn to catch to protect herself. She got a chance to join the Kenosh Comets in 1944 at the age of 15 and spent most of the season with them before being traded to the Millerettes for Lib Mahon. She played her first few seasons while still in high school. In 1947 she was named Athlete of the Year at her school. When she finally left the league she played volleyball until 1978. She planned to attend college in New York and then she met her husband. She got married to George Petrovic in 1950 and they raised two boys. She worked for Abco Markets for 15 years and also for Lederle Labs in Pearl River, New York. She played softball and volleyball on factory and traveling teams to stay active. {AAGPBL Questionnaire, National Baseball Hall of Fame; AAGPBL Newsletter, January 2002, 16.}

Meyer (Moellering), Rita "Slats"

(b. 12 February 1927, Florissant, Missouri) SS 1946–49, Peoria Red Wings

Rita Meyer played for four years with Peoria and once pitched a no-hitter but lost. She pitched in only 13 games in 1947 with a 3–6 record. The rest of her career she spent playing shortstop in 399 games. She batted .205 with 140 RBIs and 121 runs scored. {AAGPBL Baseball Cards, 1995.}

Meyers, Courtney

Courtney Meyers played third base, caught and pitched for the Harley-Allandale-Columbia Junior High baseball team at age 14. When she first tried out she was refused the chance, but she appealed the decision and the State Education Department ruled in her favor, allowing her to play.

Miami Beach Bloomer Girls

Though most of the girls playing on the Miami Beach team came from Florida, they called Philadelphia their home city. In 1933 this team traveled around the Midwest and East Coast. One trip found them in Bradford, Pennsylvania; the next day in Salamanca, New York, playing the St. Joe's club; and later in the month in Jersey City, New Jersey, and Mansfield, Ohio. They had three men on the squad: a pitcher, catcher and shortstop. There were also two women pitchers, Dot Byers and Louise Miller. Their first baseman was referred to in the papers as Ethel "Babe" Ruth because she had the strongest bat on the squad. They acquired Evelyen Speigle from the Hollywood Stars to play in the infield. Mary Weber, Kay DeBona, Ruth Carter and Mary Tumelty filled out the remainder of the roster spots. A local Mansfield paper reported that the team would be arriving in their city in mid–July to play the Westinghouse club. They were coming from a trip to Jersey City that left them undefeated for the year. {"Bloomer Girls Meet Westies," *Mansfield News-Journal*, 24 July 1933, 8; "Miami Beach Girls Play Here Monday," *Mansfield News-Journal*, 21 July 1933, 14; "St. Joseph's Players All Set for Game Here with Bloomer Girls," *Salamanca Republic-Press*, 3 July 1933, 3.}

Mickelson, Darlene "Mickey"

(b. Kenosha, Wisconsin) OF 1943, 1945, Kenosha Comets, South Bend Blue Sox

Darlene Mickelson played parts of only two seasons in the All American League before calling it quits. She played in only 50 games and hit .139 with 29 RBIs. {AAGPBL Baseball Cards, 2000.}

Mid-Atlantic Pride

Phyllis Walton started this club in 1994 to give women a chance to play baseball and not just softball. The team played on the diamond at Delaware County Community College in Media. Walton secured sponsorship for the squad from Aetna Health Plans. The team played all-men's clubs because there were no other women's teams in the area. Paul Motta, the former coach for the community college, took over as manager. In addition to running the club Walton also played. Other team members included Melissa Gibbons, Mary Kenney, Claudine Deaver (2B), Mary Alice Felt (RF), Bevin Hartnett (C), and Cindy Rabideau (SS). The players ranged in age from 15 to 40. By mid–August their record stood at 0–7. Gibbons was typical of most of the players on the roster. She had played Little League ball and then had had to turn to softball to continue to play until the

Pride started playing. {Carol Horner, "Playing Hardball: Women Eager to Play Baseball," Knight Ridder Newspapers, 26 August 1994.}

Mid-Atlantic Women's Baseball League (1999–2000)

The Mid-Atlantic league was founded in 1999 by Kelly Keller, Brenda Dyson and Ralph Zachry. The purpose was to promote women's baseball in and around the Baltimore area. The league was open to women of all ages and talent levels. The league's season was to be from April through August and all games were to be seven-inning events with professional umpires.

Middleton (Gentry), Ruth

(25 August 1930, Winnipeg, Manitoba) OF 1950–53, Chicago Colleens, Battle Creek Belles, Muskegon Belles

Ruth Middleton started in the AAGPBL with the traveling team from Chicago but then settled in the outfield for Battle Creek. She was a solid fielder with good speed. When she got on base she was always a threat to steal; she had 25 stolen bases in her career. She played in 195 games and batted .185. {AAGPBL Baseball Cards, 1995.}

Milito, Toni

(b. 1978) P

Toni Milito pitched in 1993 for the Spotswood High School baseball team in New Jersey. She finished the season with a 3–0 record, a 2.20 ERA and 26 strikeouts in only 19 innings. In 1994 she got to see the Silver Bullets in action and talked pitching with Shae Sloan. {Bill Falk, "Baseball in Purest Form, Silver Bullets Send a Message Wherever They Go," Newsday, 15 August 1994.}

Miller, Cherie

(b. 11 October 1959) 3B/Util., Queensland Rams

Cherie Miller played for the Rams at the Australian National Championship series.

Miller, Janet

OF

Janet Miller became the first female player in an all-men's league in Massachusetts in 1996, playing for the North Shore Reds. She stayed with the Reds for three seasons before the team folded. Then she joined the Boston Mets, another

over–30 men's team. Miller showed up for the first tryouts for the NEWBL and made the roster for the Boston Blitz. When not playing baseball Miller works as a sports massage therapist. {Dick Dahl, "Out of His League," Boston Globe Magazine, 22, 27.}

Miller, Melissa

3B/P, Chicago Storm, South Bend Blue Sox, Team USA

Melissa Miller grew up playing softball, as most girls did, and went on to play at Cal Baptist College on scholarship. Her high school softball jersey was retired. She was invited to try out for the Olympic softball team but chose to give baseball a try. She played three seasons with the Chicago Storm and South Bend Blue Sox in the Great Lakes Women's Baseball League. In 2003 she hit .154 in five games during the Women's World Series but fielded flawlessly. {Australian Baseball Federation, <www.baseball.org.au>; <www.baseballglory.com>.}

Milliken, JoAnn

CF, Virginia Flames

JoAnn Milliken plays for the Virginia Flames as well as serving as league commissioner for the Eastern Women's Baseball Conference (EWBC). During the 2002 season Milliken was second in hitting for the Flames, with a .467 average. She went to Arizona in October 2003 to play in a 24–hour marathon game to benefit AIDS victims in Africa. She started her team from a co-ed softball club she played for, after she discovered a number of her teammates wanted the opportunity to play baseball. {Al Mattei, "The State of Women's Baseball Found in the Washington Metro League," <TopoftheCircle.com>.}

Mills, Bonnie

(Bear, Delaware) C/IF, Parsippany Yankees, 2004 USA National Team

Bonnie Mills started playing baseball in Little League and continued through the Babe Ruth division. She played while she attended Caravel Academy and in 2003 joined the Parsippany Yankees. In 2004 she attended a tryout and was selected as a member of the USA National Team. She hit .600 for the Women's World Series and helped her club beat Taiwan on the way to beating Japan in the gold medal game. She drove in the game-winning run against Taiwan with a perfectly executed squeeze bunt. {USA Baseball 2004 Media Guide.}

Mills, Donna

(b. 1973, Lynn, Massachusetts) 3B, Waterbury Diamonds, Lowell Robins, Boston Blue Sox

Donna Mills grew up playing Little League in Pine Hill but never thought she would have the opportunity to play baseball as an adult. She set a number of offensive records playing softball at the University of Massachusetts at Lowell. Her career batting average was .438, and she knocked in 126 runs and scored another 148. Her batting was what got her noticed for Team USA. In 1996 she also received all-star and all-conference selection as the starting shortstop. She started playing during the regular season for the Lowell Robins in the New England Women's Baseball League in 1999 and travels with the Boston Blue Sox. She also spent part of her time in the NEWBL playing for the Waterbury Diamonds. In 2003 she led the U.S. team in hitting during the Women's World Series with a .471 average. She also drove in two runs and stole three bases. In the 2004 final of the World Series in Japan, Mills was 2–3 with two runs batted in. She hit .462 during the first women's World Cup event helping her team win the gold medal over Japan. When she is not playing baseball, Mills works as a court officer in the Lynn Juvenile Court system. {Chris Gasper, "Going to Bat for Her Country," *The Boston Globe*, 17 June 2004; Australian Baseball Federation, <www.baseball.org.au>.}

Mills, Dorothy Jane Seymour

Writer/researcher

Dorothy Jane Mills grew up near Cleveland, Ohio, and had a great many interests as a youngster. She majored in English while attending Fenn College (Cleveland State University today) and worked for the college's literary magazine. Dorothy also worked odd jobs for local newspapers trying to learn the trade. Shortly after her third year in college Dorothy married baseball writer and historian Harold Seymour. She transferred to Mather College and finished her degree in education. She took up teaching and continued in school to complete a master's degree. While teaching she began writing children's books and a variety of articles. Her husband retired to full time baseball writing in the 1970s, completing a series of books on baseball with Dorothy's assistance as a researcher and editor. When her hus-

band died in 1992 Dorothy began to travel more extensively but continued writing. She remarried and now lives in Naples, Florida. In addition to her own writing she established the Seymour Medal Conference and awards to honor the best baseball books written each year.

Mills, Kristin

(Bear, Delaware) P 2003, Parsippany Yankees, 2004 Team USA

Kristin Mills got her start in baseball early with Little League and Babe Ruth baseball in Bear, Delaware. In 1998 she pitched for Caravel Academy's state championship ball club, having been with the club for five years. After joining the ECWBL Mills pitched for the Parsippany Yankees to a 12–0 victory over the Angels on 4 May 2003. She held the Angels to three hits using a wicked curve and a 70–mph fastball. She finished the summer season with a 10–1 record to lead the league and also led the league with an ERA of 0.82. She pitched nine complete games and had four shutouts. She struck out 128 in 68 innings and walked only 36. In 2004 Mills played in the fourth Women's World Series and the first women's World Cup and helped her team win the gold medal by pitching a three-hit shutout in the final game. She gave up a total of four runs in two games during the series. In the World Series she combined with a teammate to throw a no-hitter in their first game of the series. She was named one of the top ten players of the tournament for finishing with an ERA of 0.81 with eight strikeouts and only giving up one earned run. In 2005 she became the assistant baseball coach at Caravel Academy. {USA Baseball 2004 Media Guide.}

Milwaukee Chicks

"A Team of Their Own"
Milwaukee Magazine, July 1994
By Tom Morgan and Jim Nitz

Fifty years ago, the Milwaukee Chicks won — and lost — it all.

Who is the only Milwaukee pitcher to win four games of a pro baseball championship series? Warren Spahn? Pete Vuckovich? Connie Wisniewski?

Connie Wisniewski? She's the right answer — the star right-hander who led the Milwaukee Chicks to the 1944 title of the All-American Girls'[sic] Professional Ball League and an athlete who left her male counterparts in the dust. The most games Spahn won in a single series was one. Vuke didn't get any while a Brewer.

Even Wisniewski's searing fastball couldn't save her team from its ultimate jam: It played its season in anonymity and red ink, then moved immediately to Grand Rapids. This year marks the fiftieth anniversary of perhaps the most successful, least loved team in Milwaukee history.

Chewing gum mogul Philip Wrigley started the league—the same one depicted in A League of Their Own—in 1943 because World War II had siphoned off more than half of the existing major-leaguers. Buoyed by good attendance in towns like Kenosha and Rockford, he added teams the next year in Milwaukee and Minneapolis.

Wrigley apparently gave little thought, though, to naming the new teams. The Milwaukee Journal dubbed the team the "Schnits," German for "little beer." After another drawing board session, the team came up with the Chicks nickname, inspired by its Hall of Fame manager, Max Carey, and a popular kids' book, Mother Carey's Chickens. Undaunted, The Journal insisted on calling the team Schnits. "I thought Chicks was a nice name," says Wisniewski. "It was a lot better than being a Schnit."

In those days, the name probably carried fewer sexist connotations than did the everyday press coverage, which sometimes referred to a player's "sturdy shanks" or other physical attributes. The players didn't seem to mind. "We had swell write-ups," says Thelma "Tiby" Eisen, the left fielder who was described as "a wisp of a thing" with "iron biceps." "They even started calling me 'Little Pigtails,' which was true. I had good legs, but I wasn't a raving beauty."

The press' favorite, Pat Keagle, was tabbed the "Blonde Bombshell." The Kenosha Evening News said the 5-foot-2-inch, 144-pound right fielder had "murder in her bat and speed to spare in her strong, sturdy shanks." (Keagle died of cancer in her 30s.)

Wisniewski wouldn't have made it out of her front door in Detroit if not for some heavy lobbying of her Polish mother, who insisted that "only bad girls leave home."

"I gave her several options," Wisniewski recalled. "I said it is either the military for four years or baseball for four months."

This cast faced a number of problems. Milwaukee native Sylvia "Ronie" Wronski loved pitching at venerable Borchert Field, but most players felt the cavernous stadium lacked intimacy. While 3,000 fans filled other ballparks, the same crowd at Borchert Field seemed lost.

The Chicks also received minimal press support. The papers wrote few feature stories on either the team or Carey's 17-year Hall of Fame career with the Pittsburgh Pirates. The most energetic coverage, in fact, was the Sentinel's sharp critiques of the 95-cent ticket prices, the

same as those for the minor-league Brewers, even though the games were shorter and sometimes satiated[sic] with errors.

The team struggled at the gate, if not at the plate. A total of 2,300 people came to the Chicks' first four games, while the higher-exposure Brewers drew 13,694 on opening day alone. "We knew as early as mid–June that Milwaukee was a bust," says Ken Sells, then league president.

The Chicks showed tenacity, however. Hours before the June 10th game, catcher Dorothy "Mickey" Maguire received notice that her husband had died in combat. She caught that night anyway, and even held off telling her teammates until after the game. Seven weeks later, Maguire received two letters, both from her husband. It turned out he'd only been mistaken for dead because he'd been burned so bad. He was shipped home after the season, but the couple divorced seven years later.

By August, the Chicks began dominating opponents, often by dint of their speed and pitching strength. As the 10-time league leader in stolen bases, Carey quickly taught the art of legalized larceny. "Max taught us how to cherry-pick our times to hit and run, steal or take a pitch," remembered Eisen, the explosive left fielder from California.

And the pitching of 5-foot-10-inch Wisniewski, later nicknamed "Iron Woman," was practically enough to win games on its own. "One or two runs was enough for her. If it was a must-win game, Connie pitched," says Viola "Tommy" Thompson, the Chicks' left-handed starting pitcher from South Carolina.

As management tried to stem the team's financial losses—even bringing in the Milwaukee Sinfonietta as a musical pre-game draw—the team kept winning. An 11-game streak in August propelled the team to the championship series. But true to form, the Chicks' luck faced a complication. Because the Brewers needed Borchert Field, all seven games were played in Kenosha, which the Chicks actually found more inviting than their own park.

Wisniewski felt especially at home, pitching an amazing five out of seven games and winning all four Chicks' victories. She yielded a miniscule two earned runs in 35 innings. "I pitched with my whole body, not just my arm," she says.

Just after the post-series corks were popped, however, the league moved the Chicks to Grand Rapids for the 1945 season, where they stayed until the league's demise in 1954. No one remembers anyone—not even Milwaukeean Sylvia Wronski—feeling homesick afterward for the town that all but ignored one of its few championship teams. {"A Team of Their Own" originally appeared in Milwaukee Magazine, July 1944. Used by permission.}

Minneapolis Millerettes

The Millerettes were a part of the AAGPBL, started by Philip Wrigley in 1943 to keep baseball alive while the men were going off to fight in the Second World War. The Minneapolis team belonged to the league for one short season, 1944. They played at Nicollet Park, which was the home park for the Minneapolis Millers. Many of the players signed by the Millerettes were locals discovered in the various softball leagues across the state, such as Lorraine Borg and Peg Torrison. Claude Jonnard acted as manager for the club. He had pitched for the New York Giants and Toledo Mudhens. A leading player for Minneapolis was Helen Callaghan, who played in 111 games and hit .287. The pitching staff was anchored by Annabelle Lee, aunt of major leaguer Bill "Spaceman" Lee and Dottie Wiltse. Wiltse finished the year with a 20–16 record and a miniscule 1.88 ERA.

The Millerettes started the season at home on 27 May 1944 and lost 5–4 to the Rockford Peaches. The crowd was entertained with the antics of Faye Dancer and Lavonne "Pepper" Paire. The Millerettes ended the first half of the year in the cellar with a record of 23–36. By the middle of the second half of the season the Millerettes found themselves playing all their games on the road because teams did not want to travel all the way to Minneapolis and then have to play in front of tiny crowds. They ended the second half with a record that nearly matched the first, 22–36. The team lost its franchise and moved to Fort Wayne in 1945. {Amy Kamenick, "'Queens of Swat': They Played Like Girls," *Minnesota Women's Press*, 2 July–3 August 1999, 1, 15.}

Mississauga Girls Baseball League

(MGBL)

The MGBL was created in 1994 to give local girls the chance to play baseball. It was open to girls from the ages of 9–21, with divisions for the different ages. The league is a part of the Ontario Baseball Association.

Mitchell, Debbie

P, Florida Lightning

Debbie Mitchell won the final game of the 1998 South Florida Diamond Classic, defeating the Hurricanes.

Mitchell, Virne Beatrice "Jackie"

(b. 1914, Chattanooga, Tennessee; d. 7 January 1987, Tennessee)

By Ryan Bucher

The 1920s were considered the golden age of sports. Sportswriters created public interest, and athletes, such as Babe Ruth and Lou Gehrig, were brought to celebrity status. Major league baseball greatly increased in popularity, so when the Great Depression hit, the major leagues remained relatively unaffected. Minor league teams, however, were not so lucky. Attendance significantly decreased, and many teams, especially in small cities, struggled to keep from going bankrupt. Team owners searched for ways to increase attendance (Berlage 1994, 73). They became innovators, trying several publicity stunts and promotional gimmicks to draw crowds. They tried everything from having the players play on donkeys or playing a game in water to changing the players' uniforms to having female ushers.

One of the greatest baseball innovators of all time was Joe Engel, who was the owner, promoter, and president of the Chattanooga Lookouts, an AA minor league team of the Southern Association. He was nicknamed Barnum Joe, and he had been involved with vaudeville in the 1920s. He was known for such antics as conducting elephant-hunting safaris in his ballpark, named Engel Stadium, and for trading his shortstop, Johnny Jones, to the Charlotte Hornets for a 25–pound turkey; he later claimed he got the worst of the deal. He even once filled the seats by raffling off a house (Gregorich 1994, 66). His greatest publicity stunt came when he got the idea to have a woman pitch in an exhibition game against the powerful New York Yankees.

In March 1931, he signed a 17–year-old southpaw who stood 5′7″ tall and weighed about 130 pounds to be the new pitcher for the Chattanooga Lookouts. Most of the newspapers claimed that Jackie Mitchell was the first woman to sign a professional baseball contract. Mitchell, however, was the second woman to sign a contract to play professional baseball, just as she was the second woman to play against a major league team. In 1898, Lizzie Arlington had become the first woman to sign a contract with the minor leagues (Gregorich 1994, 14). The first woman to play against a major league team had been Lizzie Murphy, who played against the Boston Red Sox in a benefit game for the American League All-Stars at Fenway Park on August 14, 1922 (Berlage 1994, 55). Mitchell used this opportunity to accomplish what no one thought a woman could ever do— strike out Babe Ruth and Lou Gehrig. It was an event covered by every major media source, but it was quickly forgotten.

Virne Beatrice "Jackie" Mitchell was born in Chattanooga, Tennessee, in 1914. Her father, Dr. Joseph Mitchell, was an optometrist. He and his wife, Virne, encouraged Jackie to become active. She had been a frail, sickly child, and she was encouraged to participate in sports in order to build up her health. She soon displayed an extraordinary athletic ability. She could box, run, and play tennis and basketball. Her mother and father were pleased that she was so healthy, and they wanted to see her go as far as she could in athletics (National Baseball Hall of Fame Archives).

Mitchell particularly excelled at baseball. She had become the star pitcher at the Signal School, a private preparatory school. Part of her excellence was due to the training she received as a child. Her personal coach had been Dazzy Vance, a pitcher for the Brooklyn Dodgers and a future member of the National Baseball Hall of Fame. Mitchell first met Vance when she was seven or eight. He was pitching for a team in Memphis, and Mitchell became friends with his son. When Vance was home, he would play catch with the two of them and give them pitching tips. This greatly fueled Mitchell's interest in becoming a professional baseball player. She dreamt of one day pitching in the World Series.

Mitchell first attracted the attention of baseball scouts in 1929, when she was playing for Joe Engel's Engelettes, a girls' baseball team that played games in and around Chattanooga. The team was coached by her father. Many baseball enthusiasts became impressed with Mitchell's ability. They encouraged her to get more training at Norman "Kid" Elberfeld's baseball school in Atlanta, which she attended in March 1931. This school was the only one of its kind at the time, and it was frequented by many major-leaguers, such as Luke Appling of the Chicago White Sox, who trained there during the off-season.

It was at this time that Joe Engel realized the possibilities of using Mitchell's abilities not only to launch her career, but to draw crowds. However, it was Mitchell's father who suggested to Engel that he sign his daughter. Engel had just arrived from Washington to run the Lookouts, and he was anxious to attract large crowds to the park (National Baseball Hall of Fame Archives). Mitchell was in Dallas playing in a basketball tournament, but Engel did not waste any time, quickly outfitting her with a Lookout uniform made by Spalding, and getting permission from the Yankees to agree to let her pitch one inning of an exhibition game as the team headed north from its spring training camp in Florida.

Mitchell's signing with the Lookouts grabbed national headlines. Engel reportedly took out a $10,000 life and pitching-arm insurance policy on her. Even before her first appearance on the mound, other teams in the Southern Association came to Engel with trade offers for Mitchell. The Memphis Chicks offered two players and cash for her contract, but Engel turned them down. Engel also declined offers from teams in Nashville and Birmingham, who presented him with similar proposals (National Baseball Hall of Fame Archives; Berlage 1994, 74). Engel claimed that Mitchell was just too good to be traded, but he most probably saw her as more of a novelty who would fill the stands than as an athlete.

Universal Newsreel, wire services, and reporters from all over the nation came to Chattanooga. They loved the stereotypical idea of frail, young teenager going against the big, overpowering Sultan of Swat. The sportswriters were very skeptical of how Mitchell would actually fare against the man of steel. If the best male pitchers had a tough time against Ruth, how would a 17-year-old, 130-pound girl keep him from hitting the ball out of the park? (Berlage 1994, 74).

The day before the game, reporters interviewed Mitchell and Ruth. Mitchell appeared to be calm and confident. When asked if she thought she could strike out Ruth, Mitchell replied, "Yes, I think I can strike him out" (Gregorich 1993, 74). Even Jackie's father felt she would be able to perform well. He told reporters that his daughter was "a curveball pitcher, not a smoke-ball pitcher," but she could do the job against the Yankees (Gregorich 1994, 67).

Ruth, on the other hand, seemed very skeptical. He acted extremely chauvinistic toward the fact of a woman playing baseball. He believed that Mitchell had no place on any baseball field, let alone the same field he was on. He was quoted as saying that he did not know what would happen to baseball if women were allowed to play — "Of course they will never make good. Why? Because they are too delicate. It would kill them to play ball everyday" (Gregorich 1993, 74). He then asked how big Jackie was, and when told of her size he muttered, "Well, I don't know what things are coming to" (Gregorich 1994, 68). Ruth said that he hoped his encounter with Mitchell would be the last time he was called upon to bat against a woman. It was amid this skepticism and condescension that Mitchell took the mound.

The game was originally scheduled for 1 April 1931, but was moved back to April 2 because of rain. Four thousand people showed up to watch the game at Engel Stadium. Many of them came to see Ruth and Gehrig hit one over the fence, but the majority were there to see how the southpaw would fare against baseball's best.

Mitchell warmed up while Clyde Barfoot, who had spent some time in the majors with the Cardinals and Tigers, took the mound as the starter. The first batter, Earle Combs, hit a double off the center field wall. Then, Lyn Lary singled in Combs to give the Yankees a 1–0 lead. With a man on first and nobody out, the Lookouts' manager, Bert Niehoff, took out Barfoot and brought in Mitchell to face Ruth. She was wearing the baggy, white uniform specially sewn for her by A.G. Spalding Co. and a cap with a large "C" on it.

Mitchell took her allotted warm-up pitches, and Ruth stepped into the box. He tipped his cap and drew Mitchell's attention to the fact that Lary was on first base. Jackie remembered the words of encouragement her father had given her: "Go out there and pitch just like you pitch to anybody else" (Berlage 1994, 74). She was nervous, but would quickly settle down.

Mitchell went into a long, grindy windup. She paid no attention to the man on first, as she had all her attention focused on the batter. Lary could have easily stolen second, but he stayed where he was. Ruth swung at the first pitch and missed. The next two pitches were wide. Ruth called for a new ball, then swung at the next pitch and missed. With a 2–2 count, Mitchell wound up and threw the ball as hard as she could down the middle of the plate. Ruth watched it pass over the plate, and umpire Brick Owens called the third strike. Ruth gave the umpire an angry look and headed off toward the dugout, where he threw his bat against the back wall.

The next batter was Lou Gehrig. One reporter wrote of Gehrig as he stepped up to the plate that "his knees were shaking and he cut at three fast ones ... and also sat down" (Berlage 1994, 75). As Mitchell recalled, after she struck out Gehrig, it "set off a standing ovation ... that must have lasted ten minutes" (Gregorich 1994, 69). After the crowd calmed down, Tony Lazzeri stepped into the batter's box. He swung at one pitch and fouled off another before eventually drawing a base on balls. After walking Lazzeri, Mitchell was taken out of the game and Barfoot was put back in as pitcher. Mitchell had proven that women were capable of playing against the men.

The Lookouts lost the game 14–4, but Mitchell believed that they could have won if she had been allowed to stay in the game. Unfortunately, she did not get a chance to prove that the game was not a fluke. She had planned on joining the Lookouts and pitching in every city that had a league team. Baseball commissioner Kenesaw Mountain Landis announced that women were banned from competing in baseball and that her contract was null and void. Landis claimed that baseball was "too strenuous" for a female (Gregorich 1994, 69).

With no one coming to her defense, Mitchell was taken off the club roster; however, she continued to have a role with the club, doing promotional work. She returned to the Engelettes, playing against area semipro and amateur teams. Within a month of Landis' ruling, she had joined the Junior Lookouts as the star attraction. The team was made up of former and future minor league players, and it was managed by Kid Elberfeld. Mitchell pitched the first 2–3 innings of each game. It was with the Lookouts that Mitchell returned to Engel Stadium a few months later, where she pitched three hitless innings against Margaret Nabel and the New York Bloomer Girls in front of a crowd of 4,000 (Gregorich 1994, 70).

In 1931, Mitchell signed a contract with the Lookout Mountaineers to play pro men's basketball. The next year, she returned to baseball, joining the Greensboro, North Carolina, team of the Piedmont League. Mitchell pitched for their road games only. The team was so low in the minor league systems that Landis never found out about her playing.

In 1933, at the age of 19, Mitchell signed with the House of David. The House was a barnstorming team known for its fair and exceptional play, and for the long hair and beards worn by all the men on the team. Mitchell was paid $1,000 per month, pitching an inning or two every day against minor league and semipro teams. She played in one game against the St. Louis Cardinals where she struck out a rookie shortstop named Leo Durocher. In the off-season, Mitchell played professional basketball on a men's team or toured on a team with Babe Didrikson (Berlage 1994, 77).

In 1937, at the age of 23 and with no hope of moving up to baseball's best circuits because of her banishment, Mitchell retired from baseball and returned home to work in her father's office, where she was quickly forgotten by the sports world. It was not until 1975 that Mitchell's achievements came back into the public mindset. Alan Morris, sports editor for the Chattanooga News–Free Press, received a letter asking "whatever happened to the girl who struck out Babe Ruth?" Mitchell saw the article in the newspaper and called him to retell her story. Just like in 1931, Jackie once again received hundreds of congratulatory letters about what she had accomplished.

Fifty-one years later, in 1982, Jackie was invited back to Engel Stadium to throw out the first ball on opening day. In 1984, she was honored at

Atlanta Stadium, where she watched her first major league baseball game in person. The newspaper clippings, the mail, and the honors served as a reminder that she was not forgotten. She died on 7 January 1987 at the age of 73 in Fort Oglethorpe, Tennessee (National Baseball Hall of Fame Archives).

Many still maintain that Ruth and Gehrig struck out on purpose as a publicity stunt. Several articles make it clear that both players did all they could to deliberately miss the ball. Still, Mitchell believes that they did not deliberately strike out. She knew how good she was: "I had a drop pitch. When I was throwing it right, you couldn't touch it. Better hitters than them couldn't hit me." Whether or not they were trying does not matter. Jackie never was able to achieve her dream of pitching in the World Series, but she still struck out two of the game's greatest hitters, cementing her place as "the girl who struck out Babe Ruth."

Mitchem, Shannan

(b. 17 March 1970, Decatur, Georgia) OF/3B/ DH 1994–97, Colorado Silver Bullets

Shannan Mitchem was named the top scholar athlete when she graduated from Tucker High School in 1988. Her best sport was basketball, where she was named the defensive player of the year in both 1987 and 1988. She was the starting third baseman at Florida State for four years and played in the NCAA World Series in 1990–1992. She played right field for the Silver Bullets in 19 games during their inaugural season. She drove in their first run as a new team during a game in Tucson, Arizona. Her biggest highlight came at Coors Field on May 4 when her diving catch appeared on ESPN and *Sunday Sports Center* as both a play of the day and of the week. Mitchem and fellow Bullet Ann Williams tried out for the New York Mets in 1995 by attending their camp at Port St. Lucie with 52 other hopefuls. Mitchem made it through to the second round before she was cut from the tryouts. After the Bullets folded, Mitchem went to work as a personal trainer. {*The Silver Bulletin* December 1995; David Kindred, *Colorado Silver Bullets: For the Love of the Game* (Atlanta: Longstreet Press, Inc.), 86; "For the Love of the Game," Colorado Silver Bullets souvenir program, 1995; Jennifer Frey, "Dreams Live Another Day for Players Making Mets' Cut," *New York Times*, 2 February 1995, B16; Paul Newberry, "Out of Action," *Rocky Mountain News*, 19 July 1998.}

Moczynski, Betty Jane "Moe"

(b. 30 June 1926, Milwaukee, Wisconsin) Util. OF 1943, Rockford Peaches

Before playing in the All American League, Betty Moczynski gained her athletic experience not at Pulaski High School but in the local city leagues. She played in a women's softball league, a men's fast-pitch league and a women's basketball league. In her one season of play in the All American League, the highlight of her career was driving in five runs in one game, which was one short of the record. After playing in the AAGPBL for the Peaches, Moczynski moved to Chicago to play for the Chicago Bluebirds in the National Girls Baseball League as a catcher and outfielder for four years. She worked for General Motors in Milwaukee until her retirement in 1987. {AAGPBL Newsletter, May 2001, 38; AAGPBL Questionnaire, National Baseball Hall of Fame.}

Moffet, Jane Humes

(b. 2 July 1930, Philadelphia, Pennsylvania) 1B/ OF/C 1949–52, Springfield Sallies, Kalamazoo Lassies, Battle Creek Belles

Jane Moffet graduated from Pitman High School in 1948, where there were few sports for girls, but she did play field hockey and basketball. She attended East Stroudsburg University in Pennsylvania, where she continued to play field hockey and basketball. She holds the single-game scoring record in a basketball game, with 49 points. During her first year at the university a friend saw an advertisement for tryouts for a women's baseball league and asked Moffet to go with her. Moffet went and impressed the scouts with her hitting. She did not really expect anything to come of the trial but in May 1949 Moffet got a ticket and a telegram requesting her to report for training in Muskegon, Michigan, as soon as her final exams ended. Having never traveled or played baseball before, Jane's trip turned into quite an adventure. She had to go alone because her friend did not make the league. Within a few days of her arrival in Muskegon the league decided Moffet needed practice, and she was sent to join the two traveling squads in Chicago. Her first roommates were the four Cubans who had just arrived as well. Moffet traveled in 1949 with the Sallies and did the same in 1950. In 1951 she joined the roster of the Kalamazoo club and then in mid–1952 finished her career with Battle Creek. She played in 171 games with a .240 average. She drove in only 46 runs and scored another 59.

After leaving the league Moffet finished college

and spent 42 years teaching in New Jersey. She eventually became the principal of Saddlebrook High School, a job she held for 23 years. In 1990 Moffet received word of her induction into the East Stroudsburg University Sports Hall of Fame and then in 1998 to the Pennsylvania Sports Hall of Fame. {AAGPBL Questionnaire, National Baseball Hall of Fame; Patricia Brown, "Jane Moffet," in *A League of My Own*, Patricia I. Brown, 174–179.}

Mohney, Mrs. Ethel

Owner

Mrs. Ethel Mohney was the principal stockholder of the Topeka club in the Western Association. {"Woman Owner Re-Signs Topeka Manager," *Sporting News*, 10 March 1948, 28.}

Molnar, Christine "Christy"

OF 2003–04, South Bend Blue Sox, Motown Magic

Christine Molnar graduated from Grosse Ile High School and went on to play baseball for the Blue Sox and the Magic. She helped out her teams as a switch hitter with a lot of speed. Many of her hits were infield singles, and when she got on base she ran.

Monge, Christine "Sid"

(b. 11 July 1973, San Francisco, California) P 1995–97, Colorado Silver Bullets

Christine Monge played softball at Tamalpais High School and led her team in triples, home runs, and RBIs during the 1988–89 season. She also played basketball until her graduation in 1991. She attended Bellevue Community College before joining the Silver Bullets in 1994 after turning down a basketball scholarship to Whitworth College. She led the team in appearances as a pitcher with 20 in 1995. She struck out 20 batters in just 27 innings pitched. Midway through the 1997 season, Monge was 2–2 with four saves and a 3.68 ERA and had yet to walk a batter. {*The Silver Bulletin* December 1995; Michael Kord, "Monge Excels at Back of Bullpen," *Seattle Post-Intelligencer*, 11 July 1997.}

Montalbano, Rose

2B/3B 1951–53, Muskegon Lassies

Rose Montalbano joined the Muskegon Lassies near the end of the existence of the AAGPBL.

Montgomery County (PetBarn) Barncats

The Barncats joined the EWBC/WMWBL as one of four league entrants. Their corporate sponsor was PetBarn, a pet store in Burtonville. Included on their team roster was at least one college All-American in catcher Kelly Ballentine. Ballentine also happened to be the owner of PetBarn. The team is coached by Richard Bender, who also recruits players for the club. In 1994 the Barncats won the WMWBL championship. They completed the 1999 season with a record of 4–7, tying them with the Flames for the second-best record. By 2004 the league grew to include five entrants, with Richard Bender still working with the Barncats. The club came in second in 2004. Bender also got the league and his team involved in a new venture in 2004 with the addition of the U.S. Lightning, a team for girls under age 17 in the Washington-Baltimore area who want to learn the game of baseball. This team is building on the earlier Olney Girls baseball team that had played in the area from 2002 to 2004.

Montgomery, Dorothy "Monty"

(b. 6 February 1924, Chattanooga, Tennessee) IF 1945–46, Racine Belles, Muskegon Lassies

Dorothy Montgomery played for two seasons in the All American League. Her rookie year she spent with Racine and then went on to the Lassies. Batting only .208 for the Lassies in 1946, Montgomery played in only 26 games and did not return again in 1947. She attended the University of Chattanooga and became a registered cytologist for nearly 30 years before retiring to pursue softball, bowling and riding motorcycles. {AAGPBL Baseball Cards, 1995.}

Moore, Dolores "Dee"

(b. 27 October 1932, Chicago, Illinois; d. 31 August 2000, Bensenville, Illinois) 1B/2B 1953–54, Grand Rapids Chicks

Dolores Moore gained her experience in the National Girls Baseball League in Chicago before she signed on with the All American League. She even won the MVP award one year in the national league. Dee Moore was selected for the 1954 all-star team for her all-around good play. Her fielding was what set her apart from other players, as she only made 27 errors in her career. She played in 149 games and hit .239. After playing baseball she taught in the Chicago public schools for over 30 years. {AAGPBL Newsletter, September 2000, 6;

"Obituaries," *Sports Collectors Digest*, 27 October 2000, 10.}

Moore (Walker), Eleanor "Ellie"

(b. 1 November 1933, Long Point, Illinois) P 1950–54, Chicago Colleens, Kalamazoo Lassies, Fort Wayne Daisies, Grand Rapids Chicks

Eleanor Moore played for five seasons in the All American League, three of them with Grand Rapids. She started with the touring Sallies since she was only 17 and needed some skill development. Not only did Moore become a solid pitcher, but she often helped her own cause at the bat. In one game against the Springfield Sallies she hit two home runs, but the Colleens lost 14–3. She also scored the third run, coming in on a base hit by Joan Sindelar. In 1954 she pitched a no-hitter as the highlight of her career. Her career batting average was .265 and she compiled a 49–46 pitching record with a 2.74 ERA. {AAGPBL Baseball Cards, 1996.}

Moore, Lucille

(b. March 1908, South Bend, Indiana) Chaperone 1945–48, South Bend Blue Sox

Lucille Moore worked with the Blue Sox players as their chaperone for four seasons. In addition she taught physical education and swimming at South Bend Central High School for many years. Her degree came from Indiana State Teachers College. {AAGPBL Baseball Cards, 2002.}

Moore, Mary Ann "Sis"

(b. 7 June 1932, Detroit, Michigan) 2B 1950–52, Springfield Sallies, Battle Creek Belles

Mary Moore played fast-pitch softball for Wyandotte Chemical before joining the AAGPBL's touring teams. She also graduated from Lincoln Park High School in 1950, making it possible for her to join. She learned her skills from a neighbor and former Detroit Tigers star, Eddie Lake, who often joined the local kids on the sandlots for a game. Moore participated in the AAGPBL from 1950 through 1952 before injuries cut short her career. She started with the Springfield Sallies and finished with the Battle Creek club. She got her chance to play through a teacher at her high school who introduced her to a former player, Doris Neal. After attending spring training in South Bend, Mary was sent to join the Sallies in order to get more training. In 1950 she led the Sallies in games played (77), hits (75), and RBIs (48). She also connected for three home runs and scored 65 runs to also lead the team. During the off-season she worked in an auto parts factory and then got a call to join the new team in Battle Creek. Shortly before she was to report, Mary cut off two fingers on her pitching hand and thought her career was finished. Late in the season the team called her because of injuries to other players, and she went. She finished the 1951 season, and then in 1952 her career ended with an ankle injury. She quit and went back to Michigan to work for the telephone company for 34 years, retiring in 1989. {AAGPBL Newsletter, January 1995 and September 2000, 35; Patricia Brown, "Mary "Sis" Moore," in *A League of My Own*, Patricia I. Brown, 179–184.}

Moore-McPaul, Kenya

OF 2002–04, Detroit Danger, Motown Magic

Kenya Moore-McPaul contributes to her teams as one of the fastest players in the game. Every year she is at or near the top in stolen bases, and leads in bunt singles. She also uses that speed to cover a lot of ground in the outfield.

Morgan, Constance Enola "Connie"

(b. 17 October 1934, Philadelphia, Pennsylvania; d. 14 October 1996, Philadelphia, Pennsylvania)

By Leslie A. Heaphy and Larry Lester

Connie Morgan grew up in Philadelphia with five siblings and her parents. Her father, Howard Morgan, worked as a window cleaner while her mother, Vivian Beverly, stayed home with the children. Connie Morgan attended Landreth Elementary School and John Bartrum High School before attending the William Penn Business Institute. Morgan graduated from the institute in late 1955 and got a job as a typist at Moss and Demany Furriers. Later she worked for the AFL-CIO until she retired in 1974.

When she was not in school Morgan played sports of all kinds. Later, she joined the Indianapolis Clowns after Toni Stone left in 1954, taking over her second base duties. That year, Morgan played in about 49 games under manager Oscar Charleston. Morgan was not the only woman on the 1954 team; the Clowns also signed Mamie Johnson to pitch. In her inaugural game Morgan made one fine fielding play at second to rob a Birmingham batter of a sure base hit and walked twice at the plate, thereby solidifying her place as a bona fide player and not just a gate attraction. Morgan hit one home run during her

Connie Morgan when she played for the Indianapolis Clowns (courtesy Noirtech Research).

single season in the Negro leagues when they played a game in Laurel, Kansas. Before joining the team Morgan had been a well-known amateur athlete in the city of Philadelphia. She spent five seasons with a local team called the Honey Drippers, an all-female team, where she compiled a .363 average. In addition to her baseball prowess, during the off-season Morgan played basketball with the Philadelphia Rockettes at the local YMCA in south Philadelphia. In 1995 Morgan received word that she had been selected for membership in the Pennsylvania Sports Hall of Fame. {"The Second Baseman Was a Lady," *Philadelphia Daily News*, 18 October 1997, 18; "Clowns Sell Toni Stone, Sign New Female Star," *Michigan Chronicle*, 13 March 1954; "Indianapolis Clowns List Two Women on Ball Roster," *Birmingham World*, 4 May 1954.}

Morii, Kazumi

SS/P, Japan

During the 2003 Women's World Series, Kazumi Morii had two hits in Japan's 8–4 victory over the United States. In the final versus Australia, Morii was 1–2 at the plate. For the series she hit .312 with two runs batted in. In the 2004 victory over the United States Morii scored one of the 13 runs Japan manufactured to win 13–4. {"Japan Downs United States 13–4 to Take Gold Medal in Women's World Series Baseball," *AP Worldstream*, 22 July 2004.}

Morris, Carolyn "India"

(b. 28 September 1925, Phoenix, Arizona; d. 20 February 1996, Mesa, Arizona) P 1944–46, Rockford Peaches

Carolyn Morris pitched for the A–1 Phoenix Queens beginning in 1941. She played for over 15 years with the Queens and was selected for membership in the Arizona Softball Foundation Hall of Fame in 1974 for her achievements. Two of her teammates on the Queens, Flossie Ballard and Rose Mofford, described her as an outstanding pitcher. In 1944 she signed on with the Rockford Peaches. In 1946 she was selected for the all-star team before she returned to the Queens. Her record that year stood at 29–13 with a 1.42 ERA. She struck out 240 batters while walking only 98. Her career numbers included three no-hitters and one perfect game. Morris also made a name for herself modeling for the House of Tiffany in Chicago before becoming a professional ballplayer. After her baseball career ended, she made a living as a real estate broker. {"Carolyn Morris, Ballplayer," *Washington Post*, 26 February 1996; AAGPBL Newsletter, May 1996, 8.}

Morrison (Gamberdella), Esther "Schmattze"

(b. 26 May 1931, Chicago, Illinois) C/P/OF 1950, Chicago Colleens, Springfield Sallies

Esther Morrison played for one season with the two traveling squads in the All American League. She traveled all over the country and played in a variety of places while gaining experience. She did not return in 1951 but instead went to work at Motorola and then as a postal clerk. {AAGPBL Baseball Cards, 1995.}

Morton, Kathy

OF 1996–97, Colorado Silver Bullets

Kathy Morton played softball at the University of Southwestern Louisiana in 1994 and 1995. In 1994 she hit .435 with 68 RBIs and was named a first-team All-American as a result. In 1995 she received the same honor as well as being the Louisiana Player of the Year. She joined the Silver Bullets in 1996 and 1997. During one victory in 1997, Morton helped her club beat the Shreveport All Stars 10–3 by knocking out two hits and driving in one run. {"Silver Bullets Defeat Shreveport Team," *The Advocate*, 2 June 1997, 9E; *Silver Bulletin*, March 1996.}

Motown Magic

The Magic joined the GLWBL in 2004. The manager is Jude Johnson, who used to play for the Detroit Renegades along with coach John Raniszewski. Raniszewski's wife Kris pitches for the club when she is not working for Hertz Rental Car Company. Kris started playing softball at age 11 and switched to hardball in 1997. Their home games are played at the Civic Center baseball field in Southfield while practices take place every Saturday. {Kristin Karpscuk, "Motown Magic Calling on a Few Good Women," *Daily Oakland Press*, 14 April 2004.}

Mudge (Cato), Nancy "Smudgie"

(b. 1930, New York) 2B 1950–54, Chicago Colleens, Springfield Sallies, Kalamazoo Lassies, Battle Creek Belles, Muskegon Lassies

Nancy Mudge played second base for the Lassies for parts of four seasons and even played for the league championship against the Daisies in 1954. She played in 388 games and hit just .200. She drove in 79 runs, stole 110 bases and scored 227 runs to help her teams. After baseball Mudge got married and taught for many years at the University of Minnesota. {Aron Kahn, "They Were the Girls of Summer," *St. Paul Pioneer Press Dispatch*, 9 July 1988, 6A, 8A.}

Mueller (Bajda), Dolores "Champ"

(b. 31 May 1931, Chicago, Illinois) P/3B 1949, South Bend Blue Sox

Her high school had no sports for girls, but that did not stop Dolores Mueller from playing games. She played softball, volleyball and baseball in local leagues. She even won a trophy in 1948 as the MVP in an all-star softball game. She got to play in fewer than ten games with South Bend but enjoyed her time in the AAGPBL. She continued to play softball and volleyball after she left the league. She married Chester Bajda in 1954 and they had two daughters. {AAGPBL Questionnaire, National Baseball Hall of Fame, Cooperstown, New York.}

Mueller, Dorothy "Sporty," "Dottie"

(b. 25 December 1925, Cheviot, Ohio; d. 2 June 1985) P/1B 1947–53, Peoria Red Wings, South Bend Blue Sox, Grand Rapids Chicks

Dorothy Mueller played for seven years in the All American League, starting with the Red Wings and finishing in Grand Rapids. In between she had a three-year stint in South Bend. During her career Dottie twice won 21 games and made the all-star team in 1947 when she was 21–13 with a 1.41 ERA. She followed that season with an even better record in 1948 at 21–9 with a 1.11 ERA. She also hit .211 in 318 games. {AAGPBL Baseball Cards, 1996.}

Mullen, Erin

(b. 1985, Cincinnati, Ohio) P/OF, 2004 USA National Team

Growing up in Cincinnati, Ohio, Erin Mullen started playing baseball at age four. At Sycamore High School she played freshman baseball and varsity football, earning second team all-conference honors. After joining Team USA in 2001 she received an award for her pitching against the team from Australia. She was invited back the following year and her play earned her a scholarship in 2003 to Belmont University. In 2004, coaches selected her to join the USA National Team. In the 2004 World Series she paired up with Kristin Mills to throw a no-hitter in the team's first game, against India. Mills pitched the first four innings and Mullen came in to hold on for the win. {USA Baseball 2004 Media Guide.}

Muniz, Millie

(Bridgewater, Connecticut) OF, Florida Lightning

Millie Muniz discovered early in her playing days that she had great speed; it could help her cover ground in the outfield but also at bat. She started playing baseball at age five and then moved to softball, earning a scholarship to Miami-Dade Community College. She was named the team MVP in 1997 and 1998. In 2001 she played baseball for the Florida Lightning in the South Florida Diamond League.

Murphy, Elizabeth "Lizzie"

(b. 13 April 1894, Warren, Rhode Island; d. 28 July 1964)

By Dorothy Jane Mills,
AKA Dorothy Z. Seymour

Elizabeth "Lizzie" Murphy was a serious full time ballplayer, not a dabbler or part timer. The high point of her long career came on 14 August 1922, when she was invited to play first base at Fenway Park in Boston. Murphy was asked to take part in a charity game with a group of American League all-stars, who were playing against the Boston Red Sox as a benefit for the family of Tom McCarthy, a recently-deceased local sports personality.

A woman playing with and against big-leaguers in a big-league park ... in 1922? How could that happen?

Murphy was invited to play with the American Leaguers because she was well known in Boston and throughout New England as an excellent professional player and a gate attraction. Part of the headline describing the story for the *Boston Globe* read not "Woman in Game" but "Lizzie Murphy in Game." Boston fans knew Murphy and were aware that she played first base for a reputable local men's team that challenged excellent opponents all over New England and Canada. {James C. O'Leary, "Great Benefit Nets More Than $5000 for Tom McCarthy's Family," *Boston Globe*, 15 August 1922.}

Because the term "all-stars" was used for the team of American Leaguers that opposed the Red Sox in this competition, subsequent writers have often claimed that Lizzie Murphy played in a major league All-Star Game. The series of official All-Star Games didn't begin until 1933; this 1922 game was a charity exhibition, not part of the official All-Star series. But that doesn't detract from Murphy's achievement of becoming the first woman known to play in a game with and against major-leaguers.

That day a cartoonist for the *Boston Globe* sketched the game's highlights, presenting images of the stars of the occasion: the colorful player Nick Altrock, former mayor John Fitzgerald (who entertained the crowd by warbling "Sweet Adeline"), and Lizzie Murphy, drawn by the artist as she leaned off first base to make a catch. The *Globe*'s box score listed her as "Miss Murphy 1b." {James C. O'Leary.}

Despite being labeled "all-stars," Murphy's team was hardly made up of the American League's best performers; several were near the end of their careers, and four were playing their last season in the majors. Only two members of the team were well known as excellent players: pitcher Nick Altrock and shortstop Donie Bush. Babe Ruth didn't play, nor did Walter Johnson. Perhaps they could not be persuaded to take part because they would get no income from the game; the entire proceeds were earmarked for charity.

As for the Red Sox, they were in decline, and in 1922 they landed in last place. The team on which Murphy played beat them 3–2.

In the game, Murphy shared the first-base work with Doc Johnston, and the *Globe* reporter claimed that her performance in the game was a revelation to those who hadn't seen her play before, including the big-leaguers.

How did Murphy develop her skill? By participating in industrial ball, which reached its zenith in North America during the twenties and thirties. Lizzie was born in Warren, Rhode Island, a mill town, on 13 April 1894, one of seven children of John and Mary (Garant) Murphy. As the daughter of a New England mill worker, Murphy, like many other children, became a mill worker herself at around age 12.

The mills of New England were major centers for industrial ball. Mill workers had played ball at least since the 1870s, for example at Woonsocket, Rhode Island, and in Ludlow, Massachusetts. During the 1920s, mill owners were believers in the theory of welfare capitalism. Viewing the workers as valuable commodities, they tried to reduce turnover by improving work conditions. Such improvements included the provision of recreation programs, and since baseball was one of the most popular ways of having fun, many mills sponsored baseball teams and leagues for their employees.

A government recreation survey in 1926 showed that among the leading sponsors of industrial ball, textile mills were number one. Mills all over Massachusetts, New Hampshire, Delaware, and Rhode Island established recreation associations, often docking the pay of their employees a dollar or two a month to help pay for their activities, which included baseball. Like prisons, some mills not only sponsored interdepartmental teams, they also established "varsity" (company) teams. They supported leagues in which rival mills could compete. Some mills furnished company parks, too: Textile Field, at the great Amoskeag Mill in Manchester, New Hampshire, seated 4,000 fans. In this era many cities also furnished public parks where industrial ball was played. {Harold Seymour and Dorothy Z. Seymour, *Baseball: The People's Game* (New York: Oxford University Press, 1990), passim.}

Mill teams traveled to compete with each other and to play other industrial teams. Just north of Warren, Rhode Island, in Bristol County, lay Worcester County, home of textile cities like Pawtucket and Woonsocket, where mill teams competed in the famous Blackstone Valley League. Rivalry among these mill teams remained intense for years.

Murphy's father owned baseball equipment and probably played mill ball. His daughter followed in his footsteps, both at work and at play. She was one of the nearly two million children who had to work instead of going to school in this era. The plight of working children was documented by photographer Lewis Hine, who traveled the country snapping pictures of these laborers at work, some of them shown gazing longingly at the outdoors. Sarah Cleghorn's ironic poem about these children has become famous:

> The golf links lie so near the mill
> That almost every day
> The laboring children can look out
> And see the men at play.

One of these laboring children in the years before World War I was Lizzie Murphy, who said later that even while working she was always dreaming of the outdoors and baseball. She worked as a ring spinner in Warren's Parker Mill on Metacom Avenue. In ring spinning, the yarn is twisted and drawn while passing through a small metal device traveling rapidly around a ring while winding the yarn onto a bobbin. Children

watched several of these rings at once, to make certain they did not become tangled. Factory windows had to be kept tightly shut, even on hot summer days, to preserve moisture in the thread so that it wouldn't break. "Mill work," Murphy recalled later, "could be heavy." {Dick Reynolds, "Lizzie Murphy: Queen of Diamonds," *Old Rhode Island* 4, June 1994, 11–15.}

Murphy had been participating in sports since childhood. After work and on Saturdays, like many mill hands, she played baseball, although at first she managed to get into baseball games with the boys only by bringing her father's gloves and bats to team practice. Soon, however, the boys discovered her skill and chose her to play on their teams.

Murphy was good at several sports: swimming, soccer, long-distance running, and ice hockey. She also played the piano and the violin as well as enjoying wood-carving. But baseball was her greatest pleasure. Murphy was far from a large and husky person; an average-sized woman at five-foot six, she weighed approximately 122 pounds, but she was strong, having grown up chopping wood, shoveling snow, and washing floors. Not a glamour girl, she had a pleasant face and personality.

As a teenager, Murphy played regularly on local amateur teams and gained a reputation as one of Bristol County's best. By the time World War I started, she was 18 and playing semipro baseball with the team of the Warren Shoe Company, where she worked after leaving the mill. Semipro industrial games were generally played on Saturdays and featured free admission. To get some income, the home team passed the hat and shared the take with the visitors.

When Murphy played her first Saturday game in Warren, the collection amounted to $85, but when it came time for the manager to distribute the money, Murphy was given nothing. Taken aback, she refrained from objecting immediately. Instead, she bided her time and waited until the following Saturday's game, scheduled for Newport, where crowds of sailors were expected to come out to see the new female first baseman. In fact, Murphy waited until it was time to board the bus for the game, then refused to board until the manager agreed that she would share in every game's proceeds—plus a five-dollar fee for each game she played. For this stratagem she has become known as the first female holdout in baseball. {Jane Lancaster, "R. I. woman was a Hit in a Man's Game," *Providence Sunday Journal*, 12 July 1992.}

Murphy almost didn't stay in baseball. By age 18 she had become increasingly aware that she was an anomaly among young women. After all, in the America of 1922, young ladies didn't play pro ball. "I about decided," she said later, "that baseball wasn't a game for a girl, and that I'd quit." Then she went to see a game, and "I got so excited I couldn't stay out." {Elizabeth L. Williams, "Warren Woman Recalls Life as Baseball Star," *Providence Journal*, around 1937, from clipping in Murphy File, National Baseball Hall of Fame and Library, Cooperstown, New York.} So she remained in baseball, playing with the Warren team until she hooked up with an even more important club, the Providence Independents, who toured New England towns.

How did it go for a young woman while traveling with young men? Easily, she informed her public later. "I didn't have any trouble with the boys. Of course, they cursed and swore, but I didn't mind. I knew all the words." {Elizabeth L. Williams.} From her remarks about her acceptance by the team, it seems clear that they considered her just one of the fellows. That doesn't mean she was masculine. It means merely that she was a ballplayer, and the others on the team treated her like one, not like a sex object.

Soon she found her niche with a prominent team playing out of Boston, Carr's All-Stars, a nationally known professional club. In the 1920s Boston became one of the country's focal points for baseball leagues and teams outside Organized Baseball (the name used for the major leagues and their minor affiliates). The Boston area boasted amateur, semipro, and pro teams of various types: company teams, so-called athletic clubs, neighborhood nines, town teams, pro teams, semipro teams, traveling teams, amateur leagues, and twilight leagues.

On some of these clubs a few players, usually including the pitcher, received salaries. The others shared the receipts from passing the hat — even on Sundays, although Boston's laws supposedly forbade paid entertainment on the Lord's day. Crowds at games that were referred to as "semipro" in nearby Dorchester, Revere, Cambridge, Milton, and Lexington ranged from 2,000 on weekdays to as high as 10,000 on Sundays. *The Boston Globe* gave area clubs free advertising for these games.

Ed Carr's club was fully professional and a salaried team, although Carr didn't say how much he paid Murphy and the men. Touring clubs like his earned money by splitting gate receipts with the home team, the percentage of each team's share of the take agreed upon in advance.

Besides booking Boston-area clubs, Carr's team played farther afield. The team barnstormed all over New England, at least as far north as Waterville, Maine, and toured in Canada as well, playing more than a hundred games a summer.

Canadian clubs welcomed visits from New England touring clubs. Baseball had been played since the 1840s in Ontario, Nova Scotia, and New Brunswick. Halifax, Nova Scotia, and St. John, New Brunswick, were traditional baseball rivals. In Cape Breton, baseball was played among coal miners and in Halifax among shipbuilders. London and Guelph, in Ontario, and Quebec City and Montreal, in Quebec, were baseball hotbeds, and for some years Toronto and Montreal were even in Organized Baseball's International League.

Although Murphy's father was Irish American, her mother was French Canadian. The ethnic composition of New England towns in the early part of the century included many French-speaking people who had moved there from Canada. Murphy, like her four sisters and two brothers, was bilingual, having spoken French at home from her earliest years. At least once her bilingualism paid off in baseball. Playing in Canada against a French-speaking team, she realized that the opposition's first-base coach, believing his ploy was undetected, used French to transmit the sign to steal a base. After all, would a player with "Murphy" emblazoned on her uniform understand French? So Murphy called time, set up a code with the catcher and pitcher, and had the satisfaction of helping put out five runners while they were trying to steal.

Murphy showed initiative in another manner: she promoted herself by selling postcards bearing her picture in uniform. She hawked them in the stands during games and found that she could earn as much as 50 dollars beyond her salary by the sale of these cards.

Lizzie Murphy was a drawing card. With Ed Carr's Boston team, Murphy's uniform — the regulation cap, shirt, pants, and heavy stockings— bore her full name on the front. Carr featured her picture on his club letterhead and defended his unusual choice of first baseman by saying, "She swells attendance, and she's worth every cent I pay her. But most important, she produces the goods. She's a real player and a good fellow." {Elizabeth L. Williams.}

How good was Murphy as a ball player? Reports are that she fielded well and hit around .300, a respectable figure. "She was good," recalled Charlie Burdge, a Warren teacher and athletic director, who as a child once saw her play locally. {James Merolla, "Warren's Lizzie Murphy: The Only Woman to Play Pro Baseball with Men," *Warren Times-Gazette*, 8 July 1992.} Murphy could make the plays. And she didn't stand around on the field waiting for something to happen: she chatted up the team, supporting the pitcher the way good infielders do.

Moreover, Murphy had staying power. She lasted for 17 years with Carr's team, finally becoming a mentor for younger players as they arrived to join the team.

Murphy's approach to playing ball is revealed in the guidelines she lived by: "Playing ball is the same as everything else in life. Mind your own business and concentrate on what you are doing and you will be all right. Never mind faulting the other guy for his mistakes. Just correct your own. Criticism hurts a lot more than it helps because it destroys unity." {Dick Reynolds.}

Murphy long remembered her important game with and against big-leaguers at Fenway Park in 1922. She should: Jim O'Leary, the reporter who covered the game for the *Boston Globe*, wrote, "Her work amazed even the big leaguers." {James C. O'Leary.} Obviously, the American League All-Stars hardly expected the kind of performance she gave from "a girl" (she was 28). "Naturally," Murphy recalled, "they resented a woman they had never heard of coming into the game." {Elizabeth L. Williams.}

She entered the contest in the fourth inning. The first Red Sox batter hit a slow roller to third, which third baseman Harvey McClellan went after. Murphy said he "held onto the ball as long as he could, then gunned it across—what an arm!" {Jane Lancaster.} In fact, he threw off-balance to Murphy at first base. The ball did beat the runner, but the throw was low and off-target; yet Murphy caught it with a big stretch for the putout. "I handled the ball easily," she remarked later. It was this excellent catch that the cartoonist portrayed in his sketches of the game's events.

McClellan, obviously surprised, remarked grudgingly to Altrock, "She'll do." Altrock nodded in agreement. Murphy remembered with satisfaction, "After that, we all got along fine.... Once they saw I could play baseball, they accepted me, and they were great guys." {Dick Reynolds.}

In 1937, two years after her retirement to Warren, Murphy married Warren mill worker Walter Larivee. She was 43. Interviewed by the Providence *Sunday Journal* in 1938 at her Water Street home, she was pictured exercising her homemaking skills, standing at the stove preparing pea soup. But Walter died seven years after their marriage, and at age 50 she went back to work, first in the mills and later doing clamming.

Even then, she continued as a New England baseball attraction and contributed her talent to many charity baseball events. "Everyone wanted to see the girl on first," recalled sports writer Dick Reynolds, and Murphy "raised a ton of money" for Rhode Island and New England groups by appearing in exhibition games for them. Spectators who hadn't seen her in her prime came to scoff but reputedly left admitting that she was a real ballplayer. Writers nicknamed her "Spike Murphy" and "Queen of Diamonds." {Dick Reynolds.}

But when fans tried to put on a testimonial dinner in her honor, she declined the recognition. "If you met her coming up from the river with a bucket of clams, she'd stop for a few minutes and talk baseball," recalled Burdge, but for some reason Murphy didn't want any public recognition or honors for her baseball achievements.

Her friends explained that Murphy never liked "frivolities." An occasion that made her the object of adulation may have made her uncomfortable. A plain person with plain tastes, she preferred the real thing, playing the game, to taking public bows for her accomplishments. But it's clear that she was proud of what she had done. "Eddie [Carr] used to tell me," she said in 1938, "that I was the first girl to break into baseball with a man's team as a regular player. You know, that makes me feel mighty good." {Elizabeth L. Williams.}

Murphy passed away on 28 July 1964 and was buried at St. John's Cemetery in Warren. Almost 30 years later she received public recognition by the state of Rhode Island when, because of efforts by Warren resident Charlie Burdge, along with State Representative Michael J. Urban and retired sports writer Dick Reynolds, Governor Bruce Sundlun proclaimed 1 July 1992, as Lizzie Murphy Recognition Day.

The proclamation recognized Murphy's "ability to be able to play with the best" and the fact that she "has never reached her rightful distinction as the first female ever to play major league baseball." In that respect she beats out Lizzie Arlington, Jackie Mitchell, Vada Corbus, Kitty Burke, Frances Dunlop, Babe Didrikson Zaharias, and Eleanor Engle. Most of these women were, like Lizzie Murphy, serious players who would have liked to have the chance to play regularly in the major leagues—real baseball players who were born too soon.

Murphy, Nicolle

Nicolle Murphy played baseball for one of the many Australian teams in 2002.

Muskegon Belles

The city of Muskegon got a second entrant in

the All American League when they picked up the franchise of the Belles from Battle Creek for the 1953 season. The Belles ended up in the cellar with a 38–67 record in their single season playing in Muskegon.

Muskegon Lassies

The Muskegon Lassies participated in the AAGPBL from 1946 to 1950. The Lassies were able to join the league in part because the men's Michigan State League was abandoned after the 1941 season. This left Marshall Field open for a new team, the Lassies. Organized in 1946 under L.A. Prescott, the Lassies brought in Ralph "Buzz" Boyle as their manager. Boyle was a former major league ballplayer, as many of the league managers were. *The Muskegon Chronicle* ran a contest for the team name, and about 2,000 fans showed up for the opening day game in 1946. The Lassies beat the Fort Wayne Daisies 12–0 behind the pitching of Irene Applegren. Midway through that first season, interest was heightened when local star Donna Cook joined the Lassies. Her sister also played in the league but not for her hometown team.

Before the start of the 1947 season the Lassies made a change in manager, bringing in Bill Wambsganss. Under his leadership the Lassies tied for the league pennant with Grand Rapids and Racine. The team was led by MVP Doris Sams. They lost in the first round of the playoffs to Racine. Looking forward to an exciting 1948 season, the Lassies lost over 60,000 fans with the return of men's baseball to Marshall Field. In the end only one of the teams would survive and it was not the Lassies, though the Clippers fell onto hard times by 1952 as well. The Muskegon Clippers belonged to the Central Baseball League and secured the right to share Marshall Field with the Lassies in 1948. This arrangement did not help the Lassies, so in 1949 they appealed to the city commissioners for exclusive rights to the park.

Midway through the 1950 season the Lassies were forced to transfer their franchise to Kalamazoo to save the team from financial ruin. Frank K. Leo, league president, suspended the team in June following a 3–14 start. The team averaged only about 300 fans and had significant monetary troubles. Leo gave the club owners one week to apply for a new franchise and prove they had adequate funding before the team had to move. Muskegon did see one more attempt at women's baseball in 1953 when the Battle Creek Belles moved in, but they did not last the season. The team continued to be led by Doris Sams and Donna Cook, who returned to her hometown

team. Cook and her sister are members of the Muskegon Area Sports Hall of Fame. {"Lassies Down Chicks," *Record-Eagle* (Michigan), 5 June1947, 15; "Muskegon Argues about Ball Clubs and Marshall Field," *The Holland Evening Sentinel* (Michigan), 29 November 1949, 2.}

Myatt, LuAnn

P Florida Hurricanes, Florida Lightning

LuAnn Myatt pitched the Lightning to victory in the 1997 South Florida Diamond Classic and then lost the 1998 finals to the Lightning when she switched teams.

Nabel, Margaret

(b. 27 August 1896, Perth Amboy, New Jersey) P/OF/Manager

Margaret Nabel grew up in New Jersey and attended Curtis High School. Her baseball career started in 1910 with the New York Bloomer Girls, who by 1920 were considered by some reporters to be the top woman's team in the East. The team consisted of Nabel, Helen Demarest, Maggie Riley, Ethel Condon, Toots Andies, Nina "Babe" McCatlin, Elsie Ruhnke, Florrie O'Rourke, Hattie Michaels, Mary Gilroy and Edith Houghton. Houghton and Ruhnke also played for the Philadelphia Bobbies and traveled with them to Japan. Nabel advertised regularly in the New York press looking for opponents for her club. They played any team that would sign a contract for a percentage of the guarantee for a game. In 1932, for example, they played the Jersey City Colored Athletics, a men's club. {Barbara Gregorich, *Women at Play*, 39, 42–43; *New York Age,* 17 September 1932, 6.}

Nabozny, Heather

(b. 1970) Groundskeeper

In 1999 Heather Nabozny became the new head groundskeeper for the Detroit Tigers, becoming the first woman to hold that position. Before working for the Tigers, Nabozny worked as the head groundskeeper for the Western Michigan Whitecaps, a minor league affiliate. She graduated in 1993 from Michigan State with a degree in turf management. Her first job was as a groundskeeper at the Toronto Blue Jays' spring training complex in Florida. Then she worked for the Western Michigan Whitecaps, a Class A minor league team. In 1996 she was named the Groundskeeper of the Year for the Midwest

League. {Marty Hair, "It's Not Easy Being Green," *Detroit Free Press*, 24 March 2000, 6B; Amy Kuras, "Green Queen," *Women's Health Style*, April 1999, 8–10; Jon Cook, "Nabozny Breaks New Ground," *Slam! Sports*, 17 June 1999.}

Nadeau, Martine

(b. 10 June 1971, Beauport, Quebec) P Team Canada

Martine Nadeau grew up playing baseball and softball. In 1989 she played in the Canada Games in softball, and in the 1990s became the first female to play on a Junior Elite baseball club. Nadeau pitched six innings over two games in the 2004 women's World Cup event for Team Canada. She was credited with one loss as she gave up four earned runs and seven walks. When she is not honing her pitching technique, Nadeau works as a photocopier technician. {Baseball Canada 2004 Women's National Team Media Guide.}

Nagano, Eriko

CF, Japan

Eriko Nagano took part in the 2002 Women's World Series and was named the MVP by the Japanese coaches. She led off every game for the Japanese in that series and hit .382 while playing flawlessly in center field. She played in the 2003 Women's World Series and in game five helped lead her team to a 3–0 shutout over the United States. Nagano had two hits and drove in one run. She batted .438 for the series. In the 2004 series Nagano helped her team win the gold medal over the United States by driving in two runs in the final game. {"Japan Downs United States 13–4 to Take Gold Medal in Women's World Series Baseball," *AP Worldstream*, 22 July 2004; Australian Baseball Federation, <www.baseball.org.au>.}

Nakashima, Risa

P, Japan

Risa Nakashima picked up the victory for her team in game seven of the 2003 Women's World Series. She pitched three innings against Australia, giving up two earned runs, hitting one batter and catching three trying to steal.

National Girls Baseball League

During the 1940s and 1950s a rival league to the AAGPBL developed in the city of Chicago: the National Girls Baseball League. Its president was Arch Wolfe. The NBL never achieved much national recognition because of its regional nature and the fact that it kept a closer connection with the rules of softball. The league continued to use underhand pitching and shorter base paths, as two prime examples. The league began in 1944 with four semipro teams and later added two more. The original four teams were the Parichy Bloomer Girls, the Music Maids, the Rockola Chicks and the Match Corp Queens. The teams played a 110–game schedule between May and September. In between league games the teams played a variety of exhibition contests against both men's and women's clubs. For example, in 1954 the Queens played a men's club from Compton, California, at Parichy Stadium. {"Bloomer Girls Triumph, 6–4, over Queens," *Chicago Tribune*, 15 July 1954.}

An earlier league bearing the same name had been formed in 1926 in Philadelphia, Pennsylvania. This league operated under president Edward de Poitiers, secretary Paul Barth, and treasurer Elmer Tyler Sr. There were five teams originally entered in the league with hopes of a sixth being added in Washington, D.C. The five original clubs were the Baltimore White Sox Bobbies; the Philadelphia Bobbies; the Tincies of Wilmington, Delaware; the American Bloomer Girls; and the New York Bloomer Girls. No reports of games have been discovered so far. {"Girls' Baseball Loop Seeking D.C. Entry," *Washington Post*, 9 February 1926.}

The two women's leagues signed an agreement by 1949 whereby they would not raid the rosters of teams in the other league. It had become enough of a concern that they felt a need to address the issue. In September 1949 the AAGPBL filed a $25,000 suit against the Nationals for signing Betty Tucker of Peoria, who was already under contract. {"All-American Girls File Baseball Suit," *Syracuse Herald-Journal*, 8 September 1949, 43; Chicago Historical Society.}

A number of women who played in the All American League also played for the Nationals. Sophie Kurys played second base for the Music Maids, hitting .311 for them in 1950. Terry Donahue caught for the Music Maids.

National Women's Baseball Hall of Fame

The hall was founded in 1998 in Washington, D.C., to honor female ballplayers with inductions and other awards each year. The first official inductions took place in 1999, with Claire Schillace

National Women's Baseball Hall of Fame Award Winners

Year of Award	Name	Team	Position	Years Played
1999 HOF	Claire Schillace	Racine Belles	P	1943–46
1999 HOF	Charlene Wright	N.J. Nemesis	C/Util. Inf.	1994–2000
1999 MVP	Stephanie Ciulla	Va. Flames	P	
2000 HOF	JoAnn Milliken	Va. Flames		1992–2003
2000 HOF	Susan Lukasik	Chicago Storm		1988–2003
2000 HOF	May Howard	Franklin's Young Ladies BB Club No. 1		1890s
2001 HOF	Kelly Ballentine	Md. Barncats		1992–2001
2001 HOF	Veronica Geyer	N.Y./N.J.		1980s
2001 HOF	Babe Didrikson			1930s
2002 HOF	Faye Dancer		OF	
2002 HOF	Robin Wallace	North Shore Cougars	P/IF	
2000 MVP	Kristin Guidace	North Va. Boxers	Mgr./C	
2000 MVP	Melissa Gibbons	N.J. Nemesis	P	
2000 MVP	Katy Bradford	Baltimore Stars	P	
2000 MVP	Stephanie Ciulla	Va. Flames	P	
2000 MVP	Ashley Holderman	South Bend Blue Sox	P	
2000 MVP	Robin Gelman	Md. Barncats	P	
2001 MVP	Kelli Presnell	Baltimore Stars	OF	
2001 MVP	Cindy Fereno	Va. Flames	C/Util.	
2002 MVP	Carmen Dominguez	Va. Flames	SS/P	
2003 HOF	Stephanie Ciulla	Va. Flames	P	1999–2003
2003 HOF	Dorothy Ferguson	Rockford Peaches	2B/CF	1945–54
2003 HOF	Kristin Guidace	Va. Boxers	Mgr/C/P	1990s–20003
2003 HOF	Shawn Macurio	Detroit Danger/ Renegades	Owner/IF/C	1999–2003
2003 HOF	Carol Sheldon	Detroit Danger/ Lansing Stars	1B/IF	1996–2003
2003 MVP	Andi Ermis	South Bend Blue Sox	C	2000–2003
2003 MVP	Katie Pappa	South Bend Blue Sox	P/IF	2002–2003
2003 MVP	Donna Middleton	Va. Flames	IF/OF	1990s–2003
2003 MVP	Narda Quigley	Va. Flames	OF/C	1999–2003
2004 HOF	Genevieve Beauchamp	Canada	C	2002–05
2004 HOF	Renee Hudson	Montgomery County Barncats/Va. Flames	P/1B/IF	1998–2005
2004 MVP	Donna Middleton	Va. Flames		
2004 MVP	Laura Brenneman	Va. Flames	P	
2004 MVP	Kelly Jewell	South Bend Blue Sox		
2004 MVP	Lori Bryant	South Bend Blue Sox		
2004 MVP	Katie Jagielski	Detroit Danger		
2004 MVP	Kelly Rota	Detroit Danger		
2004 MVP	Kat Shriner	Detroit Danger		
2004 MVP	Shawn Macurio	Detroit Danger	Owner	1998–2005
2004 MVP	Jessica Zawal	Detroit Danger		
2004 MGR/Coach	John Kovach	South Bend Blue Sox	Mgr.	
2004 MGR/Coach	Dave Fyfe	Va. Flames	Mgr.	

of the Racine Belles and Charlene Wright of the New Jersey Nemesis being selected. In 2000 the MVP award was added, and there were six recipients chosen that first year. The hall still had no physical building for its work by 2004, but it produces a regular newsletter and other promotional materials to raise awareness about itself.

Naum (Parker), Dorothy "Dottie"

(b. 5 January 1928, Dearborn, Michigan) P 1946–53, South Bend Blue Sox, Kenosha Comets, Kalamazoo Lassies

Dorothy Naum played in the All American League for eight seasons, the majority of them with the Comets. She pitched in 64 games and had her best season in 1951. She led the league with a 1.14 ERA that year and had a 5–4 record. Her career ERA was 2.01 with a 27–19 record. She also played in 578 games and hit only .181 but did score 184 runs and drove in 72. {AAGPBL Baseball Cards, 1995.}

Nearing (Buntrock), Myrna M. "Toddy"

(b. 13 June 1913, Eland, Wisconsin) P, Kenosha Comets

Myrna Nearing played softball for the West Allis team while she was in high school. It was her only sporting experience before joining the All American League. After her time in the league ended she continued to play softball for 11 years and won two Most Valuable Player awards. She went to work in the Briggs and Stratton Factory. {AAGPBL Questionnaire, National Baseball Hall of Fame.}

Negro Leagues

In the 1950s three women got the opportunity to play in the Negro leagues. They got the chance as the leagues were fighting to survive after the integration of baseball in 1947. Toni Stone, Connie Morgan and Mamie Johnson played for the Indianapolis Clowns, and Stone also played for the Kansas City Monarchs. While these ladies may have been brought in to help boost attendance, they were solid ballplayers as well. In addition to these three women, there were women in ownership roles such as Effa Manley, Mrs. C.I. Taylor, Ellie Stick and Hilda Bolden Shorter. These ladies became involved in the Negro leagues though their husbands, who owned teams in Newark, Indianapolis, Toledo and Pennsylvania.

Before the Negro leagues got their official start, there were a few other attempts by black women to play, such as the Dolly Vardens in the nineteenth century. There was also an attempt in 1908 to start a colored women's league in Springfield, Ohio. C.L. Mayberry owned the Springfield club and wanted to see this opportunity develop for ladies of color. Pearl Barrett, Ruth Calloway and Isabelle Baxter also played for short stints on all-men's teams between the 1910s and early 1930s. {Jean Hastings Ardell, "Mamie 'Peanut' Johnson: The Last Female Voice of the Negro Leagues," *Nine,* September 2001; "Baseball among the Fairer Sex Coming into Prominence," *Indianapolis Freeman,* 26 December 1908; Donna Britt, "Following Her Heart to Pitcher's Mound," *Washington Post,* 10 September 1999, B1, B8; Michelle Y. Green, *A Strong Right Arm* (New York: Dial Books, 2002).}

Nelson, Doris "Dodie"

(b. 12 December 1923, Los Angeles, California) OF 1944, Rockford Peaches

Doris Nelson played softball in California before joining the Peaches for one season. She played in 99 games and hit .231 with 51 runs scored. She went back to playing softball for the Phoenix A1 Queens for another 11 years after her one professional season. She made the All-American softball team for 11 consecutive years and was elected to the Arizona Softball Foundation Hall of Fame in 1975. {AAGPBL Baseball Cards, 2000.}

Nelson, Mary Ann "Nellie"

(b. 2 June 1938, Ironwood, Michigan) SS 1954, Fort Wayne Daisies

Mary Nelson only played for three games with the Daisies because she was only 15 and the league rules required players to be at least 16. She got to bat once while on the roster. She ran track and field while attending Angola High School before going on to college for a two-year certificate in data processing. She worked for 15 years with Eli Lily and then for the San Antonio school district before her health forced her to retire. {AAGPBL Questionnaire, National Baseball Hall of Fame; AAGPBL Baseball Cards, 2000.}

Nelson, Maude

(b. 17 November 1881; d. 15 February 1944) P/3B/Scout/Manager/Owner

Born Clementina Brida but better known as Maude Nelson, Nelson played for, managed, scouted for and owned baseball clubs during her career. She started as a pitcher with the Boston Bloomer Girls in 1897 and by 1911 found herself owner and manager of the Western Bloomer Girls. She then owned the All-Star Ranger Girls from 1923 to 1934. Nelson also played for the Cherokee Indian Baseball Club and the Star Bloomers during her playing career. Nelson was married twice, first to John Olson, who died in 1917, and then to Constante Dellacqua, a chef. Olson owned the Cherokee club, the Western Bloomer Girls and the Chicago Star Bloomer Girls, which Nelson also pitched for. In addition to her ball playing responsibilities Nelson also managed a resort hotel on Paw Paw Lake and her family's farm in Watervliet, New York.

An 1895 article described a game Nelson pitched in against the Sam Baldwin Jr. nine. She struck out five and fielded flawlessly in the game, though the rest of her team was less than stellar. For example, the right fielder was said to watch the ball drop and then walk after it. The team seemed more interested in displaying their new uniforms of yellow and black bloomers with black stockings than in playing. {"Base Ball in Bloomers," *The Sporting News*, 12 October 1895; Barbara Gregorich, *Women at Play* (San Diego, Ca: Harcourt Brace, 1994), 7, 9–11; Barbara Gregorich, "John Olson and His Barnstorming Baseball Teams," *Michigan History Magazine*, May/June 1995, 38–41; Barbara Gregorich, "From Bloomer Girls to Silver Bullets," *Dugout,* winter 1995, 5–10.}

Nelson and her club showed up in Mansfield, Ohio, in 1901 to play the local amateur team. The reporter who witnessed the contest stated that Nelson really was the whole show for the ladies. He said that if you did not see her hair pinned up under her hat she could pass for a male ballplayer, but that the rest of the team were not much support. The only thing that made the game a contest were the three men playing shortstop, catcher and third base. The final score was 6–3 in favor of the men. The ladies' team had eight hits, though only three were hit by the women and not the men on their squad. The fans paid 15 cents to see the game, which meant the girls made enough money to move on to their next destination. {"The Bloomer Girls Play at Baseball," *The Mansfield News*, 12 July 1901.}

In 1902 Nelson traveled with the Chicago Stars in a private railroad car. Their season opened in Tampa, Florida, in March and then they worked their way north with John Olson booking games for them. The Stars had their own canvas fence to enclose stands so they could collect an admission fee from fans who attended their games. With the canvas set up the enclosure could accommodate up to 4,000 fans. They returned to the South in 1903. One of their favorite stops was the city of Atlanta, where they could always count on a good turnout of fans. When they played the Crescents at Brisbine Park, Nelson pitched after Tom Tracy set the game up. {"The Chicago Stars," *The Atlanta Constitution*, 16 February 1902; "The Bloomer Girls" and "Bloomers to Play Here," *The Atlanta Constitution*, 25 March 1903.}

In 1927 Nelson was still pitching for the Western Bloomer Girls. She appeared as the starting pitcher against the Zanesville Greys in July 1927. The reporter who covered the game said that Nelson could be easily compared to most minor league pitchers in quality. {"Unique Attraction Booked by Local Club for Purpose of Giving Fans Rare Treat," *Zanesville Signal*, 5 July 1927.}

Nelson (Sandiford), Helen "Nellie"

(b. 13 June 1919, Toronto, Ontario; d. 6 February 1993) C

Helen Nelson came to the United States to play in the All American League. She had a great arm behind the plate and loved to talk to all the hitters. She played in 83 games and hit .210. After her short stint in the league she worked for Walgreens, rising to the rank of executive secretary to the senior vice-president. She was still working when she died in 1993. {AAGPBL Baseball Cards, 1996.}

Nereida, Alicea

Alicea Nereida was the owner of the Toa Baja Llaneros, a franchise club. She also served for eight years as the president of the Central League Confederation of Baseball.

Nesbitt (Wisham), Mary "Choo-Choo"

(b. 1 February 1925, Greenville, South Carolina) P/1B 1943–50, Peoria Red Wings, Racine Belles

Mary Nesbitt was an original member of the AAGPBL. She pitched for the Belles in the inaugural season and ended that year with a 26–13 record in 308 innings pitched. Nesbitt got married to Vester Wisham while she was playing in the league. She pitched in 129 games in her career, compiling a record of 65–49 with an ERA of 2.44. She also played first base in 498 games and hit a solid .282. She scored 209 runs, batted in 186 and stole 161 bases. She was an all-around athlete. At one point after her stint in the league, she played first base for a Rochelle team in the South Georgia Peanut League. Later she turned to softball and joined a women's league with her daughter in Palatka, Florida. They played for the Florida Trucks and Tractors team and in 1974 won the Florida state title. When not playing, Nesbitt drove a school bus and worked for the *Daily News*. A local ball field in Putnam County has been named in her honor. {AAGPBL Newsletter, September 1994; September 2000; May 2001, 23, 32; and May 2002, 16.}

Neumeier, Elizabeth

Elizabeth Neumeier has been an arbitrator since 1983, working primarily with labor-management disputes. In 1999 she became the first female arbitrator in Major League baseball history. She worked for ten years with the United States Steel Corporation and has served on a variety of boards over the years. She was also helpful in the labor disputes with the National Hockey League. She received her BA in economics from New York University and her Juris Doctor from Boston University School of Law. {"Neumeier Becomes First Female Arbitrator in Baseball." CNNSI.com, 8 February 1999.}

New England Bloomer Girls

The Frederick Baseball Club arranged a contest in 1901 with the New England Bloomer Girls. The game was to be played at Athletic Park and it was expected to be a good game since the ladies had played good ball all season. {"'Bloomer Girls' to Play," *The Daily News*, 12 September 1901.}

New England Clippers

New England Women's Baseball League

The New England Clippers played as a traveling team from the NEWBL in 1999 and 2000. They disbanded after the 2000 season because of financial troubles. A number of their players then joined the Boston Blue Sox, who took their place as an independent traveling club. {Boston Blue Sox Web site.}

New England Women's Baseball League (NEWBL/NAWBL)

The New England Women's Baseball League began in 1999 as the Women's New England Baseball League and played through 2003. The players had to be 14 or older and had to pay the $100 registration fee. The founders of the league were Chris Lindeborg, Jeri Appier, and Jerry Dawson. Dawson was a former professional ballplayer himself.

The league began in Lynn, Massachusetts, with four ball clubs: the Middlesex County Cougars, the Boston Blitz, the North Shore Navigators and the Bay State Express. There were to be 120 games played between May and August. The first two championships were won by the Bay State Express. In 2000 the league expanded to six clubs by adding the Waterbury Diamonds and the Lowell Robins. By 2002 the league had fallen to only two teams, the Robins and the Cougars, who played 11 games together with the Cougars winning seven. This was also the year the league changed its name to the NEWBL.

The new sponsor in 2003 was the owner of the men's North Shore Spirit, Nicholas A. Lopardo. In addition to sponsoring the league, he agreed to host the North Shore Lady Spirit, a traveling women's all-star team. Lopardo got involved in

Diving play being made by Seahawks shortstop Melissa Jones in front of Falcons runner Kelly Connolly (courtesy Laura Wulf).

sports while attending Susquehanna University, where he captained the baseball and football teams. He was inducted into the Susquehanna University Sports Hall of Fame. He worked as a CEO for a number of different investment companies before retiring. After retirement he bought the minor league Waterbury Spirit, and that began his involvement with baseball on the organizational side. When approached he readily agreed to help the new women's league as well.

Lopardo allowed the four league entrants to use Fraser Field in Lynn, Massachusetts, for their 12-game seasons. The first season began on June 22 and ending on August 30, 2003. Each team had 16 players and one coach. Lopardo served as the league commissioner in 2003. At the end of the 2003 season the league went through another change, becoming the North American Women's Baseball League. The league is still under Lopardo's leadership. In 2004 the new league hosted its first Labor Day Tournament, won by the Saints over the Seahawks. League commissioner Allen Melanson presented medals to the finalists as well as a number of individual awards. {Christopher L. Gasper, "Playing the Game They

Love," *Boston Globe*, 13 July 2003, 1, 11; NAWBL
Web site.}

New Jersey Bloomer Girls

A local Pennsylvania paper reported a game between the New Jersey Bloomers and a team from
their church league. The manager of the squad
was a Mrs. J.B. Livingston, and they had one man
on the team, the catcher Honus Warner. The rest
of the roster consisted of Clara St. Claire (1B),
Pearle Franklin (2B), Maggie Jones (SS), Elizabeth Martin (3B), Jennie Elworth, Mabel Clark-
son and Annie Townson (OF) and Maude Covington (P). The earliest mention of this team has
been traced to 1901 and a contest against the
Newark Nationals that Newark won 12–6 before
they traveled on to play in Utica, New York.
{*Charleroi Mail*, 6 June 1911; "Girls Won," *Newark
Daily Advocate*, 17 September 1901.}

New Jersey Nemesis

The Nemesis developed as a traveling team,
and so all their games were interleague play. In
1999 they had a perfect record at 7–0. The following season they continued their strong play, leading the Eastern Women's Baseball Conference
through July with an 8–1 record. The club was
founded by Veronica Geyer and Darlene Fiscus.
One of their leading pitchers was a ballplayer with
a lot of experience, Sue Winthrop.

New Orleans Baseball

In 2004 the Kenner Parks and Recreation Department reported the results of their girls' baseball division for 9- and 10-year-olds. They played
through the month of May at Muss Bertolino
Park. There were five teams in the division including Muss Bertolino, Wentwood, Woodlake,
Highway Park and Lincoln Manor. Some of the
top players in the league included pitchers Bri-
tani Brown, Lindsey Kimball, Crystal Freeman
and Rachel Mader. On the hitting side there were
many who helped their teams, including Jessica
Leslie, Brandi Beninate, Gabrielle Cook, Brittany
Dupre and Hali Sclafini. {Marion Bonura, "Kenner Girls Baseball Shows Its Top Hitters," *Times-
Picayune*, 17 June 2004, 7.}

New South Wales Patriots

The team from New South Wales is part of the
Australian Baseball Federation. Each year they
compete in the National Women's Champi-

onships, which began in 2000. In 2003 New South
Wales won the title but lost it again in 2004 to
Victoria by a score of 12–1. In 1998 they chose a
girls' 14–and-under team to represent them in the
first Australian Girls' Baseball Series. One player
selected was pitcher Angelique Delaney. {Inter-
national Women's Baseball Web site.}

New York Bloomer Girls

The New York Bloomers started in 1910 and
lasted through the 1935 season. When the team
began barnstorming across the entire country in
1920, they generally traveled between 3,500 and
5,000 miles a season. The team generally traveled
in two cars. Their players were paid meal money
by the day with a bonus at the end of the season
if the team made any profit. The team generally
had two male players, the pitcher and catcher.
(This was typical of bloomer teams because it was
believed by most people that this would give them
a fairer shot in any game against a men's team.)
They generally tried to play 32 games and later
added ten more per season. In 1922 their first
baseman was Stella Friss, who was described as
the Babe Ruth of female players. She received the
moniker because she had 12 home runs in 32
games that season. Friss and fellow infielder Toots
Andress gave the team solid fielding during the
1920s. Other members of that squad included
Agnes Parker (2B), Chester Friss (C/SS), Florence
Vanderburg (1B), Alma Pape (RF), Mae Schle-
icher (LF), Loretta Shanley (CF), Mildred Van-
derwall (P) and Carrie Stumph (OF).

One of their later stars was Alma Korneski,
who played centerfield from 1933 to 1935. Korneski gained her baseball experience playing second
base for a Lehigh nine. Another star was first
baseman Agnes O'Neil Rogers. A reporter once
described her play at first base as something that
made people sit up and take notice. Margaret
Nabel was the manager of the club. In the 1930s the
team advertised in white and black newspapers
for opponents to play, such as the Jersey City Colored Athletics.

Most of the Bloomers' games are hard to track
down because they played in small towns all over
America. In 1918 a local paper in Iowa picked up
a story on the Bloomers and their trip to play the
Senators at Athletic Park in Perry. The paper reported that their tour started well that year and attracted lots of fans wherever they played. In another example, the *Frederick Post* in Maryland
reported on a coming game in Buckeystown in
1925, but news of the game itself has not been
found. The game would pit the Bloomers against

New York Bloomer Girls (photograph from National Baseball Hall of Fame Library, Cooperstown, NY).

A.C. Butler and the Buckeystown Athletic Club team. The *Post* also indicated that the Bloomers had just come from beating a Bethesda club 13–1 and a Rockville squad 15–12. In 1928 they played for the title of women's baseball champion by defeating three of the leading teams of the day. They beat the Quaker City Girls of Philadelphia 49–5. The Quaker team called themselves the best women's club in the East. They also defeated the Fleischer Yarn Girls 27–8 and trounced the Baltimore Black Sox Girls 51–2. The Baltimore club was considered the best women's team in the South. Helen Demarest won that game on a two-hitter with 17 strikeouts. The roster for the 1928 squad included Helen Demarest (P), Toots Andress (C/SS), May Rohr (utility), Babe McCutten (3B), Ethel Condon (2B), Florrie O'Rourke (1B), Elsie Ruhnke (LF), Mae Knalcsek (RF), "Pep" Moran (LF), and Crane (C). Other games in 1928 included a contest against the Danville Collegians of Virginia. The game was played at Schoolfield Park with the ladies staging a practice session the day before for fans to come out and see. The Collegians brought in some extra players for the contest because they expected a tough game. The Bloomers also played the St. John's A.C. at Mc-

Curdy Field in Maryland. {"Select Site for Game with Girls' Ball Team," *The Danville Bee*, 16 August 1928, 10 and 22 August 1928, 6; "Bloomer Girls to Play," *The Frederick Post*, 7 August 1928, 3.}

According to records of the team they played 28 scheduled games and another 23 on tour throughout New York in 1934. At least part of that tour took them through central New York, where they played a team called Manlius-Pompey. Their stars Hattie Michaels and Babe McCutten leading the undefeated ball club into town. In 1935 they traveled south and played 98 games in three months. Players got a $1.25 a day for food and a bonus at the end of the season if the club made any money. {"Bloomer Girls Coming," *The Frederick Post*, 24 August 1925; "Bloomer Girls Meet Manlius and Pompey at Suburban Park," *Syracuse Herald*, 18 August 1934, 9; "Bloomer Girls Play Rex A.C. Here Sunday," *Washington Post*, 26 July 1922, 17; "Bloomer Girls to Play," *The Frederick Post*, 7 August 1928, 3; *Afro-American*, 28 July 1922; *NYA*, 17 September 1932; "Bloomer Girls to Play This Afternoon," *The Perry Daily Chief* (Iowa), 6 September 1918; Kerry Williams, "Hard Ball Was a Job for Girls," *News Tribune*, 26 May 1994; "To Play Girls Team," *Frederick Daily News*, 22 August 1925, 5.}

Others who played for the team over the years included Alma Pucci, Shank Nelson, Edna Lockhart, Mary Ontek, Mel Pearsall, Julie Gressek, Dottie Ruh, and Ginger Robinson.

New York/New Jersey Women's Baseball League

Veronica Geyer helped found this league in January 2000 with one team to begin with, the New Jersey Nemesis. The Nemesis was a traveling team that went from tournament to tournament. About two dozen players were on the roster, coming from New York, New Jersey and the Philadelphia area. The team practiced in Garwood, New Jersey. Their first chance to compete came in the Florida Diamond Classic, where they finished with a record of 0–4. They did win two games in a tournament in Washington, D.C. {Michael Gasparino, "Playing Hardball," *Long Island Sports Online*, 15 June 1999.}

New York Women's Baseball Association (NYWBA)

The goal of this association, created in 2001, is to provide instruction and competition for girls and women who wish to play baseball at all levels. The association oversees a summer league, a league for girls aged 9–17, monthly baseball clinics and various individual team events. In 2001 the first team to participate was a traveling club called the New York Traffic. During the 2002 season the Traffic disbanded, but by 2003 the association was hosting three teams from the five boroughs of New York City. The three teams were the Westchester Yankees, the Queens Cyclones and the Manhattan Giants. The teams had 15 players on their rosters and rotated their games between three diamonds in Central Park, at Eisenhower Park and at Westchester Community College. One of the league's founders, Sue Winthrop, used to coach softball at New York University. The league also has a board consisting of individuals such as former player Julie Croteau, who help keep the league afloat. Other board members include Stephanie Kung, Monique Pyle and Diane DeLucia-Mascara. In addition to playing their own games, the women in the league help out with clinics for youngsters to learn the fundamentals of the game. In 2004 the league hosted its first Labor Day Tournament, and their local team beat out a team from Philadelphia to win the title. They compiled a 4–1 record on the way to their victory. The players for the New York

team came from the two teams in the NYWBA in 2004, the Rockers and Quicksilver. In their ten league meetings the Quicksilver beat the Rockers six games to four. {Anthony Garzilli, "Recreation Baseball: Women Enjoy Playing Hardball," *The Patent Trader*, 9 September 2004; Stephanie Kornfeld, "Finding a League of Their Own," *The Rivertowns Enterprise*, 5 September 2003, 8; NYWBA Web site; Shane Miller, "Starting a League of Their Own," *Queens Ledger*, 20 March 2003; Nicholas Hirshon, "Women's Professional Baseball Takes the Field at St. Johns," *Queens Ledger*, 11 July 2002, 36.}

Ng, Kim

(b. 1968, New Jersey) Management

In 1998 Kim Ng agreed to become the assistant general manager of the New York Yankees. She moved into that position from the American League office, where she had been director of waivers and records. Ng, the oldest of five girls, grew up in New Jersey and graduated from the University of Chicago in 1990 with a public policy degree. While there, she played the infield on the university's softball team. She entered baseball's executive development program and was hired by the Chicago White Sox in 1990 to help with their computer system and offer assistance in arbitration cases. She received two promotions in 1991 and 1995 while with the White Sox. In 1997 she moved to the American League office to help with waiver rulings. After her stint with the Yankees she resigned and in 2002 joined the front office of the Los Angeles Dodgers as the assistant to the new GM, Dan Evans. Her role with the Dodgers has been in the area of talent evaluation. She had worked with Evans when they were both with the White Sox. {Buster Olney, "Woman Will Be Yankee Executive," *New York Times*, 4 March 1998, C3; Jean Ardell presentation, SABR annual meeting, 2003; Gordon Edes, "GM: A Distaff Position?" *Boston Globe*, 31 August 2003; Allison Otto, "Diamond Cutters: These Women Are Showing Careers Can Be Carved in Baseball Operations," *The Denver Post*, 16 April 2002, D-12; John Nadel, "Dodgers Hire Female Assistant GM," *AP Online*, 5 December 2001; Ben Walker, "Yanks Assistant GM Ng Resigns," *USA Today*, 2001.}

Nichols, Tina

P 1999, San Diego Stix, Orlando Dragons

During the 1997 season Tina Nichols helped her Orlando Dragons teammates win the national championship with two complete games in three days. In 1999 Nichols helped the Stix win the national championship series and she was named as a utility player to the all-tournament team. She hit .308 and was 2–0 with a 1.75 ERA for the series. Nichols worked as a tennis instructor in Hallandale, Florida, when she was not playing baseball. {"New Women's Team Flooded with Calls," *USA Today Baseball Weekly*, 29 December–11 January 1994, 6; Angie Watts, "Orlando Defeats San Diego for Women's Baseball Title," *Washington Post*, 2 September 1997.}

Nicol (Fox), Helen M. "Nicki"

(b. 9 May 1920, Edmonton, Calgary, Canada) P 1943–52, Kenosha Comets, Rockford Peaches

Helen Nicol played all sports at Western Canada High School. She also played softball in a senior ladies' league and ice hockey and speed skating in the provincial leagues. She pitched for ten years in the AAGPBL and had two no-hitters along with a career ERA of 1.89. In her rookie year in 1943 she made the all-star team for Kenosha with a 31–8 record which included 13 straight wins. She led the league again in 1944 with a 17–11 record and an 0.93 ERA. Her next highest win total came in 1945 when she won 24 more games for the Comets against 19 losses. When the league changed the rules regarding pitching in 1947 she struggled to adjust, finishing at 6–16 but each season after that she got better. She pitched 2,382 innings in her ten-year career, with 163 wins against 118 losses. She was also with the Peaches when they won the championship in 1948–50. She quit after the 1952 season because she could see things were winding down and she had a good job she did not want to lose with the Hudson Bay Company. {"Helen Nicol Still Tops Ball," *The Lethbridge Herald*, 31 August 1943.}

In addition to playing baseball she bowled, golfed and played basketball for the Ko-eds in Rockford from 1954–59. She won a number of golf championships including the Motorola Open from 1973 to 1977. Nicol also set some Canadian speed skating records and played ice hockey. In 1996 she was inducted into the Alberta Hall of Fame and in 1998 into the St. Mary's Hall of Fame. {AAGPBL Newsletter, May 2001, 34; AAGPBL Questionnaire, National Baseball Hall of Fame, Cooperstown, New York.}

Nicolls, Ashley

(b. 15 August 1982, Virginia, Minnesota) 1B, Michigan Stars, Ocala Lightning, South Bend Blue Sox

Ashley Nicolls grew up playing sports of all kinds. Her main focus was on soccer, ice hockey and fast-pitch softball, though in the summer it was always on baseball. She started playing in Little League and continued all the way through the senior division, where she ended up being the only girl playing. She also played American Legion ball when she turned 18 and was one of only a handful of women from around the state competing. Nicolls' primary position playing with the boys was first base, but since then she has played every position except catcher. Nicolls started playing with women's teams when she was 16 and joined the Michigan Stars. With the Stars she had a chance to travel and see other women playing baseball. She also played for the Ocala Lightning, the South Bend Blue Sox, the Eastern Athletics and then her own team, WIMN baseball. When she was with South Bend she received the MVP award in one of their tournament games in Toronto. In 2002 she joined the Give Back Grow Tour sponsored by the WBL. Nicolls went to Arizona in October 2003 to play in the marathon game to raise money for AIDS and played in the Give Back and Grow Tour in the summer of 2002. Nicolls established her team to give more women the chance to play baseball, and not just softball because it was the only game. She stated, "I don't want to hear the songs, 'This used to be our playground' and 'Now and Forever' and regret that there is nothing left of women's baseball." {Ashley Nicolls, correspondence with Leslie A. Heaphy, North Canton, Ohio, March 2004.} When not playing baseball, Nicolls continues to play ice hockey and is attending seminary to get her master's of divinity for the Evangelical Lutheran Church. She also has a bachelor's degree from the University of Wisconsin at Superior.

Niemiec (Konwinski), Dolores "Dolly

(b. 27 May 1931, Chicago, Illinois) 2B/3B 1948–52, South Bend Blue Sox, Springfield Sallies, Chicago Colleens, Grand Rapids Chicks

Dolly Niemiec played volleyball and basketball while attending Farragut High School. She started her baseball playing career in 1948 as a member of the barnstorming Sallies. She later joined the Grand Rapids Chicks before her career was cut short by a car accident in 1952. She then went on to become an umpire and a professional bowler. She was only 16 when she joined the AAGPBL, and she never really became much of a hitter. Her career average was only .190. Bowling became her real competitive sport; she moved into the professional ranks for four years. She also won a number of city and state titles in Michigan. As a result of those records, the Michigan Women's Sports Hall of Fame inducted her. She married Bob Konwinski in 1955 and they had four children. Dolly spent time coaching her sons' baseball teams through the Mickey Mantle League. {AAGPBL Questionnaire, National Baseball Hall of Fame; Matt VandeBunte, "Triple Play; Former Teammates Discuss Days on Diamond," *Grand Rapids Press*, 3 October 2002.}

Niland, Lily

(b. 15 September 1988, Seattle, Washington)

Lily Niland grew up playing sports that are not typically available for young ladies. In her freshman year at Ballard High School she played football and baseball. As a sophomore in 2003–04 she made the JV team and played in right field for the first two games of the season. She made the pitching staff on the JV team as a junior and even played four varsity games. Almost 100 people tried out for the JV squad, and Niland was one of 50 selected to play. She has played Little League ball every year. In 2003, during the junior division playoffs, her coach let her pitch against one of the best teams in the league. She pitched a complete game shutout. During the playoffs Niland threw 15 scoreless innings, two complete game shutouts and one save. Another highlight for Niland was

Lily Niland pitching for her high school team against Franklin High School in May 2005 (photograph by S. Kimble Niland).

striking out one of the league's best hitters to preserve her shutout. In 2004 Niland played mainly on the JV team but did get a couple of chances at varsity at the end of the season. The all-star team she played on placed third in the state. She throws in the mid–70s but her curveball and changeup are her real bread-and-butter pitches. Her advice to others wanting to play baseball is simple: "Girls can play ball with the guys! Go for it!" Her coach, Kevin Miller, says she is just one of the guys when she is on the diamond. Niland gave gymnastics a shot as well but decided it took away from her pitching, so she will stick to baseball in the future. {Lily Niland, correspondence with Leslie A. Heaphy, North Canton, Ohio, March and November 2004 and June 2005; Craig Smith, "Ballard Baseball Pitcher Proves She's One of the Guys," *Seattle Times*, 10 May 2005.}

Nine, Hayley

Hayley Nine played Greenacres Little League from 2002 to 2004. After that experience she tried out for and made her middle school team at Tradewinds Middle School, where she plays in the infield. Nine had tried out in 2003 at Christa McAuliffe Middle School but did not make that team. Her parents, Rachel and Evan, support her efforts and are involved in the league themselves.

Lily Niland hitting at the state tournament played in Vancouver, Washington, in 2004 (photograph by S. Kimble Niland).

Rachel is on the board of directors and Evan is a coach and umpire. {Julius Whigam II, "Girl Is Just Like One of the Guys out on the Baseball Diamond," *Palm Beach Post*, 15 September 2004, 12.}

Noel, Michele

2B 2004, Motown Magic

Michele Noel got her start in baseball in 2004 with the Magic in Detroit. She made the team because of her power.

Nordquist, Helen "Nordie"

(b. 23 March 1932, Malden, Massachusetts) OF/P 1951–54, Kenosha Comets, Rockford Peaches, South Bend Blue Sox

Helen Nordquist started in the All American League with Kenosha and ended her career with South Bend as the league folded. She excelled in the field and even tried her hand at pitching. She pitched in 44 games and compiled a record of 6–20 with a 5.43 ERA. Nordquist had control problems, walking 189 batters in 209 innings and only striking out 57 hitters. She caught 177 games and only hit .189 with 43 runs scored. She was not the most disciplined hitter, as she struck out 70 times compared to only 46 walks. After baseball Nordquist worked as a switch board operator, then in various accounting areas before becoming a toll collector in New Hampshire until she retired in 1994. She remained active skiing, playing volleyball and bowling. {AAGPBL Newsletter, May 2005, 27; AAGPBL Baseball Cards, 1995.}

North American Women's Baseball League (NAWBL)

This league has three divisions under its direction — the New England Division, the Ontario Division and the Florida Division. The New England Division in 2004 had four teams: the Saints, the Outlaws, the Ravens and the Seahawks.

North Carolina Baseball

Fayetteville, North Carolina, is becoming home to a new women's and girls' baseball league in 2005. In addition, an independent women's team plays in Kings Mountain, North Carolina.

North Shore Cougars

In 2002 the North Shore team won the DC Invitational, beating the DC Thunder in the final game by a score of 13–8. They also played in the Roy Hobbs Tournament in 2002 and came in fourth behind the Lightning, the Storm and the Sabres.

North Shore Lady Spirit

The Lady Spirit flew to Bonoa, Dominican Republic, for a four-game exhibition tour in November 2004 under the direction of their head coach, Ken Perrone. They played before an average of 3,000 excited fans and had to work hard to come away with four victories. They beat the Dominican national team by scores of 8–7, 6–5, 12–4 and 11–5. The Dominican team was quick and had solid hitting. While there the Lady Spirit also donated baseball equipment and visited schools to talk to the youngsters about their dreams. {Jean DePlacido, "Lady Spirit a Big Hit in Dominican Republic," *The Salem News*, 18 November 2004.}

North Shore Spirit Women's Baseball League

In 2003 the league had four competitors: the Ravens, the Eagles, the Seahawks and the Falcons. The Ravens led the league with a 10–1 record while the Falcons, Eagles and Seahawks were tied with 4–7 records. In the playoffs the Falcons reversed their fortunes and beat the Ravens, who took second place. The Eagles were third and the Seahawks took last place.

North York Girls Baseball

The North York Girls Baseball League is a part of the Central Ontario Girls Baseball League.

Nowaczewski, Annie

(b. 1978) P, Motown Magic

Annie Nowaczewski keeps herself busy playing baseball on the weekends with the Magic and attending Wayne State University. She is working on a master's in physical education. {Kristin Karpscuk, "Motown Magic Calling On a Few Good Women," *Daily Oakland Press*, 14 April 2004.}

Nyzio, Brittany

Slaterettes

Brittany Nyzio helped her team with her hitting in 1999. She finished the season with a .516 average, 4 home runs and 22 RBIs. {Greg Botelho,

"Pawtucket Slaterettes Having Another Banner Year," *Providence Journal*, 28 June 1999, C–03.}

O'Brian (Cooke), Penny "Peanuts"

(b. 16 September 1919, Edmonton, Alberta)
OF/1B 1945, Fort Wayne Daisies

Penny O'Brian stole 43 bases in only 83 games in 1945 and was one of 64 women inducted into the Canadian Baseball Hall of Fame and Museum in 1998. Her speed made her a constant threat at bat and also made her a solid outfielder who covered a lot of ground.

O'Brien, Eileen "OB"

(b. 24 May 1922, Chicago, Illinois) Util. Inf./Chaperone 1948, Muskegon Lassies

Eileen O'Brien grew up at a time when girls' sports were few and far between. She worked as a lifeguard and taught swimming lessons but never had a chance to play baseball or softball until she joined the All American League for two months. After playing in only five games she became the Lassies' chaperone and finished out the season with them in that capacity. Later she played field hockey for ten years while working as a teacher and then a librarian in the Chicago public schools until her retirement. {AAGPBL Questionnaire, National Baseball Hall of Fame; AAGPBL Baseball Cards, 1996.}

Catcher Judy O'Brien watching the game from the dugout for the New Jersey Diamonds in 1998 (courtesy Laura Wulf).

O'Brien, Judith Lynn "Judy"

(Reading, Massachusetts) C, New Jersey Diamonds, Team America, Bay State Express, Boston Blue Sox, North Shore Lady Spirit, Philadelphia Strikers, 2004 USA National Team

Judy O'Brien attended spring training for the Silver Bullets in 1994, but her playing experience on the professional level has been with the New Jersey Diamonds in 1998 and with the Bay State Express in the New England Women's Baseball League in 2001–02. She won the batting title in 2000 with a .496 average. O'Brien played for Team USA in 2000 and 2001. She made the all-tournament team in 2001 because she hit .533 for the series. In 2004 she attended tryouts for the first USA National Team and made the squad. She hit .200 in the Women's World Series with one run scored for the gold medal–winning USA team. O'Brien attended Temple University on a softball scholarship and was named an Academic All-American in 1994. {USA Baseball 2004 Media Guide; Boston Blue Sox Web site.}

Left to right: catcher Judy O'Brien, Tammy Silveira, Erin Layton (kneeling) at a tryout for the New Jersey Diamonds in 1998 (courtesy Laura Wulf).

Ocala Lightning

In the Roy Hobbs World Series the Lightning beat the

California Sabres 2–1 to win their first tournament in 2001. The team rode the pitching of Molly McKesson and the hitting and base running of Karen Hunger to win. Manager Connie McNeill guided the team to this victory. . They won again in 2002 by beating the Chicago Storm 5–4. In 2003 they made it into the semifinals before losing to the New England Lady Spirit 6–3 to end the tournament with a 3–2 record. They won the Citrus Blast tournament in 2003 by beating the Jacksonville Flames on Memorial Day.

O'Dowd, Anna Mae "Annie"

(b. 26 April 1929, Chicago, Illinois) C 1949–51, Kenosha Comets, Kalamazoo Lassies, Racine Belles, Battle Creek Belles

Anna O'Dowd graduated from Gage Park High School in 1947 with no competitive sports experience at all. She worked for the Campbell Soup Company before and after joining the AAGPBL. One of her favorite experiences from playing involved the opportunity to travel to 27 different states for ball games. She played in 97 games and hit .229. After leaving the league Anna played baseball and basketball in Chicago for a couple of years while working for Ameritech. {AAGPBL Questionnaire, National Baseball Hall of Fame.}

Ogden, Joanne "Jo"

(b. 25 April 1933, Johnson City, New York) 2B 1953, South Bend Blue Sox

Joanne Ogden hit .253 for the Blue Sox during her one season with the club. She went on to Brockport University after her playing days ended and got a BS in teaching. She taught and coached for 25 years in Lockport, New York. She retired in 1983. Her career numbers included playing in 42 games, getting 22 hits and driving in 5 runs. {AAGPBL Baseball Cards, 2000.}

O'Hara, Janice

(b. 30 October 1918, Beardstown, Maryland; d. 7 March 2001) P/Util. 1943–47, Kenosha Comets

Janice O'Hara played for four seasons with the Kenosha Comets. She could play just about any position on the field and her versatility made her a valuable person to have on the roster. She pitched in 59 games and played in 439. She compiled a 13–17 pitching record with a 3.62 ERA. She also batted only .159 with 201 hits. {AAGPBL Baseball Cards, 1996.}

Oldham, John

Manager of the San Jose Spitfires, an entry in the Ladies League in 1997. Oldham spent most of his baseball career coaching college men's teams. He served as head coach for Santa Clara University, and San Jose City College before retiring. Coaching women was different in a couple of ways, according to Oldham, in attitude and relationships as well as expectations. Most of the women were former softball players who were learning to play baseball in their 20s, 30s and even 40s. {Michael Learmonth, "Ruthless Babes," *Metroactive*, 21–27 August 1997, 1–13. }

Olinger, Marilyn "Corky"

(b. 7 June 1928, Columbus, Ohio) SS 1948–53, Chicago Colleens, Grand Rapids Chicks

After starting out with the Chicago Colleens' development team, Marilyn Olinger was assigned to the Grand Rapids Chicks and spent six seasons with them. She had a great deal of speed and used it on the base paths and in the field to dazzle the crowds. She stole 197 bases and scored 334 runs in 599 games. Her career average was only .220 but she took advantage of the times she did get on base. {AAGPBL Baseball Cards, 1996.}

Olson, Rachel

OF 2003–04, Seahawks

Rachel Olson played for the Seahawks in the North American Women's Baseball League in 2003–04 and was named the Most Improved Player in 2004.

Oppenheimer, Priscilla

Management

Priscilla Oppenheimer has worked for the San Diego Padres as their director of minor league relations since 1996. She has spent 20 years in the Padres organization. She started as a secretary who just needed a job to help pay for her sons' education. Within five years she had moved up to being an administrator for minor league relations. Her early experiences with the boardroom were not good ones, as she dealt with an all-male network. Oppenheimer vowed she would not let them drive her out and they didn't. Since taking over as director she has implemented a language program for new Hispanic players. She views all drug test results and helps with other day-to-day issues. {Allison Otto, "Diamond Cutters: These Women Are Showing Careers Can Be Carved in

Baseball Operations," *The Denver Post*, 16 April 2002, D-12.}

Orlando Dragons — AWBL/USWL

In 1997 the Orlando Dragons beat the San Diego Stix 11–1 for the USA Baseball women's national championship. The winning pitcher in the final game was Tina Nichols, completing her second game. In addition to having fine pitching in the series, the Dragons were helped by excellent fielding from players such as left fielder D.J. Johnson, who made a number of outstanding plays. The team was managed by Jeff Weaver. {Angie Watts, "Orlando Defeats San Diego for Women's Baseball Title," *Washington Post*, 2 September 1997, D05.}

Oswego Nine

The *Chicago Tribune* reported that Oswego, New York, had a traveling ladies' team in 1878 that was looking for opponents in any city. {*Chicago Tribune*, 2 June 1878.}

Ota, Sayaka

P, Japan

In the semifinals of the 2003 Women's World Series, Sayaka Ota led her team with three hits and one run knocked in as they beat the United States 4–3. In addition to her hitting contribution, Ota pitched seven-plus innings and got the victory. {Australian Baseball Federation, <www.baseball.org.au>.}

Otomo, Miyuki

LF, Japan

During the 2004 World Cup, Miyuki Otomo led all hitters with six stolen bases while batting .364 with five walks and one run knocked in. {Collin Gallant, "Women Begin Playoffs Today," *Edmonton Journal*, 7 August 2004, D3.}

O'Toole, Heidi

At age 22 Heidi O'Toole attended an open tryout for the Pittsburgh Pirates, hoping for a chance to make one of their clubs. Her previous playing experience came while growing up in Pittsburgh and from taking part in Little League, Pony League and Colt League contests. In high school she switched to fast-pitch softball to get a scholarship to West Virginia University, where she cap-

tained the team during her senior season. She attended a tryout in 1985 but got no further because the scouts said she was too slow and too small at 5 feet four inches. O'Toole was not the only woman present at the tryout, as Katie Cuddy also showed up but got nowhere either. {"Woman Tries Out for Pirates, but Doesn't Merit a Contract," *Albany Times-Union*, 31 July 1985.}

Overleese, Joanne E. "Jo"

(b. 3 October 1923, San Diego, California) 2B/SS Peoria Red Wings, Muskegon Lassies

Growing up in California provided Joanne Overleese the chance to play AAU basketball and softball while still at Herbert Hoover High School. She played only one year in the AAGPBL before going to college. Joanne attended San Diego State for one year and then spent four years at UC-Berkeley, where she played tennis, softball, field hockey, and basketball, and swam and fenced. Overleese finished her residency and internship in general surgery and went on to have a 25–year career in medicine. {AAGPBL Questionnaire, National Baseball Hall of Fame.}

Owners

By Joan M. Thomas

Ownership of a major league baseball club changes over time. Of the 112 such teams to take the field since the beginning, six women have been majority owners. (This does not include Wendy Selig-Prieb, who was president and CEO of the Milwaukee Brewers from 1998 to 2002.) Consecutively by year of their acquisition, they are Helene Britton, 1911; Grace Comiskey, 1941; Joan Payson, 1960; Jean Yawkey, 1977; Joan Kroc, 1984; and Marge Schott, 1984.

Not surprisingly, most of these women never actively sought control of a baseball enterprise; they simply inherited it. But Joan Payson, a wealthy person in her own right, was in on the financing of the original New York Mets from the outset. Moreover, she maintained her interest in the club until her death in 1975. Marge Schott relied on her own business acumen to gain ownership of the Cincinnati Reds long after her husband's death.

Owing to Marge Schott's flamboyant and notorious reputation, few people are aware of the other female big-league club owners. Schott's relatively recent regime obscures the accomplishments of her contemporaries. The first, Helene Britton, is now practically unheard-of outside the circle of baseball historians. After she inherited the St. Louis Cardinals, she stunned early twentieth century society by keeping the club. More surprisingly, she insisted on attending the owners' meetings. Prior to that, they had been men-only.

Pagliai, Leanne

GM, High Desert Mavericks

Leanne Pagliai worked as general manager for the High Desert Mavericks, an independent California club of which she also owned a minority share. Pagliai started in business as an executive for IBM before founding National Sports Placement, an agency that provides information for college students and interested professionals looking for careers in sports management. {Dottie Enrico, "Breaking the Grass Ceiling," *Newsday*, 27 March 1994; Gretchen Morgenson, "Where the Fans Still Come First," *Forbes*, 27 April 1992.}

Paine, Christina

NWBA

Christina Paine became the co-founder and CEO of the National Women's Baseball Association in 1997. In addition to her league role, Paine has also sponsored the Arizona Firebirds since 1994. Paine grew up riding horses and excelled in competitions until an accident left her disabled. She also appeared in some TV series such as *Kojak*, *Barnaby Jones* and *Big Valley*. {Tammy Lechner, "Common Threads: Baseball and Horses," *Accent on Living*, 22 March 1997.}

Paire (Davis), Lavonne "Pepper"

1944–46, Racine Belles, Minneapolis Millerettes

Scouted in 1944 while playing softball in California, Lavonne Paire was asked to join the Minneapolis Millerettes as their shortstop for $75 a week. She stayed with them for a year, and then they became the Fort Wayne Daisies. She remained in the league for ten years, primarily as a catcher. She is credited with writing the official league song in 1944. Before joining the AAGPBL, Davis played softball in Hollywood with stars such as Buddy Ebsen and Robert Preston. Davis gained a reputation in the league for being a fiery player who gave 110% all the time. On two occasions she led the league in RBIs, which made her a dangerous opponent. In 1946 with Racine, Paire hit .238 in 101 games. Davis got married in 1957 and raised three children while working as an electronics assembler. {Rose Nelson-Floto, "They Play Like Girls," *The Diamond Angle*, summer 1997, 34–36.}

Palatsides, Maryanne

Lady Mariners, Victorian Provincial Team

In the 2001 Australian National Tournament, Maryanne Palatsides hit .438 with a .625 slugging percentage. She knocked in six runs and got hit by a pitch twice in 21 at-bats. In 2002 Palatsides got the chance to play in the International Women's Championship in Geelong, Australia. Palatsides was selected after coming back from reconstructive shoulder surgery. {"Port Trio Pitch In for National Team," *Caulfield Gleneira Leader*, 9 December 2002, 50; Australian Baseball Federation, <www.baseball.org.au>.}

Palermo, Toni Ann "Peanuts"

Toni Palermo grew up at a time when sports for girls were limited, but her gym teacher encouraged her to play softball when she was only ten. At age 15 she joined the Chicago Colleens and then the Springfield Sallies as their shortstop. After playing on the two touring teams Palermo intended to sign on with South Bend, but instead she entered a convent. She earned her bachelor's degree from Alverno College in Milwaukee and three master's degrees from the University of Wisconsin at Madison. She also earned an interdisciplinary Ph.D. from the University of Wisconsin at Madison. She has continued to be active, playing tennis and teaching dancing. {Candy Czernicki, "'Peanuts' Palermo was 'Excellent Shortstop' Until God Intervened," *Catholic Herald*, 6 November 2003.}

Palesh, Shirley Ellen "Shirl"

(b. 23 November 1929, Wausau, Wisconsin) RF 1949–50, Racine Belles, Rockford Peaches

Shirley Palesh gained her experience playing fast-pitch softball, which she resumed after playing in the All American League. Her career in baseball was cut short by injuries. Her statistics include only 18 games. She hit a dismal .036 with only two hits. {AAGPBL Baseball Cards, 1995.}

Palmer, Rhonda

P 2003, Fillies

In 2003 Palmer led all batters in the California league with 14 hits in 27 at-bats. She scored 11 runs and knocked in another six. She also walked eight times while striking out six. She had five extra-base hits to also lead all batters. Palmer had a 1–1 record for the 2003 Women's World Series and a 7.94 ERA. She got two at-bats and was hitless, but she did walk twice. {California Women's Baseball League Web site.}

Pannozzo, Sharon

Media Relations, Chicago Cubs

Sharon Pannazzo worked for the Chicago Cubs in media relations starting in the mid–1980s, when there were few women in such positions. In fact, when she started she had to ride to games in a cab by herself rather than with the team. It took nearly a decade for that to change. {Dottie Enrico, "Breaking the Grass Ceiling," *Newsday*, 27 March 1994.}

Panthers

South Florida Diamond League

The Panthers joined the South Florida Diamond League in the 1990s, when it formed under the umbrella of the American Women's Baseball Association.

Papanicolaou, Paula

Paula Papanicolaou was invited to try out for the national team in 2002. Though she did not make the squad, she was placed on their development team to hone her skills for future competitions. When not playing baseball, Paula is busy raising her three children. {"Port Trio Pitch In for National Team," *Caulfield Gleneira Leader*, 9 December 2002, 50.}

Pappa, Katie

SS/2B/C 2002–2003, South Bend Blue Sox

In recognition of her excellent play in 2003, Katie Pappa was named MVP by the National Women's Baseball Hall of Fame. She became the youngest recipient of the award at the end of the 2003 season, being only 14 years old. She bats cleanup for the Blue Sox and led the team with a .400 average. She also knocked in 15 runs. Pappa is an all-around player in the field as she plays shortstop and second base as well as catching and pitching. {Blue Sox Web site; Kovach, 103.}

Parker, Andrea "Andy"

2B 1978–79, Cal Lutheran High School

As a freshman in 1978 Andy Parker played second base and right field for the Cal Lutheran High School baseball team. She hit .286 for the 3 and 8 club, and made one error in the field. Coach Rod

Frieling welcomed her on the team, along with "Sam" Collinsworth. The club only had 14 players, so they earned their spots on the roster. Returning for her sophomore season Parker raised her average to .333 under new coach Tom Del Rio. {Steve Brand, "Girls' Best Friend: Prep Diamond," *San Diego Union*, 29 April 1978; Steve Dolan, "Who's on Second?" *Los Angeles Times*, 27 April 1979, B1.}

Parks (Young), Barbara

(b. 7 February 1933, Brookline, Massachusetts) 2B/SS 1950–51, Kenosha Comets

Barbara Parks started in the league when she was only 17, so they sent her to one of the traveling teams to gain some experience in 1950. Before the season was over she had been assigned to Kenosha, returning there in 1951. She played in 66 games and hit only .170. However, she knocked in 27 runs and scored another 20 to help her ball club. {AAGPBL Baseball Cards, 1996.}

Parodi, Josephine

Josephine Parodi became better known in baseball circles as Josie Caruso. Caruso became a star attraction in 1929 and 1930 when promoter Dick Jess hired her to play exhibition baseball games. Jess had her change her name for publicity purposes and may have been attempting to play on the popularity of opera singer Enrico Caruso. The club, Josie Caruso and Her Eight Men, played all over the East Coast until she got married in 1931 and stopped playing. {Gai Berlage, "Transition of Women's Baseball," *Nine*, September 2000.}

Parr, Merrie

(b. 21 November 1979) OF/C, Detroit Danger

Merrie Parr plays for the Detroit Danger and lives in Farmington Hills, Michigan.

Parrilli, Josephine

P 1988, Florida Gators

Josephine Parilli pitched the inaugural game for the Florida Gators in 1988 as they lost to the Daredevils 11–6. The Daredevils scored seven runs off Parrilli in two innings, but most of the runs were unearned as the defense did not help their pitcher. {Bob Gordon, "Daredevils Win Women's Opener, 11–6," *Daily Herald*, 17 July 1988.}

Parsippany Yankees

The Parsipanny Yankees are a member of the East Coast Women's Baseball League (ECWBL). They are coached by player and manager Adriane Adler. In 2004 they won the ECWBL championship after finishing the season with a 12–2 record. They were led at the plate by Terri Lynn Herbst, who hit .846, and on the mound by Kristin Mills, who finished at 3–0 with an 0.88 ERA. {ECWBL Web site.}

Parsons (Zipay), Suzanne

(b. 1 April 1934, Hingham, Massachusetts) IF/OF/P 1953–54, Rockford Peaches

Suzanne Parsons only got the chance to join the All American League as it was on its last legs. She had just learned the game when the league folded, so she never got to be more than a utility player. Her statistics are incomplete as a result, but the league did have numbers for her in 53 games, where she batted only .066 and made six errors in the field. {AAGPBL Baseball Cards, 1995.}

Passlow, Kathryn "Kathy"

(b. 24 January 1975) IF 2002–03, Malvern Braves

Kathy Passlow helped the Australian team win

Kathryn Passlow of the Australian Malvern Braves (courtesy Jim Glennie).

the 2002 Women's World Series by defeating the U.S. in the semifinals and Japan in the finals. Passlow played in six games during the 2003 Women's World Series but only hit .167. She grew up playing softball and only took up baseball in 2000. {George Ierodiaconou, "Team Steal to a World Series Win," *Sunbury Macedon Leader*, 8 October 2002, 8.}

Patterson, Laura

P 1998, South Bend Belles

Laura Patterson joined the Belles for a season in the Great Lakes Women's Baseball League.

Patton, Becky

P 1998, South Bend Belles

Becky Patton joined the Belles for a season in the Great Lakes Women's Baseball League.

Paulk, Nicole

SS 1998, South Bend Belles

Nicole Paulk joined the Belles for a season in the Great Lakes Women's Baseball League.

Pawol, Jen

C/SS/OF Waterbury Diamonds, New York Traffic

In school Jen Pawol always played softball, beginning at the age of five. She tried out for the USA Olympic softball team in 1994. Her first baseball experience came with the Waterbury Diamonds. She then played for the New York Traffic. While attending Hoftra University she received Second Team All-American honors in 1997 for her play at shortstop.

Pawtucket Slaterettes

An all-girls league for those aged 5–70, located in Pawtucket, Rhode Island. The league started in the spring of 1973. It originally had four divisions: Instructional, Minor, Junior and Major. In 2003 an adult division was added. The league began when nine-year-old Alison "Pookie" Fortin wanted to try out for the local Darlington Little League team and they would not allow it because she was a girl. Her parents took the league to court, and the publicity led others to step forward and create a girls' hardball league. When the league began it was called the Darlington Pioneers and was set up for girls ages 10–16. After the first season the parents decided to rename the league

Letisha Gorman hitting in 2001. She is still playing in 2005 for the Pawtucket Women's Division.

Stephanie Phillips, pitching in 2001. She is playing in 2005 with the Women's Division.

the Slaterettes. The new league president, Peggy Massaro, guided the group to that decision after the founding presidents, Paul and Eveline Engelhardt, moved. The name was chosen because of a local men's club called the Slaters and the presence of the Slater Mill in Pawtucket.

Over the years the league's two biggest difficulties have been finding a place to play and raising funds. Because of the size of the league, the teams need multiple fields to play on, and they have always had to fight for equal time with the boys' teams. The league also requires a substantial amount of money to provide uniforms, equipment, coaches and insurance for the players.

1978 DNLL Junior Division Team with the Pawtucket Staterettes.

1978 Hasbro Junior Division Team with the Pawtucket Slaterettes.

{Dick Lee, "Girls' Baseball League Still Thriving in Pawtucket," Providence Journal, 18 July 1991, Z–01.}

Ruth Krebs showing off her pitching repertoire in 2005.

By 1991 the league developed into three divisions for girls ranging in age from 7 to 17. The league wanted to add a senior division that year but could not get enough players interested. That addition did not take place until 2003.

In 1998 the Slaterettes celebrated their twenty-fifth anniversary with a tournament involving current players and alumni. Teams represented Pawtucket, Medford, Massachusetts and Washington, D.C. {"Pawtucket Slaterettes Tournament Was a Huge Success," *Base Runner*, October 1998, 3.}

By 1999 the league claimed over 250 young women playing baseball on 21 teams in four divisions. There was no lack of interest for the game, but the problem was finding other teams to play. Without others to play it becomes difficult for the girls to give up softball where they can always find competition. {Greg Botelho, "Pawtucket Slaterettes Having Another Banner Year," *Providence Journal*, 28 June 1999, C-03.}

The Slaterettes hosted their first Roy Hobbs Tournament in 2002. They came in second after losing to the Lowell Robins 10–0 in the final game. Emily Christy got the win for the Robins while Melissa Morin and Aubrey Phanuef took the loss. The other participant in the tournament was the North Shore Cougars. {"Slaterettes Take Second in Roy Hobbs Tournament," *The Times*, 12 August 2002, B3.}

In 2003 the Slaterettes added to their Major division to allow for more adult women to play. One requirement for participation is that every player must be a member of the Amateur Athletic Union, since all games and tournaments are now sanctioned by the AAU, under the leadership of Tom Giffen.

The Slaterettes continue to operate under a board of directors that includes a president and vice-president as well as coordinators for each division, secretaries, and a series of coordinators for things such as equipment, instruction and umpires. Some of the people who have served on the board of the league over the years include Steve Cooper, Diane Cooper, Mike Cullinan, Sandie Gula, Nancy Scallin, Joseph Thibeault Jr. and others. {Sumathi Ready, "Slaterettes Shine on the Diamond," *Providence Journal*, 27 April 1998, C-01.}

Payne, Barbara "Bobbie"

(b. 18 September 1932, Shreveport, Louisiana) IF/P 1949–51, Springfield Sallies, Muskegon Lassies, Kalamazoo Lassies, Battle Creek Belles, Rockford Peaches

Barbara Payne had a short career in the All American League but played for a number of teams because she was a versatile player. A few of the teams she was traded to folded as the league began having financial difficulties. Her statistics from the league are incomplete because she spent her first year with the traveling Sallies. For the remaining two years she played in 194 games and hit .182 with 57 runs scored and 49 RBIs. {AAGPBL Baseball Cards, 1995.}

Payne, Lisa

OF/IF, Boston Blitz

While growing up, Lisa Payne played Little League but eventually switched to softball because that was the sport girls were expected to play. In 1999 she returned to baseball when she made the roster for the Boston Blitz. {Dick Dahl, "Out of His League," *Boston Globe Magazine*, 12 September 1999, 20, 22, 29.}

Peacock, Lacey "Kenora"

P 2003–04, Manitoba Taffy

Before joining the Taffy Lacey Peacock had always played behind the plate, but the coaches of her new club were impressed with her arm strength. She has learned from other pitchers and developed two fastballs, two changeups, a slider and a curveball. {Peter James, "Pitcher Shows Off Her 'Stuff' at National Baseball Camp," *Daily Miner and News*, 6 March 2004, 21.}

Pearson (Tesseine), Marguerite "Dolly," "Buttons"

(b. 6 September 1932, Pittsburgh, Pennsylvania; d. 4 January 2005) Util. 1948–54, Muskegon Lassies, Peoria Red Wings, Racine Belles, Battle Creek Belles, Kalamazoo Lassies, South Bend Blue Sox, Grand Rapids Chicks

Dolly Pearson graduated from Allderdire High School and attended Central Michigan University. She played city league basketball and softball before joining the Lassies. During her tenure in the AAGPBL Pearson played every position on the field before becoming a regular shortstop for South Bend. Her best season came during the league's final year in 1954, when she hit .327 and swatted 18 home runs. She was traded many times because she could play so many positions and play them well. She played in 541 games over seven seasons and batted .216. She had 381 hits and 279 walks to help her score 195 runs. She received her nickname on a trip with the club to Florida. She wanted to play with all the buttons in their vehicle, hence the nickname "Buttons." {AAGPBL Baseball Cards, 1996.}

After the league folded Pearson started playing slow-pitch softball in Mt. Pleasant, Michigan, where her club won 18 championships. She coached boys' baseball, girls' softball and senior girls' bowling for many years. She married Edward Tesseine in 1955 and went to work for Central Michigan University while helping her husband run the bar they owned. The Mt. Pleasant Bowlers Hall of Fame inducted Pearson, as did the Michigan Amateur Softball Association Hall of Fame in 1997. {AAGPBL Questionnaire, National Baseball Hall of Fame.}

Peninsula Peppers

The Peppers played in the California Women's Baseball League as well as enjoying independent status. They often just put together a team to play in tournaments.

Penrod, Tracy

1997, San Diego Stix

Tracy Penrod played for the Stix in the California league for one season.

Peoria Red Wings

Peoria's entry in the All American League joined in 1946 and remained active through 1951. In their first season, the Red Wings finished in the cellar with a record of 33–79. In 1947 they improved to 55–57, and then in 1948 they finally had a winning record at 70–55. They returned to the cellar in 1949 with a record of 36–73 and had losing records in their final two seasons. The Red Wings' lack of success hurt their fan attendance and accounted for the financial troubles the club had before finally folding.

Pepe, Maria

(b. Hoboken, New Jersey)

Maria Pepe gained national fame when she was 12 years old and tried out for her local Little League team in Hoboken, New Jersey. She had grown up playing ball with the boys in her neighborhood since the age of five. When she was in sixth grade at Our Lady of Grace Elementary School the chance came to sign up for the Young Democrats. Pepe did because all her friends were playing. She played three games for the Young Democrats and coach Jimmy Farina. Then, the national office said she could not play anymore. In the first game she pitched, and then she played the outfield and was a relief pitcher in the others. Coach Farina wanted her to stay on the team, but the Little League headquarters threatened to revoke Hoboken's charter if she stayed. She turned in her uniform. The National Organization for Women (NOW) heard about the situation and wanted to take the case to court. A final ruling was issued by the New Jersey Superior Court through Judge Sylvia Pressler in November 1973. Little League officials appealed the decision but it was upheld in 1974, forcing Little League organizations to let girls play. Their response was to establish Little League softball for girls. By the time the decision was made, Pepe was in high school — where she played basketball and softball — she had passed the age of eligibility for Little League play. She played softball at St. Peter's College while earning her business degree. She went on to become a CPA and works for Hackensack University Medical Center. In August 2004 she was honored at the Little League World Series for her role in changing sports for women. {Ruth Padawer, "She Came to Play," *The Record* (Bergen County, N.J.), 23 November 2003.}

Pepe had not been the first girl to play Little League ball. Kathryn Johnston of Corning, New York, played in 1950 under a nickname. This forced a change in 1951, when the national office added a rule against girls playing that stayed on the books until 1974. {Stan Grossfield, "Purpose Pitch," *The Boston Globe*, 19 August 2004, C1, C13; Dan Lewerenz, "Little League to Honor Maria Pepe, 30 Years after Lawsuit in Her Name That Let In Girls," *Associated Press*, 7 November 2003; "Little League Honors Female Pioneers," *Grand Rapids Press*, 22 August 2004.}

Peppas, June A. "Lefty," "Pep"

(b. 16 June 1929, Kansas City, Missouri) 1B/P 1948–54, Fort Wayne Daisies, Racine Belles, Battle Creek Belles, Kalamazoo Lassies

June Peppas was born in Missouri but grew up in Fort Wayne, Indiana, after her parents, George and Edna, moved the family there while she was a baby. Peppas played a variety of sandlot sports and graduated from Elmhurst High School in 1947. Her parents worked in the restaurant business, and that connection got Peppas the chance to play on a number of local softball teams sponsored by people such as Harold Greiner. Greiner not only owned the local Bob Inn restaurant but also scouted for the AAGPBL and managed the Daisies in 1949. From 1942 to 1947 Peppas played for Greiner's team, and they won the state championship in 1944 and 1945.

Peppas was signed in 1948 to pitch for Fort Wayne, but in 1949 was traded to Racine because she had control problems when the league switched to overhand pitching. At Racine Peppas worked with Leo Murphy to gain control of her pitches. Peppas was a two-time all-star selection during her time with Kalamazoo in 1953 and 1954. She split her time between first base and pitching. In the league's final season, 1954, she pitched in 13 games with a 6–4 record and a 3.32 ERA. She also helped her own cause at the plate, where she hit .333, fifth highest in the league. In the championship series after the 1954 season, Peppas hit .450 and won two games.

After the league folded Peppas went back to school to earn her bachelor's and master's degrees at Western Michigan State University. She also spent two years at Purdue University as an engineering student. She became a vocational teacher and then ran her own printing business in Kalamazoo, Michigan, until her retirement in 1988. Peppas continued to play recreational softball and basketball until 1968. Her softball team won the state championship in 1955. Later, she worked with some of the other players from the AAGPBL to reconnect with others and to host the first reunion in 1982 in Chicago. {Jim Sargent, "June Peppas and the All-American League: Helping the Kalamazoo Lassies Win the 1954 AAGPBL Championship," *National Pastime* (2002); AAGPBL Questionnaire, National Baseball Hall of Fame.}

Perado, Susan

2B

Susan Perado was one of the first two women to play college baseball before Ila Borders became the first pitcher. Perado played one game at second base for Webster College in St. Louis, Missouri, in 1985. {"Borders Makes History," *Press-Enterprise*, 16 February 1994.}

Pereira, Elyse

Elyse Pereira grew up playing Little League baseball in the City View area of Anchorage, Alaska. She got a chance to see her heroes, the Silver Bullets, when they came to town to play the Anchorage Bucs. {"Girls Meet Heroes," *Anchorage Daily News*, 27 June 1997.}

Perez, Jenny Ashley

2B, Arizona Peppers

The Arizona Peppers belonged to the Arizona league in the 1990s, and Jenny Perez played one year for the club.

Perez (Jinright), Migdalia "Mickey"

(b. 1926, Havana, Cuba) P 1948–54, Chicago Colleens, Battle Creek Belles, Rockford Peaches

Migdalia Perez came to the United States to play in the All American League. Her English was strong enough that she acted as interpreter for the other girls that came with her. The record she compiled included 173 games pitched with a 2.73 ERA. Her win-loss record stood at 67–78. Perez pitched two no-hitters during her career, in 1949 and 1953. After the league folded she stayed in America and got married. {AAGPBL Baseball Cards, 2000.}

Perez, Vicky

P

In 2002 Vicky Perez held a unique place in the history of her home county. She was believed to be the only girl playing on either a varsity or JV baseball team that year in Ventura County, California. She pitched for the Ventura High JV team in her sophomore year. She hopes to improve her pitching enough to make the varsity squad in her senior year. {Rich Romine, "Perez Proving Baseball Is Not Just a Boys' Game," *Ventura County Star*, 16 May 2002.}

Perlick (Keating), Edythe "Edie"

(b. 12 December 1922, Chicago, Illinois) LF 1943–50, Racine Belles

Edie Perlick grew up in an athletic family. She played fast-pitch softball, as did her sister Jean. Perlick played for Racine for eight seasons, patrolling the outfield and having a grand time traveling the country. She was one of the first four players signed into the new AAGPBL in 1943. One of her fondest memories is the trip the Belles took through Central America, Caracus and Managua, Nicaragua. In her first season Perlick played in 84 games and hit .268 as a rookie, her highest batting average. She hit .230 in 1946 while playing in 112 games. She also stole 88 bases and scored 72 runs. She made the all-star squad three times during her career — in 1943, 1947 and 1948 — and had a .240 average. She helped her team each year with a solid bat and the second highest career total of runs batted in, with 392. She also stole 481 bases. After her playing career ended she worked for Harris Computer Systems in Florida for 23 years. {AAGPBL Newsletter, May 2001, 31; Jim Sargent, "Edie (Perlick) Keating," <www.AAGPBL.org>; AAGPBL Baseball Cards, 1995.}

Peterboro Nine

In the small town of Peterboro, New York, a women's baseball club was created with over 50 members. From that group a traveling nine was chosen to play baseball in town and against outside competition. The captain was identified as a Miss Nannie Miller. Their first actual competition was against another nine chosen from their club, known as the junior nine. The senior nine won 29–5. The senior team wore white stockings, stout shoes, and blue and white tunics. The roster for the two teams was reported as follows:

Seniors	Juniors
Miller, Nannie — C	Clark — C
Mills, Clara — P	Haze — P
Manning, Mary — 1B	Colwell — 1B
Richardson, Fran — 2B	Sterns — 2B
Powell, Bertha — 3B	Dyer — 3B
Hand, Jennie — SS	Laing — SS
Ferris, Hattie — LF	Pratt — LF
Marshall, Maggie — RF	Gallueia — RF
Frothingham, Mary — CF	Frothingham — CF

Both Manning and Richardson scored five runs apiece for the victorious seniors. Mills, the pitcher, even scored one run so that every member of the seniors contributed to the victory. {"A Game Between Girls," *Spirit of the Times*, 29 August 1868, 26.}

Peters, Marjorie "Marge," "Pete"

(b. 11 September 1918, Greenfield, Wisconsin) P 1943–44, Rockford Peaches

Marge Peters pitched for the Peaches for two seasons and then left the AAGPBL to get married and move to Texas. She did pitch the inaugural game for the new league on 30 May 1943 against the Blue Sox. The Peaches lost 4–3 in 13 innings. She later helped organize a professional softball league in Milwaukee that included her club, the Milwaukee Jets. {AAGPBL Newsletter, May 2001, 39; AAGPBL Baseball Cards, 1995.}

Peterson (Fox), Betty Jean "Pete"

(b. 21 November 1933, Wyanet, Illinois) C 1952–53, Rockford Peaches, Muskegon Belles

Betty Jean Peterson grew up in rural Illinois, attending Wyanet High School, which had less than 100 students. Since the school did not offer sports opportunities, Peterson played softball with a variety of local teams that played one another. After she graduated Peterson went to work for a short time in a bank before going to try out for the Peaches. She got a contract with Kalamazoo but spent much of her time with Muskegon, who needed a catcher. She finished the 1953 season with an injury to her finger, and that ended her playing time. Peterson got married in 1956 to Roger Fox and had three children. She helped her husband work their farm while her children grew up and then worked for the State of Illinois in the highway department until her retirement. As a result of her contributions Peterson was selected for membership in the Bureau County Sports Hall of Fame in 1996. Her hometown of Wyanet invited her to serve as grand marshal for their parade in 1993. {AAGPBL Questionnaire, National Baseball Hall of Fame.}

Peterson, Jodie

Jodie Peterson started playing baseball when she was only six years old. In 2004 at age 15 she was still playing, but the city league in Fayetteville, North Carolina, was encouraging her to switch to softball. Peterson wants to see a women's league develop in the Carolinas like there are in other parts of the country to give girls a chance to continue to play baseball once they pass the age of about 14 or 15.

Peterson, Marie A.

Owner

Marie Peterson inherited ownership of the Miami Marlins in 1970 after her husband Robert's death. The Marlins were a Class A team in Florida. In addition to owning the team Peterson was heavily involved in the community, serving as a trustee for Resurrection Hospital and for St. Francis Hospital. {"Marie A. Peterson; Once Owned Class A Baseball Team in Miami," *Chicago Tribune*, 15 August 1994.}

Peterson, Ruth

Chaperone, Racine Belles

Ruth Peterson was an athlete herself, taking part in sports such as field hockey, track and field, and baseball. She was a physical education teacher and worked for a time as the chaperone for the Racine Belles in the AAGPBL, taking care of the ladies on the team. The role of the chaperone was to ensure the players followed the league rules and did nothing to tarnish the feminine image of the league.

Petras, Ernestine "Teeny"

(b. 17 September 1922, Haskell, New Jersey) SS 1944–52, Milwaukee Chicks, Grand Rapids Chicks, Chicago Colleens, Kenosha Comets, Battle Creek Belles

Ernestine Petras played for nine seasons in the All American League. She was named the league's best defensive shortstop in four of those years and she set a record for completing 42 double plays in 1948 while with Grand Rapids. Overall, Petras played in 834 games, hitting only .198, but she stole 420 bases, scored 359 runs and walked 342 times compared to 249 strikeouts. Her nickname had nothing to do with her size but came directly from her first name. {AAGPBL Baseball Cards, 1995.}

Petruzelli, Susan

Umpire

Susan Petruzelli attended the Harry Wendelstedt Umpire School in 1984, one of three ladies in a class of nearly 200. The other two were Perry Lee Barber and Jennifer "Jaye" Weber. When she is not umpiring Petruzelli works as an art designer in St. Louis.

Petryna (Allen), Doreen Betty

(b. 26 November 1930, Regina, Saskatchewan) 3B 1948–49, Grand Rapids Chicks, Fort Wayne Daisies, Muskegon Lassies

Doreen Petryna, better known as Betty during her playing days, spent two years in the All American League. She was discovered by a scout while she played softball for Eiler's Jewelers in 1948. She played the hot corner solidly and even set a record for the most assists in one game, with 12. Her defense is what made her a valuable addition to a team, because her hitting was weak. She batted only .139 in 122 games and only knocked in 20 runs. After retiring she and her husband had three children, whom they coached in softball and baseball. {AAGPBL Baseball Cards, 1995.}

Pettragrasso, Chris

P, Waterbury Diamonds

Chris Pettragrasso helped the Waterbury club win the 2001 Citrus Blast. She combined with Adriane Adler on a four-hit victory on the way to the finals.

Phaneuf, Aubrey

P, Pawtucket Slaterettes

Aubrey Phaneuf found herself pitching behind the "Gruesome Twosome" of Nicole Servant and Lindsay Johnston as they pitched in the junior division for Rhode Island Petroleum. Phaneuf hit .613 and had an ERA around 2.00 while being fourth in the league in strikeouts in 1999. The 2002 season found Phaneuf pitching for the Slaterettes at a Roy Hobbs Tournament where they came in second. {Greg Botelho, "Pawtucket Slaterettes Having Another Banner Year," *Providence Journal*, 28 June 1999, C–03.}

Phantoms

The Phantoms joined the Sydney Women's Baseball League in 2004 and came in second. They lost in the final to the Stealers. The club was coached by Mandi Barnao. {Sydney Women's Baseball League Annual Report 2004, 8.}

Philadelphia Bobbies

The Bobbies became part of the national phe-

nomenon of women's teams known as bloomer clubs, popular from the late nineteenth century through the early decades of the twentieth century. These teams barnstormed across the United States, playing men's clubs wherever they could. Mary O'Gara of Philadelphia formed the Bobbies, who played mainly along the East Coast except in 1925 when they journeyed to Japan for new competition. She had help from former major-leaguer Eddie Ainsmith in setting up the tour. Ainsmith had taken a group of players to Japan in 1924 and therefore knew a bit about the country and the ball playing possibilities. One of the players who made the trip with the Bobbies was Leona Kearns, a pitcher from West Union, Illinois. The group met and traveled across the West before getting to Seattle, Washington, planning to depart together for Japan. They scheduled games in places such as Fargo, North Dakota; Glasgow, Montana; and Whitefish, Montana as preparation for their tour of the Orient. {"Ball Team of Girls Coming to Montana," *Helena Daily Independent*, 24 September 1925, 9; "One of Best Girl Ball Teams in the Country," *Appleton Post-Crescent*, 15 May 1925, 21.}

The Bobbies were a group of young players ranging in age from 13 to about 20, with no veterans at all. Their strongest player happened to be Edith Houghton, who was 13 at the time of the trip. Kearns was only 17 when she joined the Bobbies. She pitched her first game in Tacoma, Washington, as the team tried to get used to playing together before leaving for Japan. The journey began aboard the *President Jefferson* on 6 October 1925, with passage paid by the Japanese promoters. Problems should have been apparent from the start when the players learned it was one-way passage, though they were assured they would make enough money playing twice a week to pay for all their expenses and their return trip. After 11 days at sea the team arrived and found themselves wined and dined in fine style before playing any ball games. They did not get off to an auspicious start, losing their first three games. Unfortunately, this trend continued. As they lost game after game it became harder to promote the club and finances became a huge problem. The on-the-field troubles finally bubbled over, causing a break between Ainsmith and O'Gara. This split the team and Ainsmith decided to try to salvage something from the trip by creating a new team with four Japanese players, Kearns, Nella Shank, Edith Ruth, himself and former pitcher Earl Hamilton. The plan was to barnstorm through Korea to make enough money to get back to America. The rest of the players stayed with

O'Gara in Kobe, hoping to appeal to others for help. Two individuals finally stepped in and helped the girls out. Henry Sanborn, owner of the Pleasanton Hotel in Kobe, housed and fed the team, while N.H.N. Mody, a banker, stepped forward to pay their passage home. O'Gara and nine of the Bobbies left Japan, arriving back in Philadelphia on 6 December 1925. This left three members of the Bobbies overseas with Ainsmith, who came up with enough money to book passage home for himself and his wife. Left on their own, the young ladies appealed to Kearns' father, who wired money. They finally left Kobe in January 1926. On the trip home Kearns was washed overboard and was unable to be saved. {Barbara Gregorich, "Stranded," *The North American Review,* May/August 1998.} The Bobbies appeared again in the newspapers when they arrived in Curwensville for a game in July 1926. The local fans were excited to have this team playing their local club.

Philadelphia Women's Baseball League (PWBL)

Narda Quigley founded the Philadelphia Women's Baseball league for the 2004 season to give women the chance to play baseball and not just softball. She grew up playing Little League but eventually switched to softball because there seemed to be no future for a girl in playing baseball. For example, scholarships are only available to play softball, not baseball, in college for women. The league has three teams, including the Clash. They play every weekend during the summer at a field in either New Jersey or Philadelphia. The players range in age but most are in their 20s and 30s. The youngest player was 13-year-old Rebecca Yuska in 2004. The other teams are the Terror and the Blue Crush. The games follow major league rules, except they play seven innings instead of nine because of the difficulty in finding good quality pitchers. {Don McKee, "She's Creating a Place to Play Hardball," *Philadelphia Inquirer,* 9 March 2004; Eileen O'Donnell, "Covering All the Bases," *Philadelphia Inquirer,* 15 July 2005.}

Phoenix Peppers

The Phoenix Peppers played in women's tournaments around the country and for a time belonged to the AWBA.

Pieper, Marjorie L. "Marge," "Peeps"

(b. 2 August 1922, Clinton, Michigan) SS/3B/RF 1946–53, Fort Wayne Daisies, Kenosha Comets, Chicago Colleens, Peoria Red Wings, Battle Creek Belles, Muskegon Lassies

While growing up in Clinton, Michigan, Marjorie Pieper played basketball, tennis and softball. She also worked in a bookstore before trying out for the All American League. She liked the chance to play but did not like the constant moving because of trades. She got traded a lot because she could play just about anywhere on the field. Teams picked her up when they needed a position filled. She played in 718 games and hit .213. Her speed led to 181 stolen bases and 256 runs scored. She also walked 286 times against only 191 strikeouts. After the seasons were over she started taking college classes at Eastern Michigan, where she got her bachelor's degree. She earned her master's from the University of Michigan and even completed 36 hours toward a doctoral degree. She continued to golf and bowl as well as coach a variety of sports. She became a teacher and taught high school and at a junior college. {AAGPBL Questionnaire, National Baseball Hall of Fame; AAGPBL Baseball Cards, 1996.}

Pietrangeli, Emil "Piet"

Umpire

Emil Pietrangeli worked for two years as an umpire in the AAGPBL during the early 1950s. The umpires of the women's games could reprimand a player for sloppy dress and kick her off the field until she fixed herself up. With this citation came an automatic fine. Pietrangeli recalls that the women often tried to throw a spitball, which was illegal, and he would have to throw them out of the game. One of the worst offenders he remembers was Jean Cione of the Peaches. During his first year in the league Pietrangeli worked eight games a week and received a paycheck of $250 a month with an additional $100 for expenses and mileage. In 1951 his pay went up to $350 a month. While he traveled to different games his wife Mary ran their grocery store, "Piet's." Following the 1951 season Pietrangeli did not renew his contract but went to work in construction, though he continued to umpire semipro ball for years. {Barbara Gregorich, "A Home run's Worth of Memories," *The Milwaukee Journal,* 28 June 1992, 20–24.}

Pirok, Pauline "Pinky"

(b. 18 October 1926, Chicago, Illinois) SS/3B 1943–48, Kenosha Comets, South Bend Blue Sox

Pauline Pirok tried out for and made the All American League in 1943. She spent three seasons with Kenosha before being traded to South Bend. In one memorable game Pirok helped the Comets beat South Bend 10–0 with four hits in five at-bats. Included in those hits were a triple and a double. In the following series against Rockford, which the Comets swept, Pirok kept up her hitting with four hits in ten at-bats. She also scored four of the eight runs her team scored in the series. Pirok got the chance to travel to Cuba for spring training in 1947. Her career average was .208 with 262 runs scored and 127 RBIs. She played in 559 games and stole 223 bases. After her playing career was over Pirok worked as a physical education teacher for 36 years in the Chicago school system. She also became an avid golfer to stay active. {AAGPBL Newsletter, May 2001, 33; AAGPBL Baseball Cards, 1996.}

Piskula, Grace Constance "Skip," "Zip"

(b. 26 February 1926, Milwaukee, Wisconsin) LF/1B 1944–45, Rockford Peaches, Milwaukee Chicks

Grace Piskula graduated from Pulaski High School in 1944. While there she played all the intramural sports offered for girls: softball, basketball and volleyball. She also participated in the school's synchronized swimming club and supported the boys' teams as a cheerleader. Piskula worked as the girls' sports editor for the high school paper as well. From 1944 to 1948 Grace attended La Crosse State University, earning a BS and playing every sport offered. Her participation earned her the Betty Belle Hutchinson Scholarship and a place on the Academic Wall of Fame. She earned her master's in 1952 from New York University and did some further graduate work at the University of Wisconsin in Madison and Milwaukee.

Grace kept herself active while in school as she played softball, volleyball, basketball and tennis for the Milwaukee Recreation Department until 1943. She played softball and basketball for the West Allis Recreation Department from 1943 and 1947. In between all that she tried out for the All American League in 1944. She hurt her leg sliding into first base while playing for Rockford and never quite recovered.

After completing her college education Grace worked as a physical education teacher at the junior and senior high level and coached intramural sports. She taught and coached for 40 years, retir-ing in 1986. With retirement came a new activity as Grace took up golfing. {AAGPBL Questionnaire, National Baseball Hall of Fame; AAGPBL Baseball Cards, 2000.}

Pitts, Pamela

Management

Pamela Pitts started working for the Oakland A's in 1981 as a secretary. Her most recent promotion in 1993 made her the director of baseball administration for the Athletics. Her job responsibilities include understanding waiver rules and dealing with all minor league contract concerns. {Casey Tefertilier, "A's Executive Pamela Pitts Wears Many Hats," San Francisco Examiner, 21 September 1993.}

Poe, Linda

P 1988, Daredevils

Linda Poe of Prospect Heights, Illinois, helped her Daredevils beat the Gators 11–6 in the inaugural game for the AWBA in 1988. She came on in relief of starter Diana Rapolz and gave up four runs after retiring nine straight hitters. Poe was helped by the excellent catching of Lee Fuchs. {Bob Gordon, "Daredevils Win Women's Opener, 11–6," Daily Herald, 17 July 1988.}

Poet, Kasey

IF/P, East Bay Furies

Kasey Poet pitched and played the infield for the Furies in the California Women's Baseball League. She played in eight games in 2003 and hit .500, 16–32 with eight RBIs.

Pollitt (Deschaine), Alice "Al," "Rock"

(b. 19 July 1929, Lansing, Michigan) SS/3B/2B 1947–53, Rockford Peaches

Alice Pollitt grew up in a home where athletics were important. Her dad had been a professional soccer player in England before coming to this country. Alice and Jackie Kelley played together in their home town and both joined the AAGPBL at the same time. Pollitt was best known in the league for her excellent fielding. Her career hitting included a .255 average with 214 RBIs and a fielding average of .914 at third base. She did have a little bit of power, as she also socked eight home runs and over 80-extra-base hits. {Susan E. Johnson, 91–92.}

Polytechnic Baseball Club

In 1907 baseball was introduced to the young ladies at Polytechnic High School in Los Angeles. Games were arranged between the daytime and evening students. A doubleheader was played the first time with each side winning one of the contests. The two teams were led by their pitchers, Miss Gray and Miss Ross. The ladies so enjoyed the competition it was decided the game would be continued the following term with both indoor and outdoor competition.

After developing their own skills, the ladies began baseball with other local area girls' teams. In their first contest they beat a Los Angeles High School team 37–9. They beat this same team again in 1908 by a score of 20–12. The winning pitcher was Miss Ruth Miller. By 1909 a number of new teams had been added and even a championship series, which was won by the team from Bonita High School in southern California.

Rosters

Day School	Evening School
Nieders—C	Meyerly—C
Ross—P	Gray—P
Espees—1B	Ross, L.—1B
Blair, N.—2B	Danizer—2B
Jones, L.—3B	Sly—3B
Blair, L.—SS	Dawson—SS
Hurd—LF	Scott—LF
Jones, E.—CF	Charbonet—CF
Rouse, Mary—RF	Johnson—RF
Charles—SS	
Bendell—RF	
Hardin—SS	
Miller, Ruth—P	
Wilhelm—LF	
Brown—C	
Larson—2B	
Evans—RF	

{"Girls' Baseball Comes to Stay," Los Angeles Times, 6 June 1907, 114; "Girls Baseball," Los Angeles Times, 3 June 1908, 16; "Sensational Playing," Los Angeles Times, 21 June 1907, 16.}

Poole, Sharon

(Haverhill, Massachusetts) CF

Sharon Poole made her local Little League team in Haverhill, Massachusetts, in 1971. She played center field for the Indians in two games before she got kicked off the team and her coach was let go. The reason for her release had nothing to do with her gender but instead happened because she had not participated in the draft. According to league rules drafted players must be used first, and there were still a few draft players who had not been assigned to teams. Therefore, Poole was an ineligible player. In the two games she played in she hit solidly and fielded without error.

Posner, Kat

P, Philadelphia Women's League

Kat Posner always loved baseball but never thought she would play the game. She grew up playing ice hockey but in 2004 joined the new Philadelphia Women's League as a pitcher. In her first game she had two hits against a local men's team. {Doug Lesmerises, "Women Trading Softball for Baseball in New League," The News Journal, 29 June 2004.}

Postema, Pamela Annette "Pam"

(b. 1955, Willard, Ohio) Umpire

Pam Postema umpired in the minors from 1977 through 1988 and for major league spring training games in 1987 and 1988. She also got to umpire the Hall of Fame game in 1987 between the New York Yankees and Atlanta Braves. Her start came in the Rookie Gulf Coast League after graduating from the Al Somer's School for Umpires in 1977 as the seventeenth student in a class of 130. During the off-season she works for UPS driving a delivery truck. She started in the Rookie league and worked her way up to the Triple A Pacific Coast League during her 11-year career. When Postema received her promotion to Triple A it was the highest a female umpire had gone. This came after six years in the Gulf Coast, Florida and Texas leagues. Bill Cutler, PCL president, rated Postema in the middle of his 15 umpires. He claimed her strength was calling balls and strikes, but said she was weak on the base paths. She then spent another five years at the Triple A level waiting for a call to the majors that never came.

Her start in umpiring did not come as easily as the simple litany of her progress would imply. Pam grew up in Willard, Ohio, the youngest of three children. She often played catch with her older brother Todd while their sister Peggy read. The town had a population of about 5,000, and there were no organized sports for girls at her school. She did catch for the city fast-pitch softball team, which traveled all over Ohio during the summers looking for teams to play. When she decided to turn to umpiring she had to write and call for six months before she was accepted.

One of the biggest controversies of Postema's career came in 1988 after umpiring an exhibition game for the Houston Astros. Pitcher Bob Knepper made the comment following the game that women should not be major league umpires or president of the United States. By the following day every paper carried the story, and NOW threatened to boycott all Astros games. When Postema was not selected that year as one of the new ML umpires, she waited for one more year and then was released after the 1989 season. She thought she had a shot at one of two NL openings in 1988, but Gary Darling and Mark Hirschbeck were chosen instead. Postema was reassigned to Triple A as a crew chief. She filed a sex discrimination suit in 1991 and ended up settling out of court. Gloria Allred, a strong woman's rights advocate, tried the case for Postema. The agreement had two requirements for Postema, that she not reveal the amount she received in the settlement and that she never apply to umpire again in a league affiliated with ML baseball. After leaving the game Postema went to work for a Honda parts factory in Mansfield, Ohio, called Newman Technology Incorporated. She also wrote a book about her experiences, titled *You Gotta Have Balls*. In 2000 Postema did receive the honor of being inducted into the Shrine of the Eternals wing at the Baseball Reliquary in California. This is a nonprofit organization that was created to honor those who have helped the game beyond just what the box scores say. Her fellow inductees in 2000 were Moe Berg and Bill Lee. {Susan Brenna, "Hey, Ump! Are the Majors Ready for You?" *Newsday*, 24 March 1988; "Female Umpire Postema Sent Back to Minors," *The Daily Star* (Oneonta, N.Y.), 29 March 1988, 7; Robin Finn, "Female Umpire Awaits Favorable Call from Majors," *New York Times*, 27 July 1987, C4; John Garrity, "Waiting for the Call," <www.SI.com>, 14 March 1988; Rich Kenda, "Ex-Ump Says Her Close Call Not in Vain," *USA Today Baseball Weekly*, 9–15 August 2000, 10; Al Pickett, "Remembering a Lost Scoop," *Abilene Reporter-News*, 30 October 1997; Pam Postema File, National Baseball Hall of Fame and Museum; Gordon Verrell, "Pam Postema Still Paying Her Dues," *The Sporting News*, 28 March 1988, 36.}

Potter, Sally

P, South Bend Blue Sox

Sally Potter pitched for the South Bend entry in the Great Lakes Women's Baseball League in 2003. She began the season with two complete games and ten strikeouts in 13 innings.

Powder Puffs

The Powder Puffs were a touring baseball squad under the direction of manager Wainstock. The team hailed from New York and played exhibitions all over the country. One of the club's stars was Mabel Sloan, who caught and played first base.

Pratt, Jeannie

Philadelphia

Jeannie Pratt grew up outside Boston and loved to play baseball. She tried out for the local Little League team with her brother when she was ten. She made the team because they thought she was a boy. When they found out she was a girl they told her she had to play softball. In 2004 she returned to baseball in the Philadelphia Women's League. {Don McKee, "She's Creating a Place to Play Hardball," *Philadelphia Inquirer*, 9 March 2004.}

Pratt, Mary "Prattie"

(b. 30 November 1918, Bridgeport, Connecticut) P 1943–47, Rockford Peaches, Racine Belles, Kenosha Comets

Mary Pratt did not get much opportunity to play competitive sports while growing up. Her junior high school offered no sports for girls, and North Quincy High School limited the girls' activities to intramural competition. As a consequence Pratt joined the Church League basketball team in 1937 and also played lacrosse, field hockey and softball in the local city leagues.

Pratt played for the Racine Belles in 1944 after playing softball in and around the Boston area. In 1939 and 1940, for example, Mary played for a club called the Boston Olympets. Playing in the AAGPBL gave her enough money to continue her college education. During her five years in the league Pratt pitched one no-hitter and had at least one 20-win season. Pratt spent 48 years teaching physical education as well as coaching and officiating basketball and softball. She went into teaching after receiving her bachelor's degree from Sargent College in 1941. While attending Sargent she tried out for every sport they offered and made every team. She played basketball, softball, volleyball, lacrosse, field hockey, tennis, sailing and archery. She earned her master's degree from Boston University and went on to play lacrosse for the United States national touring team. She taught physical education at Snug Harbor School. She was inducted into the Boston

University Hall of Fame in 1978 and the New Fund Women's Sports Hall of Fame. She also received a number of Sargent College alumni awards and induction into the National Federation of High Schools Hall of Fame. {AAGPBL Newsletter, May 2001, 38; Entry for the Boston University Hall of Fame; AAGPBL Questionnaire, National Baseball Hall of Fame; Gerard Tuoti, "No Girl Should Be Denied," *The Patriot Ledger*, 11 June 2004, 15.}

Prebble, Carrie

3B/RF, Chicago Storm

In 2002 Carrie Prebble played for the Chicago Storm. She went 0–5 at the plate in the Citrus Blast and then never showed up on the roster again that season. {Chicago Storm Web site.}

Precup, Peggy Sue "Killer"

2B 1998–2002, Chicago Storm

Peggy Sue Precup played second base for the Storm of the Great Lakes Women's Baseball League for five seasons. In 2000 she led her team in walks with 18 and stole 13 bases. At the 2002 Citrus Blast she went 1–8 at the plate although she was not in the line-up for her bat but rather for her defensive skills. She often came in as a late inning replacement. {<www.baseballglory.com>; Chicago Storm Web site.}

Presnell, Kelli

Mgr./P Baltimore Stars, Candita Banditas

Kelli Presnell pitched and managed the Baltimore Stars and pitched for the Banditas. In 2001 she received an MVP award from the National Women's Baseball Hall of Fame.

Price, Nancy

Umpire

In 1997, Nancy Price became the first woman to umpire in a Babe Ruth World Series. When she received the call for the series, Nancy had been umpiring for 21 years at all levels, from Little League to college. She also referees volleyball matches. Price's knowledge of the game started when she played softball, but a knee injury curtailed her playing. Nancy is an elementary school teacher in Huntsville, Alabama, when she is not umpiring. {Umpires—Women File, National Baseball Hall of Fame and Museum, Cooperstown, New York; "Female Umpires Game," *Albany Times Union*, 18 August 1997.}

Pryer (Mayer), Charlene Barbara "Shorty"

(b. 14 September 1921, Watsonville, California) CF/2B 1946–51, Muskegon Lassies, South Bend Blue Sox

Charlene Pryer attended Riverside Poly High for two years and then graduated from Alexander Hamilton High School. She also took classes at UCLA for two years. Batting only .202 in 1946 for the Lassies, Pryor also scored 64 runs on only 77 hits. Though that first year did not yield strong results, Pryer built a solid career for herself with the Lassies and the Blue Sox. She helped the Blue Sox win the league championship in 1951 when she led the league in stolen bases with 129. She scored 106 runs and made the all-star team. Pryer played in 704 games, hitting a respectable .255 with 510 stolen bases. Her best single season at bat came in 1951 when she hit .312. After leaving the league Pryer went to work for a local school district in a variety of roles including truant officer. She married Stuart Mayer in 1958 and raised two children. {AAGPBL Questionnaire, National Baseball Hall of Fame; AAGPBL Baseball Cards, 1995.}

Pryor, Charlotte

OF 1946, Muskegon Lassies

Psota, Kate

(b. 30 April 1986, Burlington, Ontario) SS/P/OF, Team Ontario

Kate Psota had the honor of being named the Junior Player of the Year in 2003 by Baseball Ontario. She played for and helped her Team Ontario Bantam Girls win the Western Canada tournament. Psota pitched the final game in which Ontario defeated British Columbia 2–1. She hit .524 for the tournament and was named her team's MVP. Psota also played for the Burlington Bulls during the summer of 2003 in the Central Ontario Girls Baseball League. Psota found her love for baseball at an early age when her grandmother gave her a glove and she played catch with her dad. By age six she was playing tee ball and has played at every level since then. In 2001 she played in the first Women's World Series and she received the Fair Play Award. During that series she pitched against Australia and then played shortstop in a loss to the United States. In addition to playing baseball Psota plays hockey for the Mississauga Chiefs and at Aldershot High School she plays volleyball and softball. {Alge Borusas, "Honour Catches Young Ball Player by Surprise," *Hamilton Spectator*, 23 November 2002, N07.}

Psota played second base and hit well for Team Canada in the 2004 Women's World Series. She hit the first home run for the series when Canada beat South Korea 27–0 to make it to the semifinals. In addition to her two-run homer Psota also hit three singles and a double in that same game. {"Canada Beat South Korea," *Agence France Presse*, 20 July 2004; Dan Carle, "Canuck Upset! Our Gals Down USA 2–1 at Women's Baseball," *Edmonton Sun*, 3 August 2004, SP1.}

Purser-Rose, Laura

(b. 1974, Sunrise, Florida) P 1997, Colorado Silver Bullets, 2004 USA National Team

Laura Purser-Rose played softball and soccer while attending the University of Oklahoma. She was voted an all-regional selection and helped her team win the Big 12 while there. In 1997 she pitched for the Colorado Silver Bullets and in 1998 played professional fast-pitch softball for the Durham Dragons and Tampa Bay Firestix. While with the Bullets, she pitched one of their longest outings in a 4–1 victory over a Roy Hobbs all-star team in Akron, Ohio. In 2004 she tried out and made the first USA National Team and pitched in the fourth women's World Series. She finished

Pitcher Laura Purser-Rose for Team USA (photographer John Lypian, courtesy Jim Glennie).

the series with a record of 1–1 and a 1.40 ERA with eight strikeouts in five innings. She also pitched eight innings over two games during the first Women's World Cup in 2004. She got one victory and only gave up one run. When she is not playing baseball Purser-Rose teaches and coaches. {"At Home on the Mound," *Plain Dealer*, 17 July 1997; USA Women's Baseball Web site.}

Queens of the Diamond

The Queens of the Diamond were a ladies' club from Chicago who played under the direction of Professor E.G. Johnson. In July of 1887 they competed against a local boys' team known as the Climaxes. The winner of the game depends on which scorer you believe. The news reporter claimed the women actually won and that the men cheated in reporting their victory by a score of 26–11. The best player on the women's team was the catcher Mamie Barth, who turned out to be a man in disguise. This was typical for many early women's teams, who often had two men on their roster, the pitcher and the catcher. Another member of the Queens was the pitcher, Mamie Ried, whose uniform for the day was described in great detail in the newspaper. The key focus was on the fact that her skirt was so short it did not reach her knees. While this might have appeared scandalous at the time the reporter did acknowledge this made it easier for Miss Reid and the others to run around the diamond. In the outfield were Aggie Willard, Lizzie Griscoe and Blanche Boyer. The infield had Ada Dahl at first, May Ryan at second, Lillie Russell at third and Daisy Ridton at short. It was also reported that approximately 5,000 fans showed up for the contest. {"The Girls and Boys Play Ball." *Chicago Tribune*, 5 July 1887, 1.}

Queensland Rams

Each year since 2000 the Rams have fielded a team at the Australian National Women's Championships. In 2004 they lost to Country Baseball, Western Australia, Victoria, Victoria Provincial, and New South Wales, but beat Southern Australia twice and Country Baseball once. The team was coached by David Badke with Bruce Adams helping with the pitchers. Rachel Hauwert led the team in pitching while Ann-Marie McLaughlin did all the catching.

Quigley, Narda "Pigpen"

LF/C, Virginia Flames, Philadelphia Women's League

While growing up, Narda Quigley played Little League until she was 13. She tried out for her high school baseball team and was told she could play but that she would never be able to play baseball in college because there were no women's teams. At that point Quigley switched to softball.

She got her chance to return to baseball by playing for the Virginia Flames while attending graduate school at the University of Maryland. Quigley helped found the Philadelphia Women's Baseball League in 2004 after she moved to the Philadelphia area and decided not to drive to Washington every weekend for games. Quigley teaches at Villanova University when she is not out on the diamond. {Doug Lesmerises, "Men vs. Women on the Diamond," *The News Journal*, 25 June 2004, and "Women Trading Softball for Baseball in New League," *The News Journal*, 29 June 2004; Don McKee, "She's Creating a Place to Play Hardball," *Philadelphia Inquirer*, 9 March 2004; Eileen O'Donnell, "Covering All the Bases," *Philadelphia Inquirer*, 15 July 2005.}

Racine Belles

By Grant Provance

The All-American Girls Professional Baseball League (AAGPBL) played its first season in 1943. The league consisted of four franchises: the Rockford Peaches, the South Bend Blue Sox, the Kenosha Comets and the Racine Belles. The Racine Belles were a mainstay of the AAGPBL from 1943 to 1950.

Located on the shores of Lake Superior near the southeastern tip of Wisconsin, Racine was an ideal spot to land an AAGPBL franchise. It fit the league founder's ideal: a medium sized city that had become an industrial center, producing products to contribute to the war effort. Over time the community would develop a special bond with their Belles. There are several factors that contributed to this relationship, which existed for the majority of the Belles' time in Racine. One of the most important reasons for the development of fan interest in Racine was the effort of the town's print media. The town's biggest newspaper, *The Racine Journal Times,* covered the team from its genesis, interviewing most of the players before the 1943 season began. The paper covered each game, dispatching reporters to cover the team on the road. The thorough coverage of the team by the *Times* exposed the general public to the sport, creating interest in the community. The print media was not the only means of support the Belles received from outside the organization, as the Racine business sector played a key role in supporting the team.

{Diana Star Helmer, *Belles of the Ballpark* (Brookfield, Conn.: Millbrook Press, 1993), 31.}

The business community not only provided the Belles organization with advertising revenue but also promoted the team to its workers by "closing during Belles games so that owners and customers could root for the girls." Some companies like Western Publishing, which was owned by Belles team president Bill Wadewitz, provided players with employment during the off-season. And as author Diana Star Helmer points out, "If there was no work at Western Publishing, fans all over town asked their bosses to hire a Belle." The business community of Racine helped promote the team and support its players, but the team's success on the field was what ultimately caught the fan's attention. {Helmer, 31 and 34.}

Led by manager Johnny Gottselig the 1943 Belles started strong, winning the first half of the inaugural season. Although they would not win the second-half crown, they matched up against the Kenosha Comets in the league's first championship series. The 108-game schedule had all come down to a five-game series, and the result was a three-game sweep. The Belles had easily prevailed and for their efforts were rewarded by receiving 60 percent of the gate receipts to the series. In addition they received a flag and a plaque to be displayed at city hall. There was also a $1,000 scholarship awarded to a female student to attend the University of Wisconsin in the name of encouraging women's health and recreation, credited to the Belles. There is no promotion that is better for a sports franchise than winning. The Belles championship certainly helped solidify the team's standing with the fans of Racine. {Margaret Fortunato Galt, *Up to the Plate* (Minneapolis: Lerner Publications Company, 1995), 30.}

While the team contended in the 1944 season, it was hard hit by injuries the following year. The 1945 Belles struggled early in the year, but rallied in the second half of the season to finish 40–50. They managed to make the playoffs in the fourth spot and were defeated three games to one in the opening round of the playoffs by the Fort Wayne Daisies. That same year, one-time Belles team president Don Black provided the Belles, along with the entire AAGPBL, additional exposure to potential fans by including the league in the 1945 publication *Major League Baseball: Facts and Figures.* The publication is a yearbook that chronicled statistical data for major league baseball teams.

The Racine Journal Times continued to dedicate a great deal of energy to covering the Belles. Then in 1946 another media outlet aided in publicizing the team to a broader fan base. That season, Racine's WRJN radio station began broadcasting play-by-plays of all Belles home games, along with select road games. Now both major media outlets in town were providing the team with excellent coverage, and the turnstiles reflected the team's growing popularity. By 1946 the team's attendance had mushroomed to an impressive 102,413. The league's total attendance that year was 754,000 in eight cities. The Belles were thriving as an organization, while on the field the team was again healthy and poised to win its second league championship. {Galt, 49; Helmer 75.}

The Belles returned to championship form in 1946, manager Leo Murphy guiding the team to the pennant and into the playoffs as the top seed. The Belles won their first series and advanced to play the Rockford Peaches for the championship. On 16 September 1946, the Belles and Peaches engaged in a decisive game six (Racine held a 3–2 advantage) at their home Horlick Athletic Field. That day, 5,630 fans witnessed a thriller. The Belles prevailed 1–0 as league MVP Sophie Kurys singled to lead off the bottom of the fourteenth inning, then promptly stole second, her fifth stolen base of the game. The next batter, Moe Trezza, singled into right field, scoring Kurys from second. The Belles had captured the Shaughnessy series, their second league title in four years. It would however, be the last time the team would win the championship. {Sue Macy, *A Whole New Ball Game* (New York: Henry Holt and Company), 1993, 42–45.}

The 1947 AAGPBL season saw the Belles tied for second place in the regular season standings. Racine's 65–47 record, which was identical to the Grand Rapids Chicks, ranked only behind the Muskegon Lassies, who finished with a mark of 69–43. In the first round of the Shaughnessy Playoff Series, the Belles drew the pennant-winning Lassies. The series got off to a positive start as Belles all-star pitcher Anna May Hutchison hurled a complete-game two-hit shutout in the Belles' 4–0 game-one victory. They would go on to win three of the next four, clinching a spot in the championship series against the Grand Rapids Chicks. When game one of the best-of-seven series got underway in Grand Rapids, once again the Belles relied on the right arm of ace Anna May Hutchison to gain the early advantage. She responded by tossing another gem, an 11-inning four-hitter that resulted in a 2–0 Belles victory. The Belles lost the next two games by a total of only two runs, but returned home to take two of the next three to force a decisive game seven. The Belles again turned to Hutchison to take the mound. She responded by throwing six shutout innings. Then in the seventh, the Chicks man-

aged to score what would be the game's only run. The Racine Belles had not capitalized on their opportunity to win consecutive titles; however, there were larger issues facing the team in 1948.

The Belles remained competitive on the field in 1948. The team won the pennant, posting the league's best regular season record, but again failed to win the Shaughnessy series. Despite the team's success, things off the field were not going as well. The problem facing the franchise was a matter of finance: the number of fans attending Belles games was on the decline. By the end of the 1948 season attendance had fallen off to 79,994, down 22,419 from the 1946 season. The trend continued in 1949 as the team sold only 44,912 tickets. The final straw came the following season. Attendance at Horlick field reached its lowest point in 1950 as the Belles drew only 29,000 fans to the park. The Belles front office and league officials decided to move the team to Battle Creek, Michigan, and the AAGPBL era was over in Racine. {Helmer, 76.}

The city of Racine, which once strongly supported the Belles, had seemingly lost interest. The league's operational status, that "clubs owned and operated by local and industrial leaders [are] on a non-profit community basis," meant that the city of Racine was losing money. Pundits speculate that the fall of the league was due to a number of factors, including a return to normalcy following the war, the spread of television, advances in the travel industry (including personal travel) and the rise of the nuclear family. Whatever the reason, the fact was that the team's popularity dissipated just as rapidly by 1950 as it had grown prior to 1946. {H. G. Salsinger, *Major League Baseball 1946, Facts, Figures and Official Rules*, Whitman Publishing Co., 1947, 154–55.}

From 1943 to 1950 the Racine Belles were one of the elite ball clubs in the AAGPBL. The Belles won two league championships and were in contention nearly every year of their existence. A measure of the credit for their success should be given to the team's managers. Johnny Gottselig, skipper of the Belles' 1943 title team, had the distinction of being the only one of the league's original four coaches who did not have experience playing at the major league level. He was also the only one of the four to last more than two seasons. A native of Canada, Gottselig's background was in hockey, which he played professionally. He was adept at dealing with the female players because he gained experience coaching women's softball in Canada during the hockey off-season. {Lois Browne, *The Girls of Summer* (New York and Toronto: Harper Collins, 1992), 28; Galt, 28.}

The other notable Belles manager was major

league baseball veteran Leo Murphy. He played 25 years in the big leagues with the Pittsburgh Pirates and the Cincinnati Reds. Prior to taking over as manager in the middle of the 1945 season, Murphy served on the Belles strategy board and had a vested interest in the team from the beginning. He led the team to its second title in 1946, and his Belles teams were contenders every year. To illustrate his value, when he took over the team in 1945 they were in last place; under his leadership, they made a run to the playoffs. In 1950 his successor, Norman "Nummy" Derringer, started the season 2–5 and the Belles never recovered. While he was certainly a capable manager, what set "Murph" apart from his contemporaries was his vision of how to build a team: "Murphy and the Racine directors had taken the long view, building a solid roster and resisting the temptation of seemingly advantageous quick-fix trades." An examination of the players who contributed to the team's success reflects Murphy's blueprint, as most of the Belles players who were standouts played their entire career with the Belles. {Galt, 43, 73; Browne, 162.}

Perhaps the best player in the history of the Belles franchise was Flint, Michigan, native Sophie Kurys. Born on 14 May 1925, the "Flint Flash" recorded some of the most remarkable numbers in the annals of baseball. The right-handed second baseman was a mainstay of the Belles during their time in Racine. Kurys is the AAGPBL's all-time leader in stolen bases with 1,114; she also holds the league's record for runs scored, with 688. Her ability to steal any base at any time made her one of the most formidable offensive threats in AAGPBL history, but stealing bases was not her only skill. {W. C. Madden, *The Women of the All-American Girls Professional Baseball League.* Jefferson, N.C.: McFarland and Company, Inc., Publishers, 1997), 140.}

During the inaugural season of play in the AAGPBL, Kurys proved to be a valuable part of the Belles' 1943 championship team. In her rookie year she played a solid defensive second base, and contributed offensively with a .271 batting average and 44 stolen bases. The 1944 campaign was Kurys' breakout year as a master thief on the base paths. She led the league in steals with 166 and in runs scored with 87. In 1945, Sophie led the league in steals with 115 and played excellent defense. She posted the league's highest fielding percentage at second base (.968) with 284 putouts and 168 assists. In addition to that, Kurys finished eighth in the league with a solid .239 batting average with one home run and 73 runs scored. {Salsinger, 141.}

During the 1946 season Kurys solidified her position as one of the best all-around players in the women's game. She not only led the league in steals with 201, but also in walks (93) and runs scored (117), posting career highs with 122 hits and a .286 batting average. Her fielding was once again stellar, with 295 putouts, 239 assists and only 15 errors, translating to a lofty .973 fielding percentage. Voted to the league's first all-star team and named as the AAGPBL's most outstanding player, Kurys was the catalyst for the Belles' second title. The following season the Flint Flash was named to her second all-star team. She posted good numbers in 1947 with a .239 batting average and two home runs, while leading the league with 81 runs scored and 142 stolen bases. Her defensive performance was again solid with 322 putouts, 215 assists and a fielding average of .968. Kurys continued her excellent play in 1948 and 1949. Once again leading the league in steals and runs scored, she was named to the all-star team both years. In the Belles' final season in Racine, Kurys had one of her best years. In addition to being the league's most prolific base stealer and run scorer, she also paced the AAGPBL in hits with 130 and home runs with seven. Her play in 1950 landed her yet another spot on the league's all-star team. {Galt, 53; Salsinger, 143, 148.}

When the league decided to relocate the Belles to Battle Creek, Michigan, it was the end of the Sophie Kurys era. She played only 15 games for the Battle Creek Belles before suffering a career-ending injury. A career .260 hitter, Kurys' lifetime stats include 859 hits, 22 home runs and 278 RBIs in 914 games. Her productivity, durability and consistency made Sophie Kurys one of the best players in the history of the AAGPBL. She was, however, not the only standout to don the Belles uniform.

Edythe Perlick played her entire career (1943–1950) as a left fielder of the Racine Belles. A native of Chicago, Perlick was born on 12 December 1922 and was one of the first four players to be signed to play in the AAGBPL. It did not take long for "Edie," as she was called, to make an impact on the league. In her rookie season, the right-handed slugger hit a lofty .268, leading the Belles to win the inaugural AAGPBL title. She was named to the league's first all-star team following the 1943 season. The following season, she continued to be a steady contributor for Racine. During the 1944 season Perlick posted a .229 batting average, which ranked her twenty-first in the league. In addition, she led the AAGPBL in RBIs with 61. {Jim Sargent, "Edie Perlick," <http://www.aagpbl.org/articles/arti_cd.html>, 10 February 2004.}

The 1945 season was yet another productive year for Perlick. She finished the season nineteenth in the league with a .213 batting average. She also swatted two home runs and paced the team with 41 RBIs. Perlick also established herself as a threat on the base paths, finishing sixth in the AAGPBL in steals, with 44. The following season she was a crucial member of the Belles' second championship team, finishing twenty-second in the league; batting .230 with four home runs and an impressive 88 stolen bases. In 1947 Perlick was named to her second all-star team. That year she led the league in at-bats with 436, and was again in the top 20 in the league with a .239 batting average. She swatted two home runs, finished second in the league in stolen bases with 83 and was among the top ten defensive outfielders, posting a .980 fielding percentage. {Salsinger, 141, 143, 146, 148–49.}

The final three seasons of Perlick's career were as consistent as the previous five. She was named to her third all-star team following the 1948 season, a year in which she hit .243 with 51 RBIs. In 1949 she finished seventh in the league with a .255 batting average and 41 runs batted in. Her final season she finished twenty-ninth in the AAGBPL with a .247 average with 59 RBIs. Perlick's career numbers place her in the upper echelon of AAGPBL players. She played in 851 games for the Belles, in which she hit .240 with 18 home runs, 392 RBIs, and 392 stolen bases, with a respectable .950 fielding average. {Salsinger, 4.}

Roaming the outfield with Perlick was five-foot six-inch Eleanor "Slugger" Dapkus, a right-hander. Born 5 December 1923 in Chicago, Illinois, Dapkus was a perennial league leader in several offensive categories. Like Kurys and Perlick she played her entire career, from 1943 to 1950, with the Belles. In 1943 she was named to the league's all-star team after leading the AAGPBL in home runs with ten. In 1944, she followed up her productive rookie campaign by leading the league in doubles, triples and extra-base hits. She posted excellent numbers in 1945, finishing in the top 20 in the league with a .229 batting average, and sixth in RBIs with 37. The 1947 season would be Dapkus' last as a full time outfielder. She again had a very good year, hitting .216 with two home runs and 41 RBIs. {Salsinger, 147.}

Rule changes passed down from the league's front office in 1948 altered the way pitchers were allowed to deliver the ball. The switch to overhand pitching prompted the Belles to let "Slugger" take the hill, and their decision paid off. In her first season on the mound Dapkus went 24–9, leading the league in starts with 39. In three seasons on the hill, Dapkus posted a record of 53–34, with 397 strikeouts and a paltry 1.97 earned run average.

Right-handed third baseman Madeline "Maddy" English was another career-long member of the Belles (1943–1950). Born 22 February 1925, the five-foot four-inch native of Everett, Massachusetts, was not the offensive weapon that Kurys and Perlick were, but she was a key contributor to the franchise's success. The 1943 season was not English's best. Despite the Belles' success, she committed an AAGBPL record 78 errors in her rookie season. English overcame the difficulties of her rookie season.

By the time her career ended following the 1950 season, English was named to three AAGBPL all-star teams. A career .171 hitter, she had her most productive season during the 1946 championship season, when she hit .214. In 1947 English continued the tradition of Belles base stealers as she tied the AAGBPL record for stolen bases in a single game with seven. Overall she totaled 397 steals in her career. In 832 games with the Belles from 1943–1950, English amassed 356 walks and 333 runs scored in almost 2,900 at-bats. She also became one of the best defensive third basemen in the league, finishing her career with a .896 fielding percentage.

The mainstay behind the plate for the Belles from 1943 to 1950 was five-foot two-inch spark-plug Irene "Mae" Hickson. One of the league's oldest players, Hickson was born on 14 August 1915 in Chattanooga, Tennessee. In her rookie year she was an important member of the Belles' championship team. Following a very good regular season, which earned her a spot on the league's first all-star team, she saved her best play for the AAGBPL championship series. In the three games against the Comets, "Choo-Choo" torched the Kenosha pitching staff, with a .417 batting average in the Belles' sweep of the Comets. Offensively she was productive by league standards, posting a career .171 batting average in 1,876 career at-bats. During the 1946 season Hickson set an AAGBPL record by drawing five walks in a single game. She had 316 bases on balls for her career.

Hickson was an excellent defensive catcher. In 621 games she had 2,388 putouts and 561 assists, with only 130 errors. The 1947 season was her best year behind the plate, as she finished second among all catchers in the league, with a .976 fielding percentage. That is the third-highest single-season fielding percentage at the catcher position in AAGBPL history. She holds one other league record; unfortunately it is for the most passed balls, with 23. What does not show up in her career statistics, however, was her ability to handle the talented Belles pitching staff. {Salsinger, 141.}

Anna May Hutchison, a native of Louisville, Kentucky, joined the league in the 1944 season. "Hutch" spent her first two seasons in the league behind the plate, serving as the backup to Irene

Hickson. She played sparingly: in 1945, she appeared in only 20 games. Then in 1946 when the league altered its pitching rules to allow sidearm deliveries, the Belles moved the right-handed Hutchison to the hill. She responded by going 26–14 and setting a league record for pitching appearances with 51, leading the Belles to their second championship.

The following year she had another tremendous season. Hutch again showed her durability by appearing in 40 games and pitching 360 innings, the highest total in the league. With a record of 27–13, she paced the AAGPBL in wins, and had an ERA of 1.38. Hutchison was named to the all-star team and was establishing herself as one of the best pitchers in the league. When the league again altered its pitching rules in 1948, allowing pitchers to deliver the ball overhand, Hutchison had trouble adjusting. For the first time in her pitching career she lost more games than she won. The downward spiral continued in 1949 as she again posted a sub-500 record. The following season she was moved to Muskegon, where she played only one season before retiring to Racine.

Hutchison's career as a Belle (1944–1948) was up and down, but for two seasons she was one of the most dominant pitchers in the league. Her career numbers include a record of 64–45 in 134 games, 257 strikeouts, and an ERA of 1.82 in 885 innings pitched. {Salsinger, 147.}

From 1943 to 1950, Joanne Winter was an essential member of the Belles pitching staff. Born 24 November 1924 in Chicago, Illinois, Winter was a two-time all-star whose career numbers rank at or near the top of several statistical categories. In her first three seasons, however, the right-hander amassed a less than impressive 33–56 mark. After struggling with the league's underhand delivery, she began to flourish when the pitching rules were altered in 1946. She had a remarkable season and was named to the all-star team. At one point during the season she hurled six consecutive shutouts, stringing together 63 consecutive scoreless innings. Winter earned a share of the AAGPBL record for most wins in a season in 1946, going 33–10. In 1947 she appeared in 38 games, pitching 297 innings, the second highest total in the league. In addition to her durability, "Jo" went 22–13, with 121 strikeouts and a .206 ERA. In 1948 Winter was named to her second all-star team, leading the league in innings pitched (329), strikeouts (248) and wins (25). {Gregorich, *Women at Play*, 131.}

When the league instituted the overhand pitching style in 1949, Winter, just like her teammate Hutchison, could not adjust to the new rules.

Troubled by a back injury in her final two seasons in the league, she produced a sub-500 record, and then retired following the 1950 campaign. Winter is third all-time in AAGPBL history in wins with 133, second in losses with 115, and second in games pitched with 287 and innings pitched with 2,159. She had a lifetime ERA of 2.06, in addition to recording 770 strikeouts.

Blessed with talented players, solid coaches and what at one time was an enthusiastic fan base, the Belles were one of the most successful clubs in the AAGPBL. The Belles' legacy includes three pennants, two league championships, and an impressive list of individual statistical records. The Belles were a product of the times—a team in a league that was developed to fill a void during World War II. Unfortunately, the team became a victim of the times, as the postwar economy of Racine was unable to support the team for the duration of the league's existence.

Radaker, Melissa

P 1997, Colorado Silver Bullets, New Jersey Diamonds

Melissa Radaker joined the Silver Bullets in

Melissa Radaker pitching in 1998 for the New Jersey Diamonds of the Ladies Pro League (courtesy Laura Wulf).

what turned out to be their final season, in 1997. She then went on to pitch for the New Jersey Diamonds in the Ladies Professional League. {Paul Newberry, "Out of Action," *Rocky Mountain News,* 19 July 1998.}

Rado, Jen

Pawtuckett Slaterettes

Jen Rado began playing baseball with the Slaterettes when she was nine years old. In October 2003 she went with three other Providence area ball players to Arizona to take part in the 24-hour benefit game to raise money for AIDS. {Manny Correira, "Area Players Recall 'Big Game,'" *The Providence Journal,* 5 February 2004, C-01.}

Raduenz, Patricia "Patti"

(b. 22 March 1974, Burlington, Wisconsin) SS/3B, 2004 USA National Team

Patricia Raduenz attended Michigan State University on a softball scholarship from 1993 to 1996. She hit .372 for her career, which is the best in the school's history, and was named an All-American and an Academic All-American. She also won the Big Ten Medal of Honor. She played professional women's softball for the Durham Dragons from 1997 to 1999 and for the Ohio Pride in 2000. She has been the head softball coach for the Phoenix at Elon University since 2001. Her first year as head coach saw the Phoenix finish with a 16–41 record, six more wins than in 2000. Before taking on the reins as a head coach, Raduenz served as an assistant coach at the University of North Carolina in 2000, Iowa State University, and California State University at Sacramento. {Michigan State University Web site; Press Release, Elon University, 7 June 2004.}

In 2004 she tried out for and made the 18-member USA National Team in baseball. During the series she hit .250 and drove in three runs to help her team win the silver against Japan. She had the first triple for the National Team in a 5–1 win over Australia. She also played in the first women's World Cup and hit .273 with three runs knocked in. {USA Baseball Web site and 2004 Media Guide; Kelly Wells, "Burlington Native Swinging Away for National Baseball Team," *Milwaukee Journal Sentinel,* 18 July 2004, 03Z.}

Ramsey, Barbara

Util., Arizona Cactus Wrens

Barbara Ramsey made the Wrens roster because she could play so many different positions for the club.

Raniszewski, Kris

P/IF 1997–2004, Lansing Stars, Michigan Stars, Detroit Renegades, Detroit Danger, Motown Magic

Kris Raniszewski joined the Lansing Stars in the 1990s, filling in where needed in the infield. Her versatility made her a valuable asset. She moved on to the Detroit Renegades in 1999 and then started pitching for the Danger in 2000. She not only has a strong arm and good defensive skills but can also help her team with the bat. Since she is such a strong hitter she often plays in the infield when she is not pitching. When she is not pitching for the Magic, Raniszewski works for Hertz Car Rental. She started playing softball when she was only 11 and switched to baseball in 1997. {Kristin Karpscuk, "Motown Magic Calling On a Few Good Women," *Daily Oakland Press,* 14 April 2004.}

Rapolz, Diana

P 1988, Daredevils

In the inaugural game for the AWBA, Diana Rapolz helped her team beat the Gators 11–6. Rapolz also helped at the plate by walking and scoring her first time at bat. The Gators scored their first run on a throwing error by Rapolz in the third inning. She struck out four in three innings before yielding the ball to Linda Poe. {Bob Gordon, "Daredevils Win Women's Opener, 11–6," *Daily Herald,* 17 July 1988.}

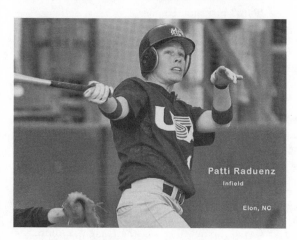

Patti Raduenz
Infield

Elon, NC

Patti Raduenz playing for Team USA (photographer John Lypian, courtesy Jim Glennie).

Rathbone, Norine

Norine Rathbone plays baseball as a member of the Men's Senior Baseball League in Las Vegas. She was the only woman in the league in 2001. In addition to playing first base, Rathbone coached her club. {"Game of Her Life," *Las Vegas Review Journal*, 5 August 2001.}

Rauner, Helen

(b. 2 August 1921, Fort Wayne, Indiana) Chaperone 1945–46, Fort Wayne Daisies

Helen Rauner chaperoned her hometown Daisies in 1945 and 1946. She gave up the job in 1946 after she got married so she could stay home and take care of her nine children and 11 grandchildren. {AAGPBL Baseball Cards, 1996.}

Rawlings, John

(17 August 1892, Bloomfield, Iowa) Mgr. 1947–48, Grand Rapids Chicks

John Rawlings came to the All American League with a world of experience, having played in the majors. Rawlings played from 1914 to 1926 for New York and Pittsburgh. He played second base on the Giants teams in the 1921 and 1922 World Series and for Pittsburgh when they won the World Series in 1925. He was a teammate on the Giants with Dave Bancroft, who also managed in the AAGPBL. Rawlings managed the Chicks to a league championship in 1948 and into the playoffs in 1947. Rawlings also scouted for the league during the winter season. {AAGPBL Baseball Cards, 2000.}

Redman, Magdalen Marie "Mame," "Minnie"

(b. 2 July 1930, Wisconsin) C 1948–54, Kenosha Comets, Grand Rapids Chicks, 1956 Allington All-Stars

Mame Redman became known as one of the best catchers in the league. She seemed to develop a knack for calling the right pitches. She was the regular catcher for Connie Wisniewski. She started in 1948 with the Comets because the team played closer to her home and she was still in high school at the time. The league traded her to the Chicks in 1950. She helped the Chicks win the league championship in 1953. She played in 369 games and hit only .172, but she did knock in 63 runs and score another 90.

After the league folded she played for the Allington All-Stars. She attended the University of Wisconsin at Oshkosh as a mathematics major with minors in biology and physical education. She won a variety of academic honors while there. After the league folded Redman played slow-pitch softball and started golfing. She even tried out for and made the roster for a man's baseball club in the Land-o-Lakes League but never got to play, because three players threatened to quit if a woman played with them. She taught math and coached girls' high school golf and fast-pitch softball. She also served as the assistant coach for the boy's baseball teams in Oconomowoc and Mukwonago, Wisconsin. {AAGPBL Questionnaire, National Baseball Hall of Fame; AAGPBL Newsletter, January 2002, 15.}

Reed, Grace

(Maine) 2B

Grace Reed played second base on a Little League team in Portland, Maine, when she was 12 years old, with the encouragement of her father Norman Reed. The national headquarters threatened to revoke the charter after learning she played on the club, but a local judge issued a temporary restraining order to allow her to play. She was later included in the suit brought against the Little League organization to allow girls to play. Later, Reed went to work for the Children's Defense Fund. {Cathleen Crowley, "Her Pitch Could Alter Male-Only Ballgames," *Eagle-Tribune*, 26 March 2000; "Most Comments Favor LL Ruling," *Newport Daily News*, 13 June 1974.}

Reeser, Sara Louise

1946, Muskegon Lassies

In 110 games in 1946 Sara Reeser batted only .207 but scored 53 runs for the Lassies.

Rehrer (Carteaux), Rita J. "Spud"

(b. 30 June 1927, Akron, Ohio) C 1946, Racine Belles, Peoria Red Wings

Though born in Ohio, Rita Rehrer grew up in Indiana. She attended St. Vincent Villa and Central Catholic High School in Fort Wayne, Indiana. She played softball in the local CYO league before trying out for the All American League in 1946. Rita married Francis Carteaux Jr. in 1947, which is why she only played for one year. She stayed home to raise their eight children. {AAGPBL Questionnaire, National Baseball Hall of Fame.}

Reid, Dorice "Dorrie"

(b. 26 February 1929, Superior, Wisconsin) OF 1948–51, Chicago Colleens, Grand Rapids Chicks

Dorice Reid played for four seasons in the All American League, spending all but one year with the Chicks. She started with the traveling Colleens and then after gaining a bit of experience got a chance to join the Grand Rapids Squad. She hit only .166 in 323 games but did score 108 runs and had a reputation as being the hitter you wanted up in a clutch situation. {AAGPBL Baseball Cards, 1995.}

Reidy (Comiskey), Grace

(b. 15 May 1893, Chicago, Illinois; d. 11 December 1956, Chicago, Illinois)

By Joan M. Thomas

Born in Chicago to Thomas and Elizabeth Reidy on 15 May 1893, Grace Reidy was raised on the city's west side with the couple's two other daughters. Biographical sketches make no reference to her formal education. She married J. Louis (Lou) Comiskey in 1913. Lou was the son of the famous "Old Roman," Charles Comiskey, founder of the American League White Sox. When his father died in 1931, Lou took over as president of the organization. Lou worked for the club in various capacities for a long time prior to that. Grace's obituary in *The Sporting News* on 19 December 1956 reported that Lou and Grace "spent their honeymoon taking a round-the-world barnstorming trip with the White Sox and Giants."

News reports of the times indicate that Grace did not take an active role in her husband's baseball concern until after his death in 1939. But she then fought valiantly to retain ownership. The White Sox were losing money at the time, and a bank that was the trustee of Lou's estate attempted to sell the Comiskeys' stock in the ball club to make up for lost earnings. Grace finally won out, and was named club president in 1941. She remained in that position for the rest of her life. She was the first woman to head an American League baseball club.

The tenacity that Grace employed in overcoming the bank's attempts prevailed throughout her years as owner of the White Sox. She was known as being somewhat tyrannical, as even her biography in the *White Sox Encyclopedia* states that she "was a tough, uncompromising dowager who ruled the ball club — and her family — with a velvet fist." {Lindberg and Fletcher, *The White Sox Encyclopedia* (Philadelphia: Temple University Press, 1997), 313.} Though her son, Charles, was given an executive position with the Sox, he was not given preferential treatment. At one point, he even resigned when she reneged on her promise to give him a raise. She allowed him to return to his job soon thereafter. Grace's daughter Dorothy, who had worked as her father's secretary, was married to White Sox pitcher John Rigney. After Grace became club president, Dorothy "served her mother as vice president and treasurer" {Lindberg and Fletcher 1997, 316} and eventually became the team secretary.

During her tenure as head of the White Sox, Grace came to be known as the "first lady of baseball." She faced the type of criticism that almost anyone in her position, regardless of gender, could expect. She was frugal when it came to the ball club, and was said to have a drinking problem. But she earned the respect of ball fans and the media. After her death, Warren Brown of the *Chicago Herald-American* wrote in a story reprinted in the *Sporting News,* 19 December 1956, that as an organizational head, she was "more in character with the founder of the Comiskey dynasty ... than his son." {Warren Brown, "Mrs. Grace Comiskey Endured...," *The Sporting News*, 19 December 1956, 22.} She must have had a good appreciation for the game of baseball, as several reports mention that she was also something of a Cubs fan.

Six years after suffering a heart attack, Grace died in her apartment on Lake Shore Drive in Chicago on 11 December 1956. A lengthy court battle over the will — Dorothy had the controlling shares in the club — eventually ended the Comiskey White Sox reign. Whether or not Grace purposely caused the legal entanglement that followed her death is a matter of pure speculation. Regardless, she was remembered fondly by most baseball people. Frank Lane, who was general manager of the White Sox from 1949 to 1953, was quoted thus: "If it hadn't been for Mrs. Grace Comiskey, I never would have been able to build the White Sox into a first-division club.... She always backed me 100 percent." {Brown, 22.} But some writers must have assumed that her position in the all-male world of major league baseball was an anomaly, not likely to be repeated. Warren Brown wrote, "Mrs. Grace Comiskey, major league baseball's First — and perhaps last — Lady, is no more." Yet, the very next decade brought another "first lady" onto the scene.

Reyna, Yazmin

2B, Virginia Flames

Yazmin Reyna played for the Flames for a short time.

Reynolds, Mary "Windy"

(b. 27 April 1921, Gastonia, North Carolina; d. 9 May 1991) OF/3B/P 1946–50, Peoria Red Wings

Mary Reynolds played for five seasons with Peoria after earning a spot on their roster in 1946. In 1947 Mary played in 113 games for the Red Wings and hit a respectable .245 with 42 runs batted in and was named to the all-star squad. By 1950 her playing days were numbered, and she spent part of her last season as a chaperone. Her career numbers included an average of .223 and a win-loss record of 30–38. {AAGPBL Baseball Cards, 1996.}

Reynoso, Miali

SS/P, San Jose Spitfires

Miali Reynoso played for the Spitfires in the California Women's League.

Rhode Island Women's Baseball League

This league began in 2004 with Deb Bettencourt as the general manager. Sarah Feeley served as the director of operations and Julie Cardin as the director of transportation. All three of these ladies have had long associations with the Pawtucket Slaterettes.

Richard, Ruth "Richie"

(b. 20 September 1928, Argus, Pennsylvania) C/RF/P 1947–54, Grand Rapids Chicks, Rockford Peaches

Ruth Richard grew up in the Ridge Valley Creek area and played softball for Sellersville-Perkasie High School. She graduated in 1946 and became a member of the Grand Rapids club in 1947. She played in 47 games in the outfield before being traded to the Peaches for the 1948 season. The Peaches turned her into their starting catcher, and she went on to have a solid career. As a catcher for the Peaches, Richard made the all-star team for six consecutive years. In 1949 enough players for two teams traveled to Central America and played one another in a series of exhibition games. This was Richard's first trip outside the country, as it was for most of the girls. Richard missed the 1950 playoffs when she broke her leg on a slide into second base at the end of the season. The fans took up a collection for her and raised just over $600.

After the AAGPBL folded in 1954, Richard joined the Allington All-Stars and barnstormed with the club through 1957. They drove across country in two cars and played local men's clubs whenever they could. They earned about $5 a game, depending on the attendance. To stay active Ruth took up golf and has continued playing to the present day. Her career stats include a .247 average with 287 RBIs and a .961 fielding percentage. She worked for 26 years at the Ametek U.S. Gauge plant making aircraft gauges. The Pennridge-Quakertown, Pennsylvania, Hall of Fame inducted Richard in 1995. {Steve Wartenberg, "Girls Professional Baseball Star Still Shines Bright," *Times Leader*, 1 January 2004; AAGPBL Questionnaire, National Baseball Hall of Fame.}

Richardson (Jessup), Marie "Rougie"

(b. Rumsford, Maine) C 1953, Fort Wayne Daisies

Marie Richardson heard about the AAGPBL in early 1953 when her brother saw an ad in the local paper. She attended tryouts for that season in Battle Creek, Michigan. She had been a catcher for the school softball team while attending Stephens High School in Rumsford. She took a Greyhound bus from Maine to Battle Creek, Michigan, for the three-day tryout and was assigned to Fort Wayne. Hearing rumors that the league would fold in 1954, Jessup took a job playing semipro softball in Arizona. Her athletic career was cut short when she broke her ankle on a slide into second base. She went to work for Reynolds Aluminum and married an air force man. {Patrick Harrington, "At Home Behind the Plate," *The Oregonian*, 19 February 2004, 01; Laura Snyder, "In a League of Her Own," *Maine Sun-Journal*, 26 September 1993, 1A, 7A.}

Richardson, Jo Ann

CF/LF 2002, Baltimore Blues, DC Thunder

JoAnn Richardson played in the EWBC for the Baltimore Blues in 2002 and hit .560 during the season. She also played for the DC Thunder in tournaments, and batted .400 for the team at a series in Maryland.

Richarz, Shannon

Team Ontario

Shannon Richarz has played baseball with boys since she was little. Finally, at age 13, she had the opportunity to join an all-girls team with the new Peewee league created in 2004. Her father Harry is the team's head coach. {Allen Pulga, "Talented Elite Girls' Baseball Team a Shock to the Boys," *Hamilton Spectator*, 14 August 2004, SP08.}

Ricketts, Joyce "Rick"

(b. 25 April 1933, Oquawka, Illinois) OF 1953–54, Grand Rapids Chicks

Joyce Ricketts started in the All American League when she was only 16 and barely got a chance to play before the league folded after the 1954 season. She played in 207 games and made the all-star team in both seasons she played. She hit .317 in her sophomore season, with 15 home runs. Her career average was .300 with 20 home runs and 143 RBIs. She was always a threat in the middle of the lineup. {AAGPBL Baseball Cards, 2000.}

Rider, Patti Jo

At age 11 Patti Jo Rider played second base in the Bristol Township American Little League along with three other girls. She became the starting second baseman for the AKC Moving Supplies team. {John Heagney, "Patti Jo's a Sluggin' Second 'Baseperson,'" *Bucks County Courier Times*, June 1974.}

Ries (Zillmer), Ruth "Boots"

(b. 20 March 1933, Walworth, Wisconsin) P, Rockford Peaches

Ruth Ries started playing baseball with her brothers when she was only six years old. She and her five sisters all liked to play after working on the farm all day. She pitched during one season for Rockford. There are no statistics available on what she did beyond three games that were recorded. She picked up the loss in one of them. {AAGPBL Baseball Cards, 1995.}

Riopelle, Christy

OF, South Bend Blue Sox, Detroit Danger

Christy Riopelle played fast-pitch softball in college before turning to baseball as her sport. She is best known for her hitting but also is a versatile fielder who can play anywhere on the field. {www.baseballglory.com.}

Rios, Georgiana

Util. 1948, Fort Wayne Daisies, Springfield Sallies

Georgiana Rios came to the United States with a group of women from Cuba who wanted to play baseball in the All American League.

Risinger, Helen Earlene "Beans"

(b. 20 March 1927, Hess, Oklahoma) P 1948–54, Springfield Sallies, Grand Rapids Chicks

Earlene Risinger grew up in Hess, Oklahoma, a town with a population of 27. Her family were sharecroppers and found their relaxation in playing baseball with the other local towns. She found herself being taught the game by her father and joining in the local contests by age six. After her high school graduation she went to work in the fields to help support the family. She read about the AAGPBL in the newspaper and went to a tryout in Oklahoma City. Earlene started her baseball career in 1948 with the traveling Springfield Sallies. When that club folded, Risinger pitched for the Grand Rapids Chicks from 1949 to 1954. Her ERA for five straight years was under 2.40. Her career ERA was 2.51. While playing for the Chicks she worked at Jordan Buick because the owner, Art Jordan, was willing to give her time off to play. The Chicks won the league championship in 1953 and she got the final win. Risinger struck out Doris Sams with the bases loaded and two outs to preserve the victory.

After her playing career ended, Risinger trained as a radiologist and worked as an x-ray technician at Butterworth Hospital from 1955 to 1969. Then she worked as an orthopedic assistant from 1972 until her retirement in 1991. In 1973 Risinger was inducted into the Jackson County, Oklahoma, Athletic Hall of Fame. {Helen E. Risinger Collection #160, Michigan and Family History Dept., Grand Rapids Public Library, Grand Rapids, Michigan; AAGPBL Newsletter, January 2001, 15; Joyce M. Smith, "Helen Earlene 'Beans' Risinger," <www.AAGPBL.org>; AAGPBL Questionnaire, National Baseball Hall of Fame.}

Robinson, Fonda

(Lacrosse, Indiana)

Fonda Robinson joined the boy's baseball team at her high school in Lacrosse because they had no softball team. Robinson became a starter in left field for the team, though she only hit .159. Robinson and her friend Jamie Campbell both made the squad as sophomores because only ten boys tried out for the team.

Roby, Kelly

(b. 1971, Crystal Lake, Illinois) C, AWBA Dare-devils, Gators

Kelly Roby caught for the Gators and the Dare-devils in the AWBA in the early 1990s. When she does not have to don her baseball gear on Saturday mornings, Roby works as the corporate training manager for the American Hotel Register Company. She has also coached boys' Little League. {Carrie Muskat, "Playing Hardball's a Down and Dirty Escape from Real Life," *Chicago Tribune*, 27 June 1993, 1, 11; Bill Beuttler, "The Girls of Summer," *Sports Illustrated*, 6 September 1993, 139.}

Rockford Ladies Club

In 1870 the *Chicago Tribune* ran an announcement for a game between the married ladies' club of Rockford and a group of single ladies. The game was played at the field of the Forest City Club and the single ladies won 33–3. Part of the difficulty in getting a full report of the game came from the order at the time of the game that no men would be permitted to watch at all. {"Ladies at the Ball," *Chicago Tribune*, 17 August 1870.}

Rockford Peaches

By Grant Provance

At its inception the All-American Girls Professional Baseball League consisted of four franchises: the South Bend Blue Sox, the Racine Belles, the Kenosha Comets, and the Rockford Peaches. Of these original franchises only the Blue Sox and the Peaches endured the endless cycle of relocation, expansion and contraction that typified the league's structure from 1943 to 1954. The Rockford Peaches became the most successful franchise in the league's brief existence. The Peaches won the AAGBPL championship four out of the league's 12 years, including three in a row between 1948 and 1950. In winning one-third of the league's titles, the Peaches established themselves as the most dominant team in AAGBPL history. The Peaches' accomplishments are even more impressive when one considers that the league's front office implemented several policies to ensure that each team would have a realistic shot at winning the pennant.

In determining the keys to success for the Rockford Peaches there are several aspects of the organization that deserve consideration. Author Barbara Gregorich states, "Three factors accounted for the Peaches' success: manager Bill Allington; fan support; and very good ballplayers who, skilled in the basics, were able to come through in the clutch." An analysis of these aspects will provide an overview of how the Peaches reached the pinnacle of their sport, and provide a historical overview of the franchise. {Gregorich, *Women at Play*, 132; Lois Browne, *The Girls of Summer*, 52.}

For the inaugural season of play in the AAGPBL, ex-big-leaguer Eddie Stumpf was tabbed the Peaches' first manager. Hiring men with major league experience was a tactic that was popular with most franchises in the league. However, Stumpf's time as skipper proved to be a fruitless endeavor. The 1943 season saw the Peaches finish at the bottom of the then four-team league, finishing the season a bleak 16 games out of first place. The following year Stumpf was replaced by Jack Kloza. The 1944 season began dismally as the team was in fifth place out of six teams. As a result, Kloza was fired midseason and the job was given to Bill Allington. A veteran of the Pacific Coast League (a minor league circuit), Allington finished out the 1944 campaign with the team finishing 53–60, good for fourth place in the league. For the next seven seasons Allington managed the team, turning it into a perennial contender. The Peaches would go on to win the Shaughnessy series (the AAGBPL equivalent of the World Series) in 1945, 1948, 1949, and 1950, and were serious contenders virtually every year.

Prior to being hired as manager of the Peaches, Bill Allington coached women's softball in Los Angeles, California. Following the success of the inaugural AAGBPL season, league mastermind Phillip Wrigley widened the scope of his scouting efforts. As a result the "Silver Eagle" (a moniker given to Allington by fans of the Peaches) and a number of talented players from the West Coast came to Chicago to take part in the 1944 season. Despite his record on the field, Allington was not always popular with his players. His motivational tactics, arduous practice schedule and rigid demands on his players made some of them uncomfortable. "Players with fragile egos— or rookies, accustomed to small-time success— made painful adjustments, or quit, or asked to be traded." In retrospect Allington's methods were justified by his team's play. During his tenure, in addition to the four world titles, the team topped the regular season standings five times and made it to the playoff finals eight times. {Browne, 75, 79.}

Following a loss to the South Bend Blue Sox in the 1952 installment of the Shaughnessy series, Allington left the Peaches to become the manager of the Fort Wayne Daisies. There is speculation that his decision to leave the Peaches was fueled by either a salary dispute or his competitive streak, as the Daisies were considered to have a better opportunity to win games. His replacement was former big-leaguer and veteran AAGBPL skipper Johnny Rawlings. By the final year of competition in the league the Peaches had come full circle, finishing their final campaign in last place. Rawlings, like Stumpf and Kloza, was unable to capture the same level of success that was achieved by the Allington-led squads. In terms of the managerial history of the Rockford Peaches it is clear that Bill Allington is the most prominent figure. While Allington displayed the traits of a great manager, it was ultimately his players who earned wins on the field. {Gregorich, *Women at Play*, 139.}

In a discussion of the key players who donned the uniform of the Rockford Peaches, the first name that should be mentioned is Dorothy Kamenshek. A native of Cincinnati, Ohio, "Kammie" was a mainstay for the Peaches from 1943 to 1951. She retired as a result of back problems following the '51 season but returned for one final year with the club in 1953. The left-hander's natural position was first base, but she also briefly played in the outfield. Standing 5'6" and weighing 136 pounds, Kamenshek was one of the most lethal hitters in the league's history. A perennial AAGPBL all-star, her .292 career batting average is among the highest in the league's history. As the rules of the AAGBPL were shifted from softball to a hybrid brand of baseball, Kamenshek's offensive numbers improved drastically. In her rookie year, playing by softball rules, she posted a .271 batting average. By the 1951 season she posted a career high .345 batting average. During her career she also belted 13 home runs, drove in 304 RBIs and stole 657 bases.

Kamenshek holds several AAGBPL records, including most hits in a career, with 1,090; putouts, with 10,440; and double plays, with 360. In addition to those records, she ranks second among AAGBPL players in at-bats with 3,736 and runs scored with 667. The statistic that best illustrates her prowess at the plate is that in nearly 4,000 career at-bats, "Kammie" only struck out 81 times. While she is remembered best as a slugger, her defensive records illustrate a proficiency in the field: she finished her career with an impressive .982 fielding average. Kamenshek's play on the field certainly establishes her as one of the best players in league history.

Another key player with the Peaches was Dorothy "Snookie" Harrell. Harrell was born in Los Angeles on 4 February 1924, and was one of the prospects who accompanied Bill Allington to Chicago following the 1943 season. Standing 5'4" and weighing 127 pounds, the right-handed Harrell was the teams shortstop from 1944 to 1952. Unlike Kamenshek, Harrell had a difficult time adjusting to play in the AAGBPL. Her rookie year was subpar, as she hit a meager .177 and committed 48 errors. However, as the years passed, Harrell's play on the field improved dramatically. Following the 1947 season in which she hit .251 and led the Peaches with 58 RBIs, "Snookie" was named to her first all-star game. A four-time all-star, Harrell finished her career with only 95 strikeouts in 2,992 at-bats, a respectable career average of .228, 306 RBIs and nine home runs. She also improved defensively, posting a career fielding average of .918. {Salsinger, 144.}

Ruth "Richie" Richard was born 20 September 1928 in Argus, Pennsylvania. An eight-year veteran of the AAGBPL, she began her career as a right fielder with the Grand Rapids Chicks in 1947, but was traded the following year to the Peaches. Richard was a fixture behind the plate for Rockford and was a valuable member of their championship teams. It did not take long for Richard to excel at the catcher position, but she struggled offensively in her first couple of years with the franchise. A left-handed hitter and right-handed thrower, "Richie" was named to six consecutive all-star teams between 1949 and 1954. In 1950 she posted a solid .251 batting average, but was unable to play in the postseason due to an ankle injury. Her career numbers are solid. A good contact hitter, she posted a .241 lifetime batting average with 15 home runs and 287 RBIs. In addition, not unlike her aforementioned teammates, Richard had a very low strikeout total, fanning only 109 times in 2,518 at-bats. She was also an excellent defensive catcher, turning 41 double plays and boasting a .961 fielding average. {Salsinger, 144.}

One of the most unique and versatile players in team history was West Virginia native Rose Gacioch. Born on 31 August 1915, Rosie was one of the league's oldest players. As a rookie for the South Bend Blue Sox in 1944, she was already 28 years old. As a result Gacioch's teammates lightheartedly dubbed her "grandma." She was acquired by Rockford the following year and with the exception of the 1950 season, which she spent with the Grand Rapids Chicks, she remained a key player for the Peaches. Gacioch began her career playing a variety of positions, which included outfield, first base, second base and third base. She was a key to the Peaches' success in the early years, contributing solid offensive numbers. She finished the 1945 season with a .211 batting average that ranked her twenty-second in the league in that category. The following year she improved her average to a lofty .257, which ranked her ninth in the AAGPBL in hitting. Her versatility would become apparent the following season, when the team decided to move her to the pitcher's mound. {Susan Macy, 75; Gregorich, Women at Play, 132.}

By the 1948 season manger Bill Allington, prompted by changes in the league's pitching rules, decided to make Gacioch a full time pitcher. She responded by posting a record of 23–7 over the next two seasons. Her best years on the mound came in 1951 and 1952. Over those two seasons she compiled 40 wins and was voted to consecutive all-star teams. In 1952 she led the league in innings pitched (259) and tied for the lead in wins (20). Her career pitching stats include a record of 94–62 and an anemic 2.48 earned run average in 1,337 innings pitched. During the 1953 season she hurled a no-hitter in a 5–1 win over her former team, the Blue Sox. Her accomplishments in all aspects of the game make Gacioch one of the most noteworthy of the former Peaches.

Patrolling the outfield for the team from 1948 to 1954 was a switch-hitting Canadian named Eleanor "Squirt" Callow. Before joining the Peaches, Callow spent her rookie season in 1947 with the Peoria Red Wings. The following year she was moved to the Chicago Colleens for a small time before landing with Rockford prior to the end of the 1948 season. Over the next seven years Callow was named to three all-star teams, establishing herself as one of league's best players.

Callow was arguably the greatest power hitter the women's game had to offer. She holds the AAGPBL career home run title with 55 and ranks second in career RBIs with 407. In addition to her power she was a solid contact hitter, boasting a career .273 average. In addition she led the AAGPBL in triples for four straight years, from 1948 to 1951. Squirt's best year came in 1951, when she also led the league in home runs and RBIs while maintaining a lofty .326 batting average. The following year she led the league in fielding efficiency with a near flawless .969 fielding average. Her defensive prowess is also reflected in her career numbers, which include 1,316 putouts and a .960 fielding average with only 80 errors.

The Rockford championship teams were blessed with an excellent pitching staff. A particular triumvirate of women contributed to the team's three consecutive titles from 1948 to 1950. The first was Canadian-born Helen "Nicki" Nicol, the all-time career wins leader in the AAGPBL. She began her career in 1943 with the Kenosha Comets, where she established herself as one of the most dominant

underhanded pitchers in the league. She struggled to adapt to the sidearm delivery adopted by the league in 1946, and was sent to Rockford in 1947. That year she posted a subpar 6–16 record, but with the switch in 1948 to overhand pitching she regained her form. She went on to post winning records in each of the next five years, including an 18–7 mark in 1951. Her career numbers place her in the upper echelon of AAGBPL pitchers. They include league records for innings pitched (2,382), games pitched (313), strikeouts (1,076), wins (163) and losses (118). Helen Nicol was perhaps the most adaptable pitcher in league history, her decade-long playing career being a testament to her skills as a pitcher.

Right-handed hurler Lois Florreich was a member of the AAGPBL from 1943 to 1950. Born in Webster Grove, Missouri, on 29 April 1927, Florreich began her career as outfielder with the South Bend Blue Sox. She was traded to the Kenosha Comets in 1945, where she was moved to third base. It was after the modified pitching rules were adopted that the "Flash," a nickname that referenced her base-stealing ability, was moved to the mound. She was acquired by Rockford in 1947 and quickly became a dominant pitcher for the team. For three years, from 1948 to 1950, Florreich amassed a record of 64–25 in leading the Peaches to three consecutive world titles.

In 1948 Flash posted an impressive 22–10 record, the first winning record of her career, and her performance earned her a spot on the league's all-star team. The following year she improved her record to 22–7 with a league-low 0.67 earned run average, and was again named to the all-star team. In her final year of play in 1950 she turned in yet another all-star performance, going 20–8, and led the AAGPBL in strikeouts with 171. Her career pitching numbers include an overall record of 86–60 in 1,304 innings pitched, 774 strikeouts and an ERA of 1.40. During the Peaches "Three-peat," Lois Florreich was arguably the most efficient pitcher in the AAGPBL, but not the only all-star caliber arm on the Peaches staff.

Louise "Lou" Erickson played only three seasons in the AAGPBL. The Arcadia, Wisconsin, native began her career with the Racine Belles during the 1948 season. She saw limited action as a relief pitcher during her rookie year and was moved to Rockford prior to the start of the 1949 season. Although she only played two seasons with the team, she was nearly as dominant as Florreich. In 1949 Erickson was named to the all-star team after posting a record of 17–6 with an impressive seven shutouts. The next year she was 16–10 on the mound and also boasted a lofty .239

batting average in limited plate appearances. Her career numbers include a record of 34–16 in 448 innings pitched, with 130 strikeouts and an ERA of 2.13. Erickson's career for the Peaches was brief, but she was a major contributor to two of the club's titles.

Alice "Rock" Pollitt was born in July of 1929 in Lansing, Michigan. She began her career with Rockford in 1947 as a utility infielder. Pollitt played in only 18 games during her rookie campaign, going 3 for 39 at the plate. She would go on to play with the Peaches until 1953, a total of seven seasons. During her career she established herself as a solid hitter and good defensive hitter. Although she did not receive the recognition that her teammates did in terms of all-star appearances, her career statistics speak to her value for the team. In over 600 games Rock had 2,177 plate appearances and a .255 batting average with 41 doubles, 35 triples, 8 home runs and 214 RBIs. Her defensive stats are equally solid with a .917 fielding average and nearly 1,000 putouts. Pollitt typifies the fundamentally sound player that comprised the Rockford teams. The quality of the teams created fan interest and as a result a unique relationship developed between the team and the community of Rockford.

The Peaches, like the majority of other AAGPBL teams, played their games in the confines of a small Midwestern city (Rockford's population in 1940 was 84,000). They were one of the few attractions in town, and by 1944 the team was drawing large crowds. On the final day of that season, 3,133 fans braved cold temperatures to witness the team's victory over the South Bend Blue Sox. Over the years the team proved to be a solid turnstile draw. The Peaches' gate receipts benefited from heavy coverage by the local print media. Newspapers, such as the *Rockford Register-Republican*, allowed baseball fans to follow the team's exploits on the field. In an era when the press was the community's source of news and information, the attention given to the team undoubtedly was a factor in the creation of Rockford's solid fan base. It was, however, not the only promotional vehicle that the team enjoyed. While newspapers brought the game to the fans, local businesses also played a part in supporting the franchise. {Macy, 75, 80; Gregorich, 139.}

The relationship between the Peaches organization and businesses in the community of Rockford was essential to the success of its ball team. Starting with the $22,500 that it cost to initially fund the franchise, businesses in the city provided economic support for the team throughout its existence. The club also benefited from advertising dollars generated by ads displayed at Bayer Field for additional income. Businesses capitalized on the notoriety of the players, using them to promote their products or services. Unlike the lucrative endorsement contracts that are common for today's athletes, the players were not usually directly paid for their services; but the team benefited from the free publicity. Some companies did provide financial rewards directly to players. One example is a promotion employed by a triad of Rockford businesses during the 1950 campaign. Hoffman and Son Jewelers and Optometrists gave players $2 per double, Mandt Brake Service offered $3 per triple, and Johnson and Burke Jewelers provided $3 to the pitching battery for a shutout, as well as $5 to any player that hit a homer. {Gregorich, 80.}

Unfortunately for the Peaches, life in post–World War Two America presented people with a variety of leisure time activities. New technology, for example the television, cut into the team's fan base and prompted advertisers to put their money behind other projects. Like the rest of the league, the Rockford Peaches were having trouble keeping the attention of the public. The final year of play began with the usual coverage by the press, who featured the team prior to and early in the season. The team played poorly, ultimately finishing in last place. As the club descended in the standings the crowds, which had been routinely in the thousands, were now barely in the hundreds. In addition, newspaper coverage of the team became significantly less prominent as the year went on. Following the 1954 season the All-American Girls Professional Baseball League fell apart and the Rockford Peaches ceased to exist as an active franchise.

Rodgers, Debbie

OF, Colorado Silver Bullets

Debbie Rodgers was one of over 950 women who tried out for the Silver Bullets in 1994. She was also among the 50 invited to spring training because of her speed. She was clocked doing the 40-yard dash in five seconds. When not playing baseball, Rodgers worked as a firefighter in Olympia, Washington. {"New Women's Team Flooded with Calls," *USA Today Baseball Weekly*, 29 December–11 January 1994, 6.}

Rodman, Kelly

P/OF, Waterbury Diamonds, Saints, Eagles, Bay State Express

Kelly Rodman played fast-pitch softball for

Eastern Connecticut State University from 1996 to 1998 before turning to baseball. In 1998 she earned Second Team All-Conference for her defense. In 2000 she played for the Bay State Express and helped her team win the New England Women's Baseball League championship. {<www.baseballglory.com>.}

Rogato, Grace

(b. 1933; d. 1 February 1993) C/3B 1951, Battle Creek Belles

Grace Rogato got a chance to join the Battle Creek Belles in 1951 after attending a tryout in New England, but she got hurt and had to return home before really getting much chance to play. She became a famous softball player, the first woman inducted into the Classical High School Hall of Fame. She coached basketball and softball as well. {"Touching Bases," AAGPBL Newsletter, January 1997, 6.}

Rohrer, Kay

(b. 29 June 1922, Los Angeles, California; d. 17 March 1962) C/OF 1945–46, Rockford Peaches

Kay Rohrer played softball in California before being recruited for the Peaches in 1945. She also appeared in a few Hollywood movies before moving to the Midwest to play baseball. In her career she played in 100 games, hit .239 and compiled a .960 fielding percentage. Her father managed the Fort Wayne Daisies in 1946. {AAGPBL Baseball Cards, 2000.}

Romance Bluebirds

This ladies' team played in Japan in 1948–1949. They were part of a women's league that only lasted two years because of lack of attendance and players. In the traditional Japanese society , the idea of women playing a game like baseball was hard to accept.

Romatowski, Jennifer "Jenny," "Romey," "Rifle Arm"

(Wyandotte, Michigan) 3B/OF/C/SS 1946–54, South Bend Blue Sox, Kalamazoo Lassies

Jenny Romatowski grew up tagging along with her brothers as they played golf, tennis and other sports. She started playing softball with Wyandotte's top girls' team. Her brother lent her his glove to play. She graduated from Wyandotte

High School in 1946 and immediately joined the AAGPBL. Romatowski started in the league as a third baseman and played a little outfield before converting to catching, where she became a standout in the field. Her hitting was never her strength, though during 1954, her last season — and her best — she hit .258 and was selected for the all-star team.

After the league ended Romatowski remained active by playing with the U.S. Field Hockey Association all-star squad that toured Europe in the 1950s and 1960s. She even played in the Netherlands at the world field hockey tournament in 1959. She graduated from Eastern Michigan with a degree in physical education, and then she taught physical education for nearly 30 years in the Van Dyke–Warren school system until her retirement in 1983. In 1999 Romatowski was selected for membership in the National Polish-American Sports Hall of Fame in Orchard Lake. She is only the fifth woman inducted into that hall. In 2001 Romatowski was also inducted into the Eastern Michigan University Hall of Fame for her career achievements. She also owns and races greyhounds. {Jo-Ann Barnas, "Romatowski: A Polish-American Pioneer," *Detroit Free Press*, 10 June 1999, 1D, 5D; "Baseball to Greyhounds," *Touching Bases Newsletter*, January 1997, 10.}

Rommelaere (Manning), Martha "Marty"

(b. 30 August 1922, Edmonton, Altoona) OF 1950, Kenosha Comets

Marty Rommelaere played softball in Altoona and in 1949 helped her team by winning the MVP award. This honor got her a tryout in South Bend in 1950, and she made the league. She played one season with Kenosha before returning home. She played in 30 games with only a .188 average. {AAGPBL Baseball Cards, 1996.}

Rose, Laura Michelle

P/IF, 2004 USA National Team

Laura Rose attended Oklahoma University and received all-regional honors while playing softball. She tried out for and made the Colorado Silver Bullets in 1997 and in 1998 played professional softball for the Durham Dragons and Tampa Bay Firestix. In 2004 she became one of 18 players selected for the USA National Team, which played in the fourth Women's World Series in July 2004. {USA Baseball Web site.}

Rosenthal, Renee

SS/P

Renee Rosenthal played baseball in Chicago. In 1992 she helped organize a four-team league in South Florida for the American Women's Baseball Association. Before taking up baseball Rosenthal played softball, as many women have done. She got involved with the AWBA to provide women with the chance to play baseball, not just softball. The four teams she organized were the Miami Thunder, the Hialeah Stingrays, the Fort Lauderdale Titans and the West Palm Beach Pioneers. The clubs would play for ten weeks and then have a league playoff. {Dave George, "Women's Baseball League Set," *Palm Beach Post*, 23 October 1992.}

Ross, Shandell Joy

(b. 26 January 1973) C, Springvale Lady Lions, Victoria, Australian National Team

In the 2001 Australian National Tournament, Shandell Ross led all hitters with a .636 average and also had a .737 slugging percentage.

Rota, Kelly "Cheetah"

(b. 11 March 1977) P/3B, Detroit Danger

Kelly Rota started her athletic career playing tee ball at age five. She played softball at Our Lady Star of the Sea and Lutheran East high schools. She was named MVP during her sophomore year at Our Lady Star of the Sea. Rota attended Macomb Community College in business and graphic design. During her college years she joined a slow-pitch softball team before hearing about the Detroit Danger in 2004. She hit .462 and was a superb player at the hot corner. She knocked in 22 runs and had 21 hits and 10 steals. Rota received an MVP award from the National Women's Baseball Hall of Fame for 2004. {Danger Web site.}

Roth, Eilaine May "I"

(b. 17 January 1929, Michigan City, Indiana) OF/IF 1948–51, Peoria Red Wings, Muskegon/Kalamazoo Lassies

Eilaine and her twin sister Elaine attended Isaac Elston High School, graduating in 1926. Eilaine played city league softball before trying out for the All American League. Eilaine and her sister played together for three years in the league. Eilaine played mainly in the outfield though she did occasionally fill in if necessary as an infielder. She played in 293 games and hit just .200. After leaving the league Eilaine played slow-pitch softball in a factory league until 1957 and worked for 21 years for Upjohn Pharmaceutical as an inspector. {AAGPBL Questionnaire, National Baseball Hall of Fame.}

Roth, Elaine "E"

(b. 17 January 1929, Michigan City, Indiana) P/OF 1948–54, Peoria Red Wings, South Bend Blue Sox, Kalamazoo Lassies

Elaine Roth joined the AAGPBL with her twin sister Eilaine in 1948, and they played together for three seasons as the "dynamic duo." Elaine spent her career as a pitcher, starting with Peoria and ending with Kalamazoo. She pitched for the Kalamazoo Lassies from 1951 to 1954. She pitched the opening game of the season in 1953, beating the Rockford Peaches 8–7. Just over 1,400 attended to witness Roth defeating Rose Gacioch and the Peaches. Roth pitched in 184 games and compiled a record of 45–69 with an ERA of 2.93. She also batted in 155 games and hit .153. {AAGPBL Questionnaire, National Baseball Hall of Fame.}

Rothchild, Susan "Susie"

1988–89, Daredevils

Susan Rothchild played in the American Women's Baseball Association in 1988 and 1989. In addition to playing, Rothchild also managed the Daredevils, one of two original entrants in the league. She helped score the first run in league history when she walked with the bases loaded against the Gators. {Bob Gordon, "Daredevils Win Women's Opener, 11–6," *Daily Herald*, 17 July 1988; Lindsey Willihite, "Women Play Hardball in Association," *Daily Herald*, 20 August 1989.}

Rotstart, Angelica M.

(Andover, Massachusetts)

Angelica Rotstart played on the freshman baseball team in 1999 at Andover High, but in 2000 she was cut from the junior varsity team because of a Massachusetts ruling barring girls from playing high school baseball. Rotstart decided to take the case to the Lawrence Superior Court to try to get the ruling changed. {Cathleen Crowley, "Her Pitch Could Alter Male-Only Ballgames," *Eagle-Tribune*, 26 March 2000.}

Rotvig, Barbara "Big Swede"

(b. Duluth, Minnesota; d. 1 December 1964) P
1948–49, 1951, Kenosha Comets

Barbara Rotvig pitched for the Kenosha
Comets for three seasons. In 1949 the highlight
of her career was a no-hitter. She pitched in 82
games and compiled a record of 28–41 with an
ERA of 2.58. Rotvig finished her career and re-
turned to college at the University of Minnesota,
Duluth. She also became a professional golfer.
{AAGPBL Baseball Cards, 2000.}

Roulet, Lorinda de

(b. 1930) Management

Lorinda de Roulet took over the running of the
New York Mets in 1975 after the death of her
mother, Joan Payson. She took the job because
her husband Vincent also died that same year. In
1978 she also became chairman of the board after
former chairman M. Donald Grant stepped down.
Born in 1930, Roulet attended Wellesley College,
raised three children and traveled with her husband to Jamaica where he served as the U.S. am-
bassador. One of her daughters, Whitney, worked
as the assistant director of public relations for the
Mets, while her other daughter, Beebe, worked in
promotions. {Joseph Durso, "First Lady of the
Mets Takes a Cram Course," *New York Times,* 13
November 1978, C6; "Mets Pick New President,"
Appleton Post-Crescent, 7 December 1975.}

Rountree, Mary "Square Bush"

(b. 23 June 1922, Miami, Florida) C 1946–52,
Peoria Red Wings, Fort Wayne Daisies, Grand
Rapids Chicks

While growing up in Florida, Mary Rountree
played a lot of softball. She caught for a Miami
team that played in the National Softball Tournament in 1938 and a St. Petersburg team that made
it all the way in 1940. Rountree was working for
the State Department in Washington, D.C., when
the AAGPBL called her in 1944. She thought it
was a joke at the time and did not join until 1946
when Max Carey called again. Rountree joined
the league in order to save money to go to medical school, which she completed in 1956. Her first
club was the newly admitted Peoria Red Wings.

After one season in Peoria, Rountree was
traded to Fort Wayne, where she stayed until her
final season in 1952. Rountree caught in 422
games and hit .206 with 105 runs scored and another 107 RBIs. She even displayed a bit of speed
for a catcher, with 89 stolen bases to go with 166

walks. Mary graduated from Wake Forest's Medical School and went on to complete her residency
at the University of Miami Medical School before
starting her own private practice. After returning for further schooling in anesthesiology Rountree again developed her own practice. {Susan E.
Johnson, *When Women Played Hardball,* 40–41,
70; "Touching Bases," AAGPBL Newsletter, September 2002, 33; AAGPBL Baseball Cards, 1995.}

Row, Catherine "Kate" Elizabeth

(b. 24 July 1979, Bentleigh, Australia) P, Springvale Lady Lions, 2004 Australian National
Team

Catherine Row joined the Australian National
Team for the first ever Women's World Series in
2001 at the age of 21. Row pitched in four innings
for her team at the 2004 women's World Cup. She
gave up four hits but no runs. Row started playing baseball when she was eight years old and
stayed with mixed teams until she turned 18 and
joined the Victoria women's league. {Kate Hagan,
"Pitching for Sport," *Moorabin Gleneira Leader,* 27
March 2002.}

Rowe, Charlene

Charlene Rowe wanted to play baseball in
Charlotte, North Carolina, and when the local
Little League organization did not let her play, her
father Ralph created a new team for her in 1966.
He recruited a group of players and they played all
challengers. In 1967 Charlene got a new sponsor
for the club, which became the Junior Hornets,
sponsored by the Charlotte Hornets of the Southern League. Coach Jack Williams took on all challengers and said the team looked great in its new
uniforms.

Roy, Patricia L. "Pat"

(b. 3 October 1938, Goshen, Indiana) 1B 1954,
Fort Wayne Daisies

Pat Roy graduated from Harlan High School in
Indiana. She played softball for the Harlan Parks
Department team and in the Fort Wayne Junior
Daisy League. In the summer of 1954 she signed
a contract to play for the Daisies but only got in
14 games before the club had to release her. According to the insurance carried by the AAGPBL,
no player under 16 could be carried by the league.
Pat was still 15. The league folded after that season so she did not get another chance to play. She
coached high school softball for 12 years and also

coached volleyball. She taught and served as an athletic administrator until her retirement. In 1994 she was added to the Lake Station High School Athletic Hall of Fame. The Indiana Coaches of Girls' Volleyball and Softball also inducted Roy in 1995 and 1996. {AAGPBL Questionnaire, National Baseball Hall of Fame.}

Royal York Baseball League

Canada

This league, as most Canadian teams are, is part of the Central Ontario Girls Baseball League. The divisions in the league are tee ball, mosquito, peewee, bantam, girls and women. The league was created in 2001 from the merger of a number of existing leagues to consolidate and create a stronger single entity. The belief was that this consolidation would help teams financially and assist in recruiting players.

Rudis, Mary

(b. 12 September 1911, Springfield, Illinois) Chaperone 1949, Springfield Sallies

Mary Rudis helped out her hometown team by serving as chaperone for the Sallies in 1949. She got the chance to see some of the United States while traveling with the club and became a part of the playing family. As a chaperone it was her duty to teach the girls decorum and deportment as well as make sure they followed all the AAGPBL rules. {AAGPBL Baseball Cards, 1996.}

Rudolph, Connie

Groundskeeper

Connie Rudolph was the head groundskeeper for the St. Paul Saints in 1999. {"Nabozny Breaks New Ground," Jon Cook, *Slam! Sports*, 17 June 1999.}

Ruelas (Bruckner), Victoria

(b. 1977, San Pedro, California) SS, San Jose Spitfires

Victoria Ruelas had the distinction of becoming the first female to play in the Little League World Series in 1989 for San Pedro, California, against a team from Latin America. She played softball at San Jose State University from 1995 to 1997 and in 1995 made the second-team NCAA All-West Regional. In 1997 she made the academic all-district team. Ruelas holds a career .353 average and a single-season record of .408 in 1997. She

also still holds the single-season RBI record, at 42 in 1997. In 1997 she joined the San Jose Spitfires at age 20 to become the starting shortstop. {San Jose State University Athletics Web page.}

Ruhnke (Sanvitis), Irene

(b. 30 March 1920, Chicago, Illinois; d. July 1999, Rockford, Illinois) SS/2B/OF 1943–47, Rockford Peaches, Minneapolis Millerettes, Fort Wayne Daisies

Irene Ruhnke grew up in a family of 13 children. She and her sister Alice played softball while attending St. Bridget's Catholic School and then continued playing at Kelly High School. After graduation they played for local semipro clubs before Irene went on to play for the Peaches and the Daisies in the All American League. In 385 games Ruhnke hit only .196, but she played because of her defensive skills.

Ruiz, Gloria "Baby Face"

OF 1948–49, Peoria Red Wings

Gloria Ruiz spent two years patrolling the outfield for the Red Wings after arriving from Cuba to play in the All American League.

Rukavina, Terry

(b. 14 May 1931, Middletown, Ohio) IF/OF 1950–53, Kalamazoo Lassies

Terry Rukavina got her start in the All American League with one of the touring teams before being assigned to the Lassies. While with the Lassies she played in Yankee Stadium. Her career numbers included 224 games with an average of .307 and 82 runs scored. After leaving the league she played basketball for the Kalamazoo team that won the 1953 Michigan State Tournament. {AAGPBL Baseball Cards, 1996.}

Rumsey, Janet J. "Rums," "JR"

(b. 16 October 1931, Moores Hill, Indiana) P 1951–54, South Bend Blue Sox

Janet Rumsey graduated from Burney High School in 1949, where she had played on the volleyball team. When she tried out for the All American league in 1951 she had no softball or baseball experience, but made the league and was assigned to South Bend. Her first season with the Blue Sox ended with them winning the playoffs. They did the same in 1952 as well. In 1954 Rumsey led the league with a 2.18 ERA in 25 games and was selected to the all-star team. Her record stood at 15–6 and she pitched a no-hitter on 24 August 1954. She pitched in a total of 105 games with a record of 39–43 and an ERA of 2.33. She batted in 115 games and hit only .169.

Rumsey continued to play fast-pitch and slow-pitch softball for 13 years after the league folded. In 1957 her fast-pitch team won the regionals and went to the national tournament. She also coached a women's industrial team for Cummins Engine Company while she worked there in a variety of positions. In 1981 Rumsey was elected to the Indiana Amateur Softball Association Hall of Fame. In 1996 she received the Jack Cramer Award for sportsmanship, dedication and athletic skill. {AAGPBL Newsletter, September 1996, 9; AAGPBL Questionnaire, National Baseball Hall of Fame and Museum.}

Russell, Debbie

CF

Debbie Russell played Little League ball while growing up in Alabama. She made an all-star team when she was 12 but was never put in the game. In October 2003 she traveled to Arizona to play in the 24-hour marathon game to raise money for AIDS research. Russell wanted to play to improve her own skills but also to make some contacts, as she hoped to develop a women's baseball league in Alabama. {Whitney McHugh, "Ozark Mom Only Alabama Player on American Baseball Team," *The Dothan Eagle*, 13 October 2003.}

Russo (Jones), Margaret Ann "Rookie"

(b. 29 September 1931, Milton, New York) 3B/SS 1950–54, Peoria Red Wings, Battle Creek Belles, Muskegon Lassies, Rockford Peaches

Margaret Russo graduated from Marlboro High School in 1949 with no sports experience at all. She worked for a while in a print shop and for a local winery before playing for the AAGPBL from 1950 to 1954. She made the all-star team in 1954, primarily due to her hitting. She hit three home runs in one game during the season. She ended the year batting .313 with ten home runs, having hit only five in all her years before that. She played in 501 games and hit .230 with 15 home runs, 166 RBIs and 251 runs scored. She also stole 104 bases and walked 251 times, compared to only 147 strikeouts. Russo was a contact hitter who was

wanted at the plate when the team needed someone to make something happen.

After the league folded she went on to Ithaca College for her bachelor's in physical education in 1955 and her master's in education in 1962. She stayed active playing basketball and softball while teaching physical education, and married Fred Jones in 1986. {AAGPBL Questionnaire, National Baseball Hall of Fame.}

Russo, Trista

P/OF, Team USA

In 1998 Trista Russo participated in the Sandy Koufax State Baseball Tournament as the first female pitcher. She pitched for the Guilderland Yankees in two games, giving up only one run on three hits in ten innings pitched. She was the winning pitcher in both games she pitched, defeating Highland and Orchard Park. Russo relies on a fastball and sweeping curve to get batters out. Also in 1998, Russo joined the American All-Stars at the South Florida Diamond Classic, pitching in two games for the club. Russo pitched for the Medford, Massachusetts, Senior All-Stars at the Pawtucket Slaterettes twenty-fifth anniversary tournament. {Matt Szefc, "Trista Russo Pitches a Piece of History," *Base Runner*, October 1998, 4.}

Russo was chosen for Team USA in 2001 because of her baseball experience. She had played the game since she was six, taking part in all the Little League divisions through the Mantle age group. Five times she was named to an all-star squad. As an eighth-grader Russo played second base for her school's softball team but made the jump to pitch for the junior varsity team as a freshman. Her coach, Gary Arpei, decided to give her the chance when he saw her pitch and realized she had some of the best stuff he had seen in a young pitcher.

During the 2003 Women's World Series, Russo pitched the first game for the U.S. against Australia. Though she lost the game 3–2 Russo pitched a complete game, giving up only three hits in eight innings. She pinch-hit in game six against Australia but did not get a hit. She pitched game eight against Japan but only went four innings, giving up five earned runs in an 11–0 loss. Her final ERA was 4.50 for 12 innings pitched. {Australian Baseball Federation, <www.baseball.org.au>.}

In addition to playing baseball, Russo played basketball and volleyball at Saratoga Springs High School. In 2001 she entered Norwich University. {Tim Reynolds, "A Diamond Is Her Best Friend," *Albany Times Union*, 7 April 1998.}

Ryaby, June "Scoop"

P, Angels

June Ryaby made her pitching debut for the Elmwood Park Angels on 27 April 2003 and lost to the Indians 16–4. Ryaby normally plays shortstop although she had pitched when she played Little League baseball. Ryaby ended the summer season at 1–4 with an 11.18 ERA. Her problem seemed to be control, as she walked 51 batters in 30 innings.

Ryan, Tess Lee

P, Chicago Storm

In 2002 Tess Ryan had a 4–0 record with a 2.80 ERA in 20 innings of pitching for the summer. In the fall she had a 2–0 record with a 2.33 ERA. Ryan continued to have no losses, with a 3–0 record in the summer of 2003. Her ERA was 1.80 and all three victories were complete games. She pitched for the Chicago Storm in the Great Lakes Women's Baseball League. At the 2003 AAU National Championship Series, Ryan pitched six innings and came away with a victory for the Storm. {Chicago Storm Web site.}

Saavedra, Cindy

(Toronto, Ontario) P/Util., Team Canada

Cindy Saavedra played in the Women's World Series when she was only 12. At 13 she played for Team Canada in the AAU National Championships. She spends most of the regular season playing on boys' Bantam teams.

Sabo (Dusanko), Juliana Rita "Julie"

(b. 22 February 1922, Regina, Saskatchewan; d. 22 August 2003) 3B/OF 1944, Milwaukee Chicks, Minneapolis Millerettes, Racine Belles

Juliana Dusanko played in the AAGPBL in 1944 and then remained in the United States to play for a time in the softball leagues in Chicago with the Parichi All Stars. She returned to Canada to play fast-pitch softball and was on two championship teams. She moved to Phoenix in 1963 with her husband Jim, an air force man she had married before joining the league. She played in 76 games and managed to hit .176 with 16 RBIs. {AAGPBL Newsletter, January 2002, 28, and May 2004; AAGPBL Questionnaire, National Baseball Hall of Fame.}

Sabres

Southern California Women's Baseball League

A southern California team based out of San Diego, the Sabres were organized to give women a chance to play competitive baseball. The team is run by Chris Hill. {Southern California Women's Baseball League Web site.}

Saggese, Lori

SS/CF 2002, Indians

Lori Saggese joined the East Coast Women's Baseball League in its 2002 inaugural season. She was assigned to play for the Indians and ended up helping manage the club as well. {Wayne Witkowski, "Pioneers Are in a League of Their Own," *Asbury Park Press*, 25 September 2002.}

St. Louis Black Bronchos

The Bronchos were a black women's team that toured the country from 1910 to 1911. The club consisted of eight women and four men under manager Conrad Kuebler. Kuebler was a white saloon keeper and horseshoer who ran regular announcements in the local paper looking for opponents. Kuebler's brother Henry owned and managed the men's St. Louis Black Stockings. In one contest the ladies played against the East St. Louis Imperials and lost 6–4. The players described in the news account were only identified by first names but were acknowledged as fine fielders and base runners. Kuebler claimed he had gathered the best lady players from around the country for his team and therefore they could play competitively against any challenger. In 1911 the club's schedule was posted in the paper and included games from May through June in Missouri, Kansas, Oklahoma and Texas. {*Indianapolis Freeman*, 2 and 16 April 1910, 5 and 18 February and 22 April 1911; Paul Debono, *Indianapolis ABCs*, 26.}

St. Louis Stars

The Stars were a bloomer team that had three men on their roster. They were listed at catcher and shortstop with an emergency pitcher. Their manager was a man named Al P. Gibbs. In one reported game the team lost to New Oxford 9–4 with about 400 fans in attendance, paying 25 cents admission.

Sakashita, Midori

P 2003, Japanese National Team

Midori Sakashita won Japan's first game in the 2003 Women's World Series over the United

THE ST. LOUIS STARS
AL P. GIBBS, Manager   Ladies Base Ball Club

St. Louis Stars from the 1910s (courtesy Barry Cheuvront and Dick Ryan).

States 8–4. She pitched four innings and only gave up two runs. She struck out four but did walk six batters. She finished with an ERA of 3.00. Sakashita helped herself with the bat, hitting .333 with one hit in three at-bats. {Australian Baseball Federation, <www.baseball.org.au>.}

Samonds, Shereen

(b. 1964) GM, Colorado Silver Bullets

Shereen Samonds graduated from the University of South Alabama in 1988 and then she worked for the Chicago Cubs front office before joining the Colorado Silver Bullets as their general manager. In 1993 she was named the Rawlings Female Executive of the Year as the only woman GM in the minors. On 9 December 1993 she gave an interview on *Good Morning America* about her experiences as an executive for the Class AA Orlando Cubs after they experienced a record-setting year in attendance. Samonds took the job with Colorado because she did not believe she would advance any higher with the Cubs and she had set a goal for herself to someday be the first female general manager in major league baseball. {Dottie Enrico, "Breaking the Grass Ceiling," *Newsday*, 27 March 1994; Television Listings, *New York Times*, 19 December 1993, 61; Jerry Crasnick, "GM Has Her Eyes on Bigger Game," *The Denver Post*, 27 June 1994, D-8; Dave Van Dyck, "Diamonds in the Rough," *Chicago Sun-Times*, 27 March 1994, 20B.}

Sams, Doris Jane "Sammy"

(b. 2 February 1927) P/OF 1946–53, Muskegon Lassies, Kalamazoo Lassies

Doris Sams grew up in family of sports stars. She played a variety of games and seemed to be a star in all of them. Her first claim to fame came at age nine, when she won the Southern Appalachian Marbles Tournament. She learned the game of baseball at an early age from her grandfather, who was a semipro pitcher. Her father had also been a semipro outfielder until he got married and settled down. She got the chance to play with her brothers Paul and Bob. She played fast-pitch softball starting at the age of 11 with Nelson's Café. That team won a couple of championships. Then Pepsi took over, and Sams played for them until 1946 when she joined the All American League.

Sams started her career as a pitcher with an 8–9 record and a 3.78 ERA her first season with Muskegon, but in 1947 her new manager, Bill Wambsganss, moved her to the outfield because of her strong hitting. In her first season Sams hit .274 with nine RBIs. She continued to split her time between the mound and the outfield. In 1947 she had the second-best record in the league at 11–4 with an 0.98 ERA. As a result of her all-around excellent play, Doris made the cover of *Dell Major League Baseball: Facts and Figures*. She made the back cover while Ted Williams graced the front. Sams set a league record in 1952 with 12 home runs; the previous high had been ten. She was selected to five all-star teams and was the Player of the Year in 1947 and 1949. In 1949 she was second in the league in batting with a .279 average, behind Jean Faut, who hit .291. Her best season at the plate was 1952, when she hit .312. Her career average was a solid .290. She pitched two no-hitters, one in 1947 and another in 1948. {Merrie Fidler, *The Development and Decline of the All-American Girls Baseball League, 1943–1954*, Master of Science thesis (Department of Physical Education: University of Massachusetts, 1976), 330–332; Jim Sargent, "Doris Sams," <www.AAGPBL.org>.}

San Diego Stix

In 1998 the Stix participated in the South Florida Diamond Classic and defeated the Michigan Stars in the consolation game. They won the 1999 USA Baseball Women's National Championship in Tucson, Arizona. They again defeated the Michigan Stars by a score of 20–4. The victory belonged to Tina Nichols, who pitched a complete game for the win. The hitting barrage was led by Chris Hill, who knocked in four runs. The only team to beat the Stix in the series was the Etobicoke All Stars from Canada. They won one game 6–2 behind the stellar pitching of Ruth Lancashire. {"Canada Shows Well in USA Baseball Championship," *AWBL Baserunner*, November 1999, 3.}

San Francisco Fillies

The San Francisco Fillies were one of four original entrants in the California Women's Baseball League.

San Jose Spitfires

The Spitfires belonged to the Ladies League operated by Michael Ribant. The manager of the club was John Oldham, and the two coaches were Jeff Perry and Toby Johnson. Perry had pitched for Oldham while he was still coaching at Santa Clara University. The team won the league in 1997 and came back in 1998 under manager Buck Taylor. Alex Sickinger caught for the club, while P.J. Brun pitched the opening day contest in 1998 against the Arizona Peppers.

Sanchez, Gina

3B 1999, Southern California Wombats

In 1999 Sanchez and her club played in the national championship in Arizona. Sanchez was selected as a member of the all-tournament team. She hit .583 with two runs scored and two stolen bases.

Sandford, Lisa

IF/P 2002–04, Montgomery County Barncats

Lisa Sandford joined the Barncats as a rookie in 2002 at the age of 13. She was named the Most Improved Player by her teammates. In addition to playing for Montgomery, Sandford played for the Germantown Athletic Club team.

Sands (Ferguson), Sarah Jane "Salty"

(b. 27 July 1935, Orangeville, Pennsylvania) C/OF 1952–54, Rockford Peaches

By Lou Parotta

Sarah Jane Sands was born on 27 July 1935 in small-town Orangeville, Pennsylvania. She attended Bloomsburg High School, where she played basketball. At an early age she became involved in baseball, despite the fact that women were not apt to participate in the male-dominated sport. At age 14, Sands was the batgirl for the semiprofessional team from Orangeville. She would take her involvement a step further by warming up the pitchers in between innings. Her love of the game was fostered during her involvement with these teams. She also played sandlot games with the boys.

During her high school days, Sands still got involved in the game in some way. During her senior year, circa 1953, Sands would warm up with the high school boys' varsity baseball team. While she could not play during a regulation game (Title VII of the Civil Rights law would not go into effect until 1972), she still caught the eye of the men who scouted for the All American Girls Professional Baseball League.

Upon graduation, Sands signed a contract to play with the famed Rockford Peaches. In her first game in May she went 4–5 with four singles to lead her teammates. She was able to see playing time under the league's rule that all teams had to play at least one rookie during each game. While she was not an exceptional hitter during her career, she was able to see action in 76 of the 110 games the Peaches played in.

Known for her exceptional defensive skills, she was also recognized for her solid fielding and strong arm. Sands played in a total of 136 total games during her two-year stint in professional baseball with the Peaches. She batted a dismal .210 over the course of 414 at-bats and garnered only 87 hits. Of those 87 hits, five were doubles and one was a home run. She scored 37 runs in her career and drove in another 29 — not too bad for a low-average hitter — and drew 13 walks. She was decent speedwise, swiping nine bases. She struck out a much-too-high 43 times, which was more than ten percent of her at-bats.

As stated above, however, Sands was in the lineup because she could field. In the 133 games she took the field (she played in 136 but three were either as pinch-hitter or pinch-runner), she amassed a strong, .933 fielding percentage, meaning she made the play over 93% of the time. She was able to make 169 putouts and assist in 27 others (a league-leading figure), and she participated in six double plays, which is difficult when playing the outfield. Over the course of those 133 games, she only committed 14 errors; about one every ten games. Because of her outstanding fielding, she made the second-team all-stars in 1954.

Despite her solid defense, the veterans on the team still rode the rookies hard. "Some of the veterans resented me," Sands said in an interview with the *Diamond Angle* of Hawaii. "After all, I was there to try and take someone's job." This was the same mentality that major league baseball veterans had when younger players joined their teams. Everyone was afraid that they would lose their job to some up-and-coming phenomenon.

Playing for the Rockford Peaches has brought Sands much notoriety since the release of the Penny Marshall film *A League of Their Own* in 1992. As a real-life consultant on the movie, Sands traveled to Cooperstown, New York, to join other former players in preparing the actresses for the movie. She instructed stars such as Rosie O'Donnell, Geena Davis and Madonna on how to look like real-life ballplayers. In an interview with Courtney A. Erickson of the Oneonta *Daily Star*, Sands said, "I showed the actresses how to stand and how to hit the baseball." With her help, *A League of Their Own* became a smash hit and a must-see for every baseball fan.

Sands has attended numerous reunions, card shows, lectures, public appearances, and special events since the movie's debut. "I do talks at schools, colleges and for organizations," said Sands. "I have been in parades, opened boys' and girls' Little League seasons by speaking and throwing out the first ball. I attended two local [Society for American Baseball Research] meetings and ... I [have] signed more autographs than I could possibly count and gave away over 1,000 of my baseball cards. I love every minute of what I do to support all girls in whatever sport they choose."

The sport of baseball is much better off because of women like Sarah Jane Sands. With their dedication to the sport and their true professionalism on and off the field, the whole experiment of women in baseball was much more than a publicity stunt; it was a success.

Sands got the chance to join the All American League at the age of 17. When her father made a contact with a scout who came and watched her pitch, they signed her to Rockford, where she earned $200 a week and then got a raise her second season to $225. This opportunity opened up many other doors for Sands that might have stayed closed were it not for her participation in the All American League.

After the league folded Sands went to work at Olmsted Air Force Base in Middletown, Pennsylvania, before moving up to the U.S. Naval Air Development Center, where she worked with a top level security clearance. Then she worked for nearly 30 years for Youngs Farm Supply and drove a school bus. She played basketball with a team called the Angels at Olmsted Air Base. She did a little coaching over the years and in 1984 her slow-pitch team won a championship. She married William Ferguson in 1957 and they had two children. {AAGPBL Baseball Card; AAGPBL Questionnaire, National Baseball Hall of Fame; Jessica Tobias, "McComb and Ferguson Were Pioneers in Women's Sports," *Williamsport Sun-Gazette*, 21 July 2004; AAGPBL Baseball Cards, 1995.}

Sanford, Lisa

(West Virginia) SS/C/P, EWBC, Team WBL

Lisa Sanford started playing baseball with the local boys when she was only seven. She played volleyball in high school and in 2002 she joined Team WBL on their trip to play in Australia.

Santiago, Taiine

CF/1B

While growing up, Tainne Santiago played Little League baseball but gave it up around age 13 because it got too hard to deal with the unfair treatment she received from her fellow players.

Santos, Susie

(b. 1972) 2B 2002, North Shore Cougars

Susie Santos started playing Little League ball at age eight and then switched to softball at Waltham High School. She also played softball for the Division II Bentley College squad until she graduated in 1994. She tried out for the Silver Bullets in 1994

Infielder Susie Santos waiting on the throw to try to tag out Eagles runner Amy Stinton (courtesy Laura Wulf).

Seahawks pitcher Ashley Cook showing off her form (courtesy Laura Wulf).

but did not make the squad. Then she finally got a chance to play baseball with the Middlesex County Cougars (North Shore) in 1999. She won a Gold Glove Award in 2000. She also tried out for Team America in 2002. Susie works as a database administrator for ENSR in Westford, Massachusetts. {Jen Salvo, "Santos Pursues Field of Dreams," <www. Townonline.com>, 30 August 2002.}

Sasaki, Maki

P, Japan

Maki Sasaki hit .250 in six games during the 2003 Women's World Series.

Saskatoon All Girls Baseball

This is the only all-girls league in Saskatchewan. In 2004 the league had four divisions for girls.

Saskatoon Ladies League

(1921)

This team is widely recognized as one of the earliest organized women's teams in that region of Canada. Unfortunately no good accounts of who played for the team or where they traveled have been found.

Satriano, Gina

(b. 27 December 1965, North Hollywood, California) P 1994–95, Colorado Silver Bullets 1994–95

Gina Satriano's love of baseball developed early since her father Tom was a major league catcher who retired in 1970 after playing for the Los Angeles Angels and the Boston Red Sox. She played Little League baseball while growing up, in 1973, becoming the first girl in California to do so after her mother Sherry threatened the league with a lawsuit. She tried out for the baseball team at UC Davis, but did not make the cut. Satriano attended Pepperdine law school and in 1993 started working as the deputy district attorney in Compton, California.

Before going to the tryouts for the Silver Bullets in 1994, Satriano kept her skills current by playing for a men's semipro team in California called the New York Heartbreakers. She also practiced with a women's semipro team known as the L.A. Gatekeepers. The Gatekeepers did not play many games because they could not find enough players regularly. Satriano became the first pitcher to start a game in a major league stadium when she pitched at Candlestick Park for the Silver Bullets in 1994. In 1995 Satriano made 14 relief appearances and earned her first save on August 23 against the Puget Sound Mariners. She developed a slider and a fastball that cuts away from hitters as her repertoire. {Harvey Araton, "The Trials of a Pro Female Pitcher," *New York Times*, 15 June 1995, B16; Andrea Higbie, "The Lady Is a Pitcher (and a Prosecutor)," *New York Times*, 4 September 1994, 30; *The Silver Bulletin*, December 1995; Steve Jacobson, "Living the Dream," *Newsday*, 8 March 1994.}

Satterfield, Doris "Sadie"

(b. 27 July 1926, Belmont, North Carolina; d. 4 November 1993) OF 1947–54, Grand Rapids Chicks

Doris Satterfield started playing ball when she was 11 years old. She joined the city league at age 15 and for three years took part in the National Softball Tournament in Detroit, Michigan. She was noticed by scouts for the AAGPBL and offered a contract, which she did not take right away. She went to school first and earned a degree in nursing before joining the Chicks in 1947. Doris batted cleanup for the Chicks because of her strong bat. During her career in the AAGPBL, Satterfield knocked in 366 runs and scored another 321. She hit .271 in 683 games. After the league folded she worked as a nurse until her retirement in 1988. {AAGPBL Newsletter, January 1994, 12; AAGPBL Baseball Cards, 2000.}

Schachter, Blanche

(b. 20 September 1926, Brooklyn, New York) C, Kenosha Comets

Blanche Schachter loved playing baseball, but shortly after joining the Comets she tore the cartilage in her right knee and her career was over before it really began. She only got to play in nine games before the devastating injury. After leaving the AAGPBL she remained active as a high school tennis coach. {AAGPBL Baseball Cards, 1995.}

Schaffrath, Pamela "Pam"

(b. 25 April 1971, Chicago, Illinois) C/1B/DH/ OF 1994–95, Colorado Silver Bullets

While growing up, Pam Schaffrath tagged along with her twin brother Mike to play baseball with his friends. She played Little League with her dad as the coach and her mom as the scorekeeper for Wells Park. She even won the MVP award one year. She received all-conference honors during her four years at St. Scholastics High School. Schaffrath attended Drake University, earning a degree in psychology. While there she played basketball and softball. She put up some strong numbers at the plate. She hit 16 home runs and drove in 115 runs. When she was chosen for the Bullets roster in 1994, she dropped her final basketball season in order to join the club. She led the team in stolen bases and doubles and finished third in batting. {Dave Van Dyck, "Diamonds in the Rough," *Chicago Sun-Times*, 27 March 1994; Susan Fornoff, "Playing Hardball," *The Sporting News*, 30 May 1994; *The Silver Bulletin*, December 1995; David Kindred, *Colorado Silver Bullets: For the Love of the Game* (Atlanta: Longstreet Press, Inc.), 90; "For the Love of the Game," Colorado Silver Bullets souvenir program, 1995.}

Scheer, Edna "Bunny"

(b. 4 November 1926, Cedarburg, Wisconsin) P 1950, Rockford Peaches

Edna Scheer played for one year with Rockford, pitching in 18 games with three wins and only one loss. She also hit .286 in 28 at-bats. After she left the AAGPBL she went to work in the restaurant business and coached Little League. {AAGPBL Baseball Cards, 1995.}

Schillace (Donahoe), Claire Joan

(b. 29 March 1922, Melrose Park, Illinois; d. 17 January 1999) CF 1943–46, Racine Belles

At the start of World War II, Claire Schillace was attending Northern Illinois University playing softball in a Chicago league. She impressed the scouts with her speed and fielding, so she was offered a contract in 1943 with Racine. By the time she finished playing, Schillace hit .202, drove in 112 runs and stole 153 bases. She later completed her degree and earned a master's in physical education from New York University. She worked as a teacher in countries including Iran, Germany and Bolivia while accompanying her husband Joe, who worked for the U.S. government. In 1965 they settled in Washington and she taught through the 1970s at Kensington Junior High. {Louie Estrada, "Claire Donahoe, Baseball Player in Women's League of 1940s, Dies," *Washington Post*, 23 January 1999, B09; J. Thomas Hetrick, "Claire (Schillace) Donahoe," <www.AAGPBL.org>.}

Schindler (Osborn), Sheila

Sheila Osborn tried out for the Colorado Silver Bullets in 1996. While she waited to hear from the club she started playing for a team in Lansing, Michigan. With her husband Don, Sheila decided to try to put together a league in Wisconsin with two teams for girls over the age of 17. Tryouts were held at a local high school. The Osborns met with Jim Glennie to get advice on starting such a league. {Shari Rampenthal, "Baseball League in Offing?" *Wisconsin State Journal*, 17 July 1996.}

Schloen, Mabel

In 1924 Mabel Schloen performed baseball skits in the vaudeville shows of Harry Linton. As a way to raise extra publicity and interest he had her play in exhibition games with local men's baseball teams. In 1926 she played in an exhibition game against the Cincinnati Reds. {Jill Agostino, "Star Quality: Schloen Was a Hit on the Diamond and in Vaudeville," *New York Newsday*, 29 September 1994; Gai Berlage, "Transition of Women's Baseball," *Nine*, September 2000.}

Schmidt (Weitzman), Violet Kathleen "Vi"

(b. 6 May 1927, Elkhart, Indiana) P 1946, Rockford Peaches, Fort Wayne Daisies

Vi Schmidt attended the St. Vincent Villa Orphanage in Fort Wayne and played sports in the CYO league. She worked for GE after school and tried out for the All American league in 1946. She only played sparingly during her one year, and did not return because she married Elmer Weitzman in December 1946. They had three children and she stayed home to raise them until her husband died in 1969. {AAGPBL Questionnaire, National Baseball Hall of Fame.}

Schmitt, Allie

Allie Schmitt played second base for the Grosse Pointe South High School boys' baseball team. Schmitt started playing baseball in the Little League system at age seven with her best friend. She played softball in 1996 but then made the decision to switch to baseball because she found it more exciting to play. Her coach, Don Cimini, was impressed with her fielding abilities and the contact she made with the bat. {Jeff Samoray, "Second Baseman Proves She's Good Enough to Make South Baseball Team," *Detroit News*, 24 April 1997.}

Schneider, Amy

Chicago Gems

Growing up in Ohio, Amy Schneider loved watching the Indians play but rarely played baseball herself. She played when she was 11–12 but then switched to softball. After junior high school, she worked as an umpire and scorekeeper rather than playing herself. She went to college at MIT and then went to work for a company making software for brain surgeries. Schneider eventually moved to Chicago and started playing softball again. She got the idea to help form a ladies' baseball team, the Chicago Gems, in 2004. In addition to that baseball experience Schneider also played in the 24-hour game in Tucson, Arizona. {"Interview with Amy Schneider," <http://independent.mostvaluablenetwork.com>.}

Schofield, June Rose "Moneybags"

(b. 1926 Toronto, Canada, d. 24 June 2002, Santa Monica, California) 1948–50, Springfield Sallies, Peoria Red Wings, Muskegon Lassies

Growing up in the Parkdale district of Toronto, June Schofield was known as a bit of a tomboy who had a great arm. She played third base for a time with a girls' club known as the Sunday Morning Class before moving south to Illinois. She signed on with the Springfield Sallies in 1948 and traveled around the United States. The next season she joined the roster of the Peoria Red Wings and then finished her playing career with a season at Muskegon. Her lifetime batting average was .232 in 234 games. In 1999 she joined 63 former all–American players as they were inducted into the Canadian Baseball Hall of Fame in St. Mary's, Ontario. {"June Rose Schofield, Ballplayer in Storied Women's League," *Toronto Star*, 12 July 2002.}

Schott (Unnewehr), Marge

(b. 1928, Cincinnati, Ohio; d. 2 March 2004, Cincinnati, Ohio)

By Joan M. Thomas

A sixth-generation resident and native of Cincinnati, Ohio, Marge Schott was the second woman (after Joan Payson) to buy a major league baseball club. Born Marge Unnewehr, she was the second eldest of a wealthy lumber dealer's five daughters. Early on, she developed a head for business through her father's example. Her later marriage to Charles Schott, also a well-to-do business man, only enhanced her cognizance of the world of wheeling and dealing. Widowed in 1968, she then took over Charles's various businesses, which included an ironworks, a brick factory and an auto dealership — but not a baseball club. Thirteen years later she became a limited partner in the National League Cincinnati Reds. By late 1984, she was the general partner of the ownership group. On 8 July 1985, she rose to the position of president and CEO. From the beginning, Schott elicited the reputation of being both a hard-nosed boss and a colorful character. Promoting her beloved pet, a St. Bernard dog named Schottzie, as the club mascot, her persona was more that of used car salesman than big league magnate. Her antics gained her much notoriety, but in the 1990s, her fame turned to infamy. Her insensitive, crude and ignorant public remarks forced her to sell her controlling shares in the club by the end of the decade. As of 2003, she continued to cling to a single share in the club, and believed that she was entitled to front row seats in the Reds' new stadium.

In the early years of her baseball ownership, Marge drew the admiration of other women who aspired to succeed in business. In 1987, while attending a women's business conference in St. Louis, she spoke with *St. Louis Post-Dispatch* reporter Virginia Hick about her role as business owner. In "She's the Boss in Baseball...," she said that when she took over her husband's businesses, as well as when she bought the Reds, she elicited the same reaction: "Lady, what are you doing here?" She said that her response was, "I own this place and I thought I'd look around."{Virginia

Hick, "She's the Boss in Baseball..." *St. Louis Post-Dispatch*, 16 March 1987.} Her aggressive attitude worked for a while. Her club even took Oakland in four games to win the World Series in 1990. However, the following year she fired the team controller, Tom Sabo. That was just the beginning of a series of unsavory news stories that sullied her reputation.

In February 1993, Major League Baseball suspended Schott from the day-to-day operation of the team for one year. She was also fined $25,000. The action stemmed from Sabo's lawsuit against the Reds, in which testimony shed light on Schott's frequent use of racial and ethnic slurs. It also revealed that she owned a Nazi swastika armband. She might have smoothed it over at the time, but her reaction to the accusations only intensified the situation. Her defense revealed her ignorance of history, as well as her dire need for sensitivity training.

Reliable chronologies {Schott Chronology 1998 & Marge Schott 2002} reveal that from then on Schott made one public gaffe after another. Following her return to power in 1994, she made her infamous remark, "only fruits wear ear rings." In 1996, she objected when umpire John McSherry's death on the field in the first inning caused the Reds' home opener to be postponed. And the rest is history. Because she continued to embarrass Major League Baseball, its executive committee again forced her to give up day-to-day operations of the club in 1996. By 1998 she agreed to sell her controlling shares. The following spring she sold 5½ of her shares, including the general partner shares, to Carl Lindner and two other limited partners. Schott considered herself a victim of the old-boys network. Some may agree, arguing that many male executives probably make bigoted remarks in private. But the fact is that if they do, they manage to keep it private. An op-ed piece that appeared in the *New York Daily News* justified Schott's expulsion, saying, "The hatred and ignorance she [Schott] purveys are shared by too many in our society. Baseball and America cannot afford to stand by in the face of prejudice." {Kenneth Jacobson, "Why the Big Deal About Marge Schott?" *New York Daily News*, 26 May 1996.}

Other uncomplimentary press releases about Schott centered on her frugality. She reportedly sent used flowers as a condolence for McSherry's death. That same year a news item said that she gave her employees candy she received free from Leaf-Donruss Co., instead of bonuses. {Hick} In addition to her reputation as a miser, there are numerous stories suggesting her heavy use of alcohol and tobacco. Yet, in spite of her forever-tarnished image, some of her accomplishments cannot be discarded.

Before her downfall, Schott received numerous honors from both local and national women's groups. In addition, she was the first woman ever to be awarded a major metropolitan area General Motors dealership. Later, she became the first woman named to the board of trustees of the Cincinnati Chamber of Commerce. Her childless marriage may account for her obsessive love for her dogs, and her soft spot for both animals and children is more than apparent. In 2002, she donated $500,000 to her home town's St. Ursula Academy, an all-girls school. She also offered to save a cow that escaped from a local slaughterhouse, saying that it could live on her farm. And, her interest in baseball was more than monetary. In an interview with *Cincinnati Enquirer* reporter Cliff Radel in 2002, she said "Baseball is America." Her thinking may be considered erroneous, but she got that one right. It is unfortunate that she could not have taken some lessons in propriety from the other two women who were big league bosses when she took on the title. {Cliff Radel, "Former Reds Owner Discusses Her Three Great Loves," *The Cincinnati Enquirer*, 26 February 2002.}

Schroeder, Dorothy Augusta "Dottie"

(b. 11 April 1928, Sadorus, Illinois; d. 8 December 1996, Urbana, Illinois) SS/P 1943–54, South Bend Blue Sox, Kenosha Comets, Fort Wayne Daisies, Kalamazoo Lassies

Dorothy Schroeder grew up on a farm with her parents and two brothers. Her father worked for the post office. Her home town was so small that she attended a one-room schoolhouse, where all the students played baseball together during recess. She wanted to be a professional ballplayer when she grew up, and so when her father saw an advertisement for the AAGPBL she wanted to try out. She had played regularly with her brothers and their friends. She went to St. Louis for her first tryout at Sportsman's Park and was invited to a second in Chicago. She became the starting shortstop for South Bend in 1943 when she was only 15 years old, making her the youngest in the league at the time and the only player to participate in all 12 years of the league's existence. She did not actually graduate from Sadorus High School until 1946.

She earned $55 a week that first season with South Bend. She played two seasons with the Blue

Sox before being traded to the Kenosha Comets. In 1947 she went to Havana, Cuba, for spring training. Midway through the 1947 season Schroeder was traded to Fort Wayne. While playing for the Daisies Schroeder's reputation really grew as one of the finest fielding shortstops in the league. She had a strong arm and good range. Her hitting got better with each season as well. Her best hitting season came in 1954, when she batted .304. In 1949 the league sent a group of players, Schroeder among them, to tour Central and South America. In the league's final season she was traded to Kalamazoo, where in her first at-bat she hit a home run. The fans bestowed on her the honor of Most Popular Player for the Lassies. She made the all-city squad as the only female, and they played against the Grand Rapids Black Sox. The Lassies ended Schroeder's career by giving her the championship she had never won. She is the career RBI leader with 431, beating out Inez Voyce with 422. She also holds the record for the most games, at 1,249; the most at-bats, with 4,129; and runs batted in with 431. Her career average was .211 and she made the all-star team three times during her career (1952–54).

After the All American League folded, Dottie joined the Allington All-Stars and played for them for three seasons. She worked for 36 years for the Collegiate Cap and Gown Company in Champaign and sang in her church choir in Sadorus, Illinois, where she grew up.

{"Baseball Star," *Parade Magazine*, 12 August 1948; "Area Woman Baseball Star Dies," *Touching Bases Newsletter,* January 1997, 7; Justine Siegal, and Rich Sangillo, *Dottie Schroeder*, <www.baseballglory.com>; Jim Sargent, "Dorothy Schroeder," <www.AAGPBL.org>.}

Schueler, Carey

As a sophomore at Campolindo High School in Moraga, California, Carey Schueler pitched for the JV baseball team. She also played basketball and set the conference scoring record, which is why she decided to go to DePaul on a basketball scholarship. She chose basketball over baseball even though she was drafted by the Chicago White Sox as a forty-third-round pick. She was the daughter of then–White-Sox-GM Ron Schueler. Schueler said it was not his idea to draft his daughter, though he did let her know they were thinking about it. {Ruda.}

Schwartz, Katherine "Kat"

OF, Knights

Kat Schwartz played for the AWBA Knights in the early 1990s. She was known for her strong hitting and strong throws from the outfield. She was one of six players from the league asked to serve as back-up players for the film *A League of Their Own*. {Michael Kiefer and Rebecca Ketcham, "Hardball," *Women's Sports and Fitness*, April 1992, 56.}

Schweigerdt, Gloria June "Tippy"

(b. 10 June 1934, Illinois) P 1950–52, Chicago Colleens, Grand Rapids Chicks, Battle Creek Belles

While attending Schurz High School, Gloria Schweigerdt played all sports available to girls. She also participated in a local bowling league. One of her fondest memories of her two years in the AAGPBL came when she got to pitch in Yankee Stadium and looked over to the stands to see the Dean Brothers sitting next to Connie Mack, watching her. She pitched in 60 games and compiled a record of 22–23 with a 2.88 ERA. After leaving the league she worked in her family's grocery store and took up golf and bowling. {AAGPBL Questionnaire, National Baseball Hall of Fame; AAGPBL Baseball Cards, 1995.}

Scott, Patricia A. "Pat"

(b. 14 July 1929, Burlington, Kentucky) P 1948, 1951–53, Springfield Lassies, Fort Wayne Daisies

Pat Scott joined the All American League in 1948 after graduating from St. Henry High School, but did not play until 1951 because she returned home to care for a sick family member. She pitched in 84 games with a record of 48–26 and an ERA of 2.46. In 1952 she pitched the Daisies to their pennant win over Rockford. After her three years in the league Scott graduated from the University of Kentucky and went to work as a medical technologist for 32 years. She was inducted into the St. Henry High School Hall of Fame in Erlanger, Kentucky, in 2000. In 2002 the city of Walton named their new ball park after her. {AAGPBL Newsletter, May 1996, 5; AAGPBL Baseball Cards, 1995; Presentation by Pat Scott at SABR Annual Meeting, Cincinnati, Ohio, July 2004; Jim Reis, "This Daisy was a Winner on the Mound," *The Kentucky Post*, 26 May 2003.}

Sears, Chrissy

(New Jersey) P 1996, Firebirds

Chrissy Sears played for the Firedbirds in Phoenix in 1996 and was one of the league's leading hitters. She hit the first over-the-fence home run for the Phoenix league, according to reporter Michael Kiefer. {Michael Kiefer, "She Ball," <PhoenixNewtimes.com>, 1996.}

Selig-Prieb, Wendy

(b. Milwaukee, Wisconsin) Management personnel

Wendy Selig-Prieb comes from a baseball family. The Milwaukee Brewers came to town when she was ten years old, and she spent many hours at the ballpark with her father. In 1990 she became the vice president and general counsel for the Brewers. Her position meant she represented the Brewers at major league meetings and helped with the daily operations of the club. In 1994 she was named to a 12-member panel to negotiate with the players' union. Her other major responsibility was to oversee the construction of the new ballpark for the Brewers. She eventually took over the running of the Brewers when her father agreed to become full-time baseball commissioner in 1998. In 2002 Selig-Prieb gave up her position as team president but remained as chairperson of the board. Selig got her bachelor's degree at Tufts University in 1982 and then went on to law school at Marquette University, graduating in 1988. She married Laurel Prieb, vice-president of the team's corporate affairs. They have one daughter, Natalie. {"Baseball: Brewers Make Changes to Front Office," *Sports Network*, 25 September 2002; Tina Lee Odinsky, "Wisconsin Pride: Interview with Wendy Selig-Prieb," *The Diamond Angle*, summer 1997, 40–41; "Selig's Daughter Prepared to Take Control of Brewers," *Capital Times*, 10 July 1998; "Selig-Prieb Named Brewers CEO," UPI, 4 August 1998.}

Seratt, Terri

(Willow Springs)

After Little League baseball had to open its doors to girls, Terri Seratt was the first to join the local Royals in her suburb of Willow Springs. Seratt had tried to sign up at the beginning of the season along with three other girls, but they were turned away. In her first game against the Twins, Seratt got up to bat three times, walking twice and singling in two runs in her final at-bat. She pitched and played first base during the game, which the Royals lost 16–10. {Ed Bruda, "Terri Plays in her 1st Little League Game," *Suburbanite Economist*, 23 June 1974.}

Servant, Nicole

SS/P, Pawtuckett Slaterettes

Nicole Servant played for Rhode Island Petroleum in 1999 in the junior league of the Pawtucket Slaterettes organization. She was second in the league in hitting, at .643. She and fellow pitcher Aubrey Phaneuf earned the nickname "the Gruesome Twosome," as they had ERAs around 2.00 and were among the league leaders in strikeouts. {Greg Botelho, "Pawtucket Slaterettes Having Another Banner Year," *Providence Journal*, 28 June 1999, C-03.}

Sexton, Karina

(b. 19 September 1984) IF/P, Queensland Rams

Karina Sexton got three at-bats in the 2003 Women's World Series and was held hitless while she handled three chances in the field without incident for the Australian National Team.

Seymour, Jade

P

Jade Seymour had the honor of being one of ten young ladies chosen for an all-star team participating in a tournament in Cooperstown. All the other teams competing have been all-boy squads. Justine Siegal took a team to the event for the first time in 2003. Seymour was invited to join the Sparks after Siegal saw her pitch in Mississauga. Seymour started playing baseball at the tender age of three and stayed with the game after a short stint in softball. Her pitching repertoire includes a fastball, a changeup and a curveball that manage to catch a lot of batters napping. {Scott Radey, " 'You Got Struck Out By a Girl,' " *Hamilton Spectator*, 6 July 2005.}

Shadic (Campbell), Lillian Evelyn "Pete"

(b. 14 June 1929, Chatham, New York) OF 1949, Springfield Sallies

Lillian Shadic attended Roeliff Jansen Central School for her entire 12 years of schooling. She got her sporting experience playing in the Hudson City Basketball and Softball leagues before joining the All American League. She toured for one year with the Sallies, playing in 26 different states. She was always a long ball threat and won at least two games with a home run for the Sallies. She stayed active after leaving the league in basketball, softball and bowling until the 1980s, when she gave up the basketball games. When her sons played Little League she coached, and later she coached and drove the bus for the girls' softball team. She drove a bus for Taconic Hills School for 17 years and worked as the manager of the Rheinstrom Hill Wildlife Sanctuary. She married Clifford Campbell in 1950 and they had seven children. {AAGPBL Questionnaire, National Baseball Hall of Fame; AAGPBL Baseball Cards, 1995.}

Shastal (Kustra), Mary

(b. 10 December 1925, Winnipeg, Manitoba; 16 May 1999) 2B 1944, Milwaukee Chicks

Mary Shastal played for one season with the Chicks before getting married and raising one son. After leaving the league she remained active in softball, bowling and curling. {AAGPBL Baseball Cards, 2000.}

Shea, Trudy

C

Trudy Shea caught for the South End Settlement House Little League team in 1960. The newspapers at the time claimed she was the only female playing in New England.

Sheehan, Kerrie

Kerrie Sheehan hit .444 in five games during the 2003 Women's World Series. She knocked in eight runs and scored four more. She did not strike out at all and only walked once. In 18 chances in the field Sheehan played flawlessly. {Australian Baseball Federation, <www.baseball.org.au>.}

Sheldon, Carol

1B/3B/P 1997–2000, Lansing/Michigan Stars; 2001, Motown Magic, Detroit Danger

Carol Sheldon played softball for a number of years before taking up baseball. She played on four world championship teams and was named Pitcher of the 1990s for the state of Michigan. In 1995 she was inducted into the Michigan USSSA Hall of Fame. In 1996 Sheldon played first base for the Lansing Stars of the Great Lakes Women's Baseball League. She joined the Michigan Stars in 1997 and even attended a Detroit Tigers Fantasy Camp in 1999. In 2003 she was inducted into the National Women's Baseball Hall of Fame. {<www.baseballglory.com>.}

When not playing baseball Sheldon is a teacher.

She uses that training to help run clinics for women's baseball. She is described by those who have seen her play as a player who knows the fundamentals; who understands the game. {Susan Smiley, "Read All About It: Sheldon in Hall," *Detroit Free Press*, 8 January 2004; Jaffeson, *Fame Forum Newsletter* 7.}

Sheldons

A team made up of nine ladies, called the Sheldons, was reported to have played two games at Lake George in 1883. They played the Kaatskills, another ladies' team, made up of women who were vacationing in the area. Though no scores were reported, the article indicated each team won one game. {*Savannah Weekly Echo*, 26 August 1883.}

Shepard, Laura

(b. 26 September 1972) P 1996, Colorado Silver Bullets

During her four-year career at Florida State University, Laura Shepard hit .315 and was selected for all-region, all-metro-conference, and all–ACC honors. Those numbers got her an invitation to try out for the Silver Bullets team in 1996. {*Silver Bulletin*, March 1996.}

Sheppard, Jen

P, Dominion Bantam Hawks

Jen Sheppard pitched for the Dominion Bantam Hawks in 2003 and has also played for four years with the Cape Breton Selects in soccer. She has been playing baseball for at least three years.

Shero (Witiuk), Doris "Baser"

(b. 22 May 1929, Winnipeg, Manitoba) OF 1950–51, Racine Belles, Battle Creek Belles

Doris Shero played in the AAGPBL in 1950 and 1951. Before joining the league she had played softball for eight years in Canada. Her claim to fame there was the fact that she did not commit an error in the outfield for three years. While with Racine and Battle Creek she played in 97 games and hit only .094. Her fielding percentage stood at .914, which is what kept her in the lineup. She married Steve Witiuk after leaving the league. He was an amateur and professional hockey player from Spokane, Washington. {AAGPBL Baseball Cards, 1995.}

Shibata, Makiko

RF, Japan

In three games during the 2003 Women's World Series, Makiko Shibata hit .250 for the Japanese National Team.

Shinen (Volkov), Kay

(b. 9 December 1921, Los Angeles, California) 3B, Kenosha Comets

Shortly after her graduation from Roosevelt High School, Kay Shinen got the chance to travel to Hawaii, Japan, China and the Philippines as part of the Good Will Tour in 1938. She spent three months traveling through these countries with other American female athletes. She spent only one year with Kenosha but played softball in the Chicago League for a number of seasons. She played in 98 games and hit .168 with 23 runs scored. She worked as a legal secretary for a number of law firms when she was not playing baseball. She married William Volkov and they had two sons. {AAGPBL Questionnaire, National Baseball Hall of Fame; AAGPBL Baseball Cards, 1995.}

Shipp, Eryn

(b. 21 July 1986) C 2003, New South Wales, Berkeley Eagles

Eryn Shipp played in the 2003 Australian National Women's Championship as the youngest member of the team from New South Wales. She was 16. She hoped to impress the coaches enough that she would be chosen for the national team that would play in the Women's World Series. She knocked in the first run in their victory against Queensland to make it to the 2003 finals. In 2004 Illawarra started their own team, and Shipp got the chance to help the new club earn their way to the Australian national championship in 2005. {Agron Latifi, "Women Playing Hardball," *Illawarra Mercury*, 17 April 2003; Peter Rowe, "Illawarra's Baseball Diamonds," *The Sunday Telegraph*, 3 April 2005, 78.}

Shively, Twila "Twi"

(b. 20 March 1922, Chicago, Illinois) LF 1945–50, Grand Rapids Chicks, Chicago Colleens, Peoria Red Wings

Twila Shively played for six years in the All American League. In 1946 Shively played the outfield for Grand Rapids and found herself in a race for the batting title with Seneida Worth of South Bend. In June she took over the lead for a short time, hitting .384. She finished the season hitting .247. It was her best year at the plate. Shively played in 614 games and hit .200. She stole 255 bases and scored 274 runs to help her clubs. When she left the league she remained active as a golfer and a hiker and in aerobics. {"Twila Shively Leads Hitters in Girls' League," *Chicago Tribune*, 23 June 1946.}

Shollenberger, Fern "Shelly"

(b. 18 May 1923, Hamburg, Pennsylvania; d. 1977) 3B 1946–54, Kenosha Comets, Kalamazoo Lassies

Fern Shollenberger was an all-star third baseman from 1950 to 1954 for the Comets. While the Comets were invariably low in the standings, their fielding was always among the best in the league, and Fern was one of the key reasons. She led third basemen in fielding percentage and number of double plays turned. After the Comets folded in 1951 Shollenberger moved on to play with the Kalamazoo Lassies. She played in 918 games over the course of her career, hitting .221 and driving in 231 runs. She struck out 155 times while walking 237. Shollenberger died in a car crash in 1977. {AAGPBL Baseball Cards, 1995.}

Shriner, Kat "Kat-Mouse"

(b. 3 May 1986) 1B, Detroit Danger

Kat Shriner grew up playing softball as a pitcher and first baseman. During her junior and senior high years in school she danced and played basketball and slow- and fast-pitch softball. Shriner did a little coaching as well. She joined the Detroit Danger in 2004 and excelled at first base defensively. She saved many a game with her stretches and digs at the bag. She also contributed a .316 average at the plate in 12 games. Shriner received an MVP Award from the National Women's Baseball Hall of Fame for her defensive play. {Danger Web site.}

Shuman (Jurasinski), Amy

(Mohrville, Pennsylvania) 1B 1946, South Bend Blue Sox

Amy Shuman played one season at first base for South Bend.

Sickinger, Alexandra "Alex"

(b. 1980, Pacifica, California) San Jose Spitfires, Cal Sabres, 2004 USA National Team

Catcher Alex Sickinger for Team USA (photographer John Lypian, courtesy Jim Glennie).

The youngest member of the Spitfires in 1997 at age 17, Alex Sickinger joined the team after graduating from Oceana High School in Pacifica. While in school Sickinger caught for the high school baseball team and received all-league honors. Her school was a liberal arts magnet school with only 350 students in the four grades. In 1994 they had no organized sports and so they started a baseball club. In 1995 three girls joined the team, including Sickinger as a sophomore. Her teammates were Gail Gamble at second base and Tiffany Bisconer at first. While Sickinger started, the other two girls played in backup roles. After her graduation in 1997, Sickinger continued to play by finding local leagues and tournament teams.

In 1997–98 she played in the Ladies League and won Rookie of the Year in 1997. By 2001 she was playing for the Cal Sabres and helped them to a second place finish at the Roy Hobbs Tournament. She was selected team MVP along with Jackie Chin. She joined Team America in 2003 and won a Gold Glove in the Women's World Series. She also received MVP honors in 2003 in the California women's league with ten hits in 24 at-bats. In 2004 she became one of 18 players selected for the first USA National Team. She graduated from San Francisco State and works as a teacher when she is not on the baseball diamond. {Merv Harris, "Playing Hardball with Gender Equity," *San Francisco Examiner*, 28 April 1995; "Local Athlete Makes USA Team," *Pacifica Tribune*, 15 July 2004; USA Baseball 2004 Media Guide.}

Siegal (Warren), Justine

(b. 1975, Cleveland, Ohio) P/C, Cleveland Quest, Toronto Lizzies, Team USA

Justine Siegal founded the Women's Baseball League (WBL) in 1998 to provide women a chance to play baseball and not just softball. Her own love of the game started when she played tee ball while growing up in Ohio. She played baseball every chance she got. As she got older those chances became harder to find. Everyone encouraged her to play softball, but she did not want to. This resulted in her switching schools during her sophomore and junior years so she could play baseball at the Brewster Academy. She graduated from Hawken High School after attending there in her freshman and senior years.

She finally decided to develop her own teams and league. Players entering the league have to pay a fee to help make the league self-sufficient and gain respectability. Coaches in the first year of the league were volunteers, but Siegal decided that they would be paid starting in 2000 to give them more authority when dealing with their players. In addition to running the league, Siegal plays and manages. The first team she pitched for was the Cleveland Quest. She also played for the Cleveland Adult Baseball League as the first woman.

She juggles all the baseball activities with raising her daughter and serving in the national guard. She earned a master's in sports studies from Kent State University to help her with her goals of promoting women's baseball.

The WBL sponsored the Citrus Blast Tournament in 2000 to make it more affordable for participants. In 2004 she helped organize a new Peewee league for girls to extend their playing down to 10- to 13-year-old players. {Douglas J. Guth, "Mothers Day, a Launching Pad to Expand Female Athletes' Scope: Justine Warren Believes Women's Baseball League Will Hit a Home run," *Cleveland Jewish News*, 12 May 2000; Daniel G. Jacobs, "A League of Her Own," *Small Business News*, June 2000, 7; Allen Pulga, "Talented Elite Girls' Baseball Team a Shock to the Boy," *Hamilton Spectator*, 14 August 2004, SP08; <www.baseballglory.com>.}

Silveira, Tammy "Timo"

OF, Bay State Express, Team USA

After growing up playing Little League, Tammy Silveira took the route of many women players when she switched to softball. She played softball while attending Bridgewater State College and majoring in physical education and sports medicine. After college Silveira joined a local men's team in New Bedford and also played

Tammy Silviera of the New Jersey Diamonds being held at first base during a game in 1998 (courtesy Laura Wulf).

for a team in New Jersey. In 2000 she joined the Bay State Express in the NEWBL. In 2002 she was invited to join Team USA in the 2002 Women's World Series in Florida. She was injured during the first round of play, and Laura Brenneman ended up subbing for her in right field. {Sam Santurf, "Injury Subs Lead Team USA Past Australia in Series," *St. Petersburg Times*, 4 September 2002, 3C.}

Tammy Silveira running the bases for the New Jersey Diamonds in 1998 (courtesy Laura Wulf).

Tammy Silveira sliding into home for New Jersey while her Diamonds teammate Judy O'Brien waits on-deck (courtesy Laura Wulf).

Simons, Sharon

Management

Sharon Simons was one member of a group who bought up 90 percent of the Texas Rangers stock from Bob Short for nine million dollars. She joined the group because her husband Pollard Simons was also a buyer; he was a Dallas investor and real estate agent.

Simpson, Louise

(Charlotte, North Carolina) OF 1944, Rockford Peaches

In her debut with the Peaches, Simpson had one hit in four at-bats and three putouts in right field as Rockford lost to Minneapolis 7–6. {"Peaches Launch Home Season," 1944 papers in Rockford Peaches File, National Baseball Hall of Fame.}

Sims, Meghan

Meghan Sims played first base and pitched for the Kentucky Owensboro Southern Little League team in the 2004 Women's World Series. She had been the team's fifth pitcher all season, and so she got a chance to pitch for her team when they needed help against Lamar National. In her game she took over in the fifth inning and walked one batter before giving up a two-run homer. {Michael Murphy, "Blowout Has Historic Footnote," *Houston Chronicle*, 23 August 2004, 9; "Little League Honors Female Pioneers," *Grand Rapids Press*, 22 August 2004.}

Sinclair, Vickey

(Manitoba, Canada) P/C/OF, Manitoba Taffy

Vickey Sinclair plays ice hockey in high school but after school she plays baseball for the Manitoba Taffy. She played for Team WBL in 2002 when they traveled to Australia to play in a women's tournament there.

Sindelar, Joan "Jo Jo"

(b. 29 August 1931, Chicago, Illinois) OF 1949–53, Chicago Colleens, Kalamazoo Lassies

Joan Sindelar played in the AAGPBL for five years and compiled a solid record, though her stats are not complete since there are none available for her in 1952. In the other four years she played in 198 games and hit .226. She had the chance to play a game in 1949 in Yankee Stadium and met Casey Stengel and Leo Durocher. {AAGPBL Baseball Cards, 1995.}

Singleton, Shanon

P, South Bend Blue Sox (Great Lakes Women's Baseball League)

Shanon Singleton holds a number of pitching records for the Blue Sox. She led the team in games pitched, with 32 at the end of the 2002 season. In 1997 she had a record of 6–1 with an ERA of 4.28. She has also hit over .400 three times and holds a career average of .385. In 2003 she started off the season hitting .667 in their first five games.

Sloan, Shae

(b. 1 August 1971, Huntsville, Texas) P/SS 1994–97, Colorado Silver Bullets

Shae Sloan had a bit of a different start than many of the Silver Bullets, since she played baseball as a junior and senior for Splendora High School in Texas. Her heroes growing up were Nolan Ryan and Joe Niekro, who both pitched for the Houston Astros. She spent four years playing softball at the University of Nebraska, where she was the starting shortstop, and hit .319 during one season. When she joined the Bullets she moved to the mound, where she started nine games and pitched 37 innings. Sloan relied on a 75-mph fastball and a series of breaking pitches to get hitters out. {Bill Falk, "Baseball in Purest Form, Silver Bullets Send a Message Wherever They Go," *Newsday*, 15 August 1994; David Kindred, *Colorado Silver Bullets: For the Love of the Game* (Atlanta: Longstreet Press, Inc.), 92.}

Smith, Bree

Pawtuckett Slaterettes

Bree Smith plays in the league along with her sister Brittany. Her parents and grandparents have all been a part of the coaching and management ranks. Smith is a first baseman who has played in all four divisions of the Slaterettes since she began in 1986. In 2002 Smith decided to travel to Cooperstown and try out for Team USA along with 12 other Slaterettes and women from all over the United States. Following her graduation from Tolman High School, Smith went on to play fastpitch softball at Elms College in Massachusetts. {Sumathi Ready, "Slaterettes Shine on the Diamond," *Providence Journal*, 27 April 1998, C-01; Terry Nau, "Slaterettes Still in Their Own League," *Pawtucket Times*, 21 May 2001.}

Smith, Brittany

Pawtuckett Slaterettes

Brittany Smith followed in her sister Bree's footsteps and joined the Slaterettes when she was five. Her father was one of her first coaches. Her mom Pat also coaches, and her grandfather was one of the league founders. {Sumathi Ready, "Slaterettes Shine on the Diamond," *Providence Journal*, 27 April 1998, C-01.}

Smith, Haley

Pawtuckett Slaterettes

In 1998 Haley Smith played for the Senior All-Stars under the direction of her coach and father Jim Smith. {Sumathi Reddy, "Girls League Celebrates 25 Years of Baseball," *Providence Journal*, 11 August 1998, C-01.}

Smith, Hazel P. "Haz"

(b. 16 February 1930, Chicago, Illinois) C/1B/SS 1951, Battle Creek Belles

Hazel Smith grew up in Chicago. She played softball, volleyball, and basketball, ran track and field, and swam in Ogden Park. She also played semipro baseball before trying out for the All American League. Smith's career in baseball was cut short when she injured her finger and could not throw properly again. She shattered her finger during spring training, catching a foul ball during batting practice. She became the chief radiologist at Holy Cross Hospital in Chicago, working there for 30 years before retiring to Florida. {AAGPBL Questionnaire, National Baseball Hall of Fame.}

Smith, Helen

OF 1946, Rockford Peaches

Helen Smith patrolled the outfield for the Peaches in their third season.

Smith, Helen Lucille "Gig"

(b. 5 January 1922, Richmond, Virginia) 3B/OF 1947-48, Kenosha Comets, Grand Rapids Chicks

Helen Smith grew up in Richmond, Virginia, with her parents, her sister Elizabeth and her brother Hugh. She graduated from John Marshall High School in 1940, where she participated in all sports available to female athletes at the time — tennis, field hockey, basketball and track and field. She received recognition as the outstanding girl athlete in her graduating class. After graduation she played fast-pitch softball in the area and worked for Thalheimer's Department Store in their photo lab. She played for five different clubs. In 1940 her team made it to the nationals. As a result of her excellence in softball Smith was voted into the National Softball Hall of Fame in 1975.

During World War II Helen joined the Women's Army Corps (WAC) where she earned the nickname "Gig." She worked for the WAC art department and played on the women's softball team at Fort Oglethorpe. In 1944 Smith moved to army intelligence and worked at the Pentagon. After the war Smith moved to New York City to attend the Pratt Institute of Art and try to make a living as an artist. In 1947, with money running short, she decided to join the AAGPBL. She spent the season at Kenosha playing in the outfield. The following year she was assigned to Grand Rapids. During her two seasons Smith never got to be a regular starter because the teams already had set lineups, and so she filled in as a reserve for players such as Connie Wisniewski. She ended up playing in only 22 games and hit .192.

After playing she returned to school and graduated with a BFA from Virginia Commonwealth University in 1950. She became an art teacher and stayed in the Richmond system until she retired in 1982. In 1999 the *Richmond Times-Dispatch* carried a special article on the top ten Virginia athletes of the twentieth century, and Smith received honorable mention. {Jim Sargent, "Helen Smith," <www.AAGPBL.org> and *Sports Collectors Digest*, 20 September 1996, 152–54; AAGPBL Questionnaire, National Baseball Hall of Fame.}

Smith, Janet Marie

By Tim Wiles

Janet Marie Smith was a key player, along with team president Larry Lucchino, on the Baltimore Orioles' front office team, which developed the revolutionary Oriole Park at Camden Yards, one of the most influential ballparks in baseball history. The success of Camden Yards, both aesthetically and economically, touched off a stadium construction boom that so far has resulted in new ballparks in approximately half of the major league markets, as well as in many minor league cities.

After growing up the daughter of an architect in Jackson, Mississippi, Smith earned a bachelor's degree in architecture at Mississippi State University in 1981 and a master's degree in urban planning at the City University of New York in 1984. Prior to joining the Orioles staff, she worked as president and chief operating officer of the redevelopment of Pershing Square in downtown Los Angeles, and as coordinator of architecture and design for the $3 billion Battery Park City project in New York City.

A lifelong baseball fan, Smith wrote to Larry Lucchino suggesting that he needed someone like her to head up the new downtown ballpark project the Orioles were considering. Lucchino agreed, and the two set about creating a new kind of ballpark, which combined modern amenities and comforts with an homage to the great ballparks and cities of baseball's past. The park's design also was influential in the way it fit in to the existing neighborhood, both architecturally and in terms of access to public transportation and parking. Fans loved the new park, and it produced revenue in a way that caused other team owners to follow suit.

To those who find it noteworthy that a woman could lead such a design effort for a baseball facility, it is worth noting that the Camden Yards project featured several other key women. Kay Lantrip was stadium project manager for the George Hyman Construction Company. Colleen Cullen was a construction project manager, Kim McCalla was assistant project manager for the Maryland Stadium Authority, and Helen Maib was the on-site representative for HOK, the Influential design firm that is responsible for many of the new ballparks.

After completing the ballpark for the Orioles, Smith moved to Atlanta, where she served as president of Turner Sports and Entertainment Development, as well as director of planning and development for the Atlanta Braves. While in Atlanta, she oversaw the conversion of the 1996

Olympic Stadium into Turner Field, the new home of the Braves. Smith also worked on a new arena for the NBA Hawks and the NHL Thrashers, renovation of the CNN Center, and improvements to Centennial Olympic Park.

When Larry Lucchino moved to Boston to become president and CEO of the Red Sox in 2002, Smith rejoined him at Fenway Park. Under the new ownership group headed by John Henry, the team committed itself to exploring renovation options that would update Fenway Park, in terms of both fan comfort and team revenue generation.

Smith and Lucchino have made major changes at the park, widening concourses, adding seats atop the left field "Green Monster," the right field roof, and behind the plate. Some administrative offices have been moved to neighboring buildings to create space within the building, and restrooms and concessions operations have been updated.

The team also added turnstiles to Yawkey Way, creating a festive team-run plaza immediately outside the ballpark itself. These changes have been generally well received by Red Sox fans, and, while the owners won't commit to permanently occupying the historic ballpark, they appear firmly committed to fully exploring all renovation options before moving to a possible new ballpark.

In naming Smith one of Maryland's Top 100 Women for 2004, the *Maryland Daily Record* commented that Smith's career projects "represent a commitment to cities and urban facilities that give us a reason to congregate as a community in a society that has precious little to bring us together." Smith has been quoted as saying, "My real interest in all of my jobs has been how you can take these facilities and rejuvenate cities— really make them come to life." Smith is an associate member of the Urban Land Institute, American Institute of Architects, and the American Planning Association. {http://www.mddailyrecord.com/top100w/2004names.html}

Smith, Jean

(b. 9 May 1928, Harbor Springs, Michigan) OF/P 1948–54, Kenosha Comets, Fort Wayne Daisies, Peoria Red Wings, Grand Rapids Chicks

Jean Smith filled the leadoff spot for her teams because she was a patient hitter. She walked 333 times against only 188 strikeouts and stole 194 bases. She made the all-star team in 1954 when she hit .252 and knocked in 56 runs. Her career numbers included a .215 average in 587 games. {AAGPBL Baseball Cards, 1996.}

Smith (McCulloch), Colleen "Smitty"

(b. 31 May 1925, Vancouver, British Columbia) 1949, Grand Rapids Chicks

In addition to her year playing in the AAGPBL, McCulloch was a standout golfer, winning all kinds of recognition in British Columbia and in Canada as large. For example, she was on the British Columbian amateur team for six years and medaled at the Canadian Open in 1961. She also played basketball, grass hockey, softball and curling. In 2001 she was inducted into the British Columbia Sports Hall of Fame. She played in 40 games in 1949 and hit .184. {AAGPBL Newsletter, May 2001, 18.}

Smith, Mrs. John L.

Management

In cooperation with Walter O'Malley, Mrs. John L. Smith, a widow, purchased Branch Rickey's stock in the Brooklyn Dodgers. His 25 percent gave O'Malley and Smith 75 percent of the club's stock. This made O'Malley the president of the ball club in 1950. Mrs. Smith took over her husband's role in the team after his death. John L. Smith had become part of a syndicate in 1944 with Rickey and O'Malley as they started to buy up the Dodgers stock. {"O'Malley, Walter Francis," *Current Biography*, H. W. Wilson, 1954.}

Smythe, Katy "Tram"

(Detroit, Michigan) 2B/SS 2000–04, Detroit Renegades, Detroit Danger, Motown Magic

While growing up in Michigan, Katy Smythe played baseball with her brothers and later attended Detroit Tiger baseball fantasy camps from 1998 to 2000. While at Redford Bishop Borgess High School she played softball and was on the varsity team for two years. In 2000 she joined the Great Lakes Women's Baseball League and played for the Detroit Renegades, who then became the Danger. She finished the 2000 season hitting .472 with eight RBIs and eight stolen bases, and she scored 12 runs. She has also played for Team USA in a variety of national and international settings. Smythe was selected to play in the first Women's World Series in 2001 in Toronto. She attended Wayne State University on a volleyball scholarship and works for Independent Engineering Laboratories as a project manager. {Kevin Ryan, "Dream Come True," *Ann Arbor News*, 2 July 2001, D1, D3.}

Somogyi, Rae-Lynn

(Willowbrook) P/SS, Team Saskatchewan

Rae-Lynn Somogyi started playing baseball for Team Saskatchewan in 2003. She had been playing on local boys' teams for years by that time. In 2004 Team Saskatchewan played in the Canadian Bantam National Tournament. {Greg Harder, "Team Saskatchewan Shooting for Gold," *The Leader-Post*, 11 August 2004, C4.}

Sopkovic, Kay

(b. 23 June 1924, Youngstown, Ohio) C 1945, South Bend Blue Sox

Kay Sopkovic played as the backup catcher for South Bend for one season. She played in 12 games with only one hit. After giving up on the AAGPBL she continued to play softball in Ohio and Arizona. {AAGPBL Baseball Cards, 2000}

South Bend Belles

Ladies Professional Baseball League

The Belles were organized in 1996 by John Kovach, reference librarian for St. Mary's College. In their inaugural season the Belles had an 8–10 record. In 1997 the Belles finished at .500 with a 9–9 record. They also started to participate in tournaments such as the national championship held in Washington, D.C., over the Labor Day holiday. The Belles have had a number of excellent players on their roster during their existence. One such player for the Belles was Joy Kroemer, who went on to play for the Colorado Silver Bullets in 1997. Another outstanding athlete who holds a variety of pitching records is Shanon Singleton. Over the years Kovach has nominated some of his players for the National Women's Baseball Hall of Fame. Kovach has also become involved in the leadership for women's baseball with others such as Jim Glennie, Tom Giffen and Justine Siegal. {AWBL Web site.}

South Bend Blue Sox

When Philip Wrigley started a new baseball league, the AAGPBL, during World War II, there were four original entrants. One of them represented the city of South Bend, Indiana. The Blue Sox joined the league in 1943 and played until the league folded in 1954. They ended their inaugural season with a record of 51–40 but the Racine club won the playoffs. In 1944 they were 64–52 and then they dropped to second-to-last place in 1945 with a record of 49–60. The year 1946 saw

them rebound to third place and then fourth place in 1947. In 1948 the league split into two divisions, and South Bend finished at 57–69. The Peaches beat the Sox in a best-of-seven series for the league championship in 1949. In 1950 they finished at an even .500 and then came their success.

Their best years came in 1951 and 1952 when they won the Shaughnessy Playoffs. In 1951 they defeated the Grand Rapids Chicks and in 1952 they beat the Fort Wayne Daisies. In 1953 they lost in the playoffs to the Kalamazoo Lassies. {"Professional Gals to Play Baseball Game Here May 13," *Zanesville Times Signal*, 8 May 1953.}

Karl Winsch steered the team through some of its best years. Winsch played for the Philadelphia Phillies in the National League before coming on board with the All American League as a manager. Dave Bancroft, a former major-leaguer with lots of fielding records, also managed the Blue Sox. Chet Grant had the dubious job of working with South Bend in their early years as they struggled to develop their skills. He stayed with the club for two years and then moved on to Kenosha. While with the Blue Sox, Grant wrote a pamphlet called the "Manual of Girls' Baseball" for the league.

The Blue Sox had a number of star players on their rosters. For example, Audrey Haine and Ruth Williams often led their pitching staff, while Betty Whiting handled first base duties almost flawlessly.

South Bend Bobbie Soxers

The Bobbie Soxers were an experiment by the AAGPBL in 1946. The league wanted to develop junior teams that would serve as feeder teams for the big league clubs. Shortly after the Bobbie Soxers' debut the other clubs followed suit. In Racine, for example, there were four junior clubs created called the Reds, Grays, Golds and Greens, named for the color of their uniforms. One of the Racine coaches was Herb Hoppe, who wanted to teach girls such as Janet Wells the fundamentals of the game. The girls ranged in age from 12 to 14, and there were 15 girls on each junior squad. The Fort Wayne Daisies developed a team called the Junior Daisies, which traveled at times with the big club. All the junior teams disappeared by the end of the 1950 season. This was a reflection of the financial difficulties the senior teams were having by that time. {Diana Star Helmer, "Kid Sisters," *The National Pastime* (Cleveland: SABR, 1993), 94–95.}

South Bend Sailors

This team of ladies played indoor baseball as a

member of the Studebaker Athletic Association League. They played 12 games in the 1932 season and an additional 24 non-league contests. All together they only lost three games. The team was managed by Ernest Harris, who taught them the fundamentals as well as stressing discipline and good moral character. {"South Bend Girl's Indoor Baseball Team Winning," *Indianapolis Recorder*, 10 September 1932, 2.}

South Florida Diamond League

The South Florida Diamond League has five teams, which play each weekend from October until June at Brian Piccolo Park in Hollywood, Florida. The league also hosts a three-day tournament. The league operates under president Lily Abello. They place two all-star teams from their league into the tournament each year. {Elizabeth Clarke, "Nothing Soft about the Play at South Florida Diamond Classic," *Palm Beach Post,* 25 April 1999.}

Sowers, Barbara

(b. 4 May 1932, Livonia, Michigan) OF 1953–54, Battle Creek Belles, Grand Rapids Chicks

Barbara Sowers played for two seasons in Grand Rapids and developed a reputation as a power hitter. One of her home runs at South Field in Grand Rapids was recorded as the longest ball hit in that park. Unfortunately for Sowers, the AAGPBL folded just as she was becoming comfortable in the league. She played in 140 games and hit .248 with 51 runs scored. She also had a .910 fielding percentage. Her experience before joining the league had all been with fast-pitch softball in Detroit. {AAGPBL Baseball Cards, 1996.}

Spangler, Elaine

Philadelphia League

Elaine Spangler had always played softball but in 2005 finally got a chance to play baseball with the new Philadelphia Women's League. When not playing, Spangler works in the areas of genetics and epidemiology. {Kathryn Levy Feldman, "A League of Her Own," *Pennsylvania Gazette*, 2 July 2005.}

Spence, Heather

C, Arizona Cactus Wrens

Heather Spence played for Arizona when they were an independent team and when they were a part of the American Women's Baseball Association.

Spiegelman, Jo B.

(b. 1958) RF, Montgomery County Barncats

Jo Spiegelman always wanted to play baseball but never got the chance until 2003, when she joined the Eastern Women's Baseball Conference. In October 2003 she went to Arizona to play in the 24-hour women's marathon game to benefit AIDS research. Her daughter Rachel went with her and played as well. They were one of only two mother-daughter teams to play in the game. Rachel has played baseball since 2001 for the Bethesda-Chevy Chase Mets, an all-girls team. Most of Spiegelman's early experiences involved playing recreation league softball, or co-ed softball, dating back to 1976. While in college at SUNY Albany and George Mason University, Spiegelman continued to play softball while majoring in biology and minoring in chemistry. She has coached her children's baseball teams in recent years. {Jo Spiegelman, correspondence with Leslie A. Heaphy, North Canton, Ohio, April and May 2004.}

Spitaleri, Camile

(b. 18 October 1970) Inf. 1996, Colorado Silver Bullets; 1997–98 San Jose Spitfires

Camile Spitaleri's softball experience before joining the roster of the Bullets was extensive. She was a three-time First Team All-American at the University of Kansas from 1990 to 1992. In 1991 she was inducted into the university's hall of fame. Spitaleri also helped the USA softball team win the gold medal at the 1991 Pan American games in Havana, Cuba. After one year with the Silver Bullets, Spitaleri joined the Ladies Professional League in 1997 and hit third in the order for the Spitfires. {*Silver Bulletin*, March 1996.}

Spradling, Jennifer

Jennifer Spradling plays Little League for East Boynton Beach. In 2004 she was the only girl chosen for the 11- to 12-year-old all-star team. She helped her team to a 5–0 victory over Delray National with a home run to left-center. {Greg Bedard, "Girl's Home run Gives East Boynton a Boost," *The Palm Beach Post*, 28 June 2004.}

Springfield Sallies

The Sallies were an expansion team created for the 1948 season of the AAGPBL. When the club looked like it would fold, the league made them a traveling squad for the 1949–50 seasons. The purpose was supposed to be player development, but the concept did not last. (The Chicago Colleens were the other traveling team.) There were 50 players, chosen by Lennis Zintak. The Sallies played 71 games in 1949 and were expected to play the same in 1950. Pat Barringer and Bobbie Liebrich served as team chaperones, while Walt Fidler drove their bus. The business manager and publicity person was Murray Howe. The young ladies received $25 a week plus $3.50 a day for meals. {AAGPBL Souvenir Program, 1986.}

During the 1950 season the Sallies traveled regularly with the Chicago Colleens. They played all over the country. Often local girls would come out and try out for the squad in hopes of getting a chance to travel and see the country.

Sroczynski, Debra

(b. 1967, Rehoboth, Massachusetts) P, Colorado Silver Bullets

After playing Little League and Pony League baseball while growing up in Taunton, Massachusetts, Deb Sroczynski moved on to softball and tennis at Dighton-Rehoboth High School. She played softball at Bridgewater State College until her graduation in 1999. Then she got the opportunity to return to her first love, baseball, with the formation of the barnstorming Colorado Silver Bullets. Sroczynski developed into a finesse pitcher with a fastball clocked in the mid–70s. In 1995 she pitched in the Donnelly Sunset League and in 1996 for the Mansfield Red Sox. She also pitched for the Buffalo Nighthawks in 1999 and was named the pitcher of the year in 1999 and 2000 in the New England Women's Baseball League for the Bay State Express. She joined the Ladies Professional Baseball League in 1997. The NEWBL started the Bay State Express in 2000. That season she helped her squad win the league title, ending the season with a 7–3 pitching record and a 1.90 ERA. After the season she helped her husband found the Boston Blue Sox, and she pitched for them in 2000 when they were a traveling team. In 2002 the Blue Sox joined a men's senior baseball league. In 2001 Sroczynski pitched one game for Team USA in the first Women's World Series. {Susan Bickelhaupt, "Diamonds in the Rough," *Boston Globe*, 7 August 2002; Chris Forsberg, "Facing World Competition, They Played Hardball." *Boston Globe*, 18 July 2001.}

In the 2001 Women's World Series Sroczynski was named the MVP, winning two games including a one-hitter in the final game. Sroczynski can be found in the classrooms at Milford Middle School East teaching physical education classes when she is not on the ballfield. {Julia Turner, "What's My Sport?" *Sports Illustrated for Women*, 1 October 2001.}

Stageman (Roberts), Donna

(b. 1 January 1926, Randolph, Nebraska) OF/SS 1946, Peoria Red Wings

Donna Stageman never played in a regular season game in the All American League. In 1946 she joined the Red Wings for spring training in Mississippi, but when all the teams started north for the regular season there was no roster spot for her. She returned to Billings, Montana, where she was a teacher for 35 years. She continued to play softball, and got married. {AAGPBL Baseball Cards, 2000.}

Stahley, Adele R. "Rustie"

(b. 10 June 1928, Schnecksville, Pennsylvania) OF 1947, Fort Wayne Daisies

Adele Stahley attended South Whitehall High School but did not play any sports there. During the Second World War all the sporting activities ceased. She did play softball in the city league for four different teams. She tried out for the All American League in 1947 and was placed on the Daisies' roster. She only played a part of one season before deciding to join the military. After leaving the Daisies, Stahley joined the WAVES and spent five years in the service. She got her pilot's license, became an air traffic specialist and worked for 25 years for the FAA. {AAGPBL Questionnaire, National Baseball Hall of Fame; AAGPBL Baseball Cards, 2000.}

Star Bloomer Girls

The first account found the Star Bloomer Girls was in 1904, when they played a local Elyria club. The Star girls were touted as the champions of the world and were traveling in their own Pullman car, secured for them by manager F.C. Schmeltz. The game was played at the local fairgrounds. The team brought their own stands to seat 2,000 fans. {"Bloomer Girls," *The Elyria Chronicle*, 23 June 1904.}

A local paper reported on what they called the Stars 10th Annual Tour around the United States in 1906. The team's entourage comprised 32 people. In addition to the players and their manager they came equipped with their own brass band to help attract fans to the game. T.E. Neer served as the club's advance publicity manager, going on ahead of the team to schedule competitions and arrange promotions. Neer gained his experience as a stage carpenter for the Faurot Opera House.

Maud Nelson was listed as being a part of this team. The Stars turned up in Maryland in 1912 to play the Cadets at Frederick High School. The boys won the contest 3–2. Both pitchers started out well, as neither team scored until the third inning. The news reporter indicated that the Stars had been traveling in the area playing local clubs for weeks. {"Bloomers," *The Times-Democrat* (Lima, Ohio), 28 July 1906, 5; "Cadets Defeat Girls in 11-Inning Game," *The Frederick Post,* 11 June 1912, 5.}

Staton, Rhonda

C/OF, San Jose Spitfires

Rhonda Staton helped her team in 2003 with nine hits in 19 at-bats. She also walked nine times while striking out only four.

Stealers

Though the Stealers started off the 2003 season of the Sydney Women's Baseball League with a loss to the Black Hawks, things steadily improved as players settled in to new positions. The team entered the semifinals with an 8–3 record. They beat the Hawks in extra innings 9–7 to make the finals. With an emphasis on the basics, the Stealers won the championship game 12–1. They repeated their success of 2003 in 2004, when they defeated the Phantoms to win the league again. They started the 2004 season with most of their players returning. One important new addition was Mel Garrett, who inspired the team with her reckless abandon on the base paths. Tracey Tyler continued to provide the big blows at the plate, including a home run in the semifinals. The team played under the direction of Kelly Griffiths and Shelley Tinworth. {League Annual Report 2003, 12; Annual Report 2004, 9.}

Steck (Weiss), Elma Mae "El"

(b. 3 May 1923, Columbus, Ohio) OF 1948–49, Peoria Red Wings, Rockford Peaches

Elma Steck started school at Northwood Elementary and then attended Indianola Junior High School and North High School. She participated in all the athletic programs offered while in school. After high school Steck went on to Ohio State University, UC-Berkeley and Arizona State. Before joining the AAGPBL Steck played softball on industrial league teams and bowled. She also taught high school in Port Clinton, Ohio, in 1943 and worked for the city recreation department in

Oakland, California. Steck played one season for the Peoria Red Wings and completed one year on a Southern touring team. She found the toughest part of playing to be getting time off from school to attend spring training. After playing in Peoria, Steck went on to teach and coach for many years at Arizona State College. {AAGPBL Questionnaire, National Baseball Hall of Fame.}

Steele, Joyce Maureen "Lucky"

(b. 25 December 1935, Wyalusing, Pennsylvania) OF/1B 1953, Kalamazoo Lassies

After graduating from Wyalusing Valley High School in 1953, Joyce Steele got the chance to play baseball for the Kalamazoo Lassies. Her sporting background included playing softball and basketball from 1949 to 1952. She joined the Lassies when she was only 17. Unfortunately for Steele, the AAGPBL was in its final seasons when she joined, and so she never really got the chance to develop her talent. After the league folded she attended East Stroudsburg State Teachers College for two years, majoring in physical education. She later became a hotel owner in Lovelton and continued to play softball. Her team won the New York State League and got to play in the Mid-Atlantic Tournament after one season. She also took up bowling and coached Little League while working as the recreation director in Wyalusing. {AAGPBL Questionnaire, National Baseball Hall of Fame.}

Stefani, Margaret "Marge"

(b. 18 December 1917, Detroit, Michigan; 13 January 1964) 2B/SS/1B 1943–48, South Bend Blue Sox, Rockford Peaches; Chaperone, 1949, South Bend Blue Sox

Marge Stefani played in the All American League for six seasons, five with South Bend. She also chaperoned South Bend in 1949. Stefani made the all-star team in the league's first year when she hit .249. Her career numbers included playing in 642 games and hitting .227. She drove in 256 runs and scored another 317. {AAGPBL Baseball Cards, 2000.}

Stegeman, Joni "Baby J"

P/SS 2000–2002, Chicago Storm; 2001 Team USA

Growing up in Skokie, Illinois, Joni Stegeman played Little League ball for 12 years. She hit a grand slam home run in her first official at-bat for the Skokie Indians. Before joining Team USA at age 17 she had played for the Chicago Storm in the Great Lakes Women's Baseball League. In 2000 she hit .438 for the Storm, leading the team in that category. She also scored 23 runs and knocked in 18. She is also noted for her strong fielding. In 2001 she played for Team USA in the first Women's World Series held in Toronto. She attended Loyola Academy in Wilmette, Illinois, while playing. {<www.baseballglory.com>; Chicago Storm Web site.}

Stephens, Ruby Lee "Stevie"

(b. 2 October 1924, Clearwater, Florida; d. 21 March 1996, Holiday, Florida) P 1946–51, Racine Belles, South Bend Blue Sox, Springfield Sallies, Kenosha Comets

Ruby Stephens grew up in Clearwater, Florida, and was working as a ship welder and softball player when a scout heard about her skills. She pitched for six seasons in the All American League. She pitched one no-hitter for Kenosha on 12 July 1950. Her single best season was 1948, when she compiled a 20–11 record with a 1.87 ERA. Her career numbers included pitching in 150 games and 961 innings. She had a 62–53 record with a 2.35 ERA. {"Ex-Standout in Women's League Dies," *The Tampa Tribune*, 30 March 1996; AAGPBL Baseball Cards, 2000.}

Stephenson, Ashley

(b. 22 November 1982, Mississauga, Ontario) 3B/P, Team Canada, Mississauga North

In addition to playing for the Canadian national baseball team, Ashley Stephenson is a hockey player at Wilfrid Laurier University where she is studying kinesiology. In 2004 while playing for Mississauga in the NAWBL, she was named Best Defensive Player in their Labor Day tournament. Her baseball experiences really began in 1999 when she played for Canada in a tournament in Florida while playing for Team Ontario, her team still. In 2002 she attended and helped Canada win silver at the Women's World Series in Australia. {Baseball Canada 2004 Women's National Team Media Guide.}

Stephenson, Marlene Renfer

Inf. 2001, USA Rockets

Marlene Stephenson played softball at East Stroudsburg University after graduating in 1994 from Pittson Area High School. She holds the records from Stroudsburg in hits, doubles, and RBIs. In 2001 she joined the USA Rockets in the Women's Professional Softball League. {Michael Lello, "Softball Star Eyes Baseball," *Times Leader*, 6 July 2001.}

Steuert (Armstrong), Beverly

(b. 27 September 1934, Maywood, New Jersey) P 1952, Rockford Peaches

Beverly Steuert pitched for Rockford while she was still in high school. She put together a 4–1 record in six games she started and three relief appearances. The AAGPBL folded before she had a chance to really play, and so she went on to play basketball and softball. She later married and raised three children. {AAGPBL Baseball Cards, 2000.}

Stevens (Fisher), Lorraine "Fish"

P/OF

Known for her defensive skills coming off the mound, Lorraine Fisher was also a solid pitcher who ended her career with 33 wins and a 2.52 ERA.

Stevenson, Emily

(Champaign, Illinois) C, Milwaukee Chicks

Emily Stevenson played for the Milwaukee franchise when she was only 18. She became the team's top pinch hitter and served as the backup catcher.

Stevenson, Rosemary "Stevie"

(b. 2 July 1936, Stalwart, Michigan) OF, Grand Rapids Chicks

Rosemary Stevenson played one season with Grand Rapids, playing in a total of 32 games. She hit .232 and the first home run she ever hit was a grand slam. In that same game she robbed Jo Weaver of an extra-base hit, catching her long fly at the fence. {AAGPBL Baseball Cards, 1995.}

Stingers

In their first season the Stingers, under the coaching of Oriel Webster, finished in fifth place as part of the Sydney Women's Baseball League. Their record stood at 3–6 with one forfeit and one draw. In 2004 they came in third in the league standings under Coach Webster. {League Annual Report 2003, 10, 17; Annual Report 2004, 8.}

Stinton, Amy

(b. 1971, Wallingford, Connecticut) OF, Waterbury Diamonds, North Shore Lady Spirit, Team USA

While growing up, Amy Stinton had the chance to play one year of Little League ball in West Hartford, Connecticut, but in high school and college she played tennis, volleyball and softball. While attending Ulster County Community College she played fast-pitch softball. Her squad made it to the National Junior College World Series. She did not return to playing baseball until she joined the Waterbury Diamonds in 2000. In the 2001 Women's World Series Stinton hit .417. She made the all-tournament team for that performance. She returned to play in the 2003 and 2004 series. In 2003 she also played in the New England league and made the North Shore Spirit all-star team.

During the 2003 Women's World Series, Stinton played center field in game three, versus Japan. Though the U.S. lost 8–4, Stinton had three hits in four at-bats and drove in two runs. In game five Stinton again played center field but had only one of three U.S. hits against the Japanese pitching duo of Masako and Matsumoto. In game six Stinton had a better day at the plate with two hits in four at-bats and one run scored as the U.S. lost to Australia 13–7. In game eight Stinton was hitless in two at-bats while the U.S. was shut out by Japan 11–0. The United States beat Australia in game nine by a score of 8–6 and Stinton had two hits in five at-bats. She drove in one run and scored two more. Japan beat the U.S. 4–3 in the semifinals and Stinton scored one run. She ended the series hitting .455 with five stolen bases. {USA Baseball Web site; Australian Baseball Federation, <www.baseball.org.au>.}

In the 2004 Women's World Series Stinton scored a run in a 3–2 victory over Canada, which put her team into the final game against Japan. Stinton was selected, along with her teammate Kristin Mills, as one of the top ten players of the tournament. Stinton hit .250 with five runs scored and solid play in left field. During the women's World Cup she hit .462 and drove in one run to help Team USA win the gold medal. {<http://www.USABaseball.com>.}

Stocker (Bottazzi), Jeanette Lillian "Jan"

(b. 13 December 1926, Allentown, Pennsylvania) C 1946, Kenosha Comets

Jeanette Stocker played basketball at Allentown High School and ran track and field when she was in junior high. She also played city league basketball and softball before she tried out for the All American League. She started with Kenosha and after four months was traded to South Bend. She decided not to report to her new club but instead went home with her future husband, Aldo Bottazzi, whom she married in 1947. To stay active she took up bowling. {AAGPBL Questionnaire, National Baseball Hall of Fame.}

Stockes, Terina

P, Team Australia

Terina Stockes led her team with two victories and no losses in the 2003 women's World Series after having played the previous season in the International Women's Baseball Championship held in Geelong, Australia. {"Port Trio Pitch in for National Team," *Caulfield Gleneira Leader*, 9 December 2002, 50.}

Stoll, Jane "Jeep"

(b. 8 August 1928, West Point, Pennsylvania; d. 27 May 2000, Phoenix, Arizona) OF 1946–54, Peoria Red Wings, South Bend Blue Sox, Grand Rapids Chicks, Springfield Sallies, Kalamazoo Lassies

During her nine-year career in the AAGPBL, Jane Stoll played in 774 games. Her career batting average was .247 and in her last three seasons she hit over .300 each year. She also knocked in 312 runs and scored another 319. Her hitting made her an invaluable asset to each club she played for. After the league folded she started a dog grooming business and then moved to Arizona to work for AT&T until she retired. {AAGPBL Newsletter, January 2001, 28; AAGPBL Baseball Cards, 2000.}

Stolze, Dorothy M. "Dottie"

(b. 1 May 1923, Tacoma, Washington) OF/SS/2B 1946–52, Muskegon Lassies, Racine Belles, Peoria Red Wings, Grand Rapids Chicks

While playing softball in California, Dorothy Stolze was discovered by Max Carey, who signed her to play for the Lassies. She also played basketball, volleyball, tennis and speedball at Alameda High School. After playing shortstop her first season, Stolze moved to second base. Then she hurt her elbow in a car accident. Stolze's best year came in 1948, when she stole 67 bases, hit .242 and scored 62 runs. Stolz developed a reputation for being a solid hitter and base stealer. Her career spanned seven seasons before she retired in 1952 and went on to be a physical education teacher and softball coach. She played in 705 games with a .219 average. She knocked in 192 runs and scored another 309. She had good speed, stealing 300 bases and walking 208 times. {AAGPBL Baseball Cards, 1996.}

She got her bachelor's and master's degrees at San Francisco State College where she excelled in field hockey, softball, basketball and volleyball at the varsity level. She continued to play softball for the Fresno Rockets, who won the ASA World Championship in 1957. She coached her high school softball team for 17 years, winning the league championship in 16 of those years. She received the highest reward by being selected Female Softball Coach of the Year six times. {AAGPBL Questionnaire, National Baseball Hall of Fame.}

Stone (Alberga), Marcenia Lyle "Toni"

(b. 17 July 1921, Bluefield, West Virginia; d. 2 November 1996, Alameda, California)

By Larry Lester

Real name: Marcenia Lyle Stone; Professional name: Toni Stone; Height: 5'7.5"; Weight: 145–50 pounds; Bat/Throw: Right/Right

Marcenia Lyle Stone was born in Bluefield, West Virginia, (Toni Stone, interview with author, 3 January 1991) the second oldest of four children (sisters Blanche and Burniece and brother Quentin). When Marcenia was only three months old, the family moved to St. Paul, Minnesota. Her father, Boykin Free Stone, a mulatto according to the 1920 U.S. census, was a mason, and her mother, Willie Maynard Stone, was a beautician. Stone attended former major league catcher Gabby Street's Baseball School in St. Paul, Minnesota, where she began her diamond career as a softball player with the Girls Highlex Softball Club. She played in the middle of the diamond at the keystone position, a position where runners come in with spikes up and the mentality of a tractor trailer. She often dusted herself off after a 6–4–3 double play.

As a high schooler, Stone lettered in tennis, the high jump and baseball, a first in Humbert High School history. Because of the lack of public acceptance of females in sports, Stone endured the typical sexist slurs, along with some racial epithets. However, she was as tough as toenails, as her rough hands revealed.

This Stone was as rugged and as durable as her

Toni Stone receiving some instructions from Jackie Robinson (courtesy of Noirtech Research).

name suggested. Although her real name, Marcenia, was cute and feminine, she changed it to Toni. "Toni was short for tom boy," Stone claimed. "I wanted my name to reflect what I was all about." The self-described tomboy walked with the bow-legged strut of a bronco rider, and talked trash that would make a sailor proud. Her rhubarbs with umpires turned the air blue and ears red.

She later pitched for the male Twin Cities Colored Giants. During the Second World War, Stone moved to the San Francisco Bay Area to play ball in the American Legion. She had wanted to play in Philip K. Wrigley's AAGPBL, which operated closer to her home town. She wrote the AAGPBL for a try-out, but never received a reply. Much like the major leagues during this period, the girls' league had their own color barrier, which operated from 1943 to 1954; it lasted seven years after the major leagues broke the tradition of segregated play.

Padlocked out of the ladies' locker room, she joined the integrated, semipro, barnstorming San Francisco Sea Lions for seasoning. After three months touring the south with the Sea Lions, she jump to the New Orleans Black Pelicans because of a financial dispute with Harold "Yellowhorse" Morris, owner of the Sea Lions and former Kansas City Monarchs pitcher.

Soon after, Stone joined the highly regarded New Orleans Creoles, making about $300 a month. From 1949 to 1952, Stone played various positions with the traditionally male New Orleans Creoles of the Negro Southern League, considered in those years a minor league. There, she honed her skills, hitting roughly .265 and developing into a better all-around infielder. Stone admitted, "They give me a fit when they started bench jockeying. They tell me to go home and fix my husband some biscuits, or anything. And they didn't spare me because of my sex. But I've heard so much cursing in my life and have been called so many bad names that now it doesn't upset me at all."

She also overcame the social hurdle of being the lone woman on a confining bus with about 15 men. "I found that this wasn't any headache," she yawned. "At first, the fellows made passes at me, but my situation in traveling around the country with a busload of guys isn't any different than that of the girl singers who traveled with jazz bands. Once you let the guys know that there isn't going to be any monkey business, they soon give you their respect."

After a tour of duty with the Creoles, she took a sabbatical from the game to marry attorney Aurelious Pesha Alberga.

By 1953, Jackie Robinson and 26 former Negro-leaguers were gracing the rosters of major league ball clubs. The lifting of the color bar by white clubs created a surplus of talent for major league clubs and a deterioration of overall team talent in the black leagues; more importantly, it weakened the black fan constituency.

With attendance dwindling around the Negro National League, clubs sought unconventional means for promotions. Perhaps the all-around highly talented Toni Stone was the solution. At the age of 32, Stone broke the gender barrier in professional baseball when Indianapolis Clowns owner Syd Pollock signed her to a $350-a-month contract (not the $12,000 reporting by Pollock to the press). The penny-wise Pollock commented, "Toni will be our regular second baseman. This girl is no freak and although I wouldn't deny that her publicity value is very great for our team and its games, we expect her playing to help us a lot" ("Woman Player Says She Can 'Take Care of Self' in Game," Ebony, June/July 1953, 48). Although Stone played for the Clowns, she was no comedian. "I went to Indianapolis to learn the fundamentals of the game," Stone remembered. "But, they hired me as a drawing card and wanted me to wear shorts." Stone skirted the issue, saying, "I cussed [Pollock] out and told him: 'No ... I came to play ball.'" And that she did.

Although married, she graced the cover of several Clown programs as "Miss Toni Stone." Lady

Stone batted a respectable .243 in 50 of the 175 games that season, with only one extra-base hit, a double ("Monarchs Win NAL Championship: Ray Neil Cops '53 Batting Title," The Kansas City Call, 12 September 1953). In most games Stone played second base for the first three innings. The Clowns' regular second sacker, Ray Neil, who won the league batting title that year hitting .397, finished the games.

Despite her limited playing time, Stone had a few Kodak moments. She often said her greatest thrill came on Mother's Day in her first year, when she got a hit off the great Satchel Paige during an Omaha, Nebraska, game. "That was the happiest moment of my life," said Toni. "I got the only hit we had against him that day."

The following year, 1954, Stone's contract was sold to Tom Baird, owner of the Kansas City Monarchs, to play for manager John "Buck" O'Neil. The defending American League champs offered her $400 a month and a $200 signing bonus (Acceptance Letter to T.Y. Baird from Marcenia L. Alberga, 15 February 1954). "We wanted Toni for a drawing card with the Monarchs and she helped," recalled O'Neil. "By then our best players were in the major leagues. The Monarchs had become a developmental team." O'Neil was unwilling to give Stone some prime time in the field, causing her to quit. She claimed she never received the signing bonus.

Meanwhile, the Clowns were replacing their original gate-attraction with two other women, 19-year-old second baseman Connie Morgan, scouted by Oscar Charleston, and 21-year-old pitcher Mamie "Peanut" Johnson. Morgan, an all-around athlete, was a local basketball star and had gained notoriety with the North Philadelphia Honey Drippers as a catcher, hitting .338 during her five-year tenure ("Clowns Sell Toni Stone, Sign New Female Star," Michigan Chronicle, 13 March 1954). For now, Mamie Johnson, the smallest of the three women at 120 pounds, was called Peanut because of her size. Contrarily, Johnson claimed her nickname was because "my fastball looked like a peanut coming to the plate." Johnson had accompanied the Clowns on a barnstorming tour after the season and impressed Syd Pollock, averaging one strikeout per inning against the local talents. Later, Johnson attended New York University, where she studied medicine and pre-engineering.

The Monarch queen and two lady Clowns gave Negro American League fans some thrills that season, with stellar play and plenty of competitive spirit. However, none of the women returned for the '55 season. Coincidentally, the AAGPBL closed its doors after the '54 season.

After playing baseball, Stone worked as a nurse, mainly caring for her husband, who was 40 years her senior, until he died in October of 1987 at the age of 103. They had no children.

Stone received many postcareer recognitions. The city of St. Paul declared 6 March 1990 as "Marcenia 'Toni Stone' Alberga Day." As part of Minnesota's Women's History Month, Stone was invited to lecture at the local schools. On 10 May 1992, the popular syndicated sports show *This Week in Baseball*, with Hall of Fame announcer Mel Allen, showcased the barrier-breaker Toni Stone.

On 4 October 1993, Toni Stone, 72, was inducted into the International Women's Sports Hall of Fame by the Women's Sport Foundation. Other inductees included Olympians Mary Lou Retton and Mary T. Meagher, the late Kit Klein Outland, a pioneer in women's speedskating, and Sharon Backus, the UCLA Bruins softball coach ("Woman's Hall of Fame Inducts First to Play in Male Pro Baseball," *The Providence Journal-Bulletin*, 5 October 1993).

Robert Nieboer wrote a play, *Tomboy Stone*, that debuted in the Great American History Theatre in St. Paul in 1997 (Obituary, *Kansas City Star*, 5 November 1996). Later that year, on October 4, about two dozen admirers gathered at the Dunning Field Complex, in St. Paul, to dedicate "Toni Stone Field."

Stone may have been hired as a novelty for a dying league, but she held her standards high, while giving her best efforts. Toni was tough — mentally and physically — with tantalizing and tenacious play. She played the game she loved with deep affection and conviction, leaving a legacy for other women to follow.

Stone (Richards), Lucille "Lou"

(b. 25 December 1925, Boston, Massachusetts) SS 1945, Racine Belles, South Bend Blue Sox

Lou Stone attended Jeremiah E. Burke High School, where there were no sports to play. Instead she played Park League basketball, softball and baseball. She gained her love for baseball from her father, who played semipro ball from the age of 17 on. She tried out and made the All American League in 1945, but only played one season before quitting because her fiancé had been killed in World War Two. She later married Joseph Richards. She played in 19 games and hit only .040. While her three children were growing up, she coached Little League with her husband for 20 years. She also drove a school bus for the Holbrook school system for 20 years. She and her husband received an award from the Massachusetts gover-

nor for their 20 years of service to youth. {AAGPBL Questionnaire, National Baseball Hall of Fame; AAGPBL Newsletter, May 2002, 21.}

Stovroff, Shirley "Shirt"

(b. 18 March 1931, Madison, Illinois; d. 16 September 1994) C 1948–52, South Bend Blue Sox

Shirley Stovroff joined the AAGPBL at the age of 17. She played for South Bend in the championship series in 1951. At the victory celebration, Stovroff told manager Karl Winsch that she had broken one of the fingers on her throwing hand about three weeks earlier but had continued to play. She caught in 455 games and hit .216. She drove in 143 runs, scored 138 and developed a reputation as a fine defensive catcher. After leaving the league she moved to California and went to work for Matel as an administrative manager. In 1986 she moved to Arizona and worked for the Arizona Racing Commission until her death in 1994. {AAGPBL Newsletter, September 1994, 22.}

Straumietis, Renee Lynne

(b. 19 October 1983) P/SS, New South Wales, Australian National Team

Renee Straumietis had seven hits and scored eight runs in the 2001 Australian National Tournament for New South Wales. She also struck out six times in 22 at-bats. She hit .375 in two games during the 2003 Women's World Series. At the 2004 National Women's Championships, she scored 15 runs and knocked in 13 to help the New South Wales club. In the 2004 women's World Cup Renee hit .250 with one run knocked in and one stolen base.

Strugnell, Claudia

(Melbourne, Australia) P, Victoria Provincial, Team Australia

Claudia Strugnell plays baseball in the Victoria Baseball Association and is working on a degree in physical education. In 2002 she participated in an international women's baseball event held in her home country. In 2004 she played for Victoria Provincial in the national championships, where she hit .667.

Studnicka (Brazauskas, Caden), Mary Lou "ML"

(b. 19 July 1931, Oaklawn, Illinois) P 1951–54, Racine Belles, Grand Rapids Chicks

Mary Lou Studnicka pitched for three seasons in Grand Rapids. In 1951, her rookie season, Studnicka finished the season with a record of 15–5, including four shutouts. Overall, she compiled a record of 38–30 in 78 games with an ERA of 2.49. After baseball she went to work in a bank in Chicago. In 1962 she became the fingerprint specialist for the police department. She got married in 1956 and raised three daughters. She also continued to play golf and softball and bowled to stay active. {AAGPBL Newsletter, September 2000, 14, and May 2005, 24.}

Stuhr (Thompson), Beverly

(b. 5 May 1932, Rock Island, Illinois) P/OF, Peoria Red Wings

Peoria's manager, Leo Schrall, signed Beverly Stuhr at the age of 16 to play for his club. Her strong throwing arm impressed him and he wanted her as either an outfielder or pitcher for Peoria. She only played one season because of injuries. She played in 27 games and hit .146. {AAGPBL Newsletter, September 1994, 23.}

Sudak, Megan

IF, Falcons, Outlaws, North Shore Lady Spirit

Megan Sudak played for the Falcons and the Outlaws in 2003–04 and received the Owners Award for Dedication, Spirit and Hard Work in 2004. Late in November 2004 she traveled to the Dominican Republic with the Lady Spirit on a goodwill tour. In addition to roaming the outfield for their four wins, Sudak also got the chance to visit an elementary school and give away supplies to the children. She videotaped the experience to share with her own students at Beverly High School, where she teaches when she is not playing baseball. {Jean DePlacido, "Lady Spirit a Big Hit in Dominican Republic," *The Salem News*, 18 November 2004.}

Sun Sox

An all-women team that applied for admission to the Class A Florida State League in 1984. The idea was the brainchild of Bob Hope, former VP for the Atlanta Braves. The financial backing was to be provided by Major Snow, Hope's brother-in-law. Snow was a real estate developer in Florida. The team's first tryouts were held at Georgia Tech under the scrutiny of Tech's baseball coach, Jim Morris. Among the players trying out were pitcher/catcher Kim Hawkins, a truck driver from

Megan Sudak playing first base for the Falcons (courtesy Laura Wulf).

Kennesaw, Georgia; Victoria O'Connell, from Norwich, Connecticut; Rosie Grubbs, from Chulafinnee, Alabama; Deb Akers, from Birmingham, Alabama; and Delores Owen, a biology teacher from Morrow, Georgia. {*Daily Star*, 18 September 1984; Furman Bisher, "Girls of Summer," n.p., 1 October 1984.}

Sunny, Stacy

(b. 13 December 1965, San Bernadino, California) 3B/C 1994–96, Colorado Silver Bullets

Stacey Sunny grew up playing baseball with her older brother and his friends in the local sandlots around San Bernadino, California. She remembers striking out 18 in six innings in one Little League game. She played softball in high school, since that was all that was available to her, and then went on to be a member of the NCAA championship squad at UCLA, after also playing at Nebraska. Later she was recognized as a member of the 1980s All-Decade Division I team. She joined the Silver Bullets as a catcher in 1994 and then moved to third base. She was moved around to keep her bat in the lineup. In the first game of their inaugural season Sunny got one of only two hits for the club, a single off relief pitcher Mark Futrell. She also knocked in three runs in their first victory in St. Paul, Minnesota. The Bullets defeated the Richfield Rockets 7–2 behind the hitting of Sunny and the pitching of Lee Anne Ketcham. She led the Bullets in games played in their first season with 43, and then in their second year she led the club in hitting at .246, with only 14 strikeouts in 130 plate appearances. When she is not playing baseball she works as a television and film producer for shows such as *Rescue 911*. {Bill Koenig, "Ouch!!! Silver Bullets Blasted, but Feel Worst Is Over," *USA Today Baseball Weekly*, 11–17 May 1994, 8; Valerie Lister, "Baseball Pro Says Push the Door Open, Have Fun," *USA Today*, 4 June 1996; Irv Moss, "Business, Not Novelty, for Bullets," *The Denver Post*, 3 July 1996, C-02; Bill Parillo, "The 4–15 Silver Bullets Are Winning Fans Over," *Tribune News Service*, 2 July 1995.}

Superkaos

This club began the 2003 season as the Superstars I but merged with Kaos to create Superkaos. Unfortunately the merger did not help the club, as they had to forfeit five of their games for lack of players. Their final record stood at 2–4 as part of the Sydney Women's Baseball League. Their 2004 season was a bit rocky as they started the year with 15 players, dropped to seven and ended with exactly nine. {League Annual Report 2003, 10, 17; Annual Report 2004, 7–8.}

Superstars II

The club had a tough 2003 season with only five or six consistent players for the year. They ended the season with a record of 3–8 with one draw as part of the Sydney Women's Baseball League. {League Annual Report 2003, 11, 17.}

Surkowski (Delmonico), Lee

(Moose Jaw, Saskatchewan) 1944–46, 1948, South Bend Blue Sox, Rockford Peaches

Lee Surkowski played softball for the Moosejaw Royals and heard about this new league, the AAGPBL, in the United States. She received a contract in the mail and went because the pay was $55 a week and she got to travel. She and her sister Anne both played for South Bend.

Surkowski (Deyotte), Anne

(b. 22 July 1923, Moose Jaw, Saskatchewan) OF 1945, South Bend Blue Sox, Rockford Peaches, Fort Wayne Daisies

Anne Surkowski remembers one of the highlights of her year in the AAGPBL as playing at various army camps. She played with her sister Lee on the South Bend squad and gained a reputation as a fearless ball player. One time she made a shoestring catch after a double somersault and still tagged out the runner. She only played in 21 games and hit a dismal .103. In 1991 she was inducted into the Saskatchewan Provincial Hall of Fame and in 1998 into the Canadian Baseball Hall of Fame. {AAGPBL Newsletter, May 2002, 22; AAGPBL Baseball Cards, 1995–96.}

Sutherland, Shirley

(b. Rockford, Illinois) C 1950, Chicago Colleens, Battle Creek Belles

Shirley Sutherland developed a reputation in the AAGPBL as a tough competitor. Her size made her the smallest catcher in the league, but she had one of the strongest arms and regularly threw out base stealers. In addition to being a fan favorite on the diamond, Sutherland played clarinet and often found a local jam session she could join while the team was traveling. {Ohio Baseball Hall of Fame Files, AAGPBL 1950.}

Swanagon, Mary Lou "Swannie"

Grand Rapids Chicks

Mary Lou Swanagon played for a short while with the Chicks in Grand Rapids.

Sydney Women's Baseball League

The league began in 2002 and by 2004 consisted of the Phantoms, the Stealers, the Stingers, the Players, the Black Hawks, the Devils, and the Kaos. Their season lasted from May through September and was capably directed by league president Janna Richert. Natalie Espinosa acted as the league secretary and kept track of all the fundraising events held by the league to keep from raising registration fees from the 2003 rate. The Stealers won the league title with the Phantoms coming in second. The Stealers had also won the 2003 championship. The MVP for the league was Alison Neasbey, while Ellen Young was named Rookie of the Year. Katherine Franklin received the distinction of being named the most improved player.

Takashima, Tomomi

C Japan

Tomomi Takashima caught for Japan at the 2004 Women's World Cup. She hit only .111 and committed one error in the field.

Tait, Michelle

Team Ontario

Michelle Tait plays for Team Ontario and is assistant coach for the 2004 elite girls' Peewee baseball team. {Allen Pulga, "Talented Elite Girls' Baseball Team a Shock to the Boys," *Hamilton Spectator*, 14 August 2004, SP08.}

Taiwan

Taiwan participated in the first women's World Cup event in the fall of 2004. The team came to Canada under the leadership of Tsai Huang-liang. Many of the players on the team played for the Shuishalien women's team before joining this national squad. They were scheduled to play Australia in their first game and then Bulgaria, but Bulgaria dropped out for financial reasons. {Deborah Kuo, "Taiwan to Compete in First World Cup," *Central News Agency* (Taiwan), 27 and 28 July 2004.}

Tamburrino, Alisa

(b. 7 January 1979) P, Doncaster Dragons, Victoria; 2004 Australian National Team

Alisa Tamburrino plays in the summer and winter leagues in Australia. Her fiancé, Dominick Ruggiero, works as the head coach for the Victoria club. {Sarah Benic, "Batter Still Swings Behind Scenes," *Moonee Valley Leader*, 16 February 2004.}

Tamura, Chika

C, Japan

Chika Tamura played in the 2003 Women's World Series. In the first game of the series she had two hits to lead her team. In game four Tamura stayed in the lineup as the designated hitter. She had two hits in two at-bats and drove in two runs while scoring another. Her hitting was not enough to bring a victory for Japan, as they lost to Australia 10–9. Tamura hit .474 for the series, with 9 hits in 19 at-bats. She also knocked in five runs and stole three bases. {Australian Baseball Federation, <www.baseball.org.au>.}

Tan, Cecilia

(b. 8 April 1967, New York City, New York)

While attending school in New York City, Cecilia Tan participated in both cross-country and track and field events. She became a ski instructor and started entering Tae Kwon Do tournaments in college. She moved on to become an instructor of Tae Kwon Do in 1998. In 2001 Tan broadened her sporting participation to include some playing with different NEWBL teams, though she was never officially on a roster. The first game she played in came on 15 July 2001 for the Boston Blitz. Tan filled in as their right fielder since the club was short a player. During the 2003 season Tan took part in the adult division of the Pawtucket Slaterettes program. She played left field for the Narragansett Electric club. Tan said that one of her favorite baseball memories was taking part in the 24 Hours for Africa baseball marathon in Arizona and watching the sun rise over the desert. When not playing baseball, Tan works as a freelance writer and editor. {Cecelia Tan, correspondence with Leslie A. Heaphy, North Canton, Ohio, February 2004.}

Tanaka, Midori

P/1B, Japan

Midori Tanaka pitched seven innings for Japan in the 2004 women's World Cup event. She gave up three earned runs but was not credited with a win or loss. Tanaka also played first base when she did not pitch and hit .400 for Japan. Fielding flawlessly, she even turned two double plays.

Tanaka, Sachika

P, Japan

Sachika Tanaka pitched in two games for Japan during the 2004 women's World Cup. She ended with a 1–1 record after giving up six earned runs in nine innings in one game but allowing none in seven innings against Canada. At the plate Tanaka is a solid hitter with good speed, stealing three bases for the club. {Collin Gallant, "Women Begin Playoffs Today," *Edmonton Journal*, 7 August 2004, D3.}

Taylor, Mrs. C.I.

By Bijan Bayne

In late February of 1922, after braving frigid Chicago weather during league meetings, C.I. Taylor of the Indianapolis ABCs lay dying. The Clark College-educated player-manager had pinch-hit for the team as recently as 1921. According to his brother Ben Taylor, C.I.'s dying wish was to have his wife Olivia control 75 percent of the team, and Ben 25 percent. C.I. died of pneumonia on 23 February 1922. He was 47.

Olivia Taylor was a Birmingham native and former schoolteacher. The widow ran the business affairs of the ABCs while Ben controlled baseball operations. Led by players such as Biz Mackey, Crush Holloway and the great Oscar Charleston, their 46–33 record in 1922–23 was their best ever. Olivia and her brother-in-law fell into dispute over control of the ball club. Ben felt cheated out of his share. Much of the inside story is murky. Marion County probate records do support Olivia's claims. (Silent partner Ryland Pyatt, a printer, owned 50 percent of C.I. Taylor's Indiana Ave. billiard hall and the ABCs.)

After a 1922 ball game, Ben Taylor complained about Olivia's 20-percent cut of the ABCs' take. He felt he and the players deserved more. He organized a Ben Taylor all-star team for a late fall game in Muncie. When the team arrived, Mrs. Taylor was there with an attorney, intent on preventing the game. Promoters had billed the all-stars as ABCs. Mrs. Taylor declared that unless she receive a share of the gate, the game should be canceled. She was overruled by a legal decision made in Muncie, and the game was played. {*Chicago Defender*, 16 December 1922.}

Two black civic groups supported Mrs. Taylor's participation in the 1923 league meetings with letters of endorsement. The groups were the Indianapolis Negro Business League and the Better Indianapolis League, and both letters were written by men. Taylor's dispute with her brother-in-law appears to have been based more upon law than gender. At the meetings, she discussed league issues with Eastern magnates such as Nat Strong, Cum Posey, and Ed Bolden.

Taylor did experience player defection. The Eastern Colored League's Washington Potomacs (managed by Ben Taylor) drew several ABCs as players in 1924. Oscar Charleston went to play in Cuba, but such winter league jumping was not uncommon during the era (powerful male owner Gus Greenlee lost some star Pittsburgh Crawfords to the Dominican Trujillo team 13 years later). In January of 1924, Taylor played down the defections. She said "Indianapolis fans will not cry over their actions." {Paul Debono, *The Indianapolis ABC's* (Jefferson, N.C.: McFarland, 1997), 99.}

From Cuba, Charleston went to the Harrisburg Giants. Apparently Dizzy Dismukes, a Birmingham native as Olivia was, chose to move to Pittsburgh. He suggested she move the club there and merge it with the Black Barons. She did not, and pressed Dismukes to return, which he did. (Dismukes eventually left to manage his hometown Barons.)

Taylor also protested a league decision to drop the ABCs and replace them with the Memphis Red Sox. Negro National League president Rube Foster cited her lack of funds, a $1,556.56 debt, a debt to Foster of more than $620, and unpaid hotel bills in Chicago.

Olivia Taylor's two-and-a-half-year ownership of the ABCs drew to a close. Fifteen years prior to Effa Manley's administration of the Newark Eagles, Taylor had faced opposing owners, litigation, defection, and quarrels with in-laws in her guidance of a largely successful ball club. She donated bats, balls and gloves to an Idaho state prison in the name of what she called "a great game, a clean game." She wrote a story about the team, "The 1–2–3's of the ABC's," which would be a wonderful resource if the self-published text could be found. Taylor was later elected Indianapolis NAACP president. She attended the 1927 national convention in Indianapolis, which was also attended by Clarence Darrow and Dr. W.E.B. Du Bois.

Taylor, Eunice "Tuffy"

(b. 12 February 1934, Kenosha, Wisconsin) C 1950–51, Chicago Colleens, Kenosha Comets

Eunice Taylor toured with the Colleens for one season in 1950 and then played one season in her home town with the Comets. Taylor caught 85 games and hit .182 while playing all over the country. {AAGPBL Baseball Cards, 1995.}

Taylor, Mary

OF/1B 1953–54, Kalamazoo Lassies

Mary Taylor hit .251 during her career in the All American League with the Lassies.

Taylor, Norma

(b. 30 March 1931, Huntington, Indiana) 1B 1950, Fort Wayne Daisies

Norma Taylor joined the Daisies when she was only 19. She played in only a few games but enjoyed the opportunity to travel and see some of the United States. {AAGPBL Baseball Cards, 1996.}

Taylor, Robynne

(b. 12 February 1983) P 2003, New South Wales

Robynne Taylor played for the Rams in the Australian National Championship series.

Team Energen

Japan

In 1999 Team Energen played in a tournament in Ft. Lauderdale and finished with a 2–2 record. Their manager, Masanori Murakami, used to play for the San Francisco Giants. Team Energen has continued to play in a variety of national and international venues since then. They have sent players from their team to play in special events such as the 24-hour benefit game in Arizona in 2004.

Japanese pitcher for Team Energen (courtesy Jim Glennie).

Japanese catcher for Team Energen (courtesy Jim Glennie).

Team Ontario

Team Ontario provides a number of divisions of women's baseball play in conjunction with the Central Ontario Girls Baseball League. Prior to 2004 the two levels were Bantam and Women's but in 2004 they added Peewee Girls. All these leagues are under the leadership of COGBL president Patrick McCauley. Team Ontario sponsors tournaments at all levels of play as well. {<www.cogbl.com>.}

Teillet (Schick), Yolande "Yo Yo"

(b. 28 September 1927, St. Vital, Manitoba, Canada) C/OF 1945–47, Fort Wayne Daisies, Grand Rapids Chicks, Kenosha Comets

Yolande Teillet caught for three years for the St. Vital Tigerettes before coming south to play in the All American League. She did not play regularly and eventually decided to give it up and return home. {AAGPBL Baseball Cards, 1995.}

Team Energen after winning in 2002 (photographer Phil Dimarzio, courtesy Jim Glennie).

Telling, Melanie

P, New South Wales

Melanie Telling started out playing tee ball and then softball. While catching for her school's team, coach Shaun Smith saw her play and recruited her for a women's baseball team he was putting together. He wanted her to pitch. Since she began playing baseball in 2003 Telling has participated in two national championship tournaments and hopes to eventually make the national team. {"Competition for a Ball Player," *Canterbury Express*, 31 May 2005.}

Tempesta, Elizabeth

Elizabeth Tempesta took part in the New England Women's Baseball League from 1999 to 2001.

Terry, Doris

P, Racine Belles

Doris Terry grew up playing baseball for a variety of amateur and semipro baseball teams in the Midwest. In 1946 she got a call from a friend, Anna May Hutchison, urging her to try out for the Racine Belles, who needed a replacement pitcher. She joined the team for only six weeks before listening to her mother and returning home to take the college scholarship she had been offered in golf at Western Kentucky State College.

She went on for a master's degree and then took up teaching at the high school and college level before working for the Maryland State Department of Education. {Susan Levine, "Still Throwing the Heat," *Washington Post*, 3 June 2004, T03.}

Tetzlaff, Doris

(b. 1 January 1921, Watertown, Wisconsin) OF/ IF/Coach/Chaperone 1944–49, 1950–53, Milwaukee Chicks, Grand Rapids Chicks, Chicago Colleens, Fort Wayne Daisies, Muskegon Lassies

Doris Tetzlaff was not known for her hitting while in the AAGPBL. For example, in 112 games in 1946 she hit under .200, finishing the season at .199, though she walked 74 times while only striking out 46 times. Over the course of her career she hit only .190 in 625 games with 161 RBIs. {AAGPBL Baseball Cards, 1995.}

Tezak (Papesh), Virginia Mae "Ginny"

(b. 22 May 1928, Joliet, Illinois) Util. 1948, Racine Belles

Growing up in Joliet, Virginia Tezak participated in sports with Catholic Youth Organization and at Joliet Township High School. While in school she earned letters in volleyball, tennis, softball and basketball. In CYO competition Tezak took part in softball and basketball. She also worked as a swimming instructor at the local YMCA. She joined the Racine Belles in 1948 but only saw playing time in four games so she did not return in 1949. Her favorite part of playing in the AAGPBL was the opportunity to travel to the different cities that had teams as well as to Florida for spring training exhibitions. After leaving the league Tezak played softball in Denver, Colorado, for four years and worked as a physical education instructor at the local parochial school. She married in 1953 and had four children. Today she is included in the exhibit at the National Baseball Hall of Fame in Cooperstown. {AAGPBL Questionnaire, National Baseball Hall of Fame; AAGPBL Baseball Cards, 1996.}

Thibeault, Karen

Slaterettes

Karen Thibeault played for the Slaterettes while her father, Joseph, served as league president. Her mother, Diane, took over the job when Karen's father died in 1994. {"Joseph L. Thibeault Jr.," *Providence Journal*, 1 March 1994, C-08.}

Thomas, Amy "Deuce"

C 1999–2000, Chicago Storm

Amy Thomas gained a reputation as a durable catcher for the Storm when she caught 209 of the 218 innings the club played. Amy hit .417 in 2000 for the Storm while also serving as the team captain. {<www.baseballglory.com>; Chicago Storm Web site.}

Thomas (Gera), Bernice "Bernie"

(b. 15 June 1931, Ernest, Pennsylvania; d. 1992)

While growing up in Ernest, Pennsylvania, Bernice Thomas lived with her parents and four siblings until the age of two. Her parents divorced and left their children to the care of relatives. All five children were split up. Bernice attended four different high schools in three different states. She always loved sports. She found out at an early age, however, that the boys did not want her playing on their teams because of her gender. At times the girls did not want to play with her either, because she played too hard. In one high school game her coach took her out because her pitches injured two catchers and she hit a line drive that hit the opposing pitcher in the face. She generally played the outfield and hit cleanup.

Thomas became known to the baseball world in the early 1960s because of her prowess in hitting a baseball for a distance. She regularly participated in home run derbies that pitted her against the likes of Roger Maris, Sid Gordon and Luis Arroyo. Many of her contests were fundraisers for children's charities and for research into hepatitis, a disease she suffered from in 1960. She also played baseball for a number of years with the Highland Parkers, an all-girl baseball team from Detroit, Michigan. She pitched and played the outfield for them. In 1967 she used her pitching skills to win 300 dolls at an amusement park. She donated the toys to the kids living at the Children's Shelter of the Queensboro Society for the Prevention of Cruelty to Children. She also helped coach the Elmjack Little Leaguers. She married Steve Gera in 1962. Steve worked as a freelance photographer, and did not have much interest in baseball until he married Bernice.

Gera gave up her job as a secretary to follow her dream of umpiring professionally. Gera became the first woman to complete the Florida Baseball Umpire School in 1967 under the direction of Jim Finley. Finley had no problem with her attending his school and was impressed with her abilities, especially when she got a perfect score on the midterm examination, the first such in the school's history. Not everyone thought this was a good thing. For example, the *New York Daily News* ran a column on 1 July 1967 asking people what they thought of a female umpire. While most responders seemed willing to accept the idea, one reader thought it a terrible idea because the diamond was no place for a woman. She would not be able to handle the language or the harassment. While she attended the school for the six weeks of training, an exhibition hitting contest was set up against Bob Feller on 27 June 1967. Three players were chosen to bat against Feller, and one of them was Bernie. She hit a couple of shots into the outfield off Feller.

Some of her early umpiring jobs included the National Baseball Congress Tournament in Wichita, Kansas, in 1967 and the Semi-pro Invitational Tournament in Bridgeton, New Jersey, in 1968. In 1969 she umpired for the YMCA Industrial League of New York City and for the Bluecoats of the New York City Police Department. From1968 to 1971 she could be found umpiring for CYO leagues such as the one in Queens.

Gera tried unsuccessfully to get a job in organized baseball. When she received no offers she decided to sue before the New York State Human Rights Commission in Manhattan under Title VIII of the Civil Rights Act. She sued on the grounds that she did not get a chance to umpire in organized baseball because of her gender. Her lawyer, Mario Biaggi, listed Commissioner Bowie Kuhn in the suit along with the National Association of Professional Baseball Leagues and the New York–Pennsylvania Professional Baseball League. Her initial request was denied on the grounds that she had not applied for jobs with the two major leagues. She did apply to the New York league and received a letter in 1968 from the president, Vincent McNamara, stating that hiring anyone other than a man would cause too many problems. On appeal she got the right to be offered a contract and received one in July 1969 from the New York league. It requested she report for duty on August 1 at a salary of $200 a month, $300 for expenses and five cents a mile for travel. On 31 July 1969 the president of the National Association, Phil Piton, rescinded Gera's contract but gave no reason for doing so. New York representative Samuel Stratton told the House of Representatives that a full investigation into the cancellation of Gera's contract should be initiated since Piton's action showed a clear violation of the Civil Rights Act. Organized baseball's justification for rescinding her contract rested on the claim she did not meet the height and weight requirements for an umpire. After another court battle before the New York State Supreme Court, where she asked for $25 million, Gera won. The final decision came down as a split vote 5–2, with the two dissenting judges being John F. Scileppi and James Gibson. On 23 June 1972 Gera signed a contract, umpired one game in the New York-Penn Class A League, and resigned.

After getting her contract Gera was assigned to umpire the bases at a game in Geneva, New York, at Shuron Park. The two teams playing that night were the Auburn Phillies and the Geneva Rangers. Gera had three contested calls in the game, one of which resulted in her throwing out Nolan Campbell, manager of the Auburn club, during the fourth inning. After the first game she decided to call it quits and left before the second game of the doubleheader. She did not immediately disappear from umpiring since she turned up at a charity event in July 1972 at Grossinger's Resort in New York.

From 1974 to 1979 she worked in community relations and promotions for the New York Mets. She worked as a group sales representative and took over the Lady Mets Club for female fans. She also traveled as a speaker, usually appearing at events for young people.

Among the many honors Gera received, one of the earliest came in 1968, when she received a citation from the Sports Lodge B'nai B'rith for her work in sandlot and Little League baseball. Peri-

odically Gera got the opportunity to write guest columns for different papers on her views about baseball. For example, in 1967 she wrote a column on the World Series for the *Long Island Post*. Her fame led to requests from various television shows for guest appearances such as the one she made on *Hotline after Dark* on Channel 11 in Indiana in 1969. On 15 October 1969 she made an appearance on the *Phil Donahue Show* to discuss her fight with organized baseball. She was inducted into the Indiana County Hall of Fame in 1988. A historical marker was also placed at Blue Spruce Park in Indiana, Pennsylvania, honoring her achievements. Gera died in 1992 of cancer after a long battle with the disease. It had been first discovered in 1985 while she worked for the Broward County Parks Department.{Bernice Gera Collection, Indiana University of Pennsylvania; Bridgeton Hall of Fame All Sports Museum, Bridgeton, New Jersey.}

Thomas, Mava Lee "Tommy"

(b. 1 September 1929, Ocala, Florida) 3B/C 1951, Fort Wayne Daisies

Mava Thomas grew up in a baseball home. Her father, Herb, played for the Boston Braves and New York Giants during the 1920s. Mava only played in a few games in 1951, giving the Daisies an extra glove and a switch-hitter at the plate. {AAGPBL Baseball Cards, 1995.}

Thomas, Stephanie

OF 1999, San Diego Storm

In 1999 Thomas played in the national championship series. She was also named to the all-tournament team. She batted .381 with six runs scored and three stolen bases.

Thompson, Annabelle "Annie"

(Edmonton, Canada; d. 1982) P 1943, Racine Belles

Annie Thompson played for a short time in the All American League during its inaugural season, with the team from Racine.

Thompson, Barbara

(b. 24 February 1934, Rockford, Illinois) 1B 1951–52, Rockford Peaches

Barbara Thompson grew up in Rockford and heard about the Peaches while in school. Her father encouraged her to try out for the ball club, which she did before the 1951 season. She spent two years playing first base for the Peaches before going back to school to become a nurse at Rockford Memorial Hospital. She only hit .204 in 18 games. She had an advantage at first since she was a lefty and she only made one error. {Diana Redmond, "Preserving the Peaches," *The Rockford Register Star,* 8 September 1993, D1; AAGPBL Baseball Cards, 1995.}

Thompson (Griffin), Viola "Tommy"

(b. 2 January 1922, Greenville, South Carolina) P 1944–47, Milwaukee Chicks, Grand Rapids Chicks, South Bend Blue Sox

Viola Thompson began playing softball when she was in the fourth grade. She stayed with the sport through her high school years at Anderson Girls High School. After graduation she pitched for a number of teams in the Greenville Textile League, and that is how she got her chance to pitch in the AAGPBL. She played for the Milwaukee Chicks in 1944 when they won the league championship. She pitched in 98 games with a 41–48 record and a 2.59 ERA. Her manager, Max Carey, was most impressed with her pickoff move to first base. In recognition of her accomplishments Griffin was inducted into the South Carolina Athletic Hall of Fame in 1997. {Ernie Trubiano, "Griffin, S.C. Hall of Fame Inductee, Remembers Women's Baseball," *The Columbia State,* 28 April 1997; AAGPBL Baseball Cards, 1995.}

Thorburn, Peggy Alonzo

Umpire

Peggy Thorburn loved baseball and tried out for her high school team in Cypress, California, but did not make the roster. In 1974 she became the manager of the varsity team at John F. Kennedy High School in La Palma, California, and in 1975 went back to Cypress to manage their varsity squad. In 1976 when a local ad went out calling for boys 16 and over to umpire, she enrolled in Bill Kinnamon's Specialized Umpire's School and became an umpire. She joined the air force in 1978 and married Ed Thorburn. When they were transferred to Germany in late 1978, Peggy found the Germans playing baseball and so she continued umpiring high school baseball games. {Women-Umpires File, National Baseball Hall of Fame and Museum.}

Tilford, Rachel

(Birch Hills, Saskatchewan) P/Util., Team Saskatchewan, Team Canada

Rachel Tilford played for Saskatchewan's Bantam team and in 2002 won the Bantam MVP Award at the Western Canadian Championship. At 17 she played for Team Canada in the 2003 AAU National Championships.

Timm, Marie

(Appleton, Wisconsin) Chaperone, 1943–45, Rockford Peaches

Marie Timm traveled with the Rockford Peaches as their chaperone during the first three years of the team's existence. When not on the road Timm worked as the physical education teacher at Nathan Hale High School in West Allis, Wisconsin. Her hobbies were golfing and reading. {1945 Rockford Peaches Program Guide.}

Tipton, Gloria

Gloria Tipton arrived in spring training in 1946 after having served in the WACs during World War II. {"200 Girls Leave on Tuesday for Spring Training," *Chicago Tribune,* 21 April 1946.}

Titus, Kate

(b. 1970, Springfield, Ohio) C, Boston Blitz

Kate Titus joined Team USA with over 12 years of baseball experience behind her. She played for the Boston Blue Sox tournament team, traveling to various places for games. In 1999 she joined the Boston Blitz in the New England league and was named league MVP. While at Muskingum College she earned academic all–American honors in 1989–1990 playing softball.

Tobias, Carol

Carol Tobias was one of the few girls who tried to play Little League before the 1970s and the changes that came out due to Title IX. She played in Rock Hill, South Carolina, on a team with her brother Neal.

Toomey, Trisha

IF, Virginia Flames

Trisha Toomey played for the Flames in the Eastern Women's Baseball Conference.

Topolie, Stephanie

(b. 18 May 1977, Mississauga, Ontario) OF, Team Canada

Stephanie Topolie graduated from Glodey-Beacom College in Delaware, where she played softball and volleyball. She received academic all–American honors in 2000 and all-conference, all-region honors in volleyball that same year. At the conclusion of the 2001 softball season Topolie earned first team all-star and all-tournament honors. In 2001 she brought her experience and skills to Team Canada, playing in the first Women's World Series in Toronto. In 2004 she played for the women's World Cup in Edmonton, Alberta. In the first game of the 2001 series, Topolie showed why she had been chosen team captain, when she had two base hits and scored three runs in Canada's opening win over Australia 8–2. {Baseball Canada 2004 Women's National Team Media Guide.}

Torres, Juanita

Umpire

Juanita Torres was the first woman to work as an umpire in the Central League Federation in Puerto Rico. This league represented the top amateur level of baseball in the country.

Towles, Caroline

(Washington) SS

Caroline Towles started playing baseball in 2002 at the age of ten as the starting shortstop for her Little League team. In 2004 she moved up to the North Seattle Pony League. She liked baseball because it was a faster game than softball. {Stephen Towles, "Girls Have Dreams of Baseball Too," *Seattle-Post Intelligencer*, 16 August 2004, B5.}

Tracy Bloomer Girls

This local team from Lorain, Ohio, traveled with another ladies' team called the Belden Bloomer Girls, defeating them regularly. {"Bloomer Girls at the Fair," *The Chronicle-Telegram* (Elyria, Ohio), 29 August 1924, 12.}

Trahan, Tina

(b. 13 January 1970, Pawtucket, Rhode Island) 1B/3B, Pawtuckett Slaterettes

Tina Trahan had the opportunity to play baseball while growing up in Rhode Island because of the Slaterettes. She started playing in 1977 and has never stopped. In high school she played softball and tennis but continued to play baseball on the Slaterettes Alumni team from 1988 to 1997. In October 2003 Trahan joined many other women in Arizona for the 24-hour marathon game. Trahan calls this one of the highlights of her career because there were so many women there and the level of play was so high. When she is not playing baseball, Trahan works as an administrative assistant at Brown University. {Tina Trahan, correspondence with Leslie A. Heaphy, North Canton, Ohio, March 2004}.

Travis (Visich), Jean "Dolph," "Rookie"

(b. 18 October 1926, Mt. Vernon, New York) 1B/OF 1948, Rockford Peaches

As a youngster growing up in Mt. Vernon, Jean Travis found many opportunities to play different sports. She attended Nathan Hale Elementary and then Washington Junior High before finding her place at A.B. Davis High School. It was in high school that Travis played volleyball, basketball and softball, earning city and county honors. She also got the chance to practice with the boys' baseball team. In addition Travis played basketball for the girls' city league and softball on a men's industrial league team. Prior to signing a contract in the AAGPBL she attended Katherine Gibbs Secretarial School and went to work as a secretary with a number of local companies until 1947. As a player she was willing to do whatever was asked of her, whether that was warming up pitchers or gathering equipment. She even taught herself to throw left-handed so she could play first base. Her favorite memory was her only home run, which she hit as a pinch hitter against the Racine Belles. She tied the game in the eighth inning. After playing in only one season, Travis did not return, because her brother was killed in an accident in September 1948. She married in 1951 and had six children. In 1993 the March of Dimes honored her as their Female Athlete of the Year. {AAGPBL Questionnaire, National Baseball Hall of Fame; AAGPBL Newsletter, May 1996, 5, and January 1997, 20.}

Tremblay, Marie-Josee

(St. Honore-de-Chicoutimi) P/3B/C, Team Quebec

Marie-Josee Tremblay started playing baseball on boys' teams and has continued to do so, even though she has also played for Team Quebec's Bantam team for girls.

Trezza, Betty "Moe"

(b. 4 August 1925, Brooklyn, New York) 2B/SS/OF 1944–50, Minneapolis Millerettes, Fort Wayne Daisies, South Bend Blue Sox, Racine Belles

Betty Trezza played for seven years in the All American League. She had a great arm, speed and solid hitting. In a game against the Kenosha Comets in 1945, Trezza helped her team by going 2–3 at the plate with one walk and two runs scored. Trezza also knocked in one run for her team's victory. Trezza did not excel at the plate but became known for her stellar fielding. She played in 717 games and hit .173. She did steal 363 bases and score 331 runs. {Betty Trezza File, National Baseball Hall of Fame, Cooperstown, New York.}

Trice, Natasha

CF, Blue Crush

Natasha Trice patrols center field for the Blue Crush in the Philadelphia Women's League. Her father comes out regularly to watch her play. {Eileen O'Donnell, "Covering All the Bases," *Philadelphia Inquirer*, 15 July 2005.}

Triolo, Sandy

CF, Montgomery County Barncats

Sandy Triolo started in the outfield for the Barncats in 1993.

Tronnier, Ellen "Cub"

(b. 28 June 1927, Cudahy, Wisconsin) OF 1943, South Bend Blue Sox

Ellen Tronnier joined South Bend in 1943, when she was only 15. She made the team after surviving two tryouts. The first was held locally at Borchert Field. Only 13 ladies were chosen from over 150 to go to Chicago for the real tryout. Tronnier was one of the lucky ones who made it, and was assigned to South Bend. After one season she decided to return to school. She earned a bachelor's degree from the University of Wiscon-

sin, LaCrosse. Upon completion of her degree Tronnier taught physical education in the Milwaukee public schools for 33 years. She kept playing softball for many years, competing in all kinds of tournaments. In 1956 her club won the National Invitational Tournament. During the 1970s she began a baseball school for girls as part of the Milwaukee Recreation Department. She was inducted into the Wisconsin Amateur Softball Association Hall of Fame in 1990. {Milwaukee Brewers Baseball Club Bulletin, 2002; AAGPBL Newsletter, September 2000, 23, and May 2001, 42.}

Tsunakawa, Ayumi

Japan National Team

Ayumi Tsunakawa played in the 2004 Women's World Series and helped Japan defeat the United States 13–4. She scored one of her club's 13 runs on a single by Eriko Nagano. {"Japan Downs United States 13–4 to Take Gold Medal in Women's World Series Baseball," *AP Worldstream*, 22 July 2004.}

Tsushima, Sayaka

CF, Japan

Sayaka Tsushima played center field for Japan in the 1998 Little League World Series. She was the sixth girl to play in a world series competition.

Tu, Fang-Yi P,

Taiwan

Fang-yi Tu pitched for her Taiwanese club in the 2004 women's World Cup. She pitched nine innings in three games and came away with an 0–1 record. Tu gave up 15 hits and eight earned runs in the series.

Tucker, Elizabeth "Betty"

(b. 28 January 1924, Detroit, Michigan) P 1946–49, Peoria Red Wings, Fort Wayne Daisies, Rockford Peaches, Grand Rapids Chicks, Chicago Colleens

Elizabeth Tucker pitched for four seasons with five different teams in the All American League. Her tenure in the league started when pitchers threw underhand. Then she made the switch to overhand, where she actually seemed a stronger pitcher. For example, in 1946 her record was 1–12 with an ERA of 3.38; her first season of overhand pitching resulted in a record of 11–17 with a 2.68 ERA. She pitched in 87 games, compiling a 16–49

record. She also developed into a pretty solid hitter for a pitcher. {"Tucker, Colleens' Hurler, Tops
Girls Baseball Hitters," *Chicago Tribune*, 18 July
1948, B3; AAGPBL Baseball Cards, 1995.}

Tucker, Melody

GM, Everett Giants

Melody Tucker worked as the general manager
in the early 1990s for the Everett Giants in Washington. The Giants are a minor league affiliate of
the San Francisco team.

Turbitt-Baker, Lisa

Umpire

Lisa Turbitt-Baker is a nationally certified female umpire in Canada who has umpired at numerous tournaments including two at the national
level. She is currently in charge of training female
umpires for Ontario. Before moving into umpiring full time, Lisa played softball and baseball for
over 20 years. Lisa also teaches sixth grade and
coaches the boys' senior high volleyball team at her
school. She got her start in umpiring at an early
age, when she tried to attend her first training at age
11 and they sent her home because she was a girl.
She had already been umpiring tee ball games for
a year. On her third visit to the clinic she finally
got to stay because of umpire Dick Willis. She
quickly moved up through the ranks and umpired
all through her college days at Brock and York universities. In 2004 at the women's World Cup she
became the first female to work home plate in an
international competition. As a result of her work
in that tournament and others she was named
Canadian Umpire of the Year for 2004, winning
the Dick Willis award. She was the first female to
ever receive that honor. {WBL Web site; Scott
Radley, "From T-Ball to World Championships,"
Hamilton Spectator, 20 November 2004, SP04.}

Twardzik, Nellie

1B

Nellie Twardzik played first base for her high
school baseball team in Webster, Massachusetts.
Some referred to her as the "Babe Ruth" of Webster. She beat out 25 young men who tried out for
the team in 1935. Her presence on the club increased fan attendance dramatically, but in 1936
her right to play was challenged by the school's
athletic council. {"Girl Baseball Star Stirs School
Wrangle by Her Presence on Bay State Boys'
Team," *New York Times*, 18 March 1936, 31.}

Ueda, Rei

3B/P

In four games during the 2003 Women's World
Series, Rei Ueda hit .364 and drove in two runs.
Ueda also pitched an inning and two-thirds, giv-
ing up one hit and one run.

Uhlir (Damaschke), Dorothy "DD"

(b. 26 August 1917, Racine, Wisconsin; d. 2000)
RF 1945, Racine Belles

Dorothy Damaschke was already married by
the time the AAGPBL came along, and so she
never got a chance to play regularly. She married
Herman Damaschke in 1938 and raised three
boys. Dorothy did get to play baseball and basketball on some local teams in Racine. She also
became city champion in badminton. She played
in only one game for Racine while filling in for a
player taking college classes. {AAGPBL Questionnaire, National Baseball Hall of Fame and Museum; AAGPBL Baseball Cards, 2000.}

Umpires

A Camp of Their Own

By Margaret Hart

With no runners on base, there is a ground ball
to the shortstop. The base umpire sets up for the
play at first and watches the ball. The ball is
thrown to first. Bang-bang ... Out! The batter-
runner leaves the field, but now the coach comes
out of the dugout yelling at the ump, "What do
you mean he's out? He was safe!" The coach is 6'4"
and 230 pounds, and the ump checks in at 5'1"
and 110 pounds. This is not a kid, but a mature,
seasoned umpire. The coach places his arm on
the ump's shoulder and a hush falls over the spectators. Everyone knows what's coming next. The
coach is advised that that is contact and is ejected,
but continues to argue the judgment call. Things
escalate. Now a second coach decides to get in on
the action, but before he has time to get there, the
plate umpire has moved in, cuts him off at the
pass and sends him back to the dugout. The base
umpire's successful ejection of the first coach
draws a cheer. Excuse me? The umpire's actions
are being supported, even applauded? You bet
they are! Twenty-one female umpires are con-
gratulating their two fellow female umpires for
their quick, decisive actions taken in just one of
many scenarios and drills enacted during a
weekend-long clinic for female baseball umpires.

In August 1996, at the Ontario Summer Games
in London, Ontario, Don Gilbert, Baseball

Canada's supervisor of umpires for Ontario and Canada, was observing Bantam games in which all participants were female, including the umpires. The players expressed a healthy respect for the umpires and the rapport was good. "I am not so sure that men accept a woman umpiring their games as easily as women are prepared to accept them," he said. "That will certainly change in the future but we're not there yet. During that tournament, there was a sense of acceptance on the part of the players and umpires that if a problem were to arise, there would not be any fear of things being said that didn't pertain to baseball."

That sparked an idea — an all-female umpires' clinic. Gilbert soon had a committee assembled to conduct the clinic, which was held in London, Ontario, in November 1997. Gilbert got things in motion by having Ray Merkley, a Baseball Canada master course conductor, and Ed Quinlan, a graduate of the now defunct Joe Brinkman Umpiring School, send out brochures to all registered umpires with names that appeared to be female. "We have no statistics currently on hand to identify female members," Merkley admitted. "We may very well have sent out invitations to men. Then again we may have missed some women as well."

"Quite frankly," said Gilbert, "I often refer to this clinic as hosting a party and not knowing if anyone was going to show up. Our goal was simple: Create a comfort zone for female officials. We felt that if we could do that, then not only would it be a better teaching atmosphere, but an easier learning milieu as well. The women proved that theory correct. It seemed they never wanted to stop hearing more umpiring information. In all my years of instructing, this was the most successful clinic."

Why hold a clinic specifically for females? More importantly, why attend an all-female clinic? Carol Giffen, a six-year Bantam and Midget umpire from Creemore, Ontario, said, "When I found out about the clinic, I was excited. I wanted to attend not only to help enhance my skills and knowledge, but I was delighted to be given an opportunity to meet others who have the same spirit and determination to go ahead and venture into what is considered a male occupation."

Those sentiments were echoed by many of the women. Lisa Turbitt was one of the clinicians. "When Don [Gilbert] asked me to be a clinician, I was excited," she said. "The other clinicians were experienced and knowledgeable umpires. I was a little concerned that my resume was not as extensive as theirs, but the clinic was an excellent experience for me as an umpire, not just as a clinician. I got a chance to network with other female umpires and that gave me the opportunity to talk about situations in which I often felt isolated."

Many of the participants were the lone females in their respective associations and found it difficult to talk with men in their associations who had never experienced sexist remarks or the perception that they need to be protected or shielded by their partners when things got hot on the diamond.

Dana Williams, an eight-year umpire from Kitchen, Ontario, was skeptical. "I didn't particularly like the idea of an exclusive all-women's clinic," she said. "I came to ensure that we were not treated 'special.' I wanted to see for myself that Lisa [Turbitt] had earned her position and was not just a token female clinician." Nikki Ross, a 47-year-old baseball and softball umpire, echoed Williams. She said she was expecting a "pink" clinic geared to ladies, not umpires. "I was afraid it would be a very toned down and sweet version of the regular clinics," she said.

Betty Opersko's officiating career spans more than 50 years and encompasses volleyball, basketball, broomball and 34 years of baseball at several levels. She has seen many "political chicks," as she calls them, and wanted to make sure the clinic didn't become a political forum for the sexes. "I was amazed," she said. "We were all treated like human beings, real people, and we belonged."

That sense of belonging is something many female umpires don't always feel. Both the clinicians and umpires recognized that female umpires experience additional situations on the field because they are female that their male counterparts do not face. The female umpires had experienced such things as sexism, blatant lack of respect for their authority due to their gender, attitudes from players' coaches and even their own partners that they could not be as good as male umpires, and the perception that they are treated as special — advancing in umpiring only due to their sex and not their ability. The clinic stressed recognizing those situations, dealing with them and striving to bring about positive change. But using them as an excuse for limited performance or lack of advancement within the profession was unequivocally condemned.

With one exception, all participants were from the Southern Ontario region. With the encouragement and support of her parents and the Nova Scotia Umpires Division, 18-year-old Shanon Archibald came all the way from Antigonish, Nova Scotia, roughly 300 miles away. She is one of only two certified umpires in her association; the other is a male. Since she represented 50 percent of her association, she thought it was indicative of female participation throughout the officiating world. Archibald was surprised to learn that there is very little female representation. "I regrettably acknowledge that politics and prejudices are part of the game," she said after attending. "Although pioneering in its goals and achievements, the clinic was only the beginning of equality in umpiring. Our experience can only serve to help other female umpires."

Acceptance by male partners appeared to be an impediment for many of the participants. What could be done to rectify that? At other clinics, there are usually only one, sometimes two, females in attendance in a group of anywhere from 25 to 40 males. At those mixed clinics, Jim Cressman, a clinician at the all-female clinic and a former minor league umpire who officiated in the 1988 Olympics in Seoul, Korea, said he had observed snickering and snide remarks when a female asked a question. Had a male asked the very same question, it would have been accepted as completely legitimate — no laughing, no problem. "Consequently," he said, "the usually lone female learned to keep her mouth shut, thereby losing the opportunity to further her umpiring knowledge."

The all-female clinic focused on developing confidence, taking constructive criticism and having a willingness to learn, change and improve. Common to officiating any sport, the women had experienced varying degrees of problems. The clinicians, however, consistently kept the group focused on solving them by developing strategies for dealing with problem situations. They focused on the usual clinic teaching points — looking professional and acting the part; knowing the rules; teamwork; communication with partners, coaches and players; approachability; maintaining control of yourself and the game; preventative officiating; and using common sense — but they stressed gaining confidence and bringing about positive change while doing it.

During the closing ceremonies, each umpire was presented with Ontario Baseball Association certification cards. Archibald, from Nova Scotia, was awarded an honorary card, and she was thrilled, she laughed, that she could now work honorary games.

To ensure the continued success and future of all-female umpire's clinics, feedback was encouraged and necessary. Said Gilbert: "We had to start somewhere to let people know that females want to and are capable of participating in higher levels of officiating baseball, and I think that this clinic was a giant step toward the recognition that is long overdue."

Meeting other umpires who had experienced and overcome similar problems was meaningful to the participants. One common complaint was the lack of properly fitting umpire uniforms. Consequently, Ross has started her own company, selling umpire wear in women's sizes.

"How has the clinic benefited women officials?" asked Gilbert. "In my opinion, it certainly proved that there is a talent pool of female officials that is no longer baseball's best-kept secret. I also feel that this clinic has opened doors to women to become more active at the provincial, national and hopefully someday international level tournaments."

The clinic was a small step toward equality of the genders in officiating. The awareness that others share similar obstacles, and the networking that arose at the clinic, were giant steps for the participants. Women working in the traditionally male field of sports officiating need no longer feel they are alone.

Article originally published in the May 1999 issue of Referee.

Reprinted with written permission from Referee *magazine. For subscription information contact* Referee *magazine, PO Box 161, Franksville, Wisc., 53216; phone 262/632–8855; e-mail: referee@referee.com.*

University of Colorado Baseball

During a game for the women's college baseball team in 1922 their catcher, Helen Blackburn, broke her nose. She caught a shot off the bat of one of the hitters while working behind the plate. The game was reported as being held on the grounds of the school to limit the attendance at the game. {"Girl Baseball Player Breaks Nose Catching," *Coshocton Tribune*, 3 June 1922, 6.}

Uwaine, Rochelle "Shelly"

OF 1997–98, San Jose Spitfires

Shelly Uwaine got her baseball start with the San Jose Spitfires in 1997 and 1998. In 1998 she also played for the national champion American All-Stars in Tucson, Arizona. The team participated in the USA Baseball Women's National Championship tournament. Uwaine attended the University of Hawaii, where she earned a BS in civil engineering in 1995 and then an MS in engineering in 1997 from UC-Davis.

Vadnais, Jessica

Jessica Vadnais joined the Hudson Boosters baseball program in 1995 at the age of 11. She helped her team get into the playoffs. In 1996 when she came back out to play, she was told the league rules had changed so that she could not play. The Boosters were privately funded and not a part of the national Little League system, and therefore could make their own rules. Rather than giving up, Vadnais found another program in River Falls that let her play in their Pony League. Vadnais pitches, plays first base and generally bats lead-off. {Bob Burrows, "Looking for Her Field of Dreams," *River Falls Journal*, 1996.}

Van Duzer, Donna Lee "D. L."

Trainer

Donna Lee Van Duzer wanted to be a trainer but discovered it was a tough field for a woman when potential employers would call and no longer be interested after learning that "D.L." was really "Donna Lee." After graduating from Long Beach State University with a degree in kinesiology, Van Duzer earned her certification from the National Collegiate Athletic Trainers Association. Those credentials got her a job as the head trainer at Los Angeles Harbor College and finally with the Texas Rangers organization. From 1990 to 1991 Van Duzer worked for the Port Charlotte Class A affiliate of the Rangers. In 1992 she moved up to their Double A club in Tulsa, but after the 1994 season the organization reassessed its needs and she was let go. In 1995 she got a job working for the Class A San Jose club of the San Francisco Giants.

Vana, Dawn

P/OF, Chicago Storm

Dawn Vana pitched for the Chicago Storm in the Great Lakes Women's Baseball League in 2002. During the Citrus Blast she won her first start 2–1 over the North Shore Cougars. When she did not take the mound, Vana could be found patrolling the outfield because she was a contact hitter. She was 7–15 in the Citrus Blast with one run scored and one batted in. {Chicago Storm Web site.}

Vanderlip (Ozburn), Dollie "Lippy"

(b. 4 June 1937, Charlotte, North Carolina) P 1952–54, Fort Wayne Daisies, South Bend Blue Sox

Dollie Vanderlip joined the AAGPBL near its end, when she was still in high school. She and her brothers had formed a local baseball league because there were no other opportunities to play.

Vanderlip was the only girl in the league. They cleared a field and built dugouts, benches and a backstop from lumber the kids stole from Vanderlip's father. She learned about the AAGPBL from Movie Tones, which played short news items before feature films. She spent two seasons with Fort Wayne and her final season with South Bend. She pitched in 43 games with a 13–12 record based mainly on her starting role with South Bend, where she was 11–4. She only hit .130 with nine base hits. After the league folded she joined the Allington All-Stars as they toured the country. She went on to work as a counselor in upstate New York before obtaining her teaching degree. {AAGPBL Baseball Cards, 1996; Jeni Leis, unpub. M. A. Thesis, 48–50.}

Van Pelt, Sallie

Sports writer

Sallie Van Pelt was the local editor of the *Dubuque Times* and also served as the paper's baseball editor. In 1879 she reported on over 60 games and showed that she had a thorough knowledge of all the rules of the game. {*Chicago Tribune*, 21 March 1880.}

Vardavas, Stephanie

Management personnel

After completing Major League Baseball's executive development program, Stephanie Vardavas worked for five years in the American League office. Vardavas managed the waivers and records department while earning a law degree at night school. Then she got a promotion to assistant counsel to the commissioner, Peter Ueberroth. She left baseball when she got a better offer but would be open to returning as a general manager or the commissioner someday. {Ken Gurnick, "It's a Field of Dream Few Have Realized," *The National Sports Daily*, 19 June 1990, 18–19.}

Vassar Resolutes

The Resolutes played at Vassar College in 1876. Their uniforms consisted of floor length skirts, long sleeved shirts, high shoes and caps. The team name was written on bands worn around the waists of the players. This team developed from two clubs that had formed as early as 1866 to give the girls at the school some physical activity. Though initially games were only played among the girls at Vassar, other schools began developing baseball teams as well. For example, Smith first created a team in 1879 and Mount Holyoke started their first in 1891. This did not mean, however, that there were suddenly lots of women's games being played between the schools. There was still great concern in Victorian society about the proper behavior of ladies, and competition did not necessarily fit in. {*Chicago Times*, 14 April 1878, 4; Barbara Gregorich, *Women at Play*, 3.}

Vecchione, Angela

(Whitman, Massachusetts) SS/C, Bay State Express, Boston Blue Sox

Angela Vecchione joined the Bay State club in 2000 and also became part of the traveling Blue Sox club when they went to tournaments. Vecchione graduated from Bridgewater State College with a degree in physical education and works as a youth program director at a YMCA when she is not playing baseball. At Bridgewater, Vecchione played softball from 1998 to 2001 and set many records that still stand. She played in the most career games, at 182, and has the second-highest career batting average, at .428. She also has the most career at-bats, hits and runs scored. {Boston Blue Sox Web site; Bridgewater State College Athletics Web site.}

Vella, Loren

Australia

Loren Vella played in the 2003 Women's World Series for Australia and hit .286 while scoring two runs. She also fielded flawlessly, handling all six attempts.

Ventura (Manina), Virginia R. "Jean"

(b. 30 November 1935, Garfield, New Jersey) 1B/Util. 1951–53, Rockford Peaches, Chicago Colleens

As a youngster growing up in New Jersey, Virginia Ventura took part in a number of recreational sporting activities while attending Washington Irving School and then Garfield High School. She played basketball, volleyball and softball at school. Later, she joined the Garfield Flashettes. Steve Eisenbergen organized the Flashettes to play city league basketball and softball. A number of other all–American players joined the Flashettes including Carol Habban, Beverly Stuart and Georgina Terkowski. They played fast-pitch softball and traveled all over for tournaments and other clubs to play.

Ventura signed with the Rockford Peaches when she was only 15. When she was not playing she attended school. Since she was so young, her playing time her first season was limited. She jumped to the touring Colleens in 1952 to improve her skills. She returned to Rockford in 1953 and played in 11 games. She did not get much chance to play, because she was the backup to one of the league's best, Dottie Kamenshek. She went on to take real estate classes at Bergen Community College. After playing in the AAGPBL Ventura stayed active by coaching for over 25 years. She was elected to membership in the Garfield Hall of Fame. Ventura married in 1960, worked in her husband's construction company and had three children. {AAGPBL Questionnaire, National Baseball Hall of Fame; AAGPBL Newsletter, May 2005, 25; AAGPBL Baseball Cards, 1995.}

Venturi (Veenema), Bridget

(b. 8 August 1966, Highland Park, Illinois) P/OF 1994, Colorado Silver Bullets, 2004 USA National Team

Bridget Venturi played tee ball, Little League and in the Deerfield Youth Baseball Association with the full support of her parents, Dominic and Dolly Venturi. At Regina Dominican High School she played softball, basketball, volleyball and tennis. One year the basketball team finished third in the state. Her softball skills earned her a four-year scholarship to the University of Michigan, where she played for coach Carol Hutchins. Venturi graduated in 1989 with an engineering degree. In 1990 she competed on *American Gladiators* and won. She tried out for the Silver Bullets in 1994 and made the inaugural squad, only to be cut the following season. After being cut in 1995 she approached the Women's Sports and Entertainment Network and got a job as a color commentator for eight Silver Bullets games. In 2004 she made the USA National Team and played in one game, where she was 3–5 with one run scored as the USA won silver. Now she works as a high school athletic director in the Chicago area. She is also continuing her contributions to women's baseball by serving on the USA Baseball board of directors. {Peggy Machak, "Ready for Another Inning," *Chicago Tribune*, 31 December 1995, 1, 4; Collin Gallant, "Former Gladiator Chases Her Dream," *The Edmonton Journal*, 2 August 2004, D1; David Kindred, *Colorado Silver Bullets: For the Love of the Game* (Atlanta: Longstreet Press, Inc.), 98; <www.USABaseball.com>.}

Vialat, Zonia

IF 1948, Springfield Sallies

Zonia Vialat had an extremely short career, playing in only one game before returning to Cuba.

Victoria All Stars

In 1999 the Victoria All Stars won the International Women's Tournament in Melbourne behind the strong pitching of Alisa Tamburrino.

Victoria Provincial Team

The Victoria Provincial team plays each year in the Australian Women's National Championships. In 2004 they won their first game 8–7 over Western Australia behind the solid pitching of Wells and Flanigan. They lost their second game to Victoria 11–5 as Copland took the loss. They trounced South Australia in their third game 22–0 as Wells won her second game. Unfortunately Victoria seemed to have their number, as they lost a second game to them, this time by a score of 20–5 with Flanigan taking the loss against Emma Binks. They lost another to New South Wales 18–0 but bounced back to defeat Queensland 21–5 with Wells again picking up the victory. They won their final two games, beating Country Baseball 21–3 and Western Australia 9–1. Campbell and Flanigan picked up the victories.

Victoria Women's Baseball

Baseball Victoria hosts a variety of teams for women in the area and has done so for ten years. Their women's team is a combination of all-stars from around the region, chosen from their local clubs to compete at the Australian championships since 2000. They are a part of the Victorian Baseball Association, which established a women's division in 1994 under the direction of Les Flower. In 2002 the team was named the women's team of the year based on their 30–1 record since 2000. They beat out the club from New South Wales for the honor. The team has been led by coach Grant Weir. The squad won the nationals for five straight years. In 2002 20 players from this squad were chosen to represent Australia at the second women's World Cup. New South Wales is the only other victor in recent years, winning in 2003. In April 2004 Victoria won again, defeating New South Wales 12–1.

At the 2004 championships the Victoria club beat New South Wales, Victoria Provincial twice, Country Baseball, Queensland, Western Australia and South Australia. The only club they lost to on the way to winning the championship was New South Wales, the runner-up. They lost 13–3 with Catherine Row taking the loss. {"Port Ladies Easily Win," *Port Phillip Leader*, 23 February 2004, 47; Women's International Baseball Web site; "Florida Lightning Win South Florida Diamond Classic Second Time," *Baserunner*, October 1998.}

In 2004 Victoria Baseball added a team and league for players age 14 and under. The new team is called the Waverly Wildcats. The new league will be run by a committee under the direction of Sandra Lording and play their games at Napier Park. {David Turner, "Lady Wildcats Ready," *Waverly Leader*, 10 August 2004, 31.}

Vidler, Megan

(b. 21 January 1984) P, New South Wales, 2004 Australian National Team

Megan Vidler played for New South Wales and then was chosen for the national team and played in the 2004 Women's World Series held in Japan.

Villa (Cryan), Margaret "Marge," "Poncho"

(b. 21 December 1924, Montabella, California) 2B/SS 1946–50, Kenosha Comets

Marge Villa started out with a bang in the All American League. She set records for the most total bases in a game, with 11, and for the most RBIs, with nine — and she was only a rookie. She got the chance to go with the touring teams that traveled to Central and South America in 1947. Marge played in 537 games with a batting average of .209. She had 168 RBIs and scored another 249 runs. {AAGPBL Baseball Cards, 1995.}

Vincent (Mooney), Georgette "Jette"

(b. 5 July 1928, Fall River, Massachusetts) P 1948–54, Racine Belles, South Bend Blue Sox

Georgette Vincent began with the Belles in 1948, pitching in 15 games. During the 1950 season Vincent often pitched the second game of the Blue Sox' many doubleheaders. For example, on 9 July 1950 Vincent beat the Red Wings in a four-hit shutout 1–0 to cap a sweep started by Jean Faut in the first game. Ten days earlier Vincent also won the second game of a doubleheader against the last place Kalamazoo club, 9–2. She struck out eight batters in that game. Her career numbers included pitching in 97 games with a 38–34 record and an ERA of 2.88. She also played in 157 games and hit .153. {OBBHOF Newspaper Collection; AAGPBL Baseball Cards, 1995.}

Violetta (Kunkel), Karen

(b. 4 March 1924, Negaunee, Michigan) Util. 1953, Grand Rapids Chicks

Karen Violetta played for one season in Grand Rapids but made her strongest contribution to the AAGPBL many years later. In 1987 she helped form the AAGPBL Players Association and served as executive director. Before taking on those roles Violetta graduated from Michigan State and Northern Michigan, where she also went on to teach. {AAGPBL Baseball Cards, 2002.}

Virginia Boxers

The Boxers have been in the Eastern Women's Baseball Conference since the 1990s. They began under player/manager Kristin Guidace. The Boxers captured the EWBC title in 2001. In 2002 they again won the league championship by defeating the Virginia Flames on 25 August 2002.

The Boxers are still an entry in the Eastern Women's Baseball Conference under the direction of manager Jody Brannon (in 2004). The Boxers won their first game in 2004 over the Baltimore Blues 8–3. They tied their second game against Montgomery 8–8 and then lost to the Flames 17–7. They lost the next two to the Banditas and the Blues before finally winning again against the Blues 13–1. By the middle of the season their record stood at 3–8 and had them in fifth place out of the six-team league.

Virginia Flames

The Flames were founded in 1992 by JoAnn Milliken and went through a number of name changes and league shifts over the years. In 1999 the Flames ended their season with a record of 4–7. This tied them for second place with the Montgomery County Barncats. In 2000 they won the first EWBC Championship by a score of 15–11 over the New Jersey Nemesis. The Flames often turned to star pitcher Stephanie Ciulla to bring them to victory. The Flames were led their first two seasons by JoAnn Milliken, who was named manager of the year in 2000. In 2001 the title went to the Boxers and then in 2002 the Boxers beat the Flames in the final to win again, even though the Flames had the best hitting team in the league. The Flames were still playing during the 2004 season under manager David Fyfe and coach Harry Simpson. The Flames led the league with a 10–2 record at the midpoint of the season.

Vonderau, Kathryn E. "Kate"

(b. 26 September 1927, Fort Wayne, Indiana) C 1946–53, Fort Wayne Daisies, Muskegon Lassies, Chicago Colleens, Peoria Red Wings, Muskegon Belles

Kate Vonderau spent her first eight years in school at Ziok Lutheran in Fort Wayne before finishing at South Side High School. While in school she took part in every intramural sport offered, since those were the only athletics available to girls at the time. She also participated in city-sponsored opportunities in softball, volleyball, basketball and bowling. Her college experience took her all the way through to a Ph.D. at the University of Iowa. Her bachelor's and master's came from Indiana University. The money the players received in the AAGPBL was not enough to pay for school, so she also worked as a bank teller. Vonderau played for a number of different teams in the AAGPBL, including being a part of the Fort Wayne Daisies' and Muskegon Lassies' championship teams. Vonderau went to Cuba in 1947 for spring training and recalled that the food was a tough adjustment. Vonderau suffered a finger injury that ended her career when she caught a foul tip off the end of her right index finger. The injury resulted in a number of surgeries that could not correct the problem completely. After retiring, Vonderau taught for 22

Virginia Flames players celebrating a tournament victory in 2004.

years, and coached softball and volleyball at the University of Wisconsin at Whitewater. In recognition of her contributions to the college's athletic program she was elected to the university's Athletic Hall of Fame in 1996. {Susan E. Johnson, *When Women Played Hardball*, p. 81; AAGPBL Questionnaire, National Baseball Hall of Fame.}

Voyce, Inez Ferne "Lefty"

(b. 16 August 1924, Rathbun, Iowa) 1B 1946–53, South Bend Blue Sox, Grand Rapids Chicks

Inez Voyze spent all her school years attending Seymour grade school and high school. She played a little softball in Lucas, Iowa, and then served as a yeoman in the navy from 1944 to 1946. She signed with South Bend in 1946 and was traded to Grand Rapids in 1947, where she finished out her baseball career. This meant she was a part of the championship team in Grand Rapids in 1947. Voyce is second in the AAGPBL for career RBIs, with 422, behind the leader, Dorothy Schroeder, at 433. She gained a reputation as an excellent fielder and was even called acrobatic by her teammates. She hit .256 in 894 games with 363 runs scored and 28 home runs. She also stole 168 bases and walked 480 times against only 144 strikeouts. After retiring from the league, Voyce worked in an office because of the skills she had acquired at the American Institute of Commerce in Davenport, Iowa. {AAGPBL Questionnaire, National Baseball Hall of Fame; AAGPBL Baseball Cards, 1996.}

Vukovich, Frances "Bebop"

(b. 30 August 1930, Smithdale, Pennsylvania) P 1950, Racine Belles

Before signing a contract with the AAGPBL, Frances Vukovich had no real baseball or softball experience. While attending Smithdale School and West Newton High School she did not take part in athletics. She pitched for the touring teams and the Racine Belles and in the off-season worked in a paper factory. She played in 21 games and hit .284. Vukovich got called Bebop because of her love of jazz music. After her baseball career ended Vukovich worked for Pacific Bell in California until she retired. {AAGPBL Questionnaire, National Baseball Hall of Fame, Cooperstown, New York.}

Waddell (Wyatt), Helen J. "Sis," "Chippie"

(b. 24 April 1930, Lemoyne, Pennsylvania) Util.

Inf./OF 1950–51, Rockford Peaches, Battle Creek Belles

While attending Lemoyne High School, Helen Waddell played basketball for three years, serving as captain during her senior season. She also played intramural volleyball and softball because there were no leagues for those sports at the time. Waddell grew up playing ball with her five older brothers whenever they needed an extra player. Before joining the AAGPBL, Waddell played softball and basketball with the Harrisburg Roverettes and worked for G.C. Murphy Company. She received a letter inviting her to tryouts in Allentown, Pennsylvania, for the AAGPBL. Waddell made the cut, and her first year in the league she played for the championship Rockford Peaches. Her teammates called her Chippie because she was always so chipper and light-hearted about everything. After two seasons in the league Waddell went back to work and coaching. She coached Cub Scout baseball and a number of girls' teams at her church. Her career numbers included playing in 123 games with an average of only .137. {AAGPBL Questionnaire, National Baseball Hall of Fame; Diana Redmond, "Preserving the Peaches," *The Rockford Register Star*, 8 September 1993, D1; AAGPBL Baseball Cards, 1995; Susan E. Johnson, *When Women Played Hardball*, 28; Brenda S. Wilson, *Nicknaming Practices of Women in a Nontraditional Occupation* (MA Thesis, University of North Carolina at Greensboro, 1991) 43.}

Wade, Heather "Boggs"

(b. January 1971) P/SS, Detroit Danger

Heather Wade played baseball on boys' teams growing up. She also played first base on her high school softball team and continued to play slow-pitch softball after graduating. In 2005 she joined the Detroit Danger. {Danger Web site.}

Wagner, Audrey

(b. 27 December 1927; d. 31 August 1984, Rock Springs, Wyoming) OF 1943–50, Kenosha Comets

Audrey Wagner patrolled the outfield for the Kenosha Comets and hit 29 career home runs. She started in 1943 when she was only 15 years old. Her father Leonard allowed her to play after school finished for the year. When she started, she pitched, but Comets manager Josh Billings quickly moved her to the outfield because of her strong hitting. In 1946 she graduated from high school and had her best year to date, hitting .281. In 1947 when sidearm pitching was introduced, Wagner improved her hitting to .305. She also knocked in 53 runs and led the AAGPBL in doubles with 25. Her best year came in 1948 when she was selected as the player of the year, with a .312 average and 130 hits to lead the league. She died in a plane crash in 1984. {"Bensenville Girls Stars on Kenosha Comets Ball Club," *The Roselle Register*, 20 August 1943; Merrie Fidler, *The Development and Decline of the All-American Girls Baseball League, 1943–1954*, Master of Science thesis (Department of Physical Education: University of Massachusetts, 1976), 332.}

Wagner, Jacqueline

2B, Cyclones

Jackie Wagner, the second baseman for the Queens Cyclones, played her first season of baseball in 2003. By trade Wagner is a personal trainer, who got involved originally to help the league with fitness issues and ended up playing. {Michael Malone, "Throwing Like a Girl," *New York Sports Express*, 28 August–3 September 2003, 15.}

Wagner, Kimberly Michele

(b. 26 March 1975, Centereach, Long Island, New York) RF/C/1B/P 2003, Cyclones

Kim Wagner has fond memories of going to see the New York Mets play at Shea Stadium with her father. This love of baseball led her to join the Brooklyn/Queens Cyclones in the New York Women's Baseball Association in 2003. She played right field, catcher, first base and pitcher depending on the needs of the team. In October 2003 Wagner participated in the 24-hour marathon game in Arizona for AIDS victims in Africa. Wagner was the only deaf player taking part. She later recalled the toughest pitcher she faced in that game: a woman from Australia whose pitches she never even got a foul tip off of. Baseball is a new sport for Wagner, who ran track and field and cross-country while in school. In 2004 she plans to go back to school at the United States Sports Academy for a degree in sports management. That decision is based on her baseball experiences. {Kimberly Wagner, correspondence with Leslie A. Heaphy, North Canton, Ohio, March 2004.}

Wagoner, Betty Ann "Waggie," "Bet," "Wag"

(b. 15 July 1930, Lebanon, Missouri) OF/1B/P 1948–54, Muskegon Lassies, South Bend Blue Sox

Though Betty Ann Wagoner attended a number of schools during her formative years, she played softball and basketball every opportunity she had. This included playing on the boys' teams in seventh and eighth grade since those were the only teams available in Phillipsburg, Missouri. She even played softball for the YMCA during her senior year in high school. Wagoner joined the AAGPBL in 1948 right after graduation. When she was not playing she worked in the office at the Bendix Corporation. After playing in four games with Muskegon, Wagoner joined South Bend and stayed there till the league folded after the 1954 season. She helped them win championships in 1951 and '52, and was selected as an all-star in 1950. One of the highlights of her career was witnessing Jean Faut pitch two perfect games. When her baseball career ended Wagoner played one year of amateur softball in Valparaiso, Indiana, and also played and coached basketball in South Bend for a number of years. She played in 665 games and pitched in 32. Her win-loss record was 8–20 with an ERA of 3.55. As a hitter she was much stronger, batting a solid .271 and driving in 191 runs, though she had no power. She came to bat 2,245 times and never hit a home run. {AAGPBL Questionnaire, National Baseball Hall of Fame; AAGPBL Baseball Cards, 1995.}

Walbancke, Kellie

1B/P 2002–04, New South Wales, Team Australia

Kellie Walbancke played in the 2004 Australian National Women's Championships, helping her club to a second-place finish behind Victoria. She had 13 hits and 15 runs in only 26 at-bats.

Waldman, Suzyn

Sports Announcer

In spring 2005, Suzyn Waldman joined the New York Yankees radio station, WCBS-AM, as their new color commentator alongside John Sterling. In doing so Waldman became the first full-time female color commentator in the major leagues. Waldman got her start on Broadway, where she worked for 15 years in *Man of La Mancha*. Following her acting career Waldman went to work for sports radio at WFAN in 1987. She spent 15 years covering the Yankees and New York Knicks. On 6 and 7 June 1993 Waldman stood in for Bob Murphy doing color commentary for the New York Mets. During the 1995 season she broadcast a network baseball game between the

Yankees and the Texas Rangers. {Rita Ciolli, "Suzyn Waldman Invades the Male Holy of Holies," *St. Louis Post Dispatch*, 17 June 1996; Raymond Edel, "Waldman Onboard in Yankee's Booth," *The Record*, 4 March 2005; Rudy Martzke, "Waldman Adds her Name to Broadcast History," *USA Today*, 24 July 1995.}

Waldman became a baseball fan at the tender age of three when her grandfather took her to watch the Boston Red Sox play. From that point forward Waldman developed a lifelong love of the game. Her perseverance paid off and with each step she has taken she won over skeptics who thought women did not know the game.

Walker, Diane

1B, Virginia Flames

Diane Walker played first base for the Flames in the late 1990s when they belonged to the Eastern Women's Baseball Conference.

Wallace, Robin

(b. 1977, Newton, Massachusetts) P/IF/C, 2004 USA National Team, North Shore Lady Spirit

Robin Wallace started playing baseball when she was five years old. She continued to play through the Babe Ruth division and also at St. Luke's Episcopal High School in Mobile, Alabama. She is believed to be the first woman to play high school baseball in Mobile. Before going to Tulane she played one year of baseball at the University of the South. At Tulane she played on a club baseball squad. In 2000 she was named rookie of the year for the New England league and in 2003 she made the North Shore Lady Spirit all-star squad. In 2004 Wallace made the roster for the USA National Team and played in the fourth Women's World Series in July 2004. She pitched two innings in the series and also drove in three runs while scoring another two to help the USA win silver. {USA Baseball 2004 Media Guide; Cassandra Taylor, "A League of Her Own," *Mobile Register*, 18 July 2004.}

Wallace has played women's baseball and been involved on the management end of the game. She was inducted into the National Women's Baseball Hall of Fame in recognition of her contributions. She also became the executive director of the North American Women's Baseball League after completing two years of law school at the University of Alabama. {USA Baseball Web site; NAWBL Web site.}

Wallick, Sierra

SS/P, San Francisco Bay Sox

Sierra Wallick grew up playing Little League baseball and then played softball while she attended Alemany High School until her graduation in 1991. After high school she played some slow-pitch softball until 1997, when she attended a tryout for the new Ladies Professional Baseball League run by Michael Ribant. Wallick made the 20-person roster for the San Francisco Bay Sox. Though she had played shortstop before, Wallick pitched for the Bay Sox. {Vincent Bonsignore, "Wallick Gets Her Chance," *Los Angeles Daily News*, 3 July 1997.}

Walulik (Kiely), Helen "Hensky"

(b. 3 May 1929, Piscataway, New Jersey) P/2B 1948–50, Fort Wayne Daisies

Growing up and attending school in Plainfield, New Jersey, gave Helen Walulik the chance to play basketball and softball for three years. As a result of her accomplishments she was named Best Female Athlete for the class of 1947. In addition to playing at school, Walulik played basketball and softball for two years with the Plainfield Bobby Sockers and for another two years with the Perth Ambey Cardinalettes. In the AAGPBL Walulik helped Fort Wayne make the playoffs in 1947. The highlight of her season was her only home run, which she hit against the Kenosha Comets. During the off-season she worked for Diehl Manufacturing since the players' salaries were not enough to live on year-round. Walulik married in 1953 and had three children. She also worked for 22 years at Ethicon as a surgical needle technician. {AAGPBL Questionnaire, National Baseball Hall of Fame; AAGPBL Baseball Cards, 1995.}

Wambsganss, William "Bill"

(b. 19 March 1894, Cleveland, Ohio; d. 8 December 1985, Lakewood, Ohio) Manager

Bill Wambsganss played for the Cleveland Indians as their second baseman from 1914 to 1923 and then for the Red Sox from 1924 to 1925. He finished his career in 1926 with the Philadelphia Athletics. His claim to fame is having completed the only unassisted triple play in World Series history while with Cleveland in 1920. He came to the All American League with a world of experience and managed the Daisies and Lassies from 1945 to 1948. His Daises lost in the 1945 championship to the Peaches. {AAGPBL Baseball Cards, 2000.}

Wanless (Decker), Betty

(b. 28 August 1928, Springfield, Illinois; d. 20 December 1995) 3B 1953–54, Grand Rapids Chicks, South Bend Blue Sox

Betty Wanless played two seasons for the Grand Rapids and South Bend clubs before the AAGPBL folded. She quickly developed a reputation as a heavy hitter after she hit a 425 foot shot as a rookie in Grand Rapids Park. The following season Betty hit 15 home runs and 13 doubles. She hit .262 in 171 games with 82 RBIs and she scored another 124 runs. Wanless had just gotten started when the league folded, otherwise who knows what her numbers might have been like. {AAGPBL Baseball Cards, 1996.}

Warawa, Leslie

(Innisfail, Alberta) P/1B/OF Team Canada

Leslie Warawa started playing for Team Canada in 2001. She played in the Women's World Series in 2002 and in the AAU National Championships in 2003.

Ward, Kris

P/C/OF Southend Raptors, Washington Stars

Kris Ward began playing in the WWBA in 2003, the year when the league began. She also served as the league treasurer from 2003-2005. She has played for the Southend Raptors and the traveling Washington Stars. Ward can play nearly any position on the field

Ward, Sarah

IF 1999–2001, South Bend Blue Sox

Sarah Ward played in the infield for the Blue Sox for three seasons. She joined the Sox at age sixteen and became a solid hitter and fielder. She hit .316, .314 and .315 during her three seasons and set a record for most chances at short in one game with 13. {Kovach, 110.}

Warfel, Elizabeth "Betty"

(b. 15 May 1926, Enola, Pennsylvania; d. 23 September 1990) P/IF 1948–49, Rockford Peaches

Betty Warfel pitched for two seasons for the Rockford Peaches and regularly filled in where needed in the infield. She could play any spot they needed her to, which made her a valuable contributor. She played in 95 games and hit only .143.

She pitched in 20 games and had a 6–5 record. After leaving the league Warfel took up bowling as her sport of choice. {AAGPBL Baseball Cards, 1996.}

Warren, Nancy "Hank"

(b. 13 June 1921, Springfield, Ohio; d. 1 June 2001, Michigan) P/2B/SS 1946–54, Muskegon Lassies, Chicago Colleens, Peoria Red Wings, Fort Wayne Daisies, Kalamazoo Lassies

Nancy Warren grew up in Springfield, Ohio, with six brothers and sisters. Warren spent nine years in the All American League. Though she moved around a fair amount it was not because she did not help her teams, especially on the mound. In 232 games pitched Warren had a record of 101–94. Her career ERA was 2.37 and she struck out 717 hitters while only walking 475. Hitting was her weakness, as she batted only .155 in 269 games. {AAGPBL Newsletter, January 2002, 22; AAGPBL Baseball Cards, 1996.}

Warwick (McAuley), Mildred Marion "Millie"

(b. 28 October 1922, Longlake, Saskatchewan) 3B 1943–45, Rockford Peaches

While growing up in Canada, Millie Warwick played softball, basketball, and volleyball and took part in track and field while attending school in Kitchener. At Commercial High School she broke the school record for the ball throw in track and won the Junior Athletic Award for track and field. To prepare for going to work, Warwick attended Alberta College for some business courses. She worked for the federal government before and after playing in the AAGPBL. She played softball in the Saskatchewan League and was named MVP in 1942. She thought that the best things about playing were all the travel and the people the players met when they moved from town to town. She returned to Canada after playing in the league and went back to playing softball. Her team won a championship in 1951. Warwick's achievements on the field led to her election to the Saskatchewan Sports Hall of Fame in 1986 and to the Saskatchewan Baseball Hall of Fame in 1991. Warwick married Kenneth McAuley in 1945 and had two boys. Her husband played goalie for the New York Rangers from 1943 to 1945. Warwick also co-founded a fast-pitch softball team known as the Edmonton Mortons. The Mortons won their league championship in 1947 and 1949 through 1951, and won the Alberta Provincial Championship the same years. In 2004 she and

Betty Dunn served as ambassadors at the first ever women's World Cup event in July 2004 in Edmonton, Canada. {Collin Gallant, "Nostalgia on the Mound to Open Women's Tourney," *Edmonton Journal*, 31 July 2004, D4; AAGPBL Questionnaire, National Baseball Hall of Fame; AAGPBL Newsletter, May 2001, 36.}

Washington Barracks Club

In 1920 two local women's teams were started in Washington. Captain Jane McKenney organized the home team, called the Washington Barracks. Their first game took place against Eunice Graham's Community Service nine. {"Girls Will Play Baseball," *Washington Post* 26 April 1920, 1.}

Washington DC Thunder

In 2002 the DC Thunder took second place in the DC Invitational and followed that with a similar finish in 2003. They lost to the North Shore Cougars in 2002 and to the East Coast Yankees in 2003. Laura Brenneman led the team in hitting in 2002 with a .633 tournament average after hitting .556 in the East Coast Women's Baseball League. Stephanie Ciulla led the way for the pitching staff.

Washington Stars

The Washington Stars were founded in 2003 by Stephanie Derouin, who also plays for the team. She began the team in order to give women in the state of Washington an opportunity to play baseball and not just softball. The 2003 season was an abbreviated one for the club, since they did not get underway until midway through the summer. Their first game was an exhibition in Tacoma against a girls' club from Canada. Then the squad played one men's team. Mainly the goal of the 2003 season was to raise awareness, interest and money for the 2004 season. The Stars also were able to send 11 members of their club to the 24-hour game in Arizona in October 2003. The Stars came back to play in 2004 and participated in tournament play as well as local games. {Stephanie Derouin, correspondence with Leslie A. Heaphy, North Canton, Ohio, May 2004.}

Washington Women's Baseball Association (WWBA)

The WWBA began in 2003 to provide baseball opportunities in the Washington State area for those young ladies 14 and older wanting an alternative to softball. One of the organizers is Jeneane

Descombes Lesko, who played in the All American League. Lesko coaches and even plays for the Washington Stars, the original team in the league. The Stars play their games in an amateur men's league in Pierce County, Washington. The long-term plan for the league is to develop eight teams. {Sherry Grindeland, "Pursuing a League of Her Own," *The Seattle Times*, 13 August 2004, B1.}

Watanabe, Hanami

P, Japan

During the first women's World Cup in 2004, Hanami Watanabe pitched a complete game for Japan, giving up three runs over nine innings but coming out with the victory.

Waterbury Diamonds

Lance Lusignan started the Waterbury Diamonds in 1999 as the team's owner and general manager. Home games have been played at Municipal Stadium in Waterbury. The Diamonds have been an entry each year in the New England Women's Baseball League (NEWBL). In their inaugural 2000 season, the Diamonds finished with a 15–7 record and were 10–6 in the NEWBL.

On 6 May 2001 the Diamonds won their first tournament, defeating the Ocala Lightning 11–8 in the Citrus Blast. To get to the final game the Diamonds beat the Orlando Fire 11–0 and the Florida Tornados 13–9 in extra innings. They also beat the South Bend Blue Sox 11–6 and the Chicago Storm 17–7. In two previous trips to the Citrus Blast, the Diamonds came in second. For their third trip the Diamonds used impressive hitting, excellent pitching and solid defense to come out on top. Leading the way were pitchers Elaine Amundsen, Adriane Adler and Chris Pettgrasso. Amundsen had two complete game victories while Adler and Pettgrasso combined for a four-hitter. On the offensive side Adler helped her own cause with good contact while Donna Mills, Danielle Ferretti and Amy Stinton hit well with runners in scoring position. {Waterbury Diamonds Newsletter, May 2001, <http://www.waterburydiamonds.com>.}

Watson (Stanton), Marion Gertrude

(b. 2 July 1923, Chatham, Ontario, Canada) P 1946–47, Peoria Red Wings, Muskegon Lassies

Marion Watson took advantage of the opportunities presented by Chatham Vocational School to play softball and to swim. She also participated in city league softball and basketball, two of the typical sports offered for women at the time. Before signing with the AAGPBL, Watson worked for the Chrysler Corporation in Chatham. Watson pitched for Peoria and Muskegon and traveled to Cuba for spring training one year. While there she broke her leg in two places while sliding in to home plate. That injury proved to be career-ending for Watson. Watson married Edgar Stanton in 1948 and had three girls. She continued to work as a secretary at Chrysler after she retired from baseball. {AAGPBL Questionnaire, National Baseball Hall of Fame; AAGPBL Baseball Cards, 1995.}

Wawryshyn (Litwin, Moroz), Evelyn Florence "Evie"

(b. 11 November 1924, Tyndall, Manitoba, Canada) 2B 1946–51, Kenosha Comets, Muskingum Lassies, Springfield Sallies, Fort Wayne Daisies

Evelyn Wawryshyn attended Tyndall Public and Tyndall High School to receive all her education. For her athletic activities she turned to city league basketball and to the Canadian Ukrainian league for softball, ice hockey and curling. In track and field she won the North Eastern Manitoba Senior Girls Champion Award in 1940. Wawryshyn signed with Kenosha in 1946 and stayed in the AAGPBL through 1951. In 1948 she was selected to the third all-star team while in 1949 she moved up to the second all-star squad. In 1950 she made the first team when she hit .311 and knocked in 50 runs. Her participation also allowed her to travel to Cuba for spring training. During the off-season she worked as a substitute elementary school teacher to make enough money to live on. After retiring from baseball Wawryshyn played golf and worked for Winnipeg's parks and recreation department. She married in 1952 and again in 1960, and had six children. In 1992 she was elected to the Manitoba Sports Hall of Fame and in 1997 to the Manitoba Baseball Hall of Fame. {AAGPBL Questionnaire, National Baseball Hall of Fame; AAGPBL Baseball Cards, 1995.}

WBL Sparks

This team was created in 2003 from girls playing baseball across North America. They were invited to play in the 64-team tournament at Dreams Park in Cooperstown in 2003 and again in 2004. The Sparks were the first female team ever invited. The girls ranged in age from 10 to 12. Justine Siegal, from Ontario, served as manager of the club. A documentary crew from Hollywood followed the team around for the week, securing footage for a film they wanted to produce of this historic event. Dreams Park is the largest 12-and-under tournament in the world. All those selected to play in the tournament are inducted into the American Youth Baseball Hall of Fame. {Justine Siegal, "Women's Baseball League E-Newsletter," May 2003 and May 2004.}

Wearne, Simone

(b. 5 December 1980, Berwick, Victoria) P, Australian National Team

Simone Wearne led her Australian teammates to victory at the Women's World Series in Florida in September 2002. She was co-winner of the tournament MVP award with her teammate and catcher Sue Fairhurst. Wearne beat the U.S. team 7-4 to get into the championship game. During the 2003 World Series Wearne pitched in two games with no decisions. Her ERA was 1.29 in seven innings pitched. Many regard her as one of the best female pitchers in the world. Wearne comes from a family of ballplayers, with her mother, father, grandfather and brother all playing baseball. She relies on four pitches when out on the mound: a fastball, a curve, a slider and a changeup. In addition to playing baseball Wearne plays tennis and likes to listen to music. {Michelle Ainley, "Pitcher Perfect, That's Wearne," *Herald Sun*, 16 December 2002, 71; Australian Baseball Federation, <www.baseball.org.au>.}

Weaver (Foss), Betty

(b. 10 May 1929, Metropolis, Illinois; d. 8 February 1998, Metropolis, Illinois) 3B/1B/OF 1950–54, Fort Wayne Daisies

While playing in the AAGPBL, Foss received an offer to come and try out for the Chicago White Sox in 1950. Scout Peter Fox saw her play and wanted to sign her to one of the Chicago farm teams. She decided to stay with the sure contract in the women's league. She convinced her husband to let her play, and she took her 14-year-old sister Joanne along with her. It seemed she made a wise choice, as she dominated the league each year in batting. In 1950 she led the league in hitting with a .346 average and was named Rookie of the Year. In 1951 she again led the league with a .368 average. She was also named the Player of the Year in 1952 and made the all-star squad in

1952 and 1953. She hit .331 with 74 RBIs and 81 runs scored. She also led the league in doubles and triples, and overall hits with 137. At the end of the 1953 season her average stood at .352 with 65 runs batted in and 99 runs scored. In 1954 she knocked in 54 runs to help her team and scored another 80. Her career numbers included a .342 batting average, 32 home runs and 312 RBIs. She and her sister Joanne dominated the league in hitting from 1950 to 1954. She toured with Bill Allington's squad from 1954 to 1957. In April 2005 Foss joined a number of former all–American players as a member of the Northeast Indiana Baseball Association Hall of Fame. {"Daisies Star Turned Down Chisox Offer," *Washington Post*, 29 April 1951, C2; Merrie Fidler, *The Development and Decline of the All-American Girls Baseball League, 1943–1954*, Master of Science thesis (Department of Physical Education: University of Massachusetts, 1976), 342–343; AAGPBL Files, OHBBHOF; AAGPBL Baseball Cards, 1996.}

Weaver, Jean

(b. 28 March 1933, Metropolis, Illinois) 3B/P 1951–53, Fort Wayne Daisies

Jean Weaver attended a one-room schoolhouse for her first eight years of school. There were no sports to participate in there. She played basketball at Metropolis High School and then played a bit of softball in Kentucky. Weaver started in the AAGPBL while she was still a senior in high school. She played with her sisters in the league, and in the course of one spring training game they all hit home runs. Weaver played in 172 games with a .246 career average. She only hit two home runs but knocked in 55 runs and scored another 71 to help her club. She pitched in 25 games with a 7–3 record over two seasons. Her problem seemed to be a lack of control, as she struck out 51 hitters but walked 100. After retiring from baseball Weaver played a bit of softball in the Chicago area and worked for Motorola as a supervisor. {AAGPBL Questionnaire, National Baseball Hall of Fame; AAGPBL Baseball Cards, 1996.}

Weaver, Joanne "The Little," "Jo"

(b. 19 December 1936; d. 26 March 2000) OF/P 1950–54, Fort Wayne Daisies

Joanne Weaver joined the AAGPBL when she was only 14, accompanying her sister Betty who went to try out for the Daisies. Weaver led the league in batting from 1952 to 1954. She was named to the all-star team in 1952. In 1954 she dominated with a .429 average in 93 games. She also stole 79 bases and hit 29 home runs. She was named Player of the Year for her achievements in 1954. Her previous two seasons she hit .344 and 346 respectively. Before Weaver led the league, her sister Betty held the honor in 1950 and 1951. In addition to her strong average Weaver also drove in 234 runs, scored 269 and stole 174 bases during her career. Her career average was .359. In 1955 she toured with the Allington All-Stars before returning to Fort Wayne and going to work. {AAGPBL Baseball Cards, 1996.}

Weaver, Rosemary

C 2000, Virginia Flames

Rosemary Weaver joined the Flames during the 2000 season, wearing the number seven. She had played fast-pitch softball for eight years and was also a prominent high school athlete. Catching had never been her position before, but Stephanie Ciulla, star pitcher, found Weaver picked up the game quickly and called good pitches. {National Women's Baseball Hall of Fame, June 2000.}

Weber, Jennifer "Jaye"

Umpire

Jennifer "Jaye" Weber attended the Harry Wendelstedt Umpire School in 1984, one of three ladies in the class of nearly 200. The other two were Perry Lee Barber and Susan Petruzelli. {Mary Ann Clayton, "For These Three Ladies Diamond Means Baseball," *The News and Observer*, 6 June 1984.}

Weddington-Steward, Elaine

Management

A graduate from St. John's University in 1984, Elaine Weddington-Steward worked for the New York Mets public relations office and then in 1990 became the assistant general manager of the Boston Red Sox, the second female minority to hold such a high level position, along with Kim Ng. She passed the bar in 1988 and is the mother of three. {Jean Ardell Presentation, SABR Annual Meeting, 2003.}

Weddle (Hines), Mary Lola "Giggles," "Shorty"

(b. 26 April 1934, Woodsfield, Ohio) SS/3B/ OF/P 1954, Fort Wayne Daisies

Mary Weddle got plenty of opportunity to play

baseball while growing up because she was one of 16 children. Her ten brothers let her play with them whenever she wanted. While attending Antioch Junior High School, Weddle played shortstop for the boys' softball team. In high school she ran track and took part in the baseball and softball throws. In 1951 Weddle played one game with the local VFW men's baseball team. She is the only woman to have done that. In 1953 she played on the A-1 Queens Softball Team in Phoenix, Arizona, and then in 1954 signed on with the Fort Wayne Daisies for the final season of the AAGPBL. Though never a regular starting pitcher for the Daisies, she did pitch a one-hitter. She hit .216 in 76 games and drove in 21 runs while scoring another 38. She had a 3–1 record as a pitcher in 15 games. Weddle got married in 1955 and had three children. After the AAGPBL ended Weddle continued to play slow-pitch softball and win all kinds of honors. Her awards included best offensive player, all-district, all-region and all-tournament. She also coached girls' softball at the junior and senior high level until 1997. {John Wickline, "Player Achieves Big League Recognition," *Wheeling News-Register*, 10 March 2002; AAGPBL Questionnaire, National Baseball Hall of Fame.}

Weeks, Rossey

(b. 7 September 1924, Jacksonville, Florida; d. 13 April 2005) C 1947, Racine Belles, Rockford Peaches

Rossey Weeks played in seven games for the Peaches and Belles. Her career was cut short by injuries before she really got a chance to play. In 1994 Weeks had her name added to the Jacksonville Sports Hall of Fame Honor Roll. {AAGPBL Newsletter, September 1994, 10; AAGPBL Baseball Cards, 1995.}

Wegman, Marie "Blackie"

(b. 1925, Price Hill; d. 20 January 2004, Delhi Township, Ohio) P/3B/SS 1947–50, Rockford Peaches, Fort Wayne Daisies, Muskegon Lassies, Grand Rapids Chicks

Marie Wegman grew up in a family of seven children and learned to play ball with her five younger brothers. He father Clem taught them all to play. Wegman attended Seton High School for three years before dropping out to go to work in a factory to help the family. She took classes at night at Western Hills High School. She played for a number of factory teams. It was while play-

ing in a softball tournament in Cleveland that she was offered a chance to play in the AAGPBL. She initially turned down the offer but changed her mind on learning the salary was more than she earned in the factory. She joined the Peaches in 1947 and played until her father died in 1950. She returned to Cincinnati and attended the university before going to work for Lodge and Shipley in 1951, where she remained until her retirement in 1988. {Rebecca Goodman, "Joined All-American Girls League in 1947," *Cincinnati Enquirer*, 23 January 2004.}

Weierman, Shirley Ann

(b. 27 June 1938, Lima, Ohio) 3B/Util. 1953–54, Fort Wayne Daisies

Shirley Ann Weierman had the distinction of being the youngest player in the All American League, as she started playing at age 14. Injuries cut her career short just as the league was folding in 1954. She remained active in golf, tennis and fishing, and graduated from Ohio State University in 1963. {AAGPBL Baseball Cards, 1995.}

Weinstock, Maia

(29 March 1977, Pound Ridge, New York) P, Manhattan Giants

Maia Weinstock grew up playing Little League (1984–88) but switched to softball after one year in the Babe Ruth division (1992). She was the MVP of her Little League team in 1988. At Fox Lane High School she played volleyball, basketball, and softball. Weinstock graduated from Brown University with a BA in human biology. While there she played varsity squash, a sport she continued to play after college. She pitched in 2003 for the Manhattan Giants in the New York Women's Baseball Association, though her previous baseball experience had all been as an infielder. Weinstock also traveled to Arizona in October 2003 to play in the 24-hour game to benefit AIDS. When she is not pitching Weinstock writes for *Discover* magazine. Her areas of expertise are physics and planetary science. {Maria Weinstock, correspondence with Leslie A. Heaphy, North Canton, Ohio, March 2004; Michael Malone, "Throwing Like a Girl," *New York Sports Express*, n.d.}

Weiss, Alta

(b. 9 February 1890, Berlin, Ohio; d. 12 February 1964, Ragersville, Ohio)

Alta Weiss uniform in museum in Ragersville, Ohio (photograph taken by Kathleen Birck).

By Kathleen Birck

Alta Weiss, a female professional baseball player in the 1800s, was born in Berlin, Ohio, on 9 February 1890, one of three daughters of Dr. and Mrs. Weiss. She grew up in the small town of Ragersville, Ohio, and at age two was said to have "hurled corncobs at the family cat with

Glove used by Alta Weiss when she played for the All-Stars (photograph by Kathleen Birck).

wrist-snap and follow-thru." Weiss despised doing housework and instead enjoyed sports, hunting, and playing music. Her father, a doctor, was a great supporter of her playing ball. He purchased a semiprofessional team, naming it the Weiss All-Stars and encouraged her high school, Ragersville High Community, to change the date of her commencement exercises to allow her to play baseball that day. At age 17, she asked to play ball with some neighborhood boys who, by the end of the game, were greatly impressed by her ability to pitch.

One day, the mayor of the town suggested she play with the semipro Vermilion Independents. After showing the manager how well she could play by striking out 15 batters in the game, she was allowed to join the club, and she played in eight games for Vermilion. Weiss threw a fastball, curveball, knuckleball, sinker, and spitball. In her first game with the team, 1,200 people saw her play; trains brought people from Cleveland just to see her pitch. During the off-season, her father built her a heated gym so she could practice. In 1908, she started at the Wooster Academy in preparation for college and then, two years later, went onto what is now the Ohio State College of Medicine, using the money she had made playing. In 1914, she graduated from medical school,

Home where Alta Weiss grew up (photograph Kathleen Birck).

Home of Alta Weiss from 1946 to 1964 (photograph by Kathleen Birck).

the only female in her class. She said that playing ball helped her to "keep her nerve and courage to get through the med course."

Bloomer teams were normally composed of women from the working class because middle class families seldom let their daughters play in the hot sun against men. However, Dr. Weiss owned her team, and this made her experience different from that of other Bloomer girls. Bloomer girls of the 1890s were considered the first professional female baseball players. These teams lasted 30 or 40 years, from the 1890s to 1920s, with some teams lasting until the 1930s. Many failed, but others such as the Boston Bloomer Girls and Western Bloomers offered exciting baseball. Teams would play men's semipro and minor league teams and were composed mostly of women, with a man often serving as the catcher, and later as shortstop or third baseman.

Being such a star from an upper middle class family, Alta drew much attention.

However, she was never was comfortable with the demands of the press. She seldom spoke out for women's suffrage, hated posing for pictures, and initially refused to wear bloomers while playing, indicating a move away from this symbol of feminism. She also never believed women would make it in baseball. However, she enjoyed the time she did play. For her, baseball offered another facet to her life in addition to her medical studies and career. Articles from the time suggest that the men really believed she could play, one paper saying, "the girl is a phenomenon — nothing more or less."

In 1925, Weiss opened her own practice in Norwalk, Ohio, and in 1927, married John Hisrich, a gas station owner. They separated in 1938 and in 1946, after the death of her father, Alta returned to Ragersville. She retired from medicine in 1948 and lived the rest of her life in a house across from her childhood home. She died 12 February 1964 in her hometown of Ragersville.

Weiss was a pioneering woman; for example, in using the money she made playing baseball to attend medical school. It is impressive to consider her accomplishments during a time when few females played ball and even fewer attended medical school. Today, in her former home, stands a display dedicated to her baseball career. Baseballs, bats, and gloves, as well as scorecards, her baseball card, newspaper clippings, and recent magazine articles detail her extraordinary playing years. She clearly was and still is a hometown hero.

Wellendorf, Chris "Tomboy"

(b. Newfoundland, Canada)

Chris Wellendorf graduated in 1983, from Basic High School where she excelled in variety of sports. She had earned the nickname Tomboy growing up because she loved to play anything. In high school she gave up most of the playing to be a cheerleader, but in 1997 she returned to the baseball diamond to try out for the new Southern California league that was starting. Due to her softball experience she had the skills needed for the league but ended up choosing not to play because the money was so poor. {W.G. Ramirez, "Wellendorf Walks Away from Dream," *Las Vegas Review Journal*, 23 July 1997.}

Welsh, Rebecca

(b. 1 September 1984) P/OF, Queensland Rams, Australia

Rebecca Welsh played for the Rams in the Australian National Championship Series.

Welton, Lisa

(b. 1966, Connecticut) P, Miracles

While growing up in Connecticut, Lisa Welton played Little League and never wanted to play softball. She joined the new Florida league in 1993 as a pitcher. When she is not pitching, Welton works in Boynton Beach as a hairstylist. {John Hughes, "Women Get a Chance to Play a Real Game of Baseball," *Fort Lauderdale Sun-Sentinel*, 4 June 1993.}

Wendall, Krissy

Krissy Wendall caught for the American Little League squad from Brooklyn Park, Minnesota, in the 1994 Little League World Series. After playing Little League Wendell went on to play hockey and participated on the U.S. team at the 2002 Winter Olympics. She also was named the 2004 Outstanding Player for her Minnesota team, which won its first NCAA Women's Hockey Championship. At the 2004 Little League World Series she and two other female former players were inducted into the Little League Hall of Excellence. {"Little League Honors Female Pioneers," *Grand Rapids Press*, 22 August 2004; "Little League Set to Honor City's Gerring," *The Journal Gazette*, 22 August 2004.}

Wendt, Kristin

Washington Stars, Southend Raptors

Kristin Wendt has played baseball for the Washington Stars under former AAGPBL player Jeneane Lesko. In 2005 she joined the new Southend Raptors in the Washington League

Wenzell, Margaret "Marge"

(b. 21 May 1925, Detroit, Michigan) Util. 1945–53, Grand Rapids Chicks, Muskegon Lassies, Peoria Red Wings, Fort Wayne Daisies, Springfield Sallies, Racine Belles, Kalamazoo Lassies, Battle Creek Belles, South Bend Blue Sox

Marge Wenzell grew up in Detroit, the youngest of four. She learned her love of baseball from her father Ed, who had played semipro ball around Detroit. She played softball for the Hudson Motor Car Company team, and they played in a national tournament in 1941 and 1943. She played in the outfield while in the AAGPBL, leading all her teams to many victories because of her solid fielding. She played in 557 games, hitting only .188. Her versatility made her a needed asset and also explained her playing for nine teams during her career. Whenever a club had an injury they traded for Wenzell. After retiring from the league, Wenzell devoted her energies to golfing and won championships at two different golf clubs. She also worked for General Motors. {AAGPBL Newsletter, May 2002, 23; AAGPBL Baseball Cards, 2002.}

Westerman (Austin), Helen "Pee Wee"

(b. 10 September 1926, Springfield, Illinois) C 1943–44, Kenosha Comets

Helen Westerman grew up playing ball with her two brothers. She played for the Madison Furniture Company team until she joined the All American League. Westerman played only one full year in the AAGPBL because when her mother became ill, she stayed home to help care for her. She played in 83 games and hit .181. She did steal 20 bases and drive in 21 runs. She stayed active playing softball for the Cardinals in Chicago and then she coached girls' softball for a few years. {AAGPBL Newsletter, May 2001, 34.}

Western Bloomer Girls

The Western Bloomer Girls were founded in 1911 by Maud Nelson and her husband John Olson. They recruited players from all over the country and then barnstormed from city to city playing mainly men's semipro clubs. At each train station they arrived at they tried to hire a local band to meet them and lead them to the ballpark. They hoped this would generate greater publicity for their games. One of the team's better players was Kate Becker, from Chicago. In 1913 at least two of their games took them to Lima, Ohio, and Danville, Illinois, for competitions. At the time the team had four male players to help make the games more competitive, though it did not always work out. They lost to the Lima team 14–0, and two of the men got hammered while pitching. Two of the men were former major league players. Kate Becker was their star pitcher and Mabel Bohle was her catcher. The team claimed Bohle was the only female catcher in the country at the time. Others on the team included Anna McCann, who pitched or played second base. Cella Doran handled some of the pitching duties while Anna Brennan patrolled left field and Cecilia Burke covered right. Another trip took them to Clearfield, Pennsylvania, to play the local nine in a contest their manager said would attract people because of the quality of their play. Their travels in 1914 landed them in Humeston, Iowa, in May to begin their annual tour of the United States. Kate Becker still led the team as their pitcher and was described by some reporters as one of the best female players in the world. {"Western Bloomer Girls Coming," *The Humeston New Era* (Iowa), 13 May 1914; "Girls Here Today," *The Lima News*, 25 June 1913, 11; "Western Bloomer Girls Slated," *The Lima News*, 26

June 1913, 11; "36 Years Ago," *The Clearfield Progress*, 23 July 1949, 4; Barbara Gregorich, *Women at Play* (San Diego, Calif.: Harcourt Brace, 1994), 32–33, 35.}

Wexford

The Wexford Baseball League has included a girls' baseball team since 1994. They belong to the Central Ontario Girls Baseball League. They came in fourth in the women's division in 2003 and then won the league championship at Wishing Well Park. In 2004 the Wexford club played 19 games between May and August.

Whalen, Dorothy "Dot"

(b. 22 July 1923, New York, New York) C 1948, Springfield Sallies

As a youngster Dorothy Whalen went to school in Richmond Hill, New York, and played a lot of basketball in the city leagues. She went to Delehany Institute to take business courses, which she used when she went to work as an insurance broker. Before joining the AAGPBL Whalen served in the U.S. Marine Corps from 1943 to 1945. She retired after one year with the Springfield Sallies but remained active in basketball, handball and golf. {AAGPBL Questionnaire, National Baseball Hall of Fame.}

Whitacre, Gina

P/SS, Virginia Flames

Gina Whitacre worked mainly in relief for the Flames in 2002 but she also hit .400 at the plate, helping the Flames earn the honor of being named the best-hitting team in the Eastern Women's league that season.

Whitaker, Melissa

(b. 18 July 1976, Victoria) IF, Malvern, Australian National Team

Melissa Whitaker played for the Australians in the 2002 Women's World Series and scored one of seven runs in their victory over Japan en route to winning the whole thing. Whitaker then played in six games in the 2003 Women's World Series but only hit .154 for her club. {Sam Santurf, "Australia Jells Fast to Capture World Series," *St. Petersburg Times*, 9 September 2002, 2C.}

White, Marcia

1949–50, Kenosha Comets

Marcia White served as the bat girl for the Kenosha Comets from 1949 to 1950. She was 14 when she got the chance to join them in breaking the barrier against women playing baseball. Her experience watching these women taught her to go after her dreams. As a result, she ended up with a 38-year career in the navy. She worked as the procurement manager for the Aegis program, a sophisticated weapons system. She started at the bottom working as a file clerk at the Great Lakes Naval Base and then in 1958 she moved to Washington as a secretary. With her involvement with the Aegis program she became the first woman to get a management position. She was handling a $4.2 billion budget annually when she retired in 1992. {Debbie Metro, "Girls League Inspired Former Bat Girl," *Kenosha News*, 30 July 1992.}

Whiteley, Jennifer

(Bronx, New York) Management

Jennifer Whiteley was born in the Bronx, but grew up in Martinsville, New Jersey, and attended Tulane University, earning a degree in management and finance in 1999. Whiteley became the general manager of the Visalia Oaks, a Class A affiliate of the Colorado Rockies, in 2001. Before joining the Oaks Whitely worked for one year with the Stockton Ports, starting as the director of finance and then moving up to assistant general manager with the Mudville Nine in 2000. As the GM for the Visalia Oaks, Whiteley has seen the team through a major stadium renovation in 2003 and helped increase their attendance by 20 percent over a three-year period. In October 2004 she received the California League Executive of the Year Award. Previously Whiteley had been nominated in 2002 for the Rawlings Woman Executive of the Year and the team won the City of Visalia Beautification Award in 2003. {Jennifer Whitely, correspondence with author, November 2004; Jennifer Whitely, Interview by Anthony Salazar, SABR, 2004; Ken Robison, "Fielding a Dream Job Visalia Oaks' General Manager Left Wall Street for a Home Plate Office," *The Fresno Bee*, 19 July 2002.}

Whiting, Betty Jane "Handy Hannabelle"

(b. 21 July 1925, Ida, Michigan) SS/1B/C/OF 1944–52, Milwaukee Chicks, Grand Rapids Chicks, Fort Wayne Daisies, Chicago Colleens, South Bend Blue Sox, Kalamazoo Lassies, Battle Creek Belles

Betty Whiting played for nine years in the All American League. She had some versatility as a fielder, which explains the number of trades in her career, though she did the majority of her playing at first base. She played hard in every game. Sometimes this led to injuries like the one she sustained in a game in June 1950, when she had a collision with Betty Trezza and had to be carried off the field. She also had the distinction of playing in a game in 1949 when South Bend set a single-game hitting record with 16 hits. Whiting was the only regular without a hit that day. She batted .190 for her career while playing in 943 games. She stole 198 bases and scored 311 runs while knocking in 232. {AAGPBL Baseball Cards, 2000; OBBHOF Newspaper Collection.}

Whitney (Dearfield), Norma Jean

(b. 29 May 1928, McKeesport, Pennsylvania)
2B 1949, Chicago Colleens

Whitney played one year for the Chicago Colleens traveling team and enjoyed the chance to see different places. She expected to join South Bend in 1950 but a detached retina prevented her from playing again. Whitney went to work at the G.C. Murphy Company warehouse and got married in 1952. She and her husband Duane had four children and ten grandchildren. Whitney stayed involved in sports by coaching the West Mifflin girls' softball team and bowling duck pins for 26 years. {AAGPBL Questionnaire, National Baseball Hall of Fame.}

Whitney (Payson), Joan

(1903–1975) Owner

By Joan M. Thomas

With a family genealogy that reads like a Who's Who of noteworthy, well-to-do Americans, Joan Whitney married multimillionaire Charles Payson in 1924. Yet, her impressive pedigree did not impel her to spend her life in pursuit of meaningless self-indulgences. A woman with varied interests, she lent invaluable support to both the arts and medical research. A fan of horse racing, she co-owned the Greentree Stables in Aiken, South Carolina, with her brother Jock Whitney. In particular, she loved baseball.

She inherited her fortune and philosophy towards life from her mother, Helen Hay Whitney. She even went with her mother to the Saratoga race track as a young girl. The men in her family had served President's Lincoln, McKinley and Theodore Roosevelt over the years.

Before she married Charles S. Payson Joan attended Barnard for a year and took a few business courses at Brown's Business College. After marrying in 1924 Joan stayed at home until 1929 when she decided to open a book store called "Young Books" which specialized in selling children's books in New York City. She merged this enterprise with Wakefield Books in 1942 creating a larger, single franchise. In the 1940s she also invested her money in art galleries, in entertainment and donated to a variety of charities.

According to an entry in the Whitney biographies found on the Internet, she first invested in baseball as a diversion after her children were grown. In 1950 she bought a single share of stock in the New York Giants. So, when in 1957 the team's board of directors approved the Giants' move to San Francisco, Long Island resident Joan Payson certainly felt the loss. A story in the *New York Times* on 5 October 1975 claimed she even tried to buy the Giants to avert the move.

After the Giants left, a special committee worked on ideas for bringing another team into New York. When the initial idea to form a third major league, the Continental League, was abandoned, two expansion teams for each league were admitted. New York, which already had an American League club, was awarded one of the National League franchises. Houston got the other. The new clubs were to be ready for the 1962 season.

Two women were among the initial group of investors in the new New York franchise. Canadian Dorothy J. Killiam was one, and Joan Payson was the other. Baseball historian Jack Lang, in *40 Years of Mets Baseball*, describes Killiam as an "avid fan of the Brooklyn Dodgers." He says, "When it became evident that [her] interest was in running the club herself, the other owners bought her out." Then some of the other investors sold out, and Payson ended up with "80 percent of the club." The new National League team, the Metropolitan Baseball Club, opened its first season in existence at the old home of the Giants, the Polo Grounds. All sources agree that the new owner wanted to dub the team the Meadowlarks. But the sportswriters who voted chose the title that was quickly shortened to simply the Mets. That was the first, and thus far only, time a new major league franchise arose with a woman as majority stockholder. {Peter Simon and Jack Lang, *New York Mets: 25 Years of Baseball Magic* (New York: Henry Holt and Company, Inc., 1986.)}

According to Lang, it was Payson who convinced Casey Stengel to manage the new club. He quotes Stengel as saying, "I couldn't say no to such a gracious lady." The Mets' first miserable seasons are legend, yet Payson stayed on. The club moved into its new home, Shea Stadium — named for William Shea, a principal force in the club's creation — in the spring of 1964. Payson became president of the Mets in 1968, and the following year she gained an extra dividend for her allegiance to her investment. Her ball club overcame the Baltimore Orioles to win the coveted World Series title.

Described as friendly, jolly and just plain down to earth by a number of people who knew her, she was more than just a figurehead for the Mets. She had a strong head for business and an intricate understanding of baseball. Attending the games often, she devised her own scoring system. One biographer relates, "When she went off sailing in the Greek islands one spring, she had her chauffeur attend all the games, and keep a running score and send her the scorecards."

Still head lady at Shea when she died in 1975, Payson was inducted into the Mets Hall of Fame in 1981. Now on the final list of executives eligible for induction into the National Baseball Hall of Fame in Cooperstown, she is also remembered by aficionados of the arts and horse racing. Probably, not all of her humanitarian endeavors will ever be known. But a *New York Times* story states that she "became director of the New York Hospital, St. Mary's Hospital in West Palm Beach, Fla., and the North Shore Hospital, Manhasset ... also a trustee of the United Hospital Fund and the Lighthouse for the Blind." {Joseph Durso, "Joan Whitney Payson, 72, Mets Owner, Dies," *New York Times*, 5 October 1975, 63.}

With her husband Charles she raised five children. Remarkably, one son enlisted in the army as an infantryman during World War II. He was killed at the Battle of the Bulge, something that might have easily been averted by someone of weaker character. Surely his family had the clout to keep him at home.

Payson's heirs sold the Mets in 1980, and today even Mets devotees might not be aware that the club's original owner was a woman. {Dave Dempsey, "Says Mrs. Payson of the Mets, 'You Can't Lose Them all,'" *New York Times*, 23 June 1968, SM28; Joseph Durso, "First Lady of the Mets Takes a Cram Course," *New York Times,* 13 November 1978, C6; "Joan Payson, Mets Principal Owner, Dies," *Nevada State Journal*, 5 October 1975, 23; "Mrs. Payson Moves Up to Mets' President," *Washington Post*, 7 February 1968, D3.}

Whittam, Claire

2003, Lady Mariners

Claire Whittam had the lowest average for her

Australian team in the 2003 Women's World Series. She only hit .143 in three games. She did knock in two runs and also walked twice.

Wiggins, Lauren

C, Blue Crush

Lauren Wiggins catches for the Blue Crush in the Philadelphia Women's League. She comes in from Connecticut every weekend to join her teammates. When she is not playing baseball Wiggins also plays hockey. {Eileen O'Donnell, "Covering All the Bases," *Philadelphia Inquirer*, 15 July 2005.}

Adriane Calenda and Lauren Wiggins at practice in 1998 for the Ladies Pro League (courtesy Laura Wulf).

Wigiser, Margaret M. "Wiggie"

(b. 17 December 1924, Brooklyn, New York) CF 1944–46, Minneapolis Millerettes, Rockford Peaches

While attending Seward Park High School, Margaret Wigiser received the Underhill Certificate for Outstanding Athlete in 1942, recognizing her achievements in softball and track and field. She attended Hunter College for her BA and MA degrees. It was while she was in college that Wigiser joined the AAGPBL. Her first highlight was being a part of the 1945 championship Rockford team. In 1946 Wigiser played in 39 games and hit .203. She played in 203 games during her three seasons and hit .227. She stole 65 bases and knocked in 88 runs. She also scored another 80 and added 63 walks to her hit total of 159. {AAGPBL Baseball Cards, 1996; AAGPBL Newsletter, January 2002, 25.}

After her baseball career ended, Wigiser achieved success as an amateur golfer. She was the Amateur Champion of Milford, Pennsylvania, from 1950 to 1955. In 1982 Wigiser was selected for membership in the Hunter College Hall of Fame and in 1997 the hall presented her with their outstanding achievement award.

Wigiser played for two years in the National Girls Baseball League in Chicago before leaving to go back to school to earn a master's degree. She taught at Martin Van Buren High School from 1956 to 1961 and then at Francis Lewis High School from 1961 to 1969.

The New York City Public Schools Athletic Association inducted her into their hall of fame in 1989, recognizing her accomplishments as director of girls' high school sports in New York City from 1969 to 1982. One of her greatest achievements was helping to rescind the rule prohibiting girls' participation in high school sports in the city. She started her campaign to get the resolution changed while working at Francis Lewis as chair of health and physical education in 1969. Wigiser wrote a new resolution that was approved, and by 1970 girls' basketball had begun along with volleyball and bowling. Though the permission was given for the girls to play, the fight was not over. Each year, the coaches and Wigiser had to ask for enough money to provide uniforms and other equipment for the teams and had to battle to get gym time. {AAGPBL Questionnaire, National Baseball Hall of Fame; Arthur V. Claps, "History of NYC Basketball," *Newsday*, 29 March 2002.}

Wiley, Charlotte

SS 2003, Alameda Oaks

Charlotte Wiley played for the Alameda Oaks in the California Women's League and had the second-highest batting average in the league behind veteran Rhonda Palmer. Wiley hit 17–30 in eight games and drove in 15 runs.

Wiley (Sears), Janet "Pee Wee"

(b. 12 October 1933, South Bend, Indiana) 1B 1950–53, Chicago Colleens, South Bend Blue Sox, Rockford Peaches

Janet Wiley grew up in South Bend, Indiana, watching the Blue Sox play at Playland Park. Before joining the AAGPBL as a player Wiley served as the bat girl for the South Bend club in 1947 and 1948 when she was only 14- and 15-years-old. She received a telegram from the team's general manager inviting her to join the club as the new bat girl. She was to report to the team chaperone, Lucille Moore. Her duties as bat girl varied from collecting the bats to keeping ice water ready for the players during games. She and her fellow bat girl alternated working for the visiting teams as well. She also participated in summer league baseball sponsored by the Blue Sox. The Blue Sox developed these teams to encourage girls who wished to play baseball but had no opportunities at their schools. While hanging around the Blue Sox to learn the game, Wiley got many chances to play first base and decided she would do that rather than pitch as she had originally planned. She tried out for the Blue Sox in 1950 and made the team even though she was still in high school. She got sent to join the traveling Chicago Colleens because the Blue Sox already had a regular first baseman. After three weeks she got called back to South Bend and finished the season with the Sox. Wiley finally retired due to recurring knee injuries after the 1953 season in Rockford. She coached her old elementary school's softball team (St. Matthew's) for eight years. She also got married and raised six children. {AAGPBL Questionnaire, National Baseball Hall of Fame; Patricia I. Brown, *A League of My Own* (Jefferson, N.C.: McFarland, 2003) 184–87.}

Williams, Ann

(b. 18 September 1970, Vero Beach, Florida) P, Colorado Silver Bullets

Before joining the Silver Bullets, Ann Williams played softball at Nicholls State, where she achieved All-Southland conference honors. As a pitcher for the Bullets, Williams struck out 23 in only 21 innings pitched in 1994, but had a 7.06 ERA. Williams used three pitches to get batters out: a slider, a circle change and a fastball clocked in the low 80s. As a pinch hitter, she also had a .333 on-base percentage at the plate. Williams attended the New York Mets training camp at Port St. Lucie with fellow Bullets player Shannan Mitchem in 1995. Both women tried out and were cut by the end of the second round. Williams did not make it past the first cut, while Mitchem made it to the second. When she was not on the baseball diamond Williams worked as a substitute teacher in Gainesville, Florida. {Gregory Richards, "Believe It: This Woman Throws Hard," *Naples Daily News*, 12 April 1995; David Kindred, *Colorado Silver Bullets: For the Love of the Game* (Atlanta: Longstreet Press, Inc.), 100;

Jeff Williams, "Well, They Tried, Mets Turned Down Silver Bullets," *Newsday*, 2 February 1995.}

Williams, Karen

Karen Williams has been a baseball executive and a baseball wife. She worked for the Houston Astros and married outfielder Billy Hatcher in 1987. She started working for the Houston Sports Association in 1983 as an intern from Ohio University. After her internship she became the Director of Promotions under Michael Storen. In 1986 the department was renamed and Williams new title became Director of Special Events. {"Karen Williams." In *Baseball Lives: Men and Women of the Game*. Mike Bryan. New York: Pantheon Books, 1989, 104–110.}

Williams (Heverly), Ruth

(b. 12 February 1926, Nescopeck, Pennsylvania; d. 10 February 2005) P 1947–53, South Bend Blue Sox, Peoria Red Wings, Kalamazoo Lassies

Ruth Williams started playing softball when she was only 12 years old. She attended a tryout in Pennsylvania in 1946 after her father saw an ad in the local paper. She went and was assigned to Fort Wayne. Williams once pitched 46 consecutive scoreless innings in her career. Her best season was her rookie year, when she was 12–8 with a 1.70 ERA in 180 innings. Her overall numbers in 162 games were solid. She had a career 2.24 ERA with a 65–69 record. She struck out 315 hitters and walked 395. She only hit .130 but she was there to pitch, not hit. {"Woman Recalls Her Years as Professional Baseball Player," *The Intelligencer and The Record*, 3 August 1992, A1, A4; AAGPBL Baseball Cards, 1995–96.}

Williams, Polly

WNEBL

Polly Williams grew up in Florida and played softball in school. She joined the WNEBL in 2000 and found she liked baseball better because the game was faster. When not on the ball field Williams worked as a social worker. {Michael O'Conner, "The Local Women Are ... Playing Hardball," *The Boston Herald*, 28 May 2000.}

Willson, Cindy

SS, Arizona Baseball

In 1994 Cindy Willson played shortstop for the Cactus Wrens and hit .514.

Wilson, Mildred

1946–49, Chaperone

Mildred Wilson acted as chaperone for the Racine Belles from 1946 to 1949. She also played some softball and baseball. She graduated from Long Island University with a physical education degree. {Merrie Fidler, *The Development and Decline of the All-American Girls Baseball League, 1943–1954*, Master of Science thesis (Department of Physical Education: University of Massachusetts, 1976), 249.}

Wiltse (Collins), Dorothy "Dottie"

(b. 23 September 1923, Inglewood, California)

By Carolyn M. Trombe

In the early 1930s, southern California teemed with stars of varying magnitudes. Aside from the conventional icons of the silver screen, those with athletic prowess also dominated the scene. Softball in particular proved a strong sport in this area of the country, drawing a significant fan base during regular games and tournaments alike. One of the most outstanding of these softball stars was Dottie Wiltse Collins, a pitcher who reached even higher levels of excellence when she was recruited for the All-American Girls Professional Baseball League.

Dottie began her sports career as a bat girl for the Mark C. Bloome softball team in southern California. During one seemingly hopeless game of the championship series in 1935, the manager of the team, John Berry, plucked the 11-year-old Wiltse from her role as bat girl and placed her on the pitcher's mound. Undaunted by the crowd of thousands, the young Dottie pitched her team to victory. From then on, she grew even more formidable.

Wiltse was born on 23 September 1923 in Inglewood, California, to Eleanor Camille Runswick and Daniel Emerson Wiltse. Her surroundings nurtured her love of baseball. Dan Wiltse, a lead burner for Standard Oil Company, played second base in an area semipro baseball league, teaming up with such future major league stars as Louis Novikoff, who went on to play outfield for the Chicago Cubs, posting a career .262 average. In addition, two of Dan's distant ancestors, Lewis DeWitt "Snake" Wiltse, who threw for the Philadelphia A's and the Baltimore Orioles in the early 1900s, and Snake's more famous younger brother, George Leroy "Hooks" Wiltse, who pitched a no-hitter for the New York Giants on the Fourth of July 1908, provided ample inspiration for future Wiltse feats. With such a background, Dottie could hardly fail to excel.

Interestingly, Dottie chose to follow the pitching path taken by Hooks and Snake rather than opting for the infield like her father. However, Dottie's father exerted the biggest influence on her baseball career. Each day after school, Dottie waited patiently for her dad to come home from work so they could enjoy a game of catch. They began practicing in the backyard of Dottie's home where Dan had built a backstop, but at times they moved to the softball field behind the high school for a more challenging venue.

Barbara White Hoffman, Dottie's best friend from childhood, recalls Dottie and her father walking by her house on their way to the school, softballs and mitts in hand. Curious as to where they were going, one day she decided to follow them. "I would watch them every night," Barbara confided. "Having been a ball player, Pop really knew what he was talking about, so I learned a lot." Inspired by her interest, Dan soon included Barbara in the practice sessions, and as a result she went on to play league softball with Dottie. {Barbara White, personal correspondence with author, November 2003.}

By the time Wiltse pitched her first game in 1935, she was well on her way to a stellar softball career. Aside from the local softball teams for which she played, Dottie also joined a co-ed baseball team in grade school. Unfortunately, no opportunity existed for her to play in high school, as scholastic sports were not available to women at that time. However, Wiltse continued to pitch not only for Mark C. Bloome, but also for Goodrich Silvertown, sponsored by Goodrich Rubber; Cantlay Tanzola, an affiliate of the oil industry; and Young's Market, an area supermarket chain. After graduation from high school in 1941, Wiltse worked as a receptionist for Payne Furnace and pitched for the company's semipro softball team. At night, when games were canceled due to the blackout enforced during World War II, she aided the war effort by assembling airplane parts in a local factory.

Three years later, in 1944, Bill Allington, Wiltse's former manager from softball teams such as Mark C. Bloome and Goodrich Silvertown, approached her after a game and suggested that she try out for the All-American Girls Professional Baseball League. Along with six other California girls handpicked by Allington, including Faye Dancer, LaVonne "Pepper" Paire, and Annabelle Lee, Wiltse boarded a train in Los Angeles to make the cross-country trip to Chicago in the spring of that year. When asked if she was scared going so far away for the first time, Wiltse said, "Heck no. It was a train full of sailors." {Dottie

Wiltse Collins, interview with author, June 2002, Ft. Wayne, Indiana.}

The tryouts were highly competitive, yet, as if to demonstrate the baseball savvy of Bill Allington, all six girls from California made the league. Wiltse, along with Dancer and Lee, began play with the Minneapolis Millerettes. Despite the team's overall poor showing, Wiltse held her own with a 20–16 record and a 1.88 earned run average. The team disbanded at end of the 1944 season, after it became apparent that teams in larger cities did not fare as well as those in mid-sized ones. In 1945, the Millerettes, including Wiltse, moved to Fort Wayne, Indiana, where the team was renamed the Fort Wayne Daisies.

Wiltse continued her outstanding play with the Daisies, where she stayed for the remainder of her career. Some of her feats include 17 shutouts in a season and two no-hitters in 17 days, both in 1945. In addition, in her first year with the Daisies, Dottie pitched 345 innings, with 293 strikeouts and 111 bases-on-balls. She ended the year with a 0.83 ERA and a .744 winning percentage. The next two years also concluded with brilliant ERAs of 2.32 and 1.33, respectively, and a solid spot on the Daisies' pitching rotation.

That first year with the Daisies also saw the beginning of the courtship between Dottie Wiltse and her future husband, Harvey Collins. Harvey's interest was piqued when he watched Dottie win both games of a doubleheader in flawless fashion. Perhaps he expected a different type of game, probably having heard more about the ladylike deportment of the players than their superb athleticism. League officials stressed the exemplary conduct of players to stem comments such as the one made by columnist Halsey Hall before the Millerettes were due to play their first home game. In a column in the *Minneapolis Tribune* in May 1944, Hall quipped, "Common courtesies and the sweet little niceties accorded ladies generally go by the board at Nicollet Park next weekend."

The uniforms the girls wore reinforced the idea of femininity. They consisted of short flaring skirts, reminiscent of the ice skating uniforms of the time, with boxer-type shorts underneath. The players also attended charm school during the first two years of the league and were issued handbooks outlining proper conduct. One of these edicts was that while slacks were allowed on the buses that took players to competing cities, the girls were to don skirts if they left the bus for any reason.

Yet despite these restrictions, the players demonstrated not only their natural aptitude but their love for the game. Even the cynical Hall gave credit where it was due when he stated in the *Minneapolis Tribune* in late May 1944 that the girls played "like genuine ballplayers." This fact so impressed Harvey Collins that he confided to his friend that he wanted to meet Wiltse after the game. To that end, Harvey's friend arranged for him to help deliver beer to the apartment Wiltse shared with five other girls. Their courtship began with a golf date the following day and culminated in their marriage in March 1946. The union lasted more than 50 years.

Harvey continued to support Dottie's playing career after their marriage. During the middle of the 1948 season, Dottie (now Collins) herself decided the time had come to stop. After pitching one game of a double-header, she handed the ball to her manager and voluntarily benched herself. She was six months pregnant at the time. Dottie's catcher, the future doctor Mary Rountree, remembers how frantic she was, calling shots to a pregnant pitcher. She recalls signaling pitches that would go to the left or the right of the soon-to-be mother. "I was so nervous every time a batter hit a ball," Rountree confided. {Mary Rountree, interview with author, October 2002, Highland Beach, Florida.} However, Collins took her pregnancy in stride. "I was healthy," she said, "and the doctor said it was all right for me to play. I know my manager was relieved, though, when I walked off the mound for the last time." {Dottie Collins, interview with author, June 2002, Ft. Wayne, Indiana.}

Thankfully, Collins only temporarily departed from baseball. Although she intended to quit the game completely in 1948 for full time motherhood, baseball lured her back for two more seasons of play. The year-long hiatus did not affect her pitching at all as she chalked up an ERA of 3.46 and a winning percentage of .619. While combining motherhood and baseball was not always easy, Collins credits a support system consisting of her teammates, her husband, and her mother-in-law, who always sat in the stands with Collins' daughter, Patty, snuggled up in her lap. The fans, too, rallied around her. One fan even made a miniature pink Daisy uniform for Patty, which Collins later donated to the archives at the Northern Indiana Historical Society in South Bend, Indiana, the largest depository of memorabilia from the AAGPBL. This uniform, along with Collins' warmup jacket, was also included in the Women in Sports exhibit, "Breaking Barriers," at the Northern Indiana Historical Society, which opened in the fall of 2002.

After the 1950 season, Collins permanently retired from baseball, intending to put the game behind her. Always sports-minded, though, she took up golf with a vengeance after the birth of her sec-

ond child, a son, Daniel, in 1954. Her feats on the green equaled those she had performed on the mound. She was twice awarded the all-city championship for women's golf, once sharing the accolade with Harvey for men's golf, the only husband-and-wife team to do so. {Dottie Collins, interview with author, June 2002, Ft. Wayne, Indiana.} Collins still enjoys an occasional game of golf today.

She also promoted youth sports through the Elks Club in Ft. Wayne during the late 1950s, the 1960s and the 1970s, organizing beginning and intermediate level golf games for children and coordinating a children's bowling league. Although these sports offered opportunities for both boys and girls, the girls in particular benefited from Collins' involvement, particularly since few sports options existed for women in the 1950s and 1960s. Her efforts, especially in the game of golf, guaranteed that the potential of many budding female athletes was realized rather than remaining dormant.

In addition to her community involvement, Collins worked part time while raising her family. Ironically, her choice of jobs ensured that the game she thought she had left behind was never far away. Dottie worked for both Vim's Sporting Goods, where she especially enjoyed helping young baseball players choose just the right bat, and for The Baseball Blue Book, headquartered at that time in Fort Wayne, where all the records of major league baseball were kept.

Dottie truly welcomed the game back into her life in 1982 with the first reunion of the All-American Girls Professional Baseball League in almost 30 years. Appropriately, the girls gathered in Chicago, Illinois, where they had first flocked for tryouts in the 1940s and early 1950s. The following year, several of the players united once again for an exhibition game as part of the Run, Jane, Run women's sports festival in Fort Wayne, an event they repeated in subsequent years. {Dottie Collins, interview with author, June 2002, Ft. Wayne, Indiana.}

Finally, in 1987, the Players Association was formed in the home of Fran Janssen in South Bend, Indiana. The association came to fruition mainly due to Collins' crusade in locating former players. For more than nine years, she also served as the treasurer and newsletter editor, guiding the organization to the force it has become today. In addition, her quest to resurrect the league after years of obscurity led to the opening of the "Women in Baseball" exhibit at the Hall of Fame in Cooperstown, New York, in 1988, an event Collins considers one of the highlights of her life.

Appropriately, Collins received the honor of opening the curtain to display the Hall of Fame's first exhibit of women's professional baseball. Her drive to gain recognition for the league extended beyond the exhibit in Cooperstown, though. Among the audience on hand to view the ceremonies was veteran actress and director Penny Marshall. Marshall's interest in the league was sparked after she viewed a documentary about the AAGPBL written by Kelly Candaele, the son of AAGPBL outfielder Helen Callaghan. Her interest grew tenfold as she witnessed the spirit these women still displayed as they celebrated their rise from obscurity to the annals of baseball history. As a result, she resolved to immortalize the league on film. *A League of Their Own* was released to great acclaim in 1992, earning the distinction of being one of the top ten grossing movies of the year and one of the top grossing movies of all time at the USA Box Office. The movie was also nominated for a Golden Globe Award in 1993. {<IMDB.com>} Collins served as a technical director on the set, helping to ensure the authenticity of the film, with a particular emphasis on the scenes where baseball is actually played.

Following the movie's release, the resurgence of interest in the league meant an expanded membership in the Players Association and an influx of fan mail for Collins. Her unflagging efforts to support the league continue today, with talks at area schools and correspondence with aspiring athletes. In 1999, her personal recognition came when she was one of the first two women, along with Daisy teammate Joanne Weaver, to be inducted into the Fort Wayne Baseball Hall of Fame.

Collins will long be remembered for her accomplishments both off and on the mound. Her dedication, her professionalism, and her tireless efforts for the sake of the league all have ensured that women's sports have a past from which to spring and a future towards which to strive. More importantly, in choosing her own path rather than the one dictated by society, Collins taught by example the rewards we reap when we dare to act upon our dreams.

WIMNZ Baseball

WIMNZ Baseball is a women's team from Wisconsin and Minnesota that began play in 2003. The founder of the team is Ashley Nicolls. Their competition was primarily boys' junior teams in the area because there were no women's teams to play. Their first game took place at Wade Stadium in June 2003 against a team from West Duluth. The first hit for the new squad came from Theresa Williams and the second from Ashley Nicolls. {Ashley Nicolls, unpublished article given to Leslie A. Heaphy.}

Wingrove (Earl), Elsie "Windy"

(b. 26 September 1923, Saskatchewan, Canada) CF 1946–47, Fort Wayne Daisies, Grand Rapids Chicks

While growing up in Canada, Elsie Wingrove had a chance to play a number of sports at school. One of her favorites was ice hockey, but she also took part in curling, track and field and fast-pitch softball. She bowled in a commercial league and played for the Saskatoon Pats in the city league. Before joining the AAGPBL she worked as a bank teller and attended Saskatoon Technical College, playing softball for their team. In 1946 she joined the Grand Rapids team but was loaned out to Fort Wayne for a couple of months. She was a part of the championship squad in Grand Rapids in 1947. She played in 119 games with a .181 career average. Her fielding is what kept her in games, as she finished with a .952 fielding percentage. After leaving the league Wingrove helped her husband coach Little League and junior girls fast-pitch softball while working for Canadian Customs. Wingrove was inducted into the Saskatchewan Baseball Hall of Fame for her contributions. {AAGPBL Questionnaire, National Baseball Hall of Fame; AAGPBL Baseball Cards, 1996.}

Winsch, Karl "Hap"

(b. 10 February 1915, Allentown, Pennsylvania) Manager 1951–54, South Bend Blue Sox

Karl Winsch managed the South Bend club from 1951 until the AAGPBL folded at the end of the 1954 season. They won two championships under his leadership, in 1952 and 1953. He had been a minor league pitcher before signing with the Phillies in 1943, though he never actually got to play a major league game. His experience in professional baseball made him an excellent teacher. Winsch's wife, Jean Faut, pitched in the league; that was his introduction to women's baseball. {"Women's Baseball Manager Is in a League of His Own," *Touching Bases Newsletter*, January 1997, 14; AAGPBL Baseball Cards, 1996.}

Winter, Joanne "Jo"

(b. 24 November 1924, Maywood, Illinois; d. September 1996, Tempe, Arizona) P 1943–1950, Racine Belles

Jo Winter grew up near Chicago and was well-known locally for her sports prowess, especially in softball. She even convinced her father to move out West to give her more opportunities. They intended to go to California but only made it to Arizona, where Winter continued her softball playing but also added golf. After attending a tryout for the AAGPBL and making one of the original teams, Winter spent eight seasons with the Racine Belles. Winter was selected by the managers for the 1946 all-star team. She had a 33–10 record with six straight shutouts and an ERA of 1.19, which was second best in the league behind Connie Wisniewski. Her scoreless innings for that season extended to 63.

To show that was not a fluke, the following season Winter was 22–13 and then in 1948 she was 25–12. Those numbers are even more impressive when you realize they came after the switch to overhand pitching. Her career numbers included 287 games pitched, with a 2.06 ERA and a 133–115 record. She struck out 770 batters while walking 759. Her best season hitting seems to have been her rookie year, when she hit .253 in 31 games. {AAGPBL Baseball Cards, 1996.}

In 1950 she returned to Chicago to play for the Music Makers, a local softball team. By 1955 she was back in Arizona playing for the Arizona A-1 Queens. A new sport became her life in 1956 as she took up golf again and became a champion, winning the 1962 Arizona Women's Amateur Championship. She tried to make the cut for the Ladies Professional Golf Association but finally gave up in 1966 and returned to teach golf in Scottsdale. In 1971 she helped organize the Arizona Silver Belle Golf Championship for female players. Winter's contributions to the game of golf were recognized in 1995 when she was awarded the Ellen Griffin Rolex Award for lifetime achievement as a teacher. {AAGPBL Newsletter, September 1996, 6.}

Winthrop, Susan "Sue"

(b. 1955, Brooklyn, New York) P, New Jersey Nemesis, Queens Cyclones

Susan Winthrop founded the NYWBA in 2001 and pitches for the Queens Cyclones. Before that she pitched for the New Jersey Nemesis in the EWBC. Winthrop developed four pitches she uses regularly: a curveball, a sidearm fastball, an overhand fastball and sometimes a knuckleball. She also used to be the head coach of women's softball at New York University and she plays the saxophone professionally. Her love of baseball came in part from going to games to watch her father pitch. At Edgemont High School Winthrop played softball and continued her playing at SUNY-Albany for one game before she tore up her elbow and thought her career was over. It was ten years before Winthrop played baseball again. {Michael Malone, "Throwing Like a Girl," *New York Sports Express*, 28

August–3 September 2003, 15; Rick Carpiniello, "A League for Those Who Say Softball Isn't Enough," *The Journal News*, 9 June 2003.}

Wirth, Senaida "Shoo Shoo"

(b. 4 October 1926, Tampa, Florida; d. 1967) SS 1946–51, South Bend Blue Sox

Senaida Wirth played all six years of her career with South Bend. She was chosen by the managers for the 1946 all-star team as a rookie. She hit .245 and stole 89 bases. She had gotten off to a great start, leading the AAGPBL in hitting as late as mid–June with a .386 average at that point. By the time her career ended, Wirth stole 359 bases in 616 games. She had 360 hits and another 313 walks and hit .248. {AAGPBL Baseball Cards, 2000.}

Wise, Brenda

SS 1999, San Diego Stix

In 1999 Wise helped the Stix win the national championship series and she was named to the all-tournament team. She hit .688 to lead all hitters and scored 12 runs while knocking in another four.

Brenda Wise at training camp in 1998 (courtesy Laura Wulf).

Wisniewski, Connie "Iron Woman," Polish Rifle"

(b. 18 February 1922, Detroit, Michigan)

By Shawn Selby

Connie Wisniewski was born in Detroit, Michigan, on 18 February 1922. As a child, she was a great fan of baseball, regularly standing outside Briggs Stadium on game days to catch balls hit out of the park, or, if she was lucky, sneaking into games to watch her idols, Charlie Gehringer and Hank Greenburg, take on their rivals in the American League. She perfected her pitching style, a dramatic "windmill" delivery, by pitching balls through a tire suspended from a tree in her back yard. Although the idea of becoming a professional ballplayer never entered her mind as a youngster, in the spring of 1944 Wisniewski saw a chance to make a living at the sport she loved. Even though she was certainly of legal age, Connie asked her mother's permission to join the AAGPBL that year. Her mother refused, believing that proper young ladies did not engage in such dirty and masculine pursuits, let alone make a living doing so. Undaunted, Connie coolly suggested that if she could not play baseball, she would join the army instead. The threat worked, and Connie signed with the Milwaukee Chicks in 1944. {Lois Browne, *The Girls of* Summer, 52.}

The Chicks were managed by Max Carey, who spent much of his 20-year career in the major leagues playing in the outfield for the Pittsburgh Pirates, where he won the World Series in 1925. He was elected to the National Baseball Hall of Fame in 1961. Carey's Chicks were one of two expansion teams in the AAGPBL during the league's second year. They were also one of only two teams in the league that were allowed to play in a stadium built for a professional team. Bill Veeck, owner of the minor league Milwaukee Brewers, allowed the Chicks to play their games in Bouchert Stadium when the Brewers were on the road. Wisniewski racked up an impressive start as a rookie pitcher, winning her first five games before being hampered by a knee injury. Even with the injury and the brace it forced her to wear, she completed the season with a 23–10 record and the highest winning percentage in the league. Her batting, on the other hand, was poor. She collected only 17 hits in 111 at-bats, compiling a meager .153 average. Her poor performance at the plate did not seriously impact the team's season, however, as the Chicks took home the league championship in Wisniewski's rookie year. But even with the team's victory in the championship, the fans in Milwaukee were lukewarm in their support for the girls.

Sparse attendance and slumping box office receipts forced the Chicks to relocate to Grand Rapids, Michigan, in 1945. They may have also helped convince the team's dynamic manager, Max Carey, to accept an invitation to serve as the AAGPBL's president beginning in 1945.

During the 1945 season, Wisniewski began to come into her own on the mound. She amassed impressive numbers in her sophomore year, and earned the nickname "Iron Woman" for starting and finishing both ends of a doubleheader. She would repeat this feat twice more, even winning both games of a doubleheader two times. Over the course of the 1945 season Wisniewski started 46 games and finished 43 of them, an unheard-of statistic in today's system of pitching rotations and platooning. Even more impressive than her starts was her 32–11 record and her 0.81 earned run average. Her overpowering performance on the mound earned her the first Player of the Year award in AAGPBL history. She continued her pitching dominance in 1946, compiling a .786 winning percentage with a 33–9 record. Such stellar pitching talent led one sportswriter to call her the "Christine Mathewson" of women's baseball. Wisniewski's hitting also improved, and by the end of the 1946 campaign her batting average was up to .250. The combination of hitting and pitching she displayed landed her a spot as the starting pitcher on the all-star team that year. {Gai Berlage, *Women in Baseball*, 166.}

Things started to change for Wisniewski during 1947. The distance from the pitcher's mound to home plate was increased two feet, from 68 feet to 70 feet, causing her pitching to suffer. Although she had always been an underhand pitcher, she began to experiment with sidearm and overhand deliveries. She managed to hold her own as one of the league's premier hurlers, racking up a 16–14 record and a 2.15 ERA; however, by the next season the fates had conspired against her pitching career. The pitching distance was increased to 72 feet and overhand pitching became official. Unable to adapt, Wisniewski posted a 3–4 record in only eight starts. Her pitching days were over.

Fortunately for Wisniewski, however, as her pitching lost its punch, her hitting steadily improved. Recognizing that she was still a valuable asset to the Chicks, manager Johnny Rawlings suggested she move to the outfield. She had a difficult time mastering the new position, but with more at-bats came more opportunity to hone her skills at the plate. Wisniewski did not disappoint. She ended 1948 with 127 hits, including a year-high seven home runs. Her .289 average ranked her as the league's third-best hitter.

After another solid year in the outfield, Wisniewski left the AAGPBL in 1950 to play in the Chicago National Girls Baseball League for more money. Her decision to jump the AAGPBL caused a crisis in the league. If Wisniewski, a bona fide star of women's baseball, should leave, what was to stop other big names from doing the same? The AAGPBL sought to prevent her departure. After an agreement was reached between the owners in both leagues to allow rosters to be exchanged well in advance of upcoming seasons, Wisniewski was free to join the NGBL's Music Maids. The NGBL was a fast-pitch softball league, so her normal underhand delivery fit in well. Her weekly wage increased from $100 to $250 in the new league, she was provided with a limousine to drive her to and from games, and she received a clause in her contract stipulating that she would be paid even if she were injured. Even with the benefits of playing in the Chicago league, Connie was disappointed with what she saw as the league's lack of professionalism as well as the almost constant atmosphere of betting that surrounded it. So, in 1951, she returned to the Chicks when they offered to equal her salary from the NGBL. Although the AAGPBL had a rule blackballing players who had played in the Chicago league, the requirement was relaxed for a player of Wisniewski's caliber. She lost no time regaining her old form. She posted a .326 batting average in 1951 with 126 hits and a career high .957 fielding average and was an all-star outfielder for the Chicks in 1951 and in 1952. {Gregorich, *Women at Play*, 105; Lois Browne, *The Girls of Summer*, 181.}

While she continued her success on the field, Wisniewski worked at General Motors. During the war she helped the automobile giant fill military contracts, and when the war ended she continued at GM, working to fill the voracious public demand for cars. In addition, Wisniewski and fellow Chick Doris Satterfield had opened a small burger joint near the Grand Rapids theater. Called the Chicks Dugout, the business was moderately successful and the partners eventually sold it for a profit. {Lois Browne, 134.}

At the end of the 1952 season Wisniewski decided to retire. She had been selected as an all-star that year, and decided to go out on top of her game. At 30 years old, she was beginning to feel the wear and tear of the game. After leaving the AAGPBL she returned to work full time at General Motors.

When Wisniewski passed away in May of 1995, she left behind her a legacy as one of the premier woman baseball players of her day. A two-position star was and is rare in baseball, but she rose to the status of a Walter Johnson on the mound and

a Stan Musial in the field. She was recognized by fans and sportswriters alike as a dominant player both on the mound and in the outfield, and she never failed to conduct herself with grace and professionalism both on and off the field.

Witt, Kim

Kim Witt was the ballplayer who tried out for the Minnesota Twins in 1982. She was one of 406 players who showed up at open tryouts. Witt's job when not playing baseball was working for the post office. Her family encouraged her to go to the tryouts and see what she could do. While not invited back, Witt showed herself and the others that she was a fine fielder. She never got to bat in the tryouts because she had to leave to go to work before getting a chance.

Wohlwender (Fricker), Marion "Wooly"

(b. 13 March 1922, Cincinnati, Ohio) C 1943, Kenosha Comets

Marion Wohlwender grew up in Cincinnati and attended Western Hills High School. She played baseball for the Vic Brown Rosebuds and the H.H. Meyer Packing Company, where she worked. She joined the AAGPBL in its inaugural year but did not return after one month because of family problems. She returned home and got married in 1945. She continued to play baseball for three more years and coached a girl's softball team for one year. {AAGPBL Questionnaire, National Baseball Hall of Fame Library, Cooperstown, New York.}

Wold, Bridget

Bridget Wold managed in the Ladies Professional League in 1997 and 1998. She started with the Los Angeles Legends and moved to Florida in 1998 with the team franchise. {Barry Jackson, "Women's League Puts Team in Homestead," *Miami Herald*, 9 April 1998.}

Wombats

Southern California Women's Baseball League

Women's Baseball Leadership

By Justine Siegal

Women have been playing baseball since before they even had the right to vote. Women played at Vassar College in 1866, as professionals for the AAGPBL during World War II, and against men on the Colorado Silver Bullets, a professional barnstorming team, from 1994 to 1997. Propelling these baseball opportunities have been the visionary leaders who create the opportunity and then execute it. These baseball leaders have created both professional and amateur chances for females to play.

"Women's baseball" is different than "women in baseball." "Women in baseball" includes managers, umpires, announcers, and any females who contribute to the game of baseball. "Women's baseball" is by my definition a league or team that is designed for females to play on. Men do administrative work (i.e., coaching) within women's baseball, but the focus in "women's baseball" is on females playing with or against other females. {Debra Shattuck, "Bats, Balls, and Books: Baseball and Higher Education for Women at Three Eastern Women's Colleges," *Journal of Sport History*, summer 1992, 91, 109.}

Women's Baseball Overview

Women have been involved in American baseball since its inception in the nineteenth century. A historical analysis of women's roles in baseball shows that their participation rate is a result of social, political, and economic times. In the beginning of the twentieth century, it was socially acceptable for women to play baseball with the men, as demonstrated by the mixed "Bloomer Girls" teams. As gender roles evolved, society steered women toward softball. It was not until 1943, after the men had gone off to war, that women were sanctioned by society to play baseball again. From 1943 to 1954, the AAGPBL operated, becoming the first professional baseball league for women. When the men returned from war, it was no longer considered popular or profitable for women to play baseball, and the league folded. Forty years later women were given another opportunity to play professionally: In 1993, the Colorado Silver Bullets were formed. The Bullets were an all-star women's team that barnstormed across the country playing men's teams. A withdrawal of sponsorship caused the Bullets to fold in 1997. In 1995, Bobby Bonds, Tom Lang, and Sal Algieri formed a short-lived professional league, the United States Women's Baseball League. The Ladies Professional Baseball League folded after a year and a half of play between 1997 and 1998. In 2004, USA Baseball and Baseball Canada both initiated their first national women's team; the teams competed in the first IBAF World Cup of Women's Baseball in Edmonton in August 2004. {Gregorich, *Women at Play*, 1993; Berlage, *Women in Baseball*, 1994; Karen H. Weiller and Catriona Higgs, "The All American Girls Professional Baseball League, 1943–54: Gender Conflict in Sport," *Sociology of Sport Journal*, 1992, 46–54.}

AAGPBL: Philip Wrigley

The All American Girls Professional Baseball League (AAGPBL), 1943–54, was the brainchild of Philip Wrigley, the owner of the Chicago Cubs. Worried that major league baseball would shut down as a result of the male players going off to World War II, Wrigley wanted to ensure that he could still fill up his stadium with fans. His idea was women's softball. The idea turned into a successful Midwest league. The softball play over the years mutated into baseball. For instance, the AAGPBL started with a larger ball (then a baseball) and pitched underhand, and by the end of the league the pitchers threw overhand with a smaller ball.

Wrigley was a businessman who felt that sex appeal would help sell his women's league. Wrigley wrote in his promotional material to potential team owners, "We will select the kind of players that people will want to see in action. Then we will groom them, to make sure they are acceptable. It won't be like the bad old days of peep shows and Bloomer Girls.... The League will be good for you and your community, good for the country, good for the war effort, and good for you." League secretary Marie Keenan explained, "We do not want our uniforms to stress sex, but they should be feminine, with emphasis on the clean American sports girl." In the end, it was Wrigley's desire to make money that fueled his interest in women's baseball. Years later after the league, Wrigley confessed to a reporter that he never saw an All-American team in action because he felt that he would have only been disappointed, as he would have only compared the women to his male players. {Browne, 25, 40, 45.}

Silver Bullets: Bob Hope

Although he created a historical baseball opportunity for women in the 1940s and '50s, Wrigley was not interested in promoting women's baseball for the purpose that women might play hardball. In the 1980s Bob Hope, a former Atlanta Braves executive, thought that women should have a chance to play baseball. In 1984, Hope tried to form a women's minor league team but could not obtain a franchise. President of Whittle Sports Properties, Hope looked to sell his sport idea to his advertising clients. Coors Brewing Company took the bait and in 1994 the Silver Bullets were formed. The Bullets barnstormed around the country and played against men's professional and amateur teams. The team ended in 1997 when Coors withdrew their sponsorship.

Wrigley wouldn't watch his women play because he would compare their play to the male style of play, but the Bullets created a stage for the world to compare the men versus the women. And that is what happened. The question became whether women could beat men at baseball. Hope and his Bullets promoted women's baseball by proving women can play hardball, but its development of women's baseball was limited. Created by a marketing company, the Bullets' foundation was the promotion of gender wars: women against men. The baseball was measured by gender ability and not just the game itself.

AWBL: Jim Glennie

The Silver Bullets did impress one man: Jim Glennie. Glennie founded the American Women's Baseball League as a nonprofit, umbrella organization in 1996, "to promote women's baseball across the country and around the world" In 1999, Glennie's goal was Olympic status for women's baseball. He explains, "The women's baseball movement must plan for the day our Sport has Olympic recognition and must develop a meaningful professional organization." In October 1999, Glennie convinced USA Baseball, under the leadership of Dan O'Brien, to host the Women's National Championships in Tucson, Arizona, at USA Baseball headquarters.

In 2001, Glennie started the Women's World Series. Japan, Australia, Canada, and the United States participated in the inaugural event. The United States team was selected by the AWBL, with Glennie covering many expenses. The annual international event has grown to eight countries in 2004 (new countries include Hong Kong, Taiwan, India, and South Korea). USA Baseball has sanctioned the first women's national team for the IBAF 2004 World Cup of Women's Baseball. Glennie and the AWBL vice-president, Jeri Baldwin, now sit on the steering committee for USA Baseball's first national team.

"Women's baseball will not develop from the grass roots and grow to maturity," Glennie predicted in 1999. He continued, "Some attention grabbing occurrences such as Olympic status or a professional league with quality that lasts for a few years is needed to snag the attention of the younger players." Glennie's top-down approach for grassroots development will be tested through the potential success of Team USA 2004 and the women's World Cup. Glennie's involvement in the women's game for the last 18 years makes him arguably the national leader with the longest tenure in women's baseball. {*Base Runner*, September 1999, October 1999.}

USWB: Tom Giffen

Being an international leader in women's baseball was financially costly for the AWBL. In May 2001, Jim Glennie officially announced his new baseball relationship with Tom Giffen of Roy Hobbs Baseball. The AWBL would merge into Roy Hobbs Baseball, using their offices and infrastructure but running under the new name — United States Women's Baseball (USWB). In theory this partnership would allow Glennie to focus on his international efforts, while Giffen would work on the everyday operations. According to USWB's "Welcome to United States Women's Baseball," letter (1 May 2001), organization objectives included the following:

- Sanction and selection of the national team to compete in the Women's World Series;
- Operation of a national women's championship as part of the annual Roy Hobbs World Series;
- Development of leagues and teams in various cities;
- Promotion of a team insurance program;
- Solicitation of a national sponsor;
- Development of a system of regional tournament;
- Participation in a software management system; and
- An annual meeting of the board of directors and advisory committee.

In the USWB's May 2001 press release, Glennie wrote, "This is a major step forward in promoting women's baseball. Tom brings a very successful men's baseball organization and an already in-place national network to this mix." By the end of 2002, Glennie and Giffen were no longer working together and the USWB was disbanded. Giffen and Glennie confided to Women's Baseball League president, Justine Siegal, that management issues were the reason for the break-up. In an effort to work together, Giffen and Siegal along with WBL vice-president Patrick McCauley met at the Roy Hobbs office in Akron, Ohio. During this closed-door meeting in the fall of 2002, they tried to work out the difficulties. Leaving that fall meeting, Siegal thought that she would be working with Giffen with the understanding of Giffen's primary motivations. In the end, Giffen chose not to work with the WBL.

AAU

Without a national women's organization to work with, Giffen went to the Amateur Athletic Union to become the chair of Women's Baseball. It was WBL board member Rick Morris who initiated the women's program at the AAU. Morris convinced Siegal to meet with the AAU and to persuade them to start a women's baseball program. On 6 March 2002, Siegal wrote AAU director of sports Mike Killpack, asking the AAU to start a girls' and women's baseball program. Siegal wrote, "The WBL offers its services to the AAU in the development of a girls baseball program. An example of this help was evident during Girls-N-Sports Event 2002. Seventeen of our coaches volunteered to introduce baseball fundamentals to over 500 girls." In 2003, the AAU welcomed women's baseball as the thirty-ninth sanctioned sport in the AAU. AAU chair Giffen wrote, in the 2003 press release, "We have a long way to go, but this is a special moment of recognition for the women playing baseball in the United States. We certainly hope that we will be able to draw everyone together [to] work towards improving opportunities for women and girls to play baseball."

The national women's AAU championship is held at the Roy Hobbs World Series tournament in Florida — the same event that USWB planned to hold their national women's event. Objectives of the AAU program (according to a 2003 press release) are to

- Establish rules and guidelines for national events;
- Establish national championship qualification and roster regulations;
- Approve the participation of foreign teams in the national championship;
- Provide committee review of national championship rules and guidelines as well as review of roster integrity issues; and
- Establish goals and plans for 2004.

Roy Hobbs Baseball is a tournament-driven organization, as is the AAU. AAU tournament directors of all sports are encouraged to make money at their sporting events. The AAU is a good match for Giffen because he can operate moneymaking tournaments within his Roy Hobbs national tournament structure. In 2005, Giffen will become the past chair of AAU women's baseball, and active player-coach and current vice-chair Chris Hill will become the head chair. Giffen was invited to be a part of the USA Baseball Women's Steering Committee but declined the invitation and sent an alternate AAU representative, Adriane Adler, in his place.

WBL

In 1997, Justine Siegal founded the Women's Baseball League. The WBL Web site (www.baseballglory.com) reads, "tired of waiting for opportunities to play, the WBL is building them. Founder, Justine Siegal, has the extra motivation to ensure that girls have a place to play baseball. Siegal explains, 'I want my six-year old daughter to have a place to play baseball ... [she] symbolizes all of the other daughters from around the world who want a chance to participate. This is what the WBL is all about; creating opportunities for the daughters of the world.'" What started out as a local four-team league in Cleveland, Ohio, became a national organization by 1999.

The mission of the Women's Baseball League is to enhance awareness, provide opportunities for female athletes to participate in the game of baseball, and promote the quality and standards of the game. Since its inception, Siegal has worked with the National Baseball Hall of Fame, the All American Girls Baseball League, Baseball Canada, and other national and international organizations. Today the WBL is an event-driven organization that promotes opportunities for girls and women in baseball. The WBL participated in events such as the Women's World Series, the AAU Girls-N- Sports event, and the Australian International Women's Baseball Championships. Teams and programs have been created such as the Give Back and Grow Tour, where players traveled by bus for ten days to six different cities to play baseball games and give clinics. The year 2003 launched the beginning of the highly successful WBL Sparks, a 12- and under girls' team that competes in boys' tournaments, such as Cooperstown Dreams Park. The 2003 WBL Sparks were the subject of an independent documentary.

Siegal has worked with both Giffen and Glennie. Having played baseball with the boys until she was 22, Siegal has playing experience with both men and women. She has a MA in sport studies, where she studied the practical possibilities of making women's baseball a mainstream sport. Ironically, Siegal, a current player, says, "the more opportunities the WBL creates for girls and women in baseball the less opportunities I myself have to play. However I receive great satisfaction knowing that we [the WBL Board] are helping girls by giving them the opportunity and the community to be both a girl and a baseball player." The WBL's growth and impact on women's baseball is limited by its lack of financial resources.

NAWBL

The latest newcomer to women's baseball is the North American Women's Baseball League. Owned by Nick Lopardo, the NAWBL has the financial backing that no other amateur league has ever had. The NAWBL started in 2003 as the New England Women's Baseball League in Lynn, Massachusetts. The four-team league held its games at New Frasier Field, the home of Lopardo's pro men's team. In addition, the New England Women's Baseball League sponsored the Lady Spirit, a league traveling all-star team whose team expenses are all paid for (i.e., plane travel, hotels, and meals). Robin Wallace was named executive director of the NAWBL and Al Melanson was named league commissioner; these two people are believed to be the only full time paid staff in women's baseball. In the 2003 program for the New England Women's Baseball League, Lopardo writes, "My goal is to have the finest female baseball players competing in the highest quality environment that we can provide for them." He continues, "In our inaugural 2003 season, we laid a solid foundation to build upon. I believe we can unite women's baseball regionally, nationally, and internationally and give women their rightful place in America's favourite pastime."

With unification on his mind, Lopardo, with the aid of Melanson and Wallace, formed the North American Women's Baseball League in 2004. The NAWBL has provided money to various leagues in the United States and Canada to help them promote and expand their women's leagues. With finances to back the league, the NAWBL broke ground with USA Baseball. The NAWBL has given a large donation to USA Baseball to help form the first national women's team for play in the 2004 women's World Cup in Edmonton.

In two years, Lopardo has catapulted the NAWBL to the forefront of women's baseball. He explains his motivation to be involved with women's baseball in the New England Spirit's 2003 program: "The opportunity came to me to be involved in men's professional baseball [New England Spirit] and we believe we have a very successful organization. It was only natural for me to offer the female baseball players the same opportunity I give the men." Unlike Philip Wrigley, who never watched the AAGPBL players compete, Lopardo is known for cheering on his team from the dugout bench. Hiring law school student Robin Wallace, a current player who has experience with both men's and women's teams, was a smart leadership move, giving Lopardo a female perspective on the women's game while also hav-

ing a qualified individual to do the day-to-day work. Separating him from the other leaders of women's baseball is his ability to back up his vision for women's baseball with the money needed to make the sport grow. Time will tell what the impact of Lopardo's NAWBL will be on women's baseball.

USA BASEBALL

The leadership of women's baseball has united as it has never done before. USA Baseball, the governing body for amateur baseball, is now onside with the growth of women's baseball. In the past USA Baseball has taken a passive role in regards to the female game, but with the IBAF's women's World Cup in August 2004 and the financial backing of Nick Lopardo and the NAWBL, they have now stepped up to the plate. To utilize the expertise of all of the national women's leaders, USA Baseball has taken a monumental step by creating the Women's Baseball Steering Committee. On this committee are leaders from each of the national organization, including Paul V. Seiler, executive director and CEO of USA Baseball; Nick Lopardo; Adriane Adler of AAU Women's Baseball; Jeri Baldwin of the American Women's Baseball League; Jim Glennie, president of the American Women's Baseball League; Bob Hope, president of and partner in the Atlanta-based marketing firm of Hope-Beckham; Justine Siegal, president of the Women's Baseball League; and Robin Wallace, executive director of the NAWBL. Nick Lopardo has been named general manager of Women's Team USA.

USA Baseball's executive director and CEO, Paul V. Seiler, says, "We are very excited to move forward with this long overdue opportunity for women in baseball. USA Baseball is excited to be working with several individuals who have shown a passion for the women's baseball movement, and our organization is proud to join them in supporting the team that will represent our nation at the 2004 IBAF Women's World Cup. USA Baseball views this as an important first step in developing a much stronger system for girls to play baseball at the grassroots level." {USA Baseball press release, 19 April 2004.}

CONCLUSION

Women's baseball has been underrepresented in America. A national governing body for women's baseball is essential for the long-term growth of the game. Through the work of the national leaders represented here and the regional work of countless volunteers, women's baseball has reached a point in 2004 where national unification is possible. It can be concluded that it takes commitment, passion, and vision for women's baseball to grow, but it also takes money to make things happen. In addition, women's baseball cannot be just a marketing gimmick, but, rather, needs to be a viable sport option. It is not reasonable to expect all of the leaders to get along or for them all to unite. However, by having a national governing body, national leaders can decide whether or not to play on the same team. USA Baseball's involvement and leadership in the women's game and its steering committee is essential to the sport's growth. While women have been playing baseball sporadically since the game's inception in the 1800s it will be the twenty-first century that allows girls and women to play baseball nationally.

Women's Baseball League (WBL)

Justine Siegal founded the Women's Baseball League in 1997 to provide opportunities for women to play baseball. One of the goals she set was to offer coordination for the many efforts that began around the country in the late 1990s. One of the ways the WBL provides help is by maintaining a Web site that keeps players up-to-date on tournament opportunities and other events in women's baseball. Clubs that need players can advertise their tryouts and players can connect with teams in their local areas. In 2001 the WBL also began hosting an annual conference on women's baseball. It has expanded each year with more clinics, more guest speakers and larger numbers of participants. The inaugural conference was held in February 2001 in Cleveland, Ohio. In 2002 the conference took place in Toronto and in 2003 it was held in Disney World. The 2004 conference took place in February 2004 in Maryland. Special guests have included such people as former AAGPBL player Wilma Briggs, minor league umpire Shanna Kook, writer Dorothy Mills, and Canadian umpire Lisa Turbitt-Baker. A forum on women's baseball was sponsored by the National Baseball Hall of Fame and Museum in April 2002. Included among the invited guests were Justine Siegal of the WBL, Patrick McCauley, vice-president of the WBL, and Nikki Ross, supervisor of WBL umpires. The WBL also hosts a tour called the Give Back and Grow Tour, which began in 2002. That year the team played five games and gave a number of clinics for prospective players.

Team WBL played in the international championship in Australia in December 2003. The team included players not just from the U.S. but recruited from Canada and Australia as well. The goal was to have a team to represent the WBL as the United States team, since that is where the WBL is located. Twelve players made the squad, ranging in age from 14 to 37. Justine Siegal managed the team and Deb Bettencourt helped coach. They both played as well. {WBL Web site; "Preserving History. Honoring Excellence. Connecting Generations," Press Release, 10 April 2002, National Baseball Hall of Fame, Cooperstown, New York.}

Women's National Adult Baseball Association (WNABA)

The WNABA was created in 1994 by Richard Hopkins and Michael Micheli as an umbrella organization to help with coordination of women's teams and leagues across the country. Micheli was the founder of the original National Association for men in 1986, and he thought they could expand it for women. According to his records, over 2,000 women were playing baseball in the summer of 1994. The Colorado Women's Baseball Association and the Phoenix league are good examples of local members of the WNABA. The teams from Phoenix started hosting the association's national championship in 1998. Hopkins also managed the Cactus Wrens. In 1994 Fort Wayne, Indiana, joined the organization with a four-team league. Cindy Sands and Brenda Dreyer were instrumental in getting the teams off the ground. They even invited some former AAGPBL players to the opening game. {Marc Johnson, "Women's Baseball Begins," *News-Sentinel*, 15 July 1994; Marlon W. Morgan, "Response to WNABA is Positive," *News-Sentinel*, 10 June 1994.}

Women's New England Baseball League (WNEBL)

The Women's New England Baseball League was founded in 1999 by Chris Lindeborg and Jerry Dawson. Lindeborg played softball at Bentley College and Dawson was drafted by the Pittsburgh Pirates in 1984. The original league had four entrants, who played weekly in Lynn, Massachusetts. The four original squads were the Middlesex County Cougars, the Boston Blitz, the North Shore Navigators, and the Bay State Express. The 1999 season began when Mary Pratt of the AAGPBL threw out the first pitch. The league employed 21 umpires to call their league games. The first league championship was won by the Express over the Blitz in a 2–0 shutout on 22 August 1999. Year two saw the league expand to six teams by adding the Lowell Robins and the Waterbury

Diamonds. The Express won the second season championship by defeating the Navigators 3–0. The four original teams got the chance to play a doubleheader at Doubleday in Cooperstown in 2000. In 2002 the league renamed itself the New England Women's Baseball League (NEWBL) and is now run by women who play in the league. Much of the funding for the league equipment came from major league pitcher Kevin Appier because his sister plays in the league. {Barbara Huebner, "A New League of Their Own," *Boston Globe*, 12 May 1999; Women's New England Baseball League Official League Program, 1999.}

Women's Professional Baseball League (WPBL)

Shawn Stiles decided to try something new in 1996 and set out to establish the Women's Professional Baseball League. There would be teams up and down the East Coast in the league, with Stiles as the commissioner. The season would last from May until August and include at least four teams from the Carolinas. In 2001 the league had teams still playing in Pennsylvania under the leadership of Mike Williams. The USA Rockets and USA Stars were two of the teams. {Marjo Rankin Bliss, "Stiles Hopes League Lets Women Take Baseball Back to the Fans," *Charlotte Observer*, 3 March 1996; Michael Lello, "Softball Star Eyes Baseball," *Times Leader*, 6 July 2001.}

Women's World Series

In 2000 the victory belonged to Team Canada as they came from behind to defeat the Waterbury Diamonds 9–8. The Canadian team had a 7–0 record in the series. In the final contest they were held hitless by Jessica Miccio until the third inning. By the seventh inning Waterbury was ahead 8–4. The tying run in the final inning was driven in by Samantha Magalas. The winning run came in on a botched play by the first baseman. Canada's manager, Pat McCauley, used all 15 of his players to win the game. {"Team Canada Rallies to Win Women's World Series," *Baseball Canada*, 20 November 2000.}

In 2001 the United States easily defeated the team from Japan for the title. The score of the championship game was 9–1. Australia came in third, beating out Canada 1–0 in the consolation game. Japan went in to the final game as the favorite with a 5–1 record and the United States came in at 3–3. Both Canada and Australia had 2–4 records.

The 2002 series went to Australia as they de-feated Japan 8–6 in the final contest in Florida. The Aussie Stars were coached by Chris Norrie, a high school teacher during the rest of the year. After finishing third in 2001 the Stars thought they would not be able to attend the 2002 series, but in the final they put together a team and arrived with nothing to lose. The Stars started their march to the championship with a 5–2 win over Japan in their first game. They followed that with a loss to the U.S. 18–6. To get to the finals the Stars defeated Canada 19–2 and the U.S. 7–4. {Sam Cleveland, "Coast Coach Spur in Aussies' World Win," *Gold Coast Bulletin*, 1 October 2002.}

In 2003 the team from Japan beat Australia in the final game 4–1 to win the series. The series started on 25 August 2003 with Australia defeating Japan 7–6 with a run in extra innings. The losing pitcher, Saori Yokoi, walked in the winning run. Terina Stokes got the win for Australia. The leading hitter in the contest was Japan's Chika Tamura. Australia immediately followed that victory with a 3–2 extra-inning win over the United States. Trista Russo was the losing pitcher while Simone Wearne got the win for Australia. In the third game the U.S. lost to Japan 8–4; Amy Stinton led the way with three hits and two runs knocked in for the Americans. Catcher Alex Sickinger scored two runs to help the U.S. cause. Miki Hotta led the Japanese batters with three hits, while Midori Sakashita knocked in two runs and was given the pitching victory.

In game four Australia beat Japan 10–9 on only seven hits. Shae Lillywhite helped the Australians with four hits in six at-bats. Terina Stokes shut down the final Japanese attempt and secured the win. Game five turned into a 3–0 shutout for Japan over the United States. The Americans only had three hits, and Ashley Cook took the loss though she only gave up five hits. Japan's victory went to Ogawa Masako. Game six was a hitter's game, as Australia beat the United States 13–7. Nicole Cain scored three runs for the Australians to lead a balanced attack while Laura Brenneman led the U.S. with a 4–4 performance at the plate and three runs knocked in. Game seven saw Japan defeat the Aussies 10–2 behind the strong hitting of Miki Hotta. The United States was shut out again in game eight by the Japanese by a final score of 11–0. Ayumi Kataoka drove in five runs for the Japanese while Chihiro Kobayashi picked up the win. The USA rallied to defeat Australia in game nine with a score of 8–6. A balanced attack was led by Alex Sickinger, who knocked in two runs and scored another. Rhonda Palmer pitched a complete game victory for the U.S. In the semifinals the U.S. forced the first game into extra innings before losing 4–3 to Japan. They scored the winning run against Trista Russo while Sayaka Ota got the victory. In the final game Risa Sakashita pitched a complete game victory for Japan while Renee Straumietis picked up the loss. {Australian Baseball Federation, <www.baseball.org.au>.}

The 2004 series took place in Japan from July 18 to 21, 2004. The championship game found Japan facing Team USA for the title. Each team entered the championship with a 4–0 record. Kim Braatz-Voisard drove in the winning run for Team USA in their victory over Canada, 3–2, to put them in the title game. The victory went to reliever Ashley Cook, her second in the series. Going into the final game Braatz-Voisard led her team with a .600 average and four runs knocked in. Japan won the final game and claimed the title with a solid 14–4 victory. They scored eight runs in the fifth inning to run away with the game. After taking a 3–0 lead in the top half of the first, Team USA surrendered the lead for good when Japan came back with five runs in their first at-bats. Laura Purser-Rose took the loss for the United States while Konishi got the win. The tournament's top ten players included Kristin Mills and Amy Stinton while Kim Braatz-Voisard was honored as the best offensive player of the series. She hit .538 with six RBIs and six runs scored.

The United States defeated India, Taiwan, Australia and Canada to make it to the finals in 2004. Japan got to the same game by defeating Canada, South Korea and Hong Kong. All together eight teams participated in this fourth Women's World Series.

Wood, Mary

OF, Kenosha Comets, Peoria Red Wings

Mary Wood grew up in Lakewood, Ohio and played in the AAGPBL from 1946–47 as an outfielder for Kenosha and Peoria.

Wood, Nadine

(Elmsdale, Canada) CF 2004, Canada

Nadine Wood tried out for the Canadian National Team in 2004 after having played softball for a Nova Scotia club and for a fast-pitch team from Halifax.

Woods, Kristen

C 2003, New South Wales

In the 2003 Australian National Champi-onships, Kristen Woods helped her club beat Queensland to make it to the finals. She had three hits including one double to help the cause. She led all hitters in the game, with Carly Kidd getting two.

Woodward, Mrs. A.H.

Vice-President

Mrs. A.H. Woodward was elected vice-president of the Birmingham Barons after the death of her husband in 1930. At the time of her election she became the only female official in the Southern Association. {"Woman Now Official of Birmingham Club," *Washington Post*, 17 January 1930, 17.}

World Cup of Women's Baseball

The first World Cup of Women's Baseball took place in 2004 in Edmonton, Canada, with five teams participating from July 30 to August 8. The 14 games were played at Telus Field. Two former players from the All American League, Betty Dunn and Millie Warwick McAuley, were named special ambassadors to the games. The event was hosted by the Edmonton International Baseball Foundation, led by chairman Ron Hayter. Originally eight teams were expected to be a part of the event, but three teams dropped out for financial reasons. India and the Dominican Republic withdrew first, and then Bulgaria. In preparation for the event, Team Canada played the USA National Team in two exhibition games the week before. They tied the first game, and the American club won the second 8–5 in Alberta, Canada. {Joanne Ireland, "Girls of Summer Take the Field," *Edmonton Journal*, 29 July 2004, D1.}

The games started with Australia and Taiwan playing in the afternoon on July 30. Australia defeated the team from Taiwan 7–5 in seven innings. Canada and Japan played that evening to round out the first day's action, with Japan defeating the Canadian team 10–8 in eight innings.

The USA won their first game in the World Cup 5–1 over Australia. Laura Purser-Rose pitched a complete game for the victory. She gave up only five hits while Laura Brenneman had a 3–4 performance at the plate to lead the offense. The first RBI of the game belonged to Sarah Gascon, who knocked in Brenneman after she had doubled. Simone Wearne took the loss for Australia.

Japan got off to a 2–0 start while Taiwan came up the loser in their first two games. Japan defeated Taiwan and Canada in their two wins. In

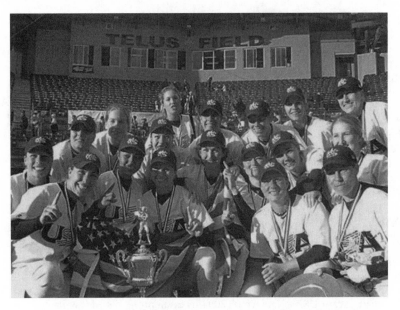

Team USA after winning gold in 2004 (photographer John Lypian, courtesy Jim Glennie).

During her first season the reporters followed her everywhere because of her sex, but she found the second year a little less chaotic. She also got an occasional chance to umpire a spring training game such as the one on 16 February 1975 between the Dodgers and Southern Cal at Dodger Stadium. During that game she was evaluated and recommended for the job in Class A. In 1977 she moved to the Midwest League. Based on her knowledge and skills she was chosen by league president Bill Walters to umpire the All-Star Game in Burlington.

Before she took up umpiring Wren had been a catcher on a number of fast-pitch softball teams, playing since she was 13 years old. She traveled all over for the Spokane Lillies and the Yakima Webcats. Though these teams were fast-pitch softball, playing on them taught her a love of the game and she decided she wanted to umpire. To fulfill her dream of umpiring professionally she attended and graduated from the Specialized Umpire Training Course in Mission Hills, California, in January 1975. Bill Kinnamon, the director of the school, indicated that while her scores were high (she graduated in the top ten out of 45) she would have a tough time due to her sex. Her path, like others who have tried to break into the men's game, was a difficult one because there have been many who thought that women did not belong as umpires. In fact, one veteran umpire claimed that women's minds did not work fast enough and they did not have the guts to deal with the flak they would get when having to make a tough call. She left the game in 1978 and never returned. She went to work for UPS after the 1977 season while she waited to hear about her next assignment. {"An Umpire Named Christine," <MWLguide.com>, 22 April 2001; Christine Wren File, National Baseball Hall of Fame and Museum, Cooperstown, New York; "Female Ump Assigned to Northwest League," *The Sporting News*, 7 June 1975, 41; "The Handwriting on the Wall," *Referee*, June 1978, 7; Jerome Holtzman, "Gals Have No Guts to Umpire," *The Sporting News*, 19 April 1975; "Lady Ump Set to Debut," *Daily News*, 23 May 1975.}

the final standings the United States won gold with a 5–1 record. The silver medal went to Japan at 3–3 while the Canadian team took the bronze medal with a final record of 4–2. Australia came in fourth and Taiwan came in last place. In the gold medal game the U.S. squad defeated the Japanese by a score of 2–0. In the bronze medal game the Canadian club came out victorious over Australia 8–3.

In the gold medal game Kristen Mills tossed a shutout to defeat Japan 2–0. Mills only gave up three hits on the way to victory. Laura Brenneman scored the first U.S. run on a single by Sarah Gascon. Donna Mills knocked in Keri Lemasters for the second run. This victory made up for the American loss to Japan a few weeks earlier in the fourth Women's World Series.

The leading hitter for the tournament was Shae Lillywhite from Australia, who hit .556. Melanie Harwood led all hitters by knocking in five runs while Miyuki Otomo stole six bases for Japan. Karine Gagne scored six runs for Canada to lead all players, and Ella Holien won two games for Australia against no losses to lead all pitchers in the series. {<www.usabaseball.com>; 2004 USA Baseball Media Guide.}

Wren, Christine

(b. 1949, Spokane, Washington) Umpire

Christine Wren began umpiring in 1975 and spent two seasons in the Class A Northwest League.

Wright, Charlene

(Torrance, California) P/OF 1999, Michigan Stars; 1997–2004, Chicago Storm; 2003 Team America

While playing for the Michigan Stars in 1997, Charlene Wright drove in the winning run for her club in the NWBA Tournament. The Stars won the series by defeating the San Diego Diamonds 11–10 in the final game. In 1999 Wright made the all-tournament team at the national championships for the stars. She was chosen as a utility player based on her pitching. She had a 1–0 record with a 2.66 ERA and eight strikeouts. Wright has also played for the New Jersey Nemesis and has been named to the National Women's Baseball Hall of Fame. In 2000 she pitched 63⅓ innings with a 2.87 ERA. In the 2003 Women's World Series Wright made four appearances, pitching in seven-plus innings. She gave up ten runs on 13 hits and walked four batters. {Australian Baseball Federation, <www.baseball.org.au>; <www.baseballglory.com>.} Wright earned her bachelor's degree from UCLA and her master's in geography from San Diego State. She works as a geography teacher and in the Martin Library of Sciences at Franklin and Marshall College. {Michael Schwartz, "Local Woman Has Wright Stuff," *Lancaster News*, 27 July 2003, C-6.}

Wright, Katie

3B/P/SS, Chicago Storm

Katie Wright joined the Chicago Storm in 2002. During the Citrus Blast she played in every game, going 5–14 at the plate. She did not appear in any other games that season. {Chicago Storm Web site.}

Wronski (Straka), Sylvia "Roni"

(b. 1925, Milwaukee, Wisconsin; d. 1997) P, Milwaukee Chicks

"WHEN THE CHICKS WERE CHAMPS, BUT NOT MANY FANS CARED"

The Milwaukee Journal, July 31, 1994

By Tom Morgan and Jim Nitz

If Milwaukeean Sylvia Straka happens to be a tad nostalgic this summer, it's no surprise. This is the fiftieth anniversary of a landmark in her life.

Back in 1944, she was, as they said in those days, a "diamond girl" — a tradition-shattering women's professional baseball player.

Then Sylvia Wronski — or "Roni," as she was called — she pitched for the Milwaukee Chicks, a team that was a rousing success on the ball field, but a bust at the box office. The Chicks won the 1944 All-American Girls' Professional Baseball League championship. But red ink and anonymity in the form of a near empty ballpark proved too much for the Chicks. The team packed up and moved to Grand Rapids, Michigan, the next year.

The 5-foot-2 Straka wasn't the Chicks' star, but she did accomplish something that no other Milwaukee hurler could manage. She came within one out of a no-hitter. Only a two-out base hit by their opponent that day, the Racine Belles, separated her from women's baseball immortality. Her 4-to-1 victory, part of a doubleheader, had been shortened to seven innings. Nine days later, she took the mound at Chicago's Wrigley Field in front of 16,000 fans. It was no pitchers' duel, but the experience, she says, was immensely satisfying. Milwaukee pounded the South Bend Blue Sox, 20–11.

The Chicks— or the Schnitts (little beers), as the media referred to them — often attracted 200 to 300 partisans at Milwaukee's old Borchert Field, which regularly drew full houses of 13,500 for Milwaukee Brewers games.

Millionaire Philip Wrigley had put up a sizable wad of his chewing gum fortune to start the women's league and keep baseball going while many of America's male major leaguers were off fighting Hitler's Nazis.

The women's league survived a decade, from 1943 to the mid–1950s, when TV and the renewed popularity of mainstream baseball spelled its doom. But the young women had carved their niche in history. The popular '92 movie, *A League of Their Own*, captured the flavor of the times, when female players were required to wear one-piece dresses and knee socks, and to have coiffed hair and freshly applied lipstick. They played a spirited brand of ball, even when sliding into bases, which was rough on their legs and anything but easy in skirts.

Straka's pro career ended almost as abruptly as the team's stay in Milwaukee. She played part of the next year in Michigan. "Then I had a chance in 1946 to play for a Chicago team," she remembers, "but my fiancé [Ed Straka] said if I played in Chicago, he would go to school in Connecticut." She chose to hang up her glove, and he didn't move to Connecticut.

At 69, she's a grandmother and great-grandmother now and remains active, going bowling several times a week and doing water aerobics. A retired factory machine operator, she takes pride that the women's league was honored in 1988 with a permanent exhibit in the National Baseball Hall of Fame in Cooperstown, N. Y.

"I was the tomboy who made good," says Straka, whose childhood home in the 2800 block of N. Hubbard St. was practically in the shadows of Borchert Field. "Whoever would have guessed that a grubby kid from Hubbard St. would end up at Cooperstown?" {"When the Chicks were champs, but not many fans cared" originally appeared in *Milwaukee Magazine* July 31, 1994. Used by permission.}

Wulf, Laura

By Laura Wulf

To say that the Silver Bullets were an inspiration to author and photographer Laura Wulf would be an understatement. Their presence made room for some lost hopes and abandoned dreams, and helped her to reconnect with her younger, passionate self. And when the Silver Bullets folded, Wulf decided that it was time to get out from behind the camera and on to the field. In the summer of 1998, after some searching, Wulf joined an organized pickup baseball game in the Boston area. She found the team because the owner of the batting cages where she practiced asked if she played. When Wulf said no, he pointed to a sign hanging by the door and suggested that she call. Sign-up for that game was ongoing, he said.

Wulf went home and called the number on the flyer, to ask if she could come down and play. Just in case it was not obvious, she explained that she was a woman, and asked if it was still ok. The man on the other end told her where the field was and said he'd evaluate her when she showed up. The following week Wulf drove to the field thinking that she would just watch and see before joining in, but as soon as she walked near enough to be seen, the organizer called her over, asked if she was there to play, and put her at first base to see how she handled the ball.

Wulf handled the throws cleanly, got a few pointers about footwork, and that was the extent of the tryout. She made the club. After four years of watching the Silver Bullets play, and 23 years after her only other baseball experience, she was finally back on a baseball diamond, shagging fly balls. She was the only woman on the field. The other players were men ranging in age from their early 20s to early 40s. Standing in the outfield, Wulf had to ask herself if she was dreaming. Her happiness was palpable, indescribable and unexpected. Wulf was 34, a grown-up, and a recent art school graduate. Why did she feel like such a kid, and why was this experience such a source of pleasure?

For the next three months Wulf played once a week. Adjusting to hitting live pitching was the hardest part. And she was not as strong as the rest of the players. But she remembers a long at-bat where she fouled off a series of pitches and heard her teammates rooting for her from the bench. She could feel the support and respect from the other players as she tried to stay alive at the plate, and it was moments like those that felt like victories. Wulf played in the outfield and pitched a number of times. Though she made mistakes, so did the other players. She tried not to feel that each mistake was glaring proof that a woman did not belong out there. By the fall, when the temperatures began to drop and the season came to a close, Wulf felt that she had proven to herself that she deserved to be out there, learning and playing the game of baseball, as much as any of the male players. She made the final out in the final game, a catch in right field of a sinking line-drive, and got some high fives from her teammates. They all ran off the field together.

That winter some players from the pickup league decided to put together a team for the 30-and-over competitive league in Boston, and when one of them called to invite Wulf to join the team she was flabbergasted and thrilled. Though she felt that she had proven to herself that she could play the game, she was not entirely sure what the other players had thought about a woman's presence on the field. This invitation erased one more of the long line of doubts and questions that she had been faced with as an aspiring amateur baseball player.

The next year, before the first game in this competitive league, Wulf watched a video, given to her by a friend, of an early 1970s ABC *Afterschool Special* called "Rookie of the Year." It was about a young girl, played by Jodie Foster, who wants to play baseball. She tags along with her brother's team until they're short a player and she gets her chance to get in the game and help them to victory. Purely the stuff of kids' fantasies, but it helped to calm the pregame jitters. Wulf does not remember much from that first game except that within the first few innings, everybody on the field seamed to know her name, even the umpire.

She remembers making a couple of catches in right field and hitting a hard line drive directly at the center fielder. She also recalls a bystander leaning against a tree, watching, who offered words of encouragement as Wulf walked past him. "You look good, 3," he said, referring to the number on her uniform, and to her abilities, not looks.

The rest of that season proved to be long and difficult. It was one of the hottest summers on record and just being in the outfield in full uniform at midday was grueling. The competition was tougher than in the pickup league, and Wulf began to understand what a difficult and complex game baseball is, and saw how much she had to learn if she wanted to continue to play. She was able to make contact at the plate, but did not get a base hit all season. She got on base with walks, scored some runs, and played in the outfield. The highlight came with the call to pitch an inning of relief against a team that had already scored eight runs against them, and not allow a run. There was one other woman playing in the league. Kate Titus was much more experienced, played catcher and first base, and continued to play in 2003 on a USA amateur women's national team.

As it happened, that same summer a women's baseball league started up in the area, so Wulf went to the tryouts, made the cut and after the morning game in the

Men's Senior Baseball League she traveled north to play in the New England Women's Baseball League. Playing two games in one day was really too much, but she wanted to take full advantage of the opportunities. Wulf was not taking anything for granted. The following season she continued to play in the women's league, but when the season ended decided that it was time to stop. She found the game hard on her body; her legs were always sore from sprinting and her arm ached steadily. Wulf also discovered that although she was a good athlete she was not all that good a baseball player. She found sitting in the dugout tedious, and missed the continuous action and movement of tennis or volleyball.

After seven years, first of photographing and then of playing, perhaps Wulf's odyssey was coming to an end. The Colorado Silver Bullets were the impetus for her to embark on a journey that she had never believed possible. The courage and determination that she saw in the eyes and in the actions of every one of the players and the coaches resonated with her and emboldened her to try something that would have been inconceivable otherwise. The Colorado Silver Bullets expanded the sense of what is possible by counteracting a long held prejudice that girls and women can not or should not play baseball. Baseball is, after all, only a game, but games are structures that help us to challenge ourselves, define our goals, and discover our abilities and our limitations. Sports are at their best when they give us hope and when their structures helps us to clarify our potential, our capacities and our spirit. Sports also reflect our society back to us, showing us our priorities and our prejudices.

Recently Wulf transferred her baseball card collection from its shoebox to a set of notebooks and archival pages. Though the disintegrating rubber bands are gone, the cards still reconnect her to the past. But now they also remind her about her more recent experiences and incite her to wonder about what the future holds for baseball.

An earlier version of this article appeared in Elysian Fields Quarterly *16, no. 4 (1999).*

Yahr, Betty

(b. 22 April 1923, Ann Arbor, Michigan) OF 1946, Rockford Peaches

Betty Yahr developed a reputation during her single season as an outfielder with speed and a good glove. She played in 22 games and added 13 hits and 8 RBIs to her other contributions. In the field she had 31 putouts and one assist for a .889 percentage. The Peaches asked her to return for a second season but she chose not to. {AAGPBL Baseball Cards, 1996.}

Yamada, Misato

P, Spitfires

With nine walks and six hits during the 2003 season, Misato Yamada helped her ball club with the bat. She also scored eight runs.

Yanagi, Shigeyo

C

Shigeyo Yanagi caught for the Wakayama High School girls' baseball team in the early twentieth century, when Japan was trying to establish baseball in the schools for young ladies.

Yang, Kai-Yu

C, Taiwan

Kai-Yu Yang caught in all the games for Taiwan at the 2004 women's World Cup event. She had only one hit in 14 at-bats, giving her a batting average of .091. In the field she had 11 putouts and no errors.

Yantz, Robin A.

Umpire

In 1979 Robin Yantz decided she wanted to continue her involvement with baseball by becoming an umpire. She had played softball in college and was teaching at John F. Kennedy High School in New Jersey when she decided to attend an umpire's school. She went to the necessary classes and took the exams and got her first chance in May. Though she got off to a dubious start, getting beamed by an overthrow in her first game, Yantz stuck with it and survived the season. She umpired 35 games on the bases and expected to umpire behind home plate in 1980. Yantz was listed as one of only three females umpires in a New Jersey Umpires Association with 120 men. {Women-Umpires File, National Baseball Hall of Fame.}

Yawkey, Jean Remington Hollander

(b. 1909, Brooklyn, New York; d. 1992)

By Joan M. Thomas

Born in Brooklyn, New York, in 1909, Jean Remington Hollander grew up in Freeport, New York, on Long Island. Little is known about her family background, other than her parents were reasonably well off. After graduating from Freeport High School, she married her hometown beau, Charlie Hiller, who was the school's star basketball player. It is uncertain whether that marriage ended as the result of divorce or Charlie's death. It is certain that in the 1930s, Jean worked "as a model and salesperson at Jay Thorpe, an exclusive women's clothing store ... in New York City." There is speculation that she met Tom Yawkey when he accompanied his first wife Elise on a shopping trip there.

Tom Yawkey bought the Boston Red Sox in 1933, and the Yawkey cognomen to Bostonians became synonymous with baseball, especially owing to his second wife's maintenance of the club for years after his death. In 1944, shortly after Tom's first marriage ended in divorce, he married Jean on Christmas Eve. Their wedding in Georgetown, South Carolina, was an informal affair at the home of friends. The happy couple said their vows dressed in their hunting clothes. That event was a precursor of the modest lifestyle they would lead for the remainder of both of their lives.

Tom Yawkey owned property on South Island, South Carolina, but according to *Boston Globe* reporter Susan Trausch, the local townsfolk claimed that he and Jean preferred staying in a small cabin instead of the family mansion. That was probably true, as other stories related over the years describe them both as down-to-earth and unpretentious. Jean liked the wilderness, usually wore pants— even to gala events— and was a chain smoker. She also had a quick temper and was somewhat vindictive, fiercely independent and shunned the press. All of this lends credence to

reports that she was a very private person. She rarely granted interviews. She could also be described as gracious, caring and generous. Despite her avoidance of publicity, she was friendly and cordial to ordinary people, especially children.

After a lengthy struggle with leukemia, Tom died in 1976, leaving Jean to decide what to do with his baseball empire. The next year a group of investors proposed a deal to purchase all of Mrs. Yawkey's holdings in the Red Sox. But the offered price failed to meet the approval of the American League. The second proposal and final agreement left Mrs. Yawkey as a general partner, and a tug-of-war for control of the club ensued. Another general partner, former Red Sox trainer Buddy LeRoux, wanted his own way — opposite to Tom Yawkey's method of running things. Jean Yawkey and the club's then-general-manager Haywood Sullivan fought LeRoux in a drawn-out legal battle that culminated with LeRoux selling his interest in the Red Sox in 1987. In Jean Yawkey's obituary in February 1992, Nick Cafardo of the *Boston Globe* states that it was then that she took over as "hands-on majority owner."

As with any good executive, Yawkey knew how to delegate authority but took an active role in making major decisions. And she never tired of going to the games or the meetings. Like Tom Yawkey, she "was passionate about baseball." Like both Helene Britton and Joan Payson, she particularly enjoyed keeping score. At each game, she sat up in her private box on the roof like a beacon for Red Sox fans and players alike. She took the game quite seriously, and shed tears when the club lost the World Series in 1986.

During her tenure as head of the Red Sox, Yawkey became the first woman board member of the National Baseball Hall of Fame & Museum. It was she who commissioned sculptor Armand LaMontagne's statue of Ted Williams for the Cooperstown museum. In 1991, the Greater Boston Chamber of Commerce inducted her into the Academy of Distinguished Bostonians.

Yawkey lived a solitary life after she lost Tom. Childless, she adopted a number of surrogate sons, two of whom ended up with control of the Red Sox when she died of complications from a stroke in 1992. One was "John L. Harrington, executor of her estate and custodian of her two-thirds interest in the club," and the other was Haywood Sullivan, who owned the remaining third. Unfortunately, like some other child-parent relationships, the bond between Sullivan and Yawkey soured during the last years of her life. Harrington was her trusted accountant and became Red Sox CEO. He was still in charge of the

Yawkey Foundation when it sold the club ten years later.

As a benefactor, Jean Yawkey's contributions are too many and too varied to summate. Much of her efforts were directed toward boys' and girls' clubs and homes, as well as wildlife conservation. The annual Jean R. Yawkey Award, to honor an outstanding woman "who significantly contributes to New England's health and community spirit," was established in 1988.

By the time of Yawkey's passing, two more women had become major league baseball heads: Joan Kroc and Marge Schott. So, for a short time, there were actually three women attending the meetings as majority owners. {Susan Trausch, "The Woman Who Owns the Red Sox Keeps Her Private Life Private," *Boston Globe Online*, 6 April 1989, 73; David Margolick, "Red Sox Are the Subject of a Custody Battle, *New York Times*, 26 February 1992, 29.}

Yeager, Cathy
OF San Jose Spitfires

Cathy Yeager played in the outfield for a couple of seasons with the Spitfires in the California Women's Baseball League. In her first game in the 2005 season she went 0-3 at the plate. {CWBL Web site.}

Yokoi, Saori
P, Japan

Saori Yokoi pitched in the first game of the 2003 Women's World Series and lost to Australia 7–6 in extra innings. Yokoi walked in the winning run. She pitched in three games, giving up four hits, three runs and walking five batters for the series. In one plate appearance she was kept hitless. {Australian Baseball Federation, <www.baseball.org.au>.}

Young Ladies Ball Club — Chicago

W.S. Franklin organized the Young Ladies Ball Club in 1889 to play during the summer months in Chicago before touring other parts of the country. The biggest crowds came out to see them when they played in Canada. Franklin answered critics of women playing baseball by claiming that women had played ball going all the way back to the Greeks and Romans. To handle the finances of the team, Franklin secured the services of G.H. Benson. The players on the club ranged in age from 17 to 22, with Emma Howard acting as captain and pitching for the club. Her sister May was

the catcher. The rest of the team included Ray Warner at first base, Belle Fuller at shortstop, Nellie Walters at second base, May Lawrence at third base and Lulu Grant, Alice Allison and Eva West in the outfield. {"Base Ball Girls," *Brooklyn Daily Eagle*, 8 September 1889, 11.}

Young Ladies Base Ball Club

The papers of South Bend reported on the expected visit of the Young Ladies Base ball Club in 1885. The papers also gave an account of the contest versus the Island Park Nine. The game lasted seven innings and the men triumphed 15–7, though the ladies held their own quite well and entertained the 1,000 fans with good baseball. They were billed in the advertising leading up to the game as the only team of their kind in the country. Ladies were especially encouraged to come out and see them play. {*South Bend Daily Times*, 8 and 10 August 1885.}

Young Ladies Baseball Club — Philadelphia

This team played in Philadelphia in 1889. The *Inquirer* indicated that they had three games booked in October of 1889 but did not say who they would be playing or how the games turned out except one. They lost 23–14 on the Athletics field to a team from Chicago called the Champeens. {*Philadelphia Inquirer*, 3 October 1889, 8 October 1889.}

Young Ladies Baseball Club — Washington

A group of nine young ladies who played at Capital Park in Washington in 1890 were known as the Young Ladies Baseball Club. One of their contests was described as a 15–10 losing effort against a group of unnamed young men. The ladies wore black stockings and a short black-and-yellow striped skirt with a black top. The uniform was selected to allow the girls the best movement on the diamond. Unfortunately, the reporter present at the game only identified the members of the team by their first names. {"Women Wield the Bat," *Washington Post*, 4 October 1890, 6.}

Young Lady Champions

The Young Lady Champions played the Fort Hamilton Nine in 1894. About 700 people showed up to watch the contest, and the men's team actually erected a temporary fence to keep the fans off the field. The ladies wore black stockings, red and white striped dresses and caps, and blue blouses. The reporter indicated that only two of the women really had any baseball skills, the pitcher and the third baseman. The team was led by manager Buckner who was also planning a trip through New England for the club. The catcher for the team was a young man, and that helped in catching errant pitches. No official score was kept after the men scored ten unanswered runs. The roster for the Young Lady Champions included Maud Nelson — P, Georgie Devere — 1B, Emily Foster — 3B, Rosie Mitchell — 2B, Lizzie Sheldon — SS, Fronie Sheldon — LF, Lottie Livingston — CF, Josie Douglas — RF, and Lillie Carroll — C. {"Girl Base Ball Players," *Brooklyn Daily Eagle*, 6 May 1894, 7.}

Youngberg, Renae "Ray"

(b. 3 April 1933, Waukegan, Illinois) 3B/P 1951–54, Grand Rapids Chicks

Renae Youngberg grew up in the years before Little League allowed girls to play, and so she joined the neighborhood kids on the sandlots. She attended Waukegan Township High School and earned a scholarship to attend Illinois State Normal University. There were no sports available there for women, but Youngberg did take part in all the extramural sports. She played basketball, field hockey, volleyball and softball. Outside of school she also played industrial league basketball, bowled and played independent softball and baseball. Youngberg became a member of the Junior Comets, local girls divided up into teams and coached by one of the regular Comet players. Through this type of play Youngberg got the opportunity in 1949 to join the traveling teams of the AAGPBL. She did not return in 1950 because she had to spend six months in a sanatorium with a confirmed case of TB. She received permission to return to the league in 1951 and joined the roster of the Grand Rapids Chicks.

Youngberg was known more for her fielding than her hitting until her final season. In 1954 she hit eight home runs and drove in 50 runs for Grand Rapids. Her previous home run total in over 800 at-bats was zero. She also batted .269. In 1953 she had an interesting season, as she was loaned out from Grand Rapids to South Bend and Muskegon for a short period. She returned in time to be a part of the championship Chicks team in 1953. After her playing days ended, Youngberg went on to earn a degree from Illinois State University in 1955. She taught physical education for 30 years and coached for 15. She stayed active ath-

letically by playing softball, basketball, volleyball and also golfed and bowled. {AAGPBL Questionnaire, National Baseball Hall of Fame; Joyce M. Smith, "Renae 'Ray' Youngberg," <www.AAGPBL.org>; AAGPBL Baseball Cards, 1995.}

Youngen, Lois

(b. 23 October 1933, Westfield Center, Ohio) C/OF 1951–54, Fort Wayne Daisies, South Bend Blue Sox

Lois Youngen grew up in a baseball household. Her father pitched for Kent State University in the 1920s and she played with all the neighborhood boys. She played softball in Ashland, Ohio, before joining the All American League in 1951. One of the best memories of her time in the league came from catching Jean Faut's perfect game in 1953. She played in 116 games, batting .255 with 39 runs scored. After leaving baseball, Youngen earned a Ph.D. in 1971 from the University of Oregon, where she headed their physical activity and recreation department. {"Lois Youngen Interview," Diamond Angle Web site.}

Yull, Carmela

P, Westside Rangers

In 1928, at the age of 15, Carmela Yull joined the Westside Rangers, an all-boys' baseball team. They played their games at Chelsea Park. She made the team because she could hit and field well. In addition she did a little pitching. {"Some Young Lady May Soon Break into Big Lineups," *The Messenger* (Athens, Ohio), 10 August 1928, 2.}

Yuska, Rebecca

(b. 1991) P, Philadelphia Women's League

Rebecca Yuska played Little League growing up and then got too old for the teams available to her. In 2004 a new league started in the Philadelphia area for women baseball players. Yuska joined the Clash and in her first appearance shut out the opposing men's team on three infield grounders. {Doug Lesmerises, "Women Trading Softball for Baseball in New League," *The News Journal*, 29 June 2004.}

YWCA Plainfield Nine

The physical education director of the Plainfield YWCA decided to add a baseball team for the young ladies of the area. Elizabeth Wetherell began conducting practices for 25 interested ladies in the spring of 1915. The YWCA claims it was the only such team in the country. The squad was led by their pitcher, Marion Mair, who had had some experience playing with her brothers. Wetherell wanted to attract enough interest to create a three-team women's league. {"Plainfield Girls Now Play Ball and Slide to Base Just Like Boys," *Washington Post*, 21 April 1915, 4.}

Zachery, Susan

3B/SS Baltimore Stars

Zajac, Mary

RF, Virginia Flames

In 15 at-bats for the Virginia Flames in 2002, Mary Zajac hit an even .400. Zajac picked up where she had left off with her hitting, after returning from active duty to rejoin the Flames in 2002.

Zammit, Jackie

New South Wales

Jackie Zammit played for three years at the Australian National Championships for women's baseball, from 2000 to 2002. During the regular season Zammit played for the Blacktown Workers, an under-18 team from Sydney. {Christianni Colussi, "Jackie Shows the Boys How It's Done," *Penrith Press*, 29 January 2002.}

Zawal, Jessica "Z"

(b. 2 June 1983, Royal Oak, Michigan) C/3B, Detroit Danger

Jessica Zawal grew up playing every sport she could. Her main motivation came from a desire to beat her younger brother. She played basketball and softball in high school, which earned her a scholarship for both sports to Rochester College, where she is studying to become a teacher. She joined the Detroit Danger in 2004. {Danger Web site.}

Zephyrs

The Zephyrs became the newest entry in the EWBC when they joined in 2004, bringing the league total to six teams. Their manager is Jen Carr.

Ziegler, Alma "Gabby," "Ziggy"

(b. 9 January 1918, Chicago, Illinois; d. 30 May 2005, Los Osos, California) 2B/P/SS 1943–54, Grand Rapids Chicks

Alma Ziegler attended school in Chicago through eighth grade and then went to high school in Los Angeles, California, after her family moved. She played in a number of softball leagues in California, which is how she found out about the AAGPBL. There were a lot of players from California recruited by Bill Allington and others. She also attended Woodbury Business School and worked as a secretary for Payne Heating when she was not playing baseball. Ziegler excelled as a second baseman and also had a good record as a pitcher. She was a three-time all-star and was voted player of the year in 1950 when she had a 19–7 record with a 1.36 ERA. She pitched three consecutive shutouts that year and had 43 scoreless innings before the streak was broken by the Blue Sox when they scored one run on 30 June. In 1951 she was second in the league in ERA at 1.26, behind Dorothy Naum. While never outstanding with the bat, she had speed and made her hits count. For example, in 1950 she had 56 hits but also scored 56 runs. Every year she was in the league Ziegler was named captain of the Chicks. In fact, in 1953 when the Chicks won the Shaughnessy Championship, Ziegler coached them in the final game after manager Woody English got thrown out of the game. She was honored in 1953 with "Gabby Ziegler Night."

After her baseball career ended, Ziegler became an avid golfer and worked as a court reporter for Los Angeles County and San Luis Obispo County Superior Courts. She also spent some time as a volunteer driver for Meals on Wheels. During the filming of *The Stratton Story*, Ziegler was a stand-in for June Allyson in a scene when Allyson's character had to catch a baseball. While making that film she had the chance to meet one of the other stars, Jimmy Stewart. {AAGPBL Questionnaire, National Baseball Hall of Fame; John Eligon, "'Gabby' Made Her Mark for the Chicks," *Grand Rapids Press*, 10 September 2001.}

Ziegler, Marie

(b. 3 July 1937, Belding, Michigan) OF 1953, Grand Rapids Chicks

Marie Ziegler got only a limited chance to play in the All American League, since she was only 15 when she played in a couple of games for Grand Rapids. Being still in high school made it difficult to travel and be a real part of the league. After the league folded Ziegler turned to softball and played on a number of Michigan state championship ball clubs. {AAGPBL Baseball Cards, 1995.}

Zinck, Aurora "Alaska"

(b. 25 February 1984, Fairbanks, Alaska) C, Detroit Danger

Aurora Zinck started playing softball as soon as she could grip a ball and has been playing ever since. She played in school and also during the summer on one of Alaska's traveling teams. In 2003 she played for Team Alaska, which placed third in the Western Big League Championship. Zinck also skied in high school, played soccer and ran cross-country. She left Alaska to attend Oakland University and plays lacrosse for the school. She joined the Danger in 2005. {Danger Web site.}

Zotara, Sharon

Umpire

Sharon Zotara became an umpire after attending the umpiring school run by Bruce Froemming and Joe Brinkman. She worked for five years as a high school and Stan Musial League umpire. After attending the school she tried to get a job, but no one called her. She tried changing her name and lowering her voice when she called but that did not help. Finally, Neil Moran of the Catholic High School Athletic Association in Manhattan called her and assigned her to a game in Central Park in 1992. When she arrived at the game she learned she would be the only umpire for the junior varsity game. {Gregg Sarra, "Following Their Call," *Newsday*, 24 September 1996.}

Zotara graduated from the University of Tulsa with a marketing degree and then returned for a master's degree in physical education in 1989. Since then she has worked as a physical education teacher and coach at Mercy High School and in the Elmont School district. {Umpires File, OBHOF.}

Zuckerman, Megan

1B, North Shore Cougars

Zuckerman served as the NEWBL co-president in 2002. She got involved in the game of baseball as a way to mentor young girls who want the chance to play baseball rather than softball. In addition to serving the league, Zuckerman coaches and plays for the North Shore Cougars. She graduated from Tufts in 1993. {J.L. Barnes, "ORR Alum Finds a League of Her Own," *The Standard-Times*, 27 July 2002, A1.}

Zurkowski (Holmes), Agnes "Aggie"

(b. 21 February 1920, Regina, Saskatchewan) P 1945, Racine Belles, Fort Wayne Daisies

Agnes Zurkowski played softball in Canada before coming to the United States. She played on championship teams in 1940 and 1941. She came down to join the Belles in 1945 and then found herself traded halfway through the season. She did not get to pitch much, and so at the end of the year she returned to Canada and continued to play softball there. In 1991 she received recognition for her playing with her induction into the Saskatchewan Baseball Hall of Fame. {AAGPBL Baseball Cards, 1996.}

Appendices

A: AAGPBL Rosters

These rosters were compiled by the editors from a variety of sources. **Bold** type indicates that there is an entry in the main text about that player.

Battle Creek Belles (1951–52)

Bancroft, Dave— Mgr.
Bush, Guy— Mgr.
Cooper, Joe — Mgr.
Cook, Donna— CF (1951)
Crawley, Pauline— LF (1951)
Heafner, Ruby— C (1951)
Keyser — RF (1951)
Krick, Jaynie— 3B/P (1951)
Kurys, Sophie "Flint Flash"— 2B
Luhtala, Shirley—1B (1951)
Moffet, Jane— C/1B/OF
Moore, Mary "Sis"— 2B
Pearson, Marguerite "Dolly"— SS (1951)
Peppas, June— P/1B (1951)
Sutherland, Shirley— C (1950–51)
Wenzell, Margaret— 2B (1951)
Young, Janet— P/OF (1951)

Chicago Colleens (1948, then touring team)

Bancroft, Dave— Mgr.
Albright, Eileen— P/2B/3B (1948)
Alvarez, Isabel— P (1950)
Barnett, Charlene— 2B (1948)

Barringer, Patricia— Chaperone (1950)
Battaglia, Fern— SS (1950)
Brown, Patricia "Pat"— P (1950)
Bukavina, Terry — RF (1950)
Callow, Eleanor— OF (1948)
Cook, Donna— P/OF
Cook, Doris— P (1948)
Courtney, Patricia "Pat"— 3B (1950)
Deemer, Audrey— Util. (1950)
Georges, Beulah— P (1948)
Hay, Florence — OF (1949)
Healy, Dorothy — OF (1948)
Johnson (Noga Stuhr), Arleene—(1948)
Johnson, Margaret — Chaperone (1948)
Kabick, Josephine— P (1948)
Luna, Betty— OF/P
Marrero, Mirta— P (1948)
Marlowe, Jean— P/RF (1950)
Moore, Eleanor— P (1950)
Mudge, Nancy— 2B (1950)
Olinger, Marilyn— SS (1948)
Perez, Migdalia— P (1948)
Reid, Dorice— OF (1948)
Schatz, Joan — CF (1950)
Schenck, Audrey — 3B (1950)
Sindelar, Joan— LF (1950)
Sutherland, Shirley— C (1950)

Schweigerdt, Gloria— P (1950)
Taylor, Eunice— C (1950)
Tetzlaff, Doris— 3B (1948)
Tucker, Elizabeth "Betty"— P (1948)
Vonderau, Kathryn "Kate"— C (1948)
Vukovich, Frances— P (1950)
Whiting, Betty—1B (1948)
Wiley (Sears), Janet "Pee Wee"—1B (1950)
Wilson, Dodie — OF (1948)

Fort Wayne Daisies (1945–54)

Allington, Bill— Mgr.
Bass, Dick — Mgr.
Carey, Max— Mgr.
Eisen, Thelma "Tiby"— Mgr.
Foxx, Jimmy — Mgr.
Greiner, Harold — Mgr.
Kellogg, Vivian— Mgr.
Rountree, Mary— Mgr.
Wambsganss, Bill— Mgr.
Adams, Evelyn— SS
Arnold, Lenna
Beare, Kathryn— C
Briggs, Wilma— RF (1950)
Brumfield (White), Miriam Delores— IF/OF/P (1952–53)

337

Callaghan, Helen— OF
Callaghan (Maxwell), Margaret "Marge"— 3B
Campbell, Georgia (1947)
Campbell, Jean (1947)
Carveth (Dunn), Betty— P (1945)
Cook, Donna— OF/P
Cook, Dorothy— SS (1946)
Dabbs, Sarah — OF (1947)
Dancer, Faye— P/OF/1B
DeCambra, Alice— 2B/SS/P
Deegan, Mildred "Millie"— P (1950)
Eisen, Thelma "Tiby"— CF (1950)
Fitzgerald (LeClair), Meryle— P
Foss (Weaver), Betty (1950)
Gates, Barbara — P (1953–54)
Georges, Beulah— P
Haine (Daniels), AudreyP
Harney, Elise— P
Heafner, Ruby— C
Hill (Westerman), Joyce— C
Jackson, Lillian— OF
Janssen, Frances— P (1950)
Johnson (Noga, Stuhr), Arleene
Kellogg, Vivian—1B (1945, 1950)
Kline (Randall), Maxine— P
Kotowicz, Irene— OF
Lee (Harmon), Annabelle— P
Leonard (Linehan), Rhoda— 2B/RF
Lessing, Ruth— C (1945)
Luna (Hill), Betty— OF/P
Marrero, Mirta— P
Meier, Naiomi "Sally"— LF (1950)
Moraty, Mary
Pieper, Marjorie— SS/3B/RF
Podolski, Bertha
Rauner, Helen — Chaperone
Rountree, Mary— C (1950)
Ruber, Gerry
Ruhnke (Sanvitas), Irene— OF/2B
Ryan, May
Schallern, Ellen
Schmidt (Weitzman), Violet— P
Schroeder, Dorothy Augusta "Dottie"— SS (1950)
Stancevic, Marian

Teillet (Schick), Yolande
Tetzlaf, Doris— 3B
Tognatti, Alice — OF
Trezza, Betty (1945)
Tucker, Elizabeth— P
Vonderau, Kathryn E. "Kate"— C (1950)
Wiltse (Collins), Dorothy "Dottie"— P (1950)
Wingrove (Earl), Elsie— OF
Wood, Trois— P (1950–51)
Zurkowski (Holmes), Agnes "Aggie"— P

Grand Rapids Chicks (1945–54)

English, Woody — Mgr.
Gottselig, Johnny— Mgr.
Meyers, Benny — Mgr.
Rawlings, John— Mgr.
Adams, Evelyn— SS
Barney, Ruth (1948)
Beans, Charlene (1952)
Berthiaume (Wicken), Elizabeth— OF (1945)
Blumetta, Catherine— P
Butcher (Marsh), Mary— P
Childress, Thelma— CF (1946)
Clapp, Louise (1954)
Cook, Donna— P/OF
Courtney, Patricia "Pat"— 3B
Earp, Mildred (P) 1947–50
Eisen, Thelma "Tiby"— CF
Fisher, Joan (1948)
Gianfrancisco (Zale), Philomena— OF
Gacioch, Rose— P (1950)
Grambo (Hundeby), Thelma
Gutz, Julia— C
Haylett, Alice— P (1948)
Hill (Westerman), Joyce— C
Hunter, Dorothy "Dottie"— Chaperone (1945)
Jamieson, Betty (1948)
Kabick, Josephine— P
Keagle, Merle— P/OF (1948)
Lee (Harmon), Annabelle "Lefty"— P
Lessing, Ruth— C (1948)
Paire (Davis), Lavonne "Pepper"— C (1948, 1950)
Pearson (Tesseine), Marguerite, "Dolly"— SS

Pechulas, Katherine — Util. (1948)
Petras, Ernestine "Teeny"— SS (1945, 1948)
Petryna (Allen), Doreen Betty— 3B (1948)
Reid, Dorice— OF
Satterfield, Doris— OF (1948)
Shively, Twila— OF (1945)
Smith, Helen— OF (1948)
Taylor, Eunice— C
Teillet (Schick), Yolande— C/OF
Tetzlaff, Doris— 3B (1945)
Thompson (Griffin), Viola (1945)
Tucker, Elizabeth— P
Voyce, Inez—1B (1946, 1948, 1950)
Wenzell, Margaret— Util. (1945)
Whitman, Vera — 2B
Whiting, Betty—1B (1945)
Wingrove (Earl), Elsie— OF (1945)
Wisniewski, Connie— P (1945, 1948)
Ziegler, Alma— 2B (1945, 1948, 1950)

Kalamazoo Lassies (1951–54)

Derringer, Norm — Mgr.
Skupien, Mitch — Mgr.
Allen, Agnes
Baker (George), Mary Geraldine "Bonnie"— C/Mgr.
Barr, Doris— P/OF
Blumetta, Catherine Kay
Carey, Mary— 3B/2B/SS
Cook, Doris— OF
Cordes (Elliott), Gloria— P/1B
Francis, Betty— OF (1950)
Hunt, Carrie — Bat girl
Liebrich, Barbara— 2B/3B
Lovell (Dowler), Jean— C/P (1950)
Luna (Hill), Betty— LF (1950)
Marlowe (Malanowski), Jean— P
Naum (Parker), Dorothy— P
Pearson (Tesseine), Marguerite "Dolly"— SS
Peppas, June— P/1B

Reeser, Sara—1B
Romatowski, Jennifer—C
Roth, Elaine—CF (1950)
Sams, Doris—P/CF (1950)
Schatz, Joan—OF (1952)
Shollenberger, Fern—3B
Whiting, Betty—1B (1950)
Williams (Heverly), Ruth—C

Kenosha Comets (1943–51)

Billings, Josh—Mgr. (1943)
Gottselig, Johnny—Mgr.
Grant, Chet—Mgr.
McManus, Marty—Mgr.
Metten, George—Coach
Petras, Ernestine—Mgr.
Shinners, Ralph—Mgr.
Stumpf, Eddie—Mgr.
Abbott, Velma—2B/3B
Anderson (Perkin), Janet—OF
Bennett, Catherine—P
Bevis, Muriel—P/OF (1950)
Brumfield (White), Miriam Delores—1B/OF/P (1948–51)
Butcher (Marsh), Mary—P
Carey, Mary—3B/2B
Cione, Jean—P (1950)
Colacito (Appugliese), Lucille—C (1944–45)
Cook, Clara—P (1943)
Fabac (Bretting), Elizabeth "Betty"—2B
Florreich, Lois—OF
Folder (Powell), Rose—P (1944)
Ganote (Weise), Gertrude—IF (1944)
Glaser, Rose Mary—OF/P (1944)
Goldsmith, Bethany—P (1950)
Hageman (Hargreaves), Johanna
Hanna, Marjorie—P (1944)
Harnett, Ann—IF (1944–45)
Harney, Elise "Lee"—P (1943–45)
Heim (McDaniel), Kay—C (1943–44)
Hickey, Lillian—OF
Hohlmayer (McNaughton), Alice—1B

Hunter, Dorothy—1B/Chaperone
Jameson, Shirley—OF (1943–45)
Jaykoski, Joan "Jake"—OF/P (1951–52)
Kabick, Josephine—P
Kazmierczak, Marie—OF (1944)
Kobuszewski, Theresa
Koehn, Phyllis—OF (1943–45)
Lenard, Josephine—LF (1950)
Lester, Mary Lou (1943)
Lovell (Dowler), Jean—P
McCreary, Ethel (1943)
Mahon, Elizabeth Bailey "Lib"—IF (1944)
Mickelson, Darlene—OF (1943)
Naum (Parker), Dorothy "Dottie"—P (1950)
Nearing (Buntrock), Myrna—P (1943)
Nicol (Fox), Helen—P (1943–44)
O'Hara, Janice—OF/1B (1943–45)
Petras, Ernestine "Teeny"—SS (1950)
Pieper, Marjorie—IF/OF
Pirok, Pauline "Pinky"—IF (1943–45)
Pratt, Mary—P (1944–45)
Ryan, Ada—Chaperone (1943)
Shollenberger, Fern—2B/3B (1950)
Schroeder, Dorothy "Dottie"—SS
Stephens, Ruby Lee—P
Tipton, Gloria—P (1946)
Villa (Cryan), Margaret "Marge"—C/2B (1950)
Wagner, Audrey—OF (1943–45)
Wawryshyn, Evelyn—2B
Westerman (Austin), Helen—C (1943)
Wood, Mary—OF

Milwaukee Chicks (1944)

Carey, Max—Mgr.
Cook, Clara—P (1944)

Davis, Gladys "Terry"—IF (1944)
Eisen, Thelma "Tiby"—OF (1944)
Figlo, Josephine—OF (1944)
Grant, Olga—OF (1944)
Hunter, Dorothy—1B/Chaperone (1944)
Kabick, Josephine "Jo"—P (1944)
Keagle, Merle—OF (1944)
Klosowski, Dolores—IF (1944)
Maguire (McAlpin), Dorothy—C (1944)
Panos, Vicki—OF (1944)
Petras, Ernestine "Teeny"—IF (1944)
Stevenson, Emily—C (1944)
Tetzlaff, Doris—IF (1944)
Thompson (Griffin), Viola—P (1944)
Whiting, Betty—IF (1944)
Wisniewski, Connie—P (1944)
Wronski (Strata), Sylvia—P (1944)
Ziegler, Alma—IF (1944)

Minneapolis Millerettes (1944)

Jonnard, Claude "Rubber"—Mgr. (1944)
Blumetta, Catherine Kay—P (1944)
Callaghan, Helen—OF (1944)
Callaghan (Maxwell), Margaret—IF (1944)
Dancer, Faye—OF (1944)
Farrow (Rapp), Elizabeth—P (1944)
Haine (Daniels), Audrey—P (1944)
Jackson, Lillian—OF (1944)
Kellogg, Vivian—IF (1944)
Kissel (Lafser), Audrey—IF (1944)
Lee (Harmon), Annabelle—P (1944)
Lessing, Ruth—C (1944)
Paire (Davis), Lavonne "Pepper"—C (1944)
Ruhnke (Sanvitis), Irene—IF (1944)
Ryan, Ada—Chaperone (1944)

Trezza, Betty— IF (1944)
Whiting, Betty Jane—1B/OF/
   C (1944)
Wigiser, Margaret (1944)
Wiltse (Collins), Dorothy
   "Dottie"— P (1944)

Muskegon Lassies (1946–50)

Bigbee, Carson — Mgr.
Boyle, Ralph — Mgr. (1946)
Cooper, Joe — Mgr.
Wambsganss, Bill— Mgr.
Zintak, Lennis— Mgr.
Applegren, Amy Irene (1946)
Bergman, Erma— OF (1946)
Berthiaume (Wicken),
   Betty— OF
Carey, Mary— 2B/3B/SS
Carlson, Phyllis (1949)
Cook, Donna— of (1946)
Davis, Gladys "Terry"—
   2B/SS (1946)
Degner, Betty — P (1949)
Dennert (Hill), Pauline
   (1947)
Fischer, Alva Jo (1946)
Francis, Betty— OF
Johnson (Goodman),
   Arleene— 3B (1946)
Kensler, M.— Chaperone
Keough, Mary
Klosowski, Theresa (1948)
Lenard, Josephine— OF (1946)
Maguire (McAlpin), Dorothy
   "Dot"— C (1946)
Marrero, Mirta— P
Martin, Mary
Metrolis, M. Norma— C
   (1946)
Montalbano, Rose— 2B/3B
Montgomery, Dorothy— 2B
   (1946)
Mudge (Cato), Nancy— 2B
O'Brien, Eileen (1946)
Overleese, Joanne— 2B
Pearson (Tesseine), Mar-
   guerite "Dolly"— SS
Pieper, Marjorie— 3B/SS/RF
Pryor, Charlotte — OF (1946)
Reeser, Sara—1B (1946)
Roylance, Juanita
Sams, Doris— OF
Schofield, June—1B/3B/SS
Stoltze, Dorothy— OF/SS

Peoria Red Wings (1946–51)

Gottselig, Johnny— Mgr.
   (1946)
Murphy, Leo— Mgr.
Rawlings, John— Mgr.
Reynolds, Mary— Mgr.
Schrall, Leo— Mgr.
Abbott, Velma— 2B/3B
Baker, Mildred
Blumetta, Catherine Kay— P
   (1946)
Bryson, Marion— P (1946)
Buccor, Kathrine
Carey, Mary— 3B/2B/SS
Cione, Jean—1B (1946)
Crawley, Pauline— OF
Daley, Elizabeth
Dancer, Faye— OF/1B/P
   (1949)
DeCambra, Alice— 2B/SS/P
   (1949)
Denoble, Jerre — OF (1947)
Donahue, Terry— C/3B/SS
   (1946, 1949)
Eisen, Thelma "Tiby"— OF
   (1946)
Faralla, Lillian— P/2B (1946)
Ferguson (Key), Dorothy—
   P/2B/3B
Flaherty, J. (1949)
Gallegos, Luisa— P (1948)
Gerring, Betty — Chaperone
   (1946)
Gilchrist, Jeanne— C
Guest, Geraldine — OF (1951)
Hoffman, Nadine (1946)
Hohlmayer (McNaughton),
   Alice— P
Hough, G. (1951)
Ives, Irene — Chaperone
Jacobs (Badini), Jane— P
   (1946)
Jochum, Betsy (1949)
Kidd, Glenna Susan— P (1950)
Lawson, Mary— OF (1946)
Lee (Harmon), Annabelle
   "Lefty"— P (1946, 1949)
Louett — P

Warren, Nancy— 2B/SS (1946)
Wawryshyn (Litwin, Moroz),
   Evelyn— 2B (1946)
Wenzell, Margaret (1946)

Machado (Van Sant),
   Helene— OF (1946)
Mandella, Lenora— P/IF
Metrolis, M. Norma— C
Meyer (Moellering), Rita—
   SS (1946)
Moriarity, Mary
Pearson (Tesseine), Mar-
   guerite "Dolly"— Util.
   (1949)
Reynolds, Mary— P/3B (1946,
   1949)
Romatowski, Jennifer— C
   (1949)
Roth, Elaine— P/OF
Rountree, Mary— C (1946)
Ruiz, Gloria— OF (1948)
Schofield, June—1B/3B/SS
   (1948–49)
Shively, Twila— OF (1949)
Sloan, Francis
Smith, Shirley— OF/2B (1947)
Steck (Weiss), Elma Mae
   "El"— OF (1948)
Stoll, Jane— OF (1946)
Terry, Betty
Tucker, Elizabeth— P (1946,
   1949)
Vonderau, Kathryn "Kate"—
   C
Waco, Ruth
Watson (Stanton), Marion—
   P
Wood, Mary— OF (1946–47)
Ziemak, Frances— P

Racine Belles (1943–50)

Derringer, Norm — Mgr.
Gottselig, Johnny— Mgr.
   (1944)
Murphy, Leo— Mgr.
Virginia Carrigg — Chaperone
   (1944)
Anderson, Marie
Barr, Doris— P
Batikis, Annastasia "Stash"—
   CF
Brody, Leola— IF (1943)
Bureker (Stopper), Geraldine
   "Gerry"— OF (1948–49)
Chiano, Clara "Gabby" (1944)
Cordes (Elliott), Gloria— P/1B
Crews, Mary Nesbitt— P
   (1944–45)

Danhauser (Brown), Margaret—1B (1944)

Dapkus (Wolf), Eleanor— OF/P (1944–45, 1950)

Dusanko, Julianna— IF (1944)

Emry, Elizabeth— P/3B

English, Madeline Catherine "Maddie"— SS (1944–45, 1950)

Ferguson, Fern — P (1945)

Figlo, Josephine— OF

Flaherty, Mary— P/3B

Heafner, Ruby— C

Hickson, Irene— C (1944)

Hood, Marjorie — OF (1943)

Hunter, Dorothy—1B

Hutchison, Anna May— P/C (1944–45)

Jacobs (Badini), Jane— P (1944)

Knezovich (Martz), Ruby— C (1943–44)

Kurys, Sophie— 2B (1944–45, 1950)

Luhtala, Shirley —1B

Montgomery, Dorothy— IF

Nesbitt (Wisham), Mary

Paire (Davis), Lavonne "Pepper"— C/3B

Pearson (Tesseine), Marguerite "Dollie"— SS (1950)

Perlick (Keating), Edythe— OF (1944, 1950)

Peterson, Ruth — Chaperone

Russell, Betty

Sabo (Dusanko), Julianna Rita "Julie"— IF (1944)

Schillace (Donahoe), Claire— OF (1944)

Smith, Charlotte — Util. (1943–44)

Stephens, Ruby Lee— P

Stone (Richards), Lucille

Terry, Doris— P

Thompson, Annabelle— P (1943)

Trezza, Betty— SS/3B (1950)

Uhlir (Damaschke), Dorothy "DD" (1945)

Walmsley, Thelma (1946)

Wilson, Mildred — Chaperone

Wind, Dorothy "Breezy"— SS (1943–44)

Winter, Joanne— P (1944, 1950)

Zurkowski (Holmes), Agnes "Aggie"— P

Rockford Peaches (1943–54)

Ainsmith, Bill — Mgr.

Allington, Bill— Mgr. (1944, 1949, 1950)

Rawlings, John— Mgr.

Stumpf, Eddie — Mgr.

Abbott, Velma— 3B/2B

Alspaugh, E. (1949)

Applegren, Amy Irene (1950)

Barnett, Charlene (1949–50)

Berger (Knebl), Joan— RF (1951)

Berkowitz, R. (1949)

Callow, Eleanor— LF/P (1949–1951)

Carveth (Dunn), Betty— P (1953–54)

Cione, Jean—1B

Cook, Dorothy— SS (1946)

Daetweiler, Louella— C

Davis, Gladys "Terry"— OF

Deegan, Mildred "Millie"— P/SS/2B

Eisen, Thelma "Tiby"— CF

Erickson (Sauer), Louise (1949–50)

Farrow (Rapp), Elizabeth— P

Ferguson (Key), Dorothy "Dottie"— 3B/2B (1949–50)

Filarski (Steffes), Helen "Fil"— 3B

Fischer, Alva Jo— P/SS

Florreich, Lois— P/OF/3B (1949–50)

Fox (Nicol), Helen "Nickie"— P (1949–50)

Gacioch, Rose— P/OF (1949–1950)

Green, Dorothy "Dottie"— C (1949–50)

Harrell (Isbell, Doyle), Dorothy Harriet "Snookie"— SS (1949–50)

Heafner, Ruby— C

Hlavaty, Lillian (1951)

Holgerson (Silvestri), Margaret— P/2B (1949)

Holloway, Marion

Jogerst, Donna — P (1952)

Jones, Marilyn (1950)

Kamenshek, Dorothy—1B (1949–1951)

Kelly, Jacqueline — 3B (1949–1951)

Kotowicz, Irene— CF/P

Lenard, Josephine— OF

Little (Bend), Olive— P

Lovell (Dowler), Jean—(1949)

Lundahl, Mildred — Chaperone

Mansfield (Kelley), Marie — P (1950–51)

Measner— P

Meier, Naomi— OF

Miller, Ruth — C (1943)

Moon, Dorothy— P

Moore, Mary Ann— 2B

Morris, Carolyn— P (1946)

Oravets, Pauline (1943)

Pollitt, Alice— SS (1949–1951)

Pratt (Deschaine), Mary— SS/P

Richard, Ruth— C (1949–1951)

Sawyer, Helen (1943)

Schmidt (Weitzman), Violet— P

Shier, Bunny —(1950)

Smith, Helen (1946)

Steck (Weiss), Elma Mae "El" (1949)

Surkowski (Delmonico), Lee— OF

Swamp, Rella (1943)

Timm, Marie— Chaperone (1944)

Towery, R. (1949)

Waddell (Wyatt), Helen— 2B (1950–51)

Wigiser, Mildred— OF

Yahr, Betty— OF

South Bend Blue Sox (1943–54)

Bancroft, Dave— Mgr. (1950)

Grant, Chet— Mgr.

McManus, Marty— Mgr.

Niehoff, Bert — Mgr. (1944)

Winsch, Karl— Mgr.

Armstrong, Charlotte

Arnold, Louise Veronica (1951)

Baker (George), Mary— C

Barr, Doris— P/OF

Beare, Kathryn— C

Bennett, Catherine— P
(1943–44)

Bird (Phillips), Nalda— P/OF

Bleiler (Thomas, Seitzinger),
Audrey (1951)

Brumfield (White), Miriam
Delores— IF/OF/P (1947)

Carver, Virginia — OF

Chester, Bea— 3B (1943–44)

Clapp, Louise (1954)

Cook, Donna — P/OF

Crigler, Idona — 3B (1947)

Dailey, Mary (1951)

Denton, Mona— P

Dunn, Gertrude (1951)

Dwojak, Loretta — 3B/OF

Faralla, Lillian (1951)

Faut (Winsch, Eastman, Fan-
try), Jean— P/3B (1950–51)

Filarski (Steffes), Helen— 3B
(1950)

Francis, Betty— OF

Froning (O'Meara), Mary
(1951)

Gallegos, Luisa

Ganote (Weise), Gertrude

Headin, Irene — P (1945)

Hill (Westerman), Joyce— C

Hoffman, Margaret Barbara
(1951)

Jamieson, Janet— C/3B
(1948)

Jochum, Betsy— OF/1B/P

Jones, Doris (1945)

Junor, Daisy— LF

Kemmerer, Beatrice (1951)

Kidd, Sue— P (1950–54)

Koehn, Phyllis— P

Kotil, Arlene "Riley"—1B
(1950–51)

Luckey, Lillian — P

Luna (Hill), Betty— P

Mahon, Elizabeth Bailey
"Lib"— 2B/OF (1951)

Mandella, Lenora— P/IF

Martin, Joan (1951)

Mickelson, Darlene

Montalbano, Rose— 2B/3B

Moore, Helen — Chaperone
(1944)

Moore, Lucille

Mueller, Dorothy— P (1950–
51)

Naum (Parker), Dorothy— C

Pearson (Tesseine), Mar-
guerite "Dolly"— SS

Pirok, Pauline— 3B

Pryor, Shorty — 2B (1950–51)

Roark, Mildred

Romatowski, Jennifer— SS/C
(1950)

Roth, Mary — P (1950)

Rumsey, Janet (1951)

Schroeder, Dorothy Augusta
"Dottie"

Shafrani, Geraldine — OF
(1943)

Sopkovic, Kay— C

Stefani, Margaret— 2B (1947)

Stephens, Ruby Lee— P

Stoll, Jane "Jeep"— CF (1950–
51)

Stovroff, Shirley— C (1950–
51)

Studnicka (Brazauskas,
Caden), Mary Lou— P

Surkowski (Delmonico),
Lee— OF

Thompson (Griffin), Viola—
P

Tronnier, Ellen— OF

Vincent (Mooney), Georgette
(1951)

Voyce, Inez—1B

Wagoner, Betty— RF (1950–
51)

Way, Rose

Whiting, Betty Jane—1B/OF/
C

Whitney (Dearfield),
Norma— 2B

Wiley (Sears), Janet "Pee
Wee"—1B/P

Williams (Heverly), Ruth— P

Wirth, Senaida "Shoo
Shoo"— SS (1946, 1950,
1951)

Springfield Sallies (1948, then touring team)

Bigbee, Carson — Mgr.

Allen, Agnes— P (1950)

Barbaze, Barbara— OF (1948)

Barr, Doris— P (1948)

Bays, Betty — C (1950)

Berger (Taylor), Norma— P
(1950)

Bergman, Erma— P (1948)

Burkovich, Shirley— Util.
(1950)

Cindric, Ann "Cindy"— P
(1950)

Cook, Doris— P (1950)

Cornett, Betty Jane— 3B
(1950)

Courtney, Patricia "Pat"— 3B

Deemer, Audrey— Util.
(1950)

Gallegos, Luisa (1948)

Gutz, Julia— C (1948)

Jamieson, Janet— C/3B (1948)

Kidd, Sue— P (1949)

Kolanko, Mary Lou— CF
(1950)

Liebrich, Barbara— Chaperone (1950)

McComb, Joanne (1950)

Marlowe (Malanowski),
Jean— Chaperone (1948)

Martinez (1950)

Mattson (Baumgart), Jacqueline— C (1950)

Meacham, Mildred—1B
(1948)

Middleton (Gentry), Ruth—
RF (1950)

Moore, Mary— 2B (1950)

Morrison (Gamberdella), Esther— LF (1950)

Mudge (Cato), Nancy— 2B

Neal, Doris— 3B (1948)

Parks (Young), Barbara— SS
(1950)

Perez (Jinright), Migdalia— P
(1950)

Rudis, Mary (1948)

Schofield, June— 3B (1948)

Stephens, Ruby— P (1948)

Stoll, Jane— OF (1948)

Stovroff, Shirley— OF (1948)

Wawryshyn (Litwin, Moroz),
Evelyn— 2B (1948)

Wenzell, Margaret— IF (1948)

Whalen, Dorothy "Dot"— C

Zonia, Violet — C (1948)

Chaperones

Baker, Hilda

Baker (George), Mary

Carrigg, Virginia

Christensen, Edna

Gerring, Betty

Green, Dorothy

Hageman (Hargraves), Jo-
hanna

Hannah (Campbell), Helen
Harrington, Helen
Hohlmayer (McNaughton),
　Alice
Hunter, Dorothy
Ives, Mrs.
Kenster, Eunice
Lindahl, Mildred
McCutchan, Mrs.
Moore, Mrs. E.T.
Moore, Lucille
Rieber, Geraldine
Ruttes, Mary
Ryan, Ada

Stancevic, Mariam
Stefani, Margaret
Tetzlaff, Doris
Timm, Marie
Wagoner, Irene
Wilson, Mildred

Allington All-Stars (1954–57)

Allington, Bill— Mgr.
Berger (Knebl), Joan— 3B
Descombes (Lesko), Jean—
　OF

Dunn, Gertrude "Gertie"—
　2B
Geisinger (Harding), Jean—
　1B
Horstman, Catherine— OF
Kline (Randall), Maxine— P
Richard, Ruth— C
Schroeder, Dorothy Augusta
　"Dottie"— SS
Smith, Jean— OF
Vanderlip (Ozburn),
　Dollie— P
Weaver, Joanne— OF
Youngen, Lois— P

B: AAGPBL Teams, League Champions and Batting Champions

Teams

1943: Inaugural Teams
　Kenosha Comets
　Racine Belles
　Rockford Peaches
　South Bend Blue Sox
1944: Expansion Teams
　Milwaukee Chicks
　Minneapolis
　Millerettes
1945: Expansion Team
　Fort Wayne Daisies
　Milwaukee moves to
　Grand Rapids
1946: Expansion Teams
　Muskegon Lassies
　Peoria Red Wings
1948: Expansion Teams
　Chicago Colleens
　Springfield Sallies
1950: Muskegon moves to
　Kalamazoo

1951: Racine moves to Battle
　Creek
1953: Battle Creek moves to
　Muskegon

Champions

1943 Racine Belles beat
　Kenosha Comets*
1944 Milwaukee Chicks beat
　Kenosha Comets*
1945 Rockford Peaches
1946 Racine Belles
1947 Grand Rapids Chicks
1948 Rockford Peaches beat
　Racine Belles*
1949 Rockford Peaches beat
　South Bend Blue Sox*
1950 Rockford Peaches
1951 South Bend Blue Sox
1952 South Bend Blue Sox
1953 Grand Rapids Chicks

1954 Kalamazoo Lassies
*Had a first- and second-half
champion who played one another
in a playoff series.

Batting Champions

Gladys Davis .332
Betsy Jochum .296
Mary Crews .319
Dorothy Kamenshek .316
Dorothy Kamenshek .306
Audrey Wagner .312
Jean Faut .291
Betty Foss .346
Betty Foss .368
Joanne Weaver .344
Joanne Weaver .346
Joanne Weaver .429

C: Other Rosters

These rosters were created by the editors from a variety of sources. They are incomplete but represent what we have been able to document so far. **Bold** type indicates that there is an entry in the main text about that player.

Australian Baseball

Aussie Diamonds (1998)

Trucchio, Frank — Coach
Trucchio, Julie — Coach
Avant, Mandi

Balzat, Katrina
Binks, Emma— P/3B
Cockbill, Kristina

Creek, Paula
Daniel, Lisa
Dobson, Laura
Forras, Maria
Frier, Deb
Gosstray, Narelle— 2B/P
Grant, Marion
Jensen, Danielle
McGarvie, Ann
Palatsides, Maryanne— C
Ross, Shandell Joy
Smith, Karen
Stainer, Janine
Stokes, Terina— P
Sutcliffe, Belinda
Taylor, Marita
Telford, Amanda
Townley, Rebecca
Williams, Jodie
Witchell, Karen
Young, Lyndal

Country Baseball, NSW

Fathers, Paul— Head coach
Smith, Sue— Assistant coach
Paton, Archie— Assistant
 coach
Allen, Sarah— Util.
Binet, Louise—1B
Burnett, Alison— OF
Butler, Belinda— OF
Coulter, Melissa— P
Dolbel, Narissa— P
Foley, Kate— OF
Friend, Lauren— 2B
Jarvis, Bronwyn
Jenkin, Glenys— IF
Jennings, Renae— P
Kidd, Carly— C
Knapton, Amy— OF
Lees, Karan— OF
McVie, Julie— P
McVie, Melanie— OF
Norman, Melanie— 2B
Norrish, Michelle— OF
Philip, Natalie— IF
Saggus, Samantha— C
Shackleton, Tania— P
Shipp, Eryn— P
Slater, Dene
Smith, Amanda— IF
Smith, Tiana— IF
Spokes, Tina— IF
Strong, Kerry— OF
Taylor, Robynne— P
Toomer, Kelly— OF

White, Jodie—1B
Whitfield, Jamie— SS
Woods, Kristen— 3B
Wright, Joanne— 3B

Falcons

Attard, Rebecca— P
Bulger, Stacey— P
Mangan, Sonia
Tingley, Danielle

New South Wales Patriots (2002–04)

Smith, Shaun— Head coach
Hills, Terrey— Pitching coach
Gaynor, John— Assistant
 coach
Adamson, Anna— OF
Bilby, Danielle— IF
 (2002–04)
Catford, Angela— OF (2004)
Cornick, Chantelle— P/OF
 (2004)
Cosstick, Rebecca— 3B
 (2003–04)
Curry, Danielle— OF/C
 (2002–03)
Fairhurst, Suzanne— C/3B
 (2002–03)
Fitzgerald, Christal— P/SS
 (2002–04)
Gaynor, Katie— OF/1B
 (2002–04)
Gosstray, Narelle— 2B/P
 (2002–04)
Grant, Krystal— OF
Gunn, Kellie— P/OF (2002–
 03)
Henry, Kylie— OF/P (2003)
Kucharova, Ella— P (2002)
Lawrence, Leigh— P (2002,
 2004)
Logan, Keiren— Util.
Lovering, Tahnee— C (2004)
Luland, Alison— P/OF (2002–
 03)
McKean, Georgina— IF
Orchard, Keiren— OF (2002)
Price, Chantelle— OF (2004)
Riley, Kelly— IF
Saggus, Samantha— C/3B
 (2002–03)
Saggus, Stacey— SS/2B (2003)
Shaw, Shanna— P (2004)
Sheehan, Kerrie— OF/P
 (2003)

Smith, Catherine— P
Straumietis, Renee— P/SS
 (2002–04)
Taylor, Robynne— P
Telling, Melanie— P (2004)
Vella, Loren— P/2B (2002–
 04)
Vidler, Megan— P/OF (2002–
 04)
Walbancke, Kellie—1B/P
 (2002–04)
Whiteford, Jessica— OF
 (2002)
Zammit, Jackie— P (2002)

Queensland Rams (2002)

Norrie, Chris— Head coach
Brockie, Scott— Pitching
 coach
Studerman, Matt— Assistant
Avery, Katie— OF
Bell, Justene— P/2B
Berry, Renee— IF
Bombell, Mindy— OF
Cooper, Annika— Util.
Cooper, Kestie— 3B/P
Dawson, Anita— P
Doherty, Terri— Util.
Fritz, Zoe—1B
Hauwert, Rachel— Util.
Kelly, Therese— Util.
Kirby, Lisa— SS/P
McKay, Claire— OF
McLaughlin, Ann-Marie— C
Miller, Cherie— 3B/Util.
Nicholson, Sandie— P/OF
Rose, Kassandra— OF
Sexton, Karina— SS/P
Smith, Renee— C
Welsh, Rebecca— P/OF

South Australia

Frick, Josh— Head coach
Holland, Tim— Assistant
 coach
Bradbury, Georgina— OF/1B
Burner, Hayley— P/SS
Collins, Keryn— 3B/P
Finch, Paula— OF/C
Haden, Kathryn— SS/2B
Haden, Sarah— OF/SS
Halliwell, Brooke— SS/2B
Phillips, Rebecca— P/C
Ross, Ashleigh— C/P
Samsonenko, Lana— 2B/Util.
Scott, Kendall—1B/OF

Sulkowski, Amy —1B/2B
Thorn, Penny — 3B/P
Thorn, Wendy — OF/2B
Wainwright, Julie — P/Util.
Wells, Sue —1B/OF

Victoria

Ruggiero, Dominick — Head
  coach
Wearne Michael — Assistant
  coach
Binks, Emma— P/3B
Brisbane, Naomi
Cain, Nicole— OF
Davidson, Alison— P
Hamilton, Samantha— IF
Holien, Ella— P
Hough, Jade— IF
Hutton, Leanne — P
Lee, Deanne— OF
Lillywhite, Shae— IF
Manzie, Kelli— C/P
Marklew, Shelli— OF/P
McCann, Amy— Util.
Palatsides, Maryanne— C
Papanicolaou, Paula— Util.
Parker, Sue-Anne — P
Row, Catherine— P
Tamburrino, Alisa— P
Walker, Allana — OF
Wearne, Simone— P
Whitaker, Melissa— IF
Whittam, Claire— Util.

Victoria Provincial

Culph, Tony — Head coach
Rice, Adrian — Pitching coach
Gaunt, Rod — Assistant coach
Adams, Sam — 2B
Balzat, Katrina — P
Busbridge, Layla — C
Campbell, Erin — P
Cook, Sonia — 3B
Coombes, Rebecca— P
Copland, Sam — P
Danaher, Sue— Util.
Finch, Paula
Flanigan, Sinead — P
Gibson, Lauren — C
Greenwood, Caroline — P
Harris, Jodie — SS
Holroyd, Samantha — P
Houson, Leanne — P
Kelly, Naomi
Lee, Vanessa— Util.
Lord, Sue-Anne — P

Marklew, Shelli— OF/P
McCann, Amy— OF
Newton, Lindsay — OF
Papanicolaou, Paula— Util.
Russell, Nicole — OF
Ryan, Angela — P
Ryan, Tess— P
Saavedra, Kathryn
Smith, Alexis— P
Squires, Prue — 3B
Strugnell, Claudia— P
Thompson, Casey — 2B
Wallis, Kym —1B
Wells, Jacinta — P
Wyatt, Marita

Western Australia

Ward, Graham — Head coach
Pittaway, Adam — Assistant
  coach
Baxter, Cheryl-Lee — Util.
Cant, Tracey — OF
Farr, Joanne
Fiorentino, Rhonda — OF
Forkin, Chelsea— Util.
Fox, Erin — OF
Foxton, Deb — P
Galus, Chelsea — P
Hirst, Jodie — P
Jardim, Carmel — IF
Kreppold, Christina— 3B
Langley, Julianne—1B/P
Leevers, Taryn
Lehane, Kerron— P
Menzies, Jenny — OF
Mirco, Amanda — IF
O'Hehir, Amanda — P
Prosper, Eyvette — OF
Rafferty, Sharon
Rath, Lisa — P
Schulbergs, Marika — C
Tassell, Stephanie — P
Thompson, Jodie — 2B
Villamagna, Nicole — SS

Willbees

Bonazza, Jess— P
Dawkins, Pam
Ihaka, Vivian "Viv"— P

AWBA

Daredevils

Bergo, Paula
Fuchs, Lee— C/Coach
Landeweer, Kathy— P

Mehrer, Darlene— League
  founder
Poe, Linda— P
Rapolz, Diana— P
Rodriguez, Gina
Rothchild, Susan—1B

Gators

Fink, Debbie
Parrilli, Josephine— P
Stickelmaier, Linda

Knights

Lammert, Sue— SS/P
Lukasik, Sue—1B
Maly, Rochelle— P
Schwartz, Katherine— OF

AWBL

Glennie, Jim— League president
Novotny, Rob — League vice-
  president

Florida Lightning

Sowell, Dave — Coach (1999)
Mazzatenta, Mike — Coach
  (1999)
Baggleman, Charles— Coach
  (1999)
Allegra, Fran — C/IF (1999)
Allen, Robin — OF (1999)
Casey, Kim — C (1999)
Chin, Jackie— OF (1999)
D'Auria, Pate — IF/OF (1999)
Estrada, Yadia — IF (1999)
Hicks, Lisa — OF (1999)
Hogan, Kim— P/IF (1999)
Kobayashi, Chihiro— |P
Levine, Michelle — IF (1999)
Mahoney, Kate— IF/C (1999)
Mazzatenta, Nicole — IF
  (1999)
Mitchell, Debbie— P/IF
  (1999)
Murray, Meghan
Neal, Andrea — IF/P
Nichols, Tina —P/IF (1999)
Purser-Rose, Laura— P/IF
  (1999)
Scocco, Sandra — IF/C (1999)
Strickland, Gina — P/IF/C
  (1999)
Tamburrino, Alisa— P
Viola, Jill — IF (1999)

Orlando Dragons

Weaver, Jeff— Manager
Johnson, D.J.— OF
Nichols, Tina— P/IF

Benefit Game—24-Hour Contest

Alley, Lani
Barclay, Jennifer
Bettencourt, Debbie
Brannon, Jody— Manager
Brownewell, Stacy
Burgess, Amber
Catarino, Jill
Chiba, Nanaei
Davenport, Mae
Delarco, Brooke
Deluccio, Justine
Derouin, Stephanie
Escker, Elizabeth
Fereno, Cindy
Fletcher, Theresa
Flores, Dee
Forrest, Alison
Frey, Lisa
Granahan, Nora
Gulley, Jen
Hammond, Jennifer
Hunolt, Alicia
Itamochi, Keiko
Johnson, Ashley
Keener, Allyson
Keyser, Allisyn
Kitta, Megumi
Kreyche, Cathy
Kung, Stephanie
Kyle, Susan
Laspina, Melanie— C
Lineberger, Sheri
Love, Amy
McNulty, Lauren
MacGregor, Theresa
Manzie, Kelli
Marchand, Michelle
Menghini, Patti
Meyer, Bronwin
Miki, Yufu
Moy, Dawn
Nicholls, Ashley
Niland, Lily
Precup, Peggy Sue
Rado, Jen
Ray, Dawn
Robertson, Elizabeth
Russell, Debbie

Ryan, Tess
Sanford, Lisa
Schneider, Amy
Shiflett, Mary
Smiley, Renee
Smith, Chris
Spangenburg, Laura
Sparks, Denise
Spiegelman, Jo
Spiegelman, Rachel
Staub, Dorothy
Tameike, Sayaka
Tan, Cecilia
Trahan, Tina
Wagner, Kimberly
Wagner, Laurie
Ward, Kris
Weinstock, Maia
Wendt, Kristin
Yeager, Cathy
Young, Colleen
Yuvan, Jan

California Women's Baseball League (CWBL)

Alameda Oaks (2003–04)

Coats, Sal — Mgr./P/2B
Cleary, Katie— P/C
Crawford, Kory — IF
Dobrint, Alexandria— IF
Fields, Bartley — OF
Garcia, Bekki— IF/P
Gary, Rachel— IF/P
Kyle, Susan —1B/P
LaFirenza, Chris— P
Lychak, Kim— OF
McHale, Carol —1B
Marshall, Michelle— 2B
Matsuda, Rachel — Util.
Mojica, Jaclyn — OF
Moy, Donna — P/IF
Ross, Michelle — OF
Schubert, Hayden — C
Wiley, Charlotte — SS
Woodard, Alicia — OF

California Sabres

Amundsen, Elaine— OF
Chin, Jackie— CF
Curone, Jo— P
Deutsch, Kelly— P
Erickson, Whitney— 2B/P
Hill, Chris—1B/util.

Hoover, Kim
Jester, Tracy —1B
Kerns, Amber
Leatherwood, Cherie — P
Lindsey, Heather — RF
Marton, Sharon
Maya, Alison — SS
Neal, Andrea — P
Ross, Cindy — 2B
Sharp, Stephanie
Sickinger, Alexandra "Alex"— C
Torres, Steph
Treat, Tammy
Valdez, Rhonda — 3B
Vaughan, Bernie
Witzigman, Sandy — RF
Young, Stephanie

East Bay Furies (2003)

Bazinni, Brianna — C/OF
Erickson, Whitney— C/P/IF
Gamulo-Owens, Maria — 2B/OF
Garcia, Lois— PF/1B/P
Hansen, Jennifer —1B/3B/OF
Kamisher, Robin — IF
Noguchi, Etsu — IF/OF
Plank, Heidi —1B/C
Poet, Kasey— IF/P
Risch, Mackenzie — 2B/OF
Schroeder, Heather — OF
Staton, Rhonda— 2B/OF

Peninsula Peppers (2004)

Ballantine, Stephen — Mgr.
Aragon, Marina — OF
Borden, Julie — OF
Brenner, Danielle — P/C
Deleon, Tamara—1B
Gibson, Lisa— IF
Hatfield, Karla— Util.
Imado, Mia — OF
Lindley, Ashley —1B
Lovett, Christina — OF
McNulty, Lauren — 2B/OF
Martinez, Claudia — IF
Mojica, Jaclyn — OF
Perez, Jenny Ashley— 2B
Raquiza, Adrienne — SS
Rentfrow, Shayna — C/3B
Schneider, Sherri — C/OF

San Francisco Fillies (2003–04)

Ed Sickinger — Mgr.

Bjorklund, Chelsea— IF
Borello, Shari — IF
Britton, Dominisha— P
Bryant, Shawna — OF
Cunanan, Susie— 3B
Emory, Anna — OF
Henley, Rocky— 3B/P
Hill, Angela— OF
Lane, Julie — IF/OF
LoBue, Katie — OF
Lonya, Julia —1B
Lovato, Tonette — IF
Mendoza, Rina —1B/OF
Name, Lynda — OF
Palmer, Rhonda— P/1B
Pyle, Lesly — OF
Robertson, Elizabeth — SS
Sickinger, Alexandra "Alex" —
  C
Tam, Tammy — 3B/SS
Williams, April — SS

San Diego Stix (1999)

Maxey, Pat — Manager
Bearup, Karie — P/OF
Borders, Leah — P/IF
Cramer, Jennifer— Util.
Deutsch, Kelly— IF
Gallina, Marita— IF
Gersztyn, Barb— P
Hickson, Leslie— P
Hill, Chris —Util./1B
Leschorn, Michelle — Util.
Thomas, Stephanie— OF
Vaughn, Bernie — OF

San Jose Spitfires (2003–04)

Piro, Dan — Manager
Cloyd, Cathy — OF
Doerer, Valerie— IF
Dowell, Viki — OF
Guasch, Celeste — 2B/OF
Hatfield, Karla— OF
Kik, Cheryl— IF
Lahl, Tami — IF
Laspina, Melanie— C/IF
Locke, Jenny — SS/P
Logan, Chrystal — P/C
McCloyd, Katy — OF
Martinez, Pat— IF
Mowry, Cheri — C/SS
Parker, Rachel — C/IF
Plemons, Tina — IF
Reynoso, Miali— SS/P
Rigoni, Jen — IF

Sisnerous, Jessica —1B/P
Staton, Rhonda— C/OF
Subia, Brenda — IF
Yamada, Misato— P
Yeager, Cathy — OF
Zinich, Layna — IF

Canadian Baseball

Birchmont Baseball

Hollingworth, Craig — Coach
Rutledge, Grant — Coach
Weatherup, Carmen — Coach

Burlington Bulls

Psota, Kate— SS/P

Dominion Bantam Girls Hawks

Price, Paul — Coach
Blois, Annaliese— C
Burgess, Sarah — SS/P
Davidson, Caelyn —1B
Dedieu, Lauren— Util.
Fleming, Chelse — 2B
Little, Aimee— 2B
MacDonald, Susan — 2B
MacNeil, Kayla — C
MacNeil, Lindsay— 3B
Prince, Nicole — OF/2B/3B
Sheppard, Jen— P
Slaunwhite, Candace — P
Stewart, Amanda —1B

Queensland Team

Studerman, Matt — Head
  coach
Adams, James— Assistant
  coach
Adams, Anne Marie — Execu-
  tive officer
Bettridge, Faye — Scorer
Bell, Justene— IF
Cummings, Jaimie — C/OF
Dark, Amanda— IF
Dawson, Anita — IF
Fritz, Zoe—1B/OF
Graham, Melissa— P/OF
Hauwert, Rachel— P/Util.
Heathcote, Kiara — 2B/OF
Hurst, Georgina — IF
Kirby, Lisa— IF
Miller, Cherie— C/3B
Nicholson, Cassandra — P/Util.
Rapley, Peta — IF/OF

Rose, Kassandra — OF/P
Sexton, Karina— IF
Squires, Prue — C/3B
Waples, Jacqui — OF

Team Ontario Bantam Girls

Psota, Kate— SS/P

Victorian Women's Baseball Team (2002)

Longstaff, Kane — Coach
Ross, Cameron — Coach
Ross, Shandelle— Mgr.
Ruggiero, Domenick — Coach
Binks, Emma— P/3B
Brisbane, Naomi
Hamilton, Samantha— IF
Holien, Ella— P
Hough, Jade— P
Lee, Deanne— OF
Lilywhite, Shae— IF
Manzie, Kelli— C/P
Marklew, Shelli— OF/P
Palatsides, Maryanne— C
Papanicolaou, Paula— Util.
Passlow, Kathryn— IF
Row, Catherine— P
Tamburrino, Alisa— P
Tompkins, Jessica
Wearne, Simone— P
Whitaker, Melissa— IF

Colorado Silver Bullets

Hope, Bob — President
Crabbe, Bruce — Infield coach
Grubb, Johnny — Outfield/
  hitting coach
Haun, Jean — Team trainer
Niekro, Phil — Manager
Niekro, Joe — Pitching coach
Blair, Paul — Coach
Jones, Tommy — Coach
Pignatano, Joe— Coach
Aguilar, Marcie— IF (1996)
Amado, Jeanette— OF
Braatz-Voisard, Kimberly—
  OF (1994–97)
Burnham, Elizabeth— C
Charpia, Billie Jo— P
Clark, K.C.— OF
Cole, Amy — OF
Conro, Pamela— P (1996)
Coombes, Melissa— P (1994–
  97)

Cress, Missy— C (1994–97)
Coughenour, Cara— IF
(1995–96)
Croteau, Julie—1B
Dalton-Hill, Jenny— 3B
(1997)
Davis, Pamela— P (1995–97)
Delloso, Michelle— 2B/Util.
Dufficy, Pat— C (1996)
Espinosa, Wendee— OF
(1996)
Espinoza-Watson, Laura— IF
(1996–97)
Geatches, Allison— OF/1B
Gouthro, Laurie— IF
Habetz, Alyson— P (1995–97)
Heisler, Toni— SS (1997)
Henry, Jenifer (1997)
Holmes, Tammy— OF (1996–
97)
Ivie, Tamara— IF (1995–97)
Ketcham, Lee Anne— P
(1994–97)
Kimberling, Shannon— C
Kroemer, Joy (1997)
Kropke, Keri— OF
Martinez, Lisa— P
Marzetta, Angie— OF (1995–
97)
McAnany, Michelle— 2B
(1994–97)
Mitchem, Shannan— 3B
(1994–97)
Monge, Christine— P (1995–
97)
Morton, Kathy— OF (1996–
97)
Purser-Rose, Laura (1997)— P
Radaker, Melissa— P (1997)
Satriano, Gina— P
Schaffrath, Pamela— IF/C
(1994–97)
Shepard, Laura— P (1996–97)
Sloan, Shae— P (1994–97)
Spitaleri, Camile— IF (1996–
97)
Sroczynski, Debra— P
Sunny, Stacy— OF (1994–97)
Venturi (Veenema),
Bridget— P
Williams, Ann— P
Williams, Julie (1997)

East Coast Women's Baseball League

Elmwood Park Angels

Barletta, Jennifer — Util.
Campbell, June— LF/P
Cervino, Marie — Util.
Coviello, Christina — 3B/1B
Deluccio, Justine — P/RF
Diprenda, Carly — C/1B, Captain
Donohue, Donna — 2B/RF
Frey, Lisa — SS/P, Captain
Hergert, Michelle — CF
Kotynski, Marlena — P/IF/OF
(Sub)
Laws, April — IF/OF
Maier, Kim — Util.
Marron, Theresa —1B/3B/2B
Martin, Jules— Util.
Mirabella, Sharon — IF
Paragios, Melissa — RF/2B
Potter, Amanda — P/OF/IF
(Sub)
Ryaby, June "Scoop"— P
Smith, Suzanne — OF/3B/P
Stone, Melissa — Util.
Tompkins, Tara — 2B/IF
Woschinko, Jennifer — Util.

Indians

Bacco, Samantha — OF/IF
Bellapianta, Fran — SS/2B/OF
Bordonaro, Michele — IF/OF
Caruk, Julia — OF (Sub)
Cleaveland, Carol — IF/OF
Cooke, Heather — OF (Sub)
Cooley, Cara — P/OF
D'Amato, Michelle—1B/Mgr.
Egan, Kathlyn — IF/OF
Ferretti, Danielle— OF/IF
Hires, Brogan — OF
Lamb, Dawn — Util.
Melasippo, Nicole — C/3B/1B
Noriega, Marlene — OF (Sub)
O'Keefe, Barbara — 2B/3B
Rinaldi, Kim — OF/IF
Ryan, Jenn — CF (Sub)
Saggese, Lori— SS/CF/Mgr.
Schock, Jennifer — P/IF/OF
(Sub)
Swiss, Carolyn —1B/3B
Tuttle, Stephanie — C/IF
Vulcano, Maria — IF/OF
Wright, Charlene— P (Sub)

Madison Mets

Avallone, Chris— Coach
Avallone, Cheryl — C (Sub)
Blake, Donna — 3B/OF/C
Caruso, Vicki — C/IF/OF
Caruso, Rayna — Sub
Chiarolanza, Stacy— IF/OF
(Sub)
Crane, Shirley — P/SS
Davis, Caroline — C/OF/IF
(Sub)
DeBenedictus, Diane — IF/OF
DeFalco, Deanna — P/1B
Dirkes, Kris— IF/OF (Sub)
Endean, Amy — Util. (Sub)
Finkeldey, Bonnie — C/3B/
OF/Mgr.
Jackson, Kim— P (Sub)
Jenkins, Joann — Util.
Kuck, Julie — OF (Sub)
McCarron, Krystle — Util.
(Sub)
McGovern-Ackerson, Laureen — IF/OF (Sub)
McKeand, Kelly
Mullins, Colleen
Palmiere, Dawn — Util.
Pappas, E. Maggie — IF
Peralta, Nancy — P/2b/OF/
Mgr.
Petruzelli, Sophia —1B/OF
Shapiro, Patrice — IF/OF
Sosa, Tracy — IF
Staats, Teresa — 2B/OF
Stracka, Leigh — Sub
Vanderberg, Vanessa —1B/OF
(Sub)
Vybiral, Missy — OF (Sub)
Whitney, Tobi — P/CF

Parsippany Yankees

Adler (Calenda), Adriane —
Coach
Beltran, Jamie — OF/2B
Bittiger, Alicia — 3B/C
Brown, Marilyn
Catalano, Angie — C (Sub)
Catanese, Carolynn — 2B/SS
Cortese, Denies— OF/P
DeLorenzo, Alisha — OF
(Sub)
Efcak, Amy — C/IF (Sub)
Fiscus, Darlene— IF/OF
Foody, Jen— IF/P
Griffith, Danielle "Skippy"—
OF/IF (Sub)

Gwinnett, Nikki —1B (Sub)
Herbst, Terri Lynn— OF/P
Hertzberg, Lauren — OF (Sub)
Hipple, Betsy — OF/3B (Sub)
Howard, Leigh — OF/1B
LaScala, Michelle — OF (Sub)
Layton, Erin —1B/C (Sub)
Lombana, Lissette —1B/3B
McCloskey, Kelly — C/OF/IF
Mills, Bonnie— C/IF/P
Mills, Kristin— P
Mills, Sarah —1B/2B
Moll, Annie — OF
Montana, Renee — IF/OF
(Sub)
Nieves, Vivian — C/IF/OF
Pawol, Jen— C/P/IF (Sub)
Petrillo, Cory — IF/OF
Rodriguez, Valerie — 3B/SS
Ryan, Tess Lee— P/IF
Sichieri, Katie — OF/IF (Sub)
Thorn, Krista — IF/OF/P
Tucci, Lori — IF/OF

EWBC Rosters (formerly the Washington Metropolitan Women's Baseball League)

Baltimore Blues

Richardson, Jo Ann— Mgr./
OF
Dyson, Brenda — Manager
Kruger, Dave — Coach
Strerig, Jan

Baltimore Stars

Keller, Kelly— Mgr./IF/OF
Albright, Marisa — IF/OF
Bouchat, Katie — SS/C
Bradford, Ellen
Bradford, Katy— P
Brooks, Terri — OF
Colvin, Kristy —1B
Day, Dinah — IF/OF
Ervine, Debbie — Util./P
Johnson, T.J.— C
Kotula, Heather — LF/SS
Levine, Felicia — IF
Powers, Sharon — OF
Presnell, Kelli — P/OF
Santone, Denise — OF
Sheckells, Cheryl —1B
Smith, Barbara — OF

Swank, Dreama — IF
Torres, Jean — OF
Zachery, Susan — 3B/SS
Young, Melissa

Cantina Banditas

Presnell, Kelli—Mgr./P

Montgomery County Barncats

Sweeney, Diane — Manager
Bender, Richard — Coach
Ballentine, Kelly— C
Garelick, Jackie — IF (2000–02)
Gelman, Robin— P (2000–02)
Goldberg, Kirsten — RF (2000–
02)
Hassell, Lori (2000)
Hudson, Renee— P/RF
(2002)
Lazur, Lisa — 3B
Martino, Nan— 3B (2000–02)
Owen, Teo
Sandford, Lisa— IF/P (2002)
Scott, Lisa — C (2000–02)
Smith, Lori
Triolo, Sandy— CF (2000–02)
Weisman, Cindy — 2B
Zifcak, Lisa

Virginia Boxers

Beatson, Nora—1B/OF
Brannon, Jody— Manager
Casey, Jim — Coach
Brenneman, Laura— SS
Carr, Jennifer — LF/C
Guidace, Kristin— Mgr.
Hoffman, Bonnie— P
Kreyche, Cathy—1B

Virginia Flames

Fyfe, David — Manager
Milliken, JoAnn — Manager
(2002–03)
Simpson, Harry — Coach
Brenneman, Laura— SS
Ciulla, Stephanie— P (2002–
03)
Cramer, Jennifer—1B
Darden, Leandra— 3B
Deleone, Gina
Dominguez, Carmen— P
(2002–03)
Fereno, Cindy— 2B (2002–03)
Hammond, Jennifer (2002–
03) IF/OF/P

Maliszewski, Danielle— C
Middleton, Donna — C
Ovington, Kay
Quigley, Narda— RF (2003)
Quigley, Paran
Weaver, Rosemary "Rosie"—
1B
Whitacre, Gina— P/SS
Zajac, Mary— OF

DC Thunder (2002)

Casey, Jim — Manager
Fyfe, Dave — Assistant man-
ager
Beatson, Nora—1B/OF
Brenneman, Laura— SS
Carr, Jennifer — LF/C
Ciulla, Stephanie— P/CF
Dominguez, Carmen— 2B/3B
Gelman, Robin— P
Guidace, Kristin— P
Hammond, Jennifer— 3B
Hoffman, Bonnie— P
Hudson, Renee— P
Kreyche, Cathy—1B
Maliszewski, Danielle— C/2B
Middleton, Donna — C
Milliken, JoAnn— Mgr./PH
Presnell, Kelli — P
Richardson, Jo Ann— OF

Florida Women's Baseball League

Florida Lightning (1999)

Baggleman, Charles— Coach
Mazzatenta, Mike — Coach
Sowell, Dave — Coach
Allegra, Fran — C/IF
Allen, Robin — OF
Casey, Kim — C
Chin, Jackie— OF
D'Auria, Pate — IF/OF
Estrada, Yadia — IF
Hicks, Lisa — OF
Hogan, Kim— P/IF
Levine, Michelle — IF
Mahoney, Katie— IF/C
Mazzatenta, Nicole — IF
Mitchell, Debbie— P/IF
Nichols, Tina— P/IF
Purser-Rose, Laura— P/IF
Scocco, Sandra — IF/C
Strickland, Gina — P/IF/C
Viola, Jill — IF

Great Lakes Women's Baseball League

Akron Fire (2002)

Flaherty, Colleen— OF
Holderman, Ashley— CF
Hughes, Lisa — 3B
Kovach, Emily — RF
Sheldon, Carol— DH
Wallace, Robin— SS

Chicago Gems (2004)

Chicago Storm/Lightning

Jason Marlin — Coach
Bason, Katie— P/3B/C
Brenneman, Laura— SS
Brownewell, Stacy— LF
Engholm, Jill — RF/LF
Fatah, Yasmine — RF
Gary, Rachell— IF/P
George, Patty "Mayo"— CF/ 3B/SS
Hughes, Jennifer— C/3B
Keener, Allyson— P
Korecek, Katie— 3B/SS
Lander, Tricia
Lukasik, Sue— 1B
MacGregor, Theresa— IF/OF/ P
Manzie, Kelli— C/LF
Marlin, Johanna — RF
McIntyre, Kelly — LF
Murillo, Gina — OF
Prebble, Carrie— P/OF
Precup, Peggy Sue— SS/2B
Ryan, Tess Lee— P/OF
Saia, Amy — 1B
Schneider, Amy— LF
Stegeman, Joni "Baby J"— SS/3B/RF
Vana, Dawn— P
Williams, Christen — RF
Wright, Charlene— P/OF
Wright, Katie— 3B

Cleveland Comets (2003–05)

Cleveland Quest (2000)

Siegal (Warren), Justine— P (2000)
Kalner, Staci

Fort Wayne Phantoms

Michigan Stars

Anderson, Lindsay (1997)
Davis, Brenda (1997–1999)
Engelbrecht, Jav — OF (1999)
Ford, Maria — IF/OF (1999)
Gaglio, Synda (1997)
Gonzalez, A.— IF (1999)
Gouthro, Laurie— IF (1999)
Hannah, Katherine— P/IF (1999)
Johnson, Jan — C/IF (1999)
Lamer, Tina — IF (1999)
LeMasters, Keri— P/IF (1999)
Miner, Jodie — IF (1999)
Murray, Meghan — C/IF (1999)
Simon, Trish (1997)
Schmitt, Allie— 2B (1997)
Smead, Kris (1997)
Switzer, Ainsley (1997)
Tanner, Fay — IF (1999)
Wilkinson, Julie — IF (1999)

Motown Magic (2004)

Johnson, Jude— Manager
Raniszewski, John — Pitching coach
Asis, Monica "Monika"— 1B/ OF
Belman, Jo Jo— DH/Util.
Bowling, Sue — OF
Civiello, Annette— IF/OF/P
Civiello, Marie— P/OF/IF
Engel, Heather "Blaze"— C/ OF
June, Kim "Kimmer"— 3B
Molnar, Christine— OF
Moore-McPaul, Kenya— OF
Noel, Michele— 2B
Raniszewski, Kris "Lefty"— P/1B/3B
Sheldon, Carol— 1B/3B/P
Smythe, Katy "Tram"— SS
Yeager, Lindsay — C/3B

South Bend Blue Sox/Belles

Kovach, John — Manager
Bryant, Lori— CF/C
Christian, D'Andre — IF/OF
Christianson, Jerrika— SS
Ermis, Andi— C
Hayes, Melissa— IF
Holderman, Ashley— P/1B
Jewell, Kelly — IF
Kroemer, Joy— IF
Mighelle, Jerrika — SS

Miller, Melissa— 3B/P
Molnar, Christine — 2B
Pappa, Katie— IF/C
Potter, Sally— P
Pratt, Kelly — RF
Riopelle, Christy— OF
Singleton, Shanon— IF/P
Tuel, Dawn — P
Wallace, Robin— 2B
Ward, Sara— IF
Younger, Christianson — CF

Manitoba Taffy (2003/04)

St. Germain, Russ— Head coach
Kuleza, Greg — Assistant coach
St. Germain, Sharon — Bench coach
Kolomic, Paul — Pitching coach
St. Germain, Adam — Bat boy
Boulloigne, Rachelle — RHP/IF/OF
Cotter, Stephanie — RHP /IF
Dokken, Cheryl — RHP/IF/OF
Knutson, Alisha — 3B/OF
Kuleza, Sara — 2B/C
MacInnis, Alex — LHP /1B/OF
Meilleur, Kim — C/SS/OF/ RHP
Peacock, Lacey— RHP/C/IF
Podolsky, Maxine — C/IF/OF
Regier, Kaila — C/IF/OF
Roy, Tamara — OF/IF/C
Ryan, Jessica — RHP/IF/3B
St. Germain, Sara — RHP/1B/ 3B
Wagner, Laurie — SS/1B/RHP
Whitechurch, Jenifer — RHP/ IF

Independent Teams

Boston Blue Sox

Sroczynski, Ron — Manager
Clark, Lisa
Goodwin, Jeanette— 1B/3B
Kapenas, Jennifer— IF/OF
LaMarine, Karen— OF
Lindeborg, Chris— P/1B
Mills, Donna — 3B
O'Brien, Judy— C
Sroczynski, Debra— P
Vecchione, Angela— SS/C

Great Lakes Fire — Roy Hobbs (2002)
Kovach, John — Manager
Beining, Tina
Johnson, Tammy
Kovach, Irina
Maurer, Sandy
Moors, Brenda
Potter, Sally
Rodman, Kelly
Schneider, Amy
West, Vanessa
Williams, Christen

Japanese Baseball

Team Energen (1999)

Murakami, Masanori — Manager
Arai, Junko— IF
Arimura, Tomoko— IF
Chiba, Nanaei — P
Hayashida, Junko— C
Ichikawa, Takako— IF
Igarashi, Tomoko— OF
Ishikawa, Kanako— OF
Kira, Kazumi — OF
Kobayashi, Chihiro— P
Kubato, Yoshiko— P
Maeno, Tae — IF
Morii, Kazumi— IF
Nakayama, Kimie — IF
Nishikawa, Junko— OF
Nori, Junko— P
Onozuka, Hanako— IF
Otani, Rui — IF
Shibata, Makiko— C/IF
Suzuki, Keiko— IF
Yamamoto, Tomomi "Tommy"— P/OF

Ladies Professional League Rosters

Long Beach Aces

Satriano, Gina

Los Angeles/Florida Legends

Brill, Mel
Chin, Jackie— OF
Gonzalez, Adrian
Hernandez, Rene
LeMasters, Keri— IF
Levine, Michelle

Nichols, Tina— P
Suzuki, Keiko
Yamamoto, Tomomi "Tommy" — P/OF

New Jersey Diamonds

San Jose Spitfires

Oldham, John— Manager
Taylor, Buck — Manager
Johnson Toby — Coach
Perry, Jeff— Coach
Bronson, Nancy — P
Brun, Patti Jane "PJ" — CF/P
Coats, Sal— 2B
Edwards, Marcetta "Skeets"— OF
Kreider, Rhoda — OF
Macer, Alicia — P
MacGregor, Theresa— OF
Martinez, Caroline — P
McCann, Rachelle "Rocky"— 3B
Palmer, Rhonda—1B/P
Perez, Melanie — IF
Ruelas (Bruckner), Victoria— SS
Schenk, Jill
Sickinger, Alexandra "Alex"— C
Spitaleri, Camile— SS
Uwaine, Rochelle— OF
Wasinger, Brenda
Windsor, Cheryl — SS

Los Angeles Legends

Satriano, Gina

Phoenix Peppers

Hughes, Dan — Coach
Bartlet, Denise— LF
Bergeson, Dawn— P
Braatz-Cochran, Leah— 3B/C/1B
Churchill, Jennifer — P/Util.
Deluca, Christina— P/1B
Kelly, Tracy— RF
Langston, Sandra— C
Lohmann, Tammy— SS
Riedel, Dana — CF
Sears, Christy — P
Thompson, Jennifer
Wooder, Rhonda — 2B

Long Beach Aces

Mid-Atlantic Pride

Motta, Paul — Coach
Deaver, Claudine — 2B
Felt, Mary Alice — RF
Gibbons, Melissa
Hartnett, Bevin — C
Kenney, Mary
Rabideau, Cindy — SS
Walton, Phyllis

NEWBL/WNEBL Rosters

Bay State Express

Needham, Paul — Head coach (1999)
Sroczynski, Ron — Head coach
Astl, Paula — IF (1999)
Britton, Dominisha— P
Coleman, Kate
Cook, Ashley— P
Fernandes, Yolanda
Gello, Phyllis— OF
Goodwin, Jenette— IF
Greuling, Jackie
Haas, Jill— IF
Hoag, Sue — OF (1999)
Kapenas, Jennifer— IF/OF
Kelly, Katharyn — IF (1999)
LaMarine, Karen— OF
Lavin, Moe — OF (1999)
Lindeborg, Chris— P/1B
Mills, Donna— 3B
Mullen, Erin— P
O'Brien, Judy— C
Pantelone, Jennifer — OF
Partanen, Karen — IF(1999)
Payne, Lisa— OF/IF
Russo, Trista— P/OF
Shibata, Makiko— RF
Silveira, Tammy— C
Sroczynski, Debra— P/Captain
Tempesta, Elizabeth— IF
Titus, Kate— C
Vecchione, Angela— SS/C
Wright, Charlene— P/OF
Wilson, Rebecca — IF/P (1999)
Wulf, Laura— OF (1999)
Zarrett, Nicole — IF

Boston Blitz (1999)

Harrington, Paul — Head coach
Appier, Jeri— OF/P/Captain
Ansell, Sandra — IF

Blumenthal, Lani — C
Boyd, Kimberly — IF
Conville, Kelly — IF
Dutily, Samantha — IF
Gibbons, Ann — IF/P
Hironaka, Carrie — OF
Kennedy, Michelle — OF
Mitchell, Nora — IF/P
Olivieri, Doreen — IF
Pashkevitch, Katia — C
Payne, Lisa— IF
Riggio-Axelson, Cloe — OF
Thompson, Cora — IF

Detroit Danger (also in Great Lakes Women's Baseball League)

Macurio, Shawn — Owner
McGlone, Greg — Manager
Garbey, Barbara — Coach
Karam, Brian — Assistant
Christian, Karstan — Hitting coach
Stewart, Mark — Coach
Macurio, Barry — Coach
Schroff, Bob — Pitching coach
Zahn, Geoff— Pitching coach
Akers, Lindsey — OF
Boggs, Heather — P/SS
Bowling, Sue — IF/OF
Carr, Deanna — OF/P
Civiello, Annette— IF/OF
Civiello, Marie— OF
Cuevas, Miriam — P/OF
Elliott, Lauren — P/OF/Coach
Engel, Heather— C/OF
Fleck, Karen— P/Util.
Flynn, Courtney — P/1B/OF
Fradeneck, Kate — OF
Galea, Michelle — P/3B/SS
Garbig, Kelly — P/2B/3B
Gravina, RoseAnne — OF/1B
Howey, Becky—1B/P
Jagielski, Katie "Jag" — 2B/SS
Johansen, Kim — 3B
Jones, Stacy — SS/1B
June, Kim— IF
Klusek, Sarah— OF/P/2B
Kwiatkowski, Melanie — P/2B/C
Lagocki, Jolene— P/IF
Lagocki, June — IF
Livernois, Kimberly— OF
Macurio, Shawn— C/P
Martin, Jessica — IF/C

McCullough, Judy — OF
Mercatante, Andrea— P/SS/3B
Moore-McPaul, Kenya — OF
Nielson, Shawn — P/OF
Nowaczewski, Annie— 2B
Parr, Merrie— OF/C/P/IF
Raniszewski, Kris— P/3B/SS
Rasmussen, Krista — OF
Riopelle, Christy— C/OF
Rota, Kelly— P/3B
Schultz, Dawn — OF
Sheldon, Carol—1B
Shriner, Kat—1B
Sivalelli, Angela — IF/OF
Smith, Mikeal — IF
Smythe, Katy— SS
Szegda, Nina "Niner"— OF
Zawal, Jessica— C/OF
Zinck, Aurora— C

Lowell Robins

Gay, Lindsey— IF

Middlesex County Cougars (1999)

Dall, Dick — Head coach
Lindeborg, Chris— IF/P/Captain
Barber, Colleen — OF
Belleville, Kristen — IF
Charron, Ann-Margaret — IF
Flaherty, Colleen— OF
Grealy, Erin — OF
Hickey, Kim — IF
Kirker, Nicole — IF
McCormack, Karen — IF
Santos, Susie— IF
Saunders, Michelle — C
Shibata, Makiko— IF
Stubbs, Kelly — OF
Yamamoto, Tomomi "Tommy"— OF/P
Zuckerman, Megan— IF

New Jersey Diamonds

Herbst, Terri Lynn
O'Brien, Judy— C

North Shore Cougars

Zuckerman, Megan— Coach
Bresse, Sue — LF
Burrill, Christina— CF/3B
Charron, Anne Margaret— SS

Cheney, Lisa — RF
Clayton, Rachel — LF
Connolly, Kelly — RF
Delaney, Christy
Esquivel, Rosalie — RF
Finn, Susan — P
Flaherty, Colleen— CF
Hanley, Kristal — 2B
Hickey, Kim — 3B/P
Mazin, Robyn— C
McGivney, Amanda — 2B
Milligan, Cheryl — 3B
Nardone, Jess— C/P
Olson, Cheryl — LF
Pederson, Shelly
Perry, Maryanne — CF
Rist, Beth — 3B
Santos, Susie— 2B
Wallace, Robin— P/C
Zewinski, Lisa — RF
Zuckerman, Megan—1B
Zarrett, Nicole

North Shore Navigators (1999)

Marden, Kevin — Head coach
Camire, Melanie — C
Durkee, Tracey — IF
Farren, Patricia— OF
Haas, Jill— P
Looney, Shelly— OF
Martini, Zabra — OF
Masiello, Karen — IF
Miller, Janet— OF/Captain
Milligan, Cheryl — IF
Morrison, Jen — OF
O'Connor, Jane — IF
Pederson, Michelle — IF
Peterson, Erica — IF/P
Sherry, Karen — IF
Titus, Kate— C

South Bend Blue Sox

John Kovach — Manager
Carol Sheldon—1B

Waterbury Diamonds (2000–02)

Lusignan, Lance — General manager
Alberto, James— Manager
Adler, Adriane— P
Amundsen, Elaine— P
Athens, Karrie
Callahan, Julie
Caron, Jaime

Faircloth, Sherrie — 2B
Ferretti, Danielle—1B
Geyer, Veronica "Ronnie"—
IF/P
Guerrera, Jo Anna
Hankey, Dawn — P/SS
Herbst, Terri Lynn— OF
Honeysett, Sharon — LF
Kupka, Jackie — P/C
McDermott, Keri
Miccio, Jessica — P/SS
Mills, Donna— 3B
Nolan, Melissa — P
Pettragrasso, Chris— RHP
Rodman, Kelly— P/OF
Shannon, Suzanne
Stinton, Amy— OF

National Girls Baseball League Rosters

Parichy Bloomer Girls

Dvorak, Betty

Chicago Queens

Beckman, Joanne
Bergman, Erma— P/OF

New York/New Jersey Women's Baseball League (2000)

New Jersey Nemesis (Traveling Team)

Faulkner, Sean — Coach (1999)
Galvach, Gary — Coach (1999)
Richardson, Kevin — Coach (1999)
Bankovich, Marjorie — OF (1999)
Beatson, Nora— IF/OF (1999)
Beishline, Jennifer "JB"— P (2000)
Fadul, Melissa— IF/P (1999)
Farren, Patricia— OF (1999)
Fiscus, Darlene— C/IF/OF (1999)
Garrett, Donna — IF/P (1999)
Geyer, Veronica— IF/P (1999)
Gibbons, Melissa— P (2000)
Guidace, Kristin— C/P/IF (1999)
Hekimian, Catherine— IF (1999)

Hoffman, Bonnie— P/IF (1999)
Meyers, Courtney— C/P/IF (1999)
Richardson, Michelle — IF/OF (1999)
Santiago, Taiine— IF/OF (1999)
Winthrop, Susan— P (2000)
Wright, Charlene— P/OF

New York Women's Baseball Association (NYWBA)

Manhattan Giants

Kirk, Claire — SS
Laurie, Jen— 3B
Weinstock, Maia— P

Queens Cyclones

Lenhart, John — Coach
Beck, Amanda— SS
Kung, Stephanie— C
Legge, Derika— SS
Roberts, Rochelle
Wagner, Jacqueline— 2B/OF
Winthrop, Susan— P/League founder

North American Women's Baseball League

Outlaws

Pollard, J.P.— Coach
Devlin, Bill — Coach
Burrill, Christina— IF/P
Carroll, Jillian — IF/P/C
Clark, Lisa — IF/OF
Cleary, Katie— C/P
Connolly, Kelly — OF
Corrozza, Jamie — OF
Esquivel, Rosalie — OF/P
Finn, Susan — P/IF
Fitzgerald, Christal — IF
Fox, Julie — IF
Hannah, Katherine "Kat"— P/IF
Kulak, Rachelle — IF/OF/C
McIntosh, Lacey— IF
Milligan, Cheryl — IF/P
Smith, Natasha — IF/OF
Sudak, Megan— IF

Ravens

Perone, Ken — Coach
Amurrio, Rosa — Util.
Bernhardt, Michelle —1B/OF
Button, Catie — Util.
Clear, Erica — P/IF
Cronin, Lisa — IF
Delaney, Christy — IF
Duggan, Courtney — P/IF
Healy, Nicole — IF
Jordon, Stacey — IF/C
Lehane, Kerron — P/C
Marconi, Jacqueline — IF/P
Masiello, Karen — OF
McCaffrey, Alex — IF/C
Miller, Janet— IF/OF/P
Mills, Donna—IF/P
O'Brien, Judy— C
Pantelone, Jennifer — P/IF/OF
Perry, Maryanne — OF/P
Slaunwhite, Candace — P/C
Sroczynski, Debra— P/IF

Saints (2003–04)

Marfione, Ron — Coach
Kerrins, Wayne — Coach
Barnes, Anita — OF/1B
Beaulieu, Allie — Util./P
Boulos, Anna — Util./P
Doherty, Darcy— OF
Finn, Susan — P/IF
Greeley, Danielle — IF/C
Hickey, Katie — IF
Hunt, Emily— P/IF
Lemasters, Keri— IF/P
Lowery, Christina — IF
Mojica, Jaclyn — OF/P
Pappas, Danielle —1B/OF
Rodman, Kelly— OF
Rogers, Wendy — OF/P
Salisbury, Brenda — IF
Sickinger, Alexandra— C/OF
Stinton, Amy— OF
Vargas, Ashley — IF/P
Vidler, Megan— P
Zuckerman, Megan— IF

Seahawks

Morgan, Mike — Coach
Brandt, Frances— OF
Carr, Tianna — OF
Cheesbro, Erika — OF/IF
Collins, Mariella — IF/P
Cook, Ashley— P/IF
Creedon, Emily — IF/C
Creedon, Lauren — IF

Dolan, Colleen — IF/OF/P
Greckol-Herlich, Naomi—
   C/P/IF
Hance, Vicki— OF
Jones, Melissa— IF
LaMarine, Karen— OF
McKay, Claire— IF/OF
Olson, Rachel— OF
Santos, Susie— IF
Silveira, Tammy "Timo"—
   OF
Wallace, Robin— P/IF/C

North Shore Spirit Women's League (NEWBL-2003)

Eagles

Marfione, Ron — Coach
Doherty, Darcy
Finn, Susan
Hunt, Emily— P/IF
Kelly, Julie
Lemasters, Keri— IF
O'Neil, Becky
Rist, Beth
Rodman, Kelly— P/OF
Stinton, Amy— P
Thompson, Amanda
Zuckerman, Megan— Captain

Falcons

Burrill, Christina— Captain
Carrozza, Jaime
Clark, Lisa
Connolly, Kelly
Cunningham, Michelle— P
Esquivel, Rosalie
Hannah, Katherine— P
Harris, Leanne
Lindeborg, Chris— P/1B
Mazin, Robyn— C
Milligan, Cheryl — Captain/SS
Sudak, Megan— IF

Lowell Robins

Sterling, Mark — Coach
Black, Beth
Christy, Emily— P
Clear, Erica
Connolly, Kelly
Delaney, Christy
Esquivel, Rosalie
Grennell, Bonnie
Gay, Lindsey— IF

Jones, Melissa
Kimball, Stephanie
Masiello, Karen
Mazin, Robyn— C
Milligan, Cheryl — 3B
Olson, Rachel— OF
Pederson, Shelley
Powers, Rachel
Scott-Delesky, Caitlin

Ravens

Perrone, Ken — Coach
Chisty, Emily— Captain/P
Collins, Katie
Cronin, Lisa
Desch, Jen
Kay, Brandi
Masiello, Karen
Mills, Donna— SS/P
Miller, Janet— OF
O'Brien, Judy— C
Pantelone, Jennifer — P/IF/
   OF
Perry, Maryanne
Scott-Delesky, Caitlin

Seahawks

Munkholm, Ekli — Coach
Carr, Tianna
Cook, Ashley— P
Dolan, Colleen
Gaudet, Nichole
Greckol-Herlich, Naomi—
   C/P/IF
Hance, Vicki
Jones, Melissa
Lamarine, Karen— OF
Lefavor, Theresa
Olson, Rachel— OF
Santos, Susie— 2B
Wallace, Robin— Captain

Pawtucket Slater-ettes—Various Divisions

Ayoub, Ed — Coach (1981)
Balthazard, Roger — Manager
   (1978)
Bergeron, Mary — Manager
   (1978)
Boudreau, John — Coach
   (1990)
Clarke, Mary — Coach (1983)
Deroche, Joanne — Coach
   (1982)

Hartzell, Fred — Coach (1983)
Janelle, Steve — Coach (1989–
   90)
Krum, Bill — Coach (1983)
Malo, Steve — Coach
O'Riley, Ray — Coach (1983)
Piatt, Richard — Coach
Potter, Bill — Coach (1981)
Pouliot, Norman — Coach
Smith, Jay — Coach (1989)
Amaral, Susan
Aquino, Lisa
Aquino, Rita
Ayoub, Lisa
Balthazard, Linda
Balthazard, Sandy
Barbeau, Elizabeth
Bartley, Sarah
Beauchamp, Chelsea
Beaupre, Karen
Bedard, Holly
Belmont, Lea
Bettencourt, Melissa
Boneventure, Martina
Boudreau, Bethanie
Boudreau, Kris
Boynes, Keri
Bryan, Katie
Buddy, Denise
Bynum, Nicole
Clarke, Mary
Costa, Jennifer
Costa, Kim
Costa, Missy
Costigan, Cathy
Coughlin, Kellie
DiPaolo, Kim
Doucette, Brenda
Doyon, Dareth
Dragon, Cheryl
Drywa, Katie
Durand, Karen
Fisher, Sandi
Fonseca, Anna
Gagne, Cathy
Garde, Jennifer
Gorman, Letisha
Gosselin, Jackie
Goyette, Deb
Goyette, Linda
Goyette, Patty
Guadette, Estelle
Guadette, Gene
Gula, Tracy
Harnois, Kristine
Hartzell, Heidi

Jarvis, Selina
Kern, Janelle
Krum, Nancy
Langlois, Jane
Langlois, Linda
Laporte, Jennifer
Lemieux, Kelly
Lippnen, Laurie
Litchman, Sara
MacLane, Mindy
MacLane, Tracy
Malo, Cindy
McKitchen, Erin
Newman, Donna
Noiseux, April
Phillips, Christine
Pickles, Laurie
Pickles, Sheri
Potter, Judy
Potter, Kim
Pouliot, Michelle
Quinlan, Lara
Scallin, Jennifer
Silva, Lynn
Smith, Ashley
Smith, Bree
Smith, Haley
St. Germain, Allie
Swistak, Andrea
Surette, Kate
Tanquay, Jessica
Taylor, Belinda
Thurber, Shirley
Trahan, Tina
Tremblay, Amanda
Trottier, Michelle
Wallin, Diana
Watjen, Amanda
Yankee, Autumn
Zarski, Laurie

Philadelphia Women's Baseball League

Buchanan, Becky
Gibbons, Melissa — 2B
Halloran, Erin — 1B
Quigley, Narda — OF
Trice, Natasha — CF
Wiggins, Lauren — C

Southern California Women's Baseball League

Bandits

Martin, Sharon — Manager
Atkins, Ashley — OF
Ayure, Liz — OF
Bejarano, Lenora — 2B
Cardoza, Bernie
Cervantes, Maria — C/OF
Cosgriff-Hernandez, Megan
    Tomasita — C/IF
Daniel, Chastity — Util.
Deutsch, Kelly — P/IF
Elliott, Carin — IF
Fitzgerald, Kelly — IF
Gagne, Chris — OF
Hershberger, Michelle — IF/C
Hoenigman, Rhonda — OF/IF
Lindsey, Heather — OF
Maldonado, Jess — OF/2B
Moore, Shelley — IF
Navarro, Lupe — IF
Pantoya, Bernadette — IF
Phillips, Heather — IF
Robles, Barbara — P/IF
Schneider, Liz — Util.
Schoenbachler, Melanie — OF
Schultze, Donna — Util.
Sexton, Sabrina — C/IF
Sharp, Stephanie — 3B/SS
Sveum, Jasmin — OF
Taverso, Tacy — Util.
Trudell, Sherry — Util.
Weinman, Windy — P/IF
Williams, Melissa — P/OF
Wilson, Michelle — Util.

Sabres

Betti, Melanie
Chin, Jackie — OF
Conro, Pamela — P
Curone, Jo — P
Deutsch, Kelly — P
Hill, Chris — 1B
Hoover, Kim
Kerns, Amber
Leatherwood, Cherie — P
Lindsey, Heather
Martin, Sharon
Maurer, Sandy
Maya, Alison — SS
Neal, Andrea — P
Ross, Cindy — C

Sexton, Sabrina
Sharp, Stephanie
Sickinger, Alexandra "Alex" —
    C
Thomas, Stephanie
Torres, Stephanie
Treat, Tammy
Valdez, Rhonda
Vaughan, Bernie — OF
Witzigman, Sandy
Young, Stephanie

Silverhawks

Cosgriff, Rich — Manager
Betti, Melanie
Cordoza, Bernie
Emmi, Nancy — IF
Ewald, Karen — Util.
Edwards, Marla
Hanson, Marcell — IF
Hernandez, Meghan
Hershberger, Michelle — C/
    OF
Hoover, Kim
Kerns, Amber — P/Util.
Martin, Sharon — P/OF
McCormick, Cathy — P/Util.
Ott, Stephanie — OF
Picozzi, Evelyn — C/Util.
Risk, Penny
Schneider, Liz — IF
Treat, Tammy
Trudell, Sherry — Util.

Waves

Blazi, Melodi — OF
Carter, Missy
Castro, Maribel — Util.
Conro, Pamela — P/IF
Hanson, Marcell
Harmon, Selena — Util.
Hughes, Lisa
Meynig, Paula — P/OF
Pantoya, Bernadette
Parks, Barbara — Util.
Romero, Lori
Ross, Cindy — IF/Manager
Thomas, Stephanie — C/IF/
    Manager
Vadasy, Eva
Valdez, Rhonda — IF
Zapolski, Gail — Util.

Rhode Island Women's Baseball League (RIWBL)

Sydney Women's Baseball League

Blackhawks

Longstaff, Kelly — Coach
Vickery, Janenne — Coordinator
Davis, Tracey — C
Dickson, Lois — RF
Halse, Simone — P

Devils

Douglass, Ken — Coach
Caruso, Lena — Coach
Adamson, Anna — SS
Fyfe, Mel — C
James, Karie — Util.
Marks, Pip — Util./Coordinator
Perry, Leanne — P
Richert, Janna — CF
Schlierick, Kae — 1b
Wise, Karly — Util.

Stealers

Tinworth, Shelley — Coordinator
Blank, Jordie — 2B
Charles, Julia — LF
Griffiths, Kelly — P

Stingers

Murphy, Mel — Coordinator

Superkaos

Miller, Yvette — 3B

Superstars II

Gentle, Amy — Coordinator

USA National Team (2004)

Scott, Marty — Manager
Croteau, Julie — Assistant coach
Green, Lance — Assistant coach
Marfione, Ron — Assistant coach
Braatz-Voisard, Kimberly — OF

Brenneman, Laura — SS
Britton, Dominisha — P
Cook, Ashley — P
Gascon, Sarah — IF
Lemasters, Keri — IF
McKesson (Gibbs), Molly — P
Mills, Bonnie — C
Mills, Donna — IF
Mills, Kristin — P
Mullen, Erin — P
O'Brien, Judy — C
Purser-Rose, Laura — P
Raduenz, Patricia — IF
Sickinger, Alexandra — C
Stinton, Amy — OF
Venturi (Veenema), Bridget — OF
Wallace, Robin — OF

USWB

Washington Metropolitan Women's Baseball League

DC Dynamite

Gelman, Robin — P
Milliken, JoAnn — OF
Triolo, Sandy — OF
Zachery, Susan — 3B/SS

WWBA (2003–04)

Washington Stars

Descombes (Lesko), Jeneane — Coach
Cherberg, Claudia — Assistant Coach (2004)
Derouin, Stephanie — Captain (2003–04)
Benton, Anna (2004)
Booth, Tish (2004)
Fletcher, Theresa (2003–04)
Forrest, Alison (2003)
Foshee, Tracy (2004)
Fraser, Mari-Jo (2003)
Halls, Janice (2004)
Imamura, Liz (2004)
Johnson, Ashleigh (2003–04)
Karlin, Anna (2003–04)
Lee, Mikkel (2003–04)
Menghini, Patti (2003–04)
Merriwood, Trinity (2003–04)
Myles, Christy (2004)

Niland, Lily — P/OF (2003)
Phelps, Kayli (2004)
Sheehy, Tracy (2004)
Shiflett, Mary (2003–04)
Smiley, Renee (2003–04)
Spangenburg, Laura (2003–04)
Thompson, Jennifer (2003)
Tricoche, Sandy (2003–04)
Ward, Kris — P/C/OF (2003–04)
Wendt, Kristin (2003–04)
Winters, Megan (2004)

Ocala Lightning

Almeida, Leah — 1B/P
Arthur, Lauri — C/OF (1999)
Ballard, Barbara — LF
Bellmore, Kris — P/OF (1999)
Brill, Mel — C (1999, 2002)
Byers, Adria — 3B
Chambless, Tammy — OF (1999, 2002)
Dennis, Christene — OF
Gardner, Tike — P (1999, 2002)
Hall, Kari — LF
Hunger, Karen — LF/C
Kaliner, Staci — 2B
Lawler, Patty — P (1999)
LeMasters, Keri — IF
Lord, Pam — OF (1999)
McChesney, Laura — IF/OF (1999)
McKesson (Gibbs), Molly — P/RF
McNeill, Connie — P/Coach (1999)
Mills, Donna — 3B
Nichols, Tina — 1B
Provenzano, Amanda — IF/C (1999)
Ray, Dawn — IF/OF (1999)
Remillard, Michelle — P/DH
Sanders, Stacy — P (1999)
Sparks, Denise — IF (1999)
Townley, Laura — RF
Turner, Bonnie — IF/OF (1999)

Women's Baseball League (WBL)

Siegal (Warren), Justine — League president

Sparks (2003/2004)

Siegal (Warren), Justine — Manager (2003–04)

McColl, Anne — Coach
(2003–04)
Barnwell, Shannon — P/IF
(2004)
Brown, Taisa — P/Util. (2003)
Carroll, Jillian — P/C/Util.
(2003)
Carter, Kate — OF (2004)
Cella, Anna— C/IF (2004)
Duffy, Lauren — C/P/Util.
(2004)
Gallardo, Mariana — P/C/Util.
(2004)
Hebert, Alex — C/P/Util.
(2004)
Hunter, Jennifer — P/SS
(2003)
Kennaley, Kathryn—
1B/P/DH (2003)
Kimbrell, Anna— C/P/SS
(2003)

Kwan, Saskia — Util. (2003)
MacPherson, Katie— 3B
(2003)
McColl, Robyn — 2B/P
(2003–04)
Mitchell, Candace — P/CF
(2003)
Patoff, Samantha — Util.
(2004)
Pearlman, Molly — IF/P
(2003–04)
Scherer, Kate — Util. (2004)
Spurr, Miller — OF (2003)
Thomas, Laura Beth — P/Util.
(2003)
Van Dusen, Jennifer — Util.
(2004)
Yoel, Natalie — Util. (2004)

Give Back and Grow Tour Team (2002)

McCaley, Patrick — Manager
Waffle, Alan — Coach
Bettencourt, Debbie— Tour
director
Beining, Tina— P/RF
Clayton, Cassie— C/P
Herman, Elise — OF
Jester, Tracy —1B/OF
Leatherwood, Cherie — P/1B
MacGregor, Theresa— Util./P
McCauley, Roxanne — OF
Maya, Alison — SS/2B
Meghiddo, Gabby —1B/OF
Nicolls, Ashley—1B
Sickinger, Alexandra— C/2B
Siegal (Warren), Justine—
P/C/3B
Sierzega, Kathy — SS/2B

Appendix D:
Women's World Series Results

2001 Women's World Series

4–8 July 2001
Toronto, Canada

July 4	Canada 8	Australia 2
July 4	Japan 5	Australia 4
July 4	USA 8	Canada 2
July 5	Japan 12	Canada 2
July 5	Japan 6	USA 5
July 5	USA 4	Australia 1
July 5	Canada 7	Australia 4
July 6	USA 7	Canada 4
July 6	Japan 7	USA 1
July 6	Australia 7	Japan 6
July 7	Japan 3	Canada 0
July 7	Australia 7	USA 6
July 8 —		
Bronze Medal	Australia 1	Canada 0
July 8 —		
Championship	USA 9	Japan 1

Tournament Records

Japan 5–1
USA 3–3
Canada 2–4
Australia 2–4

USA defeated Japan 9–1 to take gold.

2002 Women's World Series

2–8 September 2002
St. Petersburg, Florida

Australia defeated Japan 8–6.

2003 Women's World Series

25–30 August 2003
Gold Coast, Australia

August 25	Australia 7	Japan 6
	Australia 3	America 2
August 26	Japan 8	America 4
	Australia 10	Japan 9
August 27	Japan 3	America 0
	Australia 13	America 7
August 28	Japan 10	Australia 2
	Japan 11	America 0
August 29	America 8	Australia 6
August 30	Japan 4	America 3
	Japan 4	**Australia 1**
		Gold Medal

2004 Women's World Series

18–21 July 2004
Uozu City, Toyama Prefecture
Japan

July 18	Japan 10	Canada 6
	USA 11	India 0
	Hong Kong 16	South Korea 6
	Australia 10	Taiwan 9
July 19	USA 4	Taiwan 3
	Canada 12	Hong Kong 2
	Australia 20	India 3
	Japan 53	South Korea 0
July 20	Canada 27	India 0
	Taiwan 16	South Korea 6
	Japan 36	Hong Kong 0
	USA 11	Australia 1
July 21	USA 3	Canada 2
	Japan 14	Australia 4
Championship Game	Japan 14	USA 4

Japan beat the United States 14–4 in the championship game.

Women's World Series V

7–10 October 2005
Orlando, FL

Date	Team	Team
October 7	Quebec Blue 5	S. Florida Crush 3
	Aussie Hearts 12	WBL Misfits 3
	Colorado Diamonds 10	Burlington Bulls 2

Date	Team	Team
	Ocala Lightning 10	Florida Tornadoes 0
	Quebec Blues 8	Aussie Hearts 5
	Toronto Angels 13	S. Florida Crush 1
October 8	Quebec Blue 9	WBL Misfits 5
	Toronto Angels 5	Aussie Hearts 5
	Colorado Diamonds 8	Florida Tornadoes 0
	Ocala Lightning 7	Burlington Bulls 0
	Aussie Hearts 6	S. Florida Crush 4
	WBL Misfits 5	Toronto Angels 3
October 9	WBL Misfits 16	S. Florida Crush 3
	Quebec Blue 7	Toronto Angels 1
	Ocala Lightning 7	Colorado Diamonds 3
	Burlington Bulls 7	Florida Tornadoes 5
	Toronto Angels 9	S. Florida Crush 6

Quebec Blue beat Aussie Hearts 9–1 for Championship.

Appendix E:
Women's World Series Rosters

2001 Women's World Series

Australia

Weir, Grant — Manager
Longstaff, Kane — Coach
Binks, Emma — P/3B
Coombes, Rebecca — P
Donald (Clark), Pamela — OF
Gosstray, Narelle — IF
Grant, Marion — OF
Hamilton, Samantha — IF
Holien, Ella — P
Hough, Jade — IF
Kreppold, Christina — IF
Lee, Deanne — OF
Lilywhite, Shae — IF
Manzie, Kelli — C
Marklew, Shelli — OF
Papanicolaou, Paula — IF
Ross, Shandell — C
Row, Catherine — P
Stokes, Terina — P
Straumietis, Renee — IF
Wearne, Simone — P
Whitaker, Melissa — IF

Canada

Topolie, Peter — Head coach
Harwood, Mike — Assistant coach
Montgomery, Neil — Assistant coach

Cacciolottolo, Lisa — OF
Clayton, Cassie — P/C
Eckebrecht, Nikki — IF/P
Gagnon, Carole — IF/P
Grahek, Jackie — IF
Griffiths, Natalie — P/OF
Harwood, Melanie— C/P
Hazelwood, Nadine— C/IF
Hutson, Jordan "Jordi" — IF/C
Lancashire, Ruth— IF
Laperriere, Alexandra — IF/P
Leblanc, Renee — OF
Limoges, Andrea— IF
McGraw, Krista— OF
Magalas, Samantha— IF
Neal, Andrea — IF/P
Pappin, Anjelica — C/IF
Pappin, Lyra — P/OF
Prato, Stephanie — P/IF
Psota, Kate
Russell, Kelly — IF
Stephenson, Ashley— OF/IF
Topolie, Stephanie— OF/IF
Topolle, Misty — IF/C
Warawa, Leslie— P/OF

Japan

Murakami, Mashi — General
    manager
Hirose, Tesuro— Manager
Arai, Junko— IF
Arakawa, Yoko— OF
Goto, Yoko— IF
Hotta, Miki— IF
Ikeda, Haruka — P
Kashimura, Miho— P
Kawaho, Maya— C
Kowatari, Mina — P
Kuroda, Yoko— C
Matsumoto, Ayano— P
Morii, Kazumi— IF
Nagano, Eriko— OF
Okubo, Naoko— P
Sakashita, Midori— P
Ueda, Rei— IF
Yamamoto, Tomomi
    "Tommy"— P
Yokoi, Saori— P

USA

Glennie, Jim— Manager
Giffen, Tom — Coach
Adams, Allison— IF
Amundsen, Elaine— P
Chambless, Tammy— OF
Cook, Ashley— P

Dennis, Christene— IF/P
Goodwin, Jeanette— IF
Gurley, Katherine— P
Haas, Jill— P/IF
Herbst, Terri Lynn— OF
Hunger, Karen— C
MacGregor, Theresa— OF
McKesson (Gibbs), Molly— P
Miller, Melissa— IF
Mills, Donna— IF
Mullen, Erin— P
Muniz, Millie— OF
O'Brien, Judy— C
Pawel, Jen — C
Ruelas (Bruckner),
    Victoria— IF
Russo, Trista— P
Smythe, Katy— IF
Sroczynski, Debra— P
Stegeman, Joni— IF
Stinton, Amy— OF
Titus, Kate— C
Uwaine, Rochelle— OF

2002 Women's World Series

America — Bronze

Brenneman, Laura— SS
Cook, Ashley— P
Lemasters, Keri— IF
MacGregor, Theresa— OF
McKesson (Gibbs), Molly— P
Mills, Donna— IF
Russo, Trista— P
Titus, Kate— C

Aussie Stars — Gold

Bilby, Danielle— IF
Binks, Emma— P/3B
Coombes, Rebecca— P
Donald (Clark), Pamela— OF
Fairhurst, Suzanne— IF
Gaynor, Katie— C
Gosstray, Narelle— IF
Grant, Marion — OF
Gunn, Kellie— P
Hamilton, Samantha—1B
Holien, Ella— P
Kreppold, Christina— IF
Langley, Julianne— OF
Lee, Deanne— OF
Manzie, Kelli— C
Marklew, Shelli— OF
McCann, Amy— IF

O'Hehir, Amanda — P
Papanicolaou, Paula— IF
Passlow, Kathryn— IF
Ross, Shandell— C
Row, Catherine— P
Sexton, Karina— IF/P
Stokes, Terina— P
Straumietis, Renee— Util.
Tamburrino, Alisa— P
Vidler, Megan— P
Wearne, Simone— P
Whitaker, Melissa— OF

Canada

Stephenson, Ashley— P

Japan — Silver

2003 Women's World Series

America

Barton, Meredith
Brenneman, Laura— SS
Cleary, Katie
Cook, Ashley— P
Gary, Rachell
Hughes, Jennifer
Lemasters, Keri— IF
MacGregor, Theresa— OF
McKesson (Gibbs), Molly— P
Miller, Melissa— IF
Mills, Donna— IF
Palmer, Rhonda— P
Russo, Trista— P
Sickinger, Alexandra— C
Stinton, Amy— OF
Wright, Charlene— P

Australia

Bell, Justene— p
Bilby, Danielle— IF
Binks, Emma— p/3b
Cain, Nicole— OF
Gosstray, Narelle— IF
Hamilton, Samantha—1b
Hough, Jade— p
Lee, Deanne— of
Lillywhite, Shae— IF
Passlow, Kathryn— IF
Sexton, Karina— p
Sheehan, Kerrie— util.
Stockes, Terina— p
Straumietis, Renee— p
Vella, Loren— p

Wearne, Simone— p
Whitaker, Melissa— IF
Whittam, Claire

Japan

Arai, Junko— OF
Arakawa, Yoko— P
Hotta, Miki— P
Kataoka, Ayumi— IF
Kawaho, Maya— C
Kobayashi, Chihiro— P
Kon, Yukiko— IF
Masako, Ogawa— P
Matsumoto, Ayano— P
Morii, Kazumi— OF
Nagano, Eriko— OF
Nakashima, Risa— P
Ota, Sayaka— p
Sakashita, Midori— P
Sasaki, Maki— P
Shibata, Makiko— RF
Tamura, Chika— C
Ueda, Rei— P
Yokoi, Saori— P

2004 Women's World Series

Australia

Weir, Grant — Head coach
Binks, Emma— P
Cain, Nicole— OF
Catford, Angela— OF
Forkin, Chelsea— IF
Gaynor, Katie— OF
Gunn, Kellie— P
Hamilton, Samantha— IF
Holien, Ella— P
Hough, Jade— IF
Kreppold, Christina— C
Lee, Deanne— OF
Lillywhite, Shae— IF
McCann, Amy— OF
Row, Catherine— P
Straumietis, Renee— P
Tamburrino, Alisa— P
Vidler, Megan— P
Wearne, Simone— P

Canada

Lachance, Andre — Manager
Beauchamp, Genevieve— C
Campbell, Janice— 2B
Cooke, Colleen— C/P
Forman, Erin— SS
Fradette, Nathalie— 3B/OF
Gagne, Karine— SS/OF
Gilham, Kaley— P
Hannah, Katherine— P
Harwood, Melanie— P
Hazelwood, Nadine— OF
Higgins, Isabelle — 2B
Lancashire, Ruth— P
Limoges, Andrea— 2B
Magalas, Samantha— 1B/OF
Nadeau, Martine— P
Psota, Kate— P
Stephenson, Ashley— P
Topolie, Stephanie— OF

Taiwan

Juang, Lin-Guei — Manager
Tseng, Hsing-Chang — Coach
Wang, Chi-Cheng — Coach
Lin, Chu-Chun — Trainer
Chu, Yu-Chin— P
Chy, Lin-Yin— P
Hsu, Hsiu-Lin — IF
Huang, Ching-Yung— IF
Huang, Chiung-I — OF
Hung, Jui-Mei — P
Lee, Hsiao-Chi — OF
Liao, Pei-Chun — IF
Lin, Meng-Huei — IF
Liu, Hui-Fang — IF
Liu, Tzu-Hsin — P
Liu, Yi-Pei — C
Tien, Hsiang-Ping — IF
Tsai, Ming-Chen — IF
Tu, Fang-Yi— P
Wu, Mei-Ying — OF
Yang, Kai-Yu— C
Yeh, Hung-Ling — P

Japan

Hirose, T.— Manager
Okura, K.— Coach
Yoda, T.— Coach
Arai, J.— OF

Arakawa, Y.— C
Funakashi, K.— IF
Hotta, M.— OF
Imai, A.— P
Kashiwakura, F.— IF
Kataoka, Ayumi— IF
Kawaho, Maya— C
Kobayoshi, N.— P
Kon, Yukiko— IF
Konishi, Mika— P
Matsumoto, A.— P
Morii, Kazumi— OF
Nagano, Erika— OF
Nakajima, Risa — P
Nishi, T.— C
Okura, M.— P
Ota, Sayaka— P
Sakashita, Midori— IF
Tamukai, M.— P
Tamura, Chika— C
Tsunakawa, Ayumi— IF
Ueda, Rei— IF
Wada, Y.— IF
Yokoi, Saori— P

USA

Scott, Marty — Manager
Croteau, Julie— Assistant
Green, Lance — Assistant
Marfione, Ron — Assistant
Braatz-Vosiard, Kimberly— OF
Brenneman, Laura— SS
Britton, Dominisha— P
Cook, Ashley— P
Gascon, Sarah— IF
Lemasters, Keri— IF
McKesson (Gibbs), Molly— P
Mills, Bonnie— C
Mills, Donna— IF
Mills, Kristin— P
Mullen, Erin— P
O'Brien, Judy— C
Purser-Rose, Laura— P
Raduenz, Patricia— IF
Sickinger, Alexandra— C
Stinton, Amy— OF
Venturi (Veenema), Bridget— OF
Wallace, Robin— Util.

Appendix F:
World Cup Rosters, 2004

Australia

Adams, Ann-Marie — Exec. officer
Longstaff, Kane — Assistant coach
Smith, Shaun — Pitching coach
Weir, Grant — Head coach
Binks, Emma— P/3B
Cain, Nicole— OF
Catford, Angela— OF
Forkin, Chelsea— IF
Gaynor, Katie—1B/OF
Gunn, Kellie— P
Hamilton, Samantha—1B
Holien, Ella— P
Hough, Jade— IF
Lee, Deanne— OF
Lillywhite, Shae— SS
Lovering, Tahnee
McCann, Amy— OF
Straumietis, Renee— P/SS
Tamburrino, Alisa— P
Vidler, Megan— P
Wearne, Simone— P

Canada

Lachance, Andre — Coach
Lacroix, Jean-Francois— Pitching coach
Lawlor, Brad — Assistant coach
Beauchamp, Genevieve— C
Campbell, Janice— 2B
Cooke, Colleen— C/P

Forman, Erin— SS
Fradette, Nathalie— 3B
Gagne, Karine— CF
Gilham, Kaley— P
Hannah, Katherine— P
Harwood, Melanie— LF
Hazelwood, Nadine— OF
Higgins, Isabelle— 2B
Lancashire, Ruth— P
Limoges, Andrea— 2B
Magalas, Samantha—1B
Nadeau, Martine— P
Psota, Kate— P
Stephenson, Ashley— P
Topolie, Stephanie— OF

Taiwan

Juang, Lin-Guei — Manager
Tseng, Hsing-Chang — Coach
Wang, Chi-Cheng — Coach
Chu, Yu-Chin— P
Chy, Ling-Yin— P
Hsu, Hsiu-Lin — IF
Huang, Chiung-I — OF
Hung, Jui-Mei— P
Lee, Hsiao-Chi — OF
Liao, Pei-Chun— IF
Lin, Meng-Huei — IF
Liu, Hui-Fang — IF
Liu, Tzu-Hsin — P
Liu, Yi-Pei — C
Tien, Hsiang-Ping — IF
Tu, Fang-Yi— P
Wu, Mei-Ying — OF
Yang, Kai-Yu— C

Japan

Futami, Sueko— Manager
Hashimoto, Tokuji — Coach
Saito, Kataaki — Coach
Fukuda, Erika
Ikari, Mihoko
Kasagami, Yuka— 2B
Kasai, Hazuki
Kawamoto, Yu— SS
Kishimoto, Mari— P
Kitsutaka, Kazuyo — 3B
Kobayashi, Chihiro— P
Matsumoto, Kei
Otomo, Miyuki— LF
Tanaka, Midori— P/1B
Tanaka, Sachika— P
Tanamachi, Sayuri
Tsunoda, Yuki
Uehara, Arisa

United States

Braatz-Voisard, Kimberly— RF
Brenneman, Laura— SS
Britton, Dominisha— P
Gascon, Sarah— CF
Lemasters, Keri— SS
Mills, Donna— 3B
Mills, Kristin— P
Purser-Rose, Laura— P
Raduenz, Patricia—1B
Sickinger, Alexandra— C
Stinton, Amy— LF

Appendix G:
Tournament Results

1997 South Florida Diamond Classic

4–6 April 1997
Ft. Lauderdale, Florida
No Results Found

1997 USA Baseball National Women's Championship

1–2 September 1997
Prince George Stadium, Washington, D.C.

The Orlando Dragons defeated the San Diego Stix 11–1.

Participants

Brandon Typhoon	Chicago Lightning
Florida Lightning	Michigan Stars
Orlando Dragons	Philly Pride
San Diego Stix	South Bend Belles
Virginia Flames	Virginia Boxers

1997 NWBA Tournament

5 October 1997
Phoenix, Arizona

The Michigan Stars defeated the San Diego Diamonds 11–10.

Pool A	Pool B
American Eagles	Florida Hurricanes
Florida Lightning	Michigan Stars
Phoenix Firebirds	Orlando Dragons
San Diego Stix	Tampa Bay Diamondz

1999 South Florida Diamond Classic

23–25 April 1999
Ft. Lauderdale, Florida
No Results Found

1999 California Cup

3–5 July 1999
San Diego, California
No Results Found

1999 South Bend Invitational

7–8 August 1999
South Bend, Indiana
No Results Found

1999 Labor Day Tournament— Washington Metropolitan Women's Baseball League

3–6 September 1999
Maryland

Division A	Division B
Michigan Stars 3–1	N.E. Clippers 5–0
Chicago Storm 2–1	DC Dynamite 2–3
Ocala Lightning 2–3	South Bend Blue Sox 1–2
Cleveland Bears 0–2	New Jersey Nemesis 0–3

1999 Women's National Championship—USA Baseball

15–17 October 1999
Hi Corbett Field, Tucson, Arizona

October 15	Storm 1	Etobicoke 7
	Stars 12	Wombats 5
	Wombats 1	Stix 13
	Angels 12	Storm 13
	Etobicoke 0	Stars 5
	Stix 21	Angels 0
October 16	Etobicoke 6	Stix 2
	Storm 17	Wombats 1
	Stars 10	Storm 5
	Angels 15	Etobicoke 5
	Wombats 5	Angels 11
	Stix 16	Stars 2

October 17 — Consolation Game

	Stix 13	Michigan Stars 16
	Storm 1	Etobicoke 4

October 17 — Championship Game

	Stix 20	Stars 4

2000 Citrus Blast

5–7 May 2000
Orlando, Florida
No results found

2000 South Bend Blue Sox Baseball Classic

18 June 2000
South Bend, Indiana
No results found

2000 Roy Hobbs/AWBL Independence Classic

1–4 July 2000
Akron, Ohio

Game 1	Waterbury Diamonds 4	Michigan Stars 0
Game 2	Chicago Storm 8	Cleveland Quest 5
Game 3	Diamonds 4	San Diego Stix 2
Game 4	Storm 5	Ocala Lightning 4
Game 5	Team Ontario 13	Stars 3
Game 6	Lightning 8	Quest 3
Game 7	Ontario 4	Stix 2
Game 8	Ontario 5	Storm 0
Game 9	Diamonds 11	Quest 6

Game 10	Stix 8	Lightning 7
Game 11	Summit 15	Stars 5
Game 12		
Semifinals	Stix 8	Ontario 5
Game 13		
Semifinals	Storm 13	Diamonds 8
Game 14 Championship		
	Rained out — Stix vs. Storm	

2000 Roy Hobbs Women's National Amateur Baseball Championship

19 November 2000
Lee County Stadium

Team Canada defeated the Waterbury Diamonds 9–8 in the final game.

Team Canada was 7–0 in tournament play. The Waterbury Diamonds were 5–3 in tournament play.

National Women's Championship

14–21 April 2001
New South Wales

Team	Wins	Losses
Victoria	5	0
New South Wales	4	1
Western Australia	3	2
Country BB New South Wales	1	4
Victoria Provincial	1	4
Queensland	1	4

Mississauga Women's Tournament

16–17 June 2001
Canada
No Results Found

Women's All-Star Tournament

28 June–1 July 2001
Toronto, Canada

June 28	Team Ontario (W) 6	South Bend 0
	Australia 13	N. E. All Stars 0
	Team Ontario (B) 3	Chicago Storm 0
	Waterbury Diamonds 4	Ocala Lightning 1
June 29	Australia 6	Waterbury Diamonds 4
	Chicago Storm 15	South Bend 8
	Team Ontario (W) 10	Team Ontario (B) 0

	Ocala Lightning 17	N.E. All Stars 8
	Team Ontario (B) 11	South Bend 1
	Waterbury Diamonds 12	N.E. All Stars 8
	Team Ontario (w) 16	Chicago Storm 1
	Ocala Lightning 5	Australia 3
June 30	Team Ontario (w) 5	Australia 4
	Ocala Lightning 11	Team Ontario (B) 0

July 1— Championship Game
     Team Ontario 3   Ocala Lightning 1

Mississauga Girls' Tournament

21–22 July 2001
Canada
No Results Found

2001 All-Star Game

11 August 2001
Detroit, Michigan
WBL All Stars
Detroit Danger vs. Toronto All-Stars
No Results Found

2001 Roy Hobbs/USWB National Championship

November 2001
Fort Meyers, Florida

Cal Sabres 15	Washington Thunder 6
Cal Sabres 6	Ocala Lightning 0
Boston Blue Sox 3	Cal Sabres 0
Cal Sabres 9	Midwest Maniacs 7
Boston Blue Sox 11	Cal Sabres 0
Cal Sabres 3	Ocala Lightning 2
Cal Sabres 6	Boston Blue Sox 1
Ocala Lightning 2	Cal Sabres 1

Ocala Lightning beat the Cal Sabres 2–1.

2002 Roy Hobbs Citrus Blast

25–27 May 2002
Ft. Myers, Florida

May 25	Storm 2	Cougars 1
May 25	Storm 4	Eastern Athletics 3
May 26	Far East Bloomers 10	Storm 0
May 26	Storm 3	Bloomers 0
May 27	**Lightning 5**	**Storm 4**

2002 Women's All Star Tournament

28–30 June 2002
Toronto

June 28	Team Ontario (W) 3	COGBL All Stars 1
	Team Ontario (W) 16	WBL Tour Team 6
June 29	WBL Tour Team 7	COGBL All Stars 4
	Team Ontario (W) 11	Team Ontario (B) 0
	Team Ontario (W) 11	WBL Tour Team 1
	Team Ontario (B) 12	COGBL All Stars 2
	Team Ontario (W) 15	COGBL All Stars 4
	WBL Tour Team 5	Team Ontario (B) 3

June 30 — Championship Game —

| | Team Ontario (W) 13 | WBL Tour Team 0 |

2002 D.C. Invitational Tournament

6–7 July 2004
Silver Spring, Maryland

Game 1 DC Thunder 11 Akron Summa 0
Game 2 DC Thunder 11 No. Shore Cougars 6
Game 3 DC Thunder 11 Chicago Storm 8
Championship Game —
  Cougars 13 DC Thunder 8

Burlington Women's Tournament

12–14 July 2002
Burlington, Ontario

July 12	Burlington 10	Milton 0
	Royal York 14	North York 0
July 13	Mississauga 6	Ajax 0
	Wexford 12	Milton 5
	Mississauga 13	Royal York 0
	Burlington 4	North York 0
	Ajax 14	Wexford 2
	Ajax 11	Wexford 1
	Royal York 14	Milton 1
July 14	Mississauga 8	North York 7
	Ajax 10	Burlington 6
	Mississauga 4	Royal York 2

Championship Game —
  Mississauga 8   Ajax 4

2002 California Women's Baseball Festival

20–21 July 2002
San Diego, California
No Results Found

Western Canada Girl's Baseball Championship

16–18 August 2002
Kelowna, British Columbia

August 16	British Columbia 11	Alberta 10
	Saskatchewan 10	Manitoba 10
	Ontario 7	Quebec 5
	Saskatchewan 14	Alberta 13
	British Columbia 12	Quebec 2
	Ontario 10	Manitoba 3
August 17	Quebec 13	Manitoba 3
	Ontario 8	Alberta 5
	British Columbia 10	Saskatchewan 5
	Alberta 13	Quebec 7
	British Columbia 10	Manitoba 9
	Ontario 14	Saskatchewan 2
August 18	Ontario 9	British Columbia 7
	Quebec 8	Alberta 7

Women's Provincial Championship

16–18 August 2002
Scarborough, Ontario

August 16	Ajax 11	Wexford 1
	Mississauga 10	North York 0
	Royal York 10	Burlington 6
August 17	Wexford 11	North York 1
	Ajax 9	Milton 5
	Mississauga 13	Royal York 2
	Burlington 12	Wexford 9
	Royal York 10	Milton 4
	Mississauga 12	Ajax 0
August 18	Mississauga 14	Burlington 2
	Ajax 10	Royal York 0

Championship —
  Mississauga 11   Ajax 5

Peewee Provincial Championship

21–24 August 2002
Toronto

August 21	Annette 28	Milton 3
August 22	Annette 13	Burlington 12
August 23	Burlington 25	Milton 8
August 24	Burlington 10	Annette 8

August 24 — Championship —
Annette 15   Burlington 5

Great Lakes Invitational

30 August–4 September 2002
South Bend, Indiana
No Results Found

WBL National Championships

18–20 October 2002
Vero Beach, Florida
No Results Found

2002 Women's Baseball National Championship

6–10 November 2002
Fort Myers, Florida

Ocala Lightning 6–0
Chicago Storm 4–3
Cal Sabres 4–2
North Shore Cougars 3–3
East Coast Yankees 2–3
South Florida Crush 1–4
Great Lakes Fire 0–5
Championship Game: Ocala Lightning beat
   Chicago Storm 5–4.

2002 International Women's Championship

16–22 December 2002
Geelong, Australia

December 16	Aussie All Stars 16	USA 1
	Australia 13	Canada 3
	Japan 9	USA 1
	Australia 11	Japan 0
December 17	Australia 12	USA 2
	Aussie All Stars 5	Canada 4
	Australia 13	Aussie All Stars 3

	Canada 12	Japan 2
December 18	Aussie All Stars 16	Japan 5
	Canada 17	USA 11
	Japan 11	USA 1
	Australia 7	Canada 2
December 19	Australia 11	Japan 7
	Australia 16	Aussie All Stars 4
	Japan 6	Canada 4
	Aussie All Stars 25	USA 6
December 20	Canada 6	Aussie All Stars 3
	Aussie All Stars 9	Japan 5
	Canada 20	USA 3
	Australia 13	USA 0
December 21	Australia 6	Japan 2
	Canada 12	Aussie All Stars 5
December 22	Japan 8	Aussie All Stars 7
December 23	USA vs. Victoria All Stars— cancelled	

December 22 — Gold Medal —
Australia 11   Canada 0

2003 Colorado Women's Baseball Tournament

27–29 June 2003
Lakewood, Colorado

Team Colorado won the tournament by defeating the Ocala Lightning and the American Snappers.

Washington, D.C., Invitational

July 4 Weekend, 2003

The East Coast Yankees defeated the Washington Thunder.

Cooperstown Dream Park 12U Tournament

5–11 July 2003
Cooperstown, New York
No Results Found

Southern California Classic

25–27 July 2003
San Diego, California

Bay Area CWBL 5–0
Los Angeles Mavericks 3–2
Bay Area Blues 2–2
Cal Sabres 1–3
Arizona Fire 0–4

The California Bay Area CWBL beat the Los Angeles Mavericks 15–2.

Canadian Baseball Championships

Bantam Division
13–17 August 2003
Windsor, Ontario

August 13	British Columbia 14	New Brunswick 12	
	Quebec 24	Manitoba 4	
August 13	Alberta 9	Saskatchewan 7	
	Ontario 10	Nova Scotia 8	
August 14	Windsor 8	New Brunswick 7	
	Quebec 11	British Columbia 7	
	Saskatchewan 11	Nova Scotia 1	
	Manitoba 8	Windsor 4	
	Ontario 2	Alberta 0	
August 15	Quebec 9	New Brunswick 0	
	British Columbia 15	Windsor 9	
	Ontario 11	Saskatchewan 2	
	Nova Scotia 6	Alberta 4	
	Manitoba 11	New Brunswick 1	
August 16	Quebec 6	Windsor 3	
	Manitoba 11	British Columbia 7	
	Alberta 9	British Columbia 8	
	Saskatchewan 12	Manitoba 3	
	Windsor 17	British Columbia 8	
	Nova Scotia 9	Manitoba 1	
August 17	Ontario 16	Alberta 0	
	Quebec 11	Saskatchewan 0	
	British Columbia 12	Manitoba 0	
	Windsor 3	Nova Scotia 2	
	Alberta 3	Saskatchewan 1	
	Ontario 5	Quebec 4	

Great Lakes Tournament

30 August–1 September 2003
South Bend, Indiana

The New England Lady Spirit defeated the South Bend Blue Sox.

2003 Citrus Blast Tournament

Memorial Day Weekend
Florida

The Ocala Lightning beat the Jacksonville Flames.

2003 AAU Women's National Championship

5–9 November 2003
Fort Myers, Florida

Final Standings

Team	Wins	Losses
Chicago Storm	7	0
New England Lady Spirit	5	2
Ocala Lightning	4	2
Team Canada	3	3
South Florida Crush	1	4
Cal Sabres	1	4
East Coast Yankees	1	4
Cleveland Comets	1	4

The Chicago Storm won the championship 1–0 over the New England Lady Spirit.

International Women's Baseball Tournament

16–22 December 2003
Geelong, Australia
No Results Found

Australian National Women's Championship

9–17 April 2004
Tamsworth, New South Wales

Team	Wins	Losses
Victoria	7	1
New South Wales	6	2
Victoria Provincial	5	3
Western Australia	4	4
Queensland	3	5
Country BB New South Wales	3	5
South Australia	0	8

2004 AAU Tournament

22–25 April 2004
Tucson, Arizona
No Results Found

2004 Citrus Blast Tournament

27–31 May 2004
Florida
No Results Found

Great Lakes Midsummer Classic

19–20 June 2004
South Bend, Indiana
No Results Found

Washington Invitational

3–5 July 2004
Washington, D.C.
No Results Found

2004 World Cup of Women's Baseball

30 July–8 August 2004

Edmonton, Canada

July 30	Australia 7	Taiwan 5
	Japan 10	Canada 8
July 31	Japan 5	Taiwan 4
	USA 5	Australia 1
August 1	USA 5	Japan 4
August 2	Canada 2	USA 1
August 3	Australia 7	Japan 1
August 4	Canada 3	Taiwan 2
August 5	USA 8	Taiwan 1
	Canada 5	Australia 0
August 7	USA 12	Australia 2
	Japan 3	Canada 1
August 8	Canada 8	Australia 3
Gold Medal Game —		
	USA 2	Japan 0

Great Lakes Invitational Classic

30 August–6 September 2004
No Results Found

North American Women's Baseball League Tournament

4–5 September 2004
Fraser Field
Lynn, Massachusetts

The Saints beat the Seahawks 6–0.

2004 West Coast Women's Baseball Tournament

23–26 September 2004
San Francisco, California
No Results Found

Disney's Sunshine Showdown

9–11 October 2004
Florida
No Results found

The Far East Blues beat Boggy Creek 3–0.

October 9	Boggy Creek 9	Far East Red 9
	Canadian No. Stars 7	Far East Blues 9
	Boggy Creek 6	Canadian No. Stars 5
	Far East Blues 10	Far East Reds 5
October 10	Canadian No. Stars 5	Far East Red 4
	Far East Blue 10	Boggy Creek 0
October 11	Boggy Creek 7	Canadian No. Stars 0
	Far East Blue 10	Far East Red 3
Bronze Medal Game —		
	Far East Red 7	Canadian No. Stars 0
Finals	Far East Blue 3	Boggy Creek 0

AAU National Championship

3–7 November 2004
Lee County Stadium
Florida

The New England BoSox beat the Ocala Lightning 2–1.

Friday Games—

California Sabres 12	NE BoSox 10
Chicago Storm 18	So. Florida Crush 0
Chicago Storm 19	Cleveland Comets 7
East Coast Yankees 18	Cleveland Comets 2
East Coast Yankees 21	So. Florida Crush 5
N. E. BoSox 12	Detroit Danger 0
Ocala Lightning 10	California Sabres 7
Ocala Lightning 9	Detroit Danger 0
Quarterfinals—	
East Coast Yankees 13	Detroit Danger 1
Chicago Storm 13	Cleveland Comets 0

N. E. BoSox 12   So. Florida Crush 0
Ocala Lightning 10   California Sabres 4
Semifinals—
Ocala Lightning 10   East Coast Yankees 3
N. E. BoSox 7   Chicago Storm 3
Final —
N. E. BoSox 2   Ocala Lightning 1

California Women's Baseball League

Memorial Day Tournament
27–30 May 2005
Santa Clara, California

BoSox 4–0
CWBL Bay Sox 5–1
Washington Stars 2–4
San Diego Sabres 2–3
Florida 0–5

Championship game: BoSox defeated CWBL Bay Sox 8–2.

East Coast Women's Baseball 7/4 Tournament

4 July 2005
Caravel Academy
Delaware

Team	W	L
D.C. Thunder	2	1
East Coast Yankees	2	1
Phila. Independence	1	2
N.Y. Yankees	1	2

Consolation Game —
Phila. Independence 23   N.Y. Yankees 4
Championship Game —
East Coast Yankees 9   D.C. Thunder 2

Bibliography

Adams, Allison

Anderson, Craig. "A Different Game." *The Sunday Capital*, 24 June 2001, C1, C4.

Adams, Evelyn Edell "Tommie"

Buckman, Jenifer V. "'Tommie' Adams Funeral Is Today." *Richmond Times-Dispatch*, 16 August 1999, B3.

Adler (Calenda), Adriane

Adler, Adriane. Correspondence with Leslie A. Heaphy, North Canton, Ohio, 2004.

Leonard, Tim. "Women Striving to Get League Its Turn at Bat." *The Record* (Bergen County, N.J.), 11 May 2002, AO1.

Afterman, Jean

Davidoff, Ken. "Pioneering Spirit Serves Yanks Assistant GM Well." *Newsday*, 18 April 2004.

Feinsand, Mark. "Batting Around with Jean Afterman." <*www.MLB.com*>, 30 January 2003.

Nadel, John. "Dodgers Hire Female Assistant GM." *AP Online*, 5 December 2001.

"New York Yankees Promote Jean Afterman." *AP Online*, 11 February 2003.

Otto, Allison. "Diamond Cutters: These Women Are Showing Careers Can Be Carved in Baseball Operations." *Denver Post*, 16 April 2002, D-12.

"Rumours Rampant as Yankee Assistant GM Afterman Attends Yomiuri Game." *Slam Sports*, 2002.

"Transactions." *Denver Rocky Mountain News*, 15 April 2004.

"Yankees Hire Afterman as Asst. GM." *AP Online*, 5 December 2001.

"Yankees Name Afterman Assistant GM." *Baseball America News*, 5 December 2001.

Related Terms: Management Personnel

Alderfer (Benner), Gertrude

Alderfer, Gertrude. Correspondence with Leslie A. Heaphy. North Canton, Ohio, November 2004.

Alexandria Baseball

"Lee-Jackson Girls Form Ball Club." *Washington Post*, 27 March 1935, 18.

All-American Girls Professional Baseball League (AAGPBL)

AAGPBL Baseball Cards. Series 1, 2 and 3. Larry Fritsch Cards, Stevens Point, Wisconsin.

"AAGPBL Ceases Operations, While Silver Bullets Continue Tradition." National Baseball Hall of Fame Press Release, 6 September 2004.

AAGPBL Newsletters.

All American Girls Professional Baseball League, 1943–54. Fort Wayne, Indiana: City of Fort Wayne, 1986.

AAGPBL Souvenir Program. Fort Wayne, Indiana: AAGPBL, 1986.

"AAGPBL Comes to Cooperstown." *Sports Collectors Digest*, 2 September 1988, 121.

"All American Girls Baseball Teams to Open Tour May 13." *Chicago Tribune*, 11 April 1949, C2.

"All-American Girls Get a Chance to Reminisce." *Toledo Blade*, 9 August 1993.

"All American Girls League Looks Ahead." *Chicago Tribune*, 31 December 1947, 14.

"All American Girls League Stars on Cards." *Sports Collectors Digest*, 2 September 1988, 121.

"All-American Girls Loop Series Game Sought for Here." *Washington Post*, 22 April 1951, C5.

"All-American Lassies Play to Top Gate; Are Top Attraction." *Sports Review* (Omaha), July 1955.

"Arkansas' All-American Girls." *Arkansas Democrat-Gazette*, 17 September 2003, 25.

Ballantyne, Gail. "Huntsville Man Pushes for Women of Baseball to be Recognized." <WHNT.com>, 8 September 2003.

"Baseball: Babette Ruths." *Newsweek*, 29 July 1946, 68–69.

"Batter (If Still There) Up!" *Newsweek*, 3 May 1943, 82.

"Belles Get Eight New Players in Deals with Four." *The Enquirer and News*, 29 June 1951, 24.

Berghouse, Lisa C. "Former Ballplayers Are Still Working in a League of Their Own." *San Bernadino Sun*, 23 August 2002.

369

Berkowitz, George. "Casey Is a Lady!" *Los Angeles Times*, 27 August 1944, F18.

Biemiller, C.L. "World's Prettiest Ballplayers." *Holiday* 11 (June 1952) 50–51 ff.

"Big Leaguers." Washington Post, 9 May 1952, B4.

Brennan, Patricia. "'League' Has Some Powerful Plusses." *St. Louis Post-Dispatch*, 17 April 1993.

Brown, Patricia I. *A League of My Own*. Jefferson, North Carolina: McFarland, 2003.

Browne, Lois. *The Girls of Summer*. New York: Harper Collins Publishers, 1992.

Browne, Murray. "West Michigan Whitecaps Conjure the Baseball Magic of Earlier Pro Leagues." *West Michigan Senior Times*, May 1994, 1, 3, 12–13.

Brummer, Courtnay Charles. "A League of Her Own." *Brookfield News*, 16 June 1994, 1, 14.

Busby, Michael. "The Early AAGPBL: Creating Cards for the Girls of Summer." *Sports Collectors Digest*, n.d.

Canby, Vincent. "For the Girls of Summer, Pop Flies and Charm School." *New York Times*, 1 July 1992, C13, C22.

"Carey, Bancroft y Rawlings LLegan Esta Semana a Isla." *El Imparcial*, 28 February 1949.

"Carey Signs 180 Pretty Ball Players." *Washington Post*, 31 March 1948, 14.

Constable, Burt. "'League' Wins the Heart of a Skeptical Veteran." *Daily Herald*, 4 July 1992, 10.

Croatto, Pete. "A League of Their Own." <Filmcritic. com>, 7 October 2004.

Cross, Brian. "League Lives On in Memory." *Regina Free Press*, 14 June 1997, 10.

"Daisies' Star Turned Down Chisox Offer." *Washington Post*, 29 April 1951, C2.

"Dancer Inspired Madonna Character in Film." *Associated Press*, 3 June 2002.

Dematteo, Anthony. "Famous Old Women Having Fun." *St. Augustine Record*, 9 February 2002.

"Diamond Daisies." *Sport Life*, October 1949, 72–75.

"Dottie Is a Slugger." *American Magazine* 150:57 (August 1950).

Draeger, Carey L. "Girls of Summer." *Michigan History*, September/October 1997, 16, 20.

Dunn, E.W. "Stella, the Stellar Star." *Baseball Magazine*, September 1908, 58.

Eisenbath, Mike. "In Retirement Years, Women Still Cherish League." *St. Louis Post Dispatch*, 30 July 1995.

Eligon, John. "Ageless Pros Gather to Renew Old Ties." *Grand Rapids Press*, 9 September 2001.

Fay, Bill. "Belles of the Ball Game." *Colliers* 1224:44 (August 13, 1949).

Feldman, Jay. "All But Forgotten Now, a Women's Baseball League Once Flourished." *Sports Illustrated*, June 10, 1985.

Fidler, Merrie. *The Development and Decline of the All-American Girls Baseball League, 1943–1954*. Master of Science Thesis. Department of Physical Education: University of Massachusetts, 1976.

Fincher, Jack. "The 'Belles of the Ball Game' Were a Hit with Their Fans: When the Girls of Summer Played for Pay, They Proved Women Did Not Have to Sacrifice Their Femininity to Excel in a Man's World." *Smithsonian* 20 (July 1989), 88–94, 96.

"For Chicago Women, It's a Whole Different Ball Game." *Sports Collectors Digest*, 2 September 1988, 126.

"For Whom Did the Bell Toll? It Was Racine After All." *The Journal Times*, 28 June 1991, 1.

Forman, Ross. "Rockford, Ill., Exhibit to Honor AAGPBL, Peaches." *Sports Collectors Digest*, 16 July 1993, 14.

"Fred Leo of Arlington Heights Chosen to Head All American Girls Baseball." *Arlington News*, 25 November 1949, 9.

Friedman, Arnold. "Professional Women Baseball Players Bring Hope to Clifton." *Dateline Journal*, 24 November 1993, 1, 10.

Galt, Margo Fortunato. *Up to the Plate: The All American Girls Professional Baseball League*. Minneapolis: Lerner Publications Co., 1995.

Geyer, Jack. "Southland Girls Dot Middle West Rosters." *Los Angeles Times*, 14 April 1949, C2.

"Girl Baseball Stars Play Benefit Tonight for Jewish Hospital." *Chicago Tribune*, 8 September 1947, 30.

"Girl Baseball Stars Play Tomorrow." *Syracuse Herald-Journal*, 22 August 1950, 21.

"Girl Baseball Teams to Appear in Benefit." *The Marion Star* (Ohio), 5 May 1953, 17.

"Girls Almost Joined Majors during WWII." *The Lima News*, 8 June 1956.

"Girls Baseball: Midwest League Opens Its 3rd Professional Season." *Life* 18 (June 4, 1945), 63–66.

"Girls Baseball League Names Chaperone, Aid." *Chicago Tribune*, 8 March 1948, B3.

"Girls Baseball League to Hold 10 Day School." *Chicago Tribune*, 9 April 1950, A6.

"Girls' Baseball Loop Thriving." *Iowa Nonpareil*, 27 June 1948, 23.

"Girls Baseball Stars Play Benefit Tonight for Jewish Hospital." *Chicago Tribune*, 8 September 1947, 30.

"Girls Game Has Thrived Since Wrigley, Rickey Formed 'Lipstick League' as Backstop in Case War Blotted Out Majors." *Washington Post*, 7 May 1952, 21.

"Girls Games for Red Cross Attract 20,000." *Chicago Tribune*, 19 July 1944, 19.

"Girls League Inspired Former Bat Girl." *Kenosha News*, 30 July 1992.

"Girls Teams Play Tonight." *Washington Post*, 9 May 1952, B4.

"Girls' Teams Will Meet for League Lead." *Chicago Tribune*, 28 July 1946, A2.

"Gonzalez, Rose and Co. Meet the Ladies of Baseball in St. Louis." *Sports Collectors Digest*, 26 November 1993, 16.

Gordon, James. "Beauty at the Bat." *American Magazine*, June 1945, 24–25.

Grawozburn, Clement C. "The Women of the All-American Girls Professional Baseball League: Pioneers in Their Own Right." *UW-L Journal of Undergraduate Research* VII (2004), 1–7.

Gregorich, Barbara. "A Home run's Worth of Memories." *The Milwaukee Journal*, 28 June 1992, 20–24.

_____. *Women at Play: The History of Women in Baseball*. San Diego, California: Harcourt Brace, 1994.

_____. *Women in Baseball: Indiana's Dynamic Heritage*. Indianapolis, Indiana: Indiana Historical Society, 1993.

_____. "Women's League Brought Dream to Life." *USA Today Baseball Weekly*, 22–28 September 1993, 16–17.

_____. "You Can't Play Baseball in a Skirt." *Timeline*, June 1993.

Guerrero, Lucio. "Crowd's Still Rooting for Women Players." *Chicago Sun-Times*, 10 March 2003, 7.

Habib, Hal. "When Baseball Went to War." *Palm Beach Post*, 23 March 2003.

Halberstein, Joe. "On Second." *The Lima News*, 19 May 1947, 11.

Halpert, Felicia E. "Timeout: My Turn, Gold Gloves and Silver Hair." *Newsday*, 15 August 1993.

Hammer, Trudy J. *The All-American Girls Professional Baseball League*. New York: New Discovery Books, 1994.

Hardee, A. Craig. "Food Issue Collector Compulsive, Obsessive." *Sports Collectors Digest*, 8 September 1995, 162.

Helen Earlene Risinger Collection #160. Michigan and Family History Department. Grand Rapids Public Library. Grand Rapids, Michigan.

Helmer, Diana. "AAGBL Comes to Cooperstown." *Sports Collectors Digest*, 2 September 1988, 121.

_____. *Belles of the Ball Park*. Brookfield, Connecticut: Millbrook Press, 1993.

_____. "Belles of the Ballpark." *Sports Collector's Digest*, 2 September 1988, 118–121.

_____. "Force Out." *Elysian Fields Quarterly* XII (summer 1993), 18–21.

_____. "The Night the Lights Went On at Wrigley." *Sports Collectors Digest*, 2 September 1988.

_____. "The Second Career of Woody English." *Sports Collectors Digest*, 2 September 1988, 124.

Hicks, Phil. "The Girls of Summer." *The Chronicle-Telegram*, 26 July 1994, D1.

Higgs, Catriona T. "Fandom in the 40's: The Integrating Functions of All American Girls Professional Baseball League." *Journal of Sport Behavior*, June 1997.

"Honoring Women in Baseball." *New York Times*, 27 October 1992.

Hunsinger, Lou. "A League of Their Own." *Williamsport Sun-Gazette*, 21 June 2002, 12.

"In Search of the Girls of Summer." *Sports Collectors Digest*, 2 September 1988, 122.

Isaacson, Pamela. "Belles of the Ball." Senior Honors Thesis, Brandeis University, 1998.

Italie, Hillel. "Women's Baseball League Was Better Than a Gimmick." *Chronicle Telegram*, 5 July 1992, D-6.

Jackel, Peter. "For Whom the Belles Toll." *Racine Journal-Times*, 4 August 1991, 1B, 7b.

_____. "Kurys Steals Spotlight." *Racine Journal-Times*, 4 August 1991, 1B.

_____. "Movie Plans Concern Team." *Racine Journal-Times*, 4 August 1991.

Johnson, Susan E. *When Women Played Hardball*. Seattle: Seal Press, 1994.

Kahn, Aron. "They Were the Girls of Summer." *St. Paul Pioneer Press Dispatch*, 9 July 1988, 6A, 8A.

Kovach, John. *Benders: Tales from South Bend's Baseball Past*. South Bend, Indiana: Greenstocking Press, 1987.

"Ladies of the Little Diamond." *Time*, June 14, 1943, 73–74.

"Lassies Beat Rockford 8–7." *Kalamazoo Gazette*, 21 May 1953.

Laughlin, Kathleen. "Sports-Minded All Their Lives: Female Professional Baseball Players in the All American Girls Baseball League." *Feminisms* III (July 1994), 8ff.

"A League of Women." *Chicago Tribune Magazine*, 5 July 1992.

"League Reunion." *New York Times*, 10 July 1982, 32.

Leis, Jeni. "The History of the All-American Girls Professional Baseball League." Unpub. MA Thesis, 1998.

Lesar, Al. "Getting into the Game: Women Players Recall Breaking Barriers." *South Bend Tribune*, 29 September 2002, A1.

Lewis, Jerry D. "The Girls of Summer." *Sport* 81 (August 1990), 14.

"Lisbon Lass Plays Third for 'Big League' Club." *East Liverpool Review*, 30 May 1951, 10.

McGraw, Patricia Babcock. "'Girls' to Relive the Good Old Days in Rockford." *Chicago Daily Herald*, 21 September 2002, 1.

Macy, Sue. *A Whole New Ball Game: The Story of the All-American Girls Professional Baseball League*. New York: Henry Holt and Co., 1993.

Madden, W.C. *The Hoosiers of Summer*. Indianapolis, Indiana: Guild Press, 1994.

_____. *The Women of the All-American Girls Professional Baseball League: A Biographical Dictionary*. Jefferson, North Carolina: McFarland, 1997.

"Madonna Donates Baseball Uniform for Charity Auction." *Kenosha News*, 10 October 1991.

Marguerite King (Moran) Collection #121. Michigan and Family History Department. Grand Rapids Public Library. Grand Rapids, Michigan.

Marazzi, Rick. "HOF'ers and Rockford Peaches Star at New Haven Show." *Sports Collectors Digest*, 29 November 1996, 100–101.

Martelle, Scott. "Women in Diamonds." *The Detroit News*, 21 July 1992, 5C.

Masters, Jim. "There's No Crying in Softball." <NWITimes.com>, 10 March 2003.

Metro, Debbie Luebke. "In a League of His Own." *Kenosha News*, 29 September 1992, 9.

"Midland Run Fund Raiser Reunites 14 Former Players in the AAGPBL." *Sports Collectors Digest*, 9 July 1993.

"Mister Carey's Chickens: Girls' Baseball." *American Magazine* 146:104 (September 1948).

Nicholson, W.G. "Women's Pro Baseball Packed the Stands ... Then Johnny Came Marching Home." *WomenSports* 3 (April 1976), 22–24.

"The Night the Lights Went On at Wrigley." *Sports Collectors Digest*, 2 September 1988, 122.

"No League of Their Own." *St. Louis Post-Dispatch*, 10 May 1997.

Odinsky, Tina Lee. "Women's Baseball Flourishes in Flower City." *International Baseball Rundown*, July 1995, 12.

Ogden, David C. "The All American Girls Professional Baseball League: Accomplishing Great Things in a Dangerous World." In *Baseball and American Culture*. Edward J. Reilly, ed. New York: Haworth Press, 2003.

Okkonen, Marc. *Baseball in Muskegon: An Illustrated Chronology*. Muskegon, Michigan: Mice Printing, 1993.

Pearlman, Cindy. "Playing by the Rules." *Entertainment Weekly*, 31 July 1992.

"Photographs and Memories." *Seattle Times*, 6 July 2000.

Pietryga, Vickie. "All-American Girls: Hundreds Reported for Duty to America's Favorite Pastime during World War II." *Cubs Magazine*, Spring 1992, 102–06.

"Pioneers of the Diamond." *Alberta Report*, 8 June 1998.

Rader, Benjamin. *American Sports: From the Age of Televised Sports*. Upper Saddle River, New Jersey: Prentice Hall, 1999.

Railey, Joe. "Teams Play Series Finale Here Tonight." *Columbus Enquirer* (Georgia), 29 June 1950, 18.

Randle, Nancy. "Their Time at Bat: A Women's Professional League That Made Baseball History." *Chicago Tribune*, 5 July 1992, 11–15.

"Real Baseball Offered in Girls' Loop." *Syracuse Herald-American*, 26 September 1954.

Rhoden, William. "Hardly the Boys Next Door." *New York Times*, 28 October 1998, D1.

Robbins, William E. "Baseball Film's Belles Are from Racine." *Kenosha News*, 10 July 1991, 1.

Rodewald, Judy. "Getting to First Base." *Women's Sports and Fitness* IX (October 1987), 48–49.

Roepke, Sharon. *Diamond Gals*. Kalamazoo, Michigan: Sharon Roepke, 1986.

"Rookies Get Big Break in All-American Girls League." *Newark Advocate and American Tribune*, 9 May 1950, 14.

Rounds, Kate. "Where Is Our Field of Dreams?" *Ms* II (September–October 1991), 44–45.

St. Aubin, Helen, as told to Todd Gold. "This Mother Could Hit: A Women's League Baseball Star Recalls Her Days with the Girls of Summer." *People Weekly*,. August 17, 1987, 77, 78, 81.

Schnaidt, Vanessa Keilson. "Representations and Reality: Constructions of Gender in the All-American Girls Professional Baseball League." BA Thesis, Scripps College, 2003.

"She Can Beat Boys in Half-Dozen Games." *Washington Post*, 25 September 1938, PY1.

Shook, Dennis. "Baseball Movie Scores with 3 Former Players." *Kenosha News*, 27 June 1992.

Smith, Claire. "League to Test Public Acceptance." *New York Times*, 26 January 1995, B11.

Smoot-Kimble, Naomi. "Apple Pie and Thigh-Highs: Gender Roles and Women's Baseball in the 1940s." *The Sextant*, Summer 2003, 23–50.

Snider, Mike. "Penny Marshall's Field of Dreams." *USA Today*, 20 April 2004.

Stackel, L. "Old Timer's Day for Some All-American Girls." *Ms.*, October 1982, 20.

"Take to Air in All-American Girls' Baseball." *Chicago Tribune*, 30 June 1946, A3.

Tarantino, Anthony. "Time of Their Lives: Local Women Recall Their Wonder Years in Professional Baseball." *The San Diego Union-Tribune*, 7 July 2003, E-2.

Taylor-Roepke, S. "Other Major League, 1943–1954." Abstract. *North American Society for Sport History Proceedings and Newsletter*, 1981.

Theriault, John Jr. "All-American Girls Revel in Historical Baseball Role." *Daily Herald*, 20 July 2001.

"350,000 See All-American Girls' Games." *Chicago Tribune*, 21 July 1946, A4.

"Tickets on Sale for Girls' Baseball Games." *Van Nuys News*, 8 November 1948, 6.

Townsend, Brad. "Bat Girls." *The Dallas Morning News*, 18 April 1998, B9.

"200 Girls Leave on Tuesday for Spring Training." *Chicago Tribune*, 21 April 1946, A4.

Van Dyck, Dave. "Diamonds in the Rough." *Chicago Sun-Times*, 27 March 1994, 20B.

"Veteran South Side Girl Ball Players to Start Training." *Chicago Tribune*, 14 April 1949, A2.

Vignola, Patricia. "The Patriotic Pinch Hitter: The AAGBL and How the American Woman Earned a Permanent Spot on the Roster." *Nine: A Journal of Baseball History and Culture* 12, no. 2 (2004), 102–113.

"WAACS in Diamond Rally: All-Star Battle at Wrigley Field under Lights." *Chicago Herald-American*, 1 July 1943.

Wabalickis, Kris. "Dressing the Stars." *Kenosha News*, 27 November 1991.

Walters, Laura Shaper. "The Real Days When Women Went to Bat." *Christian Science Monitor*, 16 June 1992, 10.

"Weaker Sex — Who Says?" *Sport Life Magazine*, March 1949, 48–49.

Weiller, Karen H. and Catriona Higgs. "The All American Girls Professional Baseball League, 1943–54: Gender Conflict in Sport." *Sociology of Sport Journal*, 1992, 46–54.

_____. "Living the Dream." *Canadian Journal of the History of Sport* XXIII (May 1992), 46–54.

Wells, Libby. "Baseball Day to Cover Women's Role during War." *Palm Beach Post*, 18 March 2004.

"Westport Woman Remembers the Girls of Summer '51." *New York Times*, 9 August 1952.

"Winger out of Lineup for Film on Women's Baseball." *Kenosha News*, 21 June 1991.

Winter, Jeanne. "The History of the All-American Girls Professional Baseball League." AAGPBL File. National Baseball Hall of Fame and Library, Cooperstown, New York.

Wolters, Larry. "Baseball Girls Give Television Neatest Curves." *Chicago Tribune*, 24 May 1947, 17.

"Woman Player Says Could 'Take Care of Self' in Games." *Ebony*, June/July 1953, 50.

"Women and Baseball." *Elysian Fields Quarterly* 12, no. 2 (1993), whole issue.
"Women in Baseball: AAGPBL — Touring Teams." File. National Baseball Hall of Fame, Cooperstown, New York.
"Women in Diamonds." *Detroit News*, 21 July 1992, 5C.
"Women to Sign on Equal Time." *USA Today Baseball Weekly*, 11–17 May 1994, 41.
Wulf, Steve, ed. "Scorecard: The Girls of Summer." *Sports Illustrated*, August 1, 1988, 11.
Young, D. "Seasons in the Sun (All-American Girls' Baseball League)." *Women's Sports*, October 1982, 48–52ff.
Zipter, Yvonne. "The All American Girls Baseball League." *Hot Wire* IX (January 1993) 24ff.
Related Terms: General

Allard, Beatrice

Allard, Beatrice. Correspondence with Leslie A. Heaphy, October 2004, Canton, Ohio.

Allen, Peggy

McMillan, Ken. "The Double Standard." *Real Sports*, May/June 2001, 28–30.

Allington All-Americans

"All-American Girls Squad to Be in Town Sunday to Vie with Menasha." *Appleton Post Crescent*, 14 June 1958, 20.
"All-American Girls to Play at Kalida." *The Lima News*, 3 June 1956, 2-D.
"'Queen for a Night.'" *The Lima News* (Ohio), 17 June 1956.
White, Allan. "Touring All-American Girls Prove Baseball's Still Anybody's Game." *The Lima News*, 14 June 1956.

Alvarado, Linda

"Hispanic Trailblazer Breaks All the Barriers." <http://www.americandreams.org>.
"Homerunner: Linda Alvarado, Empresaria." *Latina*, August 1999.
"Linda Martinez Alvarado." File. Colorado Women's Hall of Fame.
"President Names Linda Alvarado to the President's Advisory Commission on Educational Excellence for Hispanic Americans." 17 March 1995, Press Release, Office of the Press Secretary.
Related Terms: Management Personnel

Alvarez, Isabel

"Isabel Alvarez Pitched in Women's Baseball League before Joining STO." *Fort Wayne GE News,* 24 July 1945.
"Thirty Year GE Employee in Opening Scenes of Hit Movie." *Fort Wayne GE News* 73, no. 17.
Vendrely, Nancy. "Homecoming Is Sweet for Cuban Baseball Player." *The Journal Gazette*, April 1996.
_____. "Memory Lane Takes a Ball Player to Cuba." *The Journal Gazette*, 9 March 1996.
Related Terms: AAGPBL

American Female Baseball Club

"Women Ball-Players Mobbed." *Atlanta Constitution*, 9 March 1893, 2.

American Legion Ball

"Baseball Is Held, No Game for Girls." *Washington Post*, 30 June 1929, M22.

American Women's Baseball League

Gordon, Bob. "Daredevils Win Women's Opener, 11–6." *Daily Herald,* 17 July 1988, 7.
Herbst, Terri Lynn. "The Women's Pro Game." *Elysian Fields Quarterly*, 1998.
Muskat, Carrie. "Playing Hardball's a Down and Dirty Escape from Real Life." *Chicago Tribune Sun*, 27 June 1993, 1, 11.
Shriver, Chuck. "Women's Baseball League Set to Open Fifth Season of Play." *Daily Herald*, 5 June 1992, 14.
TerHorst, Cheryl. "Women Have Few Chances to Play Ball." *Daily Herald*, 14 August 1991.
Willihite, Lindsey. "Women Play Hardball in Association." *Daily Herald*, 20 August 1989.
"Women Play Hardball." *Daily Herald*, 8 July 1992.

Anderson (Sheriffs), Vivian

"A Pro from Days Past." *Brookfield News*, 20 August 1998, 33.

Arizona Baseball

Garcia, Jose E. "Reviving Women's Baseball Is One Man's Goal." *The Arizona Republic*, 23 July 2004.

Arlington (Stroud), Elizabeth

Berlage, Gai Ingham. "Five Forgotten Women in American Baseball History: Players, Lizzie Arlington, Alta Weiss, Lizzie Murphy; Umpire, Amanda Clement; and Owner, Helen Britton." *Cooperstown Symposium on Baseball and the American Culture.* Westport, Connecticut: Meckler Publishing, 1990. Pp. 222–242.
Hanlon, John. "Queen Lizzie Plays First Base." *Sports Illustrated*, 21 June 1965, E3–E4.
"Our Bloomer Girls." *The Decatur Review*, 6 September 1901.
Related Terms: Bloomer Girls

Asian Baseball

"First Chinese Taipei Women's Baseball Championship Opens." *Xinhua News Service*, 11 February 2004.
Related Terms: World Cup

Australian Baseball

"Australian Women's Baseball Team to Visit Hall." *The Daily Star*, 28 June 2001.
Benic, Sarah. "Batter Still Swings behind Scenes." *Moonee Valley Leader*, 16 February 2004, 46.
_____. "Errors Costly for Tigers." *Melton Moorabool Leader*, 3 February 2004, 22.
_____. "Our Mission: Regain the Crown." *Manningham Leader*, 11 February 2004, 35.
"Binks, Stokes, on Vic Women's Side." *Caulfield Glen Eira Leader*, 28 February 2005, 50.

Cleveland, Sam. "Coast Coach Spur in Aussies' World Win." *Gold Coast Bulletin*, 1 October 2002.

"Competition a Ball for Player." *Canterbury Express*, 31 May 2005.

"Fairhurst Hits First Home Run." *The Gold Coast Bulletin* (Australia), 1 April 2002, 28.

Fjelstad, Jesper. "World Guns for Aussies." *Diamond Valley Leader* (Australia), 18 December 2002, 33.

Gandon, Mike. "Nicholle Strikes a First." *Illawarra Mercury* (Australia), 28 March 2002, 62.

Hagan, Kate. "Pitching for Sport." *Moorabbin Glen Eira Leader* (Australia), 27 March 2002, 401.

Hodge, Karen. "Winding Up for Success." *Manningham Leader* (Australia), 2 July 2003, 8.

"Home Diamond Final." *Melton Moorabool Leader* (Australia), 26 February 2002, 19.

"Honor for Port Ladies." *Caulfield Glen Eira Leader*, 12 January 2004, 30.

Ierodiaconou, George. "Team Steals to a World Series Win." *Sunbury Macedon Leader* (Australia), 8 October 2002, 8.

"Lady Braves Rally." *Stonnington Leader*, 3 March 2004, 44.

"Lady Lions Have Got Right Stuff." *Oakleigh Monash Leader*, 29 October 2003, 49.

Latifi, Agron. "Women Playing Hardball." *Illawarra Mercury* (Australia), 17 April 2003, 58.

Lato, Daniel. "Baseball a Force for Women in Summer Bonanza." *The Advertiser*, 18 February 2005, 77.

"Lees Sibling Rivalry." *Diamond Valley Leader*, 10 March 2004, 27.

"Lion Ladies Dominate Vics Team." *Oakleigh Monash*, 2 March 2005, 23.

"Lions Pound Out the Runs." *Oakleigh Monash Leader*, 8 October 2003, 56.

"National Title Goes to NSW." *Penrith Press* (Australia), 30 May 2003.

"Port Ladies Easily Win." *Port Phillip Leader*, 23 February 2004, 47.

"A Rooty Hill Woman Will Be Among About 60 Trying Out for the State Women's Baseball Team at a Series of Trials Starting on Saturday." *St. Marys Standard* (Australia), 19 November 2003.

Rowe, Peter. "Illawarra's Baseball Diamonds." *The Sunday Telegraph* (Sydney), 3 April 2005, 78.

"Schulte Makes State Team." *Townsville Bulletin-Sun*, 18 October 2003, 125.

Shevelove, Marty. "A Whole New Ball Game." *Oakleigh Monash Leader* (Australia), 15 October 2003, 8.

_____. "Doncaster Sinks Mariners." *Caulfield Glen Eira Leader*, 21 March 2005, 46.

"Sisters Do It for Themselves." *Whittlesea Leader*, 25 February 2004, 74.

"Teen in National Team." *Northside Chronicle*, 25 May 2005.

Thomas, Bradley. "Dragons Prevail in Well-fought Thriller." *Manningham Leader*, 22 October 2003, 35.

"Tigers Back on the Prowl." *Melton Moorabool Leader* (Australia), 16 December 2003, 24.

"Tigers Strike Out Under Pressure." *Melton Moorabool Leader* (Australia), 5 March 2002, 20.

Turner, David. "Lady Wildcats Ready." *Waverly Leader*, 10 August 2004, 31.

"Vics Glove 5th Title in Row." *The Gold Coast Bulletin* (Australia), 8 April 2002, 30.

"Vics Out to Maintain Grip on Title." *Manningham Leader* (Australia), 5 February 2003, 30.

"Victorian Women Make Their Pitch." *Diamond Valley Leader* (Australia), 14 January 2004, 26.

"Winning Formula for the Women." *Whitehorse Leader* (Australia), 3 July 2002, 78.

"Women Blast St. Kilda." *Stonnington Leader*, 22 October 2003, 43.

"Women Ready to Play Ball." *The Gold Coast Bulletin* (Australia), 30 March 2002, 126.

"Women's World Series Moves to Australia." *Associated Press Online*, 11 July 2003.

Related Terms: World Series, Kathy Passlow, Rebecca Coombes, World Cup

Autry, Jacqueline

"Angels' Owner Threatens to Move Team from Anaheim." *The Cincinnati Post*, 16 March 1996.

"Angels Readmitted to Baseball Heaven." *The Post-Standard*, 16 October 2002, D-2.

"Autry's Widow Says Singing Cowboy Would Love These Angels." *San Francisco Chronicle*, 28 September 2002.

"Giles, Autry Honorary Presidents." *The Valley Independent*, 14 June 2001.

"Jackie Autry Began with Three Strikes Against Her." *St. Louis Post-Dispatch*, 2 June 1996.

"Jackie Autry Upset, Ponders Moving Angels." *Los Angeles Daily News*, 16 March 1996.

"Remarks Honoring the 2002 World Series Champion Anaheim Angels." Public Papers of the Presidents, Vol. 39, No. 22, 2 June 2003.

Related Terms: Owners

AWBA

Battista, Judy. "Baseball Lures Would-Be Women Stars." *The Miami Herald*, 14 September 1992.

Beuttler, Bill. "The Girls of Summer." *Sports Illustrated*, 6 September 1993, 139.

George, Dave. "Women's Baseball League Set." *Palm Beach Post*, 23 October 1992.

Niedzielka, Amy. "Miami's League of Their Own." *The Miami Herald*, 9 August 1992.

AWBL

Base Runner. October 1998, November 1999.

Harrington, Patrick. "At Home Behind the Plate." *The Oregonian*, 19 February 2004, 01.

Baker (George), Mary Geraldine "Bonnie"

Browne, Lois. *Girls of Summer*. Toronto: Harper and Collins, 1992. Pp. 34, 35, 38, 44, 116, 182–83, 198.

Fay, William Cullen. "Bonnie's the Belle of the Ball Game." *Sport*, May 1947, 26, 28, 97–98.

Galt Fortunato, Margo. *Up to the Plate*. Minneapolis: Lerner Publications, 1995. Pp. 64, 72, 75.

Helmer, Diane. *Belles of the Ballpark*. Brookfield, CT: Millbrook Press, 1993. P. 18.

Macy, Sue. *A Whole New Ball Game: The Story of the All-American Girls Professional BB League*. NY: Henry Holt & Co, 1993. Pp. 25, 79.

Pontanilla, Bernice. "Little Gets Display of Her Own." *Winnipeg Sun*, 30 July 2003, 44.

Solomon, Keith. "Saskatchewan Baseball Pioneer Baker Dead at Age 84." *News Optimist*, 31 December 2003, 13.

Vanstone, Rob. "Baker Was a Star for Women's Baseball." *The Leader-Post* (Regina, Saskatchewan), 18 December 2003, C2.

Walton, Dawn. "Canadian Ball Star Gave U.S. Someone to Cheer." *Bell Globe Media*, December 2003.

Baltimore Ladies
"Girls' Nine Seeking Players and Games." *Washington Post*, 3 January 1926, 19.

Bancroft, Dave
"Manager of South Bend Blue Sox Holds Major League Record for Shortstops." *The Lima News*, 18 May 1949, 17.

Barber, Perry Lee
Brand, Madeline. "Profile: Perry Barber." NPR *Morning Edition*, 18 August 2000.

Perry Lee Barber File. National Baseball Hall of Fame and Library, Cooperstown, New York.

Sarra, Gregg. "Following Their Call." *Newsday*, 24 September 1996.

Related Terms: Collections, Umpires

Barnett, Pearl
"Woman to Play 1st Base for the Havana Stars." *Chicago Defender*, 12 May 1917.

Baseball Wives
Bouton, Bobbie and Nancy Marshall. *Home Games: Two Baseball Wives Speak Out*. New York: St. Martin's Press, 1983.

Garvey, Cyndy. *The Secret Life of Cyndy Garvey*. New York: Doubleday Books, 1989.

Hargrove, Sharon and Richard Hauer Costa. *Safe at Home: A Baseball Wife's Story*. College Station, Texas: Texas A & M University Press, 1989.

John, Tommy and Sally. *The Sally and Tommy John Story: Our Life in Baseball*. New York: MacMillan, 1983.

Battle Creek Belles
"Bush Joins Girls." *Syracuse Herald-American*, 22 July 1951, 56.

Baxter, Isabelle
"Girl Ball Player Aids Cleveland 9." *Chicago Defender*, 17 June 1933, 11.

"Girl to Play 2b Base." *Cleveland Plain Dealer*, 27 August 1932.

"Isabelle Baxter." *Cleveland Call and Post*, 29 May 1948.

Beaty, April
"A Conversation with April Beaty." *Star Magazine*, 9 June 1996.

Beauchamp, Genevieve
Spencer, Donna. "A Tournament of Their Own." *Ottawa Citizen*, 14 December 2002, C5.

Beck, Amanda
Garzilli, Anthony. "Recreation Baseball." *The Patent Trader*, 9 September 2004.

Kornfeld, Stephanie. "Finding a League of Their Own." *The Rivertowns Enterprise*, 5 September 2003, 8.

Malone, Michael. "Throwing Like a Girl." *New York Sports Express*, n.d.

Bates College Web site.

Becker, Kate
"Kate Becker, Woman Pitcher, Had Drop That Fooled Local Players." *Williamsport Sun*, 27 May 1913.

"Western Bloomer Girls Slated." *The Lima News*, 26 June 1913, 11.

Related Terms: Bloomer Girls, Western Bloomer Girls

Benefits
Correira, Manny. "Area Players Recall 'Big Game.'" *The Providence Journal*, 5 February 2004, C-01.

Haggerty, Nancy. "Women to Play a 24-hour Game to Benefit AIDS Victims in Africa." *New York Times*, 21 September 2003.

Bergmann, Erma
Bergmann, Erma. Interview with Joan M. Thomas. 23 June 2003 and 23 January 2004.

Blondes and Brunettes
"A Base-Ball Burlesque." *New York Times*, 25 September 1883, 2.

"A Baseball Sensation." *New York Clipper*, 25 September 1875, 205.

"The Female Baseball Club." *New York Clipper*, 18 September 1875.

"The Female Baseball Players." *New York Clipper*, 12 April 1884.

"The Girl Ball Players from Philadelphia." *New York Clipper*, 29 September 1883.

"Girl Baseball Players." *Atlanta Constitution*, 10 July 1884, 4.

"Novelties." *New York Clipper*, 29 December 1883.

"The Young Ladies' Baseball Club." *New York Clipper*, 22 September 1883.

Bloomer Girls
"And Canvas of Bloomer Girls Attached." *Sanduskey Evening Star*, 20 June 1909.

"Another Baseball Game for Blood Next Saturday." *The Arizona Republican*, 31 July 1901.

"Atlanta Federals Down Bloomer Girls." *The Constitution* (Georgia), 3 May 1914, 11A.

"Ball Crowd Angry When It Discovered 'Bloomer Girls' Men." *Lincoln Daily News*, 21 July 1913.

"Base Ball." *Lima Times-Democrat*, 28 July 1906, 5.

"Baseball at Blossberg." *The Wellsboro Agitator*, 21 August 1901.

"Baseball Reunion Is Held by Two Women's Teams." *Sheboygan Press*, 21 August 1958, 43.

"Base Stealing." *Cincinnati Enquirer*, 23 March 1910.

"Base Ball in Bloomers." *The Sporting News*, 12 October 1895.

"Battle over 'Girls.'" *Washington Post*, 21 July 1913, 1.

"Benefit Game Sure Success." *Los Angeles Times*, 29 October 1916, VI17.

Berlage, Gai. "Women Baseball Stars of the Swinging 1920s and 1930s." *Nine: A Journal of Baseball History and Social Policy Perspective* V (Fall 1996), 77–93.

"Bleachers Fell." *Cincinnati Enquirer*, 21 August 1911.

"Bloomer." *Sandusky Evening Star*, 27 June 1900.

"Bloomer Ball Players." *The Arizona Republican*, 30 July 1901, 4.

"Bloomer Ball Tossers." *Cincinnati Enquirer*, 20 July 1903.

"Bloomer Girl Game Tuesday Called Off." *The Messenger* (Athens, Ohio), 17 September 1928, 3.

"Bloomer Girl Team Coming." *Chillicothe Constitution* (Missouri), 9 April 1903.

"The Bloomer Girls." *Cincinnati Enquirer*, 6 October 1905.

"The Bloomer Girls." *Coshocton Daily Age*, 30 July 1900, 1.

"Bloomer Girls." *Elyria Chronicle* (Ohio), 23 June 1904, 1.

"Bloomer Girls." *Elyria Chronicle* (Ohio), 21 June 1904.

"Bloomer Girls." *The Coshocton Daily Age*, 7 August 1900.

"Bloomer Girls." *Lincoln Daily News*, 21 July 1913.

"Bloomer Girls." *Sheboygan Press*, 22 July 1913.

"Bloomer Girls." *Fort Wayne News*, 21 July 1913.

"Bloomer Girls." *Colorado Springs Gazette*, 4 August 1895, 2.

"The Bloomer Girls Again." *Cincinnati Enquirer*, 18 July 1899.

"Bloomer Girls and Beyond." Chicago Historical Society, Chicago, Illinois.

"Bloomer Girls Appear but Are Not the Kind Much Anticipated." *The Charleroi Mail* (Pennsylvania), 8 June 1911.

"Bloomer Girls Are Defeated by Locals." *New Smyrna News*, 6 March 1914, 5.

"Bloomer Girls Are Men." *Sheboygan Press*, 22 July 1913, 6.

"Bloomer Girls Are Victorious." *Oxnard Courier*, 26 November 1909.

"Bloomer Girls at the Fair." *The Chronicle-Telegram* (Elyria, Ohio), 29 August 1924, 12.

"Bloomer Girls Base Ball Team to Play Legion Here Friday." *Monessen Daily Independent,* 30 August 1920.

"Bloomer Girls Battery." *Mansfield News*, 5 July 1909.

"Bloomer Girls Beaten." *Cincinnati Enquirer*, 2 September 1900.

"Bloomer Girls, Blue Birds, and Cuties Triumph." *Chicago Daily Tribune*, 18 July 1954, A6.

"Bloomer Girls Coming." *The Frederick Post*, 24 August 1925.

"Bloomer Girls Game." *Los Angeles Times*, 21 September 1908, I12.

"Bloomer Girls Great on Squeeze Play." *Los Angeles Times*, 19 September 1908, 16.

"Bloomer Girls in Warren." *Warren Evening Mirror*, 31 August 1911.

"Bloomer Girls Lose to Rexmen." *Washington Post*, 29 August 1921, 7.

"Bloomer Girls May Play Baseball Abroad." *Cincinnati Enquirer*, 7 October 1905.

"Bloomer Girls Meet Manlius and Pompey at Suburban Park." *Syracuse Herald*, 18 August 1934, x.

"Bloomer Girls Meet Westies." *Mansfield News-Journal*, 24 July 1933, 8.

"Bloomer Girls Object to Peeping Toms." *The National Police Gazette*, 17 May 1902, 6.

"Bloomer Girls on Losing End Here." *Coshocton Tribune*, 1 July 1923, 14.

"Bloomer Girls, Outdone by Ladies of Shelbyville, IND.—Great Game." *Cincinnati Enquirer*, 19 August 1904.

"Bloomer Girls Play at Baseball." *Mansfield News*, 12 July 1901.

"Bloomer Girls Play at Local Park Tonight." *Charleroi Mail* (Pennsylvania), 7 June 1911, 1.

"Bloomer Girls Play at Normal Park Tomorrow." *Indiana Evening Gazette*, 9 June 1922, 4.

"Bloomer Girls Play Beaches on Hill Wednesday." *Coshocton Daily Age*, 6 August 1906.

"Bloomer Girls Play Feds on Saturday." *The Constitution* (Georgia), 29 April 1914, 10.

"Bloomer Girls Play Feds Today." *The Constitution* (Georgia), 2 May 1914, 10.

"Bloomer Girls Play Here on Saturday." *The Constitution* (Georgia), 23 April 1914, 10.

"Bloomer Girls Play Rex A.C. Here Sunday." *Washington Post*, 26 July 1922, 17.

"Bloomer Girls Play Rex Clubmen Today." *Washington Post*, 28 August 1921, 22.

"Bloomer Girls to Play." *The Frederick Post*, 7 August 1928, 3.

"Bloomer Girls to Play." *Los Angeles Times*, 28 May 1910, 16.

"'Bloomer Girls to Play." *Daily News*, 12 September 1901.

"Bloomer Girls to Play Here." *Washington Post*, 7 June 1913, 9.

"Bloomer Girls to Play Here June 8th." *The Chronicle-Telegram*, 20 May 1927, 21.

"Bloomer Girls to Play High School Cadets." *The Frederick Post*, 2 June 1913.

"Bloomer Girls to Play this Afternoon." *Perry Daily Chief* (Iowa), 6 September 1918.

"Bloomer Girls Trimmed." *Cincinnati Enquirer*, 18 August 1900.

"Bloomer Girls Were Chewing Navy Plug." *The Fort Wayne News*, 21 July 1913.

"Bloomer Girls Won First Game." *Newark Daily Advocate*, 4 October 1906, 6.

"Bloomers." *The Times-Democrat* (Lima, Ohio), 28 July 1906, 5.

"The Bloomers Outclassed." *Cincinnati Enquirer*, 2 July 1900.

"Bloomers to Play Here." *The Constitution* (Georgia), 25 March 1903, 9.

"Boston Bloomer Girls." *The Arizona Republican*, 27 July 1901.

"Cadets Defeat Girls in 11 Inning Game." *The Frederick Post* (Maryland), 11 June 1912, 5.

"Equitable Life's Outing." *New York Times*, 17 July 1915, 5.

"Fair Bloomer Girls to Play Ball Here." *Los Angeles Times*, 16 September 1908, 17.

"Fans Nearly Start a Riot." *Los Angeles Times*, 21 July 1913, I1.

"Female Ball Players." *Cincinnati Enquirer*, 27 June 1903.

"Filmland's Baseball Team to Arrive Tonight." *Reno Evening Gazette*, 26 May 1931, 9.

"From All Accounts." *The Frederick Post*, 21 July 1913, 5.

"Gals Win, B'Gosh." *Cincinnati Enquirer*, 23 August 1900.

"Girls in Bloomers Cannot Play Ball." *Chicago Tribune*, 22 September 1895, 1.

"Girls Lost, As Usual." *Cincinnati Enquirer*, 21 July 1900.

"Girls March in a Picnic This Year." *The Decatur Review*, 4 August 1918, 22.

"Girls Seek Baseball Game." *Washington Post*, 25 June 1922, 45.

"Girls Team Is Attraction for Friday." *Monessen Daily Independent*, 30 August 1920.

"Girls Victorious." *Los Angeles Times*, 22 November 1909, I15.

"Girls Won." Newark Daily Advocate, 17 September 1901.

Gregorich, Barbara. "Jackie and the Juniors Vs. Margaret and the Bloomers." *The National Pastime* 13 (1993), 8–10.

_____. "Jackie Mitchell and the Northern Lights." *Timeline*, May/June 1995, 50–54.

_____. "John Olson and His Barnstorming Baseball Teams." *Michigan History Magazine*, May/June 1995, 38–41.

"Group of Trenton's First Bloomer Girls." *Trenton Evening Times*, 28 June 1917.

"Hooray for the Girls." *Cincinnati Enquirer*, 24 August 1900.

"Jonesboro High School Girls." *The Decatur Review*, 26 April 1904, 3.

"Kate Becker, Woman Pitcher, Had Drop That Fooled Local Players." *Williamsport Sun*, 27 May 1913.

Kelley, Bev. "They Played to Win — Those Bloomer Girls!" *Chicago Tribune*, 16 May 1954, C23.

Lawes, Rick. "1st Female College Pitcher Has Major Goal." *USA Today Baseball Weekly*, 23 February–1 March 1994, 13.

"Look Out Mathewson." *Cincinnati Enquirer*, 25 August 1905.

"Lost Game but Made Money." *Cincinnati Enquirer*, 26 August 1900.

"Manly Maidens." *Massillon Independent*, <www.news paperarchive.com>.

"Mary." *Sandusky Daily Star*, 31 July 1901.

"Miami Beach Girls Play Here Monday." *The Mansfield News-Journal*, 21 July 1933, 14.

"Mob 'Girl' Ball Players." *New York Times*, 21 July 1913, 1.

"'Movie Star' Baseball Team to Meet F.A.C. at Local Park." *The Frederick Post*, 26 August 1931, 3.

"Nashua 16 — Bloomer Girls 1." *Nashua Reporter* (Iowa), 8 August 1907.

"New Wrinkle in Baseball." *Los Angeles Times*, 20 September 1908, 17.

"No-Hit Pitcher to Face Bloomer Girls." *The Constitution* (Georgia), 1 May 1914, 12.

"Our Bloomer Girls." *The Decatur Review*, 6 September 1901.

"Outlaw League Beat Bloomer Girls." *Los Angeles Times*, 8 September 1908, 16.

"Picked Team Plays Bloomer Girls." *Washington Post*, 20 July 1913, S3.

"St. Joe's Players All Set for Game Here with Bloomer Girls." *Salamanca Republic Press* (New York), 3 July 1933, 3.

"San Pedro Games." *Los Angeles Times*, 21 September 1908, I12.

"Second Mathewson Is Blooming in Bloomers." *Cincinnati Enquirer*, 5 May 1911.

"Select Site for Game with Girls' Ball Team." *The Danville Bee* (Virginia), 16 August 1928, 10.

"The Semi-weeklies." *Nebraska State Journal*, 2 August 1897, 2.

"A Shut Out." *Delphos Herald*, 3 September 1900.

"Shut the Bloomers Out." *Cincinnati Enquirer*, 3 September 1900.

"Some Bloomer Girls Coming." *The Decatur Review*, 2 September 1908, 4.

"Stage Set for Contest with Girls Today." *The Danville Bee*, 22 August 1928, 6.

"Star Bloomer Girls Nine to Play Jacksons." *The Syracuse Herald*, 16 June 1913.

"These Girls Can Play Ball." *Boston Herald*, 8 August 1903.

"To Nevada." *The Mansfield News*, 19 July 1901.

"To Play Girls Team." *Frederick Daily News*, 22 August 1925, 5.

"Typos and Bloomer Girls." *Cincinnati Enquirer*, 29 July 1911.

"Ungallant Pastimes." *The Syracuse Herald*, 24 January 1908.

"Wants to Play Ball, Cincinnati Girl Looking for a Job as a Center Fielder." *Cincinnati Enquirer*, 12 June 1903.

"Western Bloomer Girls Coming." *Humeston New Era* (Iowa), 13 May 1914.

"Will Show Garage Nine How to Slug Pellet." *The Nevada State Journal*, 26 May 1931, 7.

"Women Ball Twirlers." *The Fresno Weekly Republican*, 5 November 1897.

"Young Women to Play Baseball." *Charleroi Mail* (Pennsylvania), 6 June 1911, 1.

Blum, Jennifer

Chessari, Joe. "Oakland Woman Ready to Play Hardball." *The Record* (Bergen County, N.J.), 8 August 1996.

Bohle, Mabel

"Girl Baseball Player Who Saved Day for Cooke's Colts Team." *Chicago Tribune*, 20 April 1915, 10.

Borders, Ila

Ardell, Jean Hastings. "A Solitary Journey: Lefthander Ila Jane Borders." *Nine* 8, no. 2 (2000), 2–15.

_____. "Ila Borders, Pitcher." In *The National Pastime: A Review of Baseball History*. Cleveland: SABR, 2000. Pp. 10–15.

_____. "Ila Borders Retires." <http://www.wbl.com>.

_____. "On a Dream and a Prayer." *The Sporting News*, 4 April 1994.

"Baseball Player Is More Than Just One of the Guys." *Tallahassee Democrat*, 25 July 1996.

Bisheff, Steve. "A Pitcher Who Dresses Down Competition." *Orange County Register*, 16 February 1994.

"Borders a Hit with Fans, Batters." *The Miami Herald*, 24 May 1997.

"Borders' Act Not Bad." *St. Paul Pioneer Press*, 20 May 1997.

"Borders and Ketchum Play Ball with the boys." <Tabloidsports.com>, 7 May 1997.

"Borders Blazes a Female Trail." *New York Times*, 18 September 1997, C3.

"Borders Departure Overshadows St.s' Loss." *St. Paul Pioneer Press*, 26 Jun 1997.

"Borders' Debut: Ouch." *St. Paul Pioneer Press*, 1 June 1997.

"Borders Just Wants to Play Baseball." *Duluth News Tribune*, 14 June 1997.

"Borders Makes Debut." *Duluth News-Tribune*, 5 July 1997.

"Borders Makes History." *Press-Enterprise*, 16 February 1994.

"Borders Makes History." *Press-Telegram*, 1 June 1997.

"Borders Makes Seventh Appearance." *Minnesota Heritage*, 22 June 1997.

"Borders' Opening (P): Man, It's Cold out There." *St. Paul Pioneer Press*, 16 May 1997.

"Borders Shines in Relief." *Press-Telegram*, 5 July 1997.

"Borders Takes Loss but Has Her Moments." *St. Paul Pioneer Press*, 23 May 1997.

"Borders Traded to Duluth." *St. Paul Pioneer Press*, 26 June 1997.

"Borders Would Like to Forget Her History-making Debut." *The Minnesota Daily Online*, 2 June 1997.

"Borders Yields Seven Walks." *The Miami Herald*, 4 June 1997.

Brauer, David. "Throwing a Curve Ball." *Newsweek*, 10 August 1998, 60.

"Breaking Baseball's Last Barrier?" *Gettysburg Times*, 6 May 1997, B2.

Brill, Marlene Targ. "Ila Borders." In *Winning Women in Baseball and Softball*. New York: Barron's, 2000. Pp. 77–92.

"Bucking Tradition She Sticks to Baseball." *Miami Herald*, 4 July 1995.

Buscaglia, Marco. "Female Hall of Famer Plans to Pitch Her Way to the Major Leagues." *College Press Service*, n.d.

Charland, William. "A Pitcher Defies Baseball's Gender Borders." *Christian Science Monitor*, 31 August 1999.

Crouse, Karen. "Borders Finishes What She Starts." *Orange County Register*, 16 February 1994.

"Diamonds Are This (P's) Best Friend." *Wichita Eagle*, 20 May 1995.

"Dukes Female Pitcher Is More Than a Simple Publicity Stunt." *Duluth News-Tribune*, 6 July 1997.

"Dukes Need Borders for Her Pitching Not Publicity." *Duluth News-Tribune*, 27 June 1997.

"Dukes Rally against Woman." *Duluth News-Tribune*, 23 May 1997.

"Feats, Fiascoes of Three Women Make Good Gossip." *San Jose Mercury News*, 5 June 1997.

Fehr, Donald. "Show Girl." *ESPN Magazine*, 26 June 2000, 92.

"Female Pitcher Has Rocky Debut." *The Miami Herald*, 4 June 1997.

"Female Pitcher Takes First Loss." *New York Times*, 4 March 1994, B13.

Ferraro, Nick. "Breakthrough Borders Takes Act to Duluth." *St. Paul Saints*, 2 July 1997.

"Fielder's Choice." *St. Paul Pioneer Press*, 25 May 1997.

"First Woman in Men's Pro Baseball Retiring." *North County Times*, 29 May 2000.

Frey, Jennifer. "Border's Line." *Sports Illustrated*, 2 September 1997.

Gallo, Bill. "Her Turn for Sainthood." *Westword*, 15 May 1997.

Gummer, Scott. "Ila Borders." *Sports Illustrated for Kids*, August 1994, 50.

Heffernan, Donald. "Strawberry Field." *St. Paul Saints Yearbook* 1998, 17.

Heiss, Dana. "Borders Knocks Down Barrier for Women." *USA Today Baseball Weekly*, 2 December 1998, 22.

Hughes, John. "Pitcher Ila Borders Prepares for Her Second Season." *Orange County Register*, 18 May 1998.

"I Got Traded for a Girl." *Duluth News-Tribune*, 26 June 1997.

"Ila and the Odyssey." *St. Paul Pioneer Press*, 7 May 1997.

"Ila Borders Obtuvo Primer Exito." *El Universal*, 26 July 1998.

"Ila Borders Pitches Two Scoreless Innings." *The Miami Herald*, 15 July 1997.

"It Borders on Sanity." *St. Paul Pioneer Press*, 30 May 1997.

"It's the 90s and Borders Belongs." *St. Paul Pioneer Press*, 1 June 1997.

Ivory, Lee. "Try 60 Seconds." *USA Today Baseball Weekly*, 26 August 1998, 3.

Karlen, Neil. *Slouching Toward Fargo*. New York: Harper Collins, 2000.

Lawes, Rick. "Female Pitcher Eyes Pros." *USA Today Baseball Weekly*, 6 June 1996.

_____. "First Female Pitcher Has Major College Goal." *USA Today Baseball Weekly*, 23 February 1994, 13.

Lesko, Ron. "Female Pitcher Reflects on 'Dream' Season." *Associated Press*, n.d.

"Making Her Pitch." *The Macon Telegraph*, 21 February 1996.

McConnell, Jim. "Borders, Abbott Earn Induction." *Pasadena Star-News*, 19 June 2003.

Millea, John. "Big Splash Yields to the Mundane; Ila Borders' Two Northern League Managers Aren't Sure That She Has the Stuff to Stay in the League." *Star Tribune*, 20 August 1997.

Moriah, David. "Ila Borders: Brown Hair, Blue Eyes—and a Wicked Curve Ball." *Brio Magazine*, 1998.

Nadel, John. "Expanding the Borders of Baseball." *Associated Press*, 5 May 1994.

"No Special Treatment for Borders." *St. Paul Pioneer Press*, 29 June 1997.

Odinsky, Tina. "Manifest Destiny." *International Baseball Rundown*, May 1996, 16.

Penner, Mike. "Female Pitcher's Debut Is a Big Winner." *Los Angeles Times*, 16 February 1994.

"(P) Sees Future for Female Players." *Charlotte Observer*, 13 August 1995.

"Playing out Her Dream of a Lifetime." *Miami Herald*, 3 April 1995.

"Rookie Woman Snags Pitching Spot in Minors." *Lexington Herald-Leader,* 29 May 1997.

"Run with Borders." *USA Today Baseball Weekly*, 30 June 1999, 50.

"St. Paul Gives Woman a Chance as (P)." *Sun Herald*, 6 May 1997.

"Saints' Borders Gets the Best of Mitterwald." *Duluth News Tribune*, 16 June 1997.

"Saints' Borders Loses but Has Her Moments." *St. Paul Pioneer Press*, 24 May 1997.

"Saints Keep Ila Borders on Roster." *Contra Costa Times*, 29 May 1997.

"Saints Noted for Innovation." *St. Paul Pioneer Press*, 7 May 1997.

"Saints Open and Border's Watch Begins." *St. Paul Pioneer Press*, 15 May 1997.

"Saints Pitch Offer to Female Left-hander." *Aberdeen American News*, 6 May 1997.

"Saints Say Woman Will Get Tryout." *St. Paul Pioneer Press*, 6 May 1997.

"Saints Start Strong." *St. Paul Pioneer Press*, 31 May 1997.

Smith, Shelley. "Ila Borders." *Sports Illustrated*, 66–67.

"Solid Outing for Borders." *Minnesota Heritage*, 5 June 1997.

Stevenson, Samantha. "Sister Strikeout Does the Job Well." *New York Times*, 23 February 1994, B10.

"Try 60 Seconds." *USA Today Baseball Weekly*, 26 August–1 September 1998, 3.

Wallace, Robert. "Professional Baseball Player Ila Borders Is an Inspiration." *The Holland Sentinel Online*, 11 September 1998.

Winston, Lisa. "Northern League." *USA Today Baseball Weekly*, 18 November 1998, 23.

"Woman Earns Shot in Minors." *Lexington Herald-Leader*, 29 May 1997.

"Woman Earns Spot on Saints Roster." *Aberdeen American News,* 29 May 1997.

"Woman Gets Shot at Minors." *Wichita Eagle*, 6 May 1997.

"Woman Gets Tryout with St. Paul." *USA Today Baseball Weekly*, 7 May 1997, 45.

"Woman in Baseball Planned for Decades." *St. Paul Pioneer Press,* 7 June 1997.

"Woman in Majors Next? Not Quite Yet." *St. Paul Pioneer Press*, 30 May 1997.

"Woman Invited to Camp." *Akron Beacon Journal*, 6 May 1997.

"Woman Makes Minor Team, Will Make History." *Detroit Free Press*, 29 May 1997.

"Woman May be Saint." *Duluth News-Tribune*, 6 May 1997.

"Woman (P) has Rocky Outing." *Aberdeen American News,* 1 June 1997.

"Woman (P) a Hit with Fans, Opposition." *Aberdeen American News*, 23 May 1997.

"Woman Pitcher Wins Again." *New York Times*, 26 February 1994, 36.

"Woman Pitches and Wins." *New York Times*, 16 February 1994, B12.

"Woman Reaches Heaven." *Akron Beacon Journal*, 29 May 1997.

"Woman Starts." *USA Today Baseball Weekly*, 15 July 1998, 49.

"Woman to Pitch in Minor Leagues." *New York Times*, 29 May 1997, B13.

Boston Bloomer Girls

"Another Baseball Game for Blood Next Saturday." *The Arizona Republican*, 31 July 1901.

"The Semi-weeklies." *Nebraska State Journal*, 2 August 1897, 2.

Related Terms: Bloomer Girls

Boston Blue Sox

Bickelhaupt, Susan. "Diamonds in the Rough." *Boston Globe*, 7 August 2002.

O'Connor, Michael. "Battle of the Sexes." *Boston Sunday Herald*, 23 June 2002, B30.

Braatz-Voisard, Kimberly

"Brawl in Women's Game." *New York Times*, 14 June 1997, 31.

Jackson, Tony. "Role in Brawl Still Haunts Silver Bullets Outfielder." *Denver Rocky Mountain News*, 3 July 1997.

"For the Love of the Game." Colorado Silver Bullets Souvenir Program, 1995, 31.

Related Terms: Colorado Silver Bullets

Briggs, Wilma

Pontanilla, Bernice. "Little Gets Display of Her Own." *Winnipeg Sun*, 30 July 2003, 44.

Bright, Amy

Rombech, Jerry. "She Calls Strikes in Ridgeville." *The Chronicle-Telegram*, 1 July 1995, B7.

Britton, Dominisha

McKeon, Ross. "A Dream That Refuses to Die." *San Francisco Chronicle*, 26 May 2005, D7.

Britton, Helene

"Baseball Moguls Are Gathering in Gotham." *The Washington Post*, 9 February 1913.

Berlage, Gai Ingham. "Five Forgotten Women in American Baseball History: Players, Lizzie Arlington, Alta Weiss, Lizzie Murphy; Umpire, Amanda Clement; and Owner, Helen Britton." *Cooperstown Symposium on Baseball and the American Culture*. Westport, Connecticut: Meckler Publishing, 1990. Pp. 222–242.

"Bresnahan Will Manage Cards Again — Mrs. Britton." United Press, 12 September 1912.

Britton, Helene (interview). "My Experience as a League Owner." *Baseball Magazine*, February 1917, 13.

Burr, Harold C. "Women in Baseball." *Baseball Magazine* August 1933, 403–405.

Lieb, Fred. *The St. Louis Cardinals.* New York: G.P. Putnam, 1944. 46.

"Mrs. Bigsby, Owned Baseball Club, 71." *New York Times*, 10 January 1950, 29.

Steinberg, Steve. *Baseball in St. Louis, 1900–1925.* Charleston: Arcadia Publishing, 2004.

Thomas, Joan M. "Major League Baseball in St. Louis, Part Four." *St. Louis Senior Circuit*, n.d.

"$20,000 Taken by Bresnahan." *The Constitution* (Georgia), 5 January 1913, 10-B.

"Woman Who Owns a Ball Team." *The Indianapolis Star*, 1913.

"A Woman Who Owns and Runs a Big National Baseball Team." *Atlanta Constitution*, 21 May 1911, E6.

Related Terms: Owners

Broadcasters

"From Songbird to Sportscaster." *New York Times*, 3 April 1994.

Tammeus, Bill. "Big League Baseball Isn't a '90s Operation." *Mountain Democrat*, 15 April 1991, A1, A5.

Brownewell, Stacey

Kadin, Deborah. "A League of Her Own, Warrenville Teen Determined to Make It in Male-dominated Field of Baseball." *Daily Herald* (IL), 15 August 2002.

Brumfield (White), Miriam Delores "Dolly"

Lesar, Al. "Getting into the Game; Women Players Recall Breaking Barriers." *South Bend Tribune*, 29 September 2002, A1.

Bulgaria

"Bulgaria Pulls Out of Women's Tourney." *Edmonton Journal*, 27 July 2004, D5.

Bureker (Stopper), Geraldine

"AAGPBL Interview — Geraldine Bureker." <http://thediamondangle.com>.

Burke, Kitty

"This Woman Did Bat in the Major Leagues." *Albany Times-Union*, 31 July 1985.

Burnham, Kendall

"Burnham Released by Minor-League Team." *The Register-Guard* (OR), 18 June 2003.

"Colts Let Go of Burnham." *San Angelo Standard-Times*, 22 June 20003.

Kennedy, Kostya and Mark Bechtel. "For the Record." *Sports Illustrated*, 26 May 2003.

Burrill, Christina

Gasper, Christopher L. "Playing the Game They Love: Women Pursue Baseball Dreams." *Boston Globe*, 13 July 2003, 1.

Caitlin (Doyle), Emily

Carlson, Peter. "Mother-to-Be Caitlin Banished by Ueberroth." *Washington Post*, 23 August 1987, A1.

_____. "Senators Unveil Surprise Stopperette." *Washington Post*, 19 July 1987, A1.

_____. "Sex Scandal Threatens Senators' Pennant Hopes." *Washington Post*, 16 August 1987, A1.

_____. "Will Desperate Senators Shatter Baseball's Sex Barrier?" *Washington Post*, 12 July 1987, 1.

Kornheiser, Tony. "Pappy Doyle Returns; Streak Hits 20." *Washington Post*, 27 September 1987, A1.

California Women's Baseball League

Herendeen, Steve. "Women Who Love Diamonds." *Alameda Times-Star* (California), 21 February 2003.

Callaghan(Candaele, St. Aubin), Helen

Candaele, Kelly. "Gas Money." *Los Angeles Times Magazine*, 9 April 2000, 18–19.

_____. "Mom Was In a League of Her Own." *New York Times*, 7 June 1999, S9.

Helmer, Diana. "Mom Was a Major Leaguer." *Sports Collectors Digest*, 2 September 1988, 126.

Thomas, Robert McG. Jr. "Helen St. Aubin, 69, Athlete Who Inspired Films." *New York Times*, 11 December 1992, D19.

Related Terms: AAGPBL, General

Callaway, Natalie

Kreck, Carol. "The Girls of Summer Distaff Players Shortstopped by Obscure Rule." *Denver Post*, 15 May 1996, G-01.

Calloway, Ruth

"Girl Second Base Guardian Star of Former Detroiter's Nine." *Detroit Tribune Independent*, 29 July 1933, 7.

Campbell, Janice

Jewers, Jody. "Campbell Will Make History with Team Canada Tonight." *The Halifax Daily News*, 30 July 2004, 53.

Camps

"3rd Annual Women's Baseball Camp to Raise Money for Breast Cancer Research." *PR Newswire*, 15 April 2003.

Canadian Baseball

"Baseball." *The Halifax Daily News*, 19 August 2004, 60.

"Burlington Girls Get Taste of Baseball Fame; Chosen for Historic Cooperstown Tourney." *The Hamilton Spectator*, 26 July 2003, N06.

Collins, Fred. "Dream Falls Short; Young Female Pitcher Lacks Experience." *Calgary Herald*, 7 October 2002, D10.

Cowley, Norm. "At Last, a Championship of Their Own." *Edmonton Journal*, 1 December 2003, D2.

_____. "Women's Baseball Hits the Strike Zone." *Edmonton Journal*, 28 May 2002, D2.

Humber, William. *Cheering for the Home Team: The Story of Baseball in Canada.* Erin, Ontario: Boston Mill Press, 1983.

_____. *Diamonds of the North: A Concise History of Baseball in Canada.* Toronto: Oxford University Press, 1995.

Humber, William and John St. James. *All I Thought about Was Baseball: Writings on a Canadian Pastime.* Toronto: University of Toronto Press, 1996.

"Islander Invited to National Women's Camp." *The Guardian*, 2 March 2004, B3.

Pulga, Allan. "Talented Elite Girls' Baseball Team a Shock to the Boys." *Hamilton Spectator*, 14 August 2004, SP08.

Radley, Scott. "'You Got Struck Out By a Girl.'" *Guelph Mercury*, 6 July 2005, B13.

Spencer, Donna. "Baseball in December." *The Leader-Post* (Regina, Saskatchewan), 13 December 2002, C5.

_____. "A Tournament of Their Own." *Ottawa Citizen*, 14 December 2002, C5.

"Team Canada Rallies to Win Women's World Series." <www.baseballcanada>, 20 November 2000.

"Team Saskatchewan Earns Bronze Medal." *The Leader-Post*, 17 August 2004, C8.

Carey, Max

"Carey Signs 180 Pretty Ball Players." *Washington Post*, 31 March 1948, 14.

"Mister Carey's Chickens." *The American Magazine*, August 1948, 104.

Carnes, Jo Ann

"No Hits, Runs or Errors." *Los Angeles Times*, 14 May 1976, A13.

Champion Ladies Club of Cincinnati

"Girl Base-ball Players Fined." *Chicago Tribune*, 10 June 1890, 9.

Chicago Colleens

"All-American Girl Baseball Players Clash at Stadium." *Syracuse Herald-Journal*, 23 August 1950, 35.

"All-American Girls Offer Sport Treat." *Syracuse Herald-American*, 20 August 1950, 50.

"Colleens and Sallies Steam Up for Final Thriller Here Tonight." *The Austin Statesman*, 6 July 1949.

"Colleens, Comets Meet in Two Games Tonight." *Chicago Tribune*, 11 July 1948, B3.

"Colleens Games to Be Televised, Broadcast." *Chicago Tribune*, 5 May 1948, B4.

"Colleens Open Season Sunday with Rockford." *Chicago Tribune*, 7 May 1948, B2.

"Colleens Open Season Tonight at Rockford." *Chicago Tribune*, 9 May 1948, A5.

"Colleens, Sallies in Return Contest." *Portland Press Herald*, 16 August 1950.

"Colleens, Sallies to Open League Play Here." *The Lima News*, 7 June 1950, 21.

"Colleens, Sallies to Play Here." *Washington Post*, 30 July 1950, C2.

"Colleens to Play Kenosha Girls Team in Opener Tonight." *Chicago Tribune*, 13 May 1948, C3.

"Colleens Whip Muskegon, 5–4; Capture Series." *Chicago Tribune*, 25 June 1948, B3.

"Colleens Win in 14; Play Again Tonight." *The Austin Statesman*, 6 July 1949.

"Girls Baseball at Stadium in August." *Washington Post*, 16 July 1950, C4.

"Girls Baseball League to Field 4 Farm Clubs." *Chicago Tribune*, 18 April 1948, A5.

"Girls Baseball Nears Real Thing." *Chicago Tribune*, 25 April 1948, A3.

"Girls Fastball Teams to Open League Series in Lima Games." *The Lima News*, 4 June 1950, 2-D.

"Girls Teams Play at Disch Tonight: Colleens, Sallies Invade Austin for Two Day Stand." *The American Statesman*, 5 July 1949.

"Glamour Baseball Invades Stadium at 8:30 Tonight." *Portland Press Herald*, 14 August 1950.

"Grand Rapids Chicks to Open Series with Colleens Tuesday." *Chicago Tribune*, 30 May 1948, A5.

"League to Assign 18 Girl Players to Colleens Today." *Chicago Tribune*, 21 April 1948, B2.

"New Chicago Girls' Baseball Team to Get Players Today." *Chicago Tribune*, 10 April 1948, A3.

"Peaches Play Colleens in Pair Today." *Chicago Tribune*, 16 May 1948, A4.

"Rival Hurls No Hitter: Colleens Lose, 3–0." *Chicago Tribune*, 14 May 1948, B4.

"Sallies Beat Colleens, 6–4, in Fund Game." *The Post-Standard*, 24 August 1950, 17.

"Springfield Nips Colleens, 5–3." *The Austin American*, 7 July 1949.

"Springfield Shades Chicago 2–0 in Girls' Baseball Tilt." *Nashua Telegraph*, 18 August 1950, 2.

"WBKB Will Telecast Girls' Game Tonight." *Chicago Tribune*, 25 June 1948, B2.

Related Terms: AAGPBL, Springfield Sallies

Chicago Storm

"Women's Baseball Tourney Set." *South Bend Tribune*, 29 August 2002, B5.

Christy, Emily

Konecky, Chad. "Return to Pitching Reinvents Princeton Softballer." *The Somerville Journal*, 12 September 2002.

Clark, K.C.

Jacobson, Steve. "Living the Dream." *Newsday*, 8 March 1994.

Related Terms: Colorado Silver Bullets, Gina Satriano.

Clays, Adah

"Girl a Baseball Star." *Washington Post*, 11 February 1917, E9.

"Girl Baseball Star Is Two-Handed Twirler." *Washington Post*, 27 May 1917, 19.

Clement, Amanda

Amanda Clement File. South Dakota Sports Hall of Fame, Sioux Falls, South Dakota.

Amanda Clement Scrapbook. National Baseball Hall of Fame and Museum, Cooperstown, New York.

Berlage, Gai Ingham. "Five Forgotten Women in American Baseball History: Players, Lizzie Arlington, Alta Weiss, Lizzie Murphy; Umpire, Amanda Clement; and Owner, Helen Britton." *Cooperstown Symposium on Baseball and the American Culture.* Westport, Connecticut: Meckler Publishing, 1990. Pp. 222–242.

"Girl Is Strict Umpire." *Washington Post*, 17 June 1906, S3.

Kapitan, Colin. "Girl Umpire of Dakota Etched Deep in Diamond Lore; Was YC Student." *Yankton Press and Dakotan*, 1964.

Lutz, Wally. "No One Cried 'Kill the Umpire' When Miss Clement Called 'Em." *The Daily Argus-Leader*, 24 June 1951.

"Only Girl Umpire." *Washington Post*, 26 January 1906, 9.

"Queen of the Diamond." *Argus Leader*, 10 April 1979.

Roan, Sharon L. "Yesterday: No One Yelled 'Kill the Ump' When Amanda Clement was Man in Blue." *Sports Illustrated*, 5 April 1982, 81.

Related Terms: Umpires

Cleveland Quest

Heyse, Paul. "It's A Start." *The Chronicle-Telegram*, 15 May 2000, B1.

Collections

AAGPBL Files. Northern Indiana Center for History, Fort Wayne, Indiana.

AAGPBL Files. Penn State University, State College, Pennsylvania.

AAGPBL File. Canadian Baseball Hall of Fame, Canada.

Amanda Clement File. South Dakota Sports Hall of Fame, South Dakota.

Amanda Clement Scrapbook. National Baseball Hall of Fame and Library, Cooperstown, New York.

Bernice Gera Collection. Special Collections Library, Indiana University of Pennsylvania, Indiana, Pennsylvania.

Grand Rapids Chicks. Grand Rapids Public Library, Grand Rapids, Michigan.

Joyce Sports Research Collection. Hesburgh Library, University of Notre Dame, Notre Dame, Indiana.

Kenosha Comets. Kenosha Museum, Kenosha, Wisconsin.

Marguerite Moran Collection. Grand Rapids Public Library, Grand Rapids, Michigan.

Milwaukee Chicks. Oral History Project. University of Wisconsin, Milwaukee.

Perry Barber File. National Baseball Hall of Fame and Museum, Cooperstown, New York.

Racine Belles. Racine County Historical Society and Museum, Racine, Wisconsin.

Sophia Smith Collection. Smith College Library, Smith College.

Women in Baseball. Rockford Museum, Rockford, Illinois.

Women in Baseball Files. National Baseball Hall of Fame and Museum, Cooperstown, New York.

Women-Umpires File. National Baseball Hall of Fame and Museum, Cooperstown, New York.

College Teams

"American Girl as Ball Player." *Washington Post*, 5 June 1910, MS4.

"Co-eds Play Ball." *The Syracuse Herald*, 2 May 1911, 5.

"Girls at Academy Take Up Baseball." *The Erie Daily Times*, 25 May 1922, 18.

"Girls Who Play Baseball." *The Appeal* (St. Paul), 24 July 1897.

Colorado Silver Bullets

"All-Female Team Cuts Sex Impostor." *San Jose Mercury News*, 15 April 1994.

"All-Female Team Wins Friends Despite Runless, Hitless Debut." *Philadelphia Daily News*, 25 April 1994.

"All-Women's Team to Play at Coliseum." *San Jose Mercury News*, 23 June 1994.

"Alumni Stop Silver Bullets 6–4." *Wichita Eagle*, 20 May 1995.

Ames, Katrine. "A Whole New Ball Game." *Newsweek*, 9 May 1994, 58–59.

Araton, Harvey. "The Trials of a Pro Female Pitcher." *New York Times*, 15 June 1995, B16.

"Area Baseball Stars Dodge the Silver Bullets." *Philadelphia Inquirer*, 4 August 1994.

Arias, Carlos. "Experience Is, Indeed, the Best Teacher for Silver Bullets." *Orange County Register*, 18 August 1995.

"At Home on the Mound." *Plain Dealer*, 17 July 1997.

Atkin, Ross. "All-Women's Team Plays Catch-up Baseball." *Christian Science Monitor*, 26 August 1994.

_____. "Women's Baseball Makes a Pitch for Major League Recognition." *Christian Science Monitor*, 4 August 1997, 13.

Bailey, Sandra and Jack McCallum. "Level the Field." *Sports Illustrated*, 23 May 1994.

Bamberger, Michael. "The Girls of Summer." *The Chronicle-Telegram*, 9 May 1994, B1.

"Baseball Pioneer Captures Spot on Woman's Team." *Wichita Eagle*, 6 April 1994.

"A Baseball Experience Strikes Out." *Philadelphia Inquirer*, 2 August 1994.

Berlage, Gai. "The Colorado Silver Bullets: Can Promotion Based on the 'Battle of the Sexes' Be Successful?" *The Baseball Research Journal*, 1998, 40–42.

"Blasted in Debut." *Lexington Herald-Leader*, 9 May 1994.

Blumenfeld, Laura. "The Girls against the Boys." *Washington Post*, 24 April 1994, F1.

"Brawl in Women's Game." *New York Times*, 14 June 1997, 31.

Buckley, Taylor. "Silver Bullets Could Use an Image Make-Over." *USA Today*, 24 May 1994.

"Bullets Endure a Rout." *Portland Press Herald*, 1 August 1997.

"Bullets Help Women Play Hardball." *Charlotte Observer*, 20 April 1994.

"Bullets Hopeful Born Male." *Denver Post*, 13 April 1994, D-6.

"Bullets in Single A? Could Be." *Miami Herald*, 10 June 1995.

"Bullets Put on Show." *Times Leader* (Pennsylvania), 9 August 1994.

"Bullets Serious Ball Club." *Sun Herald*, 3 August 1995.

"Bullets Wrap Up First Season." *Charlotte Observer*, 4 September 1994.

"Cal Rookie Blasts Historic Home run." *San Francisco Chronicle*, 15 May 1996.

Cannon, John. "Silver Bullets Prove Golden." *The Frederick News-Post*, 9 June 1995, B-1.

Carey, Jack. "Blanks." *USA Today*, 16 May 1994.

Carter, Donna. "Beaning Barriers Silver Bullets Pitcher Strives to Open Doors so More Women May Chase Baseball Dreams." *Denver Post*, 14 May 1995, B-1.

_____. "Bullets Lose; Not to Fans, Souvenirs Are Big." *Denver Post*, 15 May 1995, C-1.

_____. "Going to Bat for Women's Baseball." *Denver Post*, 12 February 1995, B-16.

_____. "Sweating Silver Bullets." *Denver Post*, 12 February 1995, B-1.

"Chance at Bat Comes Late for Girls of Autumn." *St. Paul Pioneer Press*, 20 March 1994.

Collias, Robert. "Hawaiian League Reloads with Pair of Silver Bullets." *USA Today Baseball Weekly*, 12–18 October 1994, 8.

"Colorado Silver Bullets." *Associated Press*, 10 December 1993.

Cooper, Barry. "Pro Baseball for Women?" *Chicago Weekend*, 8 May 1994.

"Coors' Field of Stifled Dreams." *Business Week*, 24 January 1994, 8.

Crasnick, Jerry. "Bullets Learning Joys, Ills of Game." *Denver Post*, 27 June 1994, D-1.

_____. "Hall Has Classy Phil on Hold for Space." *Denver Post*, 27 June 1994, D-1.

_____. "Niekros Bond with Bullets." *Denver Post*, 27 June 1994, D-7.

_____. "Satriano Still Breaking Ground at Old Ballpark." *Denver Post*, 27 June 1994, D-7.

_____. "To a Man Ladies Were Duped by Prospect." *Denver Post*, 27 June 1994, D-7.

Cronin, Bob. "Light on Funds." *USA Today*, 22 August 1997.

"Crowd Found Cause to Cheer for the Bullets." *Charlotte Observer*, 9 May 1994.

Daugherty, Pat. "Can a Woman Ever Make It to the Major Leagues? No." *Scripps Howard News Service*, 13 May 1995.

DeSimone, Bonnie. "Playing Hardball." *Cleveland Plain Dealer*, 8 May 1994, 1D, 9D.

"Despite 19–0 Loss, Women Prove They Can Play Baseball." *Sun-Herald*, 9 May 1994.

"Diamond These Girls' Best Friend." *Press-Telegram*, 9 May 1994.

"Did Losing Help the Colorado Silver Bullets?" *San Jose Mercury News*, 8 December 1994.

Donnellon, Sam. "Silver Bullets." Knight Ridder Newspapers, 9 May 1994.

Dorsey, David. "Pro League Bolstered by Ex-Silver Bullets." *USA Today*, 9 July 1998.

Edes, Gordon. "Women Determined to Make League of Their Own Work." *Fort Lauderdale Sun Sentinel*, 20 December 1993.

"Equal Opportunity." *Denver Post*, 13 February 1994, B-12.

Falk, Bill. "Baseball in Purest Form: Silver Bullets Send a Message Wherever they Go." *Newsday*, 15 August 1994.

Farrell, Joe. "Sports Talk." *The Record* (Bergen County, N.J.), 29 May 1994.

Farrell, Mary H.J. "Say It Ain't So." *People Weekly*, 6 June 1994.

Farrey, Tim. "Women Root One Another On for Sports on Pro Baseball Team." *Seattle Times*, 17 February 1994.

"Female Baseballers Claim Men Are Cheating." *San Jose Mercury News*, 4 August 1995.

"Female Pro Baseball Team Getting Ready to Take the Field." *The Wichita Eagle*, 19 February 1994.

"Fighting for Respect." *The Florida Times-Union*, 20 July 1997.

For the Love of the Game. Silver Bullets Souvenir Program, 1995.

"For These Women, a Team of Their Own." *Philadelphia Inquirer*, 20 February 1994.

Foreman, Tom Jr. "Silver Bullets." *Associated Press*, 6 May 1994.

Fornoff, Susan. "Playing Hardball." *Sporting News*, 30 May 1994.

Friedman, Vicki L. "Silver Bullets Pay a Visit to Harbor Park Tonight." *The Virginian Pilot*, 6 June 1996.

Gallo, Bill. "Storming the Outfield Walls." <Denverwestword.com>, 2 March 1994.

"A Game of Their Own." *Detroit Free Press*, 7 May 1994.

Garcia, Jim. "Women 'In a League of Their Own': Local Players Try out for Colorado." *Sacramento Observer*, 16 February 1994.

Gay, Nancy. "Female Baseballers Claim Men Are Cheating." *San Jose Mercury News*, 4 August 1995, 1A, 24A.

Geehan, Barb and Ben Brown. "Silver Bullets: Big Plans on Deck with New Owners." *USA Today*, 23 September 1994.

Ginn, Sharon. "A Baseball Dream Come True." *The Press-Enterprise*, 27 June 1994, D5.

"Girls of Summer at Bat." *Akron Beacon-Journal*, 9 May 1994.

Goodall, Fred. "Gradually, Women Are Making Waves in Baseball." *The Gettysburg Times*, 21 December 1993, 3B.

"Guys Caught Cheating in a Game against Silver Bullets." *Detroit Free Press*, 27 July 1995.

Harasta, Cathy. "Silver Bullets Fighting for Respect." *St. Louis Post-Dispatch*, 13 July 1997.

Hart, Michael R. "Blanking the Silver Bullets." *All Hands*, August 1995.

Hay, Henrietta. "Girls Can Admire Silver Bullets." *Denver Post*, 2 October 1996, B-11.

"Headline: Bullets Blanked by Semi Pro Team." *St. Paul Pioneer Press*, 14 May 1994.

"Headline: Bullets Not Ready to Play with Pros." *St. Paul Pioneer Press*, 15 May 1994.

"Headline: Coors to Keep Silver Bullets Going." *St. Paul Pioneer Press*, 2 September 1994.

"Headline: A League of Their Own." *St. Paul Pioneer Press*, 13 March 1994.

"Headline: Mets to Hire Silver Bullets as Replacements." *St. Paul Pioneer Press*, 2 February 1995.

"Headline: Niekro's Show Women (P)'s the Fine Points." *St. Paul Pioneer Press*, 20 March 1994.

"Headline: Northern League A.S.'s Spoil Silver Bullets Debut." *St. Paul Pioneer Press*, 9 May 1994.

"Headline: Pro Baseball Teams for Women?" *St. Paul Pioneer Press*, 7 August 1996.

"Headline: She Hits Ball Underhanded." *St. Paul Pioneer Press*, 10 May 1994.

"Headline: Silver Bullets Give Women's Baseball a Shot at Success." *St. Paul Pioneer Press,* 30 April 1995.

"Headline: Silver Bullets Making Strides." *St. Paul Pioneer Press*, 20 August 1995.

"Headline: Silver Bullet's Win on No-Hitter." *St. Paul Pioneer Press*, 9 July 1994.

"Headline: Tickets Going Fast for Saints 5/27 Match with Silver Bullets." *St. Paul Pioneer Press,* 10 May 1994.

"Headline: Twin Cities Hold Warm Memories." *St. Paul Pioneer Press*, 29 July 1995.

Helser, Linda. "Ms. Baseball Lives Dream of Playing in Pros." *Arizona Republic*, 28 April 1994.

"Hey, She Took 2 and Hit to Right, What More Do You People Want?" *Akron Beacon Journal*, 16 July 1995.

Hiestand, Michael. "Plans Would Revive All-Women's Baseball League in Time for '95." *USA Today,* 12 May 1994.

Higbie, Andrea. "The Lady Is a Pitcher (and a Prosecutor)." *New York Times*, 4 September 1994, 30.

Holtz, Randy. "Niekro Searches for Answers for Silver Bullets." Scripps Howard News Service, 27 June 1994.

Holztclaw, Mike. "Silver Bullets about Giving Women a Chance at a Game They Love." *Newport News Daily Press,* 19 July 1994.

Horner, Carol. "Playing Hardball: Women Eager to Play Baseball." Knight Ridder Newspapers, 26 August 1994.

"In 2nd Year, Women's Team Shows Some Progress." *The State* (S.C.), 13 July 1995.

Jackson, Tony. "All-Stars Dodge Bullets, Escape with 4–3 Victory." *Rocky Mountain News*, 4 July 1997.

_____. "30,587 Watch Silver Bullets Just Miss Shot at Victory Against Semi-pro Team." *Rocky Mountain News*, 4 July 1996.

"John Niekro Will Replace His Uncle as (P) Coach of the Silver Bullets." *Akron Beacon Journal*, 3 February 1996.

Jordan, Ray. "Silver Bullets Raise Their Record to 6–36." *St. Louis Post-Dispatch*, 22 August 1994.

"Just Trying to Have Fun." *Chicago Sun-Times*, 27 March 1994, 20B.

Kaufman, Michelle. "In First Time Out, Silver Bullets Impress Oil Can Boyd but Still Lose, 19–0." *Tribune News Service*, 8 May 1994.

_____. "Silver Lining: Bullets Not out of Their League." *Denver Post*, 9 May 1994, C-1.

_____. "Women's Team Bites the Bullet While Gaining Experience." *Detroit Free Press*, 17 August 1994.

Keeler, Bob. "Chance for Women to Get in the Game." *Newsday*, 17 March 1994.

"Ketcham Pitches Silver Bullets to Victory." *San Jose Mercury News*, 27 July 1994.

Kindred, David. *Colorado Silver Bullets: For the Love of the Game.* Atlanta: Longstreet Pres, Inc., 1995.

Koenig, Bill. "Silver Bullets Cancel Games Against Pros." *USA Today Baseball Weekly*, 18–24 May 1994, 40.

_____. "Silver Bullets to Pierce Gender Barrier." *USA Today Baseball Weekly*, 15–28 December 1993, 29.

Kreck, Dick. "Women, Baseball Hit It Off." *Denver Post*, 16 July 1994, E-8.

Lambert, Tim. "These Girls Can Play." *Gettysburg Times*, 10 June 1995, B1, B2.

"A League of Their Own." *Toledo Blade*, 9 August 1993.

"A League of Their Own." *Greensboro News and Record*, 6 June 1996.

"Level the Field." *Sports Illustrated*, 23 May 1994, 16.

Machak, Peggy. "Ready for Another Inning." *Chicago Tribune*, 31 December 1995, 1, 4.

"Macon's Tyler to Pitch against Silver Bullets." *Macon Telegraph*, 16 August 1994.

Madden, Michael. "Women Play Hardball." *Boston Globe*, 20 December 1993.

"Maiden Effort in Debut." *Philadelphia Daily News*, 9 May 1994.

Mallory, Maria. "Coors' Field of Stifled Dreams." *Business Week*, 24 January 1994, 8.

"A Manager Returns." *New York Times*, 17 January 1995, B11.

Molinet, Jason. "Bullets Beaten, Mets Oldtimers Edge Women's Team." *Newsday*, 18 June 1995.

"Molly (P)'s in League of Their Own." *Philadelphia Daily News*, 8 April 1994.

"Morristown's Beggs Cut by Silver Bullets." *Watertown Daily Times*, 20 April 1995.

Moss, Irv. "Bullets Learn Perils of Coors." *Denver Post*, 4 July 1996, D-01.

_____. "Business, Not Novelty, for Bullets." *Denver Post*, 3 July 1996, C-02.

"Mount Clemens Woman Makes Female Pro Baseball Team." *Detroit Free Press*, 5 April 1994.

"A New Day Dawning on the Diamond." *Philadelphia Inquirer*, 8 May 1994.

"New Woman's Team Flooded with Calls." *USA Today Baseball Weekly*, 29 December 11 January 1994, 6.

Newberry, Paul. "Out of Action Former Silver Bullets Find Selves Without a Team of Their Own." *Rocky Mountain News*, 19 July 1998.

Newhan, Ross. "A Dream of Their Own." *Los Angeles Times*, April 30, 1994, C1, C11.

"Niekro, Bullets Get Game Ready." *Charlotte Observer*, 20 April 1994.

"Niekro Remains Manager of Silver Bullets." *Charlotte Observer*, 16 January 1996.

"Niekro Says His Silver Bullets Are Not Patsies." *The Wichita Eagle*, 21 May 1995.

"Niekro, Throwing a Curve, to Manage Women's Team." *New York Times*, 12 December 1993, 365.

"Nine Silver Bullets Sign to Play in Ladies Pro League." *USA Today*, 8 May 1998.

"19–0: A Loss of Their Own." *Miami Herald*, 9 May 1994.

Nobles, Charlie. "The Women of Winter: Baseball Tryouts Have Begun." *New York Times*, 19 December 1993, S9.

"Nomads No More: Silver Bullets Want Own Home." *Seattle Post-Intelligencer*, 7 August 1996.

Nutt, Amy. "Out of Her League." *Sports Illustrated*, 30 May 1994, A8.

"Opening Grade: A for Effort, L for Loss." *Press-Telegram*, 9 May 1994.

Parrillo, Bill. "The 4–15 Silver Bullets Are Winning Fans Over." *Tribune News Service*, 2 July 1995.

Phillips, Mike. "Women on Way to Major Leagues." *Miami Herald*, 7 May 1995.

"Pitching Baseballs— Against Men." *San Jose Mercury News*, 14 May 1994.

"Pro Team Holding Tryouts for Women." *The News and Observer*, 24 May 1996.

"Professional Women's Baseball Team Will Play Men." NPR *Morning Edition*, Bob Edwards, 28 March 1994.

"Professional Women's Team Gets Ready for Spring Training." *Detroit Free Press*, 19 February 1995.

"Questions for Laura Espinoza-Watson." *New York Times*, 6 October 1996, SM34.

Rapaport, Ron. "Boyd Claims He's Wounded by Silver Bullets." *Los Angeles Daily News*, 23 May 1994.

Reaves, Joseph A. "Silver Bullets Shoot Denver into 2-team Mainstream." *Chicago Tribune*, 10 July 1994.

"Relief Pitcher Stars for Colorado Bullets' Ventura Packs a Silver Sidearm." *Times Leader* (Pennsylvania), 9 August 1994.

"Response to WNABA Is Positive." *The News-Sentinel*, 10 June 1994.

Richards, Gregory. "Believe It: This Woman Throws Hard." *Naples Daily News*, 12 April 1995.

Rosewater, Amy. "Fielding Their Dreams Women Aim to Play for Colorado Baseball Team." *Cleveland Plain Dealer*, 16 April 1996, 1E.

Rounds, Kate. "Where Is Our Field of Dreams?" *Ms. Magazine*, Sept/Oct. 1991, 44–45.

Rountree, Sara Buff. "Should Women Get the Chance at Pro Ball?" *USA Today Baseball Weekly*, 20–26 November 1996, 25.

Rowe, John. "These Women Play Hardball." *The Record* (Bergen County, N.J.), 8 March 1994.

Rykiel, Boots. "Colorado Silver Bullets Misfire in First Outing." *USA Today*, 9 May 1994.

Sadler, Ruth. "Silver Bullets Merchandise Hits the Bulls-eye for Fans." *Denver Post*, 13 June 1994, D-3.

Saladino, Tom. "Battle of the Sexes." *The Chronicle-Telegram*, 14 June 1997, D6.

Sarra, Gregg. "Search for Excellence 143 Women at Army for Pro Baseball Tryout." *Newsday*, 27 January 1994.

_____. "Women Join Pro Baseball." *Newsday*, 11 December 1993.

Satriano, Gina. "Can a Woman Ever Make It to the Major Leagues? Yes." *Scripps Howard News Service*, 13 May 1995.

Shea, Jim. "An Ever Expanding Field." *The Hartford Courant*, 5 June 1994, C7.

Shearer, Ed. "Women Will Get Their Chance This Summer to Play Professional Baseball against Minor League Men's Teams." *AP News Service*, 10 December 1993.

Shuster, Rachel. "Baseball Team Opens Doors, Minds." *USA Today*, 21 February 1994.

"Silver Bullets." *Associated Press*, 9 June 1995.

"Silver Bullets Aim to Pierce Doubts on Women's Baseball." *Detroit Free Press*, 25 March 1994.

"Silver Bullets Apply for Minor League Status." *Oneonta Daily Star*, 10 June 1995.

"Silver Bullets Are First Step." *The State*, 10 June 1994.

"Silver Bullets Are Simply a Bad Act." *Knoxville News-Sentinel*, 1 June 1996.

"Silver Bullets Arrive in Charlotte Thursday." *The Charlotte Observer*, 4 May 1994.

"Silver Bullets at Candlestick." *San Jose Mercury News*, 15 May 1994.

"Silver Bullets Back for Rematch with Bombers." *Charlotte Observer*, 12 July 1995.

"Silver Bullets Beat KJR Team." *Seattle Post-Intelligencer*, 8 August 1996.

"Silver Bullets Bite at Tryout." *San Jose Mercury News*, 7 February 1995.

"Silver Bullets Call off Games." *Wichita Eagle*, 13 May 1994.

"Silver Bullets Closer to Reaching Target." *Akron Beacon Journal*, 16 July 1997.

"Silver Bullets Coming to Colorado." *Denver Post*, 12 June 1994, C-18.

"Silver Bullets Coming to Macon on 5/14." *The Macon Telegraph*, 7 February 1996.

"Silver Bullets Cover Another Mile on Road to Beating Odds." *The State*, 10 June 1994.

"Silver Bullets Drop Another." *Denver Post*, 14 May 1994, D-4.

"Silver Bullets Drop Exhibition in Asheville." *Charlotte Observer*, 6 June 1994.

"Silver Bullets Earning Their Stripes." *Akron Beacon Journal*, 13 July 1997.

"Silver Bullets End First Season." *Miami Herald*, 4 September 1994.

"Silver Bullets Enlighten, Open Doors for Women." *Miami Herald*, 21 May 1995.

"Silver Bullets Face Fort Bragg All Stars." *Fayetteville Observer*, 27 May 1996.

"Silver Bullets Foil Cheating Airmen." *Charlotte Observer*, 25 July 1995.

"Silver Bullets Forced to Lower Sights on Foes." *Charlotte Observer*, 14 May 1994.

"Silver Bullets' Future Uncertain — Baseball Team goes 23–22, but Coors to Drop Sponsorship." *Wisconsin State Journal*, 27 August 1997.

"Silver Bullets Game to Be Broadcast Live from Capital City." *The State*, 12 July 1995.

"Silver Bullets Get Historic Victory." *Akron Beacon-Journal*, 29 May 1994.

"Silver Bullets Go Gunning for a Little Respect." *Wichita Eagle*, 7 May 1994.

"Silver Bullets Held to Four Hits in 4–2 Loss." *Daily Camera*, 4 July 1996.

"Silver Bullets' Hope to go Class A." *The Record*, 10 June 1995.

"Silver Bullets Hopefuls Want Only One Thing — Opportunity." *Daily Herald*, 22 December 1993.

"Silver Bullets in Brawl with Teenage Boys' Team." *Denver Post*, 14 June 1997, C-02.

"Silver Bullets Looking for a Few Good Women." *Press-Telegram*, 29 August 1996.

"Silver Bullets Losing Sponsor." *The Frederick Post*, 22 August 1997, B-4.

"Silver Bullets Make History with Win No. 1." *USA Today Baseball Weekly*, 1–7 June 1994, 31.

"Silver Bullets May 8 Season Opener Will Be on ESPN2." The Miami Herald, 25 March 1994.

"Silver Bullets More Competitive." *The Florida Times-Union*, 24 May 1997.

"Silver Bullets Need Quick Hit." *The State*, 9 May 1994.

"Silver Bullets 9–1 Victory Shows They are Improving." *San Jose Mercury News*, 6 August 1995.

"Silver Bullets No-Hitter Blow to Charleston Team's Pride." *The State*, 10 July 1994.

"Silver Bullets Not Giving Up without a Fight." *Oregonian*, 13 July 1997.

"Silver Bullet Notes." *Akron Beacon Journal*, 17 July 1997.

"Silver Bullets Play at Jacobs." *The Chronicle-Telegram*, 12 July 1995, B5.

"Silver Bullets Play Exhibition." *The Frederick News*, 8 June 1995, D-8.

"Silver Bullets Player Felled by the Long Arm of the Law." *San Jose Mercury News*, 3 September 1996.

"Silver Bullets Rally by Ice Gators." *The Advocate*, 3 June 1997.

"Silver Bullets Return." *The State* (S.C.), 12 July 1995.

"Silver Bullets Seek More History." *Wisconsin State Journal*, 17 June 1996.

"Silver Bullets Shelled in Opener." *San Jose Mercury News,* 9 May 1994.

"Silver Bullets Stepping Down." *New York Times*, 13 May 1994, B15.

"Silver Bullets Still Looking for a Bull's Eye." *Akron Beacon Journal*, 18 July 1995.

"Silver Bullets Take Aim at Season." *Wichita Eagle*, 25 March 1994.

"Silver Bullets, Team USA Coming." *Wichita Eagle*, 21 March 1995.

"Silver Bullets to Make Stops in Oklahoma." *The Daily Oklahoman*, 21 May 1995.

"Silver Bullets Win a Game." *New York Times*, 29 May 1994, S7.

"Silver Bullets Win Big." *Contra Costa Times*, 6 August 1995.

The Silver Bulletin, March 1996, July 1996, December 1996. Whole issues.

"Silver Meets Green." *Boston Herald*, 27 July 1997.

Smith, Claire. "Swings and Misses Aren't Heart of the Matter in This Game." *New York Times*, 9 May 1994, B7.

Spencer, Sheldon. "Increasing Their Firepower Silver Bullets Add Power, Toughness in Third Season." *Seattle Post-Intelligencer*, 7 August 1996.

_____. "Silver Bullets Bring Tour Back to Area Game Tonight in Everett." *Seattle Post Intelligencer*, 6 August 1996.

"States Women Get League of Their Own." *Detroit Free Press*, 17 September 1994.

"Team Hopes for a Hit over the Gender Wall." *The Charlotte Observer*, 8 May 1994.

"Their Turn to Play." *The Charlotte Observer*, 7 May 1994.

"A Trying Ordeal." *Philadelphia Daily News*, 1 February 1994.

"Trying Out." *The Wichita Eagle*, 2 February 1995.

"Two Bullets Give Their Best Shot at Mets Camp." *Detroit Free Press*, 2 February 1995.

"An Underhand Approach to Pitching." *The Miami Herald*, 5 April 1994.

Van Dyck, Dave. "Diamonds in the Rough." *Chicago Sun-Times*, 27 March 1994, 20B.

Vecsey, George. "Niekro, Throwing a Curve, to Manage Women's Team." *New York Times*, 12 December 1993, 6.

Vecsey, Laura. "Women of All Shapes, Sizes and Addresses Try for Baseball League." *New York Times*, 11 August 1994.

Walker, Barbara. "All-Women's Baseball Team Is Both Silly and Boring." *New York Times*, 8 May 1994, 13.

Wall, Richard. "Into the Park." *Women's Sports and Fitness*, April 1994.

Walsh, Patti. "Australian Olympic Team Riddles Silver Bullets." *The Virginian Pilot*, 7 June 1996.

Warner, Jack. "They Play a Man's Game with Grace, Agility and Professionalism." *The Atlanta Journal and Constitution*, 1 June 1997.

Weir, Tom. "Nothing New in Men on a Women's Team." *USA Today*, 20 April 1994.

Whitaker, Celeste E. "Coors Dumping Silver Bullets." *The Atlanta Journal and Constitution*, 21 August 1997.

White, Carolyn. "Davis Brightens Women's Baseball Hopes." *USA Today*, 12 June 1996.

_____. "Silver Bullets Brace for Sunday's Opener." *USA Today*, 6 May 1994.

_____. "Silver Bullets Pleased Despite Shaky Start." *USA Today*, 31 August 1994.

"Who's on First?" *Detroit Free Press*, 4 February 1995.

Wilde, Jason. "Silver Bullets Taking a Crack at Status Quo." *Wisconsin State Journal,* 18 June 1996.

Williams, Jeff. "Well, They Tried: Mets Turn Down Silver Bullets. Who Are They?" *Newsday*, 2 February 1995.

Williams, Pete. "Silver Lining: Bullets Showed They Belong." *USA Today Baseball Weekly,* 7–13 September 1994, 35.

Williams-Snyder, Vanessa. "Diamonds— Baseball Diamonds That Is— Can Be a Girl's Best Friend." *Gannett News Service*, 28 May 1997.

Wilson, Jeffrey. "Silver Bullets Play Exhibition in Japan." *USA Today*, 8 November 1996.

"Winless Silver Bullets Continue to Misfire." *Detroit Free Press*, 16 May 1994.

"Women at Major League Baseball Camp Shatter Images." *The Herald*, 5 February 1995.

"Women Athletes Inspire Little Girls." *Wichita Eagle*, 10 October 1996.

"Women Bullets 0–2, but Hitting Lifts Spirits." *Lexington Herald-Leader,* 15 May 1994.

"Women Eager to Learn If They Can Cut It on Diamond." *Lexington Herald Leader*, 13 April 1994.

"Women Fail to Land Strikebreaker Jobs." *San Jose Mercury News*, 2 February 1995.

"Women Finally Get Turn at Bat." *The State*, 9 May 1994.

"Women Slowly Make Inroads in the Profession of Baseball." *Wichita Eagle*, 29 March 1994.

"Women Tryout with Mets." *Sun Herald*, 2 February 1995.

"Women Versus Women Is Better." *The Miami Herald*, 3 July 1994.

"Women's Baseball Era Dawns." *Philadelphia Inquirer*, 10 April 1994.

"Women's Baseball Makes a Pitch for Recognition." *Christian Science Monitor*, 4 August 1997.

"Women's Baseball Team Is Walloped, 19–0." *Philadelphia Inquirer*, 9 May 1994.

"Women's League in 1995." *The Miami Herald*, 15 May 1994.

"Women's Pro Baseball Team Loses Third Straight." *Charlotte Observer*, 16 May 1994.

"Women's Pro Baseball Team Ready to Hit Road." *The Charlotte Observer*, 5 April 1994.

"Women's Professional Team Begins Play Today." *Toledo Blade*, 8 May 1994, 6.

"Women's Sports Gets Money Needed to Break Through." *St. Louis Post-Dispatch*, 6 August 1995.

"Women's Team Falls in Billings." *The Cincinnati Post*, 15 August 1994.

"Women's Team Roster Filled." *Press-Telegraph*, 5 April 1994.

"Women's Team Short on Results but Long on Enthusiasm." *Detroit Free Press*, 16 August 1994.

Zipay, Steve. "Niekro Set to Prove a Point." *Newsday*, 16 December 1993, 153, 174.

Related Terms: Pam Davis, Gina Satriano

Colorado Women's Baseball Association (CWBA)

Newsletter, February 1995–October 1996. JoAn Flower, ed.

Cook, Ashley

Mullen, Maureen. "A Whole New Ballgame, Women Shine on Lynn Diamond." *Boston Globe*, 8 August 2003, E10.

Related Terms: New England Women's Baseball League

Coombes, Rebecca

"Coombes Pitches in for the Stars." *Mordialloc Chelsea Leader* (Australia), 11 December 2002, 58.

Corbus, Vada

"Girl Catcher Is on Joplin Ball Club's Payroll," *South Bend News-Times*, 20 April 1931.

"Girl of 19 Signs with Joplin as Catcher; Brother on Team." *New York Times*, 18 April 1931, 28.

"Joplin Signs Girl Catcher, 19 and Blond." *Chicago Tribune*, 19 April 1931, A2.

Cornett, Betty Jane

Lister, Harry. "You've Come a Long Way Baby." *News Record/Valley News*, 4 July 1992, B1, B4.

Cortesio (Papageorgiou), Maria "Ria"

"Baseball's Only Woman Ump Makes Single-A Debut." *Referee*, June 2001, 16.

"Baseball's Only Woman Ump Reflects on Job." *Associated Press*, 14 April 2001.

Batterson, Steve. "Calling Her Own Game." *Quad City Times*, 13 May 2001, D1, D6.

Baxter, Kevin. "For Umpire, Making the Major Leagues Is a Dream, Not a Crusade." *The Miami Herald*, 27 August 2002.

_____. "Forget Gender and Play Ball." *The Gazette* (Montreal), 9 September 2002, B5.

Bush, Joe. "Kane County Next Stop for Female Umpire." *Daily Herald* (Illinois), 2 May 2001.

Connors, Mike. "Ump Brushes Off Rhubarbs as Routine." *Press Journal* (Vero Beach, Florida), 10 August 2002, B1.

Crouse, Karen. "Female Umpire Hears All, Calls All." *The Palm Beach Post*, 19 May 2002.

Davidoff, Ken. "Boss: Clemens' Outing Beats Female Umpire's." *Newsday*, 28 July 2002.

Elliott, Jeff. "Cortesio Helps Break Up Attack on Ump." *Florida Times-Union*, 25 June 2003, E-3.

_____. "The Lady in Blue Cortesio Living Diamond Dream." *Florida Times-Union*, 25 June 2003, E-1.

Ettkin, Brian. "Lady in Blue." *Sarasota Herald-Tribune*, 2 July 2002, C1.

Gates, Nick. "Hey Lady, Smokies Swamp Mudcats." *Knoxville News-Sentinel*, 8 June 2003, D7.

_____. "Is There a Strike Against Female Umpire?" *Knoxville News Sentinel*, 24 April 2003, D1.

Luttrell, Jim. "Ump Laughs Off Steinbrenner's Remarks." *New York Times*, 23 August 2002, D6.

Manoyan, Dan. "Working with the Count against Her." *Journal Sentinel*, 9 May 2001.

Mansch, Scott. "Ria Cortesio Feature." *Great Falls Tribune*, 14 July 2000.

"Midwest League Gets Female Umpire." *Syracuse Herald American*, 8 April 2001.

"Not Just Another Umpire: The Midwest League's Ria Cortesio Is the Only Woman in Pro Baseball Calling Balls and Strikes." *Wisconsin State Journal*, 16 April 2001.

Ria Cortesio File. National Baseball Hall of Fame and Museum, Cooperstown, New York.

Victory, Dennis. "The Lady Is an Ump." *Birmingham News*, 9 May 2003.

Wiedmer, Mark. "An Umpire Trying to Be Like All Others." *Chattanooga Times Free Press*, 17 April 2003, D1.

Related Terms: Amanda Clement, Bernice Gera, Pam Postema, Umpires, Christine Wren

Coutts, Lynn

"Coutts to Play Against Silver Bullets." *Bangor Daily News*, 2 July 1996.

Cox, Theresa

Grant, Rubin. "Female Umpire Makes First Appearance." *Birmingham Post-Herald*, 4 June 1988, B1, B6.

Gurnick, Ken. "It's a Field of Dreams Few Have Realized." *The National Sports Daily*, 19 June 1990, 18–19.

Martin, Wayne. "Lady Ump Makes Successful Debut at the Met." *The Birmingham News*, 5 June 1988, 1B, 8B.

_____. "Woman Ump Set for Weekend Duty at the Hoover Met." *The Birmingham News*, 2 June 1988, 1D, 7D.
Related Terms: Umpires

Coyne, Colleen

Neimand, Josh. "Former Tabor Student Makes Baseball History." *The Sentinel* (Marion, Massachusetts), 16 June 1994, 1, 9.

Croteau, Julie

"A Battler for Baseball Equality Makes It to First Base." *Christian Science Monitor*, 12 November 1993.
"Blazing New Trail for College Baseball." *Philadelphia Inquirer*, 26 March 1989.
Brill, Marlene Targ. "Julie Croteau." In *Winning Women in Baseball and Softball*. New York: Barron's, 2000. Pp. 62–76.
"College Woman Baseball Player Quits Team, Calls Players Lewd." *San Jose Mercury News*, 7 June 1991.
Collins, Mary. "A Girl Who Plays Baseball Needs a Girls' Team." *Washington Post*, 27 March 1998, 92.
"Croteau Blazing Another Trail as a Member of Silver Bullets." *Knoxville News Sentinel*, 30 April 1994.
"Croteau: Pressure Was Intense." *Richmond Times Dispatch*, 14 September 1994.
"Croteau Turns Passion to Coaching." *USA Today Baseball Weekly*, 1–7 May 1996, 35 36.
"Croteau's Love of Baseball Exceeds Pain of Past." *Washington Post*, 21 June 1997.
Dawidoff, Nicholas. "Resigned: From the Baseball Team at St. Mary's College of Maryland, Junior First Baseman Julie Croteau." *Sports Illustrated*, 17 June 1991, 98.
Diglio, Alice. "Girl Players Say Court Case Hit Home." *Washington Post*, 6 April 1988, C1, C5.
_____. "Girl Sues to Play Ball." *Washington Post*, 17 March 1988, A1, A20.
Farrell, Mary H.J. "Say It Ain't So." *People Weekly*, 6 June 1994.
"Female Sluggers Rare on Little League Teams." *Tulsa World*, 23 July 1989.
"Feminas Hacen Historia En el Beisbol." *Nuevo Herald*, 21 December 1993.
"1st Woman College Player Quits." *The Frederick News*, 7 June 1991, B-3.
"Flawless at First." *New York Times*, 19 March 1989, S1.
"Freshman Pitcher Goes Distance for Her School." *Austin American-Statesman*, 16 February 1994.
Gibson, Edie. "Who's On First? Julie Croteau Plays Hardball." *Seventeen*, September 1989, 554.
"A Girl Who Plays Baseball Needs a Girls' Team." *Washington Post*, 27 March 1988, 92.
Gurnick, Ken. "Game 'Has Been a War.'" *The National Sports Daily*, 19 June 1990, 19.
Hartley, Charles J. "A Freshman Who Just Wanted to Play Baseball Gets Her Chance in College." *Chronicle of Higher Education*, 22 March 1989, A35.
Kornheiser, Tony. "Julie Croteau's Play Deserves to be Judged on the Baseball Field, Not in a Court Room." *Washington Post*, 19 March 1988, D3.
Leavy, Jane. "Hey, Fans, Guess Who's on First?" *Washington Post*, 16 May 1988, B1 B3.

McCarthy, Colman. "If Stanky Had Coached Julie Croteau." *Washington Post*, 2 April 1988, A19.
Murphy, Caryle. "Judge Rejects Bias Claim of Girl Cut from Baseball Team." *Washington Post*, 24 March 1988, D1, D7.
_____. "Prince William Girl Testifies on Competition for First Base." *Washington Post*, 23 March 1988, D1, D5.
_____. "Team Backs Pr. William Coach in Sex Bias Case." *Washington Post*, 19 March 1988, B1–B2.
Nelson, Mariah Burton. "Julie Croteau: Batting Down Barriers." *Women's Sports and Fitness*, September 1991, 54–55.
_____. "Profiles: Julie Croteau." *Women's Sports and Fitness*, September 1991, 54–56.
Nobles, Charlie. "The Women of Winter: Baseball Tryouts Have Begun." *New York Times*, 19 December 1993, S9.
"Parents Sue." *The Frederick Post*, 18 March 1988, C-2.
Pennington, Bill. "Sexism Has No Place Here." *The Record* (Bergen County), 28 June 1991.
Raspberry, William. "School Sports: Separate but Equal?" *Washington Post*, 6 April 1988, A25.
"Scaling the Wall: Croteau Turns Passion to Coaching." *USA Today Baseball Weekly*, 6 June 1996.
"She's Just One of the Boys Now." *Philadelphia Daily News*, 20 March 1989.
"She's Ready to be First Woman to Compete in College Baseball." *The San Diego Tribune*, 17 March 1989.
"Silver Bullets Grant First Baseman Dream." *Rocky Mountain News*, 17 April 1994.
".300 Hitter Among 37 Women out to Become Pro." *Seattle Post-Intelligencer*, 21 December 1993.
"Why I Sued Little League." *Washington Post*, 10 April 1988, 36.
Wiles, Tim. "Julie Croteau." *Letters in the Dirt*. 33 (29 May 1998).
"Woman Ball Player's Bid Postponed." *The Seattle Times*, 17 March 1989.
"Woman Can't Make Mark on Diamond." *The Record* (N.J.), 17 March 1989.
"Woman Coach Is Staying Focused." *Bangor Daily News*, 25 April 1996.
"Woman Earns College Spot in Baseball." *Charlotte Observer*, 25 February 1989.
"Women's Ball Club Planning to Return." *Pittsburgh Post-Gazette*, 14 September 1994.

Cubans

Fay, Bill. "Belles of the Game." *Colliers*, 13 August 1949.
"The Flag Not Insulted." *Washington Post*, 23 March 1893, 6.
"Marrero (Mirta) Hurls Opener Tonight at Griffith Stadium." *Washington Post*, 3 May 1951, 16.
Small, Collie. "Baseball's Improbable Imports." *Saturday Evening Post*, 2 August 1952.
"2 Cuban Girls Pitch Tonight." *Washington Post*, 4 August 1950, B5.
Related Terms: AAGPBL, Isabel Alvarez, Mirta Marrero

Dancer, Faye

"'All the Way, Faye' Dancer Dies; Women's Baseball League Star." *Washington Post*, 2 June 2002.

"Dancer Inspired Madonna Character in Film." *Associated Press*, 3 June 2002.

"'League of Their Own' Ball Player." *Grand Rapids Press*, 2 June 2002.

Martin, Douglas. "'Girl' Baseball Star Broke All the Rules." *New York Times*, 12 June 2002, S6.

Parrotta, Lou. "Faye Dancer — Classy Clown." <http://thediamondangle.com/>.

Dauvray, Helen

"Helen Dauvray Remarries." *Brooklyn Daily Eagle*, 30 April 1896, 1.

Davidson, Alison

Hodge, Karen. "Winding Up for Success." *Manningham Leader* (Australia), 2 July 2003, 8.

Davis, Pamela

"All Things Considered: Pam Davis." NPR, Noah Adams Host, 5 June 1996.

Craine, Anthony. "There's No Place Like Home — Yet." *Inside Sports*, July 1997 10.

"Davis Works Inning of Scoreless Relief." *Detroit News*, 5 June 1996.

"Female Pitcher Wins Exhibition." *Ann Arbor News*, 5 June 1996.

"Out of the Bullpen, Into the Record Books." *New York Times*, 5 June 1996, B15.

"Silver Bullets Defeat Shreveport Team." *The Advocate*, 2 June 1997, 9E.

"Such a Relief: Woman Pitcher Wins in Minors." *The Chronicle*, 5 June 1986, A3.

"A Sun with a Gun." *USA Today Baseball Weekly*, 12–18 June 1996, 27.

White, Carolyn. "Davis Brightens Women's Baseball Hopes." *USA Today*, 12 June 1996.

"Woman Takes Place in Baseball History." *Star Tribune*, 5 June 1996.

Davis, Rachel

Yap, Rizza. "Girl Gets Chance to Make Calls." *Los Angeles Daily News*, 25 June 1998.

Davis, Sherry

Floto, J.G. "Thumbnail Sketches of Female Baseball Pioneers." *The Diamond Angle*, Summer 1997, 45.

DeBenedictis, Lois

Lesmerises, Doug. "Men vs. Women on the Diamond." *The News Journal*, 25 June 2004.

Deegan, Mildred

"Finish Line." *Rocky Mountain News*, 25 July 2002.

Martin, Douglas. "Baseball Career Inspired Movie." *National Post* (Canada), 30 July 2002, S7.

_____. "Millie Deegan, 82, Pioneer in Women's Baseball League." *New York Times*, 28 July 2002, 33.

Derouin, Stephanie

Derouin, Stephanie. Correspondence with Leslie A. Heaphy. North Canton, Ohio, 2004.

Ruiz, Don. "Local Woman Looks to Start Baseball League for Women." *The News Tribune*, 26 May 2003, CO3.

_____. "Women's Baseball Pioneer Still Pioneering." *Tacoma News Tribune*, 27 July 2003.

Descombes (Lesko), Jean

Evans, Jayda. "Baseball's Women Vets Long for a League of Their Own, Again." *Tribune News Service*, 6 July 2000.

Grindeland, Sherry. "Pursuing a League of Her Own." *Seattle Times*, 13 August 2004.

"Jean Descombes Has Plenty on the Ball." *The Lima News*, 17 June 1956, 2-D.

Dettweiler, Helen

"Fifteen Year Old Girl Faces Hard Match in Golf Tourney." *Appleton Post-Crescent*, 16 June 1939.

"Golf Queen Shows How to Hit Ball." *Iowa City Press-Citizen*, 24 October 1941, 9.

"Helen Dettweiler Gives Pros Good Scrap in Exhibition Play." *Walla Walla Union Bulletin*, 30 July 1952, 13.

"Helen Dettweiler Is Leading Helen Hicks for Augusta Crown." *Syracuse Herald Journal*, 18 January 1940, 28.

"Helen Dettweiler to Appear at Country Club on Tuesday." *Walla Walla Union Bulletin*, 27 July 1952, 11.

"Helen Dettweiler to Become Baseball Announcer." *Washington Post*, 19 June 1938, X2.

Whittlesey, Merrell W. "H. Dettweiler Turns Pro for 'Good Will' Job." *Washington Post*, 11 May 1939, 21.

Dickinson, Amy

Leavy, Jane. "Amy Dickinson: A Tomboy Who Wants Out." *Womensport*, January 1977, 9, 13.

Didrikson (Zaharias), Mildred Ella "Babe"

"Babe Appears Here Sunday." *News-Journal*, 18 August 1934, 6.

"Babe Didrikson Is Exonerated." *Mansfield Journal*, 23 December 1932, 11.

"Babe in Lead of Golf Meet." *Mansfield News Journal*, 17 March 1950.

"'Babe' Premier Slated Oct. 11 in Beaumont." *Port Arthur News*, 29 August 1975, 9.

"Babe Zaharias Dies; Athlete Had Cancer." *New York Times Magazine*, 28 September 1956.

"Babe Zaharias, World's Greatest Girl Athlete, Now Weighs but 90 Pounds." *Syracuse Herald Journal*, 31 August 1956, 26.

Block, Melissa. "Marilynn Smith Remembers Babe Didrikson Zaharias." NPR, 22 May 2003.

"Didrikson a Threat in Women's Western." *Oshkosh Daily Northwestern*, 28 June 1940, 19.

Gallico, Paul. "SI Flashback: Farewell to the Babe." *Sports Illustrated*, 8 October 1956.

Murray, Jim. "Babe the Greatest." *Port Arthur News*, 7 October 1975, 10.

"Play Team of Beards under Arcs." *Mansfield News-Journal*, 18 August 1934, 6.

"Westies Host to House of David Club." *Mansfield News Journal*, 18 August 1934, 6.

Documentaries

Marshall, Penny and Elliott Abbott, producers. *A League of Their Own*. Columbia Pictures, 1992.

Olson, Gordon. *The Girls of Summer — The Grand Rapid Chicks, 1946–54*. The Grand Rapids Public Library and Museum, Grand Rapids, Michigan, 1990.

Siegel, Lois. *Baseball Girls*. National Film Board of Canada, 1996.

Taylor, Janis. *An Oral History of the All American Girls Professional Baseball League: Interviews with 40 Players*. Northern Indiana Historical Society, South Bend, Indiana, 1994.

_____. *When Diamonds Were a Girl's Best Friend*. University of Northern Kentucky, Covington, Kentucky, 1986.

_____. *When Dreams Come True*. Taylor Productions, 1989.

Wilson, Kim, Kelly Candaele and Mary Wallace. *A League of Their Own*. K and K Productions, Burbank, California, 1992.

Dole, Shawna

Hogstrom, Erik. "Baseball Diamonds Are This Girl's Best Friend." *Telegraph Herald*, 13 June 2004, E1.

Dunn, Gertrude "Gertie"

Shea, Kathleen Brady. "Friends Mourn 'A Real Pioneer' Killed in Small Plane Crash." *Philadelphia Inquirer*, 1 October 2004.

Earp, Mildred

Ivy, Darren. "No Skirting the Issue, Arkansans Like Sue Kidd and Mildred Earp Pitched in to Make Women's Professional Baseball a Short-lived Hit a Half Century Ago." *Arkansas Democrat-Gazette*, 17 September 2003, 23.

East Coast Women's Baseball League

Lesmerises, Doug. "The Mills Sisters Play Hardball." *Delaware News*, 4 July 2004.

Witkowski, Wayne. "Pioneers Are in a League of Their Own." *Asbury Park Press*, 25 September 2002.

Eastern Women's Baseball Conference

Slattery, Chris. "Diamonds Are a Girl's Best Friend." <*Gazette.net*>, 20 July 2001.

Engle, Eleanor

"Baseball Frowns on Girl Player." *The News* (Newport, Rhode Island), 23 June 1952, 12.

"Baseball: No (Wo)man's Land." *Harrisburg Patriot*, 24 June 1952.

"Bill Veeck Predicts Minors Can't Stop Girl Ball Player." *Harrisburg Patriot*, 23 June 1952.

"First Girl in Organized Baseball Is Exiled to Press Box as Pilot Calls Signing a 'Gag.'" *New York Times*, 23 June 1952, 26.

Fraley, Oscar. "Women Should Play Says Fraley, They Look Better." *Redlands Daily Facts*, 24 June 1952.

French, Ben. "Official Edict Ends Career of Girl in Baseball." *The Gettysburg Times*, 24 June 1952, 3.

"Girl Player's Brief Career in Harrisburg Over." *Gazette and Bulletin*, 24 June 1952.

"Girl's Contract Voided." *Washington Post*, 22 September 1965, D2.

"Harrisburg's Girl Player Known to Newberry Sluggers." *Williamsport Sun*, 25 June 1952.

"Minor Leagues, Trautman Strikes Out Eleanor Engle." *The Era* (Pennsylvania), 24 June 1952, 11.

Pagey, John. "Shapely Young Gal Not Cut Out to Be Star on Diamond." *Mansfield News-Journal*, 20 June 1952, 9.

"Pro Baseball Hits Signing of Women Players." *East Liverpool Review*, 24 June 1952, 13.

"Pro Team Signs Lady to Contract." *Edwardsville Intelligencer*, 23 June 1952.

"She's Back at the Typewriter." *Dixon Evening Telegraph*, 24 June 1952, 8.

"Trautman Bars Woman Players, Censures 'Travesty' on Baseball." *New York Times*, 24 June 1952, 38.

Travers, Johnny. "Gal Shortstop's Bid Given Short 'No' By O.B. Officials." *The Sporting News*, 2 July 1952, 5.

Turner, Marjorie. "Pro Baseball World Gets Shock." *Syracuse Herald-Journal*, 24 June 1952, 23.

"Woman Signs with Baseball Team, May Not Get to Play." *Redlands Daily Facts*, 23 June 1952, 7.

"Women Ball Players." *The Era* (Pennsylvania), 11 July 1952.

English, Woody

Helmer, Diana. "The Second Career of Woody English." *Sports Collectors Digest*, 2 September 1988, 124.

Espinoza-Watson, Laura

"Questions for Laura Espinoza-Watson." *New York Times*, 6 October 1996, SM34.

European Women's Baseball

Molinet, Jason. "Women's Baseball in Europe in Works." *Newsday*, 18 June 1995.

Executives

Gurnick, Ken. "It's a Field of Dreams Few Have Realized." *The National Sports Daily*, 19 June 1990, 18–19.

Exhibits

Abram, Susan. "A Woman's Place Is at Home (Plate): New Exhibit Honors Women in Baseball." *Los Angeles Daily News*, 22 June 2003.

Bergin, Mary. "Exhibits Spotlight Baseball's Role." *Capital Times* (Wisconsin), 24 May 2003, 6C.

Pontanilla, Bernice. "Little Gets Display of Her Own." *Winnipeg Sun*, 30 July 2003, 44.

"Women in Baseball: There's No Place like Home (Plate)." Burbank Central Library, Burbank, California, 2–30 June 2003.

Fans

Ardell, Jean Hastings. "Baseball No Longer Needs Ladies' Day to Lure the Female Fan." *Los Angeles Times*, 3 April 1994, B7.

"Base Ball." *Porter's Spirit of the Times*, 6 September 1856.

Chadwick, Henry. "The Sin of Kicking." *Baseball Magazine*, November 1908, 20.

Elderdice, Raymond J. "The Female Fan." *Baseball Magazine*, November 1909, 50.

Geyer, Orel. "A Fair Fan." *Baseball Magazine*, October 1909.

Goewey, Edwin A. "At the Game." *Leslie's Illustrated Weekly*, 22 April 1909, 379.

Glaser, Lulu. "The Lady Fan." *Baseball Magazine*, September 1909, 22.

Hite, Mabel. "On Just Being a Fan." *Baseball Magazine*, November 1908, 24.

Hoefer, W.R. "Ladies' Day." *Baseball Magazine*, September 1931, 451.

"The Ladies and Baseball at Danver's Center." *New York Clipper*, 20 August 1859.

"More Women Than Men Go to Ball Games in Sheldon." *Chicago Tribune*, 28 July 1907, F7.

"What Our Girls Know About Baseball." *Outing*, June 1888, 274.

Farren, Patricia

Kaster, Julie. "Baseball Diamonds This Girl's Best Friend." *Eagle-Tribune*, 25 July 2000.

Faut (Winsch, Eastman, Fantry), Jean

Sargent. "Jean Faut; The All-American League's Greatest Overhand Pitcher." *Ragtyme Sports*, March 1996, 30–32, 34, 36, 38.

Ferguson (Key), Dorothy

"Cancer Claims Canuck Peach Mordabito: Women's Baseball Player's Story Told in 'A League of Their Own.'" *The Vancouver Sun*, 12 May 2003, B7.

DeDoncker, Mike. "I'd Rather Play Ball Than Eat or Sleep." *Seattle Times*, 10 May 2003, D1.

"Dottie Ferguson Key; Woman Baseball Player with Rockford Peaches." *Pittsburgh Post Gazette*, 12 May 2003, B-6.

"Female Ball Player Who Inspired Madonna Movie Character Dead." *The Star Phoenix* (Saskatoon), 10 May 2003, B4.

"Former Peaches Star Is Dead at 80." *Milwaukee Journal Sentinel*, 11 May 2003, 02C.

"Former Women's Baseball Player Dies at 80." *Associated Press Online*, 9 May 2003.

"Madonna's 'League' Character Dies at 80." *Deseret News* (Salt Lake City), 11 May 2003, D09.

"Peach of Women's Pro Baseball Dies." *Edmonton Journal*, 10 May 2003, C6.

Field Days

"Equitable Life's Outing." *New York Times*, 17 July 1915, 5.

"Fair Athletes Faint in Vassar Field Day." *New York Times*, 13 May 1906, 7.

"Georgetown Girls' Ball Team Enters World Series Race." *Washington Post*, 13 May 1926, 22.

"Girls at Base-Ball." *New York Times*, 19 August 1883, 2.

"Girls Win in School Contest." *Los Angeles Times*, 5 April 1925, 14.

"Grammar School Games." *Los Angeles Times*, 11 December 1907, 16.

"Played Between Giggles." *Boston Globe*, 15 July 1892, 10.

"The Sportswoman." *Washington Post*, 5 May 1927, 18.

"Thrilling Plays and Close Finishes Mark Paterson Girls' Baseball Game and Meet." *New York Times*, 7 June 1925, S6.

"To Play Left-handed Boys." *Washington Post*, 9 June 1914, 14.

"Women's Varied Activities." *Washington Post*, 11 October 1920, 8.

Filarski (Steffes), Helen

Poliquin, Bud. "Diamond Celebration." *Post-Standard* (Syracuse, N.Y.), 11 September 2003.

Flaherty, Colleen

Konecky, Chad. "Somerville Resident Shines in Women's Baseball League." *Somerville Journal*, 5 September 2002.

Flaherty, Mary

Terrazzano, Lauren. "Mary Flaherty, 74, Played in WWII Women's Baseball League." *Newsday*, 4 April 2000, A67.

Florida Baseball

"Play Ball in Florida." *Washington Post*, 25 February 1914, 4.

"What, Girls' Baseball?" *Washington Post*, 8 February 1953, L7.

Florida Legends

Etheart, Pascale. "Blazing the Trail for Women in Baseball League." *Miami Herald*, 19 July 1998.

Jackson, Barry. "Women's League Puts Team in Homestead." *Miami Herald*, 9 April 1998.

Florida Women's Baseball League

Hughes, John. "Women Get a Chance to Play a Real Game of Baseball." *Fort Lauderdale Sun-Sentinel*, 4 June 1993, 47.

"Women's League in Florida Plans Opening in November." *Baseball America*, 21 February–6 March 1994.

Folder (Powell), Rose

Supine, John. "'League' Rekindles Memories for Former Ballplayer Powell." *State Journal-Register*, n.d.

Fornoff, Susan

Celizic, Mike. "Give Discredit Where Due." *The Record* (Bergen County), 11 July 1993.

Stone, Larry. "The Art of Scorekeeping." *Baseball Digest*, 1 July 2004.

Fort Wayne Daisies

"All-American Girls in Two-Game Series Here." *The Newark Advocate and American Tribune*, 2 May 1950, 13.

"Daisies Beaten in 10th; Trail Rockford by 3–2." *Fort Wayne News-Sentinel*, 15 September 1950.

"Daisies, Belles Halted by Rain." *Washington Post*, 4 May 1951, B6.

"Daisies, Belles Play Twin Bill Tonight." *Washington Post*, 5 May 1951, 13.

"Daisies, Belles to Play Monday." *Washington Post*, 9 May 1951, 18.

"Daisies Play Belles Here." *Washington Post*, 13 May 1951, C5.

"Daisies Star Turned Down Chisox Offer." *Washington Post*, 29 April 1951, C2.

"Daisy-Blue Sox Scrap Set for Saturday Night." *The Herald Press* (Michigan), 21 August 1953, 12.

Day, Dick. "Peaches Wallop Daisies, 11–0, to Clinch Play-off Crown." *Rockford Register Republic,* 18 September 1950.

"15-hit Attack Heads Daisies 3–1 Defeat." *Rockford Morning Star*, 10 September 1950.

Flynn, Terry. "Kentucky Field Named for Former Pro Female Pitcher." *Cincinnati Enquirer*, 21 March 2002.

"Fort Wayne Daisies Open AGBL Campaign Friday." *Van Wert Times-Bulletin* (Ohio), 27 May 1954, 13.

"Girls Baseball Game Called." *The Marion Star* (Ohio), 15 May 1953, 20.

"Girls Baseball Team to Appear in Benefit." *The Marion Star*, 5 May 1953, 17.

"Girl Baseball Teams Play Here Tonight." *Washington Post*, 14 May 1951, 11.

"Girls Practice in Alexandria." *Washington Post*, 30 April 1950, 9.

Halberstein, Joe. "Girls Baseball Comes to Lima Thursday." *The Lima News*, 19 May 1949, 34.

_____. "Twin Bill Booked Friday Night Between Girls Baseball Teams." *The Lima News*, 20 May 1949.

"Marrero (Mirta) Hurls Opener Tonight at Griffith Stadium." *Washington Post*, 3 May 1951, 16.

Milne, Harry D. "Daisies Blank Peaches, 8–0, Square Series." *Rockford Morning Star*, 17 September 1950.

Olofson, Phil. "Daisies Square Rockford Series, 5–3; 5th Game Tonight." *Fort Wayne News-Sentinel*, 14 September 1950.

"Peaches Take 2nd Straight from Daisies, Erickson Pitches 7–2 Victory." *Rockford Morning Star*, 12 September 1950.

"Sisters Star in Game Here." *Washington Post*, 4 May 1952, C5.

Related Terms: AAGPBL, Rockford Peaches

Frazer, Megan

Bogaczyk, Jack. "Charleston's New General Manager Has Plenty of Experience Behind Her." *Charleston Daily Mail*, 27 March 2003, 1B.

Froning (O'Meara), Mary

Hart, Joe. "Ex-Player to Net Brewers Honor; O'Meara Was a Pioneer in Women's Baseball." *Capital Times* (Madison, Wisconsin), 12 May 2003, 1D.

Gacioch, Rose

Brand-Williams, Oralandar. "Woman's Baseball Star Dies at 89." *The Detroit News*, 13 September 2004.

Garber, Jillian

Casey, Laura. "Girl Is one of the Guys Playing Baseball." *Oakland Tribune,* 22 June 2003.

_____. "High School Player Also Sports Dancing Shoes." *The Daily Review* (California), 22 June 2003.

Gascon, Sarah

"Former SLU Softball Player Helps U.S. Win Women's Baseball Gold." *The Advocate* (Louisiana), 16 August 2004, 5-D.

Related Terms: World Cup

Gay, Lindsey

Barnes, J.L. "OR Alum Finds a League of Her Own." *The Standard-Times*, 27 July 2002, A1.

General Books and Histories

Ackermann-Blount, Joan. "Really Getting Organized." *Sports Illustrated* 57 (30 August 1982), 58–63ff.

Ackmann, Martha. "Welcoming Women to Baseball's Playing Fields." *Boston Globe*, 20 July 1998.

"And Now ... the Rest of the Story." *Referee*, May 1979, 24.

Ardell, Jean. *Breaking into Baseball: Women and the National Pastime.* Carbondale: Southern Illinois University Press, 2005.

Athletic Activities for Women and Girls. American Physical Education Association, New York: American Sports Publishing Co., 1903.

Atwater, Anne Elizabeth. *Movement Characteristics of the Overarm Throw: A Kinematic Analysis of Men and Women Performers.* Thesis, University of Wisconsin, 1970.

Barak, Tal. "Men Play Baseball, Women Play Softball." <www.npr.org/templates/story/>.

Barrow, Edward Grant. *My Fifty Years in Baseball.* New York: Coward-McCann, 1951.

"Baseball Among the Fairer Sex Coming into Prominence." *Indianapolis Freeman*, 26 December 1908.

Beck, Melinda, et al. "He Hits, She Runs, He Scores: After Hours, Baseball Is Still One Wild, Wild World." *Newsweek*, 20 April 1992, 64–65.

Berkson, Susan. "America's Real Pastime — Sexism — Is Still Played." *USA Today Baseball Weekly*, 12–18 October 1994, 15.

Berlage, Gai Ingham. "Sociocultural History of the Origin of Women's Baseball at the Eastern Women's Colleges During the Victorian Period." *Cooperstown Symposium on Baseball and the American Culture.* Westport, Connecticut: Meckler Publishing, 1989. Pp. 100–122.

_____. "Transition of Women's Baseball: An Overview." *Nine: A Journal of Baseball History and Culture* 9, nos. 1 and 2 (2001), 72–81.

_____. *Women in Baseball: The Forgotten History.* Westport, Connecticut: Praeger Publishers, 1994.

Bjarkman, Peter C. "Diamonds Are a Gal's Worst Friend: Women in Baseball History and Fiction." *Elysian Fields Quarterly* XII (Summer 1993), 93–105.

"'Bonnie Brewer' Promotion Draws Feminist Fire." *Stevens Point Daily Journal*, 3 September 1977, 3.

Brownstein, Bill. "Movie Strikes Out Myth That Women Can't Play Ball." *Ottawa Citizen*, 31 August 1995, F12.

Bryan, Mike. *Baseball Lives: Men and Women of the Game Talk about Their Jobs, Their Lives, and the National Pastime*. New York: Fawcett Columbine, 1990.

Borst, Bill. "The Matron Magnate." *SABR Baseball Research Journal*, 1977, 26.

Cahn, Susan M. "No Freaks, No Amazons, No Boyish Bobs." *Chicago History*, 1989, 26–41.

Candelaria, Cordelia. *Seeking the Perfect Game: Baseball and American Literature*. New York: Greenwood Press, 1989.

Clifton, Merritt. *A Baseball Classic*. Richford, Vermont: Samisdat, 1978.

Deacon, James. "Women in Sport: Leagues of Their Own." *Maclean's Magazine*, 7 April 1997, 62ff.

Deford, Frank. "Now Georgy-Porgy Runs Away." *Sports Illustrated*, 22 April 1974, 26–28ff.

Durso, Joe. "Marianne Moore, Baseball Fan." *Saturday Review*, 52 (12 July 1969), 51 52.

Dutcher, Rodney F. "Girls to Replace Men in Baseball." *Atlanta Constitution*, 22 April 1923, B6.

Eisenbath, Mike. "Diamond Lady: St. Louisian Out to Prove Woman's Place is at Home (Plate)." *St. Louis Post-Dispatch*, 1 March 1994.

Ephron, Nora. "Women." *Esquire*, January, n.d.

Feldman, Jay. "Glamour Ball." *Sports Heritage*, May/June 1987.

"The Female of the Species." *Baseball Magazine*, July 1931, 371.

Ferrante, Karlene. "Baseball and the Social Construction of Gender." *Women, Media and Sport*. Edited by Pamela J. Creedon. Thousand Oaks, California: Sage Publications, 1994.

"Field of Dreams? Women's Baseball League for 1995." *Brandweek*, 23 May 1994, 40B.

Fornoff, Susan. *Lady in the Locker Room!* Champaign, Illinois: Sagamore Publishing, 1993.

Frost, Helen and Charles Digby Wardlaw. *Basketball and Indoor Baseball for Women*. New York: Scribner, 1950.

Frymir, Alice and Marjorie Hillas. *Team Sports for Women*. New York: A.S. Barnes and Co., 1935.

Gandon, Mike. "Nicholle Strikes a First." *Illawarra Mercury* (Australia), 28 March 2002, 62.

Gems, G.R. "Early Women's Baseball: A Case of Subjugation and Transformation." *Base Woman*, January 1989, 2–3.

"Get Stronger, Get Faster, Play Ball." *Base Woman*, October 1987, 2–3.

Giancaterino, Randy. "A Swing through History." *Women's Sports and Fitness*, April 1994.

"Girl Pitches 2 Innings For High School on Coast." *New York Times*, 8 March 1978, B7.

Gordon, Allison. *Foul Ball!: Five Years in the American League*. New York: Dodd, Mead, 1985.

Gray, Genevieve. *Stand-off*. St. Paul, Minnesota: EMC Corp., 1973.

Gregorich, Barbara. "Baseball, Women and Research." *Wilson Library Bulletin*, May 1993, 41–43.

_____. "From Bloomer Girls to Silver Bullets." *Dugout*, Winter 1995, 5, 10.

_____. *She's on First*. Chicago: Contemporary Books, Inc., 1987.

_____. *Women at Play: The Story of Women in Baseball*. San Diego: Harcourt, Brace, and Co., 1993.

_____. "Women in Baseball: Indiana's Dynamic Heritage." *Traces of Indiana and Midwestern History* V (Spring 1993), 26ff.

Guttmann, Allen. *Women's Sports: A History*. New York: Columbia University Press, 1991.

Haynes, Mary. *The Great Pretenders*. New York: Bradbury Press, 1990.

Heaphy, Leslie. "Women Playing Hardball." In *Baseball and Philosophy, Thinking Outside the Batter's Box*. Eric Bronson, ed. Chicago: Open Court, 2004. Pp. 246–256.

Hillas, Marjorie and Marian Knighton. *Athletic Programs for High School and College Women*. New York: A.S. Barnes and Co., 1986.

Himes, Cindy L. "The Female Athlete in American Society, 1860–1940." Ph.D. Dissertation, University of Pennsylvania, 1986.

Howell, Reet. *Her Story in Sport*. West Point, N.Y.: Leisure Press, 1982.

Huntington, Anna Seaton. "Sugar and Spice and Everything Nice?" *New York Times*, 7 December 1997, SP13.

Hyman, Richard and Robert Ripley. "Believe It or Not in Baseball." *Baseball Magazine*, April 1931, 487.

John, Tommy and Sally. *The Sally and Tommy John Story: Our Life in Baseball*. New York: Macmillan, 1983.

Kane, C. "Why Can't a Woman Throw More Like a Man." *Ms.*, April 1976, 88.

Ketchum, R. "Fair Ball." *Women's Sports and Fitness*, April 1992, 59.

Kiefer, Michael. "Hardball: There's Nothing Soft About the Only Women's Baseball League in the U.S." *Women's Sports and Fitness* 14 (April 1992), 56–58.

Kiersh, Edward. "Meet the Ballgirls: Jackie and Gail Are the Envy of Fans Everywhere as the Lucky Holders of the Ideal Summer Job." *Inside Sports* 7 (June 1985), 52 54.

Kovach, John. *Women in Baseball*. Charleston, SC: Arcadia, 2005.

Krasnow, Stefanie. "Profiles— Women in Baseball." *The Whole Baseball Catalogue*, 1990, 327–329.

Kreidler, Mark. "A Woman's Prerogative." *Sporting News*, 8 June 1987.

Ladd, T. "Girl Who Broke and Set the Gender Barrier in Baseball." Abstract. In *Proceedings North American Society for Sport History*. University Park, Pennsylvania: North American Sports History, 1978.

Ledden, Jack. "Gracie at the Bat." *Allsports*, June 1944, 3

Leerhsen, C. "The Greek Chorus of Baseball." *Newsweek*, 1 August 1983, 70.

"Little League Faces Suit in Girl's Ban." *Washington Post*, 26 June 1974, B2.

Lopiano, Donna. "Fair Play for All (Even Women)." *New York Times*, 15 April 1990, S10.

"Love Lyric of a Lady Fan." *Baseball Magazine*, April 1931, 496.

Lyons, S.R. "She Made the Team." *Reader's Digest*, June 1949, 85.

McPhillips, Matthew J. "The Girls of Summer: A Comprehensive Analysis of the Past, Present, and Future of Women in Baseball." *Seton Hall Journal of Sport Law* VI (1996), 301ff.

Macy, Sue. "War, Women and Pro Baseball." *Scholastic Search* 14 (30 April 1982), 8–11.

Madden, W.C. *The Hoosiers of Summer*. Indianapolis: Guild Press, 1994.

"Major League Baseball: Not for Men Only." *Ebony*, October 1998, 45.

Managan, J.A. and Roberta Park, eds. *From Fair Sex to Feminism: Sports and the Socialization of Women in the Industrial and Post-Industrial Eras*. Totowa, N.J.: Frank Cass, 1987.

McDonald, Alfred. "Sports Scrapbook, 1903–1911." Minnesota Historical Society, St. Paul, Minnesota.

McWilliams, Gary. "A Passion for Baseball and Management." *Business Week*, 16 July 1990, 58.

Mitchell, Viola. *Softball for Girls*. New York: A.S. Barnes and Co., 1943.

Myers, Robert. "Girl Cartoonist-Writer Says Sports Needs a Woman's Touch." *The Mansfield News-Journal*, 20 May 1940, 11.

Nauen, Elinor. *Diamonds Are a Girl's Best Friend: Women Writers on Baseball*. Boston: Faber and Faber, 1993.

Neff, Craig. "[Bob] Knepper's Wild Pitch." *Sports Illustrated*, 20 August 1990, 15.

_____. "Women Not Welcome." *Sports Illustrated*, 20 August 1990, 15.

Nicholson, W.G. "Women's Pro Baseball Packed the Stands ... Then Johnny Came Marching Home." *WomenSports* 3 (April 1976), 22–24.

"No League of Their Own." *St. Louis Post-Dispatch*, 10 May 1997.

"Out on this Limb." *Reno Evening Gazette*, 1 April 1942, 12.

Palmer, Gladys E. *Baseball for Girls and Women*. New York: A.S. Barnes and Co., 1929.

Parker, Kathryn. *We Won Today: My Season with the Mets*. Garden City, N.Y.: Doubleday, 1977.

Parr, Jeanne. *The Superwives: Life with the Giants Jocks*. New York: Coward, McCann and Goeghegan, Inc., 1976.

Pierce, Charles S. "Two Tough Mothers: Bettie Taylor and Bonnie Lindros Want the Best for Their Sons, Pitcher Brien Taylor and Center Eric Lindros, and They Aren't Intimidated by Major League Baseball or the NHL." *Sports Illustrated*, 9 December 1991, 110–114.

Pietrusza, David. "Grace Coolidge — The First Lady of Baseball." *Elysian Fields Quarterly* (1993)36–39.

Pogrebin, L.C. "Diamonds Are a Girl's Best Friend." *Ms.*, September 1974, 79–82.

Powell, Roberta. *Women and Sport in Victorian America*. Ph.D. Dissertation, University of Utah, 1981.

Remley, Mary L. *Women in Sport: An Annotated Bibliography and Resource Guide, 1900–1990*. Boston: G.K. Hall, 1991.

Reynolds, Tim. "A Diamond Is Her Best Friend." *Albany-Times-Union*, 7 April 1998.

Richter, Francis, ed. "Base Ball Not for Women." *The Reach Official American League Guide for 1911*. Philadelphia: A.J. Reach Co. P. 169.

Ripley, J.W. "Baseball's Greatest Song." *American Heritage*, June/July 1983, 76–79.

Rivers, C. "Girls of Summer: Why the Great Tomboy Finds Splendor in the Dirt and Grows Up to be a Woman for All Seasons." *Womensports*, August 1977, 26–30ff.

Rondina, Catyherine and Joseph Romain. *Ladies Day: One Woman's Guide to Pro Baseball*. Los Angeles: Warwick Publishing, 1997.

Rubin, Bob. "Men Against Women: The Locker Room Wars." *Inside Sports* VIII (May 1986), 15, 17.

Salsinger, H. G. *Major League Baseball 1946: Facts, Figures and Official Rules*. Whitman Publishing Co., 1947.

Samoray, Jeff. "Second Baseman Proves She's Good Enough to Make Southern Baseball Team." *Detroit News*, 24 April 1997.

Sarafin, Betty. "Women in Baseball: Destined for the Big Leagues." *Focus*, 10 July 1994, 6, 7.

"Scorecard: Women of Steal." *Sports Illustrated*, 15 April 1991, 18.

Seymour, Harold. "The House of Baseball: The Annex." *Baseball: The People's Game*. New York: Oxford University Press, 1990.

Shattuck, Debbie. "Playing a Man's Game: Women and Baseball in the United States, 1866–1954." *Baseball History 2*. Edited by Peter Levine. 1989. Pp. 57–77.

_____. *Playing a Man's Game: Women and Baseball in the U.S.* Master of Science Thesis. Colorado Springs: University of Colorado, 1993.

_____. "Women in Baseball." *Total Baseball IV*. Edited by John Thorn and Pete Palmer. New York: Viking Press, 1989. Pp. 623–625.

Shelland, Harry. "Fair Fans 'Crash' Ball Games, Cheer Plays." *The Police Gazette*, 11 July 1931, 7.

Simmons, Herbert. "Cherchez La Femme." *Baseball Magazine*, March 1944.

Somerville, Roy. "Feminine Baseball De Luxe." *Baseball Magazine*, May 1908, 18–19.

Stanley, Alessandra. "Among Baseball's Ball Girls, Fielding Skills Take 2d Place." *New York Times*, 5 July 1991, A1.

Steinbreder, John. "Let's Make a Statement: A Woman or Black Should Get the National League's Top Job." *Sports Illustrated*, 21 November 1988, 98.

Suehsdorf, Adie. "Sluggers in Skirts." *Los Angeles Times*, 31 July 1941, F4–F6.

Tempesta, Elizabeth. "Establishing Women's Professional Baseball." In *The Cooperstown Symposium on Baseball and American Culture 2001*. William M. Simons, ed. Jefferson, North Carolina: McFarland. Pp. 353–364.

"3rd Annual Women's Baseball Camp to Raise Money for Breast Cancer Research and Education." *PR Newswire*, 15 April 2003.

Tilin, A. "A League of Their Own." *Women's Sports and Fitness*, November/December 1991, 11.

Twin, Stephanie L. *Out of the Bleachers: Writings on Women and Sport*. Old Westbay, N.Y.: Feminist Press, 1979.

"U.S. Women Have Long History as Activists." *Indiana Evening Gazette*, 10 September 1976, 9.

Viles, Peter. "First for Mets, WFAN: A Woman in the Booth — [Suzyn] Waldman Does Color, Not Play-by-Play; Fans May Already Know Her Singing Voice." *Broadcasting and Cable*, 14 June 1993, 61.

Voigt, David Quentin. "Sex in Baseball: Reflections of Changing Taboos." *Journal of Popular Culture*, 1978, 389–403.

Ward, Geoffrey C. and Ken Burns. *Baseball: An Illustrated History*. New York: Alfred A. Knopf, 1994.

Weiler, Karen H. and Catriona T. Higgs. "Living the Dream: A Historical Analysis of Professional Women Baseball Players, 1943–54." *Canadian Journal of the History of Sport* 23 (May 1992).

Wilentz, Lisa Winston. "Diamonds — The Kind That Have Four Bases — Are This Girl's Best Friend." *Sports Illustrated* 63 (5 August 1985), 6–7.

Wilson, B.S. and J.K. Skipper. "Nicknames and Women Professional Baseball Players." *Names*, 1990, 305–322.

Wolff, A. "Playing by Her Own Rules." *Sports Illustrated*, 6 July 1987, 38–39.

Wollum, Janet. *Outstanding Women Athletes*. Phoenix, Arizona: Oryx Press, 1992.

"Women and Baseball: An Original Monologue." By Olive White Fortenbacher. Library of Congress, Washington, D.C.

"Women in Baseball: Should Females Play the Game?" *Collegiate Baseball*, n.d.

"Women Players in Organized Baseball." *Baseball Research Journal*, 1983, 157–161.

"Women's Baseball Team Is Forming." *Akron Beacon Journal*, 17 March 2002.

Yoder, Robert. "Miss Casey at the Bat." *Saturday Evening Post*, 22 August 1942, 48.

Young, Ina Eloise. "Petticoats and the Press Box." *Baseball Magazine*, May 1908, 53–54.

Zipter, Yvonne. *Diamonds Are a Dyke's Best Friend: Reflections, Reminiscences, and Reports from the Field on the Lesbian National Pastime*. Ithaca, N.Y.: Firebrand Books, 1988.

Zoss, Joel and John Bowman. *Diamonds in the Rough: The Untold History of Baseball*. New York: Macmillan, 1989.

Gilham, Kaley

Carle, Dan. "Tall Future for Rocky Teen." *Edmonton Sun*, 5 August 2004, SP4.

Gisolo, Margaret

"Baseball Lassie Sure Knows Game." *Reno Evening Gazette*, 4 July 1928, 5.

"Girl Baseball Player Aids in Winning Legion Tournament." *Indianapolis News*, 26 July 1928.

"Girl Infielder Gets 4 Hits in Legion Junior Tournament." *New York Times*, 27 July 1928, 15.

Ladd, T. "Sexual Discrimination in Youth Sport: The Case of Margaret Gisolo." In *Her Story in Sport: An Historical Anthology of Women in Sports*. R. Howell, ed. West Point, N.Y.: Leisure Press, 1982. Pp. 579–589.

"Plays with Boys." *The Havre News-Promoter*, 13 July 1928, 8.

"She's Eligible." *Wisconsin Rapids Daily Tribune*, 16 July 1928, 5.

"Whatever Happened to ... Margaret Gisolo." *The Sheboygan Press*, 24 March 1961, 14.

Gordon, Mildred

"Girl Star." *Muskegon Chronicle*, 1 August 1925.

Gottselig, John

"Hockey Manager Signed to Scout Girls' Loop." *Waukesha Daily Freeman*, 24 May 1946, 7.

Grand Rapids Chicks

Beardsley, Howie. "Chicks Rule as First Team in GR Sports Hall of Fame." *Grand Rapids Press*, 17 June 2001.

"Chicks Consistent." *The Holland Evening Sentinel*, 2 June 1952, 8.

VandeBunte, Matt. "Triple Play; Former Teammates Discuss Days on Diamond." *Grand Rapids Press*, 3 October 2002.

Great Lakes Women's Baseball League (GLWBL)

Karpscuk, Kristin. "Motown Magic Calling on a Few Good Women." *Daily Oakland Press*, 14 April 2004.

Green, Dorothy

Thomas, Robert McG. Jr. "Dottie Green, A Baseball Pioneer in Women's League, Dies at 71." *New York Times*, 28 October 1992, D21.

Groundskeepers

Cook, Jon. "Nabozny Breaks New Ground." *Slam! Sports*, 17 June 1999.

Hair, Marty. "It's Not Easy Being Green." *Detroit Free Press*, 24 March 2000, 6B.

Habben, Carol

"AAGPBL Star Carol Habben." *Sports Collectors Digest*, 7 March 1997, 10.

Habetz, Alyson

"Alyson Habetz." Alabama Crimson Tide Web site.

"Alyson Habetz." University of Virginia Web site, Softball Profile.

Haine (Daniels), Audrey

Hicks, Phil. "The Girls of Summer." *The Chronicle-Telegram*, 26 July 1994, D1.

Related Terms: AAGPBL

Haller, Jodi

Lawes, Rick. "Haller Was First of Co-ed Hurlers." *USA Today Baseball Weekly*, 2–8 March 1994, 32.

Halls of Fame

DiPerna, Paula. "Baseball Hall of Fame Recognizes Women's Contributions." *Gettysburg Times*, 8 January 1997, B1.

Keay, Bill. "Canadian Baseball Hall of Fame." *The Vancouver Sun*, 10 February 2001.

Hamilton, Samantha

MacKinnon, John. "No Worries for Aussies." *Edmonton Journal*, 28 July 2004, D1.

Ryan, Melissa. "World Series Holds No Fear for Local Team." *The Age* (Melbourne), 31 August 2002, 14.

Related Terms: World Cup

Hammond, Jennifer

Hammond, Jennifer. Correspondence with Leslie A. Heaphy. June–July 2005, Canton, Ohio.

Hannah (Campbell), Helen

Everett, Hap. "Helen Hannah Front Office Boss of Club." *Los Angeles Times*, 25 February 1950, B3.

Hannah, Katherine

Gallant, Collin. "Hannah Wants the Ball Again." *Edmonton Journal*, 5 August 2004, D1.

Havlish, Jean

"Ex-Shortstop Finds Baseball Is Her Link to Mainstream." *Star Tribune*, 4 April 1993.

Kahn, Aron. "They Were the Girls of Summer." *St. Paul Pioneer Press Dispatch*, 9 July 1988, 6A, 8A.

Ridden, Kathleen C. "A Win at Wimbledon in 1959." *Ramsey County History*, Summer 1998, 13–16.

Weiner, Jay. "Millennium; Top 100 Sports Figures, Jean Havlish." *Minneapolis Star Tribune*, 25 December 1999.

Henley, Rocky

Herendeen, Steve. "Women Who Love Diamonds." *Alameda Times-Star* (California), 21 February 2003.

Related Terms: California Women's Baseball League

Hollywood Stars

"Hollywood Girls Bow by 10–6." *Washington Post*, 2 September 1931, 15.

"Hollywood Girls' Team to Play in Benefit Here." *Washington Post*, 26 August 1931, 13.

"Hollywood Girls to Play Baseball at Stadium Today." *Washington Post*, 1 September 1931, 15.

"Hollywood Girls Win 35 Games." *Washington Post*, 29 August 1931, 13.

"Large Crowd Sees Maiden Tossers Bow," *Williamsport Sun*, 27 August 1931.

"Movie Girls Play Here Tomorrow." *Washington Post*, 31 August 1931, 12.

"Sobs Mark Hearing of Balm Suit." *Los Angeles Times*, 7 July 1934, A3.

Holmes, Tammy

"Cal Rookie Blasts Historic Home run." *San Francisco Chronicle*, 15 May 1996.

Murphy, Mark. "The Madwoman of Lynn: Holmes Mixes It Up with the Men on Mass. Mad Dogs." *The Boston Herald*, 6 June 1999.

Rampenthal, Shari. "Big Ten Softball Gets Four NCAA Bids." *Wisconsin State Journal*, 15 May 1996.

"Woman Signs Up to Be a Mad Dog." *The Palm Beach Post*, 6 May 1999.

Related Terms: Colorado Silver Bullets

Houghton, Edith

"Former Wave Is Named Scout for Phillies." *Syracuse Herald*, 15 February 1946.

"Phillies Hire Girl Scout." *Elwein Daily Register*, 15 February 1946.

"Phillies Sign Girl Talent Hunter." *Waukesha Daily Freeman*, 15 February 1946, 9.

"Phillies Sign Former Wave as a Scout." *Washington Post*, 16 February 1946, 8.

"U.S. Girls Stranded in Orient, Sent Home." *Washington Post*, 2 December 1925, 1.

"Woman Baseball Scout." *New York Times*, 15 February 1946, 33.

"Woman Scout Signed by Philadelphia Phillies." *Walla Walla Union Bulletin*, 15 February 1946, 6.

Related Terms: Philadelphia Bobbies

Hu, Nancy

Odinsky, Tina Lee. "Nancy Hu: From Ballet to Baseball." *International Baseball Rundown*, March 1996, 14–15.

Hughes, Jennifer

"Village Engineer Throws a Mean Fast Ball." *Lincolnshire Review*, 26 June 2003.

Hurley, Cristine

Libman, Gary. "The Natural." *Nu Magazine*, March 2002.

Hutchison, Anna May

"Anna May Hutchison, Women's Baseball Star." *Philadelphia Inquirer*, 3 February 1998.

"Ex-Belles Pitcher Dies at 73." *Associated Press*, 1 February 1998.

Ivie, Tamara

"Bullets Set for San Bernadino." *The Press-Enterprise*, 28 June 1997.

Jackson, Gloria Jean "Jackie"

O'Gara, Roger. "Gloria Jean's Tryout Proves Pretty Failure." *The Sporting News*, 4 September 1971, 41.

Jameson, Shirley

"Power Plus." *Reno Evening Gazette*, 10 August 1945, 14.

Japanese Baseball

Chuman, Kanoe. *Baseball* [*Yakyu*]. Maekawa-Buneido Publishing, 1897. Reproduced edition in *Besuboru Magazine*, Sha, 1980.

Baba, Tetsuo. "People Contributed to the Developmental Physical Education of Nippon Women's University (5)." On Shirai, K. *Review of Human Ecology* no. 37 (1990).

Dai-Nippon Shonen Yakyu Kyokai, ed. *Official Boy's Baseball Rules* [*Koushiki Shonen Yakyukisoku*]. Ikedabunseido Publishing, 1921.

Itoi, Asajoro. *Boy's Baseball Techniques* [*Shonen Yakyu-jutsu*]. Matsuda Shoyudo Publishing, 1918.

Kimishima, Ichio. "Origin of the Japanese Baseball [*Nippon Yakyu Soseiki*]." *Besuboru Magazine*, 1972.

Koshihara, Yamato. "Encouragement the Baseball to Schoolgirl [*Joshigakusei ni Yakyu o Shoreisu*]," *Yakyukai Magazine*, June 1919.

Kuwabara, Ietoshi. *Women Play Ball [Onnatachi no Purei Boru]*. Fujinsha Publishing, 1993.

Kyoto First Elementary School, Ed. . *How to Play Baseball for Little Girls [Joshitekiyo Besuboru]*. 1903.

Shirai, Kikujiro. "Gymnastics and Play in Contemporary Europe and U.S. [Obei ni genkosuru Taiso to Yugi]," *Kyuiku-Jiron Journal* no. 610 (March 1902).

Takeuchi, Michio. "The Rise of Baseball in School Education in Meiji Period–From Baseball to 'Yakyu' [Meijiki Gakko Kyoiku niokeru Yakyu no Koryu]." In K. Eto, ed., *Some Considerations on the Modernizing Education [Kyoiku Kindaika no Shoso]*. Nagoya University Press, 1992.

Tobita, Suishu. "Nogata Women's High School Baseball Team Oppressed by the Tyranny," *Undokai Magazine*, March 1990.

Watanabe, Toru. *Japanization of American Sports: A Case of Student Baseball in Japan, in Japanese Martial Arts and American Sports. Proceedings of the 1989 U.S. Japan Conference*. Nihon University, Tokyo, 1990.

Jochum, Betsy

Pontanilla, Bernice. "Little Gets Display of Her Own." *Winnipeg Sun*, 30 July 2003, 44.

Johnson (Goodman), Mamie "Peanut"

Allen, Joanne. "Black Woman Pitcher Made U.S. History." *Wichita Eagle*, 8 December 2002.

Ardell, Jean Hastings. "Mamie 'Peanut' Johnson, the Last Female Voice of the Negro Leagues." *Nine* 10, 1, 181–192.

Berlage, Gai. "Robinson's Legacy: Black Women and Negro Baseball." In *Cooperstown Symposium on Baseball and American Culture*, eds. Pp. 123–135.

Britt, Donna. "Following Her Heart to Pitchers Mound." *Washington Post*, 10 September 1999, B1.

Cottingham, Reba. "Oral History Project on Mamie Johnson." University of Baltimore, Baltimore, Maryland. 10 December 1998.

Driver, David. "Pioneer Didn't Play for Just 'Peanuts.'" *The Laurel Leader*, 13 November 1997, 31.

Green, Michelle. *A Strong Right Arm*. New York: Dial Books, 2002.

Goode, Steven. "'Peanuts' Straight Pitch." *Hartford Courant*, 30 September 1999.

"Indianapolis Clowns List Two Women on Ball Roster." *Birmingham World*, 4 May 1954.

"Interview: Mamie 'Peanut' Johnson Discusses Her Baseball Career in the Negro Leagues in the 1950s." *Morning Edition*, NPR, 18 February 2003.

Ireland, Jack. "Female Honoree Cheered." *Wilmington News Journal*, 17 August 1997.

Johnson, Mamie "Peanut." Interview with Reba Cottingham. Negro League Oral History Collection, Archives and Special Collections, University of Baltimore, Baltimore, Maryland.

Kelley, Brent. "The First Woman to Win a Pro Ballgame." *Sports Collectors Digest*, 22 October 1999, 150.

Kerr, William B. Jr. "Ball Field Memories." *The Sunday Journal*, 18 July 1999, A1, A7.

Martin, Claire. "Pitcher's Story One of Courage and Resolve." *The Denver Post*, 15 September 2002, EE-02.

Mashberg, Tom. "'Peanut' a Big Deal — Was Negro Leagues Pioneer." *The Boston Herald*, 23 July 2000.

Meyer, Eugene L. "Baseball's Proud 'Peanut.'" *Tacoma News Tribune, Sound Life Insert*, 5 April 1999, 3–4.

_____. "For the Love of the Game." *Ann Arbor News*, 14 February 1998, C1, C2.

_____. "Often Overlooked Stars Get to Shine." *Washington Post*, 17 November 1999, M3.

_____. "'A True American Athlete.'" *Washington Post*, 3 February 1999, M5.

Mizejewski, Gerald. "Old Negro Leaguers a Hit with New Fans." *The Washington Times*, 22 February 1999.

Nance, Rahkia. "Foster Little-Known Force in Negro League." *Capital Outlook*, 3–9 January 2002.

Prater, Derek. "Negro Leagues of Their Own." *The Kansas City Star*, 28 July 2002, C1, C8.

Samuels, Christina A. "Standing on a Mound of Glory." *Washington Post*, 18 February 2001, T1.

Scott, Simon. "Interview: Mamie Johnson Describes Her Time Playing Baseball in the Negro Leagues." *Weekend Edition*, NPR, 31 August 2002.

Shores, Karla D. "Negro Leagues' Trailblazer Makes Her Pitch to Children." *Sun Sentinel*, 5 April 2003.

Suchsland, Victoria. "She Was No Joke for Indy Clowns." *Indianapolis Star*, 23 July 2002.

Voorhees, Deborah. "Swing Time." *The Dallas Morning News*, 17 February 1999, 5C.

"Women Made Major Pitch." *The Sun*, 10 May 1998, 1C, 8C.

Related Terms: Negro Leagues

Kalamazoo Lassies

"Girls Baseball Game Called." *The Marion Star* (Ohio), 15 May 1953, 20.

"Girls Baseball Team to Appear in Benefit." *The Marion Star*, 5 May 1953, 17.

Sargent, Jim. "June Peppas and the All-American League: Helping the Kalamazoo Lassies Win the 1954 AAGPBL Championship." *The National Pastime*, January 2002.

Kamenshek, Dorothy

"Dotty Is a Slugger." *American Magazine*, August 1950, 57.

Gonzales, Gloria. "Baseball Hall-of-Famers in a League of Their Own." *Los Angeles Daily News*, 21 August 1997.

Kamenshek, Dottie. File. National Baseball Hall of Fame and Library. Cooperstown, New York.

"Pipp Predicts Lady Players for Big Leagues in 5 Years." *Washington Post*, 15 May 1950, 13.
"Real Pro." *Ironwood Daily Globe* (Michigan), 9 August 1950, 12.

Kato (Kosaka), Mineko
"Onetime Female Pro Baseball Player to Make Comeback." *Japan Economic Newswire*, 12 July 2005.

Kellogg, Vivian
Neely, James E. *Vivian Kellogg: In a League All Her Own*. Brooklyn, Michigan: Historical Presentations, 2002.

Kennaley, Kathryn
"Burlington Girls Get Taste of Baseball Fame." *The Hamilton Spectator*, 26 July 2003, NO6.

Kenosha Comets
Bailey, John W. *Kenosha Comets, 1943–51*. Kenosha, Wisconsin: Badger Press, 1997.
"Colleens to Play Kenosha Girls Team in Opener Tonight." *Chicago Tribune*, 13 May 1948, C3.
Flores, Terry. "Kenosha Comets Reunite for a Day of Their Own." *Kenosha News*, 29 August 2000.
Giles, Diane. "Old Kenosha." *The Midwest Bulletin*, 21 and 28 July 1987.
Kenosha News, 1943–51.
"Kenosha Will Raise a Total of $25,000 for Support of Girls' Game." *The Sheboygan Press*, 28 January 1944, 11.
Kornkven, Jim. "Cooperstown to Recognize Comets." *Kenosha News*, 23 October 1988.
_____. "1943: Women in Baseball." *Kenosha News*, 17 September 1986.
"Peaches, Kenosha Open Ball Series." *Dixon Evening Telegram*, 8 September 1948, 9.
"Power Plus." *Reno Evening Gazette*, 10 August 1945, 14.
"Sports Briefs in Wisconsin." *Wisconsin Rapids Daily Tribune*, 24 March 1945.

Ketcham, Lee Anne
Carter, Donna. "Beaning Barriers Silver Bullets Pitcher Strives to Open Doors so More Women May Chase Baseball Dreams." *Denver Post*, 14 May 1995, B-1.
"Ketcham Pitches Silver Bullets to Victory." *San Jose Mercury News*, 27 July 1994.
Related Terms: Colorado Silver Bullets

Ketola, (LaCamera), Helen
Crawford, Cindy F. "Daisies' Diamond Days." *The Daily Journal*, 6 April 2003, 1–2.

Keyes, Erma D.
Sama, Dominic. "Erma D. Keyes; Educator; Athlete." *Philadelphia Inquirer*, 28 September 1999.

Kidd, Sue
Ivy, Darren. "No Skirting the Issue, Arkansans Like Sue Kidd and Mildred Earp Pitched in to Make Women's Professional Baseball a Short-lived Hit a Half Century Ago." *Arkansas Democrat-Gazette*, 17 September 2003, 23.

Kirby, Lisa
"Lisa, Kylie Lead Way for Awards." *Redcliffe and Bayside Herald*, 4 December 2002.

Kolanko, Mary Lou
Kolanko, Mary Lou. Correspondence with Leslie A. Heaphy. Canton, Ohio, 26 May 2001.

Konwinski, Dolly
Dematteo, Anthony. "Famous Old Women Having Fun." *St. Augustine Record*, 9 February 2002.
Rademacher, Tom. "Her Generosity Helps Unlock Memories Behind Photos." *Grand Rapids Press*, 22 September 2002.
VandeBunte, Matt. "Triple Play; Former Teammates Discuss Days on Diamond." *Grand Rapids Press*, 3 October 2002.
Related Terms: AAGPBL, Grand Rapids Chicks

Kook, Shanna
Dus, Julie. "More Than a Minor Accomplishment." <Referee.com>, 28 April 2004.
Holtzman, Jerome. "Woman Umpire Set to Begin Career." <www.MLB.com>, 16 May 2003.
Related Terms: Umpires

Korean Baseball
Tae-gyu, Kim. "Female Baseballer Can't Give Up the Diamond." *Korea Times*, 25 February 2003.

Korecek, Katie
Pemstein, Bill. "Baseball Gave Korecek an Edge." *Lake Villa Review*, 22 April 2004.

Kovach, Irina
Ferraro, Julie. "Baseball for Girls?" *South Bend Tribune*, 19 March 2005, B7.

Kovalchick (Erwin, Roark), Dorothy
Berlage, Gai Ingham. "1940s Ballplayer — Dorothy Kovalchick." *The Diamond Angle Quarterly* 56 (Summer 1997), 38–39.

Kroc, Joan
Anderson, Dave. "The Cubs Fan Who Owned the Padres." *New York Times*, 5 October 1984, A23.
"Ex-Padres Owner Joan Kroc, 75 Dies." <NBCSports.com>, 13 October 2003.
Farhi, Paul and Reilly Capps. "NPR Given Record Donation." *Washington Post*, 6 November 2003, A01.
"Former Padres Owner Joan Kroc Dies at 75." *UPI*, 13 October 2003.
"Joan Kroc Makes $50 million Gift to Benefit Children." *Newswire*, 23 October 1995.
Spagat, Elliot. "Joan Kroc, Widow of McDonald's Founder, Dies at 75." *Daily Southtown News*, 13 October 2003.
"Widow Kroc Reassures San Diego." *Washington Post*, 27 January 1981, E2.
Related Terms: Owners

Kurys, Sophie

Brennan, John. "Sports Talk." *The Record* (N.J.), 15 April 1991.

"Gal Who's Going Places." *Waukesha Daily Freeman*, 30 June 1947, 7.

"Rifle Armed." *The Lima News*, 5 June 1950, 16.

Wulf, Steve. "Woman of Steal: Rickey Henderson Is Good, but He's No Sophie Kurys." *Sports Illustrated* 74 (15 April 1991), 18.

Ladies' Day

McLemore, Henry. "Mac Against Ladies' Day." *The Hammond Times*, 29 August 1937, 14.

Ladies Professional Baseball League

Keisser, Bob. "L. B. Adds Another Women's Team to Lineup." *Press-Telegram*, 5 June 1997.

"Ladies League Founder Admits to Fraud." *San Diego Union-Tribune*, 23 September 1999.

"Ladies Professional Baseball Has Struck Out." *Long Beach Press Bulletin*, 30 July 1998.

Learmonth, Michael. "Ruthless Babes." *Metroactive*, 21–27 August 1997, 1–13.

"Nine Silver Bullets Sign to Play in Ladies Pro League." *USA Today*, 8 May 1998.

Sabedra, Darren. "Women's Baseball League a Dream Come True for Many." *San Jose Mercury News*, 22 June 1998.

Townsend, Karen Denise. "Making Dreams Come True on a Diamond." *Lesbian News* 23 (September 1997).

Laspina, Melanie

Herendeen, Steve. "Women Who Love Diamonds." *Tri-Valley Herald*, 21 February 2003.

Laspina, Melanie. Correspondence with Leslie A. Heaphy. North Canton, Ohio, May 2004.

Lee (Harmon), Annabelle "Lefty"

Campbell, Katie. "She Was Famous from the Mound." *Press Journal* (Vero Beach, Florida), 5 October 2003, D6.

_____. "Take Her Out to the Ballgame." *Press Journal* (Vero Beach, FL), 2 October 2003, A1.

Pucin, Diane. "This 'Lefty' Is Right on the Mark." *Los Angeles Times*, 23 December 1998.

Lee, Deanne

Callander, Sean. "Bundoora Slugger Belts Aussies to the Gold." *Diamond Valley Leader* (Australia), 25 September 2002, 33.

Lesko, Jeneane

Grindeland, Sherry. "Pursuing a League of Her Own." *The Seattle Times*, 16 August 2004, B1.

Ruiz, Don. "Women's Baseball Pioneer Still Pioneering." *Tacoma News Tribune*, 27 July 2003.

Sherwin, Bob. "Lesko Helping Form Women's Baseball League." *The Seattle Times*, 16 March 2005, D8.

Lillywhite, Shae

"Lillywhite Shines at World Cup." *Frankston Standard Leader*, 6 September 2004, 37.

Limoges, Andrea

Spencer, Donna. "A Tournament of Their Own." *Ottawa Citizen*, 14 December 2002, C5.

Literature

Adler, David and Chris O'Leary (illustrator). *Mama Played Baseball*. San Diego: Harcourt Brace, 2003.

Bechard, Gorman. *Balls*. New York: Plume, 1995.

Bjarkman, Peter C. "Diamonds Are a Gal's Worst Friend: Women in Baseball History and Fiction." *SABR Review of Books* IV (1989), 79–95.

Bowen, Michael. *Can't Miss*. New York: Harper and Row Publishers, 1987.

Butler, Dori. *Sliding into Home*.

Carol, Bill J. *Circus Catch*. Austin, Texas: The Steck Co., 1963.

Cebulash, Mel. *Ruth Marini, Dodger Ace*. Minneapolis: Lerner Publications, 1983.

_____. *Ruth Marini of the Dodgers*. Minneapolis: Lerner Publications, 1983.

_____. *Ruth Marini, World Series Star*. Minneapolis: Lerner Publications, 1985.

Christopher, Matt. *Diamond Champs*. Boston: Little, Brown and Co., 1977.

_____. *Supercharged Infield*. Boston: Little, Brown and Co., 1985.

_____. *Wild Pitch*. Boston: Little, Brown and Co., 1978.

Cohen, Celia. *Smoky: A Romance*. Tallahassee, Florida: Naiad Press, 1994.

Cooney, Ellen. *All the Way Home*. New York: G.P. Putnam and Sons, 1984.

Dessent, Michael. *Baseball Becky*. San Diego: Oak Tree Publications, 1982.

Due, Linnea A. *High and Outside*. New York: Harper and Row, 1980.

Ellis, Lucy. *All That Jazz*. New York: Sports Illustrated for Kids, 1990.

_____. *The Girls Strike Back: The Making of the Pink Parrots*. New York: Sports Illustrated for Kids, 1990.

Ellis, Lucy. *No Hitter*. New York: Sports Illustrated for Kids, 1991.

Fowler, Karen Joy. *The Sweetheart Season*. New York: Henry Holt and Co., 1996.

Gilbert, Sarah. *A League of Their Own*. New York: Warner Books, 1992.

Gordon, Alison. *Dead Pull Hitter*. New York: Onyx Press, 1991.

_____. *Night Game*. Toronto: McClellan and Stewart, 1996.

_____. *Prairie Hardball*. Toronto: McClellan and Stewart, 1997.

_____. *Safe at Home*. Toronto: McClellan and Stewart, 1996.

_____. *Striking Out*. Toronto: McClellan and Stewart, 1997.

Gray, Genevieve. *Stand-off*. New York: EMC Corp., 1973.

Gregorich, Barbara. *She's on First*. Chicago: Contemporary Books, 1987.

Hanmer, Trudy J. *The All-American Girls Professional Baseball League*. Minneapolis: Lerner Publications, 1994.

Harper, Elaine. *Short Stop for Romance.* New York: Simon and Schuster, Inc., 1983.

Haynes, Mary. *The Great Pretenders.* New York: Bradbury Press, 1990.

Hays, Donald. *The Dixie Association.* New York: Simon and Schuster, 1984.

Holohan, Maureen. *Left Out.* New York: Pocket Books, 1998.

Hopkinson, Debra with illustrations by Terry Widener. *Girl Wonder: A Baseball Story in Nine Innings.* New York: Atheneum, 2003.

Kelly, Jeffrey. *The Basement Baseball Club.* Boston: Houghton Mifflin Co., 1987.

Leavy, Jane. *Squeeze Play: A Novel.* New York: Doubleday Books, 1990.

Michaels, Ralph. *The Girl on First Base.* New York: Nordon Publications, Inc., 1981.

Moss, Marissa. *Mighty Jackie, the Strike Out Queen.* New York: Simon and Schuster, 2004.

Palmer, Joe E. *Slide, Katie, Slide!* Los Angeles: Remlap Publishing Co., 1994.

Patrick, Jean L.S. with illustrations by Jeni Reeves. *The Girl Who Struck Out Babe Ruth.* Minneapolis, Minnesota: Carolrhoda books, 2000.

Paulos, Sheila. *Wild Roses.* New York: Random House, Inc., 1983.

Perkins, Al. *Don and Donna Go to Bat.* New York: Random House, Inc., 1966.

Rappaport, Doreen, Lyndall Callan and Earl B. Lewis (illustrator). *Dirt on Their Skirts.* New York: Dial Books, 2002.

Renick, Marion. *The Dooleys Play Ball.* New York: Charles Scribner's Sons, 1949.

Roberts, Kristi. *My Thirteenth Season.* New York: Henry Holt and Company, 2005.

Rothweiler, Paul R. *The Sensuous Southpaw.* New York: G.P. Putnam's Sons, 1976.

Ruth, Claire. *The Babe and I.* Englewood Cliffs, N.J.: Prentice-Hall, 1959.

Sachs, Marilyn. *Fleet-Footed Florence.* Garden City, N.Y.: Doubleday and Co., 1981.

Sharbono, Kaye. *Jackie Mitchell: Baseball Player.* Morristown, N.J.: Modern Curriculum Press, 1995.

Slote, Alfred. *Matt Gargan's Boy.* Philadelphia: J.B. Lippincott Co., 1975.

Sullivan, Silky. *Henry and Melinda.* Chicago: Children's Press, 1982.

Taves, Isabella. *Not Bad for a Girl.* New York: M. Evans and Co., 1972.

Testa, Maria. *Some Kind of Pride.* Yearling Publishers, 2003.

Toth, Pamela. *Fever Pitch.* New York: Dell Publishing Co., 1986.

Valentine, E.J. *Change Up.* New York: Sports Illustrated for Kids, 1991.

Walden, Amelia Elizabeth. *Play Ball.* McGill. Philadelphia: Westminster Press, 1972.

_____. *Three Loves Has Sandy.* New York: McGraw-Hill Book Co., 1955.

Little (Bend), Olive

Pontanilla, Bernice. "Little Gets Display of Her Own." *Winnipeg Sun,* 30 July 2003, 44.

Little League

Berkow, Ira. "Sexism and Little League: A Summer with Controversy." *The Herald,* 27 June 1973.

Brud, Ed. "Terri Plays in Her 1st Little League Game." *Suburbanite Economist,* 23 June 1974, 9.

Cavanaugh, John. "Girl Stirs up League." *New York Times,* 5 June 1983, CN8.

Considine, Bob. "Little League for the Gals." *Times-Herald,* 10 January 1974, 22.

Dunham, Molly. "LL Softball Doing Well in Thurmont." *The Frederick Post,* 31 July 1980.

"For Little League's Girls, A Quiet Anniversary." *New York Times,* 24 May 1999.

"Girls and Little League Baseball Creating New Women's Lib Waves." *The Sheboygan Press,* 24 May 1973.

"Girls Hurdle LL Barrier." *Bucks County Courier Times,* 13 June 1974, 67.

"Girls Making Inroads in Tenafly Little League." *Washington Post,* 15 April 1974, D12.

Grossfield, Stan. "Purpose Pitch." *The Boston Globe,* 19 August 2004, C1, C13.

Hacker, Kathy. "Baseball Battle Bypasses Bucks." *Bucks County Courier Times,* June 1974.

_____. "Girls: Softball's Our Game." *Bucks County Courier Times,* June 1974.

"Hearing Urged on Charges of Sex Bias in Little League." *New York Times,* 10 September 1972, 45.

"Jersey Diamonds Taken Over by the Pigtail Set, Age 9 to 13." *New York Times,* 24 June 1961, 23.

Johnson, C.C. "We Believe ... Little League Surrenders." *Sporting News,* 29 June 1974, 14.

Kim, Yung. "Donald Miller, 75; Let First Girl Play Little League Baseball in New Jersey." *The Record* (N.J.), 21 May 2004, LO7.

King, Ann. "Little Girls of Spring." *New York Times,* 16 May 1999, A1.

Lewerenz, Dan. "Girls, Women Featured Prominently at This Year's LL World Series." *Associated Press,* 21 August 2004.

"Little League Faces Suit in Girl's Ban." *Washington Post,* 26 June 1974, B2.

Little League File. National Baseball Hall of Fame and Library, Cooperstown, New York.

"Little League Gives In, Says Yes to Girls." *Newport Daily News,* 13 June 1974.

"Little League HQ Prodded on Girls." *New York Times,* 12 April 1974, 67.

"Little League in Jersey Ordered to Allow Girls to Play on Teams." *New York Times,* 8 November 1973, 99.

"Little League Opens Baseball to Girls." *Press Gazette* (Ohio), 13 June 1974.

"Little League Set to Honor City's Gerring." *The Journal Gazette,* 22 August 2004.

Logan, Paul. "Little League Ball for Girls! Program Formed Nationwide." *The Herald,* 18 April 1974.

"Most Comments Favor LL Ruling." *Newport Daily News,* 13 June 1974.

Murphy, Michael. "Little League World Series." *Houston Chronicle,* 23 August 2004, 9.

"Next Thing You Know It'll Be Pink Uniforms." *Burlington Times-News* (North Carolina), 11 May 1974.

Roberts, Chris. "Little League Is Big League and the Girls Want In." *The Progress* (Pennsylvania), 22 May 1974, 37.

Rosenblatt, Gary. "For 60,000 Little Leaguers, It Is Time to Play Ball." *New York Times*, 7 May 1972, 120.

Simpson, Kevin. "While Big Leagues Fiddle, One Player's Latent Desire Burns." *Denver Post*, 9 February 1995, B-1.

Stone, Judy. "City Softball League for Girls Suggested; Baseball Proponents Looking for Support." *Edwardsville Intelligencer*, 17 May 1974, 9.

_____. "Little League Rebuffs Girls." *Edwardsville Intelligencer*, 20 April 1974, 1.

_____. "Little League's Door Still Closed to Girls." *Edwardsville Intelligencer*, 11 April 1973.

Thornton, M.L. "Little League Baseball: It's Not Good Enough for Girls." *Today's Health,* July 1974, 6–7, 72.

Torg, B.G. and J.S. Torg. "Sex and the Little League." *Physician and Sports Medicine*, May 1974, 45–50.

Towles, Stephen. "Girls Have Dreams of Baseball, Too." *The Seattle Post-Intelligencer*, 16 August 2004, B5.

Treaster, Joseph B. "Girls a Hit in Debut on Diamond." *New York Times*, 25 March 1974, 67.

Turner, Craig. "Little League Family Opposes Boy-Girl Teams." *Los Angeles Times*, 20 June 1974, SG1.

Tuttle, Nancy. "Their Heart's in the Highlands." *Lowell Sun*, 30 May 2004.

Waggoner, Walter H. "Byrne Declares 'Qualified' Girls Should Play Little League Ball." *New York Times*, 28 March 1974, 81.

_____. "Byrne Supports Girls in Little League." *New York Times*, 28 March 1974, 43.

"What Future for Little League Baseball?" *Stevens Point Daily Journal* (Wisconsin), 9 September 1976, 30.

Whigam II, Julius. "Girl Is Just Like One of the Guys Out on the Baseball Diamond." *Palm Beach Post*, 15 September 2004, 12.

Related Terms: Maria Pepe, Hayley Nine

Ludtke (Lincoln), Melissa

"Clubhouse Access: Reaction Is Mixed." *New York Times*, 6 May 1979, 202.

"Judge Denies Bid to Open Yankee Doors." *Washington Post*, 28 September 1978, D7.

"Kingman Fined $3,500." *New York Times*, 25 June 1986, D26.

"Kuhn Reacts to Suit of Female Writer." *New York Times*, 31 December 1977, 24.

Ludtke Lincoln, Melissa. "Locker Rooms: Equality with Integrity." *New York Times*, 15 April 1979, S2.

Smith, Red. "Another View on Equality." *New York Times*, 9 January 1978, C4.

Lynch, Evelyn

"Girl Baseball Player to Appear in Fairfield Tilt." *Gettysburg Times*, 5 August 1937, 3.

"Girl Is Leader in Cabin John Triumph." *Washington Post*, 2 July 1934, 18.

"Girl Plays for Celtics Against St. Joe Team." *Washington Post*, 15 September 1932, 14.

"St. Joseph's Wins from Celtics, 4–3." *Washington Post*, 17 September 1932, 12.

Lytle, Eleanor

"Girl Pitcher Hurls Way to Mound Fame." *Washington Post*, 28 July 1935, 8.

McComb, Joanne

"AAGPBL Interview — Joanne McComb." <http://thediamondangle.com/>.

Tobias, Jessica. "McComb and Ferguson Were Pioneers in Women's Sports." *Williamsport Sun-Gazette*, 21 July 2004, C-1, C-3.

McKenna, Betty

"Lisbon Lass Plays 3rd for 'Big League' Club." *East Liverpool Review*, 30 May 1951, 10.

McKesson (Gibbs), Molly

"Molly McKesson." *USA Baseball 2004 Media Guide*.

LaPeter, Lenora. "Women's World Series." *St. Petersburg Times*, 7 September 2002, 1B.

Morgan, Nancy. "Gibbs Teen Plays in Women's World Series." *St. Petersburg Times*, 22 September 2002, 26.

_____. "Woman Keeps Adding to Her Baseball Success." *St. Petersburg Times*, 20 June 2004, 4.

MacPherson, Katie

"Burlington Girls Get Taste of Baseball Fame." *The Hamilton Spectator*, 26 July 2003, NO6.

Pulga, Allen. "Talented Elite Girls' Baseball Team a Shock to the Boys." *Hamilton Spectator*, 14 August 2004, SP08.

Magalas, Samantha

Carle, Dan. "Canuck Upset! Our Gals Down USA 2–1 at Women's Baseball." *Edmonton Sun*, 3 August 2004, SP1.

Tychkowski, Robert. "Canada Rules Aussies." *Edmonton Sun*, 9 August 2004, SP5.

Related Terms: World Cup

Mahon, Elizabeth Bailey "Lib"

Pontanilla, Bernice. "Little Gets Display of Her Own." *Winnipeg Sun*, 30 July 2003, 44.

Management Personnel

"Baseball Men Beware! Women Prove They Can Run a Team." *Chicago Tribune*, 20 April 1941, B3.

Bogaczyk, Jack. "Charleston's New General Manager Has Plenty of Experience Behind Her." *Charleston Daily Mail*, 27 March 2003, 1B.

"Hispanic Trailblazer Breaks All the Barriers." <http://www.americandreams.org>.

Holtzman, Jerome. "In General Terms, She Qualifies as Czar." *Chicago Tribune*, 11 November 1993, 6.

Hums, Mary A. and William A. Sutton. "Women Working in the Management of Professional Baseball: Getting to First Base?" *Journal of Career Development* 26 (1999), 147–158.

Jordan, Pat. "The Only Baseball Boss Who's Young, Female, and Black, Tracy Lewis Holds the Cards in

Savannah." *People Weekly*. 27 (May 18, 1987), 108–110.

Lapchick, Richard E. "The Color Bar Gets Raised in Baseball." *The Sports Business Journal,* 26 November 2001.

"Linda Martinez Alvarado." Colorado Women's Hall of Fame.

"Los Angeles Dodgers Hire Former Yankees Assistant GM Kim NG." AP article, 5 December 2001.

"Major League Baseball: Not for Men Only." *Ebony* 53 (October 1998), 45.

Martinez, Michael. "Yanks' Sanderson Sidesteps Women in Locker Room." *New York Times*, 2 April 1991, B10.

Otto, Allison. "Diamond Cutters: These Women Are Showing Careers Can Be Carved in Baseball Operations." *Denver Post*, 16 April 2002, D-12.

"President Names Linda Alvarado to the President's Advisory Commission on Educational Excellence for Hispanic Americans." 17 March 1995, Press Release, Office of the Press Secretary.

Smith, Janet Marie. "Putting Together a Winning Team: Janet Marie Smith of the Baltimore Orioles on Managing a Major League Project." *Working Woman* 17 (October 1992), 28, 30.

"IX to Watch." *ESPN the Magazine*, 16 June 2003.

"Yankees Name Afterman Assistant GM." *Baseball America News*, 5 December 2001.

Manley, Effa

Berlage, Gai. "Effa Manley, a Major Force in Negro Baseball in the 1930s and 1940s." *Nine: A Journal of Baseball History and Social Policy Perspectives* (Spring 1993), 163–184.

Bock, Hal. "Memories from a Different Era." *The Chronicle-Telegram* (Elyria, Ohio), 25 April 1981, B-5.

Burley, Dan. "The Senors Get in Mrs. Manley's Hair." *New York Amsterdam News*, 10 August 1946.

"Dodger Deal Protested." *New York Times*, 12 January 1949, 38.

"Effa Manley." *The Chronicle-Telegram* (Elyria, Ohio), 21 April 1981.

"Effa Manley, 81, Who Originated Newark Eagles of Negro League." *New York Times*, 22 April 1981, B6.

Essington, Amy. "She Loved Baseball: Effa Manley and Negro League Baseball." In *The Cooperstown Symposium on Baseball and American Culture, 1999.* Jefferson, North Carolina: McFarland, 1999. Pp. 275–295.

"Josh the Basher." *Time*, 19 July 1943, 75–76.

Manley, Effa. "Negro Baseball Isn't Dead." *Our World*, August 1948, 26–30.

Manley, Effa, and Leon Hardwick. *Negro Baseball ... Before Integration*. Chicago: Adam Press, 1976.

Murray, Jim. "Baseball's Last Supper." *Mansfield News-Journal*, 8 December 1976.

"Negro Ballclubs Hope to Make Comeback This Season." Ebony, May 1949, 38.

"Newark Eagles." *Our World*, September 1947, 46–50.

Overmeyer, James. *Effa Manley and the Newark Eagles*. Metuchen, N.J.: The Scarecrow Press, Inc., 1993.

Prater, Derek. "Women in the Negro Leagues." *Kansas City Star*, 28 July 2002.

Rogosin, Donn. "Queen of the Negro Leagues." *Sportscape*, Summer 1981, 18.

Skluzacek, Julianna. "Mixed Signals: The Story of Effa Manley and the Negro Leagues (A Play)." In *The Cooperstown Symposium on Baseball and American Culture, 1999.* Jefferson, North Carolina: McFarland, 1999. Pp. 261–74. .

Spink, C.C. Johnson. "A Furious Woman." *The Sporting News*, 18 June 1977, 15.

"Woman Recalls Years as GM of Newark Eagles of Negro Leagues." *Williamsport Sun Gazette*, 7 August 1973.

Marrero, Chico

"Marrero (Mirta) Hurls Opener Tonight at Griffith Stadium." *Washington Post*, 3 May 1951, 16.

Marrero, Mirta

Douthat, Bill. "League of Her Own." *Palm Beach Post*, 12 September 2003, 1A.

_____. "A Special Reunion for Women's Baseball League." *Cox News Service*, 11 September 2003.

"Marrero (Mirta) Hurls Opener Tonight at Griffith Stadium." *Washington Post*, 3 May 1951, 16.

Marshall, Theda

Johnson, Bill. "Old Baseball Player Was in a Special League." *Rocky Mountain News*, 6 August 2000.

Massaro, Gary. "Cooperstown Now on Deck." *Rocky Mountain News*, 12 October 2000.

Mattson (Baumgart), Jacqueline

Brummer, Courtnay Charles. "Girl's Baseball League Made History Decades Ago." *Brookfield News*, 16 June 1994, 1, 14.

Meidlinger, Meg

Lukat, Carl. "Dominion Pitcher's Big Win." *Loudon Times-Mirror*, 31 March 2004, A17, A19.

Meisner, Jessica

Cavanaugh, John. "Girl Stirs up League." *New York Times*, 5 June 1983, CN8.

Related Terms: Little League

Merhige, Phyllis

Martinez, Michael. "Yanks' Sanderson Sidesteps Women in Locker Room." *New York Times*, 2 April 1991, B10.

Metesh, Bernice

"Joliet Girl, 19, Wins Semi-Pro Pitching Job." *New York Times*, 22 July 1948, 28.

Mills, Donna

Gasper, Christopher L. "Going to Bat for Her Country." *Boston Globe*, 13 June 2004.

Mullen, Maureen. "A Whole New Ballgame, Women Shine on Lynn Diamond." *Boston Globe*, 8 August 2003, E10.

Mills, Dorothy Jane Seymour

<www.HaroldSeymour.com>.

Milwaukee Chicks

"Chicks Lose." *Record-Eagle* (Michigan), 23 May 1947, 11.

"Chicks Winners." *Record-Eagle* (Michigan), 23 May 1946, 10.

Draeger, Carey L. "Girls of Summer." *Michigan History*, September/October 1997.

Gardner, Charles. "Tip of the Cap to Pioneers." *Milwaukee Journal Sentinel*, 27 August 2000, 1, 4.

"Getting Back into the Swing of Things." *Milwaukee Journal Sentinel*, 27 August 2000.

"Girls Baseball Title to Chicks." *The Vidette-Messenger* (Indiana), 18 September 1944, 6.

Haudricourt, Tom. "Talented Chicks Forced to Leave Nest." *Milwaukee Journal Sentinel*, 26 August 2000, 1, 9.

_____. "Women to Take Field Again as Players Reunite in Milwaukee." *Milwaukee Journal Sentinel*, 25 August 2000, 1, 19.

"Lassies Defeat Chicks in Opener." *Record-Eagle* (Michigan), 22 May 1947, 13.

"Milwaukee Chicks Beat Kenosha 3–0; Take Title." *Chicago Tribune*, 18 September 1944, 19.

Morgan, Tom and Jim Nitz. "A Team of Their Own." *Milwaukee Magazine*, July 1994, 10–11.

_____. "When the Chicks Were Champs, but Not Many Fans Cared." *The Milwaukee Journal*, 31 July 1994, 3.

Minneapolis Millerettes

Kamenick, Amy. "'Queens of Swat': They Played Like Girls." *The Minnesota Women's Press*, 21 July–3 August 1999.

Mitchell, Virne Beatrice "Jackie"

Berkson, Susan. "America's Real Pastime — Sexism — Is Still Played." *USA Today Baseball Weekly*, 12–18 October 1994, 15.

Brandt, William. "Girl Pitcher Fans Ruth and Gehrig." *New York Times*, 3 April 1931, 32.

_____. "Ruth Will Face Girl Pitcher Today; Home Run King Alarmed at Prospect." *New York Times*, 2 April 1931, 37.

"Girl, 17, to Pitch against Babe Ruth for Chattanooga." *Chicago Tribune*, 29 March 1931, A2.

"Girl Pitcher Faces Yankees." *Los Angeles Times*, 2 April 1931, A12.

"Girl Pitcher Fans Ruth and Gehrig." *New York Times*, 3 April 1931, 32.

"Girl Pitcher for Lookouts 'Whiffed' Ruth and Gehgrig in '31 Exhibition." *The Sporting News*, 2 July 1952, 5.

"Girl Pitcher, 17, Fans Ruth, Gehrig, Walks Tony, Quits." *Washington Post*, 3 April 1931, 1, 16.

"Girl Pitcher Strikes Out Ruth and Gehrig, but Yanks Win." *Chicago Tribune*, 3 April 1931, 40.

"Girl Southpaw to Get Chance to Fan Ruth in Exhibition Today." *Decatur Herald*, 1 April 1931, 15.

Gregorich, Barbara. "Jackie Mitchell and the Northern Lights." *Timeline*, May/June 1995, 50–54.

_____. *Women at Play: The History of Women in Baseball*. San Diego, California: Harcourt Brace, 1994.

_____. *Women in Baseball: Indiana's Dynamic Heritage*. Indianapolis, Indiana: Indiana Historical Society, 1993.

"'Jack' Mitchell Graduate of Kid Elberfeld School." *The Bismarck Tribune*, 2 April 1931.

Jeanes, William. "High Jinks or High Skill?: Jackie Mitchell Fanned Ruth and Gehrig in Her Pro Debut." *Sports Illustrated* 68 (4 April 1988), 130.

Lardner, Ring. "A Night Letter." *Chicago Tribune*, 6 April 1931, 29.

Mortenson, Tom. "In Quest of the 'Girl Who Struck Out Ruth, Gehrig.'" *Sports Collectors Digest*, 16 June 1995, 12.

Phillips, H.L. "On Women Baseball Players." *Washington Post*, 3 May 1931, MF16.

Yoakam, Cy. "She [Jackie Mitchell] Struck Out Babe Ruth." *Sports Heritage* 1 March/April 1987, 23–27ff.

Mohney, Ethel

"Woman Owner Re-Signs Topeka Manager." *The Sporting News*, 10 March 1948, 28.

Monge, Christine

Kord, Michael. "Monge Excels at Back of Bullpen. Seattle Product Closes Games for Silver Bullets." *Seattle Post-Intelligencer*, 11 July 1997.

Montgomery County Barncats

Slattery, Chris. "Diamonds Are a Girl's Best Friend." <Gazette.Net>, 20 July 2001.

Moore, Dolores

Vivanco, Liz. "Dolores Moore, Athlete; Baseball Hall of Fame." *Chicago Sun-Times*, 4 September 2000, 52.

Morgan, Constance

"Batting Tips." *Great Bend Daily Tribune*, 8 September 1954, 5.

"Clowns' Girl Second Baseman Thrills Birmingham Fans with Speedy Plays." *Kansas City Call*, May 1954.

"Clowns Sell Toni Stone, Sign New Female Star." *Michigan Chronicle*, 13 March 1954.

"Connie Morgan at Shortstop for Clowns." *Birmingham World*, 25 May 1954.

"Indianapolis Clowns List Two Women on Ball Roster." *Birmingham World*, 4 May 1954.

"Monarchs Play Clowns Tonight." *Washington Post*, 13 July 1954, 24.

"The Second Baseman Was a Lady." *Philadelphia Daily News*, 18 October 1997, 11.

Related Terms: Mamie Johnson, Negro Leagues, Toni Stone

Motown Magic

Karpscuk, Kristin. "Motown Magic Calling on a Few Good Women." *Daily Oakland Press*, 14 April 2004.

Related Terms: Great Lakes Women's Baseball League

Mudge (Cato), Nancy

Kahn, Aron. "They Were the Girls of Summer." *St. Paul Pioneer Press Dispatch*, 9 July 1988, 6A, 8A.

Murphy, Elizabeth

Berlage, Gai Ingham. "Five Forgotten Women in American Baseball History: Players, Lizzie Arlington, Alta Weiss, Lizzie Murphy; Umpire, Amanda Clement; and Owner, Helen Britton." *Cooperstown Symposium on Baseball and the American Culture.* Westport, Connecticut: Meckler Publishing, 1990. Pp. 222–242.

"Funeral Today for Ballplayer Lizzie Murphy." *Washington Post*, 30 July 1964, C5.

Hanlon, John. "Queen Lizzie Plays First Base." *Sports Illustrated*, 21 June 1965, E3–E4.

Lancaster, Jane. "R. I. Woman was Hit in a Man's Game." *Providence Journal*, 12 July 1992.

"Lizzie Feted on Her Day." *Warren Times-Gazette*, 20 April 1994, 5.

"Lizzie Murphy to Have Her 'Day' on April 13." *Warren Times-Gazette*, 16 March 1994, 3.

Merolla, James. "Warren's Lizzie Murphy: the Only Woman to Play Pro Baseball with Men." *Warren Times-Gazette*, 8 July 1992.

Murphy, Lizzie File. National Baseball Hall of Fame and Library. Cooperstown, New York.

O'Leary, James C. "Great Benefit Nets More than $5000 for Tom McCarthy's Family." *Boston Globe*, 15 August 1922.

"Pioneer Remembered." *The Providence Journal-Bulletin*, 14 April 1994.

"Red Sox VP to Visit on 'Lizzie's Day.'" *Warren Times-Gazette*, 6 April 1994, 3.

Reynolds, Dick. "Lizzie Murphy, Queen of the Diamonds." *Old Rhode Island* 4 (1994), 11–15.

Seymour, Harold and Dorothy Z. Seymour. *Baseball: The People's Game.* New York: Oxford University Press, 1990.

Muskegon Lassies

Dulo, Ken. "Naum's 2-Hitter Features Girls' Loop Double-Header; Lassies Drop Windup." *The Herald-Press* (Michigan), 2 September 1953, 12.

"Lassies Cop, 3–1: AGBL Teams in Twin Bill." *The Herald-Press* (Michigan), 1 September 1953, 10.

"Lassies Defeat Chicks in Opener." *Record-Eagle* (Michigan), 22 May 1947, 13.

"Lassies Down Chicks." *Record-Eagle* (Michigan), 5 June 1947, 15.

"Lassies Lost to Muskegon." *Record-Eagle* (Michigan), 8 June 1950, 16.

"Muskegon Argues about Ball Clubs and Marsh Field." *Holland Evening Sentinel*, 29 November 1949, 2.

Nabozny, Heather

Cook, Jon. "Nabozny Breaks New Ground." *Slam! Sports*, 17 June 1999.

National Girls Baseball League

"Bloomer Girls, Bluebirds, and Cuties Triumph." *Chicago Daily Tribune*, 18 July 1954, A6.

"Bloomer Girls, Queens Play 2 Games Tonight." *Chicago Tribune*, 27 July 1954, B4.

"Bloomer Girls, Queens Split Double Header." *Chicago Tribune*, 28 July 1954, B2.

"Bloomer Girls Triumph, 6–4, Over Queens." *Chicago Tribune*, 15 July 1954, D4.

"Bloomer Girls Win, 3–1, over Desert Queens." *Chicago Tribune*, 8 August 1954, A6.

"Bluebirds Defeat Maids, 7–3; Garber Hits Two Home Runs." *Chicago Tribune*, 27 August 1949, A2.

"Brakettes Play Two Games Tonight." *The Bridgeport Telegram*, 3 August 1951, 18.

"Chicago Will Draw Best Girls' Teams." *Chicago Tribune*, 11 April 1954, A5.

Cromie, Robert. "4 Team Girls' League Opens 10th Baseball Season Tonight." *Chicago Tribune*, 28 May 1953, D7.

_____. "It's Baseball with Curves, and Some New Angles, Too." *Chicago Tribune*, 17 May 1948, B4.

Fay, William. "Home (Plate) Is the Place for Women Now!" *Chicago Tribune*, 26 July 1947, 1.

"Free-for-All Marks Game in Girls' League." *Chicago Tribune*, 17 July 1954, B2.

"Girl Baseball Champs Here May 6th, 8 P.M." *The Deming Headlight* (N.M.), 27 April 1951.

"Girl Slugger Sent to Jail." *Syracuse Herald-American*, 29 June 1952.

"Girls Fret About Base Hits Too." *Syracuse Herald-American*, 6 August 1950.

"Girls Nines Open Play Tonight in National League." *Chicago Tribune*, 21 May 1948, B5.

"Glamour Galore in Girls Loop." *Herald Sports*, 21 May 1947, 13.

"Kabich Hurls No-hit Game; Maids Win Two." *Chicago Tribune*, 2 August 1952, B4.

"Lima Girl Socks Umpire in Game." *Mansfield News-Journal*, 2 July 1952, 15.

"Lip Service." *Statesville Daily Record*, 16 July 1950, P-8.

"Music Maids Off to Fine Start in Girls Ball Play." *Northbrook News*, 3 June 1949.

"Phoenix Queens Score 5 in 1st to Beat Jax, 11–1." *Chicago Tribune*, 21 July 1949, A3.

"Phoenix Team Beats Chicago Queens, 8 to 4." *Chicago Tribune*, 9 August 1954, C4.

"Queens Deal 6 to 3 Defeat to Bluebirds." *Chicago Tribune*, 7 August 1954, A3.

"Queens Rained Out; Play Two Games Tonight." *Chicago Tribune*, 10 August 1954, B4.

"Queens Split; Play Compton Cuties Tonight." *Chicago Tribune*, 23 July 1954, B4.

"Queens Win: Bloomer Girls Beat Jewels." *Chicago Tribune*, 26 July 1954, B4.

"Rains Postpone Girls Baseball League Game." *Chicago Tribune*, 21 July 1954, B5.

"Wanless and Garber Set National Girls League Bat Records." *Chicago Tribune*, 26 August 1949, B2.

"War Flares between Baseball Officials of 2 Girls' Leagues." *Chicago Tribune*, 12 May 1948, B1.

Naum (Parker), Dorothy "Dottie"

Dulo, Ken. "Naum's 2-Hitter Features Girls' Loop Double-Header; Lassies Drop Windup." *The Herald-Press* (Michigan), 2 September 1953, 12.

"Lassies Beat Rockford 8–7." *Kalamazoo Gazette*, 21 May 1953.

Related terms: AAGPBL

Negro Leagues

Allen, Joanne. "Black Woman Pitcher Made U.S. History." *Wichita Eagle*, 8 December 2002.

"Baseball among the Fairer Sex Coming into Prominence." *Freeman*, 26 December 1908.

"Batting Tips." *Great Bend Daily Tribune*, 8 September 1954, 5.

Berlage, Gai Ingham. "Effa Manley, a Major Force in Negro Baseball in the 1930s and 1940s." *Nine: A Journal of Baseball History and Social Policy Perspectives* 1:2 (Spring 1993), 163–184.

_____. "Robinson's Legacy: Black Women and Negro Baseball." In *Cooperstown Symposium on Baseball and American Culture*. Pp. 123–135.

"Black Sox Bloomer Girls." *Baltimore Afro-American*, 16 September 1921 and 19 May 1922.

"Clowns Sell Toni Stone, Sign New Female Star." *Michigan Chronicle*, 13 March 1954.

East, Claude. "Ball Team of Negro Girls." *Wausau Daily Record*, 1907. Negro League Baseball Museum, Kansas City, Missouri.

Egan, Erin. "Toni Stone Was One of the Only Women Ever to Play With Men." *Sports Illustrated for Kids*, April 1994, 26.

Green, Michelle. *A Strong Right Arm*. New York: Dial Books, 2002.

Gregorich, Barbara. *Women at Play: The Story of Women in Baseball*. New York: Harcourt, Brace and Co., 1993.

"Girl Second Base Guardian Star of Former Detroiter's Nine." *Detroit Tribune Independent*, 29 July 1933, 7.

"Girls at Academy Take up Baseball." *Erie Daily Times*, 25 May 1922, 18.

"Lillie Mae Jenkins." *Kansas City Call*, 19 March 1926.

Lister, Valerie. "Other Leagues Shared Spotlight." *USA Today*, 3 June 1994.

Manley, Effa, and Leon Hardwick. *Negro Baseball ... Before Integration*. Chicago: Adam Press, 1976.

McShane, Larry. "The Best Team You Never Saw: Newark's Eagles." *AP Online*, 28 May 1998.

Mizejewski, Gerald. "Old Negro Leaguers a Hit with New Fans." *The Washington Times*, 22 February 1999.

Overmeyer, James. *Effa Manley and the Newark Eagles*. Metuchen, N.J.: The Scarecrow Press, Inc., 1993.

Prater, Derek. "Negro Leagues of Their Own." *The Kansas City Star*, 28 July 2002, C1, C8.

_____. "Women in the Negro Leagues." *The Kansas City Star*, 28 July 2002.

Rogosin, Donn. "Queen of the Negro Leagues." *Sportscape* Summer 1981, 18.

"St. Louis Black Bronchos." *Indianapolis Freeman*, 23 April 1910.

Stanley, D.L. "Women in Negro Baseball Leagues." *Atlanta Inquirer*, 28 April 2001.

Shores, Karla D. "Negro Leagues' Trailblazer Makes Her Pitch to Children." *Sun Sentinel*, 5 April 2003.

Thomas, Ron. "Women in the Negro Leagues." *Emerge*, May 1996.

Voorhees, Deborah. "Swingtime: Three Women Got Their Chance to Play Professional Baseball in Negro League." *Dallas Morning News*, 17 February 1999, 5C.

Weinstein, Mike. "Women of the Negro Leagues." *Appleseeds*, February 2000, 10.

Related Terms: Toni Stone, Connie Morgan, Mamie Johnson

Nelson, Maud

"Base Ball in Bloomers." *The Sporting News*, 12 October 1895.

"The Bloomer Girls Play at Baseball." *The Mansfield News*, 12 July 1901.

"The Chicago Stars." *The Atlanta Constitution*, 16 February 1902.

Gregorich, Barbara. *Women at Play*. Pp. New York: Harcourt, Brace and Co., 1993. 7, 9–11.

_____. "John Olson and His Barnstorming Baseball Teams." *Michigan History Magazine*, May/June 1995, 38–41.

_____. "From Bloomer Girls to Silver Bullets." *Dugout*, Winter 1995, 5–10.

_____. "The Girls of Summer." *NewCity*, 2 May 1996, 9–11.

Kelley, Bev. "They Played to Win — Those Bloomer Girls!" *Chicago Tribune*, 16 May 1954, C23.

Related Terms: Bloomer Girls

Neumeier, Elizabeth

"Neumeier Becomes First Female Arbitrator in Baseball." <CNNSI.com>, 8 February 1999.

New England Women's Baseball League

Barnes, J.L. "OR Alum Finds a League of Her Own." *The Standard-Times*, 27 July 2002, A1.

Dahl, Dick. "Out of His League." *Boston Globe Magazine*, 12 September 1999, 20, 22 29.

Deady, Monica. "Throw Like a Girl." *Watertown Tab*, 12 March 2003.

Forsberg, Chris. "Facing World Competition, They Played Hardball." *Boston Globe*, 18 July 2001.

Gasper, Christopher L. "Playing the Game They Love: Women Pursue Baseball Dreams." *Boston Globe*, 13 July 2003, 1, 11.

Gilgore, Adam. "A Grass Roots Campaign." *The Boston Globe*, 11 June 2004, E11.

Hallorin, Paul. "Another League of Their Own." *The Daily Item*, 30 June 2003.

Huebner, Barbara. "Baseball League Finds a New Home." *Boston Globe*, 9 May 2001.

Kaster, Julie. "Baseball Diamonds This Girl's Best Friend." *Eagle-Tribune*, 25 July 2000.

Konecky, Chad. "Somerville Resident Shines in Women's Baseball League." *Somerville Journal*, 5 September 2002.

Mullen, Maureen. "A Whole New Ballgame, Women Shine on Lynn Diamond." *Boston Globe*, 8 August 2003, E10.

Related Terms: Women's New England Baseball League (WNEBL)

New York Bloomer Girls

"Select Site for Game with Girls' Ball Team." *Danville Bee*, 16 August 1928, 10.

New York/New Jersey Women's Baseball League

Michael Gasparino, "Playing Hardball," Long Island Sports Online (LISOnline.com, 15 June 1999.

New York Women's Baseball Association

Abramowitz, David. "Another League of Their Own." *New York Newsday*, 13 August 2003.

Carpiniello, Rick. "A League for Those Who Say Softball Isn't Enough." *The Journal News*, 9 June 2003.

Hirshon, Nicholas. "Women's Professional Baseball Takes the Field at St. John's." *The Queens Ledger*, 11 July 2002.

Kornfield, Stefanie. "Finding a League of Their Own at Ashford." *Rivertown's Enterprise*, 5 September 2003.

Malone, Michael. "Throwing Like a Girl." *New York Sports Express*, 28 August 2003.

Miller, Shane. "Starting a League of Their Own." *The Queens Ledger*, 20 March 2003.

Ng, Kim

Baggarly, Andrew. "It's a New Ball Game." *Press Enterprise* (Riverside, California), 13 July 2003, C12.

Chass, Murray. "Thomas and Sheffield Showing Salary Envy." *New York Times*, 25 February 2001, SP8.

"IX to Watch." *ESPN the Magazine,* 16 June 2003.

"Los Angeles Dodgers Hire Former Yankees Assistant GM Kim NG." AP article, 5 December 2001.

Olney, Buster. "Woman Will Be Yankee Executive." *New York Times*, 4 March 1998, C3.

_____. "Yanks' Owner Speaks His Mind." *New York Times*, 18 February 2001, SP7.

Otto, Allison. "Diamond Cutters: These Women Are Showing Careers Can Be Carved in Baseball Operations." *Denver Post*, 16 April 2002, D-12.

Painterstaff, Jill. "It's Kim-possible." *Inland Valley Daily Bulletin* (California), 30 June 2003.

Related Terms: Management Personnel

Nichols, Tina

"All She Wants Is a League of Her Own." *The Tampa Tribune*, 5 March 2000.

"New Women's Team Flooded with Calls." *USA Today Baseball Weekly*, 29 December 11 January 1994, 6.

Niedzielka, Amy. "Miami's League of Their Own." *The Miami Herald*, 9 August 1992.

Watts, Angie. "Orlando Defeats San Diego for Women's Baseball Title." *Washington Post*, 2 September 1997.

Nicknames

Wilson, Brenda S. *Nicknaming Practices of Women in a Nontraditional Occupation: Female Professional Baseball Players.* MA Thesis, 1991.

Nicol (Fox), Helen

"Helen Nicol Still Tops Ball." *The Lethbridge Herald*, 31 August 1943.

Niland, Lily

Niland, Lily. Correspondence with Leslie A. Heaphy. North Canton, Ohio, 2004 and 2005.

Smith, Craig. "Ballard Baseball Pitcher Proves She's One of the Guys." *Seattle Times*, 10 May 2005.

Nine, Hayley

Whigam II, Julius. "Girl Is Just Like One of the Guys Out on the Baseball Diamond." *Palm Beach Post*, 15 September 2004, 12.

Nineteenth Century

"The American Girl." *Washington Post*, 7 April 1889, 14.

Annie Glidden Papers. Vassar College Special Collections. Vassar College, Poughkeepsie, New York.

"Baseball Among Girls." *Washington Post*, 13 September 1885, 6.

"A Baseball Burlesque." *New York Times*, 23 September 1883.

"Base-Ball Girls." *Chicago Tribune*, 9 December 1883, 16.

"Base Ball Girls." *Brooklyn Daily Eagle*, 8 September 1889, 11.

"Beauty's New Sphere." *Washington Post*, 9 May 1896, 7.

Berlage, Gai. "Sociocultural History of the Origin of Women's Baseball at the Eastern Women's Colleges During the Victorian Period." *The Cooperstown Symposium on Baseball and American Culture 1989.* Alvin L. Hall, ed. Westport, Connecticut: Meckler Publishing, 1991. Pp. 100–122.

Brooklyn Daily Eagle, 5 September 1890.

"The Champeens Win." *Philadelphia Inquirer*, 3 October 1889.

"Female Ball Players." *Brooklyn Daily Eagle*, 23 July 1889, 6.

"Female Ball Players in a Plight." *New York Times*, 8 July 1884, 5.

"Female Ballists." *South Bend Daily News*, 10 August 1885.

"A Female Baseball Club." *Washington Post,* 3 October 1890, 6.

"The Female Baseball Club." *New York Clipper*, 18 September 1875, 194.

"Female Baseball Players." *Washington Post,* 14 July 1893, 6.

"Female Base Ballists Are Angry." *Chicago Tribune*, 9 June 1890, 3.

"Feminine Base Ball." *Albany Journal*, 12 May 1879.

"Feminine Base-Ball." *New York Times*, 21 August 1883, 4.

"For and About Women." *Washington Post*, 14 October 1895, 7.

"The Ga-lorious Fourth." *Chicago Tribune*, 5 July 1887, 1.

"A Game Between Girls." *Spirit of the Times*, 29 August 1868, 26.

Gems, G.R. "Early Women's Baseball: A Case of Subjugation and Transformation." *Base Woman*, January 1989, 2–3.

"Girl Ball Players from Philadelphia." *New York Clipper*, 29 September 1883, 453.

"Girls and Baseball." *The Sporting News*, 20 September 1890.

"Girls at Base-Ball." *New York Times*, 19 August 1883, 2.

"Girl Base Ball Players." *Brooklyn Daily Eagle*, 6 May 1894, 7.

"Girls Base Ball Players Fined." *Chicago Tribune*, 10 June 1890, 9.

"The Girls and Boys Play Ball." *Chicago Tribune*, 5 July 1887, 1.

"Girls in Bloomers Cannot Play Ball." *Chicago Tribune*, 22 September 1895, 1.

"The Girls in It." *The Sporting Life*, 12 March 1890.

"Girls Play Base Ball." *Brooklyn Daily Eagle*, 4 January 1897, 12.

"Girls' Team Won." *Brooklyn Daily Eagle*, 4 August 1890, 15.

"Girls Who Play Baseball." *New York Times*, 3 September 1893, 12.

"Glen Falls Games." *New York World*, 25 April 1890.

"How Women Play Ball." *Chicago Tribune*, 18 May 1879, 7.

"Insulted Woman Ball Player." *Brooklyn Daily Eagle*, 5 September 1901, 7.

"Introducing Females into Professionalism." *The Sporting Life*, 30 August 1890, 8.

"Kankakee 'New Women.'" *Los Angeles Times*, 30 July 1895, 2.

"Ladies at the Ball." *Chicago Tribune*, 17 August 1870.

"A Ladies' Day." *Brooklyn Daily Eagle*, 4 April 1890, 2.

"Ladies' Day at Washington Park." *Brooklyn Daily Eagle*, 15 August 1884, 2.

"The Ladies of Hallsport." *Rochester Evening Express*, 21 September 1867.

McCormick, J.B. "Romance and Baseball." *Washington Post*, 3 August 1890, 9.

"McGlynn and Baseball, On the Field Not as a Player but as a Talker." *New York Times*, 21 August 1887, 8.

"Miss Harris's Baseball Nine." *New York Times*, 18 May 1883.

New York Clipper, 18 and 25 September 1875, 22 and 29 September 1883, 8 and 29 December 1883, 12 April 1884, 17 May 1884, 12 July 1884, 25 October 1884, 1 November 1884, 3 and 24 January 1885, 21 March 1885, 23 May 1885, 12 September 1885, 31 October 1885, 20 February 1886, 2 October 1886, 27 November 1886.

"Novel Ball Game." *Brooklyn Daily Eagle*, 4 August 1902, 11.

"Novelties." *New York Clipper*, 29 December 1883, 693.

"In Petticoats." *Chicago Tribune*, 15 and 16 September 1875.

"The Presence of Ladies at Base Ball Matches." *Brooklyn Daily Eagle*, 6 July 1884, 9.

"Red and Blue Legs." *Washington Post*, 12 May 1879, 1.

"Riot on the Ball Field, Cubans Attack Female Players from the United States." *New York Times*, 7 March 1893, 1.

Shattuck, Debra. "Bats, Balls and Books: Baseball and Higher Education for Women at Three Eastern Women's Colleges, 1866–1891." *Journal of Sport History*, Summer 1992, 91, 109.

Smith, Gene. "The Girls of Summer." *American Heritage*, July–August 1994, 110–111.

"The Widow Wanted Cash." *New York Times*, 13 April 1893, 3.

"Wilson's Wicked Ways." *Brooklyn Daily Eagle*, 16 August 1891, 1.

"A Woman's View." *The Sporting Life*, 5 March 1890, 3.

"Women Wield the Bat." *Washington Post*, 4 October 1890, 6.

"Women's Baseball." *Savannah Weekly Echo*, 26 August 1883.

"Young Lady Baseballists." *The National Police Gazette*, 20 September 1890.

"Young Women Play Ball." *New York Times*, 30 April 1896, 9.

North American Women's Baseball League

Erilus, Evan. "They're Taking Their Final Cuts." *The Boston Globe*, 4 June 2004, E9.

O'Brien, Judith

LaPeter, Leonora. "Women's World Series: Swinging at Acceptance." *St. Petersburg Times*, 7 September 2002, 1B.

Oppenheimer, Priscilla

"Baseball/American League." *Rocky Mountain News*, 10 January 1996.

Healey, James R. "Padres Minor Leaguer Remains on Life Support." *USA Today*, 9 April 1996.

Otto, Allison. "Diamond Cutters: These Women Are Showing Careers Can be Carved in Baseball Operations." *Denver Post*, 16 April 2002, D-12.

Related Terms: Management Personnel

O'Rourke, Florence

"Girl a Baseball Captain." *Washington Post*, 28 March 1914, 4.

O'Toole, Heidi

"Woman Tries Out for Pirates, but Doesn't Merit a Contract." *Albany Times-Union*, 31 July 1985.

Owners

Anderson, Dave. "The Cubs Fan Who Owned the Padres." *New York Times*, 5 October 1984, A23.

"Angels' Owner Threatens to Move Team from Anaheim." *The Cincinnati Post*, 16 March 1996.

"Autry's Widow Says Singing Cowboy Would Love These Angels." *San Francisco Chronicle*, 28 September 2002.

Bass, Mike. *Marge Schott, Unleashed*. Champaign, Illinois: Sagamore Publishing, 1993.

Britton, Helene. Interview. "My Experience as a League Owner." *Baseball Magazine*, February 1917, 13.

Brown, Warren. "Mrs. Grace Comiskey Endured to See Sox in Safe Keeping." *The Sporting News*, 19 December 1956, 22.

Cafardo, Nick. "Jean Yawkey Dies at 83." *Boston Globe Online*, 27 February 1992.

Capouya, John. "Queen of the Riverfront: Marge Schott Loves Her Reds, Her Dog, and Cincinnati.

Everything Else Should Get Out of the Way." *Sport* 79 (July 1988), 28–32, 37.

Hick, Virginia. "She's the Boss in Baseball..." *St. Louis Post-Dispatch*, 16 March 1987.

"Jackie Autry Began with Three Strikes Against Her." *St. Louis Post-Dispatch*, 2 June 1996.

"Jackie Autry Upset, Ponders Moving Angels." *Los Angeles Daily News*, 16 March 1996.

Jacobson, Kenneth. "Why the Big Deal About Marge Schott?" *New York Daily News*, 26 May 1996.

"Joan Whitney Payson, 72, Mets Owner Dies." *New York Times*, 5 October 1975, 63.

Jordan, Pat. "The Only Baseball Boss Who's Young, Female and Black, Tracy Lewis Holds the Cards in Savannah." *People's Weekly*, 18 May 1987, 108–110.

Klemesrud, Judy. "Marge Schott, Cincinnati Booster, Is Rooting for Her Home Team." *New York Times*, 8 March 1985, B8.

"Ladies of the Club." *New York Times*, 17 January 1985, B12.

Lanpher, Katherine. "It's No Surprise That Joan Kroc is 'Angel.'" *St. Louis Pioneer Press*, 20 May 1997, 1B.

Lieb, Frederick G. *The St. Louis Cardinals: The Story of a Great Baseball Club*. New York: G.P. Putnam's Sons, 1944.

Lindberg, Richard C. and Mark Fletcher. *The White Sox Encyclopedia*. Philadelphia: Temple University Press, 1997.

Loewenheim, Francis. "Major League Woman: Marge Schott." *Harper's Bazaar*, September 1985, 291.

Margolick, David. "Red Sox Are the Subject of a Custody Battle." *New York Times*, 26 February 1992.

Martyn, Marguerite. "Baseball Better Exercise Than Bridge." *St. Louis Post-Dispatch*, 1912.

_____. "Mrs. Schuyler Britton Tells Marguerite Martyn." *St. Louis Post-Dispatch*, 9 April 1911.

"Mrs. Havenor Chicago Girl." *Chicago Tribune*, 14 April 1912, C2.

Nuwer, Hank. "Marge Schott: Queen of Diamonds." *Modern Maturity*, June/July 1986, 40ff.

Ohio Baseball Hall of Fame, Toledo, Ohio. Baseball Files.

Pope, Justin. "Henry Leads Group to Buy Red Sox." *USA Today*, 21 December 2001.

Quintanilla, Ray. "Marie A. Peterson; Once Owned Class A Baseball Team in Miami." *Chicago Tribune*, 15 August 1994.

Radel, Cliff. "Former Reds Owner Discusses Her Three Great Loves." *The Cincinnati Enquirer*, 26 February 2002.

"Reds Are Bought by a Cincinnatian." *New York Times*, 22 December 1984, 19.

Reilly, Rick. "Heaven Help Marge Schott. The Reds' Owner, Long Ago Reduced to a Life of Loneliness, Has Further Isolated Herself by Her Spiteful Words and Witless Deeds." *Sports Illustrated*, 20 May 1996, 72–87.

Rogosin, Donn. "Queen of the Negro Leagues." *Sportscape*, Summer 1981, 18.

Rosen, Byron. "New Bosox Bosses Right at Home." *Washington Post*, 30 September 1977, D3.

Simon, Peter and Jack Lang. *New York Mets: 25 Years of Baseball Magic*. New York: Henry Holt and Company, Inc., 1986.

Spagat, Elliot. "Joan Kroc, Widow of McDonald's Founder, Dies at 75." *Daily Southtown News*, 13 October 2003.

"Status of Duquette Still Up in the Air." <ESPN-Magazine.com>, 27 February 2001.

Trausch, Susan. "The Woman Who Owns the Red Sox Keeps Her Private Life Private." *Boston Globe Online*, 6 April 1989, 73.

Van Biema, David. "A Millonairess Named Marge Proves a Schott in the Arm for the Dogged Cincinnati Reds." *People Weekly* 24 (22 July 1985), 99–100.

"Woman Owner Re-Signs Topeka Manager." *The Sporting News*, 10 March 1948, 28.

"Woman to Take Over Ball Club." *Los Angeles Times*, 3 May 1927, B1.

Related Terms: Jackie Autry, Helene Britton, Joan Kroc, Joan Payson, Marge Schott, Jean Yawkey

Pagliai, Leanne

Morgenson, Gretchen. "Where the Fans Still Come First." *Forbes*, 27 April 1992.

Paine, Christina

Lechner, Tammy. "Common Threads: Baseball and Horses." *Accent on Living*, 22 March 1997.

Paire (Davis), Lavonne "Pepper"

Briggs, Jeremy. "Another 'League' of Their Own?" *Mountain Democrat*, 16 February 1995, B-6.

Gonzales, Gloria. "Baseball Hall-of-Famers in a League of Their Own." *Los Angeles Daily News*, 21 August 1997.

Pakistan

"Women Baseball Introduces in Pakistan." *The Pakistan Newswire*, 17 February 2002.

Palermo, Toni Ann "Peanuts"

Czernicki, Candy. "'Peanuts' Palermo Was 'Excellent Shortstop' Until God Intervened." *Catholic Herald*, 6 November 2003.

Palmer, Rhonda

Herendeen, Steve. "Women Who Love Diamonds." *Alameda Times-Star* (California), 21 February 2003.

Pannozzo, Sharon

"Sharon Pannozzo." In *Baseball Lives: Men and Women of the Game*. Mike Bryan, ed. New York: Pantheon Books, 1989. Pp. 336–343.

Parker, Andrea

Dolan, Steve. "Who's on Second? For Cal Lutheran, It's Andrea Parker." *Los Angeles Times*, 27 April 1979, SD B1.

Parks (Young), Barbara

"Westport Woman Remembers the Girls of '51." *New York Times*, 16 August 1992, Sect. 13, 1.

Passlow, Kathryn

Ierodiaconou, George. "Team Steals to a World Series Win." *Sunbury Macedon Leader* (Australia), 8 October 2002, 8.

Pawtucket Slaterettes

Murphy, Bill. "Girl Power." *Providence Journal-Bulletin*, 29 April 2003, B-02.

Russell, Patricia. "Girls of Spring." *Providence Journal-Bulletin*, 29 April 2003, C-01.

Payson, Joan

"Ailing Mrs. Payson Wires Congratulations to Mets." *New York Times*, 25 September 1969, 59.

Dempsey, David. "Says Mrs. Payson of the Mets, 'You Can't Lose Them All.'" *New York Times*, 23 June 1968, SM28.

Durso, Joseph. "First Lady of the Mets Takes a Cram Course." *New York Times*, 13 November 1978, C6.

_____. "Joan Whitney Payson, 72, Mets Owner, Dies." *New York Times*, 5 October 1975, 63.

"It Was Guts, Not Destiny, Says Owner of Mets." *The Daily Times* (Maryland), 17 October 1969, 21.

"Joan Payson, Mets Principal Owner, Dies." *Nevada State Journal*, 5 October 1975, 23.

"Mets Find Women in Clubhouse." *Washington Post*, 16 May 1968, K2.

"Mets May Be Hottest Commodity in Sports." *Walla Walla Union-Bulletin*, 9 October 1969, 19.

"Mets' Owner Covered Eyes on Last Pitch." *Washington Post*, 13 October 1969, B2.

"Mets' Owner Sat and Cried When Team Clinched First Place." *Manitowoc Herald Times* (Wisconsin), 10 October 1969, 15.

"Mets Pick New President." *Appleton Post-Crescent*, 7 December 1975.

Montgomery, Paul. "Diverse Friends of Joan Payson Fill Church for Last Goodbyes." *New York Times*, 8 October 1975, 44.

Moran, Sheila. "Sweet Victory for Millionaire Owner." *Mansfield News-Journal*, 17 October 1969, 18.

"Mrs. Payson Moves Up to Mets' President." *Washington Post*, 7 February 1968, D3.

"Mrs. Payson Triumphs at Belmont, Too." *Washington Post*, 7 October 1969, D4.

"Owner of Mets Returns Too Late to See Heroes." *New York Times*, 30 September 1969, 52.

Smith, Red. "Saga of the Lady and the Star." *New York Times*, 10 May 1972, 57.

Wilson, M.J. "Joan Payson: Richest N.Y. Mets Fan." *Appleton Post-Crescent*, 12 October 1969, C-2.

Witker, Kristi. "Joan Payson 'Mother' of the Amazin' Mets." *The Lima News*, 27 October 1969, 13.

"Woman Now Official of Birmingham Club." *Washington Post*, 17 January 1930, 17.

Peacock, Lacey

James, Peter. "Pitcher Shows off Her 'Stuff' at National Ball Camp." *Daily Miner and News*, 6 March 2004, 21.

Peoria Red Wings

"Dixon to See Girls' Baseball Teams May 18." *Dixon Evening Telegraph*, 24 April 1951, 10.

"Girls' Baseball Set for 8 p.m. at Reynolds." *Dixon Evening Telegraph*, 17 May 1951.

Pepe, Maria

Grossfield, Stan. "Purpose Pitch." *The Boston Globe*, 19 August 2004, C1, C13.

"Little League." *Washington Post*, 19 March 2002.

"Little League Honors Female Pioneers." *Grand Rapids Press*, 22 August 2004.

Padawer, Ruth. "She Came to Play." *The Record* (Bergen County, N.J.), 23 November 2003.

Related Terms: Little League

Peppas, June

Sargent, Jim. "June Peppas and the All-American League: Helping the Kalamazoo Lassies Win the 1954 AAGPBL Championship." *The National Pastime*, January 2002.

Related Terms: AAGPBL, Kalamazoo Lassies

Perez, Vicky

Romine, Rich. "Perez Proving Baseball Is Not Just a Boys' Game." *Ventura County Star*, 16 May 2002.

Peterson, Marie A.

Quintanilla, Ray. "Marie A. Peterson; Once Owned Class A Baseball Team in Miami." *Chicago Tribune*, 15 August 1994.

Philadelphia Bobbies

"Ball Team of Girls Coming to Montana." *The Helena Daily Independent*, 24 September 1925, 9.

"Coming to Curwensville." *The Clearfield Progress* (Pennsylvania), 31 July 1926, 7.

"Girl Baseball Nine Invades Orient." *Atlanta Constitution*, 10 September 1925, 8.

"Girls' Baseball Loop Seeking D.C. Entry." *Washington Post*, 9 February 1926, 18.

"Girls' Team Plays Alex. Busmen." *Washington Post*, 22 May 1927, 28.

Gregorich, Barbara. "Stranded." *The North American Review*, May/August 1998, 4–9.

"One of the Best Girl Ball Teams in the Country." *Appleton Post-Crescent*, 15 May 1925, 21, and *Bismarck Tribune*, 20 May 1925, 6.

"Philadelphia Bobbies Bow at Culpeper, 20–0." *Washington Post*, 21 May 1927.

"Philadelphia Girls' Nine to Make Tour of Japan." *New York Times*, 13 August 1925, 17.

"Phillies Hire Girl Scout." *Elwein Daily Register*, 15 February 1946.

"Phillies Sign Girl Talent Hunter." *Waukesha Daily Freeman*, 15 February 1946, 9.

"U.S. Girls Stranded in Orient, Sent Home." *Washington Post*, 2 December 1925, 1.

"Womans Scout Signed by Philadelphia Phillies." *Walla Walla Union Bulletin*, 15 February 1946, 6.

Related Terms: Edith Houghton

Philadelphia Women's Baseball League

Feldman, Kathryn Levy. "A League of Her Own." *Pennsylvania Gazette*, 2 July 2005.

Lesmerises, Doug. "Women Trading Softball for Baseball in New League." *Delaware News Journal*, 29 June 2004.

O'Donnell, Eileen. "Covering All the Bases." *Philadelphia Inquirer*, 15 July 2005.

"Woman, Invading Man's Domain, Shown at Bat in a Game of Baseball Near Philadelphia." *Atlanta Constitution*, 13 June 1911, 11.

Pollitt (Deschaine), Alice

"AAGPBL Interview — Alice Pollitt." <http://thediamondangel.com/>.

Polytechnic Baseball

"Claim Championship." *Los Angeles Times*, 11 July 1909, V16.

"Girls' Baseball." *Los Angeles Times*, 3 June 1908, 16.

"Girls' Baseball Comes to Stay." *Los Angeles Times*, 6 June 1907, 114.

"Girls' Baseball Very Popular." *Los Angeles Times*, 15 December 1907, VIIII.

"Polytechnic Girls' Baseball Team Defeats Nine from Los Angeles High School." *Los Angeles Times*, 21 June 1907, 16.

Pomona High School

"Girls' Baseball." *Los Angeles Times*, 12 April 1908, VIIII.

Postema, Pamela

Allen, Maury. "Female Ump Eyes 'Big' Shot." *New York Post*, 28 July 1987, 82.

_____. "Lady Ump Gets Shot at Big Time." *New York Post*, 26 January 1988.

Baggarly, Andrew. "It's a New Ball Game." *Press Enterprise* (Riverside, California), 13 July 2003, C12.

Berkow, Ira. "What Is It Women Want?" *New York Times*, 21 March 1988, C4.

Boswell, Thomas. "Baseball: Lost Opportunity on Postema." *Washington Post*, 1 April 1988, G1, G5.

Brenna, Susan. "Hey, Ump! Are the Majors Ready for You?" *Newsday*, 24 March 1988, 3–5.

Connors, Mike. "Ump Brushes Off Rhubarbs as Routine." *Press Journal* (Vero Beach, Florida), 10 August 2002, B1.

Crasnick, Jerry. "Odd Hall Inducts New Group." *Baseball America*, 24 July–6 August 2000, 5.

Daley, Steve. "Back to the Drawing Board, CBS." *Chicago Tribune*, 25 March 1988, 5.

Durso, Joseph. "Umpire Awaiting Her Call from Majors." *New York Times*, 8 March 1988, A25.

Ettkin, Brian. "Lady in Blue." *Sarasota Herald-Tribune*, 2 July 2002, C1.

"Female Ump Eyes 'Big' Shot." *New York Times*, 28 July 1987, 82.

"Female Umpire Postema Sent Back to Minors." *The Daily Star*, 29 March 1988, 7.

Finn, Robin. "Female Umpire Awaits Favorable Call from Majors." *New York Times*, 27 July 1987, C4.

Garrity, John. "Waiting for the Call: Pam Postema, the Only Woman Umpire in Pro Baseball, Has a Chance to Make the Majors." *Sports Illustrated* 68 (14 March 1988), 26–27.

Gergen, Joe. "Will Postema's Apprenticeship Be Rewarded?" *The Sporting News*, 1 August 1988, 6.

Grow, Doug. "Baseball's Dreamkeeper Offers Opportunity to a Bitten Believer." *Star Tribune*, 16 November 1993, 03B.

Gurnick, Ken. "Postema to Test Firing." *The National Sports Daily*, 19 June 1990, 19.

Holtzman, Jerome. "Woman's Ready — Is Baseball?" *Chicago Tribune*, 28 July 1987, Sect. 4:3.

"It's Still Long Haul for Women in Baseball." *New York Times*, 27 July 1987, C4.

Keenan, Sandy. "The Umpress Strikes Back: Triple A Umpire Pam Postema Calls 'Em as She Sees 'Em, Not Hears 'Em." *Sports Illustrated*, 30 July 1984, 44–45.

Kellogg, Rick. "In a Man's World, a Woman Finds Her Place at Home Plate." *New York Times*, 21 July 1985, S3.

Kenda, Rich. "Ex-Ump Says Her Close Call Not in Vain." *USA Today Baseball Weekly*, 9–15 August 2000, 10.

"Lady Ump Gets Shot at Big Time." *New York Post*, 26 January 1988.

Lutz, Michael. "Knepper: Umpiring Isn't Woman's Work." *Times Union*, 16 March 1988, D1.

Michelini, Alex. "Ump Strikes Back." *New York Daily News*, 20 December 1991.

Nash, Jennie. "The Umpire Won't Strike Back." *New York Woman*, August 1988.

Newhouse, D. "Women in Blue: Pam Postema's Fancy Is Umpiring and She May Be Doing It in the Major Leagues Someday Soon." *Sporting News*, May 2, 1983, 49.

"Only Pro Woman Umpire Closer to the Major Leagues." *Troy Times Record*, 21 May 1983.

Pam Postema File. National Baseball Hall of Fame and Musuem, Cooperstown, New York.

"Pam Postema: On the Record. In This Exclusive Interview, She Talks About Her Sex Discrimination Charge and More." *Referee*, July 1990, 76–77.

"Postema Booted Out of Baseball." *New York Post*, 14 December 1989.

Postema, Pam. "Baseball Treating Women as Equals? Fat Chance." *The Sporting News*, 4 May 1992.

Postema, Pam and Gene Wojciechowski. *You've Got to Have Balls to Make It in This League: My Life as an Umpire*. New York: Simon and Schuster, 1992.

"Postema Heads Back to Minors." *Washington Post*, 29 March 1988, C3.

"Postema Loses." *New York Times*, 15 December 1989, A36.

"Postema Sent to Minors After Vacancies Filled." *The Frederick News-Post*, 29 March 1988, D-1.

"Postema Takes Umpiring One Step at a Time." *Albany Times Union*, 14 July 1977.

Reed, Susan and Lyndon Stambler. "The Umpire Strikes Back: Denied a Chance to Call 'Em as She Sees 'Em, Pam Postema Sues Baseball, Charging Sex Discrimination." *People Weekly*, 25 May 1992, 87–88.

Sell, David. "She's Waiting for a Major League Call." *Washington Post*, 16 August 1987, C1, C10.

"Umpire's 2d Chance." *New York Times*, 22 January 1989.

Vecsey, George. "Postema Blazed Trail for Somebody Else." *New York Times*, 17 December 1989, S3.

Verrell, Gordon. "Pam Postema Still Paying Her Dues." *The Sporting News*, 26 March 1988, 36.

Vieira, Al. "Female Ump a Natural at Hall of Fame." *Albany Times Union*, 28 July 1987.

Wahl, Grant. "Catching up with ... Baseball Umpire Pam Postema." *Sports Illustrated*, 28 April 1997.

_____. "The Lady Is an Ump." *Sports Illustrated*, 28 April 1997.

Willson, Brad. "Ohio Gal Breaks Somers Ump Barrier." *The Sporting News*, 8 January 1977, 47.

Wulf, Steve. "The Woman in Blue." *Sports Illustrated*, 3 August 1987.

Related Terms: Perry Lee Barber, Amanda Clement, Maria Cortesio, Theresa Cox, Bernice Gera, and Umpires

Pratt, Mary

Eligon, John. "Ageless Pros Gather to Renew Old Ties." *Grand Rapids Press*, 9 September 2001.

Fargan, Jessica. "Baseball Pioneer, Hall-of-Fame Lefty Pulls for Her Sox." *The Patriot Ledger*, 26 October 2004, 21.

Goulart, Karen. "Women's Baseball Star to Share Memories." *The Patriot Ledger*, 9 April 2005, 17.

Hawryluk, Margaret. "One Peach of a Player, Pratt Still on the Go." *The Enterprise*, 20 June 2005.

Tuoti, Gerard. "No Girl Should Be Denied." *The Patriot Ledger*, 11 June 2004, 15.

Webster, Katharine. "No-Hit Pitcher, at 75, Still in a League of Her Own." *Associated Press*, 3 June 1994.

Prison Baseball

"Girl Baseball Team Will Play Convicts." *Washington Post*, 6 August 1931, 4.

Psota, Kate

Borusas, Alge. "Honour Catches Young Ball Player by Surprise." *The Hamilton Spectator*, 23 November 2002, N07.

Spencer, Donna. "Canadians Show Skill." *Hamilton Spectator*, 13 July 2005, SP17.

Public Relations

Cornelius, Jennifer. "Women as Public Relations Practitioners in Major League Baseball: Why Has It Taken So Long?" BS Thesis, California Polytechnic State University, 1998.

Quigley, Narda

Feldman, Kathryn Levy. "A League of Her Own." *Pennsylvania Gazette*, 2 July 2005.

O'Donnell, Eileen. "Covering All the Bases." *Philadelphia Inquirer*, 15 July 2005.

Related Term: Philadelphia Women's Baseball League

Racine Belles

"All-American Girls in Two-Game Series Here." *The Newark Advocate and American Tribune*, 2 May 1950, 13.

Black, John H. "Racine Edges Lassies, 3–2, Win Tourney." *Racine Journal-Times*, 6 May 1947.

"Daisies, Belles Halted by Rain." *Washington Post*, 4 May 1951, B6.

"Daisies, Belles Play Twin Bill Tonight." *Washington Post*, 5 May 1951, 13.

"Daisies, Belles to Play Monday." *Washington Post*, 9 May 1951, 18.

"Daisies Play Belles Here." *Washington Post*, 13 May 1951, C5.

"Girls Practice in Alexandria." *Washington Post*, 30 April 1951, 9.

Golub, Rob. "Belles, Old Rivals Safe at Home." *Racine Journal Times*, 29 August 2000, 1A, 9A.

Michaelson, Mike. "Cross the Border to Sample the Attractions of Racine." *Daily Herald* (Illinois), 13 January 2002.

Racine Belles Records, 1946–49. Archives Division, State Historical Society of Wisconsin, Madison, Wisconsin.

"Racine Belles Take Lead in Girls' League." *Chicago Tribune*, 4 August 1946, A2.

"Racine Wins Girls' League 1946 Pennant." *Chicago Tribune*, 8 September 1946, A4.

"These Girls Could Play Ball." *Racine Journal Times*, 28 August 2000.

Related Terms: AAGPBL

Raduenz, Patricia "Patti"

Wells, Kelly. "Burlington Native Swinging Away for National Baseball Team." *Milwaukee Journal Sentinel*, 18 July 2004, 03Z.

Reds and Blues

"Women's Baseball Team Defeats the Men's— Recent Arrivals." *New York Times*, 6 August 1911, X4.

"Women's Baseball Teams Play a Closely Contested Game." *New York Times*, 21 August 1910, C11.

Reporters

Martinez, Michael. "Yanks' Sanderson Sidesteps Women in Locker Room." *New York Times*, 2 April 1991, B10.

Reviews

Bernard, April. "Women at Play." *Newsday*, 2 May 1993. Review of Barbara Gregorich's *Women at Play*.

Fosmoe, Margaret. "New Book Pitches History." *South Bend Tribune*, 3 July 2005.

Rhode Island Baseball

"Girls Were Out to Win Game." *Providence Journal*, 28 July 1902.

Harris, Rick. "Women, Baseball and Rhode Island." In *Rhode Island's Baseball Legacy, Vol. I*. Rhode Island: Rick Harris, 2001. Pp. 16–31.

Richard, Ruth

Wartenberg, Steve. "Girls Professional Baseball Star Still Shines Bright." *Times Leader*, 1 January 2004.

Richardson (Jessup), Marie

Snyder, Laura. "In a League of Her Own." *Maine Sun-Journal*, 26 September 1993, 1A, 7A.

Rochester Baseball

"Women Ball Players: A History of the Eighteen Female Ball Tossers Now in Rochester." *Union and Advertiser*, 12 August 1879, 2.

Rockford Peaches

Ayers, Diane. "No Cryin' on Camera: Rockford Peaches Share Their Memories of Pioneering League for Documentary." *Daily Herald* (Illinois), 18 June 2004.

"Colleens Open Season Tonight at Rockford." *Chicago Tribune*, 9 May 1948, A5.

"Daisies Beaten in 10th; Trail Rockford by 3–2." *Fort Wayne News-Sentinel*, 15 September 1950.

Day, Dick. "Peaches Wallop Daisies, 11–0, to Clinch Play-off Crown." *Rockford Register Republic,* 18 September 1950.

DeDoncker, Mike. "I'd Rather Play Ball Than Eat or Sleep." *Seattle Times*, 10 May 2003, D1.

_____. "Peaches Unite at Cubbies' Game Tonight." *Rockford Register Star*, 13 July 1996.

"Dixon Church Softball Loop Sponsors Game." *Dixon Evening Telegram*, 6 May 1952, 8.

"Dixon to See Girls' Baseball Teams May 18." *Dixon Evening Telegraph*, 24 April 1951, 10.

"15-hit Attack Heads Daisies 3–1 Defeat." *Rockford Morning Star*, 10 September 1950.

Gregorich, Barbara. "Women at the Plate." *South Bend Tribune*, 15 September 2002, F8.

Groves, Bob. "Hardball Pro Thrills Girls at Athletic Trophy Picnic." *The Record* (Bergen County, N.J.), 23 June 2002, A03.

Johnson, Susan. "A Peaches Fan for Life." In *Whatever It Takes: Women on Women's Sports*. Joli Sandoz and Joby Winans, eds. New York: Farrar, Straus and Giroux, 2000. Pp. 79–87.

Macy, Sue. *A Whole New Ball Game: The Story of the All American Girls Professional Baseball League*. New York: Henry Holt & Co., 1993.

Martin, Douglas. "Baseball Career Inspired Movie." *National Post* (Canada), 30 July 2002, S7.

McGraw, Patricia Babcock. "'Girls' to Relive the Good Old Days in Rockford." *Chicago Daily Herald*, 21 September 2002, 1.

Milne, Harry D. "Daisies Blank Peaches, 8–0, Square Series." *Rockford Morning Star*, 17 September 1950.

Olofson, Phil. "Daisies Square Rockford Series, 5–3; 5th Game Tonight." *Fort Wayne News-Sentinel*, 14 September 1950.

"Peaches, Kenosha Open Ball Series." *Dixon Evening Telegram*, 8 September 1948, 9.

"Peaches Play Colleens in Pair Today." *Chicago Tribune*, 16 May 1948, A4.

"Peaches Take 2nd Straight from Daisies, Erickson Pitches 7–2 Victory." *Rockford Morning Star*, 12 September 1950.

Pontanilla, Bernice. "Little Gets Display of Her Own." *Winnipeg Sun*, 30 July 2003, 44.

"Pretty Women Pro Baseball Teams to Clash at Stadium." *Zanesville Times Signal*, 10 May 1953, 2.

Redmond, Diane. "Preserving the Peaches." *The Rockford Register Star*, 8 September 1993, 1D.

"Teams Play First Rockford." *Rockford Register-Republic*, 5 June 1943.

Rogers (O'Neil), Agnes M.

"Agnes M. (O'Neil) Rogers." *Boston Globe*, 8 November 1985.

Romatowski, Jennifer "Jenny"

Barnas, Jo-Ann. "Romatowski: A Polish-American Pioneer." *Detroit Free Press*, 10 June 1999, 1D, 5D.

Chick, Bob. "HOF Honor No Biggie to Inductee." *Tampa Tribune*, 12 June 1999.

Jerzy, Buck. "Jenny Romatowski, in a League of Her Own." Biography, National Polish-American Sports Hall of Fame.

Rosenthal, Renee

Niedzielka, Amy. "Miami's League of Their Own." *The Miami Herald*, 9 August 1992.

Rotstart, Angelica

Crowley, Cathleen F. "Her Pitch Could Alter Male Only Ballgames." *Eagle-Tribune*, 26 March 2000.

Row, Catherine

Hagan, Kate. "Pitching for Sport." *Moorabbin Glen Eira Leader* (Australia), 27 March 2002, 401.

Ruhnke (Sanvitis), Irene

Craven, Karen. "Iren Ruhnke Sanvitis; Played Baseball in '40s." *Chicago Tribune*, 16 July 1999.

Russell, Debbie

McHugh, Whitney. "Ozark Mom Only Alabama Player on American Baseball Team." *The Dothan Eagle*, 13 October 2003.

St. Louis Black Bronchos

"The Black Broncho Female Baseball Club." *Indianapolis Freeman*, 22 April 1911.

DeBono, Paul. "The St. Louis Black Bronchos." *American Visions*, June/July 1993, 26–27.

"Leading Baseball Clubs." *Indianapolis Freeman*, 18 February 1911.

"Our Women to Play Baseball." *Indianapolis Freeman*, 2 April 1910.

"St. Louis Female Baseball Club Plays." *Indianapolis Freeman*, 16 April 1910.

Samonds, Shereen

Crasnick, Jerry. "GM Has Her Eyes on Bigger Game." *Denver Post*, 27 June 1994, D-8.

Sams, Doris

"No-Hitter." *Record-Eagle* (Michigan), 13 May 1948, 13.

"She Can Beat Boys in Half-Dozen Games." *Washington Post*, 25 September 1938, PY1.

San Jose Spitfires

Learmonth, Michael. "Ruthless Babes." *Metroactive*, 21–27 August 1997, 1–13.

Related terms: Ladies Professional Baseball League

Sands (Ferguson), Sara "Salty"

Kennedy, Natalie. "Former Girls League Pro Still Goes to Bat for Women's Sports." *Wellsboro Gazette*, 1 May 1996, 6.

Tobias, Jessica. "McComb and Ferguson Were Pioneers in Women's Sports." *Williamsport Sun-Gazette*, 21 July 2004, C-1, C-3.

Santos, Susie

Salvo, Jen. "Santos Pursues Field of Dreams." <*www. Townonline*>, 30 August 2002.

Satriano, Gina

Araton, Harvey. "The Trials of a Pro Female Pitcher." *New York Times*, 15 June 1995, B16.

Crasnick, Jerry. "Satriano Still Breaking Ground at Old Ballpark." *Denver Post*, 27 June 1994, D-7.

Farrell, Mary H.J. "Say It Ain't So." *People Weekly*, 6 June 1994, 63–65.

Higbie, Andrea. "The Lady Is a Pitcher (and a Prosecutor)." *New York Times*, 4 September 1994, 30.

Jacobson, Steve. "Living the Dream." *Newsday*, 8 March 1994.

Schaffrath, Pamela

Van Dyck, Dave. "Diamonds in the Rough." *Chicago Sun-Times*, 27 March 1994, 20B.

Schillace (Donahoe), Claire

Estrada, Louie. "Claire Donahoe, Baseball Player in Women's League of 1940s, Dies." *Washington Post*, 23 January 1999, B09.

Schofield, June Rose

Hauch, Valerie. "June Rose Schofield, Ballplayer in Storied Women's League." *Toronto Star*, 12 July 2002, BO4.

Schott, Marge

"Baseball: Official Says Schott Way Behind on Stadium Rent." *Orange County Register*, 7 March 1996.

"Baseball: Reds Owner Schott in Money Dispute with City." *Orange County Register*, 8 March 1996.

Bass, Mike. *Marge Schott: Unleashed*. Champaign, Illinois: Sagamore Publishing, 1993.

Brown, Tony. "Tony Brown's Journal: Do You Have a Moral Compass?" *Cleveland Call and Post*, 10 December 1992, 4A.

Browne, Wayne. "Philadelphia Sports: Racism at the Top?" *Philadelphia Tribune*, 11 December 1992, 1A.

Capouya, John. "Queen of the Riverfront: Marge Schott Loves Her Reds, Her Dog, and Cincinnati. Everything Else Should Get Out of the Way." *Sport* 79 (July 1988), 28–32, 37.

"Cincinnati Reds." *USA Today Baseball Weekly*, 16 November 1994, 16.

"Cincy Owner Schott Apologizes for Slur." *Jet*, 28 December 1992, 51.

Crasnick, Jerry. "Reds' Schott Stirs Up Trouble Again." *Baseball America*, 10 December 1991, 11.

Crayton, Grover C. "In Black and White: Cincy's Marge Schott, Demeaning Team Logos, Same Swatch of Cloth." *Cleveland Call and Post*, 10 December 1992, 5B.

Cunningham, Bill. "Beware Thought Police: Any of Us Could Be Next." *USA Today Baseball Weekly*, 10 February 1993, 5.

Davis, Ed. "Baseball Owner's Racial Slurs Draw Anger." *Pittsburgh Courier*, 2 December 1992, A1.

Davis, Samuel. "Cincinnati Reds Owner Defends Racist Remarks." *Philadelphia Tribune*, 4 December 1992, 8-C.

Dunnavant, Keith. "Reds Partners Blew Shot to Make Legal History." *National Sports Daily*, 21 May 1991, 12.

Edes, Gordon. "Running the Reds, Schott Says, Is as Easy as Getting Hair off a Dog." *National Sports Daily*, 4 March 1991, 39.

"Editorial: Baseball Race Problems Run Deeper Than Schott." *Philadelphia Tribune*, 4 December 1992, 6-A.

Farrell, Charles. "Schott Should Stay." *Washington Afro-American*, 12 December 1992, A11.

"Former Reds Owner in Jewish Hospital." *Cincinnati Post*, 3 August 2002, 5B.

Gergen, Joe. "Former Reds Owner Marge Schott, 75." *Newsday*, 3 March 2004, A52.

Goldstein, Richard. "Marge Schott, Eccentric Owner of the Reds, Dies at 75." *New York Times*, 3 March 2004, C14.

_____. "Marge Schott: Reds' Savior, but out of Step with Time, Baseball." *International Herald Tribune*, 4 March 2004.

Gura, Bob. "Big Marge Goes Unshot." *Hyde Park Citizen*, 11 February 1993, 28.

_____. "Marge, Marge, Marge." *Hyde Park Citizen*, 6 December 1992, 20.

"It's Sad That Marge Isn't in Charge." *Cincinnati Post*, 9 April 2001, 11A.

"It's Still Long Haul for Women in Baseball." *New York Times*, 27 July 1987, C4.

Jackson, Jesse. "Schott Neither Martyr nor Baseball's Scapegoat." *USA Today Baseball Weekly*, 10 February 1993, 5.

Jackson, Tony. "Marge Blasts Jr. Deal." *Cincinnati Post*, 2 August 2003, B5.

Jacob, John E. "Racism Takes a Heavy Toll on the Nation's Economy." *Los Angeles Daily Journal*, 21 April 1993, 6.

Jeffries, Eddie. "Marge 'Schott' Down by Executive Committee: Fined, Suspended." *Pittsburgh Courier*, 6 February 1993, A-1.

"Jesse, Eric Davis Slam Slurs by Schott." *Jet*, 14 December 1992, 48.

Kaplan, David A. "Congress Takes a Schott." *Newsweek*, 14 December 1992, 67.

Kay, Joe. "Schott Never at a Loss for Words: Ex-owner of the Reds, Who Died at Age 75, Always Controversial — but Won a World Series." *Vancouver Sun*, 3 March 2004, F1.

Kirshenbaum, Jerry. "Block That Schott." *Sports Illustrated*, 30 November 1992, 32.

Klemesrud, Judy. "Marge Schott, Cincinnati Booster, Is Rooting for Her Home Team." *New York Times*, 8 March 1985, B8.

Lacy, Sam. "Baseball as Usual: Problem? Form a Committee." *Richmond Afro American,* 12 December 1992, B6.

"Ladies of the Club." *New York Times*, 17 January 1985, B12.

Lawes, Rick. "Reds' Schott Defends Right to Run Her Team." *USA Today Baseball Weekly*, 27 January 1993, 27.

_____. "Schott's Plot Concerns Players." *USA Today Baseball Weekly*, 7 October 1992, 20.

Lawson, Earl. "Schott Purchases Control of Reds." *The Sporting News*, 7 January 1985, 36.

Leo, John. "Baseball Takes a Schott." *U.S. News and Weekly Report*, 15 February 1993, 32.

Lipsyte, Robert. "Sad Refrain of Schott's Rhythm and Blues." *New York Times*, 12 May 1996, S11.

Livingston, Jeffery C. "Marge Schott: Unleashed." *Nine: A Journal of Baseball History and Social Policy Perspectives*, Spring 1994, 351–354.

Loewenheim, Francis. "Major League Woman: Marge Schott." *Harper's Bazaar* September 1985, 291.

McClelland, Sean. "Former Red Owner Was Scorned by Many: Marge Schott, 1928–2004." *The Palm Beach Post*, 3 March 2004.

McCoy, Hal. "Schott, Schottzie Being Criticized." *The Sporting News*, 18 February 1995, 33.

_____. "Schott Takes Steps to Trim Expenses." *The Sporting News*, 17 June 1984, 25.

_____. "Schott Viewed Life Through Narrow Prism." *Dayton Daily News*, 3 March 2004, B7.

McGee, Todd. "Pot Schotts— Marge Bashing Getting Out of Hand." *Reds Report,* January 1994, 3.

"Major League Baseball Will Investigate Schott's Earring Remark." *USA Today Baseball Weekly*, 25 May 1994, 18.

"On Marge Schott ... Owners Must Oppose Racism." *Los Angeles Daily Journal*, 21 December 1992, 68.

"Marge Schott Stirred Controversy with Racial Remarks, Tough Talk." *Hamilton Spectator*, 3 March 2004, SP10.

"Move Over Rush, Marge Is on the Air." *Reds Report,* April 1994, 6.

Myers, Jim. "Odds Are Stacked Against Minorities." *USA Today Baseball Weekly*, 10 February 1993, 4.

Nuwer, Hank. "Marge Schott: Queen of Diamonds." *Modern Maturity*, June/July 1986, 40ff.

O'Brien, Richard. "Block That Schott." *Sports Illustrated*, 7 December 1992, 15–16.

"An Opening Day Tradition Draws to Close in Cincinnati." *USA Today Baseball Weekly*, 30 November 1994, 7.

Pascarelli, Peter. "End of the Line?" *USA Today Baseball Weekly*, 12–18 June 1996, 3.

Perry, Kimball. "Marge, Reds Settle Lawsuit, Both Sides Keep Ticket Deal Secret." *Cincinnati Post*, 24 July 2003, A8.

Plummer, William and Civia Tamarkin. "Big Red Embarrassment." *People Weekly*, 14 December 1992, 79.

Rains, Rob. "Dog Can Romp at Ballpark." *USA Today Baseball Weekly*, 10 February 1993, 4.

_____. "On-field, Reds the Same." *USA Today Baseball Weekly*, 10 February 1993, 4.

_____. "Reds CEO Uncharacteristically Quiet Back at Home." *USA Today Baseball Weekly*, 1 December 1993, 14.

_____. "Schott Committee Seeks Compromise." *USA Today Weekly*, 16 December 1992, 9.

"Reds Are Bought by a Cincinnatian." *New York Times*, 22 December 1984, 19.

Reilly, Rick. "Heaven Help Marge Schott. The Reds' Owner, Long Ago Reduced to a Life of Loneliness, Has Further Isolated Herself by Her Spiteful Words and Witless Deeds." *Sports Illustrated*, 20 May 1996, 72–87.

Rhoden, William. "Game Stays; Ballplayers Come and Go." *New York Times,* 17 September 1994, 33ff.

Ricigliano, Mike. "Marge Schott's Pulling Out All the Stops." *USA Today Baseball Weekly*, 17 May 1995, 5.

_____. "Salary Analogy Proves Players Not Reality Based." *USA Today Baseball Weekly*, 14 December 1994, 10.

Ringolsby, Tracy. "Should Marge Schott Sell the Reds? Schott Often Is on Hot Seat." *Rocky Mountain News*, 3 April 1997.

_____. "While We're At It, Is That Dog Really Necessary?" *Inside Sports,* February 1991, 40.

Sandomir, Richard. "Gathering by River and Zoo." *Sports Inc.*, 18 July 1988, 46.

"Schott Banned by Officials from Riverfront Stadium." *New York Times*, 18 July 1996, B11.

"Schott Building Unveiled." *Cincinnati Post*, 5 April 2001, 15A.

"Schott Out of the Hospital." *Cincinnati Post*, 7 August 2002, 5B.

"Schott's Seats." *Cincinnati Post*, 5 February 2003, A2.

"Schott: They're Trying to Get Me." *Star Tribune*, 15 May 1996.

Schmetzer, Mark. "The Clash: New Ballpark Debate Has Everyone Asking, Should Reds Stay or Should Reds Go?" *Reds Report*, May 1994, 16.

_____. "Déjà vu/Reds Like to Open So Much, They Do It Twice." Reds Report, May 1994, 10.

_____. "Schottzie Stay!" *Reds Report*, April 1993, 10.

Shannon, Mike. "Marge Schott." In *Tales from the Ballpark*. Lincolnwood, Illinois: Contemporary Books, 1999.

Solomon, Jolie. "Cincinnati Reds' Marge Schott Faces Problems Other Than Baseball Scores." *Wall Street Journal*, 6 June 1986, 18.

Stathoplos, Demmie. "Marge Has Them Eating Out of Her Hand." *Sports Illustrated*, 15 July 1985, 42.

Sullivan, Patricia. "Controversial Cincinnati Reds Owner Marge Schott." *Washington Post,* 3 March 2004.

Sullivan, Tim. "C'mon Bud, Make Marge Sell the Team." *Cincinnati Enquirer*, 8 May 1996.

Teaford, Elliott. "Marge Schott, 75; Ex-Cincinnati Reds Owner." *Los Angeles Times*, 3 March 2004, B10.

Teepen, Tom. "Penalty Against Schott Doesn't Infringe Speech Rights." *Los Angeles Daily Journal*, 18 February 1993, 6.

Thomas, Stephen and Amy Goehner. "Baseball Punishes Marge Schott." *Sports Illustrated for Kids,* April 1993, 12.

"Try, Try Again." *Reds Report,* December 1993, 5.

Van Biema, David. "A Millonairess Named Marge Proves a Schott in the Arm for the Dogged Cincinnati Reds." *People Weekly* 24 (22 July 1985), 99–100.

Verducci, Tom. "In Search of the Real Marge." *Newsday,* 4 December 1992.

Warren, Rick. "From the Bleachers: 1992 and Racism Back to Its Peak." *Sacramento Observer,* 9 December 1992, D2.

_____. "Is Schott the Only Racist?" *Sacamento Observer,* 2 December 1992, D3.

"Was It Just a Schott in the Dark?" *Indianapolis Recorder,* 5 December 1992, A2.

Wehr, Lindsay. "Kentucky Club Named After Schott." *Cincinnati Post,* 5 July 2001, 8A.

Wendel, Tim. "Difficult Decisions Await Reds' Schott." *USA Today Baseball Weekly,* 3 November 1993, 14.

Weston, Robert. "Schott Era Ends in Cincinnati." *AAP Sports News,* 23 April 1999.

White, Paul. "Schott and Co. Visit Champion Affiliate." *USA Today Baseball Weekly,* 21 September 1994, 26.

_____. "Star-crossed Lover's Lament." *USA Today Baseball Weekly,* 10 February 1993, 2.

"Will Alleged 'Nigger' Slur by White Owner of Cincinnati Reds Hurt Baseball?" *Jet,* 21 December 1992, 52.

Williams, Pete. "Reds' Schott Under Fire." *USA Today Baseball Weekly,* 2 December 1992, 3.

_____. "A Winning Team Should Help to Blow All Turmoil Out of Town." *USA Today Baseball Weekly,* 24 February 1993, 30.

Wright, Barnett. "Baseball Bigot? Lawsuit Discloses Racist, Ethnic Slurs." *Philadelphia Tribune,* 4 December 1992, 1-A.

Schroeder, Dorothy

"A Thrilling Time." *South Bend Tribune,* 22 September 2002, F8.

Schueler, Carey

Ruda, Mark. "Daughter of White Sox GM is First Woman Drafted." *Baseball America,* 11 July 1993, 2.

Scott, Patricia

"Diamond to Honor Patricia Scott." *The Kentucky Post,* 16 March 2002.

Flynn, Terry. "Kentucky Field Named for Former Pro Female Pitcher." *Cincinnati Enquirer,* 21 March 2002.

Reis, Jim. "This Daisy Was a Winner on the Mound." *The Kentucky Post,* 26 May 2003.

Selig-Prieb, Wendy

Baggot, Andy. "Selig-Prieb's Move Came at Right Time." *Wisconsin State Journal,* 17 August 1999.

Bamberger, Michael. "Brewers Executive 1st Woman on Owners' Negotiating Team." *Tribune News Service,* 24 August 1994.

"Baseball: Brewers Make Changes to Front Office." *Sports Network,* 25 September 2002.

Dabe, Christopher. "Marquette U. Keeps Brewers' CEO Tied to Milwaukee Roots." *University Wire,* 5 May 1999.

Foster, Kathy. "Selig-Prieb Has Passion for Baseball." *Wisconsin State Journal,* 2 March 2000.

Mulhern, Tom. "Brewers Standing Pat So far: Wendy Selig-Prieb Isn't Overly Concerned Her Team Has Failed to Pick up Anyone This Offseason." *Wisconsin State Journal,* 25 December 2001.

Riverside, Maureen Delaney. "The New Power Hitters—Women Gain off Field Too." *Capital Times,* 20 July 1999.

"Selig-Prieb Admits to Disappointment." *Wisconsin State Journal,* 14 August 2001.

"Selig-Prieb Named Brewers CEO." *UPI,* 4 August 1998.

"Selig-Prieb Not Fooling Anyone." *Wisconsin State Journal,* 21 September 1999.

"Selig-Prieb: Project Will Go On as Planned." *Capital Times,* 16 July 1999.

"Selig's Daughter Prepared to Take Control of Brewers." *Capital Times,* n.d.

Sheldon, Carol

Smiley, Susan. "Read All About It: Sheldon in Hall." *Detroit Free Press,* 8 January 2004.

Shively, Twila

"Twila Shively Leads Hitters in Girls League." *Chicago Tribune,* 23 June 1946, A3.

Sickinger, Alexandra

Harris, Merv. "Playing Hardball with Gender Equity." *San Francisco Examiner,* 28 April 1995.

"Local Athlete Makes USA Team." *Pacifica Tribune,* 15 July 2004.

Siegal (Warren), Justine

Alexander, Susanne M. "New Baseball League Has Women on Deck." *Crain's Cleveland Business,* 29 May 2000.

Guth, Douglas J. "Mothers' Day, a Launching Pad to Expand Female Athletes' Scope: Justine Warren Believes Women's Baseball League Will Hit a Home run." *Cleveland Jewish News,* 12 May 2000.

Jacobs, Daniel G. "A League of Her Own." *Small Business News,* June 2000, 7.

McLean, Steve. "For the Love of the Game." *The Toronto Sun,* 18 June 2005, S16.

Pulga, Allen. "Talented Elite Girls' Baseball Team a Shock to the Boys." *Hamilton Spectator,* 14 August 2004, SP08.

Simons, Sharon

"Woman is Major Owner of Rangers Baseball Team." *Newport Daily News,* 1 June 1974, 5.

Smith, Helen Lucille "Gig"

Sargent, Jim. "Helen Smith." *Sports Collectors Digest,* 20 September 1996, 152–54.

Smith, Helen. File and Questionnaire. National

Baseball Hall of Fame and Library, Cooperstown, New York.

Smith, Janet Marie

Masello, David. "Playing the Field: Janet Marie Smith, Vice President of New-Stadium Planning and Development for the Baltimore Orioles, Takes a Swing at Downtown Redevelopment." *Architectural Record* 178 (October 1990), 45–46.

Smith, Janet Marie. "Putting Together a Winning Team: Janet Marie Smith of the Baltimore Orioles Managing a Major League Project." *Working Woman*, October 1992, 28–30.

Related terms: Management Personnel

Smithfield Baseball

"Girls Want Games." *Washington Post*, 18 June 1926, 17.

Smythe, Katy

Ryan, Kevin. "Dream Come True." *Ann Arbor News*, 2 July 2001, D1, D3.

_____. "Women's Baseball Grows." *Ann Arbor News*, 2 July 2001, D3.

South Bend Blue Sox

"Daisies, Blue Sox Divide Two Games." *The Lima News*, 21 May 1949, 3.

"Daisy-Blue Sox Scrap Set for Saturday Night." *The Herald Press* (Michigan), 21 August 1953, 12.

"Field of Dreams." *South Bend Tribune*, 29 September 2002, F8.

Gregorich, Barbara. "Women in Baseball." *Traces of Indiana and Midwestern History*, Spring 1993.

Halberstein, Joe. "Girls Baseball Comes to Lima Thursday." *The Lima News*, 19 May 1949, 34.

_____. "Twin Bill Booked Friday Night Between Girls Baseball Teams." *The Lima News*, 20 May 1949.

Haugh, David. "Breaking a Sweat, Breaking a Barrier." *South Bend Tribune*, 28 September 2002, B1.

Kovach, John. *Benders: Tales from South Bend's Baseball Past*. South Bend, Indiana: Greenstocking Press, 1987.

"Manager of South Bend Blue Sox Holds Major League Record for Shortstops." *The Lima News*, 18 May 1949, 17.

O'Connor, Michael. "Battle of the Sexes; Diamond Club Isn't Just for Men." *The Boston Herald*, 23 June 2003, B30.

"Pretty Women Pro Baseball Teams to Clash at Stadium." *Zanesville Times Signal*, 10 May 1953, 2.

"Professional Gals to Play Baseball Game Here May 13." *Zanesville Times Signal*, 8 May 1953.

"Remembering South Bend's Playland Park." *South Bend Tribune*, 27 July 2003, F8.

"Top Gals Teams Here Tomorrow." *The Signal*, 12 May 1953, 14.

"Women's Baseball Tourney Set." *South Bend Tribune*, 29 August 2002, B5.

Sportswriters

Casey, Ed. "When Male Athletes, Female Writers Collide." *The Sunday Capital*, 7 October 1990, A15.

Springfield Sallies

"All-American Girl Baseball Players Clash at Stadium." *Syracuse Herald-Journal*, 23 August 1950, 35.

"All-American Girls Offer Sport Treat." *Syracuse Herald-American*, 20 August 1950, 50.

"Colleens and Sallies Steam Up for Final Thriller Here Tonight." *The Austin Statesman*, 6 July 1949.

"Colleens, Sallies to Play Here." *Washington Post*, 30 July 1950, C2.

"Girls Teams Play at Disch Tonight: Colleens, Sallies Invade Austin for Two Day Stand." *The American Statesman*, 5 July 1949.

"Glamour Baseball Invades Stadium at 8:30 Tonight." *Portland Press Herald*, 14 August 1950.

"Sallies Beat Colleens, 6–4, in Fund Game." *The Post-Standard*, 24 August 1950, 17.

"Springfield Nips Colleens, 5–3." *The Austin American*, 7 July 1949.

Related Terms: AAGPBL, Chicago Colleens

Sroczynski, Debra

Bickelhaupt, Susan. "Diamonds in the Rough." *Boston Globe*, 7 August 2002.

Forsberg, Chris. "Facing World Competition, They Played Hardball." *Boston Globe*, 18 July 2001.

Turner, Julia. "What's My Sport?" *Sports Illustrated for Women*, 1 October 2001.

Related Terms: Boston Blue Sox

Stageman (Roberts), Donna

Bright, Carolynn. "Helena Woman's Brief Pro Career Ends in Hall of Fame." *Associated Press*, 18 November 2003.

Staten Island

"Amateurs in Skirts on Baseball Field." *New York Times*, 2 October 1904, 7.

Steele, Joyce

Keeler, David. "Film Debut Puts Steele in League of Her Own." *The Rocket-Courier*, 13 February 1992.

_____. "Lovelton Woman to Appear in Hollywood Film." *The Rocket-Courier*, 4 July 1991, 1, 6.

Stephens, Ruby Lee

"Ex-Standout in Women's League Dies," *The Tampa Tribune*, 30 March 1996.

Steuert (Armstrong), Beverly

Groves, Bob. "Hardball Pro Thrills Girls at Athletic Trophy Picnic." *The Record* (Bergen County, New Jersey), 23 June 2002, A03.

Stolze, Dorothy

Chapin, Dwight. "Dorothy Stolze — Played 7 Years in Baseball League." *San Francisco Chronicle*, 24 July 2003, A22.

Stone (Alberga), Marcenia Lyle "Toni"

Berlage, Gai. "Robinson's Legacy: Black Women and Negro Baseball." In *Cooperstown Symposium on Baseball and American Culture*. Jefferson, North Carolina: McFarland, 1997. 123–135.

_____. "Stone, Toni." In *Encyclopedia of Ethnicity and Sports in the United States of America*, George Kirsch et al., eds. Westport, Connecticut: Greenwood Press, 2000. Pp. 443, 444.

"The Black Woman in Pro Baseball, Toni Stone!" *The African American Registry*, n.d.

"Clowns, Barons Play Tonight at Griffith." *Washington Post*, 14 July 1953.

"Clowns Play Here Tonight." *Washington Post*, 1 September 1953, 17.

"Clowns Play Here Tuesday, Have Girl Star." *Washington Post*, 12 July 1953, C2.

"Clowns Play Here Tuesday Night Against Memphis." *Washington Post*, 30 August 1953, C2.

"Clowns Sell Girl Player, Toni Stone to Monarchs Then Hire 2 Other Girls." *The Call*, 12 March 1954, 12.

"Clowns Sell Toni Stone, Sign New Female Star." *Michigan Chronicle*, 13 March 1954.

"Clowns Sign Two Top Sophomores." *The Call*, 20 March 1953, 10.

Dallas, Bill. "Female Players Here July 19 in Negro League Twin Bill." *Philadelphia Evening Bulletin*, 7 July 1953.

Dubay, Diane. "From St. Paul Playgrounds to Big Leagues, Stone Always Loved Baseball." *Minnesota Women's Press*, 3–16 February 1988.

Egan, Erin. "Toni Stone Was One of the Only Women Ever to Play with Men." *Sports Illustrated for Kids*, April 1994, 26.

"Enriching Ourselves by Honoring Our Heroes." *Minnesota Women's Press*, 17 February–1 March 1988, 4.

"Female Player Remembered by Major League Baseball." *Jet*, 1 June 1992, 50.

Forman, Ross. "Black Woman Was Alone in Own League." *USA Today*, 2 July 1992, 2C.

_____. "Marcenia 'Toni' Stone: Veteran of Negro Leagues." *Sports Collectors Digest*, 7 August 1992, 177.

Gregorich, Barbara. "1954 Toni Stone." *American Visions*, June–July 1993, 27.

_____. *Women at Play*. New York: Harcourt and Brace, 1993.

Grow, Doug. "Baseball Pioneer Never Listened to Naysayers." *Minneapolis Star Tribune*, 31 January 1997, 2B.

_____. "League of Her Own: Tomboy Stone Dead at Age 75." *Minneapolis Star Tribune*, 5 November 1996, B8.

Hawley, David. "Toni Stone, a Baseball 'Tomboy' Among Men, Dies." *Minnesota Pioneer Press*, 5 November 1996, 1A, 8A.

"Honoring a Local Hero." *Minnesota Women's Press*, 14–27 March 1990.

Keenan, Sandy. "Stone Had a Ball." *Newsday*, 5 October 1993.

"Lady Ball Player." *Ebony*, July 1953, 47–50, 52–53.

"Monarchs, Clowns Play Here Next Week." *Washington Post*, 5 July 1954, 12.

"Monarchs Face Clowns Tuesday." *Washington Post*, 12 July 1954, 13.

"Monarchs Play Clowns Tonight." *Washington Post*, 13 July 1954, 24.

Nance, Rahkia. "Foster Little-Known Force in Negro League." *Capital Outlook*, 3–9 January 2002.

"Negro Girl Second Baseman Will Oppose Rainbows Tuesday Night." *Council Bluffs Non Pareil*, June 1950.

Nelson, John. "Toni Stone." *AP Sports*, 4 October 1993, 42.

Obituary. *New York Times*, 10 November 1996.

Prater, Derek. "Negro Leagues of Their Own." *The Kansas City Star*, 28 July 2002, C1, C8.

Riley, James A. "Lady at the Bat." *The Diamond*, March/April 1994, 23ff.

"She Wasn't Afraid to Swing for the Fences." *Minneapolis Star Tribune*, 6 March 1990, 1A, 6A.

Smith, Claire. "Belated Tribute to Baseball's Negro Leagues." *The New York Times*, 13 August 1991, A1, B9.

"Speaking of People: Lady Ball Player on Male Team." *Ebony*, 1 September 1950, 4.

Thomas, Robert McG. Jr. "Toni Stone, 75, First Woman to Play Big-League Ball." *New York Times*, 10 November 1996, 47.

Thomas, Ron. "Baseball Pioneer Looks Back." *San Francisco Chronicle*, 23 August 1991, C3.

_____. "Baseball's 'Intruder' Loved Game." *San Francisco Chronicle*, 23 August 1991.

Toni Stone Collection. Minnesota Historical Society, St. Paul, Minnesota.

Voorhees, Deborah. "Swing Times." *The Dallas Morning News*, 17 February 1999.

Weaver, Mike. "Female Player Was a Minority of 1." *San Jose Mercury News*, 11 August 1991, 1D, 3D.

"Woman Player Says She Can 'Take Care of Self' in Game." *Ebony*, June/July 1953, 48.

"Woman Who Shatters Gender Barrier Dies." *Los Angeles Daily News*, 6 November 1996.

Related Terms: Negro Leagues

Sun Sox

Bisher, Furman. "Girls of Summer: An All-Female Lineup for the Sun Sox." *The Sporting News*, 1 October 1984, 7.

"A Diamond These Girls' Best Friend." *Daily Star*, 18 September 1984.

"Women Get Their Shot in Baseball." *Times Union*, 18 September 1984.

Sunny, Stacy

Farrell, Joe. "Sports Talk." *The Record* (Bergen County, N.J.), 29 May 1994.

Fornoff, Susan. "Playing Hardball." *The Sporting News*, 30 May 1994.

Lister, Valerie. "Baseball Pro Says Push the Door Open, Have Fun." *USA Today*, 4 June 1996.

Related Terms: Colorado Silver Bullets

Terry, Doris

Levine, Susan. "Still Throwing the Heat." *Washington Post*, 3 June 2004, T03.

Theses and Dissertations

Cornelius, Jennifer. *Women as Public Relations Practitioners in Major League Baseball: Why It Has*

Taken So Long. BS Thesis, California Polytechnic State University, 1998.

Garrett, Linda Andrews. *A Comparison of Role Perceptions Held by Females Participating in Little League Baseball, Girls Softball and Non-participants in the Lehigh Region of Pennsylvania.* Ph.D. Dissertation, East Stroudsburg State College, 1977.

Hensley, Beth H. *Older Women's Life Choices and Development after Playing Professional Baseball.* Ph.D. Dissertation, University of Cincinnati, 1995.

Isaacson, Pamela. *Belles of the Ball.* Honors Thesis. Brandeis University, 1998.

Schnaidt, Vanessa Keilson. *Representations and Reality: Constructions of Gender in the All-American Girls Professional Baseball League.* BA Thesis, Scripps College, 2003.

Wilson, Brenda. *Nicknaming Practices of Women in a Nontraditional Occupation: Female Professional Baseball Players.* MA Thesis, University of North Carolina at Greensboro, 1991.

Thomas (Gera), Bernice

Bernice Gera Collection. Special Collections Library. Indiana University of Pennsylvania, Indiana, Pennsylvania.

"Bernice Gera, First Woman Umpire in Pro Ball." *Newsday,* 25 September 1992.

Ettkin, Brian. "Lady in Blue." *Sarasota Herald-Tribune,* 2 July 2002, C1.

Farrell, William E. "Court Rules Woman May Be a Baseball Umpire." *New York Times,* 14 January 1972, 1.

"Woman Ump Shows Form in Court." *Washington Post,* 24 October 1969, D4.

"Woman Wins Three Year Fight to Become Baseball Ump." *Washington Post,* 26 July 1969, C2.

(Thompson) Griffin, Viola "Tommy"

Trubiano, Ernie. "Griffin, S.C. Hall of Fame Inductee, Remembers Women's Baseball." *The Columbia State,* 28 April 1997.

Tournaments

Clarke, Elizabeth. "Nothing Soft about the Play at South Florida Diamond Classic." *The Palm Beach Post,* 25 April 1999.

"Hurricane Dennis Interrupts Women's Baseball Series Between Canada and Cuba." *Canadian Press,* 10 July 2005.

Trezza, Betty

Pontanilla, Bernice. "Little Gets Display of Her Own." *Winnipeg Sun,* 30 July 2003, 44.

Related Terms: Olive (Bend) Little, AAGPBL

Tucker, Elizabeth

Tucker, Colleens' Hurler, Tops Girls Baseball Hitters." *Chicago Tribune,* 18 July 1948, B3.

Turbitt-Baker, Lisa

Radley, Scott. "From T-Ball to World Championships." *Hamilton Spectator,* 20 November 2004, SP04.

Related Terms: Umpires

Twardzik, Nellie

"Girl Baseball Star Stirs School Wrangle by Her Presence on Bay State Boys' Team." *New York Times,* 18 March 1936, 31.

Umpires

Allen, Lee. "God Speed to the Woman Umpire." *The Sporting News,* 25 May 1968, 6.

Barber, Perry Lee. "The Men (and Women) in Blue." *International Baseball Rundown,* March 1996, 12, 20.

Baxter, Kevin. "The Lady Is an Ump." *The Miami Herald,* 5 August 2002.

Berlage, Gai Ingham. "Women Umpires as Mirrors of Gender Roles." *The National Pastime: A Review of Baseball.* Society for American Baseball Research, Summer 1994, 34–28.

Boswell, Thomas. "Baseball: Lost Opportunity on Postema." *Washington Post,* 1 April 1988, G1, G5.

"Connie Says Women Could Be Umpires." *South Bend Tribune,* 9 August 1949.

Corrigan, Patricia. "In the Field of Dreams, a Would-Be Umpire Takes Strike Three Looking." *St. Louis Post-Dispatch,* 24 July 1999.

Durso, Joseph. "Umpire Awaiting Her Call from Majors." *New York Times,* 8 March 1988, A25.

Dus, Julie. "More Than a Minor Accomplishment." <Referee.com>, 28 April 2004.

Finn, Robin. "Female Umpire Awaits Favorable Call from Majors." *New York Times,* 27 July 1987, C4.

Garrity, John. "Waiting for the Call: Pam Postema, the Only Woman Umpire in Pro Baseball, Has a Chance to Make the Majors." *Sports Illustrated* 68 (14 March 1988), 26–27.

"Girl Is Strict Umpire." *Washington Post,* 17 June 1906, S3.

Grant, Rubin. "Female Umpire Makes First Appearance." *Birmingham Post-Herald,* 4 June 1988, B1, B6.

Gurnick, Ken. "It's a Field of Dreams Few Have Realized." *The National Sports Daily,* 19 June 1990, 18–19.

"It's Still Long Haul for Women in Baseball." *New York Times,* 27 July 1987, C4.

Keenan, S. "The Umpress Strikes Back: Triple A Umpire Pam Postema Calls 'Em as She Sees 'Em, Not Hears 'Em." *Sports Illustrated* 30 July 1984, 44–45.

Kellogg, Rick. "In a Man's World, a Woman Finds Her Place at Home Plate." *New York Times,* 21 July 1985, S3.

McEvoy, Sharlene A. "When the Umpire Strikes Out: Gender Discrimination in Professional Baseball." *Women Lawyers' Journal* 79 (September 1993), 17.

Magel, Jerry. "Now Mom's Umpiring in Little League." *San Diego Union,* 23 March 1958.

Martin, Wayne. "Lady Ump Makes Successful Debut at the Met." *The Birmingham News,* 5 June 1988, 1B, 8B.

_____. "Woman Ump Set for Weekend Duty at the Hoover Met." *The Birmingham News,* 2 June 1988, 1D, 7D.

Newhouse, D. "Women in Blue: Pam Postema's Fancy Is Umpiring and She May Be Doing It in the Major Leagues Someday Soon." *Sporting News*, 2 May 1983, 49.

"Only Girl Umpire." *Washington Post*, 26 January 1906, 9.

"Pam Postema: On the Record. In This Exclusive Interview, She Talks About Her Sex Discrimination Charge and More." *Referee*, July 1990, 76–77.

Postema, Pam and Gene Wojciechowski. *You've Got to Have Balls to Make It in This League: My Life as an Umpire*. New York: Simon and Schuster, 1992.

"Postema Heads Back to Minors." *Washington Post*, 29 March 1988, C3.

"Postema Loses." *New York Times*, 15 December 1989, A36.

"Queen of the Diamond." *Argus Leader*, 10 April 1979.

Radley, Scott. "From T-Ball to World Championships." *Hamilton Spectator*, 20 November 2004, SP04.

Reed, Susan and Lyndon Stambler. "The Umpire Strikes Back: Denied a Chance to Call 'Em as She Sees 'Em, Pam Postema Sues Baseball, Charging Sex Discrimination." *People Weekly*, 25 May 1992, 87–88.

Roan, Sharon. "Yesterday: No One Yelled 'Kill the Ump' When Amanda Clement Was Man in Blue." *Sports Illustrated*, 5 April 1982, 81.

Schmetterer, Jerry. "Lady Umpires a Hit in the Young League." *New York Sunday News*, 27 July 1975.

Sell, David. "She's Waiting for a Major League Call." *Washington Post*, 16 August 1987, C1, C10.

"Tank McNamara." 29, 30 March and 1 April 1988. Comic strip focuses on woman umpire.

"Umpire's 2d Chance." *New York Times*, 22 January 1989.

Vecsey, George. "Postema Blazed Trail for Somebody Else." *New York Times*, 17 December 1989, S3.

Vieira, Al. "Female Ump a Natural at Hall of Fame." *Albany Times Union*, 28 July 1987.

Wahl, Grant. "The Lady Is an Ump." *Sports Illustrated*, 28 April 1997.

Willson, Brad. "Ohio Gal Breaks Somers Ump Barrier." *The Sporting News*, 8 January 1977, 47.

Women in Baseball—Umpires File. National Baseball Hall of Fame and Museum, Cooperstown, New York.

Related Terms: Perry Lee Barber, Maria Cortesio, Theresa Cox, Bernice Gera, Shanna Kook, Pamela Postema, Christine Wren

Uniforms

Wiles, Tim. "Uniforms for All: the Advent and Evolution of Women's Uniforms." *Memories and Dreams*, Summer 2004, 18–19.

Van Duzer, Donna Lee "D.L."

Winston, Lisa. "Female Trainer Is Trying to Mend Gender Barrier." *USA Today Baseball Weekly*, 22–28 March 1995, 31.

Vardavas, Stephanie

"Stephanie Vardavas." In *Baseball Lives: Men and*

Women of the Game. Mike Bryan, ed. New York: Pantheon Books, 1989. Pp. 137–145.

Vassar

Hughes, Larry. "Ahead of Their Time." *Poughkeepsie Journal*, 18 December 1992, 1G, 6G.

Richardson, Sophia Foster. "Collegiate Alumnae." *Popular Science Monthly* 50 (February 1897), 517–526.

Smith, Gene. "The Girls of Summer." *American Heritage*, July–August 1994, 110–111.

Venturi (Veenema), Bridget

Gallant, Collin. "Former Gladiator Chases Her Dream." *The Edmonton Journal*, 2 August 2004, D1.

Machak, Peggy. "Ready for Another Inning." *Chicago Tribune*, 31 December 1995, 1, 4.

Visalia Baseball

"Visalia Girls Are Pennant Winners." *Los Angeles Times*, 12 May 1927, A10.

Wagner, Audrey

"Bensenville Girl Stars on Kenosha Comets Ball Team." *The Roselle Register*, 20 August 1943.

"Audrey Wagner." *Edwardsville Intelligencer*, 2 December 1948, 2.

Waldman, Suzyn

Ciolli, Rita. "Suzyn Waldman Invades the Male Holy of Holies." *St. Louis Post Dispatch*, 17 June 1996.

Clines, Francis X. "She Knows Her Way Around a Ball Park." *New York Times*, 13 January 1993, C1.

Edel, Raymond. "Waldman Onboard in Yankee's Booth." *The Record*, 4 March 2005.

Markowitz, Dan. "From Songbird to Sportscaster." *New York Times*, 2 April 1995, A1.

Martinez, Michael. "Yanks' Sanderson Sidesteps Women in Locker Room." *New York Times*, 2 April 1991, B10.

Martzke, Rudy. "Waldman Adds Her Name to Broadcast History." *USA Today*, 24 July 1995.

Riassman, Bob. "Suzyn Waldman Resigns from WFAN." *New York Daily News*, 16 November 2001.

Sandomir, Richard. "An Announcer Knows Her Game." *New York Times*, 23 April 1996, B13.

_____. "The Yankees Analysts Do Play by Play, Too." *New York Times*, 25 March 1997, B13.

"Side by Side by Yankees." *USA Today Sports Weekly*, 9–15 March 2005, 3.

Slater, Chuck. "Baseball Announcer Who Broke Barriers." *New York Times*, 13 February 2000, WE1.

Viles, Peter. "First for Mets, WFAN: A Woman in the Booth." *Broadcasting and Cable*, 14 June 1993.

"Waldman Leaves WFAN." *New York Times*, 17 November 2001, S4.

"Woman on First." *People Weekly*, 8 October 2001.

Wallace, Robin

Taylor, Cassandra. "A League of Her Own." *Mobile Register*, 18 July 2004.

Wallick, Sierra

Bonsignore, Vincent. "Wallick Gets Her Chance; Newbury Park Woman to Play in Baseball League." *Los Angeles Daily News*, 3 July 1997.

Wambsganss, William "Bill"

"Wambsganss Admits Girls' Baseball Has Differences." *The Sheboygan Press*, 8 August 1947.

Washington Barracks

"Girls Will Play Baseball." *Washington* Post, 26 April 1920, 1.

Washington Metropolitan Women's Baseball League

Crowley, Cathleen F. "Region Gave Birth to Women's Baseball Teams." *Eagle Tribune*, 26 March 2000.

Mattei, Al. "The State of Women's Baseball Found in the Washington Metro League." *<www.TopOfTheCircle.com>*.

Washington Women's Baseball Association

Grindeland, Sherry. "Pursuing a League of Her Own." *The Seattle Times*, 13 August 2004, B1.}

Waterbury Diamonds

Waterbury Diamonds Newsletter. May 2001. *<http://www.waterburydiamonds.com>*.

Wearne, Simone

Ainley, Michelle. "Pitcher Perfect, That's Wearne." *Herald Sun*, 16 December 2002, 71.

"She's Pitching It Up for Women." *Cranbourne Leader* (Australia), 25 September 2002, 13.

Weaver (Foss), Betty

"Daisies' Star Turned Down Chisox Offer." *Washington Post*, 29 April 1951, C2.

"Sisters Star in Game Here." *Washington Post*, 4 May 1952, C5.

Related Terms: Fort Wayne Daisies, AAGPBL

Weaver, Jean

"Sisters Star in Game Here." *Washington Post*, 4 May 1952, C5.

Weaver, Joanne

"Sisters Star in Game Here." *Washington Post*, 4 May 1952, C5.

Web Sites

AAGPBL. <http://www.aagpbl.org>.

American Women's Baseball Federation. <http://www.awbf.org.

American Women's Baseball League. *<www.womenplayingbaseball.com>*.

Baltimore Blues. *<http://www.bluesbaseball.homestead.com/>*.

Boston Blue Sox. *<http://www.bostonbluesox.com>*.

California Sabres. *<http://www.calwomensbaseball.org>*.

Chicago Gems. *<http://www.chicagogems.com>*.

Chicago Storm. *<http://www.chicagostorm.com>*.

Colorado Silver Bullets. *<http://www.coloradosilverbullets.org/>*.

Colorado Women's Baseball Association. *<http://www.coloradobaseball.org>*.

Detroit Danger/Motown. *<http://www.detroitdanger.com>*.

East Coast Women's Baseball League. *<http://scorebook.com/womensbaseball>*.

Eastern Women's Baseball Conference. *<http://home.att.net/~itsahit/home.html>*.

Light Years Photography. *<http://www.laurawulf.com/baseball/frame_baseball.htm>*.

National Women's Baseball Hall of Fame. *<http://eteamz.active.com/hallfame/index.cfm>*.

New England Women's Baseball League. *<http://www.newbl.org/>*.

New York Women's Baseball Association. *<www.nywomensbaseball.com>*.

North American Women's Baseball League. *<http://www.nawbl.com>*.

Philadelphia Women's Baseball League. *<http://www.phillywomensbaseball.com>*.

Rhode Island Women's Baseball League. *<http://www.womeninbaseball.com>*.

South Bend Blue Sox. *<http://www.sbbluesox.com>*.

Southern California Women's Baseball League. *<http://www.playwomensbaseball.com>*.

United States Women's Baseball. *<http://www.uswb.org>*.

Washington Women's Baseball Association. *<http://www.washingtonwomensbaseballassociation.com/>*.

Women's Baseball History. *<http://www.exploratorium.edu/baseball/>*.

Women's Baseball League. *<http://www.baseballglory.com>*.

Women's Baseball News. <http://www.saskbaseball.ca/women_baseball_news.htm>.

Women's International Baseball Association. <http://www.wibba.com>.

Weddington-Steward, Elaine C.

Turner, Renee D. "Introducing Elaine C. Weddington: First Woman Baseball Executive: Boston Red Sox's Assistant General Manager Breaks New Ground in the Big Leagues." *Ebony* 45 (July 1990), 25–26.

Vecsey, George. "Robinson's Legacy Reaches a Front Office." *New York Times*, 25 February 1990, S4.

Related Terms: Management Personnel

Weddle (Hines), Mary

Wickline, John. "Local Heroes." *The Intelligencer*, 5 May 2003, 1, 5.

_____. "Player Achieves Big League Recognition." *Wheeling News-Register,* 10 March 2002.

Wegman, Marie

Goodman, Rebecca. "Joined All-American Girls League in 1947." *The Cincinnati Enquirer*, 23 January 2004.

Related Terms: AAGPBL

Weiss, Alta

Baumann, J.A. "The pitcher wore a dress." *Ohio Press,* August 2003.

Berlage, Gai Ingham. "Five Forgotten Women in American Baseball History: Players, Lizzie Arlington, Alta Weiss, Lizzie Murphy; Umpire, Amanda Clement; and Owner, Helen Britton." In *Cooperstown Symposium on Baseball and the American Culture.* Westport, Connecticut: Meckler Publishing, 1990. Pp. 222–242.

Cleveland Press. 3 October 1907.

Gregorich, Barbara. "You Can't Play in Skirts: Alta Weiss, Baseball Player." *Timeline: The Magazine of the Ohio Historical Society,* July/August 1994, 39–43.

Gregorich, Barbara. *Women at Play.* New York: Harcourt Brace & Company, 1993.

Ragersville Historical Society. *Ragersville Town History.*

Ritter Public Library. Production "You can't play ball in a skirt: Alta Weiss, an Ohio hero." 2003.

Wenzell, Margaret

Gonzales, Gloria. "Baseball Hall-of-Famers in a League of Their Own." *Los Angeles Daily News,* 21 August 1997.

Western Bloomer Girls

"Bloomer Girls Tomorrow." *Stevens Point Daily Journal,* 2 August 1912.

"Famous Western Bloomer Girls to Oppose Greys Here Next Monday Evening." *Zanesville Signal,* 5 July 1927, 8.

"Muncy Is Aiding Playground Fund with Sane Fourth." *Gazette and Bulletin,* 4 July 1913.

"Western Bloomer Girls Coming." *The Humeston New Era,* 13 May 1914.

"Western Bloomer Girls Slated." *The Lima News,* 26 June 1913, 11.

Related Terms: Bloomer Girls, Kate Becker, Maud Nelson

White, Marcia

"Girls League Inspired Former Bat Girl." *Kenosha News,* 30 July 1992.

Whiteley, Jennifer

Clough, Bethany. "Break for the Winter as the Visalia Oaks' Season Ends." *The Fresno Bee,* 13 September 2002.

Griswold, Lewis. "Ballclub Promises to Remain in Visalia City." *The Fresno Bee,* 22 January 2002.

Jaffe, Matthew. "Diamond Dreams." *Sunset,* 1 June 2004.

Passan, Jeff. "It's a Winner, Visalia Opens Renovated Recreation Park with a Victory on Field, in Stands." *The Fresno Bee,* 12 April 2003.

Robison, Ken. "Fielding a Dream Job Visalia Oaks' General Manager Left Wall Street for a Home Plate Office." *The Fresno Bee,* 19 July 2002.

Warszawski, Marek. "Keep 'Em Coming." *The Fresno Bee,* 19 March 2004.

Whitely, Jennifer. Correspondence with Leslie A. Heaphy. North Canton, Ohio, November 2004.

Wigiser, Margaret

Claps, Arthur V. "History of NYC Basketball/Out of the Dark Ages/ Wigiser Led Campaign to Create Girls Sports in City Schools." *Newsday,* 29 March 2002.

Wiley (Sears), Janet "Pee Wee"

Pontanilla, Bernice. "Little Gets Display of Her Own." *Winnipeg Sun,* 30 July 2003, 44.

Williams, Ann

Richards, Gregory. "Believe It: This Woman Throws Hard." *Naples Daily News,* 12 April 1995.

Related Terms: Colorado Silver Bullets

Williams, Karen

"Karen Williams." In *Baseball Lives: Men and Women of the Game.* Mike Bryan, ed. New York: Pantheon Books, 1989. Pp. 104–110.

Williams (Heverly), Ruth

"Woman Recalls Her Years as Professional Baseball Player." *The Intelligencer and The Record,* 3 August 1992, A1, A4.

Wiltse (Collins), Dorothy

Sargent, Jim. "Pitching in the AAGPBL in the 1940s." *Sports Collectors Digest,* 3 October 1997, 156–57.

Related Terms: AAGPBL

Wirth, Senaida

"Girl Baseball Star Hits .386 to Lead League." *Chicago Tribune,* 9 June 1946, A5.

Wisconsin Baseball

"Baseball Reunion Is Held by Two Women's Teams." *The Sheboygan Press,* 21 August 1958.

Rampenthal, Shari. "Baseball League in the Offing?" *Wisconsin State Journal,* 17 July 1996.

Wisniewski, Connie

Martin, Heinie. "Connie May Be Pitching Her Last Year." *The Grand Rapids Herald,* 6 August 1946.

"25th Victory for Connie." *The Grand Rapids Herald,* 6 August 1946.

"Wisniewski, Evans Pitch 20th Victories." *Chicago Tribune,* 14 August 1950, C4.

Related Terms: AAGPBL

Women's Baseball League (WBL)

Alexander, Susanne M. "New Baseball League Has Women on Deck." *Crain's Cleveland Business,* 21, 29 May 2000.

Caldera, Pete. "Women's Baseball Coming to Baxter." *The Times Herald Record,* 23 July 1997, 63.

Women's Baseball League Newsletter, May 2003, February 2004.

Women's National Adult Baseball Association

Johnson, Marc. "Women's Baseball Begins." *News-Sentinel,* 15 July 1994.

Morgan, Marlon W. "Response to WNABA Is Positive." *News-Sentinel*, 10 June 1994.

Women's New England Baseball League (WNEBL)

Barnes, J.L. "OR Alum Finds a League of Her Own." *The Standard-Times*, 27 July 2002, A1.

"The Girls of Summer." *The Village Voice*, 28 July–3 August 1999.

Huebner, Barbara. "A New League of Their Own." *Boston Globe*, 12 May 1999.

O'Connor, Michael. "The Local Women Are ... Playing Hardball." *The Boston Herald*, 28 May 2000.

Women's New England Baseball League Official League Program, 1999.

Related Terms: New England Women's Baseball League (NEWBL)

Women's Professional Baseball League

Lello, Michael. "Softball Star Eyes Baseball." *Times Leader*, 6 July 2001.

Women's World Series

"A Swing at Acceptance." *St. Petersburg Times*, 7 September 2002.

"Baseball: Matsumoto, Nagano to Take Part in Women's World Series." *Japan Economic Newswire*, 15 June 2004.

Benic, Sarah. "Dragons Live World Series Dream." *Manningham Leader*, 25 August 2004, 34.

Callander, Sean. "Bundoora Slugger Belts Aussies to the Gold." *Diamond Valley Leader* (Australia), 25 September 2002, 33.

"Canada Beat South Korea." *Agence France Presse*, 20 July 2004.

"Canada Crushes South Korea." *Edmonton Journal*, 21 July 2004, D5.

"Canada Scores Nine in Baseball Romp." *The Star Phoenix*, 20 July 2004, B3.

"Canada Settles for Bronze." *Stratford Beacon Herald*, 9 August 2004, 9.

"Canadian Women Drop Semifinal." *The Guardian*, 22 July 2004, B1.

"Canadian Women Hit Early in Victory over Hong Kong." *Guelph Mercury*, 20 July 2004, B6.

"Canadian Women Lose to U.S. in Women's Baseball." *The Halifax Daily News*, 22 July 2004, 43.

Cowley, Norm. "At Last, a Championship of their Own." *Edmonton Journal*, 1 December 2003, D2.

_____. "Playing Women's Baseball Has Its Perks." *Edmonton Journal*, 8 June 2004, D3.

Forsberg, Chris. "Facing World Competition; They Played Hardball." *Boston Globe*, 18 July 2001.

"Girls of Summer Go for the Gold: Women's World Baseball Championships on Deck." *Edmonton Journal*, 13 December 2002, D5.

Holmes, Sam. "World Series Boosts Australian Women's Baseball." AAP *Newsfeed*, 11 July 2003.

Ierodiaconou, George. "Team Steals to a World Series Win." *Sunbury Macedon Leader* (Australia), 8 October 2002, 8.

"Japan Downs United States 13–4 to Take Gold Medal in Women's World Series Baseball." *AP Worldstream*, 22 July 2004.

"Japan Join U.S., Australia in Women's World Series Baseball Semis." *Agence France Presse*, 19 July 2004.

Jewers, Jody. "Nova Scotia Women Trying Out for National Baseball Team." *The Halifax Daily News*, 21 May 2004.

Johnstone, Andrew. "Favourites Tag Is No Obstacle." *Progress Leader* (Australia), 14 January 2003, 42.

LaPeter, Leonora. "Women's World Series: Swinging at Acceptance." *St. Petersburg Times*, 7 September 2002, 1B.

Morgan, Nancy. "Gibbs Teen Plays in Women's World Series." *St. Petersburg Times*, 22 September 2002, 26.

Mullen, Maureen. "Small World at the Series, U.S. Among 3 Teams as Event Shifts Site." *Boston Globe*, 8 August 2003, E10.

Park, Mary Jane. "Storm Dampens Visit by Japanese Official." *St. Petersburg Times*, 8 September 2002, 8.

"Port Trio Pitch In for National Team." *Caulfield Glen Eira/Port Phillip Leader* (Australia), 9 December 2002, 50.

"Royals Are Crowned Queens of Baseball." *Bayside Leader*, 23 September 2002, 46.

Ryan, Melissa. "World Series Holds No Fear for Local Team." *The Age* (Melbourne), 31 August 2002, 14.

Stanturf, Sam. "Australia Jells Fast to Capture World Series." *St. Petersburg Times*, 9 September 2002, 2C.

_____. "Injury Subs Lead Team USA Past Australia in Series." *St. Petersburg Times*, 4 September 2002, 3C.

_____. "U.S. Team Splits Its First Game in World Series." *St. Petersburg Times*, 3 September 2002, 7C.

"Team USA Takes Silver at Women's World Cup IV." <http://www.USABaseball.com>, 21 July 2004.

"Team USA to Play for Women's World Series Title Tonight." <http://www.USABaseball.com>, 21 July 2004.

Tomlinson, Julia. "Aussies Fit, Ready." *The Gold Coast Bulletin* (Australia), 23 August 2003, 156.

"Women Drop Ball." *The Toronto Sun*, 22 July 2004, 98.

"Women Open Series with Loss to Japan." *The Record*, 19 July 2004.

"Women's World Series." *Tampa Tribune*, 8 September 2002, 10.

Women's World Series Program, 2001.

"Women's World Series Baseball." *Agence France Presse*, 18, 19 and 20 July 2004.

"Women's World Series Baseball in Japan Cancelled Due to SARS." *Agence France Presse*, 24 June 2003.

"Women's World Series Cancelled Due to SARS." *Xinhua News Agency*, 24 June 2003.

Zerr, Scott. "It's a World Cup of Their Own." *Edmonton Sun*, 28 May 2002, SP8.

Related Terms: Australian Baseball, Canadian Baseball, Tournaments

World Cup of Women's Baseball

Arrowsmith, Lisa. "Six Countries to Compete in World Cup of Women's Baseball in Edmonton." *Canada Business and Current Affairs*, 8 March 2004.

"Baseball World Cup for Women Set for July." *Milwaukee Journal Sentinel*, 9 March 2004, 02C.

"Bulgaria Pulls Out of Women's Tourney." *Edmonton Journal*, 27 July 2004, D5.

"Canada Rallies Over U.S. in Women's Baseball Event." *Stratford Beacon Herald*, 3 August 2004, 9.

Carle, Dan. "Canuck Upset! Our Gals Down USA 2–1 at Women's Baseball." *Edmonton Sun*, 3 August 2004, SP1.

Cowley, Norm. "At Last, a Championship of Their Own." *The Edmonton Journal*, 1 December 2003, D2.

Davidi, Shi. "Team of 18 Women to Tune Up for World Cup." *Hamilton Spectator*, 12 June 2004, SP10.

"Dominican Women Out." *The Record*, 17 June 2004, D7.

Gallant, Collin. "Australian Bats Silence Japan" *Edmonton Journal*, 4 August 2004, D3.

_____. "Hannah Wants the Ball Again." *Edmonton Journal*, 5 August 2004, D1.

_____. "Nostalgia on the Mound to Open Women's Tourney: Wartime Pro Baseball Players Help Launch Five-Nation World Cup." *Edmonton Journal*, 31 July 2004.

_____. "Outfielder Wins Bursary, Eyes Women's Selection Camp." *The Edmonton Journal*, 9 March 2004, D5.

_____. "Women Begin Playoffs Today." *The Edmonton Journal*, 7 August 2004, D3.

Garcia, Jose E. "Women Play the Game Too." *The Arizona Republic*, 16 July 2004, 6.

Ireland, Joanne. "Girls of Summer Take the Field." *Edmonton Journal*, 29 July 2004, D1.

Kuo, Deborah. "Chinese Taipei Women's Baseball Team Ready for World Cup in Canada." *Central News Agency*, 28 July 2004.

_____. "Taiwan to Compete in First World Cup." *Central News Agency* (Taiwan), 27 July 2004.

MacDonald, Jim. "Canadian Women Win Bronze in First Baseball World Cup." *Hamilton Spectator*, 9 August 2004, SP04.

_____. "Women on Three-Game Win Streak Heading into Playoffs." *The Halifax Daily News*, 7 August 2004, 73.

MacKinnon, John. "No Worries for Aussies." *Edmonton Journal*, 28 July 2004, D1.

"Nova Scotians Selected." *The Halifax Daily News*, 10 March 2004, 48.

Specter, Mark. "Problematic Tournament Done for Love of the Game." *National Post* (Canada), 29 July 2004, S5.

Tappay, Kenneth. "Baseball Cup Organizers Real Champs." *Edmonton Journal*, 19 August 2004, A15.

Tychkowski, Robert. "Canada Rules Aussies." *Edmonton Sun*, 9 August 2004, SP5.

_____. "Extra-Inning Heartbreaker." *Edmonton Sun*, 8 August 2004, SP5.

"U.S., Japan Advance to Final at World Cup of Women's Baseball." *AP World Stream*, 8 August 2004.

"U.S. Wins Gold, Canada Bronze in First World Cup of Women's Baseball." *The Vancouver Sun*, 9 August 2004, D4.

"Women to Compete for Baseball World Cup." *Times Colonist*, 9 March 2004, B4.

Zerr, Scott. "Filling up the Cup." *Edmonton Sun*, 9 March 2004, SP9.

_____. "Just the Fundamentals." *Edmonton Sun*, 29 July 2004, SP5.

Related Terms: Samantha Magalas, World Series

Wren, Christine

"Boos Help Woman Feel Right at Home (Plate)." *New York Times*, 23 February 1975.

Christine Wren File. National Baseball Hall of Fame and Museum, Cooperstown, New York.

Dorfman, Harvey A. "Christine Wren: Another Season." *New York Times*, 6 June 1976.

_____. "Christine Wren: Woman in Blue." *Baseball Bulletin*, July 1976, 11.

_____. "Woman Umpire Story: The Perils of Christine." *New York Times*, 17 August 1975, 2S.

"Interview: Chris Wren." *Referee*, July/August 1977, 8–11, 13–15, 45.

Jensen, Dwight. "Umpire Wren Makes Her Debut Look Routine." *Christian Science Monitor*, 26 June 1975.

"They're Playing Christine Dirty." *Binghamton Paper*, 22 August 1976, 3B, 8B.

West, Karen. "Passion for Diamonds." *Seattle Post-Intelligencer*, 6 July 1975, D1–D2.

"Woman to Umpire in Dodger Game." *New York Times*, 16 February 1975, S10.

Yearbook, 1980. Cedar Rapids Reds.

Related Terms: Umpires

Wright, Charlene

Schwartz, Michael. "Local Woman Has Wright Stuff." *Lancaster News*, 27 July 2003, C 6.

Wronski (Straka), Sylvia

Cole, Jeff. "Straka, Then Wronski, Pitched in Women's League." *Milwaukee Journal Sentinel*, 1 December 1997.

Yawkey, Jean

"Died. Jean Yawkey." *Time*, 9 March 1992.

Pope, Justin. "Henry Leads Group to Buy Red Sox." *USA Today*, 21 December 2001.

Rosen, Byron. "New Bosox Bosses Right at Home." *Washington Post*, 30 September 1977, D3.

"Status of Duquette Still Up in the Air." <ESPN-Magazine.com>, 27 February 2001.

Sullivan, Jack. "Sox CEO Reaps Windfall from Yawkey Estate." *Boston Herald*, 17 March 1999.

Related Terms: Owners

Yull, Carmela

"Some Young Lady May Soon Break into Big Lineups." *The Messenger* (Athens, Ohio), 10 August 1928, 2.

YWCA

"Plainfield Girls Now Play Ball and Slide to Base Just Like Boys." *Washington Post*, 21 April 1915, 4.

Zammit, Jackie

Colussi, Christianni. "Jackie Shows the Boys How It's Done." *Penrith Press* (Australia), 29 January 2002.

Related Terms: Australian Baseball

Ziegler, Alma "Gabby"

Cornejo, Mark. "In a League of Her Own." *San Luis Obispo Tribune*, 11 June 2005.

Eligon, John. "'Gabby' Made her Mark for the Chicks." *Grand Rapids Press*, 10 September 2001.

Johnson, Greg. "Gabby's Flair Enlivened Chicks, Women's Baseball." *Grand Rapids Press*, 4 June 2005.

Related Terms: AAGPBL, Grand Rapids Chicks

Zuckerman, Megan

Gasper, Christopher L. "Playing the Game They Love: Women Pursue Baseball Dreams." *Boston Globe*, 13 July 2003, 1.

Related Terms: New England Women's Baseball League

About the Contributors

Bijan C. Bayne is author of *Sky Kings: Black Pioneers of Professional Basketball*. His essay on Black baseball in North Carolina appears in the anthology *Baseball in the Carolinas* (McFarland, 2002), and his essay on schoolyard basketball is in the book *Basketball in America: From the Playground to Jordan's Game* (Haworth, 2004)

Kathleen Birck graduated from Kenyon College in Gambier, Ohio, with a bachelor's degree in neuroscience in 2000. While there, she completed an independent study on women in baseball with Professor of History Peter Rutkoff. She also holds bachelor's and master's degrees in nursing from the University of Pennsylvania School of Nursing. She became board-certified as a family nurse practitioner in 2004 and is practicing in Mississippi at a community health center.

Kerrie Bottorff received a B.A. in history from Kent State University and completed two internships at the National Baseball Library and Archive in Cooperstown, New York. She currently works for the Orange County Library System in Orlando, Florida, and is earning a masters of library and information science from the University of South Florida.

Ryan Bucher received a B.A. in history from Kent State University in 2003, graduating with University Honors. He is currently a graduate student in the Graduate School of Management at Kent State University. In May 2005 Ryan completed his M.B.A. with a finance concentration. He is currently completing a second master's in economics.

Jim Glennie has been involved in women's baseball since 1992, but he has played and coached baseball for over 50 years. He founded and or-ganized the Michigan Women's Baseball League, the Great Lakes Women's Baseball League, the American Women's Baseball League and the Women's International Baseball Association. As president of the American Women's Baseball League, a national organization that promotes opportunities for women to play baseball in the United States, he has organized over 16 regional and national tournaments across the country, and as president of the Women's International Baseball Association, he has helped organize four Women's World Series international tournaments in Australia, Canada, Japan and the United States. Glennie has worked as an assistant attorney general for the State of Michigan for 20 years. He and his wife Jannel have two daughters.

Margaret Hart is a freelance writer as well as a baseball and football official from Mississauga, Ontario. She attended the Ontario Baseball Association's all-female umpire clinic.

Leslie A. Heaphy is an associate professor of history at Kent State University, Stark Campus. She is the author of *The Negro Leagues, 1869–1960* (McFarland, 2002) and editor of the forthcoming *Black Baseball in Chicago* (McFarland, 2006). Leslie also chairs the Women in Baseball committee for the Society for American Baseball Research. Though she has lived in Ohio for many years, she remains a devoted New York Mets fan.

Larry Lester is one of the country's leading authorities on the Negro Baseball Leagues. His first book (in collaboration with Dick Clark of Ypsilanti, Michigan) is simply titled *The Negro Leagues Book* (Society for American Baseball Research, 1994) and was billed as "the most complete collection of information on baseball's

Negro Leagues ever published." Lester serves as co-chairman of the Negro Leagues Committee for the prestigious Society for American Baseball Research, based in Cleveland, Ohio. His next four books are a part of a *Black America Series*, by Arcadia Publishing, entitled *Whistle Stops*. The stops are *Black Baseball in Detroit, Black Baseball in Chicago, Black Baseball in Kansas City* and *Black Baseball in Pittsburgh*. In 2002, the University of Nebraska Press published *Black Baseball's National Showcase: The East-West All-Star Game, 1933–1953*. This publication won the *Sporting News*-SABR Research Award and the Robert Peterson Recognition Award. McFarland will publish his latest book, *Baseball's First Colored World Series: The 1924 Meeting of the Hilldale Giants and Kansas City Monarch*, in 2006.

Dorothy Jane Mills, also known as Dorothy Z. Seymour, has been selected for inclusion in Who's Who in America. An independent scholar and the author of 17 books, she is also the widow and lifetime collaborator of Dr. Harold Seymour, the first historian of baseball.

Jim Nitz is a Milwaukee native who now lives in Marshall, Wisconsin. He and his wife, Wendee, have a son, Jeff, who plays shortstop for the Boston University club baseball team, and a daughter, Bethanee, who runs cross-country and pitches for the Marshall U14 fast-pitch softball team that Jim coaches. He has written articles on such topics as Borchert Field, the American Association Milwaukee Brewers, Happy Felsch, Ken Keltner, and the Milwaukee Chicks for *Milwaukee History*, *The Milwaukee Journal*, *Milwaukee Magazine*, SABR publications, and the SABR Bio-Project.

Lou Parotta is a social studies teacher at Thomas R. Proctor High School in Utica, New York, and is the coordinator of continuing education at the Utica School of Commerce in Utica, New York. He is a lifelong baseball fan, and has been a frequent contributor to the *The Diamond Angle* as a guest writer. Lou is currently a sports columnist with the *Boonville Herald & Adirondack Tourist* and the features writer for www.LegionBaseball.com. He was once employed by the New York-Penn League, and is a member of the National Baseball Hall of Fame and Museum, the Ted Williams Museum, the Negro Leagues Museum, and the International Boxing Hall of Fame in Canastota, New York.

Grant Provance holds a B.A. in history from Kent State University. He lives in Canton, Ohio, with his wife.

Shawn Selby is a Ph.D. student at Ohio University in Athens, Ohio. He is currently working on his dissertation dealing with Congress and the mass culture critique during the 1950s and 1960s.

Justine Siegal is the president and founder of the Women's Baseball League. She has been playing baseball for over 25 years in both women's and men's leagues. She is currently a doctoral student in sport management at the USSA. When not playing or coaching, Justine loves to spend time with her seven-year-old daughter Jasmine.

Micheo Takeuchi has a Ph. d. in Education and teaches at Kinjo Gakuin University in Japan. He has published several papers and books on topics related to both education and baseball. He manages a women's baseball team at his university and is the chair of the board of trustees for the All-Japan College Women's Baseball League. He has been a member of SABR since 1977 and is an associate member of the Player's Association of the AAGPBL.

Joan M. Thomas is a freelance writer based in St. Louis and a 15-year member of SABR. In addition to her work for SABR, she is a regular contributor to *St. Louis Parent* and *Senior Circuit* magazines. Her baseball-related essays have appeared in a number of widely distributed publications. After her first book, *St. Louis 1875–1940*, was released in 2003, she began work on another book, *St. Louis' Big League Ballparks*.

Carolyn M. Trombe is a writer from upstate New York. Her work has received awards from the Panhandle Professional Writers Association, the William Faulkner Creative Writing Competition, the National League of American Pen Women, and the Writer's Digest Writing Competition. Carolyn's biography on Dottie Wiltse Collins was published by McFarland in 2005.

Tim Wiles is Director of Research at the National Baseball Hall of Fame and Library in Cooperstown, New York, a position he has held since 1995. He is the co-editor of *Line Drives: 100 Contemporary Baseball Poems* (Southern Illinois University Press, 2002).

Laura Wulf is a photographer and artist living in Boston. Her baseball photographs have been shown at the Yogi Berra Museum in Montclair, New Jersey, the Art Complex Museum in Duxbury, Massachusetts, and are included in the photography collection of the National Baseball Hall of Fame in Cooperstown, NY. Her Web site is www.laurawulf.com.

Index

427